Oracle9*i* Web Development

Oracle Press™

Oracle9*i* Web Development

Bradley D. Brown

Osborne/**McGraw-Hill**

New York   Chicago   San Francisco
Lisbon   London   Madrid   Mexico City
Milan   New Delhi   San Juan
Seoul   Singapore   Sydney   Toronto

Osborne/McGraw-Hill
2600 Tenth Street
Berkeley, California 94710
U.S.A.

To arrange bulk purchase discounts for sales promotions, premiums, or fund-raisers, please contact Osborne/**McGraw-Hill** at the above address. For information on translations or book distributors outside the U.S.A., please see the International Contact Information page immediately following the index of this book.

Oracle9i Web Development

234567890 DOC DOC 01987654321

ISBN 0-07-219388-3

Publisher
  Brandon A. Nordin

Vice President & Associate Publisher
  Scott Rogers

Acquisitions Editor
  Lisa McClain

Project Editor
  Patty Mon

Acquisitions Coordinators
  Ross Doll
  Paulina Pobocha
  Jessica Wilson
  Athena Honore

Technical Editor
  Mike O'Mara

Copy Editor
  Marcia Baker

Proofreader
  Pam Vevea

Indexer
  Valerie Perry

Computer Designer
  Lucie Ericksen
  Michelle Galicia

Illustrators
  Michael Mueller
  Lyssa Wald

Series Design
  Jani Beckwith

Cover Series Design
  Damore Johann Design, Inc.

This book was composed with Corel VENTURA™ Publisher.

*To my great grandparents, who migrated
to the United States of America.
The land of freedom and opportunity.*

*To my grandparents, Howard and Cordelia Miles,
and Harry and Jeannette Brown.
For making my parents who they are.*

*To my parents, Birney and Julie Brown, for they made me who I am.
I know how much they love me, for I have children.*

*To my in-laws, Wes and Carol Haas,
for giving me the gift of my wife.*

To my wife, Kristen, for loving me for who I am.

*To my children, Austin and Paige, who will never know
how much I love them . . . until they have children.*

*To my children's children. Who will teach Austin
and Paige how much their mother and I love them.*

About the Author

Bradley D. Brown is chairman of the board and chief architect of TUSC, an Inc. 500 full-service consulting company—with offices in Atlanta, Chicago, Denver, Detroit, and Milwaukee—that specializes in Oracle consulting, training, and product. He has been involved with Information Technology consulting since 1982, with a focus on Oracle since 1987. Brad is recognized worldwide as a leading Oracle author and speaker, and is affectionately known as "The Dotcom of Web Technology." In June 1998, Brad authored his first book *Oracle Application Server Web Toolkit Reference,* for Oracle Press and Osborne/McGraw-Hill. In 1999, he followed that highly successful venture with *Oracle8i Web Development.*

Contents at a Glance

PART III

Modules

PART IV

Oracle Tools

PART V

Ongoing Support

Contents

PART I
Getting Prepared

PART II
Core Concepts

PART III
Modules

PART IV
Oracle Tools

PART V
Ongoing Support

Foreword

rad Brown is the Chairman & Chief Architect of TUSC, the Oracle Experts. His personal mission is to make a difference for those he touches. He's done it with this book and with his first two books, which were based on OAS. This book was a total rewrite from the prior *Oracle8i Web Development* (OAS) book, which was based on the Spyglass Listener. *i*AS is based on, and works with, the Apache Listener.

Instant gains can be achieved by upgrading to *i*AS. Performance can instantly be enhanced 2–4 times, it is scalable and reliable, and the Web cache increases performance another 2–150 times. The Internet architecture is a solid development architecture that every company should use for *all* their intranet, extranet, and Internet development.

Andy Grove was quoted in *Wired* magazine, saying, "In the future, all companies will be Internet companies. I still believe that. More than ever." AS is the software that will see your company into the future.

This book covers a wide range of topics, including: Oracle9*i*AS Architecture, Installation, Configuration and Tuning, 24×7, Disaster Planning, HTML, JavaScript, XML, WML, OAS to *i*AS Migration, Built-in PL/SQL Packages, Security, Java, PL/SQL, Perl, PHP, Designer, Portal, Developer, IFS, Caching, OEM for *i*AS, Discoverer, Troubleshooting, Debugging, Logging, and Site Analysis, Search Engines, Site Indexing, Testing, and Good Sites.

Brad is clearly the world's leading authority on 9*i*AS and Oracle Web Development. After you read *Oracle9i Web Development,* you'll know why. I highly recommend this book to everyone at Oracle, as I highly recommend it to you.

—Thomas Kurian, Vice President Oracle Server Technologies

Acknowledgments

y kids continue to get older and wiser every day. Austin and Paige are now 14 and 11. Two years ago, Austin was an inch from overtaking me height-wise, now he's about four inches beyond. Austin has incredible common sense, and tireless imagination and creativity. He is an amazing young man who cares very much for other people. Austin is confident in his own abilities, which makes me proud. I have so enjoyed the opportunity to have him as a part of my life. Amazingly, we only have about five more years with Austin before he goes away to college. I know that we will be best of friends forever. Watch for Austin on the big screen some day, he's an incredible actor.

Paige is an absolutely brilliant child, smarter than almost everyone I know. Not only is she incredibly smart and bright with a keen common sense, she's an incredible athlete. She won the state championship in the breaststroke two years ago. This year she got 2nd place—in two more years, I bet she wins again. She's extremely modest and would be very upset if anyone knew she was a state champion, so please don't say anything to her about it. She's the most amazing and fascinating child you will ever meet. Paige will give 110 percent of herself; she is always there for everyone. I am extremely fortunate to have such a special wife and children. I couldn't have written this book without their love and support.

My two prior books took a monumental chunk of my life away from my wife and children, so I didn't plan to write another book so quickly. However, when *i*AS was released, I started digging into the functionality and, I was so excited, I started writing papers, doing presentations, and holding training classes at TUSC to bring everyone up-to-speed on the new technology. But something was missing—a book to bring it all together. I felt I owed it to each of our employees and to you to share that information. So, this time I vowed it would be different—I would write a book without taking all that time from the family (and friends). I promised myself I wouldn't sit in front of my laptop at the swim meets all summer. I promised myself I would play golf or go swimming when my kids asked. Just before summer, in April, I asked Kristen, my wife, Austin, and Paige what they thought about me writing another book—I assured them it would be different this time (side note—I probably said that last time, too). It was unanimous; I was voted down. So, I thought about it for a while . . . why would it matter to them if it didn't affect them—in other words, if I kept my promise that it would be different this time? I started working on the book, a month passed and nobody noticed. Then two, and then three months—again, nobody noticed. Then one day in July, I printed off a chapter from the book. I took it with me, so I could review it. Paige noticed and recognized it was a book chapter; she asked if I was writing another book. I was busted. I replied, "yes," and she said, "I thought we all said no." I replied, "I've been working on it for three months now—I'm nearly done writing it." She said, "Oh, OK." Then she yelled to her brother, "Dad's writing another book." I could hear the sigh from the other room. She said, "And he has been for three months now." Austin didn't reply. So, this time I proved I could write a book without it negatively affecting my family. Then, again, maybe I just proved I always work too much. Seriously, I'd like to thank Kristen, Austin, and Paige for putting up with me each and every day. I do work too much, no doubt about it.

Kristen's passion for life is always energizing. She's the perfect mother of our children. We've been married now for more than 18 years. It's hard to believe it's been that long. We have enjoyed life beyond our wildest dreams. We're so privileged and honored to have such a wonderful family, friends, and each of you. I think I summed it up well in the dedication of my last book, which was to Kristen: The one I love, who makes me a better man, makes me complete, and helps me to be the best I can possibly be—I wouldn't be half the person I am without her. She has taught me more about myself than anyone ever, and edified my ability to be patient. She is my soul mate and life partner. She taught me when to stop and realize that there is always tomorrow. She helps me to put life into perspective and helps me to use all my talents (as defined in the Bible). Kristen put balance in my life and helps me to keep life in the nonurgent important box (as defined by Steven Covey), rather than the urgent important side of life—she helps me eliminate crisis from our lives. Kristen has not only given me my children, but she had them, a task I certainly couldn't bear. She always does the hard things! Kristen always helps me understand what I need to participate in and supports me 110 percent; she completes me and makes me the best person I can possibly be. She helped me finish college in three and a half years. She helped me choose my first job, supported me when we lived in my home town, and understood and supported me when it came to moving to New York or Chicago for my career. She has always supported my career over her own, all the way. Kristen supported my dream to start my own company, and then to move to Colorado (I've dreamt of living in Colorado since I visited when I was ten years old). She supports me every day in every way. Not only did Kristen support my dream to write one book, but also supported every moment of the second (and now third) book. I know she is always there for me. Our relationship grows every day, we are better friends every day and we are best friends now. I love Kristen because she thinks a lot like I do. She knows that if you do good things for others, good things will happen to you. She supports our children in every way—when they hurt, she hurts. She lives her life for others. When I say the wrong thing, she knows what I mean. I want nothing but the best for everyone I know and so does she. Kristen and I are very much alike, but she thinks more with her heart and I tend to think with my head. She is a person of feelings—I'm an ESTJ (Meyers-Briggs) and she's an ESFJ. I'm strong on the thinking side and she's strong on the feeling side. She completes me. Behind every good man, there is a great woman and Kristen is the woman behind this man! Kristen, thank you for completing me and making me a better man!

A special thank you to my family for everything you've ever done for me—my parents, Birney and Julie Brown, my grandparents, Howard and Cordelia Miles, my sisters, Michele and Pam, my in-laws, Wes and Carol Haas, my brother-in-laws, Steve and Brian Haas, Mike Scanlon, and Tom McCallum, my sister-in-laws, Patty and Kristine Haas, my aunts and uncles, cousins, nephews, nieces, and all my other relatives.

Thank you to my YPO friends (far too many to list) and forum mates, Aaron, Antoine, Bart, Dave, Jeff, John, Ken, Marc, Tom, and Will—for all you've blessed me with.

My partners, Rich Niemiec and Joe Trezzo are two of the best guys in the world. I've had the pleasure of working with them since our days together at Oracle. We were known as the three musketeers back then—all for one, one for all. In other words, whatever we learned, we shared with each other and, if one of us needed help with something, all of us were there for him. It's still that way today. Since we started TUSC in 1988, we've managed the company using consensus ruling. This means all three of us must agree on any major decisions about the company. Again, maintaining our motto: one for all, all for one. Imagine yourself founding a company more than 13 years ago with two other people. In any company, there are good times and there are bad times. We've maintained a friendship throughout all 13 years. We're like brothers to each other. Joe and I didn't have any brothers growing up, but these guys are the brothers I always wanted. It's a special bond between us. If you ever see the three of us together, you'll see what I mean. I asked Joe and Rich for their thoughts on this book.

Joe said, "Oracle has come along way from the days of introducing their first PC-based version of Oracle back in 1986 with version 4 of Oracle. Things were simpler back then, but they were also more limited. Since then, the age of terminal-host has become extinct, client-server came and went, and the Internet/intranet now are the fields of play. Oracle has catapulted to Version 9i with a myriad of complexity far deeper than any one person can ever master. Note, this complexity offers options that extend to cover the needs of most companies. That has always been the intriguing aspect of Oracle, that being, the company has always stayed ahead of the pack in the underlying flexibility and functionality of the database. Over the years, it has exceeded most competition, not only in the database aspect, but also in its toolset and applications. Oracle is a dominant force that's hard to compete with because the company succeeds time and time again when many people count them out. I have watched and monitored this company—Oracle—for my entire professional career, and I'm convinced it will continue to lead the way and define the future. Oracle's Web technology continues to advance at a rapid pace, as evidenced with versions 8i and 9i. To date, nobody has mastered the Web technology in terms of the software delivery arena, but Oracle continues to lead this arena and build technology to support, as well as define, this landscape. One thing most people don't realize is the Internet is still in its infancy. Many more evolutions are to take place until the delivery is perfected and I'm sure Oracle will continue to be a dominant player in this process."

Rich said, "The dotcom revolution helped us blaze the first trail in the Internet revolution. The next trail is the one that will carry us through the next ten years. Brad Brown provides the tools you need to be a part of the next Internet evolution, and Oracle provides the database and tools to be the Web leader. Oracle was the first relational database released in 1979, the first to have Java and XML, the first to ship on Linux. Oracle9i takes the next step with external tables, which moves us closer to the operating system. I predict we'll have a future that brings the operating system and the database together as one under some future Oracle version. External tables in Oracle9i and advances with the application server are the beginning of this future. The XML datatype shows that Oracle is also advancing this standard. The move to a 64-bit database accelerates the Internet and the information age. With 64-bit hardware, the theoretical limit of addressable memory (2 to the power of 64) becomes 16E (exabytes) or 18,446,744,073,709,551,616 bytes of memory. Because it's estimated that only 12 exabytes of information are in the entire world, 16E is a pretty healthy amount of memory (although data is growing by 2E per year). Imagine storing every single piece of information on Earth in one database and *in memory*! When we have everything in memory and the database and operating system as one, the Web developers will use this book to take all Web sites to the next level and truly deliver the Internet paradigm shift we all know is coming. Brad prepares us for this future with his best book ever!"

Even though my name is on the front of this book, a large group of people contributed to the project. This is, primarily, how this time was different. The work was spread across more than 25 people, specifically, the people mentioned here, who wrote entire chapters or made significant contributions to chapters. The following people made significant contributions to my book. After you read everyone's contributions, you might wonder what I did. As I mentioned in my introduction, this all started because I had written a number of papers on various topics that ended up in this book. I wrote a number of the chapters myself but, for some chapters, I provided the outline, for other chapters, I provided content (like my papers), and for others, I provided guidance and direction. For the subjects in which I'm not a subject matter expert, the authors wrote the vast majority of their own content. The concept was to provide expert knowledge in every subject area. I attempted to bring one voice to this book, so you don't feel like you're reading 20 writing styles. I have read and reviewed every chapter a minimum of five times. I have included biographies on everyone, so you can see the wealth of knowledge and experience that went into the writing of this book.

Lynn Agans—Assistant Extraordinaire   A special thanks goes to my faithful assistant, Lynn Agans, for everything she did to make this book a success. Her time, dedication, and commitment to this book were hard on her physically and mentally—it's a tough challenge. Lynn pulled together and organized e-mails from people like you, performed countless reviews on the chapters, coordinated efforts with the other authors, kept the review process lively and flowing, and so much more. Lynn adapted and overcame all of the difficult situations to help me create a masterpiece. Thank you, Lynn, for your work on this book and for everything you do to make my job easier.

Darren Fulton—Chapters 1, 2, and 10   Darren Fulton is a senior consultant with TUSC with 12 years of experience in application programming, and six years specializing in Oracle. While he has written and presented at various Oracle user groups, this is Darren's first effort contributing to a book project of this scope. Darren stepped up to the challenge when I initially asked him to write Chapter 10. Then I asked if anyone could take on Chapter 1 and, once again, Darren took the challenge. Chapter 2 was already assigned to two other people, but their project and travel assignments pulled them away from writing the chapter. Darren quickly volunteered to write yet another chapter. Thank you Darren—you made a huge difference in writing these chapters.

Kevin Maher—Chapter 3   Kevin Maher is a TUSC consultant. He graduated from the University of Colorado and has been working with Oracle software since 1996. Kevin has been on assignment in Portland for months now. Traveling for an extended period is difficult, especially on your personal life. Kevin not only spent months in Portland, but he was also still able to write this chapter—that's a tough task. Thank you, Kevin!

Wayne Taylor—Chapter 4   Wayne Taylor is a senior consultant with TUSC. He has been working in Information Technology for over ten years. During that time,

Wayne has been a UNIX System Administrator, Oracle developer, Oracle DBA, and architecture designer. During his career, Wayne has implemented a number of Web-based architectures based on Oracle databases and Web servers. In my last book, Venkat Devraj wrote this chapter. When I contacted Venkat to update the chapter, however, he assured me it was more than a minor update—many things had changed. Another thing that changed for him personally was he had just raised venture capital and was starting a new business. So, unfortunately, he didn't have the time to update this chapter. I asked for volunteers within TUSC and Wayne quickly offered to update this chapter. Thank you, Wayne, for stepping up to the challenge and making the updates to this chapter!

Vicky Foster—Chapter 5   Vicky Foster is an Oracle DBA at TUSC with 12 years industry experience. She has seven years experience in analysis, data modeling, database design, legacy system conversion, and general database administration using Oracle and UNIX. Vicky recently relocated to Atlanta, Georgia, from Raleigh, North Carolina. She is a certified cardio kickbox and indoor cycling instructor. She also enjoys traveling, live jazz, and ethnic foods. After I wrote my last book, Vicky sent me an e-mail asking me about disaster planning—she didn't work for TUSC at that time, but she was writing a disaster-planning document. I filed the e-mail. Then, when I started to develop the outline for this book, I found Vicky's e-mail. It struck me this would make a great chapter for the new book. So I asked Vicky if she would write this chapter for the book. Vicky responded, saying something like, "Sorry for my delayed response, I just got back from Atlanta." We had just opened our office in Atlanta, but it only entered my mind briefly that maybe she was being recruited for a position at TUSC. I didn't say anything. Vicky agreed to write the chapter. About two weeks later, I saw an H/R document stating that Vicky Foster's background check had cleared. I thought, "Are there two Vicky Fosters?" This can't be the same Vicky I've asked to write the book. It was. Thanks, Vicky, not only for writing the chapter, but for joining the TUSC team. It's a small world, isn't it?

Robin Fingerson—Chapter 6 and 17   Robin Fingerson is a technical management consultant who has been with TUSC for three and a half years. She has ten years experience with Oracle as a DBA and as a custom application developer. Robin has worked with the Oracle development toolkit from its earliest versions and is "excited about the changes and new possibilities for the tools in the 9i release." In addition to her work with Oracle, Robin has been involved in Web publishing for several years. Beyond having heavy client demands, Robin had many other things going on while writing these chapters. Her "adapt and overcome" spirit is always inspirational to everyone around her. Robin updated Chapter 6 by adding significant content. Robin wrote the Forms portion of Chapter 17 from scratch. Thank you, Robin, for adapting and overcoming!

Mark Riedel—Chapter 7 and 11   Mark Riedel is a senior consultant with TUSC and has been with TUSC since 1993, specializing in PL/SQL and *i*AS applications using JavaScript, while teaching software classes on the side. I remember when Mark joined TUSC in 1993. I still lived in Chicago at that time. I used to do a lot of our training classes and I took pride in receiving the highest marks possible from my students. Then Mark started doing training classes, and his "marks" were higher than mine. Mark is an excellent instructor and an excellent educator. He's always sharing his knowledge with the world. Mark contributed to my last book and stepped up to the challenge yet again. In fact, Mark turned in both of his chapters nearly a month early. I can assure you Mark was the only person who holds that honor. Thank you, Mark!

Jason Bennett—Chapter 8   Jason Bennett is a senior principal consultant with Oracle Corporation's South Development Services consulting group and is based out of Charlotte, North Carolina. Jason has been an employee of Oracle Corporation since 1998 and he specializes in Oracle Internet-based solutions. Jason was an employee of TUSC from 1997 to 1998, based out of the Chicago office. Jason was a contributing author for my second book, *Oracle8i Web Development,* which came out in December 1999. Jason has been published in *Oracle Magazine* and has presented several times at Oracle Open World. It was unfortunate when Jason wanted to move to North Carolina—seeing him leave the TUSC team was sad. I've kept in touch with Jason and appreciate that he's taken the time to help contribute to my last two books. Jason took on the task of coordinating Chapter 8 and making it a success. Thank you, Jason!

Vince Vazquez—Chapter 8 and 13   Vince Vazquez is a technical management consultant with TUSC and has been in the Information Engineering industry for over 16 years. Nine of those years were spent in the United States Army as a programmer analyst. Vince has been working with Oracle since 1987. He enjoys the complete software life cycle and he feels nothing is more important than the client. When Vince is at a client site, they are guaranteed to have his full and undivided attention, as well as an unbiased opinion. It seems every project Vince has worked on, Oracle is being used on the backend. With Oracle9*i*, 9*i*AS, XML, Java, JSP, EJB, PL/SQL, Forms, and Reports, a client can be assured that with Oracle, it has the capability to produce mission-critical solutions to meet any of its needs. I've known Vince personally for some time now, and he has a great relationship with me and my family. Vince has come skiing with our Colorado TUSC Day group for a couple of years in a row now. And, Vince and his two boys (Christopher and Nicolas) also went to Tijuana with a group of my YPO friends, where we built a home for a family that didn't have one. Vince is a giving and kind person. Vince's contributions to Chapters 8 and 13 made a difference. Thank you, Vince.

Mike Linde—Chapter 9   Mike Linde is a senior consultant at TUSC. He has been writing computer applications for over 15 years with the last 8 years focusing on Oracle development. Mike has traveled throughout the United States, England, and South America while developing data mining applications and training end users on the use of Oracle and UNIX in conjunction with these applications. Mike has programmed in many languages, including Assembler, C, C++, Visual Basic, Basic, and Pascal. Since switching from Client/Server development to Web development, Mike has written applications using HTML, WML, XML, ASP, Perl, JavaScript, VBScript, and Java. Mike is our resident wireless expert. After writing the wireless components of our Time Reporting System (TRS) application and for our remote DBA products, I knew Mike was a perfect fit for this chapter. Mike has done an excellent job of documenting the Oracle9iAS Wireless Edition and how to develop applications that support cellular phones with WML. Thank you, Mike, for writing this chapter.

Marlene Theriault—Chapter 12   With over 19 years experience as an Oracle database administrator, Marlene Theriault is noted for her ability to make hard concepts easily understandable. Marlene's newest book, *Oracle Security Handbook,* coauthored with Aaron Newman, Oracle Press (Osborne McGraw-Hill) is now available. She is also the author of *Oracle8i Networking 101,* Oracle Press (Osborne McGraw-Hill), coauthor of the *Oracle8i DBA Handbook* with Kevin Loney (TUSC), *Oracle DBA 101* with Rachel Carmichael and James Viscusi, Oracle Press, and coauthor of *Oracle Security* with William Heney, O'Reilly and Associates. *The Oracle9i DBA Handbook,* written by Kevin Loney (TUSC) and Marlene Theriault is due out soon. I've known Marlene for quite some time now. She's absolutely the world's leading Oracle Security expert. I was initially slated to update the Security Chapter (I wrote it last time), but when I ran into Marlene at an Oracle User group conference, I immediately knew why I hadn't started the chapter yet—Marlene should write the chapter, not me. Thank you for stepping up to the challenge, Marlene, you've done a much better job than I ever could have.

Joe Nibert—Chapter 13   Joseph D. Nibert is a senior consultant at TUSC. Joseph has over seven years experience in building Oracle Web-based database applications. Joe took on the impossible task of coordinating the Java chapter. This is such a huge topic (as you see by the size of the chapter), it took several people to make this chapter a success. But, most of all, Joe pulled all the material together, coordinated the other authors, and made this chapter what it is today. Thank you, Joe, for making the Java chapter everything it is today!

Janet Bacon—Chapter 13   Janet Bacon is a TUSC senior consultant. Janet has been working in IT since 1986 and has been a database administrator since 1988. She has been responsible for maintaining Oracle, Sybase, and RdB databases. Janet's primary focus has been database design and implementation, but she has recently been concentrating on database application performance. Janet also teaches database administration and tuning classes for TUSC. She was kind enough to take on the challenge of writing about the Java Virtual Machine within *i*AS and the Oracle9*i* database. Thank you, Janet, for making the Java chapter better. Janet also performed numerous proof reviews to make the content perfect.

Chris Piacesi—Chapter 15   Chris Piacesi is a Technical Manager for Oracle Corporation in the State & Local Consulting group. He has over 12 years of information technology consulting, most of which included using Oracle and Oracle tools. Chris specializes in building custom justice and public safety applications, and he has led successful projects for several local, state, and federal law enforcement agencies. He was also a contributing author for *Oracle8i Web Development.* Chris helped with this chapter last time but, this time, he took on the entire contribution. Thank you, Chris.

Rich Zapata—Chapter 16   Richard E. Zapata is a senior consultant with TUSC. Rich has a good deal of experience with the Oracle9*i*AS Portal product, implementing it at numerous clients, including a subsidiary of a Fortune 500 company. He regularly contributes to the Oracle Portal discussion groups and is the content owner for the TUSC Oracle9*i*AS Portal class curriculum. Rich has taught and presented Oracle9*i*AS Portal numerous times, and, currently, he helped author the Oracle9*i*AS Portal portion of this book. Rich has over six years in the IT industry, including the last three with a focus on Oracle. Rich is without a doubt our local Portal expert. Rich developed, implemented, and supported TUSC's first production Portal application, which was developed for a customer. Rich did all this while writing the chapter. I was impressed with how much I learned when I read Rich's chapter and you will be, too! Thank you, Rich.

Dan Martino—Chapter 17   Dan Martino is a senior consultant at TUSC and has been an Oracle developer for the past nine years. His experience includes Oracle Forms, Reports, PL/SQL, Java, and Web Development. Dan is one of the funniest guys I know. He wrote the Reports section of Chapter 17, but he makes everything he does fun. Check out his examples! Thank you for making a difference, Dan, and thank you making us all laugh! Dan's a stand-up comic, so if you ever have him in a training class, you're sure to be entertained.

Gregg Petri—Chapter 19 and 20   Gregg C. Petri is a Senior Consultant for TUSC in the Lakewood, Colorado office. Gregg holds an M.S. in Computer Science and has over 11 years of experience in IT, the past 7 of which were working with Oracle databases and application servers. Gregg stepped up to the challenge of writing about something he knew little about—the Web Cache. This product was new enough that no experts on the subject could be found. However, Gregg quickly studied, learned, and tested the product. I found his chapter so exciting, I devoted countless hours to learning and understanding everything he wrote. Then Gregg and I copresented on Oracle Web Cache at the Rocky Mountain Oracle Users Group. What an honor that was! Chapter 20 was slated to discuss Oracle's configuration management via OEM. However, because Oracle decided to pull back the release of its *i*AS configuration support to version 2.0 of *i*AS, I decided Chapter 20 would cover Comanche and the other GUI configuration management tools for Apache. I asked Gregg if he would mind taking on this challenge. He quickly agreed. After writing this chapter and learning that Comanche often corrupts the configuration files, Gregg pointed out that Chapter 20 is in the "Oracle Tools" section of the book and this wasn't an Oracle Tool. Gregg was correct. We moved his content to Chapter 3, by passing it on to Kevin. Then I asked Gregg if he would start over, and write about OEM and other browser-based Oracle management tools. Gregg wrote this chapter with pride. Thank you, Gregg, for making a difference every day!

John Rago   John R. Rago is a management consultant at TUSC. John has been working with management information systems for more than 14 years, including the last 6 with a focus on Oracle. When I went looking for a resident Discoverer expert within TUSC, it was clear that John was that person. John's done a wonderful job of delivering an excellent chapter that will educate you about using Discoverer in a Web environment. Thank you, John.

Bob Taylor—Chapter 22   Robert W. Taylor is a senior technical management consultant with TUSC. A graduate of the University of Connecticut, he has been creating custom solutions with Oracle products for the last 14 years. Bob is the chief architect of TUSC's various Development Standards and Toolkits, which allow TUSC consulting teams to capitalize on teamwork for the efficient creation of high-quality business solutions. Bob is absolutely the guy you want on your team when it comes to maintaining code. His proactive debugging techniques can save you countless hours. Bob wrote this chapter the last time, too. Thank you, Bob, for making a difference on this chapter once again.

Steve Hamilton—Online chapter, "Good Sites"   Steven L. Hamilton is a Senior Consultant in the Detroit office of TUSC. He has worked in database administration for 16 years using TIS, SUPRA, UNIFY, and ORACLE. Steve worked for ten years as a developer prior to becoming a database administrator. Steve was awarded the Distinguished Service Medal while at the Defense Department for his work on databases during Desert Storm. He previously contributed to *Oracle8i Web Development,* wrote a user manual for "SQL*Loader" for the Defense Department, and has also written several books on Biblical subjects. Thank you, Steve, for updating this chapter. Not only did pulling all these links together take a huge amount of work, but also testing and verifying the content of each link.

My Review Team

A special thanks goes out to my review team: Mike O'Mara who served as the Technical Editor; Lisa Price, who provided hours of reviews; and Lynn Agans, who also provided numerous edits in this process. And a sincere thank you to Sten Vesterli, who was kind enough to review Chapters 13 and 15 for me.

Michael O'Mara—Technical Editor   Michael O'Mara is a TUSC Senior Consultant. Mike has over five years experience building Oracle applications and has spent the last two years building Web-based applications. Mike will tell you he didn't do it alone—he's a very kind and giving person. Mike also joined my family and me in Tijuana building homes. In a previous profession, Mike was a drywaller—the way they hang drywall in Mexico is a bit different than he was used to. I think Mike's question was, "where's the mud?" On this project, Mike was the mud that pulled this book together into a technically edited masterpiece. Without Mike, many of the examples wouldn't have worked. Mike contributed countless hours to make this book technically correct. This meant Mike had to install *many* products on his laptop. In fact, he bought a new laptop just for this project. When something didn't work as quoted, Mike made sure it was fixed and that comments were inserted to help you better understand the components needed to make it work. When Mike offered to take on this challenge, I warned him about how demanding it would be, but he didn't back down. In fact, Mike was amazingly fast, which kept us right on track. Thank you, Mike, for taking the challenge—you made a difference in every chapter. Everyone who reads this book will thank you for examples that work!

Lisa Price—TUSC Copy Editor   Lisa Price joined the TUSC team in January 2000, as a Technical Writer, based in the Chicago TUSC office. She has over 15 years of experience in writing and editing, in both the public and private sectors. Lisa has been wonderful to work with on this project. When Lisa reviewed the first chapter of the book, it came back with about 1,000 comments attached. She didn't want to upset me, or the original author, so rather than making changes to the content, she chose to make comments and suggestions. I assured Lisa I wouldn't take offense to her comments and she should just go ahead and make the changes—that I would review and accept her changes as I saw fit. Her changes were always right on the mark. She's provided you with a book that delivers a more consistent style and excellent grammar. Lisa made the copy-editing process an absolute pleasure—an experience I hadn't achieved to this level previously. Lisa is by far the best copy editor I've ever had the pleasure of working with. Thank you, Lisa, for also making a difference in every chapter!

Sten Vesterli—Reviewed Chapter 13 and 15   Sten Vesterli is an expert on Oracle Web technology and the author of *Oracle Web Applications 101,* published by Oracle Press. He has worked with the Oracle Web/Application Servers since the first version and he frequently speaks at international Oracle conferences on the topic of Oracle Web applications. Sten currently works for IconMedialab, helping customers mainly in Switzerland and Germany implement advanced Web solutions. I've known Sten for several years now. Sten approached me to coauthor his Oracle Web Applications 101 book. Initially I said I would but, later, I decided I was going to write this book, so I reneged on our agreement. Sten was left to write the book alone, after I helped with the outline. I did write the forward for Sten's book, but he certainly had the most difficult job of writing it alone. When I told Sten I was writing this book, he offered to help review chapters. The chapters Sten reviewed are a higher quality because of his time and commitment to making a difference. Thank you, Sten!

Senior Managers of TUSC

A special thank you to all of TUSC's senior management team: Burk Sherva, Dave Ventura, Dave Kaufman, Tony Catalano, Jake Van der Vort, Dan Rabinowitz, and Bill Lewkow. Without the senior management team (and Joe and Rich, of course) holding down the fort while I was working on the book, TUSC wouldn't be where it is today. Thank you, guys!

Osborne/McGraw-Hill and Oracle

Of course, all the people at Osborne/McGraw-Hill made writing this book a pleasure as well: Lisa McClain, Associate Acquisitions Editor; Ross Doll, Paulina Pobocha, Jessica Wilson, and Athena Honore, Acquisitions Coordinators; Marcia Baker, Copy Editor; and Patty Mon, Project Editor.

A sincere thank you to Margaret Mei, Senior Product Manager, Oracle9i Application Server, Oracle Corporation for her ongoing help and support. Margaret got me prereleases of all the products, which made my life a lot easier. Margaret also convinced Thomas to write the forward for this book. Thank you, Margaret.

Team TUSC

Everyone at TUSC has contributed to this book in some way, shape, or form. Whether directly or indirectly, each person has played a role in the completion of this book. All the fine employees and friends who work at TUSC: Lynn Agans, Anwer Ahmed, Brian Anderson, Martin Andrea, Joel Anonick, Diane Ansah, Michael Ault, Janet Bacon, Kamila Bajaria, Roger Behm, Ashok "A. J." Bhuvanagiri, Gregory Bogode, Michael Bonofiglio, Dean Bouchard, James Broniarczyk, Eric Broughton, Mark Bullen, Paul Burke, Mike Butler, Damir Calic, Karen Callaghan, Patrick Callahan, Bill Callahan, Alain Campos, Peter Cargill, Brian Carignan, Michael Castro, Tony Catalano, Deqiao "David" Chen, Michelle Chesterfield, Kiran Chimata, Emily Clark, Holly Clawson, Judy Corley, Janet Dahmen, Terry Daley, Rod Davis, Susan DiFabio, Doug Dikun, Barb Dully, Jeff Ellington, Matt Engels, Brett Feldmann, Kevin Fiedler,

Dan Filkins, Robin Fingerson, David Fornalsky, Vicky Foster, Darren Fulton, Craig Gauthier, Kevin Gilpin, Steven Glubka, Gary Goebel, Joseph Graham, Jason Grandy, Chelsea Graylin, Kathleen Greenhalgh, Mark Greenhalgh, John Gregory, John Grove, Paula Hahn, Andrew Hamilton, Steven Hamilton, Ora Handy, Scott Heaton, Mike Holder, Chris Holland, Ronald Holleman, Amy Horvat, Leslie Hutchings, Bruno Ierullo, Mohammad Jamal, Celeste Jenkins, Doug Kadoski, Mohammad Kanaan, David Kaufman, Teri Kemple, Prabhjot Khurana, Mike Killough, Chuck Krutsinger, Felix Lacap, Lynn Lafleur, Ron Lemanske, Alexander Levin, Bill Lewkow, Andrew Limouris, Mike Linde, Eric Linneman, Larry Linnemeyer, Ryan Litwin, Kevin Loney, Antonia Lopez, Doug Lundin, Kevin Maher, Matt Malcheski, Daniel Marsh, Dan Martino, Kevin Marvicsin, Gillian McGee, Wayne McGurk, Edward McPhail, Charlene Mo, David Muehlius, Donald Murray, David Naimark, Joe Nibert, Rich Niemiec, Christos Nikolaides, Mike O'Mara, Chris Ostrowski, Robert Palmatier, Mark Pelzel, Allen Peterson, Gregg Petri, Cory Pfohl, Nadica Podgurski, Robin Pond, Lisa Price, Preston Price, Gilbert Quesea, Dan Rabinowitz, John Rago, Heidi Ratini, Pamela Real, Bob Reczek, Sheila Reiter, Mark Riedel, Jennifer Riefenberg, Chris Rizzo, Scott Schmidt, Alan Schneider, Sabina Schoenke, Chad Scott, Kerry Scott, Larrel Scott, Charles Seaks, Julie Shaw, Raymond Shaw, Kevin Sheahan, Burk Sherva, Mick Simenc, Anthony Solosky, Kevin Start, Jack Stein, Thomas Suhrhoff, Pitcheswararao "Rao" Surapaneni, Randy Swanson, Linda Talacki, ZhiChen "Jenny" Tao, Robert Taylor, Wayne Taylor, Christopher Thoman, John Thompson, David Trch, Joe Trezzo, Joseph Tseng, Joel Tuisl, James Turner, Razi Ud-Din, Jay Urban, Jason Van Ausdall, Jake Van Der Vort, James Vaughn, Vince Vazquez, Dave Ventura, Jon Vincenzo, Jack Wachtler, Robert Wall, James Walsh, Kimberly Washington, Michael Williams, Chuck Wisely, Dan Wittry, Thomas Wood, Bob Yingst, Amy Zahnen, Rich Zapata, and Qi Zhou.

From the Coauthors and Contributors

The following thoughts and comments are from some of the people who contributed to this book:

Darren Fulton: "Seeing a book come together from the inside has been an amazing experience. I certainly have a new respect for anyone committed and crazy enough to author a technical book. It's certainly not a job for the timid. When programming, it's easy to concentrate on the problem at hand and focus on the immediate details in front of your nose. By giving me the opportunity to contribute to this effort, Brad has certainly opened my eyes to a whole bigger world out there." Darren would like to thank his wife, Barbara, and his children, Collin and Emma, for the gift of time they gave to the project.

Kevin Maher: "*i*AS is an excellent product and I have enjoyed working with it and writing about it. I would like to thank Deb and my parents for their support."

Vicky Foster: "First thanks to God the Creator, for it is only through Him that I am able to prosper. Next, thank you to the friends who read, reread, and reread my rough drafts. Phyllis, Christopher, Veronica, and Franklin, you were most patient and honest in your feedback. Thank you to my family for their continued support in all that I do. Duane, Tinea, Vincent, Barbara, Clarence, Joan, Eddie, Mia, Kaesaan, Grandma Tynes, and Grandma Mimi, our support for one another is forever and there is power in small numbers. And, lastly, thank you to Bradley Brown for seeing enough potential in my sample templates and trusting enough in my ability to offer a never-before published author the great opportunity to participate in this book."

Joe Nibert: "I would like to thank my wonderful wife Heather for encouraging me to put in the extra effort and assisting in writing parts of this book, and my infant daughter, Alexis, who showed me how to look at everything as if I were seeing it for the first time. Sharing knowledge and experience with others is extremely gratifying, and I'm lucky to have been a part of the generation of the book."

Sten Vesterli: "When I wrote *Oracle Web Applications 101,* there were many topics that I just couldn't fit in. I'm, therefore, happy to have been able to contribute to Brad's bible of Oracle Web development that continues where my own introductory book leaves off."

Janet Bacon: "Thirteen years ago, two of the most influential people in my career, Lucia Allen-Voreis and Denny Benson, suggested I dive into what was then the latest in technology—relational database systems. They thought it would be a great career path for me, so they created a new DBA position at our company and assigned me to it. Little did I know at that point how much it would change the direction of my life. I want to say thank you, Lucia and Denny, for all your support throughout the years and your endless confidence in me."

Rich Zapata: "Writing a chapter is a tough endeavor. There are specific things I learned (the hard way) and the first is this: as soon as you're assigned the task, ATTACK! Don't let up. Because you must be sure of what you're writing, there's a *lot* of time you spend testing and making sure your examples work. Keep on it, especially if you have client obligations. Use time wisely and get a laptop. It's certainly hard work, but once you print that first draft, you'll be the happiest person alive."

"I also want to thank Master Lock Company, for its patience with the Portal product and for incredible support; and Suburban Library System, for its willingness to go beyond the boundaries and try new things, which inspired me to do the same."

Gregg Petri: "I would like to thank my wife, Aimee and my son, Chase, for all their support and patience while the book was in development. I feel fortunate to have been given the opportunity to contribute my knowledge and experience."

John Rago: "I owe a very special thanks to my mom and dad, Patricia and Angelo Rago, for providing me with everything, the least of which are values of hard work and determination, qualities that have enabled me to make this contribution to Brad's book. I'd also like to thank Brad for the opportunity and his understanding, and Joel Anonick for his timely input and Discoverer expertise."

Steve Hamilton: "I thank my parents, Lloyd and Berneice, for their help and encouragement over the years."

Jason Bennett: "I would like to thank my wife Terri and my children, Rachel and Zachary, for sacrificing valuable husband and daddy time for my writing efforts. I also want to thank Brad Brown for the honor and privilege of being a coauthor for this book"

Dan Martino: "I have been working with Oracle for the past nine years and never found myself running out of challenges. Working with Brad on this book insured I never will. Brad, thanks for the encouragement and kind words during the development of the Reports Chapter and for instilling in me the concept of "Sleep is for cowards." I would like to thank my fiancée Mary P. Skala for her encouragement and support in developing this chapter. Mary, I look forward to resuming our Saturday morning exercise walks to Dairy Queen."

Mike O'Mara: "A special thanks goes to Scott Heaton, Darren Fulton, Doug Lundin, Gregg Petri, Rod Davis, Jay Urban, Jennifer Riefenberg, Gillian McGee, and Brad Brown for helping with the technical edits, I could never have accomplished this alone. I would also like to thank my wonderful wife, Brenda and my son, Caleb, for the encouragement and support throughout the editing process. Working with the *Oracle9i Web Development* book has been a great opportunity for me."

Lisa Price: "Thank you, Brad, for your vision, support, and belief in my abilities; and Lynn Agans and Mike O'Mara for your companionship and senses of humor during this adventure. Thanks, too, to Susan DiFabio, for your encouragement and support, and Bob Reczek, for being my sounding board and cheerleader. Special thanks to my husband Jackson for all the sacrifices you made so I could work on this book, and for your unflagging encouragement, friendship, and love; and my children, Lindsay, J. T., and Spencer, for reminding me of the simple pleasures and ultimate joy in life. Finally, Brad, Rich, and Joe, thank you for putting together a company that truly defines the word 'Team.' Your leadership is inspiring."

Wayne Taylor: "My thanks go out to the many people who have worked with me over the years but, especially, to my wife Annie and my children, Heather and Jacob, for putting up with many years of reading and "playing" with computers. I would also like to thank the Information Technology teams at the following customers because they have given me many challenges to exercise the gray matter and directly/indirectly have input within my chapter: Flexben Corporation, Troy, Michigan; Interfirst Bank, Ann Arbor, Michigan; and University of Michigan (ITD), Ann Arbor, Michigan."

Vince Vazquez: "I want to thank our client, Rockwell Automation, in Milwaukee Wisconsin, for allowing us time to learn as we produced a complete state of the art Object/Relational/XML data repository."

Chris Piacesi: "I would like to thank my wife, Ann and children, Lisa and Joseph, for their support. I also want to thank Brad Brown for the opportunity to contribute to this book."

A great number of people contributed to this book by the questions they asked about *i*AS, by being a customer, or just being a friend. These people include Natalie Webb, Greg Greenwood, Ellen Robinson, Carl Cozine, Neil Bauman, Marcia Wood,

Steve Leatherman, Monty Sooter, Ron Rose, Tom Sheridan, Frank Ress, Terri Miller, Mary McGee, Dave Leonard, and so many more.

Thanks to everyone who sends me an e-mail with a question in it. These end up as Tips or information included in the chapters and are an invaluable source of information for me, and for others, who now can read them.

If I left out your name, you're in my heart and thoughts. Thank you for buying a copy of this book.

Introduction

In my Oracle8*i* Web Development book's introduction, I mentioned that Harry S. Dent predicted we would witness a strong spending wave until at least 2009, when the Dow reaches 20,500. Was Harry wrong or is the current economic situation just a bump in the road? Who could have predicted the Feds would bump up interest rates to the point that consumers would decide to save money, causing an inventory surplus, resulting in an economic slowdown that would put the vast majority of IT projects on hold? Is that what happened? What will history say? The world moved from the world of dotcom to dotbomb in less than six months. Could we have imagined that the IT professional would go from being in high demand and in an employees' market to high surplus and, therefore, an employers' market? Is this all a result of the year 2000 programmers that are now available? Is it really the Fed's fault? As of September 2001, according to some sources, there's still more demand than supply for the IT professional. One source says the sky is falling, the other says it's fallen, and yet another says things have never been better. I guess it all depends on where you stand in the food chain at this point in time. Are you better off than you were a year ago?

Is the Internet a fad, is its need dissipating? It's certainly been confirmed this isn't the case. With DSL service and cable modems in many homes across the United States, we're proving that the Evernet (always on Internet) is becoming part of our daily lives. When will we have a wireless Internet-connected electronic tablet that provides the same functionality (with handwriting and voice recognition), size, weight, and durability of a pad of paper? ViewSonic has a Tablet PC today—we're getting closer to being completely wireless every day.

My kids look everything up on the Internet. Whether we're headed to Branson, Missouri, or 215 Union Blvd in Lakewood, Colorado, we get our directions not from a printed map, but from the Internet. When I was a kid, most of my friends had CB radios at home. This was an early version of instant messaging. If you wanted a private channel to discuss something, you set up an algorithm with your friends—channel 13 really meant 28 and channel 3 really meant 7. Today's kids have instant messaging to communicate with their friends. They say it's easier to communicate with their friends and they're right. The phone doesn't ring on the other end—their parents don't intercept the call—it's OK for girls to "call" boys—and the list goes on. Do you really answer your phone at home anymore? Do you screen the calls with caller ID? Do you block solicitors from calling? In Colorado, we can register our desire to ban solicitations on the Internet (**http://www.coloradonocall.org**)—this sure strikes me as an excellent XML opportunity. We used to have an entire bookshelf filled with Oracle manuals (today it would require at least five shelves), but all the Oracle documentation is now available on the Internet (**http://docs.oracle.com**). Will the Internet become as critical as your phone (for 911) or electricity? I believe it will—it's just a matter of time.

Computers continue to get faster and faster. In fact, it was recently announced that the world's faster computer today resides at Lawrence Livermore National Lab (LLNL). This computer operates at 12.3 teraflops, contains 8192 PIII processors, has 4 terabytes of memory and more than 160 terabytes of disk space. That's a huge amount of processing power. Compaq recently announced it will have a 30-teraflop computer available for sale in 2003. LLNL plans to reach 100 teraflops by 2005.

What Is the Future of the Internet?

The Internet . . . E-commerce . . . B2B . . . B2C . . . the Wireless Web . . . high-speed Internet access . . . Internet 2. With all the facets of the Internet, how can anyone predict what the future will bring?

In a Congressional Research Service Issue Brief done by the National Council for Science and the Environment (10/24/00), Rita Tehan discusses the difficulties in measuring the Internet—its scale, the number and types of users, and so forth. One problem is many domain names are unused. Another difficulty is some sites are just synonyms for other sites. Estimates for the number of people actually using the Internet differ greatly. The difficulty here is partly because analysts use different survey methods and different definitions of "Internet access." Some companies might count users at age 2, while others might begin at age 16 or 18. It's also difficult to survey who the Internet users are. How do you measure the use of college students or workers who browse the WWW on the job? Then, there's the issue of methodology and just how the surveys are conducted.

According to this Issue Brief, "The Internet is now growing at a rate of about 40 percent to 50 percent annually (for machines physically connected to the Internet), according to data from the Internet Domain Survey, the longest-running survey of Internet hosts." In 1969, there were 4 Internet hosts; in 1989, there were 130,000. In 1999, there were 56,218,000 hosts. That's pretty impressive.

On **http://www.internet indicators.com/facts.html**, a counter shows the Global Internet Commerce Revenue since 1998. This changes at a rate of around $100,000 every ten seconds. It's amazing to watch the rate at which money is being spent! Additional facts and figures can also be found on this site, such as 10 million homes in the United States will be networked by 2003.

The International Offshore Entrepreneur has an article titled "The Internet: Road to Riches . . .or Is It?" at **http://www.goldhaven.com/ioi/Art10698.htm**. A study by eMarketer is used to show some interesting numbers. For example, consumer Internet purchases are expected to reach $26 billion by 2002. B2B is expected to reach $258 billion by 2002. This study also shows that "as in the offline world, the top 10 percent of e-commerce businesses account for more than 90 percent of sales over the Web. According to the study, while 97 percent of large corporations are connected in some way to the Net, only about a third of their small business counterparts are online today. And, while 33 percent of large companies are companies conducting sales over the net, only 4 percent of small business firms are engaged in similar transactions."

Wendy McAuliffe, in an article titled, "One billion users will drive the Internet by 2005," states that e-commerce revenues will be up to $5 trillion by 2005.

In "The 5-Year Forecast" by David Lake, he states, "annual consumer e-commerce should jump almost 500 percent to $269 billion in 2005, according to Jupiter Research."

So Who Is Correct?

In an article by Todd Phillips from Advanced Manufacturing Magazine, he starts out by saying, "Forget the numbers. It doesn't matter whether B2B e-commerce hits $5.7 billion or $7.3 billion by 2003 or by 2010. Analysts and experts all use different methods to calculate their predictions. But the only thing that is deadly consistent is their belief that the numbers are going up. Fast. That means more people spending more time online, and more money."

To back up this statement, Mr. Phillips gives forecasts from several research groups. For example, one quarter of all B2B purchases will be made online by 2003 (Source: Boston Consulting Group). According to Deloitte Research, B2B e-commerce will dominate the B2C side by a factor of six, reaching $1.3 trillion by 2003. A study by the Gartner Group estimates that B2B e-commerce will skyrocket from about $145 billion in 1999 to $7.3 trillion in 2004, accounting for 7 percent of all global sales transactions. Forrester Research predicts that global e-commerce will reach $6.9 trillion in 2004, capturing 8.6 percent of the world's sales of goods and services.

So what is the future of the Internet? It's hard to say. A couple of things are certain, though. The first one is the Internet is not a fad. The second is the future of Web Development is Java. In an article by Peter Galli from *eWeek,* a series of studies conducted by Evans Data Corp showed that "developers using Java will outnumber those using C/C++ by next year. Janel Garvin, vice president of research at Evans said that more than half of North American developers use Java today, with that number expected to rise by 10 percent next year."

Components Needed

To make everything in this book work, you need to install the following Oracle products:

Oracle Database version 8*i* (8.1.7) or 9*i*

- You need Oracle9*i* for Ultra Search (Chapter 25) and for the Oracle9*i* features discussed elsewhere

- Otherwise, version 8.1.7 will do

*i*AS 1.0.2.2 Enterprise Edition

- Starting with Chapter 2, you need *i*AS

- For the Java (Chapter 13), PL/SQL (Chapter 14), Perl (online chapter), and PHP (online chapter) modules, the standard edition of *i*AS will do

- Ideally, you'll install the Enterprise Edition, which is required for Wireless Edition (Chapter 9), Portal (Chapter 16), Developer (Chapter 17), IFS (Chapter 18), Web and Database Cache (Chapter 19), and OEM (Chapter 20)

XML Library

- For some of Chapter 8, you need to download the latest libraries from technet

- Otherwise, the standard edition of *i*AS will do

Additional optional components you may want to consider:

- HTML GUI Editor, such as Dreamweaver or FrontPage

Audience

This book is written for individuals—like you—and for businesses that are looking for a comprehensive, cost-effective development environment that easily accommodates developing and deploying applications on the Web. You should be familiar with Oracle and the Internet architecture, and you should have some experience on how an Application Server works. For extreme beginners, a perfect prerequisite to this book is my first book, *Oracle Application Server Web Toolkit Reference* (Osborne/McGraw-Hill, 1998). If you're planning to develop applications using Oracle's prior Web server technology, you'll want to consider my prior book, *Oracle8i Web Development* (Osborne/McGraw-Hill, 1999).

How this Book Is Organized

This book is full of excellent Web development information. When I planned to update my Oracle8*i* book, I estimated that about 70 percent of this content would be new content. I grossly underestimated how much things had changed—I was wrong. There are so many features and massive product rewrites, about 90 percent of the book had to be redone. Because I didn't feel it was fair to leave the remaining 10 percent unchanged, about 9.9 percent of that was updated. In other words, not a single chapter, in fact, not a single page in this book went untouched. Therefore, this isn't a revision of the Oracle8*i* Web Development book but, rather, an entirely new book, proving that technology continues to move at the speed of light, so hang on!

You might be wondering which Oracle products you should use. Figure 1 shows the strengths and weaknesses of the different Oracle products, languages, and tools. Take some time to understand which tools should be used for your application components.

You begin your journey in the "Getting Prepared" section with a look into the Oracle Web architecture in Chapter 1. Chapter 1 looks at this radically new architecture from the Web server on up. OAS used the Spyglass Web server, whereas *i*AS uses Apache. In Chapter 2, I look at the Installation of the entire *i*AS suite. I'd highly recommend reading this chapter before you touch the installation disks. This can help you avoid some pain. Additionally, you might learn you don't even need to install *i*AS separately because *i*AS is installed with the database (version 8.1.7 and beyond). Chapter 2 can help you understand the components of the different *i*AS versions. Because the configuration of *i*AS isn't as easy as it was for OAS, I'd highly recommend you read Chapter 3 to learn about configuring and tuning *i*AS. In Chapter 4, I discuss Oracle's new RAC technology that takes Oracle Parallel Server (OPS) to the next level—providing near linear scalability, but also 24×7 reliability and functionality. Chapter 4 also discusses other options to keep your databases running 24 hours a day, 7 days a week. In Chapter 5, I discuss the importance of having a disaster plan in place. What things should you consider? Do you rely on

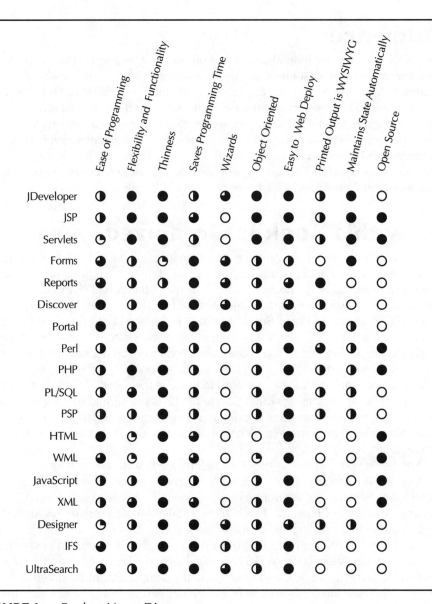

FIGURE I.   *Product Usage Diagram*

other vendors for any of your processing? What will happen to your site if those vendors suddenly go away? What if they go out of business? Or, worse, what if their site is hacked? Will you be prepared?

Next we move into the Core Concepts of Web development. Chapter 6 reviews some basic and advanced HTML tip and techniques. New browser and HTML features—such as icons on the address line to Cascading Style Sheets—are discussed. In Chapter 7, I show you some excellent JavaScript tips and techniques. If you don't know JavaScript already, this chapter can teach you the syntax of the JavaScript language—using a comparison of JavaScript to the PL/SQL language (because most Oracle developers know PL/SQL already). Chapter 8 reviews the next big thing: XML. Oracle has provided vast libraries of code to support all your XML needs. Whether you plan on using the DOM or SAX parsers, Oracle provides them both. This all results in a huge savings on programming time. You can perform database insert, update, and delete operations through XML. Oracle's XSQL functionality enables you to extract data in an XML format using a SQL query. In Chapter 8, I provide you with an XSQL generator (written in Java Server Pages). The XML processor can also incorporate XML Style Sheets Translators (XSLT) that enable you to transcode the XML data from one format to virtually any other format. No longer do you need to write countless loading scripts for each of your customers. With XML, you can publish to a standard API using XSLT to alter data to the API format. The XML Advanced Query (AQ) features offload demand from peak processing times, so you can maximize the throughput of your applications. Oracle9*i* database provides a new XML datatype as well. In Chapter 9, I discuss Wireless Web development—from WML to the Oracle9*i*AS Wireless Edition. If you plan to consider developing any applications for wireless devices, you'll be impressed by Oracle's approach to transcoding your HTML applications for delivery on a variety of wireless devices without writing any additional code. If you want to develop an application for cell phones, you'll be happy to learn about the Wireless PL/SQL Toolkit that we've written and documented in the Chapter 9. In Chapter 10, you learn how to migrate your applications from OAS to *i*AS. You'll be pleased that although the underlying architecture changed drastically, if you have OAS PL/SQL applications, the migration is easy. In Chapter 11, you learn about several of the built-in PL/SQL packages useful for Web development that Oracle provides with the database. These packages include utl_smtp, utl_http, utl_tcp, and dbms_obfuscate. Examples are provided for each of these packages. The capability to send e-mail (utl_smtp) and read Web pages (utl_http) are my two favorite built-in packages. Chapter 12 can help you learn about several security measures you could take into consideration. When it comes to publishing a server on the Web, you want to be cautious. A few security issues exist with *i*AS that could cause potential breaches or hacking on your site, so be sure to read Chapter 12.

*i*AS uses third-party modules to support extensions to the Apache server. The next section, "Modules," provides tips, techniques, and plenty of sample code for the Java, PL/SQL, Perl, and PHP modules. In Chapter 13, Java is covered extensively. Again, because most Oracle developers know PL/SQL, the chapter begins with a lesson to help you move from the world of PL/SQL into the world of Java development. As of *i*AS 1.0.2.2, Oracle replaced the Java engine to provide faster execution and an EJB-compliant engine, so they could compete directly with BEA and IBM's application servers. At the time OAS was released, Oracle hyped Java and how they were supporting Java. However, the open-source application server Java community was under rapid and constant changes. Oracle talked a lot about being CORBA- and EJB-compliant. The result was that my prior book (*Oracle8i Web Development*) was criticized in the Amazon reviews because it didn't cover enough Java. The reality was Oracle didn't have good Java capabilities with OAS. As you see in Chapter 13, this isn't true with *i*AS. Now we have JSPs, true EJB support, and much more. Also important to note is I've personally encountered a major paradigm change as a result of Oracle's true support for Java now. Java is better than PL/SQL in many ways. From the object-oriented capabilities, to the huge open-source community (lots of free libraries of code), to the huge developer base (tons of free help and support), to the power of the language (fewer limitations—such as utl_file's file size limit of 32K), to Oracle's BC4J (their extensive Java library), to the fact that you can do Java free—Java is better. This doesn't mean it's necessarily better for your organization, however. You must take into consideration your core competency as a programming unit. Do you know Java? Can you develop and support an application faster with PL/SQL? If so, you'll enjoy Chapter 14, which covers the PL/SQL cartridge extensively. You'll be excited to learn that PL/SQL isn't going away—in fact, numerous improvements have been made to the PL/SQL engine and PL/SQL module. For example, the utl_tcp, utl_smtp, and owa_cache packages have been added. The addition of PL/SQL Server Pages (similar to Java Server Pages) is a welcome addition to the PL/SQL module. You'll also be excited to learn about the UnWebAlchemy tool that I wrote. It converts previously written PL/SQL procedures into PSP files. The native compiler also adds considerable speed to the PL/SQL engine. In the online chapters, Perl and PHP, you learn about the Perl and PHP modules, respectively. These modules provide an upgrade path for the Perl and LiveHTML cartridges that were used (although infrequently) in OAS.

Next we move on to the "Oracle Tools" section, where we discuss Designer, Portal, Developer (Forms and Reports), IFS, Web and Database Caching, Oracle Enterprise Manager, and Discoverer. Although I personally am not a Designer expert, in Chapter 15, Chris has written an excellent chapter full of tips for using Designer to generate Web code. In Chapter 16, you'll be happy to learn about Portal. Although Portal is an upgrade for WebDB, the name change reflects the magnitude of differences from WebDB. This isn't WebDB with a new name. Rather, it's an important component within *i*AS. Portal provides an excellent development foundation for any Web application. From the single signon capabilities to Portlets like the powerful forms, reports, charts and calendars, you'll be impressed by Portal. In Chapter 17, you learn about Developer Forms and Reports. Whether you're deploying your Developer applications on an intranet or the Internet, you'll want to read this chapter. Developer Reports provides a powerful Web deployment platform for all your reporting needs. In Chapter 18, the long-awaited (and hyped) Internet

File System (IFS) will prove to be a welcome addition to the *i*AS family of Oracle tools. There happens to be a post-IFS installation bug in version 1.0.2.2, so be sure to refer to document 150114.1 to resolve this bug. I'm confident that by the time this book is published, this bug will no longer exist in the IFS configuration. You'll be impressed by the IFS capabilities to be mounted as a powerful file system that stores its data in the Oracle database. In Chapter 19, you'll be amazed at the power of not only the Oracle database cache, but also of Oracle's Web Cache product. Achieving 2 to 150 times the performance for your dynamically generated content will surely turn your head. This is especially true if several people will be hitting the same dynamic content at about the same time. Be sure to read about this powerful *i*AS feature. In Chapter 20, you see how you can use the Oracle Enterprise Manager (and other tools) via a Web browser. Each of the tools is discussed and demonstrated in this chapter.

Finally, we move into the "Ongoing Support" section of this book. In Chapter 21, I review various methods of troubleshooting problems you might have with your application. Chapter 22 helps you enhance your application debugging capabilities. Don't elect to read this chapter when you're ready to debug your code. Rather, read this chapter *before* you write any code. You'll want to be sure to include the generic debugging techniques shown in this chapter. In Chapter 23, you learn how to read and analyze the logs generated by the *i*AS server. This can be an important skill, so you understand what, when, and for how long people are hitting your site. If you're deploying your site on the Internet and search engine ranking is important to you, be sure to study Chapter 24. The techniques discussed in this chapter can help you to achieve a number one ranking in the search engines. I have used these techniques and, believe me, they work. Because no Web site is complete with online search capabilities within the site, you want to read Chapter 25. You previously had to purchase a separate content generation tool (such as Wisebot, which no longer exists) or build your own spider to build the search engine content. However, Oracle incorporated Oracle Text (previously Intermedia) into the database (as of 9*i*). Ultra Search is built on top of Oracle Text. It uses spider technology to read through a Web site and index content. Oracle Ultra Search is also capable of indexing data in database tables and external files. This functionality provides a powerful search engine for your Web applications. Oracle Text enables you to search text (and long) fields in the database for text-based content. A new index type was added in Oracle9*i* for document classification applications using Oracle Text. Finally, if you're not too tired tonight, you can read Chapter 26, which covers application and load testing of your Web applications. Performance is a key component of any Web application and this chapter can help you maximize your application's accuracy, performance, and reliability. The online chapter, "Good Sites," reviews a number of Web sites that might help you with your Web development.

Best of luck on your journey to reading this book! So many Web-related topics exist (such as the E-mail server and Oracle Applications 11*i*), that, unfortunately, they couldn't all be covered in this book, but I hope this book proves useful for you. It might take you more than a day to read it. Generally, although this book was ordered with the goal of being read from Chapter 1 all the way through Chapter 26, skipping around from one chapter to another should also prove successful. I hope to get this book published as an ebook, too, so if you're interested in reading this on a reader, watch for this format soon.

You'll also want to take the time to learn about all the new Oracle9*i* database features, which are extremely comprehensive. These include advanced queuing e-mail (dbms_aq), list partitioning, enhanced object relational technology, new OLAP services, fast fault recovery, OEM enhancements, database resource manager, RAC, enhanced cursor sharing, security improvements (such as predisabled accounts), better LDAP support, materialized view improvements (such as fast refresh of complex views), external tables (flat files that can be queried with SQL), online changes allowed in the database, flashback queries, user-defined events, the new log miner, data guard, and B2B integration. Amazing, isn't it?

Book Conventions

The following conventions are used in this book to help you:

- **Boldface** is used for user input.

- *Italics* is used to emphasize and to highlight the first use of important terms.

- Keys or keypresses are formatted in small caps (ESC). Keypress combinations are separated with a hyphen (ALT-F). Sequences of keypress combinations are separated by a comma (ALT-F,O).

- Numbered lists indicate step-by-step instructions.

About TUSC

Bradley D. Brown, Richard J. Niemiec, and Joseph C. Trezzo are cofounders of TUSC, an award-winning, senior-level consulting firm that provides management and technical consulting support in Oracle—the world's leading supplier of software for information management and second-largest independent software company. TUSC consultants leverage their vast experience and knowledge to provide best practices expertise, resulting in successful implementations in the core service areas of Database Services, Expert Business Solutions, Remote Database Administration, and Training & Mentoring.

TUSC is experiencing tremendous growth in both employees and clients. The Atlanta office—which opened in 2001—is the fifth location for the company, and is one of three-to-six new regional offices TUSC is looking to open in key areas around the United States.

In addition to ranking two consecutive years on the Inc. 500 list of fastest-growing companies, TUSC was previously inducted into the Chicago Entrepreneurship Hall of Fame and won Arthur Anderson-Chicago's Best Practices Award for "Emerging Technologies" and Ernst & Young LLP's Entrepreneur of the Year Award in the category of "E-Developer."

This book joins more than 20 others written by TUSC employees and is the latest addition to The Ultimate Oracle Library series of books.

About the Founders

Bradley D. Brown, Richard J. Niemiec, and Joseph C. Trezzo founded TUSC—a full-service consulting company specializing in Oracle—more than a decade ago. TUSC has evolved into a senior-level consulting company recognized as an industry leader within and outside the Oracle community.

The three energetic entrepreneurs created TUSC under "The Ultimate Software Consultants" name in late 1988, after separately leaving Oracle Corp. to pursue individual interests. Over time, they came to realize the many goals they shared and decided to combine their efforts into a top-notch consulting, software, and training company. That company became known as TUSC.

At the outset, Brown, Niemiec, and Trezzo did it all—from developing something as technical as an infrastructure and as simple as an employee handbook, while using Brown's home as an office. Today, the company is recognized as a premier player in the consulting industry.

When they were at Oracle Corp., Brown, Niemiec, and Trezzo were known as the "Three Musketeers" for their all-for-one, one-for-all approach. It's the same dedication to customer and employee satisfaction that has helped them achieve greatness with TUSC.

Bradley D. Brown

This book marks the third Brad Brown has written for Oracle Press and Osborne/McGraw-Hill. He previously authored *Oracle Application Server Web Toolkit Reference* (1998) and *Oracle8i Web Development* (1999). Brad is recognized worldwide as a leading Oracle author and is involved with numerous organizations, having served as president and membership chair of the Rocky Mountain Oracle Users Group and Executive Editor of *Exploring Oracle DBMS* magazine.

Brad now serves as chairman of the board and chief architect for TUSC. His vast experience and expertise earned him additional roles as chief information officer of Open Access Broadband Networks and board member for GeekCruises, Lantech Inc., Colorado Uplift, and Cactus Strategies. Brad is currently education chairperson for the Colorado chapter of the Young Presidents Organization after having previously served as its inventory of skills chairperson, technology officer, membership, and assistant education chairperson. Brad also was a cofounder and acting chief technology officer for Eventconnex Inc.

Joseph C. Trezzo

Joe Trezzo has been designing, developing, deploying, administering, and managing Oracle-based systems since 1985 (version 4). He's a certified Oracle DBA, an accomplished author—having served as editor in chief of *Exploring Oracle DBMS* magazine—and a VIP presenter at international conferences. Joe authored *Oracle PL/SQL Tips and Techniques* in 1999 for Oracle Press and Osborne/McGraw-Hill. He has presented papers at the last 15 international Oracle conferences; earning top honors each of the last ten years.

Joe is cofounder, president, and chief operating officer for TUSC. He has a solid business background and is a strong believer in education. His deep understanding of business can be directly linked to his undivided dedication to clients. Joe vows to do whatever it takes to reach a project's goals to ensure customer satisfaction. He also believes in people and that true teamwork is a key to any company's success. This is a proven philosophy he often shares with colleagues during expert tracks at entrepreneur and leadership conferences. Joe was inducted into the Illinois Entrepreneur Hall of Fame in 1988 and awarded the Ernst & Young Entrepreneur of the Year in 2001.

Richard J. Niemiec

Rich Niemiec is the author of *Oracle Performance Tuning Tips and Techniques*, published by Oracle Press and Osborne/McGraw-Hill in 1999. His colleagues recognize him as an expert in the industry, having delivered the top presentation at international Oracle users groups on several occasions. Rich currently serves as president of both the International Oracle Users Group-Americas and Midwest Oracle Users Group. He previously was executive editor of *Select* magazine and editor in chief of *Exploring Oracle DBMS* magazine. He was the 1998 Chris Wooldridge Award winner.

A master in database administration who often consults with members of the media on technological trends and the effect they'll have on the industry at large, Rich instills the Traits of the TUSC Leader—enthusiasm, initiative, integrity, knowledge, loyalty, moral and physical courage, respect, self-control, tact, and unselfishness. His experience in data processing ranges from teaching to consulting, with emphasis in database administration, performance tuning, project management, and technical education.

PART
I

Getting Prepared

CHAPTER
1

Architecture

ith the introduction of Oracle9*i* Application Server (9*i*AS), Oracle presents the development community with a full-featured suite of tools and applications to develop, deploy, manage, and tune applications for the Web. Oracle9*i*AS is a reliable, scalable, middle-tier application server that enables you and your organization to benefit from the true power of the Internet. As illustrated in Figure 1-1, rather than being a single product, Oracle9*i*AS is a collection of services designed to work together to deliver content dynamically to the Web. Your organization can pick and choose the services it needs, and can add new services as you grow and

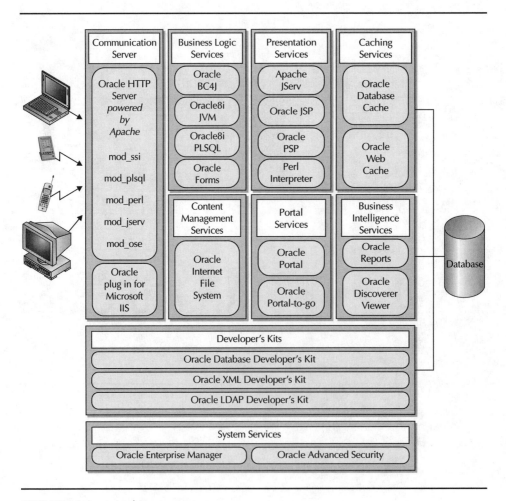

FIGURE I-I. *Architecture*

change. Oracle9*i*AS is designed to enable the newest Web development methods, tools, and standards, supporting Java J2EE, XML, PL/SQL, or Java Server Pages, and many others we cover in detail throughout this book. Oracle9*i*AS also provides services for configuring the other application services, configuring Web and database caching, and a host of other application components.

Oracle classifies the 9*i*AS services into several groups according to the type of support they provide: Communication Services, Web servers to handle requests to and from the Web; Business Logic Services, the development tools and languages for building custom applications; Presentation Services, the dynamic Web page development tools; Caching Services, tools to improve Web site performance by caching common data or pages; Content Management Services, IFS for managing documents in the database; Portal Services for publishing links, content, and applications for the end user to subscribe; Business Intelligence Services, useful for creating reports and ad-hoc queries of user activity on your sites; and, finally, Database Services, the Oracle9*i* Database for storing your application data. As part of the 9*i*AS Suite, Oracle also provides several developers kits to aid in creating dynamic, flexible applications, and tools to manage the database, and security once the Web sites are deployed.

The openness of this suite affords you and your site designers and developers tremendous flexibility and scalability in the tools and services you want to use. As your needs grow, you can add services or change development direction without leaving the integrated Oracle environment. For example, if you're well-versed in Oracle Forms, but don't have much experience with the Web, you might choose to deploy your forms and reports on the Web today, and add Java or PL/SQL Server Pages as you gain more experience. If you have static pages you want to make dynamic, you can gain management control of the static content using IFS, deploy them today, and add Java tags to create Java Server Pages (JSPs) that query their dynamic content from the database later. As your site traffic grows, you might find caching most-used data or pages beneficial to increase performance. When your Web sites become *really* popular (and I know they will), you can deploy your applications and data across multiple servers, add more caching, and manage everything using the Enterprise Manager and the Advanced Security system services. Of course, as your sites gain attention and prestige, others will want to incorporate your content, which you can easily provide through the use of XML and Enterprise Java Beans.

Oracle9*i*AS currently comes in three flavors: Standard Edition, Enterprise Edition, and Wireless Edition. *Standard Edition* provides the tools needed to get started with your application development efforts and to grow to a medium-size Web site. *Enterprise Edition* adds extra services to grow your site from a medium to a large Web presence. For deploying content to cell phones and small Web appliances using the Wireless Access Protocol (WAP) interface, Oracle provides the *Wireless Edition,* which adds Portal-to-Go.

This chapter discusses the following topics:

■ Communication Services

■ Content Management Services

■ Business Logic Services

■ Presentation Services

■ Business Intelligence Services

■ Portal Services

■ Developer's Toolkits

■ Caching Services

■ System Services

Communication Services

Communication Services provide Internet connectivity to your users. The Web is the most visible facet and interface of the Internet today, consisting of client and server computers, which can handle multimedia documents. The Internet follows a standard set of protocols and conventions, and has become a universe of network-accessible information. The communication is based on the Hypertext Transfer Protocol (HTTP). Communication Services are the components, protocols, and procedures that provide multimedia communication services—real-time audio, video, and data communications—over packet networks, including Internet Protocol (IP)-based networks. The bottom line is the Communication Services are, in effect, the Web server.

Oracle9iAS provides you with several options for your Communication Services. These services continue to expand with each minor release of 9iAS.

Communication Services—Powered by Apache

Oracle supports the following Oracle Apache Modules in this (1.0.2.2) release:

mod_ssl	Secure Sockets Layer (SSL) message encryption support
mod_perl	Support for writing Apache modules in Perl
mod_jserv	Communication with Java servlet engine (J2EE)
mod_plsql	PL/SQL toolkit support

mod_ose	Delegates URLs to stateful Java and PL/SQL servlets in Oracle Servlet Engine (OSE). This module keeps session IDs in cookies or redirected URLs routes requests to the appropriate OSE sessions communicates with OSE over Network Services (that is, SQL*Net), which gives firewall support between Oracle HTTP Server and OSE, and connection pooling
http_core	Core Apache features
mod_access	Host-based access control; provides access control based on client hostname or IP address
mod_actions	Filetype/method-based script execution; provides for CGI scripts based on media type or request method
mod_alias	Aliases and redirects; provides for mapping different parts of the host filesystem in the document tree and for URL redirection
mod_auth	User authentication using text files, Basic and Digest Authentication
mod_auth_anon	Anonymous user authentication, FTP-style
mod_autoindex	Automatic directory listings
mod_cgi	Execution of CGI scripts; processes any file with MIME type application/x-httpd-cgi
mod_digest	MD5 authentication; provides for user authentication using MD5 Digest Authentication
mod_dir	Basic directory handling; provides for "trailing slash" redirects and serving directory index files
mod_env	Passing of environments to CGI scripts; provides for passing environment variables to CGI/SSI scripts
mod_expires	Apply Expires: headers to resources; provides for the generation of Expires headers according to user-specified criteria
mod_headers	Add arbitrary HTTP headers to resources; document headers can be merged, replaced, or removed
mod_include	Server-parsed documents; provides for server-parsed HTML documents

mod_log_config	User-configurable logging replacement for mod_log_common
mod_log_common	Provides for logging requests made to the server, using the Common Log Format or a user-specified format
mod_mime	Determining and registering document types using file extensions
mod_negotiation	Content negotiation
libproxy (mod_proxy)	Caching proxy capabilities; provides for an HTTP 1.0 caching proxy server
mod_rewrite	Powerful URL-to-file name mapping using regular expressions; provides a rule-based rewriting engine to rewrite requested URLs on-the-fly
mod_setenvif	Set environment variables based on client information; provides for the capability to set environment variables based on attributes of the request
mod_so	Support for loading modules at run time; provides for loading of executable code and modules into the server at startup or restart time
mod_speling	Automatically correct minor typographical errors in URLs; attempts to correct misspellings of URLs users enter, by ignoring capitalization and allowing up to one misspelling
mod_status	Server status display; enables a Webmaster, DBA, or server administrator to find out how well the server is performing, presenting an HTML page that gives the current server statistics in an easily readable form
mod_userdir	User home directories; provides for user-specific directories
mod_usertrack	User tracking using cookies

Communication Services—IIS

Incoming requests are handled by the Oracle Communication Services, more commonly known as the *Web Server*. Oracle9iAS comes bundled with the Apache Web Server and also supports Microsoft Internet Information Server (IIS). With the Oracle Plug-in for Microsoft IIS, you can directly invoke PL/SQL and Java Web-stored objects from an Oracle database. Oracle Plug-in for Microsoft IIS provides functionality in a Microsoft IIS environment that's similar to the Oracle

HTTP Server Modules: *mod_plsql* and *mod_ose*. Using it, you can access Web application components in one of the following two ways:

- passing a preconfigured virtual directory prefix (PL/SQL access)
- passing a predefined file extension and virtual directory prefixes, which are stored in the Java configuration file (Java access)

PL/SQL Web Component Access

Oracle Plug-in for Microsoft IIS supports accessing PL/SQL server pages and PL/SQL stored procedures written with Oracle PL/SQL Web Toolkit. If you have an existing PL/SQL application, you should have no problem invoking it from IIS. PL/SQL requests are filtered using a predefined prefix and are executed using pooled database connections. Developers have the ability to configure PL/SQL component access from multiple databases.

Java Web Component Access

Oracle Plug-in for Microsoft IIS supports accessing JSPs and servlets. Java requests are filtered using a Java configuration file.

For more information, see Chapter 3, "*iAS Configuration and Tuning,*" or *Oracle Plug-in for Microsoft IIS Configuration and User's Guide* in the Oracle9*i* Application Server Documentation Library.

Content Management Services

Content Management Services make all your content, regardless of the file type, accessible in one heterogeneous file hierarchy through Web browsers, Microsoft Windows networking, File Transfer Protocol (FTP), or an e-mail client. In addition, you can use these services to configure sophisticated file searching capabilities, event alerts, and check-in, check-out functionality to support collaborative projects. On NT- or Windows 2000-based servers, many of these services are available through Microsoft IIS. To enable these same services on all operating systems, Oracle introduced Internet File System.

Oracle Internet File System

Oracle Internet File System (IFS) is a service that stores files in an Oracle8*i* or Oracle9*i* database. From the user's viewpoint, Oracle IFS appears as any other file system accessible through Web browsers, Microsoft Windows Explorer, FTP, or an e-mail client. The fact that files are stored in the database is transparent to users because users don't directly interact with the database. For more information on IFS, see Chapter 18.

Unlike other file systems, Oracle IFS stores all your document files in the same file system. For example, you can display e-mail message files and address books, Web files, and word processing or spreadsheet files within a single file hierarchy, or you can perform a single search to locate all references to a topic.

File System Management

Like most traditional operating system-based file systems, you can manage the files you own or those for which you have the proper permissions. The main file management features include:

- **Renaming files**   You can rename files you own.

- **Deleting files**   You can delete files for which you have the correct permissions.

- **Uploading files**   You can upload files using FTP, Windows Explorer (by using Server Message Block and Web Folders), and the Web.

- **Setting automatic expiration on files**   You can set an expiration date for each file you upload to Oracle IFS. The file is automatically deleted on that date.

- **Modifying file attributes**   You can view and modify file attributes such as description, filename, and the access control permissions.

Unlike most traditional operating system-based file systems, IFS is built to support collaborative team development and management of documents. These additional features include:

- **Check-in, check-out (CICO)**   For group projects, you can check out files, so others can't overwrite your work. Files remain locked until you check them back in or an administrator releases the lock.

- **Versioning**   Developers can decide to make a file versioned. Each time the versioned file is checked in, a new version is created and stored. File versions can be kept or purged as needed.

- **Searching**   Oracle IFS includes a Find utility that uses interMedia Text extensions to search across multiple file types. This advanced search utility enables you to search quickly without having to know database syntax.

- **Multiple folders per file**   This feature allows multiple folders to be assigned to files, avoiding making multiple copies of files when the same document fits into a number of categories. This feature reduces maintenance when files are updated and also saves storage space.

■ **Extensible file attributes**   Application developers can extend Oracle IFS to manage new types for custom information. For each new type, you can define custom attributes about the information, which are then used to track and search for the information. This is especially useful for tracking binary or proprietary application-owned file types that, traditionally, are difficult to search.

Ultra Search

Oracle *Ultra Search* is new in the Oracle 9*i* database release and enables you to search inside databases, as well as static HTML pages. Other search engines cannot see content inside a database and wouldn't be able to find, for example, documents, newspaper articles, and so forth stored inside a database. Ultra Search unifies search areas across heterogeneous corporate repositories, Web sites, and groupware content. Oracle Ultra Search includes a Web interface, Web crawling, and search administration facilities to provide a unified interface for enterprise and vertical portal search applications. For more information on UltraSearch, see Chapter 25.

Business Logic Services

Business Logic Services are the development tools and languages that support your application logic. With Business Logic Services, you can build and run custom Web applications. The following sections describe the major elements that provide Business Logic Services in Oracle9*i* Application Server.

Oracle Business Components for Java

Oracle *Business Components* for Java is a 100 percent pure Java and XML framework that enables productive development, portable deployment, and flexible customization of multitiered, database applications from reusable business components. Application developers can use this framework to

■ author and test business logic in components that automatically integrate with databases

■ reuse business logic through multiple SQL views of data that support different application tasks

■ access and update the views from servlets, JSPs, and Thin-Java Swing clients

■ customize application functionality in layers without modifying the delivered application

See Chapter 13 for details on building custom applications using Java.

Oracle *PL/SQL*

Oracle *PL/SQL* is a scalable engine for running business logic against data in Oracle Database Cache and Oracle databases. It enables you to invoke PL/SQL procedures stored in Oracle databases through your Web browsers. The stored procedures retrieve data from tables in the database and generate HTML pages, which include the data that is then returned to the client browser. See Chapter 14 on using PL/SQL to develop custom applications.

Oracle Forms Services

If you have the Enterprise Edition of 9*i*AS installed, you can run applications based on Oracle Forms technology either over the Internet or over your company intranet. On the application server tier, Oracle *Forms Services* consists of a listener and a run-time engine, where the application logic is stored. On the client tier, Oracle Forms Services consists of a Java applet, which provides the user interface for the run-time engine, and Oracle JInitiator (a Java plug-in), which provides the capability to specify the use of a specific Java virtual machine on the client.

In Oracle9*i* Application Server, when you submit a URL to launch an Oracle Forms-based application, the Web listener accepts the request and downloads the Oracle Forms applet to your browser. The Oracle Forms applet then establishes a persistent connection to an Oracle Forms run-time engine. All processing takes place between the Oracle Forms applet and the Oracle Forms Services run-time engine, which seamlessly handles any queries or commits to the database. See Chapter 17 for more information about Oracle Developer.

Presentation Services

Presentation Services deliver dynamic content to client browsers, supporting servlets, Java Server Pages, Perl/CGI scripts, PL/SQL Server Pages, forms, and business intelligence. You can use Presentation Services to build your presentation layer for your Web applications. While Oracle puts these services into a separate group, you can think of them grouped with the Business Logic Services, in that your application logic can reside within these components. I recommend you break your business logic into executable components, which can then be called or invoked by these services.

Apache JServ

Apache JServ is a 100 percent pure Java servlet engine that is fully compliant with the following Sun Microsystems Java specifications:

- Java Servlet APIs version 2.0
- Java Runtime Environment (JRE) version 1.1

Beginning with version 1.0.2.2 of *iAS*, Oracle offers the J2EE servlet engine (for more information, see Chapter 13). Apache JServ works on any Java Virtual Machine that's compliant with this JRE and executes any Java servlet that's compliant with this version of the Java Servlet APIs specification. When the HTTP server receives a servlet request, it's routed to mod_jserv, which forwards the request to the Apache JServ servlet engine.

OracleJSP (Java Server Pages)

JSP technology extends Java Servlet technology, and supports the use of Java calls and scriptlets within HTML and XML pages. By using JSP pages, you can create user interfaces by combining static template data with dynamic content. JSP pages support component-based development, separating business logic (usually in JavaBeans or PL/SQL-stored procedure calls) from the presentation, thus, enabling you to focus on your areas of expertise. Consequently, JSP developers (who may not know Java) can focus on presentation logic, while Java developers can focus on business logic. For more information on JSPs, see Chapter 13. For general information about JSPs, refer to the Java Server Pages Specification (available from **http://java.sun.com**).

OracleJSP is an implementation of Java Server Pages version 1.1 as specified by Sun Microsystems and extends this specification to provide the following benefits:

- **Portability between servlet environments**   OracleJSP pages are supported on all Web servers that support Java servlets built to the version 2.0 or higher specification. Consequently, you can migrate your existing JSP pages that are compliant with the version 1.0 specifications to Oracle9*i* Application Server without needing to rewrite them.

- **Support for SQLJ**   *SQLJ* is a standard syntax for embedding SQL commands directly into Java code. OracleJSP supports SQLJ programming in JSP scriptlets. This includes support for an additional filename extension, sqljsp, which causes the OracleJSP translator to invoke the Oracle SQLJ translator.

- **Oracle JSP Markup Language (JML)**   Oracle provides the JML tag set as a sample tag library, which enables developers unfamiliar with Java syntax to jumpstart by using looping, conditionals, and other high-level programming logic.

- **Extended National Language Support (NLS)**   OracleJSP provides extended NLS support for servlet environments that cannot encode multibyte request parameters and bean property settings. For such environments, OracleJSP offers the *translate_params* configuration parameter, which can be enabled to direct OracleJSP to override the servlet container and do the encoding itself.

- **Extended datatypes**   OracleJSP provides the *JmlBoolean, JmlNumber, JmlFPNumber,* and *JmlString* JavaBean classes in the *oracle.jsp.jml* package to wrap the most common Java datatypes. These extended datatypes provide a way to work around the limitations of Java primitive types and wrapper classes in the standard *java.lang* package.

■ **Custom JavaBeans** OracleJSP includes a set of custom JavaBeans for quickly accessing the Oracle database.

Oracle PL/SQL Server Pages (PSP)

Oracle *PSPs* are one of the most exciting new features offered to traditional Oracle PL/SQL developers in 9*i*AS. PSPs are analogous to Java Server Pages, but they use PL/SQL, rather than Java for the server-side scripting. Unlike the other server page offerings, PSPs are fully compiled components executed as Oracle Stored Procedures. The Oracle PSP service includes the PSP Compiler and the PL/SQL Web Toolkit.

By using this service when developing applications, you can separate page formatting from application logic. Starting with either an existing Web page or a stored procedure, you can create dynamic Web pages by imbedding PL/SQL tags. These dynamic Web pages can perform database operations and display the results as HTML, XML, or plain text. Typically, a PL/SQL server page is intended to display in a Web browser. It can also be retrieved and interpreted by a program that can make HTTP requests, such as a Java or Perl application, however, enabling you to improve you application's modular development and reuse. See Chapter 14 for more on developing with PSPs.

If you plan to use PSPs as your presentation layer solution, it's important to understand that unless you use a Database Cache Server, the PL/SQL will be executed on the database server, not on the application server. Java and most other languages execute their code on the application server, making those solutions scalable without using a Database Cache Server.

Perl Interpreter

The *Perl Interpreter* is a persistent Perl run-time environment, which is embedded in the Apache HTTP Server, thus, saving the overhead of starting an external interpreter, as in a tradition CGI call. When Oracle HTTP Server receives a Perl request, it's routed through *mod_perl* to the Perl Interpreter for processing.

Business Intelligence Services

Oracle *Business Intelligence Services* enables you to manage and analyze your business and your Web site daily by enabling you to deploy and share business intelligence over the Web or over your corporate intranet.

Oracle Reports Services

Using Oracle *Reports Services* and its *Reports Servlet Services,* you can create and run new or existing Oracle Reports on an internal company intranet, an external company extranet, or publish them to the Internet. Oracle Reports Services is optimized to deploy Oracle Reports applications (reports and graphics) in a multitiered environment. The Report Services consist of the server component, run-time engines, and the servlet runner. In Oracle9*i*AS, when a client submits a request for a report, the Oracle HTTP Server Web listener routes that request to the Oracle Reports Services server component. The server routes the request to the Oracle Reports Services run-time engine, which runs the report. The report output is then sent back to the client through the Oracle HTTP Server Web listener. Reports can be formatted as HTML, XML, Adobe Acrobat, or as plain text for the user. Developers can also easily customize the report for import into Microsoft Excel or any other commonly supported document Multipurpose Internet Mail Extensions (MIME) type. See Chapter 17 for more information about Oracle Developer.

Oracle Discoverer 4*i* Viewer

Oracle *Discoverer 4i Viewer* is a tool for running and viewing workbooks (reports) created with Oracle Discoverer 4*i* Plus over the Web. Targeted at power users, Discoverer Viewer enables you to access information from the database and embed it in your site using graphic user interface (GUI) tools and a What You See Is What You Get (WYSIWYG) data display, without being experienced SQL developers. You can publish live reports to Web sites by creating a linkable URL that indicates to Discoverer Viewer which workbooks to open. Clicking the URL invokes the workbook query to the database and returns live results to the browser. Users interact with the query results to drill up or down, to enter values into optional parameters, or to follow links to other workbooks or applications.

Portal Services

You can use *Portal Services* to build portal sites that integrate all your content on a single Web page. Portal sites give your users a single, centralized, personalized view of relevant applications and data. By using Oracle9*i* Application Server Portal Services and Portal-to-Go, you can make your portal sites accessible to both fixed and mobile clients. While building simple applications within Oracle Portal is also possible, its real purpose is in offering applications to users through a subscription model. If you've used customizable portals such as **http://my.excite.com**, **http://my.yahoo.com**, or **http://my.etrade.com**, you're familiar with this model.

Oracle Portal

An *enterprise portal* is a Web-based application that provides a common, integrated entry point for accessing dissimilar data types on a single Web page. For example, you can create portals that give users access to Web applications, business documents, business intelligence reports, charts, and links that reside both inside and outside your corporate intranet. You can manage the user experience, creating and administering portal pages that contain portlets. To users, *portlets* on a page appear as regions of an HTML page that present text or graphics as links to more information or applications. Portlets provide access to Web resources, such as applications, Web pages, or syndicated content feed. Portlets are owned by *portlet providers,* which provide the communication link between the portal page and the portlets. When an application is ready for the user, it's *published,* and the portal administrator makes it available to the intended audience. The user then *subscribes* to the portlet, effectively putting it on their personalized page. For more on portals and portlets, see Chapter 16.

Portal-to-Go

Portal-to-Go is a translation layer available on the Enterprise Edition of the database that enables Web content to be displayed on Wireless Application Protocol (WAP)-enabled devices, such as browser-enabled cell phones and hand-held devices. Portal-to-Go works by isolating content acquisition from content delivery. It works like an XSLT style sheet, providing an intermediary format layer—Portal-to-Go XML—between the source format and the target format. Portal-to-Go XML is a set of Document Type Definitions (DTDs) and XML document conventions used to define content and internal objects in Oracle Portal-to-Go. For more information on Portal-to-Go, see Chapter 9.

9i Dynamic Services

Dynamic Services uses XML, XSLT, and a common Java or PL/SQL client API to turn any Web content or legacy application accessible via the Web into a service, usable by other applications or the end user. Services are application calls or Web data sources wrapped in an XML service package that defines the input and output APIs, the properties of the data source, and the execution flow. Thinking of each dynamic service as an application component, the services can be grouped and published together to form a coherent Web application interface. Dynamic Services offer support for most Web protocols (for example, HTTP, UDDI, LDAP, SMTP, XML Schema, or SOAP) and enables developers also to wrap legacy applications with custom APIs, giving them a new standards-based interface. As part of the Dynamic Services architecture, Oracle provides a central registry for managing and defining the properties, rights, syntax, and execution flow of the applications contained within Dynamic Services. Oracle also provides a Dynamic Services Adapter to incorporate management of the Dynamic Services into the 9*i*AS Portal registry, so any services defined in Dynamic Services are immediately available for publication as a portlet.

Developer's Toolkits

To support application development and deployment, Oracle has provided in Oracle9*i*AS several toolkits containing libraries and tools. Using these *Developer's Toolkits,* you can build Web applications that can access your database.

Oracle Java Messaging Service (JMS) Toolkit

Oracle Java Messaging Service (JMS) extends the standard Sun Microsystems Java Message Service version 1.02 specification. In addition to the standard JMS features, Oracle JMS provides a Java API for Oracle Advanced Queuing (AQ). This API supports the AQ administrative operations and other AQ features including:

- **An administrative API** to create queue tables, queues, and topics.

- **Point-to-multipoint communication** that extends the standard point-to-point by using recipient lists for topics.

- **Message propagation between destinations**, which allows applications to define remote subscribers.

- **Transacted sessions** so you can perform JMS, as well as SQL operations in one common transaction.

- **Message retention** after messages are dequeued.

- **Message delay** to make messages visible after a specified time.

- **Exception handling** so messages can be moved to exception queues if they cannot be processed successfully.

- **Oracle8*i* or Oracle9*i* AdtMessages** message types, which are stored in the database as Oracle objects. Consequently, the payload of the message can be queried after it's enqueued. Subscriptions can be defined on the contents of these messages in addition to the message properties. See Chapter 8 for more on advanced queuing.

Oracle SQLJ

Oracle *SQLJ* is a preprocessor that developers can use to embed *static* SQL operations in Java code. A *SQLJ program* is a Java method containing embedded static SQL statements that comply with the ANSI-standard SQLJ Language Reference syntax.

Static SQL operations are predefined. The operations themselves don't change in real time as a user runs the application, although the data values returned can change dynamically.

Oracle SQLJ consists of a translator and a run-time component. The *translator* converts embedded SQL into calls to the SQLJ *run-time component,* which performs the SQL operations. In standard SQLJ, this is typically done through calls to a JDBC driver. In the case of 9*i*AS, it's done through an Oracle JDBC driver. When you run SQLJ applications, the run-time component is invoked to handle the SQL operations. See Chapter 13 for more on using SQLJ.

Oracle XML Developer's Kit

Extensible Markup Language (XML) is quickly becoming the new standard for Web development, especially among business-to-business (B2B) content and service providers. Oracle XML Developer's Kit (XDK) contains XML component libraries and utilities you can use to enable applications and Web sites with XML. Using Java stored procedures, the API to call the components is available to either Java or PL/SQL-based applications. See Chapter 8 for more on developing applications using XML.

Oracle9*i* features several enhanced database operations to store XML through SQL and render traditional database data as XML. These functionalities are required to support B2B and business-to-customer (B2C) e-business, packaged applications, and Internet content management. The main area of XML support in Oracle9*i* is built-in XML XDKs.

With Java preloaded and the C XDK linked into Oracle9*i*, developers can easily access World Wide Web Consortium (W3C) functionalities that generate, manipulate, render, and store XML-formatted data in Oracle9*i*. Also available in PL/SQL and C++, the XDKs offer XML/XSLT parsers, XML schema processors, XML Class Generators, XML Transviewer Beans, and the XSQL Servlet, providing basic building block features that let developers quickly enable their applications for XML.

The following sections discuss the XML features introduced in Oracle9*i*.

XMLType

XMLType stores content natively (as XML) and allows XML operations to be run from SQL. XMLType enables nonnative XML data to be treated as XML by enabling users to create an XML View over standard database tables, documents, or Web content. The same high-performance access to XML data is available whether data is natively XML or an artifact generated from existing data.

XML Generation

In response to the challenge of generating XML in bulk from a database, Oracle has moved XML generation capabilities into the database and has made application server kernels available as built-in SQL operators. This ensures massively sustainable throughputs, enough for the largest content repositories or the busiest exchanges.

Arrive Data Types

A universal content model for all kinds of data and documents can be created through a set of native *Arrive data types,* which can hold references to XML documents or fragments (inside or outside the database). Just as applications locate HTML files using URL, a set of native Arrive data types can locate XML content— native or generated, inside the database or outside—using Arrive. URI-References play a major role in creating database-backed content repositories, which can be used to feed portals, archives, or other content management systems.

Oracle LDAP Developer's Kit

The *Lightweight Directory Access Protocol* (LDAP) Developer's Kit supports client connectivity with Oracle Internet Directory, the Oracle LDAP directory server. Oracle Internet Directory combines a native implementation of the Internet Engineering Task Force's (IETF) LDAPv3 standard with an Oracle8*i* or Oracle9*i* back-end data store. Specifically, you can use Oracle LDAP Developer's Kit to develop and monitor LDAP-enabled applications. It supports client calls to directory services, encrypted connections, and you can use it to manage your directory data. See Chapter 12 for more on LDAP.

Caching Services

To scale your e-business Web site, Oracle9*i*AS provides *Caching Services* in the Enterprise Edition of the suite. These services include Oracle Web Cache and Oracle Database Cache. Oracle Web Cache is a content-aware service that improves the performance, scalability, and availability of Web sites by caching both static and dynamic pages. Oracle Database Cache is a middle-tier database cache that reduces the load between the application and database tiers by caching frequently requested data, avoiding unnecessary network round-trips for read-only data. See Chapter 19 for more information about Oracle's cache solutions.

Oracle Database Cache

Oracle *Database Cache* resides on the middle tier as a service of 9*i*AS. It improves the performance and scalability of applications that access Oracle databases by caching frequently used data on the middle-tier machine. With Oracle Database Cache, your applications can process several times as many requests as their original capacity because round-trips to the back-end database are greatly reduced. Oracle Database Cache service supports running stateful servlets, Java Server Pages, Enterprise JavaBeans, and CORBA objects in Oracle8*i* and Oracle9*i* JVM.

Who Should Use Oracle Database Cache?

If your applications meet the following criteria, you can use Oracle Database Cache to boost the scalability of your Web sites and the performance of your applications:

- Your applications access an Oracle database.

- You use a multitiered environment, where the clients, Application Server, and Oracle database servers are located on separate machines.

- Your applications communicate with an Oracle database through Oracle Call Interface (OCI) or an access layer built on OCI, like JDBC-OCI, ODBC, or OLE.

- Your Web or application users generate mostly read-only queries.

- Your applications can tolerate some synchronization delay with data in the source database. That is, the cache doesn't need to be as up-to-date as the real-time data in the master database. (You decide how often to refresh the data.)

Oracle Database Cache Environment

In the Oracle *Database Cache environment,* the cache software consists of a thin middle-tier database instance for caching frequently accessed data and running intelligent software that routes queries. The source database is on the back end running in its own tier. It is the original and primary storage for the data. Currently, Oracle Database Cache can cache data from only one source database.

Example of How Requests Are Served by Oracle Database Cache

When users request frequently accessed data, the request passes from the client to the Oracle Database Cache, through the Web Server, and the database cache returns the data. Because the data is stored on the same tier, the data is returned quickly and the request doesn't need to pass to the source database server for retrieval of the data. If a new user requests the same information, the request is again served in the middle-tier database cache, which returns the data quickly. If the data doesn't reside in the cache, the request is then routed through to the source database for resolution, cached in the middle tier, and served to the user. Any subsequent request for the same data is served from the cache.

How Oracle Database Cache Is Different Than the Source Database

Although Oracle Database Cache looks like a regular database instance placed in the middle-tier, important differences exist.

- Oracle Database Cache does cache data, but it isn't a persistent store for data.

- You cannot perform backup and recovery on it. If you need to back up your data, then you must store it on the source database.

- Oracle Database Cache cannot be used to create tables or other database objects. The only way you can put data into this environment is by caching data from the source database to the middle-tier instance.

- Oracle Database Cache doesn't provide transparent application fail-over (TAF) guarantees if it fails because Oracle Database Cache isn't a true persistent store for data. It's only a mirror of the source instance.

- Oracle Database Cache cannot be treated as an enlisted database in global transactions to avoid an unnecessary and expensive two-phase commit.

How Do Applications Make Use of Oracle Database Cache?

To take advantage of the benefits of Oracle Database Cache, you only need to configure the environment of your applications. You needn't make any modifications to your applications if they use SQL statements to access the database or are linked with OCI using dynamic libraries and are layered directly on OCI. If your applications satisfy either criterion, queries are routed to the middle-tier database cache automatically.

Oracle Web Cache

Oracle *Web Cache* is a Web Server caching service that improves the performance, scalability, and availability of busy Web sites that run on 9*i*AS and the Oracle database. Most Webmasters run statistics on their sites and have a good idea what pages are hit most often. By storing frequently accessed pages in virtual memory, Oracle Web Cache reduces the need to repeatedly process requests for those URLs on the Web server. Unlike legacy proxy servers and other Web server products that only handle static images and text, Oracle Web Cache caches both static and dynamically generated HTTP content from one or more application Web servers. Using Oracle Web Cache, Web clients experience faster page retrieval and the load on the HTTP servers is significantly reduced.

As you can see in Figure 1-2, Oracle Web Cache is positioned in front of Oracle HTTP Servers to cache their pages and to provide content to Web users that request it. When Web browsers access your Web sites, they send HTTP requests to Oracle Web Cache, which acts as a virtual server or virtual request router to the Oracle HTTP Servers. If the requested content has changed or aged off, Oracle Web Cache retrieves the new content from an Oracle HTTP Server.

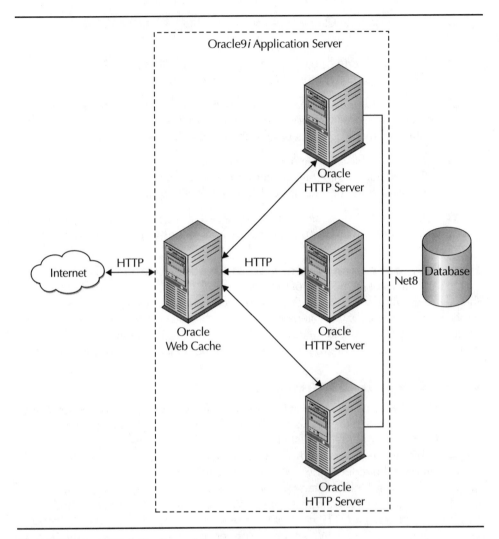

FIGURE 1-2. *Web Cache architecture*

Oracle Web Cache Main Features

The main features of Oracle Web Cache make it ideal for dynamic e-commerce Web sites that host online catalogs, news services, B2B services, and portals.

■ Static and dynamically generated content caching: Caches documents according to rules and timetables you specify.

■ Cache invalidation: Supports page invalidation as a means to keep Oracle Web Cache pages consistent with the content on 9iAS.

- Performance assurance: Built-in performance measurement handles performance issues, while maintaining cache consistency. These statistics assign a priority order to contents and determine which documents can be served old and which must be retrieved fresh.

- Surge protection: Lets you set limits on the number of concurrent requests passed to Oracle Web Cache to avoid overburdening it.

- Load balancing: Dynamically distributes requests over many Web Servers that Oracle Web Cache cannot serve itself. Oracle Web Cache is designed to manage HTTP requests for up to 100 9*i*AS server machines.

- Backend fail-over: Automatically redistributes the load over the remaining Web servers when one server fails or is taken offline. When the failed server returns to operation, Oracle Web Cache automatically includes it in the server pool.

- Session tracking: Supports Web sites that use session ID tracking to track users.

- Security: Provides password authentication for administration tasks, control over which ports operations can be requested from, and timeout for inactive connections.

System Services

Oracle9*i*AS includes Oracle Enterprise Manager and Oracle Advanced Security to provide system management and security services for your applications. These services manage your Oracle environment and network security through encryption and authentication.

Oracle Enterprise Manager

Oracle *Enterprise Manager* has been enhanced from a database administration tool into a system management tool that provides an integrated environment for centrally managing your Oracle platform. This service is also available in the Enterprise Edition, and combines a GUI console, Oracle Management Servers, Oracle Intelligent Agents, common services, and administrative tools. In Oracle9*i*AS, you use the console to manage Oracle Database Cache, Oracle Forms Services, and the host operating system. From the console, you can perform the following tasks:

- Centrally administer and diagnose Oracle Database Cache and Oracle Forms Services

- Monitor the status of your Oracle products and third-party services

- Schedule maintenance activities on multiple machines at varying time intervals

- Monitor networked services for scheduled and unusual events

- Customize your display by organizing your server components into logical groups according to your unique system architecture; as your system grows and changes, you can rearrange the services to fit the new architecture

Oracle Advanced Security

Oracle *Advanced Security* provides a "soup-to-nuts" suite of security services for Oracle Database Cache, Oracle8i and Oracle9i JVM, and Oracle8i and Oracle9i PL/SQL. Its functionality is twofold: first, network security features protect enterprise networks and securely extend corporate networks to the Internet; second, it integrates security and directory services, combining to provide enterprise user management and single sign on.

Network security features ensure data privacy, data integrity, and user authentication between the multiple servers in the network. They also provide users single sign on where the user authenticates once, and then authentication occurs transparently in subsequent connections to other databases or services on the network. Using a single sign on, users can access multiple schemas and applications with a single password.

Security and Directory Services provide your or your systems administrator tools to manage users centrally on a central directory service, rather than repeatedly managing the same users on individual databases and servers. Using Oracle Enterprise Security Manager, a tool accessible through Oracle Enterprise Manager, enterprise users and their authorizations are managed in Oracle Internet Directory or other LDAP directory services. See Chapter 12 for more information on security.

Database Services

Oracle9i *Database Services* provide distinct advantages over the Oracle8i database. The Oracle9i database contains many important new features that optimize traditional business applications and facilitate critical advancement for Web applications. Oracle9i database's new features deliver the performance, scalability, and availability essential to your applications.

The Oracle9i database offers transparent, rapid-growth clustering capabilities, along with powerful and cost-effective security measures, zero-data-loss safeguards, and real-time intelligence to deliver the power needed in today's dynamic marketplace.

Because this is a Web development book and not a DBA reference, the new availability features are covered by name only. These new features include the enhanced disaster recovery environment (LogMiner and viewer, Oracle9i Data

Guard, Data Guard Monitoring and Automation, Zero Data Loss Log Transport, Delayed Mode, Real Application Clusters: Within-seconds Failover, Oracle Application Clusters Guard, Oracle9*i* Fail Safe: Four-Node Failover, Fast-Start Fault Recovery, Fast Instance Freeze and Resume, Oracle9*i* Flashback Query, Comprehensive Log Analysis, Resumable Space Allocation) and precision database repair features (Rapid Crash Recovery, Improved Failed State Diagnostics, Faster Failure Detection, and Oracle Fail Safe Enhancements). Although we won't discuss this in detail, you'll be excited to know that 9*i* is more scalable than 8*i* was. Oracle9*i* database provides a number of new scalability features, including Increased Transaction Throughput on Oracle9*i* Real Application Clusters, Cache Fusion Architecture (Automatic "Fusing of Caches," and Reduces Disk I/O Cluster Treated as Scalable Single System). Security (Security for Data, Users, and Companies, Security API Enhancements, Directory Access Utilities, Virtual Private Database (VPD) Enhancements, Standards-Based Public Key Infrastructure (PKI), Improved User and Security Policy Management, Enterprise User Management Enhancements, Password Encryption, Secure Random Number Generator, Oracle Internet Directory Administration Improvements, Directory Services Availability Improvements, LDAP server scalability and performance, Optimization of Server-Side Caching, Oracle Label Security, and Oracle Policy Manager) and Oracle9*i* Systems Management (Self-Managing Undo Features, Memory Management, Working Memory Management, Persistent Initialization Parameters, Oracle Database Configuration Assistant, Oracle-Managed Files, Resumable Space Allocation, Corresponding Sub-Cache Configuration, Mean Time to Recover (MTTR) Specification, SQL Queryable Through V$SQL_PLAN View, Parameter Changes Persist Across Shutdowns) have been improved considerably. Many more features have been enhanced in Oracle9*i*. For further discussion of the DBA 9*i* new feature topics, see *Oracle9i Database New Features*. The information in this section was pulled primarily from that document, but has been limited to features important to Web developers.

Features that can make your Web development (and maintenance) faster are discussed in detail in the following. When I initially learned about all these new features, I thought I was dreaming. Nearly every enhancement I ever imagined is in the Oracle9*i* database!

New Online Data Evolution Architecture

Oracle9*i* contains a new online reorganization and redefinition architecture that allows much more powerful reorganization capabilities. Long awaited, administrators (and developers) can now perform a variety of online operations to table definitions, including online reorganization of heap-organized tables. This makes reorganizing a table possible while users (or your testing team) have full access to it.

Online Schema Changes

Oracle9*i* provides the mechanism to redefine the table structures, while keeping them online and fully accessible to users and applications. This has always been a challenge for rapid development environments in the past.

Online Table and Index Reorganization

Oracle9*i* also provides a simple mechanism to reorganize and redefine tables, while keeping them online and available to application users. Oracle9*i* online table and index reorganization reduces planned downtime, increases application availability, reduces disk fragmentation, and improves application performance. Now you can create and drop indexes on-the-fly!

Dynamic Database Parameters

Have you ever run into an *init.ora* parameter that affected your Web development? Sure you have, we all have. You can now reset online Oracle9*i* database parameter settings that affect database server memory use. This enables you to take databases offline and restart them for parameter settings to take effect.

Fine-Grained, Automatic Resource Management

Oracle9*i* includes several new features that enhance resource management. These features are discussed in the following sections.

Granular Control Over Resources

The *Database Resource Manager* is significantly enhanced in Oracle9*i* to allow for more granular control over resources. It adds features such as automatic consumer group switching, maximum active sessions control, query execution time estimation, and undo pool quotas for consumer groups. Administrators are able to specify the maximum number of concurrently active sessions in each consumer group. Once this limit is reached, Database Resource Manager queues all subsequent requests and runs them only after existing active sessions complete. These are welcome features in a Web development environment!

Automatic Consumer Group Switching

The *automatic consumer group-switching* feature of Oracle9*i* enables you to specify criteria that, if met, causes the Database Resource Manager to switch the consumer group of a long-running session automatically: for example, from a consumer group set up for OLTP operations to one more suited for batch reporting. This feature helps your performance.

You can also set a maximum estimated execution time for each consumer group. The Database Resource Manager estimates the approximate query execution time for each operation before it begins and will abort the operation if it exceeds the limit specified.

Undo Pool Quota

With the *undo pool quota* feature, you can specify a maximum on the total amount of rollback data generated per resource consumer group. This prevents rogue transactions from consuming excessive rollback space and affecting system operation. Watch out ad-hoc query users!

Performance

Oracle9*i* continues to demonstrate leading performance in all areas. Various performance measurement and tuning projects continue to measure, tune, and improve Oracle9*i* run-time performance in all areas. Speed makes any application king of the hill.

Native Compilation and Improved PL/SQL Optimization

A major focus of Oracle9*i* is improving performance in areas critical to Web applications. Support for native compilation and improved optimization of PL/SQL improves the performance of many of today's business applications, often significantly. The addition of memory and CPU costs to the cost-based optimizer results in better optimization plans, less resource use, and faster overall performance.

Latch Contention Improvements

Latch Contention in many areas has been eliminated or reduced, which improves performance on highly active systems. General I/O improvements, including self-tuning direct I/O, prefetching, and skip/scan row source operations on indexes also improve performance in data warehouse and OLTP environments.

Enhanced Java Performance

Oracle's new Java engine provides a fast, scalable Java environment for your Web development. Improved garbage collection, better native compilation, increased object sharing, and session pinning have all improved the performance of built-in Java executing inside the database. JDBC and SQLJ performance improvements have also improved the performance of Java in the middle tier or on the client.

Network and Distributed Database Performance

Both network and distributed database performance have been improved by the rework of database-to-database communication using OCI. In addition, specific network interface optimization, new improved virtual circuit I/O, and a unified event/wait model all substantially improve client/server communication performance. Improved distributed query optimization has also been built into the optimizer.

SQL and PL/SQL Improvements

For those who've been concerned that PL/SQL was dead (as a result of Java), you'll be happy to know that SQL and PL/SQL continue to be improved in Oracle9*i* to meet current development requirements.

Multilanguage server-side debugging has been added, allowing integrated development environments to debug both Java and PL/SQL within the same framework.

Support for inheritance and multilevel collections complete the modeling capabilities of the object-relational subsystem in Oracle9*i*. This makes building complex models inside the database possible. In addition, Oracle9*i* supports type evolution: certain changes may be made to object types, even if instances of the types exist in the database. Both types of support make it easier to deploy complex applications in real-life environments.

New ANSI requirements are also supported, including support for the CASE statement, ANSI-compliant joins, and reserved name versioning. To aid migration to Oracle9*i* from other databases, scrolling cursor support has been added, and stored procedures can now return result sets that can be easily passed and pipelined between both database and client-side processes.

SQL Improvements

The following datatypes are new for Oracle9*i*:

- TIMESTAMP

- TIMESTAMP WITH [LOCAL]TIME ZONE INTERVAL YEAR TO MONTH

- INTERVAL DAY TO SECOND

- XMLtype, native XML datatype

- SYS.UriType, SYS.UriFactoryType

- SYS.ANYType, SYS.AnyData, SYS.AnyDataSet

- MDSYS.SDO_GEOMETRY, new spatial datatype

- ORDSYS.ORDImage—media type

- ORDSYS.ORDVideo—media type

- ORDSYS.ORDAudio—media type

The following built-in SQL functions are new for Oracle9*i*:

- ASCIISTR

- COMPOSE

- COALESCE
- CURRENT_DATE
- CURRENT_TIMESTAMP
- DBTIMEZONE
- DECOMPOSE
- FIRST
- FROM_TZ
- LAST
- LOCALTIMESTAMP
- NULLIF
- NUMTOYMINTERVAL
- INTERVAL YEAR to MONTH
- NUMTODSINTERVAL
- INTERVAL DAY TO SECOND
- PERCENTILECONT
- PERCENTILEDISC
- SESSIONTIMEZONE
- SYS_EXTRACT_UTC
- SYSTIMESTAMP
- TO_DSINTERVAL
- TO_TIMESTAMP
- TO_YMLITERAL
- TZ_OFFSET
- UNISTR
- WIDTH_BUCKET

The following built-in SQL expressions are new for Oracle9i:

- DATETIME EXPRESSION
- EXTRACT
- INTERVAL

The following built-in SQL condition is new for Oracle9i:

- IS OF type condition

The following top-level SQL statements are new for Oracle9i:

- CREATE PFILE
- CREATE SPFILE
- MERGE

PL/SQL Improvements

Oracle9i includes a PL/SQL package, *DBMS_METADATA,* which provides interfaces for extracting complete definitions of database objects. The definitions can be expressed either as XML or as SQL DDL. The following two styles of interface are provided:

- A flexible, sophisticated interface for programmatic control
- A simplified interface for ad hoc querying

Other improvements to PL/SQL include the following:

- Integrated front-end for SQL compilation: PL/SQL immediately supports all SQL syntax changes to embedded SQL.
- SQL parallel query mechanism has been extended to stored procedures written in Third Generation Language (3GL) (which includes Java and external routines, as well as PL/SQL). Stored procedures can now incrementally return data to the calling SQL statement.
- Full support for ANSI-style CASE statements and expressions.
- Better support for compute-intensive applications through native compilation support.

- The SQL and PL/SQL run-time engines have been more tightly integrated to improve performance.

- The overhead of calling PL/SQL procedures from SQL has been reduced.

- PL/SQL offers improved assistance in data conversion between RAW and numeric datatypes. The UTL_RAW package offers CAST_TO_NUMBER, CAST_FROM_NUMBER, CAST_TO_BINARY_INTEGER, and CAST_FROM_BINARY_INTEGER.

SQL*Plus Improvement—*i*SQL*Plus

*iSQL*Plus* is a browser-based implementation of SQL*Plus, which can be used over the Internet to connect to an Oracle RDBMS to perform the same actions as through the SQL*Plus command line. The *i*SQL*Plus implementation uses a Web browser, an Oracle HTTP Server with the *i*SQL*Plus Server, and an Oracle RDBMS Server.

Summary

Oracle has provided the architecture for your success. The tools Oracle provides can speed your development, make better use of your hardware, and reduce your total cost of ownership. Whether you're a long-time Oracle shop or a new Oracle customer, using Oracle9*i* from end-to-end can provide a one-vendor solution that won't let you down.

CHAPTER
2

Installation

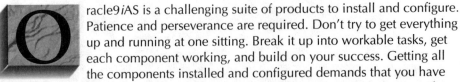racle9*i*AS is a challenging suite of products to install and configure. Patience and perseverance are required. Don't try to get everything up and running at one sitting. Break it up into workable tasks, get each component working, and build on your success. Getting all the components installed and configured demands that you have knowledge in several areas of expertise. Most individuals working with these products are likely to be DBAs because this is a natural for an Oracle product; however, installing and configuring 9*i*AS requires knowledge of configuring Apache or IIS Web servers, TCP/IP networking, advanced database features, SQL*Net, systems administration, and Web security. Only a few people have the entire range of skills and experience necessary to accomplish this individually. Do some research, ask for help in areas that are new to you, find people who can augment your skills, and work as a team.

This chapter discusses the following topics:

- Before You Begin

- Installing 9*i*AS

- Installation Tips and Traps

- Postinstallation: Configuration Assistants

- Deinstallation

Before You Begin

As with all software installations, you need to take a few steps before installing 9*i*AS.

1. Read the *Oracle Installation Guide* and Release Notes. Either read the documentation on the installation disks or download it from Oracle (**http://otn.oracle.com**). Be sure to note any minimum hardware memory and disk space requirements. Also note any particular issues for your operating system, network architecture, or database version.

2. Install all OS service packs. Make sure your operating system is current, with all service patches and upgrades in place.

3. Look online for bugs and patches for your specific hardware/OS configuration and version of the 9*i*AS software. The software versions cut on to CD are almost never the latest and greatest information available, and Oracle often posts patches before the CDs are even shipped. Oracle Metalink has a searchable bug database, Support Notes and Alerts, and Technical Forums. OTN has Discussion Groups for finding additional reported problems and solutions others have encountered. Knowing these traps in advance can

save you hours of frustration. For example, when I was testing an installation for this chapter, I ran into difficulty installing 9iAS on a brand new Intel server running Windows 2000. I fought with it for hours, and then found a Note on Metalink (Note 136038.1) indicating 9iAS versions 1.0.2.2 and lower aren't supported on Intel Pentium 4 chips because of an incompatible Apache dll file. When I moved to an older Pentium 3 server, it installed just fine.

4. Determine what components you're installing. The installation disks for 9iAS (1.0.2.2 at press time) have the entire available Standard Edition and Enterprise Edition options on them. Read through the various components and determine what features you actually need. If you miss a component or get more installed than you want, you can add or remove them later. Adding missing components is often much easier and less time-consuming, however, than removing unwanted components.

5. Check your database and drives for available space. Portal in particular, and 9iAS in general, install a lot of components into the database. Running out of extents is a sure way to mess up an installation. Also, several reported errors about underestimated space requirements are in the installation documentation. Give yourself some breathing room over the documented minimums. Nothing is more frustrating than getting almost there and having the installation fail at the last minute because of space constraints. Also, make sure the machine(s) you're installing on are up to the task. Apache is often criticized as a resource hog, as is the Oracle database. Trying to run these applications on undersized machines will only cause you frustration. For demonstration purposes, the smallest machine I successfully installed and ran all the 1.0.2.2 Enterprise Edition components on was an Intel Pentium III 500 MHz server running Windows 2000, with 320 megabytes of memory and 10 gigabytes of disk space, and it wasn't easy. I certainly wouldn't recommend this for a production deployment of any real applications.

6. Don't forget to back up the NT registry files. This is helpful if any iAS components need to be deinstalled or reinstalled.

7. Check the Installation Guide for the TCP ports used by the various Oracle components you're using. If you're installing in a network configuration that crosses firewalls or has other security measures in place, you need to work with your systems administrator to open the ports needed to allow the necessary communication channels for these features to work properly. Problems with these issues can be difficult to diagnose. Use the PING and TNSPING commands to test the ports.

8. Log in to the server with administrator rights. You might choose to install 9iAS under a distinct user or under the default server administrator, but the

user must have administrator rights to complete the software installation. I recommend installing the various components under distinct users because it makes configuring paths, permissions, and environment variables much easier to manage.

9. If you have the disk space, copying the three installation disk contents to the hard drive and installing from there can make the installation go faster.

10. Practice, practice, practice. Installing and configuring all the various available components is a hefty undertaking, especially Enterprise Edition with Portal and two different flavors of caching. These are large, sophisticated, and relatively new products, which means they're difficult to get right the first time. In writing this book, and this chapter in particular, I installed and configured all the 9iAS components several times, on different machines, and with several different configurations, and not once did I get through the whole thing without a hitch! Before installing or upgrading 9iAS on your production servers, practice on a test system that mirrors your production configuration as closely as possible.

Installing 9iAS

This section walks you through the installation process, using version 1.0.2.2 of 9iAS on an Intel Pentium III server running Windows 2000. The installation of 9iAS has improved greatly since the initial release of the product and I expect it will continue to improve. If you're installing a later version, the process will likely have changed from what I outlined here. Remember, always read the *Oracle Installation Guide* for your particular version and go online to get the latest information updates. This chapter is intended to give you an overview of the installation process. It isn't a replacement for the *Installation Guide* and Release Notes documentation from Oracle.

Begin by inserting disk 1 of 3. If the Oracle Universal Installer doesn't start automatically, begin the installation process by running iSetup.exe from the top folder. As shown in Figure 2-1, you can view Help at any time. If you select Yes here, the installer prelaunches a browser to view the *Installation Guide*. Select Next to go to the next Welcome screen.

Select Next to choose the version of 9iAS you want to install.

Determine the version of 9iAS you want to install. We installed Enterprise Edition for this chapter, as shown in Figure 2-2. For a more detailed list of the components to be installed, see the *Oracle Installation Guide* documentation for 9iAS.

The next screen that appears enables you to choose the Oracle home directory for the 9iAS 8.1.7-based components. 9iAS must live in a different Oracle home from the installed database and any other installed Oracle applications. For most production deployments, and to take advantage of the caching features, I'd expect the 9iAS components to live on a different server machine from the database. By default, the installer will create a new home called iSuites. Be sure you have enough

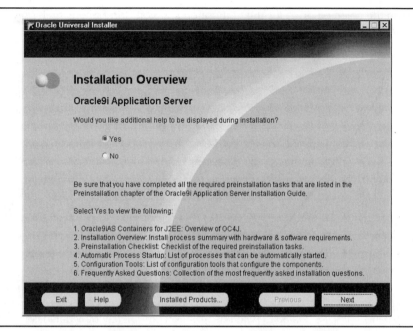

FIGURE 2-1. *Installer Start*

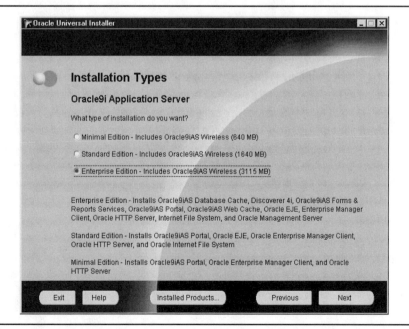

FIGURE 2-2. *Version Select*

space on the selected drive for the components. If you don't, the installer gives you an error page and makes you select a new home or directory path.

The Forms and Reports Server Home screen enables you to choose the Oracle home directory for 9*i*AS 8.0.6 (Forms and Reports Server)-based components. These components must also live in a different Oracle home from the installed database and any other installed Oracle applications, including the 8.1.7 components. By default, the installer creates a new home called Oracle_806. Be sure you have enough space on the selected drive for the components. If you don't, the installer gives you an error page and makes you select a new home or directory path.

The next screen (Figure 2-3) enables you to select the component you want to configure during the installation process. If you choose not to configure a particular component now, you'll have to configure it manually later using the configuration assistant for that component. By default, the installer selects all but the Oracle Management Server for configuration now. When you select Next from this screen, the installer begins installing components. If you're installing on an NT 4.0 server, the installer requires a reboot after installing the first set of components. If you're running Windows 2000, a reboot isn't required.

To install database caching, enter the SYSDBA password (not SYSTEM) for the source database and also enter the password of the Windows NT user who invoked the installation process. Database caching installs a completely new database instance

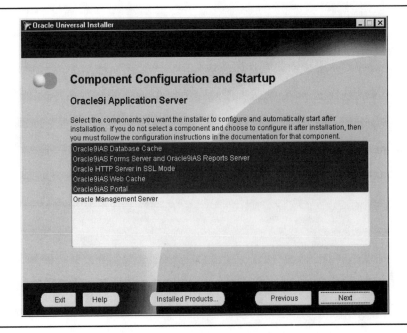

FIGURE 2-3. *Component Configuration screen*

in the 9*i*AS iSuites Home. The user must be an NT administrator and a DBA. See Chapter 19 for details on database caching.

The screen in Figure 2-4 appears only if you select Oracle9*i*AS Portal in the Component Configuration and Startup screen. Enter or accept the default Login Server Database Access Descriptor (DAD) and Schema names. This screen enables you to enter the name of the DAD to be used to access Oracle Portal via the Web server and the name of the database schema where the Portal database objects will be installed. A *DAD* is a set of values that specify how the Apache Listener connects to your Oracle database server to fulfill an HTTP request dynamically. Based on this DAD name, the installer automatically sets other DAD-related and default settings, such as the name and location of the document table. The default DAD name is portal30. Enter the name of the database schema that will contain Oracle Portal. The default schema name is also portal30. See Chapter 16 for more information about using Portal. Enter the TNS connect string for the database. The information you enter here is used to create the PL/SQL Gateway settings you can access from a Web browser after installation at the following location: **http://machine_name:port/ pls/admin_/gateway.htm**.

If you're installing 9*i*AS on the same server as the 8.1.7 database Home, an Apache HTTP server might already be running for the database. Look in the NT services to find out. If so, the installer can detect this instance and change the

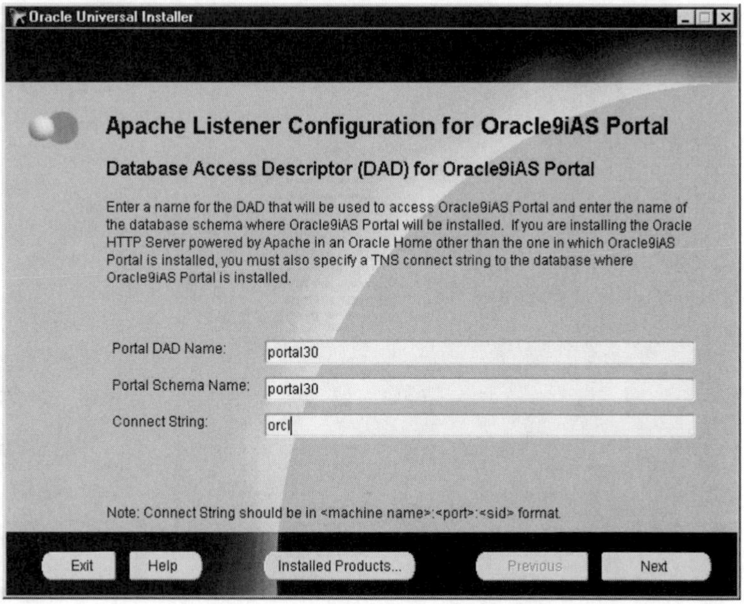

FIGURE 2-4. *Portal DAD screen*

default TCP ports in the 9*i*AS Apache configuration file (iSuites/Apache/Apache/ conf/httpd.conf) from 80 and 443, to 7778 and 4443. If you don't want this to occur, remove the database Apache instance before installing Portal, or manually change the ports in the configuration files after the installation. You cannot have both Apache instances listening on the same ports on the same machine.

In the screen shown in Figure 2-5, enter the DAD name for the Login Server. The *Login Server* provides an enterprise-wide Single Sign-On (SSO) mechanism that enables an Oracle Portal user to log in securely to Oracle Portal, as well as any partner and external applications, using a single user name and password.

Enter the SYS user name and password for the source database. Enter the NT administrator user for the destination machine where the iCache database instance will reside.

Enter the database where the wireless edition repository will reside, as shown in Figure 2-6. If you aren't using the wireless edition, you can remove this later.

In the next screen that appears, enter the schema user name and password for the wireless edition repository. Do *not* put the wireless edition repository in SYS or SYSTEM. Create a new user for the repository.

Enter the SYSTEM password for the database in the next screen to appear. The installer needs it to create the user and tablespaces for the wireless repository.

The Summary screen, shown in Figure 2-7, enables you to review all the settings and configuration options before the actual software installation proceeds. These

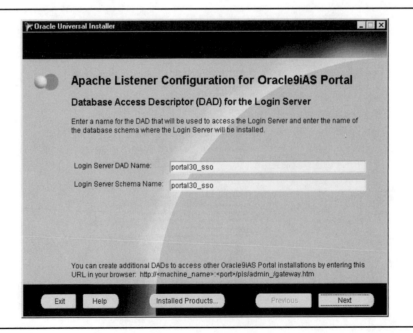

FIGURE 2-5. *Login Server screen*

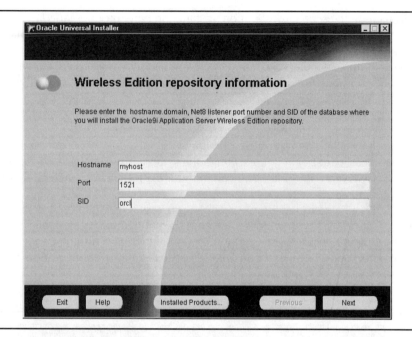

FIGURE 2-6. *Wireless edition repository screen*

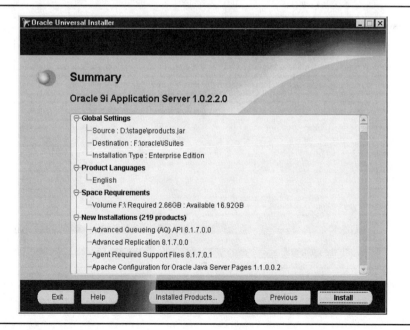

FIGURE 2-7. *Summary screen*

settings include the source, destination, installation type, product language, space requirements, and a list of software components to be installed. To make changes to any of these settings, click Previous to return to the respective option screen.

You can monitor the installation process on the following screen, shown in Figure 2-8. An installation log is created that you can look through later if you encounter any difficulties along the way. You'll be asked to swap disks during the installation, as the installer adds components. At about 43 percent complete, the installer asks for disk 2; at around 81 percent, it asks for disk 3.

After the installation is complete, the configuration assistants use the information you entered earlier to begin going through the setup of the Database Cache, Web Cache, Web Server, and Portal. You can monitor the progress as each configuration assistant progresses.

As each configuration assistant starts, the progress is reported on this screen, shown in Figure 2-9. If you choose not to run the configuration assistants at this time or if you run into difficulty, you can stop the installation and run the configuration assistants later, one at a time. If you didn't choose to run the configuration assistant, the installation is now complete.

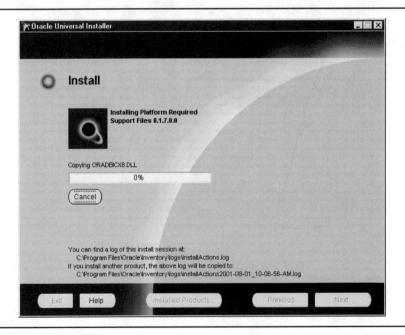

FIGURE 2-8. *Installation monitor*

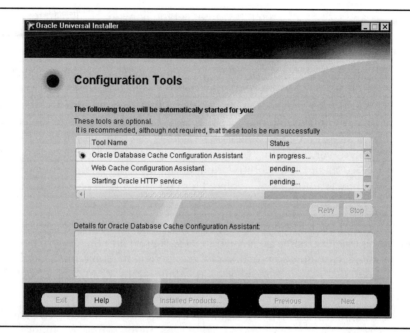

FIGURE 2-9. *Configuration assistant monitor*

Installation Tips and Traps

I included some pitfalls to avoid and things to look for if you run into trouble. Some of these I ran into myself, others I compiled from various alerts and notes available from Oracle Metalink online support (**http://metalink.oracle.com**). As always, go to Metalink or read the Release Notes for the most current information.

1. Check the network setup of each 9*i*AS server and source database server machine. In particular, check the following:

■ The machine's IP address is a fixed DNS served IP address, not a dynamic one. To find out, start up a command window, and enter the command c:> ipconfig /all. This gives you some information about the machine IP settings. If in doubt, check with the network administrators and get them to set up a permanent DNS name and IP address for you before proceeding.

■ The 'machine' name that's viewable in the control panel–network is *exactly* the same as the name by which your machine is known to the DNS networking system (case counts, watch those zeros and Os, ones and Ls). If they aren't the same, get the network administrators to change the name by which your machine is known on the DNS server to the same as you have entered locally on your computer.

■ Here's an example of what can happen if these are different: When you run a test form or report, using reports in this example, you can enter **http://dns_machine_name:80/dev60html/testrep.htm** and the test page is picked up okay. Look down the page at the page trailer—Web host—and the machine's *own* name is taken instead, for example, **myserver.tusc.com**. To cure this, fix the testrep.htm file. Also, in the D:\Oracle\806\Net80\Admin\tnsnames.ora file, the reports server entry is automatically entered for you, but myserver is the host name rather than the DNS name—change it.

2. The machine name must *not* have any spaces in it, for example, dev serv1. If the machine name does have spaces, change it in the control panel–network configuration section of the offending machine first, and then reboot and request that the network administrator change his or her DNS description of your machine to the new name.

3. Check the virtual memory setting in Control Panel | System. You should increase this to at least 200 Megabytes on all the server machines.

4. Before installing 9iAS, check to make certain the source database is installed and up-and-running, in particular

■ Check the services in the Control Panel. You should have an oracleservice<sid> service running, as well as an oracle<sid>TNSlistener service running. Also, the 9iAS installation guide suggests making the SID and the Service Name the same for the source database. Making sure you do this when installing it is easiest. If you don't, you must remember to use the correct name during the 9iAS installation process: "Which is it again, the SID or the service name? I forget."

■ Using Sql*Plus, check to make certain the installation logins are valid: sys/<password> and system/<password>. 9iAS install uses these and is unforgiving.

■ During the installation, do *not* rely on a user/pwd login strings with no database alias. You must install and test this with the full alias specified in the tnsnames.ora file—for example, *sys/<pwd>@my_database*—because this is what the 9iAS server processes use. Similarly, when the installer asks for database names in the form machine:port:sid, be careful to get it right. This is used to set up the JDBC connect strings for the Java components.

5. The 9*i*AS Installation Guide suggests you need to configure the tnsnames.ora and listener.ora files to handle external procedure requests by entering an External_procedure_listener= ... section to the files. You can do so, if necessary, but my default 8.1.7 database installation had these configured already.

Post-installation: Configuration Assistants

Each configuration assistant selected in the configuration assistance screen (Figure 2-3) comes up with its own set of wizard screens to set it up. If you did not choose to run any configuration assistants at installation time, you can run them individually after the installation. They are as follows:

- Net8 Configuration Assistant

- Database Cache Configuration Assistant

- Portal Configuration Assistant

- Database Configuration Assistant

- iFS Configuration Assistant

- Management Server Configuration Assistant

This is not the order you would run them in, just the order they are presented in the Oracle Installation Guide documentation. See the 9*i*AS Installation Guide for details on running each of the configuration assistants. One component missing from the 1.0.2.2 list of configuration assistants is Web Caching. It was added to 9*i*AS in version 1.0.2.1. It gets installed with the other 9*i*AS components automatically. The documentation for configuring and running it can be found in a text file that is included with the component Release Notes on the installation CDs or on TechNet (http://otn.oracle.com). Each configuration assistant has steps you can take for testing if the configuration was successful.

Configuration Assistant Tips and Traps

Here are a few tips and traps when running the configuration assistants. These apply to 9*i*AS version 1.0.2.2. Be sure to read the *Installation Guide* and Release Notes for your particular installation version and OS.

1. Be sure to look for manual steps in the *Installation Guide* before running the Configuration Assistant Wizards. This can save you from having many problems.

2. Make sure the correct Oracle home is selected for the particular assistant you're running.

3. If the installation fails for any reason, check the installation log for clues to the problem. In my experience, most installation errors are caused by database-naming issues, such as not following the correct format `machine:port:sid` when asked to provide the database connect string. Other errors I commonly see are path problems in the environment variables and an incorrect Oracle Home selected for the configuration assistant. The installation log can help point you in the right direction for troubleshooting the error.

4. The Portal installation documentation indicates it should take about two hours. This is wildly optimistic on most machines. Also, the tablespace size requirements are grossly underestimated. Take a look on Metalink for more realistic estimates. The progress indicator bar isn't accurate. On one installation I ran, the installation continued for another 35 minutes after the indicator bar was on 100 percent, so be patient.

5. You might have to set some init.ora parameters to get Portal to run properly. The Java_large_pool size and the sessions parameters are noted in Metalink as two in particular that may need tuning.

6. Installing IFS after Portal is installed causes Portal to stop running. See the Release Note 150114.1 (in Metalink) for a patch to this problem.

De-installation

If you have difficulty installing a 9*i*AS component, you might be forced to deinstall and reinstall it. The Oracle Universal Installer – Deinstaller doesn't do a complete job in several circumstances. This can cause you tremendous frustration as you try to reinstall and old configuration parameters and settings are picked up. Following are some recommendations to deal with this problem.

Before deinstalling, back up the NT registry files. If you're running 9*i*AS and a database on the same machine, and you intend only to deinstall 9*i*AS, this is particularly important because you'll need to be more selective about what you remove. Taking out the wrong registry listings can also cause the database to fail. If you kill the database or worse, put the registry back and start over.

If you have to reinstall Portal, drop the Portal*xx* users from the database (which could take up to an hour or more). Do *not* run the deinstaller; it will take forever to drop each installed database object one-by-one. For most other deinstalls, follow these steps:

1. Stop all Oracle NT services. Before you can delete the files in Oracle Home, make sure all the services associated with that particular Oracle

Home are stopped. To see the running services, navigate to Start | Settings | Control Panel | Services. This will list all the active services. The Oracle Services contain the word "Oracle" in the service name, so it's easy to find the Oracle services in the list of all running services. Select the services associated with the particular Oracle Home (iSuites and 806 are the most likely candidates you'll look for) and stop them all.

2. Delete the Oracle Home(s) directories. This should be done only after performing Step 1. Drive:/oracle/iSuites and Drive:/Oracle/806 are the default 9*i*AS Homes.

3. Delete 9*i*AS Oracle entries in Program Files.

4. If you intend to reinstall everything Oracle-related on the particular machine, delete the directory and all the files created under C:\Program Files\Oracle. This will take care of the Oracle Universal Installer.

5. Delete the Oracle Registry entries. To edit the registry, run the program regedit.exe. Expand the tree of registry keys and perform the following tasks:

   ■ Delete the ORACLE key under HKEY_LOCAL_MACHINE – SOFTWARE. Do *not* do this if you intend to leave the database running on the machine.

   ■ Delete the registry entries associated with the Win NT Services created by Oracle9*i* Application Server. They are under the following entries:

   HKEY_LOCAL_MACHINE - SYSTEM - ControlSet001 - Services
   HKEY_LOCAL_MACHINE - SYSTEM - ControlSet002 - Services
   HKEY_LOCAL_MACHINE - SYSTEM - CurrentControlSet - Services.

   All the NT services are listed here. As previously mentioned, most of the Oracle Services contain the word "Oracle" in the service name. Only delete the entries for the particular Oracle home(s) you're removing. Leave any entries intact for the services you want to leave running.

6. Delete the listings created in the PATH and CLASSPATH environment variables. In WinNT, right-clicking My Computer, and then selecting Properties can do this. This opens a window called System Properties. Select the Environment tab and update the PATH and CLASSPATH variables to remove the Oracle Home entries created for the Oracle9*i* Application Server product you're deinstalling. Don't just delete the PATH environment variable. That would be bad because then you wouldn't be able to access most of the programs on your machine.

7. A few other system environment variables are created, for example, WV_GATEWAY_CFG. Delete any Oracle-related variables. Remember,

you must look for these entries under the particular NT user that 9*i*AS was installed under. If you installed the software as the local system user, the entries will be set at the system level. If you installed 9*i*AS under its own NT user, it might be easier to drop and re-create the user.

8. Finally, reboot the machine. This is required any time NT services are deleted or environment variables are changed.

Summary

Now that you have 9*i*AS installed, you can continue with the rest of this book, configuring the various components and developing your Oracle Web applications. Remember, 9*i*AS is *not* a single application, but a suite of tools you can use to develop and deploy Web applications. I wouldn't expect anybody to use all the tools available, but I would expect each team of developers to pick and choose the tools that best meet their particular needs and skills. As you and members of your team become familiar with additional components, and as your applications grow and change, you can add new features to your development toolbox.

CHAPTER
3

iAS Configuration
and Tuning

AS is a highly configurable and tunable product that can meet the needs of a wide range and type of Web sites. Configuring *i*AS requires an understanding of the configuration of the Apache Web server and its various modules, such as mod_jserv and mod_plsql. To take advantage of features in *i*AS while maximizing performance, the *i*AS administrator should be well versed in all the features, and their associated costs and benefits.

In this chapter, the following topics are discussed:

- Quick Tuning and Configuration Answers
- Getting Started
- Understanding Ports
- Starting, Stopping, and Restarting *i*AS (Apache)
- Configuring *i*AS (Apache)
- GUI *i*AS Configuration Editing
- Managing and Configuring Modules
- Configuring *i*AS Security
- Monitoring Your *i*AS Web Server
- Tuning *i*AS
- Tuning Application Modules
- Hardware and Operating System Tuning

Quick Tuning and Configuration Answers

If you prefer to read the quick answer rather than the entire chapter, this section is for you. In this section, I summarize the major points of configuration for optimum performance and security. Because summarizing an entire chapter into one section is difficult, I highly recommend you read the entire chapter. If you don't have time, the following is the short version:

- Hardware
    - Size your hardware properly
    - At a minimum, distribute *i*AS, database, and FTP on to individual servers

- Hardware components should operate at no more than 75 percent to 80 percent of capacity

- Use directio for maximum disk performance

- Distribute the load

- The more RAM, the more *iAS* and module instances can be invoked

- Production servers should have at least 1GB of RAM

- Operating System

  - Use the logs and Web utilities to monitor *iAS* use

  - Use top, vmstat, netstat, sar, and ps to manage memory use, paging, swapping, and TCP/IP parameters on UNIX

  - Use Task Manager and Performance Monitor to manage memory use, paging, and swapping on NT/2000

  - Set the operating system swap file size to three times the physical memory

  - Set TCP/IP parameters per the hardware vendor's specification for a Web server

  - Obtain the latest operating system patches, especially for TCP/IP

- *iAS*

  - Tune *iAS* (Apache) directives and parameters

  - Keep logs small (1–5MB)

  - Log only warnings and errors (LogLevel warn)

  - Monitor logs for errors

  - Become familiar with the default configuration files. They provide good configuration information and settings

  - Don't use SSL unless it's a requirement

  - Turn off (comment out) modules you aren't using

  - Avoid using the rewrite, usertrack, session, and extended status modules

  - Turn off .htaccess capability

- Modules

  - PL/SQL

- Make use of OWA_CACHE for better PL/SQL performance

- Set session state to true if you have few users executing a series of PL/SQL procedures

- Use connection pooling

- Pin key packages in memory

■ Perl

- Turn on caching

■ Java

- Make use of JDBC connection pooling

- Pin key classes in memory

- Turn auto reload off

- Use the single-threaded model

- Load balance JServ

- Be sure debug mode is off

■ Oracle Database and SQL

- Tune your database

- Use Oracle9*i* rather than Oracle8*i*

- Tune your PL/SQL and SQL code

Getting Started

*i*AS is based on Apache. Entire books are written about configuring Apache. For more detailed information, I highly recommend *Professional Apache*, by Peter Wainwright (Wrox Press, 1999). This chapter's focus is specifically for *i*AS and the configuration components of primary interest to you.

Prior versions of the Oracle Application Server (OAS) included a graphical browser-based configuration tool. Apache provides no such tool and neither does *i*AS. The administrator is expected to maintain the configuration files using a text editor (such as vi, Notepad, or TextPad). Future versions of Oracle Enterprise Manager (OEM), included with 9*i*AS, are expected to include the capability to configure Apache. Until then, you need to understand these configuration files. Understanding how Apache works is extremely important.

Where *i*AS Gets Its Configuration Information

Prior to version 1.3.4, Apache used the following three configuration files located within the conf subdirectory of the server's root directory (usually the $ORACLE_ HOME/Apache/Apache/conf directory):

- Master configuration file, typically named httpd.conf, which contains the basic server configuration, including the locations of the other two configuration files.

- Resource configuration file, specified by the ResourceConfig parameter in the master configuration file, and typically named srm.conf, which contains the resource directives.

- Access configuration file, specified by the AccessConfig parameter within the master configuration file, and typically named access.conf, which contains the directory access control directives.

All three of these files are still included in the Apache installation, but the resource and access configuration files are now empty and their directives are placed in the master configuration file. Because Oracle 9*i*AS 1.0.2.2 uses Apache 1.3.19, the resource and access configuration files aren't used.

Understanding Directives

The configuration files contain directives to tell *i*AS how to operate. A *directive* or command is an instruction that tells *i*AS to perform a specific task. *i*AS responds to a specific set of commands. Generally, the directive name is followed by a series of one or more arguments. Directives typically start with an uppercase letter and each word within the directive is also capitalized. Directives that contain directives within them, *subdirectives,* are typically surrounded by a less than (<) and a greater than (>) sign, just like XML and HTML. For example, the directive for virtual hosts is <VirtualHost>. Here are some directives pulled from the httpd.conf file:

```
ServerType standalone
Port 80
ServerName tuscbdb
DocumentRoot "C:\ORACLE\iSuites\Apache\Apache/htdocs"
<Directory />
    Options FollowSymLinks
    AllowOverride None
</Directory>
```

If you're curious about the possible directives, use apache –L as defined in the following "Starting, Stopping, and Restarting *i*AS (Apache)" section.

Oracle Changes
to the Master Configuration File

The Apache master configuration file created during the Oracle 9iAS installation has changed from the standard Apache master configuration file. Some of the changes made to the configuration file include the following:

- Minor filename changes, such as for the values of the LockFile and ScoreBoardFile parameters.

- SSL support by adding a Listen 443 directive and including the mod_ssl.c module, specifying the parameters for the global context of the mod_ssl.c module, and specifying the parameters for the SSL virtual host context directive <VirtualHost _default_:443>.

- An alias named /jservdocs/ to point to the physical directory where the Apache JServ documentation is installed. Apache JServ replaces Oracle JWeb used in prior versions of the Oracle Application Server.

- A Dynamic Monitoring System (DMS) directive introduced in 9iAS 1.0.2.1 to allow a browser to access performance and resource metrics out of the shared memory scorecard. If this section is removed, DMS metrics are still collected, but cannot be accessed by a browser.

- An alias named /perl/ to point to the physical directory where Perl scripts are stored, and the appropriate directives for processing these scripts in the persistent Perl run-time environment embedded in the HTTP server.

- Directives to include two of the configuration files that contain the Oracle-specific directives.

iAS Configuration File Structure

iAS uses eight configuration files containing the required directives. Two of the Oracle configuration files—jserv.conf and oracle_apache.conf—are included at the end of the master configuration file. The other Oracle configuration files are included using directives within the oracle_apache.conf file. In other words, they're nested. See Figure 3-1 for the hierarchy of all the standard Apache and Oracle configuration files.

The following is a summary of the information contained in each of the Oracle configuration files:

- **jserv.conf**   Apache JServ configuration that loads the JServ module and specifies the appropriate module parameters.

- **oracle_apache.conf**   Includes the remaining six configuration files and defines a virtual directory for Discoverer files.

- **mod__ose.conf**   Oracle Servlet Engine (OSE) configuration that loads the OSE module and specifies the appropriate module parameters. The OSE module services requests to stateful Java and PL/SQL servlets.

- **plsql.conf**   PL/SQL configuration that loads the PL/SQL module and specifies the appropriate module parameters. This file also specifies the aliases for the /help/ and /images/ virtual directories used by Oracle Portal, plus directives specifying the handling of the /images/ and /docs/ subdirectories of the Portal installation. Note, the /images/ alias is also defined in another Oracle configuration file—6*i*server.conf.

- **ojsp.conf**   JavaServer Pages (JSP) configuration that defines the /jspdocs/ alias and associates requests containing a .jsp or .sqljsp extension to the JServ module.

- **xml.conf**   Extensible Markup Language (XML) configuration that defines the /xsql/ alias and associates requests containing an .xsql extension to the XSQL servlet.

- **6*i*server.conf**   Forms and Reports configuration that defines aliases, environment variables, and MIME types used by the Forms and Reports servers. As noted previously, the /images/ alias in this file is ignored because it's previously defined in plsql.conf.

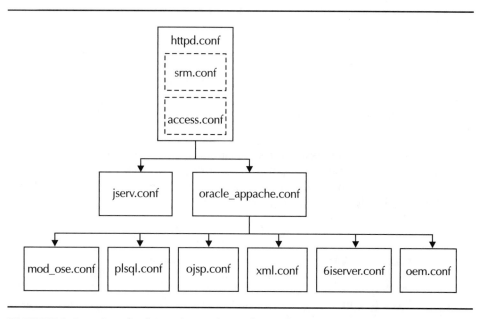

FIGURE 3-1.   *Standard Apache and Oracle configuration files*

■ **oem.conf**   Oracle Enterprise Manager (OEM) configuration that defines
the listen port (default is 3339), virtual host _default_:port, and associated
virtual host directives to use the browser-based interface of OEM.

More details about the configuration of *i*AS will be discussed shortly, but first,
let's discuss TCP/IP ports and the *i*AS (Apache) control program.

Understanding Ports

Ports are virtual divisions within an IP address on a machine. Even though a listener
can operate on any port (providing you have the privilege and the port doesn't conflict
with another service), in general, ports with a number less than 1025 are used as
system-level ports—typically assigned by the Transmission Control Protocol/Internet
Protocol (TCP/IP) commission that sets standards for these port numbers. Port 80 is
the industry standard TCP/IP port for HTTP communication.

To see which ports *i*AS has used, look at the file $ORACLE_HOME/portlist.txt.
This file shows a list of the ports, but it doesn't show what they're used for and this
isn't an inclusive list. For example, here's the portlist.txt file from my machine:

```
80
443
8007
7777
4443
7778
8008
```

The previous list doesn't include many ports, such as the Web Cache ports
(for example, 4000, 4001, 4002). To see which ports the system is using, use the
following line command:

```
netstat -a
```

The netstat command displays protocol statistics and current TCP/IP network
connections. The –a parameter displays all connections and listening ports. Executing
this command shows you an extensive listing of every port in use on your machine.
The following is only a partial listing for my laptop:

```
Active Connections
```

Proto	Local Address	Foreign Address	State
TCP	TUSCBDB:2989	TUSCBDB:0	LISTENING
TCP	TUSCBDB:8080	TUSCBDB:0	LISTENING
TCP	TUSCBDB:9001	TUSCBDB:0	LISTENING
TCP	TUSCBDB:15000	TUSCBDB:0	LISTENING
TCP	TUSCBDB:990	TUSCBDB:0	LISTENING

```
TCP     TUSCBDB:990          TUSCBDB:2985          ESTABLISHED
TCP     TUSCBDB:4900         exchange.tusc.com:smtp  TIME_WAIT
TCP     TUSCBDB:8080         TUSCBDB:4870          TIME_WAIT
TCP     TUSCBDB:8080         TUSCBDB:4889          TIME_WAIT
TCP     TUSCBDB:8080         TUSCBDB:4894          TIME_WAIT
TCP     TUSCBDB:8080         TUSCBDB:4897          TIME_WAIT
...
```

TIP
If you plan to put a listener on a port other than 80 or 443, you should use a number greater than 1024, so you don't conflict with industry standard port numbers. Most proxy servers limit users to ports 80 and 443 for HTTP and HTTPS. If you plan to deploy an application on the Internet, be aware that choosing a port outside these numbers can cause proxy issues for your users. However, because port 8080 was the de facto standard HTTP port, many proxy servers also allow access to port 8080.

The following table outlines the standard port assignments and uses:

Port Number	Standard Assignments
80	The default HTTP Listener port
443	The default HTTPS Listener (SSL—Secure Sockets Layer) port
21	The FTP (File Transfer Protocol) port
23	The telnet port
79	Finger daemon
110	POP-3
Ports 1–1024	Reserved for system level duties

Starting, Stopping and Restarting *iAS* (Apache)

The *iAS* control program is respectively named apache on NT/2000 and apachectl on UNIX. To start *iAS* on NT/2000 at the command line, check to see that the apache executable is in the system PATH environment variable. To check this, find the apache executable, typically found under the $ORACLE_HOME/Apache/Apache directory, and then check the path by selecting the system icon in the Control Panel and selecting the Environment tab (NT) or Advanced tab (2000). In most of my installations, the PATH variable wasn't set on NT/2000 for the $ORACLE_HOME/Apache/Apache directory. Add the directory for the apache executable in the PATH environment variable if it isn't set.

To start *i*AS from the command line, enter the following:

```
apache -k start
```

To stop *i*AS from the command line, enter the following:

```
apache -k shutdown
```

You can also start and stop *i*AS on NT/2000 using the Oracle HTTP Server shortcuts under the Start Button | Programs | Oracle. Additionally, the Services icon in the Control Panel has an entry for Oracle HTTP Server, which enables you to start and stop *i*AS.

To start *i*AS on UNIX, check to see if the path contains the directory holding the httpd executable, using the following line command:

```
echo $PATH
```

To start *i*AS on UNIX from the command line, enter the following:

```
apachectl start
or
httpd
```

To have *i*AS start automatically when the server is rebooted, edit /etc/rc.d/rc.local and add $ORACLE_HOME/Apache/Apache/bin/httpd

To shut down *i*AS, enter

```
apachectl shutdown
or
kill -9 'cat $ORACLE_HOME/Apache/Apache/logs/httpd.pid`
```

Command line syntax for apache and apachectl is

```
Usage: APACHE [-D name] [-d directory] [-f file] [-n service]
              [-C "directive"] [-c "directive"] [-k signal]
              [-v] [-V] [-h] [-l] [-L] [-S] [-t] [-T]
```

Command line options for UNIX and NT/2000:

- **-D name**   Define a name for use in <IfDefine name> directives

- **-d directory**   Specify an alternate initial ServerRoot

- **-f file**   Specify an alternate ServerConfigFile (good for testing configuration changes or having multiple installations of *i*AS server)

- **-C "directive"**   Process directive before reading configuration files
- **-c "directive"**   Process directive after reading configuration files
- **-v**   Show version number
- **-V**   Show compile settings
- **-h**   List available command line options (this page)
- **-l**   List compiled-in modules
- **-L**   List available configuration directives
- **-S**   Show parsed settings (currently only vhost settings)
- **-t**   Run syntax check for configuration files (with docroot check)
- **-T**   Run syntax check for configuration files (without docroot check)
- **-n name**   Name the *iAS* service for the following -k options:

    - **-k stop l shutdown**   Tell running *iAS* to shut down
    - **-k restart**   Tell running *iAS* to do a graceful restart
    - **-k start**   Tell *iAS* to start
    - **-k install l -i:**   Install an *iAS* service
    - **-k config**   Reconfigure an installed *iAS* service
    - **-k uninstall l -u**   Uninstall an *iAS* service

Configuring *iAS* (Apache)

To configure *iAS* and its many modules manually, you need to be familiar with the *iAS* directory structure and the location of the configuration files. To locate the configuration files, see the following directories, which are in $ORACLE_HOME/Apache/Apache:

- **bin**   Location of *iAS* executables
- **cgi-bin**   CGI programs
- **conf**   *iAS*/Apache
- **htdocs**   Location of Web site files, such as HTML files
- **logs**   Log files

Oracle Configuration Files

In addition to the previously defined configuration files in the "iAS Configuration File Structure" section, additional iAS configuration files include:

- **mime.types**   Multipurpose Internet Mail Extensions (MIME) mapping between MIME types and file extensions

- **wdbsrv.app**   Configuration information for Database Access Descriptors (the PL/SQL module)

- **formsweb.cfg**   Parameters used by forms CGI programs

- **jserv.properties**   Configuration for JServ engine

- **zone.properties**   Settings for servlet zone

As previously mentioned, the most important and driving configuration file in iAS is the httpd.conf file, located in the $ORACLE_HOME/Apache/Apache/conf directory. This file contains directives for the Web sites and the behavior of iAS. The file is read at the startup of iAS, so changes to this file don't take effect until iAS is restarted. The directives in iAS follow a bottom up inheritance model, in which case settings are inherited or overridden from bottom to top for the file. If two contradicting directives exist, the last directive takes precedence over the first directive. Directives also scoped into three tiers: server, container, and per-directory.

Server Directives

The server directives are global to iAS. For example, the directives specifying ServerRoot and PidFile are global directives, as follows:

```
ServerRoot "D:\Oracle\Ora81\Apache\Apache"
```

and

```
PidFile logs\httpd.pid
```

Container-Level Directives

The *container level* is limited in scope for directives and overrides server-level directives. They provide a way of limiting scope through a specific directory, URL, or HTTP request. In this example, I tell iAS to allow access to server status information from the localhost only, so if users try to find out information about the host server and their request isn't from the localhost, they'll be denied access.

```
<Location /server-status>
     SetHandler server-status
     Order deny,allow
     Deny from all
     Allow from localhost
</Location>
```

Per-Directory and File Directives

The *directory level* (per-directory) directive has directory scope, meaning it applies to a specified physical directory and overrides container and server directives. Directory level is a commonly used directive to notify *iAS* about what directories are accessible to the Web site visitors. In the following example, I enable the htdocs directory to be accessed by all, and to have symbolic links and server-side includes.

```
<Directory "c:\website/example1/htdocs/">
     Options Indexes FollowSymLinks +Includes
     AllowOverride None
     Order allow, deny
     Allow from all
</Directory>
```

Directory directives levels can use wildcards and search patterns. In the following example, I tell *iAS* to grant visibility to the docs directory and any of its subdirectories.

```
<Directory C:\website\example1\docs\*>
     Order allow, deny
     Allow from all
</Directory>
```

File directives apply to specified files. In the following example, I tell *iAS* not to allow files with the extension .ht to be viewed because .ht files contain security and directory information, and I want to limit access to that information. File directives can also use wildcards and search patterns.

```
<Files ~ "^\.ht">
     Order allow, deny
     Deny from all
</Files>
```

Some directives, like Limit and FileMatch, can be nested within a directory.

Directive Merging

When *iAS* starts up, it parses the httpd.conf file and performs directory merging. *iAS* merges the following: Directory and .htaccess, Location and LocationMatch,

Files and FileMatch. .htaccess files are unique because they are parsed and followed for every request.

Directives can be placed inside other directives. The following directives can be placed inside directory and file directives:

- **ExecCGI**   Allow execution of CGI programs

- **Includes**   Allow server-side includes (SSI)

- **Indexes**   Allow directory indexing

- **FollowSymLinks**   Allow files accessed using symbolic links

- **SymlinksIfOwnerMatch**   Allow symbolic links only if linked file is owned by the owner of the link

- **All**   Enable all options except multiview

- **Multiview**   Content negotiation

- **None**   Disable all options

Setting Your Global Directives

ServerType can be set to either inetd or standalone. inetd mode is supported only on UNIX platforms and isn't a common setting. The Default mode is standalone, which allows Apache to handle its own network connections. For example:

```
ServerType standalone
```

ServerName is the name of the server responding to the HTTP requests. It can be a hostname or IP address. For example:

```
ServerName localhost
ServerName 127.0.0.1
```

ServerRoot is the default location where the configuration, error, and log files are kept. For example:

```
ServerRoot "D:\Oracle\Ora81\Apache\Apache"
```

PidFile is the file in which the server records the process identification number for the *i*AS process when it starts. This process ID can be used to stop or restart the server. For example:

```
PidFile logs\httpd.pid
```

Timeout is the number of seconds before the server time out. For example, to timeout in 300 seconds (5 minutes):

```
Timeout 300
```

KeepAlive tells Apache whether to allow persistent connections. For example, to keep connections alive:

```
KeepAlive On
```

BindAddress is the directive used to tell the server which IP address to listen to. BindAddress can contain "*", an IP address, or a fully qualified Internet domain name. For example, to bind all addresses:

```
BindAddress *
```

Port is the default port for HTTP servers to operate. Port 80 is the default port. For example:

```
Port 80
```

Listen is a directive that can be used to replace Port and BindAddress directives. Listen can be specified multiple times for a list of ports. Listen is defaulted for port 80 and uses 443 for SSL. For example:

```
Listen 443
```

ServerAdmin is the e-mail address to which problems with the server should be sent. For example:

```
ServerAdmin Bradley_d_brown@tusc.com
```

DocumentRoot is the default location where Web pages reside. By default, *iAS* looks for the htdocs directory under ServerRoot. DocumentRoot sets the virtual root for the initial HTML document directory. For example:

```
DocumentRoot "D:\Oracle\Ora81\Apache\Apache\htdocs"
```

ErrorLog is the location of the error log file. For example:

```
ErrorLog logs\error_log
```

LogLevel is used to set the logging level condition. Error, debug, and warn are some common settings. As discussed in the following, for better performance, the preferred setting is error, but the default setting is warn. For example:

```
LogLevel error
```

The Include directive provides the capability to modularize configuration files, and allows the administrator the flexibility of containing module specific directives in separate files. Examples include jserv.conf, which contains directives for the Java Servlet Engine, and oracle_apache.conf, which has directives for additional includes, such as the plsql.conf and the ojsp.conf. Includes can be referenced using the full path or a relative path. Include files can be used for *i*AS installations supporting multiple Web sites because the file for all the Web site configurations may be dynamically generated.

*i*AS uses the following include files:

```
include "D:\oracle\ora81\Apache\Jserv\conf\jserv.conf"
include conf\oracle_apache.conf
include "D:\Oracle\Ora81\Apache\jsp\conf\ojsp.conf"
include "D:\Oracle\Ora81\Apache\modplsql\cfg\plsql.conf"
```

If you want to put your virtual hosts into a separate configuration file called virtual_hosts.conf, the directive might look like this:

```
include "C:\website\virtual_hosts.conf"
```

To define virtual directory mappings, use the Alias section of the httpd.conf file. The virtual directory *i*ASDemo is defined here and it will reference files in the physical directory c:\website\examples. Note, the ending slash must be a forward slash:

```
Alias /iASDemo/ "c:\website/examples/"
```

Including Directives Based on the Module Loaded

Conditional logic can be used in your configuration files. These conditional directives enable you to include directives if a specific *i*AS module is loaded. If the module isn't loaded, the directive is ignored. For example:

```
<IfModule mod_mime_magic.c>
    MIMEMagicFile conf\magic
</IfModule>
```

Configuring Multiple Sites Using the VirtualHost Directive

Apache can be configured to support multiple Web sites using the Port, Listen, NameVirtualHost, and the VirtualHost directives. The ports the sites are using and listening on need to be specified, and they correspond to the ports listed in the NameVirtualHost and VirtualHost container. VirtualHost information can be added using an include file (as previously demonstrated), so virtual hosts' entries can be generated programmatically. This capability of supporting multiple sites, combined with URL redirection, makes deploying a new release to production a matter of turning on a site just by redirecting the production URL to the new VirtualHost.

The following example shows the *i*AS directives supporting two Web sites, example1 at **http://localhost:80** and example2 at **http://localhost:9015**:

```
Port 80
Port 9015
Listen 80
Listen 9015
NameVirtualHost 127.0.0.1:*

<VirtualHost 127.0.0.1:80>
    ServerName localhost
    ServerAdmin admin@localhost
    DocumentRoot "c:/website/example1/htdocs/"
    ErrorLog "c:/website/example1/logs/error.log"
    CustomLog "c:/website/example1/logs/access.log" common
</VirtualHost>
<VirtualHost 127.0.0.1:9015>
    ServerName localhost
    ServerAdmin admin@localhost
    DocumentRoot "c:/website/example2/htdocs/"
    ErrorLog "c:/website/example2/logs/error.log"
    CustomLog "c:/website/example2/logs/access.log" common
</VirtualHost>
```

Using mod_rewrite

mod_rewrite is a powerful addition to the Apache Web server. It gives complete manipulation and flexibility over solving URL issues, but this flexibility comes at a cost in complexity and performance. You can use mod_rewrite to redirect obsolete URLs to new URLs, redirect failing URLs to another Web server, fix syntax issues like the trailing slash, restrict access to robots, and mitigate content issues.

mod_rewrite can be used to address the trailing slash issue, where a user requests a directory instead of a document, such as /docs/logs instead of /docs/logs/. To fix the problem, direct *i*AS to do an internal and external redirect using a mod_rewrite rule, as follows:

```
<Directory "c:\website/example1/docs/logs/">
    Options Indexes FollowSymLinks
    RewriteEngine on
    RewriteBase /logs/
    RewriteRule ^logs$ logs/ [R]
    Order allow, deny
    Allow from all
</Directory>
```

TIP
*A good article on using mod_rewrite can be found
at **http://www.engelschall.com/pw/apache/
rewriteguide/**.*

GUI *i*AS Configuration Editing

Future versions of OEM, included with 9*i*AS, are expected to include the capability
to configure Apache, but a graphical configuration tool isn't currently provided by
Oracle. Also, we've experienced problems with most of the GUI tools available today,
so my recommendation is to use a text editor as previously discussed. Many of the
graphical configuration tools are publicized by the Apache GUI-Dev project at **http://
gui.apache.org**. The Apache GUI-Dev project was formed to define a common set
of goals for developing graphical Apache configuration tools and to publicize
information on the tools.

Advantages and Disadvantages
of a Graphical Configuration Tool

*i*AS is designed for high performance and expandability and, consequently, is highly
configurable. Because the *i*AS installation doesn't include a graphical configuration
tool, several tools have been developed for this purpose. While you might be quite
comfortable manually editing the configuration file, others expect that a graphical
tool is available to maintain any system file. As with most tools, pros and cons exist
to using a graphical tool to maintain an *i*AS installation.

Advantages of a Graphical Configuration Tool

If you're new to *i*AS and, therefore, to Apache or to Web servers in general, you
might not be comfortable manually editing the configuration file or you might not
know how to implement a certain feature. A graphical interface provides a level of
comfort in knowing there's a reduced chance that you'll "break" the configuration.
A well-written tool can also guide you in the right direction, providing assistance
and recommendations on configuring the directives. By making *i*AS easy to configure
and maintain, Apache is more likely to be chosen when comparing and evaluating
the Web server choices.

Ideally, a graphical configuration tool enables even expert administrators to
configure *i*AS installations more easily than by manually editing the configuration
file. By taking all the available resources into account, the tool can reliably
recommend the optimal configuration.

If the graphical tool is browser-based, you can manage all the *i*AS servers within
the network from a central location. Allowing the user to manage the servers remotely
provides an additional level of support because the user doesn't have to be at the
physical node where Apache is installed or to connect using remote control software.

Disadvantages of a Graphical Configuration Tool

The main disadvantage of using a graphical configuration tool is it might make administering the installation more time-consuming or difficult. If the tool isn't easy to use or doesn't provide all the required functionality, it might hinder more than it helps.

Another disadvantage is if the tool isn't well written, it might break your configuration. If the configuration file contains directives the tool doesn't recognize, or contains directives where the tool doesn't expect to find them, the tool might not correctly apply the changes. In fact, our experience has shown that most of the tools do, in fact, break the *iAS* configuration files.

A third disadvantage, similar to the disadvantage of a poorly written tool, is the tool must keep up with Apache releases and should work on all platforms supported by Apache. Development of the Apache Web server is extremely active and new releases are published regularly. The tool must understand the directives available for each version and operate dynamically to allow the administrator to configure the directives applicable to the installed version.

Comanche

Comanche is an Apache graphical configuration tool that derives its name from Configuration Manager for Apache. Comanche is available in binary form from Covalent at **http://www.covalent.net/projects/comanche** for Windows NT/2000, Linux, HP-UX, Solaris, FreeBSD, and Irix. In the spirit of the open source movement, the source code is also available. If you want, you can download the Tcl/Tk toolkit and use the source code to customize Comanche to meet your needs.

In experimenting with Comanche, I found that versions 3.0b4 and 2.0b6 are available. Attempting to use 3.0b4 on Windows 2000 resulted in several registry error messages, so I used version 2.0b6 instead.

To run Comanche, simply download and extract the files into the desired directory. Because Comanche is available in executable form, execute the comanche.exe file (NT/2000) or comanche2.0 (UNIX) to start the application.

Managing and Configuring Modules

Managing and properly configuring *iAS* modules is important to provide the fastest possible performance from your *iAS* servers. This section covers the key *iAS* modules.

Configuring the PL/SQL Module (DADs)

The PL/SQL module can be administered via a browser-based configuration. You can also edit the wdbsrv.app file. Because the browser-based functionality is easy to use and provides all the needed functionality, I recommend using it rather than editing the file. The primary configuration for the PL/SQL module is to administer Database Access Descriptors (DADs) and their specific configurations.

DADs contain the information needed by *iAS* components to connect to Oracle databases. DADs can be used by any component that supports configurable database access. *iAS* provides a Web page for creating and configuring DADs.

To set up a DAD in a browser access, use the following URL:

```
http://localhost/pls/admin_/gateway.htm
```

In older versions of *iAS* prior to version 1.0.2.2, use the following URL:

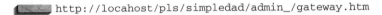

```
http://locahost/pls/simpledad/admin_/gateway.htm
```

In *iAS* version 1.0.2.2, security was added to the PL/SQL module configuration. These additions were made in the $ORACLE_HOME/Apache/modplsql/cfg/wdbsrv.cfg file. To edit the PL/SQL module configuration, it's necessary to log in to a valid database schema (such as portal30). Prior versions had a potential security bug that allowed anyone to administer the PL/SQL module through a browser, if they knew the URL.

Adding a New DAD

To add a new DAD, select Gateway Database Access Descriptor Settings, and then select Add Default (blank configuration). Enter values for the following fields:

NOTE
If Database User and Password are omitted, users are prompted for the valid database user ID and password.

- **DAD Name**   For example, example1

- **Database User**   Also known as schema name (optional)—if you leave this blank, the user is prompted for a valid database user name and password. In other words, implementing database authentication

- **Database Password**   (Optional if Database User is left blank)

- **Connect String**   The ORACLE_SID

- **Session cookie**   Used for Portal, usually left blank

- **Session state**   Preserves package/session state between requests, usually set to no

- **Connection pool parameters**   Connection pooling improves performance. The default setting turns connection pooling on. Connection pooling saves your site the expensive processing time of opening and closing database connections

- **Default Home Page**   The page to be used if no procedure or package is specified in the URL

- **Document Access Information**   Used for uploading and downloading documents in the database

- **Path Aliasing**   Map a word to an absolute path

Accessing Your New URL and DAD

After creating the previous example1 DAD, the virtual path to access database packaged procedures is

```
http://localhost/pls/example1/package.procedure
```

The components of **http://localhost/pls/example1/dbinfo** are as follows:

- **Protocol**   http or https

- **Hostname or IP address**   localhost

- **Port**   80 if omitted, default of 80 assumed

- **Module**   pls

- **DAD**   example1

- **Database Packaged Procedure**   package.procedure name

Configuring the Java Module

*i*AS comes preconfigured with the mod_jserv module. JServ has two components: the mod_jserv component written in C and the servlet engine written in Java. The mod_jserv component serves as an intermediary between *i*AS in the servlet engine, while the servlet engine contains the servlet application programming interface (API).

JServ

The JServ configuration is located in the $ORACLE_HOME/Apache/JServ/conf/ jserv.conf that contains the configuration of the JServ engine. A jserv.properties file also contains initialization settings for the Java Virtual Machine (JVM).

Java programs are compiled to class files, which can be contained within a Java Archive File (JAR). JServ uses class and jar repositories called *servlet zones*. Each zone can have its own set of classes and each zone can be configured to use a separate JVM.

TIP
*For load balancing and improved security, use
servlet zones and separate JVMs for large sites with
the majority of applications written in servlets.*

A number of settings are in the jserv.conf file. The directive

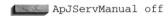
```
ApJServManual off
```

tells the JVM to start up when the Apache Web server is started up. If you need to
start multiple JVMs for security or load balancing purposes, set the ApJServManual
directive as follows:

```
ApJServManual on
```

With ApJservManual turned on, the JVM needs to start and restart scripts to run
the JVMs. In addition, each JVM needs to reside on its own port. ApJServProperties
specifies the location of the JServ properties file. This directive is ignored in a
manual startup.

```
ApJServProperties "C:\Oracle\Ora81\Apache\Jserv\conf\jserv.properties"
```

ApJServLogFile specifies the log file for the C portion of mod_jserv. In UNIX, you
need to make sure the owner of the JVM process has necessary write permissions. Log
messages are written to the Apache error log if the directive is set as follows:

```
ApJServLogFile DISABLED
```

To specify a log file, set ApJServLogFile using a path and filename, as follows:

```
ApJServLogFile "C:\Oracle\Ora81\Apache\Jserv\logs\mod_jserv.log"
```

ApJServLogLevel can be set to any of the following levels: debug, info, notice,
warn, error, crit, alert, or emerg. The default level is notice. If you change this to
debug or info, and then restart Apache, you see the following messages in the
mod_jserv.log:

```
ApJServLogLevel info
[02/06/2001 03:25:29:695] (INFO) wrapper: Shutdown done (PID=256)
[02/06/2001 03:25:29:695] (INFO) Apache Module was cleaned-up
[02/06/2001 03:25:30:206] (INFO) wrapper: Java Virtual Machine started (PID=588)
[02/06/2001 03:25:30:206] (INFO) wrapper: controller started (PID=256)
```

ApJServDefaultHost specifies the host running the JVM. To have the JVM run
on a different host than the Web server, specify ApJservManual on and start the
JVM manually.

ApJServSecretKey enables you to specify a key file that enables the administrator to restrict access to the servlet engine.

```
ApJServSecretKey C:\Oracle\Ora81\Apache\Jserv\conf\jserv.secret.key
```

If ApJServSecretKey is disabled, any process on the machine can connect to the servlet engine and execute servlets.

```
ApJServSecretKey DISABLED
```

ApJServMount sets the path mapping to a servlet zone. This directive can be set more than once, so multiple relative paths can point to the same location.

```
ApJServMount /servlets /root
ApJServMount /dev /dev
```

To test if JServ is working, reference the following URL, which calls the Java servlet IsItWorking:

```
http://localhost/servlets/IsItWorking
```

The code for the IsItWorking servlet is located in the $ORACLE_HOME/Apache/Jserv/Servlets directory.

To compile your own Java servlet, set your environment PATH variable to include

```
$ORACLE_HOME/Apache/jdk/bin
```

and set your CLASSPATH variable to include the following JAR file:

```
$ORACLE_HOME/Apache/Jsdk/lib/jsdk.jar
```

The following code sample creates a servlet using a "Hello World" example:

```
import java.io.*;
import javax.servlet.*;
import javax.servlet.http.*;
public class HelloWorld extends HttpServlet {
    public static final String MSG = "Hello World, mod_Jserv is Cool!";
    public void service (HttpServletRequest request,
                         HttpServletResponse response)
        throws ServletException, IOException
    { response.setContentType("text/html");
      PrintWriter out = response.getWriter();
      String server = getServletConfig().getServletContext().getServerInfo();
      out.println("<!DOCTYPE HTML PUBLIC \"-//W3C//DTD HTML 3.2//EN\">"
        + "<HTML> <BODY BGCOLOR=\"#FFFFFF\">"
        + "  <H1>" + MSG + "</H1>"
```

```
               + "</BODY> </HTML>");
        }
}
```

Save the file as HelloWorld.java and compile the code using the following syntax:

```
javac HelloWorld.java
```

Now to execute your HelloWorld servlet, use the following URL:

```
http://localhost/servlet/HelloWorld
```

ApJServMountCopy specifies if virtual hosts inherit the primary mount points, allowing the administrator to set up a shared mount point for servlets. This applies only to sites using virtual hosts.

```
ApJServMountCopy on
```

ApJServAction maps a file extension, such as .jhtml or .xml, contained in a URL to a servlet. For example, when I set the following in the jserv.conf file:

```
ApJServAction .jhtml /servlets/HelloWorld
```

When a document request arrives with the jhtml extension, the HelloWorld servlet is invoked.

```
http://localhost/tryme.jhtml
```

Servlet Engine

The mod_ose module enables *i*AS to communicate with the OSE by using the Net8 protocol, HTTP tunneling. It benefits from the Net 8 features load balancing, firewall support, and connection manager.

Servlets benefit from the mod_ose behavior of maintaining state between requests. State is maintained for the duration of the *i*AS process. This behavior differs from mod_jserv, which doesn't maintain state between requests.

The configuration file is located in $ORACLE_HOME/Apache/Apache/conf/mod_ose.conf file.

The default configuration file, httpd.conf, references the file oracle_apache.conf, which references the file mod_ose.conf. In httpd.conf, a file include also exists for oracle_apache.conf.

Servlet Engine Properties   The jserv.properties file contains initialization settings for the JVM. This file location is set in the jserv.conf by the ApJServProperties directive:

```
ApJServProperties "C:\Oracle\Ora81\Apache\Jserv\conf\jserv.properties"
```

When this file is updated, the JVM must be restarted to reflect the changes. The wrapper.bin directive provides the path for the JVM executable and is used only in automatic mode, which is the default.

```
wrapper.bin=C:\Oracle\Ora81\Apache\jdk\bin\java.exe
```

The wrapper.bin.parameters=[parameters] property contains parameters passed to the JVM and is used only in automatic mode. Wrapper.bin.parameters can have multiple values.

The wrapper.path=[path] is used to pass the PATH environment to the JVM. On NT/2000, delimit the statement with semicolons. On UNIX, delimit it with colons. Wrapper.path is set in the default configuration.

The wrapper.classpath=[path] property is used to set the CLASSPATH environment variable for the JVM to use. The classes you want automatically reloaded on modification cannot be in this class path or the class path of the shell in which iAS is started.

The default settings for wrapper.classpath are as follows:

```
wrapper.classpath=C:\Oracle\Ora81\Apache\jdk\lib\tools.jar
wrapper.classpath=C:\Oracle\Ora81\Apache\Jserv\ApacheJServ.jar
wrapper.classpath=C:\Oracle\Ora81\Apache\Jsdk\lib\jsdk.jar
# The following classpath entries are required to run EJBs
wrapper.classpath=C:\Oracle\Ora81\lib\aurora_client.jar
wrapper.classpath=C:\Oracle\Ora81\lib\vbjorb.jar
wrapper.classpath=C:\Oracle\Ora81\lib\vbjapp.jar
```

The wrapper.env=[name]=[value] property is used to pass environment variables to the JVM in name-value pairs. The default value is the bin directory for iAS:

```
wrapper.env=PATH=C:\Oracle\Ora81\bin
```

The wrapper.env.copy=[name] property copies environment variables for specified names. It can have multiple values.

If set to true, the wrapper.env.copyall=[true|false] property copies all environment variables to the JVM.

When debugging Java servlets, use the log option to have the servlet write events to the jserv.log file. For performance reasons, set log=false in a production environment. For example, in a development environment:

```
log=true
```

The previous setting generates log messages similar to the following:

```
[09/08/2001 15:41:52:703 PDT] IsItWorking: init
[09/08/2001 15:43:13:889 PDT] IsItWorking: destroy
```

The location and name of the log file is set using the following directive:

```
log.file=C:\Oracle\Ora81\Apache\Jserv\logs\jserv.log
```

The other directives affecting logging JServ events are

```
log.timestamp=true
log.dateFormat=[dd/MM/yyyy HH:mm:ss:SSS zz]
```

Logging is processed by a minimum priority thread. If this thread doesn't run periodically, the log queue can overflow, resulting in an out-of-memory error. The two directives that mitigate this condition are log.queue.maxage and log.queue.maxsize. *Maxage* defines the maximum time a message can stay in the queue, while *Maxsize* defines the maximum number of messages in the queue.

Servlet Zones

Configuration for servlet zones can be found in the jserv.properties file. The *port* directive specifies the port *i*AS JServ listens on. The default is 8007.

The *zones* directive contains a list of servlet zones separated by commas. For example:

```
zones=root,dev
```

Each servlet zone can have its own configuration, which is specified in the properties file.

```
root.properties=c:/Oracle/Ora81/Apache/Jserv/servlets/zone.properties
dev.properties=c:/website/example1/app/dev.properties
```

The servlet zone has a properties file named zone.properties. The zone.properties file contains the following directives. The repositories property sets the location for the servlets related to this servlet zone, as follows:

```
repositories=c:/Oracle/Ora81/Apache/Jserv/Servlets
repositories=c:/website/example1/app
```

To enable a servlet class for autoreloading (if the servlet changes), use the autoreloading.classes directive. The default value is True.

```
autoreload.classes=true
```

To enable servlet-resourced autoreloading, such as properties, use the autoreload.file directive. The default value is True.

```
autoreload.file=true
```

The *dev.properties* file specifies the servlet repository, as well as classLoader parameters, such as autoreload.classes, init.timeout, and destroy.timeout. The init.timeout parameters specify the number of milliseconds allowed for initializing a servlet. The destroy.timeout file specifies the time allowed for destroying a servlet.

```
autoreload.classes=true
init.timeout=10000
destroy.timeout=10000
```

The properties file contains session parameters, such as session.useCookies, which tells the servlet to maintain session state with cookies, as follows:

```
session.useCookies=true
```

To prevent hanging servlet sessions, set the session.timeout to a large number. For example:

```
session.timeout=1800000
```

To determine how often to check for sessions that have timed out, set the session.checkFrequency parameter, as follows:

```
session.checkFrequency=30000
```

Containers For J2EE (OC4J)

As of *iAS* version 1.0.2.2, OC4J was not installed and configured in the *iAS* installation. To test your installation of OC4J, execute the following commands from the command line:

```
cd $ORACLE_HOME/j2ee/home
java -jar orion.jar
```

The default configuration file is in $ORACLE_HOME/j2ee/home/config/server.xml. Using the –config switch, however, you can specify a different configuration file.

```
java -jar orion.jar -config /your_path/server.xml
```

Servlets written for the Tomcat servlet engine should work under the OC4J because Oracle certified OC4J as 100 percent compatible with Tomcat.

Accessing Non-Oracle Databases in Java   Type 4 JDBC drivers from Merant can be used to access DB/2, SQLServer, Sybase, and Informix. While these drivers don't ship with *iAS*, they have been certified under *iAS* as of version 1.0.2.2.

Java Development Kit (JDK) Version Oracle recommends using the J2 SDK version that ships with *i*AS. For *i*AS version 1.0.2.2, this is version 1.2.2_07 of the J2 SDK.

Configuring CLASSPATH The CLASSPATH environment variable is configured automatically to run OC4J. Java JAR and class files are loaded directly from the lib directory.

Configuring *i*AS Security

*i*AS supports both simple and easy-to-configure security solutions, from directory and digest security, to the robust and complex security using secure sockets layer (SSL).

IP and Domain Restriction

The advantage of IP and Domain Restriction is it doesn't require password maintenance. The disadvantage is its vulnerability to spoofing—where intruders falsify the IP address—to gain access to your site. IP Restriction is susceptible to spoofing, but Domain Restriction is more difficult to spoof. Under IP Restriction, requests must be issued from a specified IP address or group of IP addresses designated in the httpd.conf file.

To implement IP or Domain, use the Order, Allow, and Deny directives in the directory container. You can allow or deny from hosts, IP addresses, partial domain name, and network/netmask pair.

```
<Directory "c:\website\example1\htdocs">
    Order Deny, Allow
    All from 172.21.24.0/255.255.0.0
</Directory>
```

TIP
Use Deny before Allow to provide higher levels of security.

Directory Indexing

Use the following directives to make a list of the files in a directory available to your visitors. The Options Indexes Multiviews tells Apache to display contents of a directory if the default page, such as index.htm or index.html, isn't located in the directory.

```
<Directory "C:\website\example1\htdocs\indexed_directory\">
    Options Indexes MultiViews
    AllowOverride None
    Order allow, deny
```

```
    Allow from all
</Directory>
```

Figure 3-2 shows how Options Indexes Multiviews enables visitors to see files listed in a directory.

.htaccess

The *.htaccess* files often contain authorization information that should be kept from users. .htaccess files are great for administration of user access to certain files and directories without having to restart Apache. The .htaccess files are parsed for every request. Unfortunately, this additional parsing can cause performance problems, so the following performance section recommends you turn off this functionality. To prevent clients from viewing .htaccess files, edit httpd.conf to add the following directives:

```
<Files ~ "^\.ht">
      Order allow, deny
      Deny from all
</Files>
```

On NT/2000, .htaccess isn't a valid filename, so you must use a name like _.htaccess.

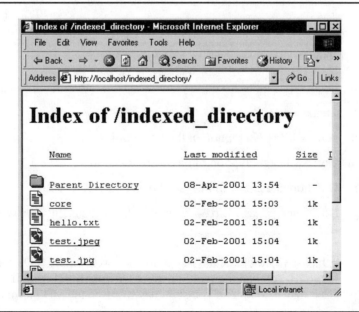

FIGURE 3-2. *Directory Indexing in browser*

Basic and Digest Authentication

Basic Authentication enables you to assign passwords to users, define groups of users, and assign users to groups. These groups can be assigned to specific files and virtual paths. When Apache receives a request for a file or directory protected with basic authentication, the requestor is required to provide a user name and a password to gain access. Basic Authentication sends unencrypted passwords across the network, making this an insecure method of security. The utility to create and maintain the password file is htpasswd. This program can be found in the $ORACLE_HOME/Apache/Apache/Bin directory.

The following command creates an authentication file named password.file and prompts for a password for the first user name (scott). The next command adds an authentication record (user name student and password of mypassword) to the file named password.file. The –p parameter tells htpasswd to add the password to file, but don't encrypt it—in other words, store it in plain text.

```
htpasswd –c password.file scott
htpasswd –pb password.file student mypassword
```

htpasswd usage:

```
htpasswd [-cmdps] passwordfile username
htpasswd -b[cmdps] passwordfile username password
htpasswd -n[mdps] username
htpasswd -nb[mdps] username password
```

htpasswd options:

- **-b** Use the password from the command line, rather than prompting for it

- **-c** Create a new file

- **-d** Force CRYPT encryption of the password

- **-m** Force MD5 encryption of password (default)

- **-n** Don't update file; display results on stdout

- **-p** Don't encrypt password (store in plain text)—note, this only works on NT/2000

By default, htpasswd automatically stores the password in the MD5 format (encrypted password). You can then add directives to your httpd.conf file or an .htaccess file. I strongly recommend you store passwords in the MD5 format, instead

of in unencrypted format. The following directives would be added at whatever level you want to perform basic authentication using the password file. In other words, if you place these directives at theVirtualHost level, they apply to the entire virtual host. If you place these directives at the Directory, File, or Location level, they apply to that specific Directory, File, or Location.

```
AuthName 'Registered'
AuthType Basic
AuthUserFile'C:\website\example\password.file'
require valid-user
```

Digest Authentication is similar to Basic Authentication, except it sends passwords encrypted across the network using a cryptographic checksum. The primary difference is you use the htdigest program to create a Digest Authentication file. The htdigest program doesn't allow passwords to be passed on the command line. You will be prompted (and reprompted) for the password. The use for htdigest is

```
htdigest [-c] passwordfile realm username
```

Where:

The -c flag creates a new file.

Once basic or digest security is configured, your Web site visitors are greeted by a screen, as shown in the following illustration, prompting them for a user name and a password.

If the incorrect user name and password are entered three or more times, or if they select the Cancel button, the user is presented with an Access Denied message in his browser, shown next.

Anonymous

Anonymous access, often used on FTP sites, can be implemented by adding Anonymous directives to the .htaccess file. Anonymous access is often accompanied by prompting for a valid e-mail address on connection to the server. Anonymous directives list valid user names. Anonymous_LogEmail requires an e-mail address to be entered for the password. Anonymous_VerifyEmail states whether the server syntactically checks for valid e-mail addresses containing a dot and @ sign. For example, the following directives can be added to the context of your choice (for example, Global, Directory, File, Location):

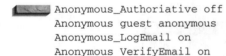

```
Anonymous_Authoriative off
Anonymous guest anonymous
Anonymous_LogEmail on
Anonymous VerifyEmail on
```

Database Authentication

Database authentication uses a database schema (that is, a user name and a password) to authenticate users. By combining database authentication with logic in your application, you can provide application-level authentication. By using the user pseudocolumn, your application logic can use database roles or table-based roles to determine a user's level of functionality. Typically, you build PL/SQL packages to support the level of application authentication you want to provide for your users.

Database authentication is recommended for a small number of users or small intranet Web sites. For large sites or Internet sites, you probably want to use the Single Signon functionality or application logic for security.

TIP

When creating a DAD, if the user name and/or password aren't entered, database authentication is enabled for that DAD.

SSL

Secure Sockets Layer (SSL) is the encryption protocol that handles HTTPS (HTTP over SSL). SSL isn't normally packaged with Apache, however, Oracle has thankfully packaged this module into the *iAS* version of Apache. SSL uses encryption called *public key cryptography.* The server sends the client a public key. The client encrypts data using the public key and sends it to the server, which can decrypt the data using the private key. SSL is the recommended security implementation for supporting e-commerce sites.

TIP

Use SSL for security of Internet applications from end-to-end.

Oracle has provided a demo certificate to be used in the development environment. In a production environment, you want to create a new key and certificate.

Steps to Create a New Key and Certificate

1. Create a new directory called demoCA.

   ```
   mkdir c:\demoCA
   ```

2. Copy the openssl configuration file into a demoCA directory.

   ```
   copy $ORACLE_HOME\apache\open_ssl\bin\openssl.cnf c:\demoCA
   ```

3. In the Command window, change directory to demoCA and set the path to include c:\oracle\ora81\apache\open_ssl\bin.

   ```
   SET PATH=$ORACLE_HOME\apache\open_ssl\bin;%PATH%
   ```

4. Edit the openssl file and comment out the following lines:

   ```
   #RANDFILE= $ENV::HOME/.rnd
   #oid_file= $ENV::HOME/.oid
   ```

5. Replace the line starting with dir:

   ```
   dir= C:\demoCA
   ```

Steps to Creating a Key

1. Create a random key by typing:

   ```
   openssl genrsa -des3 -out priv.key 1024 -config
   ```

2. Create a new certificate by typing:

   ```
   openssl req -new -key priv.key -out certreq.csr
      -config c:\demoCA\openssl.cnf
   ```

NOTE
*When openssl prompts you for the
CommonName, enter your host.domain.com.*

3. You should now have the files priv.key and certreq.csr in the
   demoCA directory.

4. Go to **www.verisign.com**, select Get a Server Certificate, and then
   select the Trial version.

5. Follow the instructions and fill out all information accurately.

6. Open certreq.csr with the editor and copy the encrypted message
   into the text box provided by Verisign.

7. Verisign will e-mail the SSL trial certificate.

8. Save the e-mail to a text file.

9. Open this text file and delete text appearing before:

   ```
   ---BEGIN CERTIFICATE---
   ```

10. Save this as cert.crt file in c:\demoCA directory.

11. Remove the password from the key file.

12. Copy the private key and register the key.

    ```
    copy priv.key priv.key.org
    openssl rsa -in priv.key.org -out priv.key
    ```

13. Edit your httpd.conf file, and then locate and replace the following two entries:

    ```
    SSLCertificateFile conf\ssl.crt\server.crt
    ```

    with

    ```
    SSLCertificateFile c:\demoCA\cert.crt SSLCertificateKeyFile
    ```

    and replace:

    ```
    conf\ssl.key\server.key
    ```

with

```
SSLCertificateKeyFile c:\demoCA\priv.key
```

14. Using the public and private key Oracle provided, test the SSL functionality. Modify the httpd.conf file's VirtualHost container. For example:

```
<VirtualHost 127.0.0.1:443>
DocumentRoot c:\website/example1/htdocs/
ServerName localhost
SSLEngine on
SSLCertificateFile conf\ssl.crt\server.crt
SSLCertificateKeyFile conf\ssl.key\server.key
Listen 443
</VirtualHost>
```

15. Restart Apache and in your browser go to **https://localhost:443/**. If SSL is working, you should see the standard Web page for your localhost server.

TIP

Secure log files and directories from read/write access. Log files contain private information about who is accessing your Web site and how they're using it.

Monitoring Your *iAS* Web Server

Knowing how to monitor your *iAS* Web Server can help you achieve better performance, improved security, and reliability. Monitoring can also help you understand how your users are using the Web site.

Monitoring Error and Log Files

Excessive or repeated errors consume the system's resources and slow response times. Check the log files regularly to detect inefficiencies in the *iAS* configuration.

For example, an image map with undefined areas might cause a repeated HTTP Error 500. Every user who clicks one of these areas generates the error. You can eliminate the problem by eliminating the "holes" in the image map. Another example is a repeated HTTP Error 404, which is usually caused by a broken hypertext link. Any repeated error slows down your entire application.

Regular monitoring of log files provides a good understanding of how users access your site. Use this information to optimize allocation of hardware and server resources. You can use tools, such as WebTrends, for detailed site use monitoring.

Don't allow your log files to grow without limit. When a log file reaches a certain size (the size greatly depends on the size of your site, but 1–5MB is a good standard rule), archive the file and start a new log file. You need to stop Apache to accomplish this. This avoids the overhead of writing to a large file.

Error Log

Using the mod_log_config module, Apache offers flexibility in terms of logging. ErrorLog specifies the location of the error.log. The default location for the error log file is $ORACLE_HOME/Apache/Apache/logs/error_log, but log files can be located wherever you specify. The error log file, unlike some other log files, cannot have a customized format. Under UNIX, the error log can be redirected to the system log daemon using the following directive:

```
ErrorLog syslog
```

Log Level and Format

Settings for log files can be placed within containers for VirtualHosts, so each of your Web sites has its own set of log files. The *LogLevel* specifies the types of errors added to the log file. See Chapter 23 for a listing of log levels. Some log files, like the access_log, can have a specified log format. *LogFormat* is the directive that can be used to modify the standard format of the log file. LogFormat takes two arguments: the format string and a name for the format (optional-). LogFormat, along with TransferLog, can be defined in the VirtualHost container to customize the format for tracking all site visits and activity. In my VirtualHost, I have the following specified:

```
TransferLog c:/website/example1/logs/access.log
LogFormat "%h %l %u %t \"%r\" %>s %b \"%{Referer}i\
   " \"%{User-Agent}i\"" combined
```

TIP

Excessive logging can cause performance problems. Set logging level and log files to capture only what your site needs.

To set the logging level to capture warnings (or worse), use the LogLevel directive, as follows. The default is warn, as discussed in the following tuning section, using LogLevel error can improve *i*AS performance by over 150 percent. If you require more detailed logs for analysis of your user community (see Chapter 23 for more information about log file analysis), however, you won't receive detailed logs if LogLevel is set to error.

```
LogLevel warn
```

Monitoring Processes and Memory Use

To monitor memory use on UNIX, various utilities depend on the flavor of UNIX. top, sar, and vmstat are all useful tools. The *ps –aef* command is useful to determine active processes in UNIX. On NT/2000, the Task Manager can provide details on process and memory use.

*i*AS mod_status and mod_info

iAS mod_status generates server status information when enabled. To enable the server status information to be available only by clients accessing the site from LocalHost, add the following directives to httpd.conf. mod_status, by default, presents standard status information to obtain additional server status information.

```
ExtendedStatus on
```

The following directives are used with mod_status:

```
<Location /server-status>
    SetHandler server-status
    Order deny,allow
    Deny from all
    Allow from localhost
</Location>
```

To access server status information in the browser, use the link **http://localhost/server-status**, as you see in Figure 3-3.

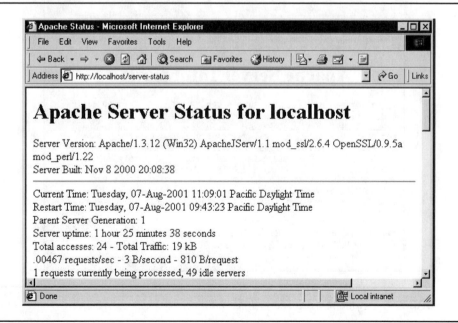

FIGURE 3-3. *Apache (iAS) Server Status*

TIP
Server status information can be used by hackers, so it's best to place the allow and deny directives in the location container where server-status is turned on.

To obtain module configuration information, showing configuration information such as what modules are loaded, use the mod_info module. Turn on mod_info by adding the following directives to httpd.conf:

```
<Location /server-info>
    SetHandler server-info
    Order deny,allow
    Deny from all
    Allow from localhost
</Location>
```

To access server status information in a browser, use the link **http://localhost/server-info**, which displays a page similar to Figure 3-4.

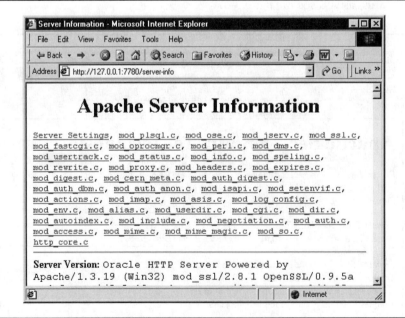

FIGURE 3-4. *Apache (iAS) Server Information*

Monitoring mod_ jserv

mod_jserv has its own set of log files and status information page. In the jserv.conf file—located under $ORACLE_HOME/Apache/Jserv/conf—uncomment the following code to enable the JServ status page:

```
<Location /jserv/>
  SetHandler jserv-status
  order deny,allow
  deny from all
  allow from localhost
</Location>
```

To see the status page similar to Figure 3-5, restart Apache and, in the browser, go to **http://localhost/jserv/**.

Select the configured hosts link on the status page to view the JServ settings for your Web site, which executes the following URL: **http://localhost/jserv/status?module=127.0.0.1** and displays a page similar to Figure 3-6.

If you select Mapped Servlet Engines, and then select the information on the current status of the servlet engine and the root servlet zone, which executes the following URL **http://localhost/jserv/engine/0/**, you see a page similar to Figure 3-7.

When you select the current status of the servlet engine, you can also see information on the location of the log file and max connections, as in Figure 3-8.

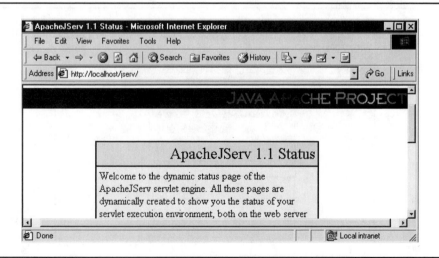

FIGURE 3-5. *Apache JServ Status*

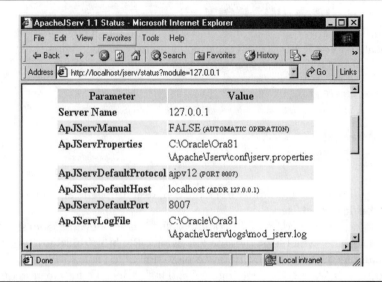

FIGURE 3-6. *Configured Hosts Parameters*

When selecting status on a servlet zone, you can determine whether autoreload is turned on and see the settings for various timeouts, as shown in Figure 3-9.

FIGURE 3-7. *JServ Engine Status*

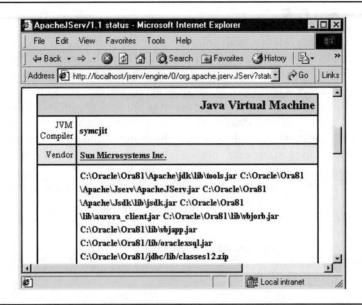

FIGURE 3-8. *Java Virtual Machine details*

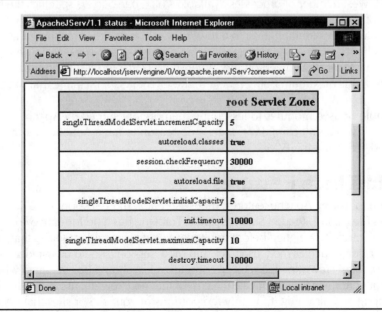

FIGURE 3-9. *Servlet Zone information*

Tuning *i*AS

The following tuning tips can help enhance your *i*AS performance.

Host name lookups occur when *i*AS performs a Domain Name Server (DNS) lookup on an IP address of the request. These lookups are slow and should be avoided using the directive `HostNameLookup off`. Also, when configuring the VirtualHost directive, use the IP address of the server versus the name of the server to prevent DNS lookups.

Use the Options FollowSymLinks directive, rather than SymLinksIfOwnerMatch, which causes Apache to evaluate whether the owner of the link is the owner of the server and also causes Apache to check the full path of the symbolic link. This checking takes processing time and should be avoided.

.htaccess files can cause Apache to run slower because, for every request, the .htaccess files in the document directory accessed are parsed. .htaccess files can be ignored using the AllowOverride directive.

```
<Directory "C:\website/example1/htdocs/">
    AllowOverride None
</Directory>
```

MinSpareServers, MaxSpareServers, and StartServers aren't as important for tuning with the latest versions of Apache. Apache has a robust algorithm for allocating and destroying server processes. *StartServers* (the number of processes Apache creates on startup) is controlled dynamically and, therefore, shouldn't be set. *MinSpareServers* sets the lowest number of processes available. *MaxSpareServers* specifies the highest number of processes available.

Set MaxClients (default 256) to a lower level if your site is reaching this level and the clients connecting are experiencing performance issues. MaxClients sets the maximum processes allowed on the server. If an HTTP request cannot be satisfied because of this maximum being reached, the client gets a message that the server is unavailable.

Disable unused modules to lessen the memory consumed by Apache. For example, if you aren't using Java, there's no reason to have Apache automatically start mod_jserv and the JVM.

Avoid These Features

Avoid the following Apache features: mod_usertrack, mod_session, URL Rewrite, .htaccess files, and Extended Status. Session Tracking has a performance cost, which should be carefully weighed before implementing it. This said, modules that facilitate session tracking, such as mod_usertrack and mod_session, should be avoided. Rewriting URLs, especially rewriting them using complex rules, should be evaluated when looking at performance. To mitigate the cost of the mod_rewrite, use it selectively by enabling and disabling it for only the portions of your site or sites that need it. Because .htaccess files are parsed for every request, they should be avoided. The extended status page generated from mod_status has a high performance cost because two system time calls are made for each request.

Tuning Your Logging

Logging can be both CPU- and I/O-intensive. If possible, log errors only by setting LogLevel error, as follows:

```
LogLevel error
```

TIP
Using LogLevel error versus the default LogLevel warning can improve performance by over 150 percent.

Tuning Application Modules

Tuning your Web applications can make or break the performance of your Web site. With a variety of applications supported by *iAS*, a number of tuning options exist. CGI applications can often be tuned by allowing the CGI scripts to be cached. PL/SQL applications can be tuned using tools like SQL trace and Explain Plan. Java database applications can benefit from SQL tuning, as well as class caching.

Tuning CGI/Perl Applications

CGI scripts written in Perl can be cached by using the mod_perl module Apache::Registry. In the default httpd.conf file, the following directives are set to turn on caching for Perl scripts. The location container is used, so I can also not have some CGI scripts cached because caching of CGI scripts can sometimes cause a problem with their execution. This is because of the wrapper Apache uses to enable CGI script caching.

```
Alias /perl/ "c:\website\example1\cgi-bin\"
<Location /perl>
    SetHandler  perl-script
    PerlHandler Apache::Registry
    AddHandler perl-script .pl
    Options +ExecCGI
    PerlSendHeader On
</Location>
```

When your URL references /perl/hello.cgi, your script is cached. When you reference your script /cgi/hello.cgi, however, your script won't be cached. This flexibility is important if your Perl CGI script is using code that can result in abnormalities when cached. To tell if a Perl script is cached or not, check the mod_perl environment variable, which is always set when handling requests. As demonstrated in Figure 3-10, to generate the status page for mod_perl, add the following directives to httpd.conf and the reference **http://localhost/perl-status/** in your browser:

```
<Location /perl-status>
    SetHandler  perl-script
    PerlHandler Apache::Status
    order deny,allow
    deny from all
    allow from 127.0.0.1
</Location>
```

Tuning PL/SQL and PSP Applications

To tune PL/SQL applications and PSPs, build your applications in a way that reduces the load on the database server and performs fast data manipulation language (DML). Tools such as the *iAS* Database Cache, and mod_plsql features, such as connection pooling, can enable you to reduce the load on the database. Explain Plan, sqltrace, tkprof, and Oracle Expert can help you tune your queries by showing you optimizer

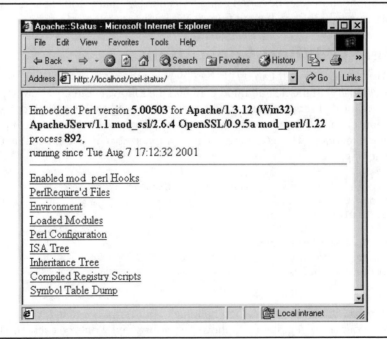

FIGURE 3-10. *Perl status page*

paths and places where you can enhance performance through index creation. Oracle9*i* provides numerous optimizer hints, new indexing options, and new PL/SQL and database features to improve DML performance.

Use Database Connection Pooling

PL/SQL programs and PSPs can be configured to use database connection pooling. When configuring the database access descriptor, make sure to leave the default setting for connection pooling option on. This tells *iAS* to pool database connections. Opening and closing database connections causes a big performance drain on the database, so I highly recommend using connection pooling.

9*i* New Features and Hints

Inserts can be faster (at the expense of some additional disk space use), using the append hint. Inserts, updates, and deletes on tables that don't need to be recoverable can be made faster by setting the affected table to nologging, so no redo log information is generated. Indexes being suppressed by functions in the where clause can take advantage of function-based indexes, which can enhance performance 100 times over.

Tuning Your PL/SQL Code

PL/SQL provides the capability to create PL/SQL tables (that is, arrays). The index of the table is the binary integer ranging from -2147483647 to +2147483647. This table index option is known as *sparsity,* and enables meaningful index numbers, such as customer numbers, employee numbers, and other useful index keys. Use PL/SQL tables to process large amounts of data.

PL/SQL tables can also be used in Oracle Call Interface (OCI) applications, enabling you to pass arrays from OCI into PL/SQL stored procedures to process large batches of data. PL/SQL tables increase performance by operating on tables rather than on single rows.

PL/SQL provides TABLE and VARRAY (variable size array) collection types. The TABLE collection type is called a nested table. *Nested tables* are unlimited in size and can be sparse, so elements within the nested table can be deleted using the DELETE procedure. Variable-size arrays have a maximum size, and maintain their order and subscript when stored in the database. Nested table data is stored in a system table associated with the nested table. Variable-size arrays are designed for batch operations in which the application processes the data in batch array style.

Use Explain Plan, Tkprof, and Oracle Expert to Improve Query Performance

To maximize performance and minimize execution time, optimize application SQL statements. Tuning SQL is often the effort of rewriting SQL statements either to do less work or to improve the parallelization factor of the query.

Explain Plans are crucial to tuning SQL and examining the execution path. The Explain Plan lists the execution path that the Oracle's Optimizer chooses for a given query, enabling you to review the execution path before it's submitted. Use Explain Plan to analyze queries and to tune the query before it's executed. If Explain Plan reveals a poor execution path, you can tune the SQL statement using hints to obtain a better Execution Path.

To use the Explain Plan utility, select permission must be granted on the tables you're attempting to explain. You must also have select and insert permissions on the PLAN_TABLE table. To create the Explain Plan table, run the $ORACLE_HOME/rdbms/admin/utlxplan.sql script.

You can also generate a SQL trace file and use it with the *tkprof utility,* which shows the different phases, including parsing, fetching, and execution. SQL trace can be turned on for an individual session or for the entire database. To turn on SQL trace for your current session, execute the data dictionary language (DDL) statement in a SQL*Plus window.

```
ALTER SESSION SET SQL_TRACE = true;
```

To turn on sqltrace for the entire database, modify the init.ora file, adding sql_trace = true, and then restart the database.

Oracle Expert provides a good analysis of DML running on your database and can generate a report on indexes it recommends creating and removing, based on the DML collected and analyzed. Oracle Expert comes with the Oracle Tuning Pack.

Caching PL/SQL   Caching PL/SQL calls eliminates additional network round trips to the database server. Caching is used by Portal. To invoke caching, make calls to OWA_CACHE package.

Tuning JSP/JServ Applications

When tuning JServ applications, consider preloading commonly accessed classes at JServ startup, which is similar to pinning PL/SQL packages in a database. Add classes to pin in the servlets.startup directive in the zone properties file.

Use Connection Pooling and Connection Caching

JDBC connections are expensive in terms of performance and, therefore, should be avoided by using connection pooling. JDBC allows physical database connections to be shared or pooled through logical connections. A *logical connection* is one in which the JDBC client borrows the physical connection and returns the physical connection when it closes the logical connection. This model has been enhanced with the Oracle extension to JDBC 2.0 that introduces database connection caching. Connection caching allows for improved connection management by associating a number of pooled logical connections with a physical database connection containing a database schema name.

Use Autoreload Only in Development, Not Production

Autoreload is an option commonly used in development because it enables you to change classes without restarting the Apache server. In a production environment, Autoreload can cause poor performance because it requires the classes to be checked for changes for each call to JServ.

```
Set Autoreload.classes = false
Set Autoreload.file = false
```

Use the Single-Threaded Model

Using the *single-threaded model* can improve application performance by more than 25 percent. This gain is the result of the decrease in synchronization bottlenecks. The single-threaded model enables you to have a pool of serially reusable servlets, which are thread safe. To implement the model, establish the servlet connection in the init() method and disconnect from the database server in the destroy method. Use the following settings when configuring applications to use a single-threaded model:

```
single ThreadedModelServlet.initialCapacity
single ThreadedModelServlet.incrementCapacity
single ThreadedModelServlet.maximumCapacity
```

Load Balancing JServ

Starting multiple JServ processes can benefit even a single processor machine because Apache won't automatically restart the process if it dies. *Load balancing* can increase the performance of Java classes that have synchronized methods by making parallelism possible. A JVM process can go down when a servlet terminates with a System.exit(), so load balancing provides reliability through redundancy. Starting multiple JServ processes allows a lot of flexibility for your site because servlet zones can be distributed on different JServ. JServ processes can be started with a different user ID than that which owns Apache. Every JServ process can be started with a unique CLASSPATH and JDK version, making it possible for sites to have some servlets that need various versions of the JDK running in their own environment. An additional script is required to start up more than one process.

JServ, by default, is automatically started each time Apache is started with ApJServManual set to auto (the default setting) in jserv.conf.

```
ApJServManual auto
```

To start JServ manually, turn the manual setting on with

```
ApJServManual on
```

Manually Start the JServ Processes in UNIX

1. Stop Apache Web server.

```
apachectl stop
```

2. Modify jserv.conf to set ApJServDefaultPort to a port other than default 8007.

3. Modify jserv.conf to set ApJServManual on.

4. Modify jserv.properties to set the old port number to the new port number specified for ApJServDefaultPort.

5. Start Apache Web server.

```
apachectl start
cd $ORACLE_HOME/bin
```

6. Create a new file called jservctl.

```
#!/bin/ksh
# This shell script manually starts the JVM.
# It is a simplified script based
# on a script found on Metalink
# http://metalink.oracle.com Note: 123533.1
function usage {
    echo " "
    echo "jservctl usage:"
    echo "To start: jservctl "
    echo "To stop: jservctl -s "
    echo "To see version: jservctl -v"
    echo "To see options: jservctl -V"
    echo "To get usage: jservctl -h"
    echo " "
}
echo "1 is $1"
if [[ "${1}" = "0" ]] then
    usage
     exit -1
fi
if [[ "${1}" = "-h" ]]
then
    usage
    exit 0
fi
JSERV_CMD=$1
APACHE_HOME=$ORACLE_HOME/Apache
```

```
JDK_HOME=$APACHE_HOME/jdk
JSDK_HOME=$APACHE_HOME/Jsdk
JSERV_HOME=$APACHE_HOME/Jserv
JSDK_JAR=$JSDK_HOME/lib/jsdk.jar
JSERV_JAR=$JSERV_HOME/libexec/ApacheJServ.jar
JSERV_NAME="org.apache.jserv.JServ"
JSERV_LOG=$JSERV_HOME/logs
JSERV_CFG_DIR=$JSERV_HOME/etc
CLASSPATH=$CLASSPATH:$JSDK_JAR:$JSERV_JAR
export CLASSPATH
LOG=$JSERV_LOG/jserv.log
PROPERTY=$JSERV_CFG_DIR/jserv.properties
CLASSES=$CLASSPATH
$JDK_HOME/bin/java -classpath $CLASSES $JSERV_NAME
    $PROPERTY $JSERV_CMD &> $LOG
```

JServ and Session Tracking   JServ uses session cookies to bind a session with a particular JServ process. When a request arrives, mod_jserv randomly chooses to which JServ process to route the request and adds a cookie trailer specifying the ApJservRoute, which is added to the session cookie before satisfying the client request. Subsequent requests are routed to the appropriate JServ process, based on the cookie value for ApJservRoute.

Turn Off Debug and Developer Flag When Deploying JSPs to Production

In the servlet zones properties file, there's a setting for the init args for developers to turn on debugging. The *Debug* mode is used to generate debugging messages. The Developer mode is used to specify whether or not at run time the JSP should automatically recompile and reload any JSPs that have changed since they were last loaded. The default setting for Developer mode is True.

Use the following directive to turn off Developer mode and Debug mode:

 `servlet.oracle.jsp.JspServlet.initArgs=debug=false, developer_mode=false`

Hardware and Operating System Tuning

You can use the operating system and Web utilities to analyze *i*AS performance, including process CPU time and memory use, and connection and request statistics. A number of other ways exist to monitor the performance of your applications, servers, and sites. The following sections cover the general tuning items.

Reviewing Hardware Recommendations

In addition to the following general recommendations, make sure your hardware resources are adequate for the requirements of your specific applications. To avoid hardware-related performance bottlenecks, each hardware component should operate at no more than 75 percent to 80 percent of capacity. In the beginning of a system's life, the 80 percent of capacity rule is common sense, but it's often forgotten once the application goes into production. Loading the last 20 percent of the system is what can cause the worst performance problems.

The following is the *absolute* minimum hardware configuration for most *iAS* deployments on the Sun Solaris platform:

- Sun UltraSparc II at 168 MHz or Pentium Pro at 200 MHz

- Memory: 128MB, recommended 1GB

- Network Connection: 100 Mbps

- Disk Space:

   - Minimal Edition: 630MB

   - Standard Edition: 1.35GB

   - Enterprise Edition: 3.60GB

Processor and memory resources should be more than adequate to handle the maximum traffic on your network connections. If your network becomes a bottleneck, you can upgrade to faster network interface cards or install multiple network interface cards on each machine.

Tuning *iAS* on Solaris

To monitor *iAS* performance on Sun Solaris systems, use the top, vmstat, sar, and ps utilities to monitor memory use, swapping, paging, and processor use by *iAS* processes.

Oracle recommends installing *iAS* on its own machine for optimum performance and monitoring. Processor use varies with each individual application. If the application is network-intensive, the listener processes consume the majority of processor cycles. If your application is code-intensive, the modules consume the majority of the work, so modules perform the majority of the processes. If the application is database-intensive and the database is on the same box as *iAS* (not recommended for a production site), the database processes consume most of the machine CPU and I/O.

Tuning the Operating System

Sun Microsystems regularly updates the Solaris operating system components (TCP/IP, subsystem). TCP/IP is heavily used by *i*AS, so be sure you've installed the latest patches.

Sun also provides the Solaris Internet Server Supplement, which is a set of add-on modules specially tailored for Solaris systems that host Web sites. Make sure to obtain this supplement from Sun. The following subsections discuss items you can set at the operating-system level for optimum system performance.

File Descriptors   Make certain the limit on file descriptors per process is set at the maximum before starting *i*AS, using the unlimit command, as follows:

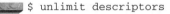

```
$ unlimit descriptors
```

Transmission Control Protocol (TCP) Settings   The following table lists the recommended TCP parameters and values for Solaris. These values are good recommendations and haven't changed in a long time, but you might want to contact Oracle support for the most current recommendations.

Parameter	Recommended Value
tcp_conn_req_max_q0	1024
Tcp_conn_req_max_q	1024
tcp_slow_start_initial	2
tcp_close_wait_interval	60000
Tcp_conn_hash_size	32768
tcp_xmit_hiwat	32768
tcp_recv_hiwat	32768

To set these TCP parameters, you must first connect to the root UNIX account (su root), and then use the following command, replacing each parameter with the suggested value of the preceding parameter:

```
# /usr/sbin/ndd -set /dev/tcp parameter value
```

Using the netstat Utility   Solaris contains a TCP/IP statistic, known as *tcpListenDrop,* that counts the number of times a connection is dropped because of a full queue. You can use the Solaris netstat utility (-s option) to report networking statistics, including tcpListenDrop. Applications that have high tcpListenDrop counts should increase the size of the queue by specifying higher values for the backlog to the listener (the listen() call). Set the maximum backlog size by adjusting the value of the tcp_conn_req_max parameter higher. In the case of an initial handshake, an incoming packet is sent with only the Synchronized Sequence Numbers (SYN) flag set. When a packet is sent, the server makes an entry in the listen queue, and then sends another packet to acknowledge the first packet. It also includes a SYN flag to reciprocate the synchronization of the sequence number in the opposite direction. The client then sends another packet to acknowledge the second SYN, and the server process is scheduled to return (from the accept() call), subsequently moving the connection from the listen queue to the active connection list.

Solaris has two TCP tunable parameters—tcp_conn_req_max_q and tcp_conn_req_max_q0—which specify the maximum number of completed connections waiting to return from an accept() call and the maximum number of incomplete handshake connections, respectively.

Use the netstat utility (-s option) to monitor TCP statistics and to determine connection-drop activity, as well as the type of drops. The tcpHalfOpenDrop statistic is incremented when an in-doubt connection is dropped. The default value for tcp_conn_rq_max_q is 128 and the default value for tcp_conn_req_max_q0 is 1,024. The default values are typically sufficient and shouldn't require tuning. By examining the statistics with the netstat utility, however, you can determine if the parameters need to be adjusted.

TCP implementations use a congestion window limiting the number of packets that can be sent before an acknowledgment. This is used to improve the startup latency and also helps avoid overloading the network. The TCP standard specifies that the initial congestion window should consist of one packet, doubled up on each successive acknowledgment. This causes exponential growth and may not necessarily be ideal for HTTP servers, which typically send small batches of packets. Solaris provides a tcp_slow_start_intital parameter, which can be used to double the congestion window from its default of 1 to 2. This improves transmission throughput of small batch sizes.

Contrary to Solaris, NT/2000 doesn't immediately acknowledge receipt of a packet on connection/start, which results in an increase in the connection startup latency. NT/2000 immediately acknowledges if two packets are sent. The difference between the NT/2000 and the Solaris implementation causes performance discrepancies, or higher response times, when NT/2000 clients are used to connect to Solaris servers with a high-speed or LAN-based network. Set the congestion window on Solaris to 2, using tcp_slow_start_initial equal to 2.

In Solaris, the tcp_conn_hash_size parameter can be set to help address connection backlog. During high connection rates, TCP data structure kernel lookups can be expensive and can slow the server. Increasing the size of the hash table improves lookup efficiency. The default for tcp_conn_hash_size is 256. This parameter must be a power of 2 and can be set in the /etc/system kernel configuration file.

Use the netstat utility to monitor the overall network traffic, as well as the network traffic for a given interface, using the (-k) option.

Monitoring Processor Use

Gather CPU statistics to determine process utilization. You can also monitor system scalability by adding users and increasing the system workload. Use the sar and mpstat utilities to monitor process use, as described in the following subsections.

Using the sar Utility   To determine process use, use the following sar command:

```
$ sar -u 1 5
```

When you use the sar command, you receive a listing similar to the following:

```
$ sar -u 1 5

SunOS Tuscco_oas3 5.6 Generic_sun4m

%usr    %sys    %wio    %idle
1       1       0       98
3       5       0       92
8       2       0       90
2       2       0       96
```

The sar command (-u option) provides the statistics identified in the following table:

CPU Statistics	Description
%usr	Percentage the processor is running in user time
%sys	Percentage of processes running in system time
%wio	Percentage the processor spends waiting on I/O requests
%idle	Percentage the processor is idle

Using the mpstat Utility   On Solaris, you can also monitor CPU processes using the mpstat command, as follows:

```
$ mpstat 1 3
```

The mpstat utility is similar to the sar command: the first argument to mpstat is the polling interval time in seconds. The second argument to mpstat is the number of iterations. The mpstat utility reports the statistics per processor.

Monitoring the Run Queue

Monitor the *run queue* to determine if processes are waiting for an available processor. Use the following sar -q command to monitor the run queue:

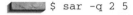 `$ sar -q 2 5`

The following table describes the statistics shown when you use the sar -q utility:

Statistic	Description
Runq-sz	Length of the run queue (processes waiting for CPU)
%runocc	Percentage of time occupied
Swpq-sz	Number of processes that have been swapped out and are now ready to run
%swpocc	Percentage of time occupied

Tuning I/O

Direct input/output (I/O) bypasses the UNIX file system cache and copies the file system-based file data directly into user space. Direct I/O on file systems is similar to raw devices. Solaris 2.6 enables direct I/O to be performed using the directio() system call. An application can use the directio() system call to perform direct I/O processing on a file. To control whether direct I/O to the file system is forced, use the mount command options: noforcedirectio and forcedirectio.

Use direct I/O to

- Improve large sequential I/O performance

- Improve performance of large files during file transfers

- Eliminate extra buffer copies and file system cache maintenance

- Reduce CPU consumption

Tuning *i*AS on Windows NT/2000

On Windows NT/2000 platforms, the available tuning options aren't nearly as extensive as on UNIX platforms. Use the Task Manager and Performance Monitor to assess hardware and operating system performance and to verify the application processes being used by *i*AS. The bottom line is you don't have the same tuning options available for Windows 2000 as you do for UNIX.

Optimizing FTP Downloads

If your site offers a large volume of data for FTP downloads, you will obtain better performance for these downloads, and for other server accesses, by hosting the downloadable data on a separate server. This releases resources on your *iAS* servers for handling HTTP and application requests.

Setting Swap Space and Distributing the Load

In setting up an *iAS* site, make sure swap space use doesn't exceed 75 percent to 80 percent. *iAS* generates new processes over time. You should set up each *iAS* machine with three times as much swap space as physical memory. If your system begins swapping or paging excessively, you might be running too many processes on your system. In this case, add more memory or additional nodes (machines) to your site to distribute the load. Another possible cause of excessive swapping and paging is memory leakage in applications.

Summary

iAS is a complex and powerful product. With a multitude of configuration and tuning options available, *iAS* is the perfect application server for any business, from a small company to the largest dot-com in the world. Invest the time to understand the Apache Web server completely and, in turn, *iAS* inside and out—and it will pay off ten times over. If you simply read the quick tips in the beginning of this chapter, and then read the summary, I highly recommend you find the time to read and understand this chapter. I hope the "Getting Started" section provided you with a basis from which to start configuring *iAS*.

CHAPTER

4

24×7 Uptime

s the old saying goes, the more things change, the more they stay the same. Nowhere is this truer than in the area of Web-enabled application availability. As many traditional brick-and-mortar companies scrambled to add the coveted *e* prefix to their operations, many painful lessons were learned along the way. Because customers can potentially access your Web site at any time of day or night, if your site is down or unavailable, this directly results in lost revenue, bad publicity, and, worst of all, customers may retain a bad impression about your site and never return. We've all read newspaper articles about companies who discovered this the hard way when their glamorous Web site was replaced with the dreaded HTTP 500–Fatal Error message.

Even after realizing the critical nature of ensuring a Web site is online and running 24 hours a day, 7 days a week, the challenge posed to the Information Technology (IT) group within a modern e-company can be a daunting one. When a Web site is functioning normally, it's seamless to the end user, but the number of hardware, software, and human components working behind the scene can be extensive. Some of the necessary steps in creating a highly available architecture include the following items:

- Identify every component connected to the Web site. Each hardware and software component must be identified and its relationship to the other components must be determined and factored into the whole architecture. The importance of this cannot be overstressed because it's often one of the smallest components within the system architecture that causes downtime.

- Identify all possible failures that might occur. Once all the components within the architecture have been identified, the next step is to determine all possible failures that could occur. Regardless of how unlikely the failure may seem at this stage, all should be considered. I'm a firm believer that O'Doul's Law frequently applies within the IT arena (O'Doul's Law states that Murphy was an optimist).

- Identify the necessary steps to handle each failure. After each of the different component failures has been identified, the next task is to determine the necessary steps to minimize or completely eliminate the possibility of failure. This is often a combination of redundant systems, and manually and automatically initiated procedures.

- Balance the business requirements with the cost. Finally, unless you happen to be an IT manager lucky enough to possess an unlimited budget, the business requirements must also be balanced against the cost of creating and supporting the infrastructure.

Table 4-1 lists various availability levels with percentage of availability, yearly minutes of downtime, and some of the architecture requirements necessary to achieve that level of availability.

Availability	Downtime (Minutes/Year)	Architecture Requirements (Increasing availability includes all previous levels)
99.0%	5,256	Server must be fully redundant including the following items: Hot swappable disks Dual or Quad Ethernet Connection Redundant power supplies Hot Backups Documented (and tested) upgrade and backup/restore procedure Full recovery must be possible within eight hours
99.25%	3,942	Documented (and tested) fast backup-restore procedure Robust monitoring of all server and application components Redundant Network Paths Archived redo logs must be available within two hours Full recovery must be possible within four hours
99.50%	2,628	Automated fast backup-restore procedure Database and Web Server failover Triple-mirrored database consisting of the following instances: Active Primary Database Current but inactive backup Database Standby Database sAll archived redo logs must be immediately available Full recovery must be possible within two hours

TABLE 4-1.   *Hardware Availability*

Availability	Downtime (Minutes/Year)	Architecture Requirements (Increasing availability includes all previous levels)

99.75%	1,314	Fully redundant disaster recovery site
		Fully redundant clustered database with the following instances:
		    Active Primary
		    Active Backup
		Recovery/site failover must be possible within thirty minutes

99.90%	526	Multiple fully redundant disaster recovery sites and remote redundancy Site failover must be possible within ten minutes
99.99%	53	Fully automated recovery/failover Site failover must be immediate
99.999%	5	Fully redundant pairs across entire architecture

TABLE 4-1. *Hardware Availability* (continued)

The following list includes some commonly classified components you'll encounter.

- **Hardware**   This includes all physical components within the Web server infrastructure, including processors, memory boards, I/O controllers, and interconnection wiring. Hardware can encompass a wide variety of different systems with the increasingly heterogeneous server environment providing a wide variety, such as Web, database, application, encryption, and user directory and system management services.

- **Operating system (OS)**   Once regarded as the lowest layer on top of the system hardware, the distinction is now blurring as ever more functionality is included within the OS. Depending on the server hardware that's in place, the range of OS that could be encountered can be diverse. Database servers can be housed on one of the traditional major Unix vendors, such as Sun, HP, Compaq, or IBM. Application servers can run on Windows NT/ 2000 and the Web servers may be on a combination of these or one of the emerging open source operating systems, such as Linux. Considering the widely diverse selection of platforms supported by Oracle, you might encounter any or all of these.

- ■ **Network** The network must be sufficiently powerful for any commercial Web site to function adequately. This category includes the various components that make up the network, such as interface cards, cables, routers, switches, firewalls, and load balancing devices.

- ■ **Server software** Server software includes all non-OS software used by the various servers. This includes the database software, such as the Oracle RDBMS, Web servers (for example, Apache Server, Microsoft IIS, Netscape), and combination Web/application servers such as Oracle Internet Application Server. As with OS, the distinction between the different types of server software is blurring as new functionality is bundled. For example, the Oracle Database now contains an integrated Web Server and Java Engine, and Oracle Internet Application Server now contains Web and database caching, and file system and mail services.

- ■ **End-user applications** End-user applications consist of various purchased applications and in-house custom developed applications. This can be as simple as an application to browse a company product catalog or a fully Web enabled ERP application like Oracle Applications. In the past, the Web-based applications were often limited to less-complex Internet/ extranet applications. Now, however, many companies are deploying intranet Web-based applications as the capabilities of Web-based development tools begin to rival that of client server tools.

- ■ **Data within the database** The actual data stored in the database. This can include company product catalogs, price lists, order details, tax information, and so on. This is the real hidden "wealth" of any site, and all the other components merely support ways to manipulate and accumulate additional data.

Not only does the failure of any single component potentially result in downtime, but the interconnections between them can also be points of failure.

The consequences of implementing an architecture that doesn't serve the availability requirements of a business can be severe. Once the Web site has gone live, the cost of lost business and emergency fixes can accumulate rapidly and possibly cause the company to go out of business. As such, the importance of doing things right the "first time" and avoiding the quick-launch-and-fix-it-later approach cannot be stressed enough. Frequently, time to market is one of the key requirements for many e-business sites as they attempt to bring their solution to market ahead of the competition. Analysts should be extremely cautious during this phase to balance the requirements of an accelerated launch with the risk of launching a flawed system.

The best approach to this problem is being familiar with many readily available options to enable the design and deployment of an appropriately robust solution. The good news is, with the release of the Oracle9*i* complement of Internet Application Server and Internet Database Server, more options exist for the rapid creation of robust solutions than ever before. In the world of Oracle, we truly are entering into an exciting time!

A complete discussion of high-availability solutions available within an Oracle Web application architecture would take far more than a single chapter. In fact, entire books have been written on the topics of configuring and managing the individual components to prevent failures. Instead, this chapter focuses on the following high-availability features provided by the Oracle9*i* suite.

- Oracle Real Application Clusters

  - High Availability using Real Application Clusters

  - Advantages of Real Application Clusters

  - Disadvantages of Real Application Clusters

- Transparent Application Failover

  - High Availability using Transparent Application Failover

  - Advantages of Transparent Application Failover

  - Disadvantages of Transparent Application Failover

- Oracle Data Guard

  - High Availability using Oracle Data Guard

  - Advantages of Oracle Data Guard

  - Disadvantages of Oracle Data Guard

- Advanced Replication

  - High Availability using Advanced Replication

  - Advantages of Advanced Replication

  - Disadvantages of Advanced Replication

- Internet Application Server

  - High Availability using Internet Application Server

  - Advantages of Internet Application Server

  - Disadvantages of Internet Application Server

- Third-party solutions

- Combining multiple solutions together

- Custom High Availability solutions

Oracle Real Application Clusters

Oracle Real Application Clusters (RAC) are the next step in the evolution of Oracle Parallel Server (OPS). In the past, deployment of an application under OPS was extremely difficult and the application had to be designed with OPS deployment in mind. Oracle RAC is designed to allow an application to take advantage of the new features without changes to the application. Oracle database applications can now be developed for a single database, but deployed on an RAC with many nodes.

Oracle RAC is a database configuration that consists of multiple database instances with shared access to the same physical set of data files. Like its predecessor, RAC is configured on specific Hardware/OS combinations capable of supporting a clustered environment.

Figure 4-1 displays the typical components within a clustered environment.

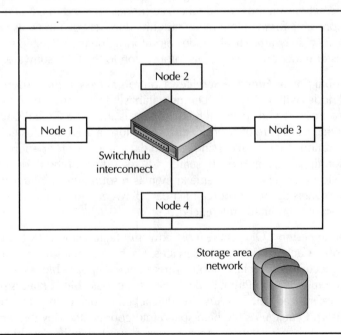

FIGURE 4-1.   *Typical cluster environment components*

The Oracle RAC is the combination of a number of different hardware and software components. The following list details the individual components and their functions:

- **Cluster Server Hardware**   The physical hardware on which the RAC database is housed. This is comprised of two or more single or multiprocessor nodes connected together in a clustered configuration with a high-speed interconnect for internode communication.

- **Cluster Shared Disks**   The physical shared disks on which the database files are stored. The shared disks must be able to support simultaneous raw disk access from all nodes within the cluster. Shared disk configurations include Storage Area Network (SAN), shared RAID, or Network Attached Storage (NAS), which can be attached either directly to the cluster nodes or to the high-speed interconnect.

- **Cluster Manager**   The Operating System Dependent (OSD) functions for the control of the cluster functionality. This is composed of two distinct modules. First, the Global Services daemon performs tasks on behalf of the RAC software, such as shutting down, starting up, and other administrative type actions on the individual cluster nodes. Second, the Node Monitor is responsible for maintaining communication between the cluster nodes and the RAC software. This includes monitoring the membership status of the cluster nodes and passing this information to the RAC software.

- **Global Cache/Enqueue Service**   Controls access to the resources on all nodes within the RAC. During database operations where the same resource must be accessed by multiple sessions, the Global Cache/Enqueue service takes care of coordinating operations across the cluster nodes. For operations such as accessing cached data blocks or for performing locking operations, this must occur seamlessly regardless of the node to which the session is attached. A scheme known as *resource mastering* is used to allow the ownership of a resource to "float" between the nodes, depending on where it is optimally referenced.

- **Cache Fusion**   One of the most powerful features of RAC. By using the Global Cache and Enqueue services, Cache fusion allows the sessions connected to one cluster node to reference database blocks that are cached in memory in a different node. When a database block read is requested, if the referenced data block is already cached by one of the other nodes in the cluster, Oracle uses the high-speed interconnect to copy the block between nodes. When a database block write is requested, if the data block referenced is already cached by one of the other nodes in the cluster, Oracle again copies the data between nodes, but now the ownership will be assigned to the node performing the data block update. Additional database block reads are able to continue on other nodes, but any database block writes are forced to wait until the first session performing the update performs a commit or rollback.

Figure 4-2 displays the typical processes associated with the RAC.

RAC offers many improvements over OPS. Whenever a failure of one of the cluster nodes occurs, the following operations must occur.

■ **Cluster Reorganization** is performed by the Global Services daemon and involves determining which nodes are no longer part of the cluster. This is achieved by instructing each database instance to update its entry in the membership map contained within the control file. At the end of this process, any nonupdated entries in the membership map are deemed to be failed nodes.

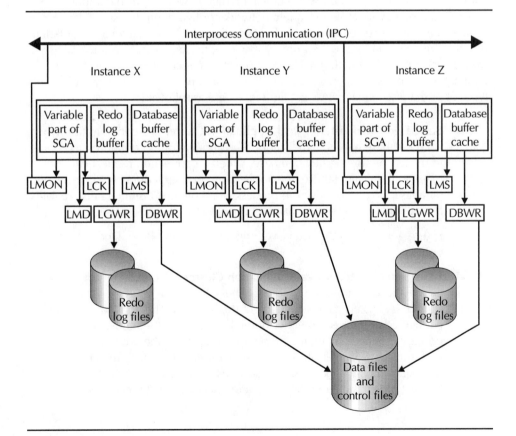

FIGURE 4-2. *RAC processes*

■ **Database recovery** involves determining which buffer cache blocks and database object locks were owned by the failed instance. Also, the ownership of the resources might need to be reassigned.

■ **Transaction Recovery** involves reading the failed node's redo log files and determining the transactions that need to be applied and the incomplete transactions that should be rolled back. Depending on the amount of recovery that must be performed, this can take an excessive amount of time. The fast-start rollback feature enables you to tune the maximum duration the recovery process should take and enables recovery to be performed in parallel.

The two simplest high-availability configurations that can be created using RAC use a two-node cluster with a primary/secondary configuration. This approach uses an active primary database that services most of the connection requests for the application. The secondary database doesn't typically service normal application requests, although with the appropriate network configuration, the secondary instance can be connected to directly for operations such as maintenance or batch reports. During the failure of the primary instance, the secondary instance takes over by performing transaction rollback and instance recovery. All subsequent connection attempts are then directed to the secondary instance. The two different types of primary/secondary RAC configurations are as follows:

■ **Basic Dedicated Listener Real Application Cluster** is a configuration where each database has its own listener. The application is configured to connect to the listener for the first database. When a connection request cannot be made to the first database, the application, instead, connects to the second database. Any transactions in process when the first instance fails are rolled back and the application must reconnect to the second instance.

Figure 4-3 displays the listener configuration for the Basic Dedicated Listener RAC.

■ **Basic Shared Listener Real Application Cluster**   A configuration where the databases share one or more listeners. When the primary database is started, it registers itself with each of the listeners. The application is then configured to connect to either of the listeners and the request is sent to the primary instance. When the primary instance fails, the secondary instance performs recovery, registers itself as the primary instance, and accepts all subsequent connections. Any transactions in process when the first instance fails are rolled back and the application needs to reconnect.

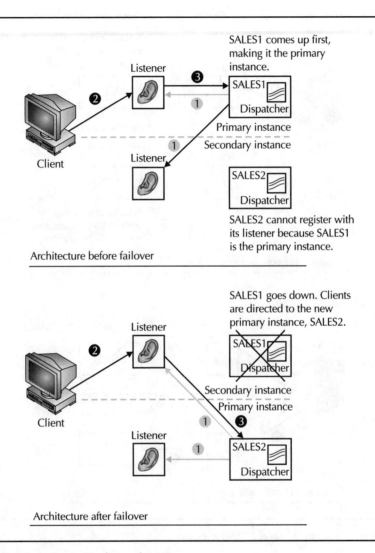

FIGURE 4-3. *Basic Dedicated RAC*

Figure 4-4 shows the listener configuration for the Basic Shared Listener RAC.

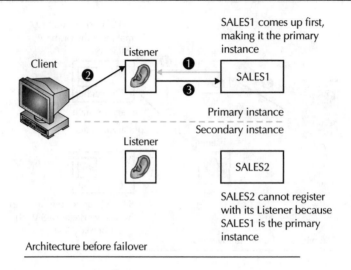

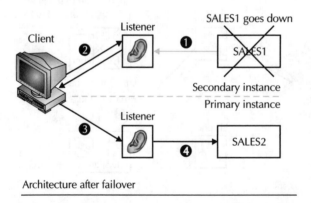

FIGURE 4-4. *Basic Shared Listener RAC*

Advantages of Real Application Clusters

Real Application Clusters (RAC) offer the following advantages:

■ Unlike OPS, minimal changes to the application are required to take advantage of the features offered by the architecture of the RAC.

- Creating a high-availability solution is extremely easy using the two-node RAC.

- In a primary/secondary configuration, automated instance recovery after the failure of a node is automatic, thus enhancing mean time to recover (MTTR).

- Combining the RAC with other features, such as Oracle RAC Guard, Transparent Application Failover, and Oracle Data Guard creates an extremely powerful architecture, which is both highly scalable and resilient.

Disadvantages of Real Application Clusters

RAC have the following disadvantages:

- Because all participating nodes share disk subsystems, the configuration is still prone to disk failures unless specific steps are taken to prevent them. Such steps include hardware mirroring (RAID 1, 0+1, and so forth), and using NAS or SAN devices.

- Because the high-speed interconnect is the central point of communication between the cluster nodes, unless redundancy can be used, it can become a single point of failure.

- RAC can protect only against localized node failure within the cluster. By itself, it doesn't offer any remote redundancy as needed for disaster prevention, such as the loss of an entire data center.

TIP
Additional improvements in high availability and scalability can be achieved by combining RAC and other Oracle9i features.

Transparent Application Failover

One of the most important design considerations for any application is transparency in that the application end user shouldn't be concerned about the application architecture. From the user perspective, frequent service disruption can quickly become frustrating. Even the most elegant high-availability solution can appear cumbersome to end users if they are required to reconnect and reenter their work.

Transparent Application Failover (TAF) is one component of Oracle Networking that can be used to minimize the disruption caused by connectivity related issues. When the connection between the application and the database is lost because of network connectivity or database problems, depending on how it has been configured, TAF performs the following functions:

- **Restore Database Sessions**   The connection to the database is restored using the same user ID and password previously used.

- **Continue SELECT operations**   Previously issued SELECT statements are reexecuted, and then continued at the same point they were at prior to being disconnect.

Because TAF cannot restore in-doubt transactions, PL/SQL variables and user session variables their status will be lost on failover. If complete transparency is required by the application, however, a combination of PL/SQL OCI functions for failover callback can be combined with writing values into a temporary table in the database for restoration after the failover.

Although not strictly a TAF feature, one additional component of Oracle Networking that can be used for multiple database instances, such as with RAC to improve application transparency, is that of load balancing. This allows the application connections to be balanced across all available database instances. Load balancing can also be used with replicated databases and Oracle Data Guard standby databases. When combined with the automatic reconnection feature of TAF, this provides significant improvements in high availability by minimizing session disruption.

Advantages of Transparent Application Failover

TAF offers the following advantages:

- Applications can seamlessly reconnect to the database without user intervention.

- Previously executed SELECT statements continue from where they left off.

- TAF can be combined with load balancing to improve scalability and availability significantly.

Disadvantages of Transparent Application Failover

TAF has the following disadvantages:

- Not all session information can be restored.

- Previous transactions are rolled back.

Oracle Data Guard

Oracle Data Guard (ODG) offers an integrated solution for configuring and managing standby databases. A standby database implementation consists of one or more databases that are separate copies of a production database. Unlike Oracle RAC databases, the standby databases can be located locally within the same data center as the production database, remotely located across the wide area network (WAN), or a combination of the two. Some of the uses of standby databases include maintaining a separate database for reporting or DSS type ad-hoc queries, an offsite database used for disaster recovery, or a copy of a production database used for development or Quality Assurance Testing.

The following list includes some of the many components that are part of the ODG architecture.

- **Primary Database**   The production database that's the source of the data for the standby instance. With ODG 9*i*, a single primary database can have multiple standby databases.

- **Standby Database**   The database that's a copy of the primary production database.

- **Log Services**   The method by which the redo logs are transferred from the primary database to the standby databases. They also control how frequently the redo log files are applied to the standby database.

- **Data Guard Broker**   The software component that handles the creation, control, and management of the primary/standby database configuration.

- **Data Guard Site**   The collection of one primary database and up to nine standby databases.

A standby database can be created using either the Data Guard Manager component of the Oracle Enterprise Manager or using the command line tools. Creating and managing an ODG site involves the following steps:

- **Configure Primary Database**   The primary database must be running in ARCHIVELOG mode and on the same hardware platform, OS version, and RDBMS software version to be used for the standby database.

- **Determine Protection Mode**   When creating the standby database, considering what the appropriate Protection mode should be is important. ODG allows a number of different Protection modes to be used.

■ **Guaranteed Protection Mode**   Ensures all changes are propagated to the standby database site after they've been committed on the primary database.

■ **Instant Protection Mode**   Ensures all changes are propagated to the standby database site after they've been committed on the primary database unless network connectivity prevents this from occurring. Once the network connectivity is restored, the redo logs are applied to bring the standby database up-to-date.

■ **Rapid Protection Mode**   Ensures all changes are propagated to the standby database site as soon as possible, without causing performance degradation on the primary database.

■ **Delayed Protection Mode**   Ensures all changes are propagated to the standby database site after a period of time. With a delayed Protection mode standby, the propagation delay can be specified to allow the database to lag behind the production database.

■ **Determine Standby Operation Mode**   Used to control how frequently the changes are applied to the standby database after propagation from the primary database. The database can be run in one of the following two modes:

■ **Managed Recovery Mode**   Allows the standby database to apply all changes as soon as they're propagated to the standby site. The database isn't available for use, however, until it has been opened.

■ **Read Only Mode**   Allows the standby database to remain open for read-only queries, allowing for reports and DSS ad-hoc queries to be run on the database. No changes are applied to the database, however, until its mode is changed to Managed Recovery mode.

Figure 4-5 shows an overview of the ODG architecture.

Once the standby databases are created and configured, ODG Broker manages and monitors the propagation and application of redo logs, depending on the selected Protection mode. Because ODG allows the creation of multiple standby instances, the best protection configuration might be to have a number of standby databases, each with different Protection modes. Because a standby database can be opened in read-only mode, consider using it for running batch reports or DSS type ad-hoc queries.

If the primary database becomes unavailable because of hardware problems on the primary database node, a failover to the standby database can be initiated. The amount of data lost during the failover operation is dependent on the chosen

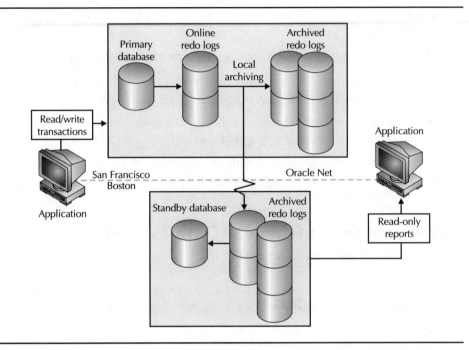

FIGURE 4-5.   *Oracle Data Guard architecture*

Protection mode. After failover has occurred, the standby database assumes the role of the primary database. Once the hardware problem on the primary database node is resolved, returning to the original configuration requires reinstantiating the database by recopying the database and reconfiguring the standby node to its original state.

ODG 9*i* allows a manually initiated switchover from primary database to standby database without the need to reinstantiated when the switchback occurs. This can be useful for performing maintenance on the database nodes.

Advantages of Oracle Data Guard

ODG offers the following advantages:

- Can be used in conjunction with RAC and Transparent Application Failover.

- Depending on the Protection mode chosen, Switchover/Failover can occur with little or no data loss.

- If a read-only standby database is used, the standby database can be used for reporting and DSS.

- With Data Guard Manager, configuration and administration is simplified.

- Data Guard provides for disaster recovery if the standby database is maintained at a remote location.

- Data Guard is flexible because a standby database can be maintained automatically or through the manual means with user input and/or scripts.

- Network bandwidth requirements are less intensive compared to other high-availability solutions because only the archived redo logs are propagated from the primary to the standby.

Disadvantages of Oracle Data Guard

ODG has the following disadvantages:

- Although ODG can be configured to run on local nodes, it doesn't offer the same scalability as Oracle RACs.

- Depending on the Protection mode chosen, Switchover/Failover can take a significant amount of time.

- The frequency of propagation depends heavily on the available network bandwidth. In an environment with a significant volume of database changes, the amount of changes propagated can cause excessive network traffic.

- No easy fallback mechanism exists to return to the original primary machine after the standby database has been activated. The standby database must be reconstructed as the original primary and a failover to the original primary (now the standby) must be initiated.

- While the standby database is open in read-only mode, it cannot be kept synchronized with the primary database (that is, the archived redo logs cannot be applied while it's open).

- Data not present in the archived redo logs (such as tables and indexes created through the NOLOGGING/UNRECOVERABLE option) isn't propagated to the standby. As such, the commands that disable redo need to be avoided or explicit measures need to be implemented to record and manually propagate such commands. Implementation of a robust database patch procedure can help to propagate such changes to all standby databases.

- User errors (accidental table deletions, and so on) and logical corruption (index keys not matching the table column values) within the primary database may get propagated to the standby database via the archived redo logs if not detected and rectified in time.

■ The standby database must be running on the same hardware, OS version, and RDBMS version as the primary database.

Advanced Replication

Advanced Replication (AR) is a sophisticated replication mechanism available in Oracle. AR enables one or more source databases, certain predetermined schemas, and even specific segments within each database to be replicated to one or more target databases in a one-way or multiway replication scheme. Thus, both the source and the target databases can concurrently handle reads and writes. From a logical perspective, AR provides a "hot" standby database. Unlike in a conventional standby database scenario, the target database is open and available for immediate failover if the source database crashes (see Figure 4-6). Ideally, the target is maintained on a separate machine at a remote location for disaster recovery purposes. Because the target is continuously open, it can be used as a reporting instance, enabling end users or DSS-type applications to use it for issuing complex queries that cannot normally be issued in the production online transaction processing (OLTP) database (for fear of hurting production performance).

Figure 4-6 shows the configuration for the AR architecture.

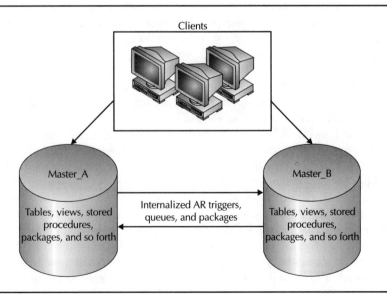

FIGURE 4-6. *Advanced Replication architecture*

Under AR, multiple copies of the entire database or specific subsets are concurrently written to and kept synchronized in nearly real-time fashion. Such a configuration is called a *multimaster configuration* (because multiple master copies exist). If immediate synchronization isn't desired, an event-based approach may be taken to propagate the transactions from each master to the others. For instance, the propagation can be time-based, with the propagation occurring during specific low-use hours. If replication were being done for failover purposes, however, synchronization would typically be immediate. Thus, each database copy should be maintained in a "peer-to-peer" manner. All writes are initially stored locally, and then forwarded to each target database through the "push" mechanism, as opposed to simple replication snapshots, which "pull" the data from the source database.

Each transaction is propagated in a consistent fashion to prevent data integrity violations. If integrity violations or conflicts occur, specific conflict resolution schemes are implemented. Conflicts can occur for a variety of reasons. For instance, if different users make conflicting changes to the same row in each database, a conflict will exist. A unique-key violation is another example of such conflicts. Conflicts need to be detected and resolved amicably. AR provides powerful algorithms for conflict detection and resolution. Conflict resolution can be consistent across the database or vary at the segment (table), or even column, level. Multiple conflict-resolution techniques are available, such as using the latest change, using the earliest change, using changes specific to a certain site/database, using the maximum value, and so on.

As transactions are forwarded, if a specific target database is unavailable, the transactions are retained at the source in the local deferred queue. When the target database is available again, the transactions are applied to it. The lack of availability of one or more target databases doesn't prevent the transactions from being propagated to the remaining database copies. Both DML and DDL statements are propagated across all the masters. AR has traditionally used triggers, asynchronous queues, and various journal tables to implement different replication schemes. Trigger-based replication is effective in certain scenarios.

In environments with large-scale concurrent DML, however, overall response time and throughput are adversely affected by high-trigger activity and the resultant recursive SQL. Traditionally, the trigger-based approach in AR is a major deterrent, preventing sites with heavy OLTP activity from efficiently using it without significant performance degradation. In an effort to avoid performance loss, however, AR in Oracle9i uses internalized triggers and packages. Internal triggers and packages are C code modules linked into the Oracle kernel. This makes the code relatively more tamper-proof (with heightened security), as well as lightweight and efficient, allowing the implementation to be speedy and scalable. No external components are configured or maintained. Because packages and triggers aren't generated, they can be instantiated and run faster. Also, since the release of Oracle8i, data propagation is handled through the direct stream protocol, rather than the equally reliable, but less efficient, two-phase commit protocol.

In the case of AR, during failure of a specific database copy, the cause of failure needs to be determined and the database recovered/rebuilt from the latest copy or from the backups. As previously mentioned, a chance of some data loss (most recent writes) exists during such failure. Whenever a specific database copy fails, the other copies continue to function unless a major disaster occurs in which all existing copies are wiped out. The chances of this are remote. During such situations, the downtime interval is significant because the database has to be rebuilt using the last available backup. All client/user traffic can be redirected through the TAF (if the applications are written in OCI9*i*) or Net8 (automatic or explicit reconnection) to surviving copies of the database.

Advantages of Advanced Replication

AR offers the following advantages:

- All databases maintained by AR can be kept open and used concurrently.

- AR can be used for disaster recovery by having a database copy maintained at a remote site.

- Hardware independence exists because the machines on which these databases are created can be of varying manufacturers, platforms, and OS versions.

- Improvements have been made to the graphical Oracle Enterprise Manager to simplify the setup and management of replicated databases.

Disadvantages of Advanced Replication

AR has the following disadvantages:

- Propagation might not always be immediate. Changes to data in one database might not be visible in all other databases immediately.

- During disasters, a distinct possibility exists of some data loss because a site's database might be destroyed prior to the latest changes being propagated. If the database at a site fails, but isn't destroyed, the data loss will be temporary and all database copies can be synchronized once the failed database comes back up.

- Conflict resolution mechanisms must be well thought out and address scenarios in which all database copies can be directly written to (in master/master and master with updateable snapshot configurations) to prevent logical data corruption.

Internet Application Server

In the creation of a completely robust application environment, the application/Web server obviously needs to be as robust as the database. Although far fewer options are available for creating a 24×7 application server, Oracle Internet Application Server (*i*AS) offers significant advancements toward this goal. Because most components within *i*AS are capable of load balancing, using several smaller application servers, as opposed to a single large application server, is often beneficial when designing an architecture around *i*AS.

With this type of configuration, *i*AS can balance particular request types, for example, Oracle Forms6*i* servlet requests, across a number of servers. If a particular server is unavailable, subsequent requests are balanced across the surviving application servers.

Another configuration that works well in combination with *i*AS is the use of external hardware/software load-balancing devices. If each of the *i*AS application servers has the identical configuration, an external load-balancing device can distribute the load across all the application servers. If a single application server becomes unavailable, the load-balancing device then redistributes the requests across the surviving nodes.

Figure 4-7 shows an overview of the *i*AS load-balancing architecture.

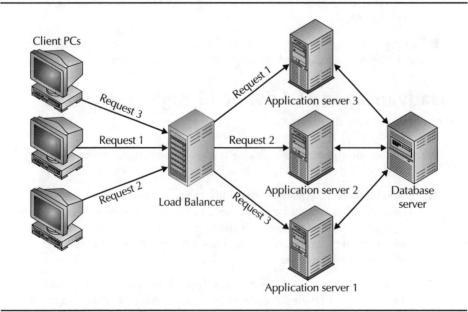

FIGURE 4-7. *Oracle Data Guard architecture*

Advantages of Internet Application Server

Internet Application Server offers the following advantages:

- significantly improved reliability with Oracle9*i*AS

- simplified management using Oracle Enterprise Manager

- most components can be configured for load balancing/failover

Disadvantages of Internet Application Server

- Limited installation options include many components that may not be needed.

- Modification of Apache modules, although possible, should be avoided as this may complicate support by Oracle.

Third-Party Solutions

A growing number of third-party hardware and software high-availability solutions are on the market. These should be considered during the initial design stage. For example, most of the NAS and SAN vendors also provide optional software solutions that provide additional local and geographically remote mirroring functionality. Each of these solutions comes with its own set of weaknesses and is probably best employed in combination with one or more of the previous solutions. *Oracle 24x7 Tips and Techniques,* by Venkat S. Devraj (Osborne/McGraw-Hill, 1999) provides an additional discussion of various third-party hardware and software solutions in further detail.

Combining Solutions

Each of the high-availability options discussed in this chapter provides protection from certain types of failure. Often the best approach is to combine two or more of the solutions to form a comprehensive "best of breed" solution and prevent a wide variety of outage-causing situations. For instance, using RAC protects against local node failure only, but using ODG with it provides additional protection from a disaster scenario, such as a complete loss of the data center.

You can also combine an Oracle solution with a third-party solution. For instance, you could use one of the SAN or NAS vendor solutions to accomplish geographical mirroring, as well as using AR. Most geographic mirroring solutions are capable of operating in both synchronous and asynchronous modes. Determining the performance implications of using synchronous mode is important, however, because this has a direct impact on the production database environment. By replicating some database objects with AR and others using the hardware-vendor geographic-mirroring solution, you can provide an appropriate level of protection without compromising performance.

Custom High-Availability Strategies

Finally, some application-specific ways exist to achieve data redundancy for failover. For instance, you can use Oracle Advanced Queuing (AQ) to allow transactions to be queued and applied to a remote database without encountering the normal delays associated with remote database operations. Implementing portions of the application this way allows all copies of the database to be synchronized. Furthermore, AQ allows transactions to continue if the primary and secondary databases become disconnected. Once the connection is reestablished, all queued transactions are then propagated to the secondary database. The application can be written to send an alert to administrative personnel regarding the failure of the write (so appropriate corrective action can be taken).

Some of the features of Oracle Net9 OCI can be used to allow the application to detect failed connection attempts to the primary database and, alternatively, connect to the secondary database until the primary database once again becomes available.

Summary

The most important consideration in avoiding downtime is recognizing the many factors that can cause downtime for your Web site and employing one or more solutions to minimize or eliminate them. After many years of working with Oracle-centric architectures, creating a plan for high availability is understanding it's not a case of if, but when, a particular failure will occur and having the foresight to handle the failure. The good news is Oracle9*i* provides significant improvements in its capability to create a truly 24×7 solution.

CHAPTER
5

Disaster Planning

I f your organization installs, upgrades, or maintains Oracle databases, applications, and/or Web sites, you really need to plan your actions toward and reactions to disasters. I cannot emphasize the importance of this enough. Disaster planning must be viewed as a fundamental task if you're going to keep your enterprise-critical systems safe from outages, which have a devastating affect on your organization. A complete disaster plan should include your Web and cache servers, as well as your database servers. This chapter focuses on Oracle database servers, but your planning should include all servers.

Disaster planning describes a methodology of safeguarding and restoring Oracle databases after outages due to hardware, software, human error, and natural disaster. A sound disaster plan needs to encompass every known scenario—within reason—that could result in a loss of critical data or services. I say within reason because each disaster is a unique occurrence and only so much planning can be done. *Best practices* are the daily routine activities that can contribute to the prevention of a disaster. Your disaster plan should outline a series of steps that establish a guideline to recovery when a disaster occurs.

Eight essential steps can help you equip your Disaster Tool Belt.

1. Select a Solid Methodology or Structured Approach Toward Recovery.

2. Organize a Strong, Well-Trained, and Influential Disaster Planning Team.

3. Categorize Your Disasters.

4. Answer Key Questions.

5. Maintain Robust Documentation and Best Practices.

6. Formulate a Detailed Disaster Plan.

7. Perform Vigorous and Frequent Testing of Your Disaster Plan.

8. Include End Users and Customers in Preparation, Participation, and Training.

Other essential ingredients include securing management support, maintaining good relationships with hardware and software vendors and technical support, and keeping current maintenance payments to Oracle and other vendors.

This chapter introduces the tools of the Disaster Plan and brings them together into a comprehensive, usable framework. You should be able to select and choose your tools as applicable to customize your own Disaster Tool Belt.

This chapter discusses the following topics:

- Initial Steps and Definitions
- Categorizing Disasters

- Key Questions to Answer When Analyzing Oracle Disaster Planning

- Robust Documentation and Best Practices

- Bringing It All Together: Formulating the Actual Plan Components, Failures, Scenarios, and Action List

- Vigorous and Frequent Testing: Analyze, Plan, Test, Repeat

- End-User and Customer Participation, Training, and Preparation

Initial Steps and Definitions

The first step in any good plan is to have a methodology. The four main segments of TUSC's Disaster Planning methodology are Components, Failures, Scenarios, and Action List (CFSA).

Components include, but aren't limited to, hardware, time zone differences, software, security, vendors, system design, Oracle Instances, documentation, geographical locations, cultural and language differences, backup strategies, database options and architecture, heating, cooling, power sources, and maintenance procedures. *Failures* are factors that relate to loss, corruption, action, or composition of components. *Scenarios* are a matrix of failures, components, and actions. And, finally, the *Action List* is composed of the resolution activities executed in the scenario.

A comprehensive disaster plan is made up of several smaller plans. A more general task list can help start any planning effort. This general approach is called a Planned Action List (PAL).

A PAL consists of the following components:

- Purpose/Requirements/Scope

- Concerns and Dependencies with Responsible Parties Identified

- Schedule

- Action List

- Worst-Case Scenario

- Backout Plan

- Actuals and Post Mortem

This approach is useful for planning everything from migrating an instance to planning your relocation from one state to another. It's an easy, adaptable checklist approach to mapping out actions for an issue of any size. It enables you to focus on the main points of the issue and it gives an at a glance view for issue summarization and reporting to all levels of management. The use of a PAL compliments the Disaster Planning methodology and is definitely a contribution to any planning effort.

The second step in the process is to determine who the members of the disaster planning and recovery team should be. In other words, who has the skills, knowledge of expertise, and foresight to add value to the effort? Value should be inclusive of, but not limited to, individuals who have prowess in the organization's political, financial, and technical fronts to "fight for the cause." Disaster Planning consistently gets a lot of lip service without any actual action. Let's face it, the best-laid plan is nothing without some clout behind it, so the need for a strong team is essential.

Disaster Team members have many areas of responsibility. Their job is to answer the key questions that comprise the components, scenarios, and actions of the disaster plan. Team members rank the disaster scenarios based on risk, probability, and effect. They ensure the team's efforts are focused on defining the most detailed actions for the riskiest scenarios. Members act as a primary contact and coordination point for disaster recovery notification and efforts. They establish emergency response procedures that help minimize the duration of disruption to operations and reduce the complexity of the recovery efforts. Team members have or know the location of keys and codes for access to buildings and systems. They also ensure the plan clearly identifies who declares an emergency situation and who instigates recovery scenarios.

The Disaster Team provides and/or verifies the organization's hardware and software architecture documentation is current and readily accessible. They make sure the vendor and technical support contact lists are current and readily accessible, and that vendor maintenance support payments are current. They always know the location of current software versions and ensure their accessibility.

Team members are responsible for remaining technically astute about the organization's hardware and software architecture. They maintain and upgrade the disaster plan as changes to configurations, architecture, and vendors occur over time. The members ensure the plan is tested and verified by current staff with regularity. They also keep communication flowing and encourage a sense of unity within the team.

These people are the key resources whose input will form the backbone of your disaster planning efforts. These are the players who will garner the proper additional resources and serve as the brainstorming core. The team should be composed of individuals like the leaders of Network Engineering, UNIX Administration, Oracle DBA, End-User and Customer community representation, and other people deemed appropriate. A strong team is the key to a sound planning approach and a successful disaster plan.

The methodology and the Disaster Team lay the foundation for your Disaster Planning effort. The next step is the categorization of disasters.

Categorizing Disasters

Oracle database disasters can span many levels. Categorizing or classifying possible disaster events that could cause a loss of critical data or services is the next step in the Disaster Planning effort. Disasters can include errors at the server, database, or user level, or natural disasters. From an incorrectly deleted row in a table to a table unable to extend because of lack of disk space to a failed UPS to a massive natural disaster, classifying these components helps refine the scope of your plan.

Hardware

Oracle databases can be housed on many hardware platforms. They can reside on hardware that embodies the less-traditional, newer emerging platforms, or the more-established, tried-and-true enterprise standard platforms. Oracle servers and disk storage arrays span many two-tier, three-tier, network, high availability, clustering, file-systems, NFS, NAS, and SAN architectures. Many vendors are also in the hardware game, ranging from the legacy players (such as SUN, HP, IBM, EMC, and so forth) to the less-experienced players trying to earn their market share. Maintaining good relationships with these vendors is essential for parts and service delivery in emergency situations.

The main hardware components are the Oracle server, the network SQL*Net communicates through, and the client. The recovery of any other hardware component should be fully addressed in the disaster plan. By applying the concepts presented, you can extrapolate a plan for all other hardware. Here is where you begin to identify the *F* in CFSA—your site's pool of failures.

Hardware Failures include disk loss or corruption issues, space limitations, server memory loss or corruption issues, and failures of various hardware components (NIC, SCSI, Boards, CPU, Controllers, and so forth). Power outages and fluctuation issues, heating and cooling issues, and sprinkler and spillage issues can also occur.

Software

Oracle databases are housed on, and interact with, many flavors of software, various operating systems, vendor specific disk storage tools, hardware management and monitoring tools, and a myriad of other third-party application tools and application front ends. The main software component is the Oracle database itself. The recovery of any other software components should be fully addressed in the disaster plan.

The failures and errors and corresponding solutions that fall into the software category have been expertly documented in *Oracle8 Backup & Recovery Handbook,* by Rama Velpuri and Anand Adkoli (Osborne/McGraw-Hill, 1998). Oracle also discusses backup and recovery issues in its documentation set and several good books on the subject are available in bookstores or online. Referring to these tried-and-true practices is your best source for the step-by-step details of what's discussed in this chapter.

Human Errors

Users of Oracle databases, as any users of computer systems do, create the errors found in this category. Users can range from the novice to the superuser to the DBA. Contrary to popular belief, DBAs do make mistakes occasionally.

Depending on the scope of the user error, and when the error is identified or confessed, probing the redo and archive logs with the appropriate third-party tools can generate the undo SQL statements to unapply the errors that are the simplest to fix.

Some common human error failures are deleting, inserting, or updating row(s); dropping or altering database objects (tables, indexes, views, database links, users, and so forth); manually removing index or datafiles; filling archive log destination; and rm -rf * .txt (remove all files in all directories) on a UNIX system.

Natural Disasters

Fire, flood, hurricanes, earthquakes, tornadoes, war, terrorism, riots, and so forth fall into this category. These disasters can be isolated, local, regional, continental, or global.

Security Attacks

Security attacks can invade your network in a number of ways. Whether it's a hacker from the outside, a disgruntled employee, or someone stealing information, being prepared for these situations is important. When one of our customer's credit card company was hacked, it took our customer out of business for over a week.

Key Questions to Answer When Analyzing Oracle Disaster Planning

So far, we've selected a methodology and an organized, strong team. We're also aware of the disaster categories we need to consider. Now we're ready to move to the next step, gathering the team to answer some key questions that add depth and breadth to your disaster plan. These key questions fall into four main groups: General, Architecture, Database, and Human Factor. The answers to these questions either begin your robust documentation process or add to your existing documentation.

General Questions

What are the enterprise-critical Oracle systems to be recovered in a disaster? How vulnerable are they? How long can you afford to be without access to them? How much is this recovery protection worth?

These key questions are extremely subjective. The team must determine the answers for your site. Once you identify these instances, once you define the vulnerability in terms of monetary or customer costs, and once you define acceptable system outage windows, then you'll have the beginning of the tangible terms of worth for your disaster recovery protection.

Does a company-wide methodology and plan currently exist? If so, when was the last time it was vigorously tested or verified by current staff members? The answer to these questions can give the team a benchmark for where you are in your disaster-recovery mindset and how far you need to go to achieve a reliable plan. No disaster plan can identify all the possible outcomes, but applying a structured approach enables you to deal with unforeseen disaster events with more confidence. Once the event is defined, this methodology gives you a better understanding of all the issues and dependencies involved, and puts you on a resolution path.

Architecture Questions

Are our critical systems local, regional, or global? Do language, cultural, or time zone barriers exist to international locations? Do other locations have similar quality in physical recovery capabilities? Are our critical Oracle systems joint ventures with Web, Internet business with multiple partners, or multiple architectures with varied levels of quality? What additional steps must be put in place and tested to ensure proper synchronization of databases across these barriers? What assurances can you implement to ensure the level of care will be consistent when dealing with second- or third-party vendors and service providers?

The answer to these questions can give you a picture of the extension and vulnerability of your organization's system architecture. If you have any of these barriers, you must define a disaster plan that incorporates actions and scenarios that are flexible, adaptable, and specific to the uniqueness of your architecture.

Is communication consistent among all critical systems' change management process and maintenance personnel? You could sit right next to the UNIX System Administrator or the Network Administrator, or be a teleworker hundreds or thousands of miles away, but if you don't communicate, any changes to the hardware, software, or architecture have the same result. In general, it could quickly spiral any recovery effort into a worse state. Think of the case of the on-call DBA restoring the incorrect version of the database because the documentation was out-of-date. What additional "opportunities" did you create for yourself, which could have been avoided during an already stressful situation, if proper communication and documentation were executed and maintained?

Are you implementing best practices in design phases of interfacing systems (tape library simultaneous data streams, parity implications, disk mirroring (RAID), and so forth) that compliment your approach to Oracle disaster recovery? For example, are you sacrificing an expedient recovery to meet your backup window limitations in your selection of hardware configurations? It can backup X amount of data in X hours at X rate of speed because of simultaneous streams during backups, but what is the restoration time for that same data? Is it the same, two times, three times, or more? Could you improve restoration time if you opt to purchase a slightly more expensive configuration that will pay off in a disaster by offering a faster restore window? Or, should you incur the additional cost of disk space to house a second mirror for your crucial instances? Are you implementing the best RAID configuration to maximize disk use, have optimal database performance, and have the best recovery options?

What security issues will you have to deal with? Security is always a challenge in disaster situations, but security is important because it relates to the vulnerability, practical enforcement of robust documentation, and best practices on daily security enforcement of your site. You must implement actions in your plan to ensure the same level of security (or better) exists during a disaster period than in a nondisaster period.

Can vendors and suppliers get you what you need, when you need it, in a timely manner? Maintaining good relationships with these vendors is essential for parts and service delivery in emergency situations. Having a collective, updated vendor contact list and "rush pricing" lists available and accessible is imperative.

If needed, do you have a secondary or tertiary disaster recovery location? Are your site's crucial systems worthy of the additional costs associated with having an idle or semi-idle standby disaster recovery location(s)? If so, your plan must include actions that accommodate this scenario. Managing multiple locations is a large undertaking and takes time and concerted effort to maintain. In a disaster situation, however, having more than one data store location can easily pay for itself by decreasing recovery time.

Database Questions

Ask yourself if you're following the Optimal Flexible Architecture (OFA) recommended principles that can assist with disk loss or failure. These include placement of redo and archive logs on separate disks and multiplexing redo logs (multiple groups, members across multiple disks) with at least three groups of two members each. You should also have multiple copies of control files on separate disks with at least three copies spread across three different disks.

Are you practicing database integrity strategies that can assist in the event of loss? Are you implementing archive log mode that can help restore database integrity during recovery because of a loss or failure? Have you used multiple destinations that span separate disks or set up a job to copy archive logs to a separate disk at certain time intervals? Have you become proficient in using a redo/archive log-probing tool?

You should regularly back up Oracle database objects and other objects, such as data and index files, control files and control files backed up to trace, redo log files, archive log files parameter files, password files, ORACLE_HOME directory structure, and logical backup files.

Physical backups and logical backups are two types of smart backup strategies you should implement to assist in the event of loss. *Physical backups* consist of cold (full) and hot backups. *Logical backups* (complete, incremental, and cumulative) are created using the Oracle export utility.

Cold backups are the most complete form of backup and are performed after a database is shutdown cleanly (shutdown normal or immediate). A cold backup is invalid if the database is open. A cold backup is the best backup format to restore from because all objects being backed up by this method are from the same point in time and have the same System Change Number (SCN) timestamp. In our ever-increasing 24×7 production environment, however, cold backups are sometimes sacrificed to meet uptime requirements.

Cold backups are best placed on disk first, and then copied to tape. This allows for quick access without tape involvement if recovery from the last cold backup will suffice, and the last cold backup required is available on disk and isn't corrupt.

Hot backups compliment uptime requirements. Hot backups copy data and index files while the database is up and running. A hot backup is impossible if the database is closed. This option can be used where 24×7 access is required.

Hot backups require archive log mode and are best done at low database activity times. Like cold backups, hot backups are best placed on disk first, and then copied to tape. Hot backups should backup only one tablespace at a time, not all tablespaces in backup mode at once. Each tablespace should be kept in backup mode for as short a time as possible. Redo and archive logs shouldn't reside on the same disk (contention) because hot backups cause a redo log overhead and redo, in turn, generates archive. With either backup method, it's important that you have sufficient disk space.

The Oracle *exports* utility is used to create logical backups. Exports are performed while the database is up and running. An export is impossible if the database is closed. Exports have many parameter options: complete, incremental, and cumulative to name a few. A complete instance, table, or user level export can be performed. In version 9*i* of the Oracle database, several additional tablespace parameters exist, which can give you more flexibility in your logical backups. Exports can be a robust recovery tool that's most effective with proper parameter selection. Exports and imports can be performed between different versions of Oracle with procedures that can be found on Metalink. Again, when using exports, ensure your disk space is sufficient. If you're running exports nightly and you want to keep more than one version, be sure to set up the appropriate scripts to archive the number of versions you want to save.

Combine the best of the available backup methods to give yourself restoration options in a disaster. For example, perform a cold backup once a week, hot backups nightly, and logical backups nightly for critical systems.

What's your database backup tape rotation schedule? Are they rotated off-site? Can you get to specific backup tapes from off-site when you need them quickly? How long do you have to wait for off-site delivery of tapes? How long are tapes kept in rotation before being written over or trashed? The answers to these questions can give you insight into the physical and time limitations of restoring. If you don't have the tape on-site, or if it takes *X* amount of time to get the tape on-site or to another designated location, you need to address these factors in the outage-time frame scenarios of the disaster plan. The age of the tape or other media used to store database backups is also relevant.

The team needs to consider the following additional questions:

- Which high-availability solution should you incorporate into your systems?

- Should you implement standby databases for your most critical systems?

- Can replication assist in your efforts?

- Do you have data marts, or operational data stores or data warehouses that contain the same information as your crucial systems? If you do, what's the "refresh" factor for them?

These options might require heavy manual intervention to restore data but, in some cases, it might be better to have some data in an open database that's a little outdated than to have no data and no database at all. If you plan to use any of these options, be sure you're cognizant of the possible setup and performance overhead, as well as any new features that may vary from version to version. In 9*i*, for example, Standby is now called Data Guard, and there will be automatic application of redo logs to the standby instance. The instance must stay in standby mode for automatic redo log application. If the standby is placed in read-only mode, redo log application is suspended until standby mode is reinstated. Parallel Server has also been renamed to Real Application Clusters in 9*i*. For more information on the features, see Chapter 4.

When attacking errors in an Oracle database restore, it's best to use existing resources to determine the best recovery details for your scenario. A few of the errors that fall into this category are loss or corruption of a data file (system, temp, index), loss or corruption of a redo log file or active/inactive group, loss or corruption of a control file, failure during a hot backup, and failure during a cold backup.

What transaction volumes exist on critical systems and what size databases are you working with (giga, tera, or petabyte)? The answer to this question defines the framework for your disk space use, your backup and recovery windows, your nondisk storage media, your hardware selections, and many other factors that play into your site's unique configuration. Each of these contributes to your disaster recovery scenarios and actions.

Human Factor Questions

Is there buy-in at all levels of management for disaster backup and recovery financing? Do personnel disaster recovery skill sets exist? Are there primary and secondary personnel?

The answers to these questions illustrate the difference between the vocalized intent of management support and the actual support received when the costs are presented. Management must be willing to invest in hardware and training of personnel to best equip its defense team in a disaster. Management must be willing to invest in IT disaster planning with an acceptance that the return on the investment might not be manifested in the same manner that customer-facing investments are. It must recognize the tangible value of the shortest downtime possible with the most data restored in crucial systems in the event of a disaster—if the proper investments in equipment and training are made. Management must also recognize that a disaster may or may not occur. With the proper equipment and input from a strong, well-trained team, the design and execution of the plan can be comprehensive, effective, and efficient. Management must understand this for a disaster plan to be successful. Putting all of these components in place provides a series of Service Level Agreements for your organization.

Robust Documentation and Best Practices

The methodology has been selected. The team is organized. The disasters are categorized. The key questions have been answered. You're now at the fifth step in the process. Ensuring documentation reflects the current state of all system architecture components and is readily available. Keep accurate and robust documentation and schedules for the following items:

- Hardware
- Software
- Vendor Contacts
- Technical Support Contacts
- Personnel Emergency Contacts
- Building Maintenance
- Security
- Backup Schedules and Backup Media Locations, see the example in Table 5-1

SERVER	INSTANCE	TYPE	DAY	BACKUP DURATION	STORAGE MEDIA	ROTATION SCHEDULE	NUMBER OF TAPES IN ROTATION	MEDIA RETENTION
Eros	CSTEST	Cold, Incremental	Mon - Sat	2–4 A.M.	Disk then Tape	Off-site weekly on Fri	14	2 weeks
	CSTEST	Cold, Full	Sun	2–4 A.M.	Disk then Tape	Off-site weekly on Fri	14	2 weeks
Poseidon	CSSTAGE	Cold, Incremental	Mon - Sat	2–4 A.M.	Disk then Tape	Off-site weekly on Fri	14	2 weeks
	CSSTAGE	Cold, Full	Sun	2–4 A.M.	Disk then Tape	Off-site weekly on Fri	14	2 weeks
Aphrodite	CSPROD	Cold, Incremental	Mon - Sat	2–4 A.M.	Disk then Tape	Off-site biweekly on Wed, Fri	21	3 weeks
	CSPROD	Cold, Full	Sun	2–4 A.M.	Disk then Tape	Off-site biweekly on Wed, Fri	21	3 weeks

TABLE 5-1. *Operating System Backup Schedule Documentation Example*

Hardware documentation should be readily accessible by users who need to reference it and should include the following details or their equivalents in your environment:

Hardware Documentation Example

Server name	aphrodite.hercules.com
Host ID	909ag8900
Serial number	LMK999987
IP address	999.99.9.99
Operating System	Sun Solaris 8
Operating System Bootstrap Information	=etc configuration directory this_host canonical master
Patch Levels	none
Server type	E6500
Hardware	(4) 500 MHz CPUs, 4GB RAM, (2) 18GB internal disks
Disk configuration	SLICE MNT PT DEVICE SIZE c0t0d0s0 /u01 xxxxx 9GB
Hardware Vendor	Sun Microsystems
Vendor Contact Information	General info, (555) 555-1212, www.sun.com
Parts Rush Delivery Instructions	(555) 555-1213, 24-hour delivery guaranteed
Purchase date	8/19/2000
Support Contact Information	Support ID: 08194104, www.sun.com/service/online
Physical location	Richmond, VA office, Secondary Data Center

You also need to document the network configurations (including the CPU number and type, and purchase date) and maintenance information, and have them available. Know the resident applications, interfacing systems, users, and dependencies, if applicable. Make sure your backup schedules and backup media locations are in place.

Before making any hardware changes, migrations, patch applications, reorganizations, or upgrades, use the PAL checklist step of a backout plan to ensure you can get back to where you started if the worst-case scenario occurs. After making hardware changes, update the documentation immediately and communicate the changes to proper personnel. Keep records of hardware failures to weed out sources of inferior parts and avoid possible future outages. Gather and maintain server statistics for growth and capacity planning. Make hardware schematics generally accessible. Where possible, maintain spare disk capacity to house data from failed servers.

Software documentation should be accurate as well. Robust use and compilation of database external metadata should occur. Don't let the database itself be the only source of documentation as to what resides in it. Have external documentation of all objects readily available. Table, index, sequence, and view definitions should be stored in a CASE tool, or other suitable venue whose repository is external from the database, and kept in synchronization with the database as part of your change management process. Using these tools as sources of metadata can be useful in re-creating the database objects if an event that demands object re-creation occurs. Some case tools can also generate good pictorial references for entity relationships and data models for developers.

Software documentation should be readily accessible by users who need to reference it and should include the following details or their equivalents in your environment:

Software Documentation Example

Software Name	Designer 6i
Category	Data Modeling
Server/Desktop Name Where It Resides	PC-DBA01
Server/Desktop Type/ OS Where It Resides	
Serial Number/Software Key	000-896-84A-99
Software Vendor	Oracle
Software Version	6.0
Vendor Contact Information	(555) 555-4321, support.oracle.com
Parts Rush Delivery Instructions	(555) 555-4321, support.oracle.com
Purchase Date	8/19/2000
Physical Location	Raleigh, NC office

Include the following category items in your software documentation:

- database reorganization
- performance tuning
- database administration
- SQL statement tuning
- data modeling
- development

Your maintenance information should include support levels, licensing information, and contact numbers. Know your resident applications, interfacing systems, users, and dependencies, if applicable. Table 5-2 shows an example of logical backup schedule documentation for backup schedules and backup media locations.

Best practices for software maintenance include implementing the procedures shown in Figure 5-1.

Use the PAL checklist before you make any software changes, migrations, patch applications, reorganizations, or upgrades to ensure you can get back to where you started from if the worst-case scenario occurs. After making software changes, back up the control file to trace, if appropriate, update the documentation immediately, and communicate changes to the proper personnel. Keep records of software failures, where appropriate, to avoid possible future outages, and gather and keep daily instance space use statistics for growth and capacity planning (see Figure 5-2).

Make software schematics accessible (see Figure 5-3).

Make a backup copy of the init.ora. Keep external documentation for database objects (see Figure 5-4).

SCRIPT AND EXPORT DUMP FILE LOCATIONS

$ORACLE_BASE/admin/scripts/expimp/export_full_*instancesid*.par

$ORACLE_BASE/admin/scripts/expimp/export_full_*instancesid*.sh

$ORACLE_BASE/admin/scripts/expimp/export_full_*instancesid*.dmp

SERVER	APPLICATION(S) RESIDENT ON SERVER	INSTANCE(S)	CRONJOB TIME	APPROX SIZE OF *.DMP
Aphrodite (Production)	Customer Service	CSPROD	24:00	1GB
	E Commerce	ECOMPROD	24:30	2GB
Poseidon (Stage)	Customer Service	CSSTAGE	24:00	500MB
	E Commerce	ECOMSTAG	24:30	1GB
Eros (Test)	Customer Service	CSTEST	24:00	500MB
	E Commerce	ECOMTEST	24:30	1GB

TABLE 5-2. *Logical Backup Schedule Documentation Example*

Oracle Database Architecture and Best Practices

■ Purpose of This Document

■ Statement of Work

References

Purpose
This document outlines the architecture of our company's Oracle databases. Architecture includes, but is not limited to:

Locations	Applications
Size	Servers
Schematics	Security
Third-Party Applications	Change Management
Data Modeling	Standards
Backups	DBA Daily Checks
UNIX Directory Structure	Other References

Our company's Oracle databases can be divided into two main categories: test instances and production instances. They all reside on an xx operating system/ platform. Test versions range from xxx to xxx and production versions range from xxx to xxx. The end-user applications that reside in them include Web-based applications xxx,xxx,xxx. These are a mixture of home-grown and third-party applications.

Statement of Work
The sizes of these instances range from xxx to xxx. There are numerous references that will give a pictorial view of our Oracle databases. These include schematics, such as xxxxx.

The UNIX directory structure...
Our data modeling tool of choice is...
Backups are...
Database security uses roles to implement...
Development is done through the following third-party tools...

FIGURE 5-1. *Database architecture Best Practices example*

Tablespace Percent Used

- // percent_used.sql
  ```
  select us.tablespace_name "Tablespace",
      df.totalspace "Total Space",
      (df.totalspace - us.Usedspace) "Free Space",
      us.Usedspace "Used Space",
      round(100 * (us.usedspace / df.totalspace)) "Pct. Used"
  from
      (select tablespace_name,
         round(sum(bytes) / 1024) TotalSpace
       from dba_data_files
       group by tablespace_name) df,
      (select tablespace_name,
         round(sum(bytes) / 1024) UsedSpace
       from dba_segments
       group by tablespace_name) us
    where df.tablespace_name = us.tablespace_name
    order by round(100 * (us.usedspace / df.totalspace))
    /
  ```

- Results of Query

Tablespace	Total Space	Free Space	UsedSpace	Pct. Used
INDEX_ONE	512,000	511,640	360	0
TEMP	1,024,000	1,013,600	10400	1
TOOLS	512,000	506,520	5480	1
USERS	204,800	201,160	3640	2
DATA_ONE	512,000	495,528	16472	3

FIGURE 5-2.   *DBA daily checks instance space usage statistics documentation example*

Tablespace	Total Space	Free Space	UsedSpace	Pct. Used
SYSTEM	512,000	479,376	32624	6
RBS	1,024,000	940,800	83200	8
RBS02	1,024,000	940,800	83200	8

Object Extent (Next, Greater > 35) Check

- // next_ext.sql
  ```
  select a.owner,a.segment_name,a.tablespace_name,a.next_extent
  from dba_segments a
  where a.owner <> 'SYS' and
      a.next_extent > (select max(bytes)
              from dba_free_space b
              where a.tablespace_name = b.tablespace_name
              group by b.tablespace_name)
  ```

- // ext_35.sql
  ```
  select owner, segment_type type,segment_name,tablespace_name tspace,
  round((bytes/1024)/1024) MB,
  extents "EXTENTS>35", max_extents
  from dba_segments
  where extents > 35
  and owner <>'SYS'
  order by extents desc, segment_name
  ```

- Results of Query

  ```
  OWNER     TYPE   SEGMENT_NAME            TSPACE      MB EXTENTS>35 MAX_EXTENTS

  ---------- ------ --------------- --------- ------------ ----- ------- ---------   ------------

  DIONYSUS TABLE  T_CUSTOMER_ADDRESS  DATA_ONE    8      84      705
  ```

FIGURE 5-2. *DBA daily checks instance space usage statistics documentation example* (continued)

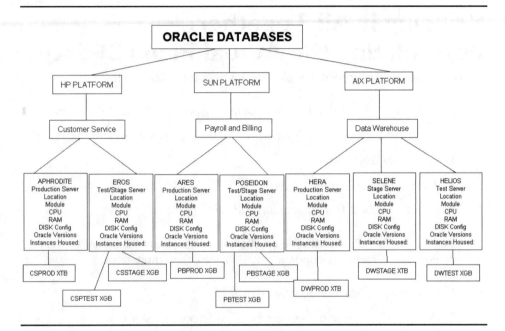

FIGURE 5-3. *Database Schematic documentation example*

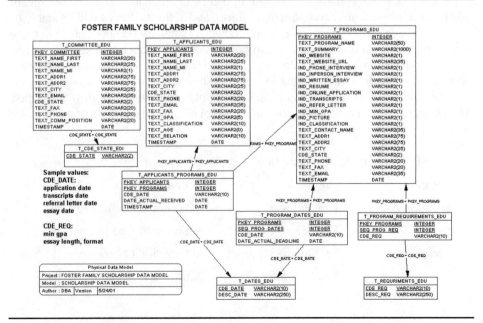

FIGURE 5-4. *Data model documentation example*

Bringing It All Together: Formulating the Actual Plan (CFSA)

To recap, a solid disaster recovery plan begins with the following five steps:

1. Select a Solid Methodology or Structured Approach Toward Recovery.

2. Organize a Strong, Well-Trained, and Influential Disaster Planning Team.

3. Categorize Your Disasters.

4. Answer Key Questions.

5. Maintain Robust Documentation and Best Practices.

Once these five steps are completed, it's time to formulate the actual disaster plan for your site. Creating (or updating) the plan involves three steps:

1. Formulate a Detailed Disaster Plan.

2. Perform Vigorous and Frequent Testing of Your Disaster Plan.

3. Include End Users and Customers in Preparation, Participation, and Training.

The first step in the actual creation (or updating) of the plan is to gather your team and make a list of all your components, failures, and actions. The list will probably be lengthy and dynamic, that is, you can add, delete, or alter the components to fit the different scenarios you develop. The components on the list become like pieces of a puzzle that has more than one solution. Combine each piece with the next until you flesh out the different disaster scenarios for your site.

The following example shows a detailed list of components, failures, and actions (see Figure 5-5). A sample scenarios matrix template and an example of a populated scenarios matrix follow:

Sample Scenarios Matrix Template

Location	Failure	Action List
Location A	F1: Failure 1	Actions and Components list
Location B	F2: Failure 2	Actions and Components list
Location C	F3: Failure 3	Actions and Components list
Location B, C	F2:, F4: Failure 2,4	Actions and Components list

- C00: Location of Disaster at Central Data Center in Richmond, Virginia
- C01: Location of Disaster at Branch Data Center in Raleigh, North Carolina
- C02: Location of Disaster at Branch International Data Center in St. Thomas, Virgin Islands
- C03: Location of Disaster at Branch International Data Center in Frankfurt, Germany
- C04: Location of Recovery Media on-site
- C05: Location of Recovery Media off-site
- C06: Geography of Disaster is Local (isolated to office building, street, city)
- C07: Geography of Disaster is Regional (isolated to state, East Coast)
- C08: Geography of Disaster is Global (database recovery is not a priority issue)
- C09: Media is readable for restore
- C10: Media is not readable for restore
- C11: Backup and Recovery Procedures are available
- C12: Backup and Recovery Procedures are not available
- C13: Time to get tapes on-site
- C14: UPS longevity at Central Data Center in Richmond, Virginia
- C15: UPS longevity at Branch Data Center in Raleigh, North Carolina
- C16: UPS longevity at International Branch Data Center in St. Thomas, Virgin Islands
- C17: Hardware Vendor's Rush Replacement Parts Delivery Timeframe
- C18: Time to Test and Configure Replacement Part
- C19: Software Vendor's Rush Replacement Delivery Timeframe
- C20: Time to Test and Configure Replacement Software
- C21: Idle Space on other servers available
- C22: Idle Space on other servers not available
- C23: Personnel contact lists are accessible and current
- C24: Vendor contact lists are accessible and current
- C25: Data Marts, Operational Data Stores, Data Warehouses contain crucial system production data
- C26: Secondary location is available
- C27: Remote access is available
- C28: Time-Zone Differences

FIGURE 5-5. *Components, Failures, and Actions List sample document*

- C29: Secondary, Tertiary Recovery Locations
- C30: System Design
- C31: SLA Terms
- C32: Size of Instance/Database
- C33: Backup, Export is applicable to situation for restore
- C34: Documentation verified
- C35: Backup, Export is not applicable to situation for restore
- C36: Incomplete Recovery
- C37: Maintain Uptime
- C38: Refer to industry standard documentation

Failures
Hardware:

- F01: Disk, Network, Router, Cable Loss, or Corruption Issues
- F02: Server Memory Loss or Corruption issues
- F03: Failures of Various Hardware Components (NIC, SCSI, Boards, CPU, Controllers, and so forth)
- F04: Power Outage and Fluctuation Issues
- F05: Heating or Cooling Issues
- F06: Sprinklers and Spillages

Software:

- F07: Loss or Corruption of a Data File (system, temp, index)
- F08: Loss or Corruption of a Redo Log File or Active/Inactive Redo Group
- F09: Loss or Corruption of a Control File
- F10: Failure During a Hot Backup
- F11: Failure During a Cold Backup
- F12: Failure During an Export

Human Error:

- F13: Incorrectly Deleted, Inserted, Updated Table Row(s)
- F14: Incorrectly Dropped, Altered Database Objects (tables, indexes, views, database links, users, and so forth)
- F15: Incorrectly Manually Removed Index or Data Files
- F16: DBA allowing filling of archive log destination
- F17: SA typing - rm -rf * .txt on a UNIX system

FIGURE 5-5. *Components, Failures, and Actions List sample document* (continued)

Natural Disaster:

- F18: Fire
- F19: Flood
- F20: Hurricane

Actions:

- A00: Initial Disaster Alarm, Recognition, or Notification
- A01: Initial Assessment, Scope of Damage by Notified Part(ies)
- A02: If warranted, contact and gather members of Disaster Recovery Team to take necessary steps to resolve failure
- A03: If warranted, contact DBA, UNIX SA, Network Admin, and so forth to take necessary detailed steps to resolve failure
- A04: Detailed Diagnosis and Assessment of Damage
- A05: Declaration of Failure and Notification of Damage Summary and Tentative PAL
- A06: Team Gather Pertinent Contact Lists, Keys, and Codes
- A07: DBA, UNIX SA, Network Admin performs restore
- A08: End Users, Customers participation in restore
- A09: Contact Vendors
- A10: Contact Authorities
- A11: Postmortem

FIGURE 5-5. *Components, Failures, and Actions List sample document* (continued)

Populated Sample Scenarios Matrix

Location	Failure	Action List
C01: Location of Disaster at Branch Data Center in Raleigh, North Carolina	F14: Incorrectly Dropped Table in Development Environment	A00: Initial Disaster Alarm, Recognition, or Notification A01: Initial Assessment, Scope of Damage by Notified Part(ies) C06: Geography of Disaster is Local (isolated to office building, street, city) A03: Contact DBA to take necessary detailed steps to resolve failure C11: Database Backup and Recovery Procedures are available C09: Media is readable for restore C33: Backup, Export is applicable to situation for restore A07: DBA imports table from export *.dmp file

Populated Sample Scenarios Matrix

Location	Failure	Action List
C00: Location of Disaster at Central Data Center in Richmond, Virginia	F14: Incorrectly Dropped Table in Development Environment	A00: Initial Disaster Alarm, Recognition, or Notification A01: Initial Assessment, Scope of Damage by Notified Part(ies) C06: Geography of Disaster is Local (isolated to office building, street, city) A03: Contact DBA to take necessary detailed steps to resolve failure C11: Database Backup and Recovery Procedures are available C10: Media is not readable for restore C34: Documentation verified, data model contains most current table structure A07: DBA re-creates table generating DDL from data modeling tool C36: Incomplete Recovery, table structure restored, data lost
C01: Location of Disaster at Branch Data Center in Raleigh, North Carolina	F07, F15: Incorrectly Manually Removed Index File in Production	A00: Initial Disaster Alarm, Recognition, or Notification A01: Initial Assessment, Scope of Damage by Notified Part(ies) C06: Geography of Disaster is Local (isolated to office building, street, city) A03: Contact DBA to take necessary detailed steps to resolve failure A05: Declaration of Failure and Notification of Damage Summary and Tentative PAL C11: Database Backup and Recovery Procedures are available C37: Maintain Uptime C34: Documentation verified, all data file indexes known A07: DBA rebuilds data file and indexes after integrity reconciliation, and notifies when complete, while database remains open to all users. Performs analyze tables, if warranted.
C00: Location of Disaster at Central Data Center in Richmond, Virginia	F08: Loss or Corruption of a Redo Log File or Active/Inactive Redo Group in Production	A00: Initial Disaster Alarm, Recognition, or Notification A01: Initial Assessment, Scope of Damage by Notified Part(ies) C06: Geography of Disaster is Local (isolated to office building, street, city) A03: Contact DBA to take necessary detailed steps to resolve failure C37: Maintain Uptime C12: Backup and Recovery Procedures are not available C38: Refer to industry standard documentation, *Oracle8 Backup & Recovery Handbook,* by Velpuri and Adkoli A07: DBA executes steps outlined in document with own experience to recover redo log while database remains open to all users

Populated Sample Scenarios Matrix

Location	Failure	Action List
C03: Location of Disaster at Branch International Data Center in Frankfurt, Germany	F18: Fire	A00: Initial Disaster Alarm, Recognition, or Notification A01: Initial Assessment, Scope of Damage by Notified Part(ies) C06: Geography of Disaster is Local (isolated to office building, street, city). Trash can fire in data center A10: Fire Dept not called A03: Everyone asked to verify systems, no damage to systems, no additional action required
C03: Location of Disaster at Branch International Data Center in Frankfurt, Germany	F18: Fire	A00: Initial Disaster Alarm, Recognition or Notification A01: Initial Assessment, Scope of Damage by Notified Part(ies) A10: Fire Dept called A02: Contact and gather members of Disaster Recovery Team to take necessary steps to resolve failure A04: Detailed Assessment of Damage C06: Geography of Disaster is Local (isolated to office building, street, city). Fire damages production server, as well as water damage from sprinklers. Database crashed, server fried and wet. Electric wiring for that panel damaged. A05: Declaration of Failure and Notification of Damage Summary and Tentative PAL A06: Team Gather Pertinent Contact Lists, Keys and Codes C11: Database Backup and Recovery Procedures are available C22: Idle Space on other servers is not available A09: UNIX SA: Contact Hardware Vendor for rush delivery of replacement server C17: Hardware Vendor's Rush Replacement Parts Delivery Timeframe C37: Maintain Uptime A07: DBA executes steps to fail over to standby production database at same location. Becomes new production server C36: Incomplete Database Recovery A08: End Users, Customers point to standby production database in interim and try to re-create last transactions C18 Electricians: Time to Test and Repair electric panel, reset sprinkler system C18,: UNIX SA: Time to Test and Configure Replacement Server A07: UNIX SA installs new operating system and configures parameters A07: DBA installs Oracle on replacement server and sets up as new standby database A05: End Users and Customers informed that current server will remain as production server A07: UNIX SA and DBA work together on establishing new backup schedule for replacement server A11: Post Mortem

Populated Sample Scenarios Matrix

Location	Failure	Action List
C02: Location of Disaster at Branch International Data Center in St. Thomas, Virgin Islands	F04: Power Surge	A00: Initial Disaster Alarm, Recognition, or Notification A01: Initial Assessment, Scope of Damage by Notified Part(ies) C06: Geography of Disaster is Local (isolated to office building, street, city). A10: Power Company called, Building Maintenance called C16: UPS longevity sustains servers with no interruption A03: Everyone asked to verify systems, no damage to systems, no additional action required

Vigorous and Frequent Testing: Analyze, Plan, Test, Repeat

"It's a bad plan that admits no modification"—Publilius Syrus, Maximum

At this point, you and the team have analyzed all the components and failures that began the disaster plan framework specific to your site. You've also incorporated the scenarios and actions for your site that rounded out that framework.

But, just as the best-laid plan is nothing without the clout and finesse of a strong team behind it, your disaster plan will fail to provide a beacon of light in an outage storm without vigorous and frequent testing, as well as confirmation of the documented scenarios and actions. You have expended time, effort, and money toward your disaster team's endeavors. Now is when you take your robust documentation and put it to the test. Verify what you thought would happen under x, y, and z conditions when x, y, and z conditions actually occur. In the words of an old Nike advertisement, "Just Do It." Do the scenarios over, over, and over again. Analyze, plan, test, repeat; analyze, plan, test, and repeat.

You can take several approaches to test your plan. However you do it, though, be as consistent, frequent, and thorough as possible. Both primary and secondary staff members should participate in the testing. If only one person or a select few primary people are responsible for testing your plan, what happens when a disaster occurs and that one person is unavailable? If your documentation is as robust as it should be, the secondary person should be able to take it and run with it, right? We know this isn't always the reality. Including both primary and secondary personnel in your test executions, ensure everyone knows the plan and is ready to play their part in its execution. People make the plan work by being familiar with it. Of course, not everyone in the company needs to be involved, but don't only include those folks in the IS or IT departments. End users and customers also need to be involved.

The disaster team members are responsible for ensuring that the plan is tested and verified by current staff with regularity. They are responsible for quality assurance of the testing process. The disaster team should verify and signoff on the thoroughness of testing and simulations, where appropriate. The team must also confirm that the test plans are accurate. They must be sure proper documentation modification and updates occur in a timely fashion, and the proper personnel are involved. Documentation updates should definitely occur. Each time a scenario and action is carried out, it serves as a check and balance or a sanity check to give you, the team, and company management verification that what you have on paper as your enterprise disaster plan will work in a time of need.

End User and Customer Participation, Training, and Preparation

Best practices and the disaster plan are designed to outline the procedures for responding to and recovering from disasters. Disaster planning and recovery is no longer only an IS and IT issue. Personnel outside IS and IT should be part of the team. The team must include end users and customers of your crucial systems.

The effects of a long-term outage can be catastrophic, so the disaster plan must have input from IS, IT, end users, and customers of the company's system services. Disaster response user and customer participation and training must be done to ensure as smooth as possible a transition in the face of interruptions of daily work procedures. The system(s) end user representative of the disaster team should ensure the following end-user customer components of the plan include the following:

- Notify end-users and customers of the disaster, if the disaster scale is large enough to warrant this, and give them a recovery time frame and/or an interim-solution scenario.

- Help end users and customers embrace change if their primary location is uninhabitable. Get them familiar with concepts such as secondary locations for workstations, secondary methods for internal and external communications, remote access capabilities, and additional security/protection issues.

- Assist end users and customers in developing procedures to function during recovery periods or long outages. The procedures might include manual processes—yes, paper.

- Assist end users and customers in prioritizing their daily work. Incorporate the high-priority tasks into the end user and customer recovery scenarios.

Summary

The question isn't *if* an outage will occur, but *when* an outage will occur. Will you be prepared to diagnose, plan, and react in a way that will minimize the impact to the bottom line of your company during a time of crisis? What are the tangible and intangible costs paid with each passing minute or hour during an outage?

If you have a predefined, detailed plan of components, failures, and actions customized for your site, and if you and your team have taken the time to brainstorm and document the pool of possible disaster scenarios and actions before a disaster actually occurs, you are equipped to respond to any disaster.

Your first thoughts during a disaster should be of surviving it with minimal negative affects on performance, availability, database integrity, uptime, end users, and customers. Your second thoughts may vary, but they should include getting the predefined disaster plan and performing the tasks from a fitting scenario and action list. You can execute this second step only if a predefined plan exists.

The first step discussed of the eight essential steps to equip your Disaster Tool Belt was adopting a structured approach that's understood and practiced by all companywide. Disaster planning is a huge, on-going effort and needs senior-level technical and experienced input. A well-trained, senior disaster-planning team is the key resource that breathes life into your plan. The team is the focal point of all efforts, which keeps communication flowing and encourages a sense of unity within the company.

Categorizing your site's pool of possible disasters, including hardware, software, human errors, and natural disasters helps refine your plan. Gather your team and answer key questions to determine the general, architecture, database, and human factors that add body to the components, failures, scenarios, and actions of your plan.

Having the team secure management support for the disaster plan and find resources that have prowess on your organization's political, financial, and technical fronts are both imperative. Maintain good relationships with hardware and software vendors, as well as technical support. Keep maintenance payments current.

Maintain robust documentation and follow best practices when doing daily activities and maintenance tasks. Keep hardware, software, best practices, backup, database architecture, and other documentation accurate and accessible to those who need it. Hardware and software vendors, personnel, and technical support contact lists should also be kept current.

The detailed disaster plan must be customized to fit your site's needs and become part of your daily thought processes and management activities. Add, change, and delete your plan as often as is appropriate. Take the defined components, failures, and actions into a plug-and-play fashion and form them into various scenarios.

Vigorous and frequent testing must be performed by all primary and secondary staff to verify that what you thought would happened under certain conditions actually does happen when those conditions occur. Staff familiarity with the plan is crucial to success and builds a highly trained team that can accurately diagnose and recover from an outage situation with confidence. This also contributes to more precise estimates of outage time frames when considering Service Level Agreements (SLA) requirements. Finally, include end users and customers of these critical Oracle systems in the process of building and testing the plan's actions to complete and balance out the plan from all perspectives.

Disaster Planning is essential for Oracle databases that house enterprise-critical systems. Customize your plan to build your company's Disaster Tool Belt framework. Balance your disaster planning effort with other company goals. Extrapolate the framework discussed in this chapter to other components in your organization outside the Oracle database. Realize that if you choose not to give disaster planning the proper energy and attention, this could mean the death of your organization. Will your organization only be a survivor in a disaster situation? Or, will it thrive with a vigorous, predefined Disaster Plan Tool Belt that can help to minimize the negative impact to your company's bottom line?

2 Cor. 4:17-18
"For our light afflictions, which is just for a moment, is working for us a far more exceeding and eternal weight of glory, while we do not look at the things which are seen, but at the things which are not seen. For the things which are seen are temporary, but the things which are not seen are eternal."

This chapter is dedicated to the memory of the victims and all those affected by the incomprehensible attack on America on September 11, 2001. The loss of life and peace far outweigh the loss of computer systems. May we all recover quickly.

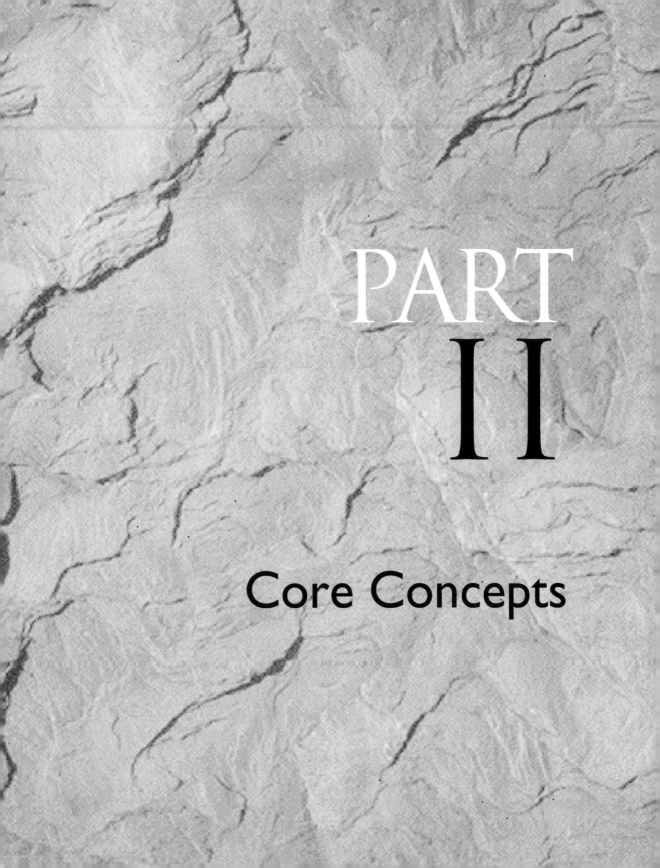

PART
II

Core Concepts

CHAPTER
6

HTML Development

ypertext Markup Language (HTML) has gained popularity as a solution to the problem of displaying output in many different formats. HTML is a document layout language that enables you to place generalized descriptive markup tags on text within documents. HTML describes how the content of the document should be displayed in users' Web browsers. HTML also describes how the document can be linked to other documents and other Internet services via hyperlinks.

HTML documents can be created using any text editor (for example, NotePad, vi, PFE, or Microsoft Word). HTML documents are typically viewed in a Web browser (for example, Internet Explorer or Netscape Navigator). HTML isn't a programming language like C, Java, or Perl, and it doesn't contain any logical structures. HTML is a markup language that provides a standard specification to describe how text and images should be displayed, and is designed to layout and structure the contents of a text document.

TIP

*You can read detailed information on the HTML specifications from the World Wide Web Consortium (W3C) Web site (**http://www.w3.org**). The organization is responsible for standardizing any software standards related to the World Wide Web.*

This chapter isn't meant as an extensive HTML reference chapter. Instead, it's meant to provide you with valuable tips and techniques for developing applications with *i*AS and using HTML in the browser. This chapter covers HTML as it relates to the development of Web applications using Oracle technology.

Numerous books give more detailed information on HTML, for example, *HTML: The Complete Reference,* by Thomas A. Powell (Osborne/McGraw-Hill, 2000).

In this chapter, you learn about the following topics:

- Writing HTML
- Providing an Icon for Your Web site
- Providing a Shortcut Link for Your Web site
- Viewing the HTML Source Without the Results
- Determining Which Browser
- Using Metatags
- Using HTML Tables

- Creating an HTML Form

- Working with URLs and Hyperlinks

- Forcing Side-by-Side Forms

- Using Cascading Style Sheets

- Creating Subject and/or Text for E-mail

- Sending E-mail from an HTML Form

- Indenting Your Text

- Placing Two Headings on the Same Line

- Determining Which Frame Is Which

- Understanding Frame Etiquette

- Creating a Window Frame Look

- Referencing CGI Scripts

- Tracking Visitors to Your Site

Writing HTML

HTML can be written by hand in any text editor; however, numerous WYSIWYG (What You See Is What You Get) GUI (graphical user interface) tools enable you to paint your pages, and then generate the HTML code without having to tag the entire document manually. These tools also enable you to open an existing HTML file for editing directly from the GUI editor.

HTML editors often extend beyond writing HTML code. Some tools aid you in developing JavaScript, Dynamic HTML (DHTML), layers, and animation. HTML editors include MacroMedia's Dreamweaver, Symantics' Visual Page, HotMetal, and Microsoft FrontPage. Most Microsoft products (for example, Word, PowerPoint, and Excel) have the capability to save documents in HTML format.

Even though you can generate HTML using a GUI editor, I highly recommend you learn how to write HTML "the long way" first. Understanding the fundamentals of HTML structure before writing HTML in a GUI tool is important. When you develop dynamic code with a programming language (for example, PL/SQL, Java, Perl, or C), you aren't able to edit the code in a GUI editor, so you need to understand the HTML tags. Take the time to understand HTML, become familiar with all versions of HTML, and then use a GUI tool. If you use a server page language (PSP, JSP, or PHP), you can use a GUI editor indefinitely because GUI editors understand the scriptlet tags. See Chapters 13, 14, and the online chapter, "PHP Module," for more information.

Understanding the standards for writing HTML tags is also important. HTML isn't a complex language, but it's important to write clean, well-formatted code that can be easily maintained. Some of the GUI HTML editors don't follow the accepted standards for writing "clean" HTML tags. For example, early versions of Microsoft FrontPage were infamous for generating code that would embarrass any HTML programmer, and MS products can produce excessive tags in a document. Generated HTML tagging should follow the most current HTML standards. If you choose to use a GUI HTML editor, be sure it writes clean HTML code.

Working with the Browsers

Even though the world seems to have standardized on two browsers (Microsoft Internet Explorer and Netscape Communicator), multiple versions of each of these browsers are available. Other Web browsers are also available, including the subset shown in Table 6-1.

Browser	Manufacturer	Description
Opera	Opera Software	User-friendly, versatile, and fast browser that's keyboard-based. Opera has a small footprint and provides features for users with disabilities. **http://www.operasoftware.com/download.html**
Amaya	W3C/Amaya	Web browser and authorizing tool designed to be a test bed for experimentation with new specifications and extensions of Web protocols and standards. **http://www.w3.org/Amaya/**
NetCaptor	Stilesoft Inc.	Enables you to display multiple Web sites at one time on separate tabs. Also has the capability to open groups of sites at the click of a mouse button. **http://www.netcaptor.com/**
NeoPlanet	NeoPlanet Inc	Customizable Web browser with a built-in Web directory. **http://www.neoplanet.com**

TABLE 6-1. *Browsers*

Browser	Manufacturer	Description
ChiBrow	KCS & Associates	Browser designed for children browsing the Web. Comes with a preselected list of safe sites and enables parents to administer a list of approved sites. **http://www.chibrow.com**
Cyberworld Viewer	Cyberworld Int'l Corp	Enables you to view the World Wide Web through photo-realistic 3-D environments optimized for the Web. **http://www.cyberworldcorp.com**
1st Choice Browse2000	Sabine Consulting	Displays multiple Web sites and can connect up to 200 URLs at a time. **http://www.ftppro.com/**
Lynx	The University of Kansas	Full-featured text-based browser intended primarily for local access. **http://lynx.browser.org/**

TABLE 6-1.   *Browsers* (continued)

TIP
*You can find more detailed information on Web browsers by visiting **http://www.browsers.com**.*

Some browsers have developed their own set of proprietary extensions to the HTML standard and browsers often interpret the standard tags differently. The support of cascading style sheets (CSS) also isn't standard. Documents may display differently in Netscape vs. IE, or even display differently in the various versions of the same browser. When it comes to developing Web applications, you have a number of decisions to make: Is your application going to support every possible Web browser? Or, are you going to support the "least common denominator" approach? Is your application going to support a specific subset of browsers, for example, version 5.0 browsers or subsequent versions? Will your application support only a specific browser, such as Internet Explorer 5.0? Will text-only browsers view your application?

The decisions you make regarding browser support can greatly affect the time it takes to develop your application. If, for example, you plan to support every possible browser and you plan on using JavaScript, you must be extremely careful about how you code your application to allow earlier versions of browsers to display your pages. To support a specific subset of browsers, you must test your application on each of the browsers within your subset and on each unique platform (operating system) for which it's deployed. For intranet application development, you can often choose only one browser version and platform to support.

TIP

*You can make a quick check for how your page will display on different browser versions at the Web Backwards Compatibility Viewer, found at **http://www.delorie.com/web/wpbcv.html**.*

If a browser doesn't understand or support a tag, most browsers ignore the tag, but display the contents of the information between the tags. If, for example, your HTML file contains <BIG>This is big.</BIG> and your browser didn't support the <BIG> tag, the browser would display "This is big." in a normal font. To avoid this, always provide alternate content for older browsers. If you plan to notify users who are using an older browser version that they need to upgrade, use tags to accomplish this task. The <NOSCRIPT>, <NOFRAMES>, <NOEMBED>, and <NOLAYER> tags enable you to display alternate content on older browsers that don't support these features, and can be included in your HTML document. The <NOSCRIPT> tag, for example, enables any message (or HTML code) between these tags to be displayed on browsers that cannot understand the <SCRIPT> tag, which is used to support scripting languages, such as JavaScript.

One of the difficulties of designing applications for the Web is the inability of the developer to control the Web environment. Users customize their Web browsing experience and may choose to access your site with JavaScript, images, Flash, or Style Sheets disabled. Don't design a Web site for general public consumption without providing an option either to exit the site politely or to view the site without the unsupported feature. You wouldn't want your site to be totally dysfunctional without these features. You should provide contact information or a link to a static Web page as an alternate site. At the least, you should display a message telling the user the feature is required to view your site.

TIP

From a user perspective, informing the users they must use JavaScript (or any other feature) to view your site is a hostile message . . . people don't like to be told they must have a specific browser or resolution. Unless you are supporting a small subset of browsers, you should—if you want to keep customers—provide an alternate procedure to access a static page or an information/contact page of some sort.

<NOSCRIPT>

The <NOSCRIPT> tag is used to inform users their Web browsers don't support the <SCRIPT> tag. Older browsers actually don't understand the <NOSCRIPT> tag. They simply ignore it, so the information between the tags is displayed. A browser that's JavaScript-compatible, however, correctly interprets the <NOSCRIPT> tag and the contents between the tags aren't displayed.

If your browser doesn't support the <SCRIPT> tag, the tag is ignored and the contents therein are treated as text. Therefore, JavaScript developers typically place their JavaScript code between HTML comment tags, so users with older browsers won't see the JavaScript code. A JavaScript-compatible browser still interprets the code appropriately inside the comment tags. The following code segment demonstrates how the <NOSCRIPT> command is used to inform the users that their browsers don't support JavaScript:

```
<SCRIPT>
<!--
[javascript code]
// -->
</SCRIPT>
<noscript>
Your browser does not support JavaScript. Please review the
<a href=/minbrowser.html>minimum browser requirements</a>
for our site. Thank you.
</noscript>
```

<NOFRAMES>

The <NOFRAMES> tag is typically used to inform users that their browsers don't support frames. The <NOFRAMES> tag can also be used to display your Web site in a nonframes-based browser. A browser that supports frames ignores content included in the <NOFRAMES> tag. If you don't use this tag and a browser doesn't support frames, the user only sees a blank page. By using this tag, you can alert your user that their browser doesn't support frames.

Although frames have been supported from Netscape v2.0 and Internet Explorer v.3.0, it may still be necessary to provide alternate content for nonframes-based browsers. The definition for a separate page can be included between the <NOFRAMES> tags, or a simple message or graphic. The following is an example of how the <NOFRAMES> tag can be used to warn users they must download an upgraded browser:

```
<noframes>
<head>
<title>Please download a new browser</title>
</head>
<body>
```

```
<font size="2" face="Arial, Geneva, Helvetica, Verdana">
Your browser does not support frames. Please review the
<a href=/minbrowser.html>minimum browser requirements</a>
for our site. Thank you.
</font>
</body>
</noframes>
```

<NOEMBED>

Executable applets can be embedded into Web pages using the <EMBED> tag.
Not all browsers support these embedded items, which are executed by plug-ins.
The <NOEMBED> tag is used to inform users that their browsers don't support the
<EMBED> tag. Browsers that don't support the <EMBED> tag display the contents
between the <NOEMBED> tags, for example:

```
<noembed>
<font size="2" face="Arial, Geneva, Helvetica, Verdana">
Your browser does not support plug-in objects. Our site uses
the MacroMedia Shockwave plug-in. Please review the
<a href=/minbrowser.html>minimum browser requirements</a>
for our site. Thank you.
</font>
</noembed>
```

<NOLAYER>

The <NOLAYER> tag is used to advise users that their browsers don't support
the <LAYER> tag. In 1997, Netscape developed the nonstandard proprietary tags
<LAYER> and <ILAYER>, enabling you to define a self-contained unit of HTML
within your document. The <LAYER> tag enables you to stack transparent sheets
on your HTML document, which can be moved around and stacked as the developer
pleases. The <NOLAYER> tag can be used to direct the user to a nonlayered version
of your HTML document.

```
<nolayer>
<head>
<title>This site is best viewed by a new browser</title>
<Meta http-equiv=refresh content=10;url=nolayer_index.html>
</head>

<body>
<font size="2" face="Arial, Geneva, Helvetica, Verdana">
Your browser does not support layers. For the best viewing
of our site, please upgrade your browser to our minimum site
requirements. If your browser does not automatically display
our non layer-based version of our site, please click
<a href=nolayer_index.html>here</a> now or review the
```

```
<a href=/minbrowser.html>minimum browser requirements</a>
for our site. Thank you.
</body>
</nolayer>
```

Providing an Icon for Your Web Site

Internet Explorer enables you to provide a small icon that will display in the address area to replace the standard Web page icon. The icon will also appear in the users' Favorites listing when they bookmark your site. To include an icon for your Web site, design a small icon using the Microsoft Icon Editor, save it as favicon.ico, and place it in your main HTML directory. Internet Explorer loads this icon when it opens your Web page and displays it in the address line.

Providing a Shortcut Link for Your Web Site

Users can add your site to their list of bookmarks (Netscape) or Favorites (IE) by right-clicking your page, which Figure 6-1 demonstrates. You can provide a shortcut link for Internet Explorer users, however, including the following code:

```
<SPAN style='color:blue;cursor:hand;'
  onClick='window.external.AddFavorite(location.href, document.title);'>
  Internet Explorer Users: Click here to add this
  page to your list of favorites
</SPAN>
```

FIGURE 6-1. *Shortcut to create a Favorite*

Viewing the HTML Source Without the Results

While developing your Web application, you can view the source code without viewing the results in the browser by putting view-source: in front of the URL for the site or the page. This is different from using the View Source menu option because it displays the code for the *generating* page code, not the displayed page. This is particularly useful when a site is under development or when you're debugging the site. The following example displays the source for the generating page code of the TUSC Web site:

```
view-source:http://www.tusc.com
```

Determining Which Browser

Newer versions of Web browsers contain quite a bit of information about themselves, which they'll gladly divulge with a little JavaScript code. Using the navigator object, users can find out specific information, including which browser, which version, which operating system, and so forth. This is useful if you want to present the user with a version of your Web site that's optimized for each browser. The following code snippet, demonstrated in Figure 6-2 prints the browser name:

```
<SCRIPT LANGUAGE="JavaScript">
<!--
bName = navigator.appName;
document.writeln(bName);
// -->
</SCRIPT>
is your current browser <p>
```

More information about this object can be found at **http://www.irt.org/xref/ Navigator.htm**. A number of excellent JavaScript examples exist online. See Chapter 7 for more information about JavaScript.

Using Metatags

Metatags can be extremely useful to developers. *Metatags,* placed in the header section of your Web page, identify the creator of the page, the document type, search keywords to assist search engines (see Chapter 24 for more information), a description of the page that may be displayed by some search engines, how long the page should remain current, and a host of other options.

FIGURE 6-2. *Showing the current browser*

Two different types of metatags exist: *NAME* and *HTTP-EQUIV*. NAME tags describe the creator, description, keywords, and the source of the page. All static Web pages should include keyword and description tags to assist their placement in search engines. HTTP-EQUIV tags control or direct the actions of Web browsers by sending additional information to the Web server.

Refreshing a Web Page After a Given Interval

You might want to refresh or reload a Web page after a given interval, for example, you would like to refresh the contents of the page every ten seconds. This makes sense, of course, only if the page's contents are dynamically generated. The following HTML example refreshes the page every ten seconds:

```
<HTML>
<HEAD>
<META HTTP-EQUIV="REFRESH" CONTENT="10">
<TITLE>Stay tuned! I refresh every 10 seconds.</TITLE>
</HEAD>
<BODY>
...Page contents here...
</BODY>
</HTML>
```

You can also branch to another page after a specified period of time. The following example branches to another page after 300 seconds (five minutes).

This type of logic is useful if you want to log users off if they don't perform an activity within a specified period of time.

```
<HTML>
<HEAD>
<META HTTP-EQUIV="REFRESH" CONTENT="300; URL=auto_logoff">
<TITLE>Keep active, otherwise I log off in 5 minutes!</TITLE>
</HEAD>
<BODY>
...Page contents here...
</BODY>
</HTML>(2)Forcing a Web Page to Expire
```

Another method of forcing the refresh of a specific page is to *age* or *expire* the page. At the desired expiration date, the browser refreshes the page and no longer displays the expired page. This method is also used when you don't want the user to be able to navigate "back" to a particular page. The following is an example of the expired metatag:

```
<META HTTP-EQUIV="Expires" CONTENT="Sun, 01 Jul 2001 22:04:00 MST">
```

NOTE
Timestamps must be in the following format:
"Mon, 30 Dec 2002 21:29:02 GMT".

TIP
Selecting an invalid timestamp (for example, 0) is
interpreted as "expire immediately."

In some cases, you want to expire a page and not cache the data locally, to ensure your page is always current. You can use a combination of the Expires metatag, and a Pragma metatag. To use Pragma, the value must be set to no-cache. When this is included in a document, it prevents Netscape Navigator from caching a page locally. Internet Explorer doesn't always respect the no-cache parameter; the parameter is really meant for proxy servers. Proxy servers cache Web pages for an entire organization or ISP (for example, AOL). Proxy servers cache pages, but they don't always take other factors, like cookies, into account.

```
<META HTTP-EQUIV="Pragma" CONTENT="no-cache">
```

Multiple HTTP-EQUIV tags can be used in a single page. Perhaps you want to refresh the page every ten seconds until it expires. HTTP-EQUIV tags can also pass keywords and content type to the browser. All metatags are placed in the head section of the document.

Using HTML Tables

HTML tables are widely used to display tabular data, but they can also be used to control your document's layout. Tables are one of the most valuable formatting features of HTML.

Web developers often use tables to enforce specific layout and spacing, instead of relying on the browser to lay out objects. Tables enforce strict sizing and placement of objects, allowing you to create complex visual interfaces that won't be affected by browser size or user settings. A non-table HTML document might look great on your browser, but may be rearranged and distorted in another user's browser. Sometimes changing your browser's window size can greatly affect the look of your site.

Drawbacks exist to using tables as layout tools, however. A Web page designed as a single table to handle layout spacing won't display until the entire table is created (that is, closed with the </TABLE> tag). You must also be careful to design your Web page so the table displays in its entirety without scrolling horizontally because it's too wide display in one screen.

HTML tables are made up of rows, columns, and cells. HTML table cells can contain images, form fields, text, rules, headings, and even another table.

In HTML, a table starts with the <TABLE> tag and *must* end with the </TABLE> tag. These two tags encapsulate a table and its elements within the HTML document. Use the following tags within the <TABLE> tags to format information in the table:

Table Tag	Definition
<TR></TR>	Defines a table row
<TH></TH>	Defines the table header cell (and will be centered and displayed in a bold font)
<TD></TD>	Defines the table's data in a cell
<CAPTION></CAPTION>	Defines the title of the table, which can appear at the top, bottom, left, or right of the table

The following example, demonstrated in Figure 6-3, creates a table using HTML:

```
<HTML>
<HEAD>
<TITLE>Sample HTML Table</TITLE>
</HEAD>
<BODY>
<TABLE BORDER=1>
<CAPTION ALIGN=TOP>HTML Table Tags</CAPTION>
<TR>
```

```
           <TH>Table Tag</TH>
           <TH>Definition</TH>
</TR>
<TR>
           <TD>TR</TD>
           <TD>Defines a table row</TD>
</TR>
<TR>
           <TD>TH</TD>
           <TD>Defines the table header cell (and will be in a bold font)</TD>
</TR>
<TR>
           <TD>TD</TD>
           <TD>Defines the tables data cell</TD>
</TR>
<TR>
           <TD>CAPTION</TD>
           <TD> Defines the title of the table which can appear
                at the top, bottom, left or right of the table</TD>
</TR>
</TABLE>
</BODY>
</HTML>
```

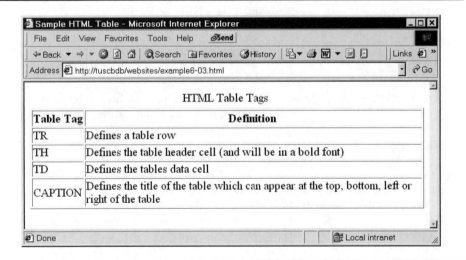

FIGURE 6-3. *HTML Table example*

Formatting Data in Tables

Tables and columns can be a fixed size, for example, <table width=300>, or they can be variably sized, such as <td width=50%>. If you omit the width attribute, the table or column will be only as wide as necessary to accommodate the widest cells. Your layout shouldn't require the user to scroll horizontally to see all the data in the table. In addition, HTML treats tables as objects, which can be centered or aligned to the margin with other text flowing around them. For example, a small table <table width=40 align="left"> will be displayed at the left margin with text wrapping around it.

Table cells span one or more columns or rows if you use <td colspan=2> or <td rowspan=4> to create complex data tables as shown here and in Figure 6-4:

Naming Conventions

Characters	Table data
	More table data
Numbers	Number naming convention

```
<TABLE BORDER=1>
<TR>
<TH COLSPAN=2 ALIGN="LEFT">Naming Conventions</TH>
</TR>

<TR>
<TD ROWSPAN=2 VALIGN="TOP">Characters</TD>
<TD>Table data </TD>
</TR>

<TR>
<TD>More table data</TD>
</TR>

<TR>
<TD>Numbers</TD>
<TD>Number naming conventions</TD>
</TR>
</TABLE>
```

Each of the cells in a table can be formatted using standard HTML tags, including font, color, and size. The border of the table can be specified, or omitted, and the spacing of the cells and within the cells can be set using attributes of the <TD> and <TABLE> tags.

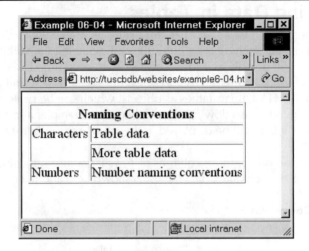

FIGURE 6-4. *Table with rows and columns spanning*

Adding Images in a Table

A number of attributes are available for each of the HTML table commands. The BORDER attribute on the <TABLE> tag, for example, defines the border thickness in pixels. If you want to turn off the border, you can leave off the BORDER attribute or you can set the BORDER attribute equal to 0 (BORDER=0). You can also set the border color, the color of the shadow, or highlight on the bevel.

In the following example, a background image has been added to the table definition. Just as you use the BACKGROUND attribute in the <BODY> tag, you can use the BACKGROUND attribute in the <TABLE> tag, as the following syntax illustrates:

```
<TABLE BORDER=1 BACKGROUND="background.jpg">
```

Images can be added to tables in two ways: using an image as the background for the entire table or each cell, or inserting an image object directly into the table cell. Using images as background for a table cell means text content for the cell can also be included. Table cells containing only images are often used to build complex layouts where each image is a hypertext link.

Netscape and IE treat the background attribute differently for tables. Netscape uses the upper-left corner of the background image in each cell and separates the cells with a blank border, even with the BORDER attribute set to 0. Explorer centers the image behind the entire table and both browsers tile small images to fill the

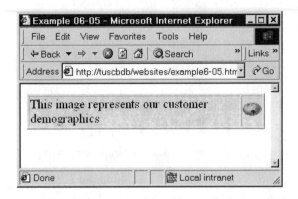

FIGURE 6-5. *Table with images*

entire cell. Test background images for your tables carefully if they're large or complex because this can make your carefully drawn tables unreadable.

In the following example, text was inserted in the table cells. Inserting an image into a table cell is accomplished by embedding the <IMG> tag in the <TD> tag. When the browser constructs the table, the image is then downloaded and inserted into that particular cell, as Figure 6-5 and the following example illustrate:

```
<TABLE BORDER=1 BACKGROUND="background.jpg">
<TR>
<TD>
This image represents our customer demographics
</TD>
<TD>
<IMG BORDER=0 HEIGHT=20 WIDTH=30 SRC="/images/world.gif">
</TD>
</TR>
</TABLE>
```

Displaying "Empty" Cells in a Table

Cells that don't have any text, but do have a background image or color specified, won't display with the correct colors or images (in Netscape) because the cell is empty. If you display your table with borders, the empty cells don't appear surrounded by the border—they look raised. This can make the table hard to read, especially if it contains many cells of data.

Use the nonbreaking space ( ) to force the cell to display properly.

```
<TD BGCOLOR="red"> </TD>
```

Netscape and IE display tables with background colors and images differently. Test these objects carefully in all versions of each browser you support to ensure the table is displayed properly.

Creating an HTML Form

HTML forms enable you to prompt a user for input, and then pass that information to an Apache module. The information is passed to the program either using a URL (the GET method) or through standard input (the POST method). The contents of the form (for example, fields and buttons) must be enclosed within the <FORM> tag.

The <FORM> tag itself contains attributes. One of the attributes is ACTION, which contains the URL of the program to execute. Another attribute is METHOD, which instructs the browser to use the GET or POST method of sending the information to the server. In addition to form elements, you must include a Submit button, which sends the information to the server. Optionally, you can include a Reset button in your form, which enables the users to reset the form input fields to their default values quickly.

The JavaScript-aware browsers have event handlers that can be used to execute a script defined in the document. Table 6-2 contains the most commonly used JavaScript event-handler tag attributes used with the <FORM> tag.

The following example demonstrates the use of the onSubmit event, which executes a JavaScript function called checkInsertForm(). When the user presses the Submit button, the onSubmit event occurs and the checkInsertForm() JavaScript function executes.

```
<form name="InsertMemberForm" onSubmit="return(checkInsertForm())"
    action="http://myserver.com/ougTool/cart1/insertMember" >
```

Event Handler	Description
onSubmit	Event is triggered when a user activates the Submit button
onReset	Event is triggered when the Reset button is clicked
onSelect	Event is triggered when the current selection on a form field changes
onChange	Event is triggered when the contents of an object, text, or text area field are changed

TABLE 6-2.   *Common JavaScript Event Handlers*

FIGURE 6-6. *HTML Form example*

The following example shows the checkInsertForm() JavaScript code. This function checks the value of each field in the form. If the value of a field is empty, an alert() message box is displayed and the cursor is placed into the empty field.

```
<SCRIPT LANGUAGE="JavaScript">
<!--
     //check valid field entries
      function checkInsertForm()
      {
          if (document.InsertMemberForm.in_FirstName.value == "")
          {
            alert("Missing First Name");
            document.InsertMemberForm.in_FirstName.focus();
            return(false);
          }
...
// -->
</SCRIPT>
```

The following example, demonstrated in Figure 6-6, is an HTML form requesting the first and last name from the user, which is then submitted in the information to the server using a Java Server Page called insertMember.jsp. This example also includes a Submit and a Reset button.

```
<HTML>
<HEAD>
<TITLE>Example HTML Form</TITLE>
</HEAD>
<BODY>
<H1> Name Verification</H1>
<FORM METHOD=POST ACTION="http://myserver.com/jsps/insertMember.jsp"  >
First Name <INPUT TYPE=TEXT NAME="first_name" size=10  MAXLENGTH=10 ><BR>
Last Name <INPUT TYPE=TEXT NAME="last_name" size=20 MAXLENGTH=20 ><BR>
<INPUT TYPE="submit" VALUE="Send Name" >
<INPUT TYPE="reset" >
</FORM>
</BODY>
</HTML>
```

Limiting Data That Can Be Entered

In the preceding example, the <INPUT> tags set up the input fields in the form. The following example form uses input fields for City, State, ZIP Code, and Country. The SIZE attribute of the <INPUT> tag limits the display size of the input fields being entered to a maximum number of characters displayed at a time. The MAXSIZE parameter limits the maximum number of characters to be entered into a field. In this example, the user can see only 20 characters in the City field. The other attribute is the TYPE attribute, which indicates the datatype. All the fields are text fields.

```
<td><input type=text name = "city"    size=20></td>
<td><input type=text name = "state"   size=2></td>
<td><input type=text name = "zipCode" size=5></td>
<td><input type=text name = "country" size=15></td>
```

The NAME attribute indicates the name of each variable or field. The TYPE attribute specifies the type of GUI control that's going to be used for the field. Many different types of controls can be used, including those shown in Table 6-3.

The NAME attribute is used as a unique name assigned to each field. The name given to a field should be treated the same way a variable field is within a coded script. The name you select shouldn't use embedded spaces or punctuation that can cause problems when passing information to and from a server-side script. When naming your input fields, use characters, numbers, or underscores, and use a name that describes the data the user is to input. The name used in the HTML document for an input form field should also be the name used on the server-side script. For example, if you name an input field password1 in your HTML form, the server-side program must accept a field called password1.

The following HTML script example, as demonstrated in Figure 6-7, creates two input fields: in_password1 and in_password2. These fields are input type=password

<INPUT> Type	<INPUT> Tag
Buttons	<INPUT TYPE="BUTTON">
Check box	<INPUT TYPE="CHECKBOX">
Radio button	<INPUT TYPE="RADIO">
Files	<INPUT TYPE="FILE">
Hidden fields	<INPUT TYPE="HIDDEN">
Images	<INPUT TYPE="BUTTON">
Text box	<INPUT TYPE="TEXT">
Password	<INPUT TYPE="PASSWORD">
Reset	<INPUT TYPE="RESET">
Submit	<INPUT TYPE="SUBMIT">
Text window	<TEXTAREA> ... </TEXTAREA>
Menus	<SELECT>...<OPTION>...</SELECT>

TABLE 6-3.   *HTML Form Input Types*

FIGURE 6-7.   *Password confirmation form*

fields and contain text titles of "*Password" and "*Re-enter Password" preceding the field.

```
<table><tr>
    <td><Font color="RED">*Password</FONT></td>
    <td><table  border=0 cellpadding=0>
      <tr>
      <td><input type=password name = "in_password1" size=10 maxlength=10>
          </td>
      <td></td>
      <td><Font color="RED">*Re-enter Password</FONT> </td>
      <td><input type=password name = "in_password2" size=10 maxlength=10>
          </td>
      </tr>
 </table></td>
</tr></table>
```

The SIZE and MAXLENGTH attributes give developers control to limit the size of the field and the maximum amount of characters a user can enter. In the preceding example, the password field's SIZE field is set to 10, so an input field the size of ten characters will display on the document. The MAXLENGTH field is also set to 10, which restricts the user from entering more than ten characters. If the MAXLENGTH attribute is set to greater than the SIZE of a field, the user can scroll in the input field and enter characters up to MAXLENGTH.

If you still need to validate your input data, write a piece of JavaScript to be called from the <FORM> tag. Two event handlers can be used at the form level: *onSubmit* and *onReset*. The name of the script specified on the onSubmit="script()" and onReset="script()" event handlers instructs the browser to invoke the script after the user presses the Submit or Reset button. The onSubmit attribute enables you to evaluate the input data on the client side before it's sent across the Internet to the server-side script for processing. The script assigned to the onReset attribute is executed once the user presses the Reset button, as the following code illustrates:

```
<!-- OnSubmit example. -->
<FORM ACTION="insertMember.jsp" onSubmit="verify_input()" >

<!-- OnReset example. -->
<FORM ACTION="insertMember.jsp onReset="clear_input()" >
```

Creating Images That Act Like Buttons

In addition to the Submit and Reset buttons created in an HTML form with the <INPUT> tag, you can also add images that act as buttons. This is supported in Explorer 5.0, but not in Navigator 4.6.

HTML 4.0 provides the <BUTTON> tag. The <BUTTON> tag is similar to the button created by <INPUT TYPE=IMAGE> with improved presentation features. This tag enables you to add an image. The button can, for example, be of a type Submit or Reset that appears and behaves identically to a three-dimensional button. The button can move up and down as it's pressed, giving the user a bit of animation. Text placed between the <BUTTON> and </BUTTON> tags displays on the button face. An <IMG> placed between the <BUTTON> and </BUTTON> tags causes the browser to display the image as the button.

TIP

Many of the graphic editors enable you to turn your image into a button.

The following code is an HTML example of the <BUTTON> tag used for Submit and Reset:

```
</HEAD>
<BODY>
<H1>Example Special Buttons</H1>
<FORM METHOD=POST ACTION=http://www.tusc.com/cgi_bin/process_name.cgi >
First Name <INPUT TYPE=TEXT NAME=first_name size=10  MAXLENGTH=10><BR>
Last Name <INPUT TYPE=TEXT NAME=last_name size=20 MAXLENGTH=20><BR>
<BR><BR>
<!-- Submit Button -->
<BUTTON TYPE=SUBMIT NAME="submit" VALUE="Submit"
   STYLE="font: 12pt Arial Blue; background:red" >
<IMG SRC="check.gif" WIDTH=30 HEIGHT=20 ALT="">
Check Me Out
</BUTTON>
<!-- Reset Button -->
<BUTTON TYPE=reset NAME="reset" VALUE="reset" "
   STYLE="font: 12pt Arial Blue; background:red" >
<IMG SRC="check.gif" WIDTH=30 HEIGHT=20 ALT="">
Clear Form
</BUTTON>
</FORM>
</BODY>
</HTML>
```

The Web page generated by this code is demonstrated in Figure 6-8.

The JavaScript-aware browsers have event handlers that can be used to create a button executing a script defined in your HTML document. Refer to Chapter 7 for further information on JavaScript and *iAS*. Table 6-4 contains a list of on event tag attributes that can be used with the <BUTTON> tag.

FIGURE 6-8. *Form with buttons*

TIP
Coding a Back button on your Web page is easy!
Simply create a tiny form: <form><input
type="button" value="back" onclick="history.go
(-1)"></form>

The following script, demonstrated in Figure 6-9 is an example of a button
executing a script when the browser detects the onClick event. The script executes

Event Handler	Event Is Triggered When the User
onBlur	Moves out of a form field that has focus
onClick	Presses down, and then releases the mouse button
onDblClick	Presses down and releases the mouse button twice
onFocus	Enters a field to makes it active
onKeyDown	Depresses a key on the keyboard
onKeyPress	Depresses and releases a key on the keyboard
onKeyUp	Releases a key on the keyboard
onMouseDown	Presses the mouse button down and before it's released
onMouseMove	Moves the mouse pointer around the display region of an HTML element
onMouseOut	Moves the mouse pointer away from the display region of an HTML element
onMouseOver	Moves the mouse pointer into the display region of an HTML element
onMouseUp	Releases the mouse button

TABLE 6-4. *JavaScript Event Handlers*

FIGURE 6-9. *JavaScript button example*

after the user has selected the display region of your image (the button), and then presses and releases the mouse button (clicks).

```html
<HTML>
<HEAD>
<TITLE>Example JavaScript for Button</TITLE>
</HEAD>
<BODY>
<H1>Example JavaScript for Button</H1>
<FORM METHOD=POST ACTION=http://www.tusc.com/cgi_bin/process_name.cgi>
First Name<INPUT TYPE=TEXT NAME=first_name size=10  MAXLENGTH=10 ><BR>
Last Name<INPUT TYPE=TEXT NAME=last_name size=20 MAXLENGTH=20 ><BR>
<BR><BR>
<!-- Submit Button -->
<BUTTON NAME="submit_button"
        onClick="alert('Submit button was pressed')"
        STYLE="font: 12pt Arial Blue; background:red" >
<IMG SRC="check.gif" WIDTH=30 HEIGHT=20 ALT="Check Me Out">
Check Me Out
</BUTTON>
<!-- Reset Button -->
<BUTTON NAME="reset_button"
        onClick="alert('Reset button was pressed')"
        STYLE="font: 12pt Arial Blue; background:red" >
<IMG SRC="check.gif" WIDTH=30 HEIGHT=20 ALT="Clear Form">
Clear Form
</BUTTON>
</FORM>
</BODY>
</HTML>
```

Suppressing the Return Key in IE Forms

Often client/server-minded users continue pressing the ENTER key in IE, which, instead of moving them to the next form field, navigates them to the nearest Submit button and performs a submit. The onKeyPress() event handler can be used to capture the keystroke by applying the following syntax:

```
onKeyPress="return DoOnKeyPress(event);"
```

DoOnKeyPress() returns True or False, based on code used inside the function. The use of the ENTER key isn't necessary in Navigator, but the preceding code works as well.

Working with URLs and Hyperlinks

The Uniform Resource Locator (URL) is the address schema of the World Wide Web. URLs are defined by RFC 1738. When you start up your browser and attempt to enter the Internet, you're using an HTTP URL to locate the home Web page you defined. Many different protocols and types of URLs exist, including, but not limited to, the following:

- **File URL** A URL that retrieves a specific file on a site.

- **File Transfer** A URL that transfers a file from one machine to another.

- **Gopher URL** A URL that pulls information from a Gopher server.

- **News URL** A URL that pulls information from a Usenet newsgroup site.

- **HTTP URL** Hypertext Transport Protocol (HTTP) URL that pulls information from an HTTP server that serves HTML documents.

- **Partial or relative URL** Once you reach a hypertext document with a URL, you can access other documents on the server by entering the document name or a relative URL (for example, myOtherDoc.HTML).

Table 6-5 shows examples of valid URLs.

Hyperlinks or hypertext links can be created in HTML with the <A> tag (*A* meaning anchor) and the HREF attribute. Hyperlinks give your visitors a road map

URL	Description
ftp://www.myftpserver.com/ myftpfile.doc	Uses the File Transfer Protocol (FTP) to download a specific file (myftpfile.doc) from a specific server (**www.myftpserver.com**).
http://www.myhttpserver.com/ myhtml.html	Uses Hypertext Transfer Protocol (HTTP) to transfer a specific document (myhtml.html) from the virtual root directory (because no directory was specified) of a specific server (**www.myhttpserver.com**).

TABLE 6-5. *Example Valid URLs*

URL	Description
http://www.myhttpserver.com/ myhttpdirectory/	Refers to a specific server (**www.myhttpserver.com**) and refers to a specific directory (myhttpdirectory), but doesn't refer to a specific file. In this case, the HTTP server uses its default initial file (usually, index.html).
myfile.html ../app/myfile.html	This URL doesn't specify a protocol or directory. Because URLs are relative to the last URL, the browser uses the prior URL's protocol, server, and directory.

TABLE 6-5.   *Example Valid URLs* (continued)

to information on the World Wide Web that you feel pertains to your topic. You can create hyperlinks to different resources on the WWW with a partial or relative URL.

When you visit a Web site with a browser, the hyperlinks are usually underlined and the hyperlink text has a different color than the text on the rest of the document. Images can also be "hot," or active, providing links to direct your visitors to other resources on the Web.

The HTML <A> tag with an HREF attribute is used to direct your visitors to an anchor within your document or to another document. The HREF can contain an absolute URL reference (including protocol, server, directory, and file) or it can include a fragment identifier or a JavaScript code fragment. Place text, an image, line breaks, and headings to mark a visible area that users can select to hyperlink, between the tags <A> and </A>.

Attributes can be set in the <BODY> tag to change and set the color of visited, unvisited, and active (currently being viewed in another browser window) hyperlinks, including the following examples:

<BODY> Attribute	Description
ALINK	Set the color of active links
LINK	Set the color of unvisited links
VLINK	Set the color of visited links
BGCOLOR	Set background color for page
TEXT	Set text color

The following HTML code segment sets the preceding links accordingly:

```
<BODY BGCOLOR="white" TEXT="black" LINK="blue"
     VLINK="red" ALINK="yellow" >
```

Colors can be referenced by name or by RGB value. The ALINK, LINK, and VLINK attributes are noted as being deprecated in the specification for HTML 4.0. Font items in the specification are replacing them for cascading style sheets (CSS), even though they'll still be supported in current versions.

Keyboard shortcuts (hot keys) and tab orders (TAB key) can also be added to your hyperlinks, giving the user keyboard control. The *hot keys* can be set with the ACCESSKEY attribute of the <A> tag. The *tab order* enables the user to tab to hyperlinks and is set with the TABINDEX attribute. The following hyperlink examples use hot keys and tab orders. Notice the LINK, VLINK, and ALINK attributes set in the <BODY> tag. The example shows HTML output containing hyperlinks.

```
<HTML>
<HEAD>
<TITLE>Hyperlinks to Web sites</TITLE>
<BODY BGCOLOR="white" TEXT="black" LINK="blue"
     VLINK="red" ALINK="yellow" >
<H1>Cool Web Sites to Browse</H1>
<BR><A HREF="http://www.internet.com"
     ACCESSKEY=w
     TABINDEX=1> Web Developers Channel (ALT-W)
   </A>
<BR><A HREF="http://www.webplaces.com"
     ACCESSKEY=g
     TABINDEX=2> Web Graphics (ALT-G)
   </A>
<BR><A HREF="http://www.inquiry.com"
     ACCESSKEY=a
     TABINDEX=3> Ask the professionals web related questions (ALT-A)
   </A>
<BR><A HREF="http://www.webdeveloper.com"
     ACCESSKEY=d
     TABINDEX=4> Resources and technical information
                 on Web Development (ALT-D)
   </A>
<BR><A HREF="http://www.webreference.com"
     ACCESSKEY=i
     TABINDEX=5> Information on web development. (ALT-I)
   </A>
<BR><A HREF="http://www.wdvl.com"
     ACCESSKEY=v
     TABINDEX=6> Web Developers Virtual Library. (ALT-V)
```

```
   </A>
<BR><A HREF="http://www.browserwatch.com"
     ACCESSKEY=b
     TABINDEX=7> Information on browsers and plugins. (ALT-B)
   </A>
<BR><A HREF="http://web1.w3.org/markup/html-spec/html-spec_13.html"
     ACCESSKEY=h
     TABINDEX=8> Document on the HTML Coded Character Set (ALT-H)
   </A>
</BODY>
</HTML>
```

The Web page generated by this code is demonstrated in Figure 6-10.

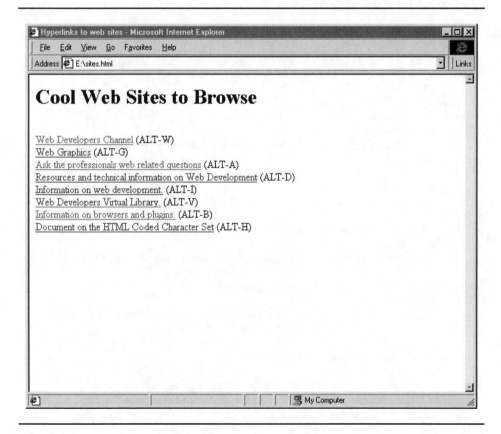

FIGURE 6-10. *Hyperlink examples*

Removing Hypertext Underline Links

For users who don't like the underlined hypertext links, the feature can be turned off through their browser settings.

- For IE users, go to Tools | Internet Options. Select the Advanced tab. Under Underline links, select the Never radio button.

- For Netscape users, go to Edit | Preferences | Appearance | Colors and unselect Underline Links.

TIP
You can use HTML 4.0 CSS to indicate the links not be underlined.

When the user passes over a hyperlink, the mouse pointer turns into a hand notifying the user that a hyperlink is present. Some feel different-colored text, an underline, and changing the mouse pointer is overkill for hyperlinks. If you're using CSS, the following technique enables you to remove the hyperlink underline. Place the following code at the head of your document to eliminate the hyperlink underlines. When the user passes over the hyperlink, the mouse pointer still changes to a hand and the text will be blue.

```
<style type="text/css">
a { text-decoration: none;
color: blue ;}
</style>
```

If the preceding HTML example, Cool Web Sites to Browse, is changed to include the preceding style tags, the page appears identical to the one shown in Figure 6-11.

If you want to eliminate the underlining on only a few links on your pages, you can either move the style declaration to each link:

```
<A HREF="page.html" STYLE="text-decoration: none">No fancy stuff on me</a>
```

or you can create two classes—one underlined and one not underlined—and apply those to each link. First, create the style declaration in the page header:

```
<style>
    a.1{text-decoration:none}
    a.2{text-decoration:underline}
</style>
```

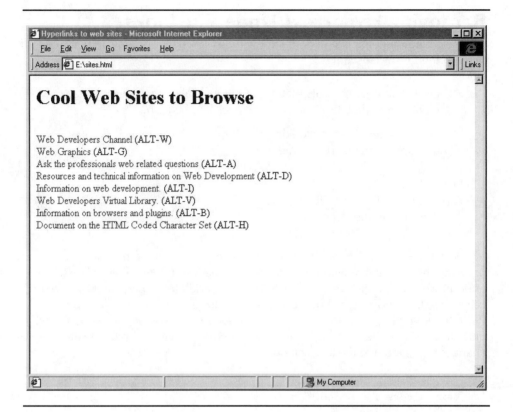

FIGURE 6-11. *Cool Web Sites*

Then specify each link using the CLASS= attribute. The following link isn't underlined.

```
<a class="1" href=page.html>Link not underlined</a>
```

Forcing Side-by-Side Forms

HTML tables can be used to force Submit buttons to be side by side for different forms. The </FORM> tag implies a new line, so if another <FORM> is opened, the Submit button for that form appears below the first form. To force the buttons to appear on the same line, use an HTML table. The following code creates two buttons and places them side by side in a table:

```
<HTML>
<FONT COLOR=#FF0000 SIZE=4>Without a table</FONT>
<FORM 1>
<INPUT NAME=Form1 TYPE=Submit VALUE=Button1>
</FORM>
<FORM 2>
<INPUT NAME=Form2 TYPE=Submit VALUE=Button2>
</FORM>
<FONT COLOR=#006010 SIZE=4>With a table</FONT>
<TABLE>
<TR>
<FORM 1>
<TD><INPUT NAME=Form1 TYPE=Submit VALUE=Button1></TD>
</FORM>
<FORM 2>
<TD><INPUT NAME=Form2 TYPE=Submit VALUE=Button2></TD>
</FORM>
</TR>
</TABLE>
</HTML>
```

TIP

The same logic can be used to display two tables or two images side by side.

Cascading Style Sheets

Cascading style sheets (CSS) enable you to change the browser defaults for page display. A CSS is a template for the look-and-feel of your site. Instead of coding individual tags for fonts and colors for objects on the page, using style sheets centralize font, size, color, and link information, so it can be applied to multiple objects. CSS can be created for individual elements, whole pages, or entire sites. You can turn off underlining on links; change the default font, size, and line spacing; control the placement of objects; and set special attributes to anything that falls within an <H1> tag or any other tag. CSS makes it easy to bring consistency to your entire Web site. Using the capabilities of CSS to design your Web site can save time, but remember, the implementation of style sheets in the two major browsers has been inconsistent.

By using static CSS, you can change the look and feel of your site in one place and change the feel of the entire site instantly. Dynamic CSS based on the user's input makes for an extremely powerful application—as Oracle Portal quickly demonstrates.

Style Sheet Support in Different Browsers

CSS was released with the version 4.0 HTML specifications. Unfortunately, the 4.0 versions of IE and Navigator were released prior to the final specification of CSS. The two browsers implement style sheets differently. This leads to the confusing mix of CSS1, CSS2, and *layers* (a Netscape-specific implementation of object placement). You must be careful regarding the browsers your site supports or limit your implementation of style sheets to the features supported by both IE 4.*x* and Netscape 4.*x*. When implementing CSS features, test the appearance and effects on both IE and Netscape 4.*x* and 3.*x*. This implementation results in enhanced effect for those with browsers that support the CSS and no diminished effect for those that don't.

TIP
Users may browse with style sheets turned off. Test your Web pages with Style Sheets turned off, as well, to make sure your pages are still readable for users who prefer to use their own fonts and colors, or those who surf with an older browser.

Don't implement unsupported features because this might make any information on your site inaccessible to users on certain browser versions. For example, DHTML is IE-centric and isn't implemented on the Netscape browser. Conversely, be careful about implementing the functionality of Netscape-specific tags that aren't supported by Microsoft. Some rework might be necessary to make all your pages appear appropriately in all browsers.

WebReview.com contains a master list of all style sheet components and information on how they're implemented in different browsers. You can find this list at **http://style.webreview.com/**. When you decide to enhance the CSS structure of your site, review this list carefully to ensure your page displays on all the browser versions you may be supporting. The master list includes the supported features for all current versions of Netscape, IE, and Opera.

The primary features that work on all major browsers are simple formatting features, such as text color, font, and size. Layers, image manipulation, and advanced text effects are supported erratically, if at all, in most browsers. Remember, while many of the CSS tags are supported in the most recent releases of the major browsers, users surfing with a browser even one revision behind might be unable to see your site properly.

Implementing Style Sheets

The Web is a fluid medium and users demand new, updated, and fresh content constantly. As a redesign of your Web site is inevitable, implementing CSS means easier maintenance: you update the colors, fonts, sizes, and backgrounds of the entire site by making the changes in a style sheet. The full benefit of CSS will be more fully realized when browsers support it more completely.

Styles can be used by Web pages in many different ways. Styles can be specified for individual elements on a page, although this isn't an improvement over using normal tags. Styles can also be local to a single page, within a <STYLE> tag in the page header. Only the current page uses this style. In the following example, which is demonstrated in Figure 6-12, the style changes the font and size for any text following a <P> (paragraph) tag:

```
<HTML>
<HEAD><TITLE>Pseudo-element example</title>
<STYLE TYPE="text/css">
     P { font-size: 14pt; line-height:16pt; font-family: helvetica }
</STYLE>
</HEAD>
<BODY>
This sentence will display in your default font
<P>This sentence will display in Helvetica, look Ma no FONT tag!</P>
</BODY>
</HTML>
```

Design, redesign, and consistency of your Web pages becomes easier by implementing the linked style sheet in all your pages. A *linked style sheet* is a single reference used by all your pages. The following example links the style sheet style1.css to the Web page. The LINK tag is added in the header of the Web page.

```
<LINK rel="stylesheet" type="text/css" href="style1.css" title="style1">
```

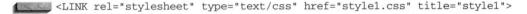

FIGURE 6-12. *Style sheet example*

The style sheet itself is a simple text document that contains template information for tags used in the Web page. The following entry in a style sheet, for example, displays paragraph text in 9pt Arial, links in lowercase Arial 9pt, and isn't underlined. Visited links are displayed in gray.

```
p    {font-family:arial;
       font-size:9pt;
       }
A:link
      {color: #660000;
       font-family:arial;
       font-size:9pt;
       text-transform:lowercase;
       text-decoration:none;
       font-weight:normal;
       }

A:visited
      {color: gray;
       font-size:9pt;
       text-decoration:none;
       text-transform:lowercase;
       }
```

This isn't particularly painful to implement. Instead of using LINK, VLINK, and FONT tags sprinkled in your HTML document, style sheets apply to any text that's marked using the specified tags. As the site grows, making mass changes becomes more difficult. Changing the link color in all Web pages linked to a style sheet is as simple as changing the style sheet reference. No compiling or relinking is required. Making modifications now and knowing they're implemented consistently throughout your site is incredibly easy when you have only one page to edit.

TIP

When implementing CSS, take the opportunity to change your links to conform to one of the standards common on the Web—unvisited links a "hot" color and visited links subdued. For example, have links on pages in maroon (or another color that works well with your color scheme) and visited links grayed out.

Perhaps the most daunting aspect of implementing CSS is the consideration of what is supported by the various browsers and the multitude of tag specifications that exist. The resources at the previously listed WebReview site—

http://www.webreview.com—are useful. Another good site for how-to information is found at **http://www.stars.com/Authoring/Style/Sheets/WDVL.html**, a part of the Web Developers Virtual Library (**http://www.stars.com**) that includes a tutorial and a wealth of resources for using style sheets effectively.

Tools for implementing CSS are also improving. Most GUI HTML development tools support style sheet implementations and a tool dedicated to style sheets is available at the Sheet Stylist page at **http://homepages.tcp.co.uk/~drarh/Stylist/**. Many tools are affordable and provide a demonstration to download and try before you purchase them.

Creating Subject and/or Text for E-mail

Did you know you can automatically enter the subject line for visitors who click a link on your site to send you e-mail? The following syntax is a standard e-mail link in HTML:

```
<A HREF="mailto:bradley_brown@tusc.com">Click here to send me email</A>
```

With only a slight modification, you can automatically enter the subject line for Web surfers who click the link, making it easier to track e-mail from your Web site:

```
<A HREF="mailto:bradley_brown@tusc.com?subject=About
        your 9i book">Click here to send me email about my book</A>
```

If the user clicks the line "Click here to send me email," the user's default e-mail program starts, which creates a new e-mail message and automatically enters the subject line with the text, "About your 9i book." Taking this one step further, if you want to populate the message for the user, this is done with the BODY attribute, used as follows:

```
<A HREF="mailto:bradley_brown@tusc.com?subject=About
        your 9i book"&body="I would like to ask you a question,
        which is:">Click here to send me email about my book</A>
```

TIP

The mailto: address wasn't supported in early versions of Internet Explorer and it isn't supported by many of the available online HTML e-mail functions. Unless you're sure all your users are using an IE or Netscape browser and a POP3 e-mail package, choose another approach.

Sending E-mail from an HTML Form

If you want the user to enter the information into an HTML form and submit that message through e-mail, the following code automatically sends e-mail that contains not only the to, from, and subject, but also the message body:

```
<FORM METHOD=POST TYPE=FILE ENCTYPE="text-plain"
      ACTION="mailto:bradley_brown@tusc.com?SUBJECT=Subject Line&=">
<INPUT TYPE=TEXT NAME="MESSAGE" VALUE="Message Body">
<INPUT TYPE=SUBMIT VALUE="Send Email?">
</FORM>
```

TIP
Note the "&=" after Subject Line.
This is needed to force the text to
display the data in the message body.

Indenting Your Text

Because tabs aren't directly supported in HTML, you can mimic indenting your text in several ways.

The simplest way to mimic standard indenting is to use the <dd> tag (definition tag) to indent a paragraph; however, you cannot control how many spaces the text will be indented using this method.

```
<dd>This text will be indented. <br> This text will
break back to the left margin.<p>
```

You can also create a placeholder by using a single-pixel GIF image. When displaying the GIF image, you can set the height and width using the respective <IMG> attributes, as the following line of code illustrates:

```
<img src="one_pixel.gif" height=1 width=20>Indented Text
```

This syntax enables you to create an exact-size placeholder. The download time isn't an issue because the GIF is small and will be cached the first time it's used. Make sure the .gif file is transparent, so any background image is still displayed.

If you're deploying your site to Netscape browsers only, you can use the Netscape tag <SPACER> to indent paragraphs. IE doesn't understand this tag and simply ignores it.

```
<SPACER TYPE=horizontal SIZE=20>Spaced Text
```

TIP

Another way to accomplish formatting in which you needn't "placehold" more than the vertical height of the character is to use several consecutive nonbreaking spaces ( ). Remember, HTML ignores multiple "normal" spaces within a document; you must use .

If you want to indent a whole section of text, use <BLOCKQUOTE> </BLOCKQUOTE>. Text between the BLOCKQUOTE tags will be indented from the left and right margins.

Placing Two Headings on the Same Line

To get two different-size headings on the same line, you cannot use the <H> (heading) tag because an implicit break (<BR>) occurs when headings are used. You can mimic two headings on the same line by using the <FONT> tag, however, as the following example illustrates:

```
<font size=+1 font=arial>Welcome to </font>
<font size=+3 font=arial>TUSC</font><br>
```

Understanding Which Frame Is Which

When using frames, it's common for a link in one frame to open a document in another frame using a TARGET attribute in the link. In addition to referencing an explicitly named frame (frames are given names in the frameset definition, such as MAIN or INDEX frames), HTML provides several relative frame references to control where a document opens:

- **_blank**   Opens the link in a new, unnamed window

- **_self**   Opens the link in the current frame

- **_parent**   Opens the link in the immediate FRAMESET parent

- **_top**   Opens the page in the full, unframed window

If you don't specify a target, the link opens in the current frame or browser window. Specifying an explicit name for the target opens the link in the frame of that name. If the frame doesn't exist, the link opens in a new window with the name you specify. Many Web sites don't explicitly set targets for their links, resulting in unpredictable behavior when you click links or navigate within the Web site. Conscientious use of these explicit and relative frame references can ensure your Web page behaves as you designed it.

TIP
Search engines reference each individual page in your Web site, but they're incapable of indexing or linking to your "master" frameset page. Including <NOFRAMES> content is critical if you want search engines to link to your frameset page.

Understanding Frame Etiquette

You have a vision of how your page should look and, typically, you spend a considerable amount of effort sizing objects, so your site is a work of art. You don't want to see your page displayed in a frame when it's accessed from someone else's site. Just as you wouldn't allow an external site to be displayed in a frame on your site, you want to ensure your site is always seen in its own browser window. You can eliminate all frames before your page is displayed in at least three ways.

First, a metatag can set the target frame to "_top", meaning wipe out all frames and open the page in the browser window itself, as the following example shows:

```
<META HTTP-EQUIV="Window-target" CONTENT="_top">
```

Second, if you have control of the link itself, you can use a target frame of "_top" to display any of your subpages, as illustrated here:

```
<A HREF="main.html" TARGET="_top">
<IMG SRC="home1.gif" alt="TUSC Main Page"
    WIDTH=90 HEIGHT=42 BORDER=0 ALIGN=bottom>
</A>
```

Finally, JavaScript can be used to move the displayed page to the main browser window, as shown in this example:

```
<script language=javascript>
if (parent.frames[1])
    parent.location.href = self.location.href;
</script>
```

Make sure you return the favor to any links you include on your site to outside Web sites. Opening another site within your own frames is considered poor form, so include the TARGET="_top" attribute for all external links you create.

TIP

If most of your links on a page are external links, you can use a <BASE TARGET = "_top"> tag in the header of your page to default all links to the main browser window, instead of adding it explicitly to each link.

Creating a Window Frame Look

One site we created contained a frame on all four sides, giving it the look of a TV screen. The reason for this appearance was to support multiple browser window sizes without recoding the application. By putting the black frames around the page, we kept the same look and feel no matter what window size was used.

TIP

If you want to butt graphics up against the edge of the window, put your HTML page in a frame and add the tag MARGINWIDTH=0 MARGINHEIGHT=0.

Referencing CGI Scripts

Static Web pages that simply present data to the user make up the bulk of the Web, but Web pages on the Internet can request user input and respond to it. This functionality is used for pages such as search engines, surveys, credit card information, and online registrations. The data can be accepted from an HTML form and sent to a program through a Common Gateway Interface (CGI) script.

A *CGI script* is a simple protocol used to communicate between a form on the Web and a program on a server. CGI scripts use UNIX/C concepts, such as STDIN (standard in), STDOUT (standard out), and environment variables. No specific programming language is required for CGI scripts, so use C, PRO*C, Perl, and/or UNIX shell scripting. The only requirement of the programming language used is it must be able to handle STDIN and STDOUT.

A CGI script has the capability to send information to and receive information from the browser. This feature gives the Web its interactive nature. A CGI program receives two types of information from the browser. The CGI script can gather pieces of information about the browser, server, and the CGI script itself. The server provides this information to the CGI script through environment variables. The CGI script can be passed information entered by the user. This information is encoded by the browser and sent through an environmental variable (specifically, QUERY using the GET method) or through the standard input (STDIN using the POST method).

The workings of a CGI script are simple.

1. The user submits input, usually by entering data and pressing a Submit button. The CGI script receives the data from the input form as a set of name-value pairs. The names are defined by the URL or by the HTML form elements in the HTML script. The input is read from STDIN.

2. The CGI script takes the data and parses the information by name. The script can also send the information off to be processed by other programs.

3. The CGI script prepares the data to be written in HTML format and sends out through STDOUT.

For example, imagine you, as the developer, are debugging a Web application and want to see what some of the environment variables contain. You also want the browser to display the environment variables and their values. The following example is a CGI script, written in C, to determine the environment variables and their values to print the results to the browser:

```c
#include <stdio.h>
extern char **environ;
int main()
 {
   char **p = environ;
   printf("Content-Type: text/html\r\n\r\n");
   printf("<html> <head>\n");
   printf("<title>CGI Environment</title>\n");
   printf("</head>\n");
   printf("<body>\n");
   printf("<h1>CGI Environment</h1>\n");
   while(*p != NULL)
       printf("%s<br>\n",*p++);
   printf("</body> </html>\n");
}
```

By using HTML you can build URLs that call other URLs. CGI programs can be used to accomplish the processing of this information. The *i*AS modules implemented by Oracle are smart CGI programs. For more information about the *i*AS modules, see Chapters 13, 14, and the online chapters.

Tracking Visitors to Your Site

Once your Web site is built, tested, and deployed, you'll want to know how well it is performing. In any application, you want to know what kind of activity your Web page is generating, such as the following:

- How many visitors has your Web page received?

- Which pages are used most often?

- What kind of response time are users experiencing?

- How many guests have registered a profile?

- Where are your visitors coming from?

- What time of the day did your visitors arrive?

- Where did they travel to from your site?

Web statistics are useful for Web administrators to get a sense of the actual load on the server. See Chapter 23 for more information about Web server logs and analysis of these logs. Collecting this information can be critical to tuning and enhancing your application on the Web. In addition to accessing the operating system-level system logs for your Web server, *i*AS provides a number of methods to gather this information. If all you want to know is how many guests have registered a profile, write a PL/SQL procedure to select the count of the profiles registered in your database and return the results to your Web page. If you want to count the number of hits to a page, use a sequence number or a counter table.

Using a Page Counter

If your Internet service provider (ISP) hosts your site, you might be unable to use *i*AS or a CGI program to generate this information, so contact your ISP and inquire if it allows page counters. If it does, you'll probably be provided with a Frequently Asked Questions (FAQ) list on how to add its page counter. If CGI scripts are allowed, you can write (or download) a CGI script that keeps a tally of your visitors and displays the counter on your Web page. A number of free page counters are available on the Web. These are usually written in C or Perl, and they come with complete instructions on implementing them for your pages.

TIP
Counters are nearly always more interesting to you, the developer, than they are to the user. Displaying counters on your Web pages isn't necessary. The data can be accessed through a private Web page or directory file.

If you cannot use a CGI program for your counter, use a public counter. Many Web-based services can provide statistics on your Web site. Usually, the "fee" for this type of page counter requires you to include their advertising on your site.

One of the public counters you can use is NBCiCounter (formerly XOOMCounter), located at **http://wwwx.nbci.com/counter/**. NBCiCounter offers a free graphical page counter that provides you with an easy, but powerful, site management tool that gives you access to stats about your site. When you attempt to incorporate these services into your site, NBCiCounter sends you a set of instructions that include an anchor tag containing an image referencing its site.

Using public or external counters can slow the response of your Web page if the counter file must be referenced on a different server. Counters also record each visit to a page and, therefore, may be inaccurate if users click through a main page several times or access a cached version of the page.

If you're using Active Server Pages (ASP), an ASP component can be used to keep track of your visitors. The ASP component is called Page Counter Component. With this component, you can determine the number of times a page from your Web site has been requested. To perform this task, use the server's CreateObject method to create an instance of the Page Counter Component. The following line of code illustrates an example of creating an instance of the Page Counter Component:

```
Set pc = Server.CreateObject( "MSWC.PageCounter")
```

Then use the Page Counter Component's methods (PageCnt.dll) to retrieve and save the number of accesses to your Web site.

Summary

Web developers have encountered many limitations with HTML. HTML is only a small part of the Standard Generalized Markup Language (SGML) specifications created for the Web. HTML only determines how the information is displayed on a browser. It doesn't describe the information in the document. This is adequate for many Web pages, but application developers demand more from their documents. Web developers are looking toward smarter documents that identify what information is in the document.

The current recommendation of the World Wide Web Consortium is XHTML 1.0, a modular HTML specification that combines the best features of the current HTML 4.01 specification and XML. XHTML is provided with its own Document Type Definition (DTD) for both a strict version for new development and a traditional version for compatibility with older browsers and HTML documents. Both HTML and XML are based on the SGML specifications. HTML is an implementation of SGML for visual presentation, while XML is a subset of SGML for writing markup languages specifying the format for expressing data content. Businesses will be able to create their own self-describing markup language. See Chapter 8 for more information on XML and its definitions.

A clear understanding of HTML is the foundation for designing Web pages; however, advances in XML and the new XHTML standards are constantly changing the landscape for application developers on the Web.

CHAPTER
7

JavaScript Development

he JavaScript language was created to add procedural power to HTML documents. Alone, HTML documents have limited capabilities: they can display data, accept data entered by the user, and send entered data to a server to be processed. HTML, however, doesn't consist of *events* associated with *actions.* JavaScript, with the capability to relate to HTML objects, manipulates data within the HTML document. JavaScript is an event-based addition to HTML.

JavaScript is a simple to learn, dynamic, and powerful object-based language. HTML is a markup (text display) language, whereas JavaScript is an interpretive scripting (almost, but not quite, a full programming) language. If you're familiar with other programming languages, you'll find JavaScript easy to learn. JavaScript is based on the C language's syntax. The initial specification for JavaScript was developed by Netscape, and then published as an open specification used by other browser vendors. Today, by and large, only two browsers are in widespread use, so we must accommodate two versions of JavaScript.. Unfortunately, the two major browsers are only semicompatible and browser implementation differences are the thorns on the JavaScript rose. Technically, Netscape's implementation of JavaScript *is* JavaScript, while Microsoft's is called *JScript.* The term JavaScript, however, is often used to denote both implementations. Microsoft developed a scripting language for the browsers, which is called *VBScript,* but it doesn't have widespread use because it isn't an open source specification.

JavaScript is not Java. In presentations, I often ask if people know the four similarities that Java and JavaScript share. As time passes, more people know the answer to this question—it's J.A.V.A. Maybe it isn't quite that simple. Similarities exist between Java and JavaScript, but not more than other programming languages. When Netscape invented JavaScript, originally called *LiveScript,* Java was also beginning to gain popularity. Netscape asked Sun if it could use the name JavaScript. The name was changed, purely for marketing reasons. In hindsight, I'm unsure if Sun or Netscape would make this choice again. In my opinion, this has caused more confusion than it's been worth (for both companies) but, then again, they fed off each other. The confusion may have been a good thing for both of them. A server-side version of JavaScript, LiveWire, is available (sometimes referred to as server-side JavaScript). To date, I've found one person whose predecessors used LiveWire. His team was converting its LiveWire application to use the PL/SQL module for performance and scalability reasons.

JavaScript runs on the client, in the browser, so your browser must support JavaScript. Netscape and Microsoft browsers support JavaScript on a number of operating system platforms. This enables JavaScript to be a portable language. JavaScript is more of a scripting language than a full-fledged programming language (for example, Java or C) and JavaScript requires less code to accomplish more. The downside of less code is it isn't as powerful or flexible as a full-blown programming language. Another disadvantage is JavaScript is inline with your HTML code, so users can view your source code, which makes protecting your code more difficult (but still possible). JavaScript can be used inside an HTML document in many ways. Before you learn JavaScript, you must learn HTML. JavaScript is embedded into your HTML document and supports events based on your HTML-based objects. Therefore, you need to obtain an understanding of HTML, its objects, and the browser's object hierarchy. In JavaScript, objects have both properties (data or information about the object) and methods (behaviors of the object, basically functions that belong to and can affect that object). Objects can also have associated events. JavaScript uses dot notation similar to the Oracle dot notation (for example, Oracle uses schema.table.column to reference a column in a specific table in a specific schema) to reference objects.

JavaScript can perform data validation, event handling, navigation, document content creation, and calculations to enhance HTML forms and frames, provide cookie management, interface with other objects (for example, Java programs), provide for complete client-side applications, generate other HTML documents in pop-up windows, and more. Using JavaScript's client-side processing can make server-side calls unnecessary, enabling HTML and JavaScript to become a useful platform for reporting and collecting data. Through JavaScript, needed functionality can be performed through the client's browser.

In this chapter, the following topics are discussed:

- Comparing JavaScript to PL/SQL

- Intricacies of *i*AS

- Handling browser incompatibilities

- Writing browser-specific code from your dynamic code

- Reusing your JavaScript code

- Using PL/SQL packaged procedures to generate JavaScript

- Programming user-defined alert processing

- Displaying properties on the screen

- Opening a new window and passing parameters to the window

- Assigning JavaScript variables

- Using the Submit button

- Validating form fields

- Working with PL/SQL code and various browsers

- Making a two-dimensional array in JavaScript

- Assigning JavaScript variables

- Invoking a PL/SQL procedure from a pick list

- Changing frames simultaneously

- Resolving the access denied error

- Passing spaces as a part of the URL

- Debugging onFocus with alert

- Using typeof to avoid the Object Expected error

- Using the eval() function

- Using dynamic function arguments

- Using Arrays of objects to simulate tables and rows

- Subscribing to the JavaScript *OnFocus* newsletter

- Reviewing visual JavaScript tools

Comparing JavaScript to PL/SQL

In version 1 through version 6 of the Oracle RDBMS, SQL was the foundation of Oracle and Oracle solutions. Version 7 brought a significant enhancement to the SQL world when PL/SQL became the basis of Oracle solutions. Oracle8*i* added some new Java components to the database, but Oracle9*i* promises to make Java the next foundation of Oracle's solutions. Based on surveys I performed at Oracle users groups, most developers have a solid knowledge of PL/SQL. In this section, I assume you know PL/SQL. If you aren't familiar with PL/SQL, I recommend reading *Oracle PL/SQL Tips & Techniques,* by Joseph Trezzo (Osborne/McGraw-Hill, 1999—an update will be available in 2002). In this section, a quick JavaScript introduction comparing JavaScript to PL/SQL is provided.

JavaScript Is Case-Sensitive

If you haven't worked with case-sensitive languages, I can assure you this fact will haunt you numerous times, so say it with me: "JavaScript is case-sensitive." Java is also a case-sensitive language, but because Java is a compiled language that requires variables and methods (that is, functions) to be declared before they're used, the Java compiler typically catches your case issues. This isn't true with JavaScript because it's an interpretive language.

TIP

When you're debugging code and you cannot figure it out, stop and think—is case-sensitivity getting the best of you? Remember, sValue isn't the same data entity as svalue.

Using Semicolons or Not

A second difference between PL/SQL and JavaScript is in JavaScript, the semicolon at the end of the line is optional. The semicolon is only required if two commands are placed on the same line. Otherwise, the newline character indicates the end of the command in JavaScript. Remember, if you use separate htp.print commands to print your JavaScript code from within the PL/SQL module of *i*AS, *i*AS will send a newline character after each htp.print command. If you use a tool, such as WebAlchemy, to convert your static HTML and JavaScript file into PL/SQL code, you'll discover many tools will convert the entire script into one htp.script or htp.print command. Use semicolons to separate every command to eliminate potential problems when using conversion tools. If you don't use semicolons, your JavaScript is likely to fail after the conversion from HTML into PL/SQL. PL/SQL Server Pages use htp.prn, which places newlines as they exist in the HTML file, so PSPs can also save you from this issue.

TIP

For consistency, use semicolons at the end of every line.

Defining Variables

In JavaScript, you can define variables used to store information within your program. Variables in JavaScript must begin with a letter or an underscore. Subsequent characters can be letters, numbers, or underscores, but cannot be spaces or hyphens. In addition, variables cannot be reserved words.

TIP

I strongly suggest defining all JavaScript variables used to avoid scope problems.

Reviewing the JavaScript Keywords and Reserved Words

As with every programming language, JavaScript contains keywords. Keywords of the JavaScript language include break, continue, do, else, false, for, function, if, in, int, labeled, new, null, return, switch, this, true, typeof, var, while, and with. Additionally, all languages contain reserved words. In JavaScript, they include abstract, Boolean, break, byte, case, catch, char, class, const, continue, default, delete, do, double, else, extends, false, final, finally, float, for, function, goto, if, implements, import, in, instanceof, int, interface, labeled, long, native, new, null, package, private, protected, public, return, short, static, super, switch, synchronized, this, throw, throws, transient, true, try, typeof, var, void, while, and with. Remember, JavaScript is case-sensitive: isvalid and isValid are two different identifiers.

Looking at JavaScript Literals

Literals in PL/SQL include text, numbers, and Boolean literals. JavaScript has more extensive literal declarations than PL/SQL. JavaScript's literal declarations include integer literals (decimal, hexadecimal, and octal), floating-point literals (decimal numbers with fractional parts), Boolean literals (1-true or 0-false), string literals (0 or more characters enclosed in single or double quotation marks), and special characters (for example, backspace (\b), formfeed (\f), tab (\t), newline (\n), and carriage return (\r)).

Be aware that one of the more obscure (and definitely less endearing) features of JavaScript is that a number defined with a leading 0 tends to be defined, not as a decimal, but as an octal (probably a carryover from C). So, using the number 014 will actually be using a decimal 12. This would most commonly occur when trying to line values up to make code more readable, in a situation something like the following code:

```
aValues[0] = new Value(012);   //octal 12; decimal 10
aValues[1] = new Value(112);
```

Separating and Beautifying Your Code

Like PL/SQL, JavaScript uses separators between characters. The interpreter removes separators and the use of separators is a matter of aesthetics. JavaScript's separators are spaces, tabs, and newlines.

Commenting JavaScript

Many programmers don't like to include comments within their source code; however, comments are an important component to a programming language. Comments make code easier to read, understand, and debug. In JavaScript, there are single-line comments (denoted by two forward slashes (//)) and multiline comments (denoted by a forward slash and an asterisk (/*) and ending with an asterisk and forward slash (*/)). As in PL/SQL, you cannot nest comments.

TIP
Remember, JavaScript is typically downloaded with the HTML document and large documents may download slowly. For this reason, sometimes it's advisable to omit unnecessary comments in production implementations to minimize the size of HTML documents.

Understanding JavaScript Operators

Like PL/SQL operators, JavaScript operators enable the programmer to act or react on variables. Operators are used to assign values, make changes, and perform calculations to variables. Unlike PL/SQL, most JavaScript operators are direct descendants from C++. For assignment, PL/SQL uses colon-equals (:=), whereas JavaScript uses equals (=). Many of the arithmetic and comparison operators are the same for PL/SQL and JavaScript, such as addition or plus (+), subtraction or minus (-), multiplication (*), division (/), not equal to (!=), greater than (>>), greater than or equal to (>>=), less than (<<), and less than or equal to (=<<). Some of JavaScript's nice C++ descendents include increment a variable (++), decrement a variable (--), and add a variable to another (+=). For comparison, PL/SQL uses equals (=), whereas JavaScript uses double equals (==). Another important operator is the concatenation operator, which in PL/SQL is the double pipe (I I), while JavaScript uses a plus sign (+).

Notice the plus sign serves two purposes in JavaScript: addition between numbers and string concatenation. If *any* of the arguments in an expression are strings, JavaScript changes them all to strings and use the + operator to concatenate them rather than performing addition. To force number conversion, you can subtract 0 from a string that represents a number.

Controlling Your Structures

JavaScript contains full control structures, including if-then-else, for, while, do, and so forth. The syntax for the if-then-else structure is a little different than in PL/SQL. In JavaScript, the condition statement must be placed between parentheses (()). The statements are placed between curly braces ({}). For example, the if-then-else syntax in JavaScript is as follows:

```
if (condition) {
    [statements]
}
else {
    [statements]
}
```

An example of actual JavaScript code follows:

```
if (a == b) {
    c = 200;
    d = 75;
}
else {
    c = 300;
    d = 5;
}
```

The c-style for loop is considerably more extensive in JavaScript than in PL/SQL.

```
for ([initializing_expression];
     [conditional_expression];
     [loop_expression]) {
     [statements]
}
```

The following is an example of actual JavaScript code using the for statement:

```
for  (x=0;x<100;x++) {
    document.write(x + " ");
}
```

The previous example initializes x to 0 as your script enters the for loop. At the end of the loop, the loop expression is executed, at which time x will be incremented by 1. The conditional statement is tested before each loop (even the first one). Important to point out is that these three components can be unrelated components (that is, x needn't be in each of the expressions).

JavaScript includes a while statement similar to the JavaScript for statement without the initializing and loop expressions. The following syntax illustrates the while statement:

```
while (conditional_expression) {
       [statement]
}
```

JavaScript labels are identical to PLSQL labels in that they can be used within a loop. JavaScript labels are supported in JavaScript version 1.2 and subsequent releases. JavaScript labels are indicated with a colon after the label. Labels are typically used with the break and continue statements referencing a specific label. The following example includes while, if, label, and break statements. The break statement enables you to reference a label outside another loop structure, in this case, the while loop used in the following example:

```
y = 0; // Set y to 0
start_loop:
y++;    // Increment y by 1
x = 0; // Set x to 0
// Check to see if y is less than 5, if so, do the while loop
while (y<5){
  x++; // Increment x by 1
  document.write(x + " " + y); // Write current x and y to browser
  // Check to see if x is equal to 20 yet, if so, break out of loop and
  // go to the start_loop label.
  if (x==20) {
    break start_loop;
  } // End if
} // End While
```

Modeling the Objects or Object Modeling?

JavaScript's object model enables you to implement powerful and versatile models for application development. The object model eases the design and implementation details of complex programs and enables the use of previously created objects in current projects. Remember, JavaScript is object-*based*, not object-*oriented*. You cannot create your own complex objects in JavaScript, but you can refer to JavaScript objects. If that isn't confusing enough, object-based versus object-oriented means JavaScript *doesn't* provide several basic functions of object-oriented languages. These basic functions include inheritance, polymorphism, and encapsulation. Java is an object-oriented language. JavaScript can use or refer to objects created in Java, and the JavaScript object model is simple to understand. The following is an example of a simple HTML script:

```
<FORM NAME=Emp ACTION="/emp/plsql/application">
<INPUT TYPE=TEXT NAME=empName>
</FORM>
```

In JavaScript, the object model to reference the value in the empName field in the Emp form would be referred to as in the following line of code:

```
window.document.Emp.empName.value
```

Although HTML is not case-sensitive, everything in JavaScript is case-sensitive! In the preceding example, the value of the field was retrieved. The value is a property of the field. Form text fields have other properties, including defaultValue and name.

While noting the preceding properties, you might wonder about the name property. Why would you need the name of the field when you had to specify the name in the object model specification (window.document.Emp.EmpName.name)? You need the name of a field because you can reference objects in JavaScript in a number of ways. For example, "this" refers to the current object; therefore, if you want to access the name of the current object, it would be referenced as follows:

```
this.name
```

You can also reference objects based on array values, for example, forms on a page or fields within a form. You could also refer to the first form and the first field on the form, as the following line of code illustrates

```
window.document.forms[0].fields[0].name
```

As the preceding syntax shows, JavaScript's object model can quickly become complex. I highly recommend you pick up at least one JavaScript book for your library. A good JavaScript book can explain the object model and describe all properties, methods, and event handlers available for each object type. I own the *JavaScript Pocket Reference,* by David Flanagan (O'Reilly, 1998), which I carry everywhere I go.

Each object type has properties and methods associated with it. For example, the methods associated with form text fields include blur(), eval(), focus(), select(), toString(), and valueOf(). Forcing these methods to occur is also programmatically possible.

Text fields also have event handlers associated with them. The events that could occur include onBlur, onChange, onFocus, and onSelect (see Table 7-1).

Object	onClick	onSubmit	onChange	onFocus	onBlur	onLoad	onUnload	onMouseOver	onSelect	onAbort	onError	onMouseOut	onReset
Button	x												
Reset	x												
Submit	x												
Radio	x												
Checkbox	x												
Link	x							x				x	
Form		x							x				x
Text			x	x	x				x				
Textarea			x	x	x								
Select			x	x	x					x	x		
Image													
Area	x							x				x	
Window						x	x				x		

TABLE 7-1. *Events Available for Each Object Type*

The Intricacies of *iAS*

JavaScript is embedded into your HTML code, so if you're using an *iAS* module, no setup is required, JavaScript is included into your HTML document. JavaScript code is typically placed in the <HEAD> section of your HTML. If you use WebAlchemy to convert your HTML code to PL/SQL, be sure to use semicolons between each line of JavaScript code. You can write your HTML and JavaScript code in your favorite visual or text editor and convert it to PL/SQL, or write straight PL/SQL using the htp.script procedure for your JavaScript or a series of htp.p commands. If you're using PL/SQL Server Pages (PSP) or Java Server Pages (JSP) to develop your *iAS* application, the JavaScript is included in the HTML code as it would normally be. No special procedures are required to write JavaScript with *iAS*.

Handling Browser Incompatibilities

Browser compatibility is the bane of Web developers. It's painfully common to develop a routine or function in JavaScript for one vendor's browser and to test it in another, only to discover the same code doesn't work because of the existence, support, or merely referencing requirements of a particular object. The bad news is that dealing with browser incompatibility is something of an art and not a science. No particular "magic" exists to solve all compatibility problems. Most of the current JavaScript books indicate command compatibility and incompatibility of the "Big Two" browsers: Netscape Navigator and Internet Explorer.

The good news is the various browsers supporting client-side JavaScript *are* compatible, at least regarding the more common and basic features of the language. As you extend JavaScript into Dynamic HTML (DHTML), style sheets, and the HTML 4.0 specifications, more incompatibilities will be evident. Documentation regarding these general features is also widely available online, at the vendors' Web sites, and in reference books, and isn't addressed in this chapter.

The simplest remedy for browser incompatibility is to avoid the issue entirely by supporting only one browser. If you have a choice in the matter, choose one browser and browser version to support. By choosing only one browser, you can completely eliminate the issue of keeping code running on different platforms. Keeping a single application running properly for one browser and version can be difficult enough, let alone adding another browser and more versions to the situation. An infinite number of factors, well beyond the developer's control, can affect browser performance including, but not limited to, firewall settings, ISPs, the user's connection to the network, the *Internet* (that is, direct or by modem, with baud rate considered), the user's operating system, the server's operating system, and even operating system settings (for example, environmental parameters). *Intranets* (for example, local applications where the user base can be strictly controlled) are easier to support than the Internet. A certain amount of control, such as user access, versions, and which browsers are supported, can be enforced. By eliminating the complication of having to support multiple browsers, support issues become simpler, and the simplest approach seems to work best.

Limiting users to one specific browser and version isn't always possible, particularly on Internet applications. This opens a whole Pandora's box of compatibility problems that must be dealt with carefully. When supporting multiple browsers, careful testing on every supported browser, platform, *and* version (as much as possible) is essential. Testing software can help to automate testing; however, testing is complicated because multiple versions of a browser often cannot exist on the same machine. At a minimum, perform testing on the least common denominator. As much as possible, stick to core items and don't implement browser-specific features. Some information on this topic can be gained from research on the Web and more from reference books but, you, as a developer, will want to find incompatibilities as they come up and might want to compile your own list of incompatibilities *with* workarounds for reference later. Generally speaking, because Navigator appears to have more rigid syntax requirements than Internet Explorer, it might be easier to develop a JavaScript application on Navigator and port it to Explorer later than to work the other way.

TIP

At a minimum, perform testing on the least-common denominator of a browser and version. By and large, developing on Navigator and porting to Explorer might be easier because Navigator's syntax requirements are more precise than Explorer's.

For those instances where incompatibilities cannot be avoided, careful coding techniques can go a long way toward making applications run universally. JavaScript is an interpretive language. It provides the capability to create objects and properties on-the-fly. With the careful use of the JavaScript tag- and browser-specific code in JavaScript itself, you should be able to work around any incompatibilities.

Creating objects and properties is a fairly elegant way to work around some browser incompatibilities, to the extent of avoiding JavaScript errors. You can implement the code in your application to check if a given object exists using the typeof operator. If the object doesn't exist, you can avoid errors when referencing the object or property later by creating it. For example, Netscape Navigator doesn't support the disabled form object property in Internet Explorer. For the affected form fields, you can create a form property called disabled. This can be accomplished within an onLoad() event handler for designated form objects. The result is the future references to that property in your mainline code *will* locate the disabled property because the defined property is now there. The end result is that a JavaScript error can be avoided neatly. Creating the form property only avoids a

JavaScript error. Merely creating a property called disabled for the appropriate objects won't cause Navigator to do anything with the new property. In other words, the object won't actually be disabled. Creating the object property will, however, enable the same code to work in both browsers without crashing.

Another way to handle incompatibilities in browser versions is to use the JavaScript tag with specific version numbers. If the browser doesn't support the appropriate version, the browser will ignore the block of code. This must, of course, be a satisfactory solution for your application. For example, to use this "feature," browsers not supporting JavaScript version 1.2 would ignore the following script:

```
<SCRIPT LANGUAGE="JAVASCRIPT1.2">
switch(Value){
  case 1:
    break;
  default:

    alert("value is not 1");

}
</SCRIPT>
```

This code, therefore, wouldn't cause problems during execution in older browsers, with the exception of the loss of processing this code, which cannot be avoided, because the browser is ignoring the entire body of code.

The most difficult and time-consuming workaround is the most powerful of the techniques—writing browser-specific code. To identify the actual browser being used by the user, use the appVersion property of the navigator object. The following line of code contains the JavaScript appVersion variable:

```
navigator.appVersion
```

This variable can identify the actual browser and version being used. The power behind this information is undeniable and shouldn't be underestimated—it enables you to write browser-, version-, and platform-specific code. The navigator.appName command can identify the browser without the version number and is often simpler to use.

TIP

Using the browser version information enables you to maintain browser-specific code with simple if-then-else logic, but your code may quickly become difficult to maintain and hard to read.

Writing Browser-Specific Code from Your Dynamic Code

You can address browser incompatibilities outside JavaScript and the HTML document by using dynamic Web pages. Although this technique references generating Web pages in PL/SQL and Java, the principles follow through to other dynamic means of generating server-side Web pages (for example, using Perl or another module).

The theory behind this process is quite simple. You can generate dynamic documents in *i*AS, so why not use if-then-else logic based on the browser the user is using to decide what to include in the document? You simply need to read the http_user_agent environmental variable and use if-then-else logic from there.

In PL/SQL, the OWA_UTIL package's get_cgi_env function can read environmental parameters. Reading the http_user_agent (which, by the way, should correspond loosely to the navigator.appVersion value), *i*AS can identify the user's browser and operating system. You can use this information to dynamically send JavaScript and HTML browser-, version-, and platform-specific information. This is useful, for example, if you want to reference the disabled property in Internet Explorer, but not within Netscape Navigator (where it doesn't exist). By querying the user_http_agent, you can write the correct if-then-else logic to accomplish this task. This function might return a value identical to "Mozilla/3.0.1 (WinNT;1)", meaning the user is using Netscape Navigator version 3.0.1 on Windows NT. The following is an example of the PL/SQL code:

```
if (owa_util.get_cgi_env('http_user_agent') =
    'Mozilla/3.0.1 (WinNT;1)') then
    field_attributes := ' onChange="this.disabled=true";';
else
    field_attributes := null;
end if;
htp.formText(cname =>> 'Name', cattributes => field_attributes);
```

The field_attributes parameter is used in the preceding htp.formText command. If the user is using any browser other than the specific version and operating system (Netscape Navigator on Windows NT), the field_attributes will be NULL (that is, empty). If the user's browser is the specified browser, the field_attributes variable will be assigned accordingly. For purists, doing the comparison and using an else clause to do the initial assignment could accomplish the same thing. In turn, correct JavaScript code is included based on the browser.

The following is an example of Java Server Page code designed to do the same thing:

```
<% if (request.getHeader("User-Agent") == "Mozilla/3.0.1 (WinNT;1)") {
    fieldAttributes = " onChange=\"this.disabled=true\";"; }
   else {
    fieldAttributes = ""; } %>
 <FORM NAME=Name <%= fieldAttributes %>>
```

As with any powerful programming technique, the advantages and the disadvantages should be considered. Advantages include increased processing power and code versatility. The main disadvantage isn't immediately obvious. The comparison in the if statement must be absolute (if the = operator is used) and countless variations of user agent values exist for even the same version of the same browser, all of which are identified by a specific string (usually with only minor variations). Maintaining lists of such browsers can be tedious and storing lists of the browsers in a database table to be checked, instead of the simple preceding hard-coded example, might be necessary. For instance, you could check the table to verify if the current browser is in the supported browsers list, and then use the if-then-else logic to check status instead of the browser identity directly. Generally, looking for "MSIE" in the user agent string can identify the browser. If "MSIE" exists, the browser is probably Internet Explorer; otherwise, the browser is probably Netscape Navigator (although other browsers, such as Opera, do exist).

With a similar technique using PL/SQL, it's possible to produce completely different dynamic documents, depending on variable values. For instance, displaying certain columns on the screen depending on a user's security level or using similar if-then-else logic to govern the display and use of entire HTML forms.

Reusing Your JavaScript Code

When it comes to JavaScript code in your HTML documents and, in turn, in your PL/SQL packages, a number of ways exist to include JavaScript. Obviously, you could hardcode your JavaScript code into your HTML document. In PL/SQL, you might use htp.script or htp.p commands. If you analyze this from a coding practice standpoint, however, does this make sense? Wouldn't you like to share your JavaScript code and reuse it? Of course you would! Many ways exist for you to share your JavaScript code. The following subsections include more reusable and modular approaches that enable you to share your code.

TIP

You can use Oracle Portal for your JavaScript repository.

Mocking Oracle Portal's JavaScript Library Functionality

If you don't have Oracle Portal, you could develop similar functionality. You would need to create a table containing the JavaScript routines. Each routine would be located in a record of this table.

Writing a PL/SQL JavaScript Library Package

You can also write a PL/SQL package full of JavaScript routines. For example, you might call the routine js_lib. In this package, you would define each of your JavaScript functions in a separate procedure. Your PL/SQL code would call each of the js_lib procedures needed for each application component.

Yet another advantage of using PL/SQL to generate the JavaScript code is the contents of the JavaScript code can be dynamically generated. For example, not only could the JavaScript be stored in a table, but the JavaScript routine could dynamically pull information from another table, offering increased development power.

Using a JavaScript Library Instead of Inline JavaScript

Instead of including your JavaScript code directly into the HTML, you can reference a source document containing the JavaScript code. This is accomplished using the SRC attribute of the SCRIPT command, as illustrated in the following line of code:

```
<SCRIPT SOURCE="jslib.js"></SCRIPT>
```

This code retrieves the jslib.js file and includes it into the current HTML source as a JavaScript routine. Remember, URLs are always relative. In other words, the directory from which the browser requests the JavaScript code be pulled is relative to the HTML source itself. If the source were a static HTML file (the relative path for the JavaScript routine in this example), it would be the same directory as the static HTML file. If a programming language, like PL/SQL, dynamically generated the HTML, the relative path would be the relative path to the PL/SQL module.

Why not develop a PL/SQL package that contains a procedure called js? Then, for all your PL/SQL-generated HTML, you can refer to your library of routines with the SRC (source) script tag option. The only downside to this method is every routine would contain all the functions, which might be overkill for your HTML documents.

To create the js procedure, make sure you established a listener MIME type for .js, which should be set to application/x-javascript. Next, create a package with a procedure name of js (for example, a package named jslib that contains a procedure called js). Your package specification and body might appear identical to the following example:

```
create or replace package jslib as
 procedure js;
end jslib;
/

create or replace package body jslib as
procedure js is begin
  htp.p('function lib1(var1){');
  htp.p('  alert("You passed " + var1 + " to me !");');
  htp.p('}');
  htp.p('function lib2(message){');
  htp.p('  if (confirm(message))');
  htp.p('    alert("You pressed ok.");');
  htp.p('  else');
  htp.p('    alert("you pressed cancel");');
  htp.p('}');
end js;
end jslib;
/
```

The following procedure illustrates the procedures to include referencing to your jslib.js library:

```
create or replace procedure javalibtest as
begin
        htp.htmlopen;
        htp.headopen;
        htp.title('Javascript Library Example');
        htp.headclose;
        htp.bodyOpen;
        htp.print('<script src="jslib.js"> </script>');
        htp.script('lib1("Hello World")');
        htp.script('lib2("This is really cool! ")');
        htp.big('Press reload or refresh to run the example again.');
        htp.bodyClose;
        htp.htmlclose;
end;
/
```

This JavaScript code could also be easily referenced from a JSP as in this example—note, you must specify the complete virtual path to the PL/SQL module and DAD:

```
<HTML>
<HEAD>
<TITLE>Javascript Library Example</TITLE>
</HEAD>
<BODY>
<script src="/pls/dadname/jslib.js"></script>');
<script language="JavaScript">
lib1("Hello World");
lib2("This is really cool! ");
</script>
<BIG>Press reload or refresh to run the example again.</BIG>
</BODY>
</HTML>
```

Referencing a Static JavaScript Library

Another possibility is to develop a set of JavaScript routines that are static .js files. Your HTML and dynamic code can refer to any libraries easily by referencing the specific .js file. The advantage to using this approach is it's faster to use static files than dynamically generated files.

Using PL/SQL Packaged Procedures to Generate JavaScript

This brings us to a rather confusing issue: when generating JavaScript from PL/SQL, which packaged procedure should be used? *i*AS offers a bewildering number of choices, from the specialized htp procedures, such as htp.headOpen and htp.script, to the more standardized and (functionally identical) htp.print, htp.prn, and htp.p procedures, which act merely as print statements to write their contents to the destination documents.

The current trend among our Web developers is to use PL/SQL Server Pages, which use htp.prn to generate the HTML and JavaScript code. The advantages to this approach are numerous and are discussed in Chapter 14.

Programming User-Defined Alert Processing

JavaScript is an interpretive language, so you might encounter run-time errors as a result of syntax errors, errors in the code, or as a result of datatypes created on-the-fly.

Syntax errors can be addressed by editing the source code. A statement that's syntactically correct can cause run-time errors, but it attempts to perform an impossible task. The most puzzling of errors are logic errors, occurring when the program doesn't perform as expected.

One of the less obvious features of JavaScript revolves around JavaScript being an interpretive language. This feature is identical to the interpretive BASIC language of old, meaning every line of code must be interpreted byte by byte as it's executed. This can be slow and noticeable pauses can occur during intense periods of processing. When this happens, therefore, raising programmer-defined alert windows can be helpful to keep users from thinking the computer has frozen.

The trick is to open a new window and use the new window's document.write() method to fill the window with a short message, do the processing, and then close the window. The JavaScript code to open, write to, and close the window is as follows:

```
var w = window.open();          //open new window. "w" is the name
var wd = window.document;       //shorthand for referencing object

wd.open();                      //open window.document
wd.write("<HTML>");             //HTML tag for new window's contents
wd.write("<BODY>");             //BODY tag to define document properties
wd.write("Working...");         //message to put in new window
wd.write("</BODY>");            //closing BODY tag
wd.write("</HTML>");            //closing HTML tag
wd.close();                     //close document
// Processing logic goes here
w.close();                      //close window when done
```

where *w* is the object assigned to the window opened by the window.open() method. Putting the return value from window.open into a JavaScript variable enables you to reference that window object later and *wd* is a variable set equal to window.document. Its only purpose is to avoid typing "window.document" a lot in the code beneath it and to improve readability. To write to the new window, you must open the new window's document object. The window document can then be written to using the document.write() method (referred to through the wd value). On completion, the document (not the window, yet) must also be closed. The actual processing occurs before the window is closed. Finally, the new window itself must be closed.

Displaying Properties on the Screen

One of the more difficult aspects of JavaScript programming is the relationship of one object to another. JavaScript is an object-based language, which means parts of the language are referred to as objects. Anything belonging to an object is called a property, even though properties can be objects in their own right and have properties of their own. Working through the object hierarchy in JavaScript can be difficult and confusing because the browsers of different vendors have differences in the built-in objects and properties. An alternative is to use a short utility to display object properties in the document or a simple alert window using a long character string of captured object properties. The short utility is defined as a function. This function can be called for any object specified.

Collecting object properties in JavaScript is possible because of JavaScript's support of associative arrays. An *array* is a collection of values that occur one after another in repeating groups. *Normal arrays* use a number or record identifier as an array index; for example, states[1], where *1* is the array index number for the states array. Associative arrays use a string as a unique identifier instead of a number. For an associative array, the reference could be similar to states['Illinois'] as a valid identifier. Object properties in JavaScript can be referenced using either normal or associative arrays. To display properties on the screen, a method of reading the object properties from the object is needed. JavaScript also provides this capability with the enumeration for loop, as the following syntax illustrates:

```
for (property in object) {
     // Do something with or to property
}
```

The preceding functionality is similar to the UNIX Bourne Shell's for loop. The properties are read from the object, put into the index variable ("property"), and then manipulated by the line of code following the for loop.

TIP
Remember, in JavaScript, only the first line after the for loop command is executed repeatedly. To execute multiple lines, enclose them within curly braces ({}). The recommendation is that you always use braces for all for, while, and if statements to prevent confusion, especially when you add statements into the statements listed.

Producing a list of supported properties for a specified object within JavaScript in an alert window is easy. In the following example, you collect the properties and put them into a long string variable. After every 20 items, the alert window is displayed in the browser, the list is reset to NULL, and the next set of items is displayed. This continues until all properties of the specified object have been displayed, as shown in the following illustration:

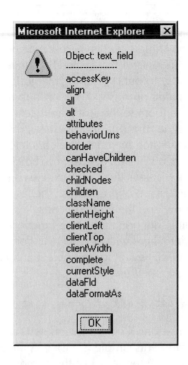

```
function show_properties(input_object){
    // "\n" is a newline; Simply puts entries on different lines
    var alert_text = "Object: " + input_object.name +
                     "\n" + "--------------------" + "\n";
    var counter = 0;
    // enumeration for loop
    for (i in input_object){
        // Build alert text string. Special handling for strings, show value
        alert_text = alert_text + i + '';
        // Increment property counter
        ++counter;
        // Modulus operator returns remainder of division,
        // if 0, every 20 items
        if (counter % 20 == 0){
            alert(alert_text);
            alert_text = "";
        }
    }
    // Print the last set
    alert(alert_text);
    input_object.blur();    // required when debugging Alert with onFocus
} //show_properties
```

Using the keyword makes passing the name of the object simple. The first declaration and assignment of alert_text is merely placing a short heading on top of the list in the first alert window, with a dashed line underneath it. The newlines ("\n") cause the alert window to put everything that follows the newline character on a separate line (for cosmetic purposes). The for loop reads the properties from the object and concatenates them to the string alert_text. After 20 items have been collected (or when the routine runs out of properties), the properties are displayed on the screen with each separated by a newline character. The modulus operator (%) returns the remainder of a division operation. The counter is divided by 20, so when the remainder is 0, it displays the alert box, clears the alert_text string, and prepares to process another group of properties. The last group of records is displayed in an alert window and the function ends.

By putting the preceding functionality into a function, you can call the show_ properties function from anywhere within an HTML document. A simple way to call the routine is to use an onFocus event for the object and call the show_properties function, as the following syntax illustrates:

```
<input type=text name=text_field onFocus="show_properties(this)">
```

This routine has its limitations. The alert window is a piece of prepackaged software, so keeping its arguments simple is easier. A method to display other attributes of the properties listed (besides just the name), such as datatype (string, object, number, and so forth) and value, would be more useful. This would be a bit difficult to arrange in an alert window as used in the preceding example. How would different values and columns be aligned for a readable display? A way does exist to do this. Instead of using an alert window to display the properties list, a pop-up window could be opened and, combining the techniques of this and the alert window discussion, an HTML display could be used to populate the new window dynamically.

The advantages of the pop-up window approach are many, and they overcome the disadvantages of having to use pop-up alert messages and Dynamic HTML through JavaScript. The power and flexibility of being able to use HTML to control the display is a substantial advantage.

The disadvantages to using the pop-up alert message approach should also be considered. Extra effort may be expended toward achieving the desired appearance of the output and, the more complex the approach, the more effort required.

The following example, illustrated in Figure 7-1, uses a pop-up HTML window to display properties. Instead of displaying generic properties, the example lists attributes of an HTML form and lists the fields defined for the specified HTML form.

```
function show_form_fields(oForm){
    var t;
    var w;
    var wd = window.document;
    // Open a window to display this information
    var w = window.open("","properties","scrollbars=yes,width=600,height=200");
    wd.write("<HTML>");
    wd.write("<HEAD>");
    wd.write("<TITLE>Show Form [" + oForm.name + "] Fields</TITLE>");
    wd.write("<BODY>");
    wd.write("<CENTER>");
    // Makes sure the form has a name before displaying it
    if (oForm.name.length >> 0) {
        t = "'" + oForm.name + "'";
    }
    // Display name of HTML form
    w.document.write("Fields in " + t + " form");
    wd.write("</CENTER>");
    wd.write("<HR>");
    // Table definition
    wd.write("<TABLE ALIGN=CENTER BORDER=1>");
    // Table headings
    wd.write("<TH>#</TH>");
    wd.write("<TH>Name</TH>");
    wd.write("<TH>type</TH>");
    wd.write("<TH>value</TH>");
    // Cycle through form fields
    for (i=0;i<oForm.length;i++){
        // Put new entry on new line
        wd.write("<TR><TD>" + i + "</TD>");
        // Name of field
        wd.write("<TD>" + oForm[i].name + "</TD>");
        // Type of field
        wd.write("<TD>" + oForm[i].type + "</TD>");
        // Value of field
        wd.write("<TD>" + oForm[i].value + "</TD>");
        wd.write("</TR>");
    }
    wd.write("</BODY>");
    wd.write("</HTML>");
    wd.close();
    // Return window object to caller
    return w;
} //show_form_fields
```

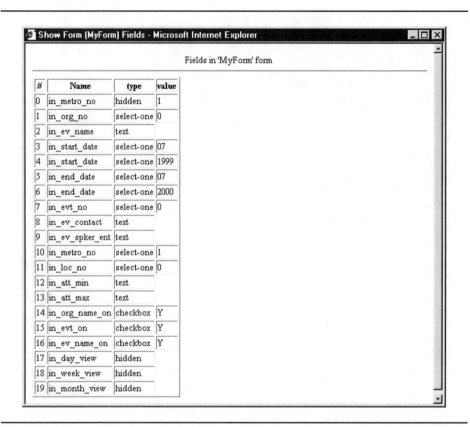

FIGURE 7-1. *Pop-up window with Field Properties*

A simple way to call the preceding routine is to use an onSubmit event for the form and call the show_form_fields function, as the following syntax illustrates:

```
<form nameansForm onSubmit"show_form_fields(this)">
```

In comparing this code to the code in the prior section, it's easy to see the code in the prior section used a for loop to traverse through the objects, taking the advantage that JavaScript represents HTML form objects as normal array objects, as well as associative array objects belonging to the specified form. JavaScript represents HTML form fields as regular (number index) array objects and associative array (named index) structures. This dual representation can be confusing. Representing the data in the easiest way for the manipulation to be performed is often less complicated. To avoid errors for dual-representation specification, walk through the form fields individually by numeric index. The length attribute of the form is used to control the loop and form.length is the number of elements in the form array. When multiple objects have the same name, JavaScript defines them as array elements, so two fields in a form called RecordStatus would *have* to be referred to as numbered array elements to tell them apart. In other words, to retrieve the value of a specific occurrence of RecordStatus in ValuesForm, the correct syntax to retrieve the first value is ValuesForm .RecordStatus[0].value. The show_properties routines are most useful for these situations.

On Internet Explorer 4.0.1, window.screen properties won't return values for the associative for loop, even though its properties can be referenced directly. Writing the properties to a pop-up window, rather than an alert window, can generally be more useful. Occasionally, certain kinds of object references might be problematic for a specific browser (cause errors during enumeration, for instance), so an easier alternative to a complex routine may be desired. Finally, certain object property values, when rendered on the screen, appear not as their actual values, but as HTML objects because of how HTML evaluates them when drawn on the page. The HTML objects can take up a lot of space in the document window.

Opening a New Window Passing Parameters

Times may occur when you want to pass parameters to a PL/SQL routine (or any CGI routine) either in the current window or in a new window. The following script can be used either to open a new page or replace the existing page:

```
<HTML>
<HEAD>
<TITLE>Passing a variable to a link</TITLE>
<SCRIPT LANUAGE="Javacript">
function CallNewWindow ()
  myWindow = window.open(
    'RoutineToCall?in_text_value=' +
    MyForm.in_text_variable.value,
    'myWin',
    'toolbar=yes,location=yes,width=500, height=300'
    );
}//CallNewWindow

function CallSameWindow()
  window.location =
    'RoutineToCall?in_text_value=' +
    MyForm.in_text_variable.value;
}
```

```
</SCRIPT>
</HEAD>
<BODY>
<A HREF="javascript:CallNewWindow()">CALL NEW WINDOW W/ TEXT VALUE</></A>
<A HREF="javascript:CallSameWindow()">CALL SAME WINDOW W/ TEXT VALUE</A>
<FORM NAME="MYFORM" ACTION="FORMCTION" METHOD="GET">
<INPUT TYPE"text" NAME="in_text_variable" VALUE="12/31/1999">
</FORM>
</BODY>
</HTML>
```

Assigning JavaScript Variables

JavaScript variables are created and handled similarly to other languages, and can be declared before they're used. For reasons of scope (which part of the application knows about a particular value), it's advisable to declare variables before using them.

JavaScript variables can have a local or a global scope. Global variables are referenced throughout the whole document. Local variables are known only in the current block of code—usually an object definition, event handler, function, or lines enclosed within curly braces ({}). Generally speaking, local variables are easier to use because global variables can be assigned anywhere and their origins can be hard to determine.

Operationally, no difference exists between local and global variables in JavaScript. The difference is where they're defined, how they're used, and where they retrieve their values. Global variables are defined outside functions and blocks, while local variables are defined inside.

In the following example, the variable myGlobal would be global, but myLocal, being defined within the current block of JavaScript code (the curly braces), would be local and recognized only within that block. A reference to myLocal outside the curly braces would produce an error. The myGlobal variable could be referenced anywhere in the document, as well as within another pair of script tags.

```
<SCRIPT>
var myGlobal;
if (typeof myGlobal == "undefined") {
    var myLocal;
}
```

Use of global variables can have unexpected consequences and should be minimized for two reasons: first, under the right conditions, global variables can interfere with one another to produce incorrect results. And, second, tracing global variables back to their source can be difficult. Consider the following example:

```
// First function
function Function1() {
  for (j=0;j<25;j++) {
    ;
  }
} // End of Function1
// Second function
function Function2() {
  for (j=0;j<10;j++) {
    function1();
  }
} // End of Function2
```

In this example, function2 calls function1, but *not* ten times as the for loop suggests. Instead, because variable j wasn't defined in either procedure, it will be defined on-the-fly in procedure 2 and the same instance of *j* will be used by procedure 1, returning 25 and immediately exiting the function 2 loop. Defining variable *j* in both functions would have kept the actual variable local and avoided the problem.

Using the Submit Button

One of the primary uses of HTML forms is to collect data from users and send it to a server to be processed. This process of sending data to a server is called the *submission.* The primary way of performing submit operations is through the use of a Submit button, from which HTML performs all submit processing for the user, as the following line of code illustrates:

```
<INPUT TYPE="SUBMIT" Value="Submit">
```

This places a Submit button on the screen that, when pressed, sends the fields in the HTML form to the server. Only *named* form fields are sent. The Submit button typically lacks the name attribute and, therefore, wouldn't be included as a value. If you supply the name attribute for the Submit button, it will send its value to the server. This can be useful if the identity of the button pressed to perform the submit needs to be known, but doesn't allow the form to be submitted for processing.

Using the built-in Submit button has disadvantages. The primary downside is pressing it is absolute, meaning once initiated, such a submission cannot be easily stopped or canceled. A more versatile approach is to define and use a submit procedure, performing the submission with an ordinary HTML button and using the form fields submit method, as the following syntax illustrates:

```
<INPUT TYPE="BUTTON" NAME="Submit" onClick"doSubmit(this.form)">
```

Consider the previous code, which defines an ordinary button invoking a JavaScript function, which, when pressed, enables presubmit processing before invoking the form's submit method. The following example illustrates this function:

```
function doSubmit(oForm){
    // Check to be sure that the district value is set to D.C.
    // If it is not, display a message and do not submit the form
    if (oForm.District.value != "D.C.") {
        alert('"' + oField.value + ' "' + " is not a valid district");
        oForm.District.focus();
        return;
    }
    // Continued pre-submit processing could occur here
    // Submit the form using the form's submit method.
    oForm.submit();
}
```

This function validates a form field and cancels the submission if the validation fails. The return statement ensures the oForm.submit() method is never invoked if the validation fails.

Validating Form Fields

One of the more useful features of JavaScript is the capability to validate form fields before sending data to a server to be processed. Validating form fields in the browser before they are sent eliminates the need for sending data to a server, validating it, and sending it back to a form for correction.

JavaScript provides several event handlers for form validation, including the onFocus() handler (invoked when a form field becomes the current field or gains focus), onBlur() (invoked when a form field stops being the current field or loses focus), and onChange() (invoked when the value of a form field changes and loses focus). The first two event handlers can be used to store and restore form field values programmatically. The onChange() event handler is used most often for validation purposes, invoked when a form field changes value (from the field itself, not when assigned programmatically). When an event handler is invoked (or triggered), the JavaScript code following the event handler—as defined in the field tag—is immediately executed, as the following line of code illustrates:

```
<INPUT TYPE"TEXT" NAME"District" onChange="alert('District changed');">
```

This code raises an alert window each time the district field is changed by entering a new value in the text field. Defining a function at the top of your HTML script and execute a JavaScript function is preferable, thus eliminating the problem of limited space in the form field tag. The following syntax makes use of the this object:

```
<INPUT TYPE"TEXT" NAME"District" onChange"onChangeDistrict(this);">
```

In this example, onChangeDistrict() is a JavaScript function defined elsewhere in the form and "this" is a reference to the current object, in this case the "District" form field.

The best way to perform field validation is to create special-purpose functions to validate each form field independently of the others. Your code is kept simple and the processing occurring in one function shouldn't affect the processing happening in other functions. Any kind of processing permissible through JavaScript can happen in these validation functions, including validation and navigation back to the offending field when data fails validation. The onChangeDistrict() function could appear identical to the following snippet of code:

```
function ChangeDistrict(oField){
  if (oField.value != "D.C."){
    alert('"' + oField.value + '"' + " is not a valid district");
    oField.focus();
    return;
  }
}
```

The field is called oField in the preceding validation function. oField is passed in as the "this" keyword in the preceding text tag, but is referenced as oField in the function. References to oField point to the field object passed to the function; in this case, the District form field. The value is compared to the valid value (D.C.) and, if not equal, the alert (which displays the incorrect value in the message) is raised. The form field's focus method is used to return focus to the field and the return command ensures the function will exit at that point.

The process of validating form fields is not *quite* this simple. Circumventing the preceding validation is ridiculous easy by exiting the field a second time. The field hasn't technically changed, so the onChange() event won't occur the second time. Prior to submission, another round of validation, this time in a submit procedure, is required to maintain data integrity. The same checks performed at the field level must again be applied to each field before submission to prevent clever users from slipping past field validation.

Working with PL/SQL Code and Various Browsers

A developer reported that he included the following JavaScript in his PL/SQL procedure, which worked fine in IE, but it doesn't show up in Netscape. Therefore, this must be a JavaScript difference, right?

```
htp.print('<input type"button" value"Return" onClick="history.back()"');
```

The problem had nothing to do with JavaScript. The problem is Netscape Navigator requires form objects to be placed between the HTML form tags or it ignores the form. Remember, HTML differences may also exist. By changing the script as follows, it works in both browsers:

```
htp.formOpen('package.procedure');
htp.print('<input type"button" value"Return" onClick="history.back()"');
htp.formClose;
```

TIP
This is further support for why I prefer Server Page technology (that is, JSP or PSP) over writing the code in programming language that generates HTML—HTML can be difficult to debug.

Making a Two-Dimensional Array in JavaScript

The way to make a two-dimensional (or more) array in JavaScript might not be obvious, but you can do it by creating a table of arrays. First, declare the initial list of values array, which will be your two-dimensional array. The following example uses states and cities. The following example demonstrates the JavaScript code to accomplish this task. You could also develop a generic procedure pulling the data from a table to load these arrays.

```
// Declare our initial array
list_of_value    = new Array();
// Now within each array element we create another array as our
// second dimension.
list_of_value ["CO"] = new Array("Evergreen","Denver","Aurora","Keystone");
list_of_value ["GA"] = new Array("Atlanta","Athens");
list_of_value ["IL"] = new Array("Naperville","Lombard","Princeton");
list_of_value ["MI"] = new Array("Detroit","Ishpenig","Flint");
list_of_value ["WI"] new Array("Milwaukee","Kenosha","Racine");
```

For the cities in Illinois ("IL"), loop through *y* for the variable list_of_value ["IL"][y].

Assigning JavaScript Variables

Did you ever wonder how to pass a JavaScript variable's value to a variable in a dynamic program in *iAS*? The following script prompts for the username and writes that name in another HTML page:

```
<HTML>
<HEAD>
<SCRIPT>
function dispname(){
  var name=prompt("Enter your name:","");
  return name;
}
</SCRIPT>
</HEAD>
<BODY>
<SCRIPT>
  var wd;
  //open window logic would go here
  wd.write(dispname());
  //close window logic would go here
</SCRIPT>
</BODY>
</HTML>
```

How do you pass this name to your dynamic code? After refining the preceding script, the following script passes the previously prompted for value on to a module:

```
<HTML>
<HEAD>
<SCRIPT>
function get_name(form) {
  var name=prompt("Enter your first and last name:","");
  document.welcome.u_name.value=name;
  return document.welcome.u_name.value;
}
</SCRIPT>
</HEAD>
<BODY>
<FORM NAME="welcome" ACTION="/jsp/myCode.jsp" onSubmit="get_name(this);">
<INPUT TYPE=HIDDEN u_name VALUE"">
<INPUT TYPE=SUBMIT value=Submit>
</FORM>
</BODY>
</HTML>
```

Invoking a PL/SQL Procedure from a Pick List

Normally, a form Submit button calls another dynamic program (or any other URL) when a user clicks the Submit button. But, what if you want to call the next dynamic program as a result of the user selecting an item from a pick list or when the user clicks a radio button, but without requiring the user to click the Submit button?

For example, suppose you want to call the getEmployee routine with the specific employee number when the user selects an employee from a drop-down list. The following HTML code is dynamically generated to pull employees from the emp table and illustrates the procedures described previously:

```
<HTML>
<HEAD>
<TITLE>Pick an Employee</TITLE>
<SCRIPT language"javascript">
function jump(page){
  if ( page != "" ) {
     self.location = page;
  }
}
</SCRIPT>
</HEAD>
<BODY>
<h1>Pick an Employee</h1>
<FORM METHOD="POST" name="vform" action="#">
<B>Employees</B>
<SELECT onchange"jump(this.options[ this.selectedndex ].value)">
<OPTION value"">
<OPTION value"/jsp/getEmployee.jsp?in_id1204">John Bull
<OPTION value"/jsp/getEmployee.jsp?in_id4023">Uncle Sam
</SELECT>
</FORM>
</BODY>
</HTML>
```

Once the employee name is selected from the list, the jump function is executed and control is passed to the stored procedure.

Changing Frames Simultaneously

What if you want to change the contents of two or more frames simultaneously on clicking a link? This task requires a snippet of JavaScript similar to the following example:

```
<html>
<head>
<title>Changing multiple frames<title>
function change_all_frames(in_emp) {
  top.frame2.location.href = "/jsp/getEmpInfo.jsp?in_emp="+in_emp;
  top.frame3.location.href = "/jsp/getHours.jsp?in_emp="+in_emp;
  top.frame4.location.href = "/jsp/getExpenses.jsp?in_emp="+in_emp;
}
</script>
</head>
<body>
...
</body>
</html>
```

Resolving the Access Denied Error

At some point, you may receive the infamous "Access Denied" message from a JavaScript routine. The "Access Denied" message occurs when you have multiple frames and you attempt to refer to a URL on another machine from one frame. This can occur when the host name is hard coded on one frame and isn't hard coded in the frame in which the relative path is used. In other words, one frame contains an absolute path (hard coded) and the other frame contains a relative path. If this error occurs, check the URLs specified.

For example, your home page contains a number of frames, which are sourced from a frameset tag displaying the initial home page. In one of the frames, you place a navigation bar, which has a source equal to the IP address of the machine (for example src=209.108), and the other frames come from the database. If I came to your site through the site's domain name, the other frames have a source pointing to the domain name. To JavaScript, this is considered two different machines, so it won't allow one page to reference another frame's source.

Passing Spaces as a Part of the URL

If you want to pass spaces in a URL, you need to convert the spaces to pluses (+) or to %20 (hex for char 32 or a space). The conversion process is performed automatically when you use the replace function in PL/SQL. In Java, you can use the Server.HTMLEncode to translate characters. If you're prompting for a parameter in an HTML form and the JavaScript is passing the parameter, you need to use your own function, identical to the following stringReplace function, to convert spaces to pluses. If the parameter is part of a form, however, and not the standard form submit functionality, the browser automatically converts spaces to pluses. If you use a specialized onSubmit event handler, you need to replace spaces in JavaScript.

The following stringReplace function converts any character in a string to another character:

```
function stringReplace(orig, find, replace) {
  var pos = 0;
  pos      = orig.indexOf(find);
  while (pos != -1) {
    orig = orig.substring(0,pos) + replace +
           orig.substring(pos+find.length,orig.length);
    pos  = orig.indexOf(find);
  }
  return orig;
}
```

To replace spaces with pluses, you could call stringReplace using the following code:

```
stringwithoutspaces = stringReplace(stringwithspaces," ","+")
```

Debugging onFocus with Alert Won't Work

An onFocus event will be called after an alert box is displayed. Don't use alert boxes for debugging when onFocus and onBlur events are present. The following is an example of a snippet of JavaScript code that could cause trouble if you add an alert (for example, for debugging):

```
/*-----------------------------------------------------------
- Function: jf_field_entry
- Purpose:  Save value of field when OnFocus event occurs
-
- WARNING!!!  WARNING!!!  WARNING!!!  WARNING!!!  WARNING!!!
- When any ALERT message box is displayed while focus is set to
- an object having this onFocus event defined, this function
- will execute!!!  If you put an ALERT anywhere, then you
- could easily get weird results.
- WARNING!!!  WARNING!!!  WARNING!!!  WARNING!!!  WARNING!!!
-----------------------------------------------------------
*/
function jf_field_entry(p1){
  if((p1.name == "in_task_id")      ||
     (p1.name == "in_subproj_id")) {

    // save values into global javascript variables for future processing
    jv_entry_value = p1.options[p1.selectedIndex].value;
    jv_entry_index = p1.selectedIndex;
```

```
      // this alert (whether in this function or another javascript
      // function) will re-save the erroneous value - wrong!
      alert("Initial value = " + jv_entry_index);
   }
   return;
}
```

Using typeof to Avoid "object expected" Errors

The most frequent cause of run-time errors in JavaScript is the act of trying to access an object that isn't there. The causes of this problem can be varied: either typographical errors in code or missing include files for otherwise perfectly good JavaScript code. These kinds of errors usually result in the dreaded "object expected" error. Tracking down the causes of such errors can be accomplished by listing the available objects one by one using the show object properties utility or by careful use of the alert() function as a debugging tool. Avoid run-time errors wherever possible, and a powerful way of doing so is to check the existence of potentially missing objects—usually functions stored in external include files—before trying to access them in code. An example of doing this follows:

```
function fnIsInteger(xInteger,bAlertSwitch){
   // ***validate dependencies
   if (typeof fnIsNumber == "undefined"){
     if (bAlertSwitch == true) {
       alert("fnIsInteger: fnIsNumber is undefined\nOperation cancelled");
     }
     return false;
   }
   // ***define variables
   var bIsInteger = true;
   var nInteger;
   var sIntegerType = typeof xInteger;
   // ***validate value
   switch (sIntegerType){
     case "string":
       if (!fnIsNumber(xInteger)){
         bIsInteger = false;
         break;
       }
       //no break to fall through to number validation
     case "number":
       nInteger = Math.round(xInteger-0);
       if (nInteger != xInteger) {
         bIsInteger = false;
```

```
    }
    break;
  default:
    bIsInteger = false;
}//sIntegertype
return bIsInteger;
}//fnIsInteger
```

In this example, two parameters are passed to the function fnIsInteger. *xInteger* is the value to be evaluated, while bAlertSwitch is merely a Boolean value used to decide whether to raise an alert window if a problem with the xInteger value is detected. Be warned, the whole purpose of the alert window is to alert the user that something is wrong and, by turning it off, the missing function situation won't be easily detected. If the routine is run in batch, however, perhaps through a constructor, with repeated calls, a continually occurring pop-up window would be extremely annoying. Use the switch to avoid that possibility when appropriate. The typeof operator is first used to validate the input data, checking to see if the fnIsNumber function—used to determine if the value is a valid number before checking to see if it's a valid integer—exists, in case the include file from which it's assumed to come isn't available. If the function doesn't exist, the evaluation isn't performed and a false result is returned. After this, the variables used by the function are defined. The sIntegerType variable is assigned the actual datatype of the xInteger input parameter and the switch command evaluates that value. If the value is a string, it's converted to a number (exiting with false if the number isn't valid). If the value is a number, the integer evaluation takes place and any other value returns false.

The eval Function

One of the more powerful (*and* dangerous!) features of JavaScript is the eval() function, which evaluates its arguments and executes them. The eval command takes a string representing a valid JavaScript command or object and performs the evaluation, dynamically executing code or interpreting a string representing an object. Be fore-warned—the object or code being interpreted by the eval() function *must* be syntactically correct or a JavaScript error will result. An example of the eval() function follows:

```
//dynamic focus function for any HTML form field
//oField  must be a valid HTML form field object
function fnFocus(oField){
  // Validate the input value - make sure it's a
  // valid HTML form field object
  if (typeof eval("document."+oField.form.name+"."+oField.name)
      == "undefined") {
    return;
  }
  eval("document."+oField.form.name+"."+oField.name+".focus()");
}
```

This example shows both uses of the eval() function: to interpret a string as an object and to interpret another string as a command to be executed. The function fnFocus takes one argument—oField. The if statement checks to see if oField is a valid HTML form field by building a string representing the object as a dynamic form field, interpreting it with the eval command, and using the typeof command to see if the on-the-fly object exists as an HTML form field. The net result should be the same as hard coding something like the following code, assuming the HTML form name is "frmForm," except the string is dynamically generated using properties of the oField object (specifically the form and name properties of the form field object) and should work with any property defined HTML form and field:

```
document.frmForm.oField.name
```

Note, this technique won't work unless both the HTML form and the HTML form field both have name attributes assigned in HTML. For this reason, giving names to HTML objects (specifically forms) is often advisable for later use in JavaScript processing even when no immediate need exists to do so. If the forms object doesn't exist (typeof against the object should yield the "undefined" value), a return is issued because the focus against a nonexistent form field won't work anyway and might yield a JavaScript error. If the validation is successful, the second eval() is executed, similarly building the object string but attaching the .focus method to the text to perform the focus.

Dynamic Function Arguments

Another powerful and lesser-known feature of JavaScript is the capability to use dynamic function arguments with the argument[] array. The argument[] array contains a list of every argument passed to the function whether or not the argument is listed positionally in the function's parameter list and is automatically populated for every function in JavaScript. This means processing parameter lists dynamically, without having to hard code them, is possible in JavaScript with careful coding. In short, parameter lists can be dynamic. Consider the following example:

```
function fnManyParms(){
  for(i=0;i<arguments.length;i++) {
    alert(arguments[i]);
  }
}
```

The declaration of fnManyParms has no arguments, but any parameter values sent can still be accessed through the arguments array as indicated in the numeric for loop. The for loop goes through the contents of the arguments array one by one, running the alert function for each one. If the function call looked like the following call statement, three alert messages would be displayed: first with the 3, and then with the 2, and then with the 1:

```
fnManyParms(3,2,1);
```

If called with four alerts would be displayed, with the values 7, 5, 3, and 1:

```
fnManyParms (7,5,3,1);
```

The function hasn't changed, but the function call is different and the output of the function will operate on the data supplied when the function is called.

When would you want to use this feature? The answer is in any situation where an operation might need to be performed on an indeterminate number of arguments. Consider, for instance, the Oracle greatest function, which takes a variable number of number arguments and returns the value that's greatest. Likewise, the *least* function takes a variable number of arguments and returns the smallest one. The arguments[] array could be used to perform this kind of functionality in JavaScript.

Using Arrays of Objects to Simulate Tables and Rows

Although JavaScript is an object-based rather than a true object-oriented language, objects can be created and used. When combined with JavaScript arrays, the table/ record layout in the Oracle database can be simulated in browser documents to avoid redrawing pages from the database.

Objects can be created in JavaScript with the new operator. The trick is first to create an object constructor (a function that creates and populates an object), and then assign it to a JavaScript array. The result is not unlike a PL/SQL (index-by) table of records or Java's arrays.

```
function Address(sName,sAddr1,sCity,sState,sZip){
    this.sName   = sName;
    this.sAddr1  = sAddr1;
    this.sCity   = sCity;
    this.sState  = sState;
    this.sZip    = sZip;
}
```

When called as a normal function using the new operator, this function creates and populates the Address object using the input values to the constructor.

Next, the array to put the objects into should be defined.

```
aAddress = new Array();
```

Finally, the array can be populated.

```
aAddress[aAddress.length] =
    new Address("TUSC","001 Main St.","Nowhere","CO","00000");
aAddress[aAddress.length] =
    new Address("TUSC","012 Main St.","Nowhere","GA","00000");
aAddress[aAddress.length] =
    new Address("TUSC","123 Main St.","Nowhere","IL","00000");
aAddress[aAddress.length] =
    new Address("TUSC","234 Main St.","Nowhere","MI","00000");
aAddress[aAddress.length] =
    new Address("TUSC","456 Main St.","Nowhere","WI","00000");
```

The length property of the array is used to assign the initial index value without having to hard code values. At the first assignment, the value will be 0, at the second, 1, and so forth. The Address constructor receives the input values and populates the array with records. To refer to the logical record value later, specify the array with subscript and the property—much like arrays of records are handled in PL/SQL. For instance, the following code displays the name "column" values of the object one by one:

```
for (j=0;j<aAddress.length;j++){
   alert(aAddress[j].sName);
}
```

Using arrays of objects is best done sparingly because arrays with more than a few hundred objects can quickly become unmanageable.

Subscribing to the JavaScript *OnFocus* Newsletter

The weekly newsletter of JavaScripts.com contains great tips and techniques, along with a library of scripts. You can subscribe to this weekly newsletter from the JavaScript site, located at **http://www.javascripts.com/**. If you're an advertiser, you can reach more than 90,000 developers with your message through sponsorship of JavaScripts.com's weekly newsletter. The advertising department can be contacted at **advertising@earthweb.com**.

Reviewing Visual JavaScript Tools

If you're more comfortable developing code using graphical development environments, tools exist that enable you to build JavaScript code graphically. Two tools worth mentioning are NetObjects Fusion and Netscape's Visual JavaScript.

Talking About NetObjects Fusion

Infuse supplied the first visual editor for JavaScript available on the market. In February 1998, NetObjects acquired Infuse. The product is called Fusion. Further information about the product can be found at **http://www.netobjects.com**. Fusion has won more than 50 industry awards. Fusion does more than simply write JavaScript, it can help you build Web sites. Fusion's Scripting Interface (FSI) is the underlying technology enabling the services components you build with Fusion. FSI exposes functionality inside Fusion as an API. From your browser, you can directly interact with Fusion using a scripting language, such as JavaScript. Third-party service providers can accept customer requests for information, conduct transactions, and then transmit the necessary data back to Fusion to complete the component installation or modification. Fusion can manage separate browser-based sessions, thus creating a unique operating environment perfectly tailored to our service provider's current business model.

Taking a Quick Look at Netscape's Visual JavaScript

Netscape's Visual JavaScript also enables you to develop JavaScript code visually. The product is written in Java. Because of the speed issues this was originally a disadvantage but, today, because of faster just in time compilers, Visual JavaScript's speed isn't as much of an issue. The advantage is the product is platform-independent. This product shows the page as it's being created.

Summary

JavaScript, a powerful scripting language that can put "life" into your site, should be a large portion of any Web project. A number of topics from data validation to pop-up windows were covered here. Great books on JavaScript are available. One of my favorite references is the *JavaScript Pocket Reference,* by David Flanagan. I carry this book with me everywhere I go.

CHAPTER
8

XML

ML stands for Extensible Markup Language. Like HTML, XML is a
subset of Standard Generalized Markup Language (SGML). XML,
which provides an unambiguous, text-based method of structuring
data, is a markup language, not a programming language. Both
humans and machines easily interpret XML. XML is also quickly
becoming the standard for electronic data interchange (EDI). Many people are
predicting XML is the next big thing. I disagree. I believe XML already is a big thing.

The data in an XML document is represented using markup tags. The *markup tags*
are defined by the user to describe the content of the data, but they don't address the
presentation of the content (as in HTML). XML identifies what the data *means* versus
how the data *looks,* as the following example illustrates:

```
<?xml version="1.0" encoding="UTF-8"?>
<BOOK>
        <TITLE>Oracle9i Web Development</TITLE>
        <AUTHOR>Bradley D. Brown</AUTHOR>
        <PUBLISHER>Osborne/McGraw-Hill</PUBLISHER>
</BOOK>
```

Why is XML important to your business? XML presents a simple, standard, and
nonproprietary means of sharing data. Manufacturers, wholesalers, retailers, consumers,
and financial institutions can share the same data. XML is a nonproprietary markup
language. The same data can be accessed through multiple devices, such as browsers,
pagers, cellular phones, and personal data assistants (PDAs). XML essentially
streamlines the process of communication between business and the consumer.

Per Oracle's marketing literature, their strategy for implementing XML is to "deliver
the best platform for developers to productively and cost effectively deploy reliable
and scalable Internet applications exploiting XML."

The Oracle9*i* RDBMS provides developers with core XML support implemented
in Java (and PL/SQL) and running on the Oracle9*i* built-in Java Virtual Machine (JVM).
Oracle9*i* RDBMS also provides many new XML features, such as a new XMLType
datatype, which can be used when defining table columns. XML support is included
in other products, such as 9*i*AS, JDeveloper, and Oracle Portal.

In this chapter, the following topics are discussed:

- Understanding the Basic Rules of XML

- Examining XML Document Syntax and Structure

- Examining XML Schema 1.0

- Examining Common XML Document APIs

- Examining XPath

- Using XML Stylesheets to Format and Display XML Documents

- XML Support in Oracle9*i*
- Oracle9*i* and Oracle Text
- Examining the Oracle XML Parser
- Examining the Oracle XML Class Generator
- Examining the Oracle XML SQL Utility
- Examining the Oracle XSQL Servlet
- XML and Advanced Queuing
- Message-Oriented Middleware (MOM)
- Dequeuing the XML Document from the Message Queue
- Parsing XML
- The Power of the XSQL Utility
- Using SOAP Regularly

Understanding the Basic Rules of XML

XML contains specific rules, which must be strictly followed when creating a document. A document must be well formed and meet the validity requirements set forth in the document type declaration (DTD).

Defining Document Type Declarations

The structure of an XML document consists of a strict hierarchy of elements with a single root. Each element consists of character data, child elements, and element attributes. The DTD formally defines the structure of an XML document based on these elements. The DTD is the blueprint for the document. Comparing DTDs to an Oracle database object, a DTD is similar to a table definition including its integrity rules.

In the following example, a DTD is created for an XML document describing a car. The root element is CAR, which has one attribute—manufacturer—which can contain the values Chrysler, Chevrolet, Ford, or Unknown. The elements MAKE, MODEL, and COLOR are children of CAR. COLOR contains two optional children: UPPER and LOWER. Let's review the car.dtd file:

```
<!ELEMENT CAR (MAKE,MODEL,COLOR)>
<! ATTLIST CAR manufacturer (Chrysler|Chevrolet|Ford|Unknown)
   #IMPLIED>
<!ELEMENT COLOR (UPPER*,LOWER*)>
<!ELEMENT MAKE  (#PCDATA)>
<!ELEMENT MODEL (#PCDATA)>
 <!ELEMENT UPPER (#PCDATA)>
 <!ELEMENT LOWER (#PCDATA)>
```

Defining "Well Formed"

The requirement that an XML document be well formed refers specifically to the document syntax. A document is said to be *well formed* if the document contains intelligible markup; in other words, it meets the rules of the DTD (that is, is well formed) or not (that is, it isn't well formed). Every tag must have a beginning and ending tag, when required, in a well-formed document. While most browsers will correctly process HTML tags that aren't closed or nested properly, XML documents have a strict tag structure, which is defined by the DTD. A tag starting within the scope of another tag must also end within the same scope.

The following is an example of a well-formed XML document, which conforms to the car DTD (that is, car.dtd) defined in the preceding section. Let's review the car.xml file:

```
<?xml version="1.0" encoding="UTF-8"?>
<CAR manufacturer="Chrysler">
    <MAKE>Jeep</MAKE>
    <MODEL>Cherokee</MODEL>
    <COLOR>
            <UPPER>Green</UPPER>
            <LOWER>Grey</LOWER>
    </COLOR>
 </CAR>
```

In this example, every start tag has an end tag, and each tag is nested correctly and conforms to the document hierarchy defined in the DTD; car.xml is well formed.

Defining Validity

An XML document is said to be *valid* if the document conforms to a DTD. Every element must be in its place within the hierarchy defined by the DTD for a document to be considered valid. The above car.xml file is both well formed and valid.

The following document is well formed because all the tags are matching, but it isn't valid because it violates the defined hierarchy of the DTD (the lower color is outside the color specification). To be valid, the <LOWER> tag must be enclosed within the <COLOR> tags, because <LOWER> is a child element of <COLOR>. Let's review the badcar.xml file:

```
<?xml version="1.0" encoding="UTF-8"?>
<CAR manufacturer="Chrysler">
    <MAKE>Jeep</MAKE>
    <MODEL>Cherokee</MODEL>
    <COLOR>
            <UPPER>Green</UPPER>
    </COLOR>
  <LOWER>Grey</LOWER>
</CAR>
```

Examining XML Document Syntax and Structure

XML, like most other languages, has strict rules for syntax. In this section, you look more closely at XML document syntax rules. For further definition of XML structure, consult any of the numerous books on XML.

Looking at Case

XML is case-sensitive. The tags <CAR>, <Car>, and <car> are treated as separate elements. If the DTD specifies an element in a particular case, all XML documents referencing the DTD must follow the case rules specified for that element. As with any case-sensitive language, defining corporate standards becomes increasingly important.

Examining Element Type Declarations in the DTD

Element type declarations define the name and content model for that element. The content model specifies what other element types are allowed inside an element of the declared type and which child elements can be present. An element can be defined as one or more of the following content models:

EMPTY

The element can be present as an empty element tag.

```
<!ELEMENT A EMPTY>
```

ANY

The element can contain any mixture of character data and elements.

```
<!ELEMENT B ANY>
```

Element-only Content Models

These elements contain only other elements as children. They cannot contain text. Special characters are used to represent element grouping.

Fixed Order Is Indicated by a Comma

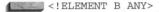

```
<!ELEMENT A (B,C)>
```

indicates element A consists of subelement B, followed by sub element C.

CHOICE Is Indicated by a Vertical Bar

`<!ELEMENT A (B|C)>`

indicates element A consists of either subelement B or subelement C.

A Repeat Rule Is Indicated by the Characters *, ?, +, or by No Character

`<!ELEMENT A (B,C)*>`

indicates element A consists of "zero or more" instances of B, followed by C.

`<!ELEMENT A (B,C)?>`

indicates element A consists of "zero or one" instances of B, followed by C.

`<!ELEMENT A (B,C)+>`

indicated element A consists of "one or more" instances of B, followed by C.

`<!ELEMENT A (B,C)>`

indicates element A consists of "one and only one" instance of B, followed by C.

Round Brackets Group Expressions for Treatment as a Unit   (B,C) indicates element B is grouped with element C.

Mixed Content Models

Mixed content model elements allow the mixture of both elements and text as content. Two forms of the mixed content model exist.

`<!ELEMENT A (#PCDATA)>`

indicates element A may only contain character data consisting of zero or more characters.

`<!ELEMENT A (#PCDATA|B|C)>`

indicates element A may contain character data, or element B, or element C.

#PCDATA stands for *parsed character data,* which means the text following the element tag is parsed for markup tag.

#CDATA can also be used. #CDATA indicates unparsed character data.

Other Rules

Only one element type declaration is allowed per element type. XML doesn't support overloading of elements.

Examining Attribute-List Declarations in the DTD

An element can have zero or more attributes. The set of attributes associated with a given element is defined by an attribute-list declaration. An attribute list declaration has the following basic form:

```
<!ATTLIST element-name attribute-definitions>
```

Element-Name

The *element-name* refers to the element type for the attribute list being defined. The *attribute-definitions* is a sequence of attribute definitions defining name, type, and default value for each attribute associated with the element type.

Attribute-Definitions

The general form of attribute definitions is attribute-name type default-declaration. The *attribute-name* is the name of the attribute. The *type* is an expression or keyword that defines the type of the attribute. The *default-declaration* defines the default value. The default-declaration can take on one of the following four values:

- **#IMPLIED**   The attribute can be specified optionally in elements of the declared type. There isn't a default value.

- **#REQUIRED**   The attribute must be specified in all elements of the declared type. There isn't a default value.

- **"attr-value"**   The attribute can be specified optionally in elements of the declared type. A default value is given by the value inside the quotes.

- **#FIXED "attr-value"**   The attribute value can't be assigned a different value in an element instance. Every element of #FIXED type has a fixed value given within quotes.

Every attribute has a type. The following examples illustrate the various possible types:

- **String-Type**   String type attributes are indicated by the keyword CDATA.

```
<!ATTLIST X  x CDATA #IMPLIED>
```

■ **Enumerated-List Type**   *Enumerated-list type attributes* are lists of predefined values. An attribute value can take only one of the listed values.

```
<!ATTLIST X  x (male|female|unknown) #IMPLIED>
```

■ **ID Type**   The *ID type attributes* define an attribute as element identifier. You can express the ID type in two ways:

```
<!ATTLIST X id ID #IMPLIED>
<!ATTLIST X id ID #REQUIRED>
```

The only default value declarations allowed are #IMPLIED and #REQUIRED.

■ **IDREF Type**   *IDREF type attributes* reference elements labeled by ID attributes.

```
<!ATTLIST X ref IDREF #IMPLIED>
```

■ **ENTITY Type**   *Entity type attributes* take a single unparsed entity reference. They are used to point to external data.

```
<!ENTITY my-car SYSTEM "images/car.jpg" NDATA JPG>
<!ATTLIST CAR-PIC car ENTITY #FIXED "my-car">
```

The attribute car refers the entity my-car.

■ **ENTITIES Type**   *Entities type attributes* take multiple unparsed entity references.

```
<!ATTLIST CAR-PIC car ENTITIES #IMPLIED>
```

■ **NMTOKEN Type**   *NMTOKEN type attributes* can take only tokens.

```
<!ATTLIST X token NMTOKEN "token">
```

■ **NMTOKENS Type**   *NMTOKENS type attributes* may take multiple tokens as values.

```
<!ATTLIST X tokens NMTOKENS "token1 token2 token3">
```

For further information regarding the syntax and structure introduced in the preceding section, refer to the XML specification found at **http://www.w3.org**.

Creating the Suspect DTD

Let's create and review an actual DTD. This DTD originated from an early Oracle XML example. This example centers on a set of suspects—presumably crime suspects. What kind of information would we need about a suspect? How about basic demographic information, such as descriptions, addresses, and phone numbers? Take the time to read through this DTD and see if you can interpret it. The complete interpretation follows the DTD. The following DTD addresses the items for our suspect data: Let's review the suspect.dtd file:

```
<!ELEMENT suspect (name*,demographics*,address*,comms*)+>
<!ATTLIST suspect id CDATA #IMPLIED>
<!ELEMENT name (first, middle*, last)+>
<!ELEMENT demographics (age*,height*,weight*)>
<!ATTLIST demographics gender (male|female|unknown) #IMPLIED>
<!ATTLIST demographics race (black|white|hispanic|asian|unknown) #REQUIRED>
<!ATTLIST demographics hair (black|blond|brown|white|unknown) #IMPLIED>
<!ATTLIST demographics eyes (blue|brown|green|hazel|gray) #IMPLIED>
<!ELEMENT address (street*,city*,state*,zip*)+>
<!ATTLIST address type (home|work|other) #IMPLIED>
<!ELEMENT comms (phone*)+>
<!ELEMENT phone (areacode*,prefix*,suffix*)+>
<!ATTLIST phone type (cellphone|pager|residential|work) #IMPLIED>
<!ELEMENT first     (#PCDATA)>
<!ELEMENT middle    (#PCDATA)>
<!ELEMENT last      (#PCDATA)>
<!ELEMENT age       (#PCDATA)>
<!ELEMENT height    (#PCDATA)>
<!ELEMENT weight    (#PCDATA)>
<!ELEMENT street    (#PCDATA)>
<!ELEMENT city      (#PCDATA)>
<!ELEMENT state     (#PCDATA)>
<!ELEMENT zip       (#PCDATA)>
<!ELEMENT areacode  (#PCDATA)>
<!ELEMENT prefix    (#PCDATA)>
<!ELEMENT suffix    (#PCDATA)>
```

An XML document based on the preceding DTD must comply with the following rules:

- It must contain one or more suspect elements.

- Each suspect element can have an optional ID attribute.

- Each suspect element consists of one or more sets of zero or more name elements, zero or more demographic elements, zero or more address elements, and zero or more comms (i.e., phone numbers) elements.

- Each name element consists of one or more sets of first elements, zero or more middle elements, and last elements.

- Each demographic element can consist of zero or more age elements, zero or more height elements, and zero or more weight elements.

- Each demographic element can have an optional gender attribute, which must be male, female, or unknown.

- Each demographic element must have a race attribute, which must be black, white, Hispanic, Asian, or unknown.

- Each demographic element can have an optional hair attribute, which must be black, blond, brown, white, or unknown.

- Each demographic element can have an optional eyes attribute, which must be blue, brown, green, hazel, or unknown.

- Each address element consists of one or more sets of zero or more street elements, zero or more city elements, zero or more state elements, and zero or more ZIP elements.

- Each address element has an optional type attribute, which must be home, work, or other.

- Each comms element consists of one or more sets of zero or more phone elements.

- Each phone element consists of one or more sets of zero or more area code elements, zero or more prefix elements, and zero or more suffix elements.

- Each phone element can have an optional type attribute, which must be either cellular phone, pager, residential, or work.

- Elements first, middle, last, age, height, weight, street, city, state, ZIP, area code, prefix, and suffix will be composed of character data.

So, how did you do at interpreting the DTD on your own? The more DTDs you see, the better you'll get at interpreting and writing them on your own. As you see in this chapter, Oracle's utilities make interpreting DTDs easy for you.

Creating the Suspect Document

The following XML document is based on and complies with the DTD defined in the preceding section; in other words, it's well formed and valid. Let's review the suspect.xml file:

```
<?xml version="1.0" encoding="UTF-8"?>
<!DOCTYPE suspect SYSTEM "http://LocOfDTD.com/suspect.dtd">
<suspect id="s1">
    <name>
        <first>joe</first>
        <last>jackson</last>
    </name>
```

```
<demographics gender="male" race="white" hair="blond" eyes="blue">
     <age>32</age>
     <height>6ft</height>
     <weight>175</weight>
</demographics>
<address type="home">
     <street>821 elm</street>
</address>
<comms>
   <phone type="residential">
     <areacode>704</areacode>
     <prefix>333</prefix>
     <suffix>1234</suffix>
   </phone>
 </comms>
</suspect>
```

Examining XML Schema 1.0

Starting with release 9*i*, Oracle supports the W3C XML Schema 1.0 recommendation. XML Schema Definitions (XSD) give developers the capability to describe and constrain the content of an XML document. With an XML schema, a developer can attach a data type to a particular XML tag or group of tags. Having the capability to constrain and assign datatypes to XML tags is powerful, especially when mapping data from an XML document directly to database tables or Java classes. XML schemas can be used in place of DTDs when defining XML documents. The following sections cover key features of XML Schema. This section is designed to familiarize you with XML Schema and to give you enough information to create a basic schema. For a complete reference of XML Schema, please refer to the XML Schema 1.0 specification found at **http://www.w3c.org**.

Looking at Namespaces

Namespaces were developed as way to segregate elements in an XML document that might have the same name, but appear at different levels. Namespaces give us a way to group elements within a specific context. Examine the following XML document. Let's review the carns.xml file:

```
<?xml version="1.0" encoding="UTF-8"?>
<car>
   <color>blue</color>
   <interior>
     <upholstery>leather</upholstery>
     <color>tan</color>
   </interior>
</car>
```

Notice the previous document contains two <color> tags. A situation such as this would likely cause some confusion for an XML parser. By defining separate namespaces, you can distinguish between the two element names. For example, let's review the carns.xsd file:

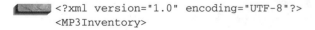

```
<veh:car
    xmlns:veh="http://mycarnamespace.com/cars/"
    xmlns:vehinterior="http://myvehicleinteriors.com/interiors/">
  <veh:color>blue</veh:color>
  <vehinterior:interior>
    <vehinterior:upholstery>leather</vehinterior:upholstery>
    <vehinterior:color>tan</vehinterior:color>
  </vehinterior:interior>
</veh:car>
```

This example references two namespaces associated with the prefixes *veh* and *vehinterior.* Now the two color tags can be differentiated with no problem. A standard prefix, *xsd,* is used to identify all the XML Schema-specific tags in a schema document.

Target Namespaces

Target namespaces allow schema creators to distinguish between declarations and definitions from other schemas. The *targetNamespace* attribute specifies a namespace containing predefined datatypes that can be used in the schema document being defined. The following document segment demonstrates how to define a target namespace for a schema document:

```
<xsd:schema xmlns:xsd="http://www.w3.org/2001/XMLSchema"
                targetNamespace="http://my.namespaces.com/mynamespace"
                xmlns="http://my.namespaces.com/mynamespace">
```

In this segment, we defined a target namespace of "http://my.namespaces.com/mynamespace". Notice the namespace declaration below target namespace declaration has no prefix defined. This indicates "http://my.namespaces.com/mynamespace" is the *default namespace.* Elements of the default namespace don't require a prefix.

Schema for a Simple XML Document

Before delving into XML Schema's key features, let's look at a schema for the following XML document. Let's review the mp3.xml file:

```
<?xml version="1.0" encoding="UTF-8"?>
<MP3Inventory>
```

```
        <artist id="1">
            <genre>Rock</genre>
            <name>Aerosmith</name>
            <song>
                <title>Pink</title>
                <album>Nine Lives</album>
                <label>Columbia</label>
                <fileName>Pink.mp3</fileName>
                <playTime>4:23</playTime>
                <dateAquired>05/05/2001</dateAquired>
            </song>
            <song>
                <title>Walk This Way</title>
                <album>Toys In The Attic</album>
                <label>Columbia</label>
                <fileName>WalkThisWay.mp3</fileName>
                <playTime>5:23</playTime>
                <dateAquired>05/05/2000</dateAquired>
            </song>
        </artist>
        <artist id="2">
            <genre>Alternative</genre>
            <name>Foo Fighters</name>
            <song>
                <title>Big Me</title>
                <album>Foo Fighters</album>
                <label>Roswell</label>
                <fileName>BigMe.mp3</fileName>
                <playTime>3:23</playTime>
                <dateAquired>05/05/2001</dateAquired>
            </song>
            <song>
                <title>Learn To Fly</title>
                <album>Their Is Nothing Left To Lose</album>
                <label>Roswell</label>
                <fileName>LearnToFly.mp3</fileName>
                <playTime>4:13</playTime>
                <dateAquired>03/05/2000</dateAquired>
            </song>
        </artist>
</MP3Inventory>
```

A schema for the previously listed XML document could take the following form. Let's review the mp3.xsd file:

```
<xsd:schema
     xmlns:xsd="http://www.w3.org/2001/XMLSchema">
<!-- The type definitions below can be referenced by other
```

```
      type using the "ref" attribute. -->
<!-- define simple type elements -->
<xsd:element name="genre"       type="xsd:string"/>
<xsd:element name="name"        type="xsd:string"/>
<xsd:element name="title"       type="xsd:string"/>
<xsd:element name="album"       type="xsd:string"/>
<xsd:element name="label"       type="xsd:string"/>
<xsd:element name="fileName"    type="xsd:string"/>
<xsd:element name="playTime"    type="xsd:time"/>
<xsd:element name="dateAquired" type="xsd:date"/>
<!-- define attributes -->
<xsd:attribute name="id" type="xsd:integer"/>
<!-- define complex type elements -->
<xsd:element name="song">
 <xsd:complexType>
  <xsd:sequence>
   <xsd:element ref="title"/>
   <xsd:element ref="album"/>
   <xsd:element ref="label"/>
   <xsd:element ref="fileName"/>
   <xsd:element ref="playtime"/>
   <xsd:element ref="dateAquired"/>
  </xsd:sequence>
 </xsd:complexType>
</xsd:element>
<xsd:element name="artist">
 <xsd:complexType>
  <xsd:sequence>
   <xsd:element ref="genre"/>
   <xsd:element ref="name"/>
   <xsd:element ref="song"
       minOccurs="0" maxOccurs="unbounded"/>
  </xsd:sequence>
  <xsd:attribute ref="id"/>
 </xsd:complexType>
</xsd:element>
<xsd:element name="MP3Inventory">
 <xsd:complexType>
  <xsd:element ref="artist"
      minOccurs="0" maxOccurs="unbounded"/>
 </xsd:complexType>
</xsd:element>
</xsd:schema>
```

This schema introduces several key features of XML Schema, which this section will address, including the following:

■ The presence of primitive datatypes in XML Schema

- The capability to define both simple and complex datatypes

- The capability for one data type to reference another datatype

- The capability to combine datatypes to form a new datatype (user-defined types)

- The capability to define a bound on sets of elements

XML Schema enables you to define integrity constraints between elements in an XML document. It doesn't take much imagination to see the power of using a schema when developing an XML-based database application. I refer to the preceding XML document and schema throughout this section.

TIP
An XML schema is much like referential integrity in the database.

Built-in Primitive Data Types

Like other languages, XML Schema contains a set of primitive data types on which other more complex data types can be derived. The following section examines each of XML Schema's primitive datatypes. The following definitions are taken directly from the W3C specification for XML Schema 1.0.

string
The *string* datatype represents strings of character data in XML.

boolean
The *boolean* datatype can be defined lexically by the set of literals {true,false,0,1} and canonically by the set {true,false}.

decimal
The *decimal* datatype is defined as the set of the values $i \times 10^{-n}$, where *i* and *n* are integers such that $n \geq 0$.

float
The *float* datatype corresponds to the IEEE single-precision, 32-bit floating point type [IEEE 754-1985]. The basic value of float consists of the values $m \times 2^e$, where *m* is an integer whose absolute value is less than 2^{24}, and *e* is an integer between -149 and 104, inclusive.

double

The *double* datatype corresponds to IEEE double-precision, 64-bit floating point type [IEEE 754-1985]. The basic value of double consists of the values $m \times 2^\wedge e$, where m is an integer whose absolute value is less than $2^\wedge 53$, and e is an integer between 1075 and 970, inclusive.

duration

The *duration* datatype represents a length of time. The value of duration is a six-dimensional space where the coordinates designate the Gregorian year, month, day, hour, minute, and second components defined in § 5.5.3.2 of [ISO 8601], respectively. These components are ordered in their significance by their order of appearance, that is, as year, month, day, hour, minute, and second.

dateTime

The *dateTime* datatype represents a specific instant of time.

time

The *time* datatype represents an instant of time that recurs every day. The value of time is the space of time of day values, as defined in § 5.3 of [ISO 8601]. Specifically, it's a set of zero-duration daily time instances.

date

The *date* datatype represents an instant of time that recurs every day. The value of time is the space of time of day values, as defined in § 5.3 of [ISO 8601]. Specifically, it's a set of zero-duration daily time instances.

gYearMonth

The *gYearMonth* datatype represents a specific Gregorian month in a specific Gregorian year. The value of gYearMonth is the set of Gregorian calendar months, as defined in § 5.2.1 of [ISO 8601]. Specifically, it's a set of one-month long, nonperiodic instances, for example, 1999-10 to represent the whole month of 1999-10, independent of how many days this month has.

gYear

The *gYear* datatype represents a Gregorian calendar year. The value of gYear is the set of Gregorian calendar years as defined in § 5.2.1 of [ISO 8601]. Specifically, it's a set of one-year long, nonperiodic instances, for example, lexical 1999 to represent the whole year 1999, independent of how many months and days this year has.

gMonthDay

The *gMonthDay* datatype is a Gregorian date that recurs, specifically a day of the year, such as the third of May. Arbitrary recurring dates aren't supported by this datatype. The value of gMonthDay is the set of calendar dates, as defined in § 3 of [ISO 8601]. Specifically, it's a set of one-day long, annually periodic instances.

gDay

The *gDay* datatype is a Gregorian day that recurs, specifically a day of the month, such as the 5th of the month. Arbitrary recurring days aren't supported by this datatype. The value of gDay is the space of a set of calendar dates, as defined in § 3 of [ISO 8601]. Specifically, it's a set of one-day long, monthly periodic instances.

gMonth

The *gMonth* datatype is a Gregorian month that recurs every year. The value of gMonth is the space of a set of calendar months, as defined in § 3 of [ISO 8601]. Specifically, it's a set of one-month long, yearly periodic instances.

hexBinary

The *hexBinary* datatype represents arbitrary hex-encoded binary data. The value of hexBinary is the set of finite-length sequences of binary octets.

base64Binary

The *base64Binary* datatype represents Base64-encoded arbitrary binary data. The value of base64Binary is the set of finite-length sequences of binary octets. For base64Binary data, the entire binary stream is encoded using the Base64 Content-Transfer-Encoding.

anyURI

The *anyURI* datatype represents a Uniform Resource Identifier Reference (URI). An anyURI value can be absolute or relative and may have an optional fragment identifier (that is, it may be a URI Reference).

QName

The *QName* datatype represents XML qualified names. The value of QName is the set of tuples {namespace name, local part}, where *namespace name* is an *anyURI* and *local part* is an *NCName*.

NOTATION

The *NOTATION* datatype represents the NOTATION attribute type from [XML 1.0 (Second Edition)]. The value space of NOTATION is the set QNames. The lexical space of NOTATION is the set of all names of notations declared in the current schema.

complexTypes and simpleTypes

XML Schema lets you define elements of two basic datatypes: simpleType and complexType. An element that has no child or attribute nodes is considered a *simpleType.* An element that has attribute nodes or child nodes is considered a *complexType.* Another way to look at the relationship between complexTypes and simpleTypes is to say a complexType is composed of one or more simpleTypes. A simpleType is based on a primitive datatype.

The following example, taken from the schema at the beginning of this section, illustrates how to construct simpleTypes:

```
<xsd:element name="genre"      type="xsd:string"/>
<xsd:element name="name"       type="xsd:string"/>
<xsd:element name="title"      type="xsd:string"/>
<xsd:element name="album"      type="xsd:string"/>
<xsd:element name="label"      type="xsd:string"/>
<xsd:element name="fileName"   type="xsd:string"/>
<xsd:element name="playTime"   type="xsd:time"/>
<xsd:element name="dateAquired" type="xsd:date"/>
```

Notice that each of the simpleTypes is based on a primitive datatype. The next example illustrates how to construct a complexType based on the simpleTypes defined in the preceding example:

```
<xsd:element name="song">
 <xsd:complexType>
  <xsd:sequence>
   <xsd:element ref="title"/>
   <xsd:element ref="album"/>
   <xsd:element ref="label"/>
   <xsd:element ref="fileName"/>
   <xsd:element ref="playtime"/>
   <xsd:element ref="dateAquired"/>
  </xsd:sequence>
 </xsd:complexType>
</xsd:element>
```

ref Attribute

The *ref* attribute in the element tag is used to reference elements of other types when constructing a type definition. If the ref attribute isn't used, the element must be defined in place. For example, the following complexType,

```
<xsd:element name="song">
 <xsd:complexType>
  <xsd:sequence>
  <xsd:element ref="title"/>
   <xsd:element ref="album"/>
   <xsd:element ref="label"/>
   <xsd:element ref="fileName"/>
   <xsd:element ref="playtime"/>
   <xsd:element ref="dateAquired"/>
  </xsd:sequence>
 </xsd:complexType>
</xsd:element>
```

can also be written as

```
<xsd:element name="song">
 <xsd:complexType>
  <xsd:sequence>
   <xsd:element name="title"      type="xsd:string"/>
   <xsd:element name="album"      type="xsd:string"/>
   <xsd:element name="label"      type="xsd:string"/>
   <xsd:element name="fileName"   type="xsd:string"/>
   <xsd:element name="playTime"   type="xsd:time"/>
   <xsd:element name="dateAquired" type="xsd:date"/>
  </xsd:sequence>
 </xsd:complexType>
</xsd:element>
```

Defining an entire XML document with every simpleType and complexType defined in the schema with references can quickly become unreadable and unmanageable. The ref attribute enables you to create complicated document structures that are organized and manageable.

sequence Element

The *sequence* element defines a repeating collection of elements within a document. The following code illustrates the use of the sequence tag:

```
<xsd:element name="song">
 <xsd:complexType>
  <xsd:sequence>
   <xsd:element name="title"      type="xsd:string"/>
   <xsd:element name="album"      type="xsd:string"/>
   <xsd:element name="label"      type="xsd:string"/>
   <xsd:element name="fileName"   type="xsd:string"/>
   <xsd:element name="playTime"   type="xsd:time"/>
   <xsd:element name="dateAquired" type="xsd:date"/>
```

```
    </xsd:sequence>
  </xsd:complexType>
</xsd:element>
```

The sequence element in this example defines a repeating collection of the elements title, album, label, fileName, playTime, and dateAquired. The equivalent definition in a DTD would have the following syntax:

```
<!ELEMENT song (title,album,label,fileName,playTime,dateAquired)*>
```

Examining Common XML Document APIs

Two popular XML document APIs currently exist. One is the Document Object Model (DOM) and the other is the Simple API for XML (SAX). The *DOM* is a tree-based API and *SAX* is event based. Tree-based means that DOM will read through the branches of the tree structure one branch at a time, processing the data as such. Later sections that discuss the Oracle XML Developer's Kit (XDK) provide sample Java classes that use both DOM and SAX parsers to traverse an XML document.

Document Object Model

The DOM is a programming API for both XML and HTML. The DOM defines the logical structure of a document, as well as the way a document is accessed and manipulated. Programmers can create documents, manipulate their structure, and add or delete elements and constructs with the DOM. DOM documents have a structure that closely represents a tree, as the following animal.xml example illustrates:

```
<?xml version="1.0" encoding="UTF-8"?>
<ANIMAL>
     <MAMMAL>
            <FOURLEGS>DOG</FOURLEGS>
            <TWOLEGS>MAN</TWOLEGS>
     </MAMMAL>
     <REPTILE>
            <AMPHIBIOUS>CROCODILE</AMPHIBIOUS>
            <DESERT>MONITOR LIZARD</DESERT>
     </REPTILE>
</ANIMAL>
```

The DOM in Figure 8-1 illustrates this example.

Each of the boxes in Figure 8-1 represents a tag or node. The rounded boxes represent the *node value,* or data between the tags. The XML document is broken

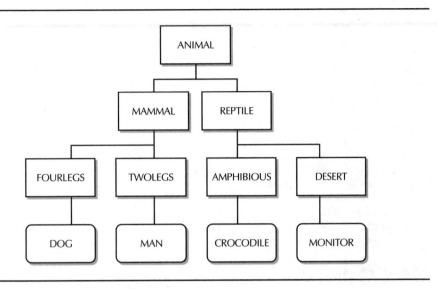

FIGURE 8-1. *Animal DOM*

down based on the hierarchical or tree structure. The items or elements in a DOM tree are referred to as *nodes* and the document's hierarchical structure is referred to as the *structure model.* The World Wide Web Consortium (W3C), which defined the DOM API specification, has the complete API specification available at **http://www.w3.org**. Oracle9*i* RDBMS supports the DOM Level 2 recommendation.

Simple API for XML

The SAX API is event based as opposed to tree based. *Event based* means the SAX API reports parsing events, such as start and end tags, directly to the parsing application through callbacks and doesn't build an internal tree. The application implements event handlers, identical to the way a GUI application handles events. The following example illustrates how an event-based API would parse the previous animal.xml document.

The event-based handler breaks the preceding XML into a series of linear events, as the following example illustrates:

```
start document
start element ANIMAL
start element MAMMAL
```

```
start element FOURLEGS
characters DOG
end element FOURLEGS
start element TWOLEGS
characters MAN
end element TWOLEGS
end element MAMMAL
start element REPTILE
start element AMPHIBIOUS
characters CROCODILE
end element  AMPHIBIOUS
start element DESERT
characters MONITOR LIZARD
end element DESERT
end element REPTILE
end element ANIMAL
end document
```

SAX Callbacks

The SAX Parser logs events through a series of callbacks. Each *callback* represents a specific event in the parsing of an XML document. In SAX callbacks are implemented programmatically through a content handler. In SAX 2.0, the class *DefaultHandler* is the default content handler. The content handler provides an implementation of each of the events or callbacks. The following table details each of methods supported by the DefaultHandler class:

Callback Method	Event
characters(char[] ch, int start, int length)	Receive notification of character data inside an element.
endDocument()	Receive notification of the end of the document.
endElement(java.lang.String uri, java.lang.String localName, java.lang.String qName)	Receive notification of the end of an element.
endPrefixMapping(java.lang.String prefix)	Receive notification of the end of a Namespace mapping.
error(SAXParseException e)	Receive notification of a recoverable parser error.
fatalError(SAXParseException e)	Report a fatal XML parsing error.
ignorableWhitespace(char[] ch, int start, int length)	Receive notification of ignorable white space in element content.

Callback Method	Event
notationDecl(java.lang.String name, java.lang.String publicId, java.lang.String systemId)	Receive notification of a notation declaration.
processingInstruction(java.lang.String target, java.lang.String data)	Receive notification of a processing instruction.
resolveEntity(java.lang.String publicId, java.lang.String systemId)	Resolve an external entity.
setDocumentLocator(Locator locator)	Receive a Locator object for document events.
skippedEntity(java.lang.String name)	Receive notification of a skipped entity.
startDocument()	Receive notification of the beginning of the document.
startElement(java.lang.String uri, java.lang.String localName, java.lang.String qName, Attributes attributes)	Receive notification of the start of an element.
startPrefixMapping(java.lang.String prefix, java.lang.String uri)	Receive notification of the start of a Namespace mapping.
unparsedEntityDecl(java.lang.String name, java.lang.String publicId, java.lang.String systemId, java.lang.String notationName)	Receive notification of an unparsed entity declaration.
warning(SAXParseException e)	Receive notification of a parser warning.

The SAX approach to XML parsing is more straightforward than the DOM, but it isn't as flexible or visual. The primary advantage of SAX over DOM is it takes less memory to parse very large XML documents. The DOM requires a tree-structure to be created in memory for a very large XML document. Depending on the size and number of concurrent documents being parsed, this could prove a costly effort. Further information concerning SAX, including the JAVA implementation of the API, is available in the Oracle XDK documentation and is freely available on the Internet at **http://www.megginson.com/SAX/index.html**. Oracle9*i* currently supports both the SAX 1.0 and SAX 2.0 implementations.

Examining XPath

XPath provides a mechanism for accessing the elements and attributes of an XML document in much the same manner we would access files on a file system. XPath allows us a way to access specific sets of nodes directly in an XML document tree. The following section details XPath syntax and the various ways elements can be accessed. XPath plays a key role in transforming XML documents using XSL, as you see later in this chapter.

Defining XPath Syntax

XPath syntax will look familiar to anyone who has navigated a Unix or DOS file system. The following table illustrates some of the various ways elements can be accessed using XPath syntax.

Syntax	Definition
/A	Select root element A.
/A/B	Select all elements B that are children of A.
//B	Select all elements B. (This will return a list of *all* B elements, regardless of ancestry.)
//*	Select all elements.
/*/*/B	Select all elements B that have two ancestors.
//B/@C	Select all elements C that are attributes of B.
//B[@C>5 OR @C=3]/*	Select all child elements of B where attribute C of B is greater than 5 or attribute C of B is equal to 3.
/A/B[1]	Select the first B child of element A.
/A/B[@C]	Select all child elements B of A that have an attribute C.
/A/B[first()]	Select the first B child of element A.
/A/B[last()]	Select the last B child of element A.
//A/[count(*) > 2]	Select all child elements of A having greater than two children.
//A/B/text()	Select all text node children of element B that are children of element A.
//*|//@*	Select the combination of all elements and all attributes.

XPath Functions

XPath provides several types of functions that can be applied while accessing elements in an XML document. The function definitions in the following sections come directly from the *W3C XML Path Language(XPath) Version 1.0* recommendation.

Node Set Functions

The following node set functions are supported by XPath and can be applied when accessing elements with an XPath path:

- **last()**   Returns a numeric reference to the last node in a node set.

- **first()**   Returns a numeric reference to the first node in a node set.

- **count(node-set)**   Returns the number of nodes in the argument node set.

- **position()**   Returns a numeric reference equal to the current position within a node set.

- **id(object)**   Selects elements by their unique ID.

- **local-name(node-set?)**   Returns the local part of the expanded-name of the node in the argument node-set that's first in document order.

- **namespace-uri(node-set?)**   Returns the namespace URI of the expanded-name of the node in the argument node-set that's first in document order.

- **name(node-set?)**   Returns a string containing a qualified name representing the expanded name of the node in the argument node-set that's first in the document order.

String Functions

The following string functions are supported by XPath and can be applied when accessing elements with an XPath path:

- **string(object?)**   Converts an object to a string.

- **concat(string,string,string*)**   Returns a concatenation of its arguments.

- **starts-with(string,string)**   Returns true if the first argument string starts with the second argument string and, otherwise, returns false.

- **contains(string,string)**   Returns true if the first argument string contains the second argument string and, otherwise, returns false.

- **substring-before(string,string)**   Returns the substring of the first argument string that precedes the first occurrence of the second argument string in the first argument string or the empty string if the first argument string doesn't contain the second argument string.

- **substring-after(string,string)**   Returns the substring of the first argument string that follows the first occurrence of the second argument string in the first argument string or the empty string if the first argument string doesn't contain the second argument string.

- **substring(string,string,number)**   Returns the substring of the first argument starting at the position specified in the second argument with length specified in the third argument.

- **string-length(string?)**   Returns the number of characters in the string.

- **normalize-space(string?)**   Returns the argument string with white space normalized by stripping leading and trailing white space and replacing sequences of white space characters by a single space.

- **translate(string,string,string)**   Returns the first argument string with occurrences of characters in the second argument string replaced by the character at the corresponding position in the third argument string.

Boolean Functions

The following Boolean functions are supported by XPath and can be applied when accessing elements with an XPath path:

- **boolean(object)**   Converts its argument to a Boolean as follows:

  - a number is true if and only if it's neither positive or negative zero nor NaN (i.e., null or nonexistent)

  - a node-set is true if and only if it's nonempty

  - a string is true if and only if its length is nonzero

  - an object of a type other than the four basic types is converted to a Boolean in a way that's dependent on that type

- **not(boolean)**   Returns true if its argument is false, and false otherwise.

- **true()**   Returns true.

- **false()**   Returns false.

- **lang(string)**   Returns true or false, depending on whether the language of the context node as specified by xml:lang attributes is the same as or is a sublanguage of the language specified by the argument string.

Number Functions

The following number functions are supported by XPath and can be applied when accessing elements with an XPath path:

- **number(object)**   Converts its argument to a number.

- ■ ***sum(node-set)***   Returns the sum, for each node in the argument node-set, of the result of converting the string-values of the node to a number.

- ■ ***floor(number)***   Returns the largest (closest to positive infinity) number that isn't greater than the argument and that is an integer.

- ■ ***ceiling(number)***   Returns the smallest (closest to negative infinity) number that isn't less than the argument and that is an integer.

- ■ ***round(number)***   Returns the number that's closest to the argument, which is an integer. If two such numbers exist, then the one closest to positive infinity is returned.

Using XPath to Access Document Elements

The XPath examples in this section access elements from the previous mp3.xml XML document. The following Java class is used to implement the XPath examples in the following sections:

```java
// XPathDemo.java
import java.io.*;
import java.net.*;
import org.w3c.dom.*;
import oracle.xml.parser.v2.*;

public class XPathDemo {
    public static void main(String args[]){
        String filename = new String();
        if (args.length< 2){
            System.out.println("Please enter: (1)Filename " +
                "and (2)XPath string.");
        }else{
          try{
            // Create an input stream for the file.
            File xmlFile = new File(args[0]);
            FileInputStream  xmlInputStream = new FileInputStream(xmlFile);
            DOMParser parser = new DOMParser();
            parser.setErrorStream(System.err);
            parser.showWarnings(true);
            parser.setValidationMode(XMLConstants.NONVALIDATING);
            parser.parse(xmlInputStream);
            // Obtain the document.
            XMLDocument doc = parser.getDocument();
            displayElements(args[1],doc);
          }catch(Exception e){
            System.out.println("Error: "+e.getMessage());
          }
        }
    }
```

```
    }
    //Display elements of XML Document given the XPath and Document
    public static void displayElements(String xpath,XMLDocument doc){
       XMLElement elements = (XMLElement) doc.getDocumentElement();
       try{
          NodeList nl = elements.selectNodes(xpath,elements);
          for (int i=0;i < nl.getLength();i++){
            //Display Text Node Values
            if (nl.item(i).getNodeType()== Node.TEXT_NODE){
              System.out.println(nl.item(i).getParentNode().getNodeName()+
                  " = "+nl.item(i).getNodeValue());
            //Display Attribute Node Values
            }else if(nl.item(i).getNodeType()== Node.ATTRIBUTE_NODE){
              System.out.println(nl.item(i).getNodeName()+" = "+
                  nl.item(i).getNodeValue());
            //Display the Text Node of an Element Node
            }else if(nl.item(i).getNodeType()== Node.ELEMENT_NODE){
              System.out.println(nl.item(i).getNodeName()+" = "+
                  nl.item(i).getFirstChild().getNodeValue());
            }
          }
       }catch(Exception e){
          System.out.println(e.getMessage());
       }
    }
  }
```

TIP

When generating your class files for the Java examples shown in this section, ensure the following .jar files are in your classpath: oraclexsql.jar, xmlparserv2.jar, classes12.zip, xsu12.jar, and classgen.jar.

The following command line syntax is used to run the XPathDemo class previously defined:

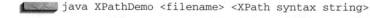
```
java XPathDemo <filename> <XPath syntax string>
```

Select All Elements in the Document

To select all the elements in the mp3.xml document, execute the XPathDemo class as follows:

```
java XPathDemo mp3.xml //*
```

The //* syntax tells the program to extract all elements. The output of this extraction is as follows:

```
MP3Inventory = null
artist = null
genre = Rock
name = Aerosmith
song = null
title = Pink
album = Nine Lives
label = Columbia
fileName = Pink.mp3
playTime = 4:23
dateAquired = 05/05/2001
song = null
title = Walk This Way
album = Toys In The Attic
label = Columbia
fileName = WalkThisWay.mp3
playTime = 5:23
dateAquired = 05/05/2000
artist = null
genre = Alternative
name = Foo Fighters
song = null
title = Big Me
album = Foo Fighters
label = Roswell
fileName = BigMe.mp3
playTime = 3:23
dateAquired = 05/05/2001
song = null
title = Learn To Fly
album = Their Is Nothing Left To Lose
label = Roswell
fileName = LearnToFly.mp3
playTime = 4:13
dateAquired = 03/05/2000
```

Select the Combination of All Elements and All Attributes

To select the combination of all elements and all attributes in the mp3.xml document, execute the XPathDemo class as follows:

```
java XPathDemo mp3.xml "//*|//@*"
```

The "*//*|//@*" syntax tells the program to extract all elements and attributes. The output of this extraction is as follows:

```
MP3Inventory = null
artist = null
id = 1
genre = Rock
name = Aerosmith
song = null
title = Pink
album = Nine Lives
label = Columbia
fileName = Pink.mp3
playTime = 4:23
dateAquired = 05/05/2001
song = null
title = Walk This Way
album = Toys In The Attic
label = Columbia
fileName = WalkThisWay.mp3
playTime = 5:23
dateAquired = 05/05/2000
artist = null
id = 2
genre = Alternative
name = Foo Fighters
song = null
title = Big Me
album = Foo Fighters
label = Roswell
fileName = BigMe.mp3
playTime = 3:23
dateAquired = 05/05/2001
song = null
title = Learn To Fly
album = Their Is Nothing Left To Lose
label = Roswell
fileName = LearnToFly.mp3
playTime = 4:13
dateAquired = 03/05/2000
```

Select the First Child of the First *song* Element of the First *artist* Element

To select the first child of the first song element of the first artist element in the mp3.xml document, execute the XPathDemo class as follows:

```
java XPathDemo mp3.xml //artist[1]/song[1]/*[1]
```

The //artist[1]/song[1]/*[1] syntax tells the program to extract the first child of the first song element of the first artist element. The output of this extraction is as follows:

 `title = Pink`

Using XML Stylesheets to Format and Display XML Documents

If XML is to become the standard for electronic data interchange, a standard must also exist for presenting the data. HTML uses cascading style sheets (CSS) to format and control the presentation of HTML documents. The same control is possible for XML documents with Extensible Style Language (XSL, also sometimes referred to as XSLT).

Defining XSL

XSL is the standard for expressing style sheets for XML. XSL is a scripting language used to describe rules for transforming XML source documents. XSL can present XML data in a variety of formats, such as HTML, speech, paper, or other media. XSL scripts are also referred to as XSL style sheets. XSL makes extensive use of XPath in accessing the elements of an XML document. The complete specification for XSL can be found at **http://www.w3.org/TR/WD-xsl**.

Using XSL to Display XML Data as HTML

The following XSL script will take an XML document and display the data in an HTML table. This example uses the previously defined suspect.xml XML document. Let's review the suspect.xsl file:

```
<?xml version="1.0" encoding="UTF-8"?>

<xsl:stylesheet xmlns:xsl="http://www.w3.org/TR/WD-xsl">
  <xsl:template match="/">
    <HTML>
    <TITLE> XML Displayed with XSL Example </TITLE>
    <BODY bgcolor="C0C0C0">
    <H1>XML Displayed with XSL Example</H1>
    <BR></BR>
    <H2>Suspect List</H2>
    <TABLE border="10">
          <TH>First</TH>
          <TH>Last</TH>
          <TH>Age</TH>
```

```
        <TH>Race</TH>
        <TH>Address</TH>
        <TH>Phone</TH>
    <xsl:for-each select="suspect">
    <TR>
        <TD><xsl:value-of select="name/first"/></TD>
        <TD><xsl:value-of select="name/last"/></TD>
        <TD><xsl:value-of select="demographics/age"/></TD>
        <TD><xsl:value-of select="demographics/@race"/></TD>
        <TD><xsl:value-of select="address/street"/>
            <xsl:value-of select="address/city"/></TD>
        <TD><xsl:value-of select="comms/phone/areacode"/>
            <xsl:value-of select="comms/phone/prefix"/>
            <xsl:value-of select="comms/phone/suffix"/></TD>
    </TR>
    </xsl:for-each>
    </TABLE>
  </BODY>
  </HTML>
 </xsl:template>
 </xsl:stylesheet>
```

The following XML document references the suspect.xsl XSL script, the suspect.dtd, and the suspect.xml files defined earlier. In other words, this xsl file pulls all the components together.

```
<?xml version="1.0" encoding="UTF-8"?>
<?xml-stylesheet type="text/xsl" href="c:\temp\suspect.xsl"?>
<!DOCTYPE suspect SYSTEM "c:\temp\suspect.dtd">
<suspect id="S1">
    <name>
         <first>Joe</first>
         <last>Jackson</last>
    </name>
    <demographics gender="male" race="white" hair="blond"
      eyes="blue">
         <age>32</age>
         <height>6ft</height>
         <weight>175</weight>
    </demographics>
    <address type="home">
         <street>821 ELM</street>
    </address>
    <comms>
      <phone type="residential">
```

```
        <areacode>704</areacode>
        <prefix>333</prefix>
        <suffix>1234</suffix>
      </phone>
   </comms>
</suspect>
```

An XML/XSL-capable Web browser, such as Internet Explorer 5.5 or Netscape 6.0, will display the preceding document as HTML. Figure 8-2 demonstrates the result of executing the preceding XML document through IE5.

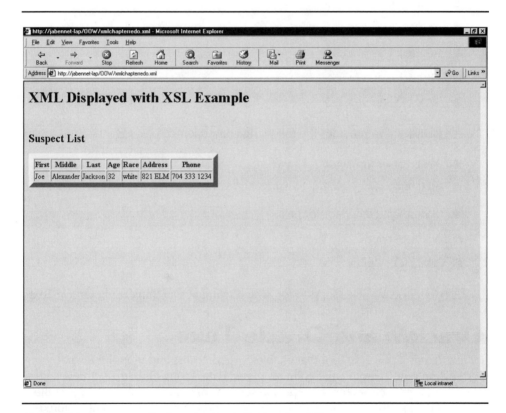

FIGURE 8-2.   *XML displayed using HTML using XSL*

XML Support in Oracle9*i*

Oracle9*i* provides a suite of XML development tools. This suite is called the XML Developer's Kit, or XDK. The XDK comes in several flavors: Java, PL/SQL, and C. This chapter covers only the Java and PL/SQL portions of the kit.

The XDK provides support for the following standards:

- XML 1.0
- XML Schema 1.0
- XML Namespaces 1.0
- XSLT 1.0
- XPath 1.0
- DOM 1.0 and DOM 2.0
- SAX 1.0 and SAX 2.0

The XDK for Java provides the following components:

- XML Parser for Java V2
- XML Schema Processor for Java
- XML Class Generator for Java
- XSQL Servlet
- XML SQL Utility

Oracle9*i* also provides support for XML document searching using Oracle Text.

Oracle9*i* and Oracle Text

Oracle Text is a powerful tool that enables you to access and pinpoint textual information quickly from large volumes of text data. Using Oracle Text, developers are able to limit their searches to specific sections of a document. XML tags in the document define these sections of a document and the entire document is stored as a Character Large Object (CLOB) in database tables. See Chapter 25 for another example of how Oracle Text is used with Oracle Ultra Search.

The following XML document could be stored in the database in a table called empReviews. Let's review the empreviews.xml file:

```
<?xml version="1.0" encoding="UTF-8"?>
<EmployeeReviews>
```

```
    <EmpId>123456</EmpId>
    <EmpName>
        <First>John</First>
        <Last>Jones</Last>
    </EmpName>
    <Reviewer>Bob Smith</Reviewer>
    <ReviewPeriod>
        <Start>01/01/1999</Start>
        <End>06/30/1999</End>
    </ReviewPeriod>
    <ReviewText>John Jones is an outstanding employee.  He is rated a
    <Rating>10</Rating></ReviewText>
</EmployeeReviews>
```

A developer can then count how many employees Bob Smith has rated a 10 in a specific review period using the following SQL statement:

```
SELECT  COUNT(*)
   FROM  empReviews
WHERE
        reviewer = 'Bob Smith'
AND     CONTAINS (ReviewText, '10 WITHIN Rating');
```

This example is simple, but imagine how powerful the XML in Oracle Text feature can be if used to search legal documents, criminal arrest reports, news articles, or corporate document databases. The XML *in context* feature also lends itself toward analyzing marketing data.

Examining the Oracle XML Parser

The *Oracle XML Parser* is implemented in Java and conforms to the XML 1.0 specification. The Oracle XML Parser can be used as both a validating and a nonvalidating parser. The Oracle XML Parser also supports both the DOM and SAX APIs. Because the Oracle XML Parser is implemented as Java, it can be executed within Java applications running outside the database. The Oracle XML Parser can also execute in Java applications inside the database using the Oracle9*i* Java VM.

Installing the Oracle XML Parser

The Oracle XML Parser is a collection of Java classes contained in a .jar file called xmlparserv2.jar. The Oracle XML Parser can be installed in two ways. The first method is to include the .jar file in the classpath of the machine to be executing Java applications that include the Oracle XML Parser Java classes. The second method is to load the .jar file into Oracle9*i* using the new loadjava utility. This method leverages the power of the new Oracle9*i* Java VM. The Oracle XML Parser .jar file is loaded into the database as part of the default Oracle9*i* database install process.

Running the Oracle XML Parser Outside the Database

The Oracle XML Parser is implemented in Java, so you can use the features outside the database. The developer has the choice of using the DOM or SAX API for parsing an XML document.

DOM

The following Java program reads an external XML document and displays its elements, attributes, and the values for both using the DOM API:

```java
// DOMDemoTraverse.java
import java.io.*;
import org.w3c.dom.*;
import org.w3c.dom.Node;
import oracle.xml.parser.v2.DOMParser;
import oracle.xml.parser.v2.XMLElement;
import oracle.xml.parser.v2.XMLConstants;
public class DOMDemoTraverse {
  //Document Object Model Parser
    public static void main(String[] args){
        try{
            if (args.length != 1){
              // Verify that an XML file was passed
                System.err.println("XML source file expected.") ;
                System.exit(1);
            }
            // Get an instance of the parser
            DOMParser parser = new DOMParser();
            // Create an input stream from the filename.
        FileInputStream  xmlInputStream
                = new FileInputStream(new File(args[0]));
            // Set parser options: validation on,
            // warnings shown, error stream set to stderr.
            parser.setErrorStream(System.err);
            parser.setValidationMode(XMLConstants.NONVALIDATING);
            parser.showWarnings(true);
            // Parse the document.
            parser.parse(xmlInputStream);
            // Get the document.
            Document doc = parser.getDocument();
            // Display document elements
            System.out.println("Document Element, Attributes, " +
                               "and values are: ");
            printElements(doc);
            // Display document element attributes
```

```java
        System.out.println("Parsing Complete. ");
     }catch (Exception e){
        System.out.println("Error: "+e.toString());
     }
  }
  public static void printElements(Document doc){
     try{
        //Get Root Element
        displayElements(doc.getDocumentElement());
     }catch(Exception e){
        System.err.println("Error printElements: "+e.getMessage());
     }
  }
   public static void displayElements(Node node){
      Node          childNode;
      NodeList      nodeChildren;
      if(node.getNodeType() == Node.ELEMENT_NODE){
         System.out.println("Element Name= "+node.getNodeName());
         //if (node.hasAttributes()){
         if (node.getAttributes().getLength() > 0){
            displayAttributes(node.getAttributes());
         }
         if (node.hasChildNodes()){
            if (node.getFirstChild().getNodeType()==Node.TEXT_NODE){
               System.out.println("Element value= "+
               node.getFirstChild().getNodeValue());
               System.out.println("");
            }
            nodeChildren=node.getChildNodes();
            for (int i=0; i<nodeChildren.getLength();i++){
               //Recursive call to displayElements method
               displayElements(nodeChildren.item(i));
             }
          }
       }
    }
  public static void displayAttributes(NamedNodeMap attNodes){
     Node node;
     System.out.println("Attribute List");
     for (int i=0; i < attNodes.getLength(); i++){
        node = attNodes.item(i);
        System.out.println("Attibute  Name  = "+node.getNodeName());
        System.out.println("Attribute Value = "+node.getNodeValue());
     }
     System.out.println("");
  }
}
```

Run the preceding program against the suspect.xml XML document, which contains data tagged within the XML tags.

After executing this syntax, the following document element, attributes, and values are displayed:

```
Document Element, Attributes, and values are:
Element Name= suspect
Attribute List
Attibute  Name  = id
Attribute Value = S1
Element Name= name
Element Name= first
Element value= Joe
Element Name= last
Element value= Jackson
Element Name= demographics
Attribute List
Attibute  Name  = gender
Attribute Value = male
Attibute  Name  = race
Attribute Value = white
Attibute  Name  = hair
Attribute Value = blond
Attibute  Name  = eyes
Attribute Value = blue
Element Name= age
Element value= 32
Element Name= height
Element value= 6ft
Element Name= weight
Element value= 175
Element Name= address
Attribute List
Attibute  Name  = type
Attribute Value = home
Element Name= street
Element value= 821 ELM
Element Name= comms
Element Name= phone
Attribute List
Attibute  Name  = type
Attribute Value = residential
Element Name= areacode
Element value= 704
Element Name= prefix
Element value= 333
Element Name= suffix
Element value= 1234
Parsing Complete.
```

SAX

The default content handler for SAX 1.0 is the class *HandlerBase*. The following Java program uses the SAX 1.0 specification, reads an external XML document, and then displays the elements and attributes, and values for both:

```java
// SAXDemoTraverse.java
import org.xml.sax.*;
import java.io.*;
import java.net.*;
import oracle.xml.parser.v2.*;

public class SAXDemoTraverse extends HandlerBase{
    // Store the locator
    Locator locator;
    public static void main(String[] args){
        try{
            if (args.length != 1){
                // Make sure name of XML file was entered.
                System.err.println("Usage: saxXMLParser filename");
                System.exit(1);
            }
            // Create a new handler for the parser
            SAXDemoTraverse saxHandler = new SAXDemoTraverse();
            // Get an instance of the parser
            Parser saxparser = new SAXParser();
            // Set Handlers in the parser
            saxparser.setDocumentHandler(saxHandler);
            saxparser.setEntityResolver(saxHandler);
            saxparser.setErrorHandler(saxHandler);
            try{
                // Create an input stream from the filename.
                FileInputStream  xmlInputStream =
                    new FileInputStream(new File(args[0]));
                saxparser.parse(new InputSource(xmlInputStream));
            }catch (SAXParseException e){
                System.out.println(e.getMessage());
            }catch (SAXException e){
                System.out.println(e.getMessage());
            }
        }catch (Exception e){
            System.out.println(e.toString());
        }
    }
    // Implementation of DocumentHandler interface.
    public void setDocumentLocator (Locator locator){
        System.out.println("Set Document Locator:");
        this.locator = locator;
    }
    public void startDocument(){
```

```
      System.out.println("Start Document");
   }
   public void endDocument() throws SAXException{
      System.out.println("End Document");
   }
   public void startElement(String name, AttributeList
         attributes) throws SAXException{
      System.out.println("Start Element:"+name);
      for (int i=0;i<attributes.getLength();i++){
         String attrname = attributes.getName(i);
         String type     = attributes.getType(i);
         String value    = attributes.getValue(i);
         System.out.println("");
         System.out.println("Attribute: "+attrname+"="+value);
      }
      System.out.println("");
   }
   public void endElement(String name) throws SAXException{
      System.out.println("");
      System.out.println("End Element:"+name);
      System.out.println("");
   }
   public void characters(char[] cbuf, int start, int len){
      System.out.print("Characters: ");
      System.out.println(new String(cbuf,start,len));
   }
   public void processingInstruction(String target, String data)
            throws SAXException{
      System.out.println("ProcessingInstruction:"+target+" "+data);
   }
   // Implementation of the EntityResolver interface.
   public InputSource resolveEntity (String publicId, String
       systemId)throws SAXException{
      System.out.println("ResolveEntity:"+publicId+" "+systemId);
      System.out.println("Locator:"+locator.getPublicId()+" "+
               locator.getSystemId()+
               " "+locator.getLineNumber()+
               " "+locator.getColumnNumber());
      return null;
   }
   // Implementation of the DTDHandler interface.
   public void notationDecl (String name, String publicId, String
     systemId){
      System.out.println("NotationDecl:"+name+" "+publicId+
      " "+systemId);
   }
   public void unparsedEntityDecl (String name, String publicId,
                        String systemId, String notationName){
```

```
        System.out.println("UnparsedEntityDecl:"+name +
        " "+publicId+" "+systemId+" "+notationName);
    }
    // Implementation of the ErrorHandler interface.
    public void warning (SAXParseException e)
            throws SAXException{
        System.out.println("Warning:"+e.getMessage());
    }
    public void error (SAXParseException e)
            throws SAXException{
        throw new SAXException(e.getMessage());
    }
    public void fatalError (SAXParseException e)
            throws SAXException{
        System.out.println("Fatal error");
        throw new SAXException(e.getMessage());
    }
}
```

If you run the preceding program against the suspect.xml XML document, you get the following output:

```
Set Document Locator:
Start Document
Start Element:suspect
Attribute: id=S1
Start Element:name
Start Element:first
Characters: Joe
End Element:first
Start Element:last
Characters: Jackson
End Element:last
End Element:name
Start Element:demographics
Attribute: gender=male
Attribute: race=white
Attribute: hair=blond
Attribute: eyes=blue
Start Element:age
Characters: 32
End Element:age
Start Element:height
Characters: 6ft
End Element:height
Start Element:weight
Characters: 175
End Element:weight
```

```
End Element:demographics
Start Element:address
Attribute: type=home
Start Element:street
Characters: 821 ELM
End Element:street
End Element:address
Start Element:comms
Start Element:phone
Attribute: type=residential
Start Element:areacode
Characters: 704
End Element:areacode
Start Element:prefix
Characters: 333
End Element:prefix
Start Element:suffix
Characters: 1234
End Element:suffix
End Element:phone
End Element:comms
End Element:suspect
End Document
```

The purpose of this example is to demonstrate how the SAX parser implements callbacks and handles events. The next SAX example demonstrates a more practical application using the SAX 2.0 parser. Notice we implement only certain callbacks. The following example loads data in to the EMP table in the SCOTT schema:

```java
// InsertSAXEmp.java
import oracle.xml.parser.v2.SAXParser;
import org.xml.sax.*;
import org.xml.sax.helpers.*;
import java.io.*;
import java.sql.*;
public class InsertSAXEmp extends DefaultHandler{
    private Locator locator;
    private static Connection conn;
    private String vElementData = null;
    private String vEMPNO       = new String();
    private String vENAME       = new String();
    private String vJOB         = new String();
    private String vMGR         = new String();
    private String vHIREDATE    = new String();
    private String vSAL         = new String();
    private String vDEPTNO      = new String();
    public static String xmlData = new String("<ROWSET>"+
                            "<ROW num='1'>"+
                            "<EMPNO>9369</EMPNO>"+
                            "<ENAME>SMITH</ENAME>"+
                            "<JOB>CLERK</JOB>"+
```

```
                                    "<MGR>7902</MGR>"+
                                    "<HIREDATE>12-APR-2001</HIREDATE>"+
                                    "<SAL>800</SAL>"+
                                    "<DEPTNO>20</DEPTNO>"+
                                    "</ROW>"+
                                     "<ROW num='2'>"+
                                    "<EMPNO>9367</EMPNO>"+
                                    "<ENAME>SMITH</ENAME>"+
                                    "<JOB>CLERK</JOB>"+
                                    "<MGR>7902</MGR>"+
                                    "<HIREDATE>11-APR-2001</HIREDATE>"+
                                    "<SAL>800</SAL>"+
                                    "<DEPTNO>20</DEPTNO>"+
                                    "</ROW>"+
                                    "</ROWSET>");
public InsertSAXEmp()
      {
            super();
      }
public static void main(String arg[]){
   try{
     DriverManager.registerDriver(new oracle.jdbc.driver.OracleDriver());
       conn = DriverManager.getConnection("jdbc:oracle:oci8:@","scott","tiger");
      // Create a new default handler for the parser
      DefaultHandler saxEmpInsert = new InsertSAXEmp();
      // Get an instance of the parser
      SAXParser parser = new SAXParser();
      // Set Handlers in the parser
      ((SAXParser)parser).setContentHandler(saxEmpInsert);
      ((SAXParser)parser).setEntityResolver(saxEmpInsert);
      ((SAXParser)parser).setErrorHandler(saxEmpInsert);
      try
      {
        StringReader is = new StringReader(xmlData);
        InputSource xmlDataIS = new InputSource(is);
         ((SAXParser)parser).parse(xmlDataIS);
      }
      catch (SAXParseException e)
      {
         System.out.println("Parse Error "+e.getMessage());
      }
      catch (SAXException e)
      {
         System.out.println(e.getMessage());
      }
   }
   catch (Exception e)
   {
      System.out.println(e.toString());
   }
}
public void setDocumentLocator(Locator locator){
  this.locator = locator;
}
public void endElement(String namespaceURI,
                       String name,
                       String rawName) throws SAXException
{
```

```
        if (name.equals("EMPNO")){
            vEMPNO      = vElementData;
        }else if(name.equals("ENAME")){
            vENAME      = vElementData;
        }else if (name.equals("JOB")){
            vJOB        = vElementData;
        }else if (name.equals("MGR")){
            vMGR        = vElementData;
        }else if (name.equals("HIREDATE")){
            vHIREDATE = vElementData;
        }else if (name.equals("SAL")){
            vSAL        = vElementData;
        }else if (name.equals("DEPTNO")){
            vDEPTNO    = vElementData;
        }else if (name.equals("ROW")){
            insertEmpRecord();
        }
        vElementData = null;
    }
    public void characters(char[] cbuf, int start, int len)
    {
        vElementData = new String(cbuf,start,len);
    }
    public void insertEmpRecord(){
      try{
        PreparedStatement stmt = conn.prepareStatement(
          "insert into EMP(EMPNO,ENAME,JOB,MGR,HIREDATE,SAL,DEPTNO) VALUES(?,?,?,?,?,?,?)");
        stmt.setInt(1,Integer.parseInt(vEMPNO));
        stmt.setString(2,vENAME);
        stmt.setString(3,vJOB);
        stmt.setString(4,vMGR);
        stmt.setString(5,vHIREDATE);
        stmt.setFloat(6,Float.parseFloat(vSAL));
        stmt.setInt(7,Integer.parseInt(vDEPTNO));
        stmt.executeUpdate();
        conn.commit();
      }catch(Exception e){
        System.out.println(e.getMessage());
      }
    }
}
```

Running the Oracle XML Parser Inside the Database

The Oracle XML Parser can be executed from within the database using the Oracle9*i* Java VM. To access the Java methods of the XML Parser, the methods must be "wrapped" in PL/SQL. Oracle provides a set of 16 PL/SQL packages whose procedures and functions map to the Java methods in the Oracle XML Parser. The group of packages is called the *Oracle XML Parser for PL/SQL*. The parser verifies the XML document is well formed and, optionally, that the document is valid. The parser will construct an object tree that can be accessed through the PL/SQL packages.

Parsing an XML Document with PL/SQL

The following example illustrates the use of Oracle XML Parser for PL/SQL by parsing an XML document and displaying the elements and attributes.

The following PL/SQL procedure reads an XML document from the operating system, parses the document, and either displays the document's elements and attributes or displays an error message:

```
CREATE OR REPLACE PROCEDURE PLSQLXML(directory VARCHAR2,
                                     inputFile VARCHAR2,
                                     errorFile VARCHAR2) is
   parser     xmlparser.Parser;
   document   xmldom.DOMDocument;
-- prints elements in a document
   PROCEDURE printElements(document xmldom.DOMDocument) is
   nodeList    xmldom.DOMNodeList;
   listLength NUMBER;
   node        xmldom.DOMNode;
   BEGIN
   -- get all elements
      nodeList    := xmldom.getElementsByTagName(document, '*');
      listLength := xmldom.getLength(nodeList);
      -- loop through elements
      FOR elements IN 0..listLength-1 LOOP
         node := xmldom.item(nodeList, elements);
         DBMS_OUTPUT.PUT(xmldom.getNodeName(node) || ' ');
      END LOOP;
      DBMS_OUTPUT.PUT_LINE('');
   END;
-- prints the attributes of each element in a document
   PROCEDURE printElementAttributeValues(document xmldom.DOMDocument) IS
      nodeList        xmldom.DOMNodeList;
      lengthList      NUMBER;
      lengthChild     NUMBER;
      lengthAttr      NUMBER;
      node            xmldom.DOMNode;
      childNode       xmldom.DOMNode;
      childNodeList   xmldom.DOMNodeList;
      nodeElement     xmldom.DOMElement;
      data            xmldom.DOMCharacterData;
      namedNodeMap    xmldom.DOMNamedNodeMap;
      attrname        VARCHAR2(100);
      attrval         VARCHAR2(100);
   BEGIN
      -- get all elements
      nodeList    := xmldom.getElementsByTagName(document, '*');
      lengthList := xmldom.getLength(nodelist);
```

```
    -- loop through elements
    FOR element IN 0..lengthList-1 LOOP
       node         := xmldom.item(nodeList, element);
       nodeElement  := xmldom.makeElement(node);
       dbms_output.put(xmldom.getTagName(nodeElement) || ':
           ');
       -- get value of elements
       childNodeList :=
       xmldom.getChildNodes(xmldom.makeNode(nodeElement));
    IF(xmldom.isNull(childNodeList)=FALSE) THEN
       lengthChild := xmldom.getLength(childNodeList);
       FOR childElement IN 0..lengthChild-1 LOOP
         childNode :=
           xmldom.item(childNodeList,childElement);
         IF xmldom.getNodeValue(childNode) IS NOT NULL THEN
           dbms_output.put_line(xmldom.getNodeValue(childNode));
         END IF;
       END LOOP;
     END IF;
     -- get all attributes of element
     namedNodeMap := xmldom.getAttributes(node);
    IF (xmldom.isNull(namedNodeMap) = FALSE) THEN
       lengthAttr := xmldom.getLength(namedNodeMap);
       -- loop through attributes
       FOR attribute in 0..lengthAttr-1 LOOP
          node := xmldom.item(namedNodeMap, attribute);
          attrname := xmldom.getNodeName(node);
          attrval := xmldom.getNodeValue(node);
          dbms_output.put(' ' || attrname || ' = ' || attrval);
       END LOOP;
       dbms_output.put_line('');
     END IF;
    END LOOP;
END;
BEGIN
-- new parser
   parser := xmlparser.newParser;
-- set some characteristics
   xmlparser.setValidationMode(parser, FALSE);
   xmlparser.setErrorLog(parser, directory || '\' || errorfile);
   xmlparser.setBaseDir(parser, directory);
-- parse input file
   xmlparser.parse(parser, directory || '\' || inputFile);
-- get document
   document := xmlparser.getDocument(parser);
-- Print document elements
   dbms_output.put('The elements are: ');
   printElements(document);
-- Print document element attributes
```

```
        dbms_output.put_line('The attributes of each element are:');
        printElementAttributeValues(document);
-- handle exceptions
EXCEPTION
    WHEN xmldom.INDEX_SIZE_ERR THEN
        raise_application_error(-20120, 'Index Size error');
    WHEN xmldom.DOMSTRING_SIZE_ERR THEN
        raise_application_error(-20120, 'String Size error');
    WHEN xmldom.HIERARCHY_REQUEST_ERR THEN
        raise_application_error(-20120, 'Hierarchy request error');
    WHEN xmldom.WRONG_DOCUMENT_ERR THEN
        raise_application_error(-20120, 'Wrong doc error');
    WHEN xmldom.INVALID_CHARACTER_ERR THEN
        raise_application_error(-20120, 'Invalid Char error');
    WHEN xmldom.NO_DATA_ALLOWED_ERR THEN
        raise_application_error(-20120, 'No data allowed error');
    WHEN xmldom.NO_MODIFICATION_ALLOWED_ERR THEN
        raise_application_error(-20120, 'No mod allowed error');
    WHEN xmldom.NOT_FOUND_ERR THEN
        raise_application_error(-20120, 'Not found error');
    WHEN xmldom.NOT_SUPPORTED_ERR THEN
        raise_application_error(-20120, 'Not supported error');
    WHEN xmldom.INUSE_ATTRIBUTE_ERR THEN
        raise_application_error(-20120, 'In use attr error');
END;
```

To execute this procedure against the suspect.xml, execute the following command from SQL*Plus:

```
SQL> exec plsqlxml('c:','suspect.xml','err.txt');
```

The elements are suspect name, first, last, demographics, age, height, weight, address, street, comms, and phone (area code, prefix, suffix). The attributes of each element are included in the following example run in SQL*Plus:

```
suspect:
id = S1
name:
first: Joe
last: Jackson
demographics:
gender = male race = white hair = blond eyes = blue
age: 32
height: 6ft
weight: 175
address:
type = home
street: 821 ELM
```

```
comms:
phone:
type = residential
areacode: 704
prefix: 333
suffix: 1234

PL/SQL procedure successfully completed.
```

Examining the Oracle XML Class Generator

The *Oracle XML Class Generator* generates a set of Java source files based on an existing DTD. The generated Java source files can be used to construct, validate, and print an XML document that conforms to the specified DTD. The Oracle XML Class Generator is written in Java and requires the Oracle XML Parser.

Implementing the Oracle XML Class Generator

The following Java application (the basis of which comes from the sample provided with the Oracle XML Class Generator) will create an XML document and a .java file for each element in the document:

```
// XmlClassGen.java
import java.io.File;
import java.net.URL;
import oracle.xml.parser.v2.XMLConstants;
import oracle.xml.parser.v2.DOMParser;
import oracle.xml.parser.v2.DTD;
import oracle.xml.parser.v2.XMLDocument;
import oracle.xml.classgen.DTDClassGenerator;
public class XmlClassGen{
  public static void main(String[] args){
      // validate arguments and display usage statement if incorrect
    if (args.length < 1){
        System.out.println("Usage: java SampleMain "+
                           "[-root <rootName>] <fileName>");
        System.out.println("fileName  Input file, XML documentor
        " + "external DTD file");
        System.out.println("-root <rootName>   Name of the root " +
                           "Element required if the input file " +
                           "is an external DTD)");
        return ;
    }
    try{
        // Try to open the XML File/ External DTD File
```

```
        // instantiate the parser
        DOMParser parser = new DOMParser();
        if (args.length == 3)
            parser.parseDTD(fileToURL(args[2]), args[1]);
        else
            parser.parse(fileToURL(args[0]));
        XMLDocument doc = parser.getDocument();
        DTD dtd = (DTD)doc.getDoctype();
        String doctype_name = null;
        if (args.length == 3)
            doctype_name = args[1];
        else
            /* get the Root Element name from the XMLDocument*/
            doctype_name = doc.getDocumentElement().getTagName();
        // generate the Java files...
        DTDClassGenerator generator = new DTDClassGenerator();
        // set generate comments to true
        generator.setGenerateComments(true);
        // set output directory
        generator.setOutputDirectory(".");
        // set validating mode to true
        generator.setValidationMode(true);
        // generate java src
        generator.generate(dtd, doctype_name);
    }catch(Exception e){
        System.out.println ("XML Class Generator: Error " +
         e.toString());
         e.printStackTrace();
    }
}
 static public URL fileToURL(String sfile){
    File file = new File(sfile);
    String path = file.getAbsolutePath();
    String fSep = System.getProperty("file.separator");
    if (fSep != null && fSep.length() == 1){
        path = path.replace(fSep.charAt(0), '/');
    }
    if (path.length() > 0 && path.charAt(0) != '/'){
        path = '/' + path;
    }
    try{
        return new URL("file", null, path);
    }catch (java.net.MalformedURLException e){
        /* According to the spec this could only happen if the */
        /* file protocol were not recognized. */
        throw new Error("unexpected MalformedURLException");
    }
  }
}
```

If the application is run for the following XML document, the Java source located following this XML document will be created.

```xml
<?xml version="1.0" encoding="UTF-8"?>
<!DOCTYPE team[
<!ELEMENT team (member*)>
<!ATTLIST team name CDATA #REQUIRED>
<!ELEMENT member (#PCDATA)>
]>
<team name="Eagles">
  <member>Joe Smith</member>
</team>
```

The resulting Java source generated from the previous XML code for the top element team follows:

```java
// Team.java
import java.io.*;
import java.net.*;
import oracle.xml.classgen.CGNode;
import oracle.xml.classgen.CGDocument;
import oracle.xml.classgen.InvalidContentException;
import oracle.xml.parser.*;

/**
 * The Document Class (for the root element Team)
 */
public class Team extends CGDocument
    public static DTD globalDTD = null;
    static
        String dtdFile = "Team_dtd.txt";
        XMLParser parser = new XMLParser();
        try
            File file = new File(dtdFile);
            String path = file.getAbsolutePath();
            String fSep = System.getProperty("file.separator");
            if (fSep != null && fSep.length() == 1)
                path = path.replace(fSep.charAt(0), '/');
            if (path.length() >> 0 && path.charAt(0) != '/')
                path = '/' + path;
            parser.parseDTD(new URL("file", null, path), "team");
            globalDTD = (DTD)parser.getDocument().getDoctype();
        catch (Exception e)
            System.out.println("Unexpected error opening DTD
            file");
    /**
     * Constructor with the required Attributes
     * @param varName for the Attribute name
```

```
 * @exception InvalidContentException  if invalid value is
 * specified for an attribute
 */
public Team(String varName) throws InvalidContentException
    super("team", globalDTD);
    try
        setName(varName);
    catch (IllegalArgumentException e)
        throw new InvalidContentException("Invalid Attribute
        value specified");
    isValidating = true;
/**
 * Prints the document to the specified OutputStream
 * @param out Java outputstream.
 * @exception InvalidContentException  if the document is not
 * valid
 */
public void print(OutputStream out) throws
  InvalidContentException
    super.print(out);
/**
 * Prints the document to the specified OutputStream
 * in the given encoding
 * @param out Java outputstream.
 * @exception InvalidContentException  if the document is not
 * valid
 */
public void print(OutputStream out, String enc) throws
      InvalidContentException
    super.print(out, enc);
/**
 * Add <code>Member</code> to <code>Team</code>
 * @param M Node of type <code>Member</code>
 * @exception InvalidContentException  if node cannot be added
 * as per the Content model of the element.
 */
public void addNode(Member M) throws InvalidContentException
    super.addNode(M);
    M.setDocument(this);
/**
 * Sets the value of attribute <code>name</code>
 * @param theData value of the attribute
 */
public void setName(String theData)
    setAttribute("name", theData);
/**
 * Returns the Team DTD.
 * @return the DTD
 * @see oracle.xml.parser.DTD
```

```
     */
    public DTD getDTDNode()
        return globalDTD;
    /**
     * Validate contents of element <code>Team</code>
     * @return true if valid contents, else false
     */
    public boolean validateContent()
        return super.validateContent();
```

The following example is the resulting Java source for the element member:

```
// Member.java
import java.io.*;
import java.net.*;
import oracle.xml.classgen.CGNode;
import oracle.xml.classgen.CGDocument;
import oracle.xml.classgen.InvalidContentException;
import oracle.xml.parser.*;

/**
 * The Node Class (for the root element Member)
 */
public class Member extends CGNode
    /**
     * Default Constructor
     */
    public Member()
        super("member");
        isValidating = true;
    /**
     * Constructor taking <code>#PCDATA</code>
     * @param theData  text for the Element
     * @exception InvalidContentException  <code>theData</code> is
     * invalid
     */
    public Member(String theData) throws InvalidContentException
        this();
        super.addData(theData);
        isValidating = true;
    /**
     * Add  a text node to <code>member</code>
     * @param theData value of the text node
     * @exception InvalidContentException  if the value of the
     * text node is invalid
     */
    public void addData(String theData) throws
        InvalidContentException
```

```
        super.addData(theData);
/**
 * Returns the Team DTD.
 * @return the DTD
 * @see oracle.xml.parser.DTD
 */
public DTD getDTDNode()
    return Team.globalDTD;
/**
 * Validate contents of element <code>Member</code>
 * @return true if valid contents, else false
 */
public boolean validateContent()
    return super.validateContent();
/**
 * Get Document Class <code>Team</code>
 * @return <code>Team</code> class
 */
public Team getDocument()
    return (Team)super.getCGDocument();
```

Examining the Oracle XML SQL Utility

The *Oracle XML SQL utility* comprises a set of Java classes that perform the following tasks:

■ Generate an XML document given a SQL query or JDBC ResultSet

■ Load data from an XML document into a database table

The Oracle XML SQL utility includes five components. Four components are Java classes: OracleXML class, OracleXMLStore class, OracleXMLQuery class, and OracleXMLSave class. The fifth component is a PL/SQL wrapper around the OracleXMLStore class called *xmlgen*.

Defining the OracleXML Class

The *OracleXML class* is the client-side front-end to the utility. The *utility* is a command-line application that contains the following two components:

■ **getXML** Generates an XML document based on a query.

■ **putXML** Loads data from an XML document in to the database.

Each of the preceding methods has a unique set of command-line parameters. Running Java OracleXML at the command-line produces the following list of command-line parameters:

```
OracleXML getXML
  [-user "username/password"]        -- the user name and password
  [-conn "JDBC_connect_string"]      -- JDBC connect string
  [-withDTD | -withSchema]           -- generate the DTD/Schema
  [-rowsetTag <rowsetTag>]           -- document tag name
  [-rowTag     <rowTag>]             -- row element tag name
  [-rowIdAttr <attrName>]            -- row-id attribute name
  [-rowIdColumn <column_name>]       -- db-column to use for the row id
  [-collectionIdAttr <attrName>]     -- collection element-id attribute
  [-useTypeForCollElemTag]           -- use type name for coll-elem tag
  [-useNullAttrId]                   -- use a null attribute
  [-styleSheet <URI>]                -- stylesheet processing instruction header
  [-styleSheetType <type>]           -- stylesheet header type (e.g.text/xsl)
  [-setXSLT <URI>]                   -- XSLT to apply to XML doc
  [-setXSLTRef <URI>]                -- XSLT external entity reference
  [-useLowerCase| -useUpperCase]     -- the case of the tag names
  [-withEscaping]                    -- if necessary do SQL-XML name escaping
  [-errorTag <errorTagName>]         -- error tag name
  [-raiseException]                  -- raise exceptions for errors
  [-raiseNoRowsException]            -- raise exception if no returned
  [-maxRows    <maxRows>]            -- maximum rows in output
  [-skipRows   <skipRows>]           -- rows to skip in output
  [-encoding <encoding_name>]        -- encoding to be used
  [-dateFormat <date format>]        -- date format to be used
  (<query>| -fileName <sqlfile>)     -- SQL query | file containing the query

  -- OR --

OracleXML putXML
  [-user "username/password"]        -- the user name and password
  [-conn "JDBC_connect_string"]      -- JDBC connect string
  [-batchSize <size>]                -- number of inserts executed at a time
  [-commitBatch <size>]              -- number of inserts committed at a time
  [-rowTag <rowTagName>]             -- the name for row elements
  [-dateFormat <format>]             -- the format of date elements
  [-withEscaping]                    -- if necessary do SQL-XML name escaping
  [-ignoreCase]                      -- ignore the case of the tag names
  [-preserveWhitespace]              -- preserves any whitespaces
  [-setXSLT <URI>]                   -- XSLT to apply to XML doc
  [-setXSLTRef <URI>]                -- external entity reference for XSLT doc
  [-fileName fileName |              -- the XML document file name  or
   -URL url |                        - URL   or
   -xmlDoc <XMLDocumentString>]      - XML string
  <tableName>                        -- the table name to put into
```

Entering *java OracleXML getXML -user scott/tiger "select * from emp"* at the command-line produces a DTD for the EMP table and an XML document containing the data in the EMP table. The table columns become tags. Now that's pretty cool, isn't it?

Defining the OracleXMLStore Class

The *OracleXMLStore class* is a noncommand-line executable utility, which is intended to be loaded into the database and wrapped by PL/SQL, but may also be called by other Java functions. The OracleXMLStore utility is the Java portion of the server-side front-end of the Oracle XML SQL utility.

Defining the OracleXMLQuery Class

The OracleXMLQuery class is the API used to generate XML documents from a query or JDBC ResultSet. The OracleXMLQuery class enables you to set the markup tags enclosing a record, as well as setting the case of the tags. The API returns an XML string or a DOM object. The DOM object can either be attached to a node passed to the API or it can be stand-alone.

The following Java example queries the EMP table in the SCOTT schema using the OracleXMLQuery API:

```
// QueryXML.java
import oracle.xml.sql.query.OracleXMLQuery;
import oracle.jdbc.driver.*;
import oracle.sql.*;
import java.sql.*;

public class QueryXML{
 public static void main(String args[]){
   try{
    DriverManager.registerDriver(new oracle.jdbc.driver.OracleDriver());
    Connection conn =
riverManager.getConnection("jdbc:oracle:oci8:@","scott","tiger");
    OracleXMLQuery query = new OracleXMLQuery(conn,
                  "select * from emp where deptno='20'");
    System.out.println(query.getXMLString());
    query.close();
   }catch(Exception e){
       System.out.println("Error:"+e.getMessage());
   }
 }
}
```

This code returns the following result:

```
<?xml version = '1.0'?>
<ROWSET>
    <ROW num="1">
        <EMPNO>7369</EMPNO>
        <ENAME>SMITH</ENAME>
        <JOB>CLERK</JOB>
        <MGR>7902</MGR>
        <HIREDATE>12/17/1980 0:0:0</HIREDATE>
        <SAL>800</SAL>
        <DEPTNO>20</DEPTNO>
    </ROW>
    <ROW num="2">
        <EMPNO>7566</EMPNO>
        <ENAME>JONES</ENAME>
        <JOB>MANAGER</JOB>
        <MGR>7839</MGR>
        <HIREDATE>4/2/1981 0:0:0</HIREDATE>
        <SAL>2975</SAL>
        <DEPTNO>20</DEPTNO>
    </ROW>
...
</ROWSET>
```

Defining the OracleXMLSave Class

The *OracleXMLSave class* is the API used to load data from an XML document into the database. The OracleXMLSave class maps the tag names in the XML document to the column names of the specified table. The OracleXMLSave utility is limited to mapping only the XML document elements to table columns. The OracleXMLSave utility contains methods for inserting, updating, and deleting data based on input from an XML document.

The following Java example saves data to the EMP table in the SCOTT schema using the OracleXMLSave API:

```
// InsertXMLEmp.java
import oracle.xml.sql.dml.OracleXMLSave;
import oracle.jdbc.driver.*;
import oracle.sql.*;
import java.sql.*;

public class InsertXMLEmp{
    // Recommended this be passed in, not hardcoded, this is for
    // demonstration purposes only.
    public static String xmlData = new String(
            "<?xml version = '1.0'?>"+
            "<ROWSET>"+
            "<ROW num='1'>"+
```

```
            "<EMPNO>7369</EMPNO>"+
            "<ENAME>SMITH</ENAME>"+
            "<JOB>CLERK</JOB>"+
            "<MGR>7902</MGR>"+
            "<HIREDATE>12/17/1980 0:0:0</HIREDATE>"+
            "<SAL>800</SAL>"+
            "<DEPTNO>20</DEPTNO>"+
            "</ROW>"+
            "</ROWSET>");
   public static void main(String args[]){
      try{
       DriverManager.registerDriver(new oracle.jdbc.driver.OracleDriver());
       Connection conn = DriverManager.getConnection("jdbc:oracle:oci8:@","scott","tiger");
       OracleXMLSave sav = new OracleXMLSave(conn,"EMP");
       sav.insertXML(xmlData);
       sav.close();
      }catch(Exception e){
          System.out.println("Error:"+e.getMessage());
      }
   }
 }
 }
```

Defining the xmlgen PL/SQL Package

The *xmlgen package* wraps the OracleXMLStore class. The functions in the xmlgen
package can be executed from SQL and PL/SQL. For example, here is the definition
for the employee table:

```
Name                              Null?    Type
------------------------------- -------- ----
 EMPLOYEE_ID                     NOT NULL NUMBER(4)
 LAST_NAME                                VARCHAR2(15)
 FIRST_NAME                               VARCHAR2(15)
 MIDDLE_INITIAL                           VARCHAR2(1)
 JOB_ID                                   NUMBER(3)
 MANAGER_ID                               NUMBER(4)
 HIRE_DATE                                DATE
 SALARY                                   NUMBER(7,2)
 COMMISSION                               NUMBER(7,2)
 DEPARTMENT_ID                            NUMBER(2)
```

Now, let's use getxml for the employee table (from SQL*Plus):

```
SQL> select xmlgen.getXML('select * from employee')
2>    from dual;
```

Here's the output from SQL*Plus:

```
XMLGEN.GETXML('SELECT*FROMEMPLOYEE')
----------------------------------------------------------------
<?xml version="1.0"?>
```

```
<ROWSET>
 <ROW num="1">
  <EMPLOYEE_ID>7369</EMPLOYEE_ID>
  <LAST_NAME>SMITH</LAST_NAME>
  <FIRST_NAME>JOHN</FIRST_NAME>
  <MIDDLE_INITIAL>Q</MIDDLE_INITIAL>
  <JOB_ID>667</JOB_ID>
  <MANAGER_ID>7902</MANAGER_ID>
  <HIRE_DATE>1984-12-17 00:00:00.0</HIRE_DATE>
  <SALARY>800</SALARY>
  <DEPARTMENT_ID>20</DEPARTMENT_ID>
 </ROW>
 <ROW num="2">
  <EMPLOYEE_ID>7499</EMPLOYEE_ID>
  <LAST_NAME>ALLEN</LAST_NAME>
  <FIRST_NAME>KEVIN</FIRST_NAME>
  <MIDDLE_INITIAL>J</MIDDLE_INITIAL>
  <JOB_ID>670</JOB_ID>
  <MANAGER_ID>7698</MANAGER_ID>
  <HIRE_DATE>1985-02-20 00:00:00.0</HIRE_DATE>
  <SALARY>1600</SALARY>
  <COMMISSION>300</COMMISSION>
  <DEPARTMENT_ID>30</DEPARTMENT_ID>
 </ROW>
...
</ROWSET>
```

The following procedure, called *xsqldemo,* processes the XML and displays the data in this example:

```
CREATE OR REPLACE PROCEDURE XSQLDemo AS
        xmlString CLOB;
        amount integer:= 255;
        position integer := 1;
        charString varchar2(255);
        i binary_integer;
        inclDTD number := 0;
BEGIN
        xmlString := xmlgen.getXML('select * from employee where
                                rownum < 3');
        dbms_lob.open(xmlString,DBMS_LOB.LOB_READONLY);
        loop
            dbms_lob.read(xmlString,amount,position,charString);
            dbms_output.put_line(charString);
            position := position + amount;
        end loop;
EXCEPTION
   when no_data_found then
```

```
        dbms_lob.close(xmlString);
        dbms_lob.freetemporary(xmlString);
END;
/
```

The xsqldemo procedure yields the following results when executed from SQL*Plus:

```
SQL> exec xsqldemo

<?xml version="1.0"?>
<ROWSET>
 <ROW num="1">
  <EMPLOYEE_ID>7369</EMPLOYEE_ID>

<LAST_NAME>SMITH</LAST_NAME>
 <FIRST_NAME>JOHN</FIRST_NAME>
  <MIDDLE_INITIAL>Q</MIDDLE_INITIAL>

<JOB_ID>667</JOB_ID>
  <MANAGER_ID>7902</MANAGER_ID>
  <HIRE_DATE>1984-12-17 00:00:00.0</HIRE_DATE>
  <SALARY>800</SALARY>
  <DEPARTMENT_ID>20</DEPARTMENT_ID>
 </ROW>
 <ROW num="2">
  <EMPLOYEE_ID>7499</EMPLOYEE_ID>
  <LAST_NAME>ALLEN</LAST_NAME>

<FIRST_NAME>KEVIN</FIRST_NAME>
  <MIDDLE_INITIAL>J</MIDDLE_INITIAL>
  <JOB_ID>670</JOB_ID>
  <MANAGER_ID>7698</MANAGER_ID>
  <HIRE_DATE>1985-02-20 00:00:00.0</HIRE_DATE>

<SALARY>1600</SALARY>
  <COMMISSION>300</COMMISSION>
  <DEPARTMENT_ID>30</DEPARTMENT_ID>

</ROW>
</ROWSET>

PL/SQL procedure successfully completed
```

Defining the DBMS_XMLQUERY Package

The DBMS_XMLQUERY package provides a group of procedures and functions that allow data to be extracted or read from database tables in XML format.

The following test_xmlquery procedure queries data from the EMP table and displays the data in SQL*Plus:

```
create or replace procedure test_xmlquery
is
  ctxsql dbms_xmlquery.ctxtype;
  clobvar1 clob;
begin
  -- define the cursor
  ctxsql := dbms_xmlquery.newcontext('SELECT * FROM SCOTT.EMP');
  -- bring back the data
  clobvar1 := dbms_xmlquery.getxml(ctxsql);
  -- print the result
  printclobout(clobvar1);
  -- close the cursor
  dbms_xmlquery.closecontext(ctxsql);
END;
```

The printclobout procedure (a similar example can be found in the Oracle documentation) is listed in the following:

```
create or replace procedure printClobOut
(result IN OUT NOCOPY CLOB)
is
  xmlsubstr varchar2(32767);
  prnline   varchar2(2000);
begin
  xmlsubstr := dbms_lob.substr(result,32767);
  loop
    exit when xmlsubstr is null;
    prnline := substr(xmlsubstr,1,instr(xmlsubstr,chr(10)));
    htp.prn(prnline);
    xmlsubstr := substr(xmlsubstr,instr(xmlsubstr,chr(10))+1);
  end loop;
end;
```

The output from the test_xmlquery procedure is as follows:

```
<?xml version = '1.0'?>
<ROWSET>
   <ROW num="1">
      <EMPNO>7369</EMPNO>
      <ENAME>SMITH</ENAME>
      <JOB>CLERK</JOB>
      <MGR>7902</MGR>
      <HIREDATE>12/17/1980 0:0:0</HIREDATE>
      <SAL>800</SAL>
      <DEPTNO>20</DEPTNO>
```

```
    </ROW>
    <ROW num="2">
        <EMPNO>7499</EMPNO>
        <ENAME>ALLEN</ENAME>
        <JOB>SALESMAN</JOB>
        <MGR>7698</MGR>
        <HIREDATE>2/20/1981 0:0:0</HIREDATE>
        <SAL>2000</SAL>
        <COMM>300</COMM>
        <DEPTNO>10</DEPTNO>
    </ROW>
...
</ROWSET>
```

Defining the DBMS_XMLSAVE Package

The *dbms_xmlsave package* provides a group of procedures and functions that
enable the user to read the contents of an XML document and insert, update, or
delete data in database tables based on content within that XML document.

The DBMS_XMLSAVE package contains a number of objects. First, you call
the newContext(targetTable) procedure, and then the insertXML, updateXML or
deleteXML procedure. Finally, you need to call the closeContext procedure. For
example:

```
create or replace procedure test_xmlsave (in_xml varchar2)
is
  ctxsql    dbms_xmlsave.ctxtype;
  results number;
begin
  -- define the cursor
  ctxsql := dbms_xmlsave.newcontext('EMP');
  -- bring back the data
  results := dbms_xmlsave.insertXML(ctxsql, in_xml);
  -- close the cursor
  dbms_xmlsave.closecontext(ctxsql);
END;
```

When you call the above test_xmlsave procedure passing in XML for the emp
table, the employee record is inserted into the database. This is power!

The Power of the
Oracle XSQL Servlet

The *Oracle XSQL Servlet* is a Java servlet. The Oracle XSQL Servlet enables the
user to easily create dynamic XML documents based on queries. The Oracle XSQL

Servlet also enables the user to transform the resulting XML document using XSLT. The Oracle XSQL Servlet is included and configured for immediate use as part of standard 9*i*AS install. The Oracle XSQL Servlet can be used with any Web server that supports Java servlets. The following sections contain a basic overview of the XSQL Servlet. Complete documentation for the Oracle XSQL Servlet can be found in the *Oracle9i Application Developer's Guide—XML*.

XSQL is a servlet that processes an XML document with SQL queries embedded in it and that produces another XML document with the results. This tool is written in Java and uses the XML Parser for Java and the XML SQL utility to perform many of its operations. It can be run from any Web server that supports Java servlets and uses the HTTP protocol as its transport mechanism.

XSQL combines the power of SQL, XML, and XSLT in the server. Because XSQL runs on the server, XSQL can perform the following duties:

- Receive Web-based requests from any client.

- Query logical views of data anywhere.

- Return the results of queries in the form of XML anywhere on the Web.

- Optionally transform the XML into other XML or HTML.

What follows is an example of a basic XML document with XSQL embedded.

```
<?xml version="1.0" encoding="UTF-8"?>
<xsql:query xmlns:xsql="urn:oracle-xsql connection="tusc">
        SELECT NAME
                FROM EMP
            WHERE TITLE='CHAIRMAN'
</xsql:query>
```

If this was an actual XML document, the query would be processed and the result would look like this:

```
<?xml version="1.0"?>
        <ROWSET>
                <ROW id="1">
                        <NAME> Brad Brown</NAME>
                </ROW>
        </ROWSET>
```

Technically, what happens is this:

1. The user enters a URL in their browser, which gets passed to the XSQL Servlet through a Java Web server. This URL contains the name of the target .xsql file and any other parameters.

2. The XSQL Servlet passes the XSQL file to the XML parser, which obviously parses the XML and creates an API for accessing the contents of the XML.

3. The XSQL Page processor then uses the API to pass the SQL statement to Oracle's XML SQL utility.

4. The XML SQL utility sends the query to the database and receives back the results.

5. The results are returned to the XSLT processor, which embeds the data in the XML in the same location as the <xsql:query> tags.

6. XSLT then sends the final XML document back to the user.

In this example, there was only one query, but any number of <xsql:query> elements can exist. For the query to be processed, the connection entry, connection="tusc", must match exactly an entry in a file named XSQLConfig.xml.

The xml document can be dynamically generated or it can be stored in an .xsql file and used again and again. This .xsql file is a template known as an *Oracle XSQL page.* An XSQL page file enables anyone familiar with SQL to assemble dynamic XML data pages based on the query or queries in the page file. Oracle XSQL pages can be used a number of different ways: you can call them from the Web via the XSQL Servlet on your Web server, use the XSQL command line utility in a batch program, call them from a java program using the XSQLRequest.process() method, or call them through a Java Server Page. The following illustration depicts the architecture of the XSQL Servlet:

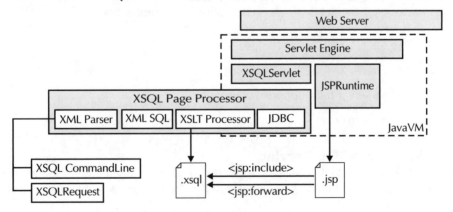

XSLT is a process used for transforming an XML document into one or more other XML documents, or transforming the XML into HTML. The transformation takes place by using a language known as XPATH. *XPATH* is similar to other programming languages in that it uses a series of commands to specify what should be done with the XML. The commands are stored in an .xslt file and used by the XSLT processor. The name of the .xslt file to use to perform any necessary transformations is supplied by the user as a parameter in the URL. A possible use of XSLT would be this: if an application is talking to a cellular phone using WML, it might need to transform the XML generated into WML or other similar standard suitable for communicating with the cellular phone. The name of the style sheet is included in the XML document in an entry that would look something like this: <?xml-stylesheet type="text/xsl" href="*name.xsl*"?>. XSLT is a subject all its own and many good books devoted only to XSLT programming are available.

TIP
TUSC has developed an application using Java Server Pages (JSP) that queries the data dictionary for schema, tables/views, columns, and the like. The output of this JSP application is it writes a series of XSQL and XSLT files. Search TUSC's site for "The Power of XML" for the complete article and the code for this application.

Examining Oracle XSQL Servlet Dependencies and Requirements

Let's look quickly at the Oracle XSQL Servlet dependencies and requirements.

Defining XSQL Servlet Dependencies

The Oracle XSQL Servlet depends on the following components:

- The Oracle XML Parser for Java V2

- The Oracle XML SQL utilities for Java

- A Web server that supports Java servlets

- A JDBC driver

Installing the XSQL Servlet

The Oracle XSQL Servlet classes are located in a .jar file named oraclexsql.jar. The .jar file must be added to the CLASSPATH of the Web server executing the servlet.

Setting Up the Connection Document

For the servlet to connect to the database, it needs to have connection data. The servlet obtains connection data through an XML document, called XSQLConfig.xml.

The following example illustrates the structure and content of the connection definition section of the XSQLConfig.xml file:

```
<connectiondefs>
  <connection name="demo">
    <username>scott</username>
    <password>tiger</password>
    <dburl>jdbc:oracle:thin:@your-server-machine:your-port:your-
    SID</dburl>
  </connection>
  <connection name="xmldemo">
    <username>xmldemo</username>
    <password>xmldemo</password>
    <dburl>jdbc:oracle:thin:@localhost:1521:ORCL</dburl>
  </connection>
</connectiondefs>
```

The connection document needs to be in the root directory of the Web server.

Generating a Dynamic XML Document

The following example demonstrates how the Oracle XSQL Servlet generates a dynamic XML document based on a query. The query is executed from a Web environment and, therefore, must be submitted in the following employeelist.xsql XML document format:

```
<?xml version="1.0"?>
<query connection  = "demo"
       doc-element = "employee-list"
       row-element = "employee"
       tag-case    = "lower">
     SELECT first_name,last_name FROM employee WHERE rownum
       BETWEEN 1 and 6
</query>
```

This document will be saved as file employeelist.xsql. Executing the file from an XML-enabled Web browser produces an XML document based on the query given between <query> tags. Figure 8-3 illustrates the resulting document in MS Internet Explorer 5.

Transcoding with XSQL

XSQL can be used to generate output to any number of devices. XSQL converts XML into the respective display device's (that is, media) required output format.

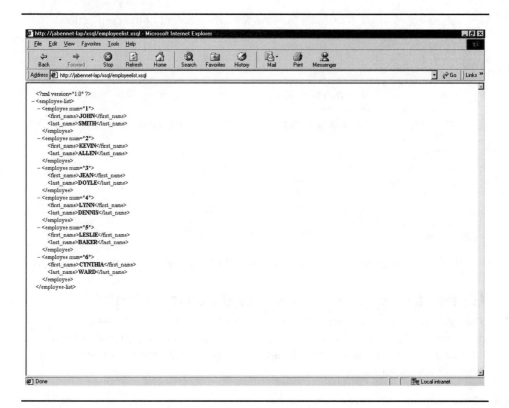

FIGURE 8-3. *Employee List in XML*

The following example is similar to an Oracle sample. Note the media attribute, which determines the XSLT (XML Stylesheet) to be used by the following flight.xsql file:

```
<?xml version="1.0"?>
<?xml-stylesheet type="text/xsl" media="Mozilla" href="FlyHTML.xsl"?>
<?xml-stylesheet type="text/xsl" media="MSIE 5.0" href="FlyHTML.xsl"?>
<?xml-stylesheet type="text/xsl" media="Motorola Voice Browser" href="FlyVox.xsl"?>
<?xml-stylesheet type="text/xsl" media="UP.Browser" href="FlyWML.xsl"?>
<?xml-stylesheet type="text/xsl" media="HandHTTP"
                  href="FlyPP.xsl"?>
<?xml-stylesheet type="text/xsl" href="FlyHTMLdefault.xsl"?>

<flightFinderResult xmlns:xsql="urn:oracle-xsql"
                    connection="fly" lang="english">
  <xsql:set-stylesheet-param name="lang" value="{@lang}"/>
    <pageTitle>Flight Finder</pageTitle>
  <xsql:query tag-case="upper">
    <![CDATA[ select F.code, F.code_from, A1.name as "depart_airport",
              F.code_to, To_char(F.schedule, 'HH24:MI') as "Sched",
```

```
                           A2.name as "arrive_airport",
                           Decode(F.Status, 'A', 'Available',
                                  'B', 'Full', 'Available') as "Stat", F.Gate
      from flights F, airports A1,  airports A2
      where to_number(To_Char(F.schedule, 'HH24MI')) >
              to_number(To_Char(sysdate, 'HH24MI'))
              and F.code_from = '{@FROM}' and F.code_to = '{@TO}'
              and F.code_from = A1.code and F.code_to = A2.code]]>
<xsql:no-rows-query>
      Select 'No more flights today from ' ||
             '{@FROM}' || ' to ' || '{@TO}' "Sorry" from dual
      </xsql:no-rows-query>
   </xsql:query>

<!-- Begin booking stuff -->
  <form action="bookres.xsql" method="post">
    <field name="CustomerName">
      <xsql:query rowset-element="dropDownList"
                  row-element="listElem">
        <![CDATA[select unique name as "listItem"
                from customers order by name ]]>
      </xsql:query>
    </field>
    <field name="FlightCode">
      <xsql:query rowset-element="dropDownList"
                  row-element="listElem">
        <![CDATA[ select F.code as "listItem",
                         F.code as "itemId",
                         A1.name as "depart_airport",
                         A2.name as "arrive_airport"
                  from flights F, airports A1, airports A2
                  where to_number(To_Char(F.schedule, 'HH24MI')) >
                        to_number(To_Char(sysdate, 'HH24MI'))
                  and F.code_from = '{@FROM}'
                  and F.code_to = '{@TO}'
                  and F.code_from = A1.code
                  and F.code_to = A2.code]]>
      </xsql:query>
</field>
    <sendRequest type="button" label="OK"/>
  </form>
<!-- End booking stuff -->
  <returnHome>index.xsql</returnHome>
</flightFinderResult>
```

The document is dynamically presented in different formats dependent on the stylesheet applied and based on the type of browser used (html, wml, and so forth).

XML and Advanced Queuing

Wouldn't it be nice to have a quick way to identify, describe, and exchange data? If only our data could identify itself. Yes, I'm talking about intelligent data. With XML, we have just that. Our applications and databases no longer have to create their own protocol to receive or send data to and from a database or application.

This section walks you through a business-to-business (B2B) application in Oracle. Our B2B application takes orders from users in XML format and passes back a response when the order is picked up and is being delivered. The response is also an XML document.

The Order XML documents are enqueued on the Order inbound queue in the database. We then dequeue the XML document, parse and process the contents, and place a response XML document on the Order outbound queue.

Here's a sample of an ItemOrder.xml document that passes in and out of the database when placed on the message queues:

```
<?xml version="1.0" encoding="UTF-8"?>
<ItemOrder itemId="12345-genA">
        <Name>Generator typeB</Name>
        <Cost>45,000</Cost>
        <Quantity>1</Quantity>
        <Vendor>Acme Generators</Vendor>
</ItemOrder>
```

Message-Oriented Middleware (MOM)

Message-oriented middleware will help you with the task of connecting your applications across unlike environments. This is accomplished by communicating through queues. One program writes to the queue and another program (or series of programs) read from the queue. MOM is defined as when products provide an assured, asyncronous, and connectionless method to exchange messages between processes. Advanced Queuing (AQ) in Oracle allows for the creation and management of message queues. For our Order Entry B2B application, we'll create three message queues. Our three queues will be called:

- **Order_inbound_Q**   The queue that accepts orders.

- **Order_outbound_Q**   The queue that sends out order statuses.

- **Order_exception_Q**   The queue that holds any orders/statuses that cannot be processed.

Advanced Queuing Features

To understand Oracle's Message-Enabled AQ feature, you need to be familiar with three AQ terms: enqueue, dequeue, and propagation.

- To *enqueue* a message is to place the message on queue.

- To *dequeue* a message is to take a message off a queue.

■ To *propagate* a message is to allow for automated coordination of enqueuing and dequeuing operations. A message can be placed in a message queue and the message then automatically dequeues and propagates to a local or remote recipient's queue.

AQ Terms and Definitions

Here is a list of terms you should also be familiar with when attempting to understand Oracle's AQ System:

■ **Message**   The smallest unit of work in the queue, consisting of the control information (metadata) and the payload (the data supplied by the user).

■ **Queue**   The storage space for a message.

■ **Queue Table**   A database table that holds one or more queues.

■ **Agent**   A user of a queue.

■ **Recipient list**   A list of one or more agents or queues you can construct to receive a message through the dequeue operation.

■ **Producer**   An agent that places messages in a queue with the enqueue operation.

■ **Consumer**   An agent that retrieves messages from a queue with the dequeue operation.

■ **Message ID**   A unique handle for a message.

■ **Message group**   One or more messages joined together logically as a group.

■ **Queue monitor**   A background process that monitors the status of a message on queue.

Order_TRANSPORT_Object

The creation of the order_transport_object object is accomplished by using Oracle's CREATE TYPE xx AS OBJECT DDL database statement. The order_transport_object has three methods that enable the developer to dequeue objects and enqueue objects or exception messages. The creation of the order_transport_object object is as follows:

```
CREATE OR REPLACE TYPE order_transport_object AS OBJECT (
    contents              VARCHAR2(30)
```

```
  , DTD_name                VARCHAR2(30)
  , operation               VARCHAR2(30)
  , destination             VARCHAR2(100)
  , transport_clob          CLOB
  , MEMBER FUNCTION enqueue ( p_queue_name IN VARCHAR2 ) RETURN RAW
  , MEMBER PROCEDURE enqueue_exception (
        p_queue_name IN VARCHAR2, p_msg_id OUT VARCHAR2)
  , MEMBER PROCEDURE dequeue ( p_queue_name IN VARCHAR2 )
);
/

CREATE OR REPLACE TYPE BODY order_transport_object AS
  MEMBER FUNCTION enqueue ( p_queue_name IN VARCHAR2 ) RETURN RAW AS
    v_enq_opt           dbms_aq.enqueue_options_t;
    v_msg_prop          dbms_aq.message_properties_t;
    v_msg_handle        raw(16);
  BEGIN
      v_msg_prop.exception_queue := 'ORDER_EXCEPTION_Q';
      dbms_aq.enqueue
        (
          queue_name            => p_queue_name
        , enqueue_options       => v_enq_opt
        , message_properties    => v_msg_prop
        , payload               => self
        , msgid                 => v_msg_handle
        );

      RETURN v_msg_handle;
  END enqueue;

  MEMBER PROCEDURE enqueue_exception
        ( p_queue_name IN VARCHAR2, p_msg_id OUT VARCHAR2) AS
    v_enq_opt           dbms_aq.enqueue_options_t;
    v_msg_prop          dbms_aq.message_properties_t;
    v_msg_handle        raw(16);
  BEGIN
      dbms_aq.enqueue
        (
          queue_name            => p_queue_name
        , enqueue_options       => v_enq_opt
        , message_properties    => v_msg_prop
        , payload               => self
        , msgid                 => v_msg_handle
        );
      p_msg_id := rawtohex(v_msg_handle);
  END enqueue_exception;

  MEMBER PROCEDURE dequeue ( p_queue_name IN VARCHAR2 ) AS
```

```
    v_enq_opt            dbms_aq.enqueue_options_t;
    v_msg_prop           dbms_aq.message_properties_t;
    v_dequeue_options dbms_aq.dequeue_options_t;
    v_msg_handle         raw(16);
BEGIN
    dbms_aq.dequeue
    (
       queue_name            => p_queue_name,
       dequeue_options       => v_dequeue_options,
       message_properties  => v_msg_prop,
       payload               => self,
       msgid                => v_msg_handle
    );
  END dequeue;
END;
```

Setting Up Oracle's AQ System

Five basic steps are involved in setting Oracle's AQ system.

1. Install Oracle AQ for use in your database and set the following INITxx.ORA parameters.

   - **AQ_TM_PROCESSES=N**   Used to create *N* number of Queue Monitors

   - **JOB_QUEUE_PROCESSES=N**   Used to set the *N* number of Jobs allowed to run at a time. AQ requires this number to be set to at least 2

2. **COMPATIBLE = 8.0.4.0.0**   Required by Oracle AQ propagation process. This is checked by the DBMS_AQADM package when certain components in the package are used. Authorize administrative and operational privileges on queues. We'll use ORDER_MANAGER as User.

   - Create an AQ administrator and an AQ user

   - GRANT AQ_ADMINISTRATOR_ROLE to ORDER_MANAGER

   - GRANT connect to ORDER_MANAGER

   - GRANT RESOURCE to ORDER_MANAGER

   - EXECUTE dbms_aqadm.grant_type_access('ORDER_MANAGER')

   - GRANT execute on DBMS_AQADM to ORDER_MANAGER

3. GRANT execute on DBMS_AQ to ORDER_MANAGER. Set up the message queue tables and corresponding queues.

Now, let's create your queues, queue tables, and subscribers to store and forward your XML datagrams. Also, start your queues and verify the creation of queues from the user_queues tables.

```
-- Create Queue Tables
begin
dbms_aqadm.create_queue_table
    (
      queue_table          =>  'Order_Inbound_Q_TBL'
    , queue_payload_type  =>  'order_transport_object'
    , multiple_consumers  =>  TRUE
    , auto_commit          =>  FALSE
    , message_grouping     =>  dbms_aqadm.NONE
    , comment              =>  'Order inbound queue table. Created on '
                              || to_char( SYSDATE, 'MON-DD-YYYY HH24:MI:SS' )
    );
dbms_aqadm.create_queue_table
    (
      queue_table          =>  'Order_Outbound_Q_TBL'
    , queue_payload_type  =>  'order_transport_object'
    , multiple_consumers  =>  TRUE
    , auto_commit          =>  FALSE
    , message_grouping     =>  dbms_aqadm.NONE
    , comment              =>  'Order inbound queue table. Created on '
                              || to_char( SYSDATE, 'MON-DD-YYYY HH24:MI:SS' )
    );
dbms_aqadm.create_queue_table
    (
      queue_table          =>  'Order_Exception_Q_TBL'
    , queue_payload_type  =>  'order_transport_object'
    , multiple_consumers  =>  TRUE
    , auto_commit          =>  FALSE
    , message_grouping     =>  dbms_aqadm.NONE
    , comment              =>  'Order exception queue table. Created on '
                              || to_char( SYSDATE, 'MON-DD-YYYY HH24:MI:SS' )
    );
end;
```

Next, you create the queues:

```
begin
    dbms_aqadm.create_queue
    (
      queue_name          =>  'ORDER_INBOUND_Q'
    , queue_table          =>  'ORDER_INBOUND_Q_TBL'
    , queue_type           =>  DBMS_AQADM.NORMAL_QUEUE
    , retention_time       =>  30 * 24 * 60 * 60
    , comment              =>  'Order Inbound normal queue. Created on '
                              || to_char( SYSDATE, 'MON-DD-YYYY HH24:MI:SS' )
```

```
  , auto_commit          =>   FALSE
  );

  dbms_aqadm.create_queue
  (
    queue_name           =>   'ORDER_OUTBOUND_Q'
  , queue_table          =>   'ORDER_OUTBOUND_Q_TBL'
  , queue_type           =>   DBMS_AQADM.NORMAL_QUEUE
  , retention_time       =>   30 * 24 * 60 * 60
  , comment              =>   'Order Outbound normal queue. Created on '
                              || to_char( SYSDATE, 'MON-DD-YYYY HH24:MI:SS' )
  , auto_commit          =>   FALSE
  );


  dbms_aqadm.create_queue
  (
    queue_name           =>   'ORDER_EXCEPTION_Q'
  , queue_table          =>   'ORDER_EXCEPTION_Q_TBL'
  , queue_type           =>   DBMS_AQADM.NORMAL_QUEUE
  , retention_time       =>   30 * 24 * 60 * 60
  , comment              =>   'Order EXCEPTION normal queue. Created on '
                              || to_char( SYSDATE, 'MON-DD-YYYY HH24:MI:SS' )
  , auto_commit          =>   FALSE
  );
end;
```

Finally, it's time to start the queues:

```
begin
  dbms_aqadm.start_queue
  (
    queue_name           =>  'ORDER_INBOUND_Q'
  , enqueue              =>  TRUE
  , dequeue              =>  TRUE
  );
  dbms_aqadm.start_queue
  (
    queue_name           =>  'ORDER_OUTBOUND_Q'
  , enqueue              =>  TRUE
  , dequeue              =>  TRUE
  );

  dbms_aqadm.start_queue
  (
    queue_name           =>  'ORDER_EXCEPTION_Q'
  , enqueue              =>  TRUE
  , dequeue              =>  TRUE
  );
```

```
end;


  -- Add subscribers
Declare
      v_subscriber          sys.aq$_agent;
begin
   v_subscriber := sys.aq$_agent
    (
      'ORDER_MANAGER'
    , NULL
    , NULL
    );

   dbms_aqadm.add_subscriber
    (
      queue_name => 'ORDER_INBOUND_Q'
    , ssubscriber => v_subscriber
    );

   v_subscriber := sys.aq$_agent
    (
      'ORDER_MANAGER'
    , NULL
    , NULL
    );

   dbms_aqadm.add_subscriber
    (
      queue_name => 'ORDER_OUTBOUND_Q'
    , subscriber => v_subscriber
    );
end;
```

4. Now you're ready to enqueue messages to a queue.

```
DECLARE
      v_my_payload     ORDER_TRANSPORT_OBJECT;
      v_my_clob        CLOB;
      v_msg_id         RAW(16);
BEGIN
   -- Load XML message Data into a CLOB
   v_my_clob :=  xmlgen.getXML('select *
                                FROM order_status
                                WHERE order_id  = 12345', 0);

   -- open the lob
   dbms_lob.open( v_my_clob,DBMS_LOB.LOB_READONLY );
```

```
    -- Instantiate a order_transport_object
    v_my_payload  := ORDER_TRANSPORT_OBJECT ( 'XML',
        'Order_item.dtd', 'INSERT',  'ORDER_MANAGER', v_my_clob);

    -- Place object on queue
    v_msg_id := v_my_pay_load.enqueue('ORDER_INBOUND_Q'  );

-- Close the lob
dbms_lob.close( v_my_clob);
END;
```

5. Dequeue messages from a queue.

```
DECLARE
    v_my_payload  ORDER_TRANSPORT_OBJECT;
    -- xml parameters
    v_parser        xmlparser.parser;
    -- DOM document
    v_dom_document xmldom.DOMDocument;
    -- Message queue options
    v_dequeue_options       dbms_aq.dequeue_options_t;
    v_message_properties    dbms_aq.message_properties_t;
    v_order_obj_handle      RAW(16);
    -- Define exceptions
    no_messages_on_queue EXCEPTION;
    PRAGMA EXCEPTION_INIT( no_messages_on_queue, -25228 );
BEGIN
    v_dequeue_options.navigation    := dbms_aq.FIRST_MESSAGE;
    v_dequeue_options.wait          := dbms_aq.NO_WAIT;
    v_dequeue_options.consumer_name := 'ORDER_MANAGER';
    LOOP
        BEGIN
            dbms_aq.dequeue(queue_name          => 'ORDER_INBOUND_Q',
                            dequeue_options     => v_dequeue_options,
                            message_properties  => v_message_properties,
                            payload             => v_my_payload,
                            msgid               => v_order_obj_handle );
            v_dequeue_options.navigation := DBMS_AQ.NEXT_MESSAGE;
            COMMIT;
        EXCEPTION
            WHEN NO_MESSAGES_ON_QUEUE
            THEN
                dbms_output.put_line( 'Inside exception WHEN ' ||
                  'no_messages_on_queue' ||
                   to_char( SYSDATE, 'dd/mon/yyyy hh:mi:ss' ) );
                -- Exit out of the Loop
                EXIT;
        END;
    END LOOP;
```

```
      -- Create a new Parser
      v_parser := xmlparser.newParser;
      -- Parse XML CLOB
      xmlparser.parseclob( v_parser, v_my_payload.transport_clob );
      -- Get XML DOM document
      v_dom_document := xmlparser.getDocument(v_parser);
   END;
```

Let's look at the new objects you create in the database.

```
SQL> desc order_transport_object;
 Name                                      Null?    Type
 ----------------------------------------- -------- ----------------
 CONTENTS                                           VARCHAR2(30)
 DTD_NAME                                           VARCHAR2(30)
 OPERATION                                          VARCHAR2(30)
 DESTINATION                                        VARCHAR2(100)
 TRANSPORT_CLOB                                     CLOB

METHOD
------
 MEMBER FUNCTION ENQUEUE RETURNS RAW
 Argument Name                  Type                    In/Out Default?
 ------------------------------ ----------------------- ------ --------
 P_QUEUE_NAME                   VARCHAR2                 IN

METHOD
------
 MEMBER PROCEDURE ENQUEUE_EXCEPTION
 Argument Name                  Type                    In/Out Default?
 ------------------------------ ----------------------- ------ --------
 P_QUEUE_NAME                   VARCHAR2                 IN
 P_MSG_ID                       VARCHAR2                 OUT

METHOD
------
 MEMBER PROCEDURE DEQUEUE
 Argument Name                  Type                    In/Out Default?
 ------------------------------ ----------------------- ------ --------
 P_QUEUE_NAME                   VARCHAR2                 IN

SQL>
SQL> desc user_queues;
 Name                                      Null?    Type
 ----------------------------------------- -------- ----------------
 NAME                                      NOT NULL VARCHAR2(30)
 QUEUE_TABLE                               NOT NULL VARCHAR2(30)
 QID                                       NOT NULL NUMBER
```

```
QUEUE_TYPE                                 VARCHAR2(20)
MAX_RETRIES                                NUMBER
RETRY_DELAY                                NUMBER
ENQUEUE_ENABLED                            VARCHAR2(7)
DEQUEUE_ENABLED                            VARCHAR2(7)
RETENTION                                  VARCHAR2(40)
USER_COMMENT                               VARCHAR2(50)


SQL> set heading off
SQL>  select * from user_queues;

AQ$_ORDER_EXCEPTION_Q_TBL_E    ORDER_EXCEPTION_Q_TBL              25542
EXCEPTION_QUEUE                0         0    NO        NO
0
exception queue

AQ$_ORDER_OUTBOUND_Q_TBL_E     ORDER_OUTBOUND_Q_TBL              25530
EXCEPTION_QUEUE                0         0    NO        NO0
exception queue

AQ$_ORDER_INBOUND_Q_TBL_E      ORDER_INBOUND_Q_TBL              25518
EXCEPTION_QUEUE                0         0    NO        NO
0

exception queue

ORDER_EXCEPTION_Q              ORDER_EXCEPTION_Q_TBL             25546
NORMAL_QUEUE                   0         0    YES       YES
2592000
Order EXCEPTION normal queue. Created on JUL-14-20

ORDER_OUTBOUND_Q              ORDER_OUTBOUND_Q_TBL              25545
NORMAL_QUEUE                   0         0    YES       YES
2592000
Order Outbound normal queue. Created on JUL-14-200

ORDER_INBOUND_Q               ORDER_INBOUND_Q_TBL              25544

NORMAL_QUEUE                   0         0    YES       YES
2592000
Order Inbound normal queue. Created on JUL-14-2001


6 rows selected.

SQL>
SQL> select * from tab;
```

```
AQ$ORDER_EXCEPTION_Q_TBL        VIEW
AQ$ORDER_INBOUND_Q_TBL          VIEW
AQ$ORDER_OUTBOUND_Q_TBL         VIEW
AQ$_ORDER_EXCEPTION_Q_TBL_I     TABLE
AQ$_ORDER_INBOUND_Q_TBL_I       TABLE
AQ$_ORDER_OUTBOUND_Q_TBL_I      TABLE
CREATE$JAVA$LOB$TABLE           TABLE
JAVA$CLASS$MD5$TABLE            TABLE
ORDER_EXCEPTION_Q_TBL           TABLE
ORDER_INBOUND_Q_TBL             TABLE
ORDER_ITEM                      TABLE
ORDER_OUTBOUND_Q_TBL            TABLE
ORDER_STATUS                    TABLE
SYS_IOT_OVER_25515              TABLE
SYS_IOT_OVER_25527              TABLE
SYS_IOT_OVER_25539              TABLE

16 rows selected.
SQL>
Queuing  XML Documents
```

Now, let's create a procedure that enables your users to put an XML document on the inbound queue. This procedure can be called by any outside source that has an XML document to put on queue. Use your JDBC or ODBC driver to call put_xml_on_que(..).

```
CREATE OR REPLACE PROCEDURE
   put_xml_on_queue     (
      p_obj_sequence_id IN OUT number,
      p_xml_string      IN VARCHAR2,
      p_dtd_name        IN VARCHAR2,
      p_operation       IN VARCHAR2,
      p_contents        IN VARCHAR2 DEFAULT 'xml',
      p_destination     IN VARCHAR2 DEFAULT 'ORDER_MANAGER')
IS
   -- Define constants
   c_start           CONSTANT NUMBER := 1;
   -- Define variables
   v_my_payload      ORDER_TRANSPORT_OBJECT;
   v_clob            CLOB := NULL;
   v_length          NUMBER;
   v_msg_id          RAW(16);
   v_string          VARCHAR2(32767);
   v_obj_sequence_id NUMBER;
BEGIN
  v_string := p_xml_string;
  v_length := length(v_string);
```

```
dbms_lob.createtemporary(v_clob,TRUE);
IF p_operation = 'INSERT'
THEN
   -- Get a new orderId from a sequence generator.  Ours is called
   -- new_obj_sequence_id  and it is simply a function we created
   -- in the database that returns a new sequence.
   p_obj_sequence_id := 12; -- new_obj_sequence_id();
END IF;
dbms_lob.writeappend(v_clob,v_length,v_string);
v_my_payload  := ORDER_TRANSPORT_OBJECT (  'XML',
      P_DTD_NAME, P_OPERATION,
P_DESTINATION, V_CLOB );
   -- Place object on queue
  v_msg_id := v_my_payload.enqueue('ORDER_INBOUND_Q'  );

END put_xml_on_queue;
```

Dequeuing the XML Document from the Message Queue

If you look at the Order_inbound_q_tbl now, you can see your XML message queued up.

```
select user_data
from order_manager.order_inbound_q_tbl
where deq_time is null;
```

You have to dequeue the message, parse the XML document, and insert the order into the Order table in the database.

```
CREATE OR REPLACE PROCEDURE order_inbound_dequeuer
IS
   -- Define constants
   p_queue_name          CONSTANT VARCHAR2(30) := 'ORDER_INBOUND_Q';
   -- Define general variables
   v_charString          VARCHAR2(4000);
   lv_exception_q_name   VARCHAR2( 50 ) :=
        'ORDER_MANAGER.ORDER_EXCEPTION_Q';
   charString            VARCHAR2(4000);
   v_exception_id        RAW(16);
   exception_id          VARCHAR2(32);
   v_sysdate             DATE := sysdate;
   xmlString             CLOB := null;
   v_xml_doc             CLOB;
   v_amount              INTEGER := 80;
```

```
    v_position              INTEGER := 1;
    amount                  INTEGER:= 4000;
    position                INTEGER := 1;
    dequeue_options         dbms_aq.dequeue_options_t;
    message_properties      dbms_aq.message_properties_t;
    l_order_obj_handle      RAW(16);
    l_order_obj             order_transport_object;
    l_order_obj_nodata      order_transport_object;
    v_msg_id                RAW(16);
    lv_return_status        NUMBER;
    v_clob_key              NUMBER;

    -- xml parameters
    p   xmlparser.parser;
    doc xmldom.DOMDocument;
    -- Define exceptions
    e_security_context_violation EXCEPTION;
    no_messages_on_queue EXCEPTION;
    invalid_transport_object EXCEPTION;
    PRAGMA EXCEPTION_INIT(e_security_context_violation, -20007);
    PRAGMA EXCEPTION_INIT( no_messages_on_queue, -25228 );
    PRAGMA EXCEPTION_INIT( invalid_transport_object, -20010 );
BEGIN
    dequeue_options.navigation      := dbms_aq.FIRST_MESSAGE;
    dequeue_options.wait            := dbms_aq.NO_WAIT;
    dequeue_options.consumer_name   := 'ORDER_MANAGER';
  LOOP
    BEGIN
        dbms_aq.dequeue(queue_name => p_queue_name,
                        dequeue_options => dequeue_options,
                        message_properties => message_properties,
                        payload => l_order_obj,
                        msgid => l_order_obj_handle );
        dequeue_options.navigation := DBMS_AQ.NEXT_MESSAGE;
        COMMIT;
    EXCEPTION
      WHEN NO_MESSAGES_ON_QUEUE
      THEN
        dbms_output.put_line( 'Inside exception WHEN
                        no_messages_on_queue' ||
                        to_char( SYSDATE, 'dd/mon/yyyy hh:mi:ss' ) );
        -- Exit out of the Loop
        EXIT;
    END;
    BEGIN
        -- Check for XML contents
        IF ( lower( l_order_obj.CONTENTS ) = 'xml')
        THEN
          -- Always commit when dequeuing - errors will be placed on
```

```
                    --  the exception_q
                    -- This procedure will be created in the Parsing
                    -- XML section below.
                      ORDER_XML_INBOUND_PARSER ( l_order_obj,l_order_obj_handle);
                ELSE
                    l_order_obj.enqueue_exception (lv_exception_q_name,
                                                   exception_id );
                    dbms_output.put_line( 'Object contents are unknown !' ||
                        to_char( SYSDATE, 'dd/mon/yyyy hh:mi:ss' ) );
                END IF;
        EXCEPTION
            WHEN INVALID_TRANSPORT_OBJECT
            THEN
                dbms_output.put_line ('EXCEPTION when INVALID_TRANSPORT ');
            WHEN OTHERS
            THEN
                dbms_output.put_line ('EXCEPTION when others order_
                                    inbound_dequeuer' );
                ROLLBACK;
                DBMS_LOB.CREATETEMPORARY( v_XML_DOC,TRUE );
                dbms_lob.copy(v_XML_DOC, l_order_obj.TRANSPORT_CLOB,
                            dbms_lob.getlength(l_order_obj.TRANSPORT_CLOB));
                l_order_obj.TRANSPORT_CLOB := v_xml_doc;
                DBMS_LOB.FREETEMPORARY(v_xml_doc);
                v_exception_id := hextoraw(exception_id);
                l_order_obj.enqueue_exception
                        (lv_exception_q_name,v_exception_id );
            COMMIT;
        END;
    END LOOP;
    COMMIT;
EXCEPTION
    WHEN OTHERS
    THEN
        dbms_output.put_line ('EXCEPTION when others order_queue_manager');
END order_inbound_dequeuer;
```

Parsing XML

Now, let's put an XML document on your order_inbound_q, so you can dequeue
the document and insert the data into the database. You'll be inserting the data into
a table called ORDER_ITEM. Here's the create statement for the order_item table.
You'll also be using an order_status table.

```
-- Table order_item
create table  order_item
      ( order_id number,
```

```
        item_id number,
        name varchar2(30),
        cost number,
        quantity number,
        vendor varchar2(30) );
-- Table order_status
create table  order_status
        (ORDER_STATUS_ID   NUMBER,
         ORDER_ID          NUMBER,
         NAME              VARCHAR2(60),
         COST              NUMBER,
         QUANTITY          NUMBER,
         ORDERED           DATE,
         SENT              DATE,
         RECEIVED          DATE,
         STATUS            NUMBER );
```

You place your item order XML document on the order_inbound_q by using the put_xml_on_queue( ) procedure and passing in the following values:

```
declare
    v_sequence number := 1;
    v_XML_string   varchar(4000);
begin
    dbms_output.enable( 2000000 );
    v_XML_string := '<?xml version="1.0" encoding="UTF-8"?>' ||
                    '<ItemOrder itemId="12345-genA">' ||
                    '<Name>Generator typeB</Name>' ||
                    '<Cost>45,000</Cost>' ||
                    '<Quantity>1</Quantity>' ||
                    '<Vendor>Acme Generators</Vendor>' ||
                    '</ItemOrder>';
    dbms_output.put_line ( v_xml_string );
    put_xml_on_queue (v_sequence, v_XML_string, 'ORDER_ITEM.dtd',
'INSERT', 'XML', 'ORDER_MANAGER' );
end;
```

To look at your XML document on queue, enter the following statement. Notice you have to select from the order_inbound_q_tbl, instead of order_inbound_q. The queue tables are where the messages persist.

```
SQL> desc order_inbound_q_tbl;
 Name                                     Null?     Type
 Q_NAME                 VARCHAR2(30)
  MSGID                 NOT NULL RAW(16)
  CORRID                VARCHAR2(128)
  PRIORITY              NUMBER
  STATE                 NUMBER
```

```
DELAY                 DATE
EXPIRATION            NUMBER
TIME_MANAGER_INFO     DATE
LOCAL_ORDER_NO        NUMBER
CHAIN_NO              NUMBER
CSCN                  NUMBER
DSCN                  NUMBER
ENQ_TIME              DATE
ENQ_UID               NUMBER
ENQ_TID               VARCHAR2(30)
DEQ_TIME              DATE
DEQ_UID               NUMBER
DEQ_TID               VARCHAR2(30)
RETRY_COUNT           NUMBER
EXCEPTION_QSCHEMA     VARCHAR2(30)
EXCEPTION_QUEUE       VARCHAR2(30)
STEP_NO               NUMBER
RECIPIENT_KEY         NUMBER
DEQUEUE_MSGID         RAW(16)
REFCOUNT             NUMBER
HISTORY               SYS.AQ$_HISTORY
USER_DATA
ORDER_TRANSPORT_OBJECT
SQL> select enq_time, user_data from order_inbound_q_tbl
where deq_time is null;
16-JUL-01
ORDER_TRANSPORT_OBJECT('XML', 'ORDER_ITEM.dtd', 'INSERT',
'ORDER_MANAGER', '< It
emOrder order_Id=12345 > < Item itemId=12345-genA > < Name>Generator
typeB</')
```

Now, you use your order_inbound_dequeuer to take the order XML document off the order_inbound_q and to pass it to the ORDER_XML_INBOUND_PARSER procedure.

```
CREATE OR REPLACE PROCEDURE Order_XML_inbound_parser
           (p_order_object IN  order_transport_object
           ,p_order_dtd    IN  RAW )
   IS
      -- Define general variables
      j                     NUMBER;
      v_execute_string      VARCHAR2(32000);
      v_length              NUMBER;
      v_sql_statement       VARCHAR2(4000);
      v_attribute_name      VARCHAR2(4000);
      v_attribute_value     VARCHAR2(4000);
      v_order_item_ID       VARCHAR2(40);
      -- xml parameters
```

```
    v_parser                xmlparser.parser;
    v_doc_type              xmldom.DOMDocumentType;
    v_dtd_clob              CLOB;
    v_str                   VARCHAR2(32000);
    v_error_file            VARCHAR2(50) := 'c:\temp\dtd_errors';
    v_string                VARCHAR2(32000);
    -- XML declarations
    v_node_list             xmldom.DOMNodeList;
    v_DONNodeList           xmldom.DOMNodeList;
    v_node                  xmldom.DOMNode;
    v_FC_Node               xmldom.DOMNode;
    v_currentNode           xmldom.DOMNode;
    v_dom_doc               xmldom.DOMDocument;
    v_child_dom_doc         xmldom.DOMDocument;
    v_child_node_list       xmldom.DOMNodeList;
    v_child_parser          xmlparser.parser;
    v_nameNodeMap           xmldom.DOMNamedNodeMap;
    v_counter               NUMBER          := 0;
    v_xml_buffer            VARCHAR2(32767);
    v_attr_node             xmldom.DOMNode;
    v_child_Length          NUMBER;
    v_nnm_length            NUMBER;
    v_nodeType              NATURAL;
    v_result                VARCHAR2(32767);
     CURSOR get_dtd (v_obj_name VARCHAR2) IS
       SELECT dtd_contents
         FROM xml_dtd
         WHERE dtd_name = v_obj_name;
BEGIN
   -- Create a new Parser
   v_parser := xmlparser.newParser;
   -- Set error file.
  -- xmlparser.setErrorLog( v_parser, v_error_file );
  -- Get the DTD for this object from our DTD table
  -- that stores our XML DTD's.
   -- You will have to create this table in order to get this
   -- part of code to work.  DTD validation is not required.
   OPEN get_dtd (p_order_object.dtd_name);
   FETCH get_dtd INTO v_dtd_clob;
   CLOSE get_dtd;
   IF v_dtd_clob is not null
   THEN
      --  Register DTD with parser
      xmlparser.parseDTDCLOB( v_parser, v_dtd_clob,
                              p_order_object.dtd_name );
   END IF;
   -- Get the document type
   v_doc_type := xmlparser.getDocType( v_parser );
   -- Set the validation mode
```

```
  xmlparser.setValidationMode( v_parser, FALSE );
  -- Parse the XML out of the CLOB
   xmlparser.parseClob( v_parser, p_order_object.transport_clob);
  -- Create the DOM Document
  v_dom_doc := xmlparser.getDocument( v_parser );
  -- Free the parsers memory
   xmlparser.freeparser( v_parser );
IF NOT xmldom.IsNull( v_Dom_doc )
THEN
     -- get all elements
     v_node_list := xmldom.getElementsByTagName(v_Dom_doc, '*');
     v_Length := xmldom.getLength( v_node_list );
     -- Check for an empty XML Document
     IF NOT ( v_Length > 1 )
     THEN
         dbms_output.put_line('We have no XML nodes to process.'  );
     END IF;
     IF NOT xmldom.IsNull( v_dom_doc )
     THEN
       -- loop through all the elements in the DOM document
       WHILE ( v_counter < v_length  )
       LOOP
          v_node := xmldom.item(v_node_list, v_counter );
          v_attribute_name := xmldom.getNodeName( v_node );
          -- Get the value from the order_id attribute in the root
          -- node
          IF ( v_attribute_name = 'ItemOrder' )
          THEN
            v_nameNodeMap := xmldom.getAttributes( v_node );
            v_nnm_length  := xmldom.getLength( v_nameNodeMap );
            FOR i IN 0..v_nnm_length -1 LOOP
               v_attr_node  := xmldom.item( v_nameNodeMap, i  );
               v_order_item_ID  := xmldom.getNodeValue( v_attr_node );
               dbms_output.put_line( 'v_order_item_ID = ' ||
                                         v_order_item_ID );
            END LOOP;
          END IF;
          -- Check to see if node has a valuefc
          IF ( xmldom.hasChildNodes( v_node ))
          THEN
            v_FC_Node := xmldom.getFirstChild( v_node );
            v_attribute_value  := xmldom.getNodeValue( v_fc_node );
             DBMS_OUTPUT.put_line( 'attribute value ' ||
                                      v_attribute_value   );
          ELSE
            v_attribute_value  := xmldom.getNodeValue( v_node );
          END IF;
          DBMS_OUTPUT.put_line( 'attribute name   = ' ||
                                   v_attribute_name   );
```

```
                DBMS_OUTPUT.put_line ( 'attribute value  = ' ||
                                        v_attribute_value   );
            v_counter     := v_counter + 1;
            v_xml_buffer := NULL;
          END LOOP;
        END IF;
      END IF;
      xmldom.freeDocument ( v_dom_doc );
    EXCEPTION
      WHEN OTHERS THEN
          dbms_output.put_line ('We have received an exception.'  );
    END   Order_XML_inbound_parser;
  /
```

Now, let's execute the order_inbound_dequeuer, which takes the order_transport_object off the order_inbound_queue. It then checks to see if the contents attribute equals xml and, if so, sends the order_transport_object to the Order_XML_inbound_parser( ), which parses and displays the contents of the XML document.

```
SQL> declare
   2     v_sequence number := 1;
   3     v_XML_string   varchar(4000);
   4   begin
   5      dbms_output.enable( 2000000 );
   6      v_XML_string := '<?xml version="1.0" encoding="UTF-8"?>' ||
   7                      '<ItemOrder itemId="12345-genA">' ||
   8                        '<Name>Generator typeB</Name>' ||
   9                        '<Cost>45,000</Cost>' ||
  10                        '<Quantity>1</Quantity>' ||
  11                        '<Vendor>Acme Generators</Vendor>' ||
  12                      '</ItemOrder>';
  13      dbms_output.put_line ( v_xml_string );
  14     put_xml_on_queue (v_sequence, v_XML_string, 'ORDER_ITEM.dtd',
'INSERT', 'XML', 'ORDER_MANAGER' );
  15   end;
  16  /
<?xml version="1.0" encoding="UTF-8"?><ItemOrder
itemId="12345-genA"><Name>Generator
typeB</Name><Cost>45,000</Cost><Quantity>1</Quantity><Vendor>Acme
Generators</Vendor></ItemOrder>
PL/SQL procedure successfully completed.
SQL> select * from order_inbound_q_tbl
   2  where deq_time is null;
ORDER_INBOUND_Q               3022830CAEC145A0A0D387275D46603B
         1          0                                                    0
0
                    19-JUL-01          42 6.38.187
                                                                      0
```

```
ITL                              ORDER_EXCEPTION_Q
0
              0                                          1
AQ$_HISTORY(AQ$_DEQUEUE_HISTORY('ORDER_MANAGER', NULL, NULL, NULL,
NULL,
1, NULL
))
ORDER_TRANSPORT_OBJECT('XML', 'ORDER_ITEM.dtd', 'INSERT','ORDER_MANAGER',
 '<?xml version="1.0" encoding="UTF-8"?>
<ItemOrder itemId="12345-genA"><Name>Gener')
SQL> exec order_inbound_dequeuer;
v_order_item_ID = 12345-genA
attribute value
attribute name    = ItemOrder
attribute value   =
attribute value Generator typeB
attribute name    = Name
attribute value   = Generator typeB
attribute value 45,000
attribute name    = Cost
attribute value   = 45,000
attribute value 1
attribute name    = Quantity
attribute value   = 1
attribute value Acme Generators
attribute name    = Vendor
attribute value   = Acme Generators
Inside exception WHEN no_messages_on_queue19/jul/2001 12:54:17
PL/SQL procedure successfully completed.
SQL>
```

Using SOAP Regularly

SOAP stands for Simple Object Access Protocol. Simply stated, *SOAP* is the protocol used for exchanging structured messages in decentralized, distributed environments. These structured messages are in the form of XML documents. SOAP was designed with the goals of simplicity and extensibility, so it doesn't define any programming model or implementation specifics. What it does provide for is a simple mechanism for expressing application-specific rules or attributes with a modular approach. This allows SOAP to be used in a large variety of systems, ranging from messaging systems to RPC.

SOAP messages are fundamentally one-way transmissions from a sender to a receiver, but can be combined to implement a request/response-type system with the response using the same connection as the request. These messages travel along what is called a *message path,* where the messages can go right to a final recipient or can stop at an intermediate recipient for some type of processing. Each recipient must know the exchange pattern of the message, that particular recipient's role in the message, how to make any required RPC calls, and how the data has been encoded. While attributes are available, no specific requirements exist as to how each recipient of a message determines what to do with it.

Each SOAP message contains up to three sections:

- **Envelope**   Defines what is in the message, who should get the message, and if the message is optional or mandatory.

- **Header**   A generic mechanism that can be used to add features to a message without any predefined specifications.

- **Body**   Contains the actual message for the recipient.

The Envelope and Body are mandatory, while the Header is optional. The following is a sample SOAP request message:

```
POST /GetName HTTP/1.1
Host: www.tusc.com
Content-Type: text/xml;
charset="utf-8"
Content-Length: nnnn
SOAPAction: "Some-URI"

<SOAP:Envelope
  xmlns:SOAP="http://schemas.xmlsoap.org/soap/envelope/"
  SOAP:encodingStyle="http://schemas.xmlsoap.org/soap/encoding/">
   <SOAP:Body>
       <m:GetEmpName xmlns:m="Some-URI">
           <position>CHAIRMAN</position>
       </m:GetEmpName>
   </SOAP:Body>
</SOAP:Envelope>
```

The response to this request is as follows:

```
HTTP/1.1 200 OK
Content-Type: text/xml;
charset="utf-8"
Content-Length: nnnn

<SOAP:Envelope
  xmlns:SOAP="http://schemas.xmlsoap.org/soap/envelope/"
  SOAP:encodingStyle="http://schemas.xmlsoap.org/soap/encoding/"/>
<SOAP:Body>
```

```
<m:GetEmpNameResponse xmlns:m="Some-URI">
<Name>BRAD BROWN</Name>
</m:GetEmpNameResponse>
</SOAP-ENV:Body>
</SOAP-ENV:Envelope>
```

SOAP provides a mechanism for reporting errors and the status of a message. These are known together as the *Fault element*. This element is optional but, if present, must appear in the body. Included in the Fault element are four subelements, which provide the error code, a human readable explanation of the error code, the cause of the fault, and any application specific error information as it relates to the body of the message.

The SOAP protocol can be bound to many other protocols, but is probably more commonly bound to HTTP with or without the HTTP Extension Framework. The reason for this is the decentralized flexibility of SOAP, combined with the rich feature set of HTTP. Using HTTP to transmit SOAP messages provides a natural mapping of SOAP semantics to HTTP semantics.

The capability to embed remote procedure calls and responses in XML is also a design goal of SOAP. RPC calls and responses are carried in the body of the message.

The encoding style in SOAP is based on a simple-type system based on common features found in other programming languages. While XML allows for a flexible style of encoding the data, SOAP defines a much narrower set of rules. The basic data types used in SOAP include integers, floating points, negative integers, and strings. Other more complex types include enumerations, arrays, and structures.

SOAP also uses namespaces. One namespace is used by the envelope and another is used for the rules for encoding. The envelope namespace is defined as **http://schemas.xmlsoap.org/soap/envelope** and the encoding rules namespace is defined as **http://schemas.xmlsoap.org/soap/encoding**.

Summary

Because of XML's simplicity and flexibility, it has revolutionized the way we exchange information in a global environment. As mentioned, Oracle's strategy for XML is to "deliver the best platform for developers to productively and cost effectively deploy reliable and scalable Internet applications exploiting XML." Starting with version 8.1.6 of Oracle8*i* and continuing with Oracle9*i*, a set of core XML support features is available to help developers marry the power of the Oracle database with the power of XML. Take the time to learn XML and you'll open the door to "the next big thing."

CHAPTER
9

Wireless Development

o you want to develop an application that can be deployed on Wireless devices, such as cell phones and PDAs? This chapter provides you with examples to get you started down the wireless Web building path. In fact, maybe this chapter should be titled "Non HTML-based Browser Development" instead. The first part of the chapter covers the Wireless Markup Language (WML) for cell phones and the second part of the chapter discusses other development options, such as Oracle9iAS Wireless Edition (OWE). OWE supports all HTML and non HTML-based browsers. This is a powerful tool!

Because many wireless providers charge by the minute, you might think testing wireless applications can be expensive (and time-consuming). You can download a wireless simulator, however, and perform your testing in the simulator. A *wireless simulator* is a browser that acts just like the browser that is installed in your cell phone or wireless device. A *wireless browser* is often referred to as a *microbrowser* or a *minibrowser*. Some of the newer HTML-based browsers also support WML.

You can find an excellent simulator (named Openwave™ Simulator) at the Openwave Web site (**http://www.openwave.com**). This site can also provide you with volumes of valuable information about wireless devices and they've created a wireless developer's portal that can be found at **http://updev.phone.com**. You must first create an account before you can visit the complete site. Most phones have the UP.Browser version 3.1 loaded on them, so you'll likely want to download the Openwave SDK 3.2, which supports the 3.*x* browsers. The Openwave SDK provides an application that runs on a PC and emulates a wireless device. Openwave SDK enables you to set the visual aspects of the phone to any one of a variety of phones. The minibrowser operates just like your wireless device, without the cost per transmission.

In this chapter, the following topics are discussed:

- Database Programming for Web-Enabled Cell Phones and Wireless Handheld Devices

  - WML Concepts

  - WML Chart of the Elements

  - Moving Between Cards and Passing Variables

  - Dealing with the Wireless Cache

  - WML GUI Editor

  - Wireless PL/SQL Toolkit

- Programming for Wireless-Enabled PDAs

- Oracle9iAS Wireless Edition

- How Oracle9*i*AS WE Works

- Services, Adapters, and Transformers

- Simple XSLT Transformer

- Converting Existing Content for Oracle9*i*AS Wireless Edition

- Testing the Service

- Configuring Apache for WML

Database Programming for Web-Enabled Cell Phones and Wireless Handheld Devices

Writing applications that run on wireless devices requires developers to consider a new set of priorities versus writing for more traditional HTML-based Web browsers, such as Internet Explorer and Netscape Navigator. The foremost wireless device concern is the size of the display for which you'll be programming, as this can vary widely among Web-enabled cell phones and PDAs. The issue of user input (that is, typing) can also be tedious on most wireless devices (especially on cell phones). To make your application more user friendly, ideally you'll need to create menus for every page displayed, so a single button press (0–9) activates a user choice. Screen design and application flow are, therefore, more crucial tasks than in more traditional Web programming.

Programming for a wireless Web-enabled personal digital assistant (PDA), such as a Palm Pilot or Compaq iPaq is easier than for cell phones for several reasons. The issue of screen size isn't as acute because PDAs almost always have larger displays than a cell phone. The PDA also has a minikeypad on its touch screen, which makes user input easier. Many PDAs, like the Palm VII, also have a built-in browser, and these browsers read and interpret most standard HTML elements. Wireless devices are stricter about the HTML syntax than a standard browser, however. This means the learning curve for creating an application designed for a PDA is considerably less for an experienced Web developer.

The language of choice for most cell phones is Wireless Markup Language (WML). WML evolved from XML (Extensible Markup Language), HTML, and Phone.com's Handheld Device Markup Language (HDML). WML was designed for developing Web pages that can be easily rendered on wireless devices with low bandwidth, small screens, and no keyboards for user input. Using WML gives you the most "bang for the buck" initially and is supported by many of the devices available today. Writing WML is also more attractive initially because the language itself has only a few elements and tags that you use for most applications. We'll look at these elements in a couple of simple examples and show you how these can be used as part of a larger application. Our ultimate goal is to create dynamic WML applications using the Oracle PL/SQL cartridge and the HyperText Functions (HTF) and HyperText Procedures (HTP) built-in package after understanding the basics of WML. Another option is to use Java and Java Server Pages (JSPs) to create WML pages. Oracle provides libraries for either method. Finally, we'll look at the Oracle9*i* Application Server Wireless Edition (OWE) and its capabilities for producing content for Web-enabled cell phones that don't use WML but, instead, use XML, HTML, or some derivative thereof. OWE was previously called Portal-to-Go.

WML Concepts

WML is a markup language based on the XML standard. In fact, WML is actually an XML application. WML is read and interpreted by a microbrowser within a Web-enabled, wireless device. WML is used for wireless environments because it requires little bandwidth, less processing power (thus, saving battery strength), and fits within the display screens of mobile phones and other wireless devices.

In other words, minibrowsers don't understand HTML; they understand WML instead. HTML is a loose markup language specification. In other words, if you forget something (like an ending tag) or if you have a syntax error or a missing tag in HTML, HTML-based browsers ignore the errors. WML doesn't ignore the error. In fact, the WML specification or Document Type Definition (DTD) outlines the exact syntax of the WML language. If you're interested in reading the complete DTD from Phone.com, you can find it at (**http://www.w3schools.com/wap/wml_dtd.asp**). Numerous good books are available on HTML today and a few good books are available about WML, but the best sources I found were all online sources. My favorite site for reference is Openwave's developer portal. Wireless devices typically support *WMLScript,* a lightweight scripting language based on ECMAScript, but modified for the wireless environment. *ECMAScript* is a standard scripting language syntax developed with the cooperation of Netscape and Microsoft. ECMAScript was derived from JavaScript (which was designed by Netscape). The official standard, ECMA-262, was developed under the European Computer Manufacturers Association—hence, the ECMA acronym. Wireless Web developers use WML and WMLScript, whereas HTML-based browser Web developers use HTML and ECMAScript (that is, JavaScript or JScript). Standard HTML-based Web browsers use the concept of "pages." WML uses the concept of a "deck of cards" for its pages. To be analogous to a standard HTML page, a card can be considered a portion of a page used to display results or ask for user input. The entire card might not be visible at one time on the display and several inputs on the same card might require several screens, displayed one at a time, to load all inputs. A deck might contain one or more cards. In summary, you can think of a deck as being all the elements currently in the phone's memory and available for other cards to use as input variables. Variables can easily be passed between cards, but not between decks without using dynamically created WML to set variables. The simplest deck consists of a single card displaying only text. As is traditional for the first application written in any language, we'll use a simple WML example to display "Hello Wireless World" on your cell phone.

Hello Wireless World

A new deck always begins with the XML header lines, which precede the opening <wml> tag. These lines must be the first lines of any file or procedure that produces WML as output.

```
<?xml version="1.0"?>
<!DOCTYPE wml PUBLIC "-//WAPFORUM//DTD WML 1.1//EN"
        "http://www.wapforum.org/DTD/wml_1.1.xml">
<wml>
```

The HelloWirelessWorld WML deck, in its entirety, is as follows:

```
<?xml version="1.0"?>
<!DOCTYPE wml PUBLIC "-//WAPFORUM//DTD WML 1.1//EN"
        "http://www.wapforum.org/DTD/wml_1.1.xml">
<wml>
  <card>
      <p>
         Hello Wireless World
      </p>
  </card>
</wml>
```

This is the simplest deck you can create. It contains the minimum number and type of elements that should be used. The tags and their purpose are as follows:

- **<wml>**   Required tag—analogous to <html>, the start of a page

- **<card>**   Required tag—this is the start of a new card, similar to <body>

- **<p>**   Paragraph tag—not require by all phones, but recommended

NOTE
The <p> and closing </p> tags aren't explicitly required, but some phones won't correctly display text without these tags enclosing all elements of a card. This isn't to imply separate <p> and </p> tags are needed for each element but, rather, an opening <p> tag at the beginning of a card (after any <do> and </do> tags) and a closing </p> immediately before the closing </card> tag. In other words, paragraph tags should enclose any text to be displayed.

WML Chart of the Elements

The most commonly used WML tags are as follows:

- **wml**   Similar to <html>—used to start a new deck
- **do**   Controls action of BACK and ENTER buttons on phone
- **go**   Jump to another card or a new URL, similar to the <a>nchor tag
- **head**   Heading section, typically used in conjunction with a <meta> tag
- **meta**   Sends directives, such as no-cache, to the phone
- **prev**   Jumps to the previous card or deck—same as the BACK button on the phone
- **p**   Paragraph—encloses textual elements to be displayed
- **img**   Indicates an image
- **a**   Anchor—works similarly to the go tag

The following tags are used for user input:

- **input**   For text input
- **select**   For a numbered list of selections (differs from HTML select tag)
- **option**   An item in the select list

The following are CGI tags:

- **postfield**   Variable submitted using the POST or GET method
- **setvar**   Passes variables among cards within the same deck

The following are character-formatting tags:

- **big**   Larger font than default
- **small**   Smaller font than default
- **b**   Bold
- **I**   Italics
- **u**   Underline

The following are commonly used character entities:

- <!ENTITY quot """>   <!— quotation mark —>
- <!ENTITY amp "&">   <!— ampersand —>
- <!ENTITY apos "'">   <!— apostrophe —>
- <!ENTITY lt   "<">   <!— less than —>
- <!ENTITY gt   ">">   <!— greater than —>
- <!ENTITY nbsp " ">   <!— nonbreaking space —>

TIP
*A great source for WML reference material is the
wap.bluedomino.com Wireless Web hosting site's
FAQ section (**http://wap.bluedomino.com/faq/**).
It has excellent reference material for you.*

Most phones can display 15 to 30 characters on a single line, depending on the size
of the screen. If you use the mode=nowrap attribute for the paragraph tag and you have
text that won't display on a single line, some phones will toggle the text left and right
every second to display all the text between the paragraph tags. For example:

```
<p mode="nowrap">A very long text string here that
will definitely wrap without the nowrap mode attribute</p>
```

Moving Between Cards and Passing Variables

Typing or entering information is extremely tedious using a cell phone. To reduce
the number of inputs or questions asked of a user, you can logically break the
questions into separate cards and jump to the next card, based on the choice made
on the prior card. In other words, you might ask users two questions if they choose
option A, versus four questions if they choose option B. To accomplish this, you
would jump to a card named "twoQ" if users press 1, and to a card named "fourQ"
if users press 2 on their phone keypad. You would then set variables accordingly
from each card.

Jumping Cards Within a WML Block

As an example of jumping to another card based on a user's choice, let's look at
the WML deck used by the TUSC Cellular*DBA Application (**http://team.tusc.com/
clients/tuscportal/cellphone.htm**). The application enables you to execute UNIX

commands and Oracle commands from a cell phone. This application prompts users for a UNIX login and a UNIX password and, optionally, three more inputs for an Oracle database login. Specifically, you need to know an Oracle login, an Oracle Password, and an Oracle SID. This is a lot of unnecessary typing if users don't need to connect to the database. You could simply use a single card and allow users to leave the other fields blank, but they would still have to push the ENTER button on the phone to respond for each of the remaining inputs. A better method is to break the deck into three cards, with the first card prompting users to find out which type of login they need, and then jumping to the appropriate card that contains either two inputs or five inputs. The WML file (login.wml) to accomplish this looks like the following:

```
<?xml version="1.0"?>
<!DOCTYPE wml PUBLIC "-//WAPFORUM//DTD WML 1.1//EN"
         "http://www.wapforum.org/DTD/wml_1.1.xml">
<wml>   <card id="main" title="TUSC Cellular*DBA">
     <do type="accept">
       <go href="$(which:noesc)"/>
     </do>
     <p>
       Select Login Type:
       <select name="which">
         <option onpick="#short">Server Only</option>
         <option onpick="#long">Server and Database</option>
       </select>
     </p>
   </card>

   <card id="short" title="Enter UNIX Login">
     User Id:
       <input name="uid" type="text" maxlength="13"/>
     Password:
       <input name="passwd" format="*M" type="password"
              maxlength="13"/>
   </card>

   <card id="long" title="Database Login">
     User ID:
       <input name="uid" type="text" maxlength="13"/>
     Password:
       <input name="passwd" format="*M" type="password"
              maxlength="13"/>
     DB ID:
       <input name="sid" type="text"/>
     DB User Id:
       <input name="dbuid" type="text"/>
```

```
   DB Password:
     <input name="dbpswd" format="*M" type="password"
            maxlength="13"/>
</card>
</wml>
```

Dissecting the Login.wml File

The following statement creates the select group named which:

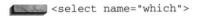 `<select name="which">`

The options are presented to the users as a numbered list on their phone with the text between each <option> and </option> tags displayed next to each successive number. The option items are numbered 1–9 (in the examples numbered 1 and 2), followed by the text between the <option> and </option> tags.

Users see the text displayed on their phone shown in Figure 9-1.

To select an item, users need only press the number on their keypad that corresponds to the item they want to select. The value of this select group is set by the onpick attribute when users press a button on their phone. This is accomplished with the following code:

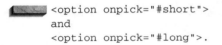
```
<option onpick="#short">
and
<option onpick="#long">.
```

FIGURE 9-1. *Wireless browser with Cellular*DBA login card*

The following line specifies that we'll jump to the card identified by the option value of the select group named "which"—note, the go statement is surrounded by the do command:

```
<go href="$(which:noesc)"/>
```

When the user presses a button, the value of the variable which is set to either #short or #long. More simply, you jump to the card named short if the user presses 1 or to the card named long if the user presses 2. This is similar to a named reference in HTML but, in WML, you jump to cards with the WML page.

Passing In-Between Cards

Sometimes it's necessary to pass information between cards. This is typically done in combination with the previous technique to limit user inputs. When the final card is posted, you might need to know the value of all variables set by user input from the previous cards. Passing variables is accomplished by using the setvar tag.

The following Newlogin.wml example WML file passes variables between cards:

```
<?xml version="1.0"?>
<!DOCTYPE wml PUBLIC "-//WAPFORUM//DTD WML 1.1//EN"
        "http://www.wapforum.org/DTD/wml_1.1.xml">
<wml>       <card id="pass1" title="Select Option Type">
         <do type="accept">
           <go href="#next1">
             <setvar name="otyp" value="$(otype:N)"/>
           </go>
         </do>
       <p>
           <select name="otype">
             <option value="short">Few Questions</option>
             <option value="long">More Questions</option>
           </select>
       </p>
     </card>

     <card id="next1" title="Select Action">
         <do type="accept">
           <go href="#next2">
             <setvar name="action" value="$(act1:N)"/>
           </go>
         </do>
       <p>
           <select name="act1">
             <option value="first">A1</option>
```

```
                   <option value="second">A2</option>
              </select>
         </p>
    </card>

    <card id="next2" title="Select Action 2">
       <do type="accept">
         <go href="#next3">
            <setvar name="action2" value="$(act2:N)"/>
         </go>
       </do>
      <p>
          <select name="act2">
            <option value="third">A3</option>
            <option value="fourth">A4</option>
          </select>
      </p>
    </card>

    <card id="next3" title="Select Action 3">
        <do type="accept">
          <go href="/pls/RDBA/srvlogin method="post">
            <postfield name="otypv" value="$(otyp:N)"/>
            <postfield name="actionv" value="$(action:N)"/>
            <postfield name="action2v" value="$(action2:N)"/>
            <postfield name="action3v" value="$(act3:N)"/>
          </go>
        </do>
      <p>
          <select name="act3">
            <option value="fifth">A5</option>
            <option value="sixth">A6</option>
          </select>
      </p>
    </card>
</wml>
```

Dissecting the Newlogin.wml File

We can see that setvar is used to pass variables and postfield is used to POST variables to the Web server. The first variable passed is named otyp. Its value is set to either short or long, depending on whether the user presses 1 (for short) or 2 (for long) on their phone pad.

The WML line that sets the variable is

```
<setvar name="otyp" value="$(otype:N)"/>
```

The list is created by the <select> and <option> tags. The option items are numbered 1–9, followed by the text between the <option> and </option> tags. The WML line is

```
<select name="otype">
```

When the choice is made, the browser jumps to the card named next1. The card is created by the line that reads

```
<card id="next1" title="Select Action">.
```

You jump to this card using a <go> tag inside of <do> and </do> tags. A <do> tag has a type associated with it, depending on whether you want to jump when the users press the designated Enter key on their phone (that is, type="accept">) or when the user presses the designated Back key on their phone (that is, type="prev">). The block of WML is

```
<do type="accept">
    <go href="#next1">
        <setvar name="otyp" value="$(otype:N)"/>
    </go>
</do>
```

When users press the ENTER key on their phone, the data posted is loaded into the QUERY_STRING environment variable. Let's assume the user selected long, first, fourth, and sixth from the respective cards. The URL that the wireless browser would send looks like this:

```
http://myserver/pls/RDBA/srvlogin?otypv=long&actionv=first
&action2v=fourth&action3v=sixth
```

To send the data to a stored procedure and display its results, note the go tag referencing the stored procedure. The code snippet to post data to a stored procedure looks like the following:

```
<do type="accept">
    <go href=" /pls/RDBA/srvlogin">
        <postfield name="otypv" value="$(otype:N)"/>
        <postfield name="actionv" value="$(action:N)"/>
        <postfield name="action2v" value="$(action2:N)"/>
        <postfield name="action3v" value="$(act3:N)"/>
    </go>
</do>
```

Supporting srvlogin Procedure

This procedure doesn't actually process the login information. It simply accepts and
prints the data back to the browser.

```
    PROCEDURE srvlogin
(otypv      IN varchar2 default NULL,
 actionv    IN varchar2 default NULL,
 action2v   IN varchar2 default NULL,
 action3v   IN varchar2 default NULL)
is
  BEGIN
        htp.prn(
                '<?xml version="1.0"?>
                <!DOCTYPE wml PUBLIC "-//WAPFORUM//DTD WML 1.1//EN"
                          "http://www.wapforum.org/DTD/wml_1.1.xml">
                <wml>');

        htp.print('<card>');
        htp.print('<p>');
        htp.print('Results of  Posting');
        htp.print('otypv    = '|| otypv);
        htp.print('actionv  = '|| actionv);
        htp.print('action2v = '|| action2v);
        htp.print('action3v = '|| action3v);
        htp.print('</p>');
        htp.print('</card>');
        htp.print('</wml>');

  EXCEPTION
    when OTHERS then
        htp.print('Error occurred:');
        htp.print('<br>'||SQLERRM||'<br>');
        htp.print('</p>');
        htp.print('</card>');
        htp.print('</wml>');
end wml_test;
```

As you can see, you can use the htp.print statement to write the WML to the
wireless browser. Another approach is to write a Wireless PL/SQL Toolkit as described
in later sections.

Dealing with the Wireless Cache

With these examples and a little imagination, you can create a wide variety of
applications for use on a wireless Web-enabled cell phone. In practice, the most

difficult task is disabling caching of pages by the phone. For your Cellular*DBA application, you always need to display the most current information. Because the pages being sent to the phone are created dynamically, two tricks seem to work for all devices.

Setting HTTP Header Parameters

The conventional method of preventing pages from caching is by setting HTTP header parameters. This is accomplished by using the owa_util package's mime_header procedure, as in the following PL/SQL example:

```
// Open the HTTP header
owa_util.mime_header('text/html', false);
// Prevent caching, HTTP/1.1
htp.prn('Cache-Control: no-cache, must-revalidate');
// Prevent caching, HTTP/1.0
htp.prn('Pragma: no-cache');
// Close up the HTTP header
owa_util.http_header_close;
```

The previous PL/SQL code generates the proper HTTP headers to prevent caching of the WML page.

Getting Really Creative

Because the "no-cache" metatags (not HTTP headers, but metatags) are ignored by most wireless browsers, the following more drastic solution has been used. This kluge technique appends a counter value to the end of a variable as part of the URL, and then increments that value for each subsequent screen sent to the phone, as in the following example:

```
<go href="http://server/pls/RDBA/wml_test?ignore=1">
```

The next page sent is as follows:

```
<go href="http://server/pls/RDBA/wml_test?ignore=2">
```

By creating a unique value to be assigned to a given variable each time, you can trick the phone into always fetching the page as if it were a new location (URL). This way, you ensure that your server program always executes to display the most current results.

Because the parameters being passed each time are changing, if you use the PL/SQL module to capture input, you'll need to use Flexible parameter passing. This technique isn't recommended but, if you see it being used, you'll know why.

WML GUI Editor

If you want to generate WML through a GUI editor, check out CoffeeCup Software's Wireless Web Builder (**http://www.coffeecup.com/download/shareware.cgi?018**). The basic concept is similar to developing HTML with a tool like Dreamweaver or FrontPage. The Wireless Web Builder generates WML by your point-and-click operations. The objects that can be inserted using the tool are somewhat limited (for example, no data input), but it provides a great start. Best of all, the tool is free and your wireless site will be hosted free.

Wireless PL/SQL Toolkit

After reviewing different WML examples, I decided I want to be able to create dynamic WML applications using the PL/SQL cartridge. So, I outlined a specification for a Wireless PL/SQL Toolkit. As discussed in Chapter 14, the HTML PL/SQL toolkit contains two primary packages: Hypertext Procedures (HTP) and Hypertext Functions (HTF). I began creating my Wireless Toolkit packages by naming them WHTP and WHTF. The following list contains my Wireless Toolkit specification. Each of the following procedures shows the input parameters and the respective output that will be sent to the microbrowser.

whtp.xmlOpen

```
<?xml version="1.0"?>
<!DOCTYPE wml PUBLIC "-//PHONE.COM//DTD WML 1.1//EN"
        "http://www.phone.com/dtd/wml11.dtd" >
```

whtp.wmlOpen

```
<wml>
```

whtp.wmlClose

```
</wml>
```

whtp.cardOpen (ctitle, cid)

```
<card title="ctitle" id="cid">
```

whtp.cardClose

```
</card>
```

whtp.comment (ccomment)

```
<-- ccomment -->
```

whtp.print (ctext)

```
ctext
```

whtp.img(csrc, calt)

```
<img src="csrc" alt="calt">
```

whtp.do(ctype, clabel, chref)

```
<do type="ctype" label="clabel"><go href="chref"/></do>
```

whtp.formInput (ctitle, cname)

```
<input title="ctitle" name="cname">
```

whtp.selectOpen

```
<select>
```

whtp.selectClose

```
</select>
```

whtp.selectOption(cpick, ctext)

```
<option  onpick="cpick">ctext</option>
```

whtp.paraOpen(cwrap,calign)

```
<p mode="cwrap" align="calign">
```

whtp.paraClose

```
</p>
```

whtp.italic(ctext in varchar2)

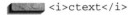

```
<i>ctext</i>
```

whtp.br

```
<br>
```

Next, you need the support package specification and body to generate the previous output when the procedures and functions are called. I've included the whtp and whtf packages as I've defined them. You can enhance these as you see fit.

whtp

```
CREATE OR REPLACE package whtp as
procedure xmlOpen;
procedure xmlClose;
procedure wmlOpen;
procedure wmlClose;
procedure cardOpen(   ctitle      in varchar2 DEFAULT NULL,
                      cid         in varchar2 DEFAULT NULL)   ;
procedure cardClose;
procedure do (        ctype       in varchar2 DEFAULT NULL,
                      clabel      in varchar2 DEFAULT NULL,
                      chref       in varchar2 DEFAULT NULL);
procedure formInput (ctitle       in varchar2 DEFAULT NULL,
                      cname       in varchar2 DEFAULT NULL);
procedure comment(    ctext       in varchar2 DEFAULT NULL)   ;
procedure img(        csrc        in varchar2 DEFAULT NULL,
                      calt        in varchar2 DEFAULT NULL)   ;
procedure paraOpen ( cnowrap      in varchar2 DEFAULT 'nowrap',
                      calign      in varchar2 DEFAULT NULL,
                      cattributes in varchar2 DEFAULT NULL);
procedure paraClose;
procedure SelectOpen;
procedure SelectOption(cpick       in varchar2,
                       ctext       in varchar2 DEFAULT NULL,
                       cattributes in varchar2 DEFAULT NULL);
procedure SelectClose;
 procedure italic( ctext in varchar2);
procedure br;

/* SPECIAL PROCEDURES */
  -- Output Procedures
procedure print (cbuf in varchar2 DEFAULT NULL);
```

```
procedure print (dbuf in date);
procedure print (nbuf in number);
  -- Output without the newline
procedure prn (cbuf in varchar2 DEFAULT NULL);
procedure prn (dbuf in date);
procedure prn (nbuf in number);
end;
/

CREATE OR REPLACE package body whtp as
procedure xmlOpen is
begin print(whtf.xmlOpen); end;
procedure xmlClose is
begin print(whtf.xmlClose); end;
procedure wmlOpen is
begin print(whtf.wmlOpen); end;
procedure wmlClose is
begin print(whtf.wmlClose); end;
procedure cardOpen(     ctitle  in varchar2 DEFAULT NULL,
                        cid     in varchar2 DEFAULT NULL) is
begin print(whtf.cardOpen(ctitle,cid)); end;
procedure cardClose is
begin print(whtf.cardClose); end;
procedure do (          ctype  in varchar2 DEFAULT NULL,
                        clabel in varchar2 DEFAULT NULL,
                        chref  in varchar2 DEFAULT NULL) is
begin print(whtf.do(ctype,clabel,chref)); end;
procedure formInput    (ctitle  in varchar2 DEFAULT NULL,
                        cname   in varchar2 DEFAULT NULL) is
begin print(whtf.formInput(ctitle,cname)); end;
procedure comment(     ctext  in varchar2 DEFAULT NULL) is
begin print(whtf.comment(ctext)); end;
procedure img(          csrc   in varchar2 DEFAULT NULL,
                        calt   in varchar2 DEFAULT NULL) is
begin print(whtf.img(csrc, calt)); end;
procedure paraOpen(     cnowrap       in varchar2 DEFAULT 'NOWRAP',
                        calign        in varchar2 DEFAULT NULL,
                        cattributes   in varchar2 DEFAULT NULL) is
begin print(whtf.paraOpen(cnowrap, calign, cattributes)); end;
procedure paraClose is
begin print(whtf.paraClose); end;
procedure SelectOpen is
begin print(whtf.SelectOpen); end;
procedure SelectOption(cpick        in varchar2,
                        ctext        in varchar2 DEFAULT NULL,
                        cattributes in varchar2 DEFAULT NULL) is
begin print(whtf.SelectOption(cpick,ctext,cattributes)); end;
procedure SelectClose is
```

```
begin print(whtf.SelectClose); end;
procedure italic(      ctext in varchar2) is
begin print(whtf.italic(ctext)); end;
procedure br is
begin print(whtf.br); end;

procedure prn(cbuf in varchar2 DEFAULT NULL) is
begin   htp.prn(cbuf);
end;
procedure print (cbuf in varchar2 DEFAULT NULL) is
begin   htp.prn(cbuf || '
');
    /* The above broken line is intentional.  Do not modify */
end;
procedure print (dbuf in date) is
begin htp.print(to_char(dbuf)); end;
procedure print (nbuf in number) is
begin htp.print(to_char(nbuf)); end;
procedure prn (dbuf in date) is
begin htp.prn(to_char(dbuf)); end;
procedure prn (nbuf in number) is
begin htp.prn(to_char(nbuf)); end;
begin
    htp.init;
end;
/
```

whtf

```
CREATE OR REPLACE package whtf as
/*function*/ xmlOpen           constant varchar2(124) :=
'<?xml version="1.0"?>
 <!DOCTYPE wml PUBLIC "-//PHONE.COM//DTD WML 1.1//EN"
         "http://www.phone.com/dtd/wml11.dtd" >';
/*function*/ xmlClose          constant varchar2(6) := '</xml>';
/*function*/ wmlOpen           constant varchar2(5) := '<wml>';
/*function*/ wmlClose          constant varchar2(6) := '</wml>';
function    cardOpen (ctitle in varchar2 DEFAULT NULL,
                      cid    in varchar2 DEFAULT NULL) return varchar2;
/*function*/ cardClose          constant varchar2(7) := '</card>';
function paraOpen (cnowrap     in varchar2 DEFAULT 'nowrap',
                   calign      in varchar2 DEFAULT NULL,
                   cattributes in varchar2 DEFAULT NULL) return varchar2;
/*function*/ paraClose    constant varchar2(4) := '</p>';
-- Like FORM tag in HTML
function     do (ctype  in varchar2 DEFAULT NULL,
                 clabel in varchar2 DEFAULT NULL,
                 chref  in varchar2 DEFAULT NULL) return varchar2;
```

```
function      formInput
                  (ctitle  in varchar2 DEFAULT NULL,
                   cname   in varchar2 DEFAULT NULL) return varchar2;
function comment(ctext in varchar2) return varchar2;
function img (csrc in varchar2 DEFAULT NULL,
              calt in varchar2 DEFAULT NULL) return varchar2;
function SelectOpen return varchar2;
function SelectOption(    cpick       in varchar2,
                         ctext       in varchar2 DEFAULT NULL,
                         cattributes in varchar2 DEFAULT NULL)
return varchar2;
/*function */ SelectClose   constant varchar2(9) := '</select>';
function italic(          ctext       in varchar2 DEFAULT NULL)
return varchar2;
/*function*/ br                constant varchar2(5) := '<br/>';
 /* Assert function purities so that they can be used in select lists  */
PRAGMA RESTRICT_REFERENCES(cardOpen,          WNDS, WNPS, RNDS, RNPS);
PRAGMA RESTRICT_REFERENCES(do,                WNDS, WNPS, RNDS, RNPS);
PRAGMA RESTRICT_REFERENCES(formInput,         WNDS, WNPS, RNDS, RNPS);
PRAGMA RESTRICT_REFERENCES(comment,           WNDS, WNPS, RNDS, RNPS);
PRAGMA RESTRICT_REFERENCES(SelectOpen,        WNDS, WNPS, RNDS, RNPS);
PRAGMA RESTRICT_REFERENCES(SelectOption,      WNDS, WNPS, RNDS, RNPS);
PRAGMA RESTRICT_REFERENCES(italic,            WNDS, WNPS, RNDS, RNPS);
PRAGMA RESTRICT_REFERENCES(img,               WNDS, WNPS, RNDS, RNPS);
 end;
/

CREATE OR REPLACE package body whtf as
function IFNOTNULL(str1 in varchar2, str2 in varchar2) return varchar2 is
begin
   if (str1 is NULL)
     then return (NULL);
     else return (str2);
   end if;
end;
function cardOpen(ctitle in varchar2 DEFAULT NULL,
                  cid    in varchar2 DEFAULT NULL) return varchar2 is
begin return('<card'||
             IFNOTNULL(ctitle,' title="'||ctitle||'"')||
             IFNOTNULL(cid,' id="'||cid||'"')||
             '>');
end;
function paraOpen (cnowrap      in varchar2 DEFAULT 'nowrap',
                   calign       in varchar2 DEFAULT NULL,
                   cattributes  in varchar2 DEFAULT NULL) return varchar2 is
begin return('<p'||
             IFNOTNULL(cnowrap,' mode="'||cnowrap||'"')||
             IFNOTNULL(calign,' align="'||calign||'"')||
             IFNOTNULL(cattributes,' '||cattributes)||
             '>');
end;
```

```
function     do    (ctype  in varchar2 DEFAULT NULL,
                    clabel in varchar2 DEFAULT NULL,
                    chref  in varchar2 DEFAULT NULL) return varchar2 is
begin return('<do '||
             IFNOTNULL(ctype, ' type="' ||ctype ||'"')||
             IFNOTNULL(clabel,' label="'||clabel||'"')||
                  '><go '||
             IFNOTNULL(chref, ' href="' ||chref ||'"')||
             '/></do>');
end;
function     formInput (ctitle  in varchar2 DEFAULT NULL,
                          cname   in varchar2 DEFAULT NULL)
return varchar2 is
begin return('<form '||
             IFNOTNULL(ctitle,' title="'||ctitle||'"')||
             IFNOTNULL(cname, ' name="' ||cname ||'"')||
             '/>');
end;
function comment(ctext  in varchar2 DEFAULT NULL) return varchar2 is
begin return('<!-- '||ctext||' -->');
end;
function img (csrc in varchar2 DEFAULT NULL,
              calt  in varchar2 DEFAULT NULL) return varchar2 is
begin return('<img '||
             IFNOTNULL(csrc,' src="'||csrc||'"')||
             IFNOTNULL(calt,' alt="'||calt||'"')||
             '/>');
end;
function SelectOpen return varchar2 is
begin return('<select>');
end;
function SelectOption(cpick       in varchar2,
                      ctext       in varchar2 DEFAULT NULL,
                      cattributes in varchar2) return varchar2 is
begin return('<option'||
             IFNOTNULL(cpick,' onpick="'||cpick||'"')||
             IFNOTNULL(cattributes,' '||cattributes)||
             '>'||ctext||'</option>'); end;
function italic(ctext       in varchar2 DEFAULT NULL) return varchar2 is
begin return('<i>'||ctext||'</i>'); end;
end;
/
```

Example Using Wireless Toolkit

Based on the previous specification and packages, I created a procedure that sends
WML to my wireless device. The WML displays a list of the TUSC books. When you
select a specific book, the minibrowser then displays the current Amazon rank and
the date the rank last changed. Now you can see how easy it is to display using the
Wireless PL/SQL Toolkit.

TIP
Important to note is WML requires a MIME type of
"text/vnd.wap.wml" not the standard "text/html."

```
create or replace procedure wml_book_sales
is
cursor book_cur is
      select * from books;
cursor book_rank_cur (in_book varchar2) is
      select to_char(date_pulled,'mm/dd/yy hh24:mi') rank_date,
            rank
      from    book_rank a
      where   date_pulled =
            (select max(date_pulled)
            from    book_rank b
            where   a.book = b.book)
      and     book = in_book;
begin
owa_util.mime_header('text/vnd.wap.wml');
whtp.xmlOpen;
whtp.comment ( ctext => 'Main menu for Book Sales' );
whtp.wmlOpen;
whtp.cardOpen ( ctitle => 'TUSC Book Sales' );
whtp.paraOpen ( cnowrap => 'nowrap' );
whtp.print ( 'Book Sales' );
whtp.br;
whtp.print(owa_util.get_cgi_env('HTTP_USER_AGENT'));
whtp.selectOpen;

for book_rec in book_cur loop
    whtp.selectOption ( cpick => '#'||book_rec.book, ctext =>
                        htf.escape_sc(book_rec.title));
end loop;
whtp.selectClose;
whtp.paraClose;
whtp.cardClose;
for book_rec in book_cur loop
    whtp.cardOpen ( cid => book_rec.book);
    whtp.paraOpen ( cnowrap => 'wrap' );
    whtp.print (htf.escape_sc(book_rec.title)||whtf.br);
    for book_rank_rec in book_rank_cur(book_rec.book) loop
       whtp.italic(book_rank_rec.rank_date);
       whtp.selectOpen;
       whtp.selectOption ( cpick => book_rec.url,
                           ctext => book_rank_rec.rank);
       whtp.selectClose;
```

```
      end loop;
    whtp.paraClose;
    whtp.cardClose;
  end loop;
  whtp.wmlClose;
  end;
```

TIP
You could extend my Wireless PL/SQL Toolkit by adding capabilities to support any browser type. In other words, by extending it to a Universal PL/SQL Toolkit. If you extend my toolkit, please send me a copy. This approach would let you easily direct which devices saw specific content and which devices didn't. For example, the following commands might be used to direct the title statement to all devices, but the header is only directed to the Wireless Palm (WP) and HTML-based devices:

```
uhtp.title(ALL, 'Universal PL/SQL Toolkit');
uhtp.header(WP and HTML, 1, 'Universal PL/SQL Toolkit');
```

Programming for Wireless-Enabled PDAs

Programming for wireless PDAs is much the same as when programming for conventional Web browsers compared to cell phones. User input (that is, typing) is much easier using a PDA because they have minitouch-screen keypads and the display is usually much larger than any cell phone display. Most PDAs have a browser that interprets standard HTML (it's more strict HTML, however) with the limitation that they don't support JavaScript. The only other difference from standard HTML is you should include a header telling the browser you're sending the page to a PDA and it doesn't need to be concerned with any elements not supported by a PDA. Note the <meta> tag used in the following example. Palm computing refers to this HTML rendering as *Web Clipping,* which is a proprietary method of providing access to online resources from a Palm OS device—including the Palm VII or Palm V with OmniSky modem. Web Clipping is built around the concept of *Application Partitioning,* where part of the application resides locally on the device, which saves on bandwidth and response time. To create your own application for the Palm platform, you need only create a simple HTML file to be converted to a Palm Query Application

(PQA) file, which is then downloaded to your PDA. Aside from an HTML editor, the only other tool you need is the Web Clipping Application Builder. Palm provides a simple utility called the *PQA Builder*—a free download from Palm at **http:// www.palmos.com/dev/tech/Webclipping/**—and available for both the PC and Macintosh platforms.

As an example of a PDA page, let's look at the login screen for the TUSC Palm*DBA Application. This is the same login screen used for the cell phone version, except you can display all login items (Userid, Password, Database Identifier, Database login, Database Password) on one screen. The user simply leaves the unnecessary items blank and presses the SUBMIT button. Our logic in the called stored procedure needs to allow for items left blank.

The Index.html file to be converted to a PQA file is as follows:

```
<html>
<head>
<title>Palm DBA</title>
<meta name="palmcomputingplatform" content="true">
<meta name="palmlauncherrevision" content="2.0.1">
<meta name="localicon" content="pdba.gif">
</head>
<body>
<h2>Login to server</h2>
<form action="/rdbacgi/hcmdexec.pl" method="POST">
<p>Userid: <INPUT type="text" name="uid">
<p>Password: <INPUT type="password" name="passwd">
<p>Oracle SID: <INPUT type="text" name="sid">
<p>Oracle Userid: <INPUT type="text" name="dbuid">
<p>Oracle Password: <INPUT type="password" name="dbpswd">
<p>Command: <INPUT type="text" name="ucmd">
<br>
<input type="submit" value="Logon">
</form>
</body>
</html>
```

Oracle9iAS Wireless Edition

As previously mentioned in the Universal Toolkit tip, if you have one application to be used by PCs, PDAs, and cell phones alike, you must develop a universal toolkit or you must write code that outputs HTML, Web Clipping, and WML, respectively. In fact, you'd need to write code specific for each of these devices. You're probably thinking, "Wouldn't it be great if I could create one set of source code that can be displayed by all devices?" Oracle answers this by saying, "Use OWE!" OWE is the name given to Portal-to-Go after it was integrated with the Oracle9iAS suite. The Oracle documentation uses Oracle9iAS WE and Portal-to-Go interchangeably.

It would be wonderful if we could simply create an application in HTML and JavaScript, and then use a "magical transcoder" that would re-create our application in WML and WMLScript. In reality, the Oracle9*i*AS WE process isn't quite as simple as specifying a URL for a Web page and expecting the page to be automatically converted into another markup language with all functionality from the original page intact. Several steps exist for converting existing pages and there's a different methodology for designing an application to be used by multiple devices.

The OWE client tools don't convert JavaScript into WMLScript and, in fact, don't even attempt to execute any JavaScript attached to elements extracted from a Web page. Oracle9*i*AS WE works best when your application relies on a database query, XML, or JSPs to retrieve information, and then returns that information as plain text to be displayed using XML. Oracle9*i*AS WE converts XML into other markup languages, thus, XML is the markup language that benefits you most in creating multiple-device applications. XML is a flexible markup language that lets tags be defined by the content developer. Tags for any data item, such as a customer name or product, can be created and used in specific applications, allowing Web pages to function like database records. Oracle9*i*AS WE transformers are designed to convert XML into other markup languages. In fact, Oracle9*i*AS WE uses its own XML definition named OWE XML. This is a well-formed, valid XML document that complies with the Oracle9*i*AS WE DTD. XML and related technologies are used by Oracle9*i*AS WE, as follows:

- XML separates presentation and content

- A DTD maps XML tags to User Interface elements

- Extensible Style Language (XSL) style sheets define rules for formatting and filtering results

In Oracle9*i*AS WE, the goal is to identify elements from an existing Web page or RDBMS source that are to be displayed by several different device types and to apply a transformer that produces the appropriate markup language based on the type of device being used by the user. For example, an input text box behaves the same on each device and is used merely to provide the user an interface for inputting information to your application, regardless of the device being used to view the application. If you define a simple input text box using XML, you need only a transformer to generate the appropriate markup language for each device to create an input text box on its display.

OWE works by separating content acquisition from content delivery. It provides an intermediary format layer—OWE XML—between the source format and the target format. Isolating the content source format from the target format enables you to plug in new content sources or target devices easily. When you create a transformer for a new device platform, all your existing content is immediately available to the new target platform.

How Oracle9*i*AS WE Works

For content to be delivered to a device, you must create an OWE service. An *OWE service* encapsulates a unit of information requested by and delivered to an OWE client. A service might display a stock quote, a map for driving directions, or flight information. For your TUSC RDBA application, you might define a service to display a specific alert message from the database. A Master service must be created to invoke a specific service. A *Master service* is an OWE object that implements a service and invokes a specific adapter. End users typically see a service as a menu item on their cell phone or as a link on a Web page. You can think of it as simply the URL needed to link a user to your application or Web site. Each Master service is based on one adapter and will create its own instance of the adapter it uses. Therefore, several services can use the same type of adapter and each can pass the adapter its service-specific parameters.

As illustrated in Figure 9-2, when end users request an OWE service from their cell phone or wireless PDA or desktop PC, the following events occur:

1. OWE's Request Manager performs user-level preprocessing, including authentication.

2. The Request Manager invokes the Master service.

3. Master service invokes an adapter to retrieve the requested content.

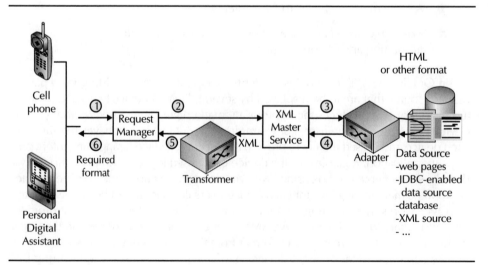

FIGURE 9-2. *9iAS Wireless Edition steps*

4. The adapter returns the content in XML to the Master service.

5. A Transformer, in the form of an XSLT (Extensible Style Language Transformations) style sheet or Java program, converts the XML content into the format appropriate for the target device.

6. The Request Manager returns the information to the device.

When you access content from OWE, you're accessing an Alias that points to a Web service. OWE provides a couple of client tools to assist in the creation of a Web service and an Alias. The first tool is the *Web Integration Developer,* also referred to as a *screen scraper,* to extract elements from existing content. The Web Integration Developer maps the selected content into OWE XML. The second tool is the Service Designer to create a Master service and an Alias that points to this service for end users to access. Once you create your services, the administrator, as well as end users, use the Personalization Portal to control what content is sent, based on the device used to access it (as determined by the Request Manager). The *Personalization Portal* is a Web-based application that users access from a desktop browser using a URL similar to the following:

```
http://myserver/papz/login.jsp
```

Oracle also provides an XML editor for anyone familiar with XML to edit content directly in the OWE repository in the database. The repository is an Oracle8*i* database that stores all OWE objects, such as users, adapters, transformers, and services.

Assuming you created a user and user group with the Service Designer, the steps to create an OWE Web service from existing HTML content are as follows:

1. Create a Web Interface Definition Language (WIDL) file from existing content using the Web Integration Developer.

2. Publish the WIDL file to the Web Integration Server.

3. Create a Master service using the Service Designer.

4. Create an Alias that points to this Master service.

5. Make the Master service available to a user or group.

You can use an Alias to create several instances of a Master service with different parameters to control behavior of the service. If you have existing WML content, you can use the Service Designer to create a bookmark to access WML content directly on the Web.

Services, Adapters, and Transformers

Let's look at each of the major components of an OWE portal.

Services encapsulate external resources, like Web pages and database information. An OWE service encapsulates a unit of information requested by and delivered to an OWE client. A service might display a stock quote, a map for driving directions, or flight information.

Adapters are APIs and tools that convert HTML and RDBMS content to XML. Adapters connect Oracle9iAS WE Services to specific types of source information and applications. Oracle9iAS WE includes Adapters for HTML content, database information (through SQL or PL/SQL), e-mail, location-based services, XML-based content, and any Java application (through an open API). Generally, an adapter performs the following functions:

- Connects to a data source

- Retrieves content

- Converts the content to an Oracle9iAS Wireless Edition XML format

Adapters return content (XML) that conforms to a Wireless Edition content DTD. The returned content can be in either the SimpleResult format or the AdapterResult format. In most cases, adapters return content that conforms to the SimpleResult DTD. The *SimpleResult DTD* contains elements that represent the components of an abstract user interface, such as text items, menus, forms, and tables. The SimpleResult DTD defines the format of deliverable service content. The *AdapterResult format* is an intermediary, user interface-independent content format. You can use it to pass raw data between Wireless Edition components. Because device transformers operate only on the SimpleResult format, a ResultTransformer associated with a Master service must convert an AdapterResult document to the SimpleResult format before the content can be delivered. When converting source content to SimpleResult format, adapters map the source content to the appropriate SimpleResult element. Likewise, when converting the content from SimpleResult format to the target format, Transformers map the SimpleResult elements to the appropriate elements in the target format (WML, HDML, and so forth).

Transformers are Java programs or XSLT style sheets that convert an XML document to the proper display format for each user's device, such as WML, HDML, or Voice XML (VoxML). They can also rearrange, filter, and add text. Oracle9iAS WE supplies transformers for the following markup languages:

- **WML 1.1**   The wireless markup language defined by the WAP Forum

- **Tiny HTML**   A minimal HTML implementation suitable for handheld devices, such as Palm Computing Platform and Windows CE devices

- **VoxML** The Motorola markup language that enables voice interaction with applications

- **TTML** The Tagged Text Markup Language is a subset of HTML developed by Nokia

- **HDML** The Handheld Devices Markup Language, a simplified version of HTML designed specifically for handheld devices

- **Plain Text** Converts content for Short Message Service-capable devices and e-mail applications

You can also create new device transformers in XSL and/or Java, making all existing services available for the new device. OWE provides tools and interfaces you can use to create your own adapters and transformers. When you create a transformer, you create a logical mapping between the abstract user interface elements represented by the SimpleResult elements and the target format (WML, HDML, and so forth).

XSLT style sheets are XML documents that specify the processing rules for other XML documents. The XSLT processor included with the Oracle XML processor conforms to the final W3C XSLT specification, Working Draft of August 13, 1999. An XSLT style sheet is specific to a particular DTD and should handle all elements declared in a DTD. When the XSLT style sheet finds the element in a source document, it follows the rules defined for the element to format its content. XSLT style sheets can include complex pattern matching and result handling logic. They typically include literal result elements, such as the target format markup tags. See Chapter 8 for more information about XML and XSLTs.

Simple XSLT Transformer

The following transformer is an oversimplified XSLT Transformer. It converts a SimpleTextItem from the SimpleResult DTD to be enclosed in paragraph tags for display output in WML.

```
<xsl:stylesheet xmlns:xsl="http://www.w3.org/XSL/Transform/1.0">
  <xsl:template match="SimpleTextItem">
  <wml>
    <card title="XSLT Text">
      <P>
        <xsl:value-of select="."/>
      </P>
    </card>
  </wml>
  </xsl:template>
</xsl:stylesheet>
```

If passed the following OWE element,

```
<SimpleTextItem>Hello Wireless World</SimpleTextItem>
```

the XSLT transformer would produce the following:

```
<?xml version="1.0"?>
<!DOCTYPE wml PUBLIC "-//WAPFORUM//DTD WML 1.1//EN"
        "http://www.wapforum.org/DTD/wml_1.1.xml">
<wml>
  <card title="XSLT Text">
<P>
Hello Wireless World
</P>
  </card>
</wml>
```

Converting Existing Content for Oracle9*i*AS Wireless Edition

The OWE documentation provides a walkthrough as an example of how to convert existing content into a Service. The example shows what the software is capable of when you have a page that divides the content into easily manageable pieces. We'd like to see what happens when a page doesn't translate as easily, and what the issues and alternatives are.

We'll create an OWE Web service from an existing HTML page.

Creating a WIDL File from Existing Content Using the Web Integration Developer

The Web Integration Developer is used to identify which elements are to be displayed for a particular service. This tool divides the page into individual HTML elements, such as anchors, tables, table data elements, and each of the various input types (text boxes, radio buttons, and check boxes). The rest of the document is grouped into a catch-all element called *doctext*. In the Oracle version of the walkthrough, the element we're interested in is the stock price for a selected stock quote at **http://quote.yahoo.com**. The stock price is displayed inside an HTML table in a table data element. You can select this element as the only thing to be displayed when a user provides a ticker symbol to look up. You're left with a service that simply prompts the user to enter a symbol and, when the form is submitted, displays only the current price for the stock such as 26.27.

In this example, we'll look up the definition for a word and display the result to the user. We'll use the URL: **http://work.ucsd.edu:5141/cgi-bin/http_Webster**.

In the Web Integration Developer, you simply choose Open URL from the File menu item and enter **http://work.ucsd.edu:5141/cgi-bin/http_Webster**. Figure 9-3 shows what this page looks like in a regular browser. Note the output used for the actual definition of the word "segue."

This page would seem to lend itself easily to translation because not much content exists to be displayed. Unfortunately, the Web page designer chose to output the text as hyperlinks, so the visitor could jump to definitions of words used in the definition itself. The Web Integration Developer enables you to select the option of displaying all the hyperlinks as a group. You can easily allow for longer definitions by editing the Reference section of the Web Integration Developer (see Figure 9-4) to create an array of anchors referenced by their index into the array using doc.html[0].body[0].p[0].a[1,2,3,4,5...n].text or simply doc.a[].text. If we create more array indexes than anchors, this is okay. The problem is the words in between the links ("in", "or", and "He") cannot be added to this group. We'll be

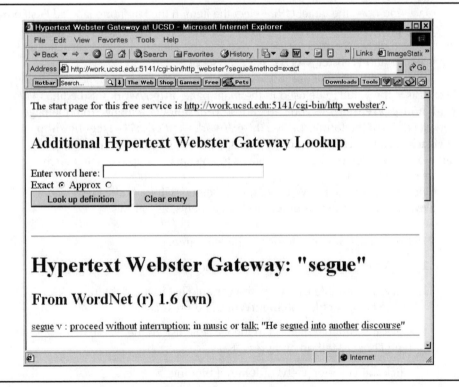

FIGURE 9-3. *Hypertext Webster Gateway in the browser*

left with a definition that doesn't read correctly as Merriam-Webster intended. The output from our service would be only anchor elements, thus, "segue v : proceed without interruption; in music or talk; "He segued into another discourse"" will be shortened to "segue proceed without interruption music talk segued into another discourse". For some definitions, we could be left with an unintelligible result. We aren't completely defeated here because we can use the last resort of the doctext element, which is all of the visible text within the document. We can create a service that displays much more information than the user needs, but it will be functional. Unfortunately, we also display extraneous information, such as the prompt for entering a new word and any other messages this site chooses to display, including advertising. The main lesson here is you must plan ahead if you want to write code once and display it on many devices. Make sure all key components of your content are contained within an HTML element, such as <TD> (table data element) tags.

We continue to create our service by generating a Web Integration Definition Language (WIDL) file for this URL.

Once you open the target URL, select the item in the left frame labeled FirstForm by clicking it. Now select WIDL File from the Generate menu item. You are now prompted to provide names for the service and the interface. Enter **WordLookup** for the interface and **Webster_GetWord** for the service.

After clicking OK, enter **segue** in the Generate New WIDL for Service dialog box. This is the value to be used in the main page (**http://work.ucsd.edu:5141/cgi-bin/http_Webster**), so you can choose your output elements from the page generated when the form is posted (**http://work.ucsd.edu:5141/cgi-bin/http_Webster?segue&method=exact**). The method=exact portion comes from a radio button choice on the main page as to an exact or approximate match on the desired word.

Once you generate the WIDL file, your screen will look like Figure 9-5. Now, select your input/output display elements, as follows:

1. Expand the Bindings folder in the left frame.

2. Click the Webster_GetWordInput binding.

3. Click the variable isindex in the variable list in the right frame. In the Name field, type **InputWord** and press ENTER.

4. Click the variable method in the variable list. In the Name field, type **LookupMethod** and press ENTER.

5. Click the Webster_GetWordOutput binding.

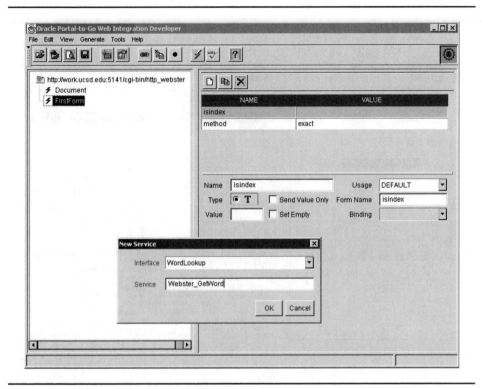

FIGURE 9-4. *Web Integration Developer Word Lookup*

6. In the variable highlighted in the right frame, you can see all the words that are HTML anchors, but we'll use only the doctext variable. Delete all other variables by clicking them and pressing the DELETE toolbar button.

7. On the sample tab, select the text, click the right mouse button, and select Create New Variable From Selection from the pop-up menu.

8. Type **Definition** in the New Variable dialog box and click OK. The Definition variable is now created in the variable list.

To test the WIDL file in the Web Integration Developer, click Webster_GetWord in the services menu in the left frame, select Test Service from the Tools menu, and type in any English word in the InputWord field. You should see the full definition, as well as the extraneous text from the HTML page.

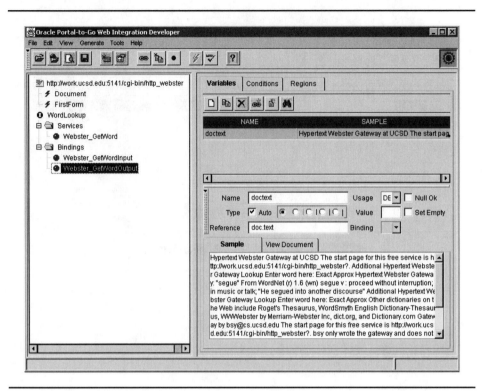

FIGURE 9-5. *Web Integration Developer binding output*

Publishing the WIDL File to the Web Integration Server

Now, you must publish this service by adding entries into the OWE Repository. The Web Integration Developer does this for you by simply selecting WordLookup in the left frame, selecting Publishing from the File menu, and selecting Publish Interface. Figure 9-6 demonstrates publishing the word lookup.

In the Specify Server field in the Publish Interface dialog box, type the name of the Web Integration Server to which you want to publish this interface and click OK. This adds the example service to the Default package.

In the User Name and Password dialog box, enter a user name and a password for the user with administrative privileges on the selected server. The Web Integration Developer copies the interface to the selected package on the Web Integration Server and notifies you that the interface is successfully published.

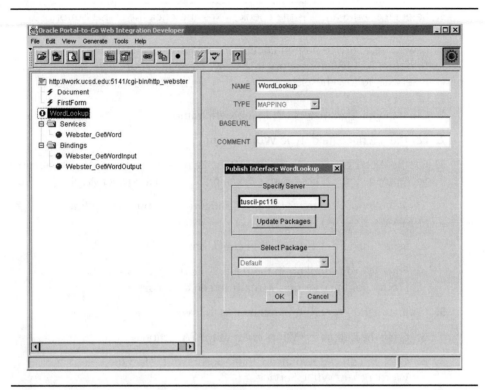

FIGURE 9-6.   *Publishing Word Lookup*

Create a Master Service Using the Service Designer

After creating the WIDL service, create an OWE service based on the WIDL service.
The Service Designer is a visual tool for creating and managing OWE objects in the
Repository. To create the Master service for the WordLookup WIDL file, follow
these steps:

1. Right-click the Master services folder in the OWE repository tree view.

2. Click Create New Master service to display the Create New Master service
    form sequence.

3. Type **Dictionary** in the Name field.

4. Click the BROWSE button next to the Adapter field, and then select
    WebIntegrationAdapter.

5. Select the Valid and Visible check boxes and click the FINISH button.

The new Master Service named Dictionary now appears under the Master services folder in the OWE repository tree view. To assign your Dictionary WIDL file to this service, follow these steps:

1. Click the Init Parameters tab in the right frame.

2. For the Interface field, type **WordLookup**.

3. For the Web Integration Server, type the machine name of the Web Integration Server in the format: host_name. domain:5555, and then click Apply.

4. Click the Input Parameter tab and configure the InputWord parameter as follows:

   a. Select the User Customizable check box.

   b. Enter **Word to lookup** in the caption field. This is used as a prompt for the user on the main screen of our service.

5. Configure the PAsection parameter as follows:

   a. Click the cell in the Value column for PAsection.

   b. Click the drop-down arrow that appears and select the WordLookup WIDL Service.

   c. Click Apply.

This creates the Master Service named Dictionary in the OWE repository. Now you must create aliases to make the Master Service available to users.

Creating an Alias that Points to this Master Service

To add a Master Service Alias to the Service Tree, first create a new folder in the Service Tree, and then add an Alias to the Master Service in this folder. The steps to create a folder and alias are as follows:

1. Right-click Service Trees in the OWE repository tree view.

2. Click Create New Folder.

3. In the Name field, type **My Folder** or any name you want. We used Mikes Folder.

4. Select the Valid and Visible check boxes and click Finish.

5. Right-click the newly created Mikes Folder in the Service Tree.

6. Click Create New Alias.

7. In the Name field, enter **Dictionary_Service**.

8. Click the BROWSE button next to the Service field. Expand the Master service folder, select Dictionary, and click OK.

9. Select the Valid and Visible check boxes and click Finish.

10. This creates an alias object in the OWE repository, as you can see in Figure 9-7.

Making the Service Available to a User or Group

As the final step, you must make this alias available to a specific user or to a group of users. Creating a user or a group is as simple as selecting the Users folder or the Groups folder in the OWE repository tree, right-clicking, and selecting Create New

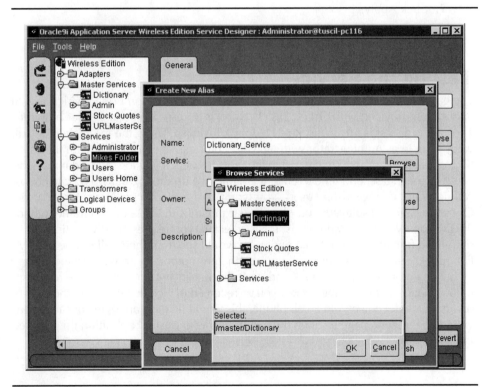

FIGURE 9-7. *Service Designer Dictionary*

User or Create New Group. For a new user, you supply a user name and a password. For a new group, you choose the list of users to be assigned to this group. For this example, I created a user named mike, a group named "Mikes Group", and a folder named "Mikes Folder" (no time was spent thinking of the names used). To allow Mikes Group to use the service we created

1. Expand the Groups folder in the OWE repository tree view.

2. Click Mikes Group.

3. Click the Service Folders tab to display the Folders panel.

4. Under Service Folders, expand the Services tree to find Dictionary_Service.

5. Dictionary_Service is in Mikes Folder—click Mikes Folder.

6. Click the RIGHT ARROW (>) button to move the folder to the Selected Folders field.

7. Click Apply.

This makes the service available to all users in the group Mikes Group.

Testing the Service

The easiest way to test this service is to use the *Personalization Portal,* which is a JSP application provided with Oracle9iAS WE and is accessed using a regular browser. The URL to access is **http://tuscil-pc116/papz/login.jsp**. Using the installation default values, log in as Administrator with a password of manager, or log in with the user ID and password of any user created in the previous step. If you log in as Administrator, you'll be asked a second time to enter the name of a user to log in as. You can choose Administrator or any existing user—you won't be asked for a password for the user. Once the page is displayed, you can expand the links in the left-hand frame to find the Dictionary_Service. When this link is selected, you're presented with (in the right-hand frame) the output that end users would see from their cell phone or PDA. For our example, as in Figure 9-8, you see the prompt to enter a word to lookup.

If you enter the word "segue" and push the SUBMIT button, you see the resulting output. Notice all the extraneous text you were forced to include because of the design of the source document. On a cell phone, this would be most annoying because you would be forced to page through the text to find your desired definition (highlighted in Figure 9-9).

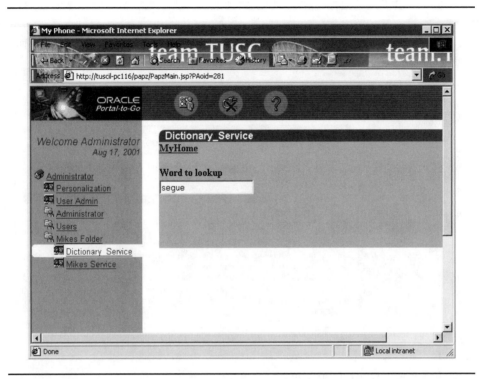

FIGURE 9-8. *Entering a Word Lookup in the browser*

Configuring Apache for WML

To display your WML pages on a wireless device without using Oracle9*i*AS WE, you must make a couple of changes to the Web server configuration files. For Apache, you need only make minor additions to the httpd.conf file. As far as Apache is concerned, it only must know how to recognize the MIME type of the file, based on the file's filename extension. Apache passes this MIME type to the receiving browser and, assuming the browser knows WML, it will know what to do with a WML type file. Recent versions of Apache can be configured entirely through the file httpd.conf, which is typically located in the apache/conf/ directory, wherever Apache is installed on the server. Older versions of Apache may require you to edit the mime.types file. If you open the httpd.conf file in a text editor, you see many Apache configuration directives. Ultimately, you'll find a section where MIME types are declared. While this

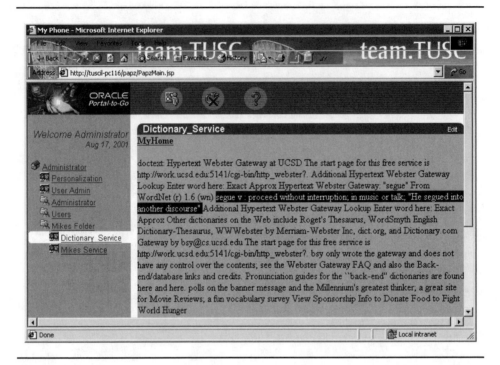

FIGURE 9-9. *Looked up "segue"*

isn't strictly necessary, this is the logical place to add WML types to Apache. In the typical Apache httpd.conf file, this section looks something like the following (depending on the version of Apache):

```
#
# AddType allows you to tweak mime.types without actually editing it, or to
# make certain files to be certain types.
```

Simply paste the following lines into your httpd.conf file, in the section previously shown:

```
#WML/WAP types
AddType text/vnd.wap.wml .wml
AddType application/vnd.wap.wmlc .wmlc
AddType text/vnd.wap.wmlscript .wmls
AddType application/vnd.wap.wmlscriptc .wmlsc
AddType image/vnd.wap.wbmp .wbmp
```

The standard WML file is delivered to the browser with MIME type text/vnd.wap.wml. The statement tells Apache to deliver this MIME type whenever the filename ends in the extension .wml. Similarly, appropriate MIME types are passed for other WML variants. The .wmlc files are compressed WML files. The extensions .wmls and .wmlsc represent WMLScript and compressed WMLScript, respectively. The .wbmp file extension represents wireless bitmap files, the graphic format that wireless devices support (as opposed to, for example, .gif or .jpg on desktop browsers).

Changes to the Apache httpd.conf file take effect only when the server is launched, so the server must be restarted to save the previous changes for the new MIME types to be recognized.

Summary

And you thought programming for two browsers was difficult! With the myriad of wireless devices available today, not to mention the variation of screen sizes and language support, we must think of new ways to manage and design our applications. Writing WML directly (even if using Oracle htp or htf functions) can be the quickest way to support many devices and get your feet wet in wireless programming. For serious development, the concepts used in Oracle9*i*AS Wireless Edition to isolate content source from content display, by using an intermediate language such as XML, are the wave of the future.

CHAPTER
10

OAS to iAS Migration

 hether you're an Oracle professional developer or a Webmaster with applications currently deployed in Oracle Application Server (OAS), this chapter provides you with an outline of the differences between the products, helps you put together a migration strategy, and points out the pitfalls you might encounter along the way. This chapter focuses largely on migrating PL/SQL-based applications because the vast majority of the OAS applications in the field were developed with PL/SQL. This chapter mentions Java, Perl, CGI, and the other application options as they're relevant. I believe most *i*AS applications will use Java as their primary development environment.

In this chapter, the following topics are discussed:

- Why Upgrade?

- Apache, Apache, Apache

- What Will Work?

- What Won't Work?

- What Has to Change?

- What's New in *i*AS?

- Before I Begin—What Do I Really Need?

- *i*AS Effects on My Deployed PL/SQL Applications

Why Upgrade?

The real question is, why not? As with all software, you have a choice whether to upgrade to *i*AS now or to continue with OAS (or, for many people, this might be OWAS 3.0 or even OWS 2.1). If you have a stable application running and are happy with its performance, you might have chosen to delay an upgrade. Maybe you chose to delay because of upgrade costs. Of course, staying put on an older version has risks as well, such as dropped Oracle product support, a more difficult future migration, and less "bang for the buck." Consider some additional factors, which the following sections discuss.

Performance

Despite its popularity among Oracle developers and improvements along the way, OAS has never lived up to its performance expectation. This is largely because of shortcomings in the Spyglass Web server and the overall architecture of the product, which became more evident as improvements were made to other Web server products in the marketplace. With later versions of OAS, installing Apache as a third-party Web listener was possible and those who did integrate Apache noticed two things: their applications weren't crashing as often and, most of all, they were seeing *big* improvements in performance. This move, however, was taken only by the brave or desperate because this configuration of OAS was neither well supported nor well documented. The positive comments from these bold Apache pioneers certainly had a big influence on Oracle's choice of Web server when it came to building *i*AS.

With Apache as the core of *i*AS, Oracle Webmasters are experiencing great improvements in overall Web site performance. My own informal testing puts the gains at about a 30 percent improvement for serving static pages, 100 percent for dynamic content, and 300–500 percent for SSL-encoded pages, over the 4.0.8 version of OAS.

Stability

Along with performance improvements, early adopters of Apache reported increased stability of their applications. Under *i*AS, the number of crashes and hung applications are well below the levels reported for OAS. Servers that were requiring daily or weekly restarts now go months without failure. In discussing *i*AS with developers at conferences around the country, I learned that Unix-based systems seem to be the most stable, NT- and Windows 2000-based systems come in next, and Linux-based systems are the least stable. To what extent these results are related to hardware versus operating system, I can't say because I haven't conducted any side-by-side tests to confirm or deny these trends. Also, testing this in a fair manner is difficult because many Linux systems are overworked older Intel machines, while many Unix and NT machines are more likely installed in higher priced equipment and in well-supported server farms.

Architecture

OAS uses persistent modules called *cartridges* to support application development using languages like PL/SQL, Perl, and Java (CGI calls to C executables are handled outside the cartridge framework). Each language uses a common API to communicate to the Web server via a cartridge backbone (called the *Cartridge Server*). Apache uses simpler third-party modules, commonly known as *mods*. *i*AS mods include mod_plsql (alternately called the PL/SQL Gateway), mod_perl (migration for Perl cartridge), mod_jserv (migration for Jweb cartridge), and mod_php (migration for LiveHTML cartridge). Having a common backbone interface from the Spyglass Web server to the cartridges seems like well-structured design. In practice, however, the common interface introduced an extra layer of code that was often a point of failure in regard to stability and required extra processes running on the server, thus bringing down performance. *i*AS eliminates this extra layer of code. If you're interested, you can find considerable documentation about the Apache Web server architecture, the run-time environment, and available third party modules at **http://www.apache.org**. Chapter 1 also provides more information about the *i*AS architecture.

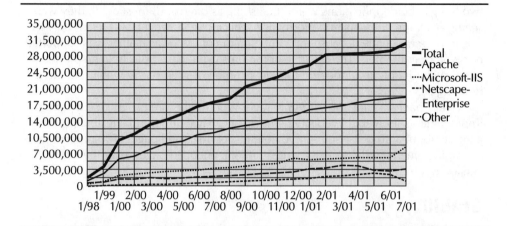

FIGURE 10-1. *Number of servers using Apache*

Popularity

As Figures 10-1 and 10-2 indicate, Apache owns the HTTP server world in both numbers and on-going market share (more than 55 percent). *i*AS is based on Apache version 1.3.

Apache installations continue to grow at a staggering pace, largely because Apache runs on most operating systems, is an open-source product, and is free. Before you get any ideas, you should know that in building *i*AS, Oracle has made modifications to the Apache kernel. This means you cannot simply download your

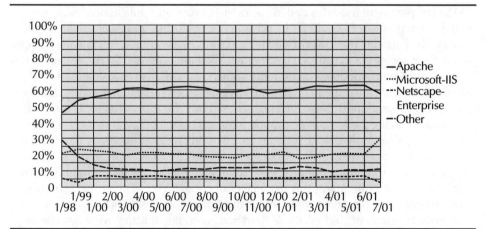

FIGURE 10-2. *Apache market share*

own Apache source from the Web, compile it, and skip paying the *i*AS license fees to Oracle. Sorry, they already thought of that.

Support

Oracle has done a good job in selecting a Web server for *i*AS that runs well and is popular and stable. If you need help, there's a tremendous amount of information, FAQs, discussion groups, and peer-to-peer support for Apache available online. Start your search with the primary Apache Web site **http://www.apache.org**. You can also search Technet (**http://technet.oracle.com**) or contact Oracle support.

Apache, Apache, Apache

The most difficult part of migrating your applications from OAS to *i*AS is learning to configure the Apache Web server. Apache can do everything the OAS Spyglass server can do and much, much more. There are many more opportunities to configure your server exactly the way you want it and many configuration parameters (called *Directives* in Apache), which are simply unavailable in OAS. As any Oracle DBA will tell you, with more control comes more complexity. So configuring Apache might look daunting and somewhat confusing at first, but don't get frustrated. Migrating to Apache is a good idea and you have three things in your favor. First, you have a working Web site already, so you only need to determine how to do the same thing using a new tool, which is much easier than rebuilding it from scratch. Second, you've done this before using Spyglass, so most of the concepts shouldn't be a surprise to you. Some different terminology exists, plus a few options you haven't seen before. Third, with the base installation of *i*AS, Oracle (actually, Apache.org) has included an excellent, well-documented, configuration file to get you started.

You've already started your Apache education by reading this book. I recommend you get any addition information you might need by any or all of the following methods:

- **Go Online** Apache's Web site, **http://www.apache.org**, is the place to start. The site has an excellent glossary, tutorials, and links to additional Apache resources.

- **Get a good Apache configuration book** *Professional Apache,* by Peter Wainwright (Wrox Press, 1999)—If you get only one book on Apache, this is the one to buy. This is the most popular Apache book currently available. Note: Some examples in the book are for Unix only.

Apache Server Bible, by Mohammed J. Kabir (Hungry Minds, 1998)—A complete reference book. Good companion to *Professional Apache.*

■ **Take a Class**   Many colleges and universities are now offering classes and even degree programs on e-commerce and Web server technology. In addition to Oracle, many consulting companies (TUSC included) teach classes on Apache and *i*AS.

Alternatives to Apache

Now that I've totally hyped Apache, as of *i*AS release 1.0.2.2, Oracle is offering IIS (Microsoft) and iPlanet (Netscape) as alternatives to the Apache Web server. If you have experience with these Web servers, you might want to consider them as an option. Otherwise, I recommend you stick with Apache.

What Will Work

The good news is that many things work exactly as they did in OAS. Some things (as noted in the following sections) work almost exactly as they did in OAS. The PL/SQL Web Toolkit and Perl work just like they did in OAS. Upgrade paths are provided for Java and LiveHTML.

PL/SQL and the Web Toolkit

Number one on the list of "must work" for porting applications to *i*AS is PL/SQL-based applications. These applications DO work, with very few exceptions, Hurray! See the "*i*AS Effects on My Deployed PL/SQL Applications" section later in this chapter for the minor changes you will need to look for in your applications.

Perl

Make sure the mod_perl module is included in your httpd.conf Apache configuration file (it's installed in the default *i*AS configuration file). Check that the environment paths are correct for the Perl executable and your Perl scripts should work like a champ. If you're using DBI or DBD-Oracle in your Perl scripts to connect to the database, you need to install these additional components that aren't part of the *i*AS standard installation.

LiveHTML—Sort of

In OAS, LiveHTML is supported by the LiveHTML cartridge and is implemented by imbedding server-side include tags (SSI) within the HTML. To convert scripted code, you must migrate from the LiveHTML SSI to the Apache PHP module. PHP was supposed to be supported by Oracle. In fact, this was mentioned in all of Apache's original documentation as the upgrade path for LiveHTML. For reasons unclear to me, however, Oracle and the PHP open source committee couldn't come to terms, so PHP isn't supported by Oracle with *i*AS. We did get the two of them working together, though.

Apache uses the mod_include module to support SSI, which is included, but not loaded, in the default *i*AS configuration file. PHP is also not included with the base *i*AS installation. The syntax for including a script is the same for both, however, Apache supports either Java Server Pages (JSPs) or PHP as a migration path for LiveHTML scripts. If you have imbedded Perl scripts in your OAS LiveHTML applications, you need to convert the script code to Java to migrate to JSP. Likewise, if you have any Web application objects in your OAS application, you need to implement them as embedded Java code or as JavaBean classes, and then change their tags to the JSP syntax. The other alternative is to migrate the Perl code to PHP. Perl and PHP are similar syntaxes; Java is less similar.

Java—Sort of

Java is supported in *i*AS, but in a significantly different form than under OAS. If you have Java as part of your OAS applications, you need to do a rewrite from the Jweb cartridge to the Jserv specification supported by the Apache Jserv module. Servlets are the migration path for Jweb in OAS. EJB and Jserver are the migration paths for the JCO, ECO, and EJB cartridges. You can find considerable documentation about available third-party modules at the **http://www.apache.org** Web site. To make a long story short, converting this is a major effort. The positive spin on this is that *very* few, if any, customers of OAS actually use the Java cartridge; it doesn't contain extensive (that is, current) Java solutions. I recommend, if you're one of the few, that you recode any Java components to JSP. I would also venture to say, however, if a company is using Java, it isn't using OAS. As of version 1.0.2.2 of *i*AS, Oracle supports the Java2 Enterprise Edition (J2EE) container to be fully Java2-compliant. See Chapter 13, "Java," for additional details.

What Won't Work

The bad news is some things don't migrate from OAS to *i*AS at all. These are discussed in the following subsections. The good news is most people didn't use these features with OAS, so these items don't affect a vast majority of applications.

PL/SQL from Files

OAS lets application developers execute anonymous PL/SQL blocks from the file system. *i*AS doesn't support this feature. If you use this feature, you need to compile these blocks into a named function or procedure in the database.

Positional Parameter Passing

OAS supports a positional parameter-passing scheme; *i*AS doesn't. This doesn't mean you have to change your procedure calls within PL/SQL to named notation (although this isn't a bad standard to adopt). Just change any calls, such as anchors, via the HTTP protocol. Again, this feature goes against the named parameter notation normally used in an HTTP URL call to a procedure, so I don't know of many developers who take advantage of this feature of OAS. If you do, change your calls to named parameter notation.

Cweb Cartridge

There's no migration from the Cweb cartridge to *i*AS. My best recommendation is to recode these modules as Java Servlets or JSPs. Other options are to do a call-out from a PL/SQL stored procedure or to convert to a CGI call to your C procedure. These options have significant performance costs, however, so use them with caution.

What Has to Change

The ugly news is some things changed in how they work, which may affect your application.

Flexible Parameter Passing Gets a New Format

Flexible parameter passing enables you to call overloaded PL/SQL procedures via a URL. Overloaded procedures are named the same in *i*AS as in OAS, but cause different behaviors, depending on the number or datatype of the parameters passed to it. Limits exist to calling an overloaded procedure via HTTP, which aren't present in internal PL/SQL calls. Because HTTP parameters aren't typed, the PL/SQL engine cannot differentiate which procedure body to call. If the number of parameters is the same and only the datatype is different, you must change the parameter name used for each overloaded procedure. If, instead, the number of parameters is used to overload the procedure, you can use the flexible parameter syntax by placing an exclamation point (!) in front of the procedure name in the URL. The call would look like this:

 `www.myhost.com/pls/examples/!my_proc?fname=joe&lname=jackson`

File Uploads and Downloads

Oracle changed the document table schema for uploading and downloading files under *i*AS. Under OAS, the files are always held in the OWS_CONTENT table in the

WEBSYS schema. Under *iAS*, the table can be owned by any schema and can have any legal table name, but files cannot be stored compressed, as they can in OAS. To migrate to *iAS*, the existing contents of the OWS_CONTENT table must be converted to the new table format. Oracle provides a tool—*oas2ias*—to do this. Please refer to the *Oracle iAS Migration Guide* for details on using the oas2ias tool. The upload/ download method is now partly set up in a special targeted DAD configuration for uploads and in a built-in package procedure, wpg_docload.download_file(file_name), for downloads. For details, see Chapter 14, or the Oracle document "Using the PL/ SQL Gateway" Product No. A86263-01, which is included in the *iAS* installation document CD. In general, Oracle recommends moving to the Oracle Internet File System (IFS) framework for this type of activity. See Chapter 18, to determine if your application requirements make this a good move for your organization.

Transaction Services

Transaction services allow a transaction to span across multiple URL requests. Transaction services in OAS are rarely used in practice because it requires a high degree of planning and foreknowledge of the application before configuring the OAS Web server. Most application developers simply find building their applications is easier using cookies or session parameters to keep track of the application state. Using these methods is still considered the preferred Web development approach because it matches the "stateless" architecture of the Web. As of press time (version 1.0.2.2), you can use the mod_ose module to build stateful applications in either Java or PL/SQL.

Application Paths

The new configuration of *iAS* and Database Access Descriptors (DADs) makes the URL to your PL/SQL applications look something like this:

```
http://www.myhost.com/pls/examples/assist.main_menu.
```

Under OAS, the application path and DAD were aliased, eliminating the need for the */pls/* piece of the application path and hiding the actual DAD name. You can work with this change in two ways. One way is to find all the references in your application and change them to the new paths. My experience is that most applications typically use relative pathing, so your applications aren't generally affected by this change. My experience is also that static pages often refer to an absolute path to reach dynamic content, however. "Impossible! It's too much work!" you say. Well, don't despair. The alternative is a simple remap of the virtual path to a one-part path. To accomplish this, you must modify the httpd.conf Apache configuration file. In the default *iAS* installation, the file can be found in the $ORACLE_HOME/apache/apache/conf directory.

1. Turn on the URL rewriting capabilities of Apache by uncommenting or adding the following line of code in the httpd.conf file:

```
LoadModule rewrite_module modules/ApacheModuleRewrite.dll
```

2. After the following line

```
AddModule mod_ssl.c
```

add the following statement

```
AddModule mod_rewrite.c
```

3. Write the logic that will rewrite URLs with a basic Unix grep and edlin string type substitution. Place the code after the following line in the configuration file,

```
DefaultType text/plain
```

and then place the following statements:

```
RewriteEngine on
RewriteRule ^/plsql/(.*)$ /pls/plsql/$1 [R]
RewriteRule ^/examples/(.*)$ /pls/examples/$1 [R]
RewriteRule ^/mts/(.*)$ /pls/mts/$1 [R]
```

Using this syntax, I'm searching for the virtual path that begins with */plsql/, /examples/* or */mts/,* and I'm replacing that syntax with */pls/plsql/, /pls/examples/,* or */pls/mts/.*

Now, when I execute the following URL,

```
http://www.myhost.com/examples/assist.main_menu
```

Apache replaces that URL with

```
http://www.myhost.com/pls/examples/assist.main_menu
```

and the URL I was using in OAS now works in *iAS*!

If you're hosting multiple Web sites on your server, the previous *ReWrite* rule entries might need to appear inside your VirtualHost directives instead of globally to the whole server. Refer to a good Apache configuration book for the details on using these directives. See the section "Apache, Apache, Apache" in this chapter for recommendations on good Apache reference sources.

What's New in *i*AS

Several things are new in *i*AS. If you're migrating applications, you'll be excited to see these new features. If you're new to *i*AS, you can still appreciate these features. The following subsections describe the new features in greater detail.

Deauthentication

Under OAS, and using database authentication, once a user logs in, there's no way to end the session unless the user closed the browser. In *i*AS, a pseudo-procedure called *logmeoff* can do this

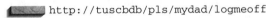

```
http://tuscbdb/pls/mydad/logmeoff
```

Variable Authentication

New options are available for setting up user authentication schemes in the DADs for your applications. Basic, Global_OWA, Custom_OWA, PerPackage, and SingleSign-On are now available.

New CGI Environment Parameters

You'll find many new CGI parameters valuable when developing your applications under *i*AS. These are accessible by calling the OWA_UTIL.get_cgi_env("param_name") built-in package procedure. See the package source code for all the available parameters. The most immediately useful additions include the following:

- **REMOTE_USER** (examples)   The Oracle username with which the user connects

- **DAD_NAME** (examples)   The name of the DAD with which the user connects

- **QUERY_STRING** (in_dept_no=10)   The parameters passed to your procedure

Logging—New Standard Log Formats

Reading and analyzing Web server logs in OAS is difficult because Spyglass doesn't output them in an industry standard format. Using common industry tools often requires Webmasters to manipulate or preparse the logs to fix the formatting. Apache's logs are configurable to output many different Web server activity details and are readable by common Web tools, such as WebTrends. Please see Chapter 23, "Logging and Site Analysis," for more information.

PSPs—PL/SQL Server Pages

Ever since Oracle came out with OAS, there's been criticism from the non-Oracle Web development world that Oracle's Web tools require too much knowledge of Oracle, namely PL/SQL. For developers with lots of Web experience, but who are new to Oracle PL/SQL, having all the HTML tags imbedded within PL/SQL procedure calls to the Web toolkit packages seems strange. And many IT shops would like to separate the page presentation from the business logic. Oracle has heard the criticism and has answered with PL/SQL Server Pages (PSPs).

WebDB has actually had PSPs for a long time—they just had a different name. In WebDB, PSPs were called "Dynamic Pages," but they were different in that they were stored in the database as uncompiled HTML with embedded PL/SQL.

I'm not a big Server Page (xSP) fan. The primary reason is because of the performance hit they typically suffer (with the exception of Cold Fusion Server Pages, JSPs and, now, PSPs). If you aren't familiar with *Server Pages,* they're simply HTML pages with embedded tags for dynamic processing at run time. The dynamic processing code is a particular programming language. PSPs use PL/SQL as the programming language. Microsoft IIS uses Active Server Pages (ASPs), which uses Visual Basic as the programming language. No surprise here, but Java Server Pages use Java.

The reason xSPs typically have performance issues is because the code can't be stored in a compiled format (it's embedded into the script tags). Therefore, they're often interpreted at run time and are, thus, slower than compiled options. HTML developers usually love xSPs, however, because they can edit the code with their favorite HTML editor, and they can easily separate the HTML visual tags and static page content from the business logic imbedded in the script language. Oracle provides the best of both worlds with PSPs. "How is that?" you ask. Because they simply convert the PSP into a compiled mod_plsql routine. In other words, the PSP is turned into a stored procedure. The PSPs are loaded into the database using the loadpsp command, which has the following format:

```
loadpsp [-replace] -user login [<page1> <page2> ...]
```

For example:

```
loadpsp [-replace] -user examples/examples mypsp.psp
```

After your PSP is loaded, you receive a message similar to the following one:

```
"mypsp.psp": procedure "mypsp" created.
```

You can now call your procedure (for example, mypsp) through mod_plsql. The loadpsp command basically turns the PSP page inside-out. What was an HTML page with imbedded PL/SQL becomes a PL/SQL procedure with imbedded HTML. Very clever! The important thing to note is there's absolutely *no* performance issue because the PSP is stored in a compiled format in the database, just like a traditional PL/SQL procedure. This is mighty powerful! See Chapter 14 for examples and more information on development strategies using PSPs.

Before I Begin— What Do I Really Need?

At conferences and presentations I attend around the country, almost half the questions I get are regarding what exactly *i*AS is, what comes with it, and what do developers need to install to replace what they currently have running? This section is intended to help clear up some of the confusion.

Database Installation Only—8.1.7 and Higher

If you're using PL/SQL only for your dynamic Web page delivery, upgrading the database to 8.1.7 or higher might be all you need to do. The Web Development Toolkit built-in packages are the same as for OAS and the database installation includes the Apache Web server. Configure the Apache Web server to replace the OAS Spyglass server, look for the minor PL/SQL pitfalls we've already discussed, and you're good to go.

The Product *i*AS Installation

*i*AS, as a product, delivered on CD, includes Oracle Portal. *Oracle Portal* is the replacement product for WebDB. Like WebDB, Portal is a lightweight Web development environment, targeted at low- to mid-intensity Web sites and intranets that need to be developed quickly. WebDB used to be licensed separately; Portal now comes as part of the Oracle's Internet Developer Suite (*i*DS). Early versions of *i*AS installed Portal by default, which caused great confusion and configuration headaches among developers and Webmasters because the Portal install defaulted to listen on port 80 of the server machine. As of *i*AS version 1.0.2.2, Oracle has improved the installation process to give the installer more options and to make installing Portal more benign. If you upgraded the database to 8.1.7 or higher, and then installed *i*AS, you'll have two installed Apache Web servers: one in the database home and another in the *i*AS home. While this configuration in itself isn't a problem, it may not be what you want, so be aware. See Chapter 16, "Portal," for more information on developing applications using Portal. See Chapter 2 and Chapter 3 for more information about *i*AS installation and configuration.

Forms Server Installation—Enterprise Edition

In addition to Portal, 9iAS Forms Services is bundled as part of the iAS, if you're running the Enterprise Edition of iAS. This is essentially a rebadge of the Oracle Forms Server in 8i. If you have Oracle Forms deployed on the Web, this is your upgrade path. See Chapter 17 for more information on deploying Forms on the Web. Oracle also has several white papers and documents available on Technet (**http://technet.oracle.com**).

iAS Effects on My Deployed PL/SQL Applications

Have you ever heard the joke about the guy who goes to the doctor, raises his hand, and says "It hurts when I go like this," and the doctor says, "Then don't do that!"? Be careful when migrating your applications—don't let the following items affect your migration.

CGI Environment Variable Differences

Under OAS, OWA_UTIL.get_cgi_env('SERVER_NAME') returns the virtual domain entered by the user (that is, partnerlink.myserver.com). Under iAS, this call returns the machine server name, no matter what the entered domain (that is, www.myserver.com). To get the expected behavior, change this to call to OWA_UTIL.get_cgi_env('HTTP_HOST') to fix the problem. HTTP_HOST also returns the port (that is, partnerlink.myserver.com:8080) if not running on port 80. This throws a small twist into your code as well because you need to parse out the port or include it into your comparison.

Application Paths

Under iAS, the DAD name is no longer aliased in the application URL, as it was under OAS. If you had an application URL like **http://www.tusc.com/myApp/welcome** under OAS, it becomes **http://www.tusc.com/pls/myDAD/welcome** under iAS. See the previous section or Chapter 3 for instructions on aliasing the two-part path.

SSL Certificates

If you're using Secure Sockets Layer (SSL) to deliver encrypted content, you should be aware that Spyglass and Apache use different file formats for their certificate and key files. You need to convert your existing SSL files to the Apache format or obtain new SSL certificates from your trusted third-party provider. Oracle provides a utility—pconvert.exe—to convert your existing certificates and keys. For more information on SSL, see Chapter 12. For instructions on converting your OAS certificates, see Oracle Support on MetaLink (**http://metalink.oracle.com**), and search for Oracle Service Bulletin 140004.1.

Summary

I strongly recommend that you upgrade from OAS to *i*AS as soon as you possibly can. The performance and reliability enhancements alone are worth the time it takes to migrate. Many Oracle shops are still using OWS, version 2.1, and OWAS, version 3.0, because when they tested OAS, they couldn't keep it running. Whether you're currently running with version 2.1, 3.0, or 4.0, make the migration straight to *i*AS. *i*AS provides the reliability you want. In addition, *i*AS also provides considerable performance improvements over prior versions. The bottom line is this: why not convert to *i*AS? Not a single reason comes to mind.

CHAPTER
11

Built-in PL/SQL Packages

T o enhance and speed up your Web-based applications, Oracle continues to provide new PL/SQL built-in packages. These packages provide you with a toolkit ready and waiting for you to use for the development of technical solutions to solve business needs quickly. Oracle provides powerful PL/SQL packages that can be used to enhance and support *i*AS applications. Some, such as HTP, HTF, OWA_COOKIE, and OWA_UTIL, were designed specifically for use with *i*AS to generate Web pages with PL/SQL, but most other built-ins have more general applicability. This chapter won't cover every possible Oracle built-in package because entire books exist on this subject. Instead, this chapter discusses the more useful built-in packages for Web development. These packages are part of the Oracle database— not Oracle*i*AS—and can be used with or apart from *i*AS.

For more information about the packages discussed in this chapter, you can check out Oracle's online documentation on their primary site (**http://www.oracle.com**) and on TechNet (**http://technet.oracle.com**). Also, check out the package headers of the packages themselves. Often the package headers, which can be read from the ALL_ SOURCE view, contain inline documentation.

Remember, any of these procedures can be called from anywhere in the database engine. In other words, you can use UTL_HTTP to retrieve information from the Internet and store the data within your database, from the database on a scheduled basis (using DBMS_JOB).

In this chapter, the following topics are discussed:

- Encrypting Sensitive Data Using DBMS_OBFUSCATION_TOOLKIT

- Reading Other Web sites Using UTL_HTTP

- Creating Dynamic Queries and PL/SQL Code Using DBMS_SQL, EXECUTE IMMEDIATE, and Reference Cursors

- Sending Electronic Mail from the Database Using UTL_SMTP

- Communicating Through TCP/IP Sockets with UTL_TCP

- Scheduling from the Database Using DBMS_JOB

- Sending Messages Via the Database with DBMS_PIPE

- Setting Session Properties with DBMS_SESSION

- Retrieving Time to the Millisecond with DBMS_UTILITY.GET_TIME

Encrypting Sensitive Data Using DBMS_OBFUSCATION_TOOLKIT

Keeping your data confidential and secure is a good idea. Passwords, to name an obvious example, shouldn't be accessible to just anyone. HTML provides the password input type to hide manually typed passwords from curious observers but, until recently, Oracle didn't provide built-in functionally to hide sensitive data from inquiring minds. True, Oracle passwords have always been encrypted and the first line of defense remains limited access (privileges) to those who need to see data elements. Occasionally, though, people can see things they aren't supposed to and hackers are out there, ready to pounce on unwary systems. In the light of such realities, it's helpful to *obfuscate,* or confuse the data as stored, so *no one* can tell what it really means when accessed from a lowly SELECT statement. Oracle has provided this functionality with the DBMS_OBFUSCATION_TOOLKIT package, which can be used to encrypt and decrypt data. Encrypted data can be stored in the database just as passwords are. This package's job is to scramble the data.

TIP
*People often refer to DBMS_OBFUSCATION_*
TOOLKIT as DBMS_OBFUSCATE.

DBMS_OBFUSCATION_TOOLKIT is an Oracle package that contains two broad kinds of routines and some supporting objects in the package header. These routines consist of procedures and function to *encrypt* (encode) data, while the others are used to *decrypt* (decode) it. For instance, the unencrypted (raw) value of a variable could be "TESTING " but, after the encryption process has been acted on, the value could be transformed to "Vdw~Zw_o", effectively hiding it. The decryption process would restore "Vdw~Zw_o" as "TESTING."

The procedures and functions can be further subdivided by data type, with a series of procedures and functions operating on raw (unformatted) data and another on regular character data.

Let's narrow our focus to character processing. A further logical subdivision can be made between the single- and multiple-*key* functions (providing different levels of security). These are discussed later. Finally, the modules themselves are divided into both procedures and functions for the developer to use as desired. The procedures and functions are pretty much the same except for how they're used. Noncode support objects in the package header include predefined values for the multiple key modes with the Des3 (multiple key) procedures.

DesEncrypt and DesDecrypt

It would be nice if we could simply call the DesEncrypt and DesDecrypt functions and retrieve the encrypted or decrypted data, but DBMS_OBFUSCATION_TOOLKIT has rules we need to understand and follow.

The character version of the DesEncrypt accepts three parameters: input_string and key_string are *input parameters,* and encrypted_string is an *output parameter.* The function version accepts only the first two values and returns the encrypted value as the function return value. All are VARCHAR2 types and *must* have lengths that are multiples of eight characters. If any of them are *not* multiples of eight characters, the procedure (or function) produces the following error message:

```
ORA-28232: invalid input length for obfuscation toolkit
```

It might not be a bad idea to use the up-until-now obsolete CHAR data type when encoding data. This has the usually unfortunate side effect of right-padding its value with spaces to the maximum length. Furthermore, encrypted values themselves cannot be encrypted again. Attempting to do so results in the following error message:

```
ORA-28233: double encryption not supported
```

The input string and key are two different data entities. The *input string* is the piece of data to be encoded: a password, Social Security number, or any data requiring encryption. The data type *must* be character (or raw, for the raw routines). If you need to encode another data type, simply convert it to character data first.

The *key* is a text value used to encode the input string. Different keys (that is, different text) applied to the same input string produce different encoded results. Note, it's *very* important not to lose a key once data has been encoded. While breaking encoded values without a key *is* possible, this is very hard and, the longer the key value actually is, the harder it is to break the encoding values. The two- and three-key modes discussed later are more secure than a single-key method. Keys must be greater or equal to eight characters.

TIP
Securing a key is just as important as securing the data it protects. You might want to use PL/SQL's capability to wrap (encode) package bodies containing key values. Also, be careful to set operating system privileges on files containing such key values.

Once you obtain the data to be encoded and define a key value, you're almost ready to encode and decode your data. In fact, you *should* be ready to go, except for one irregularity with the DBMS_OBFUSCATION_TOOLKIT package. When working with the package to develop this section, we tried to use positional parameter passing to send values to DesEncrypt. PL/SQL allows two different ways to send values to procedures and functions: positional notation and named notation.

Positional notation has the first value in the procedure/function call associated with the first value defined in the procedure/function header as described, the second with the second, and so forth. Consider the following procedure definition:

```
procedure test(one    in number, two   in number,
              three in number, four in number)…
```

Calling this procedure using position notation looks like this:

```
test(1,2,3,4)
```

Named notation, which is less commonly used, associates the *name* of the input parameter (as defined in the procedure or function header) with the value using the "=>" operator, *regardless of the position in the procedure or function call.* Because the name is associated with the value, they can be presented in any order. The order is actual parameter name => value. Calling the test procedure using named notation looks like this:

```
test(four => 41, three => 39, two => 14, one => 11);
```

Calling the desencrypt procedure could be referred to as follows:

```
dbms_obfuscation_toolkit.desencrypt(
    input_string      => v_text_c,
    key_string        => v_key_c,
    encrypted_string => v_text_encrypted_c
    );
```

Furthermore, PL/SQL allows the *overloading* of procedures and functions, meaning different procedures and functions can have the same name, as long as some difference exists in their parameter lists, which is how PL/SQL tells them apart. If you ever wondered how the TO_CHAR() function could operate on both dates and numbers, this is how—package overloading. For some reason, PL/SQL on Oracle 8.1.7.0.0 didn't like positional notation to call the DesEncrypt function (appearing to confuse the raw and char types), but *did* allow named notation. An overload issue results in the following error:

```
PLS-00307: too many declarations of 'DESENCRYPT' match this call
```

The following example encrypts the string "TESTING" using a key string (or password) of "TUSC," and places the resulting encrypted string into the v_text_encrypted variable:

```
dbms_obfuscation_toolkit.desencrypt(
    input_string      => 'TESTING',
    key_string        => 'TUSCTUSC',
    encrypted_string  => v_text_encrypted_c
);
```

The following code decrypts the string currently in the v_text_encrypted_c variable using a key string of v_key_c and places the decrypted value into the string variable named v_text_decrypted:

```
dbms_obfuscation_toolkit.desdecrypt(
    input_string      => v_text_encrypted_c,
    key_string        => v_key_c,
    decrypted_string  => v_text_decrypted_c
);
```

Des3Encrypt and Des3Decrypt

Now to move to bigger and better things. Des3Encrypt and Des3Decrypt also deal with encryption, but are a little more complicated and have more rules attached. The Des3 modules are more secure because they require longer keys, which must be precisely 128 or 192 bytes. Why 128 and 192? Because both numbers are multiples of 64 and use 2 (64×2 = 128) or 3 (64×3 = 192) 64-byte keys to encrypt the data. An extra parameter called "which" controls whether 128 or 192 bytes are used. The *which* parameter can have only one of two values. The values are conveniently hard coded in the package header for easy reference, so you can use them as self-documenting mnemonics: 0 (defined for the TwoKeyMode package variable) and 1 (defined for the ThreeKeyMode package variable). Remember, if *0* is used, the key must be 128 characters long. If *1* is used, the key must be 192 characters long. The syntax of the des3encrypt procedure is as follows:

```
dbms_obfuscation_toolkit.des3encrypt(
    input_string      => v_text_c,
    key_string        => v_key_192_c,
    encrypted_string  => v_text_encrypted_c,
    which             => 1
);
```

The syntax of the des3decrypt procedure is as follows:

```
dbms_obfuscation_toolkit.des3decrypt(
    input_string      => v_text_encrypted_c,
```

```
      key_string        => v_key_192_c,
      decrypted_string => v_text_decrypted_c,
      which             => 1
      );
```

You can also use the predefined mode variables from the package header for the which parameter. These include dbms_obfuscation_toolkit.TwoKeyMode and dbms_obfuscation_toolkit.ThreeKeyMode, which translate to 0 and 1, respectively.

Sample Procedure Using Encryption and Decryption

The following Web-based procedure accepts three keys (one for a standard encryption, one for 128-byte encryption, and one for 192-byte encryption), and a string to encrypt and decrypt. This procedure pads (with spaces) keys and text to the required length, so the procedures work without errors. You can run this procedure to demonstrate these packages.

```
Create or replace procedure test_obfuscation
(in_key            varchar2  default 'tusctusc',
 in_key_128        varchar2  default null,
 in_key_192        varchar2  default null,
 in_text           varchar2  default 'TESTING_'
)
is
 v_text_decrypted varchar2(1000);
 v_text_encrypted varchar2(1000);
 v_key             varchar2(100)
        := rpad(in_key,length(in_key) + (8-mod(length(in_key),8)));
 v_key_128         varchar2(128)
        := rpad(nvl(in_key_128,in_key), 128);
 v_key_192         varchar2(192)
        := rpad(nvl(in_key_192,in_key), 192);
 v_text            varchar2(500)
        := rpad(in_text,length(in_text) + (8-mod(length(in_text),8)));
BEGIN
  htp.header(1, 'Encryption and DeCryption Testing');
  htp.tableOpen('border=1');
  htp.tableRowOpen;
  htp.tableHeader('Unencrypted in_text');
  htp.tableData(in_text);
  htp.tableRowClose;
  BEGIN
    -- Encrypt it
    dbms_obfuscation_toolkit.desencrypt(
      input_string      => v_text,
      key_string        => v_key,
```

```
         encrypted_string => v_text_encrypted
    );
      htp.tableRowOpen;
      htp.tableHeader('Encrypted in_text using key '||v_key);
      -- If the user clicks on this link, it will attempt to re-encrypt,
      -- which could cause an error (double encryption)
      htp.tableData(htf.anchor('test_obfuscation?in_key='||
         replace_url(rtrim(v_key))||
       '&in_key_128='||replace_url(rtrim(v_key_128))||
       '&in_key_192='||replace_url(rtrim(v_key_192))||
         '&in_text='||replace_url(v_text_encrypted),
       v_text_encrypted));
      htp.tableRowClose;
      -- Decrypt it
    dbms_obfuscation_toolkit.desdecrypt(
      input_string     => v_text_encrypted,
      key_string       => v_key,
      decrypted_string => v_text_decrypted
    );
      htp.tableRowOpen;
      htp.tableHeader('Decrypted in_text using key '||v_key);
      htp.tableData(v_text_decrypted);
      htp.tableRowClose;
  EXCEPTION
    when others then
      htp.bold(sqlerrm);
  END;
  ------------------------------------------------------------------------
  --Pass through obfuscation routine using mode value 0
  -- (128 length key value)
  ------------------------------------------------------------------------
  BEGIN
    dbms_obfuscation_toolkit.des3encrypt(
      input_string     => v_text,
      key_string       => v_key_128,
      encrypted_string => v_text_encrypted,
      which            => dbms_obfuscation_toolkit.TwoKeyMode
    );
      htp.tableRowOpen;
      htp.tableHeader('Encrypted in_text using 128 byte key '||v_key_128);
      -- If the user clicks on this link, it will attempt to re-encrypt,
  --    -- which could cause an error
      htp.tableData(htf.anchor('test_obfuscation?in_key='||
         replace_url(rtrim(v_key))||
       '&in_key_128='||replace_url(rtrim(v_key_128))||
       '&in_key_192='||replace_url(rtrim(v_key_192))||
         '&in_text='||replace_url(v_text_encrypted),
       v_text_encrypted));
      htp.tableRowClose;
```

```
       dbms_obfuscation_toolkit.des3decrypt(
         input_string    => v_text_encrypted,
         key_string      => v_key_128,
         decrypted_string => v_text_decrypted,
         which           => dbms_obfuscation_toolkit.TwoKeyMode
         );
       htp.tableRowOpen;
       htp.tableHeader('Decrypted in_text using 128 byte key '||v_key_128);
       htp.tableData(v_text_decrypted);
       htp.tableRowClose;
   EXCEPTION
     when others then
       htp.bold(sqlerrm);
   END;
   BEGIN
     dbms_obfuscation_toolkit.des3encrypt(
       input_string    => v_text,
       key_string      => v_key_192,
       encrypted_string => v_text_encrypted,
       which           => dbms_obfuscation_toolkit.ThreeKeyMode
     );
       htp.tableRowOpen;
       htp.tableHeader('Encrypted in_text using 192 byte key '||v_key_192);
       -- If the user clicks on this link, it will attempt to re-encrypt,
       -- which could will cause an error
       htp.tableData(htf.anchor('test_obfuscation?in_key='||
           replace_url(rtrim(v_key))||
         '&in_key_128='||replace_url(rtrim(v_key_128))||
         '&in_key_192='||replace_url(rtrim(v_key_192))||
           '&in_text='||replace_url(v_text_encrypted),
         v_text_encrypted));
       htp.tableRowClose;
     dbms_obfuscation_toolkit.des3decrypt(
       input_string    => v_text_encrypted,
       key_string      => v_key_192,
       decrypted_string => v_text_decrypted,
       which           => dbms_obfuscation_toolkit.ThreeKeyMode
     );
       htp.tableRowOpen;
       htp.tableHeader('Decrypted in_text using 192 byte key '||v_key_192);
       htp.tableData(v_text_decrypted);
       htp.tableRowClose;
   EXCEPTION
     when others then
       htp.bold(sqlerrm);
   END;
END;
/
```

Figure 11-1 illustrates how the text "ENCRYPTED_PHRASE" is encrypted and decrypted successfully using a key string, or password, of "tusctusc."

Reading Other Web Sites Using UTL_HTTP

One of the more interesting packages Oracle provides is *UTL_HTTP*, which lets PL/SQL read Web pages like a text-only browser. UTL_HTTP reads the HTML into a PL/SQL table or a varchar2 variable. The HTML source code is then available for analysis.

Why would you want to analyze another Web site's HTML? Many reasons exist. You could read a document, analyze its contents, isolate relevant data, and load key information into your database. This is similar to the old trick of reading electronic reports and pulling key values from them. You could read a document from your own site and save the text in the database as an audit trail of what the document source looks like over time. You could read a static document from your site, use PL/SQL's pattern matching capabilities (OWA_PATTERN, LIKE operator, or INSTR()

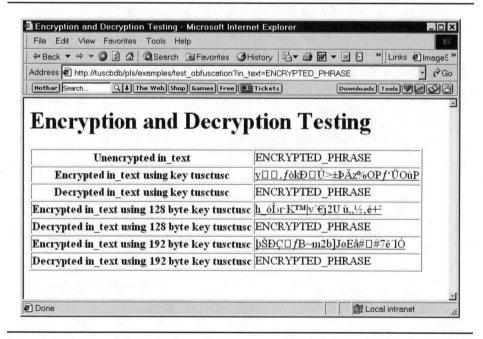

FIGURE 11-1. *Browser executing test_obfuscation procedure*

functions), or perhaps the advanced pattern-matching capabilities of PL/SQL to stream edit and replace the page automatically with the UTL_FILE package (which lets PL/SQL read from and write to operating system files). You could even use DBMS_JOB to run such applications automatically.

You need to consider two things when using UTL_HTTP. Oracle documentation suggests that if you have trouble connecting to a site using UTL_HTTP, you need to place a browser on the same machine (the database server) and see if you can connect using the browser. If you cannot connect to the Web site using a browser, you won't be able to connect to the site with UTL_HTTP. UTL_HTTP also doesn't accept cookies, so be sure to turn cookies off in the browser for testing.

TIP
If UTL_HTTP won't work for your needs, consider using Perl's LWP or Java, which are both considerably more capable than UTL_HTTP.

TIP
*Basic and digest authentication can be passed in the URL using a syntax of **http:// username:password@host/virtual_path/program**.*

UTL_HTTP Functions

UTL_HTTP comes with two functions: REQUEST and REQUEST_PIECES. The difference between the two is *REQUEST* returns a 4,000-character string and *REQUEST_PIECES* returns a VARCHAR2 PL/SQL table (array) of 2,000-byte pieces. Because REQUEST only returns a 4,000-byte string and most documents are longer than 4,000 bytes, I recommend you use REQUEST_PIECES and concentrate on that function in this section. If the page is longer than 4,000 characters, REQUEST truncates the results—potentially missing some of the important document contents. Otherwise, they're quite similar. In previous versions of the database, REQUEST_ PIECES was called REQUEST_LINES.

To use REQUEST_PIECES, you must first define the local PL/SQL table that receives the resulting data. For example:

```
v_page_table utl_http.html_pieces;
```

To populate the PL/SQL table with the HTML from the **http://www.tusc.com** Web site, simply call the REQUEST_PIECES procedure as in the following example. REQUEST_PIECES accepts several input parameters. The first parameter—the URL—is mandatory. The URL value is a string that contains the URL of the document to be read—just like the one you would use in a browser window. For instance, you could use

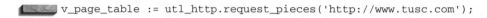

```
v_page_table := utl_http.request_pieces('http://www.tusc.com');
```

TIP
Be sure to include the transfer protocol, specifically http://, in the URL.

The other input parameters are optional and are described only briefly. *MAX_PIECES* can be used to specify the maximum number of pieces (array records) *REQUEST_PIECES* returns before truncating the page. The default is 32K (about 17 pieces or array records) and needs to be specified only if the document storage exceeds this, or lowered if memory is scarce (and the page will fit in the newly sized array). The *PROXY* parameter can be used to tell UTL_HTTP the IP address or domain of your proxy server (the default—NULL—indicates none is required). *WALLET_PATH* and *WALLET_PASSWORD* have default values and are used when using secure transmissions, so you can safely ignore them.

One other bit of information about the REQUEST_PIECES function isn't immediately obvious: the pieces are put together in byte order, one at a time, with every array element a full 2,000 bytes (not quite 2K) long, except the last one. Thinking that REQUEST_PIECES will return the document with clean line breaks, one per piece, is tempting, but that isn't what it does. Physical lines in the document are put together to a maximum length of 2,000 bytes, one after another (including new line characters), with the next piece picking up immediately where the previous piece left off. This is probably why the procedure was renamed from lines to pieces!

UTL_HTTP Test Application

The following procedure is an example of how UTL_HTTP can be used to read a document from a Web site—this could be displayed in a frame or a table data cell, or printed using SQL*Plus.

```
Create or replace procedure test_utl_http
(in_url      varchar2  default 'http://www.tusc.com')
is
  v_page_table utl_http.html_pieces;
BEGIN
  htp.header(1,'Retrieving and Printing '||in_url);
  htp.print('<BASE HREF='||in_url||'>');
  v_page_table := utl_http.request_pieces(in_url);
  for i in 1..v_page_table.count loop
     htp.prn(v_page_table(i));
```

```
  end loop;
  htp.header(1,'Done Retrieving and Printing '||in_url);
END;
/
```

Note the previous BASE tag. Figure 11-2 shows the output in a Web page
without the BASE tag—notice the images are broken. Figure 11-3 shows the output
including the BASE tag. Remember, references are relative. In a browser, when you
directly type **http://www.tusc.com**, all images are relative to the virtual root of the
server. In Figures 11-2 and 11-3, the base URL, by default, is **http://tuscbdb/pls/
examples**. Therefore, no images can be found in Figure 11-2 because the base
relative reference is **http://tuscbdb/pls/examples**. To fix this problem, we must
set the base URL to **http://www.tusc.com**.

FIGURE 11-2. *Web page without BASE tag*

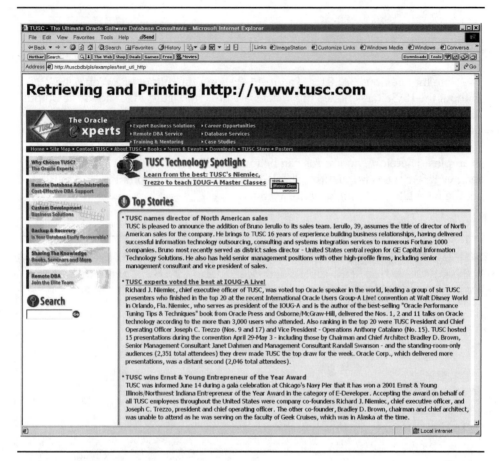

FIGURE 11-3. *Web page with BASE tag*

This function was released in the database as of Oracle RDBMS version 7.3.3. As noted, all the packages in this chapter are executed from the database engine, not *iAS*.

Exceptions

Two exceptions should be declared when using the UTL_HTTP function. If you don't declare the exceptions, you receive an ORA-6510 error indicating a PL/SQL unhandled user-defined exception occurred every time any other error is received. The following exceptions are the two exceptions that should be declared:

```
declare init_failed    exception;
declare request_failed exception;
```

The init_failed exception will occur when initialization of the http callout subsystem fails. This happens when an environmental failure, such as lack of available memory, has occurred. The request_failed exception occurs when the HTTP call fails. This happens when a failure of the HTTP daemon has occurred or if the url argument cannot be interpreted as a URL because it's NULL or has non-HTTP syntax. If the site is down or doesn't respond, you'll receive a request_failed error.

Other Possible Uses of UTL_HTTP

A number of possible uses of UTL_HTTP exist. For example, you can use UTL_HTTP for stock price tracking, to gather your competitors' price lists, to collect vendor comparison price lists as a cyber robot (gathering keyword and URL information), to create semistatic pages (such as a static home page from data like weekly news), to read templates, to call other CGI programs, or even for load testing. The possibilities are endless.

Collect Current Stock Prices and Saving in the Database

You can use UTL_HTTP to collect Oracle's stock price, track your portfolio, track your company's stock price, or to provide real-time and historical stock information on your company's Web site. Where can you gather stock information? From about a thousand different sites, so pick your favorite. To view a stock quote from Yahoo! (as HTML), use the browser to traverse down to the stock price for Oracle. The following code retrieves the current stock price for Oracle:

```
http://quote.yahoo.com/q?s=orcl&o=t
```

View the source code for that page, which appears similar to the following subset of code:

```
...
<a href="/q?s=ORCL&d=t">ORCL</a>        Nov 25         <b>34 5/8</b>
<font color="#ff0020">-3/8</font>
<font color="#ff0020">-1.07%</font>  4,019,400 <small>
...
```

Using UTL_HTTP, you can retrieve the HTML for this page using a statement similar to the following:

```
html := utl_http.request_pieces('http://quote.yahoo.com/q?s=orcl&o=t');
```

Once executed, the results of the query from Yahoo! are placed into a PL/SQL table called HTML, which can be parsed to extract key information like the following:

```
start_pos        := instr (html(x), '>orcl</a>');
end_pos          := instr (html(x), '<small>', start_pos+1);
key_information := substr(html(x), start_pos,
                          end_pos - start_pos);
```

You can break down the key_information variable further, as you see fit. The key_information variable could be stored in the database, written to a file (using UTL_FILE), or used to perform other tasks. You can schedule this procedure to execute regularly using DBMS_JOB.

Collecting Competitor Price Lists or Vendor Price Comparisons

You can gather your competitors' price lists or collect price lists from all your vendors to enable vendor price comparisons directly from your data. In other words, anything containing key information on a specific URL uses logic similar to the preceding procedure logic. You can even develop a generic routine to extract this key information from any page.

Cyber Robot

Use UTL_HTTP as a cyber robot to read through an entire site or site component to build data for searches, site maps, "what's new" pages, and so forth. Collect tables containing keywords and URLs with an intersection entity containing the keywords in each URL. The pseudo logic might appear similar to the following:

- Loop
  - Read page
  - Ignore tags (from < to >)
  - For each keyword
  - Does keyword exist in table?

    Yes   insert keyword_url record

    No   insert keyword and keyword_url
  - Find all anchors, insert url, site_tree records
  - Read next unprocessed url record

Poor Man's Web Cache

Yet another use of UTL_HTTP is creating what's referred to as a *semistatic home page,* which is useful if you want a page to contain dynamic content, but you don't want to generate that content dynamically every time someone requests the page. If you're going to experience thousands of hits every hour or minute, you certainly don't want to generate the home page dynamically for each user, do you? Even if the content on the page only changes every minute, every five minutes, or hourly, using UTL_HTTP as a "poor man's Web cache" can save valuable processing power. You might also have daily updates, a weekly news page, or even a monthly manager's report that can be created in a similar manner. The less frequently the data changes, the more powerful this function is. You can drive the re-creation of the page by a database event, such as an update. Use UTL_HTTP to dynamically generate the page's contents and retrieve the HTML for the page; then write the HTML to a static file, which can be accomplished using UTL_FILE; then determine the method of regeneration. To regenerate manually, simply execute the procedure whenever necessary. If this is a frequency-based regeneration, use DBMS_JOB to execute your procedure on whatever frequency you choose. To base regeneration on a table event, use a table-based trigger to execute your procedure or use DBMS_PIPE to queue the execution.

Executing Any Operating System Command from PL/SQL

One of my favorite uses for UTL_HTTP is to execute CGI programs directly from PL/SQL. Remember, you can call any valid URL using this procedure. This obviously includes a URL executing a CGI program that executes and returns HTML. By using UTL_HTTP to execute the CGI program, the information (HTML) is returned to PL/SQL. For example, you can have a CGI program performing credit card processing, Notice to Airman (NOTAM) information for airlines, access to Transmission Control Protocol/Internet Protocol (TCP/IP) ports, and so forth. This enables you to write the complex code in another language (for example, C, Java, or Perl) and to save PL/SQL for the graphic user display of information.

TIP
Most languages, including Java and Perl, can directly access the operating system.

Benchmarks

You can also use this functionality to establish performance benchmarks of your applications (or your competitor's) or for testing. You can execute this procedure on a scheduled basis (using dbms_job) and collect statistics. For testing purposes, you can put the call into a for loop, as illustrated in the following syntax:

```
for i in 1 .. 10000 loop
    html_pieces := utl_http.request_pieces(url_to_call);
end loop;
```

You can also store a set of URLs in a table and loop through the table using the following syntax:

```
for i in 1 .. 10000 loop
    for test_urls_cur in test_urls_rec loop
        html_pieces := utl_http.request_pieces(test_urls_rec.url);
    end loop;
end loop;
```

Dynamic Queries and PL/SQL Code Using DBMS_SQL, EXECUTE IMMEDIATE, and Reference Cursors

The capability to execute dynamic queries and PL/SQL code is nothing new in Oracle. This functionality has been around for years in the DBMS_SQL package and, more recently, reference cursors. The relatively new *EXECUTE IMMEDIATE* command is a friendly interface to perform this kind of work, however, in direct contrast with DBMS_SQL, which has been well documented elsewhere, but usually isn't as friendly or easy to use.

The purpose of dynamic code is to take a string containing a syntactically correct piece of SQL or PL/SQL code—a query, SQL DML command, or even a block of PL/SQL code—interpret it, and execute it from within the PL/SQL run-time environment. Using one of the various forms of dynamically executing code (DBMS_SQL, reference cursors, or EXECUTE IMMEDIATE), use either a string literal *or* a string variable. You can write routines that are put together according to existing conditions without having to modify code after it's written, tested, and debugged. The effect is similar to that of the exec() command in the various UNIX shells and in JavaScript.

Remember, the strings used in dynamic SQL must be syntactically correct. A typographic error using dynamic SQL can cause a run-time error just as surely as it can cause a compilation error in static code. For this reason, it's vital that you include error handling when using dynamic code.

The *EXECUTE IMMEDIATE* command in PL/SQL provides an elegance and ease of use toward writing dynamic code that previously was sorely missed. To use the DBMS_SQL package for a DML command, you have to define the command as text, run the text through a prepare function, parse it, open the cursor, execute it, and close the cursor. For a query, you have the additional steps of setting up buffers for the query data one by one (per column), and after the query, transferring the data from the buffers to your destination variables (*again,* one by one), for every row retrieved. It works, and works well once all the *T*s have been crossed, *I*s dotted, and *X*s crossed, but it's painful to implement and can be somewhat slow to develop and debug. As with any application, performance can be an issue if the dynamic SQL statements aren't well tuned. EXECUTE IMMEDIATE does away with the tedium of setting up DBMS_SQL, although it too often performs worse than hard code. A few instances exist where DBMS_SQL will still do things EXECUTE IMMEDIATE cannot, such as run with extremely large text strings. DBMS_SQL also contains a package describe procedure that could come in handy—but, by and large, EXECUTE_IMMEDIATE is a welcome substitute for the DBMS_SQL package. You might argue that extremely large pieces of dynamic code shouldn't be used anyway because such constructs are problems waiting to happen. Experienced developers know that just because you *can* do something doesn't mean you *should* do it.

But power and flexibility always have tradeoffs. The capability to use dynamic code (termed Native Dynamic SQL in its latest Oracle incarnation) is no exception. The cost of using dynamic code is the complexity of your code and slower run-time versus versatility. Hard-coded routines are always easier to write and maintain, and run faster than the equivalent dynamic routines doing precisely the same thing because the latter require more processing power to do the same work. Hard-coded routines are compiled once, they store the explain plan in a compiled form, and they always execute the same way. Dynamic routines, by their very nature, do different things once compiled and are frequently recompiled on-the-fly. Dynamic routines are also *much* more complex and require the developer not only to think about what the routine is doing under one circumstance, but to project how it will run under every conceivable condition. On the plus side, careful use of Native Dynamic SQL can save the developer a great deal of time and effort duplicating existing functionality—the very thing Native Dynamic SQL is for.

In the following section, you see the various ways of using dynamic code in PL/SQL.

DBMS_SQL

The traditional way of executing dynamic code in PL/SQL was to use the DBMS_ SQL package. DBMS_SQL can perform both queries and DML and, until recently, was the only way to perform from within PL/SQL. EXECUTE IMMEDATE has superceded DBMS_SQL and reference cursors are considerably easier to use to perform dynamic SQL. The following code demonstrates a procedure that uses DBMS_SQL to call any DDL statement dynamically:

```
CREATE OR REPLACE PROCEDURE exec_ddl(p_statement IN VARCHAR2)
IS
```

```
   exec_cursor INTEGER := DBMS_SQL.OPEN_CURSOR;
   rows_processed NUMBER := 0;
   lv_statement VARCHAR2(30000);
begin
   lv_statement := p_statement;
   DBMS_SQL.PARSE( exec_cursor, lv_statement, DBMS_SQL.V7 );
   rows_processed := DBMS_SQL.EXECUTE ( exec_cursor );
   DBMS_SQL.CLOSE_CURSOR ( exec_cursor );
EXCEPTION
   WHEN others THEN
      IF ( DBMS_SQL.IS_OPEN ( exec_cursor ) )
      THEN
         DBMS_SQL.CLOSE_CURSOR ( exec_cursor );
      END IF;
   RAISE;
END exec_ddl;
/
```

The previous procedure could be used to turn SQL_TRACE on or off, as follows:

```
...
-- Turn SQL_TRACE on
exec_ddl('alter session set sql_trace true')
...
-- Turn SQL_TRACE off
exec_ddl('alter session set sql_trace false')
```

Or, the exec_ddl could be used to enable or disable a trigger or constraint, as follows:

```
...
-- Disable the constraints
exec_ddl('alter trigger BU_ORDER disable')
exec_ddl('alter table S_EMPLOYEE disable constraint S_EMPLOYEE_TITLE_FK')
...
-- Re-enable the constraints
exec_ddl('alter trigger BU_ORDER enable')
exec_ddl('alter table S_EMPLOYEE enable constraint S_EMPLOYEE_TITLE_FK')
```

This code creates a procedure which, when executed as in the previous PL/SQL procedure snippets, dynamically executes the supplied string. The exec_ddl procedure receives the string as the p_statement variable. By supplying different strings, you can run different DDL commands! Local variables include *exec_cursor*, which defines an integer value to be used to identify the cursor after opening with the PARSE function to other dbms_sql modules. The rows_processed variable accepts the return value from the EXECUTE function and holds the number of rows processed by a DML statement (basically, the SQL%ROWCOUNT attribute of an implicit cursor that would do the same thing if hard coded). The *lv_statement* variable contains a copy of p_statement (and could be manipulated, if desired). You use the PARSE procedure to parse the SQL command (lv_statement). You use EXEC_CURSOR to receive the cursor ID. DBMS_SQL.V7 is a constant in the procedure that identifies the compatibility mode to use during execution (that is, Version 7). The *EXECUTE* function actually executes the DDL (or DML) command, returning the number of rows processed to the rows_processed variable. Finally, the CLOSE_CURSOR procedure closes the opened cursor used to process the command.

EXECUTE IMMEDIATE

Thanks to the addition of the EXECUTE IMMEDIATE command, executing dynamic code in PL/SQL is much easier. We can dispense with almost all the overhead and setup required by DBMS_SQL and simply use the EXECUTE IMMEDIATE command to execute the desired code as defined within the string text. The entire previous EXEC_DDL procedure that uses DBMS_SQL can be replaced by the EXECUTE IMMEDIATE command. For example:

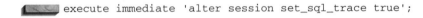

```
execute immediate 'alter session set_sql_trace true';
```

TIP
Although EXECUTE IMMEDIATE is sometimes referred to as EXECUTE_IMMEDIATE, the proper syntax in PL/SQL code is to use a space between the two words.

Although a simple command is indicated in the previous example, blocks of code of varying complexity can be executed, not to mention dynamically assigned. The example here dynamically builds and executes a block of PL/SQL code. Safe EXECUTE IMMEDIATE implementations use an exception handler, as follows:

```
BEGIN
   v_block_c :=
     'BEGIN '||
     '  if (to_char(sysdate,''D'',1) in (''1'',''7'') then ' ||
     '      process_weekend; '||
     '    else '||
     '      process_weekday; '||
     '  end if;'||
     'END;';
   execute immediate v_block_c;
EXCEPTION
```

```
when others then
   log_error(v_procedure_name,sqlerrm);
END;
```

The exception handler logs the error using an error-handling routine defined elsewhere. For more information on event handling, see Chapter 22, which discusses debugging.

EXECUTE IMMEDATE has a few additional features worth mentioning. The *USING* and *RETURNING* clauses can respectively be used to include bind variables into and receive return values from predefined string values. Place markers for the bind variables, where the specified value will be substituted in the string before processing actually occurs, are indicated by a colon (:) and an identifier, something like :1 or :value. The RETURNING clause is used to specify returning data structures, supporting a little-used feature in SQL that allows DML statements to return values from affected rows.

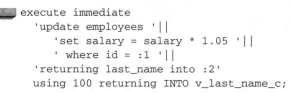

```
execute immediate
    'update employees '||
       'set salary = salary * 1.05 '||
       ' where id = :1 '||
    'returning last_name into :2'
    using 100 returning INTO v_last_name_c;
```

In this example, the using value replaces *:1* with *100* before executing the statement and *:2* returns the value into v_last_name_c after executing. The formatting of the update statement text was intended to look like a normal update in PL/SQL code and, if desired, a CHR(10) value could have been included to provide line breaks after each line for debugging purposes.

Finally, although EXECUTE IMMEDIATE can be used to perform single-row queries, it is usually easier to use reference cursors to perform dynamic queries. Note, queries returning more than one row will result in the infamous too many rows error.

Reference Cursors

Like DBMS_SQL, *reference cursors* (also called *cursor variables*) have been around for a while. Reference cursors are easier to use than dbms_sql to perform queries and, once opened, can be passed between procedures for generic processing. The declaration and opening of a reference cursor is somewhat specialized, but the fetch and close operations are identical to standard (or normal) cursor fetch and close statements. Reference cursors are the easiest way to perform dynamic select operations in Oracle.

Tradeoffs between reference cursors and normal cursors should be considered. Reference cursors are a little bit slower, are much more versatile, cannot accept parameters as regular cursors do (but can be dynamically built and can accept bind variables to accomplish the same thing), can be passed as arguments to procedures to do generalized processing, but cannot be used with implicit cursor for loops. Regular cursors are faster and require less work to set up, but are more rigid in their use.

To build a reference cursor, first declare a type in the declare section of the PL/SQL block in which it's to be used. The type is always ref cursor. For example:

```
type v_ref_cursor_type is ref cursor;
```

Once the type is established, you can create the reference cursors themselves.

```
v_ref_cur v_ref_cursor_type;
```

The reference cursor is opened using the OPEN FOR command with the query text. The query can be either a literal or a string variable. Reference cursor open strings—even when using variables—can accept bind variables, in which case a USING clause listing the substitution bind values must be supplied. For example, you can build the query in a string variable, as follows:

```
v_query_c := 'select  product_name, product_code '||
             'from    products '||
             'where   vendor_id = :1';
```

As with any string, you can dynamically build the SQL statement. You can also use if-then-else logic to vary the text of the query. For example, to use a dynamic table name:

```
v_query_c := 'select  product_name, product_code '||
             'from    '||v_table_name_c||' '||
             'where   vendor_id = :1';
```

Now you're ready to open the cursor using the OPEN FOR command, as in this example, where we're passing in a vendor_id of 1000:

```
open v_ref_cur for v_query_c using 1000;
```

From here on, the cursor handling is identical to what you can do with normal cursors (except you cannot use an implicit cursor). So, next, you use fetch statements to retrieve each record and close when done with the cursor. As mentioned, 1,000 is the value that will be bound into the text once parsed (in the place of :1). If the cursor is opened again, a different value can be used. We could also hardcode the 1,000 directly into the query text by concatenating it directly to the where clause as a string, which is sometimes easier than using the bind variable.

```
v_query_c := 'select product_name, product_code '||
             'from   '||v_table_name_c||' '||
             'where  vendor_id = '||TO_CHAR(v_vendor_n);
```

This syntax, however, forces Oracle to reparse the query internally whenever the value of v_vendor_n changes. Using bind variables avoids this. In Version 8*i* of the RDBMS and above, however, the RDBMS tuning engine automatically creates bind variables.

Select List Example

One of the more interesting features of the reference cursor is it can be passed to functions and procedures. Let's say you want to have a generic routine to write select lists for *i*AS. Every select list in HTML has the same structure: a display value and a code value, which the display value represents. You could code different procedures to generate the select lists because the data they display usually comes from different database tables. But why write largely repetitious code over and over again, when only the table and column names will be different? Cutting-and-pasting is easy, but gets old after a while and updating pasted code properly is often tricky and tedious. To avoid this, write a routine to accept a reference cursor as a parameter and generate the select list according to the supplied cursor's output. Here's an example of the actual procedure:

```
CREATE OR REPLACE PROCEDURE write_select_list(
    p_value_c      IN varchar2,        --default value for select list
    p_field_name_c IN varchar2,        -- select list to be generated
    p_cursor_ref   IN sg_ref_cur_type  --type defined in package header
    p_first_null_b IN boolean,         --create a null first item?
    p_attributes_c IN varchar2         --any HTML attributes to use
    ) IS
    ------------------------------------------------------------------
    --Procedure variables
    ------------------------------------------------------------------
    v_selected_c        varchar2(8);
    v_select_tag_c      varchar2(128);
    v_text_selected_c   varchar2(80);
    v_value_selected_c  varchar2(80);
BEGIN
    ------------------------------------------------------------------
    --initialize variables
    ------------------------------------------------------------------
    --build the select tag
    v_select_tag_c := '<SELECT';
    if (p_field_name_c is not null) then
        v_select_tag_c := v_select_tag_c || ' NAME="'||p_field_name_c||'"';
    end if; --select list name is null
```

```
if (p_attributes_c is not null) then
    v_select_tag_c := v_select_tag_c || ' ' || p_attributes_c;
end if; --attributes are null
v_select_tag_c := v_select_tag_c || '>';
----------------------------------------------------------------------
--main processing routine
----------------------------------------------------------------------
htp.p(v_select_tag_c);
--first, empty form select option
IF (p_first_null_b) THEN
    htp.p('<OPTION VALUE="" '||p_attributes_c||'>');
END IF; --first null switch = TRUE
FETCH p_cursor_ref INTO v_value_selected_c, v_text_selected_c;
WHILE p_cursor_ref%FOUND
LOOP
  IF (v_value_selected_c IS NOT NULL) THEN
      v_selected_c := NULL;
      IF (p_value_c = v_value_selected_c) THEN
          v_selected_c := 'SELECTED';
      END IF;
      --rtrim used to eliminate extraneous space in tag
      htp.p(RTRIM('<OPTION VALUE="'||v_value_selected_c||'"
        '||v_selected_c)||'>'||
        LTRIM(v_text_selected_c));
  END IF; --selected value is not null;
  FETCH p_cursor_ref INTO v_value_selected_c, v_text_selected_c;
END LOOP;
htp.p('</SELECT>');
END write_select_list;
```

Use the following code to call the procedure:

```
open v_ref_cur for v_query_c;
write_select_list(null,'p_product_c',v_ref_cur,false,null);
close v_ref_cur;
```

The actual processing occurs in the write_select_list procedure. The cursor is defined, opened, and closed outside the procedure, but the work to use the cursor is performed inside. Several enhancements to the write select list routine can be made. An additional input parameter puts leading spaces before the generated HTML tags because all tags will be left-justified and sometimes developers like to indent HTML for readability when debugging pages. Also, why force it to generate select lists? Repeating groups of radio buttons and check boxes would require similar logic, so why not add another parameter to tell the routine which kind of object to write? Oracle Portal offers this very functionality in its document generation screen. For more information, see Chapter 16, which discusses Portal in greater detail.

Totally Dynamic *Where* Clause Example

The following example builds a where clause for the Web-based PL/SQL procedure. This procedure demonstrates the power of reference cursors.

```
CREATE OR REPLACE PROCEDURE get_emp (
 min_sal  varchar2 default null,
 max_sal  varchar2 default null,
 empno    varchar2 default null,
 order_by varchar2 default null,
 order_ad varchar2 default null)
IS
type    nbt_ref_cur is ref cursor;
emp_cur nbt_ref_cur;
emp_rec scott.emp%rowtype;
nbt_sql varchar2(1000) := 'select * from scott.emp';

-- Set where yet?  If not, use where, if so, use AND
nbt_wca varchar2(20)    := ' where ';

-- Values passed in
nbt_qs  varchar2(1000) := owa_util.get_cgi_env('QUERY_STRING');

-- Query string without order by
nbt_qs2 varchar2(1000) := nbt_qs;

-- Employee Manager Name
nbt_mgr varchar2(100);
BEGIN
    -- Build the where clause
    if min_sal is not null then
        nbt_sql := nbt_sql || nbt_wca || 'sal >= ' || min_sal;
        nbt_wca := ' and ';
     end if;
    if max_sal is not null then
        nbt_sql := nbt_sql || nbt_wca || 'sal <= ' || max_sal;
        nbt_wca := ' and ';
     end if;
    if empno is not null then
        nbt_sql := nbt_sql || nbt_wca || 'empno = ' || empno;
        nbt_wca := ' and ';
    end if;
    if order_by is not null then
        nbt_sql := nbt_sql || ' order by ' || order_by;
        if order_ad = 'D' then
              nbt_sql := nbt_sql || ' desc';
        end if;
    end if;
```

```
-- Remove the order by statement
nbt_qs2 := replace(nbt_qs2, 'order_by='||order_by, '');
-- Remove the ascending
nbt_qs2 := replace(nbt_qs2, 'order_ad=A', '');
-- Remove the descending
nbt_qs2 := replace(nbt_qs2, 'order_ad=D', '');
-- Remove double &&
nbt_qs2 := replace(nbt_qs2, '&&', '&');
-- Just an order by?
if nbt_qs2 = '&' then
   nbt_qs2 := '';
end if;
if length(nbt_qs2) > 0 and
   substr(nbt_qs2,length(nbt_qs2),1) != '&' then
   nbt_qs2 := nbt_qs2 || '&';
end if;

-- Now output the page (in HTML)
htp.htmlOpen;
htp.headOpen;
htp.title( 'List of Employees');
htp.headClose;
htp.bodyOpen(  cattributes => ' bgcolor="#6666FF" text="#FFFF00"' );
htp.header( 1,'List of Employees' );
htp.tableOpen(  cattributes => ' width="75%" border="1"' );

-- Print the header above the rows - with links to reorder data
htp.tableRowOpen;
htp.tableHeader( htf.anchor('get_emp?' ||
                            nbt_qs2 || 'order_by=ename',
   'Employee Name')||' '||htf.anchor('get_emp?' || nbt_qs2 ||
   'order_by=ename&order_ad=D', '\/'));
htp.tableHeader( htf.anchor('get_emp?' || nbt_qs2 || 'order_by=mgr',
   'Manager')          ||' '||htf.anchor('get_emp?' || nbt_qs2 ||
   'order_by=mgr&order_ad=D', '\/'));
htp.tableHeader( htf.anchor('get_emp?' ||
                   nbt_qs2 || 'order_by=hiredate',
   'Hire Date') ||' '||htf.anchor('get_emp?' || nbt_qs2 ||
   'order_by=hiredate&order_ad=D', '\/'));
htp.tableHeader( htf.anchor('get_emp?' || nbt_qs2 || 'order_by=sal',
   'Salary')          ||' '||htf.anchor('get_emp?' || nbt_qs2 ||
   'order_by=sal&order_ad=D', '\/'));
htp.tableRowClose;

-- Process our dynamically built reference cursor
open emp_cur for nbt_sql;
fetch emp_cur into emp_rec;
while (not emp_cur%notfound) LOOP
```

```
        htp.tableRowOpen;
        htp.tableData( htf.anchor('get_emp?empno='||emp_rec.empno,
            emp_rec.ename));
        if emp_rec.mgr is not null then
            select ename
            into   nbt_mgr
            from   scott.emp
            where  empno = emp_rec.mgr;
        else
            nbt_mgr := '';
        end if;
        htp.tableData( nbt_mgr);
        htp.tableData( emp_rec.hiredate);
        htp.tableData( emp_rec.sal);
        htp.tableRowClose;
        fetch emp_cur into emp_rec;
    END LOOP;

    -- Wrap it up
    htp.tableClose;
    htp.bodyClose;
    htp.htmlClose;
END;
```

Sending Electronic Mail from the Database Using UTL_SMTP

The UTL_SMTP package can be used to send e-mail from PL/SQL applications and from the database. UTL_SMTP follows the Simple Mail Transfer Protocol (SMTP) standards. *SMTP* is the Internet e-mail standard and is meant to provide an Application Programmer Interface (API) to the SMTP mail systems. This simply means you can make procedure or function calls to send e-mail directly from the database. UTL_SMTP only sends mail, though, it doesn't receive mail.

We suggest you develop your own "wrapper" procedure to do the actual work of sending an e-mail. The UTL_SMTP package provides you with the building blocks to send e-mail from the database, but doesn't provide a wrapper program, however, a wrapper is built and demonstrated in the following. This procedure can be called from other applications to greatly simplify sending e-mail from the database. Generally speaking, to send e-mail with UTL_SMTP, you have to perform the following steps:

1. Open a connection

2. Identify the domain of the sender

3. Start the mail process

4. Identify the recipient

5. Open the mail body

6. Write the mail message

7. Close the mail body

8. Close the connection

The previous steps are encapsulated in the following procedure. These requirements could conceivably deter developers from using this powerful feature, particularly those trying to meet deadlines. No particular reason exists to have a dozen or so lines in applications to perform the previous with needless repetition when a simplified one-line procedure call identifying the recipient and message should suffice. The following send_mail procedure simplifies this process for all developers:

```
CREATE OR REPLACE PROCEDURE send_mail(
    sender     in varchar2,
    recipient  in varchar2,
    subject    in varchar2,
    message    in varchar2) is
    mail_conn      utl_smtp.connection;
    v_procedure_c constant varchar2(30) := 'send_mail';
BEGIN
    mail_conn := utl_smtp.open_connection(MAILHOST, 25);
    utl_smtp.helo(mail_conn, MAILHOST);
    utl_smtp.mail(mail_conn, sender);
    utl_smtp.rcpt(mail_conn, recipient);
    utl_smtp.open_data(mail_conn);
    utl_smtp.write_data(mail_conn, 'From: "' ||
                    sender || '" <' || sender ||
                    '>' || utl_tcp.crlf);
    utl_smtp.write_data(mail_conn, 'To: "' || recipient || '" <' ||
       recipient || '>' || utl_tcp.crlf);    utl_smtp.write_data(mail_conn, 'Subject: ' ||
                    subject || utl_tcp.crlf);
    utl_smtp.write_data(mail_conn, utl_tcp.crlf);
    utl_smtp.write_data(mail_conn, message || utl_tcp.crlf);
    utl_smtp.write_data(mail_conn, utl_tcp.crlf);
    utl_smtp.close_data(mail_conn);
    utl_smtp.quit(mail_conn);
END send_mail;
```

The *open_connection* and *quit* functions establish and eliminate a mail connection; the *mail_conn* variable is returned by *open_connection* as a handler for that connection to be used by the other modules. The *helo* procedure identifies the sender's domain; *mail* starts the mail and identifies the sender; *close_data* closes the mail body; *rcpt* specifies the recipient (a standard e-mail address, like abc@bcd.com); *open_data* starts the e-mail body and *close data* closes it and actually sends the e-mail; and *write_data* is used to create the text of the e-mail. The input for the previous procedure is greatly simplified over the process of sending the entire e-mail. The input parameter names should be self-explanatory.

Of course, things can go wrong with the previously described process. What would PL/SQL be without exceptions? Potential exceptions include calling routines other than write_data or close_data after open_data and calling write_data or close_data without first calling open_data (imagine trying to write to a file that isn't open).

After setting up the procedure (which could be in a package) and debugging it, sending the e-mail from another application is a snap. A call to send_mail might look like this:

```
v_text_c := 'Testing UTL_SMTP interface';
send_mail('bradley_brown@tusc.com',
          'your_address@your_host.com',
          'Good Times',
           v_text_c);
```

These examples show just the tip of the iceberg of what can be done with UTL_SMTP. Many other procedures and functions exist beyond those mentioned in the package that weren't used here because they weren't needed to perform the simplest-case example. A technique used successfully is to put HTML tags in message text for browser-compatible mail programs for specialized formatting. Numerous examples and practical pieces of code for UTL_SMTP can be found on the TUSC site (**http://www.tusc.com**).

Communicating Through TCP/IP Sockets with UTL_TCP

You've seen how PL/SQL can read HTML documents across a network, like a browser, and send e-mail. Both of these capabilities reflect a reliance on the TCP/IP protocol, which is the standard for Internet applications. PL/SQL also has the *UTL_TCP* package, which enables you to make low-level calls using TCP/IP functionality directly. The difference between UTL_TCP and the other packages is UTL_TCP works at a more basic level and is, therefore, somewhat more difficult to use and requires some understanding of TCP/IP itself. With the lower level interface, however, comes better programmatic control over what's happening, greater flexibility, and more power.

The UTL_TCP Package

The whole purpose of the UTL_TCP package is to allow developers to take advantage of the capabilities of the TCP/IP from within PL/SQL. The nuts and bolts of how TCP/IP works are well beyond the scope of this chapter but, generally, the package (an interface, actually) uses a *socket* (an Internet address plus a port number) to establish a connection. Once the connection is open, a request can be sent through the connection and responses can be received. Both the request and the response can be multiple calls, depending on the circumstances. The *request* is as simple as an HTTP request method (GET, POST, and HEAD), and the response is the connection's reply. This can be actual data coming back, depending on the request or various errors (for example, the infamous 404 error when the request cannot be fulfilled for some reason). When finished, the connection must be closed. To say this description of TCP/IP has been oversimplified is an understatement. Those who want more information should pick up a good primer on the subject.

The previous steps mock the steps required for the UTL_TCP package. A connection is established using the open_connection function, which takes an Internet address and a port as its input and returns a connection ID. Requests are made using the write_line function, using the connection ID and a command string. Depending on the nature of the request, different information is written and multiple writes may take place one after another. Responses are received using the get_line function, which uses the connection ID to receive the data. This may need to be done in a loop to continue retrieving records until no more records exist. Finally, the connection must be closed.

TIP
The UTL_TCP function can be used to create your own UTL_SMTP or UTL_HTTP but, more practically, they can be used to create interfaces with other legacy servers.

Reading Web Pages with UTL_TCP

You can use UTL_TCP to perform similar functionality to both the UTL_HTTP and UTL_SMTP packages. The reason this can be done is both packages ultimately use the TCP/IP protocol to perform their functionality anyway. Actually, Oracle documentation hints that UTL_SMTP may use UTL_TCP directly. The UTL_SMTP mail API is somewhat easier to use than the direct UTL_TCP method of doing the same thing, but some tangible benefits exist from using UTL_TCP to read documents from the Web instead of using UTL_HTTP. The main advantage is you can get a clean series of line breaks because the page is laid out instead of written one byte after another until the document ends. The tradeoff is complexity and exception handling because UTL_TCP routines break somewhat more easily than UTL_HTTP routines do.

Interestingly, during the writing of this section, an ORA-20002 error was received when I used the URL of the document I wanted to open instead of the domain name in the open_connect function. The fix was only to use the domain name in the open call and to put the document specification within the GET command.

Another exception to watch out for is the venerable value error. HTML documents consisting of *very* long lines of code can cause havoc with the routine and need to be handled.

In the following example, we'll open port 80 on the **http://www.tusc.com** server and process these results with a SQL*Plus script. This is an expanded version of an example given in the text of the UTL_TCP package header from the ALL_SOURCE view.

```
set serveroutput on size 100000

DECLARE
  -- TCP/IP connection to the Web server
  v_connection_a utl_tcp.connection;
  v_bytes_n       binary_integer;       --return value for utl_tcp.write_line
BEGIN
  v_connection_a := utl_tcp.open_connection('www.tusc.com',80);
  v_bytes_n := utl_tcp.write_line(v_connection_a,
    'GET /pls/cast/cast_list_pkg.list_all HTTP/1.0'); -- send HTTP request
  v_bytes_n := utl_tcp.write_line(v_connection_a);
  BEGIN
    loop
      --nested block for exception handling within loop
      DECLARE
        -------------------------------------------------------------
        --block exceptions
        -------------------------------------------------------------
        e_application_error exception;
        pragma exception_init(e_application_error,-20000);
        -------------------------------------------------------------
        --block constants
        -------------------------------------------------------------
        v_substring_length_n constant pls_integer := 255;
        -------------------------------------------------------------
        --block variables
        -------------------------------------------------------------
        v_record_c        varchar2(32767);
        v_substring_c     varchar2(255);
        v_start_position_n pls_integer;
      BEGIN
        --read the result
        v_record_c := utl_tcp.get_line(v_connection_a,TRUE);
        --write the result
        if (nvl(length(v_record_c),0) <= v_substring_length_n) then
            --write short record
            dbms_output.put_line(v_record_c);
          else
            dbms_output.put_line('<!--utl_tcp.sql: Warning!  Record > '||
```

```
                                '255 characters below was parsed-->');
                        --parse and write long record
                        v_start_position_n := 1;
                        v_substring_c := substr(v_record_c,v_start_position_n,
                          v_substring_length_n);
                        while (v_substring_c is not null) loop
                          dbms_output.put_line(v_substring_c);
                          v_start_position_n := v_start_position_n +
                                            v_substring_length_n;
                          v_substring_c := substr(v_record_c,v_start_position_n,
                            v_substring_length_n);
                          --safeguard against endless loop
                          if (v_start_position_n > 32767) then
                            exit;
                          end if;
                        end loop;
                        dbms_output.put_line('<!--utl_tcp.sql: end of parsed text-->');
                  end if;
            EXCEPTION
                when e_application_error then
                    dbms_output.put_line('<!--utl_tcp.sql: Application error '||
                      'during dbms_output.put_line-->');
                when value_error then
                    dbms_output.put_line('<!--utl_tcp.sql: Value error during '||
                      'utl_tcp get_line-->');
            END;
        END loop;
    EXCEPTION
        when utl_tcp.end_of_input then
            null; -- end of input
    END;
    utl_tcp.close_connection(v_connection_a);
END;
/
```

This PL/SQL script reads and displays to the screen the contents of an HTML document read from a specified domain. The logic is fairly simple, but is confused somewhat by the need to do exception handling. The pseudo logic is

- open the connection
- write the request
- continue while something is returned
- get response
- close the connection

We must detect the end of the response condition by using the end_of_input exception defined in the package (not unlike the UTL_FILE package where the end of file condition is reached through the no_data_found exception).

One other difference exists between the pages retrieved by UTL_TCP and those retrieved by UTL_HTTP—the UTL_TCP documents contain the header information that browsers don't display. Notice the header information in the following output:

```
SQL> @utl_tcp
HTTP/1.1 200 OK
Date: Thu, 10 May 2001 14:35:35 GMT
Server: Apache/1.3.3 (Unix) FrontPage/4.0.4.3
Last-Modified: Tue, 01 May 2001 21:48:02 GMT
ETag: "2c012-3ac4-3aef2f12"
Accept-Ranges: bytes
Content-Length: 15044
Connection: close
Content-Type: text/html
<HTML>
<HEAD>
<TITLE>TUSC - The Ultimate Oracle Software Database Consultants</TITLE>
. . .
```

You can also retrieve only the header by using the HEAD method instead of the GET method in the previous example.

Scheduling from the Database Using DBMS_JOB

Have you ever wanted to execute an Oracle procedure every hour? You can execute scripts from the operating system using the UNIX cron utility, but what if you want to use Oracle to schedule the execution of your package? The DBMS_JOB package is Oracle's version of the cron utility. DBMS_JOB can be used to schedule the execution of specific Oracle packaged procedures at a specific time and on a recurring basis. DBMS_JOB makes use of a number of parameters, including the following:

- **job**   The number of the job being executed

- **what**   The PL/SQL procedure to execute, including the final semicolon

- **next_date**   The date at which the job will be executed

- **interval**   A date function, evaluated immediately before the job starts executing

If the job completes successfully, the new date is placed in next_date and no_
parse, indicating not to parse this statement before execution. Examples of legal
intervals include the following:

- **'sysdate + 7'**   Execute once a week

- **'next_day(sysdate, "tuesday")'**   Execute once every Tuesday

- **'null'**   Execute once, and then the job will be deleted from the queue

Other parameters include force and instance. If force is true, a positive integer
is acceptable as the job instance. If force is false, the specified instance must be
running. Otherwise, the routine raises an exception.

For Web development, you can use DBMS_JOB to execute a package that uses
UTL_FILE to output an HTML file (the "poor man's Web cache," as discussed earlier).
This can be used to write a static HTML file dynamically, often referred to as *semistatic*
Web pages. Creating semistatic pages is more efficient than creating dynamic pages
because dynamically creating content (HTML pages) takes more processing power
than does reading a static HTML file. Creating static HTML files can save you valuable
processing power and make your application more scalable.

What if you want to use UTL_HTTP to pull data periodically from another Web
site? You can use DBMS_JOB to schedule the periodic querying of another Web site.
When it comes to developing Web applications, requests will arise to run a PL/SQL
procedure periodically. DBMS_JOB can perform this task for you.

You can specify the job number or allow Oracle to assign a job number. The
isubmit procedure submits a new job with a specific job number. The *submit*
procedure submits a new job and allows Oracle to choose the job number from
sys.jobseq. The *remove* procedure removes an existing job from the job queue.
Removing the job from the dbms_job queue doesn't stop the execution of a job
once it begins. The *change* procedure changes the job parameters. Parameters
defined as NULL will remain NULL. The change procedure can be used to alter
the execution or frequency of the job execution. The *what* procedure changes
only the command being executed, not the schedule or any other parameters. The
next_date procedure changes when an existing job will next execute. The *instance*
procedure changes the instance or force parameters. The *interval* procedure changes
the interval (how often the job executes) of an existing job. Jobs can be broken if
they've failed to execute after 16 tries or they can be manually set to broken to
prevent them from running. Because broken jobs are never executed, use the *broken*
procedure to set the broken flag back to False (not broken). The *run* procedure forces
a job to execute immediately (even if broken). Executing the job will recompute the
next_date parameter.

TIP
The status of jobs in the queue can be viewed by querying the DBA_JOBS or USER_JOBS table, and currently running jobs can be seen in DBA_JOBS_ RUNNING.

Sending Messages Via the Database with DBMS_PIPE

The *DBMS_PIPE* package provides a mechanism to enable messages to be sent between sessions. Messages aren't stored in a table, they're stored in the SGA. You can think of a pipe as a message queue. The first message in will be the first message pulled out. Each pipe can be uniquely named, similar to calling a unique phone number. Unlike a phone call, however, when the sender sends a message, the recipient won't receive the message unless he checks the pipe to see if any messages exist in the queue.

You can imagine how useful this package could be in a Transactive Content site, a concept discussed in further detail in *Oracle Application Server Web Toolkit Reference* (Osborne/McGraw-Hill, 1998). You can enable users to converse directly with a live operator for site direction using the DBMS_PIPE package. The DBMS_ PIPE package is commonly used to send a command to a job execution process. If you want to execute a report on the server, send the message of the job to be executed through DBMS_PIPE. When the job is complete, you receive a URL pointing to the report's output. A process running on the database server typically handles the recipient end of the request. This process cycles (loops indefinitely), waiting for requests to come in through a specific DBMS_PIPE message, and then acts accordingly. Messages are sent to a specific pipename using SEND_MESSAGE and messages are received from a specific pipename using RECEIVE_MESSAGE. Before sending a message, it must be "packed," or placed in to the static buffer. To read the message, you must "unpack" it, extracting the message from the static buffer.

The pipename used can be any name you choose. For example, the pipename could be a user name, enabling private user-to-user communications or it could be a generic name, such as "messages," enabling all database users with executes privilege on DBMS_PIPE and knowledge of the pipe to read or write to the pipe.

Pipes operate independently of transactions. They also operate asynchronously. Multiple readers and writers can reside within the same pipe, but pipes only operate between sessions in the same instance and cannot be used for cross-instance messages. Pipes can be explicitly created using CREATE_PIPE and removed using REMOVE_ PIPE. A pipe created using the explicit Create command should be removed explicitly using the remove function. A pipe can also be created implicitly. Pipes automatically come into existence the first time they're referenced. Pipes disappear when they contain no more data, although some overhead remains in the SGA until it's aged out. As previously mentioned, pipes are stored in the SGA, so pipes take up space in the SGA.

As Oracle suggests, other potential applications are available for the DBMS_PIPE function, including the following:

- **External service interface**   You can provide the capability to communicate with (user-written) services external to the RDBMS. This can be accomplished in a multithread manner, so several instances of the service can be executing simultaneously. The services are available asynchronously; the requestor of the service needn't wait for a reply. The requestor can check (with or without time-out) for a reply at a later time. The service can be written in the 3GL languages supported by Oracle, not only in C.

- **Independent transactions**   You can use the pipe to communicate to a separate session performing an operation in an independent transaction, such as logging an attempted security violation detected by a trigger.

- **Alerters (nontransactional)**   You can post another process without requiring the waiting process to poll. If an after-row or after-statement trigger alerts an application, the application treats this alert as an indication the data has changed. The application then reads the data to retrieve the current value. Because this is an after trigger, the application performs a SELECT for update to ensure it read the correct data.

- **Debugging**   Triggers and/or stored procedures can send debugging information to a pipe. Another session can read out of the pipe, display it on the screen, or write it out to a file.

- **Concentrator**   Useful for multiplexing large numbers of users over a fewer number of network connections or improving performance by concentrating several user transactions into one RDBMS transaction.

Suppose you write a C program performing a number of calculations based on a pricing algorithm used to price products for your customers. You must provide this routine with the customer number, the product number being purchased, the cost for the product, and the pricing algorithm for this customer. This would typically all be information you gathered from the database. Because of the complexity of the pricing algorithm, this operation is performed using a C program. The following code calls the pricing algorithm:

```
customer_price := pricing_routine.get_price(cust_no,
                 item_no, unit_cost, cust_price_algorithm);
```

The following code calls the pricing_routine:

```
create or replace function pricing_routine
                              (cust_no                 number,
                               item_no                 number,
                               unit_cost               number,
                               cust_price_algorithm varchar2)
return number is
sts          integer;
price        number;
errormsg     varchar2(512);
begin
     dbms_pipe.pack_message('1');  -- protocol version
     -- return pipe
     dbms_pipe.pack_message(dbms_pipe.unique_session_name);
     dbms_pipe.pack_message('getprice');
     dbms_pipe.pack_message(cust_no);
     dbms_pipe.pack_message(item_no);
     dbms_pipe.pack_message(unit_cost);
     dbms_pipe.pack_message(cust_price_algorithm);
     sts := dbms_pipe.send_message('get_customer_price');
     if sts <> 0 then
        raise_application_error(-20000, 'Error:'||to_char(sts)||
                                         ' sending on pipe');
     end if;
     sts := dbms_pipe.receive_message(dbms_pipe.unique_session_name);
     if sts <> 0 then
        raise_application_error(-20000, 'Error:'||to_char(sts)||
                                         ' receiving on pipe');
     end if;
     dbms_pipe.unpack_message(errormsg);
     if errormsg <> 'SUCCESS' then
        raise_application_error(-20000, errormsg);
     end if;
     dbms_pipe.unpack_message(price);
     return price;
end;
```

Procedures and Functions

The *PACK_MESSAGE* procedure packs an item into the message buffer. The procedure is overloaded to handle all data types. The only input parameter is *item,* which contains the name of the item to be packed.

The *UNPACK_MESSAGE* procedure unpacks an item from the local message buffer. This procedure is also overloaded to retrieve all datatypes. The only output parameter is *item,* containing the argument to receive the next unpacked item from the local message buffer.

The *NEXT_ITEM_TYPE* function retrieves the type of the next item in the local message buffer. It will return one of the following values:

- **0** no more items
- **9** varchar2
- **6** number
- **11** rowid
- **12** date
- **23** raw

The *CREATE_PIPE* function creates an empty pipe with the name provided and returns the status of the new pipe. The first input parameter for this routine is *pipename,* which is the name of pipe to be created. The next parameter is *maxpipesize,* which is the maximum allowed size for the pipe. The total size of all the messages in the pipe cannot exceed this amount. The maxpipesize for a pipe becomes part of the pipe and persists for the lifetime of the pipe. Callers of send_ message with larger values will cause maxpipesize to be increased. Callers with a smaller value will use the larger value. The specification of maxpipesize enables you to avoid its use in future send_message calls. The private parameter contains a Boolean value indicating whether the pipe will be True for private (and for the use of the creating user ID only) or False if the pipe is public. A private pipe can be used directly through calls to this package by sessions connected to the database as the same user as the one that created the pipe. It can also be used through stored procedures owned by the user who created the pipe. The procedure can be executed by anyone with execute privilege on the pipe. A public pipe can be accessed by anyone who has knowledge of its existence and has execute privilege on dbms_ pipe. The only return value is a 0, which means the pipe creation was successful. This is returned even if the pipe was created in a mode that permits its use by the user executing the create call. If a pipe already exists, it isn't emptied. If the pipe fails to create, your procedure receives an exception.

TIP

Don't use pipenames beginning with ORA$. These are reserved for use by procedures provided by Oracle Corporation. Pipename shouldn't be longer than 128 bytes and is case-insensitive. The pipename cannot contain NLS characters.

The *REMOVE_PIPE* function removes the named pipe. The input parameter is pipename, and should contain the name of pipe to remove. The only return value is 0 (the pipe was removed successfully). Calling the remove function on a pipe that doesn't exist also returns 0. If the remove_pipe function fails, your procedure then receives an exception.

The *SEND_MESSAGE* function sends a message on the named pipe and returns a status code. The message is contained in the local message buffer, which is filled with calls to pack_message. A pipe is created explicitly using create_pipe or implicitly the first time it's called. The following input parameters are used:

- **pipename**   Name of pipe on which to place the message

- **timeout**   Time to wait while attempting to place a message on a pipe, in seconds

- **maxpipesize**   Maximum allowed size for the pipe

The return values include 0 (the message was sent successfully), 1 (the send_message timed out, either because a lock on a pipe cannot be established or the pipe stays too full), and 2 (an interruption has occurred).

The *RECEIVE_MESSAGE* function receives a message from a specified pipe, copies the message into the local message buffer, and returns a status. You need to use the unpack_message function to access the individual items in the message. The pipe can be created explicitly using the CREATE_PIPE function or it will be created implicitly. The input parameters include pipename (the name of the pipe from which to retrieve a message), and time-out (time to wait for a message—a time-out of 0 enables you to read without blocking). The return status values can be 0 (the message was received successfully), 1 (the function timed out), 2 (the record in the pipe is too big for the buffer), and 3 (an interruption has occurred).

The *RESET_BUFFER* procedure resets the pack and unpack positioning indicators to 0. This routine isn't generally needed, but can be used if an error occurs or if special processing to clear the buffer is needed.

The *PURGE* procedure empties the named pipe. An empty pipe is a candidate for least-recently used (LRU) removal from the SGA; therefore, purge can be used to free all memory associated with a pipe. The only input parameter is pipename, which is the name of the pipe from which to remove all messages.

The *UNIQUE_SESSION_NAME* function retrieves a name unique among all sessions currently connected to this database. Multiple calls to this routine from the same session always return the same value. No input parameters exist: call the procedure and it returns a unique name. The returned name can be up to 30 bytes long.

Setting Session Properties with **DBMS_SESSION**

In any client/server application, times will occur when you want to set a user's role on-the-fly. This type of operation is often used when users have minimal privileges under their default role, but a particular procedure or function requires additional privileges to execute the procedure/function.

The DBMS_SESSION package provides access to the SQL alter session statements and other session information from stored procedures.

Procedures and Functions

The *SET_ROLE* procedure is equivalent to the SQL set role statement. The only input parameter is role_cmd, which contains the text to be appended to set role and executed as SQL. This procedure is useful in assigning a user a role only when it's required and removing the privileges of that role when it's no longer needed.

The *SET_SQL_TRACE* procedure is equivalent to the SQL alter session set sql_ trace statement. The only input argument to this procedure is *sql_trace,* which is a Boolean variable (True or False) indicating whether to turn tracing on or off.

The *SET_NLS* procedure is equivalent to the SQL alter session set <nls_parameter> = <value> statement. The input parameters to this procedure are param and value. *Param* is the NLS parameter and must begin with NLS. *Value* is the value to which the NLS parameter is set. If the parameter is a text literal, it needs embedded single quotes, as illustrated in the following syntax:

```
set_nls('nls_date_format','''DD-MON-YY''')
```

The *CLOSE_DATABASE_LINK* procedure is equivalent to the SQL alter session close database link <name> statement. The only input parameter to this procedure is *dblink,* which is the name of the database link to close.

The *RESET_PACKAGE* procedure frees all package states and releases memory used by packages in the current session. All package states are free at the beginning of a session.

The *UNIQUE_SESSION_ID* function returns an identifier unique for all sessions currently connected to the database. Multiple calls to this function during the same session return the same result. The return value from this function, unique_session_ id, can return up to 24 bytes.

The *IS_ROLE_ENABLED* function returns a Boolean value (True or False) indicating whether the named role is enabled for this session. The only input argument for this function is *rolename,* which indicates the name of the role.

The *IS_SESSION_ALIVE* function determines if the specified session is alive. The return value is a Boolean value (True or False). The only input argument to this procedure is *uniqueid,* which is the unique ID of the session to check.

The *SET_CLOSE_CACHED_OPEN_CURSORS* procedure is equivalent to the SQL alter session set close_cached_open_cursors statement. The only input argument is *close_cursors,* which is a Boolean value (True or False) indicating whether to turn close_cached_open_cursors on or off.

Retrieving Time to the Millisecond with DBMS_UTILITY.GET_TIME

The DBMS_UTILITY package contains a number of utility routines to assist in your Web development. This section discusses the aspects of one of them: DBMS_UTILITY.GET_TIME.

The *get_time* function returns the current time in hundredths of a second and is useful for performance measurements. The return variable, *get_time,* is the time, in hundredths of a second, from some arbitrary epoch. To measure time to the hundredth of a second, you must use *get_time* at the beginning and at the end of the procedure, and then subtract the two numbers.

The following code is an example using the get_time function. The *call_url_100_times* procedure starts by retrieving the current time. It then calls another routine, which could be any URL. Perhaps you want to verify how quickly your competitors handle 100 requests. At the end of the 100 calls, it prints the total amount of time it took to retrieve the page 100 times. In the following example, call_url_100_times calls the get_employees procedure to calculate the amount of time the routine takes to execute, along with the concurrent user count:

```
procedure call_url_100_times
is
timer_start  number := dbms_utility.get_time;
timer_end    number;
html utl_http.html_pieces;
begin
for x in 1 .. 100 loop
    html := utl_http.request_pieces(
            'http://hp1.tusc.com/plsql/get_employees');
    htp.print(html(1));
end loop;
htp.hr;
timer_end := dbms_utility.get_time;
htp.header(5,to_char((timer_end - timer_start)*
            .01, '999,990.99')||' seconds');
end;
```

```
procedure get_employees
is
cursor emp_cur is
       select *
       from   emp;
cursor cnt_cur is
       select count(*) user_count
       from   v$session
       where  program like '%wrks%'
       and    status  =    'ACTIVE';
today varchar2(50) := to_char(sysdate,'mm/dd/yy hh:mi:ss pm');
timer_start  number := dbms_utility.get_time;
timer_end    number;
user_counter number;
begin
htp.header(1,today);
for cnt_rec in cnt_cur loop
    htp.header(6,to_char(cnt_rec.user_count,'999')||
                ' concurrent users at start');
end loop;
select counter.nextval into user_counter from dual;
htp.header(2,user_counter);
htp.tableOpen;
for emp_rec in emp_cur loop
htp.tableRowOpen;
htp.tableData(emp_rec.emp_name);
htp.tableRowClose;
end loop;
htp.tableClose;
timer_end := dbms_utility.get_time;
htp.header(5,to_char((timer_end - timer_start)*
                .01, '999,990.99')||' seconds');
for cnt_rec in cnt_cur loop
    htp.header(6,to_char(cnt_rec.user_count,'999')||
                ' concurrent users at end');
end loop;
htp.hr;
end;
```

Summary

PL/SQL provides a wide set of tools that can be used to enhance the functionality of *i*AS applications. While the surface was barely scratched in this chapter, you learned about the possibilities of using several of them.

To review: DBMS_OBFUSCATION_TOOLKIT encodes and decodes data. UTL_ HTTP retrieves documents as text across networks. Dynamic code is supported by the

EXECUTE IMMEDIATE command and reference cursors. The UTL_SMTP package can be used to send e-mail. The OWA_UTIL package contains miscellaneous useful routines. UTL_TCP can be used to use the TCP/IP protocol to communicate with other servers. Finally, PL/SQL can be tuned and timed using the DBMS_UTILITY package utilities. Scheduling from the database can be accomplished using DBMS_JOB. Sending e-mail messages directly via the database is accomplished with DBMS_PIPE and setting session properties with DBMS_SESSION. To retrieve time to the millisecond, you can use the DBMS_UTILITY.GET_TIME utility.

CHAPTER
12

Security

any levels of security are involved in protecting a Web-based system from the operating system, through the database, across the network, and out on to the Internet. As security mechanisms get more sophisticated, the people intent on breaking into your system also become more expert. Every day, more tools are created to assist hackers in their endeavors and your job is to thwart their attacks successfully and protect your company's data.

In this chapter, the following topics are discussed:

- General Security Concepts and Basic Security Approach

  - Common Security Problems

  - Some Security Terms and Approaches

- RDBMS Security

  - Virtual Private Database

  - Encrypting Database Columns

  - Using the DBMS_OBFUSCATION_TOOLKIT

  - Fine-Grained Database Auditing

- Application-Level Security

  - Protecting the Oracle9*i*AS Directories

  - Oracle9*i*AS Built-In Security

  - Using the PL/SQL Package OWA_SEC

  - Configuring Authentication Services

  - User Security Considerations

- Network Security

  - Oracle Net and the Oracle Advanced Security Option

  - SSL/HTTPS Basics and Setup

  - Protecting Digital Certificates

  - Using the Oracle Internet Directory (LDAP)

General Security Concepts and Basic Security Approaches

Where do security holes come from? What forms of security holes can you protect your company's data against? This section discusses the most common security holes and what actions you can take to help close them.

Common Security Problems

The single most common security breaches occur because the security features haven't been properly turned on within your operating system. It's easy to install a new server and forget to modify or disable default operating system settings. You might be unable to do anything about securing your system, but you can ask the systems administrator if the encryption and certificate features have been enabled.

Approach to Securing Applications

As an Oracle developer or software vendor, you want to field your software with as easy an installation and configuration process as possible. You want to implement as many new features within your products as you can to ensure that your products will help earn money for your company. Unfortunately, ease of installation and configuration generally run counter to proper security standards. A vendor or developer often requires the program or system being delivered to be installed with the highest privileges available.

The best approach to take to ensure your data is protected is to allow your software to be installed with all permissions set as restrictively as possible. As you identify a needed privilege, enable and track that privilege. When you have the software working 100 percent, you'll have a list of exactly what privileges are required to field your software in the most protected environment possible. If you can, begin your software development cycle with the most restrictive privileges you can and use the same approach of identifying and tracking the privileges as you determine that you need them for your code to work properly. This approach is more effective in the long run because you have the entire list of required privileges as you initially field your application.

Avoid Allowing Buffer Overflows

Poor programming practices can invariably lead to inadvertent security holes. Some programming techniques are now known to cause security problems. As you write your code, ensure that you consider all potential areas where a hacker could introduce a buffer overflow. A *buffer overflow* results from a program filling up a buffer of memory with more data than the buffer can hold. Once the program begins to write beyond the end of a buffer, the program's execution path can be changed.

Buffer overflows cause a real problems when they can be exploited remotely before authentication occurs. Here's an example of how a buffer overflow might work in a Web server. When you enter a request to search a Web site for the topic "oracle," your Web browser submits the request as follows:

```
http://www.domainname.com/search.idc?search=oracle
```

This command says to submit the word "oracle" to the parameter search through the Web page search.idc. The code behind search.idc processes the parameter. This code sets up a variable, or buffer, to hold the value you passed in.

If the Web server software is coded correctly, the code will check the length of the parameter and copy only a limited number of characters. If the programmer forgets to validate the length of the string, the code may copy the parameter passed in over other memory.

Now, a malicious user sends the following command:

```
http://www.domainname.com/search.idc?
search=xxxxxxxxxxxxxxxxxxxxxxxxxxxxx0x230x150x170x450x560x00
```

Notice the hexadecimal numbers embedded in the string. These numbers are placed there to overwrite specific places in memory with new machine language code to perform some kind of potentially harmful action. The Web server, which is probably running with escalated privileges, will execute the code in the URL string instead of its own code.

To avoid this form of attack, always check the size of the buffer or verify the data being received is in a valid format. In software development, it's easy to fall into the trap of knowing what parameters you expect to be returned and not considering the results if a user submits a different set of parameters to the program. "Out of bounds" parameters should always be part of your application testing.

Some Security Terms and Approaches

One of the most common problems in maintaining security is ensuring the users attempting to enter your system are who they claim to be. If you are face-to-face with someone, ensuring that the person is who she says she is isn't a problem because you can request photographic proof. Over at telephone line, you can request a prearranged piece of information, such as a phrase, keyword, or the maiden name of the person's mother. Once the phrase or fact is presented, however, you must accept the person's identity. This procedure is known as *authentication*. In cyberspace, digital authentication enables you to prove your identity when physical means cannot be used. Unfortunately, authentication is far from perfect and someone other than the correct person can present the proper credential, such as a password.

Private Key Encryption

Private key encryption uses a symmetrical algorithm to encrypt and decrypt data. A *symmetrical algorithm* is one in which the keys used to encrypt and decrypt the data are the same or are derivable from each other. If you know the key, you can encrypt or decrypt any message, so the key must be kept secret, or private, as its name implies. Both sides of a conversation must have the shared secret key. Some of the problems with private key encryption are as follows:

- Each person you want to communicate with must get a copy of the key.

- You must find a safe and secure way to distribute the key.

- Anyone who obtains a copy of your key can read your private communications.

- You must have a different private key for each person with whom you communicate.

- Keeping track of which key belongs to each person can become problematic.

In 1973, the National Institute of Science and Technology (NIST) started the selection process for a standard symmetrical algorithm to use in encryption. The algorithm had to be flexible, secure, fast, and royalty-free. IBM's candidate algorithm, known as the Data Encryption Standard (DES) was accepted. The biggest problem with DES was its 56KB key length.

With the improvement in processor speeds and the advent of DES cracking machines, the encryption method became too weak. A search for a new algorithm produced the Advanced Data Encryption (AES). In October 2000, NIST selected the algorithm Rijndael (pronounced *Rhine-doll*), designed by two Belgian cryptographers, as the new standard. A period of analysis by the academic community must take place before the algorithm is officially accepted as the standard. AES has been selected based on the same factors as DES—flexibility, speed, security, and royalty-free licensing.

Public Key Encryption

In 1976, a new form of encryption based on asymmetrical keys was discovered. The idea was to find an algorithm that could encrypt data using one key and decrypt the data using a different key. To use this method, you first need to choose a decryption key, and then calculate an encryption key from the decryption key. This is commonly known as *Public Key Encryption*. The most important part of the algorithm would be that knowing the encryption key wouldn't allow you to know the decryption key. In other words, the algorithm had to make finding the encryption and decryption keys themselves easy, but finding the decryption key from the encryption key computationally infeasible.

With symmetrical encryption, you can't make the decryption key public because anyone could decrypt as well as encrypt any of your messages. Using asymmetrical encryption, you can make the encryption key public. Anyone is allowed to encrypt messages using your encryption, or "public," key, but only you can decrypt the message using your decryption, or "private," key.

Ron Rivest, Adi Shamir, and Leonard Adleman discovered a new public key algorithm. Named after the initials of the discoverers, *RSA* was the first public key algorithm to implement encryption, authentication, and digital signing. RSA Data Securities, Inc., held the RSA patent until it expired in October 2000. Even though the RSA algorithm wasn't free of licensing fees for its first 25 years, it still became the industry standard. Because of the licensing issues, RSA was never officially mandated as a NIST standard. Now that RSA is in the public domain, use of public key encryption should become more prevalent.

RSA encryption is based on the difficulty of factoring large prime numbers. Before you see an example, remember that a prime number is only divisible by itself and 1. For example, the numbers 17 and 19 are prime numbers. To understand RSA encryption, choose two large 56-bit prime numbers. These two values are put through a formula to generate the private key. Next, multiply these two numbers together. The result is a number divisible by only the two original prime numbers. This number is the public key that can be safely published for anyone to view. An attacker can determine the private key from the public key only if he determines the initial prime numbers used. When the numbers are large enough, finding the only two numbers that are factors of the large number becomes a monumental task.

Hybrid Encryption
Historically, the biggest problem with public key encryption has been that it's slow. To solve this problem, hybrid versions of encryption have been used. Hybrid technology uses public key technology to negotiate a shared secret session key, which is then used as the key for a symmetrical algorithm. A typical example of a hybrid system uses a combination of the DES and the Diffie-Hellman algorithm.

In this example, the client and the server want to maintain a connection that's safe from eavesdroppers. First, a random number is generated and shared between the parties using the Diffie-Hellman algorithm. Now both sides, but no eavesdroppers, know the random number. Using the random number as the key for DES, you can safely pass messages back and forth. This random number has, in effect, become a session key for this connection. The next time a connection is established, a new key will be used.

Digital Signatures
Because you can't sign your name in cyberspace, a mechanism known as a *digital signature* is used as a way to authenticate yourself to a server. Digital signatures rely

on the same principles as public key encryption, but serve to satisfy a different need. Digital signatures provide a numerical method to prove you created or signed a document. To sign a document electronically, you first hash the document into a unique value using a one-way function. The hash value is then encrypted with the private key and attached to the document as the signature. Once your document is signed, anyone can verify you sent the document by decrypting the signature using your public key and hashing the document. If the decrypted signature and the document hash match, you must have sent the document, because only you could have calculated a signature that matched the document with your public key.

RSA provides the capability to digitally sign messages. NIST adopted a different algorithm for digital signing known as Digital Signature Algorithm (DSA). Digital signatures are important in online transactions. In the not-too-distant future, we may all be able to vote electronically from the comfort of our own homes using digital signatures to validate our identities.

About Authorization

Now that you understand the different encryption algorithms available, let's look at how the system determines what privileges you have and what data you have the right to access. *Authorization* is based on matching an identity with a list of rights, privileges, or areas of access.

Your identity in the digital world is typically stored as an *access token.* When you log in to a system, a token that indicates who you are is created. As you access objects, your access token is checked against a list of users. This access control list (ACL) indicates who has the right to access specific software, directories, files, or other objects on a system. These access tokens and access control lists must be protected to ensure proper authorization.

Another approach, used by Oracle9*i,* is to create an initial cookie in which your authentication information is stored and then, based on the authentication cookie, create a second cookie to store your authorization access token.

Using SSL to Encrypt Data

When talking about data encryption, you should be familiar with a few terms. The first is the term *cipher suite,* which is a set of authentication, encryption, and data integrity algorithms used for exchanging messages between network nodes. The next term is Secure Sockets Layer (SSL), which is an industry standard protocol for securing network connections. SSL provides authentication, encryption, and data integrity using Public Key Infrastructure.

During an SSL handshake, for example, the two nodes involved negotiate to see which cipher suite they will use when transmitting messages back and forth.

SSL, which contributes to a Public Key Infrastructure, is used to secure communications from any client or server to one or more other servers or from a server to any client. You can use SSL alone or with other authentication methods, and you can configure SSL to require server authentication only or both client and server authentication.

Oracle Internet Directory (LDAP) Approach

Oracle Corporation has created a general-purpose directory service called the Oracle Internet Directory (OID) that combines the LDAP version 3 structure with the Oracle server. OID provides information about network resources and users by communicating with a database that can be either on the same operating system or a different one.

You see more about OID toward the end of this chapter.

Third-Party Supplied Authentication Tools

With the number of computers used to support today's businesses and the Internet, the number of passwords a user is required to keep track of and remember can be staggering. To help alleviate this problem, an approach called *single signon* was developed to enable users to log on to a system once with one password, and then gain access to various databases or systems based on that initial authentication. The industry-standard protocol, called *Kerberos,* is the most-often chosen product to support this capability.

Kerberos is designed to provide strong client/server application authentication by using public-key cryptography. You can get a free copy of this protocol from the Massachusetts Institute of Technology Web site. Because URLs change frequently, simply do a search on the word "Kerberos" to get to the correct MIT site.

A product called *CyberSafe* provides single signon and centralized password storage, database link authentication, and enhanced PC security using the Kerberos protocol. Kerberos is a trusted third-party authentication system that relies on shared secret keys and assumes the third party is secure. CyberSafe *TrustBroker* is a commercial Kerberos-based authentication server. To use these products, the Kerberos authentication server must be installed on a physically secure machine.

Oracle supports several third-party products that provide single sign-on capabilities in your system. Table 12-1 shows the most popular third-party authentication products, with a brief description of each one.

Oracle's Approach

To review and summarize a bit, RSA uses an algorithm called the RSA Data Security RC4 encryption algorithm, which uses a secret, randomly generated key that's unique for each user session. All network transmissions for a session between the client and server are protected because the encryption key is changed each time a session begins. The encryption key has already changed by the time the current key can be broken. Therefore, if a hacker breaks one encryption key, no advantage is gained because the key has already changed for the next session.

Product	Description
Secure Sockets Layer (SSL)	An industry standard protocol for securing network connections, SSL provides authentication, data encryption, and data integrity and contributes to a Public Key Infrastructure (PKI).
Remote Authentication Dial-In User Service (RADIUS)	This client/server protocol enables remote authentication and access using a variety of authentication mechanisms, such as token cards, smart cards, and biometrics.
Kerberos and CyberSafe	Used with Oracle Advanced Security, these provide single signon and centralized password storage, database link authentication, and enhanced PC security.
Smart cards (RADIUS-compliant)	A *smart card* is a device similar to a credit card with an embedded integrated circuit read by a hardware device at a client or server. The smart card generally stores a user name and password for user identification. A user can log in from any workstation equipped with a smart card reader because the card itself contains the authentication values.
Token cards (SecurID- or RADIUS-compliant)	*Token cards* look like a small calculator and have a keypad. Some token cards dynamically display a one-time-use password synchronized with an authentication server, while other forms of token cards work on a challenge-response basis. The server presents a challenge. The user enters the challenge into the token card and presses a key. The token card furnishes a response the user types in to the server.
Biometric authentication (Identix- or RADIUS-compliant)	Identix biometric authentication is used to communicate fingerprint-based authentication data between the authentication server and client. This form of authentication is used on both the clients and Oracle servers. Other RADIUS-compliant biometric authentication devices can be integrated with Oracle Advanced Security for authentication.

TABLE 12-1. *Third-Party Authentication Methods*

The client and server can either request or require encryption be used. The performance penalty for the overhead of encrypting and decrypting any transmission between the client and server is said to be minimal. Oracle supports keys that are 40 bits, 56 bits, or 128 bits in length but, the longer the encryption key, the more difficult it will be to compromise the encrypted message.

The session key is generated using the Diffie-Hellman algorithm, and then either DES or RC4 are used to do the actual encryption. RSA has a public key algorithm, which we discussed previously and a stream cipher algorithm that's used to encrypt data, much like DES.

Thus, the RC4 algorithm, developed by RSA Data Security, Inc., has quickly become the de facto international standard for high-speed data encryption. Despite ongoing attempts by cryptographic researchers to "crack" the RC4 algorithm, the only feasible method of breaking its encryption known today remains brute-force, systematic guessing, which is generally infeasible. RC4 is a stream cipher that operates at several times the speed of DES, making it possible to encrypt even large bulk data transfers with minimal performance consequences.

DES is required by most financial and many other institutions. The current standard is a 56-bit encryption key, but a 40-bit encryption key is provided for backward-compatibility.

Oracle9i supports all these approaches through its Oracle Advanced Security product, which is discussed in the following sections.

A Brief Examination of the Oracle Advanced Security Option

The action of examining packets as they flow through a network is commonly called *packet sniffing,* or local area network (LAN) monitoring. Please realize that packet sniffing is just viewing the packets without modifying them in any way. The harm in packet sniffing is the potential for a hacker to view compromising information. If a user name and password are sent across the network in plaintext format, a hacker sniffing the packets could obtain this information and, therefore, gain access to your system.

Far worse than just sniffing packets, though, is the potential for someone to intercept a packet and change its contents. For example, if you were using an ATM to transfer funds from your savings account to your checking account and someone intercepted the packet, the amount you were transferring and the account to which you were sending the money could be compromised.

Oracle provides a suite of tools to protect data integrity as information travels around the network. The tools, known as the Oracle Advanced Security Option (ASO), provide several different features. For example, to ensure a message isn't tampered with in any way, Oracle Advanced Security features enable a cryptographically secure message digest to be generated and attached to the message. The message digest is generated using an algorithm known as MD5 to create a cryptographic checksum. This *checksum* is different from the normal, standard checksum that operating system hardware generates and is included with each packet sent across the network. If any of the packets are tampered with, the checksum won't match the packet contents.

Use of another option, known as the Secure Hash Algorithm (SHA), is allowed through the Oracle Advanced Security Secure Sockets Layer feature. The SHA option is slightly slower than MD5, but the message digest it produces is larger. Thus, the message is more secure against *brute-force collision* (an attack that requires trying all (or a large fraction of all) possible values until the right value is found; also called an *exhaustive search*) and *inversion attacks* (an attack that involves interchanging positions of adjacent objects in a sequence).

Oracle supports three primary encryption approaches: RSA, DES, and triple-DES. Oracle's implementation of RSA's RC4 supports 40-bit, 56-bit, 128-bit, and 256-bit encryption, while its DES encryption supports an optimized 56-bit key encryption with a 40-bit version for backward-compatibility. In triple-DES, three passes of the DES algorithm are made to encrypt message data. Although a high degree of security is obtained using triple-DES, there's a penalty in performance based on the speed of the processor on which the encryption is being performed.

As was true in Oracle8*i*, the Oracle Advanced Security option's encryption and decryption are provided at the Oracle Net level as add-ons and include the following:

- DES, RSA, and triple-DES for encryption

- Kerberos, RADIUS, and CyberSafe for authentication

- MD5 and SHA for data integrity

Each of these features has been improved and enhanced for Oracle9*i* to provide more in-depth security features, and an easier configuration and implementation approach through Oracle's Advanced Security Option.

Configuring a Third-Party Product for Use with ASO

Oracle9*i* supplies the Oracle Net Manager GUI tool to provide an easy way to configure the Oracle Advanced Security option to work with a third-party product. You can also use the Oracle Enterprise Manager to perform the configuration. When a database administrator selects the Oracle Net Manager option from an Oracle Windows installation, the initial tool screen provides two options: Local and Oracle Names Servers. Expanding the Local option, you see Profile, Service Naming, and Listeners areas. When you select the Profile option, the Naming screens are presented, as shown in Figure 12-1.

The option of interest in configuring third-party vendor tools is the Oracle Advanced Security option screens. When you click the arrow next to the Naming entry on the right side of the screen, as shown in Figure 12-1, you're presented with four choices: Naming, General, Preferred Naming Methods, and Oracle Advanced

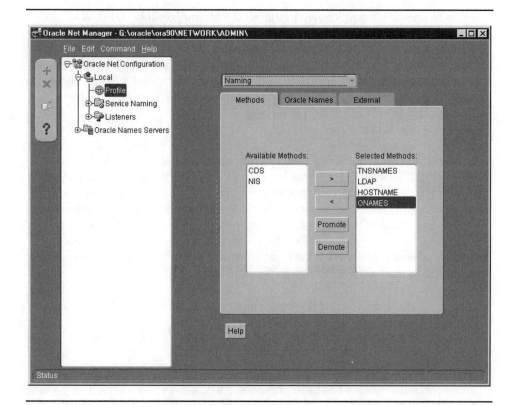

FIGURE 12-1. *Oracle Net Manager Profile Naming options*

Security. Selecting the Oracle Advanced Security option gives you the screen shown in Figure 12-2.

In Oracle9i, the available products you can specify are KERBEROS5, CYBERSAFE, RADIUS, and NTS. Based on the product you select, you can add other parameters using the Other Params tab. The Integrity tab provides you with a way to specify either SHA1 or MD5, while the Encryption tab provides you with a way to specify the encryption approach to use. Finally, the SSL tab offers you the option to configure either client or server SSL. When you click your choice, the SSL tab presents the configuration options and parameters including the capability to declare a wallet configuration method: File system, Microsoft Certificate, Microsoft Registry, or

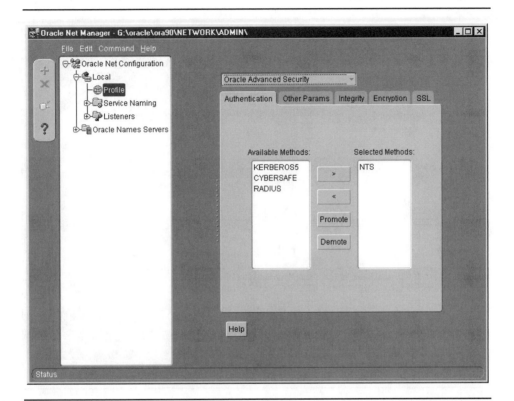

FIGURE 12-2.   *Oracle Net Manager Oracle Advanced Security option*

Entrust. You can configure the Cipher Suite and declare the SSL required version.
Figure 12-3 shows the SSL configuration screen.

NOTE
*To use SSL for server connections, you must choose
the protocol, select TCP/IP with SSL, and configure
the listener accordingly.*

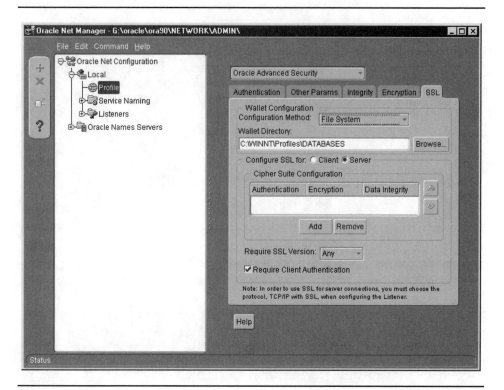

FIGURE 12-3. *Oracle Net Manager SSL Configuration option*

RDBMS Security

Oracle provides the following options for securing the RDBMS:

- Through privileges granted to individual users or roles

- Through the use of both standard and materialized views

- Through using enhanced password features, such as automatic password aging and expiration, password history, composition, complexity enforcement, and account lockout

- Through PL/SQL routines to create and enforce the Virtual Private Database (VPD) option, column encryption, and the DBMS_ OBFUSCATION_TOOLKIT

In this section, I focus on the PL/SQL routines you can use to enforce fuller data protection.

Virtual Private Databases

Oracle introduced the Virtual Private Database to provide fine-grained access control, coupled with a secure application context in Oracle8*i,* Release 3. With VPD, you establish policies that Oracle can impose on your database users. Using this approach, an organization needs only to build a security structure once in the data server. Because the security policies are attached to the data instead of the application, security rules are enforced at all times and from any access approach. Thus, the data a user has access to is the same whether she connects to Oracle from an application, from SQL*Plus, or any other database connection transport.

VPD was meant to solve the problem of maintaining data from many different departments, companies, or organizations in one central database. The VPD relies on several mechanisms to ensure data privacy for each user. To accomplish data separation, you must first ensure you designed your tables so you can restrict data access according to the values in one or more columns.

One common approach for ensuring privacy of data where several companies are involved is to define a company key field on each table, so you can identify each individual organization. You can associate users with a particular key, and then establish a policy that says users can only access rows that correspond to their designated key. When a query is submitted, the appropriate where clause is automatically attached, restricting the user to see and manipulate only her data. Thus, fine-grained access control is automatically implemented and assured.

For example, let's say you select from the Human Resources database using the following query:

```
select * from ALL_EMPLOYEES;
```

If the ALL_EMPLOYEES table has a security policy associated with it that restricts employees to view only their own company information, the query would be automatically rewritten as

```
select *
from  ALL_EMPLOYEES
where EMPLOYEE_ID = sys_context('HR_CONTEXT','ALL_EMP_ID')
/
```

In this example, the where clause automatically appended to the user's query by the policy ensures users can only see their data from their company, no matter what data is in the table or how they construct their queries. The employee's ID is obtained from the user-defined application context, HR_CONTEXT. The system function sys_context returns the value for the attribute ALL_EMP_ID in the HR_CONTEXT.

Within VPD, you must still grant users the appropriate privileges for each table, but you needn't create views and procedures to prevent users from accessing other users' data. Thus, using VPD, you no longer have to worry about users accessing the database through SQL*Plus with different privileges than they have through an application.

Creating a VPD

Creating an Oracle VPD is different from installing and configuring most other Oracle tools. The VPD isn't an application unto itself but, rather, is installed with the database. With most other Oracle tools, you use the Oracle Universal Installer to install from a CD-ROM. With the VPD, the configuration is significantly different and encompasses several steps. The steps are as follows:

1. Determine the database objects and their relationships.

2. Define your security policy objectives.

3. Create the application context.

4. Create a package that sets the context.

5. Create the policy function.

6. Associate the policy function with a table or view.

You can perform several of these steps in different ways. The approach outlined here is the one I believe will yield the most robust, scalable, and secure implementation.

Determine the Database Objects and Their Relationships

To begin creating your VPD, you must determine the database objects to be involved, their relationship to each other, and the keys on which your security approach will be built. Let's work through an example to see the steps more clearly. In the interest of keeping the example simple, let's say you work for a research facility that has several doctors working on different drug studies. Each doctor should see only the test results for his project. In this example, assume each doctor works on only one project at a time.

Keeping each project's information secure and private is of major importance. The primary key that links all of each project's information together is the project ID. Therefore, each project has its own unique ID and each doctor's ID is linked to the appropriate project or projects with which the doctor is involved.

In this simple example, let's say data is stored in only two tables: PHYSICIAN_INFORMATION and PROJECT_INFORMATION. The PHYSICIAN_INFORMATION table stores information about each doctor involved in the various studies, while the PROJECT_INFORMATION table, as the name implies, stores the associated project data. Within the physician's information is the PROJECT_ID value for each project with which the doctor is involved. By limiting the query by PROJECT_ID, you can ensure everyone querying the database sees only the information for his or her projects. The value for PHYSICIAN_USERNAME is used to obtain the physician's PROJECT_ID number.

Let's create the tables, so you can see what's to be stored within each of them.

```
create table PHYSICIAN_INFORMATION
(PROJECT_ID            number(10) primary key,
 PHYSICIAN_ID          number(6) not null,
 PHYSICIAN_USERNAME    varchar2(10),
 PHYSICIAN_NAME        varchar2(20),
 PHYSICIAN_ADDRESS1    varchar2(20),
 PHYSICIAN_ADDRESS2    varchar2(20),
 PHYSICIAN_PHONE       number(10)
);
create table PROJECT_INFORMATION
(PROJECT_ID            number(10) primary key,
 PROJECT_NAME          varchar2(20),
 PROJECT_DESCRIPTION   varchar2(80),
 TEST_RESULTS          varchar2(2000)
);
```

Define Your Security Policy Objectives

The security policy for our example is simply stated as "Doctors can only see the project information for their specific projects."

Your policy objectives will generally be more complex than this and you can have several security policies associated with a table or view. Be extremely clear on how you phrase your policies because each security policy you define must be translated into PL/SQL function code to be attached to the specified application table or view.

Create the Application Context

An *application context* is a named set of attributes and values you set, and then associate with the current user's session. Oracle provides the default context, USERENV, which contains system information about the current session, such as the user name, host, and program name. If you want to define other attributes for a user, such as employee ID or customer ID, you can do so using application contexts.

Using the Create Any Context privilege, you can create the application context. You supply a unique context name, and then associate the name with the package that implements the context. Context names must be unique across the entire database, so if you attempt to create a context using a name that already exists, you'll receive an error.

To create the context, you must have the Create Any Context privilege granted to you. For this example, you create a context called PROJECT_SEC_CTX that belongs to the PL/SQL package stored in the RESEARCH schema and named PROJECT_SEC. The syntax you use is as follows:

```
create context PROJECT_SEC_CTX using RESEARCH.PROJECT_SEC;
```

Create a Package That Sets the Context

Once you create the context, the next step is to create the package and functions that set the context. The following example shows how you set the PROJECT_ID context attributes using the current user's name obtained from the default context, USERENV. The function uses the user name to look up the necessary attributes in the table.

```
create or replace package PROJECT_SEC is
    procedure GET_PROJECT_ID;
end PROJECT_SEC;
/
create or replace package body PROJECT_SEC is
    procedure GET_PROJECT_ID
    is
    PROJECT_ID_VAR number;
    begin
     select PROJECT_ID
       into PROJECT_ID_VAR from PHYSICIAN_INFORMATION
      where PHYSICIAN_USERNAME = SYS_CONTEXT('USERENV','SESSION_USER');
     dbms_session.set_context('PROJECT_SEC_CTX', 'PROJECT_ID', PROJECT_ID_VAR);
    end GET_PROJECT_ID;
end PROJECT_SEC;
/
```

Oracle supplies the predefined function SYS_CONTEXT and the built-in context USERENV, so you can return the name of the user executing the procedure. You can obtain many other values from the SYS_CONTEXT function. Table 12-2 outlines some of the more security-oriented values.

To set the context for a user session, you need to call the function associated with the context when the context was created. You can do this from the application or by using a login trigger. Using a login trigger ensures the context is set, no matter how the user logs in to the database. To set a login trigger, use the on logon trigger, which became available in Oracle8i, version 8.1.7.

Attribute	Value Returned
AUTHENTICATION_DATA	The data being used to authenticate the login user.
AUTHENTICATION_TYPE	The method used to authenticate the user. The available values are as follows: Database: user name/password authentication OS: operating system external user authentication; Network: network protocol or ANO authentication Proxy: OCI proxy connection authentication
BG_JOB_ID	If an Oracle background process established the current session, the Job ID of the job will be returned.
CLIENT_INFO	Used in conjunction with the DBMS_APPLICATION_INFO package to store information, this parameter returns up to 64 bytes of user session information.
CURRENT_SCHEMA	Name of the default schema being used as the current schema.
CURRENT_USER	Name of the user whose privileges the current session is under.
CURRENT_USERID	ID of the user whose privileges the current session is under.
DB_DOMAIN	Database domain as specified in the DB_DOMAIN initialization parameter.
DB_NAME	Database name as specified in the DB_NAME initialization parameter.
ENTRYID	Available auditing entry identifier. Set if the AUDIT_TRAIL parameter is set to TRUE in the initialization parameter file.
EXTERNAL_NAME	External name of the database user. The distinguished name stored in the user certificate is returned for SSL-authenticated sessions using v.503 certificates.

TABLE 12-2. *SYS_CONTEXT Parameters*

Attribute	Value Returned
FG_JOB_ID	If an Oracle foreground process established the current session, the Job ID of the job will be returned.
HOST	Name of the host machine the client connected from.
INSTANCE	The instance identification number of the current instance.
ISDBA	If you have the DBA role enabled, TRUE will be returned. If you don't, FALSE will be returned.
NETWORK_PROTOCOL	Network protocol being used for communication.
OS_USER	Operating system user name of the client process that initiated the database session.
PROXY_USER	Name of the database user who opened the session on behalf of the SESSION_USER.
PROXY_USERID	Identifier of the database user who opened the session on behalf of the SESSION_USER.
SESSION_USER	Database user name by which the current user is authenticated. This value remains the same throughout the session.
SESSION_USERID	Identifier of the database user name by which the current user is authenticated.
SESSIONID	Auditing session identifier.
TERMINAL	Operating system identifier for the client of the current session.

TABLE 12-2. *SYS_CONTEXT Parameters* (continued)

Create the Security Policy Functions

Next, a PL/SQL function to implement the policy is required. The function is associated with the PROJECT_INFORMATION table.

Here is the process that occurs to impose fine-grained security on a query once the function is in place. By the way, the word "query" as used here means any form of information access from a table or view, including, but not limited to, select,

insert, delete, update, and subquery statements. Once a security policy is associated with a table or view, the query processor calls the policy function, and the function returns a value in the form of an access control condition, or predicate, when a user presents a query.

In reality, the *predicate* is a where clause that's appended to the user's SQL statement to limit the rows to be returned, updated, or deleted, depending on the type of statement used. The modified query is evaluated and optimized during statement parse time, and can be shared and reused to help improve performance.

Because our goal is to restrict the viewing of project information to only the doctor involved with the project, a predicate that contains the correct PROJECT_ID for the specific doctor must be returned. Here's a sample PL/SQL procedure to accomplish that goal:

```
create or replace package PROJECT_SEC as
 function PROJECT_ID_SEC return varchar2;
 END PROJECT_SEC;
/
create or replace package body PROJECT_SEC as
/* LIMITS SELECT STATEMENTS BASED ON PROJECT_ID VALUE */
function PROJECT_ID_SEC return varchar2
 is
   MY_PREDICATE varchar2 (2000);
   begin
     MY_PREDICATE := 'PROJECT_ID=SYS_CONTEXT(
                     ''PROJECT_SEC_CTX'',''PROJECT_ID'')';
     return MY_PREDICATE;
   end PROJECT_ID_SEC;
end PROJECT_SEC;
/
```

NOTE
To conserve space, no error handling is shown here.

In this code example, you retrieve the PROJECT_ID from the application context PROJECT_SEC_CTX and generate the predicate to be appended to a query on the PROJECT_INFORMATION table. To see how the predicate will look, let's say the PROJECT_ID is 2435678987. The returned predicate reads as follows:

```
PROJECT_ID = 2435678987;
```

This predicate is used in the where clause to ensure the only information this doctor will see is data that matches the correct PROJECT_ID.

Associate the Policy Function with a Table or View

Oracle provides a PL/SQL package called DBMS_RLS to enable you to manage security policy administration easily. Anyone creating or administering policies must have execute rights granted for this package through the SYS user. Table 12-3 shows the four procedures available in the package.

Use the DBMS_RLS package to tie a policy function to a table or a view. You use different arguments with each procedure. Table 12-4 shows the arguments and the procedure with which the argument is used.

Object_schema, object_name, and policy_name are required for the DROP_POLICY, REFRESH_POLICY, and ENABLE_POLICY procedures. Enable is the only other required parameter for the ENABLE_POLICY procedure.

For this example, you add the policy named PROJECT_POLICY to the PROJECT_INFORMATION table as follows:

```
execute DBMS_RLS.ADD_POLICY
        ('RESEARCH','PROJECT_INFORMATION','PROJECT_POLICY',
         'RESEARCH','PROJECT_SEC.PROJECT_ID_SEC','SELECT',FALSE,TRUE);
```

The statement creates the PROJECT_POLICY policy, which causes the PROJECT_SEC.PROJECT_ID_SEC function to be run when select statements are executed against the PROJECT_INFORMATION table in the RESEARCH schema.

Remember, statements are parsed and placed in the shared pool for use by other users with the same access privileges. Say, for instance, one of your business policies

Procedure	Function
DBMS_RLS.ADD_POLICY	Add a policy to a table or a view.
DBMS_RLS.DROP_POLICY	Remove a policy from a table or a view.
DBMS_RLS.REFRESH_POLICY	Force a reparse of open cursors associated with a policy to take advantage of a new or changed policy immediately.
DBMS_RLS.ENABLE_POLICY	Enable or disable a policy that has been previously added to a table or a view.

TABLE 12-3. *DBMS_RLS Package Procedures*

Parameter	Description
object_schema	Name of the schema containing the table or view.
object_name	Name of the table or view.
policy_name	Name of the policy to be added or dropped. Must be unique for the table or view.
function_schema	Schema of the policy function.
policy_function	Name of a function, which generates a predicate for the policy. If the function is defined within a package, the name of the package must be present.
statement_types	Statement types to which the policy will apply. Can be any combination of select, insert, update, and delete. The default is to apply to all these types.
update_check	When set to TRUE, the value is checked against security policies after insert or update. (Optional argument.)
Enable	Indicates whether the policy is enabled when added. Default is TRUE.

TABLE 12-4.   *DBMS_RLS Parameters for ADD_POLICY*

says a table can be accessed only during regular business hours, say, from 9 A.M. to 5 P.M. Along with coding your procedure to limit access to the table, you want to set up a job to run each evening at the close of business to invalidate the shared SQL code. You can have your job run code like the following:

```
execute DBMS_RLS.REFRESH_POLICY
('<schema where policy is stored>','<table_name>','<policy_name>';
```

In this example, the policy function is in the same schema as the actual application tables. In practice, you should keep your policy functions in a schema area owned by your company's security officer to prevent anyone from inadvertently or intentionally removing a policy from a table or a view.

Create the Trigger

Once all the pieces are in place, you must create a trigger to enforce the policy. I recommend using an on logon trigger, so the policy is activated, regardless of the approach a user takes to connect to the database.

CAUTION

One word of warning: if your on logon trigger doesn't function properly, you could end up in a situation where no one can log on to your database. In that case, you must connect as a user with SYSDBA privileges, and then remove the trigger until you can correct the error. In Oracle9i, the syntax you use from the SQL*Plus GUI logon box is shown in the following illustration. In this example, the SYSTEM account with the password MANAGER is used. The required phrase "as sysdba" is appended after the connect string.

Log On	
U̲ser Name:	system
P̲assword:	*******
H̲ost String:	mydb9.world as sysdba
OK	Cancel

Encrypting Database Columns

Along with the Virtual Private Database, Oracle offers a Label Security option. Both these features help provide multiple layers of security mechanisms to create an environment where no single failure can result in a compromise of the entire system. This approach is referred to as *deep data protection*. Along with VPD and Label Security, Oracle9*i* also provides you with the capability to encrypt data columns selectively within the database.

By encrypting sensitive data within columns in the database, you can ensure even super-privileged users, or users trying to view data through examination of database columns or the operating system files, are unable to see or compromise the secured information.

Using the **DBMS_OBFUSCATION_TOOLKIT**

Oracle supplies a PL/SQL package called the DBMS_OBFUSCATION_TOOLKIT to provide a mechanism for use in encrypting and decrypting stored data within the database. This feature is most beneficial in the protection of extremely sensitive data, such as credit card numbers, salaries, and passwords.

Bulk data encryption is supported in Oracle9*i* using the DES algorithm. The procedure DESEncrypt is used to encrypt data, while DESDecrypt is used for decryption. A cryptographic checksum capability using MD5 and a secure random-number generator procedure called *GetKey* are provided.

The encryption key used in the encryption and decryption must be provided programmatically. Therefore, the application developer must create a secure method to store and retrieve keys. The method developed must ensure the key is easy enough to retrieve to enable the user or application to decrypt the requested data without performance degradation. The key storage must also be strong enough to withstand malicious attacks. One approach is to use the wrap utility to obfuscate the PL/SQL package body performing the encryption. You put the key in the PL/SQL package body, and then wrap it, thereby making it unreadable to anyone attempting to compromise the database, including the most highly privileged DBA. To wrap a package body called MANAGEKEY, use the following syntax:

 `wrap iname=/tuscdir/managekey.sql`

Because wrapping isn't 100 percent unbreakable, you can also break up the key within the package body, and then have a separate routine reassemble it prior to use. You can develop other approaches to protect the keys effectively.

The DBMS_OBFUSCATION_TOOLKIT requires a 64-bit key, but the DES algorithm itself only provides a 56-bit key length. To get around this problem, Oracle supplies the procedure GetKey, which calls the secure random number generator.

The DBMS_OBFUSCATION_TOOLKIT package contains four procedures—two procedures that encrypt varchar2 and raw data types, and two procedures that decrypt varchar2 and raw data types. You must first install the package in the database, so you need to log in to SQL*Plus with the SYS user name and password as SYSDBA.

NOTE
If you don't include the phrase "as sysdba", you will not be connected and you'll be reminded to connect with the higher privileges.

The scripts you must run to create the package are found in $ORACLE_HOME/ rdbms/admin on UNIX, and ORACLE_HOME\rdbms\admin on Windows. From SQL*Plus, run the scripts dbmsobtk.sql and prvtobtk.plb.

Next, you have to grant Execute on DBMS_OBFUSCATION_TOOLKIT to PUBLIC, as follows:

```
grant EXECUTE on DBMS_OBFUSCATION_TOOLKIT to PUBLIC;
```

The procedures accept two parameters—the data to encrypt and the key used for the encryption or decryption algorithm.

The following is a simple call to the encryption procedure:

```
DBMS_OBFUSCATION_TOOLKIT.DES3Encrypt
(input_string => customer_encrypt.unencrypted_credit_card_no,
key_string => customer_encrypt.customer_key,
encrypted_string => encrypted_credit_card_no);
```

In this example, the customer's unencrypted credit card number is presented, along with the encryption key (customer_encrypt.customer_key). The output is the encrypted string called encrypted_credit_card_no.

Fine-Grained Database Auditing

In Oracle9*i*, fine-grained auditing is offered to let you more easily track who is accessing information in your database and how the information is being modified. You can now review redo log files and archived redo log files to determine who has interacted with or modified data and what the before image of the data was so you can repair maliciously modified data within your system.

Although Oracle's auditing solutions have been fairly robust, some areas haven't been addressed until recently. Oracle has enhanced its auditing approach to enable you to fine-tune your auditing implementation more easily by including the DBMS_ FGA package to enable fine-grained auditing capabilities.

With the DBMS_FGA package, you create conditions under which auditing records are generated. This approach seems similar to the VPD implementation because you create a policy for each package type, but a basic difference exists. With VPD, a predicate is attached to each query presented to the database to control the data to which a user has access. With FGA, a condition is examined to determine if the query meets the requirements to generate an audit action.

For example, let's say you have a table named *ALL_EMPLOYEES* that houses, among other information, the salaries for every employee in your organization. With Oracle's approach up through Oracle8*i*, you could only capture that the table had been viewed or something was changed, the user selecting on the table or making a change, and the time and date of the query or change. Without writing a trigger on the table to obtain the before and after image of the data, you couldn't capture what the data looked like before a change.

Using the DBMS_FGA package within Oracle9*i*, you attach an audit policy to a table or view to capture a defined user action. Say you want to know if any user selects information from the YEARLY_SALARY column that's a higher amount than a specific value. You can have the audit mechanism notify you that a violating query has occurred. You can specify an auditing policy by using the SQL predicate parameter audit_condition and supplying the column to audit with the audit_column attribute. An audit policy's values could look like the following:

```
AUDIT_CONDITION = where YEARLY_SALARY > 100000
AUDIT_COLUMN = YEARLY_SALARY
```

In this example, you're looking for anyone who tries to look at yearly salaries greater than $100,000. If someone attempts to view salaries that exceed the specified value, you can have the audit mechanism write a record to the audit log or even notify you by sending an e-mail or pager message.

Four procedures are included in the DBMS_FGA package: ADD_POLICY, DROP_POLICY, ENABLE_POLICY, and DISABLE_POLICY. The parameters used with the DBMS_FGA.ADD_POLICY package are shown in Table 12-5.

The DROP_POLICY, ENABLE_POLICY, and DISABLE_POLICY parameters are object_schema, object_name, and policy_name. The ENABLE_POLICY adds the fourth parameter, enable. You run the SQL script dbmsfag.sql as the SYS user to enable the DBMS_FGA package. The script creates the public synonym DBMS_FGA and grants execute to the EXECUTE_CATALOG_ROLE role.

Parameter	Description
object_schema	Schema owning the table/view. If the value is NULL, the current user is assumed.
object_name	Name of table or view.
policy_name	Name of policy to be added.
audit_column	Column to be audited.
audit_condition	Predicates for this policy.
handler_schema	Schema where the event handler procedure is located.
handler_module	Name of the event handler.
enable	Policy is enabled by DEFAULT.

TABLE 12-5.   *DBMS_FGA.ADD_POLICY Parameters*

Let's create the policy to audit for anyone selecting from the ALL_EMPLOYEES table any YEARLY_SALARY value greater than $100,000 per year. Create the error handler first, so it exists when you create the policy, as follows:

```
/* create audit event handler */
create procedure SECURITY.CAPTURE_ACTION(
  schema varchar2, table varchar2, policy varchar2)
AS BEGIN
  -- send an alert note to a pager
  UTIL_ALERT_PAGER(schema, table, policy);
END;
/* add the policy */
exec DBMS_FGA.ADD_POLICY(
object_schema   => 'HR',
object_name     => 'ALL_EMPLOYEES',
policy_name     => 'CHK_EMP_SAL',
audit_condition => where 'YEARLY_SALARY > ''100000'' ',
audit_column    => 'YEARLY_SALARY',
handler_schema  => 'SECURITY',
handler_module  => 'CAPTURE_ACTION',
enable          =>  TRUE);
```

When the audit conditions are met, an entry is placed in the DBA_FGA_AUDIT_TRAIL to capture the SQL text, policy name, and other information.

Application-Level Security

Security can be implemented on many different levels with 9*i*AS, beginning with the need to protect the software code itself through administrative security and encompassing user access security.

Using Oracle Portal, you can build, deploy, and monitor Web database applications. You can use an Oracle-supplied, HTML-based tool to create and view database objects, and to develop performance tracking and database security interfaces, as well as robust Web applications. Oracle Portal consists of an Oracle database, an HTTP server built on Apache Web server technology, and development tools that enable you to build applications using Java Servlets, Java Server pages, Perl, PL/SQL, and CGI.

TIP
Installed with the PL/SQL Web Toolkit packages, several OWA_UTIL procedures can inform you of database schema objects and other database metadata. These procedures are, by default, available from the Web. While a hacker cannot directly damage anything by calling these procedures, it could give him potentially damaging information about your database, which he can then use to attack your site. See Chapter 16 for the Apache directives needed to disable calls to these utilities.

Protecting the Oracle9*i*AS Directories

When the Oracle Portal product set is installed, the directory structure default home is Oracle\iSuites\. Within the file system is an \Apache directory and, below that, is a second \Apache directory. This naming convention is a little confusing until you get used to it.

The Oracle\iSuites code tree must be carefully protected because, in its current iteration (version 3.0.9), one of the files stored in the Oracle\iSuites\Apache\modsql\ cfg directory contains the Database Access Descriptors (DADs) for the entire Oracle Portal configuration. A DAD is normally used by the lightweight directory access protocol (LDAP) to resolve user names, passwords, machine locations, networking parameters, and so on much as the information in the Oracle Net tnsnames.ora file is used. Oracle Portal doesn't rely on the OID, Oracle's version of LDAP, to be installed to run correctly. Instead, a file called wdbsvr.app is used to store the required DAD information in plaintext. Because the Portal directory structure is well known, if someone can hack into your system and get to the file location, both your Web site and database can be easily compromised.

NOTE
In earlier versions of Oracle Portal, the file name is wdbsvr.env.

Here's a sample of the contents of the most current version of the wdbsvr.app file. This file uses the default user name and password options on a machine called TUSC, with a listener listening for connections on port 1521 to connect to a database called TUSCPORT.

```
;
[WVGATEWAY]
defaultDAD = portal30
```

```
administrators = all
adminPath = /admin_/
admindad = portal30
;upload_as_long_raw =
;upload_as_blob =
;debugModules =
;
[DAD_portal30]
connect_string   = tusc:1521:tuscport
password   = portal30
username   = portal30
default_page   = portal30.home
document_table   = portal30.wwdoc_document
document_path   = docs
document_proc   = portal30.wwdoc_process.process_download
upload_as_long_raw   =
upload_as_blob   = *
reuse   = Yes
connmax   = 10
enablesso   = Yes
pathalias   = url
pathaliasproc   = portal30.wwpth_api_alias.process_download
;name_prefix   =
;always_describe   =
;after_proc   =
;before_proc   =
;
[DAD_portal30_sso]
connect_string   = tusc:1521:tuscport
password   = portal30_sso
username   = portal30_sso
default_page   = portal30_sso.wwsso_home.home
document_table   = portal30_sso.wwdoc_document
document_path   = docs
document_proc   = portal30_sso.wwdoc_process.process_download
upload_as_long_raw   =
upload_as_blob   = *
reuse   = Yes
connmax   = 10
enablesso   = Yes
pathalias   = url
pathaliasproc   = portal30_sso.wwpth_api_alias.process_download
;name_prefix   =
;always_describe   =
;after_proc   =
;before_proc   =
;
[DAD_sample]
```

```
connect_string   =  sample-tcp
password    =  sample
username    =  sample
default_page    =  sample.home
document_table    =  sample.wwdoc_document
document_path    =  docs
document_proc    =  sample.wwdoc_process.process_download
upload_as_long_raw    =
upload_as_blob    = *
reuse    =  Yes
connmax    =  10
enablesso =  Yes
pathalias    = url
pathaliasproc    =  sample.wwpth_api_alias.process_download
;name_prefix    =
;always_describe    =
;after_proc    =
;before_proc    =
;
```

On a UNIX system, permissions on the file are restricted to read/write by the file owner, but the file is still clear text, so you want to ensure that only administrator and the Oracle/http server/Portal processes have access to the file. The files and the directory the files are in should be owned by the account the Oracle process runs under (usually the user oracle). Permissions on both the directory and file should be 700 to prevent anyone outside the administration group from accessing the file.

If the HTTP server process runs under a different account, create a group, assign the group as the file group, and make the permissions 770. In a Windows environment, things become dicier because the code tree is generally installed with access to the "Everyone" user. Take special care not to destroy Oracle's capability to access the code by revoking the Everyone grants. Check with Oracle for the latest directions on securing your Windows environment.

Using the PL/SQL Package OWA_SEC

Oracle offers a utility to provide security to procedures accessed via the PL/SQL Agent. When a Web client attempts to access a PL/SQL procedure, the utility—OWA_SEC—can be used to access the client's authentication information to perform an authorization check before allowing access to the procedure. You can either use the utility within the authorization callback procedure or the execution procedure, although the former method is more commonly used.

The OWA_SEC package contains the functions in the order they're created in the pubsec.sql script located in the $ORACLE_HOME/rdbms/admin directory. The OWA_SEC package initializes the four constants described in Table 12-6.

Constant	Value	Description
NO_CHECK	1	Any user can access any package in a DAD schema and will *not* be prompted by a custom authentication login. If NO_CHECK is used, you can use types of authentication other than the custom authentication. This is referred to as the *no check custom authentication scheme.*
GLOBAL	2	Before any user can access any package in any DAD schema, the user is subject to pass the criteria in the authorize function of the OWA_ CUSTOM package.
PER_PACKAGE	3	Before any user can access procedures in a package, the user is subject to pass the criteria in the authorize function of the package executed. If the procedure executed isn't in a package or if the package doesn't contain an authorize function, the user is then subject to pass the criteria in the OWA_CUSTOM package's authorize function.
CUSTOM	4	Only selected users can access any package in certain DAD schemas, requiring a login— referred to as the *custom authentication scheme.*

TABLE 12-6. *OWA_SEC Constants*

The procedures and functions available in the OWA_SEC package are shown in Table 12-7.

Configuring Web Authentication Services

Oracle9*i*AS Authentication Services provide for the authentication of client requests based on a specific virtual path request. Authentication may not be required, based on the virtual path requested. When you perform the installation and configuration, specify the authentication requirements for each path.

The Security forms enable you to use several authentication schemes to protect specific files and directories. *i*AS also provides authentication for *i*AS modules to authenticate users before they can use a module.

Depending on the authorization scheme, when a file or directory is protected, a client requesting access to it must provide a user name and password, be a member

Procedure or Function Name	Arguments	Description
SET_AUTHORIZATION	scheme integer	Procedure to specify the PL/SQL Agent's authorization scheme.
GET_USER_ID	varchar2	Returns the user's ID.
GET_PASSWORD	varchar2	Returns the user's password.
GET_CLIENT_IP	calls: owa_util. ip_address	Returns the user's IP address in a PL/SQL table, in which the first four elements are the numbers of the IP address.
GET_CLIENT_HOSTNAME	varchar2	Returns the user's host computer name.
SET_PROTECTION_REALM	realm varchar2	Procedure to specify the dynamic page's protection realm.

TABLE 12-7. *OWA_SEC Procedures and Functions*

of the appropriate domain, and/or have an authorized IP address. The Basic and Digest authentication schemes enable you to define named groups of user name/ password combinations, called *realms,* and groups of these realms. You can then assign user, group, and realm access to files and directories, requiring any client requesting access to input one of the specified user name/password combinations.

The following five authentication methods are available under each of the Listener and security options:

- **Basic Authentication** Uses an unencrypted user name and password prompt to authenticate the user.

- **Digest Authentication** Same as Basic Authentication, except the password is slightly encrypted.

- **Database Authentication** Uses the Oracle DBMS schemas (users) to authenticate the user.

- **Domain-Based Restriction** Based on a specific domain group. You may instruct the authentication to include or exclude specific domain groups, for example, +*.tusc.com or -*.microsoft.com.

- **IP-Based Restriction**   Based on a specific IP class level. You may instruct the authentication to include or exclude specific IP groups, for example, +205.204.102.* or -24.3.*.

Configuration of each of the previous authentication methods is discussed in detail in Chapter 3.

More About Basic, Digest, and LDAP Authentication

When accessing a directory protected by basic, digest, or LDAP, the user is prompted for a user name and password in a dialog window. Not very exciting, is it? Several limitations exist to this method of authentication. For example, you might want to use an HTML form to prompt for the user name and password. You might want to do this for many reasons, including the following:

- To provide password hint functionality for users
- To provide support information on the login page
- To customize handling of login failure
- To display custom graphics, look and feel for login page
- To avoid forcing users to adhere to a limit of three failed login attempts
- To allow for case-insensitive user name and password
- To detect browser incompatibility prior to login
- To allow for guest access (without them knowing user name/password)

As you can see, you might want to provide such functionality for many reasons. If the user specifies the user name and password as a part of the URL in the following syntax, the dialog box won't prompt her:

 `username:password@www.tusc.com/...`

By using a JavaScript function (or simply a redirect command), you can pass the previous URL on to the authentication server. This enables you to provide the previous functionality and still use basic, digest, or LDAP authentication.

User Security Considerations

One of the on-going problems developers and database administrators have faced in the past is not having the capability to track individual users who have authenticated to a middle-tier application. In many Web-based applications, the client authenticates to the middle-tier Web application, and then the application using a pool of previously established connections, queries the database on behalf of the client. In Oracle8*i*, this capability was available only to a program using the Oracle Call Interface (OCI). In Oracle9*i*, this capability can also be accomplished through the JDBC interface. When this form of connection is used, the client is said to be *proxied* in to the database server.

In Oracle8*i*, if you want to audit the individual actions of a specific user who was proxied in to the database, you couldn't do so effectively. In Oracle9*i*, the identity of each client is preserved throughout all tiers, so you now have the capability to track and audit the actions taken on behalf of a specific client. To accomplish this, use the by <proxy> clause in your audit statement. Using this clause enables you to audit all the SQL statements issued by the proxy on its own behalf, on behalf of a specified user, or on behalf of all users.

To enable auditing of proxied users, issue a command using the following syntax:

```
audit <SQL_command_type> by <application_name>
on behalf of <client_name>;
```

If you want to audit all select table commands issued by the WEBAPP server on behalf of a client named MONGO, for example, you'd use the following:

```
audit SELECT TABLE by WEBAPP
on behalf of MONGO;
```

The type of proxy authentication has also been expanded in Oracle9*i*. Oracle8*i* allowed proxy authentication only for database users providing password credentials. Oracle9*i* allows proxy of accounts based on the Distinguished Name (DN) or the full X.509 certificate. This provides a method of identifying, not authenticating, accounts using SSL credentials. The capability to use credentials can even be extended to the Virtual Private Databases to allow filtering of data based on the proxied user's identity.

Network Security

If your company's computers were never configured to interact with computers outside your installation, you could still face data compromise because your users are distributed throughout your company and, therefore, access the company databases via a network. Any company connected at least in part to the Internet faces the challenge of ensuring that malicious individuals are prevented from gaining access to private data or damaging the integrity of the computers on which their data resides. Beyond software-level network security measures, hardware and firewalls can be used to provide such security.

This section discusses the following topics:

■ Basic Oracle Net configuration

■ SSL/HTTPS basics and set up

■ Oracle Internet Directory (LDAP)

Oracle Net and the Oracle Advanced Security Option

When Oracle introduced the client/server architecture in the late version 4 and early version 5 of the RDBMS, the product was called SQL*Net. When Oracle8 was introduced, the name SQL*Net was changed to Net8. With the advent of Oracle9i, Oracle's networking functionality has undergone yet another name change, this time to Oracle Net.

With Oracle Net, the emphasis for network security has been enhanced to include stronger firewall access control (in other words, Oracle Net supports accessing a database through a firewall) through the Oracle Advanced Security Option. In an intranet environment, you can use the Oracle Connection Manager as a firewall for Oracle Net traffic. Using the Oracle Connection Manager, you can configure enabling or disabling specific client access by establishing filtering rules based on the following criteria:

■ Source host names or IP addresses for clients

■ Destination host names or IP addresses for servers

■ Destination database service name

■ Whether the Oracle Advanced Security option is being used by the client

The Oracle Connection Manager is used to enhance your firewall security by filtering out client access based on one or more aspects of the filtering rules you create.

To establish a firewall between the Internet and your application gateway and application Web server, and a second firewall between the gateway and server and your corporate intranet and databases, Oracle has worked with some firewall vendors to provide the Connection Manager software in a firewall-vendor solution. Contact your Oracle representative (or reseller) for specific vendor recommendations.

In Oracle9i, the Oracle Connection Manager acts in the same way as the listener has in prior releases using the multithreaded server option. The Connection Manager accepts requests from the Web application server and passes the requests on to dispatchers. Just as with MTS, the dispatchers pass the requests on to the Shared Server Processes for processing within the database. Figure 12-4 shows the flow

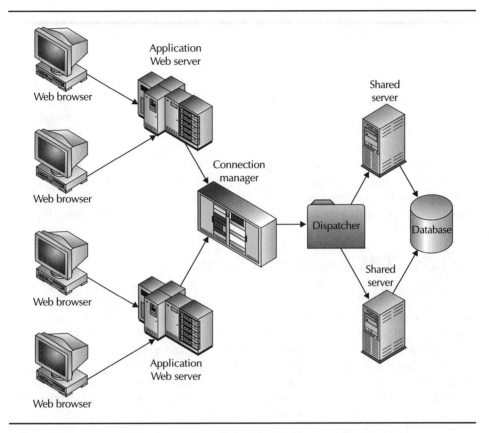

FIGURE 12-4. *Oracle Net Web Browser to database request flow*

from Web Browsers through the Web application servers to the Connection Managers, and over to the Dispatchers and Shared Server Processes. In this way, Oracle Net supports connection load balancing for dedicated server configurations, as well as across shared server configurations.

To support a large body of users, you can configure multiple Connection Managers to support the query load.

You can also use the sqlnet.ora file to specify configuration parameters that describe the criteria the software should use to determine whether a client can connect to your databases. The parameters you can use are as follows:

- TCP.EXCLUDED_NODES to specify those nodes that aren't allowed access

- TCP.INVITED_NODES to designate specific nodes that are allowed access

■ TCP.VALIDNODE_CHECKING to check for the values for TCP.INVITED_
NODES and TCP.EXCLUDED_NODES to determine who should be
permitted or denied access

To ensure your firewall is functioning optimally, don't ever "poke a hole" through
it. In other words, never leave Oracle's default listener port of 1521 available for
connections from the Internet. You also want to ensure that each of your listeners is
password protected, so no one can compromise your system by obtaining information
about the databases your listener is supporting through banner information, database
or service names, or trace and logging information.

Another step you can take to help protect your listener is to enable security
configuration parameters by setting the ADMIN_RESTRICTIONS_<listener_name>
value to ON. By enabling this parameter, you help to prevent unauthorized listener
administration.

SSL/HTTPS Basics and Setup

SSL is a protocol on top of HTTP that encrypts all messages sent between the
browser and the Web server. SSL is used to secure communications from any client
or server to one or more Oracle servers, or from an Oracle server to any client. You
can use SSL alone or with other authentication methods, and you can configure SSL
to require server authentication only, or both client and server authentication.

URLs that require SSL use HTTPS in place of HTTP. The Listener must be configured
to accept an SSL connection, and the system administrator must have a certificate for the
Listener (often obtained from VeriSign). SSL is available to secure FTP and secure telnet
in 40- and 128-bit flavors. Because the United States is now relaxing its export
restrictions, I recommend using 128-bit encryption whenever possible.

SSL also provides for authentication. When the browser connects to the server, the
server presents its certificate. The browser then either accepts that certificate (if it's
included in the site certificates in the browser) or prompts the user to decide whether
to accept the certificate. The certificate enables the user to be sure the server is what it
claims to be. However, the simple fact that a server has a certificate doesn't mean the
user must or should permit access.

In addition to the server being authenticated, the server can request the client
be authenticated. The client must have obtained its own certificate and present that
certificate to the server when prompted. Client authentication isn't required as part
of the SSL protocol and most Listeners enable this to be configured.

SSL encryption and authentication can be used for static HTML pages, CGI
programs, and cartridges. If a request for a cartridge uses SSL, the resulting HTML
page generated by the cartridge is encrypted. Application programmers don't have
to know anything about SSL and its associated encryption methods to develop an
application.

Setting Up SSL

The instructions within the online documentation and those listed in my first book, *Oracle Application Server Web Toolkit Reference* (Osborne/McGraw-Hill, 1998) can help you configure SSL. When referring to the online documentation, you might find enough ambiguity that it will be difficult to make SSL work with *i*AS.

The following tips should help you through this process. The process of registering and obtaining a certificate is performed online. You receive your trial certificate immediately.

- Do *not* abbreviate. For example, you must specify the exact state (the location your business is in, such as Illinois). For the most secure keys, use a file and random keys.

- Use filenames that make sense (for example, privkey.der).

- Previously, the genreq utility generated the key files on the server. You might need to do a system-level file find to locate the files.

- The genreq utility will ask for the distinguished name. The distinguished name is the fully qualified domain name (fqdn) registered on the Internet. Thus, only boxes with a "publicly" shared domain name can use SSL. You cannot register SSL to an IP address. You could use an internal domain name, if this is your intent.

- The security entries requested want exact paths leading to the key files, such as c:\orant\owa\bin\cert.der.

- Be careful what you do with the key file. VeriSign sends back the file in e-mail. We had a situation once where someone had forwarded the file to someone else. Exchange (e-mail) added a greater than (>) character to every line forwarded, but this wasn't obvious to the person implementing the key file because it was her first time implementing SSL. The file (and SSL) was unusable until the alterations were removed from the file.

- Prior to *i*AS, when a new port was added for SSL, you needed to alter the PL/SQL cartridge so it could use the new port.

- Netscape handles cookies differently than Microsoft Internet Explorer does. In an application, we had a session cookie that suddenly became unavailable to the SSL portion in Netscape Navigator 4.0, whereas within Explorer it worked fine. After further research, we discovered the Netscape cookie file in C:\Program Files\Netscape\User\Default\cookies.txt. Explorer's cookies live in C:\Windows\cookies in several different files. After further examination of the Netscape cookie file, we found Netscape included a port number with the cookie information, suggesting Netscape cookies are port-dependent.

■ Cookies can be marked as secure, which means they're only accessible if the user is using the HTTPS protocol. Otherwise, the cookie won't be available to the server.

■ Set up SSL on port 443 (this is the default https port, just as port 80 is the default http port) and proxy servers are likely to limit your remote (Internet-based) clients to these ports.

■ iAS supports certificates issued from other certificate authorities (CAs), such as Netscape.

Protecting Digital Certificates

Public Key Infrastructure continues to grow, as does the use of PKI along with Oracle. Of course, Oracle has been allowing the use of PKI with the database since version 8.1.5. In Oracle9i, the integration with PKI standards has increased.

Oracle worked with the following vendors to include CA trusted roots with Oracle9i. By including the CA trusted roots, you're saved from having to install a certificate for these well-known CAs on every client.

■ VeriSign

■ Entrust

■ Baltimore Technologies

There has also been an extension of the support PKI standards in Oracle. These extensions are listed as follows:

■ PKCS#12 support

■ Storage of wallet credentials in an OID

■ Multiple certificates per wallet

■ Strong encryption of wallet files

Once the CA trusted roots are in place on your system, you must ensure the certificates are kept safe because of sensitivity of your certificate files for SSL. The method chosen to provide protection is largely determined by your system administrator's philosophy on physical file protection.

Normally, all VeriSign files are stored in a single directory. The Listener account must have read-and-write access to the files in that directory. Access to the directory can usually be accomplished with the use of access control lists (ACLs), but you or your system administrator should ensure no other access is enabled to that directory by other users.

The password to the Listener account should be secure, so only your operating system Web administrator knows the password. If the VeriSign certificate is stolen or altered, it might compromise system security. Outside of protecting file access to this directory, further steps aren't available. On UNIX, the security level for these files should be set to 700 permissions (read, write, execute by the owner only) on your system.

Using Oracle Internet Directory (LDAP)

Oracle Corporation created a general-purpose directory service called the Oracle Internet Directory (OID) that combined the LDAP version 3 structure with the Oracle8*i* server. Oracle9*i* has implemented many improvements and enhancements to the product set. OID provides information about network resources and users by communicating with a database that can be either on the same operating system or a different one.

OID Security

OID provides the administrator with flexible access control by implementing three levels of user authentication, as shown in Table 12-8.

SSL version 3 is used for certificate-based authenticated access and data privacy in one of three modes: no authentication, one-way authentication, or two-way

Authentication	Description
Anonymous	Requires no user name or password for directory access. Enables the user to access all information and privileges allocated to the anonymous user.
Simple or password-based	Client uses a domain name and plain-text password to identify itself. The server verifies the sent DN and password match the DN and password stored in the directory.
Certificate-based (used with SSL)	Client and server use certificates for authentication to ensure the entity's identity information is correct.

TABLE 12-8. *OID User Authentication Levels*

authentication. The components that make up the SSL authentication for OID
are as follows:

- **Certificate**   The component used to ensure the entity's identity information
  is correct. The certificate comprises the entity's name, public key, serial
  number, and expiration date, and is signed by a CA.

- **Certificate Authority (CA)**   A trusted third party that certifies the other
  entities are who they claim to be. The CA uses its private key to sign the
  certificate once it verifies the entity's identity. CAs use varying criteria to
  establish an entity's identity and each network has a list of CAs it trusts.
  The CA publishes its own certificate, including its public key.

- **Wallet**   An abstraction used to store and manage authentication data
  required by SSL. A wallet within the Oracle environment using SSL contains
  a private key, an X.509 version 3 certificate, and a list of trusted certificates,
  known as *trustpoints.*

Oracle supplies a tool called the Wallet Manager to manage security credentials
on both the server and clients. You can use the Wallet Manager to generate public/
private key pairs and create certificate requests that can be submitted to a CA. You
can also install a certificate and configure trusted certificates for an entity using the
Wallet Manager. Figure 12-5 shows the initial Wallet Manager screen.

When a user begins an LDAP connection using the SSL port, a mechanism known
as a handshake is performed to begin communication between a client and the OID.
During the *handshake,* the client and server decide what cipher suite should be used.
Table 12-9 shows the available cipher suites that OID supports and the algorithms
supported for each suite.

Once the cipher suite is determined, the server sends its certificate to the client.
The client verifies a trusted CA signed the certificate. If client authentication is
required, the client sends its own certificate to the directory server and the server
verifies a trusted CA signed the client's certificate. The client and directory server use
public-key cryptography to exchange material to enable them to generate a session
key. Once the session key has been created, it and the cipher suite are used to encrypt
and decrypt all session communications. If the handshake is successful, the user's
authorization is verified to confirm the user has the right to access the directory.

When SSL is used, each transmission from the client to the server and back
includes a cryptographically secure message digest containing checksums within
each packet sent across the network using either the MD5 or SHA algorithm. OID
supports two levels of encryption: DES40 and RC4_40. Both encryption algorithms
use a 40-bit key size.

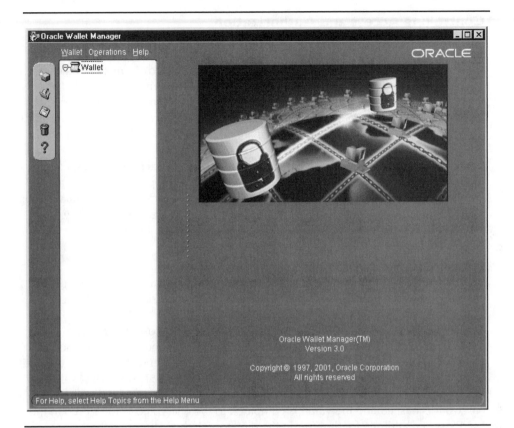

FIGURE 12-5. *Oracle Wallet Manager initial screen*

Cipher Suite	Authentication	Encryption	Integrity
SSL_RSA_EXPORT_WITH_DES40_CBC_SHA	RSA	DES40	SHA
SSL_RSA_EXPORT_WITH_RC4_40_MD5	RSA	RC4_40	MD5
SSL_RSA_WITH_NULL_SHA	RSA	None	SHA
SSL_RSA_WITH_NULL_MD5	RSA	None	MD5

TABLE 12-9. *Cipher Suites Supported by OID*

Controlling Access and Authorization

OID ensures a user's identity by verifying the authorization ID associated with the session has the required permissions to perform the requested operation. If the user doesn't have the correct privileges, the operation is disallowed. As mentioned earlier in this chapter, the mechanism used to determine a user's privileges is called access control. The administrative policies are captured in the directory metadata and describe the access control information (ACI) used to determine the correct access control for each user. The attribute values on the list control the access policies for the directory objects within the specific directory.

ACIs are attributes stored as text strings in the directory. Each ACI represents a distinct access control policy and each individual policy component is called an *ACI Directive.* You can set a security directive's access control policy to apply from a starting point downward within a directory structure, known as an access control policy point (ACP), to all entries below the ACP in the directory information tree (DIT).

About OID Passwords

When you install OID, you're prompted to specify if you want user password encryption enabled. Figure 12-6 shows the user-encryption selection screen. Your choices are either Yes or No.

The next screen prompts you for your choice of encryption schemes for passwords. By default, passwords are encrypted using the one-way hash function MD4 to produce a 128-bit hash value or message digest. Figure 12-7 shows the OID hashing algorithm options: MD4, MD5, SHA, or UNIX CRYPT, with MD4 selected.

When the client presents a password, usually in clear text, to the directory, the password is hashed and the value is compared to the encrypted value stored in the userPassword attribute for the user in the directory. If the values match, the user gains access to the directory based on the privileges the user holds. If the values don't match, an Invalid Credentials error message is returned to the user.

You aren't locked in to the encryption method chosen at installation time and you can modify the initial configuration using either the Oracle Directory Manager or the command line package ldapmodify, if you have superuser status on the system. Your choices for password encryption are as follows:

- No encryption
- MD5, an improved, more complex version of MD4
- Secure Hash Algorithm (SHA), which produces a 160-bit hash
- UNIX Crypt, the UNIX encryption algorithm

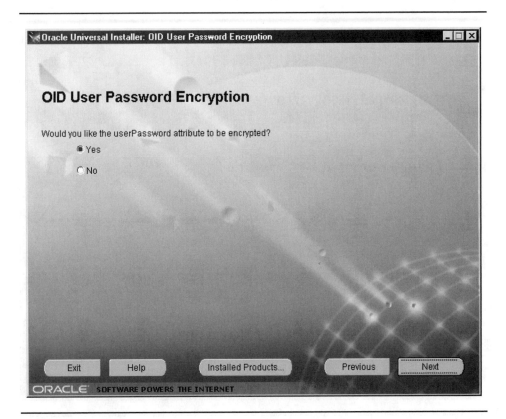

FIGURE 12-6. *OID User Password Encryption screen*

The specified value is stored in the attribute orclCryptoScheme in the root DSE as a single value.

SSL Configuration for OID

The directory reads a set of configuration parameters each time the directory server instance is started. If you're going to run the directory with SSL enabled, you need to examine the SSL parameters in the configuration set entry. By default, the secure port Oracle has registered for SSL is 636, while the regular, unsecured OID port is 389. To accommodate clients with differing security needs, you can create and modify multiple sets of configuration parameters with differing values. Each set has a different configuration set entry.

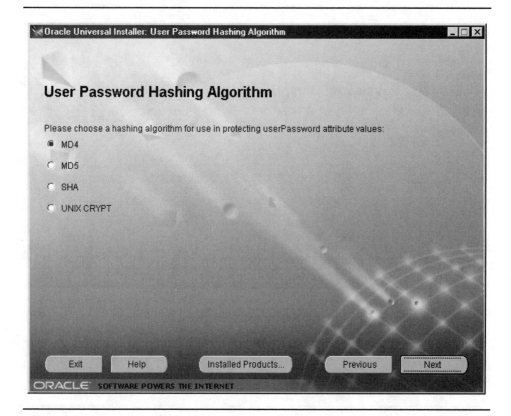

FIGURE 12-7. *User Password Hashing Algorithm screen*

NOTE
Oracle recommends you create separate configuration sets instead of modifying the SSL values in the default configuration set so, if you ever have a problem that involves Oracle Support Services, the technician can use the default configuration set while diagnosing the problem.

Audit Logging

OID provides the capability to audit critical events in the OID audit log. To query the audit log, you need administration privileges, and you use the ldapsearch command. The OID server is the only entity that can maintain or add entries to the audit log. One regular directory entry for each audit event is made to the audit log.

Audit logging is turned off by default. Because the audit log is made up of regular directory entries, you can enable auditing by modifying the DSE attribute orclaudit level to the level you want. The audit options and levels, reproduced here from the *Oracle Internet Directory Administration Guide,* are shown in Table 12-10. Notice the level values are shown in hex.

Event	Description	Audit Level Mask
Superuser login	Super user bind to the server (successes or failures)	0x0001
Schema element add/replace	Adding a new schema element (success and failure)	0x0002
Schema element delete	Deletion of a schema (successes or failures)	0x0004
Bind	Unsuccessful bind cases	0x0008
Access violation	Access denied by access control policy point	0x0010
Directory-specific Entry (DSE) modification	Changes to a directory-specific entry (DSE) (successes or failures)	0x0020
Replication login	Replication server authentication (successes or failures)	0x0040
ACL modification	Changes to an access control list (ACL)	0x0080
User password modification	Modification of user password attribute	0x0100
Add	ldapadd operation (successes or failures)	0x0200
Delete	ldapdelete operation (successes or failures)	0x0400
Modify	ldapmodify operation (successes or failures)	0x0800
ModifyDN	ldapModifyDN operation (successes or failures)	0x1000

TABLE 12-10. *OID Audit Events*

If an audit value is set to 0, auditing is disabled. You can use either the Oracle Directory Manager or the command ldapmodify from the operating system command line to enable auditing. Once you modify the audit level, the change won't take effect until you stop and restart the directory server. To search the audit log, you can use the ldapsearch command. To purge entries from the audit log, you use the bulkdelete command.

Summary

Like many of the chapters in this book, entire books are written on the topic of this chapter, Oracle Internet security. In fact, the *Oracle Security Handbook,* by Marlene L. Theriault and Aaron Newman (Osborne/McGraw-Hill, 2001) was used heavily as a reference for this chapter.

When we opened up our companies to the Internet, security exposed an entirely new world of opportunity for hackers and people just "having fun." When it comes to applications deployed to the general public, as on the Internet, security becomes a serious topic. As you collect and/or distribute information on the Internet, you must consider its confidentiality and privacy liability. If you don't consider security of the data distributed, as well as stored in your database, you should be concerned. The bigger your company is, the more publicity would be received by cracking your systems, the more people will attempt to break your security.

PART
III

Modules

CHAPTER
13

Java

I n the last few years, the Java language and platform have become the technical approach of choice for building complex, distributed Web-enabled applications across enterprises around the world. Thanks to its cross-platform run-time environment, object-oriented development model, and facilities for working with object request brokers and other code components, Java is well equipped for building applications.

The design of Java began in 1990, and the first public release and official naming (that is, Java) was in 1994. JavaSoft wasn't formed by Sun until 1996, and then the first Java Development Kit (JDK) was released. Today, more than 200,000 people worldwide consider themselves Java programmers.

Java is a powerful programming language for Web developers that can be used for anything from generating simple HTML pages to full-fledged Web-based applications. While most people are confused because they consider Java a client-side tool (they're thinking of applets that run in the browser), Java today is primarily used for server-side application development. This entire book is focused on server-side development, which is where the real power of Web development exists.

Another point of confusion is JavaScript. JavaScript was originally called LiveScript, but was strategically renamed when Netscape saw the popularity of Java growing. This strategic move has also been painful, however, because many people confuse JavaScript and Java by thinking these tools must have something in common. But Java and JavaScript only have four letters in common: *J, a, v,* and *a*. Both languages are object-based and have a syntax based on the C programming language, but neither is based on the other.

Java is a programming language. Its open specification was first created at Sun, but many companies support it. Java is capable of running on every tier in the Web world. Larry Ellison once said Java would be Oracle's programming language of choice (that is, 100 percent of its code) on the client, application server, and database server; therefore, Oracle would be 300 percent Java. Larry apparently forgot about the presentation layer, so I guess Oracle is 400 percent Java!

Applets are client-side (that is, they run in the browser) Java code. JavaServer Pages (JSPs) run on the presentation layer or tier. Servlets, Enterprise JavaBeans (EJBs), and SQL for Java (SQLJ) also are server-side/application layer programs and Java Stored Procedures are database-tier Java programs.

The Java language syntax itself is pretty easy to learn. Object-oriented programming (the C++ side of Java) is more difficult to learn, but it's easier than C and C++ because many of the complex structures, or pointers, were removed or simply don't exist in Java. Therefore, people sometimes refer to Java as C++-- (pronounced *C* plus, plus, minus, minus). In fact, Bill Joy, one of the founders of the Java Language said this himself.

Many Java code libraries are available—many come with the Java development kit (J2EE), many more are available as open source, and more still are available for sale. Many programmers use Java, so a large user community exists to draw on for support. Java is a hot language. Developers like it and they want to say they're doing Java development. Many Java editors and tools are also available.

As Java continues to gain more acceptance, and as developers embrace this technology from the database and Internet arenas, the options and information about this powerful language can become overwhelming. Why has Java exploded on the scene as the choice for developing and deploying Web-based applications? Java provides a portable solution that can be implemented on simple, lower-cost operating systems, and it's platform-independent. Java also permits applications to meet business goals by being highly available, secure, reliable, and scalable. Also, compared to C++, Java is relatively quick to develop.

Oracle's Java strategy, shown in Figure 13-1, is dedication to Java. Oracle made a strategic commitment to Java, which is evident in its integration of Java into a number of different platforms and products, such as the database, application server, and integrated development environments. Oracle supports the Java2 Enterprise Edition (J2EE) standard methodology for developing and deploying Java applications. And Oracle has provided Java developers with a rich set of Java tools to assist developers in reducing time-to-market for building applications. Oracle provides a high performance, scaleable, and available server infrastructure to deploy Java applications.

Oracle9*i*AS supports the complete Java2 Enterprise Edition, shown in Figure 13-2, with containers for J2EE—referred to as Oracle Components for Java (OC4J). *OC4J* is 100 percent Java and executes on the standard J2EE platform and Virtual Machine (Java VM). The OC4J container includes a JSP Translator, a Java servlet engine, and an EJB container.

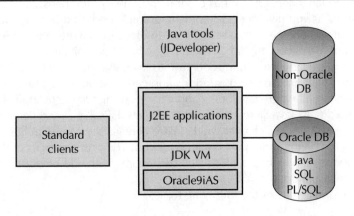

FIGURE 13-1.   *Oracle's Java strategy*

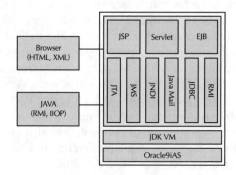

FIGURE 13-2. *Summary of Oracle 9iAS J2EE facilities*

TIP

Version 1.0.2.2 of 9iAS brought considerable new Java functionality (that is, the EJB container) and significant performance improvements over the prior versions. The entire Java engine was replaced at this version.

This chapter breaks down all the buzzwords and features associated with Java and Oracle. Because Java has become the premier language of Internet server-side development and has shown developers the real value of an object-oriented programming language, Oracle has embraced Java's comprehensive J2EE specification. As you dive deeper into developing Web-based Java applications, you'll definitely become inundated with all the Java buzzwords from the Oracle documentation and you might be wondering where each piece fits.

This chapter starts with an introduction to Java, the syntax of the language, and its functionality. Practical demonstrations and code are presented for Java that can be extremely useful when developing applications using Oracle9i Application Server (9iAS). I also discuss Java Stored Procedures, servlets, JSPs, JServ module, and PL2JAVA. If you're new to Java, this chapter will be extremely valuable for you. Discover which tools can offer the optimum performance for you. The primary focus of this chapter is the JSP technology because most Web development should be done using JSP—at least in my opinion.

This chapter discusses the following topics:

- J2xE

- Java for the PL/SQL Developer

■ Oracle's Java Virtual Machine (JVM)

■ Java Servlets

■ JDBC (Java Database Connectivity)

■ SQLJ

■ JavaServer Pages (JSPs)

■ Java Stored Procedures

■ Business Components for Java (BC4J)

■ JDeveloper

■ Deploying JSPs on Tomcat, Apache, and Oracle8*i*

■ PL2JAVA—Using PL/SQL in Java

■ Recommended Reading

■ Recommended Web sites

J2xE

J2SE, J2EE, J2ME—have you seen these terms and wondered what they're all about? I know I had. I heard and saw J2EE a great many times without understanding what it meant. J2EE is simpler than I envisioned: *J* stands for Java, which you probably guessed. 2 stands for Java platform 2, which includes versions 1.2 and later of the JDK. Version 2 is currently the latest and greatest version of Java. The first *E* stands for Enterprise or the "full-blown" version, the thickest library, and the final *E* stands for Edition. In J2xE, the *x* represents *S*, *E*, or *M*, representing the extensiveness of the Java libraries included with the edition. *S* stands for Standard—this is the middle-of-the-road version, *E,* again, stands for Enterprise, and *M* stands for Micro, or the thinnest version of the libraries.

Oracle9*i*AS and Oracle9*i* database support all the J2EE APIs. The J2EE implementations are identical in both the 9*i*AS and database server, which lets you move your code freely between the Application tiers and the Oracle9*i* data tier.

In addition to J2EE, 9*i*AS supplies several Java libraries, or frameworks, such as the XML development toolkit and the Wireless Edition framework (previously known as Portal-to-Go) to support Wireless Application Protocol (WAP) devices. The Oracle Business Components for Java (BC4J), is an object-relational mapping tool and application framework targeted to the SQL-savvy Java programmer. *BC4J* enables you to define Java objects representing the results of various SQL queries and can help share data between Java objects coming from the same rows, even if they're fetched by unrelated SQL queries. This model, for Java programmers with a

SQL background, complements the EJB entity bean implementation of 9*i*AS. BC4J enables the expert programmer to optimize SQL queries and data access patterns. You learn more about BC4J later in this chapter.

Java for the PL/SQL Developer

As you saw in Chapter 7, when I'm learning a new language, I like to compare the new language first to a language I already know. Because most Oracle developers know PL/SQL, let's cover some basic terminology of PL/SQL versus Java. If you're currently a PL/SQL developer, this section is just the touch you'll need to get you started with Java. You'll quickly understand how easy it is to write programs in Java. If you already know Java, you can skip this section—or read it as a refresher.

Learning Java

You might ask, do I need to know Java? Absolutely. So, what is Java? As previously mentioned, many people refer to Java as C++-. In other words, it's similar to C++ (which is an object-oriented version of C), without the complexity of the pointers of C++ and other constructs. Object-oriented programming languages are difficult to learn. You need to take the time to learn Java to develop a Web-based Java application. If you know C (or Perl), you can quickly understand the syntax of the Java language. Three books I recommend to help you learn Java include *Java in a Nutshell: A Desktop Quick Reference, Third Edition,* by David Flanagan (O'Reilly, 1999), *Web Development with JavaServer Pages,* by Duane K. Fields and Mark A. Kobb (Manning, 2000), and *Professional JSP, Second Edition,* by Simon Brown et al. (Wrox Press, 2001).

Program Units

In PL/SQL, program units at the lowest level are called *procedures* and *functions.* Procedures and functions can be grouped into packages in PL/SQL. In Java, the lowest level of program units is called a *method.* No distinction exists between procedures and functions in Java—what would be considered a procedure in PL/SQL is simply a method that returns nothing (indicated with the reserved word "void"). In Java, methods must be grouped into a class. Java can group classes into a higher level yet, called *packages.* You might consider Java packages similar to a database schema within PL/SQL.

PL/SQL terminology	Java terminology
Schema	Package
Package	Class
Procedure/function	Method

Terminators, Literals, and Quotes

Both PL/SQL and Java end program lines with a semicolon (;). In PL/SQL, *literals* are quoted with a single quote, whereas Java uses a double quote. In PL/SQL, a double quote indicates the text within is case-sensitive. In Java, everything is case-sensitive.

	PL/SQL	**Java**
Terminator	;	;
Literal	'	"
Quoted	"	N/A

Case-Sensitivity

As already mentioned, *everything* in Java is case-sensitive. PL/SQL, however, is *not* case-sensitive (unless you double quote the text). When you begin working with a case-sensitive language, this will probably bite you a few times. So, take a few minutes and write this down 100 times and you'll still forget it—Java is case-sensitive. Fortunately, Java is a compiled and strict language, meaning you must declare variables before using them. This means the Java compiler usually catches any case-sensitivity errors you might have overlooked. So the fact that Java is case-sensitive isn't as bad as it might first appear. Additionally, de facto naming standards exist that can also help you.

Packages Versus Classes

Because case doesn't matter when it comes to naming packages in PL/SQL, text is usually separated by underscores. In Java, however, class names should begin with a capital letter and you should capitalize each word within. Also in Java, it's recommended you don't use special characters, like the underscore. Here's an example of each:

	PL/SQL package name	**Java class name**
Example	brad_brown	BradBrown

When it comes to declaring packages in PL/SQL vs. classes in Java, the following table shows the syntax of each. I'll review some specific examples of these shortly.

PL/SQL package syntax	**Java class syntax**
create or replace package package_name...	public/private/protected class ClassName {}

Procedures/Functions Versus Methods

When naming procedures and functions in PL/SQL, words are usually separated with an underscore. In Java, however, method names should begin with a lowercase letter and you should capitalize each word within. Like class naming, you don't use special characters (like the underscore) in Java. For example:

	PL/SQL procedure/ function name	**Java method name**
Example	brad_brown	bradBrown()

The following table shows the syntax for declaring procedures and functions versus methods:

PL/SQL declaration	**Java declaration**
procedure/ function procedure/ function_name	public/private/protected static void/ int/boolean/char/byte/short/ long/ float/double methodName

The following table shows an example syntax for an actual PL/SQL procedure versus a Java method definition:

PL/SQL procedure example	**Java method example**
procedure procedure_name (in_session integer, in_name varchar2);	public void procedureName (int inSession, String inName)

Note the word "void" in the Java code, which means the method doesn't return anything (that is, it corresponds to a PL/SQL procedure).

The following table shows an example of an actual PL/SQL function vs. a Java method definition:

PL/SQL function example	**Java method example**
function *functionname* (in_session integer) returns number;	public long functionName (int inSession)

The following is an example declaration of an entire Java class and method specification:

```
public class MyClass {
    public static void main (String[] args) {}
    public int misc(String s) {}
    private boolean getFlag() {}
}
```

NOTE
*Angle brackets in Java indicates an array—in this
case, an array of String objects named args.*

The following table shows an example of the syntax for calling procedures and
functions versus calling methods:

PL/SQL call syntax	Java call syntax
package_name.procedure_name;	class.method();
a number := package_name.function_name;	int a = class.method();

Comments

Although we often joke that many programmers don't seem to like using
comments, they are very important! In PL/SQL, a single-line comment is started
with two dashes (--). In Java, a single-line comment is started with two forward
slashes (//). Multiple-line comments in both languages begin with a forward slash
and an asterisk (/*) and end with an asterisk and a forward slash (*/). Java also
supports special "documentation comments," which begin with /** and end with
*/. Documentation comments are extracted by the javadoc program, as shown
in the following line for documentation comment.

PL/SQL comments	Java comments
-- Single Line	// Single Line
/* Multiple Lines for a Comment */	/* Multiple Lines for a Comment */
N/A	/** Documentation Comment */

Variable Declaration

Variable declaration in Java is a bit cleaner than that of PL/SQL, as you can see from
the following table:

Data Type	PL/SQL declarations	Java declarations
String	mysql varchar2(100) := 'This is text'; s2 varchar2(100) := 'xxx';	String mysql = "This is text", s2 = "xxx";
Number	myint integer := 100;	int myInt = 100;
Boolean	mybool boolean := true;	boolean myBool = true;

Note, Java's declaration specifies the datatype first, and then each of the
variables separated by commas. This results in a shorter code that accomplishes the
same thing. Java also doesn't require you to define the length of your strings, which
makes it easier for you as a programmer.

Referencing Code Libraries

When it comes to referencing code libraries, you'll probably think PL/SQL is easier than Java. In fact, in PL/SQL, you can reference anything within your schema's granted access list. In Java, you must either use both the package and class name (like oracle.jdbc.driver.OracleDriver) or start the class with an import statement (like import oracle.jdbc.driver.*) to refer to a Java class without the package name. The referenced code must exist in your CLASSPATH. If you're compiling and executing Java from the command prompt, CLASSPATH is passed on the command line or can be set as an environmental variable. In JDeveloper, CLASSPATH is set up in the project properties. For 9iAS applications, the CLASSPATH is established in the jserv.properties file, as the following discusses in more detail.

TIP

*Check Technet (**http://technet.oracle.com**) for the latest libraries available. Oracle continues to publish new Java libraries for Forms developers, BC4J, Oracle Text, XML, and more. The main page shows you the latest additions to its library. Click the Downloads link or use the search box to find the Java library you want.*

Oracle continues to develop libraries and publish them for your development. The Oracle XML library (often referred to as the Oracle XDK) continues to be upgraded all the time. The beauty of Java is you can include a new (meaning the latest and greatest) library without installing a whole new version of the product or Java.

TIP

Oracle has an excellent charting and graphics library (written in Java) called Oracle Chart Builder available for download on Technet. Chart Builder is capable of displaying bar (vertical, horizontal, stacked, or clustered), line (with or without markers), area (can annotate a section), pie (with or without external labels), and stock (high/low/close, open/high/low/close, candlestick) charts. You can develop multiseries charts. You can also mix chart types and frequencies together. Charts can even be interactive (that is, drill-down). The real power comes from accessing the database to generate the charts dynamically. Chart Builder generates a GIF, JPG, or wireless BMP as its output. The image file is all that's sent to the browser, so the client-side response is fast! This is a server-side library that can be used by your JSP programs.

Operators

As you're likely aware, operators give you the means to act on variables. They are used to assign values, make changes, and perform calculations to variables. Most of Java's operators are direct descendants from C. For example:

Operator	PL/SQL	Java
Assignment	:=	=
Arithmetic	+,-,/,*	+,-,/,*
Increment	X:=X+1	X++ or ++X
Decrement	X:=X-1	X-- or --X
Add two variables	X:=X+Y	X+=Y
String Concatenation	||	+
Equal to (comparison)	=	==
And	And	&&
Or	Or	||
Decode	sts := decode(sign(in_check-100),-1,'good','bad');	sts = (inCheck < 100 ? "good": "bad");

Note, the Java *test ? trueResult : falseResult* syntax doesn't correspond exactly to the PL/SQL DECODE. The test in the Java syntax must be evaluated to either true or false, so if you need to test for multiple values, as is possible in PL/SQL, you must nest several *test ? trueResult : falseResult* Java statements within one another.

Control Statements

Java provides a number of control statements, as does PL/SQL. To name and discuss a few control statements, these include the for and while loops and the if, then, else control statements.

For Loop

Excluding PL/SQL's cursor for loop, the numeric for loop in PL/SQL isn't very versatile. The numeric for loop simply counts up or down from a starting point to an ending point. Java's for loop isn't limited to numeric (or sequential) comparisons or loop increment. For example:

PL/SQL for loop	Java for loop

```
for x in 1 .. 100 loop          for (int x = 1; x <= 100; x++) {
   -- Iterations here               // Iterations here
end loop;                        }
```

The parameters in the Java for loop include the initialization string (*x* = 1), the Boolean comparison clause (*x* <= 100), and the incremental clause (*x*++).

While Loop

The while loop in PL/SQL is similar to the while loop in Java. The only real difference is Java requires you to wrap the comparison clause in parentheses. For example:

PL/SQL while loop	Java while loop
while a=b loop	while (a == b) {
-- Iterations here	// Iterations here
end loop;	}

If, then, else

A few differences exist between the syntax of PL/SQL and Java's if, then, else statement, but you see the differences quickly. Most of the differences in the following example are operator differences. Like the while statement, Java's if statement also surrounds the comparison with parentheses. For example:

PL/SQL if statement	Java if statement
if a = b and b = c then	if (a == b && b == c) {
-- xx	// xx }
elsif c = d then	else if (c == d) {
-- yy	// yy }
else	else {
-- zz	// zz
end if;	}

Standard Output

When it comes to printing to standard output ("the screen") in PL/SQL, we typically use dbms_output.put_line, which doesn't truly write to standard output, but it's as close as you can get with PL/SQL. Java's println command does output to standard output. Using println, the information is sent directly to the standard output. For example:

PL/SQL	Java
dbms_output.put_line ('Text to Output');	System.out.println ("Text to Output");

If you're frustrated by having to type too much, you can create a *p* method, as follows:

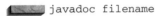

```
public static void p (String s) {
    System.out.println(s);
}
```

Program Unit Specification

In PL/SQL, you can view the specification of a procedure or package name using the describe command in SQL*Plus. If you want to view the source code of the PL/SQL program unit, you can select this information from the dba_source, all_source, or user_source view. To view the documentation associated with a Java class, you can run the javadoc command, as follows:

```
javadoc filename
```

The javadoc program extracts the documentation comments (that is, /** comment */) from the respective class file and produces a collection of HTML pages documenting the class. With Jdeveloper, however, you can view a considerable amount of information about any Java class by using the symbol-browsing feature. Right-clicking the object and selecting Browse Symbol accomplishes this.

Try, Try, Try Again

When it comes to exception handling, PL/SQL uses an exception block to handle the logic. Java uses a similar concept, which is the catch block with the try statement, as follows:

PL/SQL	Java

Begin
-- Logic
exception when
  exception_name then
  -- Exception logic;
end;
	try {
	  // Logic
	}
	catch (exceptionName e) {
	// Exception logic
	}
	finally {
	// Always executed if the try block is executed,
	regardless if an exception was caught
	}

While the code structure is similar, Java exception handling has one important difference: class methods can be defined as throwing certain exceptions, making it mandatory for the programmer to handle the error. For example, many of the methods used when connecting to the database with JDBC throw a SQLException that must be handled.

Code Libraries

When it comes to libraries of code, considerably more Java routines are available in the world than PL/SQL, many of which are available as open source. For example, Java's java.io class library is similar to, but more powerful and easier to use than PL/SQL's utl_file package. Oracle provides a Java class library named oracle.html for generating HTML. Oracle's PL/SQL Web toolkit (for example, htp package) serves a similar need for PL/SQL.

Label Example

Both PL/SQL and Java support labels, and continue and break (named "exit" in PL/SQL) statements. The following code listing is an excellent example of a block of Java code that contains each of these statements. The source of the example is from the book *Thinking in Java, Second Edition,* by Bruce Eckel (Prentice Hall PTR, 2000).

```
public class LabeledFor {
public static void main(String[] args) {
   int i = 0;
   outer: // Can't have statements here
   for(; true ;) { // infinite loop
   inner: // Can't have statements here
   for(; i < 10; i++) {
      prt("i = " + i);
      if (i == 2) {
         prt("continue");
      continue;
      }
      if (i == 3) {
         prt("break");
         i++; // Otherwise i never
              // gets incremented.
         break;
      }
```

```
        if (i == 7) {
            prt("continue outer");
            i++; // Otherwise i never
                 // gets incremented.
            continue outer;
        }
        if (i == 8) {
            prt("break outer");
            break outer;
        }
        for(int k = 0; k < 5; k++) {
            if (k == 3) {
            prt("continue inner");
            continue inner;
          }
        }
      }
    }
// Can't break or continue
// to labels here
    }
    static void prt(String s) {
        System.out.println(s);
    }
} ///:~
```

The previous Java program outputs the following data, which can help you read through and follow the previous code:

```
i = 0
continue inner
i = 1
continue inner
i = 2
continue
i = 3
break
i = 4
continue inner
i = 5
continue inner
```

```
i = 6
continue inner
i = 7
continue outer
i = 8
break outer
```

Arrays

PL/SQL supports arrays as PL/SQL table structures (now referred to as *index-by tables*—PL/SQL also supports varrays in Oracle8*i* and higher, which are more like Java arrays). Java also supports arrays. Java enables you to create, initialize, and copy single and multidimensional arrays, as the following examples illustrate:

```
// Create and initialize an array called myArray
int[] myArray = {1,2,3,4,5};
// Create an array called copyArray
int[] copyArray;
// Set the contents of copyArray equal to the contents of myArray
copyArray = myArray;

// Create a multi-dimensional array and initialize it
int[][] multiDimension = {
  {1,2,3,4},
  {5,6,7,8},
};
```

Sample Cursor for Loop

Everything you've seen so far makes Java look pretty easy. In fact, Java looks like it might be better than PL/SQL for most everything. Well, PL/SQL is considerably better and easier to use when it comes to selecting data from the database. Think about this for a minute. PL/SQL stands for Procedural Language (PL) Structured Query Language (SQL). In other words, it adds the programming logic to SQL. Java is a more generic programming language developed for widespread use. When it comes to selecting from the database, PL/SQL is easier and more efficient to use. The following example shows a Cursor For loop. In the following, I've only shown a small set of the Java code required to do this—a full example follows later in this chapter. The point is that PL/SQL is excellent at selecting data from an Oracle database and Java requires more code to do the same thing. As you'll discover in the following, though, you can create a JavaBean to simplify your Java code. As the following discusses in detail, Java Beans enable you to modularize your Java code. For example:

PL/SQL	Java
cursor emp_cur is	DriverManager.registerDriver(new
select * from emp;	oracle.jdbc.driver.OracleDriver());
begin	Connection conn = null;
for emp_rec in emp_cur loop	connString = new String("jdbc:oracle:thin:
htp.print(emp_rec.ename);	@hostname:1521:ORCL");
end loop;	conn =
	DriverManager.getConnection(
	connString,"scott","tiger");
	PreparedStatement pstmt =
	conn.prepareStatement("select * from emp");
	ResultSet rset =
	pstmt.executeQuery();
	...

Object-Oriented Programming

Object-oriented programming (OOP) is a complex topic. In fact, as you probably noticed after reviewing the Java language and syntax, Java is easy to learn. The object-oriented part of Java makes it a bit more complex, however. Unfortunately OOP can't be covered in great detail in this chapter. To learn more about this topic, pick up *The Object-Oriented Thought Process,* by Matt Weisfeld and Bill McCarty (Sams, 2000).

To simplify the concept, first think of modular programming. In other words, break programs down into modules or objects. You've probably done this in other programming languages, but Java is much more powerful and flexible than other non-object-oriented programs in this regard. You can think of a *program* as a bunch of objects telling each other what to do by sending messages. Each object has its own memory made up of other objects and every object has a type.

Object Thinking

Think of an *object* as a fancy variable. An object stores data, but you can also ask it to perform operations on itself by making requests. In theory, you can take any conceptual component in the problem you're trying to solve (dogs, buildings, services, and so forth) and represent it as an object in your program.

Another way to think of objects is to visualize objects as smart soap bubbles. You create a new one at will, with a name to tell one bubble from another, which is called *instantiation*. The object has color, position, size, and shape, or *attributes*.

You can tell it what to do, as can other bubbles, which means you can call its methods. When you finish with it, it simply pops (Java garbage collection). You can have one soap bubble enclose another (that is, inheritance from a base class). You can't get to the inside the bubble directly, you can only call its methods, which is called *encapsulation.*

To make a request of an object, you send a message to that object. More concretely, you can think of a message as a request to call a function that belongs to a particular object.

When it comes to memory management with Java, you make a new kind of object by creating a package that contains existing objects. Thus, you can build up complexity in a program while hiding it behind the simplicity of objects.

Every object has a type, in object-oriented terms, each object is an instance of a class, where *class* is synonymous with *type.* Type is a much more limited idea in PL/SQL, referring only to the description of a data structure. OO extends this idea to include behaviors and methods. The most important distinguishing characteristic of a class is what messages you can send to it.

Class Example

Let's look at a simple class definition for a Television. You'll recognize features of a standard television set.

```java
   import java.io.*;
public class Television {
   public static void main(String args[]) {
   }

   //these are global fields
   private           String tvName        = "Brad's Big Screen";
   private          boolean power          = false;
   private              int currentVolume  = 0;
   private              int currentChannel = 1;
   private static final int MIN_VOLUME     = 0;
   private static final int MAX_VOLUME     = 10;
   private static final int MIN_CHANNEL    = 2;
   private static final int MAX_CHANNEL    = 135;

   //these are methods
   public String getTvName () {
      return tvName;
   }
   public void on() {
```

```
        power = true;
    }
    public void off() {
        power = false;
    }
    public void volumeUp() {
        if (power && currentVolume < MAX_VOLUME) {
            currentVolume++;
        }
    }
    public void volumeDown() {
        if (power && currentVolume > MIN_VOLUME) {
            currentVolume--;
        }
    }
    public void channelUp() {
        if (power && currentChannel < MAX_CHANNEL) {
            currentChannel++;
        }
    }
    public void channelDown() {
        if (power && currentChannel > MIN_CHANNEL) {
            currentChannel--;
        }
    }
    public void setChannel(int inChannel) {
        if (power) {
            currentChannel = inChannel;
        }
    }
}
```

Creating a Handle for a Class

To *instantiate* a class, in effect creating a segment of memory for the class and its
variables, you must create a handle for the class. To do so, simply declare a variable
name (that is, tv) for the identifier and make an object of the desired type (Television)
with the new operator. In Java, objects are created with the new operator, which is
followed by the type of object to be created along with a parenthesized list of
arguments to be passed into the object's constructor. A *constructor* is a special
method that initializes a newly created object. Assign the variable with the equal
sign (=), as follows:

```
Television tv = new Television();
```

Sending a Message to an Object

After the class has been instantiated, you can reference any of the class's methods as previously discussed. In our example, we use the stated handle name and connect it to the message name (or method name) with a period (.), as follows:

```
// Turn the TV on
tv.on();

// Crank the volume up one notch
tv.volumeUp();

// Set the TV to channel 10
tv.setChannel(10);

// Turn the TV off
tv.off();
```

Setting Boundaries (Access Specifiers)

In PL/SQL, privilege boundaries for packages and procedures are defined by database roles and granting access. Because Java classes are stored at the operating system level and can be published as class files (versus Java source files), Java enables you to define the boundaries or scope for each variable, class, and method as follows:

Boundary	Description
public	Definition is available to everyone
protected	Only the class itself and other classes in the same package have access
private	No one can access the definition except the class itself

Static Modifier

Java methods can be defined with the static modifier. When the *static* modifier is used, the method is *not* tied to any particular object instance of that class. In other words, the object is shared. Static objects also needn't be instantiated. Static methods are also called *class methods*.

Encapsulation

By defining the scope, you can encapsulate your Java classes. This helps you write programs that are easily reused. This also lets you make public the features of objects that are important to the users of the objects, while hiding internal implementation details, which only the developer needs to know.

Inheritance

In many languages, you can include source code from an operating system source file, such as a library. To take advantage of changes to a referenced set of code, however, you typically must recompile the source code of all programs referencing the library code. In Java, all referenced code is maintained in its source format and compiled into the calling programs the first time it's referenced. In other words, all calling programs automatically inherit all changes to the library code. If you think about it, this is also true for PL/SQL. When you reference another procedure or function in PL/SQL, you aren't referencing the code as it stands at the point of compilation but, instead, at the time of execution. In other words, when the PL/SQL program unit executes, it uses a current copy of the referenced procedure or function. In loose terms, therefore, the functionality is inherited.

In Java, you can use any class as a base set of code and extend or enhance it easily. In other words, you can clone an object and make additions or modifications to the object. This is very powerful! You cannot do this in PL/SQL. The original class is called the *base, super,* or *parent* class. The cloned class is called the *derived, inherited, sub,* or *child* class. Java uses the extends keyword to add on to the base class. Changing the behavior of the base class in Java is called *overriding.*

Polymorphism

Java's polymorphism feature allows objects to change their form based on the calling program's object type. The term *polymorphism* means many shapes. For example, the Train, Plane, and Automobile classes have start and stop methods associated with them. The super class (in this case, also known as the *abstract class*—because Vehicle wouldn't have a start or stop method of its own, it would only have an empty method for each) called Vehicle also has start and stop methods associated with it. The runPlan method starts and stops a Vehicle, regardless of whether the vehicle is a Train, Plane, Automobile, and so forth. In other words, the runPlan method knows if the vehicle passed is a Train, it must call the start and stop methods of the Train class. This is the power of polymorphism! The following example illustrates polymorphism:

```
Train       t = new Train();
Plane       p = new Plane();
Automobile a = new Automobile();
runPlan (t);
runPlan (p);
runPlan (a);
void runPlan (Vehicle v) {
  v.start();
  // Do a bunch of other stuff to run the plan
  v.stop();
} // runPlan
```

Obfuscation

Java lets you distribute only your compiled Java classes without the source code. This enables you to write programs that are less open to the public's eyes. Be aware, however, that special software tools enable others to reverse-engineer your compiled classes into more or less readable source code. If you're concerned about other people reading and possibly using your code, use an obfuscation tool to make your compiled classes difficult to reverse engineer.

In PL/SQL, obfuscation (i.e., encrypting the PL/SQL program) is called *wrapping* (or *encrypting*) a package—as discussed in Chapter 14. With Java, compiling the program into a class file (using javac) is typically effective enough to protect your source code.

Oracle's Java Virtual Machine (JVM)

The Java Virtual Machine (JVM) is the program that interprets and executes your Java code, which means JVM is the reason your Java code is portable. You compile your Java source into bytecode, producing a class file. *Class* files are platform-independent, meaning they can run on any vendor's JVM. The class file is interpreted by the JVM and translated to machine code, (that is, class files or class files compressed into a Java Archive, jar file).

Developers commonly partition their Internet application code by function, such as Web presentation logic, business logic, and data manipulation logic. Each function might run on a separate platform. For example, the Web presentation logic can execute via a browser or the presentation tier, the business logic can execute on the Application server tier, which can be running on a high-end Intel system with Microsoft Windows 2000, and the data manipulation logic can be executed from within the database running on a Unix platform. Using Java, the same set of tools can be used to develop each of these code modules. Java enables you to keep your options open, so you aren't locked into a single architecture. To accommodate this type of distributed code environment, Oracle provides two different Java server environments: a J2EE container, which typically runs on the Oracle9i Application Server, and a Java environment inside the Oracle database. The Oracle9iAS J2EE container usually handles the Web presentation logic and business logic. For data manipulation using Java code, such as Java stored procedures, Oracle provides a JDK-compatible JVM in the database that's integrated with SQL and PL/SQL. Figure 13-3 illustrates these two implementations.

The JVM that executes within the Oracle database is a complete, Java2-compliant execution environment. It runs in the same process space and address space as the RDMS kernel. This JVM is tightly integrated with the shared memory architecture of Oracle.

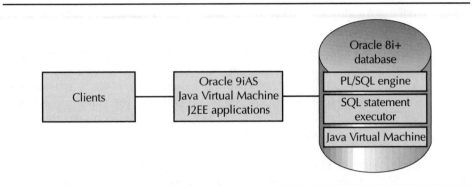

FIGURE 13-3. *JVM tiers*

Differences Between Client JVM and Oracle Database JVM

The Oracle database JVM is similar to the JVM that executes client or server-side Java code, but you should note these few differences:

- **main()** Java code within the Oracle database has no main() (top-level) method to define the profile of the application so, in Java terms, they aren't really applications. Instead, the client directly calls methods in the Java classes in the database.

- **GUI** You cannot execute Java code that provides graphical user interfaces (GUIs) inside the Oracle database. This makes sense because no user is involved with server-side code. The Oracle JVM doesn't supply the basic GUI components found in the JDK's Abstract Windowing Toolkit (AWT). Your programs can use the AWT functionality, but cannot attempt to display a user interface on the server.

- **Multithreading** When running Java inside the Oracle database, Oracle RDBMS—not Java—handles scheduling of multiple Java processes. The Oracle database server can handle thousands of simultaneous connections and the Oracle JVM uses the RDBMS facilities to schedule Java execution concurrently for multiple processes. This is good news because as a developer you needn't worry about managing threads. Before you upload a multithreaded Java application into your database, be aware that threads operate differently in this environment. You can write multithreaded applications, but they won't increase the performance of your server.

■ **JDBC**   Java applications executing within the Oracle database can access local data using a specialized JDBC driver. This JDBC driver complies fully with the Sun JDBC specification, and it supports Oracle-specific datatypes, international character sets, and stored procedures. The client and server-side APIs are identical, making it easy to move your applications from client to server. One important difference in the JDBC driver is the mechanism used to communicate between the Java application and the Oracle database. Because the JVM executes in the same memory space as the database and the SQL and PL/SQL engine, SQL*Net is circumvented when JDBC calls occur within the server. The JDBC driver performs a local, in-process (that is, internal), call to access SQL. Because of this efficiency, moving data-intensive Java code to the database server can improve the performance of your application.

To establish this local JDBC connection, simply use the default connection inside your Java Stored Procedure, as shown in the following example. Note the highlighted connection statement.

```java
// OrdCount.java
import java.sql.*;
import oracle.jdbc.driver.*;

public class OrdCount {
    public static double getOpenOrd (int prodId) {
        double          ordCnt = 0;
        try {
        Connection          conn    = new OracleDriver().defaultConnection();
        ResultSet           rs      = null;
        PreparedStatement ps        = null;
            String          query   = " SELECT count(*) " +
                                      " FROM    orders " +
                                      " WHERE   ord_status = 'O' " +
                                      " AND     prod_id  = ?";
        ps = conn.prepareStatement(query);
        ps.setInt(1,prodId);
        rs = ps.executeQuery();
        if (rs.next()) {
            ordCnt = rs.getDouble(1);
        }
```

```
        rs.close();
        ps.close();
        conn.close();

}
catch (Exception error) {
    /// handle the error
}
    return ordCnt;  } /// getOpenOrd} /// OrdCount
```

Before installing the JVM on the database, you need to check that the following init.ora parameters and database settings are set appropriately:

- SHARED_POOL_SIZE at least 65MB

- JAVA_POOL_SIZE at least 50MB

- 50MB free space in the SYSTEM tablespace

- 250MB rollback segment

The JAVA_POOL_SIZE indicates the size of the area within the SGA allocated to holding shared parts of each Java class. The default size is 20MB. This area of memory is consumed during class loading, which occurs during the installation of the JVM. Increase this parameter to 50MB for the installation. Each class consumes 4–8KB. Common Object Request Broker Architecture (CORBA) and EJB require a larger JAVA_POOL_SIZE, about 200KB per session during run time, and even more during deployment. Also, if you're compiling your Java Stored Procedure while loading it (using the `loadjava -c`), you probably need to increase the default value of JAVA_POOL_SIZE. The compiler is extremely memory-intensive. You're better off compiling the code on the client, and then loading the class on to the server. You can monitor and decrease this pool after you're in production.

Natively Compiled Code (NCOMP)

The JVM interprets bytecode and converts it to machine code. Overhead is associated with this extra layer of abstraction. Beginning with Oracle 8.1.7, it's possible to load natively compiled code into the database, so it doesn't need to be converted to machine code on execution. In versions 8.1.5 and versions 8.1.6 of Oracle, the core classes shipped with the JVM were natively compiled, or in NCOMP format. This feature is now available for user classes as well, using the Accelerator command-line tool ncomp. To use this tool, you must have a compiler for your database server and your jar (Java Archive) file must be loaded into the database.

Java Servlets

The use of Java has been transformed over time. Java was first introduced to make interactive Web pages by developing client-side (or, browser) Java applets. As applets grew, so did download times. Another problem that surfaced was poor browser reliability with Java, in which the browsers crashed or hung when Java loaded. Unfortunately, because of these problems, some people still have a negative connotation regarding Java.

The client-side problems with Java forced businesses to look at server-side Java and get back to a true thin client. In other words, server-side Java is used simply to generate HTML (and JavaScript) that's sent to the user's browser. Servlets are only one option for writing server-side Java code. Servlets are Java code executed on a server, thus, completely eliminating the issues of browser JVM compatibility, hanging/ crashing browsers, and excessive download time that applets presented.

Many reasons exist to use servlet-based technology over Common Gateway Interface (CGI), proprietary server APIs, server-side JavaScript, or Microsoft's Active Server Pages (ASP). These choices are all viable solutions for developing Web-based applications, but servlets are efficient, persistent, portable, robust, extensible, secure, and have gained widespread acceptance.

The efficiency in servlets is because they're loaded from disk and started/initialized only once, when the Web server first executes the servlet. Once loaded, servlets remain persistent by default, but you can specify otherwise, of course. *Persistence* is the capability to maintain state between requests being sent from the browser to the server. A servlet stays persistent in memory when loaded. Storing items that were loaded into a "shopping cart" is an example of a *persistent state application,* thus maintaining which items were selected without managing persistence on your own via browser cookies or URL parameters. *Servlets* are Java programs that contain specific methods. Because servlets are developed using Java, they're portable (you can move a servlet from one operating system to another without recompiling). Because of the Java-based development of servlets, they have complete access to the entire JDK, which makes them powerful and robust. Many APIs and a large user community are available to help support servlet development, which contributes to the power and robustness of servlets.

Using an object-oriented language, such as Java, gives servlets another advantage because they can be extended and polymorphed into other objects. Because servlets are server-side application code, they inherit the security of the Web server and can take advantage of the Java Security Manager.

Using servlets is the hard way to build Web-based applications using Java, however. Using JSPs is the easy way to use Java to build Web-based applications and is especially favored by Web designers. JSPs are simply HTML with Java embedded within the JSP. The real beauty of writing JSPs is the JSP engine converts your JSP in to a servlet automatically, so you get the ease of writing JSP code, and the power of servlets and servlet performance.

NOTE
Contrary to my belief, some people recommend against using JSPs over servlets—their experience is that PL/SQL programmers with PL/SQL Web Toolkit experience easily convert to servlets, but write poor JSPs full of snippets and don't use Beans properly. When it comes down to the bottom line, this is a personal decision, but choose a standard for your organization and stick to it.

The following Example1 servlet example demonstrates the basic parts of the servlet and the code necessary to write and compile it:

```java
// Example1.java
import javax.servlet.*;
import javax.servlet.http.*;
import java.io.*;
import java.util.*;

public class Example1 extends HttpServlet {

    public void init( ServletConfig config )
       throws ServletException {

           //Always pass the ServletConfig object to the super class
           super.init(config);
    } /// init

    /**
    * Process the HTTP Get Request
    */
    public void doGet(HttpServletRequest request,
                      HttpServletResponse response)
     throws ServletException, IOException {

       // Set the content type to text/html
       response.setContentType("text/html");
       PrintWriter out = response.getWriter();
       // Write out the HTML header
       out.println("<HTML>");
       out.println("<HEAD><TITLE>EXAMPLE SERVLET</TITLE></HEAD>");
       out.println("<BODY>");

       //  Print the request method sent by the browser
       out.println("Your request method was " + request.getMethod() + " \n");
       out.println("</BODY></HTML>");
       out.close();

     }/// doGet
```

```
/**Process the HTTP Post Request
 *
 */
public void doPost(HttpServletRequest request,
                   HttpServletResponse response)
  throws ServletException, IOException {
     // Set the content type to text/html
     response.setContentType("text/html");
     PrintWriter out = response.getWriter();
     // Write out the HTML header
     out.println("<HTML>");
     out.println("<HEAD><TITLE>EXAMPLE SERVLET</TITLE></HEAD>");
     out.println("<BODY>");

     //  Print the request method sent by the browser
     out.println("Your request method was " + request.getMethod() + " \n");
     out.println("</BODY></HTML>");
     out.close();
}/// doPost
/**
 * Returns a string back to the calling page.
 */
public String getServletInfo() {
    return "Example Servlet Information";
} /// getServletInfo
} /// Example1
```

After writing a servlet, you must compile the code and install the servlet where the Web server can find it, such as in a physical directory that's mapped to a virtual directory in 9*i*AS. To compile the servlet, you need to make sure the Servlet Development Kit (SDK) is in your CLASSPATH (the lib/jws.jar file). Once the servlet is compiled, the SDK jar file needs to be placed in the Web server's CLASSPATH, and then added to the servlet Web Service. For example, the $ORACLE_HOME/Apache/ Jserv/servlets directory is a predefined servlet directory for 9*i*AS. After compiling the Example1.java source file (that is, javac Example1.java) into Example1.class, you must copy or move the class file to a servlet directory. To invoke the Example1 servlet, reference the servlet by name in the URL. Assume the Example1.class file is located on your Web server in a directory called /servlet. To reference the servlet, invoke the following URL:

```
http://localhost/servlet/Example1
```

Servlets contain methods that follow the servlet standards. The previous URL forces the servlet to call the doGet() method (because this is an implicit get operation), so your HTML page will display the GET request method. To invoke the doPost() method, we must explicitly call the URL with a POST method from an HTML form. You must first create an HTML page to call the Example1 servlet with the POST method, as the following example illustrates:

```
<!-- Example1.html -->
<HTML>
<HEAD>
<TITLE>Calling Example1 Servlet with a POST method</TITLE>
</HEAD>
<BODY>
<FORM ACTION="http://localhost/servlet/Example1" METHOD="POST">
Press the button to launch the Servlet
<BR><BR>
<INPUT TYPE="SUBMIT" VALUE="Invoke Servlet">
</FORM>
</BODY>
</HTML>
```

When you invoke the servlet using this technique, the resulting Web page displays the message, "Your request method was POST". Now let's review one more servlet to prepare you for information that's covered later in this chapter. This next example displays parameter names and values once the servlet is submitted.

```
// Example2.java
import javax.servlet.*;
import javax.servlet.http.*;
import java.io.*;
import java.util.*;

public class Example2 extends HttpServlet {
    public void init (ServletConfig config) throws ServletException {

        super.init(config);
    } /// init

    public void doGet(HttpServletRequest request,
                    HttpServletResponse response)
      throws ServletException, IOException {
      //the doGet method calls the doPost to eliminate the redundancy
      // of writing the same code in each method.
            doPost(request,response);
    }

    public void doPost(HttpServletRequest request,
                    HttpServletResponse response)
      throws ServletException, IOException {
        // Write HTTP header
        response.setContentType("text/html");
```

```
      PrintWriter out = response.getWriter();
      // Write HTML header
      out.println("<HTML>");
      out.println("<HEAD><TITLE>Example 2</TITLE></HEAD>");
      out.println("<BODY>");

      //Get all the parameters
      Enumeration paramNames = request.getParameterNames();
      String param = null;

    //Iterating over the parameter names and retrieving the values
    while (paramNames.hasMoreElements()) {

        param =(String)paramNames.nextElement();
        out.println("<B>" +param+ " : "
        +request.getParameter(param)+"</B><BR>");
    } /// while paramNames.hasMoreElements()
    out.println("</BODY></HTML>");
    out.close();
  }/// doPost

    public String getServletInfo() {

        return "Example Information";
    }/// getServletInfo
}/// Example2
```

Now, let's use the following HTML to call our Example2 servlet, passing a number of parameters into our servlet:

```
<!-- Example2.html -->
<HTML>
<HEAD>
<TITLE>Example2 - Submitting a Form</TITLE>
</HEAD>
<BODY>
<FORM ACTION="http://localhost/servlet/Example2" METHOD="POST">
<TABLE>
<TR>
   <TD>Last Name:</TD>
   <TD ALIGN="left"><INPUT NAME="Last Name" TYPE="TEXT" SIZE="15"></TD>
</TR>
```

```
<TR>
    <TD>First Name:</TD>
    <TD ALIGN="left"><INPUT NAME="First Name" TYPE="TEXT" SIZE="15"></TD>
</TR>

</TABLE>
<INPUT TYPE="submit" NAME="Submit" VALUE="Submit">
<INPUT TYPE="reset" VALUE="Reset">
</FORM>
</BODY>
</HTML>
```

After building and deploying Example2 servlet, and then accessing and executing the Example2.html file in the browser, the HTML page should look like the one shown in Figure 13-4.

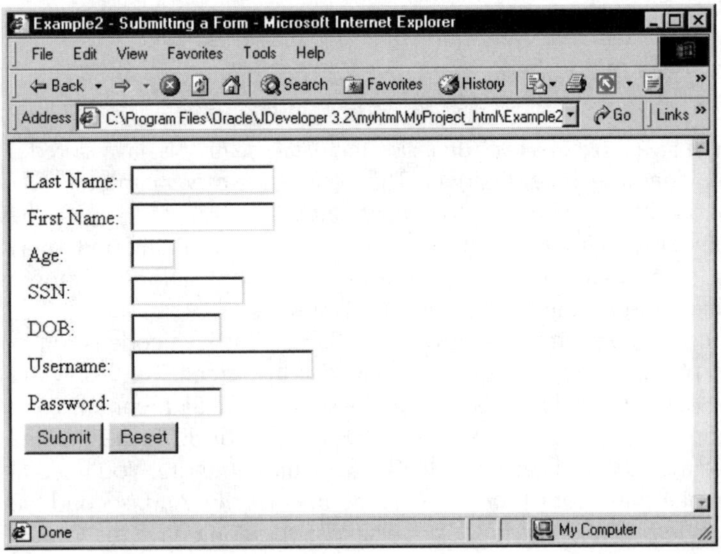

FIGURE 13-4.   *Example2 HTML page*

JDBC (Java Database Connectivity)

Java Database Connectivity (JDBC) is a standard set of classes that enables developers to access and manipulate databases from within Java programs. Oracle provides three types of JDBC drivers: thin, fat, and server-side. The driver you choose depends on the placement of the application you're building. The *thin JDBC driver* is written completely in Java and is small, making it ideal for Web-based, client-side applications (applets). The thin driver uses a TCP/IP port on the client-side to connect to SQL*Net on the server-side. SQL*Net does *not* need to be loaded on the machine that's using the thin JDBC driver. The *fat driver,* sometimes called the JDBC/OCI (Oracle Call Interface) driver, uses Oracle's client libraries (that is, SQL*Net) to access the remote (or local) Oracle database through SQL*Net. The OCI drivers are primarily used for Java client/server applications or middle-tier applications running on an application server. This is the driver you'll typically use for Servlets, JSP, and so forth. The fat driver is faster than the thin driver because it calls the database using native DB calls that use OCI.

NOTE
You must *install SQL*Net on the machine that uses the fat driver (9iAS).*

Because Java programs can run inside the database (that is, Java stored procedures), Oracle provides a server-side driver. This *server-side driver* can be used only from inside the database. It connects to a local database.

All three drivers implement the same JDBC API, permitting portability and flexibility in development and deployment of Java applications. In other words, the API (like most Java interfaces) uses polymorphism.

Let's look at an example of how to use JDBC. This Java code is run from the command prompt and the output is displayed to the screen. To display the output to a Web page, simply drop this code into a servlet or a JSP program. To find more information about the APIs provided for JDBC, go to **http://java.sun.com**. If you don't have the JDK, you can download it from the same site. You need to do this first and make sure your CLASSPATH is set up correctly. And, second, you need to obtain at least one of the JDBC drivers, so if you don't have the Oracle JDBC driver, you can download it from **http://technet.oracle.com**.

NOTE
The following example uses the thin JDBC driver connecting through port 1521 on a machine named hostname with a database SID of ORCL to a user/ schema of scott and a password of tiger.

```java
// Example3.java
import java.sql.*;
public class Example3 {

    public static void main(String args[])throws SQLException {

        try {
         Class.forName("oracle.jdbc.driver.OracleDriver");
        }
        catch(ClassNotFoundException e) {
         e.printStackTrace();
        }

        String connString = "jdbc:oracle:thin:scott/
              tiger@hostname:1521:ORCL";
        //connection_string:userid/password@machine_name:port:SID
        //connection_string can be jdbc:oracle:oci8 or oci7 or thin.
        Connection conn = DriverManager.getConnection(connString);

        Statement stmt = conn.createStatement();
        ResultSet rset = stmt.executeQuery("select * from emp");
        ResultSetMetaData meta = rset.getMetaData();

        //Returns the number of columns selected;
        int cols = meta.getColumnCount();

        for(int i = 1; i < cols; i++) {

            System.out.println(meta.getColumnLabel(i));
            System.out.println("\t\t");
        }

        System.out.println(".");
        while(rset.next()) {

          for(int i = 1; i < cols; i++) {

            String value = rset.getString(i);

            if (value == null) {
               value = "No Data";
            }
            System.out.println(value + "\t\t");
          } /// for  i < cols

          System.out.println("\n");
        } /// while  rset.next()

        rset.close();
```

```
    stmt.close();
    conn.close();
} /// main } /// Example3
```

This example uses the Statement object, which you can use if your statement doesn't contain any bind variables. In the JSP section of this chapter, you can see an example using the PreparedStatement class and binding variables.

JDBC Performance

The driver you use depends on the placement of the specific Java program. If the program is located on a server that doesn't have SQL*Net loaded on it, you need to use the thin JDBC driver. If SQL*Net is loaded on the server, the fat driver should be used. If the Java program is inside the database (that is, a Java stored procedure), you want to use the server-side driver for the optimum performance. The JDBC drivers will perform fastest based on the following list:

1. Internal JDBC driver

2. Fat Driver (oci8)

3. Thin Driver (thin)

Proxy Connections

A strong argument to use the fat JDBC driver is that it supports proxy connections. This makes it possible for the application server to establish a connection with the application username/password, and then connect "on behalf of" a specific user. This overcomes the classic problem with Java Web applications: the Java guys insist on granting DBA rights to the application server, so they can handle everything from the application.

SQLJ

What is SQLJ? If you're familiar with Oracle's precompilers, like Pro*C, Pro*Fortran, and Pro*COBOL, you can look at SQLJ as basically Pro*Java. Like the other Oracle precompilers, SQLJ replaces embedded SQL statements with the appropriate JDBC statements (note, precompilers use OCI). SQLJ is often preferred by the SQL programmer jumping into the Java world (or the Java programmer jumping into the SQL world). SQLJ complements the dynamic JDBC SQL model with a static SQL model. All the leading database vendors, including Oracle, IBM, and Sybase, support SQLJ. SQLJ enables developers to write efficient and compact programs. If you're a SQL (or Java) programmer, this might be the way you'd prefer to write your Java database applications, instead of chugging through the JDBC APIs. Some advantages of using SQLJ over JDBC: SQLJ's code is significantly more compact compared to JDBC,

SQLJ permits the use of typed cursors, and the SQL statements are checked at compile time instead of run time when JDBC SQL statements are checked. The following code line is an example of using SQLJ to update (that is, increase by 10 percent) the salaries of all employees with a specific name:

```
#sql {UPDATE emp SET sal = sal * 1.1 WHERE ename = :aName};
```

If you were using JDBC, the line of code would translate to the following:

```
String preparedString = "UPDATE emp SET sal = sal * 1.1 WHERE ename = ?";
PreparedStatement stmt = conn.prepareStatement(preparedString);
stmt.setString(1, aName);
stmt.executeUpdate();
stmt.close();
```

For SQLJ to work, you must have the Oracle JDBC drivers installed (classes12.zip for JDK 1.2) and they must be placed in your CLASSPATH. Follow the JDBC installation and make sure JDBC works (you can use the previous samples). If you obtained SQLJ from an Oracle Database installation, you should find the sqlj.exe file in the $ORACLE_HOME /bin directory and this directory should already be in your PATH. You must put the $ORACLE_HOME /sqlj/lib/translator.zip and the runtime.zip files in your CLASSPATH. The connect.properties file specifies how JDBC (via SQLJ) should connect to your database, if your program specifically references the connect.properties file. Otherwise, SQLJ uses the command line specification for the connect string. Make sure your connect.properties configuration is set up, if you want to use the connect.properties file, you need to call the Oracle.connect method, as follows:

```
Oracle.connect(ClassName.class, "connect.properties");
```

For more information on installing SQLJ, see Oracle's *SQLJ Developers Guide and Reference*.

Now that everything is up and running, let's look at an example of connecting to the database using SQLJ instead of the JDBC calls. This example displays all the employees from the emp table:

```
// Example4.sqlj
import java.sql.*;
import oracle.sqlj.runtime.Oracle;
import sqlj.runtime.ref.DefaultContext;

#sql iterator MyIterator (int empno, String ename);
public class Example4 {

    public static void main (String args[]) throws SQLException {

//set the default connection to the URL, user, and password.
//specified in your connect.properties file.
```

```
    Oracle.connect(Example4.class,"connect.properties");
      MyIterator rset = null;

    #sql rset = {SELECT empno, ename FROM EMP};

      // Note that the rest of this code is the same as Example3.java
    while (rset.next()) {
        System.out.println(rset.empno());
        System.out.println("\t\t");
        System.out.println(rset.ename());
        System.out.println("\n");
    }
//Always close an iterator to release its resources.
        rset.close();
    } /// main
} /// Example4
```

TIP
*Whenever you use multirow query result sets in
SQLJ, you must create an iterator. The use of a SQLJ
iterator replaces the use of the ResultSet class that
was required with JDBC calls.*

How do you run your SQLJ program? Your SQLJ program must first be converted
to a standard Java program using the sqlj command from the prompt. In other words,
your SQLJ program must be precompiled. Once you convert your SQLJ file to Java, you
run the javac command from the prompt. Using the Example4.sqlj source code, you first
use the sqlj translator and tell the translator what database to use.

To convert the SQLJ program to a Java program with JDBC, use the sqlj command.
We've connected to the scott user with a password of tiger. We're using the thin
JDBC driver connecting to the localhost machine on port 1521 for a SID of orcl.

```
sqlj –user=scott/tiger  –url=jdbc:oracle:thin@hostname:1521:ORCL Example4.sqlj
```

If you want to perform offline checking of SQL statement, use the following
statement:

```
sqlj Example4.sqlj
```

This translates the SQLJ file into a Java source file. Now you can compile and
run the Java program generated from the translator. To compile the Java program,
type the following at the command prompt of your operating system:

```
javac Example4.java
```

To run the Java program, type the following:

java Example4

The following example demonstrates a complete SQLJ file that updates a database table. Remember, SQLJ doesn't support dynamic SQL statements.

```
// SqljExample.sqlj
import java.sql.*;
import oracle.sqlj.runtime.Oracle;
import sqlj.runtime.ref.DefaultContext;
public class SqljExample {

    public static void main(String[] args) throws SQLException {

    Oracle.connect(SqljExample.class,"connect.properties");
        String name = "SCOTT";
        #sql {UPDATE emp SET sal = 5500 WHERE ename = :name};
        #sql {COMMIT};
    } /// main
} /// SqljExample
```

JavaServer Pages (JSPs)

With the boom of a service-driven Internet, Web sites are becoming more dynamic and powerful. A technology was needed to handle the demands of an interactive, customized, personalized, and dynamic Web application. Java servlets and JavaServer Pages (JSPs) are complementary technologies that handle the demands of dynamic content for the next generation of Internet and intranet applications. Oracle provides servlet and JSP technology functionality through tools and servers, making it easier for developers to meet the demands of the dynamic Internet.

So what is a "Server Page" anyway? You might have heard or read about Active Server Pages (ASPs), PL/SQL Server Pages (PSPs), or JSPs, and wondered what they are. *Server Pages* are simply HTML with a programming language embedded within them. *ASPs* are HTML pages with Visual Basic as the embedded language. *PSPs* are HTML pages with PL/SQL as the embedded language. A *JSP* is a standard HTML or XML page with zero or more JSP-specific tags or Java language code embedded in it. ColdFusion uses a Server Page technology as well. *ColdFusion* pages are HTML with ColdFusion tags embedded within them. *PHP* is another Server Page technology. PHP stands for Personal Home Pages, but they are HTML pages with an embedded Perl-like language. Oracle Application Server (OAS) has a LiveHTML cartridge, which uses HTML pages with embedded Perl, similarly to PHP.

JSP is a technology that simplifies the process of building Web-based applications by providing a framework to create dynamic applications using HTML, XML, and

Java. JSPs solve the issues facing Web developers, such as scalability, integration of back-end applications, and manageability and personalization of Web sites. Dynamic scripting for Web pages through JSP technology is obtained by embedding Java and JSP tags into a Web file (for example, HTML/XML, and so forth). JSP builds on the Java servlet technology, can generate Web pages with dynamic and static content, and takes full advantage of Java's platform independence and "Write once, Run anywhere" motto. In addition, JSPs can contain references to standard Java Beans components or other Java code resident on the server. This enables you to leverage the power of Enterprise Java components. In other words, JSP lets you encode fragments of Java code into an HTML document. Figure 13-5 shows how JSP requests are sent to the Web server.

With the availability of servlets and JSPs on all the major Web servers in the market, both technologies are positioned as a superior alternative to using proprietary HTTP server APIs.

Why Use JavaServer Pages?

If you like developing Web pages with a GUI editor, such as Dreamweaver or FrontPage, server page technologies enable you to do this, not only at the beginning of the project, but forever. What do I mean by this? When we develop code using mod_plsql (or the PL/SQL cartridge as it was called in OAS), we typically use a GUI editor to create our initial HTML layout, and then use WebAlchemy to convert the HTML to PL/SQL Toolkit code. The final step is to add the dynamic portion of the PL/SQL—the cursors, for loops, and so forth. After that, we're stuck maintaining PL/SQL code, forever. No longer can we turn our pages over to graphic designers and ask them to make modifications, unless your graphic designers also know how to program with PL/SQL.

With JSPs, however, we can ask our graphic design team to create the look and feel of the page(s) using their favorite GUI design tool. Then, we can add our Java

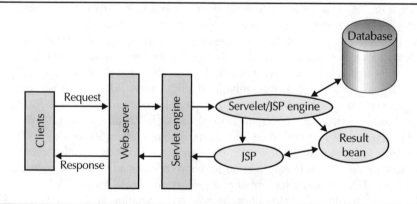

FIGURE 13-5. *Flow of the JSP request from a browser (client) to the Web server*

code to the page. Maintenance is always performed by editing the JSP (with HTML) file. Now this is powerful stuff! This is the best of all worlds, isn't it?

Another reason to choose JSP is how it compares with existing server-side technologies. JSPs offer the only high-performance, cross-platform environment, and if Beans are used properly, complete separation of application/business logic and presentation logic can be achieved.

JSP Versus CGI (Common Gateway Interface)

The CGI for server-side applications is the simplest and oldest way to handle HTTP requests and responses. CGI uses an external script (that is, Perl, C++, and so forth) to handle the request. However, CGI uses valuable system resources to process requests because the script is loaded, run, and unloaded once a response is sent. On the other hand, JSPs use threads and servlet persistence for requests for improved performance and scalability. CGI also doesn't maintain state, so you're required to handle the maintenance user information between requests.

Other advantages to using JSPs over CGI are as follows:

- JSPs maintain state because they're extensions of servlet sessions. CGI programs don't automatically maintain state.

- JSPs spawn new threads for each request. CGI creates a new process for each request, so JSPs use less resources—CPU and memory.

- JSPs are loaded only the first time after instantiation. CGI scripts are loaded each time.

- JSPs run in a JVM as an extension of a Web server. CGIs run outside the application server.

JSP Versus ASP

By providing their own APIs, Web servers such as Microsoft IIS (with ISAPI) and Netscape (NSAPI) work well, but lack the portability of JSPs by using server-specific APIs. Microsoft's ASP is the primary competitor to JSP. Using HTML templates, scripting code, and business component logic, both JSPs and ASPs support the generation of dynamic Web pages and interface with an enterprise application framework. The following list compares JSPs and ASPs:

- JSPs are interpreted once. ASPs are interpreted for each instance.

- JSPs run on most Web servers. ASP runs on Microsoft or Personal Web Server (PWS) servers. Third-party companies also exist that sell software to allow ASPs to run on other servers.

- JSPs use JavaBeans, Data Tags, and EJBs to separate page content. ASPs don't.

JSP Versus Servlets

Because JSPs are built on the servlet API, anything that can be done with a servlet can be done with JSPs. The benefits of using JSPs over servlets are the separation of presentation from business logic, the cleanliness of the code, and the fact that JSPs are easier to write. Also, JSPs and servlets interact seamlessly.

Advantages of JavaServer Pages

The JSP architecture offers the following advantages:

- *Separation of business logic from presentation logic*   Using the JavaBean component architecture is a powerful attribute of JSP. The JavaBean specification encapsulates the application logic in reusable software components written in Java. Using JavaBeans removes the bulk of the otherwise Java scriplet code from the JSP, and makes the separation of business logic and presentation logic uncluttered and easier to maintain.

- *Partitioning of developer skill sets*   Encapsulating your business logic in JavaBeans lets you focus on the presentation design without the knowledge of the application logic, so a Web designer can do the presentation and developers can build the application logic.

- *Rapid development*   Applications can be built in modules and released to the Web server, because of the Web server automatically compiling and running the JSPs when the first request arrives. For deployment and release of JSP applications, it's as simple as copying your new/modified JSP to the proper directory on the Web server.

- *Cross-platform development and deployment*   Because JSPs extend servlets, JSPs reap the benefits of belonging to the Java Platform, including "Write Once, Run Anywhere" cross-platform functionality. JSP applications can be deployed to any platform that adheres to the JSP specification (including Oracle9*i*AS).

- *Advanced performance and scalability*   JSP applications inherit the performance and scalability advantages of Java servlets.

What Happens When I Run the JSP File?

Here's the good news: the JSP file isn't parsed and compiled each time it's run. Rather, the JSP engine creates a class file (that is, the servlet) on the first execution. Every execution thereafter 9*i*AS' JSP container uses that compiled and operating system-specific class file, so the results are *fast*.

Figure 13-6 shows the JSP technology process when you execute a JSP through a JSP engine that's installed on a Web server or a JSP-enabled application server, such

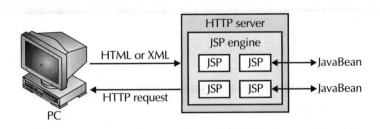

FIGURE 13-6.   *JSP engine produces HTML/XML*

as 9*i*AS: the browser directly invokes a JSP page through HTTP. The JSP can reference JavaBeans or Java programs to access an Oracle database. The JSP then formats the information in HTML or XML and sends it back to the browser.

Each JSP page is automatically compiled into a servlet by the JSP container on the first access to the JSP code. Depending on the behavior of the Web server, the servlet is saved for some period of time to be used over and over without the need to re-create and recompile it, so subsequent accesses are faster than the first.

JavaServer Pages Architecture

JSPs consist of HTML or XML with embedded Java scriptlets and JSP-specific tags. A JSP engine compiles and executes the JSP into a servlet. The compilation and execution of JSPs has two phases:

- *Translation phase*   The Web server recognizes the .jsp extension and immediately transfers the request to the JSP engine, which performs each step of the translation phase. If the JSP hasn't been instantiated or has been modified, the JSP engine translates the JSP page into Java source code, and then compiles it into an executable Java class file. This intermediate step of using servlets is transparent to the JSP author and the end user. This translation and compilation phase only occurs when a JSP is first called or has been changed, and a slight delay might be apparent. If the JSP page has already been translated, however, this phase is skipped.

The following illustration shows the flow of the translation phase.

If a servlet is already loaded, the same servlet object is used to respond to the request. The response is quick because subsequent requests go to the servlet bytecode already in memory. Otherwise, the servlet class file is loaded and a new servlet object is created to respond to subsequent requests. Response latency is minimized because Java servlets can persist across multiple requests (from the same or different browsers).

Difference Between JavaServer Pages and Java Servlets

JSPs are HTML or XML files embedded with Java. JSPs move the presentation focus to HTML and separate the business logic, but Java servlets focus on Java for both the presentation and logic.

To demonstrate the difference between JSPs and servlets, let's look at an example that retrieves a parameter passed from a form, and then prints the parameter as a Web page header level 1. First, the JSP code:

```
<H1><%= request.getParameter("name") %></H1>
```

Notice the HTML tags and the scriptlet tag (as discussed in the following, tags starting with <% are scriptlets). In comparison, Java servlets have to embed the HTML or XML into a String, and then print the String. The following servlet code will produce the same effect as the previous JSP code snippet:

```
out.println("<H1>" + request.getParameter("name") + "</H1>");
```

These two approaches are identical in their output, but in Web development, the JSP is more convenient because it uses standard HTML and XML. The JSP also reduces the need to write large amounts of Java code to produce the HTML or XML.

JSP Servers

Where do you begin? You must be able to run JSP code, right? Oracle9iAS provides the functionality to run JSP code. You can install either 9iAS or Oracle Portal to implement a JSP server. Your other option is to implement Oracle's JDeveloper product, which contains its own JSP server.

If you don't like the Oracle approach, consider using the JSP-compatible Web server available free of charge from Sun. You can use this server to test your sample JSP programs. You can download the server at **http://java.sun.com/products/jsp/** —click Download. You can download the Tomcat 3.2.3 or Tomcat 4.0 server from here.

In addition to Oracle9iAS and Tomcat, Alaire Jrun, Apache Jserv, Netscape iPlanet, and many more application servers support JSP. If you're interested in learning about other JSP engines, see **http://www.serverpages.com/Java_Server_Pages/Servlet_Engines/**.

Element Data

Element data can be classified into the following categories, discussed in detail in the following, include:

- Directives
- Declarations
- Scriptlets
- Expressions
- Standard Actions

Directives

Directives have scope throughout the entire JSP file, so they can be used to set global variables, class declarations, methods to implement, output content type, and so forth. The distinguishing feature of Directives is the @ character. Three types of Directives exist, each of which is discussed in detail in the following:

- page
- include
- taglib

The *page* Directive   The *page directive* affects the entire JSP page with a number of attributes. A JSP page can contain many page directives, but only one occurrence of any attribute value pair can exist. The exception to this rule is the *import attribute,* which can contain a list of classes to import into the page. The attributes of the page directive are as follows: language, extends, import, session, buffer, autoFlush, isThreadSafe, info, isErrorPage, errorPage, and contentType.

   The complete syntax for the page directive is (the defaults are underscored)

```
<%@ page [language="Java"]
    [extends="fully qualified superclass"
    [import="comma separated list of classes"
    [session="true|false"
    [buffer="none|24kb|nkb"
    [autoFlush="true|false"
    [isThreadSafe="true|false"
    [info="informative string for Servlet.getServletInfo()"
    [isErrorPage="true|false"
    [errorPage="errorPage.jsp"]
    [contextType="text/html|content type"] %>
```

The following example code illustrates the page directive:

```
<%@ page language="java" import="java.rmi.*,java.util.*"
         session="true" info="my page directive"
         errorPage="Error.jsp" isErrorPage="false"%>
```

The *include* Directive   The *include* directive tells the JSP engine to include the content of the resource that's being included. Note, the resource must be accessible and available to the JSP engine. The include directive parses the included resource at translation time. There is an include action that includes the resource at run time, rather than at compile time. Also, the included resource shouldn't be a dynamic page. The attribute of the include directive is file.

The following example code illustrates the include directive:

```
<%@ include file="/myJsp/myfile.html" %>
```

The *taglib* Directive   The *taglib* directive permits the JSP page to use custom-defined tags because it points to the tag library within which the tags are located. The tag library concept mechanism was implemented in JSP 1.1. The attributes of the taglib directive are uri and prefix.

The following example code illustrates the taglib directive:

```
<%@ taglib  uri="/webapp/DataTags.tld"  prefix="jbo" %>
<jbo:ApplicationModule configname="bc4j. bc4jModule. bc4jModule"
     id="bc4jModule"  username="test"  password="test"  />
<jbo:DataSource id="ordersds"  appid="bc4jModule"
     viewobject="OrdersView"/>
```

Scripting Elements

Scripting elements are used to include Java code in your JSP. You can include code, evaluate expressions, and declare variables using scripting elements. The three scripting elements are discussed in the following.

- Declarations
- Scriptlets
- Expressions

Declarations   *Declarations* are used to define class-wide variables and methods within a JSP page in the generated class file. Declarations have *class* scope, which means they can be used throughout the entire class.

NOTE
There are different levels of scope (for example,
block *scope is a variable defined in a for loop that
can only be referenced inside the for loop).*

The syntax for a declaration is enclosed between `<%!` and `%>`. The following code example illustrates a declaration:

```
<%!
    private String phrase = "Hello World";

%>
```

Scriptlets   A *scriptlet* is a block of Java code that's executed at request-processing time and enclosed between the `<%` and `%>` tags. The scriptlet can do anything you develop it to do. A scriptlet is Java code that you implement within the JSP page. Multiple scriptlets can appear in a JSP page.
The following code example illustrates scriptlets:

```
<%
    String phrase = "Hello World";
    for(int j = 0; j <= 10 ; j++){
        out.println("<BR>" + phrase + " number : "+j);
    }
%>
```

Expressions   An *expression* is a type of scriptlet. An expression is shorthand notation for displaying a result in String format back to the browser when the expression is evaluated. You must use the `toString()` method when the expression you're evaluating is an object. The syntax for an expression is enclosed between `<%=` and `%>`.
The following code example illustrates expressions:

```
<HTML>
<BODY>
<%!
    public String phrase = "Hello World";
%>
This JSP wants <%="to say " + phrase + " !!!!!!" %>
</BODY>
</HTML>
```

Standard Actions

The JSP Specification 1.1 lists action types that are standard actions and must be supported by all JSP engines. These action types are specific tags that affect the run time and response sent back by JSPs. The standard action types are described in detail in the following:

- <jsp:useBean>;<jsp:setProperty>;<jsp:getProperty>

- <jsp:param>

- <jsp:include>

- <jsp:forward>

- <jsp:plugin>

jsp:useBean; jsp:setProperty; jsp:getProperty   The useBean, getProperty, and setProperty JSP action tags are used with JavaBeans. The *jsp:useBean* action tag is used to establish an association with a JavaBean, so the object can be referenced using its ID. The *jsp:setProperty action tag* sets values of properties of the Bean. Complementing the jsp:setProperty action, the jsp:getProperty action tag returns the values of the properties of the referenced Bean.

The attributes of the <jsp:useBean> action tag are id, scope, class, beanName, and type. The attributes of the <jsp:setProperty> action tag are name, property, param, and value. The attributes of the <jsp:getProperty> action tag are: name and property.

The syntax for the useBean directive is

```
<jsp:useBean id="name"
             scope="page|request|session|application"
             class="fully qualified class name"
             beanName="name of bean"
             type="type of class" />
```

A very simple Bean with one property might look like something like the following:

```
package example.test;

public class myBean extends Object {
  String sportParameter;

  // constructor
  public myBean () {
  }
  // setter
  public void setSport(String s) {
    sportParameter = s;
```

```
  }
  // getter
  public String getSport() {
    return sportParameter;
  }
}
```

To use jsp:useBean, jsp:setProperty, or jsp:getProperty your JSP might look like the following:

```
<jsp:useBean id="bradsBean" scope="session"
             class="example.test.myBean" />
<jsp:setProperty name="bradsBean"
                  property="sport" value="soccer" />
<HTML>
<BODY>
This JSP wants to play
<jsp:getProperty name="bradsBean" property="sport" />
</BODY>
</HTML>
```

A more detailed JavaBean example, the ConnectionBean, is demonstrated in the "Moving JDBC Code to a Bean" section.

jsp:param   The *jsp:param* action tag is used to create information for other tags by using name-value pairs, in particular, the jsp:include, jsp:forward, and jsp:plugin action tags. The attributes of the jsp:param action tag are name and value.
The following code example illustrates the jsp:param action tag:

```
<jsp:param name="fullName" value="Bradley D. Brown" />
```

jsp:include   The *jsp:include* action tag includes dynamic or static resources in the JSP at request time. The resource is defined in the URL format of the tag attributes. An included page cannot set cookies or headers, but does have access to the JspWriter. The attributes of the jsp:include action tag are page and flush.
The syntax for the include directive is

```
<jsp:include page="urlSpec"
             flush="true" />
```

The following code example illustrates the jsp:include action tag:

```
<jsp:include page="index.html" flush="true" />
```

jsp:forward   The *jsp:forward* action tag forwards, or redirects, the request to another resource. When the jsp:forward action tag is reached in a JSP page, execution of that page is halted. The resource page must be in the same Context as the invoking page. The attribute of the jsp:forward action tag is page.

The following code example illustrates the jsp:forward action tag:

```
<jsp:forward page="index.html" >
<jsp:param name="username" value="brownb" />
…
</jsp:forward>
```

jsp:plugin   The *jsp:plugin* action tag is used to ensure the Java plug-in software is available by generating the browser-specific tags. The *jsp:param* and *jsp:fallback* tags can support the jsp:plugin action tag. The attributes of the jsp:plugin action tag are type, code, codebase, align, archive, height, hspace, jreversion, name, vspace, title, width, nspluginurl, and iepluginurl.

The following code example illustrates the jsp:plugin action tag:

```
<HTML><BODY>
<jsp:plugin type="applet"
            code="oracle.TestPlugin"
            codebase="/classes/oracle/applet"
            width="75" >
    <jsp:params>
        <jsp:param name="firstname" value="Bradley" />
        <jsp:param name="middlename" value="D." />
        <jsp:param name="lastname" value="Brown" />
    </jsp:params>
    <jsp:fallback>
        Sorry your browser can't handle applets
    </jsp:fallback>
</jsp:plugin>
</BODY></HTML>
```

Implicit Objects

JSPs provide implicit objects to assist in code development. Being *implicit* means these objects don't have to be declared or instantiated. Implicit objects are available only to scriptlets and expressions, not to declarations. A number of implicit objects are listed and described in the following. We mention implicit objects because if you're new to JSP programming, you'll see them in the code and might wonder where they came from.

NOTE
You needn't define or declare any of the implicit objects. The JSP engine handles this for you automatically.

request Object

The *request* object is passed to the JSP by the container and encapsulates the incoming request from the browser. It corresponds to the HttpServletRequest object that's part of the header of a servlet. The request object is used to pass and retrieve information from one page to a JSP or servlet. If you had a form on a Web page and the action of the form was to call a particular JSP, you would use the JSP to parse the data passed from the form. This is illustrated in the following example source:

```
<!-- This is the HTML Form to call a JSP Page -->
<HTML><BODY>
<FORM METHOD="POST" ACTION="submitform.jsp">
<INPUT TYPE="TEXT" NAME="FirstName">
<INPUT TYPE="TEXT" NAME="LastName">
<INPUT TYPE="SUBMIT" VALUE="Submit Form">
</FORM>
</BODY></HTML>
```

The source code for the submitform.jsp page is shown in the following. Notice the getParameter method calls the parameter with the same name as the parameter in the submitting form.

```
<%@ page contentType="text/html"
         errorPage="errorpage.jsp"%>
<HTML><HEAD>
<%
    String sLastName = "";
    String sFirstName = "";
    sLastName = request.getParameter("LastName");
    sFirstName = request.getParameter("FirstName");
%>
</HEAD><BODY>
First Name = <%= sFirstName %><BR>
Last Name = <%= sLastName %>
</BODY></HTML>
```

The request methods include

- **getAttribute(String)**   Gets a named attribute's value.

- **getCharacterEncoding()**   Gets the character encoding of the request data.

- **getContentLength()**   Gets the size in bytes of the request.

- **getContentType()**   Gets the MIME type of the request.

- **getInputStream()**   Creates an inputstream from which servlets can read client request data.

- **getParameter(String)** Gets the value of a named requestparameter.

- **getParameterNames()** Gets all parameter names.

- **getParameterValues(String)** Gets an array of Strings containing all the request parameter's values whose name matches the name of parameter queried.

- **getProtocol()** Gets the protocol of the request as Proto/Major.Minor ("HTTP/1.1").

- **getReader()** Creates a BufferedReader from which servlets can read client request data.

- **getRealPath(String)** Translates the given path to the real path on the server's file system, using the server's DocumentRoot.

- **getRemoteAddr()** Gets the IP address of the client that sent the request.

- **getRemoteHost()** Gets the hostname of the client that sent the request.

- **getScheme()** Gets the scheme of the request as defined by RFC 1783 (ftp, http, gopher, news).

- **getServerName()** Get the name of the server receiving the request.

- **getServerPort()** Gets the portnumber the server receiving the request is running on.

- **getAuthType()** Returns the name of the authentication scheme used to protect the servlet, for example, BASIC, or SSL, or null if the servlet wasn't protected.

- **getContextPath()** Returns the portion of the request URI that indicates the context of the request.

- **getCookies()** Returns an array containing all the cookie objects the client sent with this request.

- **getDateHeader(String)** Returns the value of the specified request header as a long value that represents a Date object.

- **getHeader(String)** Returns the value of the specified request header as a String.

- **getHeaderNames()** Returns an enumeration of all the header names this request contains.

- **getHeaders(String)** Returns all the values of the specified request header as an Enumeration of String objects.

- **getIntHeader(String)**   Returns the value of the specified request header as an int.

- **getMethod()**   Returns the name of the HTTP method with which this request was made, for example, GET, POST, or PUT.

- **getPathInfo()**   Returns any extra path information associated with the URL the client sent when it made this request.

- **getPathTranslated()**   Returns any extra path information after the servlet name, but before the query string, and translates it to a real path.

- **getQueryString()**   Returns the query string contained in the request URL after the path.

- **getRemoteUser()**   Returns the login of the user making this request, if the user has been authenticated, or null if the user hasn't been authenticated.

- **getRequestedSessionId()**   Returns the session ID specified by the client.

- **getRequestURI()**   Returns the part of this request's URL from the protocol name up to the query string in the first line of the HTTP request.

- **getServletPath()**   Returns the part of this request's URL that calls the servlet.

- **getSession()**   Returns the current session associated with this request or, if the request doesn't have a session, creates one.

- **getSession(boolean)**   Returns the current HttpSession associated with this request or, if no current session exists and create is true, returns a new session.

- **getUserPrincipal()**   Returns a java.security.Principal object containing the name of the current authenticated user.

- **isRequestedSessionIdFromCookie()**   Checks whether the requested session ID came in as a cookie.

- **isRequestedSessionIdFromURL()**   Checks whether the requested session ID came in as part of the request URL.

- **isRequestedSessionIdValid()**   Checks whether the requested session ID is still valid.

- **isUserInRole(String)**   Returns a Boolean indicating whether the authenticated user is included in the specified logical role.

response Object

The complement of the request object is the response object, which corresponds to HttpServletResponse in a servlet. The *response* object is the response back to the client that made the request. The response object has page scope. Use the response object in the same way you use the request object in a page. The following is a code snippet of some of the methods available for the response object:

```
...
<%
    response.setHeader("Cache-Control","no-store"); //HTTP 1.1
    response.setHeader("Pragma","no-cache"); //HTTP 1.0
    response.setDateHeader("Expires", 0); //prevents caching at a proxy server
%>
...
```

The response methods include

- **getCharacterEncoding()**   Returns the name of the charset used for the MIME body sent in this response.

- **getLocale()**   Returns the locale assigned to the response.

- **getOutputStream()**   Returns a ServletOutputStream suitable for writing binary data in the response.

- **getWriter()**   Returns a PrintWriter object that can send character text to the client.

- **isCommitted()**   Returns a Boolean indicating if the response has been committed.

- **reset()**   Clears any data that exists in the buffer, as well as the status code and headers.

- **setBufferSize(int size)**   Sets the preferred buffer size for the body of the response.

- **setContentLength(int len)**   Sets the length of the content body in the response. In HTTP servlets, this method sets the HTTP Content-Length header.

- **addCookie(Cookie cookie)**   Adds the specified cookie to the response.

- **addDateHeader(java.lang.String name, long date)**   Adds a response header with the given name and date-value.

- **addHeader(java.lang.String name, java.lang.String value)**   Adds a response header with the given name and value.

- **addIntHeader(java.lang.String name, int value)**   Adds a response header with the given name and integer value.

- **containsHeader(java.lang.String name)**   Returns a Boolean indicating whether the named response header has already been set.

- **encodeRedirectURL(java.lang.String url)**   Encodes the specified URL for use in the sendRedirect method or, if encoding isn't needed, returns the URL unchanged.

- **encodeURL(java.lang.String url)**   Encodes the specified URL by including the session ID in it or, if encoding isn't needed, returns the URL unchanged.

- **sendError()**   Sends an error response to the client using the specified status.

- **sendRedirect(java.lang.String location)**   Sends a temporary redirect response to the client using the specified redirect location URL.

- **setDateHeader(java.lang.String name, long date)**   Sets a response header with the given name and date-value.

- **setHeader(java.lang.String name, java.lang.String value)**   Sets a response header with the given name and value.

- **setIntHeader(java.lang.String name, int value)**   Sets a response header with the given name and integer value.

- **setStatus(int sc)**   Sets the status code for this response.

- **flushBuffer()**   Forces any content in the buffer to be written to the client.

- **getBufferSize()**   Returns the actual buffer size used for the response.

- **setContentType(java.lang.String type)**   Sets the content type of the response being sent to the client.

- **setLocale(java.util.Locale loc)**   Sets the locale of the response, setting the headers (including the Content-Type's charset), as appropriate.

pageContext Object

The *pageContext* object has page scope and permits the use of server-specific features. The pageContext object provides access to server-specific attributes via a class to permit a JSP to be implemented on any JSP container. The pageContext instance provides access to all the namespaces associated with a JSP page and to several page attributes. The pageContext implements a number of features to the page author, such as a single API to manage the various scoped namespaces; APIs to access various public objects; and mechanisms to obtain JspWriters for output, manage session use, expose page directive attributes, forward or include current requests, and handle error page exceptions.

TIP

If you want to view the HTTP headers, you can use the telnet program, as described in Chapter 19 under the "Viewing the Page Headers" section. Another way to view the HTTP headers is using a utility such as GETURL, which can be found at **http://www.4p8.com/geturl***. For example, by typing* **geturl -h -d http://tuscbdb***, I can view the headers for my laptop's main page. GETURL is a useful command line utility that enables you to retrieve a Web page (or any file that's accessible under the HTTP protocol). It's more useful than a browser in many ways because it can help automate tasks, such as sending a file to a remote Web server using the HTTP POST protocol. The HTTP features that are explicitly supported are GET and POST, with or without the use of a firewall/proxy, and with the capability to use the basic authentication scheme.*

The pageContext methods include

- **findAttribute(java.lang.String name)**   This searches for the named attribute in page, request, session (if valid), and application scope(s) in order and returns the value associated or null.

- **forward(java.lang.String relativeUrlPath)**   This method is used to redirect, or "forward" the current ServletRequest and ServletResponse to another active component in the application.

- **getAttribute(java.lang.String name)**   This returns the object associated with the name in the page scope or null.

- **getAttributeNamesInScope(int scope)**   This is an enumeration of names (java.lang.String) of all the attributes within the specified scope.

- **getAttributesScope(java.lang.String name)**   This is the scope of the object associated with the name specified or 0.

- **getException()**   This is any exception passed to this as an ErrorPage.

- **getOut()**   This is the current JspWriter stream being used for client response.

- **getPage()**   This is the Page implementation class instance (Servlet) associated with this PageContext.

- **getRequest()**   This is the ServletRequest for this PageContext.

- **getResponse()**   This is the ServletResponse for this PageContext.

- **getServletConfig()**   This is the ServletConfig for this PageContext.

- **getServletContext()**   This is the ServletContext for this PageContext.

- **getSession()**   This is the HttpSession for this PageContext or null.

- **handlePageException(java.lang.Exception e)**   This method is intended to process an unhandled "page" level exception by redirecting the exception to either the specified error page for this JSP or, if none was specified, to perform some implementation dependent action.

- **include(java.lang.String relativeUrlPath)**   This causes the resource specified to be processed as part of the current ServletRequest and ServletResponse being processed by the calling Thread.

- **initialize(Servlet servlet, ServletRequest request, ServletResponse response, java.lang.String errorPageURL, boolean needsSession, int bufferSize, boolean autoFlush)**   This is the initialize method called to initialize an uninitialized PageContext so that it may be used by a JSP Implementation class to service an incoming request and response within its _jspService() method.

- **popBody()**   This returns the previous JspWriter "out" saved by the matching pushBody() and updates the value of the out attribute in the page scope attribute namespace of the PageConxtext.

- **pushBody()**   This returns a new BodyContent object, saves the current "out" JspWriter, and updates the value of the out attribute in the page scope attribute namespace of the PageContext.

- **release()**   This method shall "reset" the internal state of a PageContext, releasing all internal references, and preparing the PageContext for potential reuse by a later invocation of initialize().

- **removeAttribute(java.lang.String name)**   This removes the object reference associated with the specified name.

- **removeAttribute(java.lang.String name, int scope)**   This removes the object reference associated with the specified name.

- **setAttribute(java.lang.String name, java.lang.Object attribute)**   This registers the name and object specified with page scope semantics.

■ **setAttribute(java.lang.String name, java.lang.Object o, int scope)**   This registers the name and object specified with appropriate scope semantics.

session Object

The *session* object maintains session information and has session scope. A *session* is a continuous connection from a client/browser to the application server. This isn't a connection to the database, but rather a session the application server has defined and understands. For example, if you want to maintain a user's name and not use cookies or URL parameters, you could set a session attribute to maintain the name, as the following example illustrates:

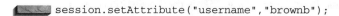

```
session.setAttribute("username","brownb");
```

To retrieve the attribute from any JSP, you would get only the attribute, as the following code example illustrates

```
String sUserName = session.getAttribute("username");
```

The session methods include

■ **getAttribute(String)**   Gets a named attribute's value.

■ **getAttributeNames()**   Returns an Enumeration of String objects containing the names of all the objects bound to this session.

■ **getCreationTime()**   Returns the time when this session was created, measured in milliseconds since midnight January 1, 1970 GMT.

■ **getId()**   Returns a string containing the unique identifier assigned to this session.

■ **getLastAccessedTime()**   Returns the last time the client sent a request associated with this session, as the number of milliseconds since midnight January 1, 1970 GMT.

■ **getMaxInactiveInterval()**   Returns the maximum time interval, in seconds, the servlet container will keep this session open between client accesses.

■ **invalidate()**   Invalidates this session and unbinds any objects bound to it.

■ **isNew()**   Returns true if the client doesn't yet know about the session or if the client chooses not to join the session.

■ **removeAttribute(java.lang.String name)**   Removes the object bound with the specified name from this session.

■ **setAttribute(java.lang.String name, java.lang.Object value)**   Binds an object to this session, using the name specified.

■ **setMaxInactiveInterval(int interval)**   Specifies the time, in seconds, between client requests before the servlet container will invalidate this session.

out Object

The *out* object is of the JspWriter class. The out object is the output stream opened back to the client. It sends the output back to the client, as the following example illustrates:

```
out.println("Hello World");
```

The out method includes:

■ **clear()**   Clears the contents of the buffer.

■ **clearBuffer()**   Clears the current contents of the buffer.

■ **close()**   Closes the stream, flushing it first.

■ **flush()**   Flushes the stream.

■ **getBufferSize()**   Returns the size of the buffer in bytes, or 0 is unbuffered.

■ **getRemaining()**   Retrieves the number of bytes unused in the buffer.

■ **isAutoFlush()**   Will be true if this JspWriter is auto flushing or throwing IOExceptions on buffer overflow conditions.

■ **newLine()**   Writes a line separator.

■ **print()**   Prints a variety of values.

■ **println()**   Prints and terminates the current line by writing the line separator string.

Other Implicit Objects

Other implicit objects you may come across are the application object, config object, page object, and exception object. The implicit objects previously listed are the objects you'll definitely see most often and potentially need to use to make your Web site/ application better suited to fit your needs. If you need more information on the methods available or details on the APIs, please use reference *i*AS JSP documentation.

Oracle JML Tags

Because JSPs separate the dynamic (Java) from the static (HTML) during development, learning Java can still be a hindrance. Oracle provides a solution for the development teams that might not have a Java expert, but that want to take advantage of using JSPs. The JSP Markup Language (JML) consists of custom tags provided by the Oracle JSP container (OracleJSP). The Oracle JML tag library provides many tags that handle Java statements and eliminate some of the need to learn Java. JML tags exist for writing Java statements that declare variables, as well as controlling flow, conditional branches, iterative loops, parameter settings, and calls to objects. The JML tag library also supports XML functionality.

The following example shows the jml:for and jml:print tags used to generate a for iterative loop, instead of writing the Java equivalent:

```
<jml:for id="i" from="1" to="5" >
    <H1><jml:print eval="i" />
      Hello World!
    </H1><jml:print eval="i" />
</jml:for>
```

The following code is the equivalent Java code in a JSP Page:

```
<%
    for (int i = 1; i <= 5; i++) {
            out.println("<H1>"+ i +" Hello World! </H1>" + i);
    }
%>
```

JSP technology is intended for two separate developer skill sets. One set consists of developing in Java and another set is used to design static content, particularly in HTML. The JML tag library is a welcome addition for Web developers with little or no knowledge of Java. The JML library is designed to help those without Java knowledge to develop JSP applications with a full complement of program flow-control features.

A Simple JSP

Let's try developing a JSP page. Remember, JSP is only HTML with Java embedded within. If you leave the Java out of the page (which you could do, but it wouldn't make much sense to do), it's just a static HTML page being generated by Java. In Java, how would you create a loop that displays a counter of numbers from 0 to 10? The following code illustrates how to program this using a for loop:

```
for (int i = 0; i < 11; i++) {
    System.out.println(i);
}
```

To embed a server language (that is, Java) into HTML, you must use the scriptlet tag, which, as previously discussed, is the **<%** to begin the code and **%>** to end the code.

The following JSP page includes the previous Java code, with a minor modification for printing (<%= is the same as out.println) and some additional HTML code:

```
<HTML>
      <HEAD>
      <TITLE>My First JSP Page</TITLE>
      </HEAD>
      <BODY>
      <H2>Welcome to the JSP world!</H2>
      <H3>I can count to 10…</?></H3>
      <% for (int i = 0; i< 11; i++) { %>
          <BR>
          <%= i %>
      <% } %>
      <H3>Are you impressed?</H3>
      </BODY>
</HTML>
```

Figure 13-7 shows what this code looks like in the browser.

FIGURE 13-7.   *Sample output from first JSP*

Passing Parameters to Your JSP

What if I want to allow a parameter to be passed into my JSP file and display this information back to the user? If the user doesn't pass a parameter, the program will use the word "World." Here is what the code might look like:

```
<HTML><HEAD><TITLE>Hello World</TITLE></HEAD>
<BODY>
<% String visitor = request.getParameter("name");
   if (visitor == null) {
       visitor = "World";
   } %>
Hello <%= visitor %>!
</BODY>
</HTML>
```

If I pass a parameter of Brad, the output will appear as it does here:

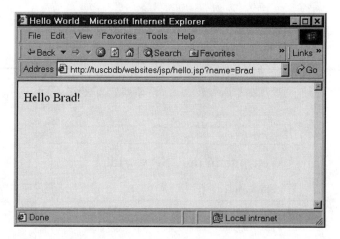

Now Can I Call the Database?

Here's a sample JSP that uses JDBC to pull data from the emp (employee) table. The JSP takes a parameter, department number (deptno), that must be a valid department number. You can either write an HTML page with a field to enter this or add the parameter at the end of the URL.

For example, to call the following JSP passing in department number 20, the URL would look like this:

```
http://localhost/JSP/GetDeptEmps?deptno=20
```

Let's look at the JSP:

```
// GetDeptEmps.java
<%@ page language="java" contentType="text/html"
         import = "java.sql.*, java.util.*, oracle.jdbc.driver.*" %>
<HTML>
<HEAD>
<TITLE>
Employee List
</TITLE>
</HEAD>
<BODY>
<H1>All Employees in department <%= request.getParameter("deptno") %> </H1>
<TABLE BORDER=1>
<TR>
<% String sql = "select * from emp where deptno = ? order by ename" ;
   String connString;
   try {
     DriverManager.registerDriver(new
        oracle.jdbc.driver.OracleDriver());
     Connection conn = null;
     connString = new String(
                "jdbc:oracle:thin:scott/tiger@hostname:1521:ORCL");
     conn = DriverManager.getConnection(connString);
     PreparedStatement pstmt =
        conn.prepareStatement(sql);
     pstmt.setInt(1, Integer.parseInt(request.getParameter("deptno")));
     ResultSet rset = pstmt.executeQuery();
     ResultSetMetaData meta =  rset.getMetaData();
// Retrieves the number of columns returned
     int cols = meta.getColumnCount(), rows =  0;
     for (int i = 1; i <= cols; i++) {
        String label = meta.getColumnLabel(i);
%><TH><% out.println(label); %></TH>
<%    }  %>
</TR>
<%    while (rset.next()) {
        rows++;
        out.println("<TR>");
        for (int i = 1; i <= cols; i++)    {
         String value = rset.getString(i);
         if (value == null) {
             value = " ";
         }
%><TD><% out.println(value); %></TD>
<%    }  %>
</TR>
<%    }
     if (rows == 0) {
         out.println("No data found!\n");
     }
```

```
      // Close up the record set
      rset.close();
      pstmt.close();
      conn.close();
   }
   catch (SQLException e) {
        out.println(e.getMessage());
   }
%>
</TABLE>
</BODY>
</HTML>
```

The beauty of using Server Pages is you can still edit the HTML with a GUI editor. For example, if I use Dreamweaver (or FrontPage) and apply a template that includes an image or banner on top, I can quickly modify the look of the page.

Moving JDBC Code into a Bean

You might think the previous code is considerably longer than the code required to do the same thing using PL/SQL. Rather than including the JDBC code into every routine, this code can be moved into a JavaBean. Once we do this, it shortens our JSP considerably. I created the following JavaBean, called ConnectionBean, that handles JDBC for our future JSPs. You'll notice I declared a default connection, but this can be overridden by any JSP program using the DbURL setter (setDbURL).

```
import java.sql.*;
import javax.servlet.http.*;

public class ConnectionBean implements HttpSessionBindingListener {
  public  Connection conn;
  private Statement stmt;
  private String dbURL=
         "jdbc:oracle:thin:examples/examples@hostname:1521:ORCL";
  public ConnectionBean() {
  try {
     DriverManager.registerDriver(new oracle.jdbc.driver.OracleDriver());
     conn = DriverManager.getConnection(dbURL);
     statement = conn.createStatement();
  }
  catch (SQLException e) {
     System.err.println("ConnectionBean: driver not loaded: " + e);
     conn = null;
  }
} /// ConnectionBeanconstructor

  public void setDbURL (String d) {
```

```
      dbURL = d;
   } /// setDbURL

   public Connection getConnection() {
      return conn;
   } /// getConnection

   public void commit() throws SQLException {
      conn.commit();
   }

   public void rollback() throws SQLException {
      conn.rollback();
   } /// rollback

   public void setAutoCommit (boolean autoCommit) throws SQLException {
      conn.setAutoCommit(autoCommit);
   } /// setAutoCommit

   public ResultSet executeQuery(String sql) throws SQLException {
      return stmt.executeQuery(sql);
   } /// executeQuery

   public int executeUpdate(String sql) throws SQLException {
      return stmt.executeUpdate(sql);
   } /// executeUpdate

   public CallableStatement prepareCall(String sql) throws SQLException {
      return conn.prepareCall(sql);
   } /// prepareCall

   public void valueBound(HttpSessionBindingEvent event) {
      try {
      if (conn == null || conn.isClosed()) {
         conn = DriverManager.getConnection(dbURL);
          stmt  = conn.createStatement();
      } /// if conn == null
}      catch (SQLException e) {
      System.err.println("ConnectionBean: in the valueBound method");
      conn = null;
     }
   } /// valueBound

   public void valueUnbound(HttpSessionBindingEvent event) {
      try {
         conn.close();
      }
      catch (SQLException e) {
      }
```

```
      finally {
          conn = null;
      }
  } /// valueUnbound

  protected void finalize() {
    try {
      conn.close();
    }
    catch (SQLException e) {
    }
  } /// finalize
} /// ConnectionBean
```

Now let's look at how the JSP code is simplified by using the Bean to manage the JDBC information. The following code is considerably more extensive than the previous example, which simply selected all the records for a specific department from the emp table. This routine accepts input parameters and dynamically builds the where clause to extract the information, so it's much more complex in terms of functionality, but with considerably less code. At the top of the JSP file, notice the reference to the ConnectionBean and how we set the connect string using the dbURL setter.

```
<%@ page import="java.sql.* "%>
<jsp:useBean id="connection" class="ConnectionBean" scope="session"/>
<jsp:setProperty name="connection" property="dbURL"
value="jdbc:oracle:thin:examples/examples@hostname:1521:ORCL" />
<HTML>
<TITLE>Select Employees</TITLE>
<BODY>
<TABLE border="1">
<TR><TH>Employee</TH><TH>Department</TH><TH>Salary</TH></TR>
<%
  String where = "";
  // Minimum salary
  String inMinSal = request.getParameter("in_min_sal");
  if (inMinSal != null) {
     where = "where sal >= " +inMinSal;
  }
  // Maximum salary
  String inMaxSal = request.getParameter("in_max_sal");
  if (inMaxSal != null) {
      where = where + ((where == "") ? "where " : " and ") +
         " sal <= " +inMaxSal;
  }
  // Department Number
  String inDeptNo = request.getParameter("in_dept_no");
  if (inDeptNo != null) {
      where = where + ((where == "") ? "where " : " and ") +
```

```
            " deptno = " +inDeptNo;
    }
    String sql = "SELECT ename, deptno, sal FROM emp " + where;
    ResultSet results = connection.executeQuery(sql);
    while (results.next()) { %>
<TR>
<TD><%= results.getString("ename") %></TD>
<TD><%= results.getString("deptno") %></TD>
<TD><%= results.getString("sal") %></TD>
</TR>
<% } %>
</TABLE>
</BODY>
</HTML>
```

How Do I Run This Stuff?

Using JDeveloper is an easy way to run your JSP code. I also highly recommend using JDeveloper as your development environment because of the built-in JSP features. Some developers feel JDeveloper simplifies the JSP development considerably.

To run the code with 9*i*AS, you simply place the code into the directory of your choice, and then tell 9*i*AS where to find the Beans you referenced. This is accomplished with the CLASSPATH directives in the jserv.properties file. If you don't have any Beans, you needn't modify the jserv.properties file. If you do modify the file, be sure to restart 9*i*AS.

Creating New JSPs with JDeveloper

To create new JSPs using JDeveloper, from the File menu, select New | Web Objects | JSP, as shown in Figure 13-8.

This creates a blank JSP from which you can start developing.

JSP Wizard

JDeveloper provides a complete JSP development environment. The *JSP Wizard* is a cool feature that uses a toolkit Oracle refers to as Business Components for Java (BC4J), discussed in detail in the following.

Let's start with the following example of JSP code. This little program simply prints some information about today's date and time, as you can see in Figure 13-9.

```
<%@ page language = "java" errorPage="errorpage.jsp"
         import = "java.util.*"
         contentType="text/html" %>
<HTML>
<HEAD>
<META HTTP-EQUIV="Content-Type"
      CONTENT="text/html">
```

```
<META NAME="GENERATOR" CONTENT="Oracle JDeveloper">
<TITLE>Hello World - <%= new Date() %></TITLE>
</HEAD>
<BODY>
<H1>How are you today?</H1>
It is now
<% Date myDate = new Date();
   String[] dow = new String[] {"",
"Sunday","Monday","Tuesday","Wednesday","Thursday","Friday","Saturday"};
   String[] ap  = new String[] {"AM", "PM"};
   out.println(myDate);
   Calendar cal = Calendar.getInstance();
   cal.setTime(myDate);
   out.println("<BR>It's currently day " +
               cal.get(Calendar.DAY_OF_YEAR) + " of this year.");
   out.println("<BR>It's day " + cal.get(Calendar.DAY_OF_WEEK) +
               " (" + dow[cal.get(Calendar.DAY_OF_WEEK)] +
               ") of the week.");
   out.println("<BR>It's now " + ap[cal.get(Calendar.AM_PM)] +
               ". Good ");
   if (cal.get(Calendar.AM_PM) == 0) {
      out.println("Morning.");

   } else {
      out.println("Afternoon/Evening.");
   }
   out.println("<BR>To be precise "
       + Integer.toString(
             cal.get(Calendar.HOUR_OF_DAY) * 3600000 +
             cal.get(Calendar.MINUTE) * 60000 +
             cal.get(Calendar.SECOND) * 1000 +
             cal.get(Calendar.MILLISECOND)
         )
       + " milliseconds have passed today");
   out.println("<BR>It's currently week " +
               cal.get(Calendar.WEEK_OF_YEAR) + " of this year.");
%>
</BODY>
</HTML>
```

JDeveloper's JSP Wizard enables you to insert JavaBeans quickly into an existing JSP file. First, place the cursor at the point of insertion in your JSP file, and then click Wizards | JSP Element. The wizard prompts you through the insertion of a JavaBean from the library.

As shown in Figure 13-10, you then select the Bean you want to insert. After selecting the Bean, you need to specify the various properties for the object, as shown in Figure 13-11. The JSP Wizard feature of JDeveloper is a powerful feature that simplifies your JSP development.

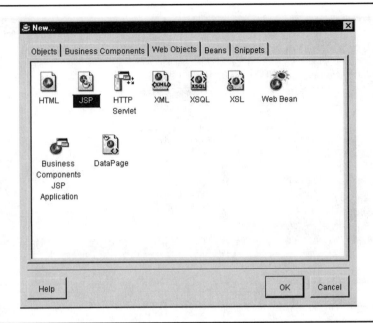

FIGURE 13-8. *New JSP*

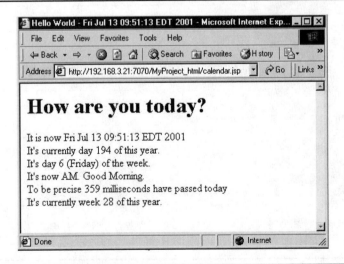

FIGURE 13-9. *Information about today*

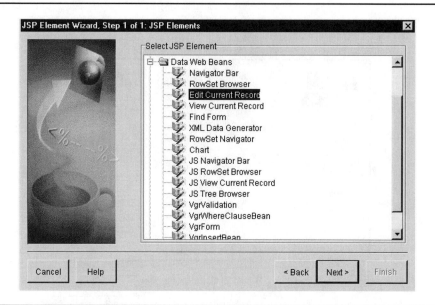

FIGURE 13-10. *Picking the JavaBean*

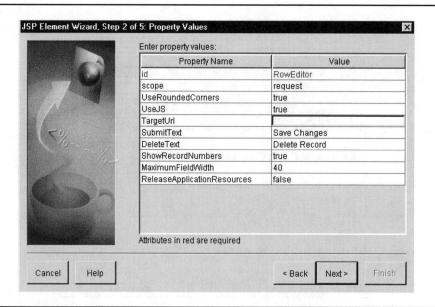

FIGURE 13-11. *Specifying data for the Bean*

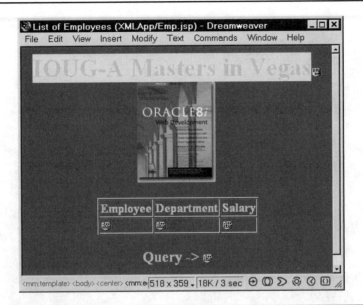

FIGURE 13-12. *JSP in Dreamweaver*

Figure 13-12 shows what this JSP looks like in Dreamweaver.
Figure 13-13 shows what the JSP now looks like in the browser when we run the JSP.

JSP Programming Strategies and Traps

You have several strategies, tips, and traps to consider when building JSP applications.

■ *Separation of business logic from presentation* This is a key advantage to using JSP. Instead of writing JSP code snippets, write a JavaBean and access the methods from the JavaBean. Using JavaBeans over code snippets cleans up your code, eases maintenance, and enables the HTML expert to focus on the page layout, and the Java expert to focus on the Java. A typical JSP page should contain only small snippets of Java code, and most of these snippets should be for handling request-processing information.

■ *Use an EJB in a JSP page* EJBs provide another avenue of using the power of Java. To use EJBs in your JSP, call the EJB directly from the JSP page or use a JavaBean wrapper for the EJB, and then call the JavaBean from the JSP page as you would any other JavaBean. This is the preferred method of calling EJB.

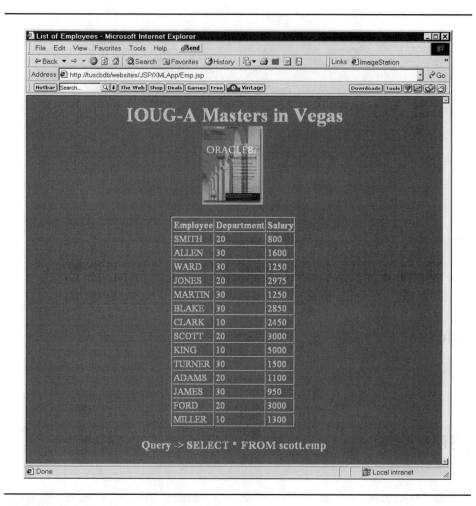

FIGURE 13-13. *JSP with the template applied*

- *Performance enhancement features, supported through Oracle JDBC extensions* Oracle provides many JDBC features to enhance performance. Things to remember and that you can do when dealing with database connections are caching database connections, caching JDBC statements, batching update statements, prefetching rows during a query, and caching rowsets.

- *When to consider creating and using JSP tag libraries* When working with the generation of JSP applications, sometimes the developer recognizes the advantages of developing JSP tag libraries. Two situations where building a tag library are areas where you have significant amounts of Java logic handling the presentation, and when you need special manipulation or redirection of JSP output. Tag libraries benefit developers who might not be Java experts, but who still need to use Java logic to handle the presentation layer.

■ *Use a Central Checker Servlet* For handling your JSP application, you might want to write a Central Checker Servlet to check session status, login status, use profile, or any other application-specific information.

■ *Large JSP pages* If you have large static JSP pages, you might notice you have slow translation or execution issues. A workaround for this is to write an HTML page, and then use the <jsp:include> tag to include your JSP code in the HTML page.

■ *JSP preservation of white space* JSP preserves white space in the source code, including carriage returns and linefeeds, in the response to the browser. JSP technology is a poor choice for generating binary data because of this white space preservation. There aren't any methods for writing raw bytes in the *JspWriter* object.

JSP Tips

There are many programming techniques that will improve your JSP coding. The following tips will be helpful to get you eating, sleeping, and thinking in JSP:

■ *Choosing the right include mechanism* Two *include* mechanisms notify the JSP engine to include the contents of the resource being referenced: the include directive and the include action. Developers might wonder which one to use. The *include directive* (<%@ include file="filename.inc" %>) includes the content of the specified resource when the page is converted to a servlet. The *include action* (<jsp:include page="pagename.jsp" flush="true" />) includes the resource at run time. The rule of thumb for when to use the different mechanisms is as follows:

■ Use the include directive if the file changes rarely because it's the fastest mechanism.

■ Use the include action only for content that changes or if the resource filename is unknown at run time.

■ *Working with buffer flushing issues* Headers and a body are contained in HTTP responses. Headers contain overall page information and must be sent to the browser before the body. The JSP engine writes all static and dynamic generated content to a buffer to allow parts of the Web page to be produced before the headers are set. Eventually, the buffer becomes full (as defined by the page's buffer size, which defaults to 24KB) or the end of the page is hit, and the response becomes committed. Once the response is committed, headers cannot be set and you cannot forward the request to another page. Flushing the buffer doesn't usually happen in most cases. But when using the <jsp:include> (the action include), the buffer is always flushed before the target page is invoked. Unfortunately, this might cause a run-time error when using the <jsp:include> tags. I suggest using the include directive until issues are resolved.

■ *Passing data between pages processing the same request* You can pass data from one page to another in two ways: either using the request parameters or the request attributes. The page invoked using the <jsp:include> or <jsp:forward> tags must have access to the HTTP request information.

```
<jsp:forward page="login.jsp">
    <jsp:param name="errMsg"
     value="The name or password is not valid" />
</jsp:forward>
```

The target page (login.jsp) must have access to the original or additional request parameters, but request parameters can hold only string values. You, therefore, must pass an object as a request attribute, session, or application scope Bean. The invoking page can create an object and set its properties for a request attribute because it's the same thing as a request scope object.

```
<jsp:useBean id="userInfo" scope="request"
    class="com.mycompany.UserInfoBean">
    <jsp:setProperty name="userInfo" property="*" />
</jsp:useBean>
...
<jsp:forward page="nextpage.jsp" />
```

The <jsp:useBean> action must be included in the page that was invoked using <jsp:forward> or <jsp:include> to use the Bean created in the invoking page. You must be able to associate the Bean from the first page with the second page. Then, using scripting code or another action, such as <jsp:getProperty>, you can pull the attributes from the Bean in the first page.

```
<jsp:useBean id="userInfo" scope="request"
    class="com.mycompany.UserInfoBean" />
<jsp:getProperty name="userInfo" property="firstName" />
```

■ *Choosing between forward and redirect* Both the forward and redirect mechanisms move you to a next page, but each works in a different way. Forwarding processes the same request. Redirecting makes a new request to the target page. Forwards are faster. Also, redirects lose any request scope objects so, if you want to pass data, you need to set and get request parameters. One other note: when you forward, the URL doesn't change. If you believe the Web site might be reloaded, resized, or refreshed and there's information you don't want to lose, you might want to use the redirect.

■ *Choosing between beans and data tags* JavaBeans and Data Tags (custom actions) are components used to encapsulate Java code and create reusable code. These two types of component-based programming exist in the JSP specification 1.1 and higher. Deciding when to use either is a matter of preference. JavaBeans are better used for carrying information, whereas Data Tags are used for processing information. On the other hand, for cosmetic reasons and maintenance of code, you might want to use Data Tags because they're based on the HTML and XML tag structure.

■ *Using packages for bean classes* Beans should be put in packages if you're going to use them in JSP applications. If a Bean isn't part of a package, you must explicitly import the class that contains the Bean. Therefore, you must use both a page directive to import the class and the <jsp:useBean> action to make it available.

```
<%@ page import="UserInfoBean" %>
<jsp:useBean id="userInfo" class="UserInfoBean" />
```

If the Bean is packaged, the <jsp:useBean> action is all you need:

```
<jsp:useBean id="userInfo"
    class="com.mycompany.UserInfoBean" />
```

■ *Mixing scripting variables and scope variables* Where possible, avoid embedding Java code in your JSP pages. Writing code directly into a JSP page can cause maintenance and debugging issues in the future. Take advantage of the framework of JSP and create Beans or Data Tags to separate the business logic. You might also run into confusion when dealing with scripting code and action tags within a JSP page.

■ *Setting properties to nonstring data type values* Request parameters are sent as Strings. So what happens when you want to use the request parameters in a Bean and the datatype of the Bean attribute you're setting isn't of type String? Using the <jsp:setProperty> tag, the JSP container converts the request parameter to the most common data type as in the following table:

Property Type	Conversion Method
boolean or Boolean	Boolean.valueOf(String)
byte or Byte	Byte.valueOf(String)
char or Character	String.charAt(int)

Property Type	Conversion Method
double or Double	Double.valueOf(String)
int or Integer	Integer.valueOf(String)
float or Float	Float.valueOf(String)
long or Long	Long.valueOf(String)

If your data type isn't listed in the previous, you must convert the datatype. The String class has many methods written to convert to other datatypes.

■ *Accessing a database*   Some general guidelines for accessing the database include the following:

  ■ Use the JDBC APIs and all the available methods it contains.

  ■ Don't put the database access code directly in the JSP page. Instead, create a Bean that connects to the database.

  ■ Use a connection pool of database connections because database connections require a lot of system resources.

  ■ Cache database query information. If you use Oracle's JDeveloper and take advantage of the BC4J, however, your database connection details are already handled quite well.

Java Stored Procedures

Java Stored Procedures aren't JSPs. Java Stored Procedures are Java programs that are stored and compiled into the database. Until Oracle8*i*, PL/SQL was the only procedural language that could be used in the database. But Java Stored Procedures provide the capability to build applications using both PL/SQL and the power of Java. This permits the seamless interoperability between PL/SQL and the ever-increasingly popular Java language. Java Stored Procedures can be executed in three different run-time contexts: stored procedures and functions, database triggers, and object relational methods.

Use Java Stored Procedures or PL/SQL?

Maybe you've been asking yourself what Java Stored Procedures are and when they're used. The following guidelines are intended to help you decide when to use Java or PL/SQL.

Java has the following characteristics:

■ Optimized for computational operations

■ Needs complex object-oriented or high-transaction processing operations

- Supports native numeric operations

- Can expand the clients to communicate with the server to include CORBA, EJB, and HTTP/browsers, in addition to Net8. Also, users can extend and write their own protocol drivers

- Develops functionality PL/SQL cannot provide (that is, host/system calls and e-mail with attachments)

- Object-oriented (inheritance, polymorphism, and components models)

- Uses JDBC or SQLJ to talk with database, which is slower than SQL

PL/SQL has the following characteristics:

- Extends SQL efficiently and safely by supporting datatypes

- Building SQL-intensive applications

- Optimized for operations surrounding the database (inserts, updates, deletes, and selects)

Java database procedures are useful for programs that are light database users and heavy operating system users, heavy string parsing procedures, or are computationally intensive—all things PL/SQL isn't particularly good at performing. Although Java and PL/SQL appear to have the same disadvantages in that they are both interpreted and are running in the database kernel, Java does run faster for these types of operations. One difference between Java servlets and Java Stored Procedures is simply the tier on which they run. Java Stored Procedures tend to fatten the data server layer and Java servlets tend to fatten the middle tier.

Don't get me wrong: Java Stored Procedures are useful. In fact, they are *very* useful. People often ask me, which language—PL/SQL or Java—is better? The answer is it depends on the operation you're performing. If you want to perform truly intense database operations, PL/SQL is likely better. If you want to perform complex calculations (like you would in a C program), Java is probably better. Any Java class or method that's written can become a Java Stored Procedure.

Accessing Java Stored Procedures from the Database

You can access Java from the database in six basic steps:

1. Identify the Java functionality you want to use in your database application (in this example, we're concatenating a string).

2. Write a Java class that contains the method of the functionality you want.

   For example:

   ```
   // JavaStoredProcedure.java
   import java.sql.*;
   import java.io.* ;


   public class JavaStoredProcedure {

      public static String makeString
        (String beginString, String endString) {
        return beginString + endString;
      } /// makeString
   } /// JavaStoredProcedure
   ```

3. After you create the Java class, compile, test, and load the Java file into the database. Loading a Java Stored Procedure into the database can be completed in two ways: using the loadjava utility or manually using the CREATE JAVA DDL syntax. The loadjava utility can load source files, resource files, or class files. The syntax for the loadjava command is as follows:

   ```
   loadjava -user scott/tiger@hostname:1521:ORCL -r -o oci8
           -f -v JavaStoredProcedure.class
   ```

   To load Java from SQL*Plus manually, use this code (note, you must first create your bfile_dir using a statement similar to the following: CREATE OR REPLACE DIRECTORY BFILE_DIR AS 'C:\TEMP'):

   ```
   CREATE OR REPLACE JAVA CLASS USING
   BFILE(BFILE_DIR, 'JavaStoredProcedure.class');
   or
   CREATE OR REPLACE JAVA SOURCE NAMED "JavaStoredProcedure" AS
   import java.sql.*;
   import java.io.* ;


   public class JavaStoredProcedure {
      public static String makeString
     (String beginString, String endString) {
        return beginString + endString;
      } /// makeString
   } /// JavaStoredProcedure
   /
   ```

4. Publish the Java Stored Procedures by building a PL/SQL Call Specification, sometimes referred to as a *PL/SQL wrapper,* after you load them into the database. All Java classes loaded into the database aren't visible to SQL. To publish a stored procedure means to create a PL/SQL procedure/function that

relates to the Java method you want to invoke through SQL or PL/SQL. You don't have to publish every method of the Java Stored Procedure, only the Java methods you want to call from SQL or PL/SQL (note, they must be public methods). Because the method makeString returns a String, you make this a function. Publish the JavaStoredProcedure.makeString method as follows:

```
CREATE OR REPLACE FUNCTION build_String
(string1 IN VARCHAR2,string2 IN VARCHAR2)
RETURN VARCHAR2
AS LANGUAGE JAVA
NAME 'JavaStoredProcedure.makeString
(java.lang.String, java.lang.String)
return java.lang.String';
/
```

The syntax for publishing a Java Stored Procedure as a Function or a Procedure is as follows:

Call Specification for a Procedure

```
CREATE OR REPLACE PROCEDURE procname (pname mode ptype, ... )
AS LANGUAGE JAVA NAME 'javaname ( javatype, ... )';
/
```

Call Specification for a Function

```
CREATE OR REPLACE FUNCTION
funcname (pname mode ptype,... )
RETURN rtype AS
LANGUAGE JAVA NAME 'javaname ( javatype,
    return javatype';
/
```

5. Set the Oracle Database privileges. If you want the user to perform any Java-related operation, issue the following command from the SYSDBA account:

```
GRANT JAVASYSPRIV TO SCOTT;
```

The JAVASYSPRIV role gives the user the capability to perform the following tasks:

- open a TCP/IP socket
- read from or write to any file
- create subprocesses
- listen on specific network ports
- set the socket factory
- set the stream handler

If you want to place some restrictions on the user, use a GRANT, as follows:

```
GRANT JAVAUSERPRIV TO SCOTT;
```

The JAVAUSERPRIV role gives the user the capability to perform the following tasks:

- open a TCP/IP socket

- read from or write to files using the PL/SQL UTL_FILE_DIR package

6. Invoke the Java Stored Procedure like any other stored procedure/function. Remember, you use the name defined for the database stored procedure/function (in this case build_String is the function name).

From SQL*Plus prompt

```
SQLPLUS> var temp varchar2(100)
SQLPLUS> EXECUTE :temp := build_String
                ('Java Stored Procedures',' are great')
```

Invoking from PL/SQL

```
set serveroutput on size 5000
Declare
  temp varchar2(100);
Begin
  temp := build_String('Java Store Procedures ',' are great');
  dbms_output.put_line(temp);
End;
/
```

Business Components for Java (BC4J)

BC4J is the business logic of accessing and manipulating data from the database. BC4J is JDeveloper's programming framework for building multitier database applications from reusable business components. BC4J provides a framework to map relational database objects to an object-oriented view of the data—it hides the relational implementation of the entities. The following table outlines the five types that classify as BC4J:

Business Components	Description
Entity Object	Encapsulates business logic for a database table, view, or synonym.
View Object	Uses SQL queries to specify filtered subsets of attributes from entity objects.

Business Components	Description
Association	Defines the relationship between two entity objects.
View Link	Defines the relationship between two view objects.
Application Module	Provides a logical container for view objects, view links, and transactions.

Entity Objects

Entity objects are the object representations of a row of data from a database table, view, synonym, or snapshot. These are the entity objects with the column names being attributes of the object (read the documentation in the VgrApplicationsImpl.Java file for more information). An entity object encapsulates the business logic and database storage details of your business entities. An association is a relationship between two entity objects (that is, foreign keys). Entity objects data is accessed through view objects. Clients use view objects to get and set attribute values.

TIP
You can optionally generate the accessor, data manipulation, create, and remove methods using the wizard when creating entity objects. This is discussed in more detail in the "Editing Business Components" section.

The wizard can generate the following optional methods:

- Accessor methods provide type-safe access to the corresponding attribute fields and a place to add your own custom code for validation (for example, getAppId and setAppId).

- Data manipulation methods (including lock) customize the entity object's locking behavior and update, insert, and delete logic. The framework calls the lock method whenever an entity's row in the database is locked for modifications. The framework, with the appropriate DML command to insert, update, or delete the row corresponding to the entity instance during the Transaction-Commit cycle, calls the doDML method. This method can be overridden to modify the update behavior. For example, instead of directly updating through a SQL statement as the framework does, update through a procedure call to the database.

- Create method customizes or adds additional initialization features to the entity object's create logic, for example, setting default values for attributes.

■ Remove method customizes or adds clean-up code to the entity object's remove logic, for example, deleting child objects in a composition.

The VgrApplicationsImpl.Java file has the default create (which generates a sequence number), remove, accessor, and data manipulation methods, which are used to enter the desired logic for each method, as the following example illustrates:

```java
// VgrApplicationsImpl.Java
package package2;
// -------------------------------------------------------------
// ---    File generated by Oracle Business Components for Java.
// -------------------------------------------------------------
import oracle.jbo.server.*;
import oracle.jbo.RowIterator;
import oracle.jbo.domain.Number;
import oracle.jbo.domain.Date;
import oracle.jbo.Key;
import oracle.jbo.server.util.*;
import oracle.jbo.AttributeList;

public class VgrApplicationsImpl extends oracle.jbo.server.EntityImpl {
  protected static final int APPID = 0;
  protected static final int APPNAME = 1;
  protected static final int APPDESC = 2;
  protected static final int APPMILESTONEDATE = 3;
  protected static final int APPDISCUSSIONID = 4;
  protected static final int APPCREATEDBY = 5;
  protected static final int APPCREATEDDATE = 6;
  protected static final int APPUPDATEDBY = 7;
  protected static final int APPUPDATEDDATE = 8;
  protected static final int VGRAPPLICATIONVERSIONS = 9;
  private static EntityDefImpl mDefinitionObject;

  //--------This is the default constructor (do not remove)
  public VgrApplicationsImpl() {
  }
  //------------ Retrieves the definition object for this instance class.
  public static synchronized EntityDefImpl getDefinitionObject() {
    if (mDefinitionObject == null) {
      mDefinitionObject = (
      (EntityDefImpl)EntityDefImpl.findDefObject("package2.VgrApplications");
    }
    return mDefinitionObject;
  }
  //--------- Gets the attribute value for AppId, using the alias name AppId
  public Number getAppId() {
    return (Number)getAttributeInternal(APPID);
  }
  //------ Sets <code>value</code> as the attribute value for AppId
  public void setAppId(Number value) {
```

```
      setAttributeInternal(APPID, value);
  }
//…other get and set of attributes
  public void create(AttributeList attributeList) {
      super.create(attributeList);
    //   Generating a sequence number on an insert
      SequenceImpl s = new SequenceImpl("vgr_app_id_s", getDBTransaction());
      Integer next = (Integer)s.getData();
      setAppId(new Number(next.intValue()));
  }
  //--------Add entity remove logic here.
  public void remove() {
    super.remove();
  }
  //------------Add locking logic here.
  public void lock() {
    super.lock();
  }
  //----------Custom DML update/insert/delete logic here.
  public void doDML(int operation, TransactionEvent e) {
    super.doDML(operation, e);
  }
  //------------ Creates a Key object based on given key constituents
  public static Key createPrimaryKey(Number appId) {
    return new Key(new Object[]{appId});
  }
  }
}
```

View Objects

View Objects encapsulate SQL code and metadata that map columns in the SELECT statement to attributes of one or more entity objects. View objects use SQL to make data available for presentation.

TIP
You can define more than one view object for the same entity object.

View Objects are often used to

- Provide an additional level of security by restricting access to a predetermined set of rows and columns. For example, you can create a view where columns containing sensitive data (such as salaries) aren't selected.

- Hide data complexity. For example, a view can display columns or rows from multiple entities. Such a view hides the fact that the data is coming from several tables.

■ Customize presentation. Using a view, you can rename columns without affecting the entities on which the view is based.

■ Store complex queries. A query can perform extensive calculations on table data. By saving this query in a view, the calculations are performed only when the view's query is executed.

■ Improve efficiency of the application by using fast-executing, optimized SQL, selecting only the data you need.

Associations

Associations are relationships between two entity objects based on common attributes. They permit the access of data from one entity object to another. Associations don't need to have referential integrity constraints from the database because they can exist regardless of integrity constraints. Associations are bidirectional and are navigable from master to detail and detail to master.

View Links

View Links specify relationships between two View Objects. A View Link specifies source and destination View Objects, and links them using attributes selected by those View Objects. A View Link can be traversed from master to detail, but not from detail to master.

Benefits of BC4J

Many benefits exist for using BC4J's in building your application. For instance, in a multitier application built with the BC4J framework, clients share the views, business rules, and custom code within components. Therefore, you can easily build, maintain, reuse, and customize components. Also, you don't need modifications to deploy components to supported platforms. The following table lists the features and benefits of BC4J framework:

Features	Benefits
Encapsulated Business Logic	Business logic, including validation, resides and executes in the middle-tier. This enables truly thin client customization and reuse.
Flexible Views of Data	Views of data are SQL-based and completely separate from the underlying entities, enabling flexible presentation schemes.

Features	Benefits
Thin Clients	BC4J supports the thin client's windows to business logic and views of data processed by the middle-tier.
Flexible Deployment	Deploy locally Oracle8*i* as CORBA servers and EJB Session Beans.
Database Interaction	BC4Js component-based coordination and locking.
Transaction Framework	Handles many repetitive coding tasks, such as master-detail management. BC4J manages changes in its cache and handles posting of changes to the database.

Oracle's BC4J dramatically reduces the time-to-market for the development of Web-based applications or any Java application that accesses databases. BC4J provides the framework that simplifies development and design of reusable database access components for applications. BC4Js can be deployed as JSPs, EJBs, Java servlets, or CORBA components, and can be called from Java, HTML, and XML.

Simply put, from the Oracle Java Roadmap document, "BC4J is the culmination of years of design and development work to pragmatically implement Oracle's vision for how to build scalable, multitier Enterprise Java applications." But the big question is this: do you want to be locked into an Oracle-specific framework in these open source J2EE times? The decision is yours to make.

JDeveloper

Oracle JDeveloper is a robust J2EE- and XML-integrated development environment with end-to-end support for building, debugging, and deploying component-based applications. JDeveloper offers wizards, editors, and visual design tools to develop applications and components according to the J2EE specification. You can build a number of Java-related applications using JDeveloper, including applets, Java applications, JavaBeans, JSP, servlets, CORBA objects, and EJBs.

JDeveloper makes application development more productive. It offers the BC4J server-side framework for creating scalable, high-performance applications. The BC4J component of JDeveloper provides design-time facilities and run-time services to simplify the task of building and reusing business logic drastically, which, in turn, reduces the time-to-market on developing a Java application.

By using JDeveloper, Java, and the BC4J, an application can be deployed as JSPs, EJBs, or CORBA components without modification to the application code. The flexibility gained when using Java permits the deployment of an application

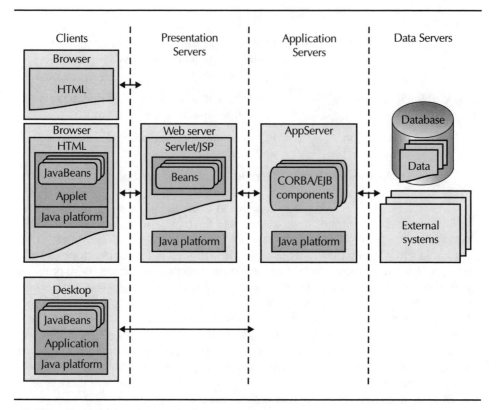

FIGURE 13-14. *Architecture for tier configuration of Java applications*

on to a variety of servers without changing the business logic or application (that is, clients could be Web browsers, or handheld wireless devices).

Figure 13-14 shows the logical architecture of applications built with JDeveloper. You can physically deploy this architecture to a tier configuration of your choice.

JDeveloper provides the necessary features to implement this application architecture. The primary features of JDeveloper are Oracle BC4J, Web Application Development, Java Client Application Development, Java in the Database, and Component-based Development with JavaBeans.

Building Business Components with JDeveloper

To create business components, you need to create a connection to the database using the Connection Manager Wizard in JDeveloper. Double-click the Connections node icon and the Connection Manager dialog box will appear, as shown in Figure 13-15.

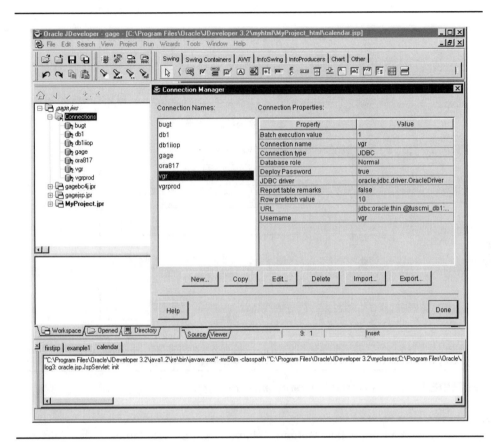

FIGURE 13-15. *JDeveloper 3.2 GUI with the Connection Manager Dialog Box invoked*

Choose New and another Connection dialog box appears, as shown in Figure 13-16. Fill out the following information:

- **Connection Name**   Name to reference your database connection

- **Connection Type**   Use JDBC for thin client connections and use IIOP for EJBs or Remote Method Invocation (RMI) connections

- **Security Information: Username/Password**   Database user name and password

- **Select a JDBC Driver**   Choose the driver you want (thin for Web applications, OCI7 or OCI8 for an Oracle Database 7/8, or another driver)

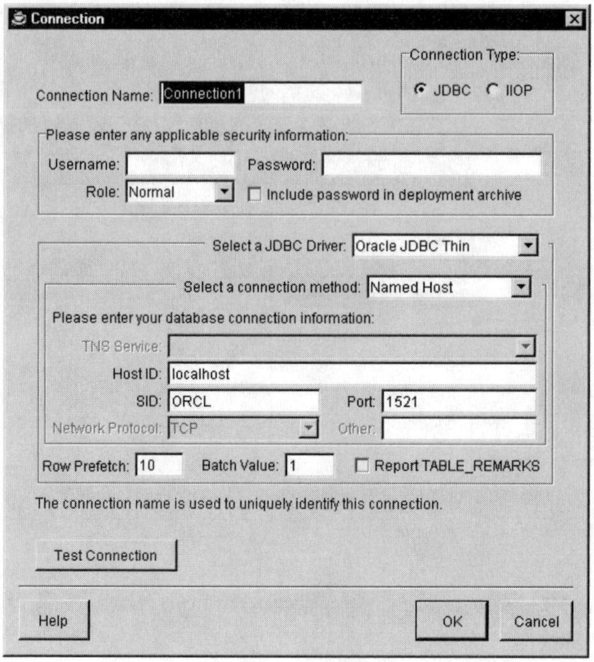

FIGURE 13-16. *Connection Information dialog box*

- **Select a Connection Method** Named Host or Net Name—Value Pair permits you to enter in the database connection information; Existing TNS Names provides you with a list of TNS names to choose from

- **Test Connection** Tests the Database Connection information entered

Generating Business Components

To generate the Business Components, from the Navigator menu bar, select File | New Project and a Projects Wizard appears, as shown in Figure 13-17. Give the project a name with the .jpr extension (projectname.jpr). What type of project would you like to create? Choose a project containing Business Components. This will take you through the wizard. You can select Next to continue with changes or Finish, if you want to use the default package name and default paths. You can change the name of the package, the path of the source code or compiled class code, and user information. After you click the Finish button, another dialog box appears, as shown in Figure 13-18. This is the Business Component Project Wizard, where you select your connection and table information for the Business Components.

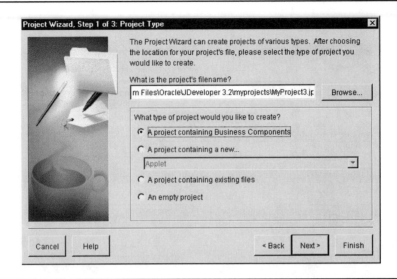

FIGURE 13-17. *Project Wizard*

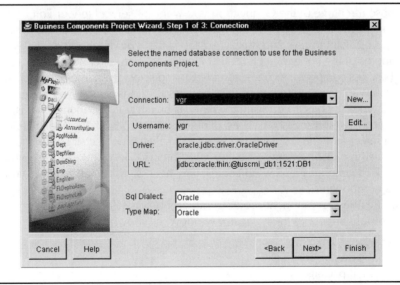

FIGURE 13-18. *Business Component Projects Wizard*

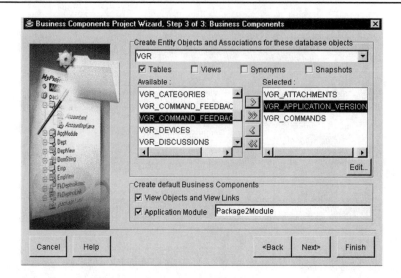

FIGURE 13-19. *Step 3 of the Business Component Projects Wizard*

Choose the name of the Connection you want, or select New or Edit to change the connection information. The *Sql Dialect* is the type of SQL data manipulation language you want to use, and the *Type Map* is the type of mapping you want on the attributes of the entity objects. Select Next, and then enter in the package name for the business components code. Select Next, and select the name of the schema for which you want to create entity objects and associations, as shown in Figure 13-19. Check all types of objects you want to create as business components (that is, tables, views, synonyms, and snapshots). A list of objects will appear in the Available: window (you can select individual objects or click >> to select all objects). Under the Create default Business Components, check View Objects, View Links and Application Module. This generates a view object and any necessary objects to build your business components.

Your Business Component project, with all objects selected in Step 3 of the wizard, should appear in the navigator window, as shown here:

Each business component you create consists of an XML file and one or more Java files (in Figure 13-19, the Entity Objects and View Objects have an XML and a Java file associated with them). The XML file stores *metadata* (the descriptive information about features and settings of an application you declare using wizards at design time) and the Java file stores the object's code (which implements application-specific behavior).

Editing Business Components

I'll bet you're thinking, "Wow, I created business components. That's easy!" And it is. But you can do substantially more with the wizards to help in the building of applications. Double-click (or right-click and choose Edit your Entity Object Name) one of the Entity Objects (the objects with your table name) and a dialog box appears, as shown in Figure 13-20.

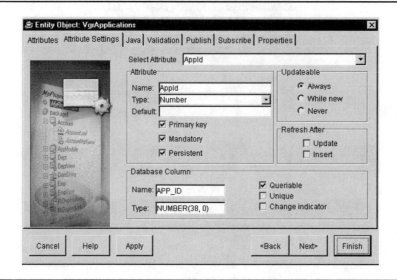

FIGURE 13-20. *Entity Object Wizard for Business Components*

As the following table indicates, you have control over many different attributes of the entity object:

Attributes:	Add or remove attributes from the object
Attribute Settings:	Modify the attributes settings (name, datatypes, mapping column, and so forth)
Java:	Generate Java files and optional methods
Validation:	Add or remove validation rules for the object
Publish:	Publish events to the entity object (you must press Apply to subscribe)
Subscribe:	Subscribe to events that are published
Properties:	Provide hints, UI formatting clues, notes to users, and so forth

Editing View Objects

To edit a View Object, double-click one of the View Objects, or right-click the View Object and choose Edit your View Object Name. A dialog box, shown in Figure 13-21, pops up.

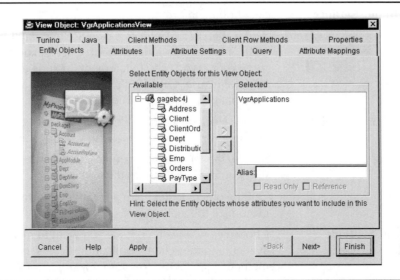

FIGURE 13-21. *View Objects Editing Wizard*

The View Object Wizard enables you to display the information of your choice. You can work with more tabs/attributes, compared to the entity object.

TIP
I recommend controlling the Attribute Settings, such as the Updateable (Always, While New, Never), in the View Object and not in the Entity Object. You might define many View Objects for an Entity object and you might want one View Object to update always and another View Object to update never. If you defined the Attribute Settings in the Entity Object to update never, you'll have conflicts.

The following table outlines the tabs and attributes available through the View Object Wizard:

Entity Objects	Select the entity objects whose attributes are needed in the view
Attributes	Select the actual attributes you want included in the view or also add new attributes

Attribute Settings	Set attribute information
Query	Add a WHERE or ORDER BY clause to default the SELECT statement or, if you're in Check Expert mode, write your own SELECT statement (include any WHERE clause, ORDER BY clause, or bind variable information in the query block)
Attribute Mappings	If you selected Expert mode, control which query attribute is mapped to which view-defined attribute
Tuning	Specify the fetch size parameter, which affects how the business logic fetches data
Java	Tell the object to generate a Java file you want to customize the view object
Client Methods	Choose view object methods you want to make available to thin-client applications. Adds the methods you choose to your view object implementation class and permits remote clients using the view object to call them
Client Row Methods	Choose row accessor methods you want available to client applications. Accessors are available for any row retrieved by the view object. Adds the methods you choose to your view object row implementation class and permits remote clients using the view object to access specific row instances, rather than require them to access the view object's row collection
Properties	Supply your own name/value pairs of business component metadata the framework can access at run time. Properties are often user-supplied data that provide hints, UI formatting clues, notes to users, and so forth. You can set custom properties on entity objects, view objects, domains, and application modules, as well as the individual attributes of an entity or a view object. Set labels for Table headers, Form Fields, and so forth (as demonstrated in Figure 13-22)

By mastering the BC4J, you will see the true value added to building Java-based applications. The implementation of Business Components gives you the time to focus on developing the core functionality of the application and not worry about the database transaction. Business Components provide the capability to add the

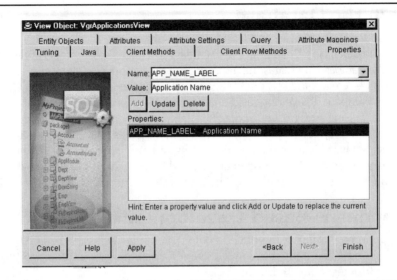

FIGURE 13-22. *Setting the default label for the APP_NAME attribute*

business logic from attribute validation, to joining tables, to everything in between in an efficient and timely manner.

Web Application Development

JDeveloper has features to help you build dynamic Web pages using either Java servlets or JSPs. Wizards can help create servlets or JSPs and also to test and debug them. The JSP Element Wizards provide even more functionality for JSPs. The JSP Wizard has an array of data Web Beans developed to minimize your efforts in building JSP applications. JDeveloper has wizards to help you build your custom Web Beans to be used in a JSP page. JDeveloper is JSP 1.1compliant and enables you to use data tags.

Java Client Application Development

JDeveloper has code-generating wizards and industry standard data-aware controls (DAC) for developing Java-based applications. DACs provide access to the database without writing any of the JDBC information. The data-aware controls can be added to a Java application using the drag-and-drop technique from a tool palette. These DACs are extremely powerful, yet easy to implement. The data-aware controls are implemented as JavaBeans and are easily extended. Because they're written as Java Beans, applications can be deployed in multitier environments without making modifications to the code.

Java in the Database

Java Stored Procedures, EJBs, and CORBA server objects are all objects that can be stored in the database. JDeveloper makes it easy to create these objects and deploy them in the database. It creates the appropriate SQL wrappers, determines dependencies, creates the JAR package, and performs the installation in an Oracle8i (or higher) database. JDeveloper also enables you to browse the Oracle database for Java objects. Using an Oracle8i or higher database, you can develop and deploy industry-standard EJBs. The JDeveloper EJB Wizard creates new Enterprise Beans or turns existing Java classes into Enterprise Beans and also generates the required EJB deployment descriptor, EJB Home interface, and Remote interface for you. JDeveloper assists you in creating and deploying any Java class as a server-side CORBA object.

Component-Based Development

JDeveloper provides a user interface to help develop Java classes. The GUI does everything from generating the source code for a new class, to adding, editing, or deleting attributes or methods from a class.

Now that I've shown you what JDeveloper can do, let me show you how to build a JSP application building on the Business Components we already created. Note, recommendations exist to save you some trouble when developing applications. First, develop and save a workspace. Second, add each new component as a New Project (that is, your business components should be a project and your JSP application should be its own project under the same workspace). This enables you to compile projects separately and to organize your application. Assuming you went through all the steps to create a project containing business components, it's now time to use the other feature JDeveloper provides. Now is the time to build your JSP applications (recall that JDeveloper can build many different components and applications, and JSP is only one piece to help you in learning the tool). I'll build on the Business Components project you created in the previous section "Building Business Components with JDeveloper."

Start by adding a new project under your workspace (File | New Project | A Project Containing a new.../ Business Component JSP application) and continue to follow wizard prompts.

NOTE
On Step 3 of 4 on the Business Components for JSP Application titled Application Template, choose Oracle to get the same look and feel as this example. The default template will lack the colors.

Now you should have been walked through two dialog interfaces. In your JDeveloper Navigator area, your JSP project should appear with all the necessary folders and structures underneath, as shown in the following illustration. Notice there's a separate folder for each table view that exists. If you expand the folder, you see a variety of JSP pages, ranging from views of the data, to edit, and insert forms for the data. After you go through the wizard to generate your JSP application, check its syntax and execute it by first Rebuilding your business components project, and then your JSP project (or you can Rebuild the entire workspace).

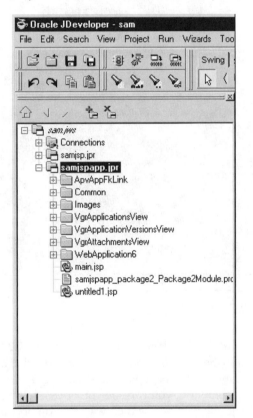

After you Rebuild the necessary projects, you're ready to run your application. Right-click main.jsp and select Run (this will run your JSP application from JDeveloper). A browser window should appear, as shown in Figure 13-23. You see all the views of the business components you created. If you had any master-detail relationships from the database, you will see master-detail relations. At this point, you have a complete working JSP application that enables the user to browse data in tables, edit data, insert data, query data, and delete data.

Select one of your business components views. I selected VgrApplicationsView URL. You'll see a navigator bar and tabs that enable the different actions to take

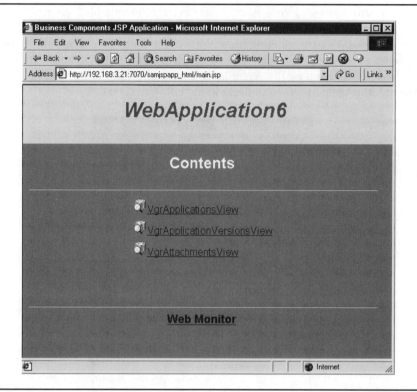

FIGURE 13-23. *JSP Application, Main.jsp*

place and to browse through the data, as shown in Figure 13-24. As you can see from the navigator bar in the window, you have action icons that take you to different rows, delete records, insert records, edit records, and query records. If you take the time to activate each button, you can see you have a full-fledged working JSP application that talks to the database, which was built on only a few clicks!

Now that you have the basics down for building applications using JDeveloper, here are some hints to show you how to build a JSP page from scratch using JDeveloper. After you highlight the samjspapp.jpr folder icon (or *node* as JDeveloper refers to it), go to the menu bar and select File | New. A dialog box should appear. You can see five tabs: Objects, Business Components, Web Objects, Beans, and Snippets. Under each tab, you see icons for all types of objects you can create in JDeveloper. Choose the Web Objects tab, select a JSP object, and click OK. This creates an untitled.jsp file under the selected project. Open this jsp file in JDeveloper. Right-click between <BODY></BODY> tags. A drop-down menu should appear. Select JSP Element and another dialog box appears, as shown in Figure 13-25.

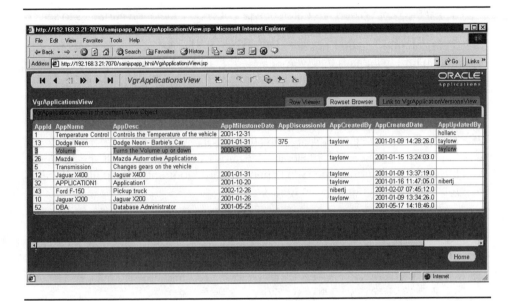

FIGURE 13-24. *JSP displaying the Applications Table with navigator bar and tabs*

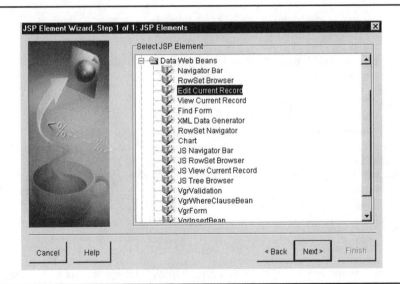

FIGURE 13-25. *JSP Element Wizard for selecting a pre-defined JSP element*

The JSP Element Wizard has different types of code generation attributes to select from: Data Tag Library, JSP Tags, Data Web Beans, Web Beans, and Themes. *Data Tag Library* enables the user to select JSP data tags. The *JSP tags* insert the correct information for the JSP tags that were selected. *Data Web Beans* are predefined Java beans that deal with accessing and viewing data (that is, viewing a table of data, viewing an entry form, and so forth). *Web Beans* are predefined JavaBeans that build nondata-related Web information (that is, toolbars, tables that don't access views, static tables, and so forth). *Themes* insert the code for style sheets. The JSP elements all insert code into your JSP application to eliminate the need to type in the unnecessary reusable code. In essence, the JSP Element Wizard is a code generator. If you continue with the code generation of the JSP Element Wizard, your untitled.jsp file will get the proper information inserted in to it.

```
<!-- Untitled.jsp -->
<%@ page contentType="text/html"%>
<HTML>
<HEAD>
<META HTTP-EQUIV="Content-Type" CONTENT="text/html">
<META NAME="GENERATOR" CONTENT="Oracle JDeveloper">
<TITLE>
Application RowSetBrowser
</TITLE>
</HEAD>
<BODY>
<jsp:useBean class="oracle.jbo.html.databeans.RowSetBrowser"
             id="rBr"  scope="request" >
<%
  rBr.setUseRoundedCorners(true);
  rBr.setShowCurrentRow(true);
  rBr.setVisibleRows(10);
  rBr.setAlternateColors(true);
  rBr.setShowRecordNumbers(true);
  rBr.setReleaseApplicationResources(false);
  rBr.setDisplayAttributes("AppName,AppDesc,AppMilestoneDate,AppCreatedBy");
  rBr.initialize(pageContext,
     "samjspapp_package2_Package2Module.VgrApplicationsView");
  rBr.render();
%>
</jsp:useBean>
</BODY>
</HTML>
```

Without typing anything, a JSP that can display a table/view as a Web page was built. The RowSetBrowser JavaBean class has other methods to permit more control over the displayed table. The development of a simple JSP demonstrates some of

JDeveloper's potential. All the wizards work similarly and you can develop, in a timely manner, any type of Java application using JDeveloper. The benefits of choosing JDeveloper over other Integrated Development Environments (IDEs) is Oracle's implementation of the BC4J. This added feature, along with the predefined JavaBeans, drastically reduces development time.

To discover the methods or more information on a particular class, select Help | Help Topics from the menu bar of JDeveloper, and a window will appear. On the left frame, select Contents | Reference folder, and a list of different reference types will be listed. Choose the appropriate reference. Another route is to select Search and type in the class or method you want. The difference between these two types of Help is that for the search, you must know what you're looking for. The other help lists all available classes and methods. The online help and documentation for JDeveloper is a great resource and helps developers reach the true potential of JDeveloper:

JDeveloper Tips and Tricks

As you learn JDeveloper, you'll find not everything works the way you want it to work. Most of the following tips and tricks refer to building JSP applications:

- Find the file jbohtmlsrc.zip (the source code for all the Web Beans JDeveloper contains), make a new folder, and unzip the file, maintaining the folder structure. The default location for this file is in the \Program Files\Oracle\JDeveloper 3.1\lib directory. Now that you have the source code of the JavaBeans, you can manipulate, extend, and fix any Bean that doesn't fit your requirements.

- jbohtml.zip—Find and unzip this file (this is the compiled class file of all the files in jbohtmlsrc). The default location for this file is in the same directory as the jbohtmlsrc.zip file. Now you have the class files, so when you make changes to the source code, the compiled code also gets changed.

- To point to these unzipped files from JDeveloper, right-click any project you created and select Properties | Libraries | Add | New. Now give a Library name and set the CLASSPATHs to point to the source and classes folders. To make sure you're viewing the correct JavaBean files, remove the JBO HTML Library from the list.

- One other potential headache is the rewriting of the webapp.zip file (this file is in JDeveloper3.2/redist folder). It controls the images, JavaScript, style sheets, and so forth—all the Web application functionality. I recommend you unzip this file to have more control over these elements and rename this file because JDeveloper will overwrite any changes you make to the webapp files.

- Creating a Web application with tabs might also cause problems if you put your tabs inside a Web page that has frames. The solution: if you unzipped the webapp.zip file, you can see a folder called webapp/jsp. Under the jsp folder, you can see two files: container_tabs.jsp and container_bottom.jsp. Open these files and replace any occurrence of top with parent.

PL2JAVA—Using PL/SQL in Java

The pl2java program generates Java wrapper classes for PL/SQL procedures and functions in PL/SQL packages. Like javac, pl2java is a part of *i*AS. After creating these classes, you can call the wrapper classes from your Java applications to invoke the PL/SQL program units. This method enables you both to implement database logic in PL/SQL, which ensures proper control of data in your databases, and to invoke existing PL/SQL code from Java applications.

Note, before you can run pl2java, you must install the DBMS_PACKAGE package in the SYS schema. The installation script dbpkins8.sql is in the $ORACLE_HOME/ows/cartx/jweb/sql directory.

You might notice pl2java isn't an executable as I thought it might be. On NT, pl2java is a command (cmd) file—on Windows 2000 pl2java is a batch (bat) file, and on Unix, it's a shell script. The command file can be found in the $ORACLE_HOME/ows/cartx/jweb/bin directory. You might want to add this directory to your path. The syntax to run pl2java is

```
pl2java username/password@connect-string plsql_package
```

After executing pl2java, you'll find a class file has been created for your package. For example, Assist.class was created after I executed the following statement (note the case of Assist because this is the case in which the class file will be created):

```
pl2java examples/examples@tcp-loopback Assist
```

Each of the procedures and functions in the Assist package can now be called from the Assist class file. You cannot call the PL/SQL packaged routine's class file directly from the browser—you need to call the class file from another Java program.

TIP
Remember, Java doesn't support default values like PL/SQL does.

The PL/SQL Definition—Ask Question

Now let's look at how you might call a procedure (or function) from another Java program. The following shows an example that calls a PL/SQL procedure from the Assist class. The Assist package contains a procedure with the following definition:

```
procedure ask_quest
(in_question      in     varchar2)
```

Calling the pl2java Class—AssistUser

The following code example calls the Assist package's ask_question procedure:

```java
// Input/output
import java.io.*;

// Oracle classes that deal with database session
import oracle.rdbms.*;

// Oracle classes that deal with PL/SQL data types
import oracle.plsql.*;

public class AssistUser {
  public static void main (String args []) throws SQLException {
    try {
      // Define ORACLE_HOME
      Session.setProperty("ORACLE_HOME", System.getProperty("oracleHome"));

      // Create a new database session and logon
      Session session = new Session();
      session.logon("examples", "examples", "tcp-loopback");

      // Instantiate Assist wrapper class:
      Assist assistMe = new Assist(session);

      // Declare question
      PStringBuffer myQuestion = new PStringBuffer(100);
      myQuestion.setValue("What is the color of money?");

      // Call the ask_question procedure
      assistMe.ask_quest(myQuestion);
    }
    catch (Exception e) {
       e.printStackTrace(System.out);
    }
  } /// main
} /// AssistUser
```

Recommended Reading

- *Java in a Nutshell: A Desktop Quick Reference, Third Edition,* by David Flanagan (O'Reilly, 1999)

- *Oracle8i Java Component Programming with EJB, CORBA, and JSP,* by Nirva Morisseau-Leroy, Martin K. Solomon, and Julie Basu (Osborne/McGraw-Hill, 2000)

- *Professional JSP, Second Edition,* by Simon Brown et al. (Wrox Press, 2001)

- "SQL Embedded in Java Part 1 Starting Out," by Ekkehard Rohwedder. *Java Developers Journal,* May 2000 Volume 5, Issue 5: 34–40

- *Developing Java Servlets,* by James Goodwill (Sams, 2001)

- *Hans's Top Ten JSP Tips,* by Hans Bergsten

- *Thinking in Java,* by Bruce Eckel (Prentice Hall PTR, 2000)

- "Oracle Java Roadmap: Java Stored Procedures" (Oracle white papers/reference)

- "Oracle Java Roadmap: Business Components for Java" (Oracle white papers/reference)

- "Oracle Java Roadmap: JavaServer Pages" (Oracle white papers/reference)

- "Oracle SQLJ Developers Guide and Reference" (Oracle white papers/reference)

- *Oracle JavaServer Pages Developer's Guide and Reference Release 8.1.7*

- "Servlets and JavaServer Pages" (Oracle white papers/reference)

Summary

PL/SQL was the primary development language of OAS. The majority of OAS applications used PL/SQL as their programming language of choice. Will that also be true for *i*AS? Does Java have a future? Will the standards continue to change? Will 4GL tools soon be generating Java code? Only time will tell. My prediction is JDeveloper will continue to morph itself into Oracle's primary 4GL development tool—generating Java source code. The Java standards will be less important as time passes. Do you worry about the TCP/IP standard and how its evolving today? Not likely. For the first time in the history of my programming career, I found a language that provides a true and remarkable advantage over other programming languages. Java can make your development faster. Java itself continues to get faster at execution. I believe server-side Java is the technology of today. Take the time to learn Java, train your programming staff, and begin maximizing your productivity.

CHAPTER
14

PL/SQL Module—
mod_plsql

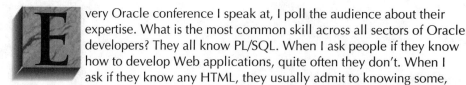very Oracle conference I speak at, I poll the audience about their expertise. What is the most common skill across all sectors of Oracle developers? They all know PL/SQL. When I ask people if they know how to develop Web applications, quite often they don't. When I ask if they know any HTML, they usually admit to knowing some, but not a lot. I then tell them they actually do know how to develop Web applications. Believing this is difficult for them at first, but when I walk them through a little exercise to develop a Web page, they get excited. You can quickly see the fire in their eyes.

If the previous scenario describes you, rest assured, you too can develop Web applications using the *i*AS PL/SQL module (mod_plsql)—you just didn't know it. The first part of this chapter provides a little exercise I go through with my students. This can help you understand how to move from knowing PL/SQL and HTML into knowing how to use the PL/SQL module to develop Web applications. The next section of this chapter talks about *i*AS's new method of developing Web applications using PL/SQL—PL/SQL Server Page (PSP). PSP provides a powerful solution for developing Web applications using PL/SQL. This chapter assumes you know both HTML and PL/SQL (refer to Chapter 6 for further information about HTML). I recommend *Oracle PL/SQL Tips and Techniques,* by Joe Trezzo (Osborne/McGraw-Hill, 1999) as an excellent reference on PL/SQL.

This chapter doesn't cover each of the Toolkit commands. My first book, *Oracle Application Server Web Toolkit Reference* (Osborne/McGraw-Hill, 1998), covers the Toolkit in detail.

In this chapter, you learn about the following topics:

- Going from PL/SQL and HTML to Web Development

- Web Toolkit Installation

- Passing Parameters to Your PL/SQL Procedures

- PL/SQL Server Pages (PSPs)

- Retrieving CGI Environment Variables

- Maintaining Source Code History

- Storing Cookies

- Referring to Pseudocolumns

- Calculating Time to the Hundredth of a Second

- Making External Calls from PL/SQL

- Wrapping or Securing Your Procedures from Source Viewing

- Redirecting Users to Another URL

- Querying Multiple Selects from List Box

- Wrapping Text Without Using <PRE>

- Clearing the Buffer

- Debugging PL/SQL

- Deauthenticating Users

- Disappearing Sessions

- Encrypting Key Information

- Ordering Data Based on User Requests

- Editing PL/SQL Code

- Catching the Domain Name from an IP

- Missing Radio Buttons

- Overdefining Actions

- Converting Numbers to Words—Literally

- Getting Information About Your Users

- Understanding Why htp.linkrel Is Now Useful

- PL/SQL Optimization

Going from PL/SQL and HTML to Web Development

This section focuses on what it takes to go from knowing a little HTML and PL/SQL to turning that knowledge into Web development knowledge.

Understanding the PL/SQL Web Toolkit

Oracle *i*AS comes with a group of PL/SQL packages called the *PL/SQL Web Toolkit*. As of version 8.1.7 of the Oracle RDBMS, the Toolkit is included as part of the built-in packages. This Toolkit generates HTML and sends it to the user's browser. For almost every HTML command, there's a corresponding Toolkit command. By using the Toolkit, you can generate Web pages. You can also pull data stored in an Oracle database and display that information in your Web page. Using PL/SQL logic, you can dynamically calculate the contents of the Web pages. The Toolkit PL/SQL packages enable you to create your own customized PL/SQL program units (packages and procedures) to access and process the Oracle data you want to place on the Web. From within your customized program units, you can call the PL/SQL Web Toolkit packaged procedures and functions to create the HTML (and any other client-side code such as JavaScript) comprising your Web page. The procedures you write are stored in the database, just as with other PL/SQL procedures.

While the PL/SQL Web Toolkit minimizes your need to know HTML syntax, you're required to have a working knowledge of HTML. For example, you need to understand hyperlinks and know they're created with the anchor tag, but you won't need to know the exact sequence of characters needed to generate an HTML anchor tag. You should also know the constructs of an HTML table because this can save you a lot of time when you display your pages. By using the Web Toolkit, you needn't hardcode the exact HTML syntax for the HTML tags. You do, however, need to know the parameters to pass the Toolkit's procedures and functions. Using PSPs and a GUI HTML editor, you needn't know the exact HTML syntax (because the editor generates the HTML for you), but you do need a good working knowledge of HTML and its capabilities.

The main package that generates HTML to send to the browser is HyperText Procedures (HTP). A corresponding package—HyperText Functions (HTF)—contains functions generating HTML as their character output. Most HTML tags have matching HTP and HTF procedures that generate the HTML tags. For example, the HTML <TITLE> tag's matching HTP procedure is called "title." The title procedure is referenced as htp.title. There is one input parameter to the htp.title procedure, which is ctitle. The letter *c* stands for character; this is a varchar2 input parameter. The word "title" is the actual title of the HTML document. The htp.title syntax is as follows:

```
htp.title('My First Page Title');
```

This syntax generates the following HTML code and sends it to the browser:

```
<TITLE>My First Page Title</TITLE>
```

Calling the htf.title function returns the HTML code as a varchar2 variable. You can store that value in a PL/SQL variable, for example:

```
title := htf.title('My First Page Title');
```

You can also nest the call to the HTF functions within an HTP procedure. Let's build an example. First, use the following code to print an HTML header (Level 1):

```
htp.header(1, 'My First HTML Header - Level 1');
```

This line of syntax generates the following output:

```
<H1>My First HTML Header - Level 1</H1>
```

To center the heading in the browser, nest the call to the heading procedure inside the center procedure. You cannot nest a *procedure* in a procedure, but you can nest a *function* inside a procedure. To center the heading, use the following syntax:

```
htp.center(htf.header(1, 'My First HTML Header - Level 1'));
```

This syntax generates the following output:

```
<CENTER><H1>My First HTML Header - Level 1</H1></CENTER>
```

A catchall procedure called *print* in the HTP package (for example, htp.print) sends whatever is placed inside the quotation marks back to the browser; for example:

```
htp.print ('<span class=major>This is a major division</span>');
```

This PL/SQL command sends the following text to the browser:

```
<span class=major>This is a major division</span>
```

Although I wouldn't recommend bypassing all the HTP and HTF, some developers choose to do so. In my opinion, the code becomes fragmented and difficult to read because all the information is concatenated together. Additionally, you must know the specific HTML syntax to embed within your PL/SQL code. You must also run the PL/SQL code through a browser to verify the HTML is generated properly, for example, to make certain you didn't forget a space or another character. Consider the future compatibility of HTML, XML, or whatever new standards come out. If you embedded HTML in htp.print statements, you need to go back and revisit your code when new standards are published. If you use the Toolkit, as the Toolkit is upgraded, you can take advantage of new HTML versions with little or no effort, thereby eliminating the need to be intimately familiar with Web technology and syntax. Some programmers consider the choice as a personal preference. Whatever path you choose, picking a standard and adhering to it is important. Using PSP also eliminates this issue because PSP uses HTML code in its native form.

If you find a specific HTML tag isn't in the Toolkit, you can build your own procedure using the htp.print tag. This tag enables you to build the HTML command that will be sent back to the browser. For example, a span procedure isn't in HTP or HTF. Although you can modify the HTP and HTF packages to add the new procedures and functions, as the following code illustrates, I recommend creating your own version of the HTP and HTF extensions to ease future *i*AS upgrades.

This code makes changes to the HTP package—the HTP procedures use the print procedure (*p*) to call the embedded HTF function:

```
procedure spanOpen (cclass varchar2)
is
begin
  p(htf.spanOpen(cclass));
end;

procedure spanClose
is
begin
  p(htf.spanClose);
end;
```

Changes to the HTF package—the functions use the ifnotnull function, similar to a DECODE statement, to determine if the value is NULL. If the value isn't NULL, additional HTML attributes are included. Otherwise, the attributes aren't included, as the following example shows:

```
function spanOpen (cclass varchar2)
returns varchar2
is
begin
  return ('<span'||
          ifnotnull(cclass,' class="'||cclass||'"')||
          '>');
end;

function spanClose
returns varchar2
is
begin
  return ('</span>');
end;
```

You also need to modify the package specifications to include the new procedures and functions.

TIP
*Oracle used to provide a free quick reference guide for the PL/SQL Web Toolkit along with each copy of Oracle Application Server (OAS), but because most software is now distributed in a mass CD kit, the quick reference guide is no longer free. If you want to purchase copies of the quick reference guide, the part number is A60119-02. TUSC (**http://www.tusc. com**) also provides a Web Toolkit poster free—you only pay for the shipping.*

You might wonder if your application will be faster if you use the Toolkit commands or the htp.print command for all your code. If you look at the underlying Toolkit, you'll find calls to the htp.print command, so using the htp.print directly would be faster. However, we're talking about milliseconds here, so this is an issue of personal preference.

Using Your HTML Knowledge

You might wonder if there's an easier alternative to using the Toolkit. For example, let's assume you already created the following HTML file using a GUI HTML editor, such as FrontPage or Dreamweaver:

```
<html>
<head>
<title>Employee List</title>
</head>
<body bgcolor="#FFFFFF">
<p>Here is a list of our employees:</p>
<table border="1" width="75%">
  <tr>
    <th>Employee Name</th>
    <th>Manager's Name</th>
    <th>Salary</th>
  </tr>
  <tr>
    <td>ename</td>
    <td>mgrname</td>
    <td>sal</td>
  </tr>
</table>
```

```
<p>Total salary for all employees $totsal</p>
</body>
</html>
```

This HTML appears identical in the browser to Figure 14-1.

In this HTML file, an HTML table containing employee information and a total salary figure is included at the end of the page. A list of employees is typically not static information, so this information needs to be dynamically pulled from the database. Notice I included column names from the emp table, which are part of the demonstration tables provided by Oracle in the scott/tiger schema.

Using WebAlchemy

WebAlchemy is a GUI tool written in Microsoft Visual C++ to reverse-engineer HTML pages to PL/SQL procedures containing HTP and HTF commands. An Oracle consultant in Australia created WebAlchemy and it's free from your Oracle representative (and the TUSC site). WebAlchemy converts HTML into PL/SQL Toolkit code. Figure 14-2 shows the WebAlchemy GUI interface after opening the preceding HTML example. By clicking the Generate PL/SQL icon (the beaker), WebAlchemy generates the code in the following subsection.

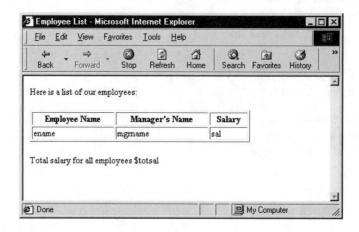

FIGURE 14-1.   *Static Employee List*

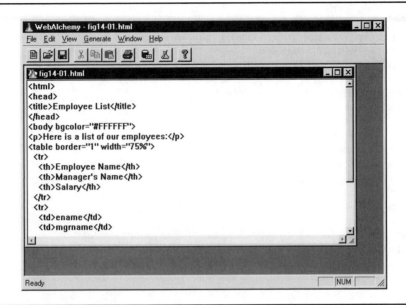

FIGURE 14-2. *WebAlchemy at work*

Performing Magic

By clicking the Generate PL/SQL icon, WebAlchemy generates the following
PL/SQL code. Now, that is magic!

```
-------------------------------------------------------
--
--  fig14_01
--  ========
--
--  Author: Bradley D. Brown
--  Date:    03 September 2001
--
--  Copyright (C) Oracle Services
--
-------------------------------------------------------
CREATE OR REPLACE PROCEDURE fig14_01 AS
BEGIN
    htp.htmlOpen;
    htp.headOpen;
    htp.title( 'Employee List');
    htp.headClose;
```

```
    htp.bodyOpen( cattributes => ' bgcolor="#FFFFFF"' );
    htp.para;
    htp.print( 'Here is a list of our employees:' );
    htp.tableOpen( cattributes => ' border="1" width="75%"' );
    htp.tableRowOpen;
    htp.tableHeader( 'Employee Name' );
    htp.tableHeader( 'Manager''s Name' );
    htp.tableHeader( 'Salary' );
    htp.tableRowClose;
    htp.tableRowOpen;
    htp.tableData( 'ename' );
    htp.tableData( 'mgrname' );
    htp.tableData( 'sal' );
    htp.tableRowClose;
    htp.tableClose;
    htp.para;
    htp.print( 'Total salary for all employees $totsal' );
    htp.bodyClose;
    htp.htmlClose;
END;
/
```

Adding Your PL/SQL Logic

You can modify the PL/SQL code in the previous example to select data from the
database using cursors and to extract individual records from the database using a
for loop. You can then change the hardcoded text to field names from your cursors.
The following code sample highlights the changed code:

```
CREATE OR REPLACE PROCEDURE fig14_01 AS
    cursor emp_cur is
    select a.ename, b.ename mgrname, a.sal
      from emp a, emp b
     where a.mgr = b.empno(+);
    tot_sal number(10,2) := 0;
BEGIN
    htp.htmlOpen;
    htp.headOpen;
    htp.title( 'Employee List' );
    htp.headClose;
    htp.bodyOpen( cattributes => ' bgcolor="#FFFFFF"' );
    htp.para;
    htp.print( 'Here is a list of our employees:' );
    htp.tableOpen( cattributes => ' border="1" width="75%"' );
    htp.tableRowOpen;
    htp.tableHeader( 'Employee Name' );
    htp.tableHeader( 'Manager''s Name' );
    htp.tableHeader( 'Salary' );
    htp.tableRowClose;
```

```
    for emp_rec in emp_cur loop
        htp.tableRowOpen;
        htp.tableData(emp_rec.ename);
        htp.tableData(emp_rec.mgrname);
        htp.tableData(to_char(emp_rec.sal,'999,999,999.99'),'RIGHT');
        htp.tableRowClose;
tot_sal := tot_sal + emp_rec.sal;
end loop;
    htp.tableClose;
    htp.para;
    htp.print( 'Total salary for all employees $'
               ||to_char(tot_sal,'999,999,999.99'));
    htp.bodyClose;
    htp.htmlClose;
END;
/
```

The bold text represents the changed code. As you can see, the changes in the procedure were minimal. Next you must compile this procedure in a database schema (for example, the examples schema).

Calling Your Web Procedure

At the completion of the preceding steps, the procedure is ready to be called from the browser. After establishing the DAD, the procedure can be executed. For example, if your host name is tuscbdb, your virtual path to the PL/SQL module is pls/ (the default) and your DAD name is examples. See Chapter 3 for more information about creating and configuring the examples DAD. Your URL would be as follows:

http://tuscbdb/pls/examples/fig14_01

That's it! By calling this URL, your first dynamically created PL/SQL procedure using the PL/SQL Web Toolkit appears, as illustrated in Figure 14-3.

The PL/SQL module calls stored procedures and passes the appropriate values to the stored procedure. The PL/SQL code facilitates the generation of HTML, which is sent back to the browser. Having your code executed within the database has performance, security, and portability benefits. These benefits are the main reasons you should design your dynamically generated Web pages to produce URLs that call PL/SQL procedures in response to user actions.

Web Toolkit Installation

As of version 8.1.7 of the RDBMS, the PL/SQL Web Toolkit is part of the standard built-in packages that come with the database, such as dbms_output, dbms_job, and the like. The Toolkit can be found in the SYS schema. The Toolkit contains packages

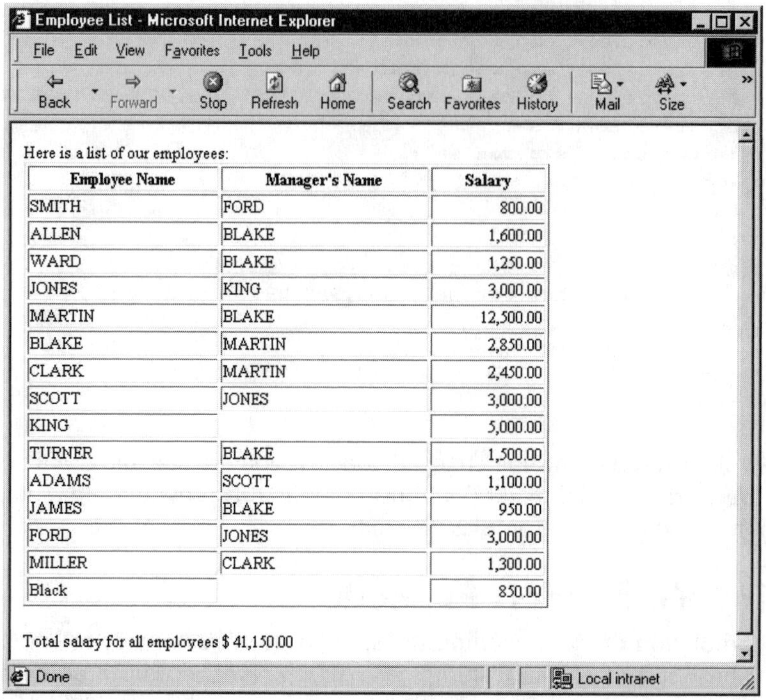

Employee Name	Manager's Name	Salary
SMITH	FORD	800.00
ALLEN	BLAKE	1,600.00
WARD	BLAKE	1,250.00
JONES	KING	3,000.00
MARTIN	BLAKE	12,500.00
BLAKE	MARTIN	2,850.00
CLARK	MARTIN	2,450.00
SCOTT	JONES	3,000.00
KING		5,000.00
TURNER	BLAKE	1,500.00
ADAMS	SCOTT	1,100.00
JAMES	BLAKE	950.00
FORD	JONES	3,000.00
MILLER	CLARK	1,300.00
Black		850.00

FIGURE 14-3. *Output from Fig14_01 example procedure*

such as HTP, HTF, OWA_UTIL, OWA_COOKIE, and more packages. For databases prior to 8.1.7, you must run the owaload.sql script in the SYS schema.

Passing Parameters to Your PL SQL Procedures

Passing parameters to a PL/SQL procedure is easier than it might first appear. If you know how HTML forms work, then you'll understand the GET and POST methods. Any anchor (or hyperlink) implicitly uses the GET method of sending information to a Web server. Only HTML forms use the POST method; however, for every HTML form you create, you can choose the GET or POST method. To understand parameter passing, you must first understand a standard URL and its composition. Let's break down the following URL to get a better understanding of this information:

`http://host:port_no/virtual_path/program?param1=value1&param2=value2`

This URL can be broken down into the following components:

- **http://**   Indicates that we wish to use the Hypertext Transfer Protocol. https:// indicates to use HTTP with secure sockets (SSL), as discussed in Chapter 12.

- **host**   The host name, this is also known as the server name

- **port_no**   The number of the TCP/IP port the Web Listener is on. If the port is 80 (for http) or 443 (for https), it needn't be specified in the URL.

- **virtual_path**   The virtual path of the program (for example, a PL/SQL module and DAD)

- **program**   The name of the program (or, for this chapter, a procedure name)

- **param1** and **param2**   The names of the parameters to pass

- **value1** and **value2**   Respective values for param1 and param2

To be more specific, look at the following URL, which is used to call a procedure to log in and pass a user name (brad) and password (brown) to the procedure (login):

`http://tuscbdb/pls/examples/login?username=brad&password=brown`

When using the GET method, the parameters of an HTML form show up on the address line in the browser (unless the form is in a frame but, by viewing the properties for the frame, the user can view the full URL). With sensitive data, such as the user name and password, therefore, I suggest you use the POST method. The POST method sends the data through standard input, so the information isn't displayed in the address line or in the URL. A user cannot bookmark a POSTed form's data because the information doesn't appear in the URL. But, because GET passes the parameter as a part of the URL, users could bookmark those pages. This can be an important security consideration.

TIP
Using the GET method builds a visible URL, so it can be useful for testing and debugging.

In the previous example, the PL/SQL procedure's input variables must match the name of the preceding variables used exactly, specifically, username and password, as the following syntax illustrates.

```
create or replace procedure login
(username varchar2,
 password varchar2)
is
begin
…code here…
end;
```

If the information wasn't passed through an anchor but, instead, used an HTML form using the POST method, the HTML would appear as follows:

```
<FORM ACTION="http://tuscbdb/pls/examples/login" METHOD=POST>
Enter Username: <INPUT TYPE=TEXT NAME=USERNAME><BR>
Enter Password: <INPUT TYPE=PASSWORD NAME=PASSWORD><BR>
<INPUT TYPE=SUBMIT>
</FORM>
```

The attribute METHOD can be GET or POST.

■ **GET method**   Through the QUERY_STRING environment variable; if the browser uses the GET method, *i*AS passes the parameters to the PL/SQL module in this environment variable.

■ **POST method**   Through standard input (STDIN); if the POST method is used, *i*AS passes the parameters to the PL/SQL Agent using standard input.

TIP
HTML's default form method is GET, whereas the PL/SQL Web Toolkit's default method is POST.

To create the above HTML form dynamically using PL/SQL code, your code would look identical to the following:

```
htp.formOpen( curl => 'http://tuscbdb/pls/examples/login',
              cmethod => 'POST');
htp.print( 'Enter Username: ' );
htp.formText( cname => 'USERNAME');
htp.br;
htp.print( 'Enter Password: ' );
htp.formPassword( cname => 'PASSWORD');
htp.br;
htp.formSubmit;
htp.formClose;
```

TIP
Some Web Listeners experience difficulty and crash when URLs exceed roughly 1,000 characters—not iAS, but some operating systems also restrict this. When creating HTML forms to accept a large number of fields, remember that when using the GET method, the URL is composed of the host name, virtual path, program name, each parameter name, and the corresponding parameter values. This can quickly lead to URLs over 1,000 characters in length. For this reason, unless you specifically need to use the GET method, we recommend using the POST method for passing parameters.

Whether your HTML form uses the GET or POST method doesn't matter to your PL/SQL procedure because the PL/SQL module handles the translation from the QUERY_STRING or standard input automatically. The PL/SQL procedure is unaware of the method used to pass the parameters from *i*AS to the PL/SQL module. This is an important feature of the Oracle PL/SQL module because the PL/SQL programmer needn't to know whether GET or POST is used and the programmer needn't be concerned with parsing either the QUERY_STRING environment variable or standard input. The PL/SQL programmer can concentrate on what he or she knows best—developing the logic to extract data from the Oracle database based on previously parsed parameters passed by the Oracle PL/SQL module.

PL/SQL Server Pages (PSPs)

*i*AS provides the capability to implement PL/SQL Server Pages or PSPs. This is a powerful new feature available for developers. This feature enables you to separate the presentation layer (site design) from the application (code development) layer. This section provides a step-by-step how-to guide for developing PSPs and a PSP development environment.

PSPs are database procedures that run on the database server to produce dynamic content in your Web applications. PSPs use mod_plsql to generate their output. PL/SQL procedures and packaged database procedures are executed to generate HTML. These procedures can execute SQL queries to extract data from any Oracle database. The beauty of PSPs over the straight PL/SQL packaging method is this: PSPs provide a friendlier programming interface. PSPs are simply HTML code with PL/SQL code embedded in them, so PSPs can be edited with a GUI HTML tool such as FrontPage, Dreamweaver, and the like. This helps separate the presentation layer from the business component layer and also aids in separation of duties for your IT group. This section discusses

- When to use PSPs
- What PSPs are
- Loading PSPs into the Database
- Sample PSP
- Server Page Technologies
- Script tags
- Naming the procedure
- Passing Variables
- Declarations

When to Use PSPs

HTML developers prefer using PSPs to writing PL/SQL code. Oracle says if you already have applications using the PL/SQL Web Toolkit to keep using them that way and, if you have existing HTML files you want to make dynamic, use PSPs. What about your new development, from scratch? What if a tool existed that could enable you to convert your existing PL/SQL code into PSPs? This tool could be called UnWebAlchemy. WebAlchemy is a tool Oracle provides to convert HTML into PL/SQL Toolkit code. The problem with HTML code that's run through WebAlchemy is, once this conversion is done, you can no longer edit the HTML in a GUI editor. You're stuck editing PL/SQL code. So what if you could unconvert your code? The good news is you can! TUSC has developed UnWebAlchemy and published it for free downloads from our Web site. You can find this tool in the Documents section of the site.

UnWebAlchemy converts procedures to PSPs. This tool was written with JavaServer Pages. So contrary to Oracle's documentation, my recommendation is you use PSP for all PL/SQL-based development.

Dynamic Web code development falls into three categories. Each of these categories is outlined here and includes the downside to using each category:

- **Category 1** Generating HTML from code (such as PL/SQL, Perl, or Java). The problem with this category is this: when the HTML look and feel is spread across many procedures, it's hard to separate developer roles (User Interface (UI) from the coder), and you end up with verbose, hard-to-read code. Because the HTML is encoded, you can't edit or fix it easily. Web programmers must painstakingly incorporate simple layout changes made by graphic designers back into the code. Many versions and variations of the visual design eventually creep in. Code often isn't reusable and is too tightly integrated with the UI. These difficulties lead to poor UIs and an early lock-in of the UI.

- **Category 2**   Tools that generate HTML or code from specifications (such as Oracle Designer or Oracle Portal). The problem with this category is these tools create inflexible page layouts, making it hard to make precise adjustments. The tools are difficult to master and involve many "tricks of the trade." The code is inaccessible and the end product can be difficult to export and reuse.

- **Category 3**   Tools that let you place code within the HTML, such as all server page technologies like ASP (Active Server Pages), JSP (Java Server Pages) and PSP (PL/SQL Server Pages). The problem with tools in this category is the application look and feel can be spread across many pages, but you can solve this with cascading style sheets, as discussed in Chapter 6. Managing ongoing development is hard because page design and application logic coding must be done serially. Code within the page often isn't reusable, but using database packages and procedures to modularize code can eliminate this problem.

TIP

The loadpsp command turns the HTML into htp.prn statements. Going back to a previous discussion, using htp.print instead of the PL/SQL Web Toolkit is faster. In addition, PSPs end up bundling multiple HTML statements into one htp.prn statement. Therefore, PSPs will be more efficient (faster) than your Toolkit code. Again, we're talking about milliseconds.

What PL/SQL Server Pages Are

PSPs are similar to, but better than, Dynamic Pages in WebDB. Previously, we often deployed a similar concept by using WebAlchemy to convert HTML to PL/SQL code. As previously mentioned, that route didn't provide a backdoor for editing. When I first heard about PSPs, I was concerned about their efficiency. Why? I was concerned because most Server Pages are inefficient and the reason is that most Server Page technologies are neither compiled nor cacheable. Well, Oracle came through on this one. PSPs provide the best of both worlds. You can edit the PSP code in an HTML editor but, better yet, the code is stored as compiled PL/SQL code! This means it's cached in the database. As discussed in Chapter 19, Oracle9*i* Application Server Web Cache will cache dynamic Web pages, too! PSPs are fast and powerful stuff.

Loading PSPs into the Database

To load a PSP file into the database, which is loaded as a stored procedure, use the loadpsp program from an operating system prompt. Each PSP file corresponds to one stored procedure in the database. The pages are compiled and loaded into the database in one step.

The syntax for loadpsp is as follows:

```
loadpsp [-replace] -user login [<page1> <page2> ...]
```

This is an example that loads a PSP file, called mypsp.psp, from the file system into the examples schema of the database:

```
loadpsp -replace -user examples/examples@tuscbdb mypsp.psp
```

You can load multiple PSPs at once. Oddly enough, PSP files cannot have an extension other than PSP, and you cannot leave off the .psp extension from the loadpsp command.

TIP
You cannot include the directory path to the PSP file in the loadpsp command.

Sample PSP

Consider the following sample PSP file:

```
<%@ plsql parameter='minsal' type='number' default='0' %>
<%@ plsql parameter='maxsal' type='number' default='99999' %>
<%! cursor emp_cur(minsal emp.sal%type, maxsal emp.sal%type) is
          select * from emp
                    where sal between minsal and maxsal; %>
<html>
<head>
<title>My First PSP</title>
</head>

<body>
<h1>Employee List</h1>
<table border=1>
<tr><th>Name</th>
```

```
<th>Salary</th></tr>
<% for emp_rec in emp_cur(minsal, maxsal) loop %>
<tr><td><%= emp_rec.ename %></td>
<td><%= emp_rec.sal %></td></tr>
<% end loop; %>
</table>
</body>
</html>
```

This PSP file accepts two parameters (minsal and maxsal) that have default values associated with them (0 and 99999, respectively). The PSP extracts the employee name and salary based on the salary range provided, as shown in Figure 14-4.

Server Page Technologies

You might wonder what other server page technologies exist and if PL/SQL Server Pages follow the server page standards. All server page technologies look like

FIGURE 14-4. *Sample PSP*

standard HTML and employ a standard scriptlet tag (<% language code here %>) to include a scripting or programming language that generates the dynamic content. OAS uses a server page technology called LiveHTML and its scripting language is Perl. PHP is an open-source server page technology that uses a Perl-like language as its scripting language, so LiveHTML has been replaced by PHP in *i*AS. However, PHP isn't officially supported by Oracle with *i*AS. ASP is Microsoft's server page technology (supported by its IIS Web Server). ASP uses Visual Basic as its scripting language and, obviously, JSP uses Java as its scripting language.

Standard Scriptlet Tag

All scripting languages use the same standard scriptlet tag, which begins with a less-than symbol followed by a percent sign (<%) and ends with the opposite (%>). The code goes inside the script tag. In the case of PSPs, the code can be any valid PL/SQL statement. In other words, the code can be a specific PL/SQL statement or it could call any PL/SQL package, procedure, and so forth. You can also intersperse PL/SQL and HTML in your PSP file.

The syntax for the scriptlet tag is as follows:

```
<% PL/SQL code goes here %>
```

An example of a scriptlet tag that calls a procedure called *myHeader* follows:

```
<% myHeader; %>
```

Special Script Tags for PSP

A number of special scripting tags (called *Directives*) are supported by PSP. Actually, most server page technologies support directives. In other words, although the underlying language is different, they all follow similar standards. The following discusses these special script tags:

- Page Directive
- Procedure Directive
- Parameter Directive
- Declaration Directive
- Print Directive
- Include File Directive

Page Directive

Use the *page directive* to specify the characteristics of the PSP. Page directive is used to indicate the scripting language (because it's a PSP, the default is PL/SQL), the type of information being produced (that is, MIME type), and the exception PSP file.

The syntax of the page directive is as follows:

```
<%@ page [language="PL/SQL"]
        [contentType="content type string"]
        [errorPage="file.psp"] %>
```

Important to note is that directive attributes (for example, contentType and errorPage) are case-sensitive. The default contentType is text/html. Other content types include text/html (the default, text/plain, image/jpeg, application/pdf, application/msword, application/excel, application/vnd.ms-powerpoint, application/rtf, and so forth.

The following is an example of the page directive:

```
<%@ page language="PL/SQL" contextType="text/html" errorPage="errors.psp" %>
```

Use the following page directive to open the dynamically generated page in Microsoft Excel:

```
<%@ page contentType="application/vnd.ms-excel" %>
```

Procedure Directive

When you load a PSP file, by default, the name of the procedure is the same as the PSP file name (without the .psp extension, of course). If you want to name the database procedure that's created, use the procedure directive.

The syntax of the procedure directive is as follows:

```
<%@ plsql procedure="procedure name" %>
```

The following is an example of the procedure directive:

```
<%@ plsql procedure="my_header" %>
```

In this example, the stored database procedure is given the name my_header.

TIP
Unfortunately, you cannot package your procedures, so you must move them manually if you want to include them in a database package.

Parameter Directive

Use the parameter directive to define the parameters to be passed into the procedures. The *parameter directive* specifies the name of the parameter, the datatype, and the default value. If the type attribute isn't specified, the parameter defaults to a datatype of varchar2. You must specify a default value for all your parameters. The parameters you define can be passed to the procedure by a GET or POST request method. The attributes values must be placed inside double quotes. Within the double quotes, text values must be placed within single quotes.

The syntax for the parameter directive is as follows:

```
<%@ plsql parameter="parameter_name" [type="PL/SQL datatype"]
        [default="'value'"] %>
```

The following is an example of the parameter directive:

```
<%@ plsql parameter="minsal" type="varchar2" default="0" %>
```

Declaration Directive

Use the declaration directive to define variables and cursors to be used in your PL/SQL code. The delimiters for the declaration directive are <%! %>. Follow the standard PL/SQL declaration syntax within the delimiters. You needn't use the DECLARE keyword.

The syntax for the declaration directive is as follows:

```
<%! PL/SQL declaration;
  [ PL/SQL declaration; ] ... %>
```

The following is an example of the declaration directive:

```
<%! cursor emp_cur(minsal emp.sal%type, maxsal emp.sal%type) is
        select * from emp
                    where sal between minsal and maxsal;
    nbt_name varchar2(100) := 'BRAD'; %>
```

Remember the semicolon at the end of the declaration. You can specify each variable on a line of its own or you can enclose all of them within the one set of delimiters, as shown in the following. All variable declarations are merged into a single block when the PSP file is loaded into a stored procedure using loadpsp.

Expression Directive

Use the htp.print("Text to print") command to print text from PL/SQL. The command looks like this in PSP code:

```
<% htp.print('Text to Print');
   htp.print( emp_rec.ename ); %>
```

The expression directive enables you to print from any scripting language without using the specific print command for the language, using an equal sign (=) instead, as the following shows. The content between the delimiters <%= %> is processed by the htp.prn packaged procedure (htp.prn is similar to htp.print). Any leading or trailing white space is trimmed. Any literal strings (that is, text) require you to use single quotes. You can also use concatenation, as you would in PL/SQL (two pipes (||) for concatenation). A semicolon isn't used at the end of the print variables.

The syntax for the expression directive is as follows:

```
<%= variable_to_print %>
```

The following are examples of the expression directive:

```
<%= emp_rec.ename %>
<%= 'The employee name is '||emp_rec.ename %>
```

Include File Directive

Server page technologies enable you to include other files into a script file, letting you easily reference libraries of code, such as a toolbar, a page footer, and the like. The *include directive* specifies the file name to be included at a specific point in the PSP file. This file can have any extension except .psp. The files you include can contain HTML, PSP script elements, or a combination of both. The file inclusion occurs at the time the PSP file is loaded into the database with loadpsp. Substitutions aren't like they are in Java (that is, no inheritance exists). In other words, substitutions are performed once (at the time of creation/loading), not when the page is served by *i*AS. This means changes to the included file after the PSP page was loaded aren't reflected when the stored procedure is run. All included files must be specified at the time the loadpsp command is executed.

The syntax for the include directive is as follows:

```
<%@ include file="path name" %>
```

The following is an example of the include directive:

```
<%@ include file="my_toolbar.html" %>
```

If you want to call PL/SQL procedures, this might be an easier approach than using include files. Changes to the called PL/SQL code will, in fact, be reflected at the time of serving. To call a PL/SQL procedure in a PSP, the syntax is as follows:

```
<% procedure_to_call; %>
```

Special Characters

PSP uses double quotes to delimit data. PL/SQL uses a single quote to indicate literal or text data, so a text literal must be surrounded by both double and single quotes. For example, the following is a text literal default value:

```
<%@ plsql parameter="in_ename" default="'Bradley Brown'" %>
```

As you can see, the value for the default attribute needs to be double quoted for PSP and because it will be a PL/SQL string (or varchar2), the variable must also be single quoted.

Most characters and character sequences can be included in a PSP file without being changed by the PSP loader, but some character sequences must be delimited with the special backslash character. The following table outlines the character sequences that must be delimited with a special character:

Character Sequence	Escape Sequence Required
%>	%\>
<%	<\%.
'	\'

The following is an example of how special characters are used in a command:

```
<%@ plsql parameter="in_phrase" default="'It'\'s a wrap'" %>
```

Handling Script Errors

If your PSP program contains any syntax errors in the PL/SQL code, loadpsp aborts and displays the line number, column number, and a brief message about the error (similar to a PL/SQL error from SQL*Plus). To handle database errors from your code, include an exception block within your PSP files. You can include a WHEN OTHERS clause to handle any unhandled exceptions, but following generally accepted PL/SQL programming practices is important.

PSPs Are the Best of Both Worlds

PSP really does provide you with the best of both worlds. HTML developers like editing PSP files in their standard GUI HTML editor (like Dreamweaver) and PL/SQL developers can maintain their PL/SQL code as they normally would. Most Oracle developers know PL/SQL very well. PSP leverages these skills for PL/SQL developers who can use their existing experience to create Web pages. For an experienced PL/SQL programmer, PSPs offer a quick way to add dynamic content to existing HTML files. They also allow for the division of labor between the Web (PL/SQL) developer and the Web (HTML) designer because the PL/SQL code can be inserted into any existing Web page.

Retrieving CGI Environment Variables

All Common Gateway Interface (CGI) environment variables conforming to the CGI 1.1 specifications are passed from *i*AS to the PL/SQL module.

The following table shows what would be retrieved from these CGI variables if you executed this URL **http://tuscbdb/pls/examples/mypsp?minsal=1000**:

Variable	Variable Meaning
GATEWAY_INTERFACE	The revision of the CGI specification to which the server complies, for example, CGI/1.1
HTTP_USER_AGENT	The browser the client is using to send the request, for example, Mozilla/4.0 (compatible, MSIE 5.5, Windows NT 5.0, Hotbar 2.0, Conversa Web 3.1.0)
PATH_INFO	Extra path information given by the client, for example, =/pls/examples/mypsp
REMOTE_METHOD	Method of accessing the program, such as GET or POST. For example, GET
REMOTE_HOST	Host name making the request if it can be determined, for example, tuscbdb
REMOTE_ADDR	IP address of the remote host making the request, for example, 192.168.0.2
REMOTE_USER	Used to authenticate user
REMOTE_IDENT	Set to the remote user name retrieved from the server
SERVER_PROTOCOL	Name and revision of the information protocol used in the request, for example, HTTP/1.1
SERVER_SOFTWARE	Name and version of information server software answering the request, for example, Apache/1.3.12 (Win32) ApacheJServ/1.1 mod_ssl/2.6.4 OpenSSL/0.9.5a mod_perl/1.22
SERVER_NAME	The server's host name, or IP address; for example, tuscbdb

Variable	Variable Meaning
SERVER_PORT	Port number on which the server is running, for example, 80
SCRIPT_NAME	Virtual path to the script being executed, used for self-referencing URLs, for example, /pls
HTTP_ACCEPT	The types of HTTP that will be accepted, for example: image/gif, image/x-xbitmap, image/jpeg, image/pjpeg, application/vnd.ms-powerpoint, application/vnd.ms-excel, application/msword, */*
HTTP_REFERER	Contains the URL that called this URL
HTTP_COOKIE	All of the raw cookie values
REMOTE_USER *	The Oracle user name the user connects with, for example, examples
DAD_NAME *	The name of the DAD the user connected with, for example, examples
QUERY_STRING *	Accesses the parameters passed to your procedure, for example, minsal=1000

TIP
The variables noted with asterisks (*) are new in iAS. Also, note, SERVER_NAME isn't what is used to be in OAS. Previously, when you used OWA_ UTIL.get_cgi_env('SERVER_NAME'), OAS returned the virtual domain entered by the user, for example, partner.myserver.com. With iAS, the same call returns the actual sever name, regardless of what URL was entered, for example, mysite.server.com. To get the desired results, change to OWA_ UTIL.get_cgi_env('HTTP_HOST'). This fixes the problem. Note, however, HTTP_HOST also returns the port (that is, partnerlink.myserver.com:1550) if you aren't using port 80.

The previous contains the available CGI environment variables. These environment variables can be accessed from within PL/SQL using the OWA_ UTIL.GET_CGI_ENV function, which is defined as follows:

```
owa_util.get_cgi_env( param_name in varchar2) return varchar2;
```

where param_name is the name of the CGI environment variable as defined in table. The following code retrieves the IP address of the remote node (the client's PC):

```
remote_ip := owa_util.get_cgi_env('REMOTE_ADDR');
```

Maintaining Source Code History

Maintaining a history of the source code enables you to roll back a change at any point. By extending this example, you could build an entire source code control application within the database. This trigger works only as of the release of Oracle8*i*. This statement assists in placing a trigger on the source$ table.

Oracle8*i* gives you the capability to create triggers on database events and on complex views. The following example shows a trigger on the CREATE event. This trigger fires for all CREATE or REPLACE statements for tables, triggers, procedures, and so forth. Because the trigger written queries the dba_source view, it only tracks the history of packages, functions, and procedures.

Each time a procedure is created or modified, a snapshot of its source code is saved and time-stamped in the source_history table.

The current implementation of the following example doesn't store trigger source, type source, or method source, but you can enhance it to the desired levels. First, create your source_history table, which stores your prior source code versions:

```
create table source_history
(change_dt date        not null,
 owner      varchar2(30) not null,
 name       varchar2(30) not null,
 type       varchar2(20),
 line       number       not null,
 text       varchar2(4000))
```

Once the source_history tables has been created, use a DBA-authorized account and execute the following syntax to create the source_history trigger:

```
create or replace trigger source_history
after   create on database
/* Maintain history of source code */
declare
v_sysdate date := sysdate;
begin
insert into source_history
        (change_dt,   owner,    name,    type,    line,    text)
(select v_sysdate, ds.owner, ds.name, ds.type, ds.line, ds.text
  from    dba_source ds
  where   sys.dictionary_obj_owner = ds.owner
  and     sys.dictionary_obj_name  = ds.name
```

```
and     sys.dictionary_obj_type  = ds.type)
;
end source_history;
/
```

Storing Cookies

Cookies enable any site to store information on a Web browser's hard disk for semipermanent storage (cookie.txt file) or in the browser's memory for short-term use. This information is sent back to the originating site whenever your application requests it.

To set a cookie on the browser, use the following PL/SQL code:

```
owa_util.mime_header ('text/html', FALSE);
owa_cookie.send ('cookie_name', cookie_value, sysdate+5);
owa_util.http_header_close;
```

Cookies must be set in the MIME header of the HTTP request. The preceding PL/SQL code opens the MIME header sent to the browser defining the HTTP request as text/html MIME type. The mime_header procedure doesn't close the MIME header yet (False). The cookie is sent to the browser, with the name cookie_name, and the value is set to the value of the PL/SQL variable named cookie_value. The expiration date for this cookie is today, plus five days. Until that time, the cookie remains "alive," or active, even if the user closes the browser and opens it later for a five-day period (down to the second).

To retrieve the cookie from a browser, include the following code in your PL/SQL procedure. The owa_cookie.get function needn't be called as part of the HTTP header.

```
read_cookie_value := owa_cookie.get ('cookie_name');
```

Referring to Pseudocolumns

Oracle provides a number of potential pseudocolumns to pull information from the database. For example, if you want to know the user name currently executing the procedure, retrieve the user pseudocolumn. The sysdate pseudocolumn returns the current date and time down to the second. If your application uses database authentication, user will contain the Oracle user name of the person who logged in to *i*AS. The ROWID pseudocolumn contains a value that uniquely identifies a single row in a table. The ROWNUM pseudocolumn returns the relative position of the current row.

TIP
ROWNUM is assigned at selection time,
prior to any order by clause.

To retrieve pseudocolumns within PL/SQL, select the information in your
SELECT statement (for example, ROWID and ROWNUM). If the information isn't
related to the data in the table (for example, sysdate and user), select the information
from the dual table. For example:

```
select  ename, sal, emp.rowid
into    nbt_ename, nbt_sale, nbt_rowid
from    emp
```

The following is another example using the dual table:

```
select  sysdate, user
into    todays_date, current_user
from    dual
```

Calculating Time to the Hundredth of a Second

To calculate time to the hundredth of a second, use the dbms_utility.get_time function.
This function returns a reference number. By retrieving this number at the beginning
of your timer and again at the end, and then subtracting the two numbers, you can
effectively calculate execution time. For example:

```
create or replace procedure get_employees is
cursor emp_cur is
  select ename
  from emp;
start_time number;
end_time   number;

begin
start_time := dbms_utility.get_time;
htp.print('Start Time:'||start_time);

for emp_rec in emp_cur loop
    htp.print(emp_rec.ename);
    htp.br;
end loop;
```

```
end_time := dbms_utility.get_time;
htp.print('End Time:'||end_time);
htp.br;

htp.print('Time to run this procedure and select all employees: '||
    to_char((end_time - start_time)/100, '99999.999')||' seconds. ');
end get_employees;
```

Making External Calls from PL/SQL

Have you ever needed to make a call to an external routine from PL/SQL? For example, what if you want to call a C program from PL/SQL? In Chapter 11, the PL/SQL UTL_HTTP package is covered in depth. One of the suggested uses of UTL_HTTP is to make calls to CGI programs, such as a C program. This makes calling external programs from PL/SQL easy. Then again, Java can handle this without issue.

Wrapping or Securing Your Procedures from Source Viewing

There are times when you don't want other developers to view the source code in your packages, procedures, or functions. Oracle provides the capability to offer PL/SQL code to someone, yet not allow that person to see what's in it. This technique is called *wrapping*. To wrap a procedure within Oracle8, use the following wrap program:

```
wrap iname=input_file.sql [oname=output_file.sql]
```

For example, to wrap send_mail.sql into send_mail.plb, use the following code:

```
wrap iname=send_mail.sql oname=send_mail.plb
```

If you omit the oname parameter from the command execution, the default output file name will be the input file name (minus the extension) with an extension of .plb. The following command produces the same results as the preceding command:

```
wrap iname=send_mail.sql
```

Once a procedure is wrapped, the output file is readable only by the Oracle database engine. If you look at the .plb file (that is, open in an editor), you'll notice the text within the file is ASCII text, but isn't decipherable into any meaningful information. You can execute the following script in SQL*Plus, however, just as you would have executed the SQL script:

```
SQLPLUS> @send_mail.plb
```

Anyone who attempts to view the source from a tool, such as TOAD, receives the following message instead of viewing the source code:

```
package body exa12a wrapped
```

TIP
Be sure to secure the source code by placing it in a directory to which other developers don't have access.

Redirecting Users to Another URL

If you're unfamiliar with the PL/SQL language and are wondering if it's possible to perform redirection like in Perl, it is. To redirect the user to **http://www .somewhere .com** in Perl, the code would appear identical to the following:

```
print "Location: http://www.somewhere.com\n\n";
```

Redirection is possible with PL/SQL using the owa_util.redirect_url procedure, as follows:

```
owa_util.redirect_url('http://www.somewhere.com');
```

Rather than using the owa_util.redirect_url procedure, you could write your own procedure using the refresh metatag, as the following example illustrates:

```
create or replace procedure my_redirect(clocation in varchar2) is
begin
    htp.htmlOpen;
    htp.headOpen;
    htp.print('<meta http-equiv="refresh" content="0;url=' ||
            clocation || '">');
    htp.headClose;
    htp.htmlClose;
end;
```

To execute the previous example, the URL call would be

http://tuscdbd/pls/examples/my_redirect?clocation=http://www.tusc.com

The following procedure verifies the user is logged in by checking a cookie. If the user isn't logged in, another procedure, start_login, is sent, passing that procedure the name of the procedure it needs to branch to once the user is logged in. If the user is already logged in, the procedure branches the user directly to the URL passed, which is contained in the variable in_url.

```
create or replace procedure check_logged_in
(in_url varchar2 default '/index.html')
is
user_no owa_cookie.cookie;
begin
   user_no := owa_cookie.get('user_no');
   -- If the user is logged in, branch to in_url
   if user_no.num_vals != 0 then
      htp.htmlopen;
      htp.headopen;
      htp.meta('refresh',null,'0;url='||in_url);
      htp.headclose;
      htp.bodyopen;
      htp.bodyclose;
      htp.htmlclose;
   else
      -- Otherwise call start_login
      start_login(in_url);
   end if;
end;
```

Querying Multiple Selects from List Box

Let's say you built an HTML form that displays a list box of departments. When the user selects a department, and then clicks the Execute Query (Submit) button on the form, you call a routine returning information about the employees in that department. The HTML to display the list of departments might appear similar to the following:

```
<form action=/pls/examples/query_department>
<select name=in_dept_no>
<option value=10>Sales
<option value=20>Consulting
<option value=30>Training
<option value=40>Administration
</select>
</form>
```

The query in the procedure, query_department, returning the information, might appear as follows:

```
create or replace procedure query_department (in_dept_no varchar2)
is
cursor dept_cursor is
       select emp_no, ename, mgr, sal, comm          from    emp
       where  dept_no = in_dept_no;
begin
  ...
end;
```

The problem comes when you want to expand the functionality of the HTML form to enable you to report on multiple departments. When you alter the list box to enable the return of multiple values, you must also pass that information to PL/SQL. PL/SQL supports this functionality through a PL/SQL table (an array of values). The only change to the HTML is to the SELECT tag, as follows:

```
<select multiple name=in_dept_no>
```

Now you need to change the declaration within PL/SQL to a PL/SQL table, as follows:

```
create or replace procedure query_department
(in_dept_no owa_util.ident_arr)
```

If you leave the cursor as defined, it won't work. If you change the query to an IN clause, it still won't work. You could use dynamic SQL, but that would be a lot of work. One option is to change the query to loop through each of the departments, as follows:

```
create or replace procedure query_department
(in_dept_no owa_util.ident_arr)
is
cursor dept_cursor (nbt_dept_no emp.deptno%TYPE) is
       select empno, ename, mgr, sal, comm
       from    emp
       where  deptno = nbt_dept_no;
begin
  for x in 1 .. in_dept_no.count loop
      for dept_rec in dept_cursor(in_dept_no (x)) loop
         ...
      end loop;
  end loop;
end;
```

If you need to sort the information by anything other than department and a value (for example, salaries across all selected departments), this method won't work. If you need to sort by another value, you need to use the dbms_sql package or you could insert the PL/SQL table values into a table, and then use a subquery, as the following shows:

```
create or replace procedure query_department
(in_dept_no owa_util.ident_arr)
is
cursor dept_cursor is
        select empno, ename, mgr, sal, comm
        from    emp
        where   deptno in (select deptno
                                from    temp_dept_no
                                where   userid = uid)
        order   by sal desc;
begin
  -- Purge prior uses of this Unique ID (uid)
  delete temp_dept_no
  where   userid = uid;
  -- Now insert the values into a temp table
  for x in 1 .. in_dept_no.count loop
      insert into temp_dept_no
      (deptno,userid)
      values (in_dept_no (x),uid);
      end loop;
  -- Now select the data
  for dept_rec in dept_cursor loop
      ...
  end loop;
end;
```

Wrapping Text Without Using <PRE>

You might have formatted text in a column of an Oracle table. By formatted, I mean the text is stored in the database with embedded carriage returns. Within your Web application, you might then want to show the data in that text column in an HTML table on a Web page. HTML, however, ignores all special characters (including carriage returns) unless you embed the text within the <PRE> tag (using htp.preOpen and htp.preClose in PL/SQL), so the users can see the carriage returns, but some lines of the text might be too long for the user to see them. Also, the <PRE> tag makes the text look rather boring. You might have even attempted to use the WIDTH attribute in htp.tableData and the COLSPEC attribute in the htp.table command without success.

This problem is best solved replacing carriage returns with the break tag (<BR>) in PL/SQL, rather than with HTML, as follows:

```
htp.tableData(replace(text_field,chr(13), '<BR>'));
```

Using this method, you aren't forced to use the <PRE> tag. By replacing the carriage returns with a <BR> tag, the browser wraps the text where you want it. You can also use the <WBR> tag, if it's optional to break at that point.

Clearing the Buffer

Have you ever been in the middle of your PL/SQL procedure (for example, writing HTML) and wanted to clear the buffer of HTML commands (so you could write a clean error page)? A command specifically designed to clear the buffer doesn't exist. The owa_util.showpage procedure does the trick, however, by moving any previous commands from the HTML buffer (a PL/SQL table) into the dbms_output PL/SQL table. In effect, this clears the HTML buffer. The syntax is as follows:

```
...
htp.htmlClose;
exception
   when no_data_found then
       owa_util.showpage;
       htp.htmlOpen;
       ...
       htp.print('Go back and make a selection');
end;
```

Debugging PL/SQL

If you go back about five years, the number (and type) of tools was *very* limited for debugging PL/SQL. Today, though, a number of firms sell PL/SQL debuggers. Chapter 25 also discusses techniques for debugging your PL/SQL code. The following table lists the companies that provide PL/SQL debuggers.

Company	Web Site	PL/SQL Debugger
Sylvain Faust	http://www.sfi-software.com	SQL-Programmer
Allround Automations	http://www.allroundautomations.com	PL/SQL Developer
Qwest Software	http://www.qwest.com/	TOAD
Compuware	http://www.compuware.com/	XPEDITER/SQL

Deauthenticating Users

When using OAS, you can use database authentication to allow a user to log in to the database to run a query, but you cannot log the user off. iAS, however, added a new pseudoprocedure to log off a database-authenticated DAD. With OAS, the user had to exit the browser. iAS provides the capability to log off the Oracle DAD using logmeoff, in the following format:

```
http://myhost/pls/myDAD/logmeoff
```

Disappearing Sessions

If you look in the v$session table, sessions will appear, and then disappear. The following is an excerpt from an e-mail about this issue:

> Here is something interesting. The other day we, the people in IT, were debating about the connection to the database from iAS. Does the Web server maintain the connection to the database for a user's session? Or does it disconnect once it sends the dynamic page back to the browser and then reconnect again when the user needs more info from database? How can you test this? Even though the v$session table has the records regarding active/inactive sessions, there is no record for our Web user in the v$session table. Does that mean iAS is no longer connected to the database?

The individual who asked this question obviously has his database on a fast processor. Sessions will show up in the v$session table for at least the life of the session. The default behavior of the iAS PL/SQL module is that when a procedure is executed (through a URL), the PL/SQL module will perform the following tasks:

1. Log in to Oracle (using the user name/password in the DAD or the user name/password specified through database authentication)

2. Execute the procedure

3. Log the user out

Although the life of the session may be short, it appears in the v$session table for a period of time. You might notice the session in the table, and then watch it disappear shortly thereafter. The next session might use the same session number, which may give the impression a session is appearing, and then disappearing, when it's really two different sessions. If you set the DAD configuration variable to Stateful Sessions, the PL/SQL module will perform the following tasks:

1. Check a cookie to see if the user has already been logged in

   ■ If so, the user is reconnected to their prior database session

   ■ If not, the user is logged in to Oracle and the cookie is set on their browser

2. Execute the procedure

3. The user isn't logged out until the session times out

Encrypting Key Information

When it comes to sensitive information, encrypt the information in PL/SQL and, more important, in the database. If you're storing credit card numbers in the database, you don't want a user to be able to query those numbers (and expiration dates) directly from an Oracle table. Multiple approaches can encrypt key information. For example, you could take the spy decoder ring approach and use the TRANSLATE statement to turn As to Zs, Bs to Gs, and so forth. You could also use an external program, such as a C program, to convert values through utl_http, as described in Chapter 11. Going through dbms_pipe, you could execute an external program. Another approach is to use the encryption and decryption functions (DBMS-OBFUSCATE-TOOLKIT), as described in Chapter 11. Oracle provides you with numerous methods of encrypting your key information.

Ordering Data Based on User Requests

Let's say your page displays a list of orders your customer currently has in progress. The current_orders procedure displays the priority of the order, the date the order was placed, the total order value, the current status of the order, and so forth. By default, you might choose to order this information by the priority, order date, and dollar value, or to pull the default order by from your user's profile record. After you accomplish the default order by, maybe the user should be able to change the sorting order. At the top of each column in the table, provide a link that enables the user to click the column heading to order by. You could handle the underlying PL/SQL logic in many ways, as the following describes.

You could use EXECUTE IMMEDIATE to build your query dynamically. This is the least-preferred method because the execution plan isn't stored in the pcode (binary compiled PL/SQL code) and DBAs typically frown on dynamic SQL. For example,

```
create or replace procedure current_orders
   (in_customer_no varchar2,
    in_order_by    number default 1)is
```

```
sql_string varchar2(1000);
sql_order_by varchar2(1000);

begin
  sql_string := 'select priority, order_date, order_total, status' ||
                'from    order_header order by ';
  if in_order_by = 1 then
     sql_order_by := 'priority, order_date, order_total';
  elsif in_order_by = 2 then
     sql_order_by := 'order_date, priority, order_total';

  end if;
  sql_string := sql_string || sql_order_by;
  -- EXECUTE IMMEDIATE call belong here
  execute immediate sql_string;

end;
```

You could define the cursor with *n* variations (one per sort order method), and then pass in the sort order using the corresponding order by clause. DBAs typically prefer this method because the execution plans are stored and this method doesn't use dynamic SQL.

The final method is by using a DECODE statement on the order by. This method is the easiest to implement. If you have multiple datatypes to order by (numbers, characters, and dates), however, this method won't be as efficient as the second method because all values must be converted to the least-common denominator (character date) prior to the order by. If you're retrieving a large number of rows, this could be an issue. Otherwise, you probably won't notice a problem. Another issue to consider is that dates and numbers are easier to handle than character data in this case. For dates, you can subtract the date from 10,000. For example,

```
to_char(10000 - order_date, 'yymmddhh24miss');
```

With the following syntax, you can multiply by –1:

```
to_char(order_total * -1, '099999999.99'));
```

With the following syntax convert character values, you need to use the TRANSLATE statement to turn an *A* to a *Z*, a *B* to a *Y*, and so forth:

```
translate(last_name, 'ABCDE...', 'ZYXWV...');
```

The following code is a complete example:

```
create or replace procedure emp_details
   (in_order_by    number default 1)
is
```

```
cursor emp_cur is
    select ename, hiredate, mgr, sal
    from    emp
    order   by decode(in_order_by,
                          1, ename,
                          2, to_char(hiredate, 'yymmddhh24miss'),
                          job),
               decode(in_order_by,
                          1, to_char(hiredate, 'yymmddhh24miss'),
                          2, ename,
                          to_char(sal, '099999999.99')),
               decode(in_order_by,
                          1, to_char(sal, '099999999.99'),
                          2, to_char(sal, '099999999.99'),
                          job);


begin
--opening of cursor etc. here…
end;
```

Editing PL/SQL Code

When editing PL/SQL code, you can certainly use good old Windows's Notepad
or UNIX's vi, but a number of excellent PL/SQL editors exist, some of which have
context-sensitive editors. For example, TOAD by Quest Software, PL/SQL Developer
by Allround Automations, and several others are excellent PL/SQL editors. You can
also use an editor such as TextPad (**http://www.textpad.com**) by Helios Software
Solutions. On the TUSC Web site (**http://www.tusc.com**), we placed a number of
add-ons for the TextPad editor. These include a script that sets up the registry to use
TextPad as the default editor in Forms.

To make TextPad your default editor in SQL*Plus, execute the following line
into the glogin.sql in $ORACLE_HOME\Plus33 or $ORACLE_HOME\Plus80
directory (depending on which version you're using):

```
define _editor="C:\Program Files\TextPad 4\TextPad.exe"
```

The macros and add-ins available from the TUSC site for download make
TextPad easier to use with PL/SQL code. Dayle Larson, a developer at Resorts
Computer Corporation in Denver, Colorado, put these together. These scripts only
work with TextPad version 4.0 (or higher).

One macro changes SQL keywords in selected text blocks to uppercase. You'll
want to save the macro files in the c:\Program Files\TextPad 4\User directory. In
TextPad 4, under Configure | Preferences | Macros, select Upper Selected SQL from
the list and add it to the menu.

If you want the same kind of syntax-coloring SQL code found in the Forms 6.0 editor, perform the following steps:

1. Copy the file into C:\Program Files\TextPad 4\Samples (It contains the syntax information for the SQL document class).

2. Double-click the registry script.

3. Choose Open (this tells your registry about the PL*SQL document class).

The .syn file contains the keywords for PL/SQL and for Forms, so it can be used as a default editor for Forms.

Catching the Domain Name from an IP

If you ever need to retrieve the domain name from which your user is originating, you can first attempt to obtain this using the following syntax:

```
remote_host_name := owa_util.get_cgi_env('remote_host');
```

Quite often, however, this will return only the IP address of the remote host. If you need to perform a reverse domain name lookup, you can perform this using the operating system command traceroute (abbreviated as tracert on NT).

Missing Radio Buttons

Have you ever tried to display a form containing some radio buttons, only to have nothing appear in the browser? For example, to display two radio buttons, you might have written the following code:

```
htp.print('<TD>');
htp.formRadio(cname=>'summdet',cvalue=>'YES',cchecked=>'TRUE');
htp.print( 'Summary' );
htp.formRadio(cname=>'summdet', cvalue=>'NO');
htp.print( 'Detail' );
htp.p('</TD>');
```

Do you notice anything missing from the preceding HTML? What about the <FORM> tag? Without the <FORM> tag, the radio buttons will be MIA. On a side note, the missing radio buttons might disappear only in certain browsers—for instance, IE is more forgiving than Netscape, so it's imperative to test your code in each browser your application will use.

TIP
*Similar ghostly issues occur if you inadvertently
forget the ending tag, </table> .*

Overdefining Actions

What's wrong with the following HTML form's action clause?

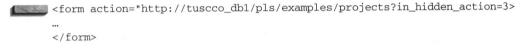

```
<form action="http://tuscco_db1/pls/examples/projects?in_hidden_action=3>
...
</form>
```

When you call your HTML routine, the same error appears as if the in_hidden_
action field doesn't have a default value (if it has a default value, the value of the
field is always equal to the default value). This error occurs because the browser
strips off all the information past the question mark (?) to build its own URL with
parameters. To pass a value, like in_hidden_action, you need to define a hidden
field identical to the following:

```
<input type=hidden name=in_hidden_action value="3">
```

Hidden fields will be placed into the URL by the browser.

Converting Numbers
to Words—Literally

When it comes to printing checks or other documents, such as a letter, converting
some numbers into the words that represent the numbers becomes necessary, for
example, turning 100 into one hundred or 402 into four hundred two. The following
function automatically performs this task. You must pass the function a value and it
then returns the number as words:

```
create or replace function number_to_words (p_number number)
return varchar2
is
   t_char_number  varchar2(64)  := to_char(p_number);
   t_integer      varchar2(8);
   t_mantissa     varchar2(128)  := ' point';
   t_return_value varchar2(128);

function digit_to_word(p_digit varchar2)
return varchar2
is
   t_return_value varchar2(8);
begin
```

```
   if    p_digit = '1' then t_return_value := ' one';
    elsif p_digit = '2' then t_return_value := ' two';
    elsif p_digit = '3' then t_return_value := ' three';
    elsif p_digit = '4' then t_return_value := ' four';
    elsif p_digit = '5' then t_return_value := ' five';
    elsif p_digit = '6' then t_return_value := ' six';
    elsif p_digit = '7' then t_return_value := ' seven';
    elsif p_digit = '8' then t_return_value := ' eight';
    elsif p_digit = '9' then t_return_value := ' nine';
    elsif p_digit = '0' then t_return_value := ' zero';
    end if;
    return t_return_value;
end digit_to_word;

begin
  if instr(t_char_number, '.') <> 0 then
    t_integer     := substr(t_char_number, 1, instr(t_char_number, '.') -1);
    t_char_number := substr(t_char_number, instr(t_char_number, '.') +1);
    while t_char_number is not null loop
      t_mantissa    := t_mantissa ||
                        digit_to_word(substr(t_char_number, 1, 1));
      t_char_number := substr(t_char_number, 2);
    end loop;
    t_return_value := to_char(to_date(t_integer, 'j'), 'jsp') || t_mantissa;
  else
    t_return_value := to_char(to_date(p_number, 'j'), 'jsp');
  end if;
  return t_return_value;
end;
```

The following example illustrates the use of functions in a SELECT statement:

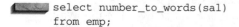

```
select number_to_words(sal)
from emp;
```

Getting Information About Your Users

A number of queries can be executed to analyze your database statistics. In addition to covering some important scripts that can help you as a PL/SQL developer, however, this section describes an application built using the PL/SQL module; an application that enables you to run any SQL statement and graph specific information within the browser.

Before addressing the application, create a table containing each of your key analysis SQL scripts. You can add records to the table as desired. The syntax for creating the table is as follows:

```
create table www_dba.top_dba_scripts (
   script_no     number(10)       not null ,
   short_desc    varchar2(4000),
   long_desc     varchar2(4000),
   cat_no        number(10),
   text_script   varchar2(4000),
   graph_script  varchar2(4000),
   header_sql    varchar2(4000),
   refresh_rate  number           default 0);
```

The following script inserts SQL statements. This example includes only one SQL statement as an example and you can add more statements at any time. You can download the entire script from the TUSC Web site.

```
insert into www_dba.top_dba_scripts
(script_no, short_desc,
 long_desc,
 cat_no,
 text_script,
 graph_script,
 header_sql,
 refresh_rate)
values (
 10, 'Users Logged On',
 'This query will return a listing of users that are
  currently logged into the Database.',
 1,
 'SELECT username, count(*) FROM v$session
  WHERE username NOT IN (''SYS'', ''SYSTEM'')
  GROUP BY username ORDER BY count(*) DESC',
 'SELECT null, username, count(*)
  FROM v$session
  WHERE username NOT IN (''SYS'', ''SYSTEM'')
  GROUP BY username ORDER BY count(*) DESC',
 'select ''<B>Username</B>'',
         ''<B>Number of Times Logged On</B>''
  from dual',
 10);
```

The following procedure enables you to pick a script from the top_dba_script table and is called from your browser:

```
create or replace procedure pick_top_dba_script
as
    cursor script_cur is
        select *
        from   www_dba.top_dba_scripts
        order  by script_no;
    refresh_it varchar2(2000) := '';
begin
    htp.htmlopen;
    htp.headopen;
    htp.title('Top DBA Scripts for Web Developers');
    htp.print('<style type="text/css">');
    htp.print('body {font-family: arial; margin-left: 100px;}');
    htp.print('h1 {background-color: blue; color: white;
                   font-size: 28pt; font-family: arial;}');
    htp.print('</style>');
    htp.headclose;
    htp.bodyopen('/img/ivybackground.gif');
    htp.header(1,'Top DBA Scripts for Web Developers');
    htp.tableopen('border=2');
    htp.tablerowopen;
    htp.tableheader('Short Description');
    htp.tableheader('Long Description');
    htp.tablerowclose;
    for script_rec in script_cur loop
        htp.tablerowopen;
        if script_rec.refresh_rate > 0 then
           refresh_it := '&in_refresh_at=' ||
                            to_char(script_rec.refresh_rate);
        else
           refresh_it := null;
        end if;
        htp.tabledata(htf.anchor(
         'run_top_dba_script?in_script_no='||
          script_rec.script_no||
          refresh_it,script_rec.short_desc));
        htp.tabledata(script_rec.long_desc);
        htp.tablerowclose;
```

```
    end loop;
    htp.tableclose;
    htp.bodyclose;
    htp.htmlclose;
end;
```

This procedure displays a page, as illustrated in Figure 14-5, containing links to run any of the reports in the top_dba_scripts table. The link runs a specific query by executing the run_top_dba_script procedure, as illustrated in the following example. Rather than using dbms_sql to execute the query, this procedures uses cellsprint to

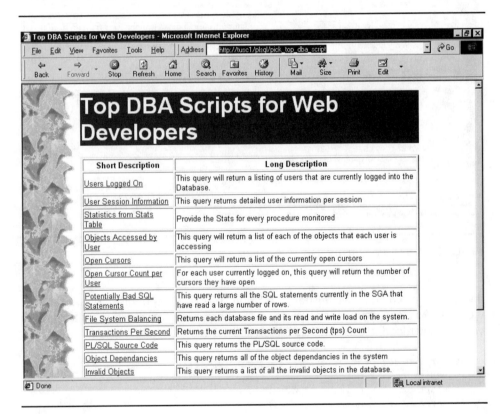

FIGURE 14-5. *Top DBA Scripts for Web Developers*

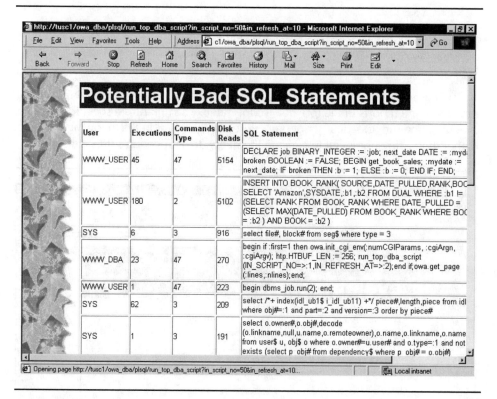

FIGURE 14-6. *Potentially Bad SQL Statements*

display the information, as illustrated in Figure 14-6. To graph this information, use the owa_chart package, which Oracle says your representative will provide free—or you can download it from the TUSC Web site.

```
create or replace procedure run_top_dba_script
   (in_script_no      varchar2,
    in_start_at       number    default 0,
    in_refresh_at     number    default 0)
as
   cursor script_cur is
   select *
     from www_dba.top_dba_scripts
    where script_no = in_script_no;
   more_records boolean;
   max_rows        number(10) := 100;
begin
   htp.htmlopen;
```

```
htp.headopen;
htp.title('display script results' );
if in_refresh_at > 0 then
    htp.print('<meta http-equiv="refresh" ' ||
              'content="' || in_refresh_at || ';URL=run_top_dba_script' ||
              '?in_script_no=' || in_script_no ||
              '&in_start_at=' || in_start_at ||
              '&in_refresh_at=' || in_refresh_at || '">');
end if;
htp.print('<style type="text/css">');
htp.print('body {font-family: arial; margin-left: 100px;}');
htp.print('h1 {background-color: blue; color: white; ' ||
          'font-size: 28pt; font-family: arial;}');
htp.print('</style>');
htp.headclose;
htp.bodyopen('/img/ivybackground.gif');
for script_rec in script_cur loop
    htp.header(1,script_rec.short_desc);
    htp.tableopen('border=2');
    owa_util.cellsprint(script_rec.header_sql);
    owa_util.cellsprint(script_rec.text_script, max_rows,
                    null, in_start_at, more_records);
    if in_start_at > 0 then
        htp.anchor('run_top_dba_script'||
                    '?in_script_no=' || in_script_no ||
                    '&in_start_at=' ||
                      to_char(in_start_at - max_rows) ||
                    '&in_refresh_at=' || to_char(in_refresh_at),
                    htf.img('/img/previous.gif', null, 'previous ' ||
                          to_char(max_rows) || ' records'));
    end if;
    if more_records then
        htp.anchor('run_top_dba_script' ||
                    '?in_script_no=' || in_script_no ||
                    '&in_start_at=' ||
                      to_char(in_start_at + max_rows) ||
                    '&in_refresh_at=' || to_char(in_refresh_at),
                    htf.img('/img/next.gif', null, 'next ' ||
                          to_char(max_rows) || ' records'));
    end if;
    htp.tableclose;
    -- display arrows top and bottom
    if in_start_at > 0 then
        htp.anchor('run_top_dba_script' ||
                    '?in_script_no=' || in_script_no ||
                    '&in_start_at=' ||
                      to_char(in_start_at - max_rows) ||
                    '&in_refresh_at=' || to_char(in_refresh_at),
                    htf.img('/img/previous.gif', null, 'previous ' ||
```

```
                    to_char(max_rows) || ' records'));
        end if;
        if more_records then
            htp.anchor('run_top_dba_script'||
                    '?in_script_no=' || in_script_no ||
                    '&in_start_at='    ||
                      to_char(in_start_at + max_rows) ||
                    '&in_refresh_at=' || to_char(in_refresh_at),
                    htf.img('/img/next.gif', null, 'next ' ||
                        to_char(max_rows) || ' records'));
        end if;
        if script_rec.graph_script is not null then
            htp.br;
            htp.br;
            htp.hr;
            owa_chart.show_chart(
                q               => script_rec.graph_script,
                chart_type      => 'hbar',
                bar_image       => 'multi',
                image_locat     => '/img/',
                chart_title     => script_rec.short_desc,
                font_size       => '-2',
                show_summary    => 'camxvs');
        end if;
    end loop;
    htp.formopen('run_top_dba_script', 'get');
    htp.formhidden('in_script_no', in_script_no);
    htp.formhidden('in_start_at', in_start_at);
    htp.print('refresh data every ');
    htp.formtext('in_refresh_at', 4, 4, in_refresh_at);
    htp.print(' seconds');
    htp.formsubmit(null, 'change refresh rate');
    htp.formclose;
    htp.bodyclose;
    htp.htmlclose;
end;
```

Understanding Why htp.linkrel Is Now Useful

In prior versions of HTML, the <Link> tag didn't play a significant role, so the PL/SQL htp.linkrel procedure didn't have an impact—it wasn't useful. However, with the creation of cascading style sheets (CSS), which are discussed in Chapter 6, the <Link> tag and, therefore, the htp.linkrel procedure become important. To refer to a style sheet called navdata.css with HTML, the syntax would be as follows:

```
<link rel=stylesheet href="navdata.css" type="text/css">
```

Unfortunately, the htp.linkrel command doesn't support the type attribute and it doesn't support additional attributes. The PL/SQL call for the same reference as the preceding HTML is as follows:

```
htp.print('<link rel=stylesheet href="navdata.css" type="text/css">');
```

Or, you can disillusion the linkrel procedure, as follows:

```
htp.linkrel(crel=>'stylesheet', curl=>'/navdata.css" type="text/css');
```

TIP
You must place a slash (/) before the style sheet name or the file will be assumed to come from the same virtual path as your PL/SQL procedure and likely cause a file not found error.

You can also modify the underlying linkrel procedure in the htp and htf packages, but it's typically unwise to modify the vendor's packages. Another option would be to create a linkrel procedure of your own.

PL/SQL Optimization

One of the trickier aspects of *i*AS development is that Web document generation needs to be as fast as possible. Users and developers both dislike lengthy periods of time waiting for Web pages to render. It would also be handy to have a way to measure the amount of time pages take to generate between the moment a page request is received and when that request finishes. Tuning PL/SQL and queries to achieve the goal of optimal code is beyond the scope of this chapter, but this section does briefly discuss optimizing PL/SQL code.

Optimizing PL/SQL Code

Tuning PL/SQL code is the most basic way you can improve performance. The slowest component in PL/SQL code is database access (queries and DML) and tuning DML is the most important tuning technique you can perform for fast applications. SQL tuning is beyond what we want to discuss here though, so, instead, we'll focus on improving native PL/SQL code. You'll probably gain only slight performance gains by tuning the PL/SQL code itself, but when generating Web pages, every second counts.

What can be done to improve PL/SQL performance is the same kind of tuning techniques that can be used for other programming languages: minimize database access as much as possible, including selects from the dual table. Remember, functions like sysdate and user do implicit selects when invoked, so instead of repeated calls during code execution, call the function once and put the result in a variable. When writing compound if-else statements, put the expressions most likely to be encountered first to avoid unnecessary comparisons. Avoid unnecessary looping (including unnecessary database access). Also avoid unnecessary datatype conversions, which can happen automatically and invisibly. When writing document tags, htp.p appears to be the most efficient procedure to use. We saved about four seconds on a large document generation by replacing the specialty HTML tags with htp.p calls, about a third of a 12-second load and render process.

Using the proper data types for math is also a good idea. PL/SQL offers several different numeric subtypes, each of which perform differently. Integers perform dismally in arithmetic expressions. Numbers are surprisingly faster than integers to perform computations, but not quite as fast as they might be. Binary integers are slightly faster than numbers. And, finally, pls integers perform computations the fastest. Avoiding implicit datatype conversions as often as possible is best. These conversions slow things down. Making all number values the same type is one way to avoid these conversions. PL/SQL converts pls integers in procedure and function argument definitions to binary integers. Also, using the modulus mod() function can be somewhat slow, although it is getting better with each release of PL/SQL.

Optimizing HTML Document Generation

Three distinct if-related issues are at work to optimize download times. The first is *document generation,* which is how long PL/SQL takes to generate the page physically. The second is how long it takes to download the generated document. The third is how long it takes the browser to render the generated document once it has been received. Document-generation time is largely a function of server considerations. Factors include SQL, PL/SQL, operating system and hardware, and taking into account what else is running on the system at the moment of document generation. Is download time a function of the networking (that is, Internet or intranet)? What path is the document taking to get to the browser? What physical communications hardware is being used? The slowest modems for rending the browser user interface and browser platform (operating system, available memory, CPU speed, and so forth) by anybody's standards are 2400-baud modems. Having an automated way to measure the times such things take would be nice.

The Stop Watch Utility

Oracle PL/SQL Tips & Techniques, by Joseph Trezzo (Osborne/McGraw-Hill, 1999), contains, amid other useful PL/SQL information, a stopwatch utility that can be used to time PL/SQL application execution. This stopwatch utility uses a useful routine

from the DBMS_UTILITY package in several packaged procedures to capture a starting time and an ending time to determine how long a particular routine takes to run, to hundredths of a second. The following code demonstrates the utility:

```
CREATE OR REPLACE PACKAGE stop_watch AS
    pv_start_time_num       PLS_INTEGER;
    pv_stop_time_num        PLS_INTEGER;
    pv_last_stop_time_num PLS_INTEGER;
PROCEDURE start_timer;
PROCEDURE stop_timer(
  p_output_procedure_c varchar2 := null
  );
END stop_watch;
/

CREATE OR REPLACE PACKAGE BODY stop_watch AS
PROCEDURE start_timer AS
BEGIN
    pv_start_time_num      := dbms_utility.get_time;
    pv_last_stop_time_num := pv_start_time_num;
END start_timer;
PROCEDURE stop_timer(
  p_output_procedure_c varchar2 := null
  ) AS
  ---------------------------------------------------------------
  --procedure variables
  ---------------------------------------------------------------
  v_text_c      varchar2(512);
BEGIN
  ---------------------------------------------------------------
  --set-up
  ---------------------------------------------------------------
  pv_stop_time_num := dbms_utility.get_time;
   --determine & execute output type
  if (p_output_procedure_c is not null) then
      v_text_c := 'Total Time Elapsed: ' ||
        TO_CHAR((pv_stop_time_num - pv_start_time_num)/100,
        '999,999.99') || ' sec    Interval Time: ' ||
        TO_CHAR((pv_stop_time_num - pv_last_stop_time_num)/100,
        '99,999.99') || ' sec';
      v_text_c := 'BEGIN ' || CHR(10) ||
        '   ' ||p_output_procedure_c || '(''' ||
        v_text_c || ''');' || CHR(10) ||
        'END;';
      execute immediate v_text_c;
  end if;
  ---------------------------------------------------------------
```

```
   --set global & exit
   ------------------------------------------------------------------
   pv_last_stop_time_num := pv_stop_time_num;
END stop_timer;
END stop_watch;
```

The *start_timer procedure* accepts no parameters and is merely called; its purpose is to record the start time in a global variable in the package header. The *stop_timer procedure* accepts one input value, a string representing what output program to use for the stop time message. The *p_output_procedure_c* value expects either values of dbms_output.put_line or htp.p (without any parentheses), but should accept *any* valid PL/SQL output routine. This routine can be used by both SQL*PLUS applications (dbms_output.put_line) *or* iAS applications (htp.p), as long as the output procedure specified is valid.

To use the stop watch, all you have to do is call the start procedure at the beginning of a procedure and the stop procedure at the end. The end-time message should be written to the bottom of the document once it's loaded for normal HTML rendering.

```
PROCEDURE write_menu IS
BEGIN
  stop_watch.start_timer;
--all other actions
  stop_watch.stop_timer('htp.p');
END write_menu;
```

Hiding the information within HTML comments might be more convenient, embedding them inside an HTML document for later reference, as the following code illustrates:

```
PROCEDURE write_menu IS
BEGIN
  stop_watch.start_timer;
--all other actions
  htp.p('<!--');
  stop_watch.stop_timer('htp.p');
  htp.p('-->');END write_menu;
```

This last idea, hiding information within HTML comments inside a document, is also a useful trick for HTML debugging. When a page doesn't render properly, you can include PL/SQL variable values inside HTML comments to see what's happening during page generation. This is especially valuable when a procedure works in development, but not in production. Most users will never know the comments are there.

Minimizing Download Time

The most effective way to minimize download time for documents is to use faster hardware. Phone lines provide generally slow access even with 56K modems, while optical lines with cable modems are faster.

Sometimes new hardware isn't going to happen, so less-effective measures must be employed. In such cases, minimizing the download document size can be helpful. Eliminating all excess tags and unused JavaScript code can do this. Also, certain closing tags (</TR>,</TD>, and </TH>, for example) can sometimes be omitted and save a surprising number of bytes. Dispensing with comments (gasp!) inside HTML documents can also save space. Spiffy features like animated images look really cool, but take a while to download, as can even static images. The fewer special features you include, the faster the document—especially a large document—will load.

Optimizing Browser Rendering

Users won't care if a document takes several long moments to render after the first bytes have been received by the browser because it has a table containing hundreds of cells, and will unfairly blame the database. A way of measuring rendering time would also be helpful. I won't go too deeply into the specifics of HTML and JavaScript solutions, but I'll touch on related issues.

In JavaScript (see Chapter 7), it's possible to capture the time the document starts loading in a global portion of code to capture a start time and later (or more elegantly in an onLoad event handler) capture start- and end-loading times. Large HTML tables can take a while to render, above and beyond the physical document load time. The browser being used has to process and draw HTML tables in the browser window interactively and this can be a slow process. Netscape Navigator has no quick fixes for this problem, but Internet Explorer 4.x and above supports a table tag attribute for inline style sheets of the value table-layout:fixed that can help improve HTML table rendering. The syntax of the attribute is as follows:

```
<TABLE STYLE="table-layout:fixed">
```

Now, to say this improves rendering time would be untrue. To be perfectly honest, full rendering time appears slightly longer when the table-layout attribute is used, but the table itself starts being rendered much sooner (almost immediately). The user should generally be distracted by this and (putting it bluntly) fooled into thinking the document is loading faster than it is.

If the document contains JavaScript using the defer script tag option, it can also be used to improve document rendering time. The *defer* option tells the browser not to interpret JavaScript until it's executed, improving document load and rendering time slightly.

```
<SCRIPT DEFER>
```

Summary

Is PL/SQL going away? I doubt it; at least not any time in the near future. Will developers move away from PL/SQL in favor of Java? I believe so. A number of applications exist today using PL/SQL as their core language, including the Oracle applications, which contain more than 4 million lines of PL/SQL code. Invest the time to understand the PL/SQL module and the power it can provide to your existing (and new) applications. You'll be amazed at the potential and possibilities. Oracle's newest PL/SQL feature, PL/SQL Server Pages, is a powerful and robust answer to the issues OAS developers faced. Previously developed PL/SQL cartridge-based applications can be converted to PSPs using UnWebAlchemy. If you already knew PL/SQL, but not how to develop Web applications using the PL/SQL module, I hope this chapter provided you with the basis to understand and begin developing Web applications.

PART
IV

Oracle Tools

CHAPTER
15

Designer

I f you're familiar with Oracle's toolset, you might be curious if Designer's generators can help you with Web code development. You might want to become familiar with the capabilities of the Oracle Designer Web PL/SQL Generator. You might also be interested in what Java support is available with Designer. This chapter provides an overview of these features to help answer these questions and assist in evaluating Designer for your situation. The learning curve for Oracle Designer is steep. To take full advantage of Oracle Designer, you must be committed to investing in yourself and learning the entire tool. This typically requires training from an Oracle Designer training provider like TUSC or Oracle Education. After gaining some experience in Designer, this chapter might help with some ideas in how to get the most out of the tool.

What are the advantages of using Designer 6i for Web development? As with all software construction, Web development requires a structured life-cycle process to ensure successful implementations. It should follow a planned process and allow for planned reuse of components, where possible. The more code written from scratch, the more expensive the full lifecycle process of building, testing, and fixing will be. Designer provides for the construction of reusable modules and can generate a lot of code that works the first time. Another advantage is centralized code with robust version control and configuration management capabilities. This centralized code, with the use of project-defined templates, style sheets, and generator preferences helps build applications with a consistent look and feel.

Using Oracle Designer Web PL/SQL Generator, developers can create fully functional Web applications that enable users to query, update, enter, and delete information in an Oracle database using Internet architecture. These generated applications are based on module- and database-design specifications recorded in the Oracle Designer Repository.

The main input to the generation process is a module-design specification. This is created using the Application Design Transformer to transform a function model or directly in the Oracle Designer Design Editor. The module definition records the tables and columns used by the module, the links between them, and detailed information on how the module uses data.

Other inputs to the generation process includes called modules and generator preferences. Called modules define the navigation between modules in a multiple-module application. Preferences determine the general appearance and behavior of the generated application. The preferences can be customized to suit your particular requirements. Figure 15-1 shows the components of Web PL/SQL Generation from design to implementation.

During generation, the Web PL/SQL Generator creates a set of PL/SQL packages, which are then compiled into the database to enable the execution of the application from a Web browser via the Oracle9i Application Server. These packages call the Web PL/SQL Generator Library, which makes use of the Oracle Web PL/SQL Developer's Toolkit—both are collections of PL/SQL packages provided by Oracle. The application communicates with the database through a set of Designer-generated packages, known

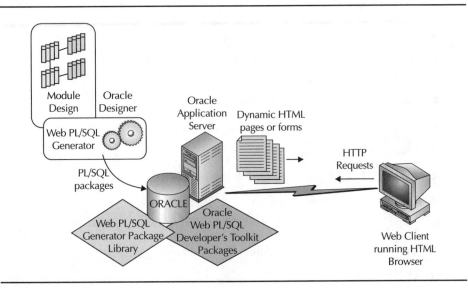

FIGURE 15-1. *Web PL/SQL Generation Components*

as the *Table API*. These PL/SQL API packages provide insert, update, delete, and lock procedures for each application table.

So does this mean Web PL/SQL Generator is the answer for all your Web development needs? No. While Web PL/SQL Generator does a good job for generating basic data entry and retrieval forms, it wouldn't be suited for building, for example, a Web portal. Web PL/SQL Generator also might not serve your needs for building complicated data retrieval forms. While the most recent version has improved navigation capabilities, you might need to develop a custom navigation framework.

Another issue is getting good-looking forms. The default forms aren't that polished and require some practice with various generator preferences, templates, and style sheets to improve the look. This is where the learning curve referred to earlier comes into play. You need experience and knowledge with Designer to get this accomplished and, even then, by using generated code, you are compromising flexibility for the sake of fast, functional, bug-free code. The bottom line is Web developers must evaluate requirements and select the appropriate development tools, as they would with any other project.

The following topics are discussed in this chapter:

- Exploring the Form Layout Options of Web PL/SQL Generation
- Accessing Master Component Item Values in Detail Components
- Creating LOV Components
- Defining Action Items

- Understanding the Packages Generated by Designer

- Incorporating Views into Generated Modules

- Building an Effective Database Security Scheme When Using Generated Modules

- Using Events and Named Routines

- Leveraging Key Web PL/SQL Generator Preferences and Attributes

- Using Frames and Style Sheets

- Using Unbound Items

- Leveraging the User Text Area

- Using JavaScript

- Overriding Designer's Default Functionality

- Using Arguments

- Managing the Software Development Life-Cycle with Configuration Management Tools

- Generating Java Source Database Objects

Exploring the Form Layout Options of Web PL/SQL Generation

Web PL/SQL Generation has three basic Layout Styles, however, many properties and generator preferences enable you to manipulate the User Interface (UI) to suit your needs. This section is intended to get you started in experimenting with these options to find the ones that best deliver applications to suit your end users' needs.

Setting the Module Layout Style

The most basic decision in designing your modules is choosing a layout style. All modules can have query forms, view forms, and insert forms. If desired, a module can also use the record list form. Choosing a layout style determines where these forms appear and the navigation between them. The following layout styles are available on the module component property sheet:

- **List**   The Query form, Record list, View form, and Insert form appear on separate pages. This style presents module components having a large amount of information to display. Use this style if you anticipate users running the application with browsers that don't support HTML frames. A detailed component of the style List can be embedded in its master's View form.

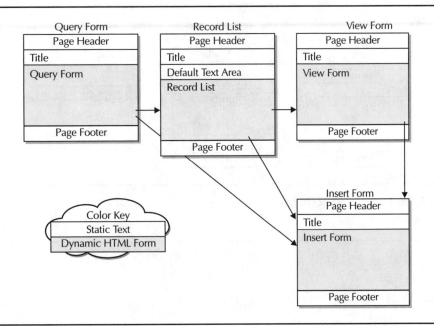

FIGURE 15-2. *List layout style*

The diagram in Figure 15-2 illustrates the default content and sequence of pages generated from a module component where the layout style is set to List.

Each HTML document appears on a separate page. When you select a record from the record list, the details are displayed within a View form on a new page.

- **List/Form** The Query form, Record list, View form, and Insert form can appear within HTML frames on the same page. Choose this style if the browsers used to run the application support HTML frames and the content of each frame can be displayed effectively within a smaller area.

The diagram in Figure 15-3 shows the default content and sequence of pages are generated from a module component when the layout style is set to List/Form.

- **Form** No Record list is created. A View form is displayed with a set of navigation buttons for navigating through record details, one at a time. This style can be efficient in presenting read-only information. Form style doesn't imply read-only. These modules can have insert/update/delete, as the figure also shows.

The default content and sequence of pages are generated from a module component when the layout style is set to Form, as shown in Figure 15-4.

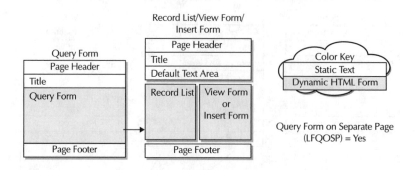

FIGURE 15-3. *List/Form layout style*

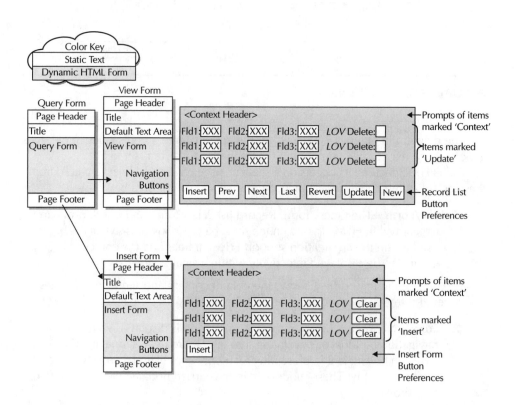

FIGURE 15-4. *Form layout style*

Generating Multiple Record Insert and Update Forms

One technique for improving the Web PL/SQL-generated user interface is the capability to create multiple record insert and update forms. These forms enable users either to insert or update multiple records without having to navigate to a new form each time. The new module component property "Rows Displayed" controls how many rows are displayed for forms with either the Form or List/Form layout style. The following table lists generator preferences that are related to multiple record forms:

Category	Preference	Description
View Form	ZONVTC	Specifies the number of items that appear on each line.
View Form	ZONVSD	Specifies whether to display a summary of deleted records.
Record List	ZONLMV	Display Record List and Multirow view form. By default, the record list doesn't display for a multirow view form.
Insert Form	ZONIBR	Specifies the number of blank rows that appear on the form.
Insert Form	ZONITC	Specifies the number of items that appear on each line.

An icon appears at the end of each row on the insert form indicating whether the record will be included in the insert when the Insert button is pressed. The Web page displays a check mark when the record is entered and displays a blank if the user clears the record. These icons must be copied on to the Internet application server from the $ORACLE_HOME\cgenw61\cvwimg directory. The virtual path to the directory on the application server should be set at the application system level in the System Image Location (SYSIMG) generator preference.

Figure 15-5 shows an example of a multirow update List/Form.

Building Break Reports and Summary Fields

Record Lists provide the results to table queries in the Web PL/SQL environment. They also provide hyperlinks to the view form where users can update database records. A problem that might arise is the duplication of data on the record list screen. Figure 15-6 shows an example of this problem. Each record displays the department name and department number.

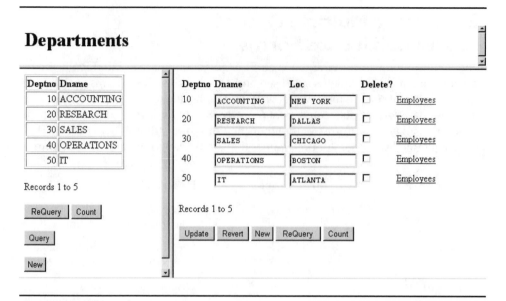

FIGURE 15-5. *Multirow update List/Form*

Employees By Department

Dname	Deptno	Ename	Job	Empno
ACCOUNTING	10	CLARK	MANAGER	7782
ACCOUNTING	10	KING	PRESIDENT	7839
ACCOUNTING	10	MILLER	CLERK	7934
RESEARCH	20	SMITH	CLERK	7369
RESEARCH	20	ADAMS	CLERK	7876
RESEARCH	20	FORD	ANALYST	7902
RESEARCH	20	SCOTT	ANALYST	7788
RESEARCH	20	JONES	MANAGER	7566
RESEARCH	20	WILSON		9873
SALES	30	ALLEN	SALESMAN	7499

Records 1 to 10

Next Last ReQuery Count

Query New

FIGURE 15-6. *Duplicate data problem*

This screen can be improved with the use of a break report by creating break groups in the Design Editor. Placing the department items in one group and the employee items in a second group, as shown here, causes the record list to display as a break report.

Note, the hyperlink is no longer the first item in the record list. The hyperlink is now the first item, which isn't a member of a break group. In cases where all items are members of break groups, the first item in the last break group becomes the hyperlink.

A summary field can also be added to record list screens. You can do this by creating a computed unbound item and defining the SQL Expression that computes the summary. For example, a count field that displays the number of employees in each department can be added. Figure 15-7 shows the unbound item definition. The following illustration shows the break report with the summary field added:

Employees By Department

Dname	Deptno	Ename	Job	Empno
ACCOUNTING	10	CLARK	MANAGER	7782
		KING	PRESIDENT	7839
		MILLER	CLERK	7934
	Emp Count			3

Records 1 to 3

ReQuery   Count

Query   New

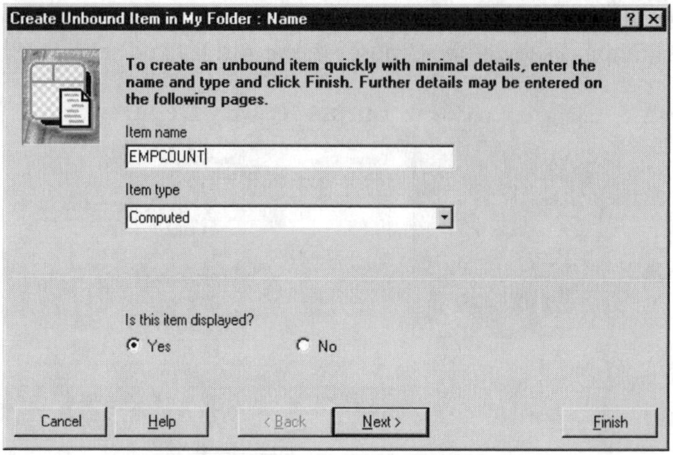

FIGURE 15-7. *Unbound item definition*

These are the basic capabilities for laying out your Web PL/SQL forms. Many properties and generator preferences can affect the look and feel of your applications. Other techniques for defining the look and feel of your applications are covered later in this chapter.

Accessing Master Component Item Values in Detail Components

In Web PL/SQL modules, referencing master component items in detail components is often necessary. In a master-detail form, you might want to display context information from the master component on the detail component form. If you're using an LOV component, you might need to restrict the list by using the value of a master component item. This feature is now available for all user-defined PL/SQL. Previously, developers had to query the master table using the foreign key data but, now, developers can reference master component items in the format of module_component.item_name. Figure 15-8 shows an example of using this feature. In this example, the list of values provides a list of managers. This list should display only those managers in the same department as the employee, so the additional restrictions property can be used to add this restriction. In the additional restrictions property, we indicate that the manager's deptno must be equal to the current employees deptno using the module_component.item_name reference syntax. Here MC_EMP is the module component and DEPTNO is the item.

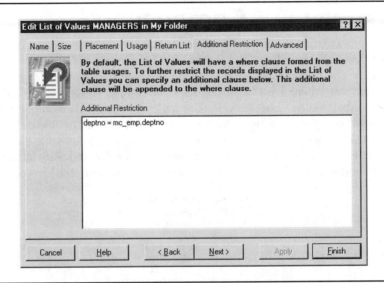

FIGURE 15-8. *Referencing master component item values*

This technique can be used in User text, LOVs, SQL expressions for unbound items, SQL text properties (WHERE, HAVING, and CONNECT BY clauses), and user-defined application logic. The generator preferences in the following table are related to this new feature:

Category	Preference	Description
Container, Module	MCNAAC	Use this preference to ensure that code for maintaining master context is always added to a module, even when the module makes no use of it.
Container, Module, Module Component	MDNDPK	Use this preference to define the name of the PL/SQL package that displays the master context information.
Container, Module, Module Component	MCNMDP	Use this preference to make available master context for the module components. A positive value means this number of master module component contexts will be maintained.

Creating LOV Components

In addition to creating a traditional Designer Lookup table usage within a module, a generated list of values can be created by defining LOV components. By creating LOV components, you gain more control over LOVs and you aren't limited to those situations where a foreign key exists. *LOV components* are models of an LOV based on a table and any associated lookup table uses. The LOV component can be defined either as a Reusable List of Values component or as a specific List of Values component within a module. The advantage to creating it as a Reusable List of Values component is the same LOV definition can be created once and associated to items of various modules. The following illustration shows two Reusable Lists of Values.

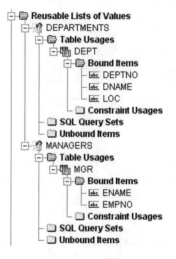

Including and Associating a LOV Component

Once defined, a LOV can be used in a module as an inclusion and associated with a bound or unbound item. The inclusion forces Designer to generate the LOV within the generated module. If the LOV isn't associated with an item, application logic is required to invoke the LOV. The association with a particular item causes the application logic to call the LOV to be generated. The following illustration shows the module diagram depiction of an inclusion and association of a Reusable LOV Component.

Mapping the LOV Return List

The return list of the LOV specifies which items receive the values returned from the LOV. The generator can map corresponding items that are linked by a foreign key by default but, in other situations, they must rely on the manual return list mapping. This shows the mapping of the empno item from the LOV with the mgr item in the module component.

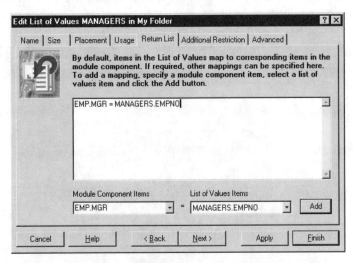

Refining the LOV WHERE Clause

By dynamically building the WHERE clause, the displayed list of values can be created in context with the user's current situation. If you were adding an employee, the manager list of values should only contain managers in the same department as the employee. Adding this type of restriction to the WHERE clause can be done in either of the two following places:

- LOV component base table or lookup table usage

- Additional Restriction clause of LOV association with an item

Where you make the WHERE clause refinement depends on your intentions. If the WHERE clause refinement is global to all modules that use it, it should reside in the LOV component. If the WHERE clause is specific to your module, it should be placed in the LOV association. Remember, component items can be referenced in the LOV association Additional Restriction clauses by using the module_component.item_name syntax.

Defining Action Items

Action Items provide two important functions within a module. The first function is allowing navigation to another module or module component in a manner similar to Called Modules. The second, more powerful, function is providing a way to initiate user-defined application logic. Defining the type of action item is done when first defining the action item. Use custom action items to initiate user-defined application logic. The following illustration shows where the developer defines the type of Action Item. Here, navigation within the module was selected.

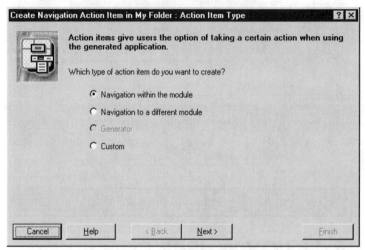

If the Action Item type is set to navigation within the module, the user must select a module component from the list. The following illustration shows the module component selection list.

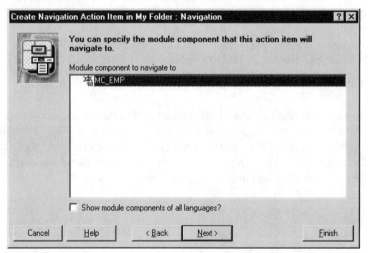

If the Action Item type is set to custom, the user must define the custom action using events and, perhaps, Named Routines. The following two illustrations show the OnClick event that uses JavaScript to navigate to **http://www.tusc.com**.

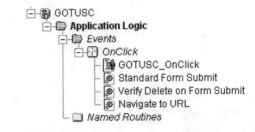

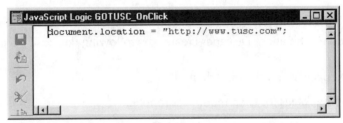

Action Items can be displayed as buttons, hyperlinks, or image links. The properties for defining the display type are as follows:

Display Option	Property	Value
Button	Create Button?	Y
Hyperlink	Create Button?	N
Image Link	Icon Name	Enter image filename

The placement of action items is controlled through generator preferences, as outlined in the following table:

Category	Preference	Description
Action Item	ZONAIP	Specify where the action items are positioned on the page.
General Layout	AILFRM	Specify which Forms display the Action Item.
General Layout	AILLDS	Set the display style of the Link Action Item.
General Layout	AILNLN	Display the Action Item on new line.
General Layout	AILTFN	Set the target frame name.

Understanding the Packages Generated by Designer

Web applications that use the Web Developers PL/SQL Toolkit are made up of PL/SQL packages stored in the database. These packages produce dynamic HTML and JavaScript Web pages from user requests made through the Apache HTTP Server and the PL/SQL Apache module, which are components of the Oracle9i Application Server. Knowledge of the procedures, functions, record structures, and parameters used in these packages enables the developer to enhance applications through the various means described later in this chapter.

Understanding Module Package Procedures

During module generation, Designer creates the following database packages:

- One package for the module itself
- Two packages for each module component
  - One package for the main PL/SQL procedures and functions
  - One package containing PL/SQL to generate JavaScript

The package for the module itself serves as a starting point for the module. The name of this package is the module implementation name (or module name, if no implementation name is given), with a dollar sign ($) concatenated to the end. For example, if the module name is myModule, the package name is myModule$.

The main module component package does most of the work. It contains procedures to display the different Web pages, as well as procedures to handle the user's actions. Its name is composed of the module implementation name, a dollar sign, and the module component name. Extending the preceding example: a module component myModuleComponent in the module becomes the package myModule$myModuleComponent.

The JavaScript package contains PL/SQL that generates the JavaScript used by the module component. Its name is the module implementation name, the string JS, and the module component name. With the previous names, this produces the package myModuleJSmyModuleComponent.

For ease of reference, the module package is referred to as the module$ package and the latter as the module$moduleComponent and moduleJSmoduleComponent packages, respectively. The most important functions and procedures contained in these packages are described in the following sections.

The Module Package

The main package for the module (the module$ package) contains the following procedures:

Procedure Name	Description
Startup	Entry point for the module. Calls the FirstPage procedure to build the page and/or the Startup procedure of the first module component.
FirstPage	Creates the first page of the module.
ShowAbout	Shows the about page for the module.
TemplateHeader	Creates the contents of the <HEAD> section for various documents within the generated application.

The Main Module Component Package

The procedures and functions comprising the module$moduleComponent package can be classified into four groups: Screen Form Procedures, Action Submit Procedures, Event Functions, and Miscellaneous Procedures and Functions.

Screen Form Procedures   Screen Form Procedures produce the HTML screens that comprise the module. This includes the startup procedure that calls one of the other procedures (for example FormQuery) to display the Query Web page.

The following table outlines the Screen Form Procedures:

Procedure Name	Description
Startup	Is the entry point for the module component.
FormQuery	Builds an HTML form for entering query criteria.
FormInsert	Builds an HTML form for inserting data.
FormView	Builds an HTML form for viewing/updating a record.
QueryList	Builds the record list screen resulting from a query.
FormDelete	Builds the form to confirm deleting a record. Only used if the browser doesn't support JavaScript. If the browser supports JavaScript, a pop-up dialog box is used to confirm deletion instead.

Action Submit Procedures   Action Submit Procedures are called from the application Web pages whenever the user clicks a button, that is, submits a particular

HTML form. They normally perform some kind of processing, and then invoke one of the Screen Form Procedures to display the next Web page to the user.

The following table outlines the Action Submit Procedures:

Procedure Name	Description
ActionQuery	Called when the query form is submitted.
ActionInsert	Called when the insert form is submitted.
ActionView	Called when the view form is submitted.
ActionDelete	Called from the ActionView procedure or when the delete confirmation form is submitted.
ActionUpdate	Called from the ActionView procedure when a record update is requested.

Event Functions   Event Functions serve as placeholders for PL/SQL code to be entered into the module component events. If you define an event on a module component, the code you enter is included in these functions.

The following table outlines the Event Functions:

Function Name	Description
PreUpdate	Contains the code entered for the module component PreUpdate event.
PostUpdate	Contains the code entered for the module component PostUpdate event.
PreInsert	Contains the code entered for the module component PreInsert event.
PostInsert	Contains the code entered for the module component PostInsert event.
PreDelete	Contains the code entered for the module component PreDelete event.
PostDelete	Contains the code entered for the module component PostDelete event.
PreQuery	Contains the code entered for the module component PreQuery event.
PostQuery	Contains the code entered for the module component PostQuery event.

Miscellaneous Procedures and Functions   The following table outlines other important functions:

Procedure Name	Description
QueryView	Selects the appropriate record and calls FormView to build the screen to display the record.
QueryHits	Returns the number of records matching a specific query. Called by QueryList to display the number of records on the list screen.
BuildSQL	Called by QueryList and QueryHits to build the SELECT statement for a particular query.
Validate	Validates the items of a module component before they're saved to the database. Performs case conversion, number conversion, validation against domains, and so forth.

The Module Component JavaScript Package

The moduleJSmoduleComponent package consists of the following procedures:

Procedure Name	Description
CreateQueryJavaScript	Creates JavaScript necessary for the Query form.
CreateListJavaScript	Creates JavaScript necessary for the Record List form.
CreateViewJavaScript	Creates JavaScript necessary for the View form.
CreateInsertJavaScript	Creates JavaScript necessary for the Insert form.

Understanding How Named Routines Are Handled

Designer's named routines can be defined at the module level, module component level, and item level. They can be either PL/SQL routines or JavaScript routines. The PL/SQL routines can be either public or private, and the JavaScript routines must have a target location defined. How the named routine is defined dictates the location in which the generated package will be handled.

All public PL/SQL named routines are declared in the appropriate package specification. A module-level PL/SQL named routine is declared in the module$ package specification. Public module-component-level and item-level PL/SQL named routines are declared in the appropriate module$moduleComponent package specification. All private PL/SQL named routines are declared within the appropriate package body.

Based on the defined target location, the generator places the defined JavaScript code in the moduleJSmoduleComponent package. The following table lists the specific procedures for each target location:

Target Location	Specific Procedure
Insert/view	CreateViewJavaScript and CreateInsertJavaScript
Record list	CreateListJavaScript
Query form	CreateQueryJavaScript

Understanding How Events Are Handled

Designer's events can be defined at the module level, module component level, and item level. At the module level and module component level, Designer only enables PL/SQL code to be used. At the item level, all events must be defined as one of the provided JavaScript events. The following table lists the location Designer will place the event code for each type of event:

Event Type	Specific Procedure
Module-level event—Private Declarations	module$ package body
Module-level event—Public Declarations	module$ package specification
Module component—PreUpdate	module$moduleComponent.PreUpdate
Module component—PostUpdate	module$moduleComponent.PostUpdate
Module component—PreInsert	module$moduleComponent.PreInsert
Module component—PostInsert	module$moduleComponent.PostInsert
Module component—PreDelete	module$moduleComponent.PreDelete
Module component—PostDelete	module$moduleComponent.PostDelete
Module component—PreQuery	module$moduleComponent.PreQuery
Module component—PostQuery	module$moduleComponent.PostQuery

Understanding How User Text Is Handled

The following table indicates which module$moduleComponent procedure handles the text entered into the user text areas. The text is simply wrapped in an htp.print call at the top or bottom of the appropriate Screen Form Procedure. Refer to this table for a listing of procedures handling each of the user text locations.

User Text Area	Procedure Handling User Text
Top of record list	QueryList
Bottom of record list	QueryList
Top of Query form	FormQuery
Bottom of Query form	FormQuery
Top of View form	FormView
Bottom of View form	FormView
Top of Insert form	FormInsert
Bottom of Insert form	FormInsert
Top of Delete form	FormDelete
Bottom of Delete form	FormDelete

Understanding Procedure Parameters

Each of the screens that make up a generated module is produced as an HTML form. When the user requests a form, the values of all the HTML input items are passed to the Action Submit Procedure. The Action Submit Procedures, ActionInsert, ActionView, ActionQuery, and QueryList, have parameters to receive these values. The P_, O_, U_, and Z_ parameters are the four types of parameters passed to the procedures.

The P_ parameters contain the current values of the HTML input items on the screen.

The O_ parameters are used on updates to hold the previous values of the HTML input items. The previous values are needed to verify that no other user has updated the record in the database since it was queried into the HTML form.

The U_ parameters are used in procedures performing queries with date items. The upper bounds of the date range query are contained in these parameters.

The Z_ parameters pass mode information to procedures, such as what action was requested by the user.

The developer can add parameters to the module$moduleComponent.startup procedure by creating module arguments and defining the argument item usage. This enables the passing of arguments to the startup procedure as part of the URL. Module Arguments are described in more detail later in this chapter.

Understanding the Package-Defined Record Types

The module$moduleComponent package declares several record types, including FORM_REC, CURR_REC, PREV_REC, and NBT_REC. For each of these types, a variable is declared global to the package with the corresponding names of FORM_VAL, CURR_VAL, PREV_VAL, and NBT_VAL. These record variables are global to the package, so they can be referenced by named routines and in user text.

The FORM_VAL record variable holds all the items passed from the HTML form to the Action Submit Procedures. Its structure maps to the bound items in the module. The CURR_VAL record is used to pass values to the appropriate Table API. This record maps to the actual structure of the module component base table. The FORM_VAL values are moved into the CURR_VAL record by the Validate procedure, performing all the necessary validation and conversion. The PREV_VAL record variable is used for updates. Identical to the CURR_VAL record variable, its structure maps to the structure of the module component base table. This record holds the previous values of an update and verifies that another user hasn't made changes to the record between the time the record was selected and an update was issued. The NBT_REC maps to nonbase table values passed to the Action Submit, including unbound items and items displayed from a lookup table usage type.

Understanding How the Generated Code Works

The entry point to a generated Web PL/SQL module is the startup procedure of the module package. If your module is called myModule, the entry point is the procedure myModule$.startup. To understand how the application works, you can start at this point and read through the generated PL/SQL code in the execution order or you can use a PL/SQL debugging tool to follow the flow of the application through the different procedures.

You'll notice many calls to the Web PL/SQL Generator Library (the WSGL package). This package comes with Designer and is used extensively to produce the HTML used in the application. Advanced developers have been known to change this package to gain more control over the generated application, but this isn't for the faint of heart. And, of course, once you start changing the packages supplied by Oracle, you are cutting yourself off from Oracle support.

Incorporating Views into Generated Modules

Using views as base tables in generated modules is a logical method in providing needed functionality. Views are often used to restrict access to certain records in a base table or to provide a logical view of multiple tables. Using views with generated modules isn't as straightforward as one might think, however, because of dependencies the generated modules have with using the Designer-generated Table API. All base tables must contain the Table API packages for proper execution and therein lies the problem. Designer doesn't generate Table APIs for views with the click of a button or from a menu selection.

To "fool" Designer into generating the desired view API, you must create a table in a separate Designer folder with the same name and structure as the view. Once the view has been generated in the appropriate schema, the table with the same name can be used to create a table API. This table API will get compiled against the view in the data owner's schema.

TIP
*By creating a Table API on a table with the same
name and structure as the desired view, you're
effectively creating the view API. This increases the
maintenance effort and can cause some confusion.
It might be good to avoid using views as base tables.*

Building an Effective Database Security Scheme when Using Generated Modules

Database security is a primary concern when developing any application. For Oracle applications, security is typically handled by assigning a user specific roles, which have been granted certain privileges on a set of database objects. By providing direct privileges on database objects, a database administrator might unintentionally provide access to data the user shouldn't have. While possibly not the best design, security rules are often embedded in the application logic, perhaps because of their complexity. A user connecting to the database with one of many data-browsing tools available could circumvent these rules. The best method to ensure application users cannot gain undesired access to database objects is not to grant privileges to them.

With Web PL/SQL applications, ensuring that users cannot gain undesired access to database objects can be achieved easily. The key is to understand two facts:

■ Web PL/SQL applications consist of database PL/SQL packages. These access database objects through DML (for SELECT operations) and through the Table API packages (for all other operations).

■ A user can access a database object by executing a stored procedure owned by a user who has direct privileges on the database object.

Using these facts, a recommended security scheme is presented in the following table:

Database User	Database Objects Owned	Privileges Granted
Data owner	All tables, views, sequences, and indexes	Resource
Application owner	Web PL/SQL application packages and Table API packages	All privileges on the database objects owned by data owner
Application user	None	Execute on specific application owner packages

In effect, you must give the application users access to database objects by granting them execute rights on the PL/SQL packages that make up the Web PL/SQL applications. You don't give the users any privileges to access the database tables themselves.

By limiting access to the data owner and application owner accounts to database administrators, the capability of application users to gain direct access to database objects is eliminated.

Using Events and Named Routines

Events and named routines in Web PL/SQL Generator modules serve the same purpose that triggers and program units serve in Oracle Forms modules. Events and named routines are defined at the module level, module component level, and bound item level (shown in the following illustration). Events are generally used for controlling navigation or performing validation. Named routines have a general purpose: they are used for coding routines that can be used in multiple locations throughout a module.

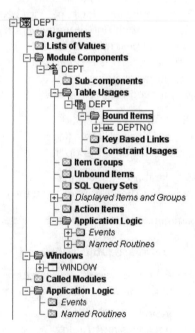

Using Named Routines

Named routines can be coded in either JavaScript or PL/SQL. JavaScript routines are executed on the client side and the PL/SQL routines are executed on the server side.

The only choice offered for a PL/SQL routine type by the Named Routine dialog is Procedure. To change the named routine to a function with the Code Editor, simply change Procedure to Function, and then add the Return clause.

Using Events

Events follow a different set of rules than do named routines. The following table details the types of events supported at each level:

Event Scope Level	Event Name	Implementation Language
Module, module component	Public declarations	PL/SQL
Module, module component	Private declarations	PL/SQL
Module, module component	Pragma declarations	PL/SQL
Module component	PreQuery	PL/SQL
Module component	PostQuery	PL/SQL
Module component	PreInsert	PL/SQL
Module component	PostInsert	PL/SQL
Module component	PreUpdate	PL/SQL
Module component	PostUpdate	PL/SQL
Module component	PreDelete	PL/SQL
Module component	PostDelete	PL/SQL
Module component	ServerValidate	PL/SQL
Module component	Validate	JavaScript
Module component	OnLoad	JavaScript
Module component	OnUnload	JavaScript
Bound item	OnBlur	JavaScript
Bound item	OnChange	JavaScript
Bound item	OnClick	JavaScript
Bound item	OnFocus	JavaScript
Bound item	OnSelect	JavaScript

Leveraging Key Web PL/SQL Generator Preferences and Attributes

As with all Designer generators, the Web PL/SQL Generator contains a multitude of generator preferences, enabling a developer to influence the appearance and behavior of a generated application. Preferences can be set at the application level, the module level, or the module component level.

In the following table, the Web PL/SQL preferences are grouped into categories. Each preceding category contains a set of preferences. The following subsections focus on a few key preferences in some of the preceding categories. The key preferences address the use of custom HTML in modules, registering PL/SQL packages external to the module, integrating frames into a module, and setting up security features.

Category	Description
Action Item	Options for where action items appear on the screen
DBA	Reference database objects
Document Attributes	Add color and background images to *i*AS applications
Document Templates	Define style templates for generated HTML documents
Frames	Options affecting the appearance and behavior of pages containing HTML frames
Frames – Custom	Define custom frameset templates
Frames – Default	Define the relative sizes of frames in the default frameset
General Layout	Options governing various aspects of the user interface
Headers and Footers	Define page headers and footers
Insert Form	Options determining the appearance of the Insert form
Links	Options determining the appearance of hyperlinks
List of Values	Options determining the appearance of lookup LOVs
Master Context	Options for displaying and maintaining master context information
Option ConText	Options for supporting the use of the Oracle ConText cartridge
Popup Calendar	Options determining appearance of the pop-up calendar
Query Form	Options determining the appearance of the Query form
Record List	Options determining the content and appearance of the record list

Category	Description
Security	Add security features
Startup Page	Options determining the content and appearance of the startup page
Text Handling	Options determining how to process user text
View Form	Options determining the appearance of the View form

Using HTML Tags in Module Components

When adding custom HTML tags to a Designer-generated module is necessary, two obvious methods exist. The first is to alter the PL/SQL packages generated by Designer. This is considered to be a postgeneration change and can cause version control headaches. Additionally, the code is difficult to maintain because it's generated code, not handwritten code. The second, preferred method, is to add the HTML directly to the module component through the user text areas. The user text areas are the artist's palettes for generated module design and are covered in a later section. If the module's preferences aren't set correctly, the HTML tags show up as plain text on the Web page. To make the HTML tags take effect, you must set the MODSUB (substitute HTML reserved characters) preference in the Text Handling category to No at the module level, as shown in the following illustration:

⊟ Text Handling	
▫ Substitute HTML Reserved Characters	No

⊟ Text Handling	
▫ MODSUB	N

Registering and Using External PL/SQL Packages in User Text

PL/SQL packages are an effective method of implementing libraries of reusable code over a large application. A single code change propagates itself over the entire application. If you plan on using PL/SQL packages in your user text area, you must register them with the module through the PKGLST or PL/SQL package list preference in the Text Handling category, as the following illustration shows:

⊟ Text Handling	
▫ Substitute HTML Reserved Characters	No
▫ PL/SQL Package List	Format, Util

⊟ Text Handling	
▫ MODSUB	N
▫ PKGLST	Format, Util

The module$moduleComponent package refers to the package that defines a module component. If you want to reference a PL/SQL named routine, defined in the module component, the module component's package must be added to the PL/SQL package list.

Using Frames and Style Sheets

A Web PL/SQL Generator module consists of several Web pages, including a page for inserting records, a page for updating, and a record list page. By default, these pages appear singularly. What if you want to show the record list at the top of the page and the update screen on the bottom using two frames? How would you do this? All you need is a frame template (see Figure 15-9 and Figure 15-10) and the correct generator preferences.

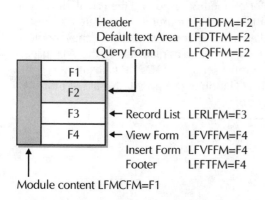

```
Header          LFHDFM=F2
Default text Area  LFDTFM=F2
Query Form      LFQFFM=F2
```

```
F1
F2    ◄
F3    ◄ Record List  LFRLFM=F3
F4    ◄ View Form    LFVFFM=F4
        Insert Form   LFVFFM=F4
        Footer        LFFTFM=F4
```

Module content LFMCFM=F1

```
<HTML>
<FRAMESET COLS="20%, *">
<FRAME NAME=F1">
<FRAMESET ROWS="20%,40%,40%">
<FRAME NAME="F2">
<FRAME NAME="F3">
<FRAME NAME="F4">
</FRAMESET>
</FRAMESET>
</HTML >
```

page contains two columns.
first column is a single frame named F1 (FRAME).
second column contains three rows (FRAMESET).
first row is named F2.
second row is named F3.
third row is named F4.

Frameset template file (LFFSTP) =d:\custom.htm

FIGURE 15-9. *Custom frame layout diagram*

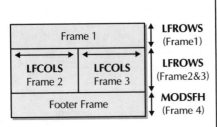

Use the HTML <FRAMESET> syntax to control the Default Frameset (Frames 1, 2 & 3)

",2"	First row (or column) is half the size of the second.
25%, 75%	First row (or column) is 25% of space available and the second uses 75%
100,*	First row (or column) is 100 pixels, the second fills remaining space.

FIGURE 15-10. *Default frame layout diagram*

Designer provides a number of preferences to enable the implementation of frames in a module, as shown in the following table.

Using Style Sheets

Style sheets contain HTML formatting information. They can be coded directly into the source of the Web page using the <STYLE> tag or they can be called externally with the <LINK> tag. More than one style sheet can be used in a single Web page. Including a style sheet in a Web PL/SQL Generator application is simple. The developer includes them through the use of templates or a global generator preference, or simply codes them in the user text areas. The following is a simple example of a style sheet:

```
H1      {font-size:    20px;
         color:        red;
         }
BODY    {color:        blue;
          background:   white;
          font-size:    12px;
         }
TABLE   {border:       4;
         }
H2,B,TH,TR,TD,SELECT:OPTION,INPUT:type   {font-size:12px;}
BIG,UL,LI{font-size:15px;
         }
```

This code can exist within an external file, a PL/SQL procedure, or a <STYLE> tag. The following sections detail the different methods of deployment.

Preference Set	Preference and Usage
Frames	**<u>Use Custom Frameset (LFCUST)</u>** Use this preference to define whether you want to use a custom frameset for pages containing HTML frames. **Default:** No **Values:** Yes, No **Levels:** Container, table, module, and module component **Value Definitions:** **Yes** The custom frameset template is used (defined using the template filename (LFFSTP)). **No** The default frameset is used.
Frames	**<u>Place Query Form on Separate Page (LFQOSP)</u>** Use this preference to define whether the Query form appears on the same page as the record list and View form (in a frame). This preference is only relevant if the layout style of the module component is List/Form. **Default:** Yes **Values:** Yes, No **Levels:** Container, table, module, and module component **Value Definitions:** **Yes** A separate page is created for the Query form. **No** The Query form, record list, and View form appear within frames on the same page. The contents of the View form won't change if the record list is requeried because HTML frame functionality enables multiple frames to be populated only at the point when the page is originally created.

Preference Set	Preference and Usage
Frames—Custom	**Module Content Frame (LFMCFM)** Use this preference to identify which frame displays the module content. If a custom frameset is used and this preference is left blank, or it doesn't specify a frame in the frameset definition, the module content is placed in the first (top) frame. Refer to Figure 15-9. **Default:** None **Values:** Up to 20 characters **Levels:** Container and module
Frames—Custom	**Default Text Area Frame (LFDTFM)** Use this preference to identify which frame is used for the default text area. If a custom frameset is used and this preference is left blank, or it doesn't specify a frame in the frameset definition, the record list frame is used as the default text area. Refer to Figure 15-9. **Default:** None **Values:** Up to 20 characters **Levels:** Container, table, module, and module component
Frames—Custom	**Record List Frame (LFRLFM)** Use this preference to identify which frame displays the record list. If a custom frameset is used and this preference is left blank, or it doesn't specify a frame in the frameset definition, the record list is placed in the first (top) frame. Refer to Figure 15-9. **Default:** None **Values:** Up to 20 characters **Levels:** Container, table, module, and module component
Frames—Custom	**Query Form Frame (LFQFFM)** Use this preference to identify which frame displays the Query form. This preference only takes effect if the Query form isn't being displayed on a separate page (Place Query Form on separate page (LFQOSP) = No). If a custom frameset is used and this preference is left blank, or it doesn't specify a frame in the frameset definition, the Query form is placed in the record list frame. Refer to Figure 15-9. **Default:** None **Values:** Up to 20 characters **Levels:** Container, table, module, and module component

Preference Set	Preference and Usage

Frames — **Auto Query View Form (LFVFAQ)**

Use this preference to choose whether the View form frame displays the details of the first record when the page is initially opened (or created). This preference is only relevant if the layout style of the module component is List/Form. This preference only determines the behavior of pages when they're first opened (or created). If the page contains a Query form (Place Query Form on separate page in Frames (LFQOSP) is set to No) and the record list is requeried, the contents of the View form won't change.

Default: Yes

Values: Yes, No

Levels: Container, table, module, module component

Value Definitions:

Yes When the page is first opened, the View form frame displays the details of the first entry in the record list.

No The first record isn't automatically queried. The View form frame is empty when the page is first opened.

Frames — **Align Center Text Frame (ZONTAC)**

Use this preference to determine whether the content of a frame containing just text is aligned to the center of the frame.

Default: No

Values: Yes, No

Levels: Container, table, module, and module component

Frames — **Top level frame name (LFTLFN)**

When you're using actions items in framesets, use this preference to specify the name of the top-level frame for the target of the hyperlink or button.

Default: _top

Values: A string of up to 20 characters

Levels: Container, table, module

Frames—Custom — **Template Filename (LFFSTP)**

Use this preference to specify the name and file extension of the HTML file where the custom frameset is defined. The full pathname must also be specified. The template file is only read during generation. It isn't required when the application is executed. Refer to Figure 15-9.

Default: None

Values: Up to 100 characters

Levels: Container, table, module, and module component

Preference Set	Preference and Usage
Frames—Custom	**View/Insert Form Frame (LFVFFM)**

Use this preference to identify which frame displays the View form, Insert form, and Delete Confirmation form. If a custom frameset is used and this preference is left blank, or it doesn't specify a frame in the frameset definition, these forms are placed in the frame after the record list (if one exists). If the record list appears in the last frame, all three forms are then displayed in the same frame (but not at the same time). Refer to Figure 15-9.

Default: None
Values: Up to 20 characters
Levels: Container, table, module, and module component

Frames—Custom	**List of Values Frame (LFLVFM)**

Use this preference to identify which frame displays the list of values. This preference only takes effect if LOVs are being placed in frames rather than windows (LOV style (LOVSTL) = FRAME). If a custom frameset is used and this preference is left blank, or it doesn't specify a frame in the frameset definition, the frame following the View/Insert form frame is used.

Default: None
Values: Up to 20 characters
Levels: Container, table, module, and module component

Frames—Custom	**Header Frame (LFHDFM)**

Use this preference to identify which frame displays the page header (MODSHD). The frame name you specify must appear in the frameset definition. If a custom frameset is used and if this preference is left blank, or it doesn't specify a frame in the frameset definition, the page header is placed in the first frame.

Default: None
Values: Up to 20 characters
Levels: Container, table, module, and module component

Frames—Custom	**Footer Frame (LFFTFM)**

Use this preference to identify which frame displays the page footer (MODSFT). The frame name you specify must appear in the frameset definition. If a custom frameset is used and if this preference is left blank, or it doesn't specify a frame in the frameset definition, the page footer is placed in the last frame.

Default: None
Values: Up to 20 characters
Levels: Container, table, module, and module component

Preference Set	Preference and Usage
Frames—Default	**Column Widths (LFCOLS)** Use this preference to specify the width (or relative width) of frame 2 and frame 3, shown in Figure 15-10. If the module component contains any enterable foreign key lookup columns and the style of the LOV window is set to FRAME, an additional frame will be created. If this is the case, you should consider the width required for the LOV frame when choosing a width for frames 2 and 3. **Default:** None **Values:** Any valid COLS attribute for the HTML <FRAMESET> tag, up to 20 characters in length (<Width of Frame 2>,<Width of Frame 3>) **Levels:** Container, table, module, module component **Examples:** 100,* 25%,75%
Frames—Default	**Row Heights (LFROWS)** Use this preference to specify the height (or relative height) of frames 1, 2, and 3, shown in Figure 15-10. **Default:** None **Values:** Any valid ROWS attribute for the HTML <FRAMESET> tag, up to 20 characters in length (<Height of Frame 1>,<Height of Frame 2 & 3>) **Levels:** Container, table, module, module component **Examples:** 100,* 25%,75%
Frames—Default	**Standard Footer Frame Height (MODSFH)** Use this preference to define the height of the footer frame, in pixels. This preference is only used if the standard footer must be placed on a page containing frames. Refer to Figure 15-10. **Default:** 50 **Values:** 1 to 1,000 **Levels:** Container, module

Including a Style Sheet That Uses the <STYLE> Tag

Including a style sheet that uses the <STYLE> tag is simple. In the user text area or in a template, include the following:

```
<STYLE>
H1    {font-size:    20px;
       color:        red;
      }
```

```
BODY    {color:       blue;
         background:   white;
         font-size:    12px;
        }
TABLE   {border:      4;
        }
H2,B,TH,TR,TD,SELECT:OPTION,INPUT:type  {font-size:12px;}
BIG,UL,LI{font-size:15px;
         }
</STYLE>
```

The new formatting characteristics will be applied to any of the referenced tags, followed by the <STYLE> tag. This method is simple, but it isn't a practical method for application-wide deployment. Therefore, the following method, external style sheets, is preferable.

Referencing External Style Sheets

Using external style sheets is the preferred method for including a style sheet in a Web PL/SQL application. Style sheets can be stored as files with a .css extension or coded in a PL/SQL package procedure. The latter method can also be referred to as a *dynamic style sheet library*. The package should contain a public procedure called css. The Web server interprets the reference to the packaged procedure, package_name.css, as an external file reference. The following code illustrates both constructs.

The following code illustrates a cascading style sheet (CSS) as it would be coded in a physical file. The file resides in a directory on some server.

```
H1      {font-size:   20px;
         color:        red;
        }
BODY    {color:       blue;
         background:   white;
         font-size:    12px;
        }
TABLE   {border:      4;
        }
H2,B,TH,TR,TD,SELECT:OPTION,INPUT:type  {font-size:12px;}
BIG,UL,LI{font-size:15px;
         }
```

The following code represents a CSS that's coded into a PL/SQL package and stored in the database:

```
create or replace package styleSheetLibrary as
      procedure css(p_library varchar2 := null);
end styleSheetLibrary;
/
create or replace package body styleSheetLibrary as
```

```
procedure generalModule is
begin
    htp.print('H1      {font-size:    20px;
                        color:        red;
                        }
              BODY     {color:        blue;
                        background:    white;
                        font-size:     12px;
                        }
              TABLE    {border:       4;
                        }
              H2,B,TH,TR,TD,SELECT:OPTION,INPUT:type {font-
                                                     size:12px;}
              BIG,UL,LI{font-size:15px;
                       }');
    end generalModule;
    procedure css(p_library varchar2 := null) is
    begin
        generalModule;
    end css;
end styleSheetLibrary;
/
```

External style sheets are referenced with the <LINK> tag, which is included within the <HEAD> tag (see the following illustration). Two preferred methods can be implemented to include external style sheets in a Web PL/SQL application. The first method is through the MODSHD, or standard header generator preference. The second method is simply to include the code in a template.

⊟ Headers And Footers	
🞲 Standard Footer On All Pages	No
🞲 Standard Footer	
🞲 Standard Header On All Pages	No
🗀 Standard Header	<LINK href="styleSheet.css"></LINK>

Using Unbound Items

Unbound items are module component items not directly tied to a column in a table. The developer uses unbound items to manipulate data and to control screen layout. This enables the developer to employ creativity in module design by providing additional flexibility that isn't available using bound items alone.

The following are six types of unbound items:

■ **Computed** An unbound item used to generate an HTML form element, such as a subtotal or grand total, that's performed on the values of a single item. Computed unbound items can be displayed only on Record Lists.

- **SQL aggregate**   An unbound item used to generate an HTML form element that computes a value by applying a SQL aggregation function to a column. SQL aggregate unbound items can be displayed only on Record Lists.

- **Client-side function**   An unbound item, used to generate an HTML form element that derives its value from a function held on the client browser.

- **Server-side function**   An unbound item used to generate an HTML form element deriving its value from a function held on the server. The derivation calculation can take place only on the server. The changes to derived fields are displayed only after a record is refreshed.

- **SQL expression**   An unbound item used to generate an HTML form element that derives its value from a SQL expression.

- **Custom**   A custom unbound item provides the capability to create an item totally under your control. Using the events defined on the client side and/or the server side, you can process the value of the item in the appropriate manner.

In addition to using unbound items as a means to perform calculations and display summary information (such as totals), unbound items can also be used in other useful methods. For example, unbound items can be used to insert HTML in a form by calling either client-side JavaScript named routines or server-side PL/SQL named routines. The usage sequence can then be changed to insert the unbound item between bound items on the View/Update form. This is useful because while the user text areas can also be used to insert HTML in a Web page, they can only place the HTML at either the top or bottom of the page. Unbound items enable control over the appearance and behavior of generated Web pages.

Leveraging the User Text Area

The user text area is the artist's palette for generated module design. Not only does it enable creativity and flexibility during module design without making postgeneration changes, it also serves as the glue for most of the advanced techniques presented in this chapter. The user text area is essential to obtain a solid understanding of what it is and how it works.

Despite the powerful capabilities of user text areas, they're easy to understand and use. The user text area is simply a method of using Designer to add custom HTML to generated pages. While custom HTML can take the form of plain text, it can also be created using named routines and PL/SQL functions, as long as they return valid HTML syntax. Similarly, the text can be formatted directly with HTML syntax, as long as the Designer preference MODSUB (substitute HTML reserved characters) is set to No. By using these methods, any structure that can be rendered using HTML can be added to your application.

User text can be added at both the module level and the module component level. Module-level user text can be placed on the first page and/or the about page. Module-component-level user text can be placed on any of the HTML documents generated for a module component, such as a Query form, a record list, a View form, an Insert form, or a Delete form. If a location isn't specified, the user text is placed in the default area. The default area is the top of the first page for module-level user text and the top of the record list for module-component-level user text.

You can also specify whether the user text is inserted at the top or the bottom of the particular page. At first glance, this may appear straightforward, but subtle, yet important, implications exist in where you place user text. If user text is placed at the top of a page, be careful not to reference items that will be defined in the lower-half of the HTML document (unless the reference is within a JavaScript function definition). HTML pages are interpreted line-by-line, top to bottom. Most Designer-generated items (forms, bound items, unbound items, and so forth) won't exist yet when the HTML and JavaScript in the top user text is interpreted. In most cases, this won't raise concerns. Many of the advanced techniques, such as overriding Designer's default functionality, won't work because they manipulate items on the Web page after it's created, but before it's displayed to the user. Remembering this is important when you work with cookies and server-side JavaScript libraries.

The following two sections are excerpts from Designer's Help feature on formatting user text with PL/SQL and HTML.

Formatting Text with PL/SQL Functions

Within user text, you may reference any PL/SQL procedure or functions defined in either the HyperText Procedures (HTP) or HyperText Functions (HTF) packages within the Oracle Web Developers PL/SQL Toolkit, the Web PL/SQL Generator Library package (WSGL and WSGFL), or any custom packages specified within the PL/SQL package list (PKGLST) preference returning valid HTML.

During generation, user text is scanned for function calls and the appropriate PL/SQL is generated to combine the HTML generated by the Web Toolkit function calls with the rest of the static text. For example:

- **Sample user text**   Welcome to the htp.bold('ACME Corporation') home page. Send comments on this page to htp.MailTo('jbloggs@acme.com','Joe Bloggs').

- **Generated PL/SQL**   htp.print('Welcome to the '||htf.bold('ACME Corporation')||' home page. Send comments on this page to '||htf.MailTo('jbloggs@acme.com','Joe Bloggs')).

- **Generated output**   Welcome to the **ACME Corporation** home page. Send comments on this page to Joe Bloggs.

Formatting Text with HTML

Normally, HTML reserved characters (< > " &) within user text are replaced with escape characters (< > " &). This behavior ensures no formatting problems occur with generated Web pages.

If you have HTML experience, you might prefer using the HTML syntax to format user text directly. Two methods of deployment exist with the Design Editor.

- Add HTML syntax to user text
- Add entire HTML documents in their native format, through an HTML editor

Adding HTML Syntax to User Text

Add HTML syntax to user text for simple formatting requirements. The assistance of an HTML editor isn't required to create or view the formatted text. During generation, the user text is placed between the <Y></Y> tags of the appropriate HTML document.

If you use this method, set the substitute HTML reserved characters (MODSUB) preference to No, as the following output illustrates:

```
Welcome to the <b>ACME Corporation</b> home page.
```

The generated output of this statement is

```
Welcome to the ACME Corporation home page.
```

You must take care to use escape characters where they are appropriate. For example:

```
This shows employees with a salary &lt; $5000. For more details, click
on the <b>Employee Name</b>:
```

The generated output of this statement is

```
This shows employees with a salary < $5000. For more details, click on
the Employee Name:
```

The substitute HTML reserved characters (MODSUB) preference affects all pages generated from a particular module, not only an individual HTML document.

Adding Entire HTML Documents via an HTML Editor

You can add an entire HTML document by using an HTML editor when more complex formatting is required. Sometimes the assistance of an HTML editor to create or view the formatted text is extremely beneficial.

Your preferred HTML editor can be invoked from the user text property in the Design Editor, and then you can create, view, and test the required content. Save the entire source of the HTML document back to the Repository as User/Help Text.

When using an external HTML editor, an HTML document is treated as text containing the following strings: "<HTML>", "<BODY>", "</BODY>", and "</HTML>". The Design Editor isn't case-sensitive for these tags, but the tags must be in the correct order.

If modifications are required, the entire HTML document can be loaded back into the HTML editor and the changes made in a native HTML editing environment. The following code is generated if MODSUB=NO:

```
<html>
<head>
  <title>TUSC</title>
</head>
<body>
Welcome to the <b>ACME Corporation</b> home page.
</body>
</html>
```

During generation, the Web PL/SQL Generator extracts the user text between the <BODY> and </BODY> tags, and places it into the appropriate HTML document. In the preceding case, the value of MODSUB is ignored and assumed to be No.

The following are several examples of methods used in user text areas:

Example 1: Loading a Server-Side JavaScript Library

```
<SCRIPT SRC="javacriptlibrary.js"></SCRIPT>
```

Example 2: Using Server-Side PL/SQL Procedures (Oracle Web Developers PL/SQL Toolkit)

```
htp.hr
htp.tableopen
htp.tablerowopen
htp.tabledata(htf.big('Row 1, Column 1'))
htp.tabledata(htf.big('Row 1, Column 2'))
htp.tablerowclose
htp.tableclose
```

Example 3: Using Server-Side PL/SQL Functions (Custom)

```
myPackage.myFunction
```

Example 4: Using HTML Formatted Text

```
<HR>
<TABLE>
<TR>
<TD><BIG>Row 1, Column 1</BIG></TD>
<TD><BIG>Row 1, Column 2</BIG></TD>
</TR>
</TABLE>
```

Example 5: Calling Named Routines

```
<SCRIPT>    myNamedRoutine();</SCRIPT>
```

Example 6: Adding JavaScript

```
<SCRIPT>
    function doNothing(){
        return true;
    }
</SCRIPT>
```

Using JavaScript

JavaScript is to Web development as PL/SQL is to Oracle Forms development. See Chapter 7 for JavaScript examples. As with PL/SQL, JavaScript is used to handle or control events behind the scenes. JavaScript isn't Java, even though the names are similar. Microsoft browsers use their own form of JavaScript called *JScript*. JavaScript and JScript aren't always compatible and have some proprietary quirks. This section discusses methods of avoiding proprietary pitfalls, loading external JavaScript libraries, and creating and loading Oracle dynamic server-side JavaScript libraries. It also discusses several Designer-specific topics, including the Web PL/SQL Generator JavaScript object and parameter naming conventions. I cover only some specific points concerning the use of JavaScript in Web PL/SQL applications. Designer's built-in help covers this subject in greater depth.

Avoiding the Proprietary Pitfall

As previously discussed, two versions of JavaScript exist. JavaScript is the original version, created by Netscape and supported by Netscape browsers. The other widely implemented version is called *JScript,* created by Microsoft and supported by Internet Explorer browsers. With many of the same features, the subtle differences can become cumbersome. Some of these differences include array index referencing of form elements, the default value of an undefined variable, and proprietary features among commonly named objects. How do you avoid these pitfalls? The easiest method is to choose a particular browser as the standard for deployment. While that's acceptable for an intranet application, what about an application designed for Internet deployment? The application must determine what browser has initiated the call. The following code segment checks the browser type:

```
function checkNavigator(nav){
    var returnVal   = false;
    if (navigator.appName == "Netscape" &&
        nav.toUpperCase() == "NS4"){
        returnVal = true;
    }
    else if (navigator.appVersion.indexOf("MSIE") != 1 &&
            nav.toUpperCase() == "IE5"){
        returnVal = true;
```

```
   }
   return returnVal;
}
```

This function returns True for NS4 (Netscape) or IE5 (Internet Explorer). Otherwise, all other browsers return False. The following code segment illustrates how to apply this function:

```
function setFocus(itemName,form) {
   var undefined;
   if(form==null || form==undefined)
      form = 0;
   }
   var itemIndex = getItemIndex(itemName,form);
   if (itemIndex != -1) {
      if (checkNavigator("NS4")){
         document.forms[form].elements[itemIndex].focus();
      }
      else
         document.forms[form].elements(itemIndex).focus();
      }
   }
   return true;
};
```

In this code, if the browser is Netscape Navigator, the elements array is referenced using square brackets and, otherwise, it's referenced using parentheses. The code assumes the other browser is Internet Explorer. The same method can be applied where other implementation discrepancies occur.

Using External JavaScript Libraries

External JavaScript libraries are loaded into a Web-based application through the SRC attribute of the <SCRIPT> tag. The following code illustrates how this is accomplished:

```
<SCRIPT SRC="javascriptlibrary.js"></SCRIPT>
```

In a Web PL/SQL Generator application, this tag can be placed in the user text area of the module component or in the standard header generator preference. In most cases, javaScriptLibrary.js is a file. It can also be a packaged procedure, with the help of the *i*AS. Once the library is loaded, any of its functions can be used in events, such as onBlur, or in module-specific JavaScript routines. The library's functions aren't visible to the user if the page source is displayed.

Creating Oracle Server-Side JavaScript Libraries

Using the Oracle9*i* Application Server's PL/SQL module, you can fool the browser into seeing a packaged PL/SQL procedure as a regular file. If this concept is applied to creating JavaScript libraries, you can control the content of the library at run time based on parameters such as the user's role, the date, or a number of other factors. It makes the libraries dynamic. The following steps outline the process to complete this task.

Step 1: Configure Your Web Listener

Ensure your Web listener is configured to map files with the extension of .js, to MIME type application/x-javascript. Otherwise, the reference loading the library will appear in your Web page as plain text. See Chapter 3 for more configuration information.

Step 2: Create the Library

Create a PL/SQL package with any name and include only one public procedure called js. The procedure js is to an Oracle package what the file extension .js is to a browser. Optional parameters can be added to the procedure. The actual library routines should be coded in private procedures accessed through the js procedure, as illustrated in the following example:

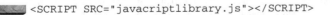

```
create or replace package javaScriptLibrary as
    procedure js;
end javaScriptLibrary;
/
create or replace package body javaScriptLibrary as
    procedure generalModule is
    begin
        htp.p('function  .........'); /* Some set of functions . */
        htp.p('function  .........');
    end generalModule;

    procedure js is
    begin
        generalModules;
    end js;
end javaScriptLibrary;
/
```

Step 3: Add the JavaScript Library to Your Module

To add the JavaScript library to your module, include the following line of code in the user text area of the module component:

```
<SCRIPT SRC="javacriptlibrary.js"></SCRIPT>
```

Understanding Web PL/SQL Generator Naming Conventions

The Web PL/SQL Generator uses specific naming conventions when creating JavaScript functions that handle item-level events or perform application-level validation.

Naming Convention for Event Handlers

Events in a Web application are comparable to triggers in a Forms application. A displayed item or document form element on a Web page can have the following events: onBlur, onChange, onClick, onFocus, and onSelect, which are the only item-level events supported by the Web PL/SQL Generator.

Designer uses a simple naming convention for JavaScript functions that are assigned to handle events. The convention is <item name>_<event name>(this, index). For example

```
MY_ITEM_OnChange(this, 0)
```

The second parameter is an index to the array if multiple record inserts and updates are being used.

Understanding the ctl Parameter

As you start digging through the code the Web PL/SQL Generator generates, you'll frequently encounter references, such as ctl.name or ctl, in the parameter list. The ctl (control) parameter is the standard parameter for all JavaScript generated by Designer. In a Form element, ctl.name refers to document.forms[0].element(<index>).

Overriding Designer's Default Functionality

Designer provides basic capabilities by enabling custom code to be added through named routines and events at the module, module component, and item levels. Sometimes it's necessary to add functionality that cannot be implemented using these methods. For example, Designer doesn't provide a method to add code behind the buttons that are automatically generated for inserting, updating, and deleting.

Even though Designer doesn't provide a means to add custom code to every aspect of a generated form, experienced programmers can manipulate them. The following technique is powerful and can be expanded to provide additional capabilities.

To override Designer's default functionality/actions with your own, use the user text area to manipulate a Web page after it's built and before it's displayed. This can only be performed at the bottom of the appropriate user text area because the form won't have been built yet. However, after the form is built, using HTML and JavaScript, the page can be manipulated before it's displayed. You can simply traverse the document and form elements, and then make the desired modifications to accomplish this.

To understand more clearly how this is done, consider the following procedure, which overrides the routine behind the Submit button with custom code.

Step 1: Create a JavaScript Routine

The following function creates a JavaScript routine:

```
function customRoutine() {
    <custom code>
    document.forms[0].submit();
    return true;
}
```

Step 2: Create a JavaScript Routine to Override Designer's Routine

The function defined in the following searches all elements on the form until it finds the Submit button. It then sets the onClick method to call your function, instead of the function originally assigned to the Submit button by the Web PL/SQL Generator.

```
function setFormValidation {
    for (var i=0; i < document.forms[0].elements.length; i++) {
        if (checkNavigator("NS4")) {
            e = document.forms[0].elements[i];
        } else {
            e = document.forms[0].elements(i);
        }
        if (e.type == "button" && e.value == "Submit") {
            e.onclick = new Function("customRoutine();");
            break;
        }
    }
    return true;
}
```

Step 3: Call the setFormValidation function at the bottom of the module form that will use your validation routine (for example, bottom of View form)

```
<SCRIPT>
    setFormValidation();
</SCRIPT>
```

Step 4: Generate the module

When you access the View form Web page, the JavaScript library loads, the page loads, and your validation function overrides Designer's default routine for the Submit button with the routine you created.

Using Arguments

Arguments can be used to pass parameters between modules. These arguments can then be bound to items on a form to automatically populate the form with the records where the argument value is equal to the value of the bold item. One useful technique is to create a master-detail relationship between modules without using Designer's key-based links. Compared to Designer's key-based links, a master-detail relationship offers a greater degree of control over the appearance, behavior and navigation between modules. It also enables a module to be used as a detail module by more than one master module by simply passing the arguments specific to the relationship between the master and the detail.

To use arguments in the creation of a master-detail relationship between modules, the underlying base tables must contain the appropriate foreign key relationships. It is then simply a matter of adding arguments to the detail module and binding them to the foreign key items on the form. When the master module calls the detail module, it passes the appropriate parameter as an argument creating the relationship. Any arguments not used will default to NULL, effectively enabling a detail module to be used by more than one master module.

To understand more clearly how this works, suppose you want to capture address information for people and businesses. Your database is normalized, so the address table contains foreign keys to the person and business tables. You create three modules: one to capture person information, one to capture business information, and one to capture address information. Two master-detail relationships with the address module serve as the detail module for both the person and the business modules. To accomplish this task, simply create two arguments in the address module and bind them to the foreign keys of the person and business tables as argument item usages. When the person and business modules call the address module, they simply pass a parameter as an argument to the address module. When the address information is saved, the parameter is saved along with the address information creating the appropriate relationship.

Assuming "per" and "bus" are the names of the arguments in the address module, the following syntax calls to the address module (where xx is the value of the parameter) would be (from the person module):

```
addressModule$addressModuleComponent.queryview?p_per=xx
```

and (from the business module):

```
addressModule$addressModuleComponent.queryview?p_bus=xx
```

Managing the Software Life Cycle with Configuration Management Tools

The inability of past releases of Designer to provide granular version control and build configurations was a severe limitation. Designer was a good tool for analysis, design, and development, but third-party tools were required to manage the software life cycle of any significant project. Designer 6i includes these tools, which provide an integrated environment for the entire software life cycle. Many projects blend the use of Designer objects with outside source code and scripts. Designer's version control manages both and creates configurations that include both Designer Objects and system files.

The following five basic components comprise configuration management in the Oracle Repository:

- Workareas
- Version Control

■ Branching

■ Comparing and Merging

■ Configurations

Defining Workareas

Workareas are configuration management containers that provide a view to the repository. These views are a single version of a collection of objects and may be shared or private. They can be used to group objects based on a phase of the development life cycle, (for example, current version of database objects in the test environment). They can also be used to restrict access to objects. Examples include a workarea to hold database objects that only DBAs can access and a workarea that contains modules only developers can access.

Configuration managers, as part of their configuration management plan, should define appropriate workareas for the project. You create Workareas using the Workarea Wizard in the Tools menu of the Repository Object Navigator (RON). Once the workarea is created, privileges must be granted to appropriate users through the Grant Access Rights utility from the RON under the File | Access Rights menu.

Working with Version Control

Working with objects under version control is done through the check-out and check-in functions from a particular workarea. When an object is checked out, it might be locked or it might remain unlocked. Another user cannot check out a locked object until the object is checked back in. Any number of users can check out an unlocked object at the same time. Once one user checks in a new version of an unlocked object, other users must merge their objects at check in.

Once an object is under version control, users can view the history of the object with either the Version History viewer or the Version Event viewer. The *Version History viewer* is a graphical tool that uses nodes and a hierarchical tree to show the history of an object. The *Version Event viewer* provides detail information about each event the object has gone through. These items include the following:

■ Object Version

■ The Version Status (checked in or checked out)

■ User Performing the Event

■ Version Date

■ Branch Information

■ Event Type (check in or check out)

■ User Notes

Developing in Parallel with Branches

The capability to work in parallel is a powerful tool that enables you to make changes in one set of objects without affecting another set of the same objects. Perhaps you need to make a small change to a production object that has been significantly modified for a future release. This can be done with *branching,* where the user checks out the version of the object currently in production, makes the update, and checks the object back in to a new branch.

To check objects into a new branch, the user must create the branch. To do this, the user must have been given the privilege to allow management of branch labels within the repository. This privilege is assigned through the Repository Administration Utility (RAU). Once the branch is created, the user must modify the default check in branch of the workarea to specify the new branch. This can only be done if the edit policy for versioning is set to allow Automatic Branching.

Comparing and Merging Objects

Comparing and merging objects is another component of parallel development. Using the earlier example of the small change needed to the production version of an object that had been enhanced for a future release, you can see a simple example of why this is important. Assume, for example, you want to ensure the small change to the production version is added to your future release. You could make the change manually, but a better way to make the update would be using the compare and merge tools that Designer provides.

Using the Version History viewer, you can compare any two versions of an object. If the small update isn't found in the future release version, the object versions need to be merged. Version merges may be performed from the Version History viewer or the RON.

Creating Configurations

You might be ready to move some portion of your application from development to test. And what's the best way to package the various repository objects needed to create the database objects, modules, source code, and scripts that make up your release? Use a configuration. A *configuration* is a collection of specific versions of objects.

Use the Configuration Wizard under the Tools menu in the RON to create your configuration. With the wizard, you can add, remove, and change the version of members for a configuration. The final step of using the wizard is to check in the configuration itself. Like other repository objects, configurations are under version control.

Generating Java Source Database Objects

You cannot talk Web development without mentioning Java. Java is an object-oriented programming language that compiles into bytecode, which allows it to run on any platform that has a Java Virtual Machine (JVM). This "write once, run anywhere" architecture is ideal for the heterogeneous network of computers that constitutes the Internet. The Oracle database includes an integrated JVM as part of its Internet computing technology. This enables programmers to develop server-side Java objects and call them from outside of the database by using PL/SQL or CORBA. Chapter 13 provides more details on using server-side Java objects. While Designer won't generate Java code, it will help you manage your server-side Java objects by storing them in the Oracle Repository and generating the DDL to create the Java objects in your database. The Designer Logic Editor handles Java source code, as well as PL/SQL and JavaScript.

Creating Java Definitions

Java Definitions are simply another type of object within the server model and are stored in the repository. They're similar to PL/SQL Definitions. With PL/SQL, users can define functions, procedures, and packages. With Java Definitions, users can define Java Source, Java Class, and Java Resource objects. Figure 15-11 shows a Java Class Definition in the server model and its property sheet.

Once the Java object is defined in the server model, the implementation details need to be defined using the DB Admin tab. This is where you define the source of your Java object. Java objects can reside within a user defined LOB column, within the CREATE$JAVA$LOB$TABLE table, or in an external BFILE. Figure 15-12 shows the Java implementation for TUSC's Java class.

Once the Java implementation details are completed, the Java database object is generated like any other Server Model object. This produces the DDL necessary for creating the source, class, or resource database object. The DDL for loading the Java class is shown in the following illustration:

```
-- C:\ias\dbjava2.jav
--
-- Generated for Oracle 8.1 on Sat Jul 14  14:11:49 2001 by Server Generator 6.5.46.1.0


PROMPT Creating Java
CREATE OR REPLACE JAVA CLASS
  USING BFILE (JAVA, 'helloWorld.class')
/
```

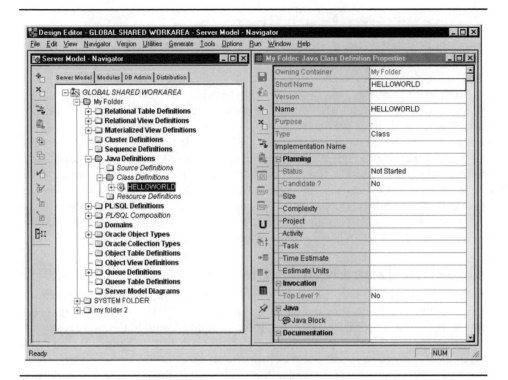

FIGURE 15-11. *Java Class Definition*

Creating a Java Call Spec

Once a Java object is loaded into the database, the simplest way to call it from outside the database is by calling server-side PL/SQL. Create a Java Call Spec by defining a PL/SQL element that accesses Java using the IS LANGUAGE JAVA specification. This is done in Designer by creating a new PL/SQL definition and setting the appropriate Java parameters, as the following illustration shows.

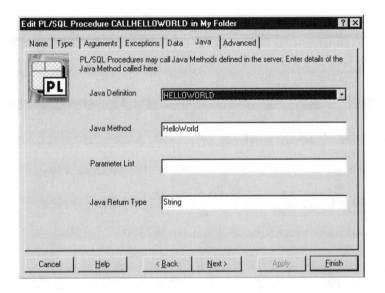

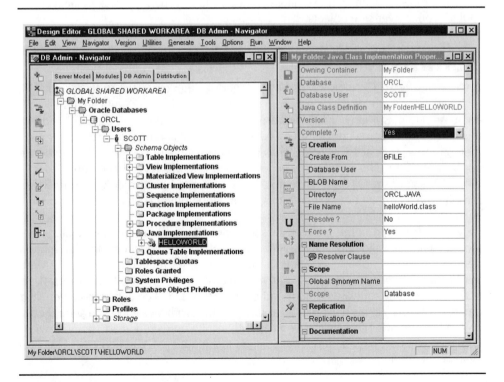

FIGURE 15-12.   *Java implementation*

Under the Java tab on the property dialog box for the PL/SQL definition, the user specifies the Designer Java Definition, the Java method, parameter string, and return type to create a PL/SQL procedure that can call a Java method. The following illustration shows the DDL generated to create the PL/SQL call specification:

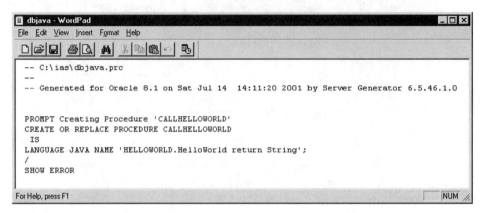

These tools for defining Java database objects and call specs provide a management tool for your server-side objects.

Summary

A vast majority of "Oracle shops" use Designer's design components to design logical database models, translate them to physical models, and then generate database schemas. Many companies drop off here and don't use Designer beyond this functionality. Some companies go beyond this level and use Designer to capture their business processes. The next step is to use the generator components to generate applications using Designer. In my experience, it is at this level that companies are either "Designer shops" or they are not. There seems to be no middle ground. The reason? The learning curve to get to this point. Hopefully this chapter helps you to get to this point faster.

As we discussed in this chapter, Designer provides a repository and declarative tools for managing and building Web-enabled database objects and application module definitions. This chapter has covered a variety of topics related to generating Web applications. It discussed generating dynamically created HTML forms using Web PL/SQL, managing software versions and configurations, and creating server-side Java database objects. At this point, if you weren't familiar with Designer, you should now have an overview of Designer's Web capabilities. If you were already familiar with Designer, you now have a number of tips and techniques you can implement for your Web applications.

CHAPTER
16

Oracle9*i*AS Portal

owadays, it's hard to imagine a site on the Web without some type of "my" page or a page that's personalized or customized just for you. This is something you're used to and it's something you now see more of in the corporate environment. You hear just as much about my.sap as you do of My.Yahoo! or my.excite. But, there's a problem with all this: what happened to the Oracle data? Where's my.oracledata? Well, the problem is solved with Oracle9iAS: the solution is Oracle Portal.

Oracle Portal is what used to be known as Oracle WebDB, but don't let that fool you. This is much more than a simple name change. This is a leap from where WebDB used to be to where it should have been. For starters, Oracle has abandoned the use of the Thin OAS/SpyGlass HTTP listener in favor of the widely accepted Apache HTTP Server. With Apache, comes the introduction of modules, one of which is mod_plsql, which replaces the OAS PL/SQL cartridge.

This chapter discusses the basics of Oracle Portal, as well as some of the advanced features. This chapter isn't designed as a step-by-step tutorial but, rather, as a general guide and introduction to Oracle Portal. This chapter demonstrates some of Portal's most useful features.

The official product name for Oracle Portal is Oracle9iAS Portal but, for the sake of brevity, I refer to it as Oracle Portal throughout this chapter.

This chapter discusses the following topics:

- From WebDB to Oracle Portal
- Oracle Portal Architecture
- Oracle Portal Installation
- Oracle Portal Basics
- Oracle Portal Security
- Oracle Portal Monitoring
- Oracle Portal Advanced Concepts

From WebDB to Oracle Portal

Oracle Portal is much more than a name change. Oracle Portal integrates many new components, such as Charts, Hierarchies, Calendars, and Menus (among others). All these components are available for Web developers, intranet developers, and even end users, to place on their own (or other users') portals. These components can be placed on pages in the form of portlets. (*Portlets* are reusable content areas, which essentially means they're a miniversion of the application components you create.) You can place these portlets on a page or let your users do it themselves. One interesting note is Oracle Portal itself is a portlet provider. In other words, the tool itself uses the concept of portlets and pages. If you already use the tool, you probably noticed how the administration pages are organized into regions and that these regions have portlets in them representing the actual tools for running Oracle Portal. Portal is a recursive product—Portal was built using Portal.

Oracle Portal is an outstanding tool, but it's somewhat misunderstood as to whether the tool is a user's tool or a developer's tool. In my mind, it's a combination of both. Up to a certain point, Portal is a user tool. Beyond that point, Portal requires the knowledge of a developer to get tasks done. You can reach a certain point using Portal as a user tool where little, if any, programming is necessary, but it's hard to build an application without some degree of programming involved. This is where Oracle Portal becomes a developer tool. It enables you to create your Portals in a highly interactive and sophisticated way.

Oracle Portal Architecture

Before you start creating applications using Oracle Portal, you should first understand the Oracle Portal architecture. Oracle Portal works in tandem with other components, including 9iAS and the Login server.

Overview

Oracle Portal is a combination of three components: Oracle Portal, the Login server, and Oracle9iAS (including Oracle HTTP server powered by Apache). Each of these components can be installed on separate machines, hence, the different architectures. Each architecture takes advantage of a different component. Figure 16-1 shows an overview of how the three work together.

Integrated Server (Two-Tier Approach)

The two-tier configuration is the simplest to install and is best suited when you want to present Portal applications from a self-contained machine. In it, all three components are integrated on to one machine.

During the installation process, you needn't specify connect strings or reference external applications, so the installation is relatively simple. In this configuration, no advantages exist for any of the components because they all share the same resources

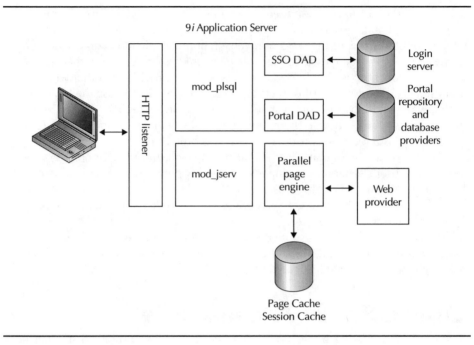

FIGURE 16-1. *Portal, Login server, and 9iAS working in harmony*

on the same machine. This configuration, illustrated in Figure 16-2, is best suited for low-traffic applications, development environments, and Oracle Portal presentations.

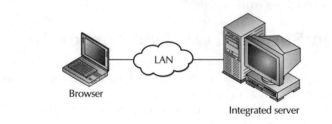

FIGURE 16-2. *Single server approach*

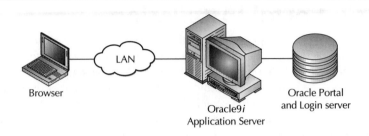

FIGURE 16-3. *Dual server approach*

The Traditional Three-Tier Approach

The three-tier approach is the most popular architecture configuration. In this configuration, shown in Figure 16-3, 9iAS is installed on Machine A and Portal, and the Login server is installed on the same database instance on Machine B. During the 9iAS installation, you specify the connection string for the database on Machine B.

The Three-Tier Split

The three-tier split is shown in Figure 16-4. The term *three-tier split* is one I use to describe the configuration of Oracle Portal and the Login server on separate database instances. This configuration is best suited if you want to use the Login server for authentication across many external and/or partner applications.

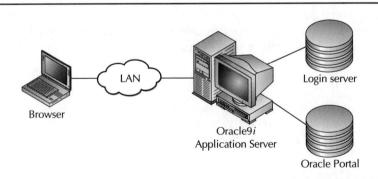

FIGURE 16-4. *Three-tier split*

Oracle Portal Installation

Oracle Portal isn't one component but, rather, a series of components. Oracle Portal itself is part of Oracle9iAS. You can choose three installation options for Oracle9iAS: Minimal, Standard, and Enterprise. Regardless of which installation option you choose, Oracle Portal will be installed. The choice you can make is whether or not you want to configure Oracle Portal via the Oracle Portal Configuration Assistant at the end of the installation. The following sections discuss some of the requirements to remember when you install Oracle Portal. One of the caveats of installing 9iAS and configuring Oracle Portal is that the installation takes a relatively long time. Experiences vary, but none of mine have ever been less than two hours and some have been as long as four hours. Laptop installations can take significantly longer, depending on the system capabilities.

TIP

If your Portal page will not load after an upgrade or installation, check the zone.properties file, located in IAS_HOME\Apache\JServ\servlets. Duplicate entries in this file can stop the page from loading. Remove these duplicates by commenting out or removing lines that start with "repositories=". If you receive a "servlet could not be contacted" error, comment out the "Parallel .jar entry" line in the zone.properties file.

Installation Overview

The Oracle Portal configuration assistant creates several schemas to support Oracle Portal. These schemas provide access to different objects that provide different services. The following tables describe these schemas in addition to the default Oracle Portal accounts created during the installation.

TIP

All passwords are set to the user name by default. These passwords should be changed immediately on completion of the installation.

Schemas Created

As of version 3.0.9, six schemas are created in an Oracle Portal installation. During the configuration of Oracle Portal, you can select the base schema name. The default base is PORTAL30. Note the base name of the schemas listed in the following table. This name will change if you select another base name. The Login server's default name is PORTAL30_SSO. PORTAL30_SSO is also a base schema name you select during the configuration of Oracle Portal. The following table shows the schema names and purpose.

Schema Name	Definition
PORTAL30	The product schema for Oracle Portal, which contains the installed Portal database objects.
PORTAL30_PUBLIC	The schema the Portal users map to when executing procedures in the Oracle Portal product schema. The schema name is constructed from the base schema with _public appended to it.
PORTAL30_SSO	The product schema for the Login server. This schema can be renamed in the installer. If unspecified, it defaults to the base schema name with _sso appended to it.
PORTAL30_SSO_PS (as of version 3.08)	The schema on the Login server database instance used to access the password store for external applications. This schema is named by appending _ps to the Login server schema name. The portal accesses the Login server's password store for external applications through this schema, either directly, if it resides on the same database instance, or over a dblink, if the Login server and the Portal are on different database instances.
PORTAL30_SSO_PUBLIC	The schema the Portal users map to when executing procedures in the Login server product schema. This name is constructed from the Login server schema name with _public appended to it.
PORTAL30_DEMO	The schema installed with the Oracle Portal demonstration code. The name of this schema is the base schema name with _demo appended to it.

Oracle Portal Accounts Created

When installed, Oracle Portal creates several default accounts that serve several purposes. These are Portal accounts, not schemas. DBAs will be happy to know that Portal accounts are stored in a Portal user table, not as actual database schemas. The following table shows these accounts and what they're used for.

Account Name	Use
PORTAL30	This account is created for the Database Administrator (DBA) with the highest privileges in Oracle Portal.
PORTAL30_ADMIN	This is the account created for the Portal administrator. This account is similar to the DBA account, but it doesn't have privileges that provide access to database administration features, such as creating and managing schemas and other database objects.
PORTAL30_SSO	This account is created for public users for unauthenticated sessions. This is the account all sessions are associated with prior to authentication.
PORTAL30_SSO_PS (as of version 3.08)	This account is created for the Login server application. The Login server is implemented with significant reuse of Oracle Portal infrastructure code and this user account is created as a result of the reuse.
PORTAL30_SSO_PUBLIC	This account is an administrative account created in conjunction with the Login server installation. It has Login server Full Administrator privileges, but it doesn't have any Portal administrative privileges.
PORTAL30_DEMO	The schema installed with the Oracle Portal demonstration code. The name of this schema is the base schema name with _demo appended to it.

System Requirements

The following subsections outline the system requirements for a successful Oracle Portal installation.

Oracle Database Requirements

Oracle Portal can be installed on a minimum of version 8.1.6.2.0 Enterprise Edition of the Oracle database. As of database version 8.1.7 and above, you can use the Standard or Enterprise Edition. This is something for WebDB users to remember. If you plan to upgrade your WebDB schema, you should ensure the database meets this requirement.

Oracle Home Requirements

Oracle Home issues used to be the source of much chagrin to people performing Oracle installations. Installer be warned, you must install Oracle9*i*AS in a separate home other than your database (if they're on the same machine).

Web Browser Requirements

The browser requirements for Oracle Portal are Netscape 4.0.8 and 4.72, or Internet Explorer 4.0.1 (with Service Pack 1) and 5.0.1.

Tablespace Requirements

Oracle Portal requires 150MB free space on the default tablespace. To view free space in the tablespaces, enter the following query in SQL*Plus using an account with sufficient privileges:

```
SELECT    tablespace_name,
          sum(bytes)/1024 free_space
FROM      dba_free_space
GROUP BY tablespace_name
```

If you encounter an out of tablespace error during the installation, open a SQL*Plus window. Log in to the database on which you're installing Portal, with an account that has DBA privileges. Enter the following query:

```
SELECT    bytes,
          name
FROM      v$datafile;
```

This should return something similar to the following:

```
    BYTES NAME
---------- ----------------------------------------
559939584 D:\ORACLE\ORADATA\ORCL\SYSTEM01.DBF
 52428800 D:\ORACLE\ORADATA\ORCL\RBS01.DBF
 70008320 D:\ORACLE\ORADATA\ORCL\USERS01.DBF
 20971520 D:\ORACLE\ORADATA\ORCL\TEMP01.DBF
 10485760 D:\ORACLE\ORADATA\ORCL\TOOLS01.DBF
 20971520 D:\ORACLE\ORADATA\ORCL\INDX01.DBF
 20971520 D:\ORACLE\ORADATA\ORCL\DR01.DBF
```

In this example, the default tablespace is the USERS tablespace, so you want to add 150MB to the 70MB already there. You do this by executing the following statement:

```
alter database datafile 'D:\ORACLE\ORADATA\ORCL\USERS01.DBF' resize 220008320;
```

Now you'll have enough space to continue the installation. For additional DBA help, refer to *Oracle9i DBA Handbook,* by Kevin Loney.

Troubleshooting and Diagnostic Tools

Depending on your configuration, you might run into issues after the installation has taken place. Luckily, several tools (including this book) can help you through them.

Find the Cause of the Problem

When troubleshooting the installation, you first need to determine the cause of the problem. To do this, use the troubleshooting ADEs by considering Apache, DADs and the Oracle Portal Enabler tables.

A: Apache   Is Apache running? First, try to access the Apache server by typing **http://<hostname>/** (assuming you have Apache running on port 80) in your browser. Do you see a page similar to the default Apache page shown in Figure 16-5?

If Apache is running, did you check the log files?

TIP

Apache Logs can offer a wealth of information. The error_log file, located in IAS_HOME/Apache/ Apache/logs, gives you error information about users accessing the Apache server. In version 3.0.9, the Apache error logs take on even greater significance. Version 3.0.9 now has a default setting (which can be changed) that will not display errors to the browser. In the past, if your DAD was incorrect, you would get a "DAD error page"; now you will see the generic "Page Not Found" error page. The real error can be found in the logs.

D: Database Access Descriptors   Is the DAD configured correctly? Did you enter the correct user name, password, and connection string in the DAD configuration? Do you have a TNS Names entry for the connection string specified in the DAD? For more information on configuring DADs, see the following section "Configuring Database Access Descriptors."

E: Enabler Configuration Tables   Are the enabler configuration tables populated correctly? Do you need to run ssodatan? What about ssodatax?

For the most part, the error you receive is an indication of what action you need to take. For example, the error "You cannot log in because there is no configuration information stored in the enabler configuration table (WWC-41439)" is generally caused either by a lack of entries in the enabler configuration tables or by an incorrect entry in the table. Running the ssodatan script usually resolves this error. This command line script can be found in the IAS_Home/portal30/admin/plsql directory.

TIP

If you change your host name, use the ssodatan script to resolve the infamous 41439 error, which can occur when porting from development into production.

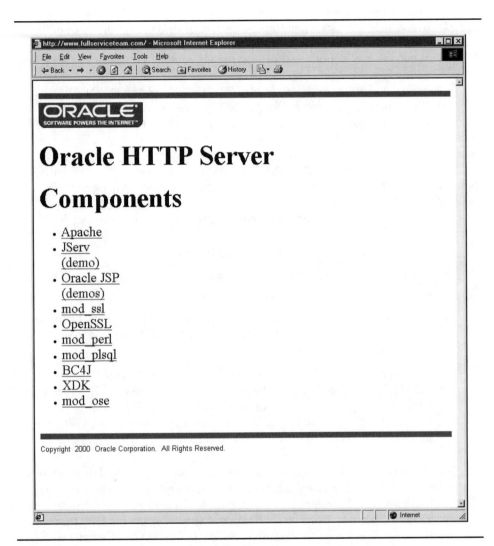

FIGURE 16-5. *Default Apache page*

Oracle Portal really is several applications working together. If you look at the Administer Partner Application screen on the Login server after a default installation, you see two applications listed: Oracle Portal and the Login server. This is because Portal itself is a Partner Application and you can have many Portal applications all sharing the same Login server. To do this, you need to tell the Login server about these new Partner Applications. This is done via the ssodatax script. The difference between the two is the *ssodatan* script is used to populate the enabler configuration table by overwriting the existing entries, while the *ssodatax* script appends to the table, leaving the current entries intact. To add additional Partner Applications to Portal, first add the application via the configuration screen to obtain a site ID, token, and encryption key, which will be used in the ssodatax script.

Both scripts update the WWSEC_ENABLER_CONFIGURATION_INFO$ table, which is the configuration table for the Single Signon enabler stack. Each Partner Application to the Login server has a table for configuration information. This table defines the login URL for the Login server with which this Partner Application is associated.

Understanding how the LSNR_TOKEN column is used in the enabler configuration table is important to plan what entries are required. This table may have more than one entry.

The following sequence illustrates what happens when a user <does what?>

1. Someone enters your site's URL from a browser.

2. The request is redirected to the Login server for authentication and the user is presented with a log in screen.

3. On a successful log in, the request is redirected to Oracle Portal's success URL (wwsec_app_priv.process_signon), which then redirects the user back to the requested URL.

4. The Login server (SSO) partner enabler APIs read the WWSEC_ENABLER_ CONFIG_INFO$ table for configuration information. Similarly, in the Login server, the Login server's private APIs read the WWSSO_PAPP_ CONFIGURATION_INFO$ table. The latter table contains the URL that should be redirected to each Partner Application.

Because each Partner Application's success URL is stored in the Login server's Partner Application configuration table, to support multiple host names for the Partner Application each distinct host name requires its own Partner Application entry on the Login server. This is so each one can specify a success URL that has the same host name as the Partner Application, so the session cookie can be scoped appropriately. Furthermore, the domain to which cookies are scoped includes the server name (ServerName) and port, so server.domain.com:80 is treated as a different cookie domain from server.domain.com:8080.

The ssodatan syntax (full use) is as follows:

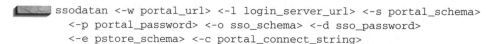

```
ssodatan <-w portal_url> <-l login_server_url> <-s portal_schema>
   <-p portal_password> <-o sso_schema> <-d sso_password>
   <-e pstore_schema> <-c portal_connect_string>
```

The ssodatan example (abbreviated use) is as follows. Notice the URLs end with a slash (/):

```
ssodatan -w http://your.portalserver.com/pls/portal30/ -l
   http://your.portalserver.com/pls/portal30_sso/ -s portal30
-p portal_password -o portal30_sso -d sso_password -c ORCL
```

The ssodatax syntax (full use) is as follows:

```
ssodatax <-i portal site id> <-t portal site token> <-k encryption key>
   <-w portal url> <-l login server url> <-s portal schema>
   <-p portal password> <-v cookie version> <-o sso_schema>
   <-e pstore schema> <-r pstore password> <-b pstore dblink>
   <-c connect string> <-n ps_connect_string>
```

The ssodatax example (abbreviated use) is as follows:

```
ssodatax -i 90993829 -t KFH219S8 -k JD384HFHJS842 -w
   http://your.portalserver.com/pls/portal30/ -l
   http://your.portalserver.com/pls/portal30_sso/  -s portal30
   -p portal_password -o portal30_sso -c ORCL
```

Diagnostics Script (diag.csh/diag.cmd)

If you aren't sure why things aren't working, tools are available that can help you in your troubleshooting. One of these is diagnostics script. The *diagnostics script,* located in `IAS_Home/portal30/admin/plsql`, uses SQL*Plus to determine all the configuration parameters and to ensure they're all correct. The parameters for the diagnostics script are the same for both versions of the script (diag.csh and diag.cmd). You must set the ORACLE_HOME environmental variable before you can run the diagnostics script. The syntax for the diag script is as follows:

```
diag.csh -s <portal schema> -p <portal password> -c <connect string>
```

The following sample shows the output from diag.csh:

```
SM2.wwsecenabler_config_info$
Login Server URL : http://webdbsvr.us.oracle.com:3000/pls/sm2_sso/
                   sm2_SSO.wwsso_app_admin.ls_login
DAD                 : sm2_sso
Host connection     : successful.
mod_plsql           : working.
JServ               : working.
Schema name         : sm2_sso
Connect string      : w817dev6
Authentication mode : Single Sign-On

sm2_sso.wwsec_enabler_config_info$
Login Server URL    : http://webdbsvr.us.oracle.com:3000/pls/sm2_sso/
```

```
                        sm2_SSO.wwsso_app_admin.ls_login
DAD                   : sm2_sso
Host connection       : successful.
mod_plsql             : working.
JServ                 : working.
Schema name           : sm2_sso
Connect string        : w817dev6
Authentication mode : Single Sign-On
*********************************
Partner Application Information

**** Oracle Portal (sm2) ****
Home URL              : http://webdbsrv.us.oracle.com:3000/pls/sm2/sm2.home
Success URL           : http://webdbsrv.us.oracle.com:3000/pls/sm2/sm2.wwsec_app_
priv.process_signon
DAD                   : sm2
Host connection       : *** FAILED ***

**** The Login Server (sm2_SSO) ****
Home URL              : http://webdbsvr.us.oracle.com:3000/pls/
                        sm2_sso/sm2_SSO.home
Success URL           : http://webdbsvr.us.oracle.com:3000/pls/sm2_sso/
                        sm2_SSO.wwsso_home.process_signon
DAD                   : sm2_sso
Host connection       : successful.
mod_plsql             : working.
JServ                 : working.
Schema name           : sm2_sso
Connect string        : w817dev6
Authentication mode : Single Sign-On
***********************************************
Recommendations:
Oracle Portal (sm2):
Please check the host name.
```

As you can see, an error occurred when the script attempted to connect to the host. Check the host name and ensure the entry in the Apache configuration file is correct.

What will the diagnostics script do for you?

■ Checks to see if the protocol is correct (currently only checks HTTP)

■ Checks whether the host name and port are correct

■ Checks to see if mod_plsql is working

■ Checks whether Apache JServ is working

■ Reads and verifies DAD information

IsItWorking Servlet

The IsItWorking servlet is another, lesser tool to help you in troubleshooting. This is a lesser tool because it's more of a yes/no tool than a tool like the diagnostics script, which gives you useful information.

To invoke the IsItWorking servlet, enter the following URL in your browser:

```
http://<host>/servlet/IsItWorking
```

The result should look like Figure 16-6.
If you see this screen, it means Apache JServ is working properly.

FIGURE 16-6. *Apache JServ is working*

Configuring Database Access Descriptors

Database Access Descriptors (DAD) contain the connection information for connecting to databases. The DAD configuration isn't something unique to Oracle Portal, but it is something inherent to mod_plsql or the PL/SQL Gateway. If you choose to install Oracle 8.1.7 with the HTTP server, you can configure DADs because the HTTP server uses mod_plsql. Configuring DADs can be done with the configuration interface, which can be accessed by the following URL:

```
http://www.yourserver.com/pls/admin_/gateway.htm
```

Entering this URL brings you to the configuration screen shown in Figure 16-7.

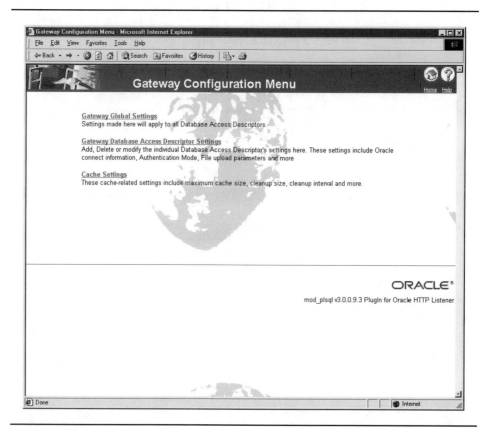

FIGURE 16-7. *DAD configuration screen*

Use this interface to create, edit, or delete DADs. You should create DADs for any database schema you need to connect to. The database can be local or remote.

In addition to the DAD interface, you also have the DAD configuration file (wdbsvr.app) that can be edited. This file can be found in the IAS_HOME\Apache\ modplsql\cfg directory. The following text is a subsection of that file. In the file, you can see the DAD definitions for PORTAL30 and PORTAL30_SSO.

```
;
[PLSQL_GATEWAY]
administrators = all
adminPath = /admin_/
admindad = portal30
;debugModules =
defaultDAD = portal30
;upload_as_long_raw =
;upload_as_blob =
;timingsTable =
;timingsModules =
;enablesso =
;servletroot =
;stateful =
;custom_auth =
;
[DAD_portal30]
;connect_string    =
password    =  !cG9ydGFsMzA=
username    =  portal30
default_page   =  portal30.home
document_table   =  portal30.wwdoc_document
document_path   =  docs
document_proc   =  portal30.wwdoc_process.process_download
;upload_as_long_raw   =
upload_as_blob   =  *
;name_prefix   =
;always_describe   =
;after_proc   =
;before_proc   =
reuse    =  Yes
connmax    =  10
pathalias    =  url
pathaliasproc    =  portal30.wwpth_api_alias.process_download
enablesso    =  Yes
;sncookiename    =
;stateful    =
;custom_auth    =
```

```
;response_array_size   =
;exclusion_list   =
;cgi_env_list   =
;
[DAD_portal30_sso]
;connect_string   =
password   =   !cG9ydGFsMzBfc3Nv
username   =   portal30_sso
default_page   =   portal30_sso.wwsso_home.home
document_table   =   portal30_sso.wwdoc_document
document_path   =   docs
document_proc   =   portal30_sso.wwdoc_process.process_download
;upload_as_long_raw   =
upload_as_blob   =   *
;name_prefix   =
;always_describe   =
;after_proc   =
;before_proc   =
reuse   =   Yes
connmax   =   10
pathalias   =   url
pathaliasproc   =   portal30_sso.wwpth_api_alias.process_download
enablesso   =   Yes
;sncookiename   =
;stateful   =
;custom_auth   =
;response_array_size   =
;exclusion_list   =
;cgi_env_list   =
;
```

As you can see, the user name and password are in the file. In previous versions (prior to version 3.08), the user name and password were stored in this file in plain text. In versions 3.08 and above, the password is encrypted.

Other version-specific issues include DAD security. In versions prior to 9*i*AS 1.0.2.2 (Portal 3.0.8), DADs were left unsecured by default, meaning anyone with access to the machine via a browser could edit your DADs via the DAD configuration interface. The way to secure prior versions of *i*AS is by editing the top portion of the DAD configuration file. In the WVGATEWAY (PLSQL_GATEWAY in current versions) portion, add the following line:

```
admindad = portal30
```

Notice in the previous file, the current versions add this line for you. What this does is, any time an authenticated user invokes the DAD configuration menu, she is asked to log in prior to being redirecting to the configuration page.

You can further secure this by setting the administrators to actual Portal users, as in the following example:

```
;
[PLSQL_GATEWAY]
administrators = PORTAL30
adminPath = /admin_/
admindad = portal30
;debugModules =
defaultDAD = portal30
;upload_as_long_raw =
;upload_as_blob =
;timingsTable =
;timingsModules =
;enablesso =
;servletroot =
;stateful =
;custom_auth =
;
```

Finally, as you can see in the configuration file, we hard-coded the user name and password to connect to the database. At times, however, you might want to connect to a database as different users, without having to create DADs for each of those users. This is known as *database authentication*. In that case, leave the user name and/or password blank, and you'll be prompted for this information when you connect. This only works in DADs where the authentication is set to Basic. If you authenticate via the Login server, leaving the user name and password blank will result in an error.

TIP
If you need to create many DADs and you don't want to use the provided GUI, edit the wdbsvr.app file. Editing this file is faster and you achieve the same results. This is particularly useful in a class or demonstration where you assign a DAD for each user who connects to the machine. Be aware that Oracle support won't support the direct editing of this file, though, so be sure to back it up prior to making changes.

Apache Configuration File (httpd.conf)

The httpd.conf file is the heart and soul of the Apache HTTP server. Many books explain the capabilities of this file and attempting to do so here would go beyond the scope of this chapter. However, some key configuration items fall within the scope of Oracle Portal and need to be understood. Chapter 3 provides more information on configuring 9*i*AS. The file itself is well documented, and contains examples and explanations for most of the directives in it.

The httpd.conf file contains directives that set the parameters and options for your Apache server configuration. The following subsections discuss the basic configuration directives and what they do.

ServerName   The *ServerName* is the name of your server, for example, *www.tusc.com.* As stated in the documentation for the httpd.conf file, you cannot simply make up a name and hope it works. This must be a valid name that's registered in your host's file. If your machine doesn't have a valid hostname entry, use localhost (or the IP address for the server).

Port   By default, the port for HTTP servers is port 80. If you want to use a port other than port 80, specify the new port with the port directive. As of *i*AS 1.0.2.2, the default port number is 80, during installation, if port 80 is busy, the installation will attempt port 7777, then 7778, and so on. During the installation, be sure nothing is running on port 80. If something was running on port 80 during the installation, you'll want to change *i*AS to use port 80.

ServerRoot   *ServerRoot* is similar to ORACLE_HOME, but it's for the HTTP Server. It serves as the root for all relative URL requests and is the place where all the essential Apache files and folders are kept.

ErrorLog   Apache has the capability to generate several logs, such as an access log and a referrer log. However, the most important log is the *error_log.* You have the option to specify where this file resides. The default location is the logs directory.

DocumentRoot   *DocumentRoot* is where Apache will start looking for files to serve clients requesting pages from the server. This directory can be any directory on the host (and even one on the network). This DocumentRoot directive works in conjunction with the *DirectoryIndex,* which tells Apache which files to serve from each directory.

Understanding the Apache configuration file is important because it will enable you to do such things as assigning aliases. For example, say you have an Oracle Portal implementation with three different applications. Application *A* is for the Executive staff, Application *B* is for the Sales staff, and Application *C* is for Customers. Each application has a different Home Page. Using aliases, you can designate a specific URL for each.

- Application A's URL: **http://my.portalserver.com/executives**

- Application B's URL: **http://my.portalserver.com/sales**

- Application C's URL: **http://my.portalserver.com/customers**

You could also have two URLs pointing at different DADs, for example, **www.serverA.com** pointing to www.portalserver.com/pls/PORTAL30 and **www.serverB.com** pointing to www.portalserver.com/pls/PORTAL308.

When you combine the power of Apache with Portal configurations, the possibilities are endless.

TIP
Want to get rid of the /pls/DADNAME after your site's URL? Edit the index.html file in the Apache/ htdocs directory with the following code:

```
<HTML>
<SCRIPT>
  document.location="http://<yourhostname>/pls/DADNAME/";
</SCRIPT>
</HTML>
```

Oracle Portal Basics

This section discusses some basic Portal terminology and features.

Pages

Portal Pages are used for the presentation of your application. They represent the canvas where you bring all the elements together. The elements are the layout, the style, and the components. Think of pages as blank HTML documents. When you create your page, you apply the layouts and styles of your choice, and then you add all the application components that make up your application. Pages also help you customize the Portal look for your users. For example, you can define a page named CUSTOMER_SERVICE for your Customer Service representatives and a page named SALES_REPS for the Sales representatives. SALES_REPS and CUSTOMER_SERVICE can have totally different layouts, styles, and even application components.

You should familiarize yourself with the two default pages in Oracle Portal: Oracle Portal Home Page and the Oracle Portal Navigator.

Oracle Portal Home Page

The *Oracle Portal Home Page* is the main page for Portal if no other page is designated as the default home page. This is the first page you see when you log in to Oracle Portal. This page is divided into four tabs: Build, Administer, Administer Database, and Monitor.

Build   The *Build* tab contains portlets that enable you to create components for your Portal, as illustrated in Figure 16-8. You can create pages, styles, layouts, applications, and so forth.

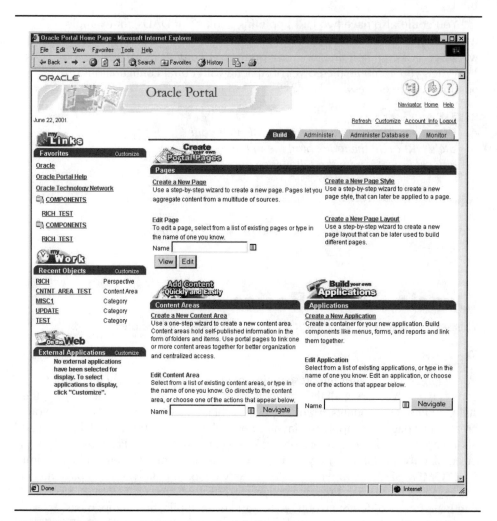

FIGURE 16-8. *Portal Home Page Build tab*

Administer   The *Administer* tab contains portlets that enable you to create, or to edit users or groups. It also contains the Services portlet. The *Services portlet* contains links to the Global Settings, the Log Registry Administration, and the Login server. The *Global Settings* enable you to set general options for your portal, in addition to enabling the beta components. The *Log Registry Administration* enables you to configure what actions you want Portal to log or keep track of (the default is everything). The *Login server* is one of the three main components of Oracle Portal.

Administer Database   The *Administer Database* tab contains portlets geared toward a DBA. It contains the Database Information portlets, as well as the

Database Memory Consumption, and Transaction and Locks portlet. It also contains portlets that enable you to edit existing schemas and objects in the database.

Monitor   The *Monitor* tab contains all the reports you can generate for Oracle Portal. A time might occur when you want to see who is logging in to your portal, when they're logging in, how frequently they're logging in, and so forth. This is the tab to go to for that information.

Figure 16-9 shows the Portal Home Page with the Monitor tab selected.

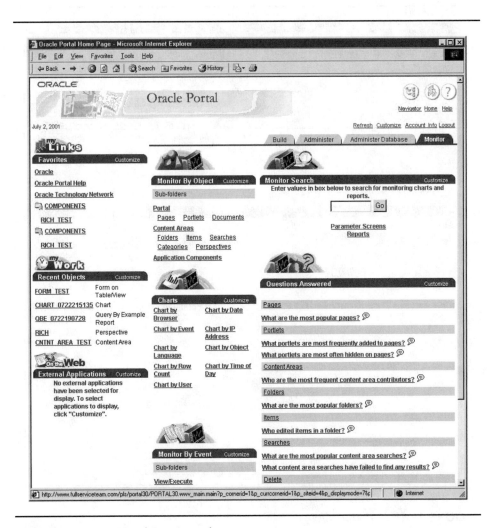

FIGURE 16-9.   *Portal Monitor tab*

Oracle Portal Navigator

If you're the Portal administrator, you'll get to know the Navigator well. The
Navigator is a generalized view of all the items contained in your Portal
implementation. Think of it as your Portal Explorer. It contains quick views to
the pages, content areas, applications, and database objects. All these items
are displayed in a hierarchical fashion, making it easy to find what you want.
Figure 16-10 shows the Navigator page.

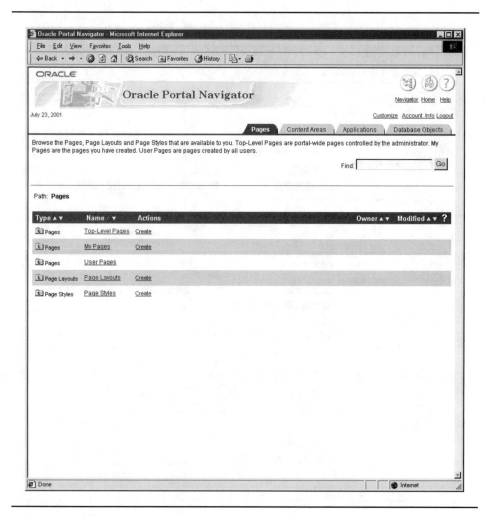

FIGURE 16-10. *Portal Navigator*

Page Styles

Page styles are nothing more than the look and feel of your page. Using the style editor, you can designate the colors for your page header, page footer, page border, portlet headers, and portlet bodies. You can also specify font faces and sizes for certain objects. All these items can be changed with an interface that's easy to use. As Figure 16-11 shows, you simply pick the element you want to change and change it. You can also preview the changes immediately using the preview page on the right.

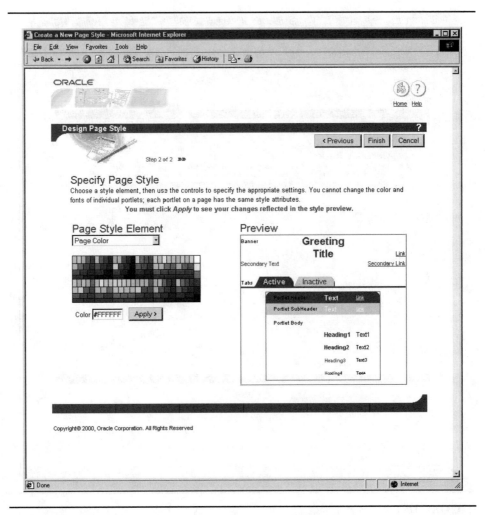

FIGURE 16-11.   *Portal page styles*

Page Layouts

A *page layout* gives you the capability to designate regions before creating your page. Think of layouts as region templates. For example, if your site has a consistent header, you can design a page layout that includes a region across the top of the page to accommodate a header portlet. Doing this saves you time when creating pages. Figure 16-12 illustrates the page layout feature.

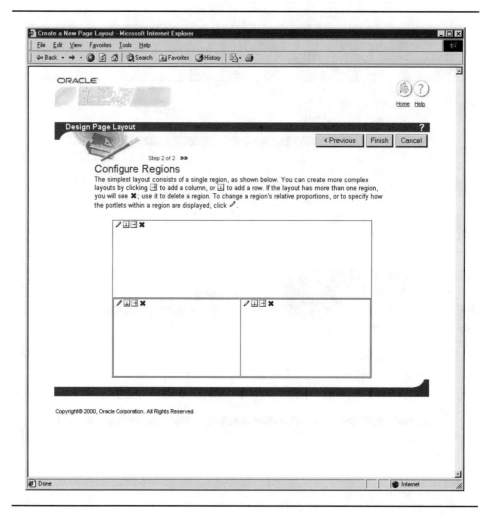

FIGURE 16-12. *Portal page layout*

Page Hierarchies

When you view the Pages tab in the Navigator, notice a hierarchy of pages is there: Top, My, and User.

- Top Level Pages are accessible to everyone as long as users have privileges to view them.

- My Pages are the pages owned by the logged-in user.

- User Pages are pages whose owners have granted privileges for you (the current logged-in user) to view.

Accessing Pages

You can access a page in several ways. One way is by setting the page as a default for a particular user or group. For example, if you have an Executive group whose page has a series of Chart portlets indicating Key Performance Indicators, you can designate the page default in the Groups configuration.

Another way to access pages is via Direct Access URLs. Direct Access URLs are URLs you can specify to access certain objects. The following syntax enables a direct access URL to a page:

```
http://<yourhostname>/pls/<DAD>/url/page/<page name>
```

For example:

```
http://www.tusc.com/pls/PORTAL30/url/page/WELCOME
```

Remember, the name used here is *not* the display name, but rather the page name. Be sure your objects are carefully and meaningfully named.

TIP
A good practice when naming your objects is to set the name, and this display name the same, to avoid confusion. There can be numerous display names that are identical, but no two names can be the same. Save yourself a portlet-placing headache—name them the same.

Direct Access URLs aren't limited to pages. You can also access folders, categories, perspectives, and documents. Use the following syntax to specify each Access URL:

```
http://<host name><port>/pls/<DAD>/url/folder/<folder name>
http://<host name><port>/pls/<DAD>/url/category/<category name>
http://<host name><port>/pls/<DAD>/url/perspective/<perspective name>
http://<host name><port>/pls/<DAD>/docs/<document name>
```

Setting Default Pages

Default pages can be set globally, for a group, or for a specific user.

Global Default Pages   The *Global default page* is the page displayed if no user or Group default page has been specified. For example, if for security reasons you do not want anyone to have access to the default Oracle Portal pages, create a blank page with a security message on it and set it as the global default. Therefore if, during the user creation, you forget to add them to a group, they will be taken to the security page, instead of the Portal pages where they have potential to change your Portal pages, and components. If you set up an administrator, set their USER default page to the Portal page and they will gain access to the Portal pages upon login.

Group Default Pages   The *Group default page* is displayed when members of the specified group log in. Users cannot simply be members of the group, however, they must also have the group set as their default group. Group default pages override Global default pages.

User Default Pages   The *User default page* is the page displayed when a user logs in. These settings override all other default page settings. If you assign a Global default page, a Group default page, and a User default page, when the user logs in, she is redirected to the page specified in the User default page setting.

Creating Pages

It's easy to create a page. Click Create New Page from the Portal Home Page's under the Build tab. You're then walked through the process using the Create Page Wizard, which is a four-step process. You have the opportunity to name your page, apply the style and layout of your choice, add portlets to your page, and specify access privileges to your page.

Regions

Regions are the distinct areas on your page where components reside. All pages have at least one region. If you don't define regions on your page, the entire page is considered a region. Regions are important because Oracle Portal enables you to set distinct properties for each region. For example, you can select to display portlet headers and borders in one region, but not in another.

Remember these facts about Regions. First, when creating regions, you can only add columns to the right and rows to the bottom. Second, you need to work from the outside in, which means you need to think about the larger regions, and then think about the smaller ones contained within them. For example, if you create three regions in the form of three columns, and then want to create a consistent header across the top, you have to delete some regions to get that header region where you want it.

Another thing to remember about regions is that tabs also represent regions. Tabs can be a bit of a nuisance, though. For example, if you place portlets in a normal region and you delete the region, Portal will ask you if you want to delete the portlets or move them. This isn't the case with tabs. If you have portlets on the tab and delete the tab, the regions (and portlets) are gone.

Applications

Applications, like pages, can be thought of as containers, but applications contain application components, such as Forms, Reports, and Charts. You cannot create application components without first creating an application to put them in. By creating an application, you are associating the application components with a particular database schema.

Application Schemas

All applications are associated with a database schema, so it's worth noting that not all your schemas will be available when you create your application. Let's say, for example, you have a data schema that contains a subset of tables from an order entry system. By default, this schema isn't available to Portal. To make this schema available as a Portal Application schema, you must designate it as such. You can do this via the Database Objects tab on the Oracle Portal Home page, where you can edit an existing schema. Figure 16-13 shows the editing options for a schema.

Notice the Application Schema check box. Once this is checked, you can use this schema to create your applications.

TIP

I strongly advise you do not load data tables into the PORTAL30 schema.

Creating Applications

Creating applications is simple and you can do it in a number of ways. One way is to use the Create Application link on the Build tab of the Oracle Portal Home Page. Another way is to click Create Application from the Oracle Portal Navigator. Regardless of which you pick, you'll invoke the Create Application Wizard. The wizard is straightforward. It asks you to name the application, associate the schema to the application, and then you set security for the application.

TIP

When creating an application, you must expose the application as a provider if you want to place the application components on a page. You can find the Expose As Provider check box on the Access menu.

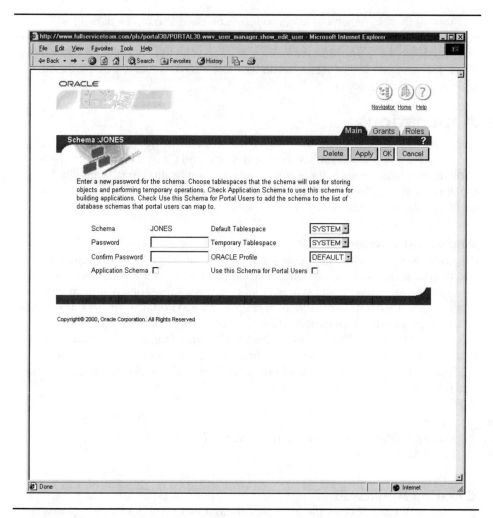

FIGURE 16-13. *Schema editing options*

Content Areas

According to Oracle, the difference between Pages and Content Areas is Pages present information in a brief format, whereas *Content Areas* provide a more detailed presentation. I think of it more or less along the same lines but, in Content Areas, you lose the concept of portlets, but gain folders, categories, and perspectives. How you use each is entirely up to you.

Folders

As previously mentioned, Content Areas introduce the concept of folders. *Folders* are containers for storing information. In this case, however, the information stored is limited to the following:

- Files
- Text
- URLs
- Other Folders
- PL/SQL
- Application Components
- Images
- Java Applications
- ZIP Files
- PDF Files (Adobe Acrobat Reader)

Even though the list is limited, don't be fooled. A great many things can be accomplished with the items on this list. For example, the Check In/Check Out feature enables your users to check an item out, edit it, and then check it in again. They can also audit folder transactions. In the example shown in Figure 16-14, I created a folder with several of the items previously described. As you can see from the example, certain items are displayed differently. For instance, the image is displayed in the folder, but you must click the item links to view them.

Categories

Categories enable you to organize your Content Areas. They provide you with the capability to categorize your items. For example, you can set up categories for Sales, Customer Service, and Marketing.

Navigation Bars

Navigation bars enable your users to access the information they need quickly. Typical navigation bars include search capabilities, links to take you back home, and links to other objects. When you create a content area, a default navigation bar is created for you. Navigation bars can be published as portlets and, therefore, can be placed on pages, so you can allow your users to access your content areas from a page.

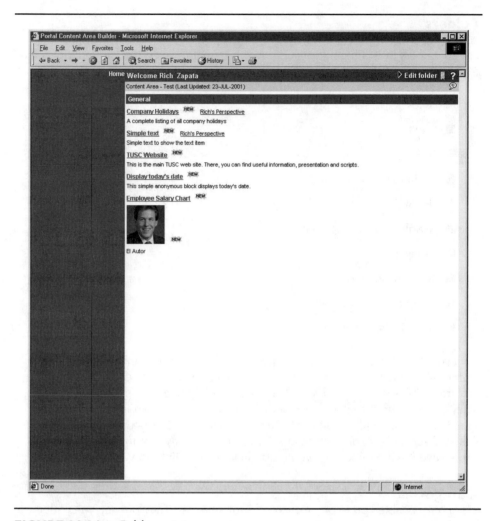

FIGURE 16-14. *Folders*

Perspectives

Perspectives can help you further organize your data. For example, common items can be grouped into the Sales Department and other groupings can be for the Customer Service Department. The purpose of the perspective is to display a subset of items quickly that are pertinent to them.

Styles

Content area styles follow the same principle as page styles, and they represent the look and feel of your content area. Using styles, you can define the font color, the font type, the background color, the background image, and so forth. Figure 16-15 shows a style.

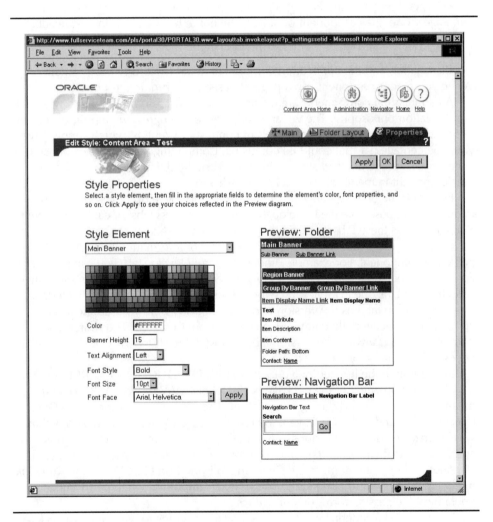

FIGURE 16-15.   *Content area style definition*

Application Components

Application components enable you to create a variety of objects for your users easily and quickly. As of version 3.0.9, you can create 12 application components, with the possibility of two beta components if you enable them.

Components such as Forms, Calendars, Charts, and Reports can be run in one of two ways: Full Page and Portlet. When running an application component in *Full Page* mode, the component populates the entire browser window. A header and footer are displayed, with the component name across the top. When viewing application components in *Portlet* mode, no header or footer exists, the font is usually smaller, and the application component items are also typically smaller. When you place components on a page, you see them running as portlets.

All application components are created via wizards, reinforcing the easy and rapid creation philosophy. The wizards indicate your progress via a progress bar in a "Step *x* out of *n* steps" fashion. This is in contrast to WebDB, which simply gave you a percentage bar that could be confusing. Completing the entire wizard isn't necessary. After the first few steps, you can accept the default settings and create the component immediately by clicking Finish.

Finally, some of the greatest tools you can use for developing, as well as for information purposes, are the Develop, Manage, and Access tabs for each component. You can access these tabs by clicking Manage from the Navigator.

On the *Develop* tab, you can find a great deal of information regarding a particular component. For example, under the *Form Develop* tab, you can see the Form name, the application it belongs to, the versioning information, the last change date, the Run Link, the PL/SQL source for the spec and body, and the call interface.

The Develop tab has the version information. Every time your application component is successfully compiled, a new version is created. The source code currently in use is always the version labeled PRODUCTION. This version isn't necessarily the latest one created.

In addition to the link telling you whether it's PRODUCTION or ARCHIVE, the tab also tells you whether the package is VALID or INVALID. INVALID, of course, means errors were found during compilation. The versioning portion of the Develop tab comes in handy when you want to create a new edition based on a copy that was created two or three versions ago. If this is the case, simply click an old version and Portal asks if you want to create the new version based on the prior copy.

Another important item on the Develop tab is the Run Link. While the *Run Link* might not be of great importance to you now, it's important when performing operations like passing forms default values.

You might be wondering what package Portal is referring to when it lists a package body and specification on the Develop tab. When you create an application component, this is generated as a package within Oracle Portal. The package source can be seen by clicking the Package Body link on the Develop tab. As you view the package source, you might also notice documented sections exist for the PL/SQL code you specify on the last step of almost all components. During this last step, you have the option to specify that PL/SQL be executed at different break points, such as before the page, after the header, before the footer, and so forth. This can come in handy for troubleshooting. Because you're generating PL/SQL within a package, you'll sometimes get errors that might be cryptic to you. Viewing the code within the package might help debug your objects.

Finally, the *Call Interface* gives you all the information you need to call your application component. Clicking the Call Interface shows you a parameters table, as well as call examples from PL/SQL blocks and URLs. These come in handy when your component interacts with other components.

TIP

When creating application components, maintain a standard prefix for components. For example, RPT for Reports, FRM for Forms, and so forth. If your application contains a lot of components, losing track of your object types is easy. Keeping the prefix consistent helps keep your components organized. The Navigator enables you to sort by name, but not by type.

Forms

If you're familiar with the Web, you're familiar with HTML-based Forms. *Forms* represent the link between your programs and the user, so Portal's Forms are extremely important. Oracle Portal recognizes this and has created many useful tools you can implement with your Forms, as well as integrate into your Forms. As such an important part of your Web applications, no wonder this application component is the most widely covered.

Portal's forte is easily and rapidly creating application components. Forms are a great example of this concept. You can easily create Forms via the Forms Wizard. You can also select the custom layout, which enables you to edit the layout using HTML, although the customization is limited. You can also place validation options on the Form itself, which is a great advantage. A collection of JavaScript functions is designed to catch null values, nonnumeric values, and so forth, all of which are at your disposal to use with your Form. If you want to make a check or validation in your Forms that isn't in the library, you can design your own. You even have the option to design a JavaScript function based on an existing one or to design one from scratch.

Three types of Forms can be created in Portal: Forms based on table or view, Master-Detail Forms, and Forms based on procedures.

Form Based on a Table or View   A *Form based on a table or view* is the easiest Form you can create and is most useful when you want to create a Form to update data in a particular table or through a view. Using this Form, you can query the table and insert, update, and delete data. You should know a few things prior to running this type of Form. For starters, the querying capabilities are simple. For another, the deletions are committed immediately, meaning once the user deletes a record, the record is gone. No undo option exists.

Master-Detail Forms   The *Master-detail Form*'s novelty lies in that you create a Master Form, displaying certain information and the Detail Form's data will display according to what was selected in the Master Form. A good example of this is orders and line items. You select the order number in the Master Form that will display the order header information and the Detail Form displays the order line items.

Forms Based on Procedures   Being able to create forms based on procedures is, in my opinion, one of the best features in Oracle Portal. The days of coding forms by hand are over. Using this type of Form, you can design a procedure that accepts parameters and, using Portal, you can create the Form that accepts the parameters from the user. The great thing about this is you can place validation on the Form itself.

Form Operations   Because Forms are perhaps the most-used application component, you should understand how to invoke them in a variety of situations. For example, one common operation is to open a Form in Update mode. Another is to pass the Form a set of values and have the Form autoexecute the query. The following section describes how to do some of these operations using a Form you already created. This section demonstrates these operations with a Form based on the infamous EMP table.

Calling a Form and Passing Default Values   Calling a Form and Passing Default Values Calling a Form and passing values is a relatively easy thing to do. First, you must get the parameter names of the values you want to pass. To obtain a listing of parameters, use the Call Interface screen. For example, you want to invoke a form based on the EMP table and pass a value to the EMPNO field. That field (or parameter) is named "empno". Now that you have the parameter name, you must determine how you're going to invoke the form, from a URL or a stored procedure. If you want to call it from a URL, you would use something similar to this:

```
http://myhostname/pls/portal30/PORTAL30.wwa_app_module.link?
   p_arg_names=_moduleid&p_arg_values=1207292797&p_arg_names=_show_header
   &p_arg_values=YES
```

Notice I specified the module ID in the URL. You need this in any case where you want to perform operations on application components, otherwise, wwa_app_module.link has no clue what you're trying to reference. In this example, I'm only going to pass an employee number, so I altered the URL to the following:

```
http://myhostname/pls/portal30/PORTAL30.wwa_app_module.link?
   p_arg_names=_moduleid&p_arg_values=1207292797&p_arg_names=empno
   &p_arg_values=10
```

Doing this places the numeral 10 in the Employee Number field (empno) when the Form is displayed. Likewise, you can fill in all the fields if you want. You simply add "name, value pairs" after the module ID in the call. If you were generating this URL from PL/SQL (or Java), you then pass in dynamic values.

Calling a Form and Passing It a Query Condition for Automatic Execution
Use the PORTAL30.wwa_app_module.link procedure for Insert mode. You must add the following argument for querying records.

You must add the p_arg_names parameter for each column passed as a query condition. The parameter name is the column name prefixed by an underscore ("_") and with the suffix "_cond". For example, the parameter name for the column "deptno" is "_deptno_cond".

Using the previous example (passing default values), reconstruct the URL as follows:

```
http://myhostname/pls/portal30/PORTAL30.wwa_app_module.link?
   p_arg_names=_moduleid&p_arg_values=1207292797&p_arg_names=DEPTNO
   &p_arg_values=10&p_arg_names=_deptno_cond&p_arg_values=%3D
```

When the called Form is started, it executes a query with the supplied condition (in this case, "where deptno=10"). If the query is successful, the matching rows are displayed in Update mode. If no matching rows are found, the Form starts in Insert mode.

A corresponding p_arg_values parameter specifies the query operator to use with the column. Allowable operators are "=", "<", ">", or valid combinations.

Because the query operators are nonalphanumeric characters, they must be encoded to be contained within a URL. The encoding is shown in the following table:

Query Operator	Encoding
=	%3D
>	%3E
<	%3C
>=	%3E%3D
<=	%3C%3D
<>	%3C%3E

You can also use the function portal30.wwutl_htf.url_encode('*any string*') to convert a string to its encoded equivalent.

The following example adds a query condition on the deptno column and uses a PL/SQL block-calling method:

```
PORTAL30.wwa_app_module.link (
    p_arg_names => '_moduleid', p_arg_values => '1255137853',
    p_arg_names => '_show_header',p_arg_values => 'YES',
    p_arg_names => 'deptno',p_arg_values =>  LTRIM(TO_CHAR(v_deptno))
    p_arg_names => '_deptno_cond',
    p_arg_values => portal30.wwutl_htf.url_encode('='));
```

Specifying Sequence Number Generator or Variables as the Default Value for a Form Column   On occasion, you might pass dates to a Form, but you don't want your users to have to enter a date every time the Form is generated. If you could just define the default date value as SYSDATE, this would be nice. Well, you can, but you must prefix SYSDATE with a pound sign (#). The same can be done if you want to specify a sequence. In this case, you would do something similar to the following:

```
#<schema name>.<sequence name>.nextval
```

If, for example, the schema name is "SCOTT" and it contains a sequence named "CUSTOMER_SEQ", the default value entry is as follows:

```
#SCOTT.CUSTOMER_SEQ.NEXTVAL
```

To pull today's date into a field, you can use the following:

```
#SYSDATE
```

Reports

Reports enable you to display data in a predefined format. You can develop reports in a Table, Form, or Custom format. Reports are another component of Oracle Portal that you'll use frequently and, for example, you might use them to display employee information. Reports are relatively easy to create. Figure 16-16 shows a report in creation.

QBE Reports   Query By Example (QBE) reports are a quick way to generate reports. The QBE Wizard guides you through the creation of your Report. During the steps of the wizard, you're prompted for the table name and table columns. After you select the columns you want to see from the particular table, you can

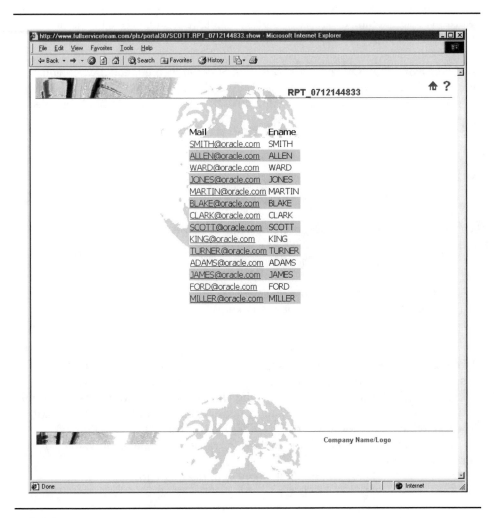

FIGURE 16-16. *Report creation*

format the Report according to these columns. A QBE Report is, perhaps, the easiest way to create a Report in Oracle Portal.

Reports from Query Wizard The Report from *Query Wizard* is the second easiest way to create a Report in Oracle Portal. In contrast to the QBE Report, the Report from Query Wizard guides you in creating a query for the Report. In other words, you're building a SQL query and you can, therefore, create things such as *joins,* where data for the Report is obtained from two different tables.

Reports from SQL Query   *Reports from SQL Query* are created when you provide a SQL query. Portal parses the query and determines the columns needed to generate the Form. Prefixing the variable with a colon passes in bind variables. For example:

```
SELECT *
FROM SCOTT.EMP
WHERE deptno = :department_number
```

TIP
When using bind variables, use a descriptive name. Otherwise, during your linking, you won't know what the Report expects. The value you specify as your bind variable will be the label for your customization screen. If you name the previous variable ":x", for example, you won't know what field data the Report expects.

Linking Data from a Report   At times, you'll want to link directly to the data displayed in the Report. For example, if you have a Report that displays a URL and an e-mail address, you want to turn the URL and e-mail address into hyperlinks. This can be done using the htf.anchor function from the PL/SQL Web Toolkit. The following example shows how you can hyperlink data from the Report.

You can add an e-mail column to the EMP table and populate it with valid e-mail addresses.

Next, create a Report from a SQL query with the following query:

```
select htf.anchor('mailto:'||email, email) mail,
       ename
from SCOTT.emp
```

You want to display the column as HTML under the Column Formatting tab or wizard step. Next, run the Report. You now have a Report with a hyperlinked e-mail address. When the link is clicked, it invokes the default e-mail client using a "to" address for the user-clicked object.

The same functionality can be used for URLs, as well as any other links in the SELECT query.

Charts

Charts are useful tools in Oracle Portal. Using *charts,* you can create key performance indicator charts, Portal usage charts, dollars saved charts, and so forth. The beauty of these is the numbers are queried every time the Chart is invoked, so the charts are real time! By using links, you can link charts to other more-detailed charts or reports. Charts are created via a SQL query, in the following format:

```
select [the_link], [the_name], [the_data], from [table]
```

Where

the_link	Specifies a link from the values represented by the_name in the Chart to another component or URL using wwv_user_ utilities.get_url (see the following links). This field is optional and always appears first in the SQL Query.
the_name	Text from this column is displayed as the label for each bar in the Chart. This field is required and always appears second in the SQL Query.
the_data	This column is used to determine the length of the bar for each name. This field is required and always appears third in the SQL Query.

As of version 3.0.9, a new chart component is available in beta. See Figure 16-17 for an example of this new Chart type.

Calendars

Calendars are yet another great tool provided by Oracle Portal. Granted, they aren't perfected yet, but they're quickly approaching that point. By specifying a SQL query that includes dates, the *calendar* component generates a GUI calendar complete with items within the date cells. Perfect examples of using this are a "Company Calendar of Events," where you display all company-sponsored events in a well-designed GUI calendar. The calendar feature makes use of the owa_util.calendarprint procedure from the PL/SQL Web Toolkit discussed in Chapter 14. Calendars, like Charts, are drawn from a SQL query in the following syntax:

```
select [the_date],       [the_name],
       [the_name_link], [the_date_link], [the_target_frame]
from    [table]
```

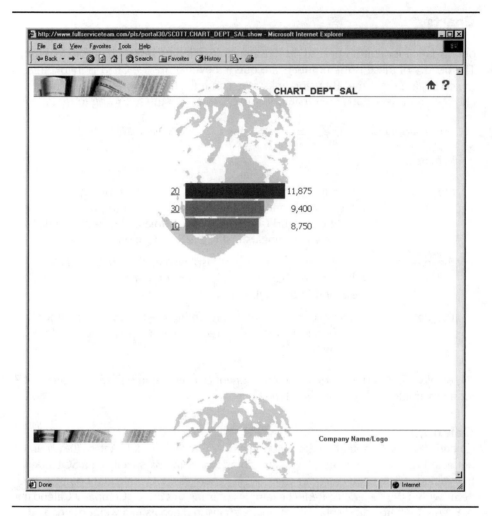

FIGURE 16-17. *New chart type example*

The variables, and their definitions, are discussed in the following table:

Variable	Definition
the_date	Displays text on the calendar on the dates contained in this table or view column. This field is required and always appears first in the SQL Query. The values in this column must have the DATE datatype.

Variable	Definition
the_name	Displays cell text from this table or view column according to the dates in the_date column. This field is required and always appears second in the SQL Query.
the_name_link	Specifies a link from the values in the_name column to another component or URL using wwv_user_utilities .get_url (see the following links). This field is optional.
the_date_link	Specifies a link from the values in the_date column to another component or URL using wwv_user_ utilities.get_url (see the following links). This field is also optional.
the_target_frame	Specifies the URL of a frame in a Web page. Enter this column if you want to link to a specific frame in a URL. This field is also optional.

Figure 16-18 shows an example of a calendar.

Dynamic Pages

Dynamic Pages are components that enable you to embed PL/SQL and SQL into HTML using <ORACLE> tags. This gives you the capability to execute SQL blocks or make calls to PL/SQL stored procedures. Dynamic Pages are similar to PL/SQL Server Pages (PSPs), which are discussed in Chapter 14. As you can see in this example, Dynamic Pages don't require you to include only PL/SQL; they also support direct SQL statements. Using a Dynamic Page, you can do the following:

```
<HTML>
<HEAD>
<TITLE>Example</TITLE>
</HEAD>

<BODY>
<H2>Example of A Dynamic Page</H2>
<ORACLE>select * from scott.emp</ORACLE>
</BODY>
</HTML>
```

Once the <ORACLE> tags are in place in your HTML, Oracle Portal parses out the PL/SQL and enables you to edit your PL/SQL code.

FIGURE 16-18. *Example calendar*

Figure 16-19 shows an example of a Dynamic Page.

XML Component

The *XML* component displays XML pages. When creating an XML component, you have the option of providing a URL to an XML file or entering the XML code into the wizard. Like dynamic pages, XML components allow the use of <ORACLE> tags and, therefore, allow the use of PL/SQL in your XML code. During the creation of the XML component, you also have the option to specify an XSL style sheet (either

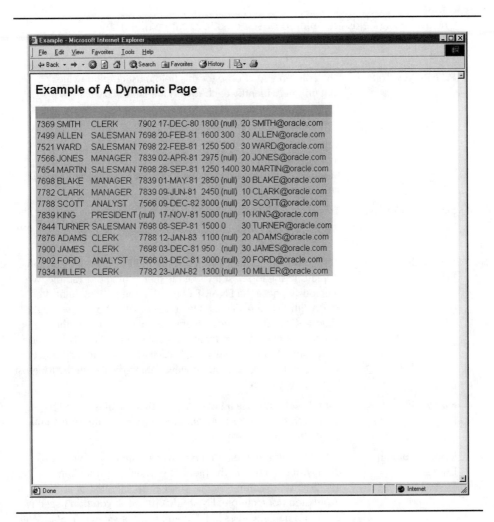

FIGURE 16-19. *Dynamic Page*

by URL or code) and a DTD. A sample XML component is provided with Oracle Portal for your reference.

Hierarchies

Hierarchies enable you to create Hierarchical Charts based on a SQL query. In SQL terms, this is a CONNECT BY statement. When creating hierarchies, bear in mind that to create one, you must have a recursive relationship in the data. For example, in an employee table, you could have an employee ID as well as a manager ID, meaning some employees are also managers and, therefore, a hierarchy is established.

The following fields are entered or selected to create a hierarchy:

Field	Definition
Primary Key Column	The column you choose for this field must contain values that uniquely identify each row in the table. For example, the employee number (EMPNO) column of the EMP table.
Parent Key Column	The column you choose for the parent key must contain values that refer to the primary key. For example, the manager's employee number (MGR) column in the EMP table. This column contains values that refer to the EMPNO column of the EMP table.
Start With Column	This column contains a value that will be used to determine the topmost level in the hierarchy. For example, the ENAME column of the EMP table.
Default Start With Value	This column determines which value in the Start With Column displays in the topmost level of the hierarchy. For example, we previously chose the ENAME column of the EMP table as the Start With Column. For the Default Start With Value, we might choose King. This creates a hierarchy that displays on the topmost level data from table rows containing King. This option is equivalent to specifying a SQL WHERE clause in a connect by statement that selects table or view data to display in the topmost level of the hierarchy.
Start With LOV	For this field, choose a List of Values that enables end users of the hierarchy to choose a Default Start With Value from a table on the hierarchy's customization Form.
Display Column Expression	Enter a column name (or names) whose values you want to display in each box in the hierarchy when it's printed. In addition to the column name, you can specify text or an expression (for example, ENAME||'-'||JOB). If you don't specify a column name, values in the column you specified in Start With Column display in the hierarchy boxes.
Link	Choose a link from the drop-down list. This link is for the text you specified in the previous Display Column Expression. Click the icon to display the Set Link Parameters window. You can set the values of the link parameters to pass to the target component here. You can enter a static value (for example: 10, KING) or you can select a column from a table. If you don't set link parameters, the default values of the link are used.

Figure 16-20 shows an example of a hierarchy.

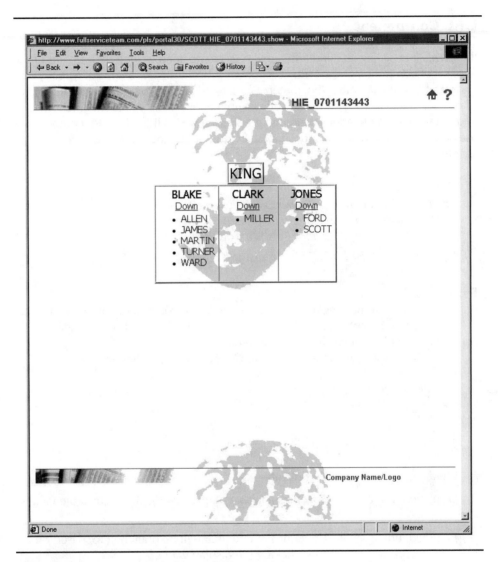

FIGURE 16-20. *Example hierarchy*

Menus

Menus are among the simplest components. They provide your users with a portlet that contains hyperlinks to the object of your choice. One example of the use of a menu is *intranet links,* where the URLs point to Web sites of a common group's interest. Menus aren't limited to URLs, however. Using direct access URLs, you can also have a menu of reports.

URL Component

The *URL component* is a tool, which in the early versions, was only available via the PDK. After seeing its popularity grow, Oracle decided to include it as part of the core set of components. The URL component is useful because you can specify a URL, and Portal will gather the content of that URL and display it in a portlet. This, of course, opens the door for many other applications, such as Flash animations, and many other applications that can be accessed via a URL. The URL component uses UTL_HTTP (as discussed in Chapter 11) to retrieve the HTML from the specified URL.

TIP
The URL component enables you to include content from any URL. This content can be placed on any page within your application. This is a powerful feature provided by Oracle Portal.

Frame Drivers

Frame drivers are something that, if you use the Web, you're familiar with, although they're decreasing in popularity. A *frame driver* in Oracle Portal simply means an action in one frame affects the data in another.

Frame drivers are generated via a SQL Query using the following syntax:

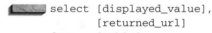

```
select  [displayed_value],
        [returned_url]
from    [table]
```

The fields in the query include the following:

Field	Definition
Displayed_value	Specifies a table column that displays selectable values in the driving frame.
Returned_url	Contains the URL that will be branched to, based on a user clicking the display value.
Table	Specifies the table or view from which to select the previous columns.

Links

Links enable you to bring application components together. As the name implies, they link things. If you want to link a Report to another Report (such as drill-through reporting), for example, you use a link to do so. Creating links is as easy as describing what they do. You can link to three things: Oracle Portal Component, Oracle Portal

Component Customization Form, and a URL. If you link to a component, Oracle Portal enables you to choose the component from a pop-up list. For a URL, enter the URL in the provided field. When linking to a component, the link component verifies the target component for bind variables. If the target accepts bind variables, the link also inherits these.

Another method of linking is using the wwv_user_utilities.get_url function. This function uses predefined links and is used with components based on SQL queries, such as charts and calendars.

The syntax to call the wwv_user_utilities.get_url function (in a select statement) is as follows:

```
<portal schema name>.wwv_user_utilities.get_url(
'<app name>.<link name>',
'<link parameter name 1>',<link parameter value 1>,
'<link parameter name 2>',<link parameter value 2>,
...
'<link parameter name n>',<link parameter value n>)
```

n may *not* be larger than 30. In other words, you can pass no more than 30 parameters to a link.

The following example demonstrates the use of the get_url function in a chart. This example assumes the components are in an application called APP_PORTAL_CHAPTER.

1. Create the target application component. In this case, create a Chart that displays all the employees' salaries for a particular department. Your Chart query should look like the following select statement. Name the Chart CHART_EMP_SAL.

```
Select
        null        the_link,
        ename       the_name,
        sal         the_data
FROM    SCOTT.EMP
WHERE deptno = :department_number
ORDER BY SAL desc;
```

2. Now create a link to this Chart (set the target to CHART_EMP_SAL). Name the link LINK_TO_CHART_EMP_SAL.

3. Create the Source Chart with the following query:

```
select PORTAL30.wwv_user_utilities.get_url(
        'APP_PORTAL_CHAPTER.LINK_TO_CHART_EMP_SAL',
        'department_number',
        DEPTNO )   the_link,
        DEPTNO         the_name,
```

```
        sum(SAL)      the_data
from    SCOTT.EMP
group   by deptno
order   by the_data desc
```

4. Name the Source Chart CHART_DEPT_SAL.

5. Run the CHART_DEPT_SAL Chart.

What you generate is a Chart similar to the one shown in Figure 16-21, where clicking the department number takes you to the target Chart displaying all the people within the selected department.

List Of Values (LOVs)

If you've used Developer Forms before, you're familiar with a List Of Values (LOVs). A *LOV* enables you to create a list of values from which the user can select one or multiple values. The great thing about LOVs in Oracle Portal is they can accept bind variables, which makes the LOV dynamic.

The syntax for a dynamic LOV is as follows:

```
select [display_column],
       [return_column]
from   [table]
```

where display_column identifies selectable values to be displayed in the LOV and return_column identifies the actual values to be passed into the component.

The following example is a dynamic LOV. This LOV displays the menu items for the logged-in user. You retrieve the logged-in user by using the get_user API.

```
SELECT menu_id,
       menu_item
FROM   menu
WHERE  user_id = portal30.wwctx_api.get_user
```

Beta Components

As of version 3.0.9, two beta components are available only if you enable them. To enable these beta components, go to your Oracle Portal Home Page. Make sure you're on the Administer tab. In the Services portlet, click Global Settings. Toward the bottom of the page, you'll see the two components and the check boxes to enable them.

Image Charts from Query   Image Charts from Query can be considered a "next generation" charting component. Image Charts enable you to create Pie Charts, Area Charts, Bar Charts, Line Charts, and 3-D Charts. The process for creating Image Charts is similar to that of Charts, with the exception that now you can select a series of

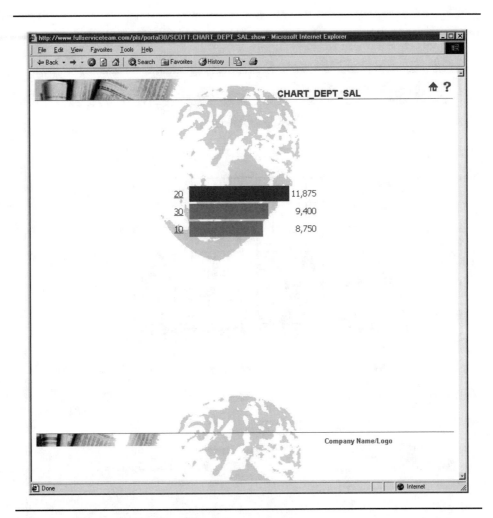

FIGURE 16-21. *Chart salaries by department*

data versus one value. In other words, where Charts enable you to graph employees and their salaries, Image Charts from Query enables you to chart employees and their salaries, commissions, and a combination of both. Figure 16-22 shows a Line Chart created from Image Charts from Query.

Data Component   The *data component* enables you to create a HTML/JavaScript-based spreadsheet for data analysis. Although this is a great concept, I'm not sure it's ready for prime time and I haven't yet figured out where you might use it.

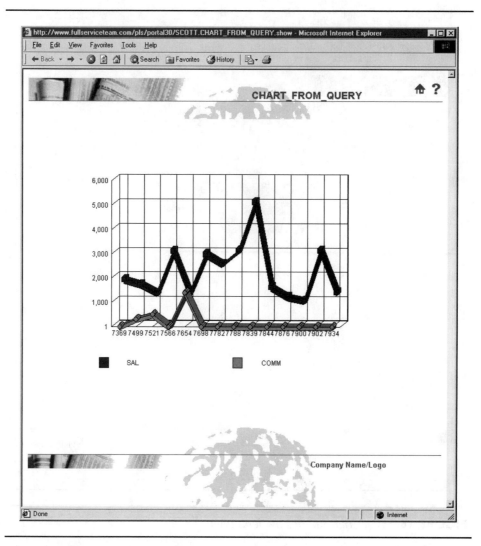

FIGURE 16-22.   *Image Line Chart*

Oracle Portal Security

Another great feature of Oracle Portal is its integrated security. Oracle Portal allows
security at the item or component level. Virtually all the components you create
in Oracle Portal have an Access tab, enabling you to specify privileges for a user,

or a group of users. The following section briefly discusses security regarding users, groups, and applications.

Users

Portal users can be added, deleted, or modified. WebDB used database schemas to manage Portal users, which drove DBAs crazy. Fortunately, Oracle Portal stores Portal user and security information in tables. DBAs love this!

Creating Users

Creating users in Oracle Portal is a relatively simple task. From the Oracle Portal Home Page, click the Administer tab. Then click Create New Users in the Users portlet. You will be prompted for the user name, password, and Login server privileges. Once these are entered, click the Create button, and your user will be created. The user you just created can now, by default, log in to Oracle Portal. However, because that user isn't assigned to a particular group and he doesn't have a Home Page assigned, on logging in, he will start at the Oracle Portal Home Page. To change this, click the Edit User link provided immediately after creating the user. Clicking this link enables you to specify personal details, group membership, organizational details, default group, and several other preferences for this user.

TIP
Users can be created en masse using the User APIs provided with Portal.

Deleting Users

Deleting users from Oracle Portal isn't as straightforward a process as creating them because of the nature of the Login server. As mentioned previously, Oracle Portal is a series of components working together. Users who log in to Oracle Portal are authenticated through the Login server and, on successful log in, are redirected to the requested Oracle Portal page. Therefore, you can probably guess more Login server users exist than Portal users. The process for deleting users from Oracle Portal is to click the Login server Administration link found on the Oracle Portal Home Page under the Administer tab. Clicking this should take you to the Login server Administration page, similar to the image in Figure 16-23.

From here, click Administer Users and edit the user you want to delete. Once in Edit mode, you can delete the user. You have now deleted the user from the Login server. The profile remains in the Portal tables, however, meaning that if you create a user with the same user name, you'll automatically bring up that profile and the personal information will be populated with the information from the previous user.

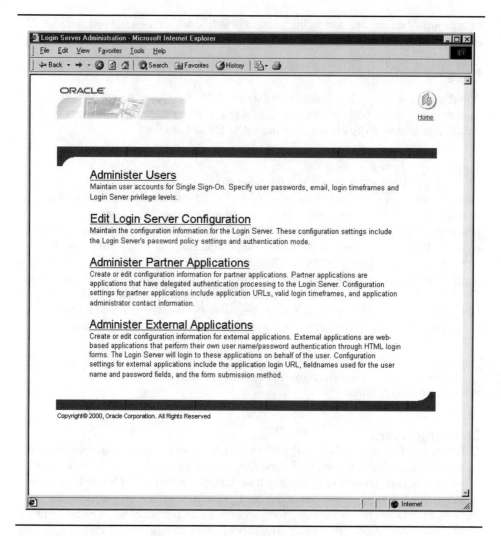

FIGURE 16-23. *Login server Administration page*

You can reset the profile by editing the user in Portal. Click the Reset To Defaults button in the user's profile, as shown in Figure 16-24.

Resetting the PORTAL30 Password

Believe it or not, forgetting the PORTAL30 password or not knowing the password can be frustrating. After all, this is a privileged account (it has DBA privileges). So

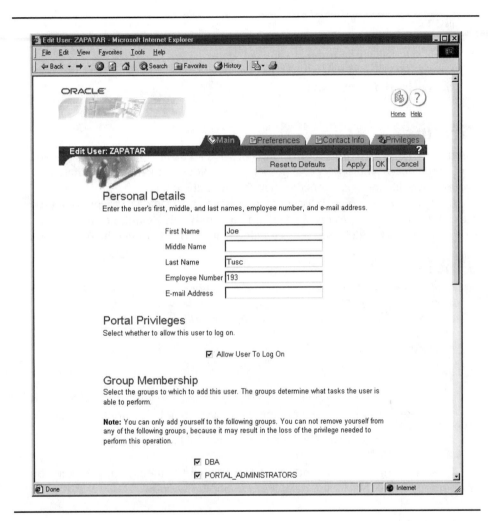

FIGURE 16-24. *Reset to Defaults*

what do you do when this happens? There's what could be called the "brute strength" method. To use this method, you need access to the wwsec_person$ table. Once you get this level of access from your DBA, you can change the password with the following update statement in SQL*Plus:

```
UPDATE  wwsec_person$
SET     password = WWSSO_UTL.HASH_PWD('NEWPASSWORD')
WHERE   USER_NAME = 'PORTAL30';
```

NOTE
In versions prior to 3.0.9, the password passed to HASH_PWD is case-sensitive. If you enter the previously shown password, the lowercase "newpassword" won't work.

Groups

Groups help organize users. Using Groups, you can assign default pages, set and revoke privileges, and set general properties, so different members of different groups have different experiences when they visit the page.

In Oracle Portal, you can assign many users to a specific group and one user can belong to several groups. A user can have only one default group, however. The user inherits this default group's privileges and properties once he or she logs in.

NOTE
Assigning a user to a group and setting a default group are two separate operations. A user must be a member of the group to set the group as a default. If you want to set a new user to a specific group, follow these steps:

1. Create the user.

2. Make the user a member of the particular group by editing the group.

3. Assign the group as the default group for the user.

These steps must be followed. If the user isn't part of the group, you won't be able to see the group from the default group pop-up window.

Creating Groups

Creating groups is as simple as creating users. From the Oracle Portal Home Page, click Create New Groups. This takes you into a three-step wizard where you can add members to your new group and set preferences for this new group.

Deleting Groups

Deleting a group can be done from the Edit menu. Select a group for editing and, once in Edit mode, you can delete the group by clicking Delete.

Application Security

You have the capability in Oracle Portal to set security at the item level. Typically, this is done via the Access tab on the application component or item. Security settings vary per item. For example, on application components, two modes exist for privileges: inherited or individual. *Inherited* mode means the component security is inherited from the application level. *Individual* mode means privileges are granted to specified individuals.

Oracle Portal Monitoring

Occasionally, the need will occur to find out information about Oracle Portal itself: information such as who's accessing it, when they're accessing it, with what browser they're accessing it, and so forth. Oracle Portal enables you to find this information by providing an extensive collection of charts organized in a content area. To use these charts, you must tell Portal what to log or what to keep track of. This is done via the Log Registry. The Log Registry can be found on the Oracle Portal Home Page under the Administer tab. By default, Oracle Portal installs with one registry entry, which logs all events. You might think this is unnecessary and choose only to log certain events. As shown in Figure 16-25, you have the option to log events by domain, subdomain, name, user name, action, browser, and language.

One item overlooked in this registry is the capability to log by group. In other words, you cannot log events by the user groups you specify. Workarounds exist to getting this information. By using the APIs and accessing the log tables, you can retrieve the information you need.

Oracle Portal Advanced Concepts

Let's look briefly at the advanced concepts of Oracle Portal, including the PDK and APIs. These concepts are intended for advanced users, who have some understanding of the PL/SQL language.

PDK

Like many applications on the market today, Oracle Portal has its own Development Kit. Using the Portal Development Kit (PDK), you can develop your own portlets to perform a variety of tasks.

The PDK enables you to create portlets in two main languages: Java and PL/SQL. You can incorporate several portlets, which are designed by others, into your Portal. Portal Studio (**http://portalstudio.oracle.com**) has several examples of these and explains their installation.

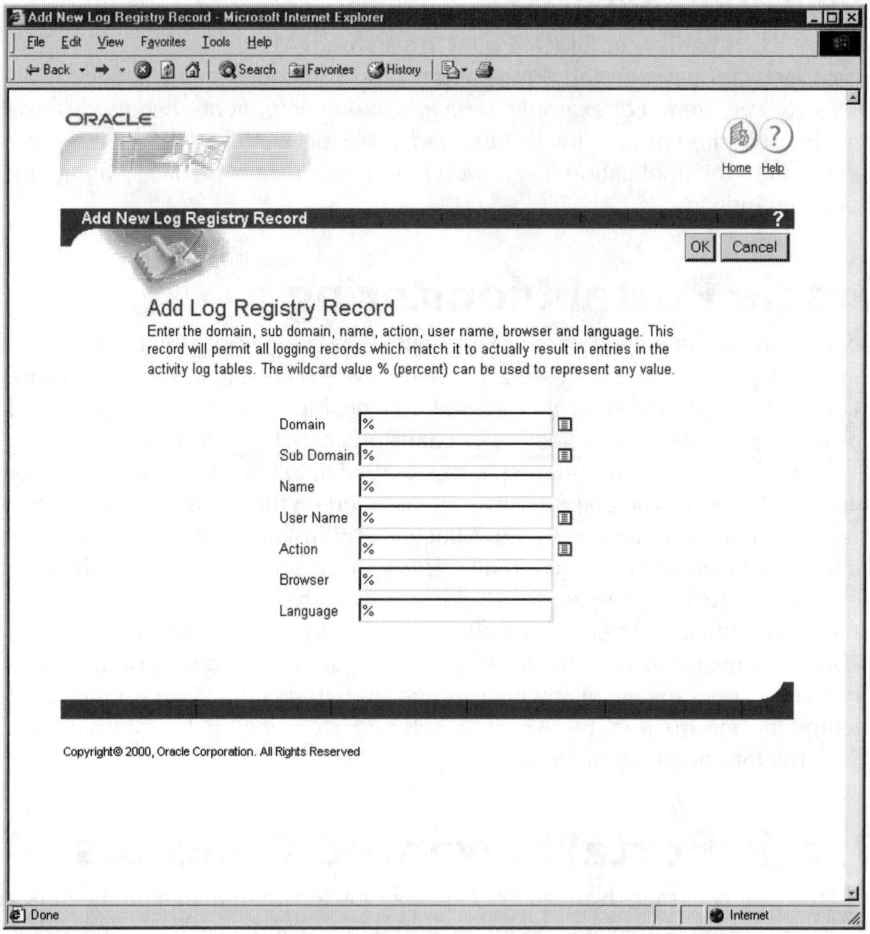

FIGURE 16-25. *Portal monitor options*

Several portlets have been introduced since Portal's release and they can be implemented into your portal relatively easily. You need to follow some rules when you build portlets, but we'll get to those later. For now, here are some examples on how to incorporate portlets built using the PDK into your portal.

The first example is relatively simple and is available on Portal Studio. This shows you how to implement a portal of your own into Oracle Portal. The sample demonstrates the Hello World portlet, which is distributed in a ZIP file that contains the following files:

- **HELLOWORLD_PORTLET.pks**   Hello World portlet specification

- **HELLOWORLD_PORTLET.pkb**   Hello World portlet body

- **SNOOP_PORTLET.pks**   Snoop portlet specification

- **SNOOP_PORTLET.pks**   Snoop portlet body

- **STARTER_PROVIDER.pks**   Starter Provider specification

- **STARTER_PROVIDER.pkb**   Starter Provider body

- **insintpr.sql**   Installation script (runs above scripts)

For those familiar with PL/SQL, these are simply packages you're going to create in a schema of your choice (in this example, we call it PDK). The first step, therefore, is to create that schema. Once we create that schema and allow it access to log in/connect, we can grant it access to the APIs. We do this by running a script called provsyns.sql.

1. Connect as the schema where you installed Portal (connect PORTAL30/ PORTAL30@ORCL;).

2. Run the provsyns.sql script, located in IAS_HOME/portal30/admin/plsql/ wwc (@provsyns.sql pdk).

3. Connect as the schema you created, in this case, PDK (connect pdk/pdk).

4. Run the installation script (@insintpr.sql).

Once you install the package(s), you need to register your provider to implement it on to pages. Do this by logging in to Portal as the administrator. Under the Administrator tab, select adding a portlet provider. Fill in the information, as follows:

- **Name**   Starter_Provider

- **Display Name**   Starter Provider

- **Timeout**   100

- **Timeout Message**   Application Timed Out

- **Implementation Style**   Database

- **Provider Login Frequency**   Never

- **Register on Remote Nodes**   No

- **Owning Schema**   STARTER (or the name of the schema you created for this provider)

- **Package Name**   STARTER_PROVIDER

Once this is done, you have the packages installed and a provider created. You should now be able to see the portlet and add it to pages.

Other portlets you can download will have a set of instructions for you to follow for installation and configuration.

TIP
*Additional portlets are available at **http:// portalstudio.oracle.com**. These include a Calendar portlet, an AltaVista Search Enterprise portlet, Scheduling portlets, and hundreds more.*

Portlet Development Guidelines

If you want to develop your own portlets for the public-at-large, Oracle has supplied the "Guidelines for Writing Portlets." Oracle provides a series of check lists for each Portlet mode as specified in these guidelines. Take the time to read this document.

APIs

After working with the Portal Development Kit, you may already be familiar with APIs because they're extremely useful, especially when creating portlets with the PDK. Using APIs, you can determine who is logged in (and display information accordingly), you can determine what group they belong to, and determine to what group, if any. You can also update their personal information, disable their accounts, enable their accounts, and so forth. You can perform many operations using the APIs. Dozens of APIs also enable you to do a variety of operations. This section discusses a subset, according to usefulness.

wwctx_api.get_user()

The get_user API is the API you'll probably use the most. This is used frequently because it returns the user ID for the logged-in user. The get_user API is often used to pass this user ID to other APIs. The syntax for get_user is as follows:

```
function get_user return varchar2;
```

An example using get_user to print the current user's username to the Web page is as follows:

```
htp.print(wwctx_api.get_user);
```

In the previous example, the logged-in user ID is displayed in the browser. Another example of its use is as follows:

```
if (wwctx_api.get_user = 'PUBLIC') then
   htp.print('This user is NOT authenticated');
else
   htp.print('This user is logged in');
end if;
```

In this example, check to see if the user is PUBLIC, meaning you check to see if the user has logged in. If he has, wwctx_api.get_user returns his user ID. If he hasn't, wwctx_api.get_user returns 'PUBLIC'.

wwsec_api.person_info()

The person_info API is also useful. This API enables you to obtain all the personal information in the wwsec_person$ table. The syntax for this API is as follows:

```
function person_info(p_person_id in number) return wwsec_person%rowtype;
```

Example:

```
declare
   l_person_rec wwsec_person%rowtype;
begin
   l_person_rec := wwsec_api.person_info(p_person_id => '784214');
   htp.print('Hello there, '||l_person_rec.first_name);
end;
```

This example prints the first name of the person whose ID is 784214. By the same logic, you could display all the information for that person, such as her telephone number, maiden name, and so forth.

If you want to display this information for the current user (instead of hardcoding the ID), you can replace the assignment of the l_person_rec variables as follows:

```
l_person_rec := portal30.wwsec_api.person_info(p_person_id =>
   portal30.wwsec_api.id(portal30.wwctx_api.get_user));
```

wwsec_api.modify_portal_user()

The modify_portal_user API enables you to edit the information stored in the wwsec_person$ table for a particular user. This comes in handy if you don't want users to edit their information via the default Portal screens. The syntax for modify_portal_user is as follows:

```
procedure modify_portal_user(
   p_user_name              in varchar2,
   p_db_user                in varchar2 default null,
```

```
p_portal_user              in varchar2,
p_display                  in varchar2,
p_display_personal_info,   in varchar2 default 'N',
p_notification_preference  in varchar2,
p_empno                    in varchar2 default null,
p_last_name                in varchar2 default null,
p_first_name               in varchar2 default null,
p_middle_name              in varchar2 default null,
p_known_as                 in varchar2 default null,
p_maiden_name              in varchar2 default null,
p_date_of_birth            in varchar2 default null,
p_email                    in varchar2 default null,
p_work_phone               in varchar2 default null,
p_home_phone               in varchar2 default null,
p_mobile_phone             in varchar2 default null,
p_pager                    in varchar2 default null,
p_fax                      in varchar2 default null,
p_office_addr1             in varchar2 default null,
p_office_addr2             in varchar2 default null,
p_office_addr3             in varchar2 default null,
p_office_city              in varchar2 default null,
p_office_state             in varchar2 default null,
p_office_zip               in varchar2 default null,
p_office_country           in varchar2 default null,
p_home_addr1               in varchar2 default null,
p_home_addr2               in varchar2 default null,
p_home_addr3               in varchar2 default null,
p_home_city                in varchar2 default null,
p_home_state               in varchar2 default null,
p_home_zip                 in varchar2 default null,
p_home_country             in varchar2 default null,
p_organization             in varchar2 default null,
p_title varchar2           in varchar2 default null,
p_spending_limit           in number default null,
p_hiredate                 in varchar2 default null,
p_source                   in varchar2 default null,
p_manager_user_name        in varchar2 default null);
```

An example of its use is as follows:

```
wwsec_api.modify_portal_user(
        p_user_name    => 'JOHNSONJ',
        p_db_User      => 'ADMIN',
        p_portal_user  => 'Y',
        p_organization => 'Information Technology');
```

The delete_user, activate, and deactivate APIs perform the respective action on given Portal users. The syntax and examples for each are as follows:

wwsec_api.delete_portal_user()

Syntax:

```
procedure delete_portal_user(p_user_name in varchar2);
```

An example of its use is

```
wwsec_api.delete_portal_user(p_user_name => 'DAVIDF');
```

wwsec_api.activate_portal_user()

Syntax:

```
procedure activate_portal_user(p_user_name in varchar2);
```

Example of use:

```
wwsec_api.activate_portal_user(p_user_name => 'LEVINEJ');
```

wwsec_api.deactivate_portal_user()

Syntax:

```
procedure deactivate_portal_user(p_user_name in varchar2);
```

An example of its use is

```
wwsec_api.deactivate_portal_user(p_user_name => 'PERFECTOV');
```

wwsec_app_priv.get_login_link()

The login link API can be used in a Dynamic Page. The login link returns the URL link for the login page.

The syntax is as follows:

```
function get_login_link(
            p_nls_link_text  in varchar2 default null,
            p_image_filename in varchar2 default null,
            p_requested_url  in varchar2
              default wwctx_api.get_product_schema || '.portal')
return varchar2;
```

Example:

```
Declare
  l_url varchar2(100);
begin
  l_url := wwsec_app_priv.get_login_url;
end;
```

Oracle Portal Applications and Samples

Portal lets you create applications. In this section, I discuss applications and various sample Portal applications.

Applications

The following are a series of applications you can use to practice or to use within your Portal.

Voting Application   This sample application enables you take a real-time poll of your users. This application assumes the following:

- Your users can log in to your Portal server.

- You have administrator privileges on your Portal server.

The steps to making the Portal application work include the following:

1. Create the voting table in a schema of your choice, as the following code illustrates:

```
CREATE TABLE portal_vote(
user_name     varchar2(100),
vote          varchar2(100));
```

2. Create the procedure that will perform the DML in the schema you created the table, as follows:

```
CREATE OR REPLACE PROCEDURE cast_vote (p_vote_choice IN varchar2) is
v_count number;
v_user varchar2(50);

cursor check_cast_votes(cp_user IN varchar2) is
select count(*)
from portal_vote
where user_name = cp_user;
BEGIN
--The user is the logged in user
```

```
v_user := portal30.wwctx_api.get_user;

-- First thing we do is see if the user has voted before.
open check_cast_votes(v_user);
fetch check_cast_votes into v_count;
close check_cast_votes;
--If the user HAS voted, then update the users vote
if(v_count > 0) then
update portal_vote
set vote = p_vote_choice
where user_name = v_user;
commit;
else
--If the user HAS NOT voted, insert the vote
--into the table.
insert into portal_vote
values (v_user, p_vote_choice);
commit;
end if;
END cast_vote;
/
grant execute on cast_vote to public;
/
```

3. Create an application based on the schema in which you created the table and the procedure.

4. Create an LOV with the vote choices.

   In this example, I create a LOV with several colors for the users to pick their favorite. I named the LOV LOV_CHOICES.

5. Create a Form, named FORM_VOTE, based on the cast_vote procedure, to accept votes. Set the USER_NAME, named p_user, to a hidden field and the VOTE, named p_vote_choice, to a combo box. Set the LOV to LOV_CHOICES. Remove all buttons except the Submit button.

6. Create the Chart, named CHART_VOTE, based on the table. Use the following SQL query:

```
select null        the_link,
       vote        the_name,
       count(vote) the_data
from   portal_vote
group  by vote
order  by the_data desc
```

7. Create the page.

8. Create a page with two tabs. One tab should contain the Form and the other tab should contain the Chart for viewing the results. Name the page VOTING_PAGE. The page should look similar to Figure 16-26.

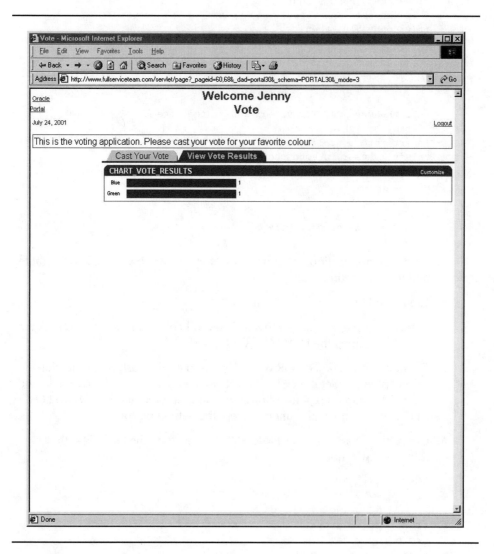

FIGURE 16-26. *Voting page*

9. Create a group.

10. Create a group to which all your voters will belong. Set the VOTING_PAGE as the default home page. Name the group VOTES.

11. Set privileges.

12. On the Grant Access tab for the Voting application, allow the VOTES group to MANAGE the application. You can also set the privileges on the two tabs, so users can see the Form tab, but not the Results tab.

13. Set the VOTES group as the users default group.

14. Set the group as the default group, so when the users log in to Portal, they are defaulted to the VOTING_PAGE.

15. Have your users log in and vote.

16. View the results.

Samples

This sample section is intended to show you how some actions are performed in Oracle Portal.

Passing Parameters Between Portlets   This example shows how to pass parameters from one portlet to another. Create one page with two portlets on it. Clicking a value in the top portlet changes the values displayed in the lower portlet. First, create a report from SQL query with the following query:

```
SELECT  htf.anchor('http://www.yourserver.com/servlet/'||
        'page?_pageid=XXXX&_dad=PORTAL30&_schema=PORTAL30'||
        '&_mode=3&dept='||deptno, deptno) department,
        dname,
        loc
FROM    scott.dept
```

You must substitute **www.yourserver.com** with the actual name of your server, and XXXX with the page ID you're going to place these portlets on. The page ID can be determined by editing the page. Once you're in Edit mode, the page ID is displayed in the address bar.

Create the second Report with the following query:

```
SELECT *
FROM    scott.emp
WHERE   deptno = :department_number
```

Add the following PL/SQL to the "Before Displaying the Page" section of the Report:

```
PORTAL30.wwv_name_value.replace_value(
     l_arg_names,
     l_arg_values,
     p_reference_path ||'.dept',
     PORTAL30.wwv_standard_util.string_to_table2(
      nvl(get_value('dept'), 10)));
```

Build a page and include these two portlets. When you click the link of the summary Report, the page will be refreshed, and the Detail Report will change, based on the data from the Summary Report.

Calendar Navigator   Passing parameters between portlets has many uses and opens the door, if you will, for many useful tools. One such application is that of a Calendar Navigator. If you use the calendar components in Oracle Portal, you're aware of how tedious it can be to navigate around the calendar by pressing the NEXT and PREVIOUS buttons. It's quite a task if you want to see what's going on six months from now, especially if you have months with many entries! The *Calendar Navigator* helps you by setting a Dynamic Page portlet on a page containing a calendar. The Dynamic Page displays a dynamic list for the next six months. In other words, if you're in June, the portlet displays July, August, September, October, November, and December. The month names are hyperlinked: clicking them reloads the calendar to the appropriate month.

1. Create the table in a schema of your choice, as follows:

```
CREATE TABLE calendar_events(
event_id       number,
event_name     varchar2(500),
event_desc     varchar2(4000),
event_date     date);
```

2. Create the Calendar Navigator by placing two components on a page: a calendar and a Dynamic Page.

First, create the page. You create the page first because you need the page ID. While no "About" section exists for pages as it does for application components, you can still easily obtain the page ID. One way—perhaps the quickest—is to look at the page hyperlinks when you're in the Navigator. The page ID is passed as a parameter.

After you have a page (complete with page ID), create a calendar that accepts a date parameter. Use the following query:

```
Select CALENDAR_EVENTS.EVENT_DATE the_date,
       CALENDAR_EVENTS.EVENT_NAME the_name,
```

```
       null                              the_name_link,
       null                              the_date_link,
       null                              the_target
from   CALENDAR_EVENTS
where  display_field_flg = 'Y'
and    to_char(event_date,'YYYYMM') >= :month
order  by the_date
```

As you can see, the calendar accepts one parameter called "month" in the format YYYYMM (for example, 200107, 200008, and so forth).

Add the following PL/SQL to the Before Displaying Page section on the calendar:

```
PORTAL30.wwv_name_value.replace_value(
    l_arg_names,
    l_arg_values,
    p_reference_path ||'.month',
    PORTAL30.wwv_standard_util.string_to_table2(
      nvl(get_value('month'), to_char(sysdate,'YYYYMM') )));
```

This passes the current month to the calendar for displaying.

Finally, create the Dynamic Page, as follows:

```
SELECT htf.anchor('http://your.portalserver.com/servlet/page'||
        '?_pageid=30&_dad=PORTAL30&_schema=PORTAL30&_mode=3&month='||
        to_char(sysdate,'YYYYMM'),to_char(sysdate,'Month')) month_1,
      htf.anchor('http://your.portalserver.com/servlet/page'||
        '?_pageid=30&_dad=PORTAL30&_schema=PORTAL30&_mode=3&month='||
        to_char(add_months(sysdate,1),'YYYYMM'),
        to_char(add_months(sysdate,1),'Month')) month_2,
      htf.anchor('http://your.portalserver.com/servlet/page'||
        '?_pageid=30&_dad=PORTAL30&_schema=PORTAL30&_mode=3&month='||
        to_char(add_months(sysdate,2),'YYYYMM'),
        to_char(add_months(sysdate,2),'Month')) month_3,
      htf.anchor('http://your.portalserver.com/servlet/page'||
        '?_pageid=30&_dad=PORTAL30&_schema=PORTAL30&_mode=3&month='||
        to_char(add_months(sysdate,3),'YYYYMM'),
        to_char(add_months(sysdate,3),'Month')) month_4,
      htf.anchor('http://your.portalserver.com/servlet/page'||
        '?_pageid=30&_dad=PORTAL30&_schema=PORTAL30&_mode=3&month='||
        to_char(add_months(sysdate,4),'YYYYMM'),
        to_char(add_months(sysdate,4),'Month')) month_5,
     htf.anchor('http://your.portalserver.com/servlet/page'||
        '?_pageid=30&_dad=PORTAL30&_schema=PORTAL30&_mode=3&month='||
        to_char(add_months(sysdate,5),'YYYYMM'),
        to_char(add_months(sysdate,5),'Month')) month_6 FROM dual
```

After you have both components good and ready, place both on the page and test your navigator.

Custom Login Screen

Even though you can create a custom login screen, there's still a flaw when you use it. The flaw is in the on_error redirect. Unfortunately, all your hard work to customize the login screen will be moot because, as soon as someone enters an incorrect user name and password, you'll be right back at the Oracle Portal built-in login page. Several people have found ways around this, one of which is to create a custom login screen. The following is a short description on how to incorporate your own custom login screen in to Oracle Portal.

The first thing you need is the actual login page. The following procedure creates a login screen. Installation instructions follow the procedure.

```
create or replace procedure custom_login_page(
    site2pstoretoken in varchar2 default null
   ,ssousername      in varchar2 default null
   ,p_error_code     in varchar2 default null
   ,p_cancel_url     in varchar2 default null
   ,p_submit_url     in varchar2 default null
   ,subscribername   in varchar2 default null) is
begin
    htp.htmlOpen;
    htp.headOpen;
    htp.title('Customized Login Page');
    htp.headClose;
    htp.bodyOpen;
    htp.header(1, 'Login');
    htp.print('This is the custom login screen <p>');

    -- If an error is passed to the custom login form,
    -- then display that error
    if p_error_code is not null then
        htp.print ('This is the error returned by the login form: ' ||
                  p_error_code );
    end if;

    htp.formopen(curl => p_submit_url );

    htp.print ('Username: ');
    htp.formText(cname => 'ssousername',csize => 30,cmaxlength => 30);
    htp.br;
    htp.br;
    htp.print ('Password: ');
    htp.formPassword(cname => 'password',csize => 30, cmaxlength => 30);

    -- pass back the mandatory parameters

    htp.formHidden(cname  => 'site2pstoretoken',cvalue => site2pstoretoken);
    htp.formHidden(cname  => 'subscribername',cvalue => subscribername);

    -- end of exclusion for versions prior to 3.0.8
```

```
    htp.br;
    htp.br;
    htp.formSubmit(cvalue => 'Login');
    htp.formClose;
    htp.bodyClose;
    htp.htmlClose;
end custom_login_page;
/
grant execute on custom_login_page to public
/
```

Compile this procedure into the SSO schema. Then update the LOGIN_URL column in the WWSSO_LS_CONFIGURATION_INFO$ table, followed by UNUSED, as the following shows

```
UPDATE wwsso_ls_configuration_info$
SET    login_url = 'http://www.yourservername.com/pls/portal30_sso/'||
                   'portal30_sso.custom_login_page UNUSED';
COMMIT;
```

In this example, the custom login page will look like Figure 16-27.

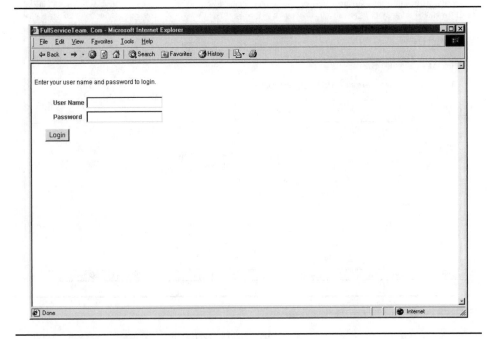

FIGURE 16-27.   *Custom login page*

When you enter erroneous login information, you now get the customized login page instead of the default login page. The procedure also displays the error passed to it, as shown in Figure 16-28.

Additional Oracle Portal Help and Information

Nearly unlimited sources can provide you with additional information about Portal. This section outlines a few such sources.

Discussion Groups

The Oracle Portal discussion groups haven't been around for a long time (then again, neither has Portal), but they're an invaluable resource when it comes to Oracle Portal questions and answers. Users from around the world come into these discussion groups to post questions and answers regarding the Oracle Portal product. The discussion groups are divided into different components of Portal. Figure 16-29 shows several groups available to you.

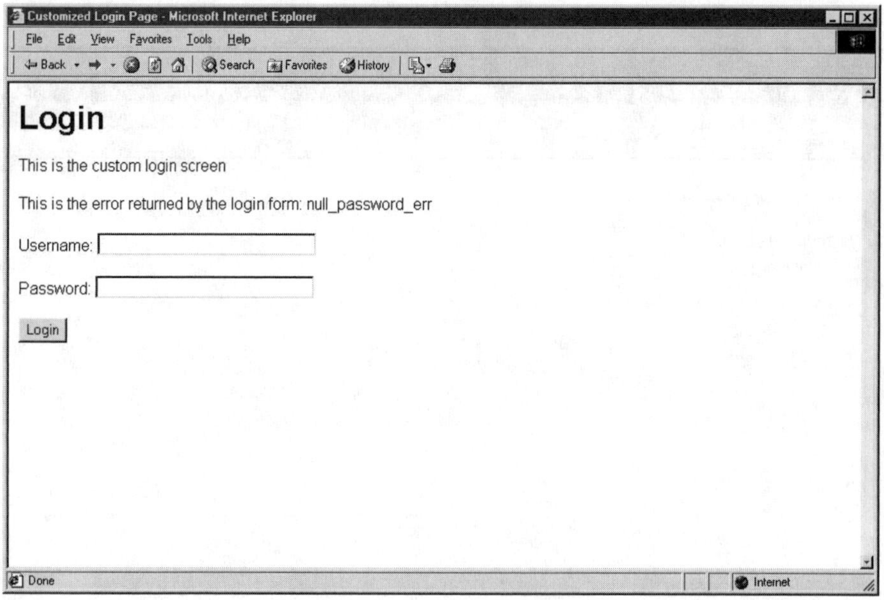

FIGURE 16-28. *Login error page*

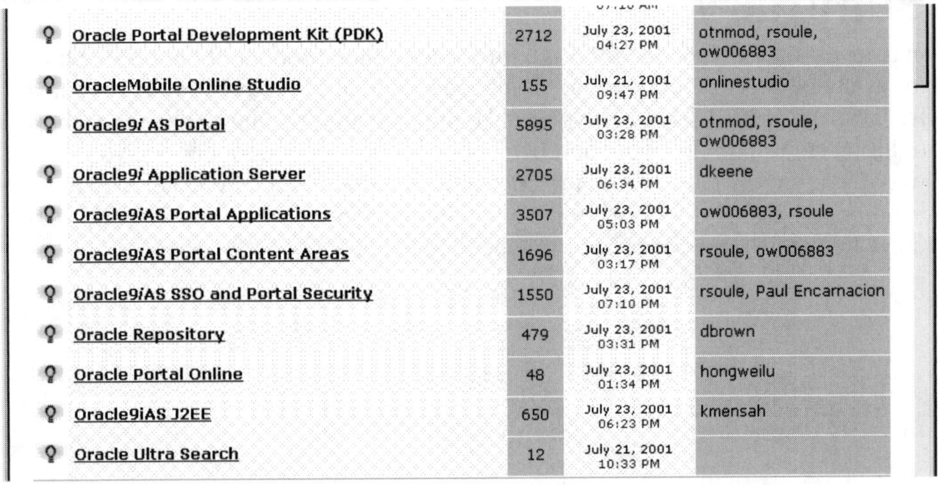

		07:10 AM	
🔍 **Oracle Portal Development Kit (PDK)**	2712	July 23, 2001 04:27 PM	otnmod, rsoule, ow006883
🔍 **OracleMobile Online Studio**	155	July 21, 2001 09:47 PM	onlinestudio
🔍 **Oracle9i AS Portal**	5895	July 23, 2001 03:28 PM	otnmod, rsoule, ow006883
🔍 **Oracle9i Application Server**	2705	July 23, 2001 06:34 PM	dkeene
🔍 **Oracle9iAS Portal Applications**	3507	July 23, 2001 05:03 PM	ow006883, rsoule
🔍 **Oracle9iAS Portal Content Areas**	1696	July 23, 2001 03:17 PM	rsoule, ow006883
🔍 **Oracle9iAS SSO and Portal Security**	1550	July 23, 2001 07:10 PM	rsoule, Paul Encarnacion
🔍 **Oracle Repository**	479	July 23, 2001 03:31 PM	dbrown
🔍 **Oracle Portal Online**	48	July 23, 2001 01:34 PM	hongweilu
🔍 **Oracle9iAS J2EE**	650	July 23, 2001 06:23 PM	kmensah
🔍 **Oracle Ultra Search**	12	July 21, 2001 10:33 PM	

FIGURE 16-29. *Portal discussion groups*

Portal Studio

Portal Studio (found at **http://portalstudio.oracle.com/**) is the home of the Portal Development Kit (PDK). On this site, you can find all things PDK. From sample portlets to the MS Exchange 2000 portlets, you can find them all here. You can also find a wealth of PDK documentation and API reference.

Oracle TechNet

Oracle TechNet (**http://technet.oracle.com/**) has always been a great source for information, downloads, and documentation. This holds true with Oracle Portal. On TechNet, you can find documentation, samples, and downloads.

Oracle Metalink

Oracle Metalink (**http://www.oracle.com/support/metalink/**) is also a great source of information on Oracle Portal, even though I've had more luck getting my questions answered in the discussion groups than through Metalink.

Apache.org

Apache.org (**http://www.apache.org/**) is the Web site for the Apache HTTP server project. On this site, you can find a good deal of information concerning the Apache HTTP server (also see other chapters in this book to understand the many aspects of Apache).

Summary

In a general sense, Oracle Portal is a truly outstanding product. If there's one thing to say about Oracle Portal on the "challenges" side, it's that the product does take learning and getting used to. If you're like me, you aren't going to like the feeling of losing control of the layout and behavior of your Web pages. I assure you, you won't. You simply have to find the control within Portal. Once you get over that learning curve, Portal is going to make a difference in your organization and your users are going to thank you for using it.

CHAPTER 17

Oracle Developer—
Forms and Reports

orms and Reports are a natural combination because Forms are often used to run Reports. This chapter is divided into two distinct sections: first you learn about Forms, and then you learn about Reports.

Almost everyone who has developed an application for Oracle has used Oracle Forms. In the client/server environment, Oracle Forms is the core Development toolset. *Oracle Forms Builder* is a tool used for developing interactive GUI screens with robust data validation capabilities. With Oracle Forms, you can quickly develop an application that automatically manages the inserting, updating, and deleting of the underlying data through SQL. Forms applications can be as simple as a few data entry screens or as complex as applications with hundreds of screens that communicate with other software systems and support thousands of transactions each hour. Applications might perform only basic inserts, updates, and deletes of data in a few tables or they might handle complex business procedural logic.

Oracle Forms Builder has been a primary application development tool in the client/server world. One of the most powerful features Oracle Developer contains is its capability to be ported to many different platforms, specifically UNIX, Windows, and Linux. With the latest releases of Oracle Forms, the list of platforms also includes the Web browser. Making business applications available to users through a Web browser with the same complex logic and user interface that your users have come to expect is one of the major benefits of running Forms on the Web. Web applications aren't limited to simple data entry forms with little data validation or business processing; Forms brings the same applications you've been using in your client/ server world to the Web with few changes.

The process of deploying Oracle Forms on the Web is a little more complex than deploying in a client/server environment, but the results of this type of implementation are tremendous. Just think, you can take a form or report and deploy it to your corporate client/server users, and then take the same form and make it available to employees over the corporate intranet, an extranet, or even the Internet—code modifications aren't even necessary!

Oracle Forms

This section of the chapter discusses the following topics:

- Deciding to Use Oracle Forms on the Web
- How Forms Server Works
- Installing and Configuring Oracle Forms Services
- The Forms Listener Servlet

- Configuring Forms CGI

- Configuring Oracle Forms as a Static Implementation

- Using a Non-Oracle Web Server

- Generating and Placing FMX Files

- Making Sure Your Icons Appear on the Web

- Closing the Browser Window When Exiting Forms

- Running Forms in a Separate Browser Window

- Setting Up Forms Server as a Windows NT Service

- Setting Up Multiple Services on Windows NT

- Starting and Stopping the Forms Server Listener

- Configuring the Forms Client

- Load Balancing

- Automatically Disconnecting Inactive Users

- Designing Web Applications

- Look and Feel

- Feature Restrictions for Forms on the Web

- Using Java in Forms

- Resolving Signature Issues

- Future Directions and Obsolete Functionality in Forms Release 9*i*.

Deciding to Use Oracle Forms on the Web

Oracle technologies are continually changing, and the move toward robust Web applications is supported by Oracle and its development toolsets. If you're already using Oracle Forms in a client/server environment, you might be considering deploying these forms on the Web.

Users are familiar with your Forms interface, and Oracle Forms deployed on the Web are virtually indistinguishable in behavior from Forms deployed via the Oracle Forms Server Runtime Engine. Simply moving the Forms to the Web environment and running them using a Java applet is a quick, intuitive way to move into the new technology, but your client/server-designed application might need some work before it can work seamlessly in a browser. Deploying *on* the Web is quite different than developing *for* the Web.

Should you use Oracle Forms to deploy your applications on the Web? Using the native development tools for Oracle has some distinct advantages: Oracle Forms Builder has a robust and easy-to-use graphical user interface (GUI), powerful data validation capabilities, and automated data manipulation language (DML) management is built in. Interaction with the database is built in to the toolset, errors are propagated cleanly, and support for PL/SQL and Java is available. Oracle Forms Builder6i is a mature and stable development environment that is tightly integrated with the new technologies released in the Oracle RDBMS. New features in Oracle8i and 9i are fully supported in the new development environment.

What are the alternatives to deploying Oracle Forms on the Web? One alternative is to use HTML Forms and a scripting language (such as JavaScript) for the client-side validation and a CGI (with iAS or other Web servers) or an Apache module to manipulate the data accordingly. To create forms functionality without using Oracle Forms, your HTML forms need to be dynamically created with a CGI or module (for example, Java, PL/SQL, or Perl). Front-end HTML-based interfaces can be designed by any number of third-party tools, including Dreamweaver, FrontPage, or ColdFusion Studio.

Another alternative is to develop the front end and procedural code with Oracle Portal (formerly WebDB). These options are detailed in Chapter 16. Finally, you can develop a Java applet that provides the same capabilities using a tool like JDeveloper, which is covered in Chapter 13. None of these methods, however, is nearly as easy as developing a form with Oracle Forms Builder.

How Forms Server Works

As you can see in Figure 17-1, Forms Server uses a three-tier architecture to deploy your applications.

- The client tier contains the Web browser, where the application is displayed and used.

- The middle tier is the application server, where application logic and server software are stored.

- The database tier is the database server, where enterprise data is stored.

Developers can build new applications with Oracle Forms Developer and deploy them to the Web with the Forms Server. Developers can also take existing applications that were previously deployed in client/server and move them to a three-tier architecture without changing the application code.

A common misconception is that you create the form in the Oracle Forms Builder module, and then run it through a converter to generate a Java applet that runs in the browser. While this seems like a logical solution—and one that might involve a smaller footprint, as well as provide many other advantages—this isn't how it works.

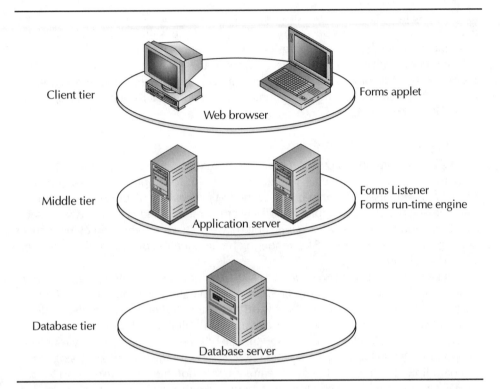

FIGURE 17-1. *Forms Server tiers*

While the same form can be used in client/server and on the Web (only one source file is required), the Web deployment of Oracle Forms is a bit more complicated than a simple conversion.

To oversimplify Forms for the Web, you could say the Forms run-time program was split into two components: a presentation layer component, which is the applet that runs in the browser, and the business logic component, which runs on the application server. This component reads the FMX (compiled version of the Form) of your Oracle Forms in their native form.

To be more specific, what happens is the client requests a URL to begin a Forms session on the Web. A Java applet is then downloaded to the browser. The generic applet is capable of painting the form canvas, performing data validation, and communicating with the Forms Server. A single applet runs all forms and must be downloaded only once for each browser. The Forms Server Runtime Engine reads and executes a standard FMX file. The Forms Server Runtime Engine performs the same functions as the Client/Server Runtime Engine—it maintains a connection to the database for the session, and runs the same Forms, Menus, and Library executables that are deployed in Client/Server mode. The difference is the Forms Server performs this function from the middle tier instead of the client machine.

The "communication" part of this scenario is the addition of the *Forms Server Listener,* which negotiates the connection between the browser request and the Forms Server Runtime Engine. Communication is addressed through sockets, HTTP, or HTTPS (Secure) protocols.

JInitiator

To display the form in a browser, Forms Server requires a Java environment to paint the screens and handle user interaction. This is accomplished by using a Java Virtual Machine (JVM) that can interpret the FMX served up by the Forms Server Runtime Engine. The Java applet handles user interaction and visual feedback, such as information generated when navigating between items or when checking a check box. The applet is responsible for rendering the application display and contains no specific application logic.

JInitiator is a specific version of the JVM that can be run by Netscape and Internet Explorer (IE) browsers. In addition, IE 5.*x* also runs a native JVM that supports Oracle Forms 6*i,* Patch 2. The IE Native JVM is restricted to intranet deployments. In other words, it won't function properly through a firewall. JInitiator doesn't replace or overwrite the default JVM in the browser. Instead, it's merely an alternate environment. Support for Oracle Forms using a native JVM can be somewhat quirky. Using the standard JInitiator provides the most seamless transition from client/server to Web.

When a user first accesses a form that requires the JInitiator applet, it's downloaded and installed as a plug-in to the browser. The same Java applet code can be used for any form, regardless of size or complexity. You needn't write custom Java code for each individual form you want to deploy on the Web.

A key element of the Java client is the use of JAR file caching. A *JAR file* is a standard Java archive that contains a series of Java class files used by the Java application. This function is used by JInitiator to improve performance on the client side. Oracle Forms Services use Oracle JInitiator to perform persistent client-side caching of the applet after the initial download. Any subsequent access to the application pulls the JAR file directly from the persistent client-side cache, significantly minimizing startup time.

State and Memory

One of the issues that every Web application deployment faces is the concept of "state." The standard transaction on the Web (that is, serving up a URL) is "stateless," which means every request is a discrete transaction and the server doesn't know or retain any information about previous requests. In a database application, maintaining a consistent connection to process complex transactions or multiple actions within a single session is often critical. Just like it does in a client/server session, Oracle

Forms maintains state (an active connection throughout the life of the session) over the Web. If your application is written using another module, such as the PL/SQL module, a connection to the database is only open on each request from the time the requested procedure starts until it ends. In these cases, you must maintain state on your own and you often need to pass extra information to the server with each request, so you can keep transactions related to each other. This can result in a significant difference in the concurrent user count between using Oracle Forms and the PL/SQL module, and an increase in traffic.

A Forms-based application connects users to the database from the beginning of the session to the end, nonstop. This results in significant concurrent user-count differences that, in turn, result in higher RDBMS licensing differences. Some of the options can make your vendors, such as Sun, Compaq, and Oracle happy: selecting Oracle Forms over PL/SQL results in considerably heavier server memory requirements (your hardware vendor likes this) and higher concurrent user licensing requirements (Oracle likes this). You can respond with something like "We already have an unlimited user license and memory's cheap."

The memory requirements for deploying Forms on the Web (vs. HTML forms using Java or PL/SQL) are obviously higher because the concurrent user count is higher. The footprint of the Forms cartridge is about 3–12MB per user. This can make a substantial difference in a large system. Each version of Developer is, however, improving the memory requirements per user. As toolkits are more tightly integrated and optimized for the Web, each version shares memory more effectively. Because the processing of the form occurs within the Forms Server, the key to scalability and performance in Web forms is memory on the Forms Server machine.

Another consideration is the requirements for the client machines. Even though the JInitiator is a "thin" Java applet, my experience is the minimum requirement for the client PC is 200 MHz with 64MB RAM. Oracle has been vague on the subject and the last recommendation is 166 MHz. Startup times and screen refreshes were reduced noticeably, however, when moving from 166 to 200 MHz. The more client memory and CPU, the better.

Performance is also a concern when deploying to the Web. Because of the scalability requirements of a typical application, my general rule for PL/SQL module applications is this: absolutely no procedure should take longer than one second to run or you (as the developer) need to talk to the resident tuning expert. In general, the average procedure time should be subsecond. For more information on PL/SQL performance, see Chapter 14.

What About Existing Forms?
Designing and developing new applications for the Web offers a huge array of options (and acronyms!): Oracle Forms, HTML forms, ASP, JSP, XML, Portal, ColdFusion, and so forth. But what if you have hundreds of existing Oracle Forms that have been developed and you want to deploy your application on the Web? What about large,

complex applications with code in Forms and libraries? You certainly wouldn't want to rewrite all this code. Existing applications that have been migrated to Forms 6.0 or 6*i* can be run on the Web simply by configuring the Forms Server and moving the executable files to the appropriate directories. You needn't make any code changes to allow the forms to work on the Web. Of course, some functionality that works well in Client/Server mode isn't well suited to the Web, but even the most complicated application can be ported with few problems. (See the "Designing Web Applications" section for detailed information.)

How easy is it? Oracle was able to Web-enable its entire suite of products, including Oracle Financials, literally overnight! If your application is large and complex, be sure to take into account the cost of rewriting large portions of your code when deciding which toolset to use on the Web. Deploying your application on the Web using Oracle Forms might be more feasible than rebuilding it in a new tool.

Issues to Consider

The following questions are instrumental in your decision-making process:

- Do you have control of the browser?

- Can you instruct the users that they must run on a specific browser version?

- Can your users download an 8–10MB program (that is, JInitiator) and install it locally?

- Do you have *enough* bandwidth?

- Do you have heavy/intensive user interface requirements?

- Is it okay if some things, such as a status line, don't work?

- Is the concurrent user count a concern?

- Do you have enough memory to support the concurrent user requirements of Forms?

- Is total memory use a concern?

If your answer to any of these questions is "No," Oracle Forms may not be a candidate for your Web solution. The other issue you need to consider is how many existing forms you have. Assuming you don't have hundreds of forms to convert, you should explore the numerous Web development (for the browser) options currently available.

If you have a large client/server application you want to move to the Web, however, or you're deploying in a controlled intranet environment, deploying Oracle Forms on the Web is the fastest and most efficient way to Web-enable your application. Also consider that Oracle is focused strongly on the Internet environment; their direction for the Forms tools is moving into a Web architecture deployment model. Designing and developing GUI applications must take into consideration both the limitations and flexibility of the Web environment.

Installing and Configuring Oracle Forms Services

Installing and configuring the Forms Server is simple. Oracle Installer now cleanly handles much of the detailed and complex configuration that was required in earlier versions. A number of default installation options are provided that set up Forms Server for a single machine or multiple machines utilizing load balancing. All of the options can be manually configured after installation, as well.

Oracle Forms Services included in 9*i*AS provide the following features:

- application infrastructure and the event model for scalability and performance over a network

- support for integrating technologies such as PL/SQL, Java Stored Procedures in the Oracle8*i* database, Enterprise JavaBeans, XML, and CORBA

- extensible user interface through native Java with Pluggable Java Components

- services for building and optimizing Oracle8*i* transactional database applications

With the release of 9*i*AS, Forms Server 6*i* has been renamed Forms Services 6*i*. Oracle 9*i*AS also has moved to a "servlet" model, replacing the Forms Server Listener with the Listener servlet, and providing a Forms Servlet. The Forms Listener Servlet is a Java servlet running in a servlet engine. The Web server routes the client requests directly to the servlet instance, which eliminates protocol restrictions required when working through a firewall. The Listener servlet is strongly recommended (by Oracle and TUSC) for deploying Forms on the Web.

Forms Services are installed automatically with the Enterprise Edition of the 9*i*AS installation—in fact, the EE version of the database is required too. Forms Services can be installed as a static implementation, cartridge (named dynamic with OAS) implementation, or using the Forms CGI. Forms CGI is available starting with 6i and is recommended because it is more scalable than the static implementation. Forms CGI provides the same functionality as the cartridge implementation, but is faster. Oracle strongly recommends the Forms CGI implementation for all Web deployment.

TIP
*On the Windows platforms, a shortcut to
run a standard test form was created for you
in the Forms Server program group. The shortcut's
name is "Run Form on the Web." The target for
the shortcut is C:\ORANT\tools\web60\html\
runform.htm. After the 9iAS installation, you can
test this immediately to confirm the automated
configuration worked.*

The Forms Server also supports a number of different modes: sockets, HTTP, and
HTTPS. For intranet installations (inside the firewall), the default socket connection will
work fine. If you require the Secure Sockets Layer (SSL), use the mode HTTPS. If you
run Forms Server through a firewall, the HTTP mode works. Oracle has tested Forms
Server6i with a number of common firewalls and proxy servers. The following firewall
implementations are supported in both HTTP and HTTPS mode: Raptor 6.0 and
Gauntlet 5.0. Neither Netscape Proxy Server 3.5 nor Microsoft Proxy Server 2.0
supports Forms Server in HTTP mode, although both support HTTPS mode.

TIP
*If a proxy server is required, the forms heartBeat
parameter must be set to < 1 minute to retain the
connection between the Java applet and the
proxy server.*

Creating the Virtual Directories on the Web Server
Whether you choose to run your forms using the Forms CGI or static method, virtual
directories must be created on your Web server to be used by Forms Services (see
Chapter 3 for the configuration of your Web server). These virtual directories are
maintained at a Listener level. Because the Java applet code is in the same physical
directory as the Java archive code (JAR files), you can elect to create only one virtual
directory for the Java code. If you separate the applet files from the JAR files, however,
two virtual directories need to be created.

In addition to a virtual directory for the applet and JAR files, a virtual directory,
containing the HTML file your browser will reference, needs to be created. This can
be an existing HTML virtual directory, but it's preferable to keep the Forms Services
HTML files separate from your other HTML files to maintain a clean system. As noted
in the following tip, another directory contains your Forms icon images. The virtual
directories that need to be created are as follows:

Virtual Directory Path	Physical Directory	Example
/java_code/	$ORACLE_HOME/ forms60/java/	c:\orant\forms60\java\
/forms_html/	An application directory for your Forms HTML files	c:\apps\forms\html\

Virtual directories must be added to the Apache server by editing the Apache configuration file for Forms, which is found in the $FORMS_HOME\conf directory in the 6*i*Server.conf file by adding the following Alias directives:

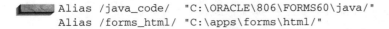

```
Alias /java_code/  "C:\ORACLE\806\FORMS60\java/"
Alias /forms_html/ "C:\apps\forms\html/"
```

Forms Listener Servlet

The Forms Listener servlet is a Java servlet introduced in the Forms 6*i* Patch 4 that improves the functionality of the Forms Listener. The pre-Patch 4 Listener is still available, but the Listener servlet should be used when deploying applications using HTTP and HTTPS modes.

The listener controls the creation of the Forms Server run-time process for each user, and handles communication between the client and the run-time process. The servlet supports more firewalls and proxy services, and isn't limited to a single HTTP protocol (HTTP 1.1). The servlet supports both HTTP 1.0 and HTTP 1.1. However, the listener servlet neither supports forms-specific load balancing nor is managed through the Enterprise Manager console window, like the Forms Listener.

TIP
JInitiator version 1.1.8.6 or greater is required. Trying to run Web forms using the previous version while implementing the Listener servlet will result in errors.

The Forms Listener servlet is supported in the 9*i*AS Enterprise Edition and requires the Apache Web server. It also requires Patch 4, which instantiates the Developer Oracle Home.

If you're running Patch 4 and the Enterprise Edition of 9*i*AS, the servlet can be configured as follows.

- The jserv.properties file ($9*i*AS_ORACLE_HOME/apache/jserv/conf/) must be edited to include the following variables at the end of the file:

```
wrapper.classpath=C:\oracle\806\forms60\java\f60srv.jar
wrapper.path=C:\oracle\806\bin;C:\oracle\iSuites\bin;
```

```
        C:\winnt;C:\winnt\system32
wrapper.env=ORACLE_HOME=C:\Oracle\806
wrapper.env=FORMS60_PATH=C:\Oracle\806
\forms60
```

Don't change the jserv.properties file that exists in the Oracle Developer Home. Change only the 9iAS file (in the previously mentioned directory).

■ If you're implementing Forms CGI, add the following entry to the formsweb.cfg file (which can be found in the $FORMS_HOME\forms60\ server directory):

```
ServerURL=http://machine_name/servlet/oracle.forms.servlet.ListenerServlet
```

Once the serverURL property is set, the values of serverPort and connectMode are ignored. Servlets use their own port numbers (starting with 903) and connectMode uses HTTP 1.1 automatically.

■ If you're using a static implementation, add the following entry to the static HTML file:

```
param name ="serverURL" value= "servlet/oracle.forms.servlet.ListenerServlet">
```

■ Finally, stop and restart the iAS HTTP server. Wait a minute for everything to start up, and then test the configured servlets by accessing the following URL:

```
http://machine_name/servlet/oracle.forms.servlet.ListenerServlet
```

Configuring Forms CGI

The Forms CGI provides the same features as the OAS cartridge implementation (although performance is better) and can be used with any Web listener that supports CGI. Using the CGI method creates the HTML page required to run a form at run time. It does this by merging a static HTML file containing standard and default parameters (basejini.html) with the parameters in a configuration file (formsweb.cfg) to determine how to run the specified form.

The Oracle Installer sets up the Forms Server with a complete set of initial configuration files. Whether you install this using the Deployment option or as a custom installation, you can customize your configuration after you install it. Forms CGI requires the following files: base.htm, basejini.htm, and formsweb.cfg. The base HTML file is read by the Forms CGI program when a user accesses the applications (by requesting the application's URL). Any variables (%variablename%) in the base HTML file are replaced with the appropriate parameter values specified in the formsweb.cfg file and form query parameters in the URL request (if any exist).

The base.htm and basejini.html files shouldn't be changed, but the Forms configuration file can be modified to provide the behavior you require. Base.htm contains the tags necessary to run a file on a browser using the AppletViewer or in a browser that can run its own certified JVM (IE 5.x, for example). Basejini.htm contains the configuration to run the Forms applet using JInitiator.

The formsweb.cfg file contains the information that determines the look and feel of the application, Java behavior, HTML page specifications, and other information about the application. The default formsweb.cfg file contains a number of parameters—open the file and check it out.

The default values can be overridden by defining a named configuration (set of parameters) by adding sections to the formsweb.cfg. For example, a configuration named emp_app would be declared as follows:

```
[emp_app]
lookandfeel=Oracle
colorScheme=Purple
pageTitle=Employee App
```

The config parameter is passed to the URL to incorporate the explicit configuration, as follows:

```
http://www.acme.com/dev60cgi/ifcgi60.exe?config=emp_app
```

NOTE
*You must add a new environment variable—
FORMS60_WEB_CONFIG_FILE—to the NT registry
in the Oracle Forms Server 6i home if you move or
rename the formsweb.cfg file (that is, FORMS60_
WEB_CONFIG_FILE = c:\temp\myfile.cfg).*

The basejini.html file contains variables defined in the formsweb.cfg file. The preference is to make changes in the formsweb.cfg where possible and to leave the basejinit.html file untouched because it will be overwritten if you reinstall the Forms Server. If you want to make changes to this file, you should make a copy of it and save it with another name.

Forms CGI Parameters in formsweb.cfg

The following parameters contained in the formsweb.cfg file allow you to configure the path to a number of files, the JVM to use, delimiters, and load balancing parameters:

Parameter	Required or Optional	Description
baseHTML	required	Physical path to HTML file that contains applet tags
baseHTMLJInitiator	required	Physical path to HTML file that contains JInitiator tags
ie50	optional	Jinitiator or Native
HTML delimiter	required	Delimiter for variable names Defaults to %
MetricsServerHost, MetricsServerPort, MetricsServerErrorURL, MetricsTimeout, leastloadedhost	optional	These parameters are for load balancing—see the documentation for more information

All the following parameters can be specified in the base HTML file as *%parametername%*. For example: <PARAM NAME="connectMode" VALUE=" %connectMode%">.

All variables in the base HTML file are replaced with the appropriate parameter values specified in the formsweb.cfg file.

Parameter	Required or Optional	Description
codebase	required	Virtual directory for <ORACLE_HOME>\ forms60\java
code	required	oracle.forms.engine.Main
connectMode	depends	Required for HTTP and HTTPS connections; optional for socket connection
archive	optional	Comma-separated list of archive files to preload
width	required	Width of form in pixels
height	required	Height of form in pixels
align	optional	left	center	right	top	middle	bottom

Parameter	Required or Optional	Description
alt	optional	Text displayed instead of applet (if browser doesn't support applets)
hspace	optional	Horizontal gutter, in pixels
vspace	optional	Vertical gutter, in pixels
type	required	"application/x-jinit-applet" for JInitiator; no value required for AppletViewer
name	optional	Applet instance name
title	optional	Advisory title string
border	optional	Border to display
standby	optional	Text to display when loading
codetype	optional	Defaults to type

Parameters specific to the Forms applet (in PARAM tags):

Parameter	Required or Optional	Description
serverHost	optional	Host on which the Forms Server, ifsrv60.exe runs (defaults to Web listener machine)
serverPort	required	Port on which the Forms Server, ifsrv60.exe listens. In most cases, the port number will remain 9000 (the default)
serverArgs	required	Command line argument for run time
splashScreen	optional	GIF file that should appear before the applet appears NO for no splash Empty to use the default splash
background	optional	GIF file that should appear in the background NO for no background Empty to use the default background
clientDPI	optional	Specifies the dots per inch (DPI) for the display
separateFrame	optional	TRUE or FALSE
lookAndFeel	optional	Oracle or Generic

Parameter	Required or Optional	Description
colorScheme	optional	Teal, Titanium, Red, Khaki, Blue, Olive, or Purple
serverApp	optional	Your application class (if any)
heartBeat	optional	Client polling period
imageBase	optional	Location of icon file: n **codeBase**, which indicates the icon search path is relative to the directory that contains the Java classes. Use this value if you store your icons in a JAR file (recommended) n **documentBase**, which is the default. In deployments that make use of the Forms Server CGI, you must specify the icon path in a custom application file
registryPath	optional	Virtual directory where the application file named in the serverApp parameter is located
webformsTitle	optional	Title of Forms window

Runform parameters (serverArgs parameters):

Parameter	Required or Optional	Description
MODULE	required	Form module name (optionally includes path)
USERID	optional	Login string, such as scott/tiger@ORA8

Configuring Oracle Forms as "Static"

The setup option of creating a "static" deployment is still supported, but you need to configure the virtual directory mappings and create a static HTML file to point to each form that can be accessed through a URL. The initial form in your application is typically the main menu that branches to all the other forms.

The easiest way to create the static HTML file for each application deployed on the Web is to modify the static HTML file template provided by Oracle. This static.html file is located in the $ORACLE_HOME/806/tools/web60/html/ directory. Make a copy of this file, placing the copy in the /forms_html/ directory. Rename this file to a name relating to your application's name. For example, if your application is a call-processing application, you might name the HTML file callproc.html.

Based on the virtual directories previously described and assuming the run time form file (FMX) is in the physical directory of c:\apps\forms\fmx\, the callproc.html is identical to the following (if you compare this file to the standard file Oracle provides, you'll see the primary differences have to do with the modification of the text and applet tags):

```
<HTML>
<!-- FILE: static.html -->
<!-- Oracle Static (Non-Cartridge) HTML File Template (Windows NT) -->
<!-- Rename and modify tags and parameter values as needed -->
<HEAD><TITLE>Oracle Developer for the Web</TITLE></HEAD>
<BODY><BR>Please wait while the Forms Client class files download and run.
     <BR>This will take a second or two...
<P>
<!-- applet definition (start) -->
<APPLET CODEBASE="/codebase_vdir/"
        CODE="oracle.forms.engine.Main"
        ARCHIVE="/jars_vdir/f60all.jar"
        HEIGHT=20
        WIDTH=20>
<PARAM NAME="serverPort"
       VALUE="9000">
<PARAM NAME="serverArgs"
       VALUE="module=fmx_name userid=user/password@sqlnetalias">
<PARAM NAME="serverApp"
       VALUE="default">
</APPLET>
<!-- applet definition (end) -->
</BODY>
</HTML>
```

Static URL

The URL you provide to your end users simply points to the page previously defined. For example, to announce the availability of your new call processing application, the company ACME would broadcast the following URL:

```
http://www.acme.com/forms_html/callproc.html
```

ACME's URL consists of the following components:

- Protocol: http

- Domain: www.acme.com

- HTML files virtual directory: /forms_html

- Static HTML file: callproc.html

Using a Non-Oracle Web Server

You may elect to use a non-Oracle Web server, in which case you have a few different choices when using Developer Server. The Web server you use must support CGI—every Web server I've ever seen supports CGI. Some common Web servers include Apache, Enterprise Server from Novell, and Microsoft IIS. The Web server deployed with 9iAS is a custom version of Apache, perhaps the most robust and reliable Web server being used on the Web. In addition, your application may run in an environment that includes a firewall or proxy server.

More information on Web servers can be found at Web Server Compare (**http://webservercompare.internet.com/**). Information about the Apache Web server can be found in the Apache FAQ at **http://www.apache.org/docs/misc/FAQ.html**.

Generating and Placing Your FMX Files

When creating a form, Forms Builder automatically creates a form definition file or Form Module Binary (FMB). The FMB file is the binary source code for the Form and it isn't usable by the run-time engine. To run a form through a browser or on your PC, you must first generate a form into a run-time executable or Form Module Executable (FMX) file. FMX files are platform-specific in both client/server and Web environments. Because FMX files are platform-specific, you *must* generate the FMX on the platform on which iAS is running. To generate the run-time executable, use File | Administration | Generate File or CTRL-T in Forms Builder or use the ifcmp60 utility to generate the FMX. For example, if your development work takes place in a Windows environment, but your Web deployment is on UNIX, you must use ifcmp60 on the UNIX machine to generate executables for that environment.

Place the FMX file into a directory that your Forms Server can access. The Forms Server itself will search the $ORACLE_HOME/bin directory first, and then the $FORMS60_PATH directory. If you don't want to specify the exact directory location of your run-time executable, place your form into one of the two previously named directories. You can also modify the $FORMS60_PATH environmental variable (on UNIX) or registry entry (on NT).

Forms Builder 6i on NT also enables you to run a form directly from Forms Builder using Run Form Web on the toolbar. Run Form Web displays the form as it appears in a browser window, without having to deploy the executables to a server during development. This is useful to developers who are working in a traditional client/server environment to create forms, but who still need to test the Web deployment of the form from the development environment.

Making Sure Your Icons Appear on the Web

Several steps are involved to make icon buttons work on the Web. First, when running a form over the Web, all icon files must be converted from ICO files (in MS Windows) or XPM files (on UNIX) to JPG or GIF files. Many image converter utilities can be found on the Web to accomplish this task.

If Forms applications are deployed on the Web, the icons won't be displayed unless you inform the Forms Server of the location—or if you modify the FORMS60_PATH. To view the icons, either put them into a directory that currently has virtual mapping or create a new virtually mapped directory. Also, create a temporary directory for the boilerplate images and use run_product.

To illustrate how this is done, let's add a new directory map, using the values in the following table:

Virtual Directory Path	Physical Directory	Example
/forms_icons/	Any application directory	c:\orant\forms60\oracle\forms\handler\icons\
/forms_temp/	Any temporary directory	c:\apps\temp\

Again, virtual directories must be added to the Apache Server by editing the Apache configuration file for Forms, which is found in the $FORMS_HOME\ conf directory in the 6iServer.conf file by adding the following Alias directives:

```
Alias /forms_icons/   "C:\ORACLE\806\FORMS60\oracle\forms\handler\icons/"
Alias /forms_temp/    "C:\apps\temp/"
```

Next, you need to edit the registry.dat file (Note: this isn't the Windows registry). On NT, the registry.dat file is located in the $ORACLE_HOME\forms60\ java\oracle\forms\registry directory. You cannot edit this file with Notepad (Notepad won't wrap the lines properly). You need to use another tool, like Textpad (or Write).

The following two entries must be modified in the Registry.dat file:

- *default.icons.iconpath=/forms_icons/,* where /forms_icons/ is a virtual directory for your Web server where all the icon image files will be stored. The path may be a fully qualified URL, relative directory, or virtual directory.

- *default.icons.iconextension=jpg,* where jpg or gif is the chosen file type.

"Default" simply references the default value in the static.html file. You can set this value to any valid application class referenced by your Web application.

Using this example, let's set the entries as follows:

```
default.icons.iconpath=/forms_icons/
default.icons.iconextention=jpg
```

where /forms_icons/ is the virtual directory created in the 6iServer.conf file and points to the location of the icon files.

Using Images in Forms

If you want to use image items on the Web in your forms, you need to set environment variables in your registry (NT) or UNIX environment. The following table describes the required entries:

Environment Variable	Example
FORMS60_OUTPUT	c:\webforms\ Must be a physical directory on the host machine
FORMS60_MAPPING	/form_map/

Closing the Browser Window When Exiting Forms

You can close the browser by using JavaScript in an HTML file and displaying it by using Web.Show_Document when you exit the main form. The contents of the close.html are as follows:

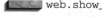

```
<html>
<body onload="closeit()">
<script> function closeit()
     { window.close(); }
</script>
</body>
</html>
```

In the POST-FORM trigger, call web.show_document to execute this HTML file, as follows:

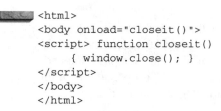

```
web.show_document('http://mywebserver.com/close.html','_self');
```

Running Forms in a Separate Window

Oracle Forms can be invoked in a separate browser window by passing the parameter separateFrame = TRUE (in the URL).

TIP

When using SeparateFrame=True, a black area is shown in the browser where the Forms applet normally resides. To prevent this, set the width and height to 1.

Setting Up Forms Server as a Windows NT Service

On Windows NT, the Forms Server is best run as an NT service, even though you can also run the Forms Server as a nonservice as the following notes. As with any other NT service, you can configure the Forms Server service to start manually or automatically when the system is brought up. The EE installation of *i*AS automatically installs the Forms Server as an NT service, but to set up the Forms Server manually as an NT service, execute the following code at the command line after installing Oracle Forms:

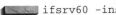
```
ifsrv60 -install fsrv60 port=9000
```

At this point, your Forms Server is registered as an NT service with the name fsrv60. You can set the service name to anything you want. You can now go into the Control Panel's Services page and look for the entry Forms Server60 for fsrv60. Click Startup. *This next step is critical.* From the Startup dialog box, select This Account on the Log On As section and type in your operating system user name and password. This specifies the Forms Server be run under a specific operating system account (this account can be the administrator, but you simply need a valid account that also has a default printer established—we need to establish a default printer because Oracle Reports are generated using the default printer's driver). You can also set the service to start automatically (when the system is booted up) or manually. If you want the Forms Server to start after each system boot, set this value to Automatic.

Setting Up Multiple Services on Windows NT

In most projects, setting up an environment for different applications or phases of development, such as a Development environment and a Test environment, is preferable. In some cases, these environments must be supported on the same machine. To access multiple sets of forms modules on the same machine, you have to start up multiple Forms Server Listener processes, each with its own path variables and default behavior. The default behavior is to use the environment variables present in the HKEY_LOCAL_MACHINE\Software\ORACLE registry keys, but these can be overridden for an application user.

You must set up the Forms Server as a service on NT. You must create a Windows NT user for each application environment you support. It's critical that the new user (for example, TEST_APP) belong to the Administrators group to read the parameters from the registry.

TIP
Always back up your registry before making any changes manually!

Log on as the new user and add the appropriate registry keys to the HKEY_
CURRENT_USER registry entries. These settings will override the variables set in
the HKEY_LOCAL_MACHINE\Software\ORACLE keys. Create the HOME*x* key under
HKEY_CURRENT_USER\Software\ORACLE, where *x* is the value of the HOME key
used by your Forms Server installation. You might have multiple homes in the registry,
so be sure to select the key for the Forms Server.

You also might need to create the ORACLE key. In the HOME*x*, you can create
variables for FORMS60_PATH and any other environment variables you want to set
for your application. For example, you can set icon paths or NLS variables.

Finally, create the Forms Server service in NT by installing the server for a specific
port (the ports must be different for the different application environments) and edit
the created service (see the previous) to use the appropriate user under Log On As:
in the Startup parameters for the Forms Service. This way, the service will be started
as the application user you created (TEST_APP) and will reference the registry keys
for the current user.

To access the different environments, edit the HTML file that starts your application
to refer to the specific PortNumber you created.

Starting and Stopping the Forms Server Listener

With the introduction of the Forms Listener servlet, starting and stopping the Listener
is no longer necessary. With earlier installations, however, the Forms Listener service
could be stopped and started at will. The Forms Server Listener can be run as a simple
process or it can be run as a Service under NT. Oracle recommends the Listener be
run as an NT service.

The Forms Server runs on an individual port. The communication from the browser
to the Web server is made through the standard HTTP port (usually port 80). The
Web server communicates with the Forms Server through the Forms Server's port
(port 9000). The Forms Server is in the $ORACLE_HOME/bin directory and is named
ifsrv60 on NT, and ifsrvm60 on UNIX. This process accepts a parameter of *port*, which
specifies the port on which the Forms Server is listening.

To start this process on NT, select Start | Programs | Oracle Developer R6.0 from
the NT taskbar, and then run the Forms Server Listener. Under UNIX, ensure the process
is executed as a background process. Assuming $ORACLE_HOME/bin is in your path,
the command from a shell prompt would be ifsrv60 -listen &. You should consider
using nohup (no hangup) for the startup of the UNIX processes, so if you log off the
UNIX account you used to start the process, the Forms Server process doesn't die.

TIP
*The default port number is 9000. If you don't specify
the port parameter, the Forms Server Listener will
start on port 9000. You need to change this port
number only if it's conflicting with another process
using port 9000 on your system.*

To check the status of the Forms Server Listener under NT, go to the Process tab in the Task Manager and find the IFSRV60 processes. Each active connection will have a Forms Server running. Under UNIX, type **ps -ef | grep ifrunw60** at a shell prompt. This displays an ifrunw60 process for each active connection. One ifsrvm60 process will also be running.

To stop the process on NT, view the status of the process and click End Process. Under UNIX, `kill` each of the ifrun60w processes and the ifsrvm60 process as listed when you viewed the process status.

Controlling the Listener from the Command Line

The NT process can be started or stopped by issuing the command net start servicename and net stop servicename from the command line. In this case, *servicename* is the name of the service found in the registry key HKEY_LOCAL_ MACHINE\SYSTEM\CurrentControlSet\Service. It might not be exactly the same name as the name displayed in the control panel. These commands can be used in a batch file to perform automatic shutdown and restart of the Listener process.

Configuring the Forms Client

When an end user starts up a Web-enabled Forms Builder application, the Forms Client (and related Java class files) are downloaded from the application server to the user's browser. As the user continues interacting with the application, additional Java class files are downloaded on an as-needed basis. You can, however, control how class files are downloaded to the user's browser using one of two methods: *incremental* (the default), in which only those class files required to render the initial state of the application are downloaded at startup, and *bundled,* where one or more bundles of class files are downloaded to the client machine at application startup. The advantage of the bundled option is each bundle downloads in a single network roundtrip. The disadvantage is the initial download might take longer than under the incremental method.

A number of class files can be collected into a JAR file. To determine how to create your own JAR files or bundles, read the Oracle documentation on Javasoft's Web site at **http://www.javasoft.com**. The latest versions of JInitiator have introduced the concept of caching the JAR files in an "extracted" state. The JAR file is first downloaded from the server, and then opened and uncompressed. Once the classes are uncompressed, they are validated and cached. Each subsequent request for that JAR file references the local cached and extracted version. This makes the caching mechanism more efficient in terms of network traffic, as well as local processing because less work has to be done to load the classes into memory.

TIP
A progress bar for downloading the JAR files is available in JInitiator 1.1.7.30 or greater. Display the progress bar by adding the parameter java_ showprogress="true" to your HTML file.

Load Balancing

The *load-balancing* feature enables you to balance the load of multiple Forms Servers dynamically across systems. Load balancing directs a Forms client to connect to a Forms Server running on the least-loaded system available. Which system is least loaded is determined by a count of the total number of processes running on that system.

TIP
Form-specific load balancing isn't supported under the architecture of Forms 6i Patch 4 and above. A hardware/OS-based load balancer must be used.

Automatically Disconnecting Inactive Users

Because Forms on the Web retain their connection to the database (state), many developers and system administrators want the capability to disconnect users if they haven't interacted with the database in a certain period of time. Disconnecting users can keep your concurrent user count under control and ensure users don't leave their browser sessions hanging.

The Forms Server has a simple mechanism called *heartBeat* to check if the Forms Java Client is still connected. If the Runtime Engine doesn't hear from the client within the specified timeout period, it shuts down and frees the resources it was using. By default, the Forms Server allows 15 minutes to pass without a signal from the client before it closes. However, you can set the timeout period and heartBeat parameter to force Forms Server to shut down sessions after a specified period of time.

If you're running Oracle Forms 6i (6.0.8.8 or higher), you can define a timeout period that forces a disconnection of the form and release the resources, as follows:

1. Create an NT registry entry called FORMS60_TIMEOUT with a value between 1 and 1,440. The value of FORMS60_TIMEOUT is the number of minutes before the session is terminated. The value will default to 15 minutes. *NOTE: This must be a DWORD value, not a string.*

2. Create a parameter in your HTML file called *heartBeat*. This parameter defines how often the client checks in to the server to determine if it's still alive. Set the value (in minutes) higher than the value set in FORMS60_TIMEOUT.

Setting the timeout period to a shorter period than the heartBeat parameter means when the Forms Server doesn't get a reply from the client every 15 minutes, the Web process is terminated. Terminating the Web process behind the form, however, doesn't give any indication to the user that the form is "dead." The form remains onscreen and any attempt to interact with it will result in errors. Users have to close and restart the form to continue using it.

Designing Web Applications

One of the benefits of deploying Oracle Forms on the Web is the same executable files (FMX) can be used for both client/server and Web deployments. Developers don't have to design and maintain multiple versions of each form, and migrating an existing client/server application to the Web doesn't generally require rewriting the forms. Just because the same file can be deployed on the Web, however, doesn't mean the design of the form or the performance of the form will be adequate in a Web environment. You need to consider a number of critical factors when moving forms to the Web or designing new applications for the Web environment.

Performance Considerations

Even though a form deployed on the Web has the same general look and feel of the client/server version of the form, Web applications are different than client/server applications. Designing Forms for a Web implementation means you have to be much more careful of your use of resources and bandwidth. Web applications imply a thin client. Not only should the requirements on the client be thin, but the bandwidth requirements should be even thinner. As Web access becomes faster outside the business arena (just look at the increase in broadband Internet connections!), users expect fast interfaces for all Web interactions. Your Oracle application is no exception.

When developing client/server applications, you should be concerned about frequent network roundtrips from the client to the server. For Web applications, the number of roundtrips from the application to the database servers is even more important. Your forms should be fast, transfer data in as few trips as possible, and interact with the database server cleanly. Because everything displayed on the screen is transferred over the network, it's important to limit the number of images (page and background) included in your forms and reports. Images increase bandwidth requirements and each time an image is required, it must be downloaded from the application server. This can burden the application server during heavy loads. To display a company logo, for example, include the image in the HTML page that downloads at application startup instead of retrieving it from the database. The image will then be cached locally in the browser, instead of fetched each time it must be displayed.

When developing Web applications, seriously consider network factors that could affect the performance of your Web applications. Consider how your application will interact with a security firewall or what will happen under heavy user loads. In addition, optimize your network connections where possible. For more information about SQL*Net, see the SQL*Net documentation.

Finally, as with any Oracle application, you should design your queries to execute as efficiently as possible and ensure PL/SQL program units are compiled. For further information regarding PL/SQL, refer to *Oracle PL/SQL Tips & Techniques,* by Joseph Trezzo (Osborne/McGraw-Hill, 1999). Bad SQL code can pull down the entire performance of your database server and, in turn, your entire Web application. For more information on performance tuning, refer to *Oracle Performance Tuning Tips and Techniques,* by Richard J. Niemiec et al. (Osborne/McGraw-Hill, 1999).

Reducing Network Traffic

With a three-tier environment, communication exists not just between the application server and the database, but also between the client on the desktop machine and the application server. Anytime a user performs an action on the form (pressing a button, navigating from one field to the next, and so forth), the Forms Server is contacted to determine if that action requires some code to be executed. In a Client/Server mode, this is handled locally on the PC. On the Web, however, this requires a message sent to the Forms Server for almost every action the user takes.

The reduction of network use, therefore, becomes an even more important area on which to focus. In general, try to avoid any form activities that require frequent screen redraws or frequent database fetches to perform. To cut down on the number of network roundtrips required for users to operate your Forms application, consider the following suggestions:

- **Mouse triggers**   Including When-Mouse-Click, When-Mouse-DoubleClick, When-Mouse-Down, and When-Mouse-Up triggers in your forms affects speed and performance. The Forms Client must communicate with the Forms Server (necessitating a network roundtrip) each time one of these triggers fires. The When-Mouse-Move trigger isn't supported because of the high number of network roundtrips required each time it fires.

- **Repeating timers**   If your form includes a repeating timer that fires every 1/100th of a second, end users face the performance ramifications of 6,000 network roundtrips every minute. Either reduce the number of timers in your forms or change the timing interval on which your timers fire. Generally, timers shouldn't expire less than once per minute. Slower connections (dialup, for example) may have problems with even minute-long timers. Whenever possible, try to design forms so actions are triggered by the user, not by a timer.

- **Images**   Images increase bandwidth requirements and each time an image is required, it must be downloaded from the application server. Be sure to keep image sizes (and the number of images) to a minimum.

■ **Remove boilerplate items**   Use Prompts instead of boilerplate items whenever possible. Prompts are retrieved with their objects, instead of being fetched separately. Remove any unnecessary boxes and lines on the canvas.

■ **Changes to the user interface**   Try to minimize dynamic changes to the user interface, such as changing prompts, using current record highlighting, and enabling and disabling objects on the form. Change the navigation to avoid having to tab through unused items and simplify the display of your forms as much as possible.

■ **Perform validation at the highest level possible**   Field-level validation might be user-friendly, but it can result in high-network traffic. If possible, validate items at a higher level (that is, record or form) to reduce traffic.

■ **Eliminate "catch-all" triggers**   Many applications use a when-new-item-instance or when-button-pressed trigger placed at the form or block level to control behavior of all items in the form. If the action is limited to a few items in the form, write a procedure and individual triggers placed on each item, so the Form Server doesn't need to process the code each time an item is touched. Don't force a trigger to fire unless it's actually required.

■ **Avoid multimedia objects**   Because multimedia objects consume considerable processing power and bandwith, use multimedia objects only when absolutely necessary.

■ **Hide objects that aren't initially required**   Many Forms applications have visible multiple stacked canvases or tab canvases, even if they're hidden behind the current canvas. Don't force Forms to fetch every item on every canvas. Instead, fetch the items only when the canvas is brought to the front or when the tab is activated. Use visible=NO to control what's loaded.

Key Mappings

Key mappings (function keys and <ctrl>/<alt> combinations) aren't the same between the Web and the client/server. Because a Web browser can run on nearly any platform, the key mappings are "generic." You can, however, customize the resource files that specify key mappings either to mimic your client/server environment or match an existing key mapping with which your users are familiar.

The key mapping used by the Web is located in the FMRWEB.RES file in the $ORACLE_HOME\form60 directory. A FMRPCWEB.RES file can also be edited to customize your key maps. It's in the same directory and contains instructions on how to remap the keys in the Web environment.

Code Partitioning

Because of the three-tiered architecture, you might have to reconsider how your application logic is partitioned. The application logic that was on the client PC under a client/server model is now running on the middle tier in the Web architecture model. Client-intensive operations that weren't a problem under the client/server model might become an issue when running the application on the middle tier. Additionally, it will become even more important under this model to partition database-intensive tasks to the database server tier.

Moving as much code as possible to the database removes some of the load from the Forms Server, which already handles the bulk of the application work. Referencing libraries and extensive code in a Forms module will definitely affect performance. As with all other interaction with the Forms Server, the fewer network trips to process code, the better.

Selecting Fonts

Most fonts aren't supported across all platforms. For example, sans serif is a commonly used font in Microsoft Windows applications, but it isn't available in UNIX. When a font isn't available on a platform, Forms attempts to use a similar font. In a client/ server environment, uifont.ali file manages the font translations. This file isn't used in the 6i deployment. Instead, a registry.dat file is referenced for the Java fonts.

An excerpt of the default registry.dat file, showing the font information and Java font mapping, follows:

```
#
# Defaults for the Font details, all names are Java Font names. Each of
# these parameters represents the default property to use when none is
# specified.
#
# defaultFontname represents the default Java fontName.
# defaultSize      represents the default fontSize. Note that the size is
#                  multiplied by 100 (e.g. a 10pt font has a size of 1000).
# defaultStyle     represents the default fontStyle, PLAIN or ITALIC.
# defaultWeight    represents the default fontWeight, PLAIN or BOLD.
#
default.fontMap.defaultFontname=Dialog
default.fontMap.defaultSize=900
default.fontMap.defaultStyle=PLAIN
default.fontMap.defaultWeight=PLAIN
#
# Default Font Face mapping.
#
# appFontname  represents a comma delimited list of Application Font Names.
# javaFontname represents a comma delimited list of Java Font Names.
#
# Note that this file uses the Java 1.1 Font names in order to be able to
# handle the NLS Plane (BUG #431051)
```

```
#
default.fontMap.appFontnames=Courier New,Courier,courier,System,
Terminal,Fixed,Fixedsys,Times,Times New Roman,MS Sans Serif,Arial
default.fontMap.javaFontnames=MonoSpaced,MonoSpaced,
MonoSpaced,Dialog,MonoSpaced,Dialog,Dialog,Serif,Serif,Dialog,SansSerif
```

At run time, the Forms Server maps the form's fonts to their Java equivalents. Java then renders the font in a font predefined for the deployment platform. To convert your form's fonts into Java equivalents, Java uses an alias list located in the registry.dat file. The following table lists the Java fonts and their generally accepted equivalents on the major deployment platforms:

Java Font	Windows Font	X Windows Font	Macintosh Font
MonoSpaced	Courier New	adobe-courier	Courier
Dialog	MS Sans Serif	b&h-lucida	Geneva
Dialog	MS Sans Serif	b&h-lucidatypewriter	Geneva
SansSerif	Arial	adobe-helvetica	Helvetica
Symbol	WingDings	itc-zapfdingbats	Symbol
Serif	Times New Roman	adobe-times	Times Roman

If a font from your form doesn't map to a Java font (through the Forms Builder font alias table), Java automatically assigns a Java font to the unmapped application font. To change the Java font alias scheme, edit registry.dat. The best bet is to follow the font guidelines, discussed in the online documentation, when you're designing forms to deploy on the Web.

TIP
Oracle recommends you use MS Sans Serif 9pt as your "base" font in all Forms applications. This font maps cleanly to the Java Dialog font and will result in the fewest problems displaying your application.

Look and Feel

The Java applet presents a number of different displays for your forms. If you use the "Oracle" look and feel, the application on the Web will look much like the form does in a client/server environment. If you use the "Generic" look and feel, the application will be closer to a Windows application. Look and Feel controls the way buttons, text entry fields, labels, and alerts are displayed. The parameters are set in the formsweb.cfg file or in the HTML file. The following table shows the parameters that can affect the way the form is displayed on the Web:

Variable Name	Notes	Valid Values
lookAndFeel	Controls how the Java applet displays the form.	ORACLE or GENERIC
colorScheme	Applicable to ORACLE lookAndFeel only. Controls the color scheme for the application (header bars, buttons, title and menus, and so forth).	Teal, Titanium, Red, Khaki, Blue, Olive, or Purple
darkLook	Applicable to ORACLE lookAndFeel only. Makes the background colors slightly darker, so data entry fields are easier to see.	TRUE or FALSE

Figure 17-2 shows the Oracle look and feel for a Form.

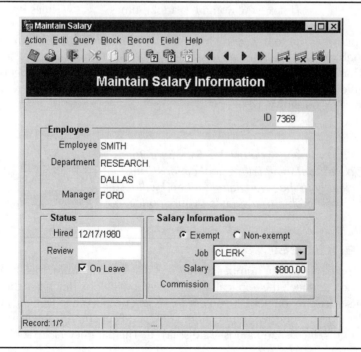

FIGURE 17-2. *Oracle look and feel*

Understanding Feature Restrictions
for Forms on the Web

If your application will be deployed to a middle-tier application server and run as a
thin-client application through a Web browser, you need to avoid using functionality
that the Web-based application doesn't support. Examine your application for
components that don't work when the application is run through a Web browser.
For instance, OCX (aka ActiveX Control) controls and mouse navigation triggers
might not work in an application deployed as a Web application. Even if such
features work (some mouse triggers do work in version 6), they might significantly
affect the performance of the Web application and you should eliminate them from
the application.

The following table lists Form Builder features, whether the feature is supported
on the Web, and any notes or guidelines about the feature (see also the following
Obsolete Components):

Feature	Supported?	Guidelines and Notes
ActiveX, OCX, OLE, DDE, VBX	No	Third-party controls that display screen output on the application server aren't supported because end users cannot view the output. If the functionality is available, use a JavaBean to mimic these features.
Console	Yes	To display the console (including the status and message lines) to end users, set the form-level property Console Window to the window in which you want to display the console.
HOST, ORA_FFI, USER_EXIT	Yes	Calls to these functions often display visual output or GUI elements on end-users' machines in client/server mode. In a Web implementation, the same calls will display the output and GUI elements on the application server (where end users cannot see or interact with them).
TEXT_IO	Yes	Reading and writing files takes place on the middle tier. A "local" file cannot be read off the PC, unless the drive is shared and visible from the Forms Server machine. Use Pluggable Java Components (PJC) to read and write files on the client machine.
Iconic buttons	Yes	Icon image files must be in GIF or JPG format (and not in ICO format) and must reside in the same directory as the HTML page.
NLS, BIDI	Yes	Supported for 8-bit languages only.

Feature	Supported?	Guidelines and Notes
When-Mouse-Enter/ Leave/Move triggers	No	Each execution of the trigger requires a network roundtrip, creating a negative effect in performance.
Magic Menu Items	No	Cut, Copy, and Paste magic menu items don't work in a Web environment. CTRL-X, CTRL-C, and CTRL-V do work, however.
Sound Items (5.0 and 6.0)	No	Sound items aren't supported in Web deployment.
Local Devices, such as barcode readers or other input devices	No	No way exists to programmatically access the 'local' machine from the browser.
WIN_API built-ins, calls to Windows DLLs	No	These are Windows-specific and all calls will attempt to run on the Forms Server, which might not be a Windows machine.
System Editor	No	Use the standard Forms editor. The System Editor is supported by JInitiator.

Using Java in Oracle Forms

As Oracle embraces the Internet platform, Java is supported in the database, in JDeveloper, and within Forms. Not only can Forms call Java Stored Procedures in the database, Java can be incorporated into Web Forms through *JavaBeans,* small, self-contained Java classes. You can write your own JavaBean classes or find dozens of examples of Beans that can be incorporated into your Forms. A Slider Bean and a Calendar Bean come with Forms demos, for example. JavaBeans are available only with Web Forms.

Beans are called from the application at run time and can replace standard user-interface components in the form with your own customized versions. You can also add your own components. JavaBeans use a special interface method called *IView* and they are called via a wrapper class that's accessible to the Form. The procedure to add JavaBeans to the form is simple and is as follows:

1. Create a JavaBean class file. You can either write your own class or find one of the many Beans available on the Web.

2. Write a container class that extends VBean to "wrap" the JavaBean. For example:

```
public class      JugglerWrapper
       extends     VBean
       implements MouseListener
          { …java code here…}
```

3. Create a Bean Area as an item in the form.

4. Set the Implementation Class property for the Bean Area to the container class name you created in Step 2. This must be a fully qualified name, that is, oracle.forms.demos.JugglerWrapper.

The JavaBean must be stored where the Forms Server can access it. Handle user interaction with the Bean Area using custom events generated by the JavaBean. These custom events are captured by a WHEN-CUSTOM-ITEM-EVENT trigger and controlled with the SET_CUSTOM_ITEM_PROPERTY built-in.

Extensive examples of implementing JavaBeans are available in the online help for Oracle Forms.

Resolving Signature Issues

Developers working in multiple environments have invariably encountered an ORA-04062 error. This is a Signature error, the result of Forms attempting to access stored procedures in the database that no longer match the specification against which they were compiled. This is usually a problem when package headers change. Adding a new procedure or function to the package specification or changing the order of the specification can result in the form not recognizing the procedure version.

If a package specification originally has functions A and B, but then C is added between them (the package specification now says A, C, B), any forms that use this package must be recompiled against the new structure. Forms "remembers" the sequence number of the function it was compiled against and when it tries to run function B, it runs C instead, and the specification doesn't match.

The only true solution is to ensure the package headers are identical on all deployed databases. Compiling the forms against the target database ensures they run correctly, but may mean recompiling forms at all production sites. While case or comment changes won't change the signature of a package, ordering and parameter list changes will. In some cases, if a package calls another package, the error message shows the calling package to have signature errors. Make sure to validate all procedural calls within the package to avoid these errors.

Future Directions

The release of Forms Builder6*i* enhanced the Web-deployment capability of Oracle Forms. The pending release of Oracle Forms9*i* introduces some major changes to Forms development, however. Oracle Forms6*i* is the last version of the Forms Builder geared toward a client/server environment. Oracle Forms, from its earliest incarnation as IAG, has tried to provide backward-compatibility for earlier versions with each upgrade and has gracefully phased out functionality within the toolset. A number of features are to be dropped in the 9*i* release, although, as before, Oracle continues to offer support for Forms 6*i* installations through at least 2002.

Obsolete Functionality

Perhaps the most important change is that Oracle Forms9i no longer supports the conventional client/server run-time environment. Web deployment is quickly becoming the focus of new development work and Oracle intends to move the Forms Development process into a strictly Internet deployment model. Character mode support is also being dropped, as is support for any V2-style functions in Forms (V2 triggers and V2 LOVs).

VBX, OLE Container, and OCX/Active X components are no longer supported. These are Windows-specific technologies that aren't applicable over the Web. JavaBean support replaces OCX/Active X controls. In addition, sound items aren't supported because they're client/server items only. All built-ins and properties for these items are, of course, removed.

RUN_PRODUCT is only supported to integrate graphics. Use RUN_REPORT_OBJECT instead to invoke Reports from within Forms on the Web. Menus are restricted to drop-down style and menu parameters are no longer supported. Most current applications don't use full-screen menus, which are entirely unsupported in 9i.

Trigger placement is more strongly controlled in 9i than in previous releases. Currently, some triggers that are logically block or form level triggers were placed at the item level. These triggers (when-clear-block, when-create-record, when-database-record, when-new-record-instance, and when-remove-record) are no longer allowed at the item level in 9i. The when-new-form-instance trigger is restricted to the form level.

Obsolete Components

The Developer suite of tools has incorporated a number of secondary components that will be removed from the Forms Builder suite with the new release. Most of them either support obsolete technology or are supported by a smaller, more streamlined Web deployment. Graphics, Procedure Builder, Project Builder, Translation Builder, Query Builder, Schema Builder, and Oracle Terminal are no longer shipped as independent modules within the Forms suite of tools.

The separate Oracle Forms Listener is dropped in favor of the Forms Listener servlet, which directs all traffic through the HTTP or HTTPS ports. Both the Oracle Forms Server cartridge and Forms CGI are removed in favor of the Forms servlet. The servlet was introduced with Forms 6i, Patch 2.

Performance Event Collection Services (PECS) are no longer supported in 9i.

More Information

White papers and technical documents about Web-enabling Forms can be found on Metalink (**http://metalink.oracle.com**), OTN (**http://otn.oracle.com**), and within the release notes and documentation for Forms Developer 6.0/6i. Documentation can be found at **http://www.oracle.com**. The Developer 6i and Oracle9iAS document provides guidelines and techniques for moving your applications on to the Web.

Additional information can be found in the user documentation for Forms and 9*i*AS. Specifically, see *Oracle Forms Developer Release 6i: Deploying Forms Applications to the Web with Forms Server* and *Oracle Forms Developer and Reports Developer Release 6i: Guidelines for Building Applications* for Web-deployment options and guidelines.

Oracle Reports

Oracle Reports has, for some time, been the most reliable way to produce output via the Web. You can easily propagate almost every report you created in the Client/ Server mode and instantly put it on the Web. In the latest version of Reports 6*i*, not only can you propagate reports to a Web environment, you can perform modifications dynamically using Extensible Markup Language (XML), which gives you the capability of modifying Reports in the following ways:

- Change attributes of a report at run time

- Dynamically add format triggers and attach them to objects within a report

- Use conditional formatting and apply decision logic at run time

You can also develop an entire report in XML (by editing a Reports configuration file as the following defines) without ever using the Report Builder tool and still run it through the Reports Server. With XML, another dimension has been added to Web reporting using Oracle products. XML is only one of the powerful features Oracle Reports brings to the table. For more information on XML, see Chapter 8.

In this section, the following topics are discussed:

- The Power of Oracle Reports Server

- Important facts to know about Reports Server

- New Features in Reports 6*i*

- Oracle Reports Architecture

- Reports Server Configuration File

- Identifying Reports Server Error Messages

- Configuring the Default Printer for Oracle Reports on UNIX

- Using a Key Map File

- Performance Tuning

- Using the Parameter Form

- Using JavaScript in Reports
- Using XML in Reports 6i

The Power of Oracle Reports Server

You can publish Reports with Oracle9i Application Server (Oracle9iAS) Reports Server throughout your enterprise via a standard Web browser and choose from many format options, including HTML, HTML cascading style sheets (HTMLCSS), Adobe's Portable Document Format (PDF), XML, Rich Text Format (RTF), PostScript, PCL, or Delimited text. Reports also gives you the capability to schedule reports for execution when you want them and for delivery by a method you choose, including e-mail or other means. Oracle Reports provides the most complete and comprehensive enterprise-reporting environment available anywhere.

Important Facts to Know About Reports Server

Before we delve into the nuts and bolts of Reports Server, here are some things to remember.

- The Reports Server is part of Oracle9iAS Enterprise Edition.

- Oracle Reports can dynamically display information via a Web browser using the following industry standard formats: Adobe's Portable Document Format (PDF), HTML, HTML Cascading Style Sheets (HTMLCSS), and XML.

- With Reports 6i, you can write PL/SQL stored procedures in the database that uses the UTL_HTTP package (available in 7.3 or later) to issue the HTTP request to the server to run the report. In the next release of Oracle Reports (Reports 9i), however, some PL/SQL procedures will be supplied to accomplish this.

- Oracle Reports imposes no limits on the size of the cgicmd.dat file.

- When you purchase Oracle9iAS Reports 6i as part of Oracle9iAS, you also receive a license for Oracle Portal. This enables the administrator to enter all the access control information where Reports Servers and RDFs are registered. This access control data can be used to authenticate users running reports outside a Portal Site.

- In Reports 6i, you have the capability of outputting XML, which is powerful. Additionally, you can also specify customizations to the reports in XML, either as a file that's read in as a customized command-line parameter or directly to the report while it's executing. In Release 9i, XML will be supported as a data source (including XML-Schema and xsql result sets). In addition, you can describe an entire report definition in XML and Reports Developer will save the definition to either an RDF or an XML file.

■ Reports can be called from within a Java application by specifying a URL to run a report request and open a socket. In Reports 9*i*, several plug-in interfaces will be written in Java, allowing data from multiple sources in a report. Additionally, Reports 9*i* is adopting JSPs to produce high-fidelity Web output (in addition to the "paginated HTML" it currently produces), so customers can code Java within the JSP. The Reports Server will also permit customization via Java in the way the cache and jobs in the job queue are managed.

New Features of Reports 6*i*

Report 6*i* comes with new features that help simplify the development and deployment process. The following table shows some of the new features of Reports 6*i*:

New Feature	Description
Chart hyperlinks	Chart values can be hyperlinks. For example, you can have a report with a chart that lists all the departments and number of employees within your department. You can click a part of the graph that states the department number and this could launch another report (drill down) that lists all the employees within that department.
Delimited output	Delimited output enables you to specify a delimiter (a character or string of characters) to separate the data in your report output.
HTML page streaming	You can view select parts of your report without downloading the entire report.
Report sectioning	You can have a single report with multiple layouts. This means you have a header, main, and trailer section, each producing its own report. And, if you combine the report with the report distribution feature, you can have one report with a department breakdown, employees by department, and an employee salary report in one rdf file that can be sent to separate locations.
Reports Runtime JavaBean	Report Builder now comes with a JavaBean run-time engine that can be run by a Java applet or a Java-enabled Web browser.
XML output	Report Builder can generate XML to modify an existing report dynamically. With XML, you can create and run a complete report without ever opening Report Builder.
Parameter Form HTML extensions	Parameter Form HTML extensions enable you to enhance your Runtime Parameter Forms with HTML tags and JavaScript for reports that are run via the Web.

New Feature	Description
Reports Server clustering	As information delivery becomes more demanding, server clustering is an easy, cost-effective solution that improves performance and load balancing.
Integration with Oracle Portal	Oracle Portal makes it more convenient and secure to publish reports via the Web. System administrators use wizards in Portal to control user access to reports.

Oracle Reports Architecture

There are two basic models of how Oracle Reports Server can be configured within a Web architecture. Figure 17-3 shows how Oracle Reports Server processes reports in two- and three-tier systems.

To describe Figure 17-3 verbally:

1. The client requests a report from her Web browser.

2. To process the request, the Web server invokes the Reports Server (either CGI or servlet).

3. The Reports Server parses the request and converts it to a command line that can be executed by Oracle Reports services. At this point, if no user ID or password ID was passed in, the user is prompted to provide one.

4. The Oracle Reports Server checks its output cache (if the request includes a Time Tolerance) to determine whether it already has output that satisfies the request passed in. If the server finds output similar to what was requested, it resends the file instead of executing the report.

5. The request is received and queued. When a report engine becomes available, the command line is sent to that engine to be executed.

6. The run-time engine runs the report.

7. The Reports Server receives the output from the engine and sends it to the Web server.

8. The Web server sends the request back to the client.

Reports Server Configuration File

The Reports Server configuration file specifies the parameters for the Reports Server. When the Reports Server is started, it retrieves a tns name to listen to from the installation or the command line. The server then identifies the configuration file with the tns name as its filename and .ora as its file extension in $ORACLE_HOME\ report60\server directory. If the configuration file isn't present, a default one is created.

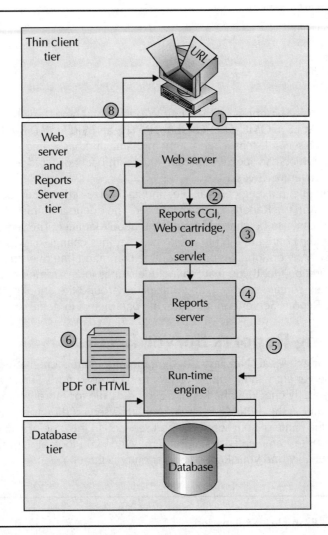

FIGURE 17-3. *Reports Server architecture*

The following directives are in the Reports configuration file:

```
identifier=string
maxconnect=number
sourcedir=path
cachedir=directory
tempdir=directory
cachesize=number
```

```
minengine=number
maxengine=number
initengine=number
maxidle=number
security=number
englife=number
```

If two servers are running on the same Windows machine, they have to share the same $ORACLE_HOME, $REPORTS60_PATH, and $REPORTS60_TMP logical directories. Each server listens to a different tns name and has a unique configuration file, however, which can specify different sourcedir, cachedir, and tempdir settings, optionally on different drives.

The minengine, maxengine, maxidle, and cachesize settings can be viewed and changed from the Reports Queue Manager. The queue administrator user ID and password can also be changed from the Queue Manager. The server process can overwrite the configuration file when these settings change or when it needs to be overwritten. Any optional arguments on the command line override the settings in the configuration file. If you want to include strings in a parameter, they must be in quotes if they contain spaces. Don't put spaces around the equal sign. Table 17-1 describes the Reports Server configuration file parameters in detail.

Identifying Reports Server Errors

Sometimes using the SQL*Net Easy Configuration tool can accidentally remove the Reports Server entry in the file. If you try to start the Reports Server and receive a 186 error, start by checking the Reports Server log file for more information. This file can be found in the $ORACLE_HOME/report60/server/ directory and is named rptsrv.log (or the name of your server's report service). In the case of 186 errors, it's most likely your tnsname entry has a problem. When you look at your tnsnames.ora file, you'll probably find your Reports Server entry is gone.

Parameter	Example	Explanation
identifier	N/A	An internal setting that contains the encrypted queue administrator user ID and password. You shouldn't attempt to modify it. If an identifier isn't specified, or is deleted, or the configuration file isn't present, anyone can supply any user ID and password from the Reports Queue Manager to log on as the queue administrator. Once someone has logged on in this way, the specified user ID and password become the queue administrator's user ID and password until changed from the Queue Manager.

TABLE 17-1. *Reports Server Configuration File Parameters*

Parameter	Example	Explanation
maxconnect	100	The maximum number of processes that can communicate with the server process at any one time. This setting is the sum of the number of engines and clients and must be greater than two (at least one engine and one client).
sourcedir	c:\apps\ reports\	A path to be searched before $REPORTS60_PATH when searching for reports and other run-time files. This setting is useful when you have more than one Reports Server sharing the same $ORACLE_HOME because each Reports Server can search different directories.
cachedir	c:\orant\ report60\ server\ cache\	report60\server\cache\The cache for the Reports Server. The cachedir parameter can be set to any directory or logical drive on the machine. If it isn't specified, the default is $ORACLE_ HOME/report60/server/cache. Assuming the Reports Server and *i*AS are on the same physical server, this parameter should be set to the physical equivalent of the REPORT60_WEBLOC directory.
tempdir	c:\temp\	A directory that will be used instead of $REPORTS60_TMP when creating temporary files. The tempdir parameter can be set to any directory or logical drive on the machine.
cachesize	100	The size of the cache in megabytes. If you expect to store the output of many of your reports in the Reports Server cache, you may want to increase this setting. If you don't expect to store a lot of output in the cache and have limited system resources, you might want to reduce it.
minengine	5	The minimum number of run-time engines the Reports Server should have available to run reports. The server process will attempt to keep at least this many engines active. Ensure that you have sufficient memory and resources available to accommodate the specified number of engines.
maxengine	100	The maximum number of run-time engines available to the Reports Server to run reports. The server process will attempt to keep no more than this many engines active. Ensure that you have sufficient memory and resources available to accommodate the specified number of engines.
initengine	5	The initial number of run-time engines started by the Reports Server. The server process will spawn this many engines when it's started. It will wait two minutes for these engines to connect to it and will shut itself down if they fail to do so. If the engines cannot connect in this amount of time, usually some setup problem exists.

TABLE 17-1. *Reports Server Configuration File Parameters* (continued)

Parameter	Example	Explanation
maxidle	5	The maximum amount of time an engine is allowed to be idle before being shut down. The Reports Server won't shut down the engine if doing so would reduce the number of available engines to less than the value of minengine.
security	1	The security level (0, 1, 2, or 3) for accessing cached output files through the Reports Queue Manager. The default level of security is 1. This setting only controls access through the Queue Manager. Accessing output files through other methods (for example, opening an output file in a browser or an editor) is controlled by the security you have in place for your file system. If a job writes an ASCII output file to a particular directory, for example, users who have privileges on that directory can look at the output in a text editor or viewer. Valid entries, and their definitions, are as follows: 0—anyone can access a job's cached output 1—only a user whose user ID is identical to that of the user who ran the job can access the job's cached output 2—only the same process that sent the job can access the job's cached output 3—the cached output cannot be accessed *Note, when someone uses the Reports Queue Manager to access output, the output isn't encrypted when it's being moved across the network. In addition, with security level 1, anyone who has administrator privileges on any machine can fake a user ID to retrieve someone else's output.*
englife	20	The maximum number of reports an engine will run before shutting itself down. The Reports Server will bring up fresh engines for new requests if the engine is shut down.

TABLE 17-1. *Reports Server Configuration File Parameters* (continued)

Configuring the Default Printer for Oracle Reports on UNIX

If you don't have a default printer defined for Oracle Reports, you'll receive an error message that Reports is unable to initialize the printer (error REP-3002) in Reports 6.0 or a REP-1800: Formatter error in Reports 3.0. This error indicates you don't have a default printer defined. After installing Oracle Reports on UNIX platforms, therefore, you must perform some postinstallation tasks. First, you must generate a PostScript print queue on your UNIX machine to the operating system. Even if you don't have a physical printer, you still need to generate this queue. Reports uses the presence or absence of a PostScript print queue to determine whether your UNIX box is capable of handling graphical (bitmapped) output.

The following code is an example of a valid uiprint.txt line:

```
"lp1:PostScript:1:LNO printer on np3:default.ppd:"
 | |            | |                    |
 | says it's a| +- cosmetic name |
 | Postscript |    for the queue is the Name of the PPD
 | Printer    |                    (Postscript Printer Definition)
 |              says it's a         file which gives details about
 Operating      Postscript Level 1 the fonts available on this
 System Print Printer              printer. Don't change this
                                   Unless
    queue name                     you know what you're doing.
```

When Oracle Reports starts up, the toolkit layer reads the uiprint.txt file, finds the line for each print queue, and gives the report a print queue name and a PPD filename. The toolkit then interrogates the operating system to ensure each queue exists and determines if the queue is a PostScript print queue. Reports loads the list of fonts in each PPD file for each print queue and, for each font, then loads the corresponding Adobe Font Metric (AFM) file to obtain sizing information.

If this process doesn't happen as described or if no PostScript print queues are found, Reports produces only character-mode output and refuses to run in bitmapped mode when forced (giving the previously mentioned error messages). The easiest way to test printing your report is to run a report from the demo directory under reports and try to get postscript output. You can verify if the output file is a flat ASCII or PostScript file by running the report. The following command runs the report (in UNIX):

```
r30runm module=test.rdf userid=scott/tiger destype=file
desname=test.lis batch=yes
```

Remember, the previous command must be entered on one command line with no carriage returns. You can view the output file using the previous command:

```
more test.lis
The beginning of a PostScript file appears similar to the following:
%!PS-Adobe-3.0
%%Creator: Oracle Toolkit 2 for Motif 2.1.5.6.2 PRODUCTION
%%Version: 2.1 5
%%CreationDate: (Fri May 24 15:46:29 1996)
%%For: Brad Brown (brownb@tusc2))
%%Routing: (Brad Brown,RPS,x6889)
%%Title: 'TEST.LIS' (Oracle Toolkit Application)
%%LanguageLevel: 2
%%Requirements: numcopies(1)
%%DocumentData: Clean7Bit
%%PageOrder: Ascend
%%Pages: (atend)
%%Orientation: Landscape
    % NOTE: This file was generated with the PPD file default.ppd
```

Using a Key Map File

Remember this: when you call Reports Server, you are calling an external program that needs to establish an independent connection to a database (in this case, Oracle). This is different than calling Reports as a cartridge, as in some versions of OAS. For all practical purposes, a cartridge maintains a persistent connection to the database at all times.

With this in mind, you have to realize a problem exists. To call a report request, you have to pass in the name of the report, the userid, the password, and the report format. How secure would your application be if you had our userid, password, and SID in the link of your report? All users would have to do is view the source of your Web page and they can see the following:

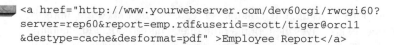

```
<a href="http://www.yourwebserver.com/dev60cgi/rwcgi60?
server=rep60&report=emp.rdf&userid=scott/tiger@orcl1
&destype=cache&desformat=pdf" >Employee Report</a>
```

This tells users who access our page what your server name, database, userid, and password are. This is the equivalent of securing your database with bubble gum. To get around this problem, you need to use a key map file.

What Is a Key Map File?

A *key map* file is a way for you to specify a "key" that can be used on the command line to be interpreted only on the server side. This key means nothing to anyone viewing the source from the HTML side, but it has all the relevant information for the Reports Server to process the request supplied.

With key mapping, we rewrite the URL above to process our request, with the user ID and password hidden, as follows:

```
<a href="http://www.yourwebserver.com/dev60cgi/rwcgi60?
empreport" >Employee Report</a>
```

The key empreport means nothing to anyone, except the Reports Server. The key file is called cgicmd.dat and is stored in the $ORACLE_HOME/bin/reports60/server directory. All you need to make this example come to life is the following line in that file:

```
Empreport:server=rep60&report=emp.rdf&userid=scott/
tiger@orcl1&destype=cache&desformat=pdf"
```

This way, no one but the Reports Server knows your user ID and password.

Benefits of Using a Key Map File

The following list outlines some of the benefits of using a key map file:

■ It shortens the URL

■ You can remap the URL without having to change any code on the HTML page

■ It hides certain parameters from users

Performance Tuning

Performance tuning is important to Oracle Reports, whether you're accessing reports through the Web or in a client/server environment. No one wants to wait a long time for something to process. In an ideal world, Reports would take seconds to run and would require no tuning at all (90 percent of reports are basic and take only a few moments to produce output). But, in the real world, Reports can take from seconds to minutes to hours. A lot depends on the environment you're running, the way you're accessing reports (Web or client/server), and the platform you're running against. With most of these out of your control, it's important you make your Reports as efficient as possible.

The following items outline some settings and methods you can use to make your report run as quickly and efficiently as possible.

ARRAYSIZE

Make this field as big as you can. This is the measure of kilobytes Report Builder can use per query in executing your report.

Rationale: Report Builder uses Oracle's array processing, which fetches multiple records in batches instead of one record at a time. The larger the array size, the more rows that can be fetched simultaneously, therefore, fewer calls to the database will be made.

COPIES

When printing to PostScript, specify COPIES=1.

Rationale: If COPIES is set to something greater than 1 for a PostScript report, Report Builder must save the pages in temporary storage to collate them. This can significantly increase the amount of temporary disk space used by Report Builder and the additional writing to files can slow performance.

Local PL/SQL Versus External PL/SQL Libraries

Use Local PL/SQL as often as you can.

Rationale: When you reference an object in an external PL/SQL library, the library has to be brought in and compiled at run time. If all the code is kept within the report being executed, no external calls need to be made, so the report runs more efficiently. This doesn't mean external libraries have no place in reports. External libraries are an excellent way of sharing code across many reports, thereby making maintenance a lot easier. Weighing the benefits and performance overhead of sharing code across many applications is important.

File Searching

Specify path variables to speed file searching and creation/access of temporary files. (Recall Report Builder provides two environment variables (REPORTS60_PATH and REPORTS60_TMP), which govern where to search for files and where to store temporary files.) For REPORTS60_PATH, specify the path in which files referenced by the report are located. For REPORTS60_TMP, specify a path that has sufficient free space for temporary files and is on a device with fast response time (for example, a RAM disk).

Rationale: REPORTS60_PATH is the default path in which Report Builder will search for files (for example, link file boilerplate). By specifying the path in which the files referenced by the report are located, you can reduce the amount of searching Report Builder needs to do to retrieve the files. (By using REPORTS60_PATH instead of hard-coding the paths in the report definition, you also maintain the portability of your report.) REPORTS60_TMP is the path in which Report Builder will create its temporary files.

Format Triggers

Placing format triggers at the lowest frequency possible is important.

Rationale: You want to get the desired effect of the format trigger with it being executed the fewest amount of times. PL/SQL in the format trigger of a frame, instead of a field, typically makes the report run faster. The PL/SQL in format trigger is executed for each instance of its object. The lower the frequency of the object, the fewer times the PL/SQL will be executed and the faster the report will run.

Indexes

Indexes are an important part of performance. When you are doing a master detail report, it's more important to have indexes in the detail query than the master query. Records in the master query are queried only once, but records in the detail query are referenced many times through the report.

Another good idea is also to have indexes in the master query. Even though master query is accessed once, it still has to be parsed and generated. Thus, the faster the Reports Server can generate the master query, the faster it can start on the detail query.

Stored Procedures Versus Local PL/SQL

Knowing when to use local PL/SQL versus Stored Objects is important. Use Stored Objects when you want to access/perform database operations.

Rationale: Because Stored Procedures run in/on the database, they can access data more quickly (because they're already there), where local procedures are perfect for performing tasks/calculations that require no database interaction. This is important to remember when working in an environment with very slow response time.

Number of Queries

Reduce the number of queries in your report as much as possible.

Rationale: In general, the fewer queries you have, the faster your report will run. While multiquery data models are often easier to understand, single-query data models tend to execute more quickly.

RUNDEBUG

Turn off the RUNDEBUG executable argument.

Rationale: RUNDEBUG causes Report Builder to perform more error checking when it runs your report.

Sizing for Nongraphical Objects

Defining any nongraphical layout objects without horizontal or vertical elasticity, in other words, fixed in size, is important.

Rationale: As a report runs in a repeating frame, it continuously has to calculate the sizes and placements of all objects in relation to their size. If nongraphical objects (boilerplate text or fields with text) have a fixed size, the report engine needn't perform all these unnecessary calculations, thereby saving time.

SQL Statements

SQL statements are the heart of every relational database system, especially the reporting piece. Before tuning any other aspect of the report, first look at what's driving the data. Here are some ways you can use SQL to improve the speed of your reports:

- Perform calculation directly in your query, rather than a formula or summary column at the group level.

- Use the where clause to exclude records instead of a group filter or a format trigger. Let the database do the work.

- If you have to do any text manipulation, do it within the SQL. This can include SUBSTR, RTRIM, LTRIM, INSTR, UPPER, LOWER, and concatenations.

Rationale: The database engine is powerful and is specially designed to handle these operations. Once data is sent from the database to the report, all your functions (previously listed) are already completed. All the report must do is to print it on the screen.

Unused Frames

All frames should have a transparent border and fill pattern.

Rationale: If Reports Server doesn't have any physical attributes to manage, it doesn't have to be printed, making the report faster.

Word Wrapping

Remove any unnecessary frames from the layout. When Report Builder creates a default layout, it puts frames around virtually everything. The reason for this is to protect the objects in the frames from being overwritten by other objects in the output. If you know from experience that the objects in a frame aren't in danger of being overwritten, you can eliminate the frame without adversely affecting your report output.

Rationale: The fewer objects in the layout, the fewer objects Report Builder must format at run time. As a result, performance is better when you reduce the number of objects in the layout.

One Line per Record

Make fields that contain text one line long and ensure their contents fit within the specified width (for example, by using the SUBSTR function).

Rationale: If a field with text spans more than one line, Report Builder must use its word-wrapping algorithm to format the field. Ensuring a field takes only one line to format avoids the additional processing of the word-wrapping algorithm.

Using the Parameter Form

A time may occur when you need to pass in parameters that aren't available on a generated HTML page. When using PL/SQL to generate a page, you can dynamically create a link and put whatever parameters the argument needs in the parameter string. But, what if you need to pass some user-supplied values into a report? And, what if, for some reason, you don't want the parameters to be supplied on the hyperlink (for example, user ID and password)? One way around this is to make the user type in his ID and password on report run time.

It's important to know that when running a report in Client/Server mode, the parameter form comes up automatically. When you run the report through the Web, however, the parameter form doesn't come up by default. If you add the following text into the URL, Reports prompts the user with your parameter form:

```
paramform=yes
```

The following is a complete example:

```
http://www.acme.com/reports?server=rptsrv&
report=sales&userid=acme/roadrunner@sales&destype=cache
&desformat=html&paramform=yes
```

Magically, your parameter form will appear, as shown in Figure 17-4.

Remember, you have only limited control over the parameter form Oracle Reports creates. You can modify it visually, by changing fonts, sizes, and colors, but you have little control over the fields it puts on the screen. In the previous example, the password field isn't encrypted. When the form is sent across the network, it won't be encrypted there either. Remember, when you create your parameter form, you're merely allocating fields to this screen. Reports doesn't support a field of type "password."

Parameter forms are great tools when you need a quick way to enter parameters into a report. If you want to make vast customizations, though, you might want to develop an HTML form and throw in some JavaScript to make it adhere to your specifications.

Using JavaScript in Reports

Remember, even though you're using reports on the Web, all you're really doing is generating a report in HTML through a browser (except while using PDF format).

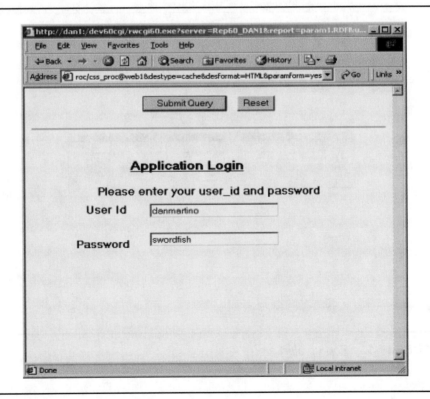

FIGURE 17-4.   *Parameter form login screen*

Because you're generating HTML, you have the capability to use a scripting language (in this case, JavaScript).

In Web development, JavaScript is used mostly for validating and processing form items (of course, JavaScript can do many other things). Because it's a rarity to use Reports to create an input form (although this is definitely possible), you might wonder "What can I use JavaScript in reports for?" The following sections discuss ways JavaScript can be implemented with Reports 6*i*.

You can create an alert that pops up when a report is generated. This can be helpful when you want a message to pop up as soon as the report is generated, saying "This report is considered confidential, please do not distribute." If you use a JavaScript alert, the viewer has to click (acknowledge) something before she reviews the report. Figure 17-5 shows an example of such an alert.

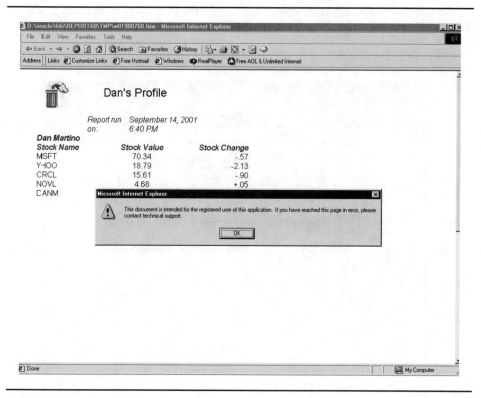

FIGURE 17-5. *Pop-up alert*

By modifying the BeforeReport Value (this is a report-level property) to contain the code shown in the following, you can get the output shown in Figure 17-5.

```html
<html>
<script language="JavaScript">
  function display_message() {
    alert("This document is intended for the registered
user of this application. If you have reached this page in
error, please contact technical support.");
  }
</script>
<body  onLoad="display_message()" dir=&Direction bgcolor="#ffffff">
```

Maybe you want another window to pop up while your main window is populating. A lot of retail sites use this philosophy on loading their page. When you go to a catalog site, usually as the first page is loading, the site pops up a smaller window advertising something they have on sale at this particular time. An example of this is shown in Figure 17-6.

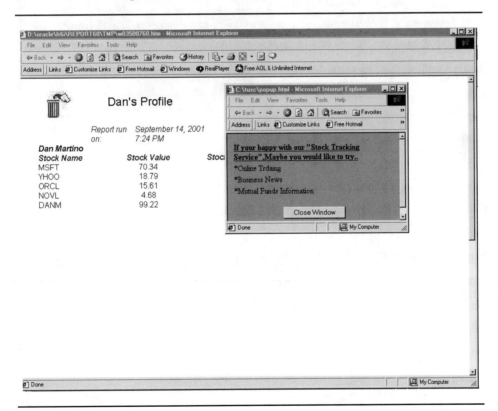

FIGURE 17-6. *Pop-up browser window*

Another way to take advantage of JavaScript within Oracle Reports is to make a record act like a link. In Reports, you can do this using the Hyperlink property at the field level. You can use JavaScript to verify you want to go to the specified record by throwing up a window that makes you confirm your decision, as shown in Figure 17-7. If you click the Oracle link, you automatically go to **http://www.oracle.com**. If you click the Yahoo! link, you automatically go to **http://www.yahoo.com**.

Once you click OK, you should get the page shown in Figure 17-8.

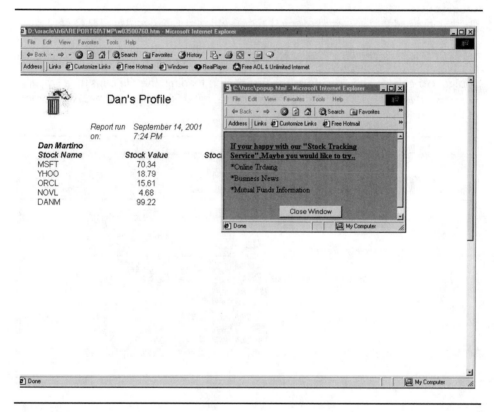

FIGURE 17-7. *Using JavaScript to launch a Confirmation dialog box*

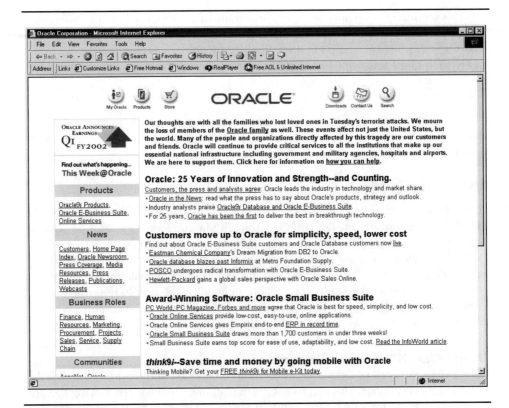

FIGURE 17-8. *These are the results of clicking a link in Figure 17-7.*

To get the previous example to work, all you have to do is modify the Before report value property to include the following code:

```
<html>
<script language="JavaScript">
function show_alert(new_window) {
  if (confirm("Are you sure you want to launch a new browser session.")) {
      window.open("http://"+new_window);
  }

}
</script>
<body dir=&Direction bgcolor="#ffffff">
```

This section of code appears at the beginning of the report when it's generated within the Web browser. It contains the function show_alert, which, when executed, asks the user if he wants to open the home page within a new browser session.

Next, add the following line to the format trigger for the stock_name field:

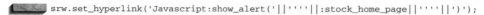

```
srw.set_hyperlink('Javascript:show_alert('||''''||:stock_home_page||''''||')');
```

This section of code sets the hyperlink property for the :stock_name field. This is needed because every stock name launches to a new home page. You wouldn't want to click Motorola and go to Novell's home page.

What Is XML?

As discussed in detail in Chapter 8, XML stands for Extensible Markup Language. Like HTML, XML is a subset of Standard Generalized Markup Language (SGML). XML is fast becoming the universal standard for electronic data exchange.

XML provides an unambiguous, text-based method of structuring data. XML is easily interpreted by both humans and machines. Data in XML documents is represented using markup tags. The tags are defined by the user to describe the content of the data, but they don't address the presentation of the content (as HTML tags do).

What Can XML Do in Reports 6*i*?

All previous versions of Oracle Reports had to be created and modified through the Oracle Reports builder. This means every small change involved modifying the .rdf file. If you had to run a report for a certain client that wanted its output to have a specific formatting technique applied to it, you would either have to modify, execute, and unmodify your report, or have multiple versions of your report, each one addressing each customer's particular needs. Either way, you'd have talked yourself into a cumbersome task and a maintenance nightmare.

With XML, you can solve this problem without having multiple versions of the source file or modifying the source code. XML lets you perform the following tasks:

- Apply customizations at run time without changing the original report.

- Apply batch updates to existing reports (basically modifying and saving the source code, without ever opening a single .rdf file).

- Create complete report definitions (that can be run using reports run time) without ever touching the Oracle Reports builder.

At this point, you're probably wondering, "How can I possibly modify a report without even opening the source code?" The answer is through an XML definition file (another way exists that still involves an XML definition routine, but this is discussed later).

What Is an XML Definition File?

Two types of XML definition files exist: full and partial. A *full XML definition file* contains the entire report definition with all the required tags and components (discussed later in this chapter) and can run independently without ever being touched by the Oracle Reports viewer, while a *partial XML definition file* only needs a few required tags (along with some specialized tags) to accomplish your task.

The following shows a simple example of a partial report definition. This definition changes the font of the F_SSN field to Arial and the size to 12 points.

```
<report name="employee" DTDVersion="1.0">
<layout>
  <section name="main">
     <field name="F_SSN" font="Arial" fontSize="12"/>
  </section>
</layout>
</report>
```

In plain English, this partial definition file says the following: "Change the font to Arial and the font size to 12 for the F_SSN field in the main section of the layout."

You can implement this definition when you call your report. On the command line, use the command line argument CUSTOMIZE and set it equal to the text file that holds the XML partial definition, as shown in the following:

```
Rwcli60 report=employee.rdf userid=username/password@mydb
destype=file desformat=PDF destype=file
customize=e:\production\reports\xml\employee.xml
```

Again, we can apply this formatting to this report without touching the source code (RDF) of the report.

Examples of What XML Definition Files Can Do

In this section, you see how you perform the following tasks:

- Change physical attributes of a field on a report (similar to what you saw earlier)

- Base formatting of fields on conditions (exceptions)

- Add program units to reports

■ Change the data model of a report

■ Create a full report definition

Test Case   The XYZ Web site provides the service of enabling users to view all the stocks they selected for their profile. Users can set up a profile of the stocks they want to track. When users sign on, a list of the stocks they have selected appears on the screen along with their stock price. The users' IDs, along with a list of their preferred stocks, are stored within our database, and we use reports to show them dynamically.

The following is our control example for scenarios we'll demonstrate. Figure 17-9 is what the report looks like with no XML definitions applied to it. This was created using Oracle Reports and is fresh off the Web site.

Now, let's look at three different scenarios and see how you can apply XML to them.

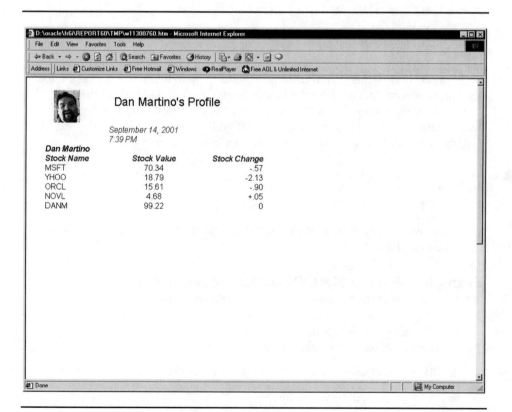

FIGURE 17-9.   *Our original report*

Scenario #1 In this user's preferences, he has specified he wants his stock name, value, and change difference to be in Courier font, 20 point, and italicized. You can use the following XML code to make this happen without opening the source code:

```
<report name="control" DTDVersion="1.0">
 <layout>
  <section name="main">
    <field name="F_STOCK_NAME"   font="Courier" fontSize="20"
fontStyle="italic"/>
    <field name="F_STOCK_VALUE"  font="Courier" fontSize="20"
          fontStyle="italic"/>
    <field name="F_STOCK_CHANGE" font="Courier" fontSize="20"
          fontStyle="italic"/>       </section>
 </layout>
</report>
```

This code looks similar to HTML. It has starting and ending tags (report, layout, and section), and all tags are placed in brackets (<>). Let's look at the code line by line.

Line Number	Description
1	Starts off the XML code with the name of the definition and the version number.
2	Tag that tells the control file we'll be making changes within the layout section of the report.
3	Dictated what section in the layout will have definitions applied to it.
4	Dictates we will modify the F_STOCK_NAME field and change the default values for font name, font size, and font style to Courier, 20, and italic, respectively.
5	Dictates we will modify the F_STOCK_VALUE field and change the default values for font name, font size, and font style to Courier, 20, and italic, respectively.
6	Dictates we will modify the F_STOCK_CHANGE field and change the default values for font name, font size, and font style to Courier, 20, and italic, respectively.
7	XML tag that indicates we're at the end of the section we're modifying.
8	XML tag that indicates we're modifying the layout section of the report.
9	XML tag that indicates we're at the end of the report definition file.

The new output based on the XML definition is shown in Figure 17-10.

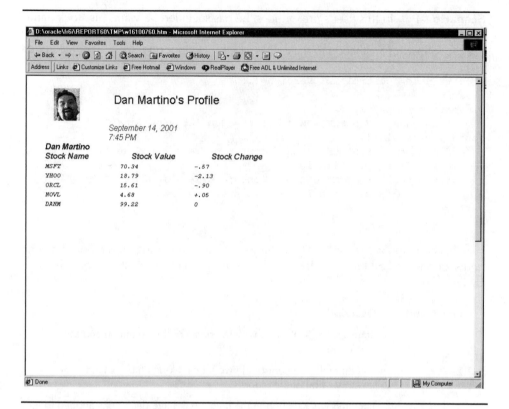

FIGURE 17-10. *Original report with the XML file assigned to it from Scenario 1*

Notice that once you've modified the font size and type to be used within the file definition, there's no guarantee anything will be affected within the Reports layout. When you created and saved the report through Report Builder, all properties and sizes were predetermined. When using XML to modify a few settings, no guarantees exist that all of the settings will be adjusted accordingly. You must make sure you allow enough variances in your layout to accommodate all the expected settings.

Scenario #2   Now let's look at how to change elements of the report based on a condition(s). This particular user wants the stocks that show a gain to appear in bold. The output is shown in Figure 17-11.

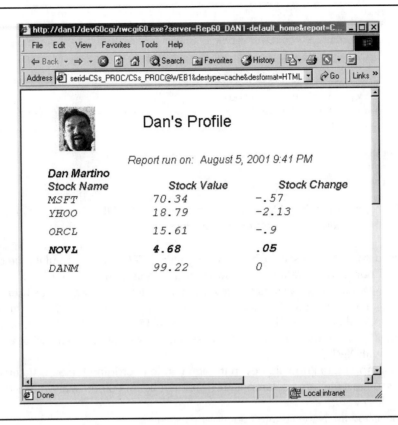

FIGURE 17-11. *Original report with the XML file assigned to it from Scenario 2*

The following is the XML source code for this output:

```
<report name="control" DTDVersion="1.0">
  <layout>
   <section name="main">
     <field name="F_STOCK_NAME"   font="Courier" fontSize="20" >
       <exception fontStyle="bold">
         <condition source="stock_change" operator="gt" operand1="0" />
       </exception>
     </field>
```

```
        <field name="F_STOCK_VALUE"  font="Courier" fontSize="20" >
          <exception fontStyle="bold">
            <condition source="stock_change" operator="gt" operand1="0" />
          </exception>
        </field>
        <field name="F_STOCK_CHANGE" font="Courier" fontSize="20" >
          <exception fontStyle="bold">
            <condition source="stock_change" operator="gt" operand1="0" />
          </exception>
        </field>
      </section>
    </layout>
</report>
```

Notice, by using the <EXCEPTION> and <CONDITION> tags, we can make the output vary, depending on certain logical operators.

Scenario #3   In this scenario, shown in Figure 17-12, we manipulate the data model of our report to return only rows based on a certain condition. In this case, we only want to show rows that have a stock changed value > 0. If this user wants to request information for the stocks prior to 1-1-2000, we can easily do this using an XML partial definition file. All we do is specify the new SQL statement and the report will run and override the old SQL statement, replacing it with what was derived with XML.

It's important to know that even though you're overriding the SQL statement, it still has to have the same column names and number of columns, as well as adhering to all rules of SQL.

The following is the source code for this scenario:

```
<report name="control" DTDVersion="1.0">
  <data>
    <dataSource name="q_1">
      <select>
        SELECT EMP_NAME,
               STOCK_NAME,
               STOCK_VALUE,
               TO_NUMBER(STOCK_CHANGE) STOCK_CHANGE
        FROM   DAN_MASTER,DAN_DETAIL
        WHERE  (MASTER.EMP_ID = DETAIL.EMP_ID)
        AND    STOCK_CHANGE > 0
      </select>
    </dataSource>
  </data>
  <layout>
    <section name="main">
      <field name="F_STOCK_NAME"    font="Courier" fontSize="20" >
        <exception fontStyle="bold">
```

```
        <condition source="stock_change" operator="gt" operand1="0" />
      </exception>
    </field>
    <field name="F_STOCK_VALUE"  font="Courier" fontSize="20" >
      <exception fontStyle="bold">
        <condition source="stock_change" operator="gt" operand1="0" />
      </exception>
    </field>
    <field name="F_STOCK_CHANGE" font="Courier" fontSize="20" >
      <exception fontStyle="bold">
        <condition source="stock_change" operator="gt" operand1="0" />
      </exception>
    </field>
  </section>
 </layout>
</report>
```

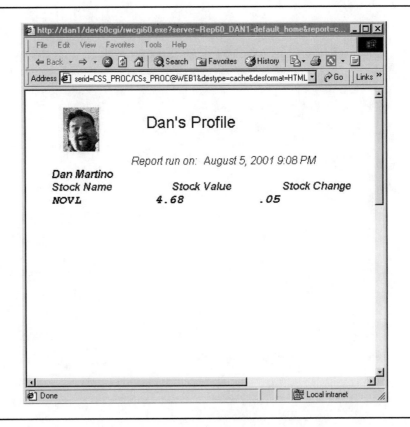

FIGURE 17-12.   *Original report with the XML file assigned to it from Scenario 3*

In this example, all you have to do is add seven lines of code and you've specified an entire SQL statement for the data model.

Summary

With earlier releases of Oracle Web servers, the deployment of Oracle Forms on the Web was inconsistent and immature, at best. The latest releases of Oracle Forms, however, have brought the robust and stable functionality from the client/server environment to the Web. The future direction of Oracle Forms development is Web-focused, and the toolset and supporting functions are constantly improving the experience of designing, developing, and deploying Forms on the Web.

Oracle Reports has been a proven Web technology for some time now. As you can see from the new XML enhancements, Oracle continues to enhance and improve the Reports capabilities for the Web.

CHAPTER
18

IFS—Internet
File System

traight from Oracle—it's IFS! IFS (Internet File System) is a repository supervisor and application development environment. IFS enables you to access an Oracle database as if it were a file system. It lets you place operating system files in the database, replacing many complex tasks usually performed by an operating system. IFS added these new features to the Oracle9iAS:

- Accesses the repository via standard protocols, such as HTTP, FTP, and IMAP4

- Seamlessly integrates with Windows Explorer and Network Neighborhood

- Supports the Internet Explorer and Netscape browsers

IFS acts like a bridge between your PC and the database. You can map a network drive to the IFS server and the rest of the work is done by IFS. When you move a file on to the IFS drive, IFS converts the file into a database object and transfers it to the repository. When the user opens the file on the IFS drive, IFS converts the file into a form the PC can read and transfers it back.

IFS is an excellent tool that enables you to share files not only on a standard intranet network, but over the Internet as well. All the advantages of a database (backup, recovery, centralized repository, search capabilities, and so much more) as well as all the advantages of the Internet, are in one simple component. We heard a lot of hype about IFS for quite some time and when it arrived, I certainly wasn't disappointed. You should know, though, that IFS requires version 8.1.7 of the database.

In this chapter, the following topics are discussed:

- Online Documentation

- Installation of IFS

- Reconfiguring IFS

- Starting IFS

- Accessing IFS

Online Documentation

Who reads the instruction manual first? If you don't, you should. You definitely want to read through the IFS documentation before installing it. The documentation can be found in the $ORACLE_HOME/IFS1.1/doc directory, in the index.html file. The documentation includes information on the following topics:

- New things in release 1.1

- Installation, setup, and administration guides

- A quick tour
- User and developer guides
- XML samples
- Class, XML, and API reference

Another great source of information on IFS is Technet (OTN). Here's a great URL for IFS help on the Technet discussion board: **http://technet.oracle.com/support/bboard/discussions.htm**

Installation of IFS

IFS isn't impossible to install, but it certainly isn't the easiest installation I've performed. Many prerequisites are in the installation guide, so be sure to read the specifications. The following are some of the main prerequisites:

- You *must* be running version 8.1.7 of the RDBMS
- 500MB of disk space for IFS
- 2GB for the database (or more)
- You need a fast machine (for example, 750 MHz+)
- Be sure to bump up (increase or at least check) some init.ora parameters (as defined in the installation guide)

Before installing IFS, I was running 8.1.6 of the Oracle database. I had some difficulties getting to the 8.1.7 version of the Oracle RDBMS. No matter how much I tried, I couldn't seem to upgrade the database. Exporting the database turned out to be a very good thing so I could migrate my data. You must set job_processes to 0; I even removed it, but that didn't work. I rebooted and the installation process got 60 percent done, but then it crashed. I blew everything away and created a new database, and then imported my data, which seemed to work fine.

I installed IFS 1.1.9 once I upgraded to version 8.1.7 of the database. The initial IFS page simply welcomes you to the configuration assistant. From this initial page, you read the text and click Next.

Selecting the Database

As shown in Figure 18-1, you next need to tell IFS what database you plan to use to store the IFS objects.

Once you select the database into which IFS files are to be placed, IFS runs a series of checks on your machine. As each item is completed, it's checked off the list.

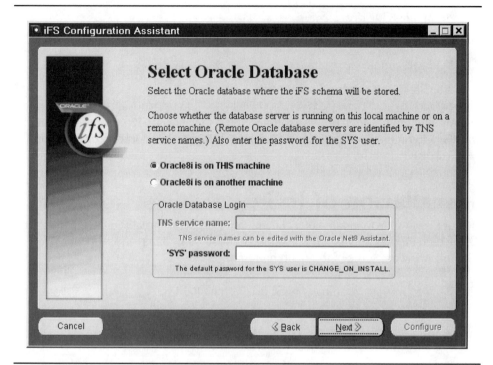

FIGURE 18-1. *Selecting an Oracle database to store IFS files*

Creating the IFS Schema and Setting Options

You next need to enter the schema (and the new password) that IFS will use to store
the IFS schema and data. You can leave the schema as IFSSYS if you want, but please
be sure to use a unique password.

After choosing a schema name, you need to make some decisions about the
configuration of your IFS schema tablespace parameters. Again, you can leave these
parameters as defaulted (recommended settings) if you want.

The IFS installation verifies that interMedia (Oracle Text) is configured properly.
You needn't do anything at this point.

Creating an IFS Protocol Instance

Next, you need to determine the instance to be created for the IFS protocols,
such as e-mail. Again, you can leave this alone and use the default if you want.

Unless you need to change the default language, choose a language and
character set and off you go!

Picking Your IFS Protocols and Ports

Next, as you can see in Figure 18-2, you're asked to select the protocols you want to have IFS support. Deselect any protocols you don't want to support with IFS. Otherwise, leave all protocols checked.

After selecting the ports you want to support, you need to indicate the ports on which you plan to support these protocols as shown in Figure 18-3. The default industry standard protocol/port combinations are displayed as the defaults. You might need to change some of these port numbers. For example, if you already have an e-mail server running on this machine, you need to change the port associated with IFS e-mail, so IFS uses a unique e-mail port number.

Next, IFS verifies each of these protocol ports is available for the corresponding IFS protocols. If a problem occurs, such as with using port 80, you see an error message and you're asked to change the port number.

Wrapping Up

The final splash screen indicates you completed the installation questions and analysis. Now is the time for the installer to install and configure IFS.

A checklist shows you the progress of installation as it occurs. Installation can take a while.

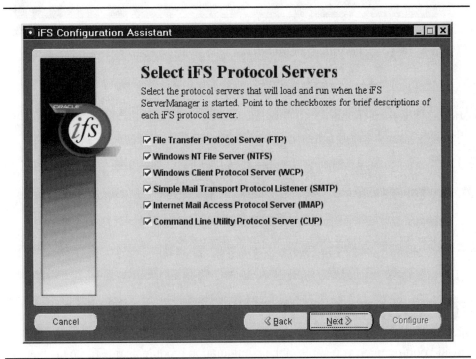

FIGURE 18-2. *Choosing IFS Protocol Servers*

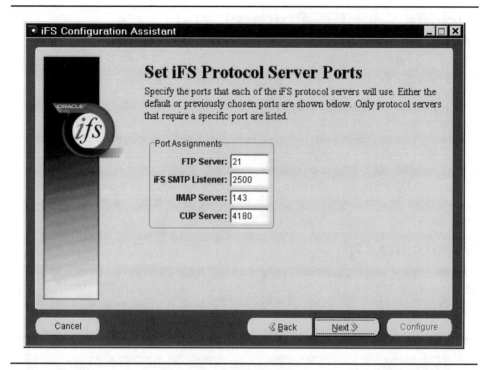

FIGURE 18-3. *Choosing port numbers*

On completion, you should see a completion page congratulating you on your success. If you reach this point, congratulations! You then need to reboot your machine at this point.

TIP
After the installation, notice no new menu options were added for IFS.

TIP
If you receive an error about a servlet zone problem, see doc ID 150114.1 on Metalink. There is a bug that existed with version 1.1.10 of the IFS installation.

Reconfiguring IFS

If you need to change a parameter after the configuration, such as specifying an invalid port number, you can run the configuration module again. To change or reset a parameter, run ifsconfig from the IFS bin directory.

Starting IFS

After installing IFS, you might expect to find a service in the Services Manager on Windows 2000, but IFS doesn't use a service manager to start. Start the IFS file services by running the ifsstart program (from the IFS/bin directory). This program prompts you for two passwords, as shown here:

The IFS user name isn't a database user name, but a user name and password stored in the IFS database. By default, the password for the IFS system account is manager. Leave the IFS user name as system and specify manager as the password. You can leave the IFS service name (ServerManager) as the default. The password of the IFS schema (IFSSYS) is the password you specified previously at the time of installation—not ifssys, I hope. Assuming you specify the correct passwords on this page, the IFS server should start up and then run.

NOTE
This step is not required to access IFS through a browser. This step is required to access as a file system on your network as discussed in the next section "Accessing IFS from the Network Neighborhood."

Accessing IFS

You can access IFS any one of the following three ways:

■ Through a browser

■ From the Network Neighborhood

■ By installing the plug-in for Windows

The following sections detail each of these methods of accessing IFS.

Accessing the Web-Based IFS— Through a Browser

To access IFS from your browser, execute the IFS login JSP program. For example:
http://tuscbdb/ifs/jsps/login.jsp. The following illustration shows you what the IFS login looks like in the browser.

By default, IFS provides two accounts (stored in the IFSSYS schema as records). The accounts are system (with a password of manager) and scott (with a password of tiger). After logging into IFS (as you can see, I logged in as system), you see a page similar to that shown here:

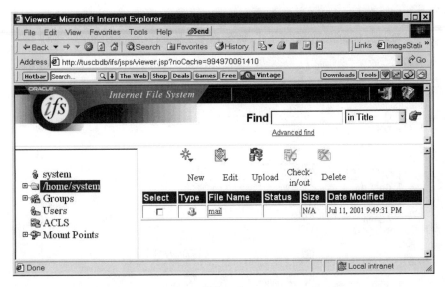

IFS provides a powerful Web-based interface. As you can see, you can administer users, groups, access control lists (ACLs), mount points, e-mail, and more. The icons across the top of the right frame (new, edit, upload, check-in/out, and delete) are context-sensitive. When I click on the word "users" in the left frame, the right frame shows a list of users, shown in the following illustration. When I click the New icon, a drop-down menu appears, enabling me to add a new user (other options are grayed out or unavailable).

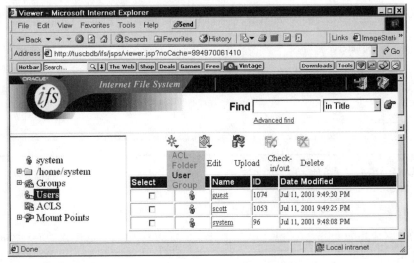

If I choose to add a new user, a page similar to Figure 18-4 displays. Creating a new user is as simple as filling in the blanks on this page (password, home directory, and so forth). Choose the groups in which to include this user and you create a new IFS user.

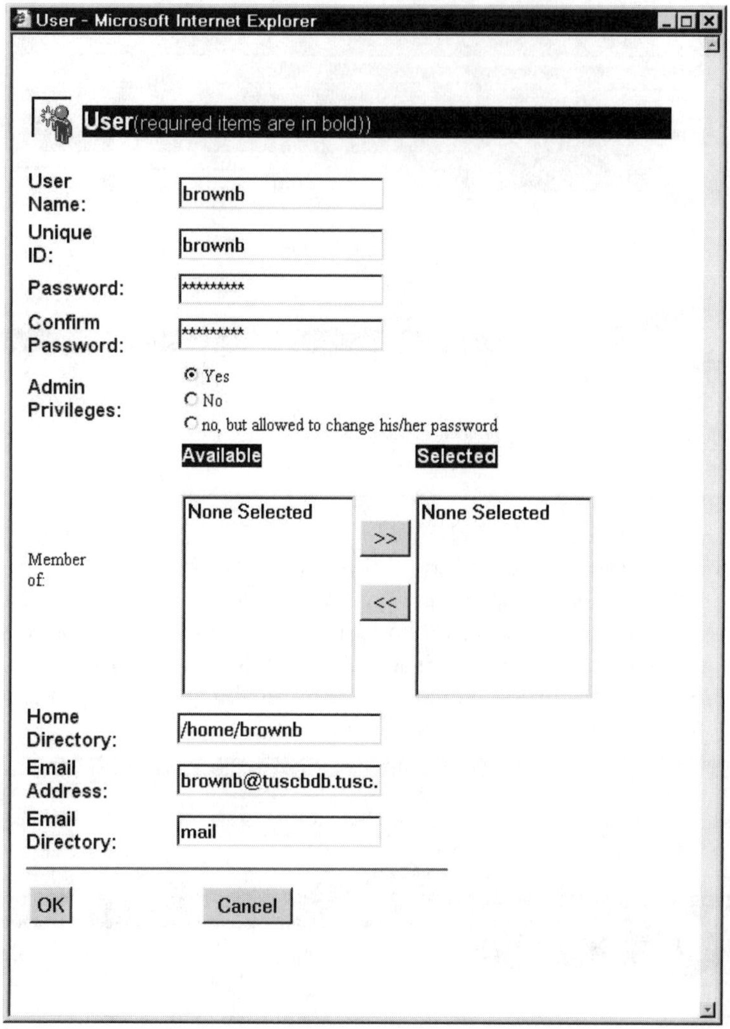

FIGURE 18-4. *Add a new user*

After creating a new user (brownb), I logged out of the IFS system account and immediately logged back in as brownb. I then clicked Upload via Browse (see the following illustration). As you can see, you can also drag-and-drop files through this browser interface.

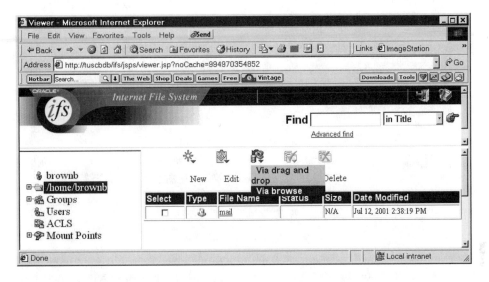

The following window shows some of the options available when you upload a file. I chose a file to upload and selected Parse File on Upload. When you click Browse, the browser enables you to select a file from the client O/S, which I did, and then I clicked Upload File.

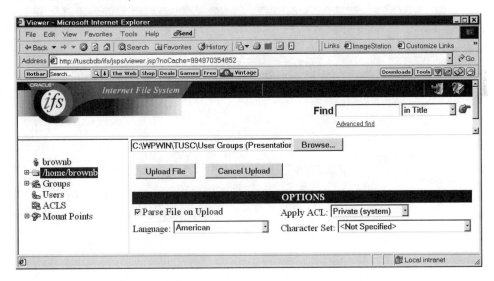

After the file was uploaded, it appears in my list (shown next). As with any file system, if I click the file (the Word documentation, in this example), it comes up right in the browser!

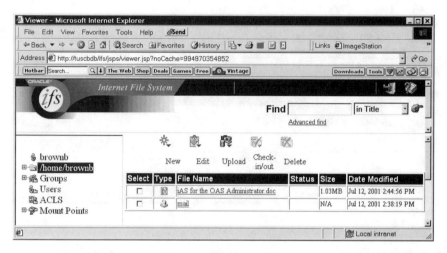

You may have noticed the Check-in/out icon. IFS is a smart file system because it enables you not only to store a file within IFS, but it also lets you maintain separate versions of a file. To use this feature, I first selected my Word document by clicking in the Select check box, and then clicking Check-in/out as you can see in Figure 18-5. To make this a versioned document, I clicked Make Versioned.

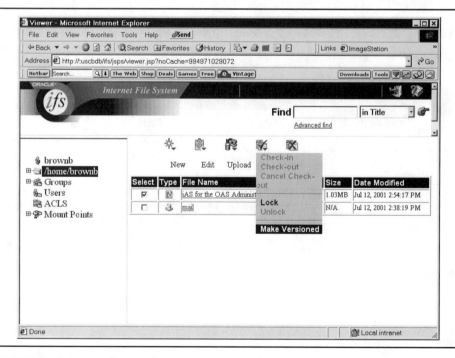

FIGURE 18-5. *Making a document versioned*

For each version of a document, you can type a comment to be stored in the database, as shown here:

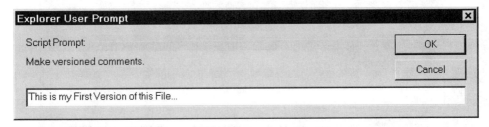

After making the document version, when you select it, you can then check the file out as demonstrated in Figure 18-6.

Once a file is checked out, its status changes to checked out, and a comment is attached to the checkout to indicate who checked the file out as you can see in the hint text in Figure 18-7.

As you continue using IFS through the browser, you see how powerful IFS is. I checked my Word document back into IFS. IFS enables me to view the history (under the Edit menu) for any file as shown in Figure 18-8.

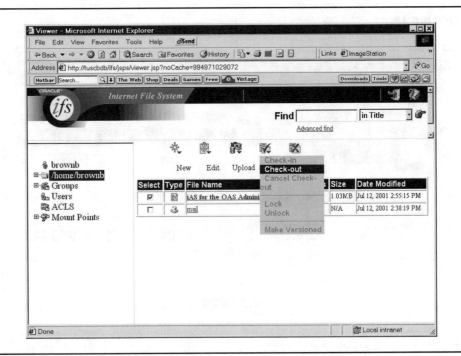

FIGURE 18-6. *Checking out the file*

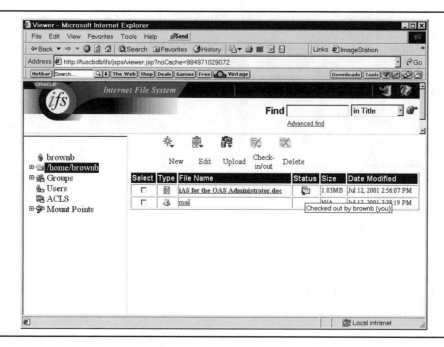

FIGURE 18-8. *The Changed status of the file*

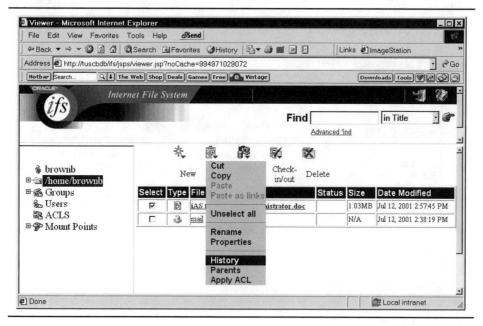

FIGURE 18-7. *Choosing View History*

When I view the history for a document, I can see the date and time the file was uploaded into the database, as well as the comments I typed during check in and check out as shown in Figure 18-9.

If you don't specify any comments, IFS fills in comments for you.

Accessing IFS from the Network Neighborhood

After I started IFS as previously described, I went to the Network Neighborhood on my machine and saw IFS as if it were another file system on my Network—amazing! I could even access this "IFS machine" from any machine on my network. As you can see in Figure 18-10, it's right there in broad daylight, showing the available amount of disk space and the home, IFS, and public directories. I was also impressed to see the index.html page there. This page shows the documentation for accessing the IFS.

I can access this file system, just like any other file system.

Install the Plug-in for Windows

If you drill through the directories, you find the \ifs\winui\install directory. This directory has the setup files needed to install the Windows UI (user interface) component. From this directory, simply run the setup.exe, which is a standard Windows installation. First, you need to pick a language. Next, the InstallShield

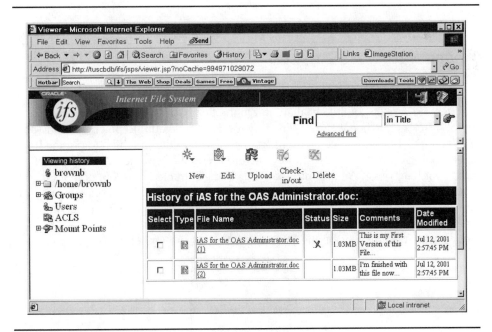

FIGURE 18-9. *History*

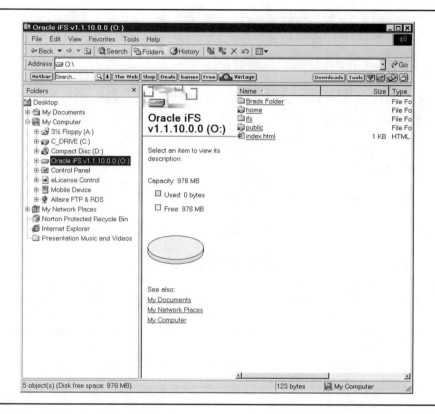

FIGURE 18-10. *IFS as a file system*

software analyzes your system. Once this is complete, InstallShield guides you through the six steps of the installation. On the first page, no input is required, so simply click next. Then, select a directory (or use the default) to place this software into your PC. In the next step, you need to choose a folder in which to put the IFS client tool. During the final step, the software is copied from the CAB files on IFS onto your hard drive. All this information is being extracted right out of IFS! Once you finish with the installation, you need to restart your machine. I once heard that the goal of Windows 2000 was you would never have to restart your machine. I guess that goal was dropped at some point, wasn't it?) After rebooting, you'll notice some new options on the Programs menu, as shown here:

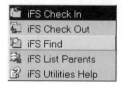

For these new options to work, you first must mount an IFS drive on your machine. You can also do this directly through the interface. If you're running IFS on the same machine on which you're testing the client UI, remember also to restart the IFS server after you reboot.

You can use these options (in the Windows plug-in) to check files in and out of IFS.

Managing the IFS Drive

By default, IFS is a shared drive, which is called *root*. You may want to add a comment for the shared drive.

By default, everyone has full privileges for this drive. You might want to change this for your environment. The default caching level is set to manual. You may want to change this, too. If you don't like the default mount name (root) for IFS, you can create a new shared directory.

Go to another computer on the network and access the machine. Through the Web interface, you can upload and download files into the public folder.

Summary

IFS is a powerful tool that enables you not only to share files (like any file system does), but also to add version control and a Web interface for the file system. These are powerful features. IFS also includes a huge array of APIs to enable you to write your own software interface to IFS. The IFS truly puts power at your fingertips!

CHAPTER
19

Web and Database
Caching

he use of various caching methods is an important part of developing responsive Web applications. The goal of caching is simple: reduce latency and minimize network traffic by filling a request for an object (such as a Web page) with an existing cached copy of the object, if a suitable copy is available. By reusing the existing copy to satisfy the request, less traffic is generated on the network, and resources on the various Web, database, and application servers aren't required to re-create the page. The end results are that the requested object is returned to the client more quickly and, because there are fewer timeouts, an overall increase occurs in reliability and performance.

The overwhelming success of the World Wide Web's architecture and the ever-increasing number of e-business Web sites has resulted in heavy volumes of network traffic and high demands on Web and database servers. Consequently, browsing the Internet is often referred to as the World Wide Wait. Several caching techniques have been incorporated into each link within the request/response chain, where a browser requests an object from a Web server, and the server responds to the client with the requested object. These caching techniques aim to eliminate the need to send requests if the object exists in a local nonshared cache. They also reduce the number of requests to the origin server for objects available in shared caches.

Your application may be using one or more forms of caching and you might not even know it. While caching plays an important role in developing responsive Web-based applications, it can also be a thorn in the side of programmers developing applications that create dynamic Web pages. In this chapter, you learn about the various types of available caching and how to get the most out of caching, while ensuring that pages returned to end users contain accurate information. In addition, you learn about the Oracle9iAS Web Cache and Database Cache products to assist you in maximizing application performance.

TIP

A precursor to Web Cache was the Web Publishing Assistant (WPA), which is no longer available—the product is considered obsolete. The last release of the product came with the 8.1.5 database. WPA was a powerful tool that enabled developers to create static versions of dynamic content on a scheduled basis. WPA is outdated and limiting because it isn't "live" data. Additionally, WPA had some Y2K issues. The product came out back when accessing tables in the database and displaying to the Web was new. Now, there's so much more technology and better ways exist to do the same thing.

This chapter discusses the following topics:

- What is a cache?
- Types of caches
- Advantages of caching
- Disadvantages of caching
- How to configure caching within a browser
- How to control caching from your applications
- Oracle9*i*AS Web Cache, including Edge Side Includes (ESI)
- Oracle9*i*AS Database Cache

What Is a Cache?

In general terms, a *cache* is a hiding place to store valuables, provisions, arms, and so forth. Extrapolating this concept to application development, a *cache* is an area of storage existing "behind the scenes," which is used to store copies of previously requested objects that can be quickly accessed when needed.

Caches are placed at various locations along the request/response chain, including Web browsers, proxy servers, Application servers, and database servers. In general, any data created by a server that can be reused to satisfy future requests by the same client or other clients is eligible for storage within a cache.

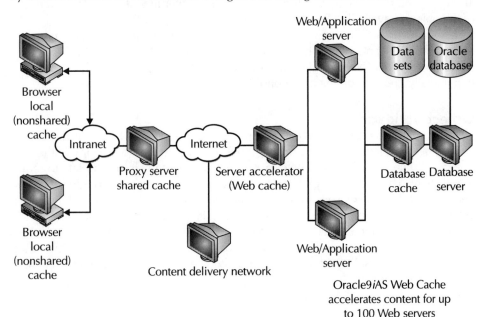

In this chapter, with the exception of the Oracle9iAS Database Cache section, *cached objects* consist of files returned from a Web server, such as HTML documents and images.

Cache Rules

Caches use a set of rules to determine how to handle requests for objects. The rules define if the cache is allowed to store a copy of a requested object, if a cached copy of a requested object is suitable to return to the client, or if the client's request cannot be satisfied by the cache. Requests that cannot be satisfied by the cache are forwarded to the origin server. If the cached object satisfies the client request, the request is a "hit," otherwise the request is a "miss." Cache effectiveness is measured by the ratio of the number of hits to the number of requests.

The two main methods of determining if a cached copy can be returned to the client without first checking with the origin server are expiration and validation.

Object Expiration

The origin server, or the application dynamically creating a Web page, can define the life of an object stored in a cache. The object might contain the expiration date and time, the time the client last accessed the object, or the time the object was modified on the server. Objects that haven't reached the expiration date are considered "fresh" and can be returned to the client without checking with the origin server. Objects requested after the expiration date are considered "stale" and the cache must check with the origin server to determine if an updated version of the object is available.

Expiration dates are useful for objects that have a known lifetime, such as images or static content, which are updated on a periodic basis. With Web-based applications, however, portions of the requested pages frequently contain dynamically created content and, consequently, should expire immediately.

Object Validation

An object that has exceeded its expiration date may or may not be the most current version of the object. The cache must, therefore, validate the stored copy of the object with the origin server to determine if the cached copy is appropriate to return to the client. The cache can perform a conditional request from the origin server to determine if the server's version of the requested object is different from the cached version. This is accomplished by issuing either a HEAD or GET request with the If-Modified-Since parameter as defined in the HTTP/1.1 specification.

The origin server responds to the conditional request with either a response that the cached copy is still valid or with the updated version of the object if the cached copy is no longer valid.

Types of Caches

Because any type of information that's eligible for reuse to satisfy future requests is cacheable, caches can exist anywhere along the request/response chain between the client and the server. In the effort to use the various network and server resources efficiently, several different types of caches were developed.

The different types of caches discussed in this chapter include Web caches, both nonshared local caches and shared proxy caches, content delivery networks, server accelerators, and database caches.

Web Caches

Web caches are a method of storing copies of objects transmitted over the Internet, such as HTML documents and images. In terms of the Web, the client is usually a browser, such as Microsoft's Internet Explorer or Netscape. Origin servers are usually a Web server, such as Apache, iPlanet, Microsoft's Internet Information Server, or Netscape Enterprise Server. A cache can exist anywhere between the browser and the Web server where it can intercept HTTP requests.

Nonshared Local Caches

Current versions of most Web browsers provide a method of caching objects on the local computer in an area known as a *nonshared cache* or *browser cache*. If a copy of a requested object exists in a local cache, the request is serviced almost immediately because no need exists to transmit the request over the network. The local cache is useful when a Web site contains the same graphics on many of the pages.

Users can customize the cache settings specific to their computers. Customizable options include the amount of disk space to dedicate for caching purposes, the location of the local cache, and when the browser should look for objects stored locally, instead of sending the request to the Web server. You, as a developer, should remember users have control of the local cache and can direct the browser always to use cached pages. This can result in users viewing a stale copy of a dynamically created Web page containing information that's no longer valid.

As an example, consider a banking application where users can transfer funds between accounts. Users select the accounts and the amount to transfer, and then click the Submit button to send the request to the server. The application program processes the transfer and returns a confirmation page to the browser. If the funds transfer page was cacheable, users can inadvertently resubmit the transfer request by simply clicking the Back button, and then clicking the Submit button again.

This example illustrates how important identifying the Web pages and objects that shouldn't be cached by the browser, and using the appropriate directives to inhibit the browser from displaying an obsolete page are when you develop Web-based applications.

Most browsers support a history mechanism to enable users to return to a recently viewed page quickly. Although history mechanisms and caches perform similar functions and may store the pages in the same location, their functionality is different. *Browser history mechanisms* show the page as it existed at the time the page was originally retrieved from the Web server, or possibly a shared cache, and ignore any expiration date. Caches, on the other hand, show a semantically transparent view of the requested page, so a page from the cache appears the same as if the Web server returned the object itself.

Internet Explorer   Within Internet Explorer 5.5, the local cache is stored in the Temporary Internet Files directory. This directory is also used to view Web pages offline and was known as "subscribing" in prior versions of Internet Explorer.

To access the cache settings, users select the Internet Options menu item in the Tools menu. The cache settings are located on the General tab in the Temporary Internet Files section, as shown in Figure 19-1. Users can remove all files from the cache by clicking the Delete Files button or configure the cache by clicking the Settings button.

Users can configure Internet Explorer's behavior for when to retrieve pages from the cache by selecting the appropriate radio button in the Check for newer version of stored pages section. Setting choices, as seen in Figure 19-2, are as follows:

- **Every visit to the page**   Bypass the local cache and always request an updated copy of the page from the Web server or a shared cache.

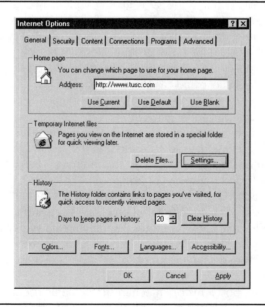

FIGURE 19-1.   *Internet Explorer—Internet Options*

- **Every time you start Internet Explorer**   Until you close the browser, Web content is only retrieved from the server for the first visit to a page within a session. If users request a page previously requested in the same session, the cached copy of the page is returned without requesting a new page from the Web server. This was the default option in Internet Explorer 4.

- **Automatic**   The Automatic option was first introduced in Internet Explorer 5 as the new default option. This option functions the same as the Every time you start Internet Explorer option, except in the way the browser handles cached images. The browser analyzes whether an image is changing over time and, if the image appears static, the browser checks less and less frequently for a newer version of the image. The cached image is returned even if the page content itself is updated regularly, resulting in reduced latency for dynamically generated pages.

- **Never**   The Never option specifies the browser always displays a cached copy of the page, if available. This option returns Web pages in the shortest amount of time, but can result in users viewing stale content.

Two methods refresh the current Web page:

- Press F5 or CTRL-R, or click the Refresh button to refresh the current page only if the timestamp on the local copy of the page is different from the timestamp on the server.

- Press CTRL-F5, or hold down the CTRL key while clicking the Refresh button to refresh the current page even if the timestamps on the local copy and the

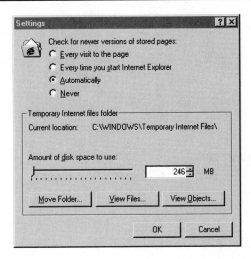

FIGURE 19-2.   *Internet Explorer—temporary Internet files settings*

Web server copy of the page match. This is useful when developing Web-based applications. During development, be sure to hold the CTRL key during refresh to ensure the requested page is re-created by the application and you aren't viewing a cached copy.

Netscape   To access the cache settings using Netscape 6, users select the Preferences menu item in the Edit menu. Then expand the Advanced branch and click the Cache menu item to view the settings. Similar to Internet Explorer, users can specify the size and the location of the cache, and configure the browser behavior regarding when to return cached items. Unlike Internet Explorer, however, users can also configure the size of the memory cache.

Users can configure Netscape's behavior on when to retrieve pages from the cache by selecting the appropriate radio button in the Compare the page in the cache to the page on the network: section. Setting choices, as shown in Figure 19-3, are the following:

- **Once per session**   Similar to the Every time you start Internet Explorer option in Internet Explorer, the first time each page is requested by a user, the request is sent to the Web server. Subsequent requests for the same

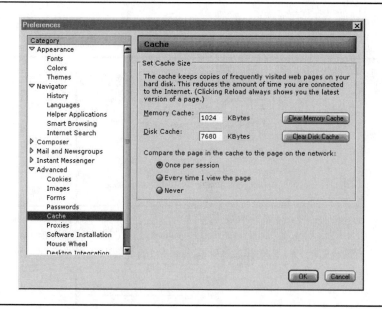

FIGURE 19-3.   *Netscape—Cache Preferences*

page during the duration of the session are fulfilled using the cached copy. This is the default option.

■ **Every time I view the page**   Similar to the Every visit to the page option in Internet Explorer, pages are always requested from the Web server and never retrieved from the cache.

■ **Never**   Similar to the Never option in Internet Explorer, pages are always retrieved from the cache if available and may result in stale content being returned.

Like Internet Explorer, two methods refresh the current page:

■ Click the Reload button to refresh the current page only if the timestamp on the local copy of the page is different from the timestamp on the server.

■ Press the SHIFT key (the OPTION key on Macintosh) while clicking the Reload button to force the browser to retrieve the page from the Web server, even if the timestamp of the cached copy is the same as the timestamp on the Web server.

Proxy Caches
Proxy caches perform a function similar to browser caches, except a proxy cache is a shared cache that serves many clients. Each browser within a network is configured to direct all requests to the proxy cache, rather than directly to the requested Web server. The proxy cache either returns the requested page to the client or forwards the request to the Web server.

Older versions of Web browsers required users to enter the proxy cache address information, but current versions of the popular Web browsers automatically locate the proxy cache and no longer require manual configuration.

Proxy caches, also called proxy servers, are useful as firewalls in enterprise intranets because only the proxy cache actually connects to the Internet provider. Many ISPs, such as America Online (AOL) use proxy servers. AOL's use of proxy servers reduces its need to go to the Internet for content. Accessing the proxy servers allows it to service the content directly from within its own network.

Content Delivery Network
Content delivery network (CDN) services provide a method of offloading static content to separate Web servers. CDN service providers install Web servers at strategic geographic locations at the "edge" of the Internet to reduce the number of network hops required to deliver the content to a large group of users. Moving these objects to the CDN service provider's server removes the burden of having to respond to these resource-intensive requests from the organization's Web server.

The Web pages are simply updated to modify the source attribute (`src`) within the `<IMG>` and `<EMBED>` tags to the new location within the CDN service's domain. For example:

```
<!-- Base URL is www.localdomain.com -->
<HTML>
<HEAD><TITLE>CDN Example</TITLE></HEAD>
<BODY>
<!-- Local content -->
<IMG src="smalldynamic.jpg" alt="small, dynamic image">
<!-- Content served by a CDN -->
<IMG src="http://www.cdndomain.com/largestatic.jpg"
     alt="large, static image">
</BODY>
</HTML>
```

Server Accelerators

Server accelerators provide a method of deploying a cache server, also known as a *reverse proxy server,* which is dedicated to caching content for a specific set of Web servers. Unlike a proxy cache that caches objects from any Web server for a specific set of browsers, a server accelerator is dedicated to caching objects for one or more specific Web servers.

A server accelerator intercepts browser object requests for Web servers managed by the server accelerator. If the server accelerator contains a fresh copy of the requested object, the server accelerator responds directly to the request, thereby saving resources on the Web server. Similar to a proxy cache, if the server accelerator doesn't contain a fresh copy of the requested object, the request is forwarded to the Web server. The Oracle9iAS Web Cache is a type of server accelerator.

Database Caches

Many database management systems use internal caching schemes to store data and query plans for recently processed queries. For example, Oracle uses the Library Cache within the Shared Pool and the Database Buffer Cache to process identical queries quickly.

Some database vendors have developed products to create a separate cache of data that's frequently requested, but infrequently updated. One such product is the *Oracle9iAS Database Cache,* which contains copies of tables the administrator chose to include in the cache, along with recently processed queries accessing the cached tables. If a query is submitted to the database and it exists in the Database Cache, the result set is retrieved using the cached data instead of sending the query to the database. Because the database wasn't needed to check the syntax and parse the query, the result set is returned more quickly to the user. Changes to the data in the cache are periodically updated using a schedule defined by the administrator. The administrator can also define an expiration date for the data during which time the cached data can be used to satisfy queries even if it's no longer current.

Advantages and Disadvantages of Caching

The complexities involved in implementing a useful caching scheme would be worthless if a significant performance benefit didn't exist. As with most complex solutions, though, caching has pros and cons to consider when developing Web-based applications.

Advantages of Using a Cache

The main advantage of using a cache is performance improvements in terms of reduced latency, reduced network traffic, and reduced loads on Web servers. In short, users requesting a page receive a quicker response.

Without the benefits of caching, the Web would be much slower and less reliable, and server administrators would be constantly configuring new hardware to keep up with demand. Sites with popular content would be overloaded with requests and network traffic would be more congested, resulting in users experiencing timeouts and streaming content delivered at slower rates.

Disadvantages of Using a Cache

The main disadvantage of using a cache is the possibility that users will receive a stale copy of a requested page. When writing an application that generates dynamic Web pages, including the appropriate HTTP headers within the pages is extremely important to ensure they're cached, or not cached, according to the application's requirements.

Another disadvantage of using a cache is a cache now services requests instead of the Web server that originally created the page, so the Web server is no longer able to maintain accurate statistics on the site use. One solution to this issue is to include a small image, such as a one-by-one clear pixel that isn't cacheable, forcing all requests for the image to be serviced directly from the Web server—if statistics are that critical for your site.

The third disadvantage of caching is the caches contain copies of pages requested by clients, which could be an invasion of privacy. Cache administrators must take reasonable steps to ensure the cache contents and logs aren't available for viewing by unauthorized persons. Users should also remember to delete the contents of the browser cache, as well as the contents of the history mechanism when they'll no longer be using the browser.

How to Control Caching from Your Applications

The caching rules for each Web page are contained in the HTTP headers and, on older browsers, within the heading section of an HTML document. The HTTP/1.1 specification provides several elements to cache the pages of your application effectively. These elements include eliminating the need to send requests to the server if the cached copy of the page isn't expired and eliminating the need for a server to send a full response if a cached page is still valid.

META Tags in the HEAD Section

Older versions of the popular browsers supported the use of <META> tags within the heading section of an HTML document to specify particular HTTP headers. For example,

```
<HEAD>
<META HTTP-EQUIV="Pragma"  CONTENT="no-cache">
<META HTTP-EQUIV="Expires" CONTENT="-1">
</HEAD>
```

Note the use of -1 for the value of the Expires parameter. This value is an invalid date and, consequently, the browser would treat the page as noncacheable because it didn't have a valid expiration date.

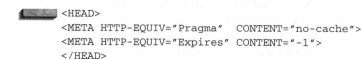

TIP

Develop your own no_cache PL/SQL procedure or noCache Java class. This program would be referenced by all your pages that shouldn't be cached by any (or specific) cache servers.

Newer versions of Web browsers usually ignore these tags and the pages end up in a cache, so the use of the HTTP headers is the preferred method of controlling caching for a Web page. If your Web server isn't HTTP/1.1-compliant, however, you should still include the no-cache pragma whenever you include the Cache-Control HTTP header directive (discussed in the next section) with a no-cache parameter for backward-compatibility.

HTTP Headers

Web servers usually generate cache-control directives in the HTTP headers, but many application development tools let programmers specify their own directives.

All date and time values in the HTTP headers must be in Greenwich Mean Time (GMT), which, for purposes of HTTP, is equal to Coordinated Universal Time (UTC). HTTP/1.1 defines three date formats, which all HTTP/1.1 clients and servers must accept, but these clients and servers can only generate one of the three formats as defined in RFC 1123. When specifying dates in the HTTP headers, therefore, always use the following full-date format:

```
wkday, dd month yyyy hh:mi:ss GMT
```

Component	Valid Values
wkday	Mon, Tue, Wed, Thu, Fri, Sat, Sun
dd	two-digit day (01-31)
month	Jan, Feb, Mar, Apr, May, Jun, Jul, Aug, Sep, Oct, Nov, Dec
yyyy	four-digit year
hh	two-digit hour in 24-hour format (00-23)
mi	two-digit minute (00-59)
ss	two-digit second (00-59)

To reuse the example in the HTTP/1.1 specification

```
Sun, 06 Nov 1994 08:49:37 GMT
```

Refer to Chapter 10 for more information about setting headers at the 9*i*AS configuration level—such as for AOL.

Viewing the Page Headers

HTTP headers are a key component of controlling caching and are of particular interest when writing Web applications. Even though the headers are located at the top of a Web document, the headers don't appear when you view the page source in the Web browser.

Netscape provides the value of the Last-Modified header when users select the Page Info menu item in the Edit menu, but users cannot view the other headers. Internet Explorer doesn't provide a means of viewing any of the page headers.

Developers view the headers using a telnet application to simulate a Web browser requesting a page. For example, to retrieve an unsecured HTTP document from the **www.tusc.com** Web site on the default port 80 (making sure to specify the HTTP port instead of the default telnet port 23), type the following commands from the command prompt:

```
telnet www.tusc.com 80
GET /index.html HTTP/1.1[RETURN]
Host:  www.tusc.com[RETURN] [RETURN]
```

Note, the Web server must be specified following the `Host:` request-header field per section 14.23 of HTTP/1.1 specification. If you leave this information out of your request, the request will fail.

The server returns the entire requested object with the HTTP headers at the top, separated by a blank line before the HTML source. Make sure you turn on spooling to capture the output of the Web page. Other headers not related to caching might be included in the response, all of which are defined in the HTTP/1.1 specification.

```
HTTP/1.1 200 OK
Date: Wed, 13 Jun 2001 17:12:00 GMT
Server: Apache/1.3.3 (Unix) FrontPage/4.0.4.3
Last-modified: Wed, 13 Jun 2001 17:12:00 GMT
Expires: Wed, 13 Jun 2001 17:13:00 GMT
Cache-control: private,max-age=60
ETag: "2c012-3f73-3b27711c"
Content-Length: 16243
Content-Type: text/html

<HTML>
...
```

All HTTP/1.1-compliant Web servers are required to send a `Date` header with each response to indicate the date and time the response was generated. Try this against your own servers to see the variety of HTTP headers that get retrieved for PL/SQL, Java, or static HTML.

Expires

The `Expires` header contains the date and time the cached page becomes stale. Local and proxy caches shouldn't return a stale page to a browser without first checking with the Web server—or with another proxy cache that has a more current copy of the page—to validate the cached copy of the page.

Note, the `maxage` parameter of the `Cache-Control` header performs similar functionality to the `Expires` header and, if present, overrides the value of the `Expires` header.

Cache-Control

The `Cache-Control` header, introduced in the HTTP/1.1 specification, provides several parameters to control how caches handle Web pages. All HTTP/1.1-compliant caching mechanisms in the request-response chain are required to obey the parameters included in the `Cache-Control` header. HTTP/1.0 caches might not recognize and, therefore, might ignore these directives, however. You can include more than one parameter in the `Cache-Control` header by separating the parameters by commas.

The following are some of the common parameters used with the `Cache-Control` header.

public, private, or no-cache   One of three following parameters can be included to determine which type of caches can save a copy of the object:

- **public**   The page can be cached by any cache, even if it isn't normally cacheable (that is, the `Authorization` header is included).

- **private**   The page can not be cached by a shared cache, but a local cache can cache the page.

- **no-cache**   The cache must revalidate the page with the origin server before returning the page to the client. This parameter doesn't mean the page isn't cacheable; it means the server must validate the cache is current before sending it to the browser (or before first retrieving it from the origin server).

no-store   The `no-store` parameter directs that no cache, either local or shared, can cache the page. History mechanisms can still store the page (that is, users can set their nonshared/browser cache to Never).

s-maxage, max-age, must-revalidate, proxy-revalidate

- **s-maxage**   Contains the number of seconds a copy of a page in a shared cache (but not a local cache) is considered fresh. This value overrides the value of the `Expires` header or the `max-age` parameter for a shared cache.

- **max-age**   Contains the number of seconds a copy of a page is considered fresh from any caches. You can set `max-age=0` to force all caches to revalidate their copies of the page.

- **must-revalidate**   Because caches can be configured to ignore expiration dates on Web pages, you can use the `must-revalidate` parameter to force all caches to validate the cached copy with the Web server to determine if the cached copy is still fresh.

- **proxy-revalidate**   The `proxy-revalidate` parameter provides the same functionality as the `must-revalidate` parameter, except it only applies to shared caches.

You can use the `proxy-revalidate` parameter with the `public` parameter as a method of caching pages that require authentication.

Cache Validators

If a cache contains an object it wants to validate to ensure it's still fresh, the cache uses certain HTTP headers called validators. *Cache validators* contain information that can be used to compare a specific Web server's page information. The HTTP header validators are usually generated by the Web server, and not by a Web application.

Responses that don't contain validators are still cacheable, but responses without validators have no information to perform a conditional retrieval from the Web server and cannot be refreshed once they expire.

Last-Modified   The `Last-Modified` validator contains the date and time the server determines the object was last modified. This value can be used to determine if the Web server's copy of the same object has been modified since it was sent to the browser.

Entity Tag (ETag)   An *ETag validator* is a server-generated value that's unique every time a server generates a new copy of a page. If a cache contains a current copy of a Web page, the ETag can be used when comparing pages when the one-second granularity limitation of the `Last-Modified` validator might be insufficient.

Oracle9*i*AS Web Cache

Many of the server-side caching products available today are designed to cache static content. These products separate a Web site's content generation mechanism from the content delivery mechanism and decrease the demands on the Web server by offloading the burden of returning frequently requested pages. With the rapidly increasing number of new Web applications, however, more and more of the HTML pages are built dynamically to satisfy specific requests and these products are not well suited to caching the custom-built pages.

As more transactions are conducted using the e-business model, Web sites must keep up with the increasing demands on their server and database resources. One solution is to add Application servers to continue to meet the growing demand. This can become an expensive solution, however, that isn't acceptable for a business searching for ways to control costs (that is, everyone on the planet today). A more cost-effective solution is to use a Web cache that can service dynamic content. The Oracle9*i*AS Web Cache, included as part of the Oracle9*i* Application Server Enterprise Edition, provides a server-side caching solution for dynamic content.

Dynamic Content Generation Overview

The addition of the Common Gateway Interface (CGI) extended the functionality of Web servers by allowing a browser to request a page from a Web server where the URL consists of a program name and parameters. The Web server passes control to the requested program that creates the dynamic page to return to the browser.

The requested program is frequently executed using an Application server and a database server manages the data used to construct the Web page dynamically. Any or all of the servers required to complete the request (Web, Application, and database) might reside on the same or different physical servers. Installing multiple servers on the same computer could lead to resource contention, but installing the servers on separate computers requires additional overhead for the time to transfer the data over the network.

TIP
If you put the Web Cache on the same server as the Database server, don't cache the static content (that is, HTML, GIF, JPG) unless you have large files that compression will help—only cache dynamic content, such as PL/SQL and JavaServer Pages, so it's not regenerated unnecessarily.

Once the dynamic page is returned to the browser, the browser initiates requests to retrieve any static objects on the page, such as images. If the browser has previously retrieved the same static objects, these objects might already exist in the local cache.

Dynamic Caching and Oracle Web Cache

In some ways, the requirements for caching dynamic content are similar to the requirements of caching static content. For example, caches that service dynamic content are also able to service static content. Caches servicing dynamic content have several unique requirements to ensure the cache is returning fresh content within acceptable response times.

Keeping the Cached Content Current

Similar to setting expiration dates on static content, caches servicing dynamic content must have a mechanism to keep the contents in the cache consistent with the contents in the database. Pages returned by the cache should appear the same as if the application program created the page itself using live data, or data that's sufficiently current (as defined by the administrator).

Whenever the data used to create a cached page is modified in the database, the Oracle Web Cache uses mechanisms to invalidate and refresh the cached content. If the data changes occur faster than the Oracle Web Cache can apply the updates, the administrator defines the amount of time, and optionally, a priority level that stale content can be returned to the browser, if at all. For a small number of updates, the changes are typically applied incrementally. For a large number of updates, however, the invalidation mechanism can process multiple cached pages at once. The Oracle Web Cache uses a combination of expiration policies and HTTP invalidation requests to manage the cached contents.

Cacheability Rules and Content Awareness

Like other caches, the Oracle Web Cache uses cacheability rules to determine if it's allowed to cache a page. The administrator defines cacheability rules based on information stored in the HTTP request headers, cookies, or parameters passed on the URL. Each different value of a header, cookie, or URL parameter is stored as a separate document within the cache. The supported HTTP request headers are `Accept`, `Accept-Charset`, `Accept-Encoding`, `Accept-Language`, and `User-Agent`. The Oracle Web Cache doesn't interpret the value of the header fields, but simply creates a separate cached entry for each different value of each supported header. Of course, browsers can be configured not to accept cookies. When a cacheability rule is based on the value of a cookie, you can specify whether to cache a copy of the document if no cookie is available.

Because HTTP is a stateless protocol, the Oracle Web Cache uses unique session identifiers to maintain the session state. Session information can either be stored in cookies or passed on the URL. If the session identifier is stored in a cookie, these session cookies are treated differently than cookies used to pass parameter values. When a page is cached based on a rule using a cookie, a separate page is stored in the cache for each unique cookie value. If the cookie is a session identifier, though, a single copy of a page can be stored in the cache, regardless of the value of the session identifier cookie.

Even the dynamically created cached content can itself be dynamic. By using in-cache personalization, you can embed special tags within an HTML page that are only recognized by the Oracle Web Cache. These tags are replaced with the associated session parameter values before returning the page to the browser. Personalized attributes are placed between any valid HTML tag pair that has a corresponding open and closing tag, such as <P> and </P>, within the <!-- WEBCACHETAG="*session parameter*" --> and <!-- WEBCACHEEND --> (note the space after <!--) tags. The administrator maps session parameters to specific URL parameters or cookies.

Load Balancing and Surge Protection

Because most Web sites use multiple Application Web servers to distribute the load of servicing HTTP requests, the Oracle Web Cache supports load balancing for up to 100 Application servers. If load balancing is in place, the Oracle Web Cache supports session "stickiness" by allowing requests from a single browser to be serviced by the same Application Web server to ensure the integrity of a transaction. The administrator defines the number of concurrent requests each Application Web server can handle.

If an Application Web server stops responding to requests, the Oracle Web Cache provides a failover mechanism. An Application server that hasn't responded to five continuous requests (failover threshold) is considered to have failed and the load on the responding Application servers is rebalanced. The failed server is polled every 10 seconds (60 seconds in version 1.0.2.1), known as the *polling interval,* to determine when it's once again responding to requests. The failover threshold and polling interval values are the default values, and are customizable by the administrator.

Deploying Oracle Web Cache

The *Oracle Web Cache Administration and Deployment Guide* details several different methods of configuring the Oracle Web Cache in relation to *i*AS. This section outlines several of the possible methods.

One Application Server

In the simplest case, you can deploy the Oracle Web Cache on the same node as the Web server. In this scenario, both the Web Cache and the Web server have the same host name.

The Oracle Web Cache can reside on a separate server from the Web server, as seen in Figure 19-4. In this scenario, the domain name is registered to the IP address of the Oracle Web Cache. All requests, therefore, are sent to the Oracle Web Cache. The Web server is given an internal name, possibly with a unique number, if the Oracle Web Cache is servicing many Web servers.

Using a Transport Layer Switch to Forward HTTPS Requests

As of version 1.0.2.2, Oracle Web Cache cannot cache secure requests sent using the HTTPS protocol. You can, however, use a Layer 4 (Transport) switch to route secure requests directly to the Web server, as shown in Figure 19-5. In this scenario, the domain name is registered to the IP address of the L4 switch and the Oracle Web Cache is set up with an internal name similar to the Application Web server.

Load Balancing Among Application Servers

Most Web sites use multiple Application Web servers on separate computers to increase reliability and distribute the load of servicing incoming requests. The Oracle Web Cache provides the capability to balance the load of requests that

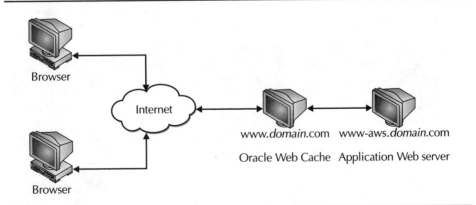

FIGURE 19-4. *Oracle Web Cache and Application Web server on different nodes*

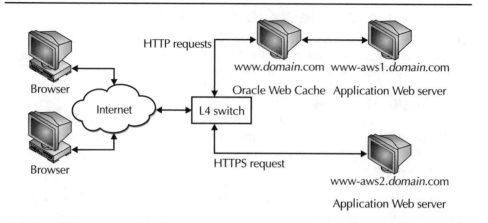

FIGURE 19-5. *Forwarding HTTPS requests not serviced by the Oracle Web Cache*

cannot be serviced by the cache for up to 100 Application Web servers, as shown in Figure 19-6. The administrator defines the weighted load percentage for each Application Web server based on the server's capacity.

If you prefer, you can use a third-party load balancer to distribute the incoming requests among the Application Web servers, as seen in Figure 19-7. The Oracle Web Cache sends all requests it cannot service to the load balancer, which distributes the requests among the Application Web servers.

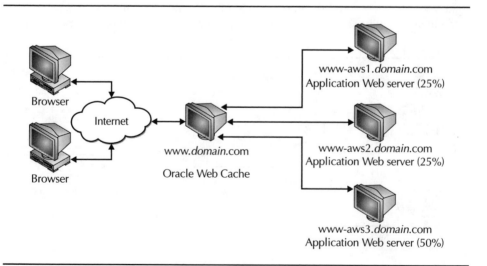

FIGURE 19-6. *Load Balancing using Oracle Web Cache*

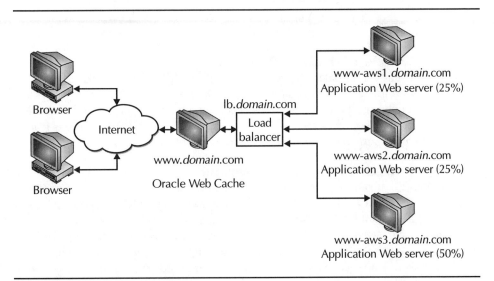

FIGURE 19-7. *Load balancing using a third-party load balancer*

Using an Application Layer Switch

If only a portion of the site's content should be cached, a Layer 7 (Application) switch can be set up to intercept all requests. In this scenario, the IP address of the L7 switch is the registered domain name, as shown in Figure 19-8. The L7 switch

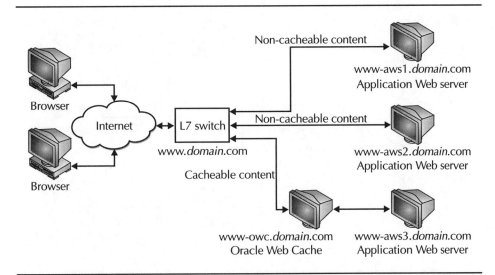

FIGURE 19-8. *Oracle Web Cache servicing a subset of Application Web servers*

can route all requests for cacheable content to the Oracle Web Cache and all requests for noncacheable content directly to the appropriate Web servers.

Multiple Oracle Web Cache Servers

Using a third-party load balancer, you can set up multiple Oracle Web Cache servers, as seen in Figure 19-9. Using multiple Oracle Web Cache servers provides a failover mechanism if one of them fails. The domain name is registered to the IP address of the load balancer and all Oracle Web Cache servers sent requests from the load balancer are configured with the same cacheability rules.

Deploying Inside or Outside a Firewall

Oracle Web Cache can be set up either inside or outside a firewall, as shown in Figure 19-10. If the Oracle Web Cache is deployed inside a firewall, you can ensure that only the Application Web servers have access to the database servers.

If the Oracle Web Cache is deployed outside a firewall, as seen in Figure 19-11, the Oracle Web Cache must send all requests through the firewall and requires additional security to ensure the cached content is secured. This option is considered a higher security risk than placing the Oracle Web Cache inside the firewall.

Distributed Network

Within a *distributed network,* as shown in Figure 19-12, you can deploy an Oracle Web Cache server at several data centers hosting the Web site.

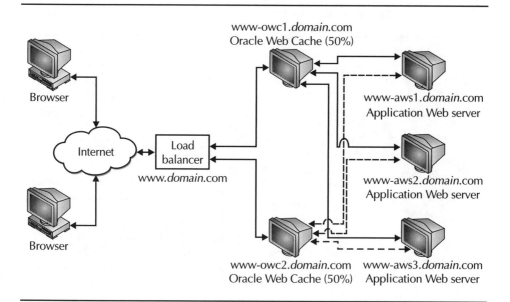

FIGURE 19-9. *Multiple Oracle Web Cache servers*

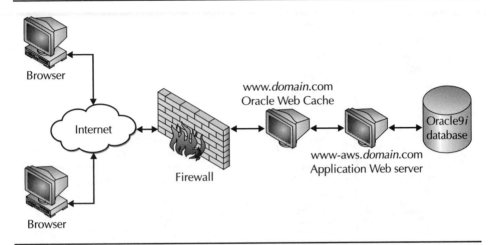

FIGURE 19-10. *Deploying Oracle Web Cache inside a firewall*

If a browser sends a request to a Web site that's hosted at more than one data center, the requested domain name is resolved into the IP address of an authoritative DNS server. Based on information such as the browser's IP address, the topology model, and the loads of the Oracle Web Cache servers within the distributed network, the authoritative DNS server returns the IP address of the selected Oracle Web Cache to the browser.

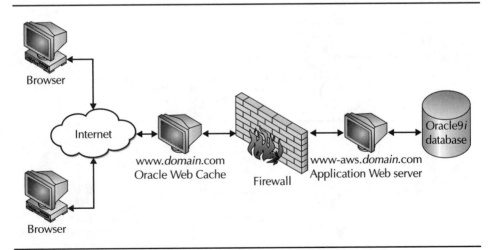

FIGURE 19-11. *Deploying Oracle Web Cache outside a firewall*

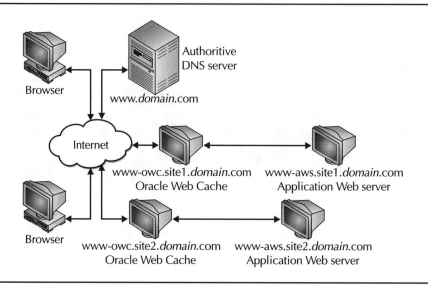

FIGURE 19-12. *Oracle Web Cache within a distributed network*

Within a distributed network, you can also centralize the data source. In this scenario, as seen in Figure 19-13, all the Application Web servers are located at a single data center, although the Oracle Web Cache servers are at separate data centers.

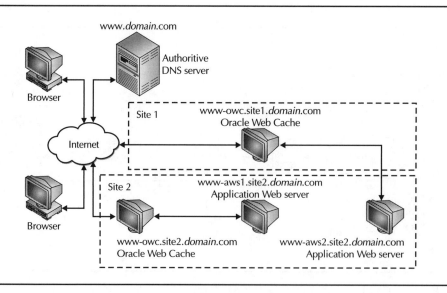

FIGURE 19-13. *Centralized data source within a distributed network*

Administering the Oracle Web Cache

The browser-based Oracle Web Cache Manager tool is used to administer the Oracle Web Cache. The administration server process must be running to use the administration interface. Once the Oracle Web Cache is configured, the cache server process performs the actual caching function. An optional watchdog server process can be started to automatically detect if the Oracle Web Cache fails and to attempt to restart the failed processes.

The `webcachectl` command-line utility is used to start and stop the server processes. If you're running the Oracle Web Cache on Windows NT, you can also start, stop, and view the status of the server processes using the Services window. Once the administration server process is running, you can use the Oracle Web Cache Manager to stop and start the cache process.

The webcachectl Utility

The `webcachectl` utility is used only to administer the server processes and doesn't provide the configuration functions available using the Oracle Web Cache Manager. The `webcachectl` utility is passed as a single parameter. The valid values are start, stop, status, and repair.

- **start** Start the administration and cache processes.

- **stop** Stop the administration and cache processes, and the watchdog process.

- **status** Display messages for the administration, cache, and watchdog processes, showing whether each process is running.

- **repair** Restore the previous version of the configuration. The Oracle Web Cache Manager doesn't provide the same level of consistency checking as the administration process. Consequently, it's possible for the administrator to enter bad configuration values that can prevent the administration process from starting. If this occurs, use `webcachectl repair` to restore the previous version of the configuration.

For example, to start the Oracle Web Cache processes, enter **webcachectl start** at a command prompt.

Starting and Stopping Processes in Windows NT

Within Windows NT, the Oracle Web Cache services have the value of the associated Oracle installation identifier as part of the process names. The administration service is named 'Oracle{ORACLE_HOME_NAME}WebCacheAdmin'; the cache service is named 'Oracle{ORACLE_HOME_NAME}WebCache'; and the watchdog service is named 'Oracle{ORACLE_HOME_NAME}WebCacheMon'. For example, if the Oracle installation home identifier is *i*Suites, the service names, respectively, are OracleiSuitesWebCacheAdmin, OracleiSuitesWebCache, and OracleiSuitesWebCacheMon.

Oracle Web Cache Manager

Once the administration server process is running, start the Oracle Web Cache Manager using your Web browser. For example:

```
http://webcachehost:4000/webcacheadmin
```

When prompted for the administrator ID and password, enter **administrator** for the user ID and the administrator's password. A separate invalidation administrator user named `invalidator` is set up with an initial password of `invalidator`.

From within the Oracle Web Cache Manager, select the desired option on the navigator frame to configure, administer, and monitor the performance of the Oracle Web Cache and the Application Web servers for which it accelerates content delivery. The main categories are:

- Administering Oracle Web Cache

- Administering Web Sites

- Monitoring Oracle Web Cache

- Monitoring Application Web Servers

You need to click Apply Changes after modifying any configuration parameters and restart the cache process.

Administering Oracle Web Cache   The first option within the Administering Oracle Web Cache section, Web Cache Operations, enables the administrator to stop and start the cache process, as shown in Figure 19-14. This doesn't affect the administration process.

The administrator changes the administration port used by the Oracle Web Cache Manager by clicking the Administration Port link, as seen in Figure 19-15. The default value is 4000.

The administrator can also change the invalidation port used to invalidate pages in the cache, and the statistics port used to monitor Oracle Web Cache performance. Both of these ports are configured using the Invalidation/Statistics Port link, as seen in Figure 19-16. The default values of the invalidation and statistics ports are 4001 and 4002, respectively.

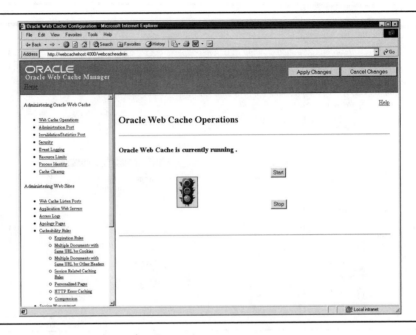

FIGURE 19-14. *Web Cache Operations*

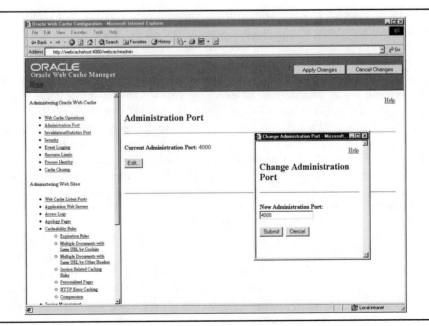

FIGURE 19-15. *Administration Port*

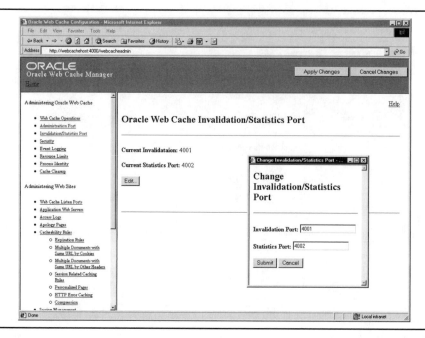

FIGURE 19-16. *Invalidation/Statistics Port*

Using the *Security link,* the administrator can change the passwords for the `administrator` and `invalidator` users, as shown in Figures 19-17 and 19-18. This option also enables the administrator to change the trusted subnets that define the computers from which the administrator can administer and invalidate cached objects (all subnets, this machine only, or a list of IP addresses), as seen in Figure 19-19.

Events and errors are stored in an event log that's configured using the *Event Logging* option. The event log is located in `{ORACLE_HOME}/webcache/logs` and is named `event_log`. All events are in the format `timestamp Information/ Warning/Error Message`. The administrator configures whether the `timestamp` values are in the local time zone or GMT. The *Oracle Web Cache Administration and Deployment Guide* recommends using GMT to improve performance. The administrator can also select whether to use Verbose Logging to log only typical events (set to No), or to log typical events plus Application Web server events (set to Yes). Figure 19-20 shows the Event Logging options.

To tune the Oracle Web Cache performance, the administrator uses the *Resource Limits* option to configure the cache size and connection limits, as shown in Figures 19-21 and 19-22. The cache size defines the amount of memory in which the Oracle Web Cache can store documents. Once the cache is full, the Oracle Web Cache performs garbage collection to remove the less popular and less valid documents. To minimize swapping documents in and out of the cache, set the cache size as large as possible within the operating system resource limit. The

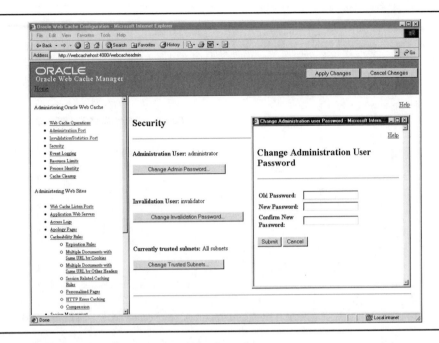

FIGURE 19-17.   *Administration User Security*

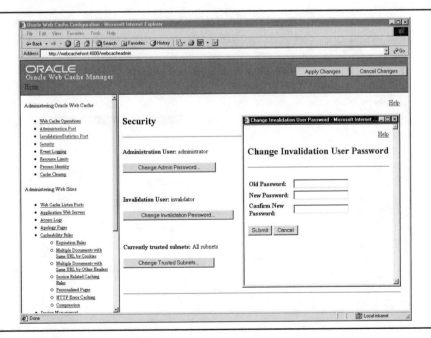

FIGURE 19-18.   *Invalidation User Security*

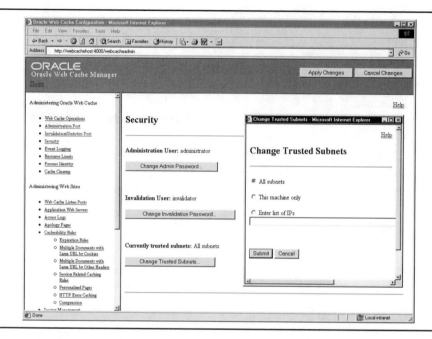

FIGURE 19-19. *Trusted Subnets*

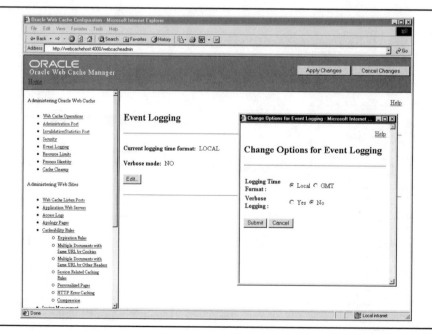

FIGURE 19-20. *Event Logging*

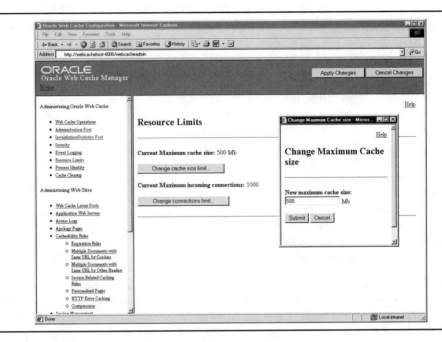

FIGURE 19-21.   *Maximum cache size*

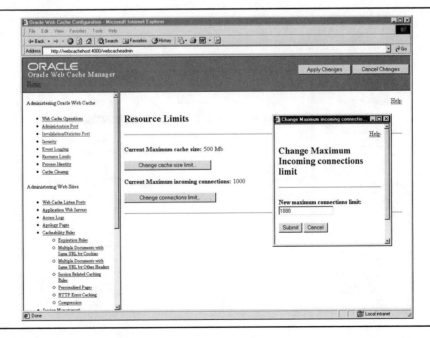

FIGURE 19-22.   *Maximum incoming connections*

connection limit is the sum of the number of incoming open connections to the Oracle Web Cache and the number of outgoing open connections to the Application Web servers. Carefully analyze site use to configure an appropriate connection limit because setting the value too low causes refused connections and setting the value too high causes performance degradation.

If the Oracle Web Cache is running on a UNIX platform, the administrator can select the *Process Identity* option to change the user ID and group ID values of the Oracle Web Cache executables, as seen in Figure 19-23. The values aren't changeable if the installation is on Windows NT.

Finally, the *Cache Cleanup* option, as shown in Figure 19-24, provides a simple means to invalidate cached pages manually. The administrator can select to invalidate all pages in the cache, pages for a specific URL, or pages that begin with a specified URL prefix. This option generates the HTTP POST invalidation requests to reduce the chances of error. Entering the HTTP header fields, especially the Base64 encoding values, plus the XML can be tricky, so the cache clean-up feature can isolate the administrator from the low-level protocol details.

Administering Web Sites   By default, Oracle Web Cache listens for browser requests on port 1100. The first option in the Administering Web Sites section, *Oracle Web Cache Listen Ports,* enables the administrator to configure an additional listening port, as seen in Figure 19-25, from which Oracle Web Cache receives browser requests.

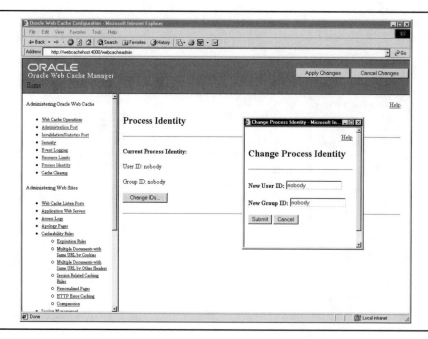

FIGURE 19-23.   *Process Identity*

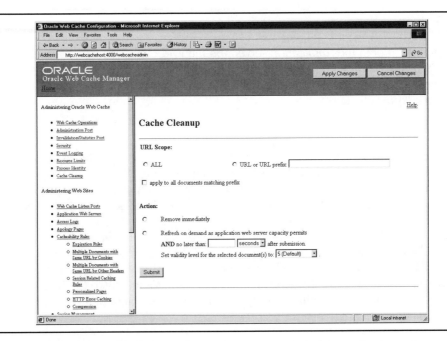

FIGURE 19-24. *Cache Cleanup*

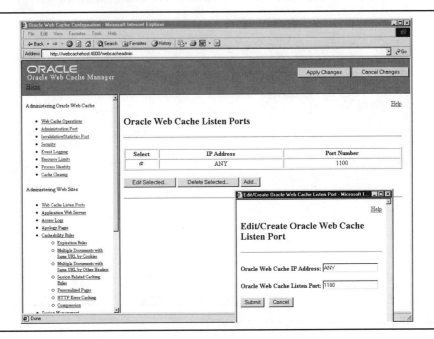

FIGURE 19-25. *Listen Ports*

TIP
You typically want to change this from port 1100 to port 80. If both the Application server and the Web Cache are on the same server, move your iAS default port to 8080 and make the Web Cache's default port 80.

The *Oracle Wallet* option enables you to locate the Oracle Wallet resource file.

The *Application Web Servers* option, as shown in Figure 19-26, is used to manage the Application Web servers for which the Oracle Web Cache accelerates content. You can use this option to configure up to 100 Application Web servers. For each server, enter the host name of the Application Web server, listening port, capacity in terms of the number of connections that the server can sustain at one time, failover threshold, ping URL, and the ping interval. The *failover threshold* determines the number of times the Application Web server doesn't respond to a request before it's considered to be down/has failed. Once an Application Web server has failed, it no longer sends requests, and the Oracle Web Cache pings the specified URL periodically as defined by the ping interval until it resumes responding to requests.

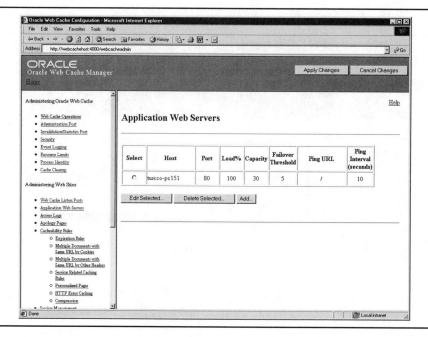

FIGURE 19-26. *Application Web Servers*

TIP
*This is where you configure Web Cache to point to
all the servers for which it should serve as a cache.*

The *Access Logs* option, as seen in Figure 19-27, is used to store information
about HTTP requests sent to the Oracle Web Cache. The default location for the
access log is in the same directory as the event log, {ORACLE_HOME}/webcache/
logs, and is named access_log. Requests are buffered in memory until they're
written to the log when the buffer is full. Define whether logging is enabled, the
logging directory, whether times are in the local time zone or GMT, the rollover
frequency in which the log is archived to access_log.*yyyymmdd,* and the
desired fields to include in the log entries. Several available fields are part of the
Extended LogFile Format (XLF), a superset of the Common LogFile Format (CLF).
The default fields are c-ip (browser IP address), cauth-id (user name if
authentication required), clf-date (date and time), request line (the HTTP
request), sc-status (status code), and bytes (content length). See Chapter 23
for more information about the *i*AS logs.

The *Apology Pages* option, as seen in Figure 19-28, enables you to configure
the pages returned to the browser when an error occurs.

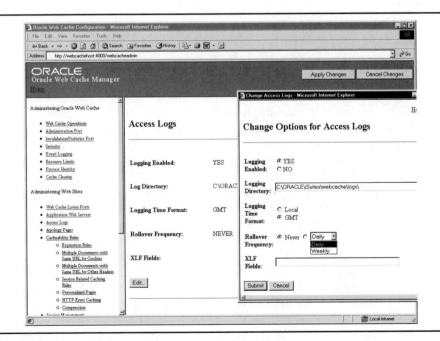

FIGURE 19-27. *Access Logs*

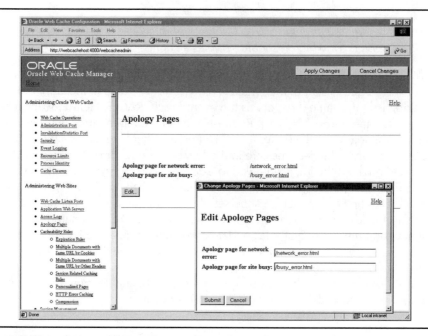

FIGURE 19-28. *Apology Pages*

As with all caches, a set of cacheability rules defines which pages are cached and which aren't. You should work closely with the Oracle Web Cache administrator to define a complete set of cacheability rules to optimize the number of cached pages and to ensure content that shouldn't be cached is excluded. If a page request isn't covered by one of the cacheability rules, the page is cached according to the HTTP header information, which typically only caches static pages.

The cacheability rules are defined within the Oracle Web Cache Manager, as shown in Figure 19-29, using a series of prioritized, POSIX 1003 regular expressions. These expressions are similar to the pattern-matching expressions used by UNIX utilities, such as `sed`. ^ denotes the start of a URL, $ denotes the end of a URL, . is a wildcard for any single character, * denotes any number of the previous characters, ? indicates the previous character is optional, and the backslash \ is used to escape special characters, such as the period (.), asterisk (*), and question mark (?). For example, to cache all files that end in `.htm` or `.html`, enter a URL expression as `\.html?$`. In this example, the backslash escapes the period to indicate a URL matching the pattern must contain a period. If the period is followed by `htm` and, optionally, an `l`, at the end of the URL ($), the page should follow the cacheability rule.

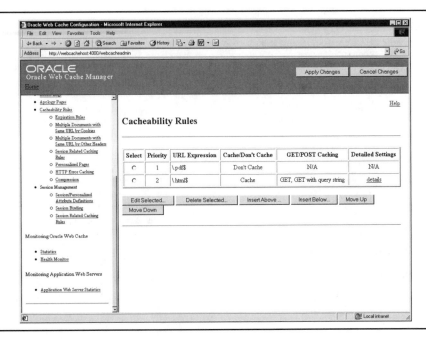

FIGURE 19-29. *Cacheability Rules*

TIP
Be sure to add a cache rule to cache JavaServer Pages (that is, \.jsp) and/or PL/SQL code (that is, ^/pls/examples/) for your dynamic pages.*

For each regular expression, specify whether a URL matching the expression is cached or isn't cached. If the URL should be cached, specify whether documents are retrieved from the cache in response to GET, GET with query string, POST, or any combination of these three HTTP methods. Also, specify an Expiration Rule, as seen in Figures 19-30 and 19-31, for matching documents, whether to cache multiple copies of a document based on the contents of a cookie or HTTP headers, how to track sessions using a session cookie or URL parameter, how to process personalized in-cache content, the HTTP error codes to cache, and whether to compress the documents in the cache.

TIP
Don't cache documents requested through GET with query string or POST if these documents update the database.

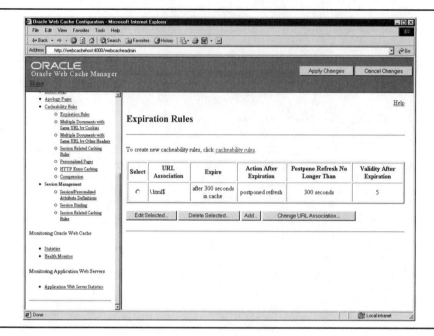

FIGURE 19-30. *Expiration Rules*

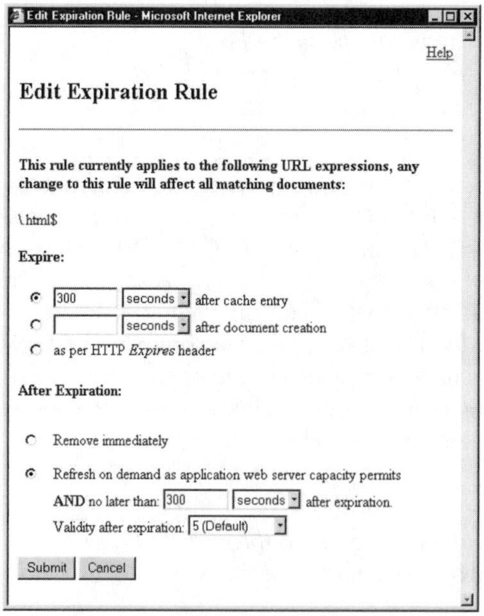

FIGURE 19-31. *Edit Expiration Rule*

You have three choices to define an expiration date on the cached content:

■ **Expire after cache entry**   Enter the number of seconds after the document is placed in the cache for when the document expires.

■ **Expire after document creation**   Enter the number of seconds after the document is created for when the document expires.

■ **Expires per HTTP Expires header**   Set the expiration date in the HTTP `Expires` header. This is the default option.

You have two choices for specifying how to handle expired documents in the cache. Expired documents are assigned a validity level that defines the time the cache could return a stale document before receiving an updated page from the Web server. The choices are:

■ **Remove immediately**   Expired documents are removed from the cache and a stale cached copy is never returned to the browser, equivalent to a validity level of 0.

■ **Refresh on demand as Application Web server capacity permits *and* no later than the specified number of seconds after expiration**   Allows the Oracle Web Cache to return stale cached copies of the requested document while waiting for the application server to create a fresh copy of the document. Returning stale documents only occurs if the document's expiration date, plus the number of seconds allowed, is still within the specified window. Documents with a lower validity level (1 is the lowest) are returned stale for less time than documents with a higher validity level (9 is the highest).

The Multiple Documents with Same Selector by Cookies area, as shown in Figure 19-32, is used to configure pages where different versions of the page should be cached, based on the contents of a cookie. Enter the cookie name, whether to cache a copy of the page for browsers that don't send the cookie with the request, and the URLs associated with the cookie.

The Multiple Documents with Same Selector by Other Headers area, as seen in Figure 19-33, is used to configure pages where different versions of the page should be cached, based on the contents of a HTTP request header. You must specify the HTTP headers for pages containing the selected header that can be served from the cache if available.

The Session/Personalization Attribute Related Caching Rules area, as shown in Figure 19-34, is used to configure caching behavior of session parameters. For each rule, select or create a new session parameter associated with a cookie, URL parameter, or both, as seen in Figure 19-35. Define whether to cache documents whose requests contain the session parameter and whether to cache documents whose requests don't contain the session parameter. Specify the URLs associated with this rule.

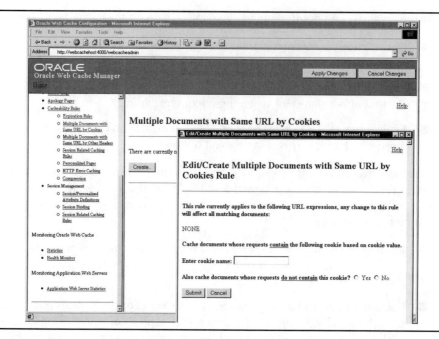

FIGURE 19-32. *Multiple Documents with Same Selector by Cookies*

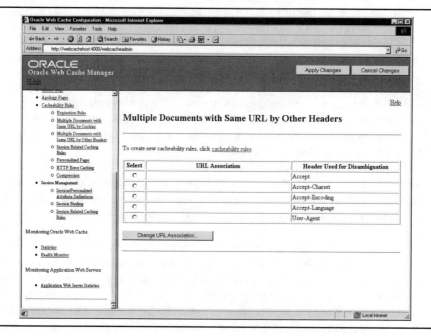

FIGURE 19-33. *Multiple Documents with Same Selector by Other Headers*

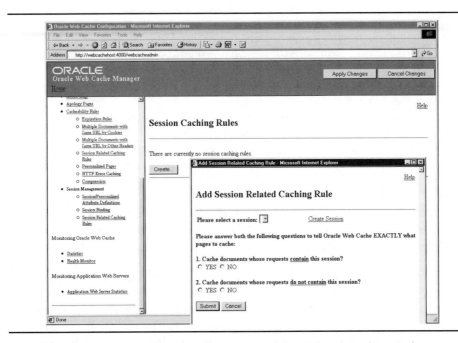

FIGURE 19-34.   *Session/Personalization Attribute Related Caching Rules*

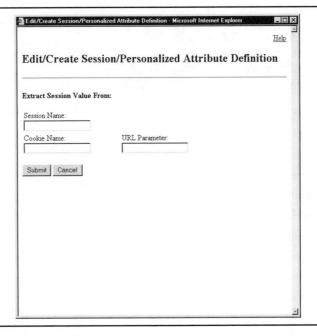

FIGURE 19-35.   *Edit/Create Session/Personalized Attribute Definition*

The Simple Personalized area, as shown in Figure 19-36, is used to enable or disable caching pages with in-cache personalization. For the rule, specify whether to cache substitution instructions for personalized attributes only or for both personalized attributes and session-encoded URLs.

The HTTP Error Caching text input, as seen in Figure 19-37, enables you to enter the error codes to cache.

Finally, select whether to compress the pages within the cache that meet the requirements of the cacheability rule, as shown in Figure 19-38.

The Session Management section contains links for defining the session parameters, enabling "stickiness" by session binding, and defining the session-related cacheability rules.

The Session/Personalized Attribute Definitions area, as seen in Figure 19-39, enables you to define session parameters. Each session parameter is associated with a cookie name, a URL parameter, or both. You can enter up to 20 session parameters for each cached page.

The Session Binding option, as shown in Figure 19-40, is used to ensure that requests from a browser are always forwarded to the same Application server to maintain state. Select or create a session parameter based on a cookie, URL parameter, or both. For the selected session parameter, use the Inactivity Timeout field to enter the number of minutes the Oracle Web Cache will continue to forward requests to the same Application Web server before timing out an inactive session.

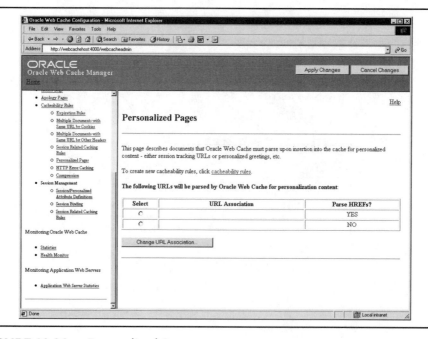

FIGURE 19-36. *Personalized Pages*

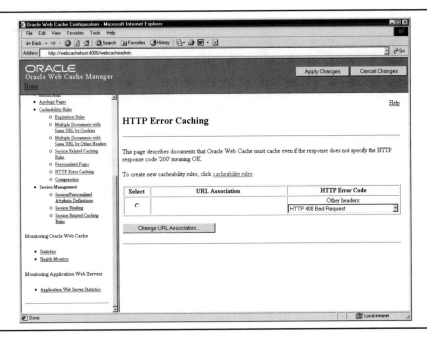

FIGURE 19-37. *HTTP Error Caching*

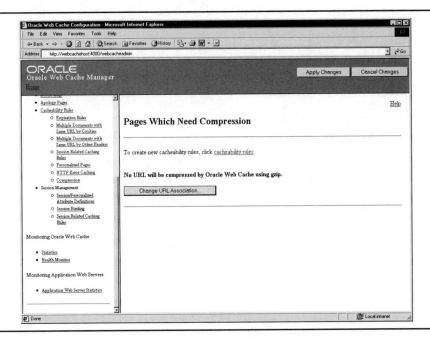

FIGURE 19-38. *Pages Which Need Compression*

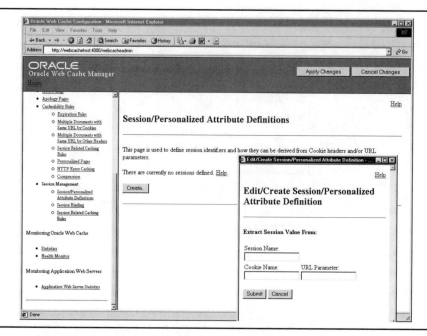

FIGURE 19-39. *Session/Personalized Attribute Definitions*

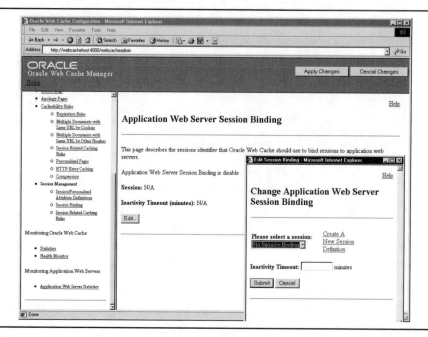

FIGURE 19-40. *Application Web Server Session Binding*

Monitoring Oracle Web Cache The Monitoring Oracle Web Cache section, as shown in Figure 19-41, contains options to gather performance statistics on the Oracle Web Cache and to monitor the overall Oracle Web Cache health.

"Performance Statistics" include the following:

- **Last Modified** The time the statistics page was created.

- **Oracle Web Cache Start Timestamp** The time the Oracle Web Cache was started.

- **Time Since Start** The elapsed time since Oracle Web Cache was started, expressed as `days/hours/minutes/seconds`.

- **Number of Documents in Cache** The number of documents stored in the Oracle Web Cache, plus the number of documents that are in transit and may be cached, depending on the cacheability rules.

- **Cache Size (in bytes)** The current size of the cache.

- **Total Number of Bytes Written** The total number of bytes written to the cache.

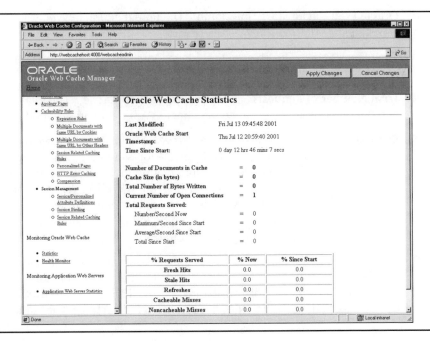

FIGURE 19-41. *Oracle Web Cache Statistics*

■ **Current Number of Open Connections** The sum of the number of incoming open connections from browsers and the number of outgoing open connections to the Application Web servers.

■ **Total Requests Served** A table containing information on the total number of requests served to the browsers. Information includes the number of current requests for each second, maximum number of requests for each second since the Oracle Web Cache was started, the average number of requests for each second since the Oracle Web Cache was started, and the total number of requests served since the Oracle Web Cache was started.

■ **Percentage Requests Served** A table containing information on the cache performance in terms of the hit ratio. Information includes the percentage of fresh hits, the percentage of stale hits, the percentage of documents refreshed with new information from the Application Web servers, the percentage of missed requests for cacheable documents, and the percentage of requests for noncacheable documents.

The Health Monitor, as seen in Figure 19-42, provides information on overall cache performance. Statistics include the following:

■ **Current Time** The time the statistics page was created.

■ **Oracle Web Cache Start Timestamp** The time the Oracle Web Cache was started.

■ **Time Since Start** The elapsed time since Oracle Web Cache was started, expressed as days/hours/minutes/seconds.

■ **Total Number of Requests Served by Oracle Web Cache** The total number of requests served since the Oracle Web Cache was started.

■ **Requests Served by Application Web Server** A table containing information on the Application Web servers for which the Oracle Web Cache accelerates content delivery. Information includes the name of the Application Web server, whether the Application Web server is up, how long the Application Web server has been up, the total number of requests resolved by the Application Web server, and the average amount of time required for the Application Web server to resolve requests.

■ **Serving Requests/Second Now** A graphical bar that shows the number of browser requests resolved for each second. The bar shows the number of documents in the cache that are expired or invalidated and are waiting to be refreshed, and the number of documents in the cache that are still valid.

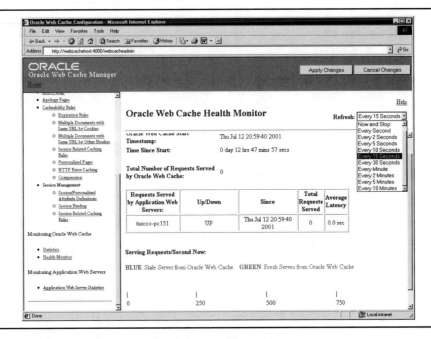

FIGURE 19-42. *Oracle Web Cache Health Monitor*

Monitoring Application Web Servers The Oracle Web Cache lists detailed statistics about the Application Web servers it services. The Application Web Server Statistics table, as shown in Figure 19-43, contains columns including the following:

- **Application Web Server** The name of the Application Web server.

- **Up/Down Time** The status of the Application Web server (up or down) and the time the Application Web server was started or stopped.

- **Completed Requests** The current, maximum, and average number of requests the Application Web server is processing for each second, plus the total number of requests processed by the Application Web server.

- **Latency** The average time to process requests in ten-second intervals and the overall average time to process requests since the Application Web server was started.

- **Load** The current and maximum number of connections from the Oracle Web Cache that the Application Web server has open, or has had open at one time.

- **Active Sessions** The current and maximum number of active sessions from the Oracle Web Cache to the Application Web server.

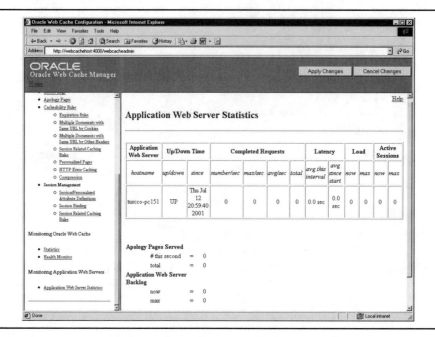

FIGURE 19-43. *Application Web Server Statistics*

The Apology Pages Served information shows the current number of apology pages being returned to browsers this second, plus the total number of apology pages returned to browsers. Apology pages are sent when a network error occurs or a site is too busy.

The Application Web Server Backlog information shows the current number of requests the Application Web server is processing, and the maximum number of requests the Application Web server has processed, for the Oracle Web Cache.

Invalidating Cached Documents

When the data in a database is updated, any cached documents built on the changed data must be invalidated. The pages can still be returned stale for the amount of time defined in the cacheability rule while waiting for the Application server to create a fresh copy of the document. The Oracle Web Cache listens for HTTP requests whose request method is POST on the defined invalidation request port. The default invalidation request port is 4001, and can be changed on the Oracle Web Cache Invalidation/Statistics Port page.

Invalidation requests are written in XML, where the XML message body contains the instructions for marking the appropriate cached documents as invalid. These HTTP POST requests can be sent manually using the Oracle Web Cache Manager or using the command line, or they can be generated automatically using triggers, scripts, or application code.

Manual Invalidation Using the Command Line   You can telnet into the Oracle Web Cache's invalidation port and directly enter the contents of the POST request.
    The format of the XML message is as follows:

```
<?xml version="1.0"?>
<!DOCTYPE INVALIDATION SYSTEM "internal:///invalidation.dtd">
<INVALIDATION>
    <URL EXP="url" PREFIX="YES|NO">
        <VALIDITY LEVEL="validity" REFRESHTIME="seconds"/>
        <COOKIE NAME="cookie_name" VALUE="value" NONEXIST="YES|NO"/>
        <HEADER NAME="HTTP_request_header" VALUE="value"/>
    </URL>
</INVALIDATION>
```

The EXP parameter specifies one or more URLs to invalidate. If the value of the PREFIX parameter is YES, the URL can contain a regular expression. Otherwise, the URLs listed in the EXP parameter must match exactly.
    The format of the XML response is as follows:

```
<?xml version="1.0"?>
<!DOCTYPE INVALIDATIONRESULT [
<!ELEMENT INVALIDATIONRESULT (URL+)>
<!ELEMENT URL    EMPTY>
<!ATTLIST URL
          EXPR         CDATA     #REQUIRED
          ID           CDATA     #REQUIRED
          STATUS       CDATA     #REQUIRED
          NUMINV       CDATA     #REQUIRED
>
]>
<INVALIDATIONRESULT>
    <URL EXPR="url" ID="id" STATUS="status" NUMINV="number">
</INVALIDATIONRESULT>
```

The ID specifies a sequence number if multiple URLs are in the invalidation response. The STATUS attribute returns SUCCESS, URI NOT CACHEABLE, or URI NOT FOUND. The NUMINV attribute contains the number of documents invalidated by the request.

Manual Invalidation Using the Oracle Web Cache Manager   A simple method of invalidating cached documents is the Oracle Web Cache Manager. Select the Cache Cleanup option within the Administering Oracle Web Cache section.

Automatic Invalidation Using Triggers   Any database that supports triggers can automatically send invalidation messages to the Oracle Web Cache when data is inserted, updated, or deleted. If you're using Oracle, the UTL_TCP package can be used to generate the invalidation messages automatically.

Automatic Invalidation Using Scripts   If you use a script to load data into the database, you can add logic at the end of the script to create and send the appropriate invalidation messages to the Oracle Web Cache. Performance assurance mechanisms built into the Oracle Web Cache allow the script to send general invalidation messages without having to specify each row that's changed in the database.

Automatic Invalidation Using Applications   Oracle Web Cache includes a Java source file named Invalidate.java, which you can compile and import into your custom JSPs and servlets to generate the necessary invalidation messages automatically. Automatic cache invalidation is expected to become a common, transparent component of the e-business content management infrastructure with the evolution of the Web-based Distributed Authoring and Versioning standard (WebDAV). See **http://www.webdav.org** for more details.

Detailed Statistics Monitor
The default detailed statistics monitor port number is 4002. This port can be changed in the Oracle Web Cache Invalidation/Statistics Port page. When you access this port at **http://localhost:4002**, you can drill into many of the statistics outlined in the performance statistics.

Edge Side Includes (ESI)
Oracle teamed with Akamai Technologies, Inc. to develop an open standard for assembling dynamic Web pages named edge side includes (ESI). ESI is a simple markup language used to define how Web page fragments are dynamically assembled at the edge of the data center or the edge of the Internet. The Oracle9*i* Application Server supports both ESI and edge side includes for Java (JESI). JDeveloper also enables the development of ESI-compliant Java applications.

The ESI assembly model is composed of a template containing fragments. The template contains the ESI tags to include, or conditionally include, each fragment and how to continue if the fragment is unavailable. Each fragment can be configured as noncacheable or cacheable. If a fragment is cacheable, it's assigned its own expiration date and maintained separately in an application server cache, content delivery network cache, or both. Fragments can be conditionally assembled and returned to the browser based on in-cache personalization parameters set in cookies or HTTP request headers.

Once the templates containing the ESI tags are developed, create a cacheability rule using the Oracle Web Cache Manager to designate whether the Oracle Web Cache or an upstream edge server should process the ESI tags.

Additional information on ESI is available at **http://www.oracle.com/start** and entering the keyword "esi", or at **http://www.edge-delivery.org**.

ESI elements are XML-based in an ESI-specific XML Namespace. The XML Namespace for ESI 1.0 is **http://www.edge-delivery.org/esi/1.0**.

ESI consists of tags designed to support the following features:

- **Inclusion**   Include the fragments used to create a Web page, where each fragment contains its own cacheability profile.

- **Conditional processing**   Conditionally include a fragment on a Web page using environment variables and Boolean comparisons.

- **Environment variables**   Access a subset of the CGI variables, including cookies.

- **Exception and error handling**   Enables the developer to specify a default page if a fragment is unavailable and the page cannot be built.

\<esi:include\>

```
<esi:include src="url" alt="url" onerror="continue" />
```

The `include` statement tells the ESI process to retrieve the resource specified in the `src` attribute. The `src` attribute can be a static address or the value can contain variables that evaluate to a valid URL. The optional `alt` attribute specifies an alternate URL if the URL in the `src` attribute isn't found. If neither the URL specified in the `src` nor the `alt` attributes can be found, the server returns a status code greater than 400, unless the optional `onerror="continue"` attribute is specified, in which case the `include` tag is deleted.

The `include` tag doesn't have a corresponding end tag.

\<esi:inline\>

```
<esi:inline name="url" fetchable="{yes|no}">
    fragment
</esi:inline>
```

The `inline` statement is used to demarcate ESI fragments. The ESI processor extracts all inline fragments included in a HTTP response and stores them independently under the specified URL.

<esi:choose>

```
<esi:choose>
    <esi:when test="…">
       …
    </esi:when>
    <esi:otherwise>
      …
    </esi:otherwise>
</esi:choose>
```

The choose statement allows for conditional logic based on expressions in when elements. One or more when elements is required and an optional otherwise element can be included as a default case if none of the when element conditions evaluate to true. The first successful when statement (a statement whose conditions result to true) will be executed. If no when elements conditions are satisfied (none of the conditions are true), the otherwise element is executed.

<esi:try>

```
<esi:try>
    <esi:attempt>
       …
    </esi:attempt>
    <esi:except>
       …
    </esi:except>
</esi:try>
```

Exception handling is implemented using a try statement with exactly one attempt and one except statement block.

The commands within the attempt block are executed. If the commands within the attempt block fail, then the commands within the except block are executed.

<esi:comment>

```
<esi:comment text="…" />
```

The comment statement enables you to include comments in the ESI tags. These tags are deleted before the HTML is retrieved, so regular HTML/XML comments should be used if the comments should be included in the assembled page.

The comment statement doesn't have a corresponding end tag.

<esi:remove>

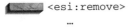
```
<esi:remove>
  ...
</esi:remove>
```

The remove statement is used to specify HTML that should be included in the assembled page if ESI isn't supported. If ESI processing is supported, the HTML within the remove statement is deleted. If ESI processing isn't supported, however, the browser doesn't understand and, consequently, ignores the opening and closing <esi:remove> tags, and simply displays the HTML within the tag block.

<esi:vars>

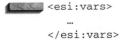
```
<esi:vars>
  ...
</esi:vars>
```

The vars statement allows for the use of an ESI variable outside an ESI block.

<!--esi ...-->

```
<!--esi
  ...
-->
```

This special statement enables you to add HTML that's dependent on ESI processing. If the Web server doesn't support ESI, the tags are treated like an HTML/ XML comment and the enclosed text is ignored.

ESI Variables ESI supports reading the following CGI variables: HTTP_ACCEPT_ LANGUAGE, HTTP_COOKIE, HTTP_HOST, HTTP_REFERER, HTTP_USER_ AGENT, and QUERY_STRING.

To access the value of variables that contain a substructure, enclose the substructure argument in braces. For example, $(HTTP_COOKIE{mycookie}). The supported CGI variables that contain substructures are HTTP_ACCEPT_ LANGUAGE, HTTP_COOKIE, HTTP_USER_AGENT, and QUERY_STRING.

JESI Tags You can use seven JESI tags within JSPs to create ESI tags in the resulting HTML:

■ **<jesi:include>** Defines how the fragments are to be reassembled; creates the <esi:include> tag.

- ■ **`<jesi:control>`**   Assigns an attribute to templates and fragments.

- ■ **`<jesi:template>`**   Used to contain the entire content of a JSP container page within its body.

- ■ **`<jesi:fragment>`**   Encapsulates individual content fragments within a JSP page.

- ■ **`<jesi:codeblock>`**   Specifies that a particular piece of code needs to be executed before any other fragment is executed.

- ■ **`<jesi:invalidate>`**   Invalidates cached objects.

- ■ **`<jesi:personalize>`**   Inserts personalized content into a page.

Oracle9*i*AS Database Cache

Whereas the benefit of the Oracle Web Cache is to improve Web server performance and cache Web pages, a companion product included in 9*i*AS Enterprise Edition, the *Database Cache,* provides the benefit of improving database performance by caching tables.

The Oracle Database Cache (formerly known as the Oracle8*i* Cache) builds on Oracle's replication technology by storing snapshots of the data in the middle tier—this is only a licensing name for a scaled-down version of the Oracle database (with some GUI tools to administer the cached tables). Using a shadow connection to the Oracle Database Cache for each database connection, the Oracle Database Cache determines if the data needed to create a result set for a read-only query is available in the cache (a cache "hit") or if it must be retrieved from the database. This query routing is transparent to OCI applications provided the applications use dynamic linking to the `libclntsh.so` library, which references the new library `wtc8.so` containing the routing logic. Applications with this library statically linked must be relinked to use the enhanced version of this library.

How the Database Cache Works

The Oracle Database Cache contains *data sets,* which consist of replicas of tables from the origin database. The Oracle Database Cache also stores information on previous queries to determine which queries were satisfied by data available in the cached data sets. Using the Java-based DBA Studio Cache Manager component of the supplied DBMS_ICACHE PL/SQL package, you define the tables to cache, the cache properties, and the synchronization policy.

The synchronization policy determines how often the cached data sets are refreshed with current data in the origin database. For each table, specify whether the cached object is updated with incremental changes or completely refreshed. You can also choose to schedule the incremental or complete synchronization, or perform the task manually.

When a query or PL/SQL subprogram is executed, the Oracle Database Cache attempts to execute the query using the data sets stored in the cache. When the query can be satisfied using the cached data sets, the Oracle Database Cache returns the result set without using resources on the source database. If the query cannot be satisfied using the cached data sets, the query is routed to the origin server. INSERT, UPDATE, and DELETE statements are always routed to the origin database for processing.

Developers should work closely with DBAs to determine which tables contain the most frequently requested data, which PL/SQL objects should be cached, and whether each data set should be refreshed using incremental updates or completely recopied from the corresponding table in the origin database.

Configuring Applications to Use the Oracle Database Cache

The Oracle Database Cache is designed to be transparent to applications, but the OCI library contains functions to allow individual applications to specify whether a connection is cached or not cached. This provides an additional level of granular control.

Enable Caching for All Applications

To enable the Oracle Database Cache to service all applications that reside on the same server, simply define the ORA_OCI_CACHE environment variable with a value of 1.

Specify Connections to Cache or Not Cache

To allow caching by the Oracle Database Cache for any connection, the ORA_ OCI_CACHE environment variable must be defined. Within an OCI application, you can specify whether caching is enabled or disabled for a connection using the mode parameter of the OCIEnvCreate() function. You can either set the mode to OCI_CACHE to specify the connection uses the Oracle Database Cache, or to OCI_ NO_CACHE to specify the connection doesn't use the Oracle Database Cache.

For example, to specify a connection uses the Oracle Database Cache:

```
OCIEnvCreate((dvoid**)&envhp,
    (ub4) OCI_DEFAULT | OCI_CACHE,
    (dvoid *)0,
    (dvoid * (*)(dvoid *, size_t))0,
    (dvoid * (*)(dvoid *, dvoid *, size_t))0,
    (void (*)(dvoid *, dvoid *))0,
    (size_t)0,
    (dvoid **)0))
```

Specifying Statements Not to Cache

For an even lower level of control, you can use the `OCIAttrSet()` function to specify which statements should be routed directly to the database, even if the connection specifies the cache should be used.

For example, to specify a statement doesn't use the Oracle Database Cache:

```
OCIAttrSet((dvoid *)stmthp1,
    (ub4)OCI_HTYPE_STMT,
    (dvoid *)&rem,
    (ub4)0,
    (ub4)OCI_ATTR_NO_CACHE,
    errhp1)
```

Summary

The use of various caching methods is an essential part of developing responsive Web-based applications. Caches reduce latency and minimize network traffic by keeping copies of objects at various locations along the request/response chain. If a cache contains a fresh copy of the requested object, the cache responds to the client's request, thereby reducing the load on the origin server, as well as the traffic on the network.

Until recently, only static content was considered cacheable. Using products such as Oracle9iAS Web Cache and technologies such as ESI, caches can store dynamic pages and even personalize the cached content before serving the cached object to the browser.

Although most caching technologies are transparent to the application developer, care should be taken to ensure all Web pages returned to the browser are "fresh enough," as determined by the business rules. Set an appropriate expiration date for each page, if it's possible to determine the useful life of the page. Additional performance gains can also be realized if you're willing to analyze and modify your programs to configure specific database connections or individual statements to use the cache.

Caching is a ubiquitous part of the World Wide Web and has enabled the use of the Internet to grow while still providing acceptable response times. With a little care and analysis, you can develop Web-based applications that maximize the benefits of caching to minimize the negative effects of sharing the medium with the rest of the world.

In benchmarks, we've found that Oracle Web Cache speeds our Web performance by 3 to 150 times. The incremental performance enhancements occur based on hired traffic accessing the same dynamic content. In other words, the more people attempting to access the same dynamic content, the closer you'll get to 150 times the noncached environment's performance. Also, as you can see in the following, the longer your dynamic content takes to generate, the better Web Cache will perform. The following performance benchmarks show three different JSPs being executed 100 times in a row—with and without Oracle Web Cache.

	JSP A	JSP B	JSP C
Without Cache	128.62 seconds	64.28 seconds	176.06 seconds
With Cache	6.75 seconds	5.43 seconds	6.01 seconds
Times Faster	19	12	29

100 concurrent requests

The bottom line is this: by using Web Cache, you'll need less hardware or you'll achieve better use of existing hardware.

CHAPTER
20

Oracle Enterprise
Manager

racle Enterprise Manager (OEM) 9.0.1 is an integrated suite of tools included with the Oracle9*i* database that enables administrators to manage Oracle resources centrally. OEM 2.2 comes with the 8*i* Release 3 (8.1.7) of the database and 9*i*AS. Resources managed by OEM include databases, as well as listeners, nodes, Web servers, and Developer servers. OEM is implemented using a three-tier architecture as shown in Figure 20-1, with the following components: first tier—Console, second tier—Management Servers, and third tier—Intelligent Agents. The *Console* is the graphical interface through which administrators manage the resources under their control. The Console communicates with one of the available *Management Servers,* all of which share a central repository containing information on the current state of the managed resources. The *Intelligent Agents* are processes running on the managed resources that periodically populate the repository tables. Depending on the size of your installation and hardware capabilities, you can install all three tiers on the same node or each tier on separate nodes. All the OEM components are included

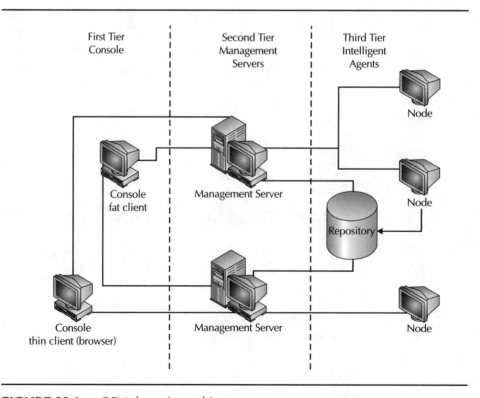

FIGURE 20-1. *OEM three-tier architecture*

with both the Enterprise and Standard editions of the 8*i* and 9*i* database. If you're installing OEM as part of 9*i*AS, however, the 9*i*AS Enterprise Edition is required to install the Management Server.

Because the Management Servers share a central repository, multiple administrators can manage the same resources. Each administrator is granted the specific permissions needed to administer the resources under his or her control. In addition, OEM supports *lights out* administration by automatically running jobs and notifying administrators when an unexpected event occurs. Because several key areas of the Console are accessible using a Web browser, authorized administrators can administer the required resources from anywhere on the network. OEM is powerful enough to allow experienced administrators to perform complex tasks, yet simple enough for a less-experienced administrator to perform basic database administration functions. Best of all, you needn't purchase an additional product to obtain this centralized management functionality.

Future releases of OEM are expected to enable the administrator to configure the Oracle9*i* Application Server. Until this functionality is available within OEM, the administrator must maintain the 9*i*AS configuration files using a text editor or third-party graphical configuration tool. See Chapter 3 for information on some of the available graphical configuration tools available to configure the 9*i*AS installation.

This chapter covers several aspects of installing, configuring, and using OEM, including the following topics:

- Intelligent Agents

- Management Servers

- Console

- Accessing the Console Using a Web Browser

- Installing Paging and E-mail Services

NOTE
If you plan on building the repository in a 9i database, you must install OEM 9.0 instead of version 2.2 that ships with 9iAS. See the OEM Technical Forum document labeled "OEM and Oracle9i Upgrade" for more information.

Intelligent Agents

The first step in using OEM is ensuring the Intelligent Agents are installed on the target nodes in the third tier. *Intelligent Agents* are processes that monitor the managed resources and communicate this information to the Management Servers in the middle tier. Agents also support the Simple Network Management Protocol (SNMP) that allows third-party monitoring tools to access Oracle's database Management Information Base (MIB) variables. Configuration and log files relating to the Intelligent Agent are located in the $ORACLE_HOME/network/agent directory.

Agents are autonomous and neither rely on a database nor require that a Management Server is running. This independence enables the Agents to perform such tasks as starting and stopping databases, performing backups, and executing job and event scripts written in Tool Command Language (Tcl) with OraTcl extensions. *Jobs* are scripts executed once or scheduled to run periodically and they perform operations such as database startups, shutdowns, and backups. Job scripts can also read from and write to files. *Events* are scripts executed when an exception occurs. For event scripts, the Tcl interpreter state and global variables are saved, so the same event isn't raised repeatedly. If the Management Server isn't running, the Agent queues the messages in files with a .q extension within the Agent's directory on the Agent's node, to be delivered once the Management Server is restarted.

Intelligent Agents are included with all Oracle 7.3.2 and later databases, although the Agent that shipped with 7.3.3 was the first version to use an automated service discovery process. Depending on the selected configuration or custom options, each installation of an Oracle database or 9*i*AS on a node may create a new Intelligent Agent. Because only one Agent is required per node to service all the Oracle resources on the node, you should disable all but one of the Intelligent Agents.

Intelligent Agent User Account

When creating a database, the catsnmp.sql script is executed to create the DBSNMP user account, the SNMPAGENT role, and the OEM_MONITOR role. The script also grants the CONNECT, RESOURCE, and SNMPAGENT roles to the DBSNMP user. The password is initialized to 'dbsnmp', but both the user name and password can be changed by editing the catsnmp.sql file and rerunning the script as SYS or INTERNAL. An Agent user account must be granted the CONNECT, RESOURCE, and SNMPAGENT roles in each database the Agent will monitor.

TIP
Change the password for the DBSNMP user to prevent a security hole in your database.

Intelligent Agent Operations

The procedures for starting, stopping, and checking the status of the Agent differ between UNIX and NT systems.

On UNIX systems, the Agent is named dbsnmp and the listener control utility—lsnrctl—is used to control the Agent operations, as shown in the following table:

Operation	Listener Utility
Start the Agent	lsnrctl dbsnmp_start
Stop the Agent	lsnrctl dbsnmp_stop
Check Agent Status	lsnrctl dbsnmp_status

On NT/2000 systems the Agent service is named Oracle<ORACLE_HOME_NAME>Agent. To start, stop, and check the status of the Agent on an NT/2000 system, use either the Services console or enter the appropriate net commands at a command prompt, as shown in the following table:

Operation	net Command
Start the Agent	net start Oracle<ORACLE_HOME_NAME>Agent
Stop the Agent	net stop Oracle<ORACLE_HOME_NAME>Agent
Check Agent Status	net start

Automatic Service Discovery Process

For agents shipped with Oracle 7.3.3 or higher, the automatic service discovery process begins when the Agent is started. The Agent discovers services using Tcl scripts located in the Agent directory.

Discover Basic Services

The main script—nmiconf.tcl—locates basic services, including listeners and databases. Basic services are defined in the appropriate network files, such as listener.ora, tnsnames.ora, oratab (UNIX systems), and the Registry (NT/2000 systems).

The script processes the Oracle home directories defined in the oratab file or in the Registry. For each Oracle home directory, the script determines all databases and services within the directory.

Discover Nonbasic Services

After discovering basic services, the agent runs the Tcl scripts listed in nmiconf.lst to discover nonbasic services, such as Web servers, paging services, other database management systems, and Oracle applications. The administrator can also develop custom Tcl scripts to monitor other resources.

Services Files

After collecting the necessary information on the services to monitor, a connect string is established for each service and the results are written to one of the following three files:

- **$ORACLE_HOME/network/admin/snmp_ro.ora**   Information on the services the Agent will monitor. The administrator shouldn't change the contents of this file.

- **$ORACLE_HOME/network/admin/snmp_rw.ora**   Index information on the services the Agent will monitor. The administrator can edit this file to specify desired parameters, or update the user name or password values for the Agent user account if they were changed from the default values of DBSNMP/DBSNMP. For example: SNMP.CONNECT.<service>.NAME = <USERNAME> or SNMP.CONNECT.<service>.PASSWORD = <password>.

- **$ORACLE_HOME/network/agent/services.ora**   Aliases for all the services the Agent discovered. Don't change the contents of this file because it's re-created each time the Agent is started.

Intelligent Agent Log Files and Tracing

The Agent writes information to several log files to aid the administrator in diagnosing problems in the automatic discovery process, Agent operations, jobs, and events. The default location of the Agent log files is in the $ORACLE_HOME/network/log directory. In addition, the administrator can specify parameters in the snmp_rw.ora file, such as specifying file locations and names, and the level of information to trace.

The first log file contains summary information of the Agent and the current parameters. This information is written every time the Agent is started, regardless of the trace settings. On UNIX systems, by default, the summary information is logged to two files whose names are dbsnmpc.log and dbsnmpw.log. On NT/2000 systems, the summary information is logged to a single file whose default name is nmi.log. The administrator can change the name of the summary log file using the nmi.log_ file parameter and can change the directory where this file is written using the nmi.log_directory parameter. Note, if the log file parameter is set on UNIX systems, messages generated by the Agent processes are written to a single file, making it difficult to determine which process generated each message.

The second log file contains information created during the automatic discovery process, and is named nmiconf.log on both UNIX and NT/2000 systems. This log file is also written every time the Agent is started, regardless of the trace settings. The administrator can change neither the directory where this file is written nor the filename.

To enable Agent tracing, set the nmi.trace_level parameter to 4 (limited logging), 8 (extensive logging), or 16 (all messages). The default value of 0 doesn't generate any trace messages. If you set the trace level to 16, expect to capture a large amount of detailed information, including the contents of the TCP/IP packets the Agent sends and receives. By default, the trace file is stored in the $ORACLE_HOME/network/ trace directory. However, the administrator can change this value using the nmi.trace_directory parameter. On UNIX systems, the trace information is stored in two files—dbsnmpc.trc and dbsnmpw.trc—and on NT/2000 systems the file is named dbsnmp.trc. The filename can be changed using the nmi.trace_file parameter.

The nmi.trace_unique parameter determines the disposition of the trace file when the Agent is started. If the value is FALSE, the existing file is overwritten. Otherwise, if the value is TRUE, the trace information is written to a new uniquely named file that includes the process identifier. The default value is FALSE, however, you should set this value to TRUE if you're having difficulty starting the Agent. To assist the administrator in managing the unique trace files, two new parameters were introduced in Oracle 8.1.7: *nmi.trace_filecnt,* which limits the number of trace files, and *nmi.trace_filesize,* which limits the maximum file size in KB. For example, if the process identifier is 1234, the first file is named dbsnmp1_1234.trc, the second file is named dbsnmp2_1234.trc, and so forth. If the maximum number of files is reached, the Agent cycles through the trace files starting with reusing the first file.

Discovering Services in an Oracle Parallel Services Environment

Within an Oracle Parallel Services (OPS) environment, all OEM commands are passed to the one Intelligent Agent running on the node. When using OEM to discover resources in an OPS environment, Oracle recommends first discovering a non-OPS database, typically the database hosting the repository, before discovering the OPS instances.

Oracle Data Gatherer

Installing an Intelligent Agent also installs the Oracle Data Gatherer. Even though Intelligent Agents were first used in version 7.3.2, the Oracle Data Gatherer didn't appear until version 8.0.4 for NT and Sun Solaris systems, and 8.0.5 for other platforms. The Oracle Data Gatherer collects performance data, such as file I/O and CPU use, which is used by the Capacity Planner, Performance Monitor, Lock Manager, and SQLServer Monitor tools included in the Oracle Diagnostics Pack, an optional add-on for OEM.

On UNIX systems, the Data Gatherer process is named vppdc and on NT/2000 systems, the service is named Oracle<ORACLE_HOME_NAME>DataGatherer. The $ORACLE_HOME/odg directory contains the Data Gatherer configuration and log files. You can use the vppcntl command line utility to control the Data Gatherer process, as shown in the following table:

Operation	Command Line Utility
Start the Data Gatherer	vppcntl -start
Stop the Data Gatherer	vppcntl -stop
Check the Data Gatherer Status	vppcntl -ping or vppcntl -status
Re-read the Data Cartridge Registry	vppcntl -refresh

TIP
If you aren't running the Oracle Diagnostics Pack,
you can disable the Oracle Data Gatherer process to
save system resources.

Management Servers

The second step in using OEM is to install one or more Management Servers in the second tier.

Configuring a Management Server

All the Management Servers share a central repository to store information gathered from the Intelligent Agents. During the Management Server installation, the installer is prompted to select an existing repository or to select an existing database where the installation program will create a repository. If a repository hasn't been created and a database to house the repository is unavailable, create a new database before proceeding with the Management Server installation.

Installing a Management Server

If you're installing 9*i*AS Standard Edition, you can install the Management Server using the 9*i* (or 8*i*) media. Start the Universal Installer, select the Oracle Management and Integration radio button, and click the Next button to continue.

The next dialog box prompts you to select an Installation Type. Select the Oracle Management Server radio button and click the Next button to continue.

In the next dialog box, select whether the Management Server will use an existing repository or create a new repository. If the installation needs to create a repository or you need to migrate a release 1.*x* repository, select the radio button for which a new repository is required and click the Next button. If you're migrating a release 1.*x* repository, use the OEM Migration Assistant after the installation completes to migrate the repository to the new version 2.2. If the Management Server will access an existing version 2.0.*x*, 2.1, or 2.2 repository, select the radio button to use an existing repository and click the Next button. Note, the repository version must match the Management Server version. If the existing repository is for version 2.0.*x* or 2.1, you must manually upgrade the repository once the installation completes using the OEM Configuration Assistant.

When all selections are complete, the Summary dialog box will show the components to be installed. If you're satisfied with your selections, click the Install button to begin installing the Management Server and dependent components.

Configuration Tools

During the installation of 9*i*AS Enterprise Edition, or following the Management
Server installation using the 9*i* (or 8*i*) media, the Configuration Tools dialog box appears
and automatically starts one or two assistants. If Oracle Net8 isn't in the Oracle home
directory specified for the Management Server installation, the Oracle Net8 Configuration
Assistant is started to configure Oracle Net8. Existing Oracle Net versions 8.1.6 or
earlier will be upgraded. In all cases, the Configuration Assistant is started either to
create a new repository or to select an existing repository.

Create a New Repository   The *Configuration Assistant* steps the installer
through the windows that capture the information to create a new repository. The
first step prompts the installer to enter a user name with DBA privileges, a password,
and the connect string of the database where the repository will be created. In the
example shown in Figure 20-2 the user is SYS, and the connect string points to the
service named tuscdemo listening on the default port 1521 on the tuscco-pc151

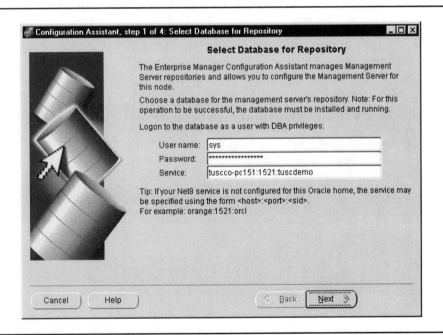

FIGURE 20-2.   *Configuration Assistant—Select Database for Repository*

host. Click the Next button to continue. The wizard will connect to the target database using the supplied credentials.

The second step prompts the installer to enter a user name and password for the repository owner. All the OEM repository objects will be created in the repository owner's schema. In the example shown in Figure 20-3, the repository owner's user name is OEM_REPOSITORY. After entering the repository owner information, click the Next button to continue.

The Configuration Assistant determines if the repository owner is an existing user in the database. If the user already exists, a confirmation window prompts the installer to confirm that the repository objects will be created in the existing user's schema. In this case, click the Yes button. Otherwise, a window opens where the installer can select the default tablespace and temporary tablespace values for the new user, as shown in Figure 20-4. The recommended tablespace is OEM_REPOSITORY. Don't install the repository in the SYSTEM, ROLLBACK, or TEMPORARY tablespaces. Once the tablespaces are selected, click the Next button to continue.

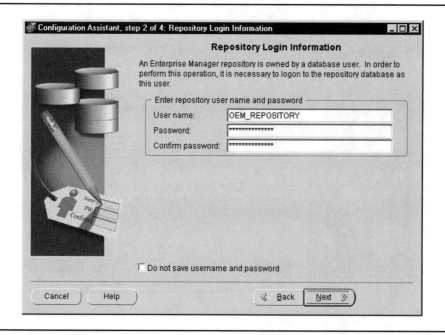

FIGURE 20-3. *Configuration Assistant—Repository Login Information*

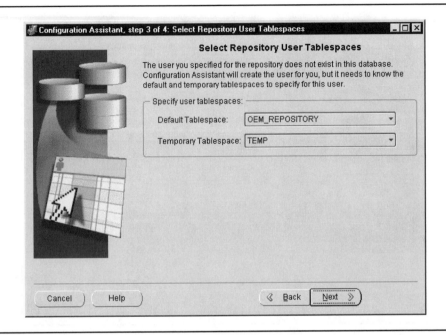

FIGURE 20-4. *Configuration Assistant—Select Repository User Tablespaces*

The last page of the wizard displays a summary of the repository creation process, as shown in Figure 20-5. At this point, you can click the Back button to step through the prior pages and change any of the values. Once you're satisfied the information is correct, click the Finish button to create the repository. A progress meter displays the current step and percent complete. If you want to view the actual SQL statements being processed, click the Show Details button. After the processing completes, click the Close button on the progress meter window. A final window appears displaying that the installation is complete.

Select an Existing Repository If the radio button to use an existing repository is selected, a window opens prompting you to enter the repository connection information. Enter the repository owner, password, and connection information on where to locate the existing repository, as shown in Figure 20-6, and then click the Next button.

After the information needed to access the repository information is complete, a summary window confirms the information. If the repository information is correct,

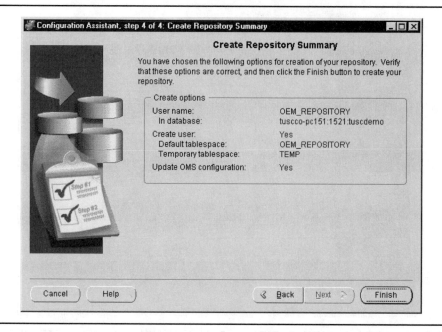

FIGURE 20-5. *Configuration Assistant—Create Repository Summary*

click the Finish button, as shown in Figure 20-7. A progress meter appears, detailing the progress of updating the configuration parameters. After the processing completes, click the Close button on the progress meter window.

Oracle Management Server   The Management Server installation process performs several steps:

■ Creates the repository owner, assigning the user's default tablespace and temporary tablespace as directed, if the owner doesn't exist

■ Grants the required role (CONNECT) and system privileges (CREATE PROCEDURE, CREATE TRIGGER, EXECUTE ANY PROCEDURE, and SELECT ANY TABLE) to the repository owner

■ Creates the repository tablespace to store the repository objects, if the tablespace doesn't exist

■ Loads the required information into the repository

■ Creates or updates the Management Server configuration file located at $ORACLE_HOME/sysman/config/omsconfig.properties

■ Creates the Management Server process, if it didn't already exist and, on NT/2000 systems, configures the service to start manually

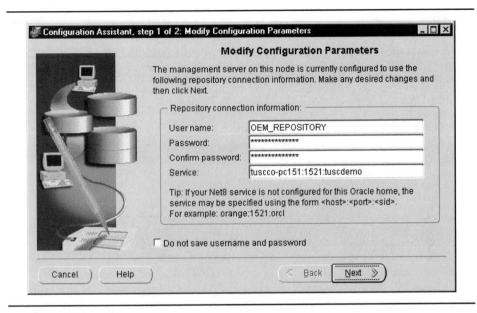

FIGURE 20-6. *Configuration Assistant—Modify Configuration Parameters*

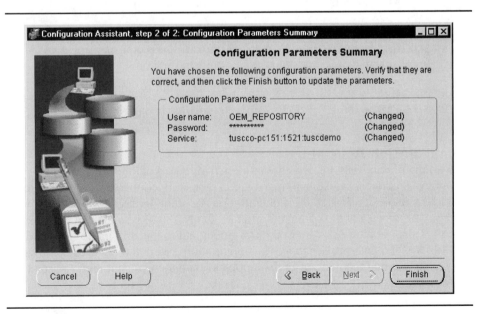

FIGURE 20-7. *Configuration Parameters Summary*

TIP
If the Management Server is installed on the same node as the database hosting the repository on an NT/2000 system, create a dependency to prevent the Management Server service from starting until the database has opened. Edit the Registry using regedt32 to add the dependency. For example, in the HKEY_LOCAL_MACHINE\System\CurrentControlSet\Services\Oracle<ORACLE_HOME_NAME>ManagementServer branch, add a value named DependOnService of type REG_MULTI_SZ with value OracleService<SID>.

On UNIX systems, the Management Server is controlled using the oemctrl utility. On NT/2000 systems, the service is named Oracle<ORACLE_HOME_NAME>ManagementServer, and can be controlled using the Services console or the oemctrl utility at the command prompt. The following table lists common commands available using oemctrl:

Operation	Command
Start the Management Server	oemctrl start oms
Stop the Management Server	oemctrl stop oms
Management Server status Check Management Server status	oemctrl status oms or oemctrl ping oms
Start the Paging Server	oemctrl start paging
Stop the Paging Server	oemctrl stop paging

Configuration Assistant

The Configuration Assistant, which was launched as part of the Management Server installation, is available to manage the repository configuration used by the Management Server. To start the Configuration Assistant on UNIX or NT/2000 systems, enter **emca** at the command prompt. On NT/2000 systems, you can also find the Configuration Assistant in the Start menu at Programs | Oracle—<ORACLE_HOME_NAME | Enterprise Manager | Configuration Assistant. Figure 20-8 shows the Configuration Operation page that appears when the Configuration Assistant is started.

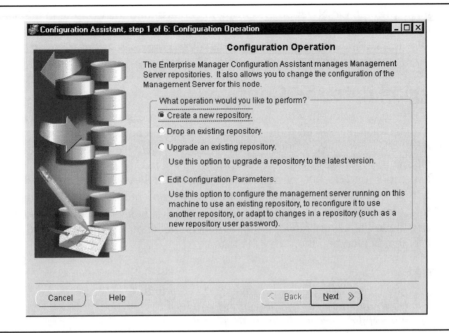

FIGURE 20-8. *Configuration Assistant—Configuration Operation*

The Configuration Assistant enables the administrator to manage repositories. The available options are the following:

■ Create a new repository

■ Drop an existing repository. You can choose to drop the owner and all repository objects, or only to drop the repository objects and leave the owner account and nonrepository objects intact

■ Upgrade an existing 2.0.*x* or 2.1 repository to version 2.2

■ Edit any or all the configuration parameters, such as the repository owner name, password, or connect string to access the repository database

Console

After creating the repository and starting one or more Management Servers and an Intelligent Agent, complete the third step in using OEM by configuring the Console. To start the Console on UNIX or NT/2000 systems, enter **oemapp console** at the command prompt. On NT/2000 systems, you can also find the Console in the Start menu at Programs | Oracle—<ORACLE_HOME_NAME> | Enterprise Manager | Console. The Console is also available using a Web browser, as described in the "Accessing the Console Using a Web Browser" section.

Logging in to the Console

To access the Console, enter the administrator user name and password, and then select a Management Server. If the desired Management Server isn't in the drop-down list, click the network button next to the drop-down list to add it. Once all the information is entered, click the OK button to log in.

Remember, on NT/2000 systems, the Management Server is configured with startup type set to "Manual" by default. If the Management Server isn't running, or if the administrator name or password is incorrect, you receive a VTK-1000 error showing the login attempt failed. If the Management Server isn't running, start the Management Server, and then retry the login step.

TIP

If you receive a VTK-1000 error saying you couldn't connect to the Management Server and you're sure you entered the correct administrator user ID and password, verify the Management Server is running.

Logging in to the Console for the First Time

You must use the Super Administrator account the first time you log in to OEM:

■ Super Administrator = sysman

■ Password = oem_temp

For security reasons, you're prompted, but you aren't required, to change the sysman password. The window to change the sysman password automatically appears if the password is set to the default value. Enter a new Super Administrator password, if desired, and then click the Change button, or click the Cancel button to leave the sysman password unchanged, to log in to OEM.

Using the Console Application

On starting the Console for the first time, the services (such as databases and listeners) on the node where the Management Server is running are set up within the Console if the Intelligent Agent is also running on the same node. After the service discovery process completes, the Console window opens, as shown in Figure 20-9.

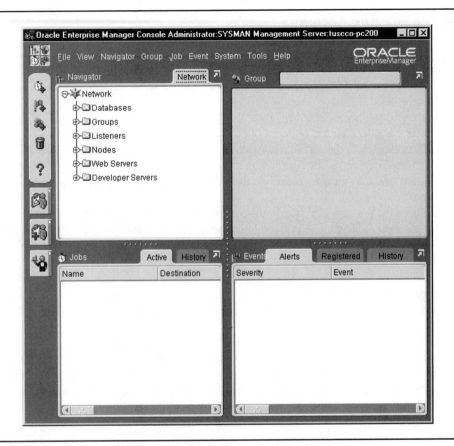

FIGURE 20-9. *Oracle Enterprise Manager Console*

Discovering Additional Nodes

To discover additional nodes, start the Discovery Wizard using the Navigator-Discover Nodes... menu item. The summary window appears, giving a brief overview of the discovery process. Click the Next button to start the wizard.

In the input area, enter one or more node names or IP addresses to discover, and then click the Next button. The discovery process begins and the window displays the progress of the search for services on each node. At the end of the discovery process, the search results for each node are shown with a check mark, indicating the node was successfully discovered, or an *X*, indicating the wizard failed to discover the node. Click the OK button to close the message window and return to the Console.

Administrator Accounts

OEM supports multiple administrators, so you should create separate accounts for each administrator before using the Console to manage your services. The default Super Administrator account sysman shouldn't be used for daily operations. Rather, new Super Administrator and Regular Administrator accounts should be created as needed.

Super Administrator accounts have the privileges required to manage all objects in the system, similar to the root account on UNIX systems or the Administrator account on NT/2000 systems. Super Administrators can perform any task within the Console.

Regular Administrator accounts have access to the nonadministrative Console operations and can view or modify only the jobs, events, and groups for which they have permission.

Select the System-Manage Administrators... menu item to view the list of current administrators and to create a new administrator account. Initially, the default Super Administrator sysman is the only account in the list. Super Administrators are denoted by a red star next to the image of the person in front of the administrator name.

Create an Administrator   Click the Add... button to create a new administrator using the Create Administrator Account window. Enter the administrator name and password.

To create a Regular Administrator, make sure the Super Administrator account check box isn't checked. Check the Access to job system check box if the administrator can manage jobs, and check the Access to event system check box if the administrator can manage events. See the following illustration for an example of creating a Regular Administrator named oem_regadmin, who can access both the job and event systems. Click the OK button to add the Regular Administrator.

To create a Super Administrator, check the Super Administrator account check box. Because a Super Administrator can perform any task, the Access to job system and Access to event system check boxes are automatically checked and disabled. Click the OK button to add the Super Administrator.

Edit Administrator Preferences   Each administrator account has several configuration options, including the following:

■   Preferred notification method (no notification, pager only, e-mail only, or pager and e-mail) that can vary by time and day of the week

■   Which event and job occurrences should trigger notification

■   Permissions to set on new objects created by the administrator

■   Preferred credentials for logging into each service

To configure an administrator account, click the Edit... button on the Manage Administrator Accounts window. The Edit Administrator preferences window opens with five tabs: General, Notification, Schedule, Permissions, and Preferred Credentials.

The *General* tab allows a Super Administrator to change the administrator's password and access (Super or Regular Administrator, access to job and event systems), and to add a description of the administrator.

The *Notification* tab defines how the administrator is notified during status changes in events and jobs, either by e-mail, pages, neither, or both. On the left side, a hierarchical control is used to select the various components necessary to send e-mail messages or pages. For e-mail messages, enter the administrator's e-mail address and an optional subject prefix. For pages, select a predefined carrier and, optionally, enter the pager's PIN. Refer to the "Installing Paging Servers and E-mail" section for information on configuring paging carriers and paging servers. For both e-mail messages and pages, use the Subject and Message Body items under the E-mail and Paging headings to select the information to be included in the message.

Click the *Schedule* tab to set the administrator's notification preferences, as shown in Figure 20-10. For each hour time slot and each day of the week, click the appropriate notification method and "paint" the method into the time slot. In the subset of hours visible in this example, the administrator is notified as follows:

■   Pager only between 7:00 A.M. and 4:00 P.M. on Sunday, and between 1:00 P.M. and 4:00 P.M. on Friday

■   Pager and e-mail between 7:00 A.M. and 8:00 A.M., and between 12:00 P.M. and 1:00 P.M., on Monday through Friday

■   E-mail only between 8:00 A.M. and 12:00 P.M., and between 1:00 P.M. and 4:00 P.M., on Monday through Thursday; and between 8:00 A.M. and 12:00 P.M. on Friday

■   No notification on Saturday

The *Permissions* tab is used to share objects between administrators. When an administrator creates an object, such as an event or a job, he defines whether other

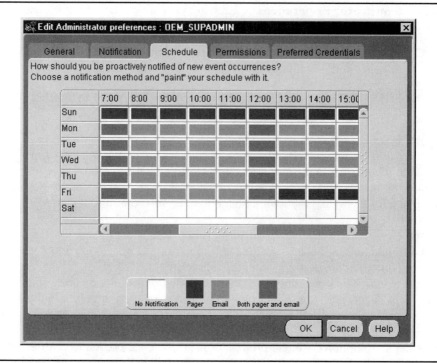

FIGURE 20-10. *Edit Administrator preferences—Schedule tab*

administrators can view, modify, or manage the object. The administrator also can check the Notify check box to select the administrators to notify by e-mail or pager when the object triggers the notification process. Click the Administrator heading to sort the administrators by name or click a permission heading to assign the selected permission to all eligible administrators.

The *Preferred Credentials* tab enables an administrator to define the credentials for each managed service, such as a database, listener, node, Web server, and so forth. For database services, supply a user name, password, and role (NORMAL, SYSDBA, SYSOPER). Either the SYSDBA or SYSOPER role is required to start up or shut down the database. For listener services, only supply a password. For node services, supply both a user name and password. Click the OK button to save the credentials and close the window.

For each service type, a service name of <DEFAULT> exists. The default service is used to supply the credentials for all services of that type for which credentials haven't been set. Services for which specific credentials are set are indicated by a green check mark. Nondefault services whose credentials are supplied by the default service are indicated by a gray check mark. The example in Figure 20-11 shows both services where the default credentials are used and nondefault services with specific credentials.

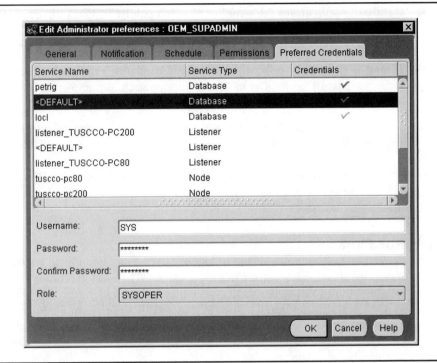

FIGURE 20-11. *Edit Administrator preferences—Preferred Credentials tab*

When you finish managing the administrator accounts, click the Close button on the Manage Administrator Accounts window to close the window and return to the OEM Console.

Console Components
The Console window consists of several components, including the following:

- **Navigator pane**   Hierarchical control to navigate services

- **Group pane**   Groups objects logically and displays a graphical view of the network

- **Job pane**   Lists jobs accessible by the administrator

- **Event page**   Lists events accessible by the administrator

- **Toolbar**   Buttons to create a job object, create an event set, create a group, remove an object, or obtain help

- **Database Applications "drawer" or "launch palette"** Click the arrow to expand the toolbar to access buttons such as DBA Studio and SQL*Plus Worksheet

- **Extended Database Applications "drawer" or "launch palette"** Click the arrow to expand the toolbar to access buttons such as interMedia Text Manager and Spatial Index Advisor

- **Service Management "drawer" or "launch palette"** Click the arrow to expand the toolbar to access buttons such as Internet Directory Manager

Each of the four panes can be maximized by clicking the icon of the arrow at the top-right corner of each pane or resized by dragging the line of dots between the panes to the desired width.

Navigator Pane

The *Navigator* pane, shown maximized in Figure 20-12, is a hierarchical control used to access the managed objects. Click a plus sign (+) to expand a branch or a minus sign (-) to collapse a branch. Objects are placed in the hierarchy by different groupings, such as databases, groups, listeners, and nodes. For example, to access a database, you can locate the database in the Databases branch, within the logical group, within the listener responding to requests for the database, or within the node that contains the database.

When accessing an object, the Console prompts the administrator to enter the necessary login information if the preferred credentials aren't configured for the current administrator. As part of entering the credentials, the administrator can check the box labeled Save as Preferred Credential to store the information for future login requests.

Depending on the type of object you're accessing, different items are available to configure by expanding the object branch or right-clicking the object.

Databases Several administrative tasks are available within each database. Expanding a database branch reveals several tools to administer a database, grouped into categories:

- Instance

- Schema

- Security

- Storage

- Replication

- JServer

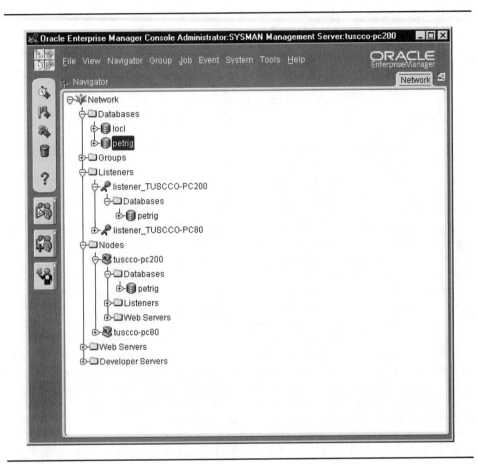

FIGURE 20-12. *Console Navigator pane*

Within the *Instance* branch, you can control the database operations; manage stored configurations, sessions, and in-doubt transactions, as well as set up resource consumer groups, resource plans and the resource plan schedule.

Right-click the Database option within the Instance branch and select the Edit… option to configure the database. Click the All Initialization Parameters… button to view the current initialization parameters. The credentials for the selected database must have the SYSDBA role to configure the database. Otherwise, the Database State and Restricted mode options are disabled. The initialization parameters are displayed in a table that can be sorted by any column by clicking the respective column heading. If the credentials have the SYSDBA role, the administrator can change parameter names and values, otherwise, the values are view only. Using the *Memory* tab, an administrator connected with the SYSDBA role can adjust the sizes of the various memory pools in the System Global Area (SGA), define the maximum number of concurrent users, and set the sort area size. Memory values are entered in units of MB (megabytes), KB (kilobytes), or B (bytes). The *Archive* tab is used to define whether the database is in Archive Log mode. If the database is in Archive Log mode, the Archive tab specifies whether automatic archiving is enabled, and the locations and name mask of the archive files. Finally, the *Resource Monitors* tab shows the current Resource Plan and the associated performance statistics generated by the plan.

The *Schema* branch contains several branches to manage all the components within each schema. For each component branch under the Schema branch, select the particular schema owner and, below the owner branch, the particular object. Manageable schema components include all object types within an Oracle database.

The *Security* branch is used to manage users, roles, and profiles. Expand a user branch to access options for roles, system privileges, object privileges, and consumer groups granted to the user. Similarly, expand a role branch to access options for roles, system privileges, object privileges, and consumer groups granted to the role. Finally, expand a profile branch to view the profiles, and expand a profile to access the users assigned to the profile.

The *Storage* branch manages all the physical storage used by the database, such as the control file, tablespaces, datafiles, rollback segments, redo log groups, and archive logs. Right-click the *Controlfile* branch to manage the control file. To change the control file, select the Backup Controlfile to Trace option. A message appears that says that a text version of the control file is now in the udump (trace) directory. This file can be edited and used when starting the database used to create a new control file set. The Controlfile branch, as well as the Tablespaces and Datafiles branches, enables you to manage the database backups. Select the Backup Management cascading menu item to perform backup and recovery operations using either a predefined or a custom backup configuration. Preferred credentials must be set up on the node to perform these operations. The last menu item for the Controlfile branch, Edit..., displays information on all the control files in the set, plus the contents of the record section of the control file. Expand the branches of the other storage components to manage the items within each particular component or right-click the branch to manage the component type.

The *Replication* branch manages database replication. Expanding the Replication branch provides an overall administration option, plus branches to manage both multimaster and snapshot replication.

The *JServer* branch manages Oracle's enterprise class platform for developing and deploying server-based Java applications. Expanding the JServer branch lists all the contexts within JServer. Right-click the JServer branch or a context to create, edit, or remove a context, create a link, or show the Java worksheet. Expand a context branch to list the objects within the context. Right-click an object to edit or remove the object, create a link, or show the Java worksheet.

Groups   The *Groups* branch provides a method of organizing the managed resources into logical groups. Groups are defined using the Group Pane. Expand the Groups branch to select a group and expand a group branch to access the resources that are members of the selected group.

Listeners   Expand the *Listeners* branch to view all the Oracle listeners running on the managed nodes. Right-click a listener to access listener-specific options, including defining a blackout period. A Super Administrator can define a blackout period for specific resources or a total blackout period covering all resources. During a blackout period, such as a planned outage, administrators aren't sent pages or e-mail messages when events are triggered for the resources covered in the blackout definition. Blackout periods can be single or recurring. *Recurring blackouts* can occur on specific days of the month, specific days of the week, within a specified hour or minute interval, and for a predefined start date and optional end date.

By expanding a specific listener branch, the administrator can access options for each of the databases serviced by the listener. These are the same options as if the database was accessed using the Databases branch.

Nodes   The *Nodes* branch lists all the nodes discovered during the Discover Nodes process. Right-click the Nodes branch to discover new nodes, refresh the list of resources available on the current nodes, or view the node blackout periods.

Right-click a specific node to manage the node and discover resources for only the selected node. A Super Administrator can also define one or more blackout periods for the node. In addition, an administrator can expand a specific node to access the resources on the node such as databases, Forms listeners, listeners, Web servers, and so forth.

Web Servers   All the Web servers discovered are available under the *Web Servers* branch. Right-click a Web server to start, stop, or ping the server to verify it's running. Clicking the Edit... menu item displays summary information about the Web server and allows the administrator to shut down or start the Web server.

Group Pane
The administrator logically groups services to display the current state of the services graphically in the *Group* pane. To create a new group, either click the New Group button on the toolbar or select the Group | Create Group... menu item. The Create Group window appears, as shown in the following illustration. Enter a group name.

Optionally, select a background image to display in the pane and select either large or small icons. Click the OK button to create the group. You receive a confirmation message that the group was created successfully. Click the OK button to close the confirmation dialog window.

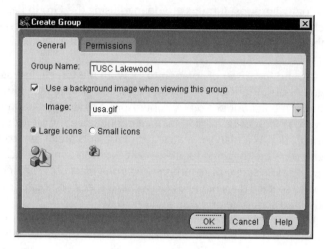

The initial background images are located in the $ORACLE_HOME/classes/ oracle/sysman/resources/images directory. New images should be created in GIF or JPG format and placed in this directory, instead of specifying a directory name in the Image input box.

The administrator can use the Permissions tab within the Create Group or Edit Group window to define whether other administrators can view or modify the group, or change the group owner.

Drag services from the Navigator pane to the new Group pane and place the icons at the desired locations on the image, or on the blank pane if no image was selected. See Figure 20-13 for an example of the maximized Group pane with two databases and one Web server. Once a database is placed on the Group pane, the administrator can right-click the database to open the floating context menu. In short, the Group pane is an alternate method of locating services by using a background image, rather than the hierarchical control in the Navigator pane.

Job Pane
The *Job* pane lists all the jobs available to the administrator. Before you can create a batch job, you must create or select an operating system user who is granted the appropriate permissions to execute batch jobs. The user must have read and write permission in the $ORACLE_HOME/network directory, plus read, write, update, and delete permission in the $ORACLE_HOME and $TEMP directories.

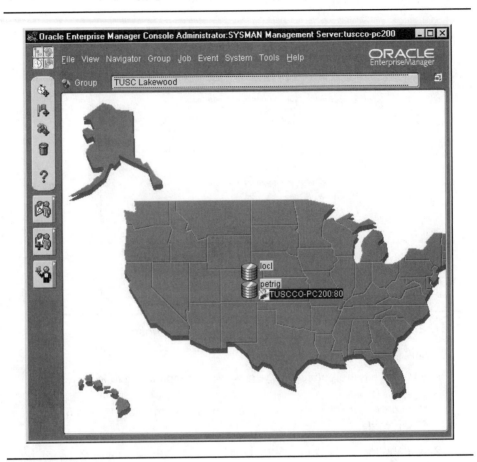

FIGURE 20-13.   *Group pane*

NOTE
*This is documented in Metalink note 151610.1, but
only the temp directory requirement has been proven.*

Windows 2000 Job Account   For Windows 2000 users, ensure the Intelligent
Agent service is set to log in as the Local System account and the account can log in
as a batch job. Create a new user, as shown in Figure 20-14. Make sure User must
change password at next logon isn't checked. The user cannot be named SYSTEM or
system. Click the Create button to create the user, and then click the Close button to
close the Create User window.

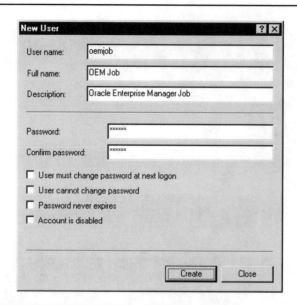

FIGURE 20-14.   *Create Job User on Intelligent Agent node*

To grant the required policy to the new user, complete the following steps:

1. Open the Local Security Policy tool in the Control Panel | Administrative Tools folder.

2. Expand the Local Policies branch.

3. Click the User Rights Assignment folder.

4. Right-click the Log on as a batch job policy and select the Security... menu item, as shown in Figure 20-15. The Local Security Policy window opens, displaying the users currently granted the policy.

5. Click the Add... button to open the Select Users or Groups window.

6. Select the OEM job user (named oemjob in this example), click the Add button, and click the OK button to grant the policy to the user and close the Select Users or Groups window. The Local Security Policy Setting window shows the user is granted the policy.

7. Click the OK button to close the Local Security Policy Setting window.

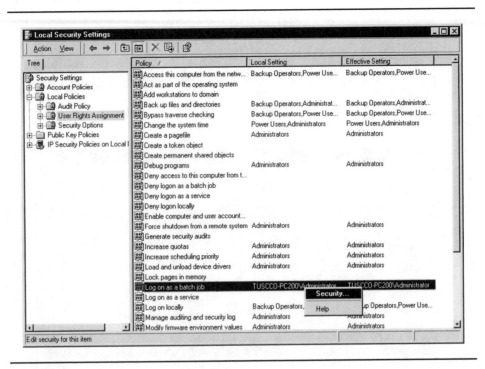

FIGURE 20-15. *Windows 2000 User Rights Assignment*

TIP
If you didn't grant a policy or group to the job user that provides the required access to the $ORACLE_HOME, $ORACLE_HOME/network, and $TEMP directories, grant these permissions directly to the user.

Update the Preferred Credentials for the node where the Intelligent Agent executes the batch job with the new user information, as shown in Figure 20-16.

Create a Job *Jobs* are used to perform various database administration activities, such as backups, or reorganizing tables and indexes. To create a new job, click the Create a new job object button on the toolbar or select the Job | Create Job... menu item to open the Create Job window at the General tab. Enter a job name, description, and select one or more destinations available in the right-half window based on the

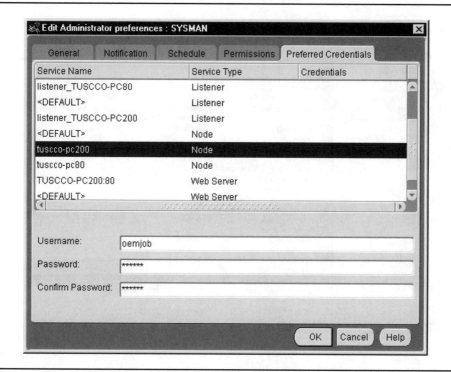

FIGURE 20-16. *Set Preferred Credentials for Intelligent Agent node*

selected destination type, as shown in Figure 20-17. Check the Fixit Job check box if this job will be executed to correct an event condition. Otherwise, leave the check box unchecked to schedule the job. Select the appropriate radio button indicating whether to submit the job to run by the Intelligent Agent, only to add the job to the library for other administrators to select, or both.

TIP
In a UNIX environment, OEM executes jobs using shell scripts. When manually canceling a job, make sure to cancel the shell process, in addition to the job process.

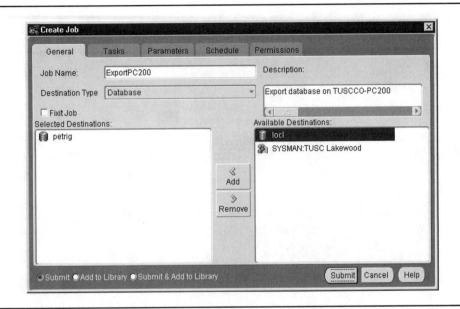

FIGURE 20-17. *Create Job—General tab*

On the Tasks tab, select one or more tasks to execute using the Add button and order the tasks using the UP ARROW and the DOWN ARROW, as shown in Figure 20-18.

Enter the parameters required by the tasks on the Parameters tab. Each task has a specific wizard to help you define the parameters. For example, click the Load Wizard... button to open the Export Wizard to export the database. Follow the wizard prompts until you reach the summary window. Schedule the job execution using the Schedule tab, as shown in Figure 20-19.

If desired, select which administrators can view, modify, or manage the job using the Permissions tab. Click the Submit button to create the job. The job appears in the Job pane, as shown in Figure 20-20.

Job History   The *History* tab in the Job pane lists the jobs that have executed. Click the orange circular arrow icon to refresh the job history list or click the trashcan icon to clear all the history. To view details for a specific job, double-click the associated job history entry. When viewing the details, use the Progress tab to view any output messages generated by the job.

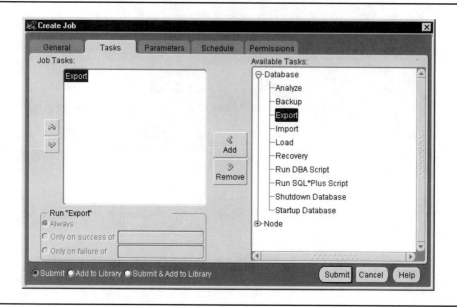

FIGURE 20-18. *Create Job—Tasks tab*

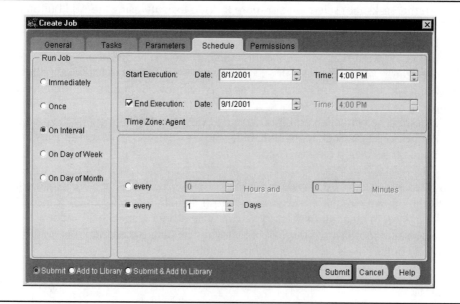

FIGURE 20-19. *Create Job—Schedule tab*

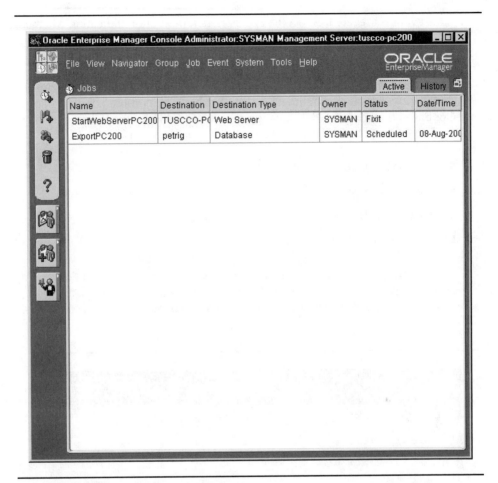

FIGURE 20-20. *Job pane*

Event Pane

Whereas the Job pane defines scripts executed for a predefined schedule or when required by an event, the *Event* pane defines scripts executed as a reaction to an occurrence within a service. To use a database analogy, jobs are like explicitly executed procedures or functions, whereas events are like implicitly executed triggers.

Creating an Event   Click the Create a new Event Set button on the toolbar or select the Event | Create Event... menu item to open the Create Event window. Enter an event name, description, frequency (in seconds, minutes, or hours), and one or more destinations based on the selected destination type. If any Fixit Jobs were created in the Job pane for the specific resource, optionally select a job to execute when the event is triggered. Select the appropriate radio button indicating whether to submit the event to run by the Intelligent Agent, only add the event to the library for other administrators to select, or both. The example shown in Figure 20-21 creates an event to check every 60 seconds if the Web server is running. If the Web server isn't responding, the event runs a Fixit job to attempt to restart the Web server.

On the Tests tab, as shown in Figure 20-22, select one or more conditions to monitor based on the selected destination type. OEM includes the following standard event tests for determining if a resource is up or down:

■ Database UpDown

■ Node UpDown

■ Listener UpDown

■ WebServer UpDown

Optional management packs provide additional advanced test conditions.

Click the Add button to add the WebServer UpDown condition to test if the Web server is running, and click the UP and DOWN ARROWS to order the selected conditions.

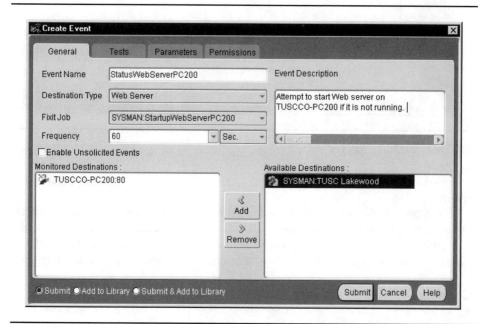

FIGURE 20-21. *Create Event—General tab*

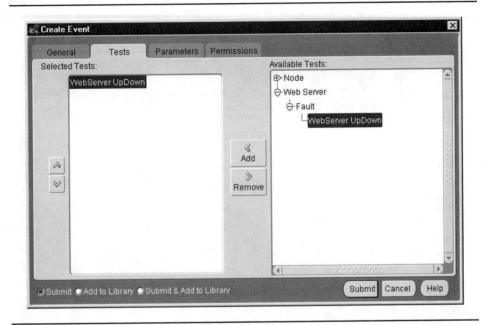

FIGURE 20-22. *Create Event—Tests tab*

The registered events are shown on the Registered tab within the Event pane, as shown maximized in Figure 20-23.

To test this event, use OEM to stop the Web server by right-clicking the Web server in the Navigator pane and selecting the Shutdown menu item. A job is submitted as shown in the Jobs pane to perform the shutdown process. Within the next 60 seconds, another job is submitted by the new event to restart the Web server.

NOTE
On Windows NT/2000, OEM starts and stops the Web server processes directly. The Services console may show the Web server service is Started, even if the Apache processes aren't running or vice versa.

Event Alerts   The *Alerts* tab in the Events pane shows alerts triggered by an event test. Alert severity is depicted as an icon, with the following definitions:

- Red flag (critical)
- Yellow flag (warning)

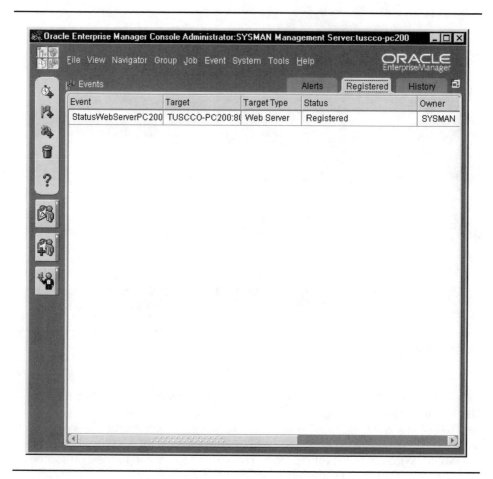

FIGURE 20-23. *Event pane*

- Green flag (clear)
- Gray flag (unknown)
- Yellow hexagon (error state)

Double-click an event alert to show the details of the failed test. While viewing the details, click the Log tab to add a journal entry to enter information you found while investigating this issue.

Event History The *History* tab in the Events pane lists the events moved to history by an administrator or cleared by an Intelligent Agent. Click the orange circular arrow icon to refresh the event history list or click the trashcan icon to clear all the history.

To view details for a specific event, double-click the associated event history entry. When viewing the details, use the Log tab to add a journal entry on the history of this alert.

Database Applications

The *Database Applications* drawer contains buttons to start database administration tools. The standard installation of OEM includes DBA Studio and SQL*Plus Worksheet. These are standalone applications that can be executed independently of OEM. On Windows NT/2000 systems, the applications are available using the Start menu at Programs | Oracle—<ORACLE_HOME_NAME> | Database Administration. On both UNIX and NT/2000 systems, you can start DBA Studio at a command prompt using oemapp dbastudio, and start SQL*Plus Worksheet at a command prompt using oemapp worksheet.

Because these applications are available either through OEM or standalone, when launched as standalone and a Management Server is available, the administrator is prompted to select whether to log in to the Management Server or to connect directly to a database. Logging in to the Management Server provides the benefits of OEM automatically supplying the databases previously discovered, as well as the preferred credentials to access the databases.

DBA Studio   *DBA Studio* provides all the features of the DBA Management Pack with the exception of the features in SQL*Plus Worksheet. DBA Studio enables the administrator to manage one or more databases using a graphical interface to create and execute DDL statements. The features available in DBA Studio are the same features available in the Databases branch of the Navigator pane.

SQL*Plus Worksheet   *SQL*Plus Worksheet* provides a graphical interface to SQL*Plus. The interface consists of two panes: the top pane is used to enter SQL*Plus and SQL commands, and the bottom pane displays the results. Most, but not all, SQL*Plus commands are supported. Review the online help for unsupported commands, such as GET, EDIT, SAVE, SPOOL, and START.

When you start SQL*Plus Worksheet, the bottom pane shows the database banner information and a message showing you're connected. If only the banner appears, connect to a database by clicking the cord and plug icon in the toolbar and entering the appropriate credentials. Once you're connected, enter one or more SQL commands delimited using normal SQL*Plus delimiters (semicolons and slashes), and click the lightning bolt icon to run the commands. To rerun a previous command, click the Command History button, select the desired command, and click the Get button.

Extended Database Applications and Service Management

The *Extended Database Applications and Service Management* drawers contain buttons to start standard and optional management packs. Depending on the applications installed, the standard installation of OEM includes one or more of the following applications:

- Oracle Applications Manager
- Oracle Enterprise Security Manager
- Oracle Text
- Oracle Parallel Server Manager
- Oracle Spatial Index Advisor
- Oracle Directory Manager
- Oracle Distributed Access Manager
- Oracle Developer Server Forms Manager

Optional management packs include the following:

- Oracle Diagnostics Pack
- Oracle Tuning Pack
- Oracle Change Management Pack
- Oracle Standard Management Pack
- Oracle Management Pack for Oracle Applications
- Oracle Management Pack for SAP R/3

Accessing the Console Using a Web Browser

One of the major benefits of the Console is it's accessible either as a standalone application (fat client) or through a Web browser (thin client). Although most of the Console functionality is available using a browser, several of the management packs won't run in the browser. Management packs that require the fat client are Oracle Tuning Pack, Oracle Diagnostics Pack, Oracle Change Management Pack, Oracle Management Pack for Oracle Applications, Oracle Management Pack for SAP R/3, and Oracle Standard Management Pack.

The Management Server listens on port 3339. Connect to the Management Server using the following URL:

```
http://managementserver:3339/
```

The default page named EMWebSite.html appears, as shown in Figure 20-24.

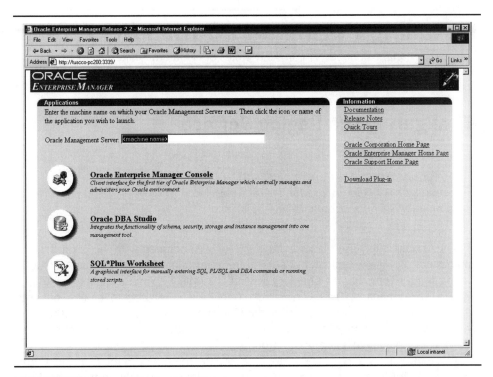

FIGURE 20-24. *OEM from a Web browser*

Enter the name of the node where the Management Server is running and select the desired application from the following options:

- Oracle Enterprise Manager Console
- Oracle DBA Studio
- SQL*Plus Worksheet

If the Management Server is running, the requested applet is launched in a separate browser session.

TIP
If this is the first time you're using Oracle's Java applications within a browser, you must install the JInitiator plug-in. New versions of Netscape and Internet Explorer automatically prompt you to install the plug-in. If you aren't prompted to install the plug-in or the applications don't open when you click the application links, click the Download Plug-In link.

Installing Paging and E-mail Servers

Before the Management Server can send pages or e-mail messages to notify administrators of an event occurrence, the paging server or e-mail server must be configured using the Console.

Configuring the Paging Service

TIP

If your pager supports using e-mail, such as pin@pagerservice.com, use the instructions in the next section, "Configuring E-mail."

The Oracle Enterprise Manager Paging Server is included with the 9i (or 8i) database as part of the typical, but not minimal, installation for Windows NT/2000. The paging service is named Oracle<ORACLE_HOME_NAME>PagingServer and is set up to start manually. The paging service only runs on NT/2000 platforms, but you can configure the paging service using the Console on either UNIX or NT/2000 systems. Start the paging service using either the Services console or by entering **oemctrl start paging** at a command prompt.

Once the paging service is running, add the paging server in the Console. Only a Super Administrator has permission to add a paging server. Within the Console, select the System-Preferences... menu item and click the Notification tab. Select the Paging Servers item and either right-click the item to select Add Server or click the Add Server button at the bottom of the page. Within the Add Paging Server dialog box, enter the host name running the pager server and click the OK button. The host name appears in the list of Paging Servers.

After adding a paging server, the Super Administrator must add a paging carrier. On the Notification tab, expand the Paging Servers branch and select the paging server. Right-click the paging server and select Add Carrier or click the Add Carrier button at the bottom of the page. Within the Add Paging Carrier dialog box enter the carrier name, pager type (alphanumeric or numeric), and for alphanumeric pages, the protocol. Supported protocols are Telocator Alphanumeric Protocol (TAP), Global System for Mobile Communications (GSM), and FLEXTD. In the Connection Properties section, enter the country code, area code, telephone number to access the pager, and, for numeric pagers, an optional suffix. Click the OK button to add the paging carrier.

After the paging server and paging carrier are configured, all administrators can configure their notification preferences to use the pager server and carrier. Within the System | Preferences... menu item, select the Notification tab. Click the Paging item in the hierarchical control to configure the paging details. Select the appropriate carrier, enter the pager's PIN if the pager is alphanumeric and, optionally, limit the message length and change the message template. Click the Test button to confirm the paging notification setup. Once all the information is entered, click the OK button to close the window.

Configuring E-mail

OEM supports sending e-mail notification using SMTP. A Super Administrator configures the SMTP gateway in the Console using the System | Configure SMTP Gateway... menu item. Within the SMTP Configuration window, enter the name of the SMTP server and a text description of the sender, and then click the OK button to close the window.

After the SMTP gateway is configured, all administrators can configure their notification preferences to use e-mail. Within the System | Preferences... menu item, select the Notification tab. Click the e-mail item in the hierarchical control to configure the e-mail details. Enter the administrator's e-mail address and, optionally enter a subject, limit the message length, and change the message template. Click the Test button to confirm the e-mail notification setup. Once all the information is entered, click the OK button to close the window.

Summary

Oracle Enterprise Manager is a powerful, comprehensive suite of tools that provides database administrators with a graphical interface to administer resources such as databases, listeners, and Web servers. OEM's three-tier architecture provides flexibility and scalability to effectively manage resources in both small and large enterprises. In addition, the browser interface enables administrators to manage the resources from anywhere in the network where the Management Server is accessible. To provide centralized administration capabilities, multiple Management Servers share a single repository and multiple administrators can administer any or all of the resources for which they're granted the proper access. Each administrator configures her notification preferences for what times she wants to be notified of a system event, how she will be notified at different times and on different days, and for which events she wants to receive notification.

In the future, OEM is expected to manage even more resources and will continue to provide administrators with helpful tools to perform their job functions.

PART
V

Ongoing Support

CHAPTER
21

Troubleshooting

any questions need to be answered when you troubleshoot your application. What is the problem? How do you fix it? Where do you start? Is there an easy way to approach the problem?

The simplest technique combines basic knowledge with common sense. If you can identify the possible problem, the rest will fall into place.

When you're developing an application and an error occurs, a number of thought-process paths can be taken to resolve the error. You must know where to begin to discover the solution. What steps should you take down the troubleshooting stairway? The following four scenarios suggest how you might deal not only with problems in your code, but also with problems in general. I hope one of the following scenarios will occur when you encounter an error during application development:

- You know the answer

- You know how to find the answer

- You know who knows the answer

- You know when to ask for help

You Know the Answer

You might already know why your application won't work. If not, you still might know how to approach resolving the problem. Review your existing knowledge base. More than likely, you've had some formal education on problem solving. And, possibly, you learned an approach in school or in an adult education course you took after you graduated. Remember, on-the-job-experience is an invaluable tool. Your life experiences—book learning, on-the-job training, technical training, soft skills training, and personal and professional experiences—can assist you as you search for the answer. Mundane solutions sometimes hold the key to make the impossible possible.

You Know How to Find the Answer

With the rapid changes in technology, the problem you're facing could be one you've never faced before. While you might not know why an error occurred, chances are you know where to start looking for the reason. Knowing where to find the answer can be as helpful as knowing the answer. You might not know this yet, but you have at your disposal a wealth of information and resources, all of which are explained in detail in the following subsections.

Log Files

Log files are located in your *i*AS directories and can be of great assistance in identifying the problem.

The error.log file (in the Apache/logs directory) states the type of error that occurred. The access.log file shows you the entire URL that was called by the browser. Double-check that the variables are all present and named correctly. In addition to the error.log, you can check the specific log for the module executed. For example, JSP pages and servlets write additional errors in the jserv.log and mod_jserv.log files. Severe system errors are logged by the operating system, such as the Event Viewer in an NT environment.

Log files and site analysis are discussed further in Chapter 23.

Exception Handling

Exception handling in your code is similar to performing the job of the error log files, except the information provided is more accessible. In fact, you can send the error handling directly back to the browser. Refer to Chapter 22 for further information about debugging your code.

If you're on a LAN, WAN, or the Internet, you might not have access to the *i*AS log files. If you write the errors to a table on which you have insert and select privileges, you can mimic the logging of errors. Obtaining the last error that occurred in a system_errors table is easier than looking through a 3MB log file. You can also pinpoint the exact location (line number) in your code where the error occurred. The log files don't provide information that's nearly as detailed as your own exception logic can provide.

Books and Other Media

You should establish an arsenal of books you can reference for your Web applications. Remember, other forms of media, including magazines, documentation, theoretical material, and technical support can provide valuable information. Books in your library should include each of the topics of which your application is composed, for example, books on *i*AS, HTML, JavaScript, Java Server Pages, PL/SQL programming, database and application tuning, and so forth.

Oracle Support

Oracle offers many technical avenues to explore in your search for answers, including online *i*Seminars, video tapes (many of which are free), and Oracle

Support (including MetaLink). The following are some of TUSC's favorite Oracle and Oracle-related Web sites:

Oracle's Technet (Technical Network)	**http://technet.oracle.com**
Oracle Support online	**http://metalink.oracle.com**
Oracle's partner network	**http://partner.oracle.com**
International Oracle Users Group	**http://www.ioug.org**
Orafans	**http://www.orafans.com**
Underground Oracle FAQ's	**http://www.orafaq.org**
TUSC (The Ultimate Software Consultants)	**http://www.tusc.com**

Oracle Support—MetaLink

With MetaLink, you can search for prior issues that were submitted online or over the phone. You can submit a TAR online by going to the MetaLink Web site, located at **http://metalink.oracle.com/**. If you're a frequent visitor, you can click the Login to MetaLink! link. If this is your first time at MetaLink or if you haven't visited in a while (since Version 1), you'll need to register.

To register, perform the following steps:

1. On the MetaLink home page (**http://metalink.oracle.com/**), click the Register for MetaLink! link.

2. When you join Oracle Support, it gives you a support identifier, such as a CSI number, a SAC, or an access code. Enter your support identifier, choose the appropriate country, and click the Proceed button.

3. On the next screen, enter your pertinent personal information. Once you enter information in the appropriate fields, click the Proceed button.

4. The subsequent screen enables you to choose a user name and password. Once you select a user name and password, click the Proceed button.

5. The next screen contains the legal disclaimer. After you read the text, click the Accept button.

6. When the registration is complete, click the Oracle's Web-based support services link to enter MetaLink. A dialog box then appears. Enter the user name and the password you chose in previous steps. MetaLink's main page will be displayed.

If you're looking for information on upgrading OAS or any other Oracle-related topic, perform the following steps.

1. In the search text box, input the phrase you want to search for (for example, upgrading to *i*AS).

2. The results are listed in the Query Result section, just below the search box.

3. If you see an entry of interest, click that entry's title link. The document will appear in the browser's current active window.

4. If you want to search for a specific word, press CTRL-F within the browser and enter what you're looking for in the text box that appears.

Search Engines and Web Sites

Search engines and Web sites provide valuable sources of information when you're troubleshooting a problem. The online chapter, "Good Sites," contains a list of Web sites (including several search engines) that can help you find the information you seek. Many sites include their own internal search engine, similar to the search engine previously described within MetaLink. Google Groups (**http://groups.google .com**) also provides a search engine to help you by searching list server documents.

You Know Who Knows the Answer

You probably know someone who knows the answer—maybe it's a friend at work or, possibly, someone that person knows. Use all the resources (including coworkers, contacts, and consultants) you can before you move to the next step. As you're probably aware, if you call Oracle Support, it could be hours, days, or weeks before a resolution to your problem is offered. Oracle isn't going to say, "John Smith needs help, so let's create a patch today to solve his specific dilemma." At the same time, you need to know when to say when. If your problem truly is an Oracle bug, contact Oracle Support.

You Know When to Ask for Help

You have an error and you don't know how to resolve it. You aren't sure who to ask for help or where to begin looking. Now is the time to ask for help. You're on the clock and you can't waste time spinning your wheels.

You need to act. I use an escalation path when I ask for help. First, I ask a specific person, based on that person's history of solving related problems, known expertise, or working relationships. If necessary, I then query our local office, and then TUSC's various offices around the country through an e-mail. I ask if anyone has encountered the problem, knows how to fix it, or knows where I can find the answer. If that fails to return a response, I turn to Oracle Support.

Take a little time to establish an escalation policy for your company.

Summary

Troubleshooting isn't as difficult as it might first appear. Remember the four scenarios that can occur when you develop Oracle applications: You know the answer; you know how to find the answer; you know who knows the answer; you know when to ask for help.

Once you pinpoint the problem area, all you need to know is when you need help, where to look for help, and when to ask for help.

The most effective troubleshooting is done proactively. Don't let problems and error messages paralyze you. Consider ongoing education (for example, learn before you need to know). Join a "knowledge network," such as your local Oracle user's group, so you have a resource you can always turn to for help. Keep proven Web sites and resources handy, so they're available when you need them.

CHAPTER
22

Debugging Your Code

ebugging is a necessary evil in all software development. The capabilities and complexities of modern development tools almost guarantee something won't work correctly the first time. To many people, debugging and tweaking code to make sure it runs properly is what makes software development interesting and challenging. Once a piece of code moves into production, however, most of these same people would prefer it run indefinitely without problems. Look at the Y2K issue. Obviously, none of us expected the programs written 20 or more years ago to be in operation on January 2000, but they were.

This chapter focuses on development and coding techniques to decrease the total life-cycle cost of an application by guaranteeing robustness and reducing the time needed to recover from production problems. Although the coding examples in this chapter are PL/SQL examples, the principles of this chapter apply to any programming language.

In this chapter, you learn about the following topics:

- Reviewing General Debugging Techniques

- Displaying HTML Screens with PL/SQL Applications

- Determining Who Holds the Lock on a Row

- Buying PL/SQL Debugging Tools

- Debugging Without Interfering with User's View

- Looking Up General Oracle Errors

- Reviewing the Log Files

- Using Proper Error-handling Techniques to Decrease Bug Recovery Time

- Sending Error Messages to a User Interface Using raise_application_error

- Preparing for Production Problems by Designing Enhanced Debugging/ Tracing Logic into Application

- Presenting All Validation Errors Simultaneously Using an Error Array

- Confirming Proper Code Installation Using Version Reporting Packages

- Marking Your Trail with Application Tracing

- Keeping Production Code Wrapped

Reviewing General Debugging Techniques

Maybe you've experienced a situation where you changed the PL/SQL, recompiled it, opened a new browser window to load that page—yet the change isn't reflected in the newly generated HTML source. After clearing the memory cache and the disk cache, and then turning off caching all together, nothing works. If you're experiencing any "interesting" issues like these, beyond checking the log files, try the following debugging techniques:

From the browser, hold down the SHIFT key and click Reload. The major browsers have a caching issue that makes Reload not quite the Reload you might expect. If this is your issue and you're doing a lot of development, use the no cache metatag, as illustrated in the following syntax:

```
<meta http-equiv='pragma' content='no-cache'>
```

Use the preceding syntax in the head section of your HTML pages. Remember to remove it when that page is stable, unless you never want this page to be cached.

Make sure you're compiling the PL/SQL code into the correct schema. Trace this information from the PL/SQL logical path to the module, to the DAD, and then the schema and database SID. If you're using a SQL*Net connect string, check your tnsnames.ora file. If all the previous criteria match up, confirm the stored procedure is generating the desired code (select text from user_source where name='XXXXX' order by type, line). If all this fails, log in (using SQL*Plus) as the schema user and enter the following syntax:

```
SQL> set serveroutput on
SQL> execute your_web_procedure
SQL> execute owa_util.showpage
```

Is the HTML code you expected displayed? Confirm your DAD isn't pointing to an alternate schema and/or you don't have a synonym defined overriding what you think is being called (select * from all_objects where object_name = 'XXXXX').

TIP

*The owa_util.show_page procedure can produce misleading errors. The Web pages you develop are assumed to be called from a Web browser. When called from a SQL*Plus prompt, commands, such as owa_util.get_cgi_env (among others), have no meaning and return a fatal error.*

Displaying HTML Screens with PL/SQL Applications

If you ever run into a situation where the browser paints only part, if any, of the screen, first look at the HTML source. Is it there? Most likely it is, and you forgot an ending tag, such as the end of an HTML table (</TABLE>). Newer browsers, such as Netscape v4.x, color-code the underlying HTML syntax to identify inconsistencies in colors.

The issue might also be less predictable, such as a network issue that's losing a portion of your HTTP transmission, or it could be as simple as an IP address conflict. If the issue isn't one of these problems, resolving it is more involved. You can set up a sniffing program (like Snoop) and capture the packets being sent to and from a test machine to your Web server. Try one request/response session or you'll get lost in the packet information and encapsulation. Review the log of your request/response test and identify the last packet being sent from your Web server to your test machine. If the packet isn't there, modify htp.htmlClose in the Toolkit, pad the end of the tag with spaces equivalent to the packet size on your network, and recompile the Toolkit.

Determining Who Holds the Lock on a Row

If you're unsure who's locking rows in the database, you can execute the following script to identify the lock holder:

```
rem locks.sql - shows all locks in the database.
set linesize 132
set pagesize 60

column object         heading 'Database|Object'  format a15 truncate
column lock_type      heading 'Lock|Type'        format a4 truncate
column mode_held      heading 'Mode|Held'        format a15 truncate
column mode_requested heading 'Mode|Requested'   format a15 truncate
column sid            heading 'Session|ID'
column username       heading 'Username'         format a20 truncate
column image          heading 'Active Image'     format a20 truncate

spool locks.lis

select c.sid,
       substr(object_name,1,20) OBJECT,
       c.username,
       substr(c.program,length(c.program)-20,length(c.program)) image,
       decode(b.type,
              'MR', 'Media Recovery',
              'RT', 'Redo Thread',
```

```
                   'UN', 'User Name',
                   'TX', 'Transaction',
                   'TM', 'DML',
                   'UL', 'PL/SQL User Lock',
                   'DX', 'Distributed Xaction',
                   'CF', 'Control File',
                   'IS', 'Instance State',
                   'FS', 'File Set',
                   'IR', 'Instance Recovery',
                   'ST', 'Disk Space Transaction',
                   'TS', 'Temp Segment',
                   'IV', 'Library Cache Invalidation',
                   'LS', 'Log Start or Switch',
                   'RW', 'Row Wait',
                   'SQ', 'Sequence Number',
                   'TE', 'Extend Table',
                   'TT', 'Temp Table',
                   b.type) lock_type,
       decode(b.lmode,
                   0, 'None',               /* Mon Lock equivalent */
                   1, 'Null',               /* NOT */
                   2, 'Row-SELECT (SS)',      /* LIKE */
                   3, 'Row-X (SX)',         /* R */
                   4, 'Share',              /* SELECT */
                   5, 'SELECT/Row-X (SSX)',  /* C */
                   6, 'Exclusive',          /* X */
                   to_char(b.lmode)) mode_held,
       decode(b.request,
                   0, 'None',               /* Mon Lock equivalent */
                   1, 'Null',               /* NOT */
                   2, 'Row-SELECT (SS)',      /* LIKE */
                   3, 'Row-X (SX)',         /* R */
                   4, 'Share',              /* SELECT */
                   5, 'SELECT/Row-X (SSX)',  /* C */
                   6, 'Exclusive',          /* X */
                   to_char(b.request)) mode_requested
from   sys.dba_objects a, sys.v_$lock b, sys.v_$session c
where  a.object_id = b.id1 and b.sid = c.sid
and    owner not in ('SYS','SYSTEM');
```

Buying PL/SQL Debugging Tools

A number of tools are available to debug PL/SQL code. You can find these tools on Oracle's Web site, at local, regional, or international conferences, and in magazines.

GUI products can also assist in the debugging process by color-coding your syntax, thereby helping to identify basic errors early in the coding process. An example of a GUI tool is PL/SQL Developer by Allround Automations.

Debugging Without Interfering with the User's View

Occasionally, you need to track certain information from your site to debug your code. To avoid interfering with the users who are using the system, put your debug write statements in as HTML comments (that is, htp.comment when using the PL/SQL Web Toolkit), so the system can still run visually. This way, you can view the HTML source to see the "I got here" flags and values while still testing changes.

Looking Up General Oracle Errors

If you have access to a UNIX server, receive an Oracle error, and don't have an error manual handy, Oracle provides an Oracle Error utility (oerr) to assist in identifying the symptom, cause, and recommended solution. To execute oerr, you need the name of the product and the specific error number, as the following syntax illustrates:

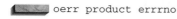
```
oerr product errrno
```

For example:

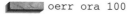
```
oerr ora 100
```

Reviewing the Log Files

Remember to review *all* the log files for errors that may occur. *i*AS provides consolidated error information in the access and error files. See Chapter 23 for more about log files.

Using Proper Error-Handling Techniques to Decrease Bug Recovery Time

One of the largest frustrations of debugging a production problem is determining what went wrong and why. Once the problem is identified, the resolution isn't far behind. Before the resolution can be implemented, a few basic questions must be answered:

- What procedure was running?
- Who executed it?

- What browser (and version) were they using?

- What platform are they on?

- What (virtual) host did they come in on?

- When did they run it?

- What record was being processed?

- What error was generated?

Although the list of questions to be answered is relatively small, the time it takes to answer these questions can be quite lengthy. We all have spent hours tracing simple bugs, like a primary key violation, which, in the end, was being caused by something simple, like the use of an incorrect sequence number. Many applications aren't written with problem resolution in mind so, to resolve bugs, you naturally start by working through the user interface until the error occurs again just to identify the troublesome module. After you identify the module, you typically gut the entire module components to identify the source of the problem.

When it comes to Internet applications, you're likely to get considerably less information from your users than you need. For example, if a user can't place an order on your site, he might send you an e-mail (if you're lucky) saying, "Here's my order, which I couldn't place on your Web site—please fix your site."

The overall time and frustration spent solving a production problem can be greatly reduced if the time it takes to identify the problem can be reduced, if not completely eliminated. This may sound like a major undertaking, but it's quite simple if sound error handling is used throughout the application.

Two simple rules can be applied to accomplish this:

1. Use exception handlers in every program unit

2. Record *all* abnormal errors—those a program unit isn't specifically written to handle

The following sections describe the two rules and how they come into play in a total error-handling solution.

Rule 1: Use Exception Handlers in Every Program Unit

An active exception handler is the *only* way to respond programmatically to a run-time error. Without an active exception handler, the program unit terminates abnormally and immediately. By using exception handlers, the program unit can remain in control when problems arise, thereby wrapping things up gracefully—displaying a user-friendly message, logging the error, and continuing the user's session. Is including exception handlers necessary in *every* program unit? Absolutely!

Consider the following function that computes the line item total of an order to the nearest, but lowest, whole dollar, and records it in the order header table:

```
create or replace function web_total (in_order in integer)
return integer
is
  nbt_running_total integer := 0;
  cursor order_detail_cur (in_id in integer) is
    select qty, amount
    from    order_detail
    where   order_id = in_id;
begin
  for order_detail_rec in order_detail_cur(in_order) loop
    nbt_running_total := nbt_running_total +
                         floor(order_detail_rec.qty *
                         order_detail_rec.amount);
  end loop;
  update order_header
  set     order_total = nbt_running_total
  where   order_id    = in_order;
  return nbt_running_total;
end web_total;
```

This function is so basic and short, a need doesn't seem to exist for exception handling. Unfortunately, this function generates a run-time error once the order total exceeds the precision of the integer data type.

Rewriting the preceding function to accommodate this potential problem yields the following program unit:

```
create or replace function web_total (in_order in integer)
return integer
is
  nbt_running_total integer := 0;
  cursor order_detail_cur (in_id in integer) is
    select qty, amount
    from    order_detail
    where   order_id = in_id;
begin
  for order_detail_rec in order_detail_cur(in_order) loop
    nbt_running_total := nbt_running_total +
                         floor(order_detail_rec.qty *
                         order_detail_rec.amount);
  end loop;
  update order_header
  set     order_total = nbt_running_total
```

```
   where  order_id    = in_order;
   return nbt_running_total;
exception
   when value_error then
      raise_application_error(-20000,  'Max order total exceeded.');
end web_total;
```

With the addition of the exception handler, the function remains in control during the identified possible problem: a calculated value that exceeds the precision of the result variable. But is this the only error that needs to be accommodated?

Absolutely not! Many other potential problems could generate a run-time error, for example:

- The precision of the order_total column could be less than the integer data. An error occurs if the calculated total is near the maximum value of the integer data type.

- The UPDATE statement may require another database extent be added to the database for the table to continue to grow. A problem can arise if the tablespace contains insufficient room for the new extent required.

- The UPDATE statement may violate a table constraint.

- A database trigger may reject the update.

- A database or hardware error may be encountered during the table update.

It is imperative that the function be protected against *any* possible run-time problems, not only the ones we identified so far in our error routine. The resolution of any possible run-time problem can be accomplished using the *OTHERS* exception. The *OTHERS* exception enables the exception handler to accommodate all other errors not specifically handled.

Rewriting the function to accommodate all potential problems yields the following program unit:

```
create or replace function web_total (in_order in integer)
return integer
is
   nbt_ora_error       varchar2(4000);
   nbt_running_total integer         := 0;
   cursor order_detail_cur (in_id in integer) is
      select qty, amount
      from   order_detail
      where  order_id = in_id;
begin
   for order_detail_rec in order_detail_cur(in_order) loop
```

```
    nbt_running_total := nbt_running_total +
        floor(order_detail_rec.qty * order_detail_rec.amount);
    end loop;
    update order_header
    set    order_total = nbt_running_total
    where  order_id    = in_order;
    return nbt_running_total;
exception
    when value_error then
      raise_application_error(-20000, 'Max order total exceeded.');
    when others then
      nbt_ora_error := sqlerrm;
      raise_application_error(-20000, nbt_ora_error);
end web_total;
```

While this function compensates for all possible run-time errors, it still has a severe limitation: it relies on the user to scribble the error on to a piece of paper and deliver it to the proper authority. If this is an end user Web-based procedure, the user sees the Request Failed page, which seems to contain gibberish (to the end user). The calling procedure needs to process the error and display a user-friendly error message. Rather than raise an exception, call your generic error display page. The generic page can be as simple as the following procedure, displaying a message providing the phone number of the support personnel for unexpected errors and the passed message for expected errors (data-entry type errors):

```
create or replace procedure user_error_message
    (in_type    number,
     in_message varchar2) is
begin
  htp.htmlOpen;
  if in_type = 'U' then
    htp.title('Support Required - Unexpected Error');
    htp.header(1,'Unexpected Error, Please Call Support');
    htp.header(3,'Please contact I.T. support at extension 2043');
  else
    htp.title(in_message);
    htp.header(1,in_message);
    htp.bodyOpen;
    htp.print('Please press the BACK button and fix the problem');
    htp.bodyClose;
    htp.htmlClose;
  end if;
end user_error_message;
```

To call our newly created *user_error_message* routine, our *web_total* procedure changes as follows:

```
create or replace function web_total (in_order in integer)
return integer
is
  nbt_ora_error      varchar2(4000);
  nbt_running_total integer         := 0;
  cursor order_detail_cur (in_id in integer) is
    select qty, amount
    from   order_detail
    where  order_id = in_id;
begin
  for order_detail_rec in order_detail_cur(in_order) loop
    nbt_running_total := nbt_running_total +
      floor(order_detail_rec.qty * order_detail_rec.amount);
  end loop;
  update order_header
  set    order_total = nbt_running_total
  where  order_id    = in_order;
  return nbt_running_total;
exception
  when value_error then
    user_error_message('E', 'Max order total exceeded.');
  when others then
    nbt_ora_error := sqlerrm;
    user_error_message('U', nbt_ora_error);
end web_total;
```

Rule 2: Record All Abnormal Errors

The second rule of effective error handling is to record all abnormal errors. Rather than writing the same generic error-logging logic in every routine, write a procedure geared to handle and record these abnormal errors. This approach not only ensures the error is recorded, but also that the error is recorded accurately. In addition, a program unit that records all run-time errors offers the following key advantages:

- The arguments passed to the program unit can be recorded, identifying errors caused by logically invalid arguments.

- The database record being processed can be recorded, identifying errors caused by data anomalies.

- The current settings of any environmental variables can be recorded. This is especially important when working with Web applications because capturing the environment (system) variables can provide a wealth of knowledge regarding the interface at the time of the error.

- The call stack (dbms_utility.format_call_stack) can be recorded, identifying the chain of events that led to the calling of the subject program unit.

- The error stack (dbms_utility.format_error_stack) can be recorded, providing a complete error list that was automatically generated by the problem.

- The section of code in which the failure occurred can be recorded. When working with large program units, it's beneficial to break the code into small, logical, uniquely identified sections. A section should be roughly one to thirty lines long. By recording the section identifier in the error log, the time spent finding the troublesome statement in a large program unit can be reduced.

To support our generic error-logging routine, we need to create the system_error table, system_error_id sequence number, and log_error procedure. To minimize the potential problems when writing to our system_error table, the table shouldn't contain constraints or triggers. Also, by sizing the table to be relatively large, we reduce the possibility of taking out a new extent during inserts. The following is an example to create the system_error table:

```
-- DDL creates the system_error table.
create table system_error(
      system_error_id          number(10),
      program_unit_name        varchar2(4000),
      unit_type                varchar2(4000),
      unit_owner               varchar2(4000),
      execution_location       varchar2(4000),
      browser                  varchar2(4000),
      server_software          varchar2(4000),
      server_name              varchar2(4000),
      server_port              varchar2(4000),
      remote_host              varchar2(4000),
      remote_addr              varchar2(4000),
      path                     varchar2(4000),
      script_name              varchar2(4000),
      oracle_error_text        varchar2(4000),
      additional_information   varchar2(4000),
      call_stack               varchar2(4000),
      error_stack              varchar2(4000),
      insert_time              date,
      insert_user              varchar2(30))
tablespace any_big_one
storage    (initial 1M next 100K pctincrease 0);
```

The following example creates the *system_error_id* sequence number:

```
-- This DDL creates the sequence number for the primary key
-- values for the system_error table
create sequence system_error_id
```

```
        increment by 1
        start      with 1
        minvalue   1
        nocycle
        cache      100
        order;
```

The following script creates the *log_error* procedure to record the errors to the *system_error* table. Note the use of autonomous transactions to allow the error data to be written to the database without interfering with any transaction that might currently be open.

```
-- Name: log_error
-- Description: Records an error in the error logging table.
-- Syntax: log_error (in_location,
--                    in_error,
--                    in_text)
--
-- Where: in_location   = The reference to a physical location within
--                        the procedure/function in which the error
--                        occurred.
--         in_error      = The Oracle error message.
--         in_text       = Any additional information provided by the
--                         developer to aid in identifying the problem.
--                         For example, this might be a rowid/account
--                         number.

create or replace procedure log_error (
                     in_location in varchar2 default NULL,
                     in_error    in varchar2 default NULL,
                     in_text     in varchar2 default NULL) is
  pragma autonomous_transaction;
  pu_failure            exception;
  pragma                exception_init (pu_failure, -20000);
  nbt_ora_error         varchar2(4000);
  nbt_id                number;
  nbt_program_unit      varchar2(4000);
  nbt_unit_type         varchar2(4000);
  nbt_unit_owner        varchar2(4000);
  nbt_unit_line         number;
  nbt_call_stack        varchar2(4000);
  nbt_error_stack       varchar2(4000);
  nbt_browser           varchar2(4000);
  nbt_server_soft       varchar2(4000);
  nbt_server_name       varchar2(4000);
  nbt_server_port       varchar2(4000);
  nbt_remote_host       varchar2(4000);
  nbt_remote_addr       varchar2(4000);
```

```
   nbt_script_name      varchar2(4000);
   nbt_path             varchar2(4000);
   cursor sys_err_id_cur is
     select system_error_id.nextval
     from   dual;

begin
   -- Probe the environment for critical data to be stored with the
   -- the error as this may aid in problem resolution.
   -- Avoid the urge to initialize these variables in the declaration
   -- section as that creates a failure point for this procedure which
   -- cannot be trapped by this procedure's exception handler. Such
   -- a failure of your error logging routine could interfere with the
   -- normal execution of the application, and this must never be allowed.
   nbt_call_stack    := substr(dbms_utility.format_call_stack, 1, 4000);
   nbt_error_stack   := substr(dbms_utility.format_error_stack, 1, 4000);
   nbt_browser       := substr(owa_util.get_cgi_env('HTTP_USER_AGENT'),
                              1, 4000);
   nbt_server_soft   := substr(owa_util.get_cgi_env('SERVER_SOFTWARE') ,
                              1, 4000);
   nbt_server_name   := substr(owa_util.get_cgi_env('SERVER_NAME') ,
                              1, 4000);
   nbt_server_port   := substr(owa_util.get_cgi_env('REMOTE_HOST') ,
                              1, 4000);
   nbt_remote_host   := substr(owa_util.get_cgi_env('REMOTE_ADDR') ,
                              1, 4000);
   nbt_remote_addr   := substr(owa_util.get_cgi_env('SERVER_PORT') ,
                              1, 4000);
   nbt_script_name   := substr(owa_util.get_cgi_env('SCRIPT_NAME') ,
                              1, 4000);
   nbt_path          := substr(owa_util.get_owa_service_path, 1, 4000);

   open  sys_err_id_cur;
   fetch sys_err_id_cur into nbt_id;
   close sys_err_id_cur;

   owa_util.who_called_me(nbt_unit_owner, nbt_program_unit,
                          nbt_unit_line, nbt_unit_type);

   -- If the pseudo column user isn't the "user" that you want, you can
   -- retrieve the correct user now. For example, if your application
   -- is using a cookie to store the real user or if you're using basic
   -- or digest authentication, you could retrieve the username
   -- at this point.

   insert into system_error
     (system_error_id, program_unit_name,  unit_type,
      unit_owner,      execution_location, browser,
      server_soft, server_name,          server_port,
```

```
        remote_host,      remote_addr,       path,
        script_name,      oracle_error_text, additional_information,
        call_stack,       error_stack,       insert_time,
        insert_user)
    values
        (nbt_id,                 nbt_program_unit,    nbt_unit_type,
        nbt_unit_owner,          in_location,         nbt_browser,
        nbt_server_software,  nbt_server_name,        nbt_server_port,
        nbt_remote_host,        nbt_remote_addr,      nbt_path,
        nbt_script_name,        in_error,             in_text,
        nbt_call_stack,         nbt_error_stack,      sysdate,
        user);
    commit;
exception
    when others then
        -- Suppress all errors as the error logging routine should never
        -- interfere with normal program flow.
        rollback;
        NULL;
end log_error;
```

Once the *log_error*-creating procedure (creating our supporting tables and sequence numbers) is implemented, identify the impacts to the web_total function. Note, the *code_section* variable is added and set accordingly throughout the function.

```
create or replace function web_total (in_order in integer)
return integer
is
    nbt_code_section  varchar2(4000);
    nbt_ora_error     varchar2(4000);
    nbt_running_total integer;
    cursor order_detail_cur (in_id in integer) is
        select qty, amount
        from   order_detail
        where  order_id = in_id;
begin
    nbt_code_section := 'Beginning';
    nbt_running_total    := 0;
    for order_detail_rec in order_detail_cur(in_order) loop
        nbt_code_section  := 'In cursor loop';
        nbt_running_total := nbt_running_total +
                            floor(order_detail_rec.qty *
                            order_detail_rec.amount);
    end loop;
    nbt_code_section    := 'Before update';
    update order_header
    set    order_total = nbt_running_total
```

```
    where  order_id    = in_order;
    nbt_code_section    := 'After update';
    return nbt_running_total;
exception
  when value_error then
    user_error_message('E', 'Max order total exceeded.');
  when others then
    rollback;
    log_error (nbt_code_section,
                sqlerrm,
                'Runtime error calculating total for Order '||
                  to_char(in_order));
end web_total;
```

Sending Error Messages to a User Interface Using raise_application_error

When writing stored program units to support a user interface written for the Web, you might need to send error messages back to the user interface, for example, validation errors that are within the user's capability to correct. Errors originating from system problems or logic errors should always be written to an error log to assist in problem resolution.

Using either the return value of a function or an OUT parameter of a procedure to communicate validation error messages back to the interface can solve error handling to the user level. These techniques rely on properly constructed front-end logic to make the interface "aware" of the validation error. This can result in numerous problems. In the following code snippet, the conditional statement returns the execution from this routine to the stored program unit performing the user interface.

```
create or replace procedure web_payroll_calc(in_emp     in number,
                              out_gross  out number,
                              out_ded    out number,
                              out_net    out number,
                              out_error  out varchar2) is
  nbt_timesheet_found boolean     := false;
  nbt_code_section    varchar2(4000);

  cursor timesheet_cur (in_id in number) is
    select *
      from  web_timesheet
      where emp_id       = in_id
      and   processed_flag = 'N';
begin
  --Access all outstanding timesheet entries for the employee
```

```
--and process.
nbt_code_section := 'Before timesheet_rec loop';
for timesheet_rec in timesheet_cur(in_emp) loop
  nbt_code_section := 'In timesheet_rec loop';
  nbt_timesheet_found := true;
  --Call incremental payroll logic here...

end loop;
nbt_code_section := 'After timesheet_rec loop';

--Prevent check creation if no timesheet records were found.
if not nbt_timesheet_found then
  out_error := 'Check not created - no timesheet records found.';
end if;
exception
  when others then
    rollback;
    log_error (nbt_code_section,
               sqlerrm,
               'Runtime error doing payroll calculation for emp #'||to_char(in_emp));
end web_payroll_calc;
```

This code performs payroll calculations for a specific employee, setting the error code, if necessary. The following code is the Web procedure called from another procedure to gather the employees to be processed. The *accept_emp_info* program unit is the procedure called from the user's browser displaying the employee information:

```
create or replace procedure accept_emp_info
   (in_emp varchar2) is
nbt_gross_amt      number(10,2);
nbt_ded_amt        number(10,2);
nbt_net_amt        number(10,2);
nbt_error_msg      varchar2(4000);
nbt_code_section   varchar2(4000);
begin

   -- Perform payroll calculations and populate the payroll tables.
   -- The gross, deduction, and net check amounts will be returned.
   -- Use these to complete the payroll check record and display
   -- to the browser
   web_payroll_calc(to_number(in_emp), nbt_gross_amt,
                    nbt_ded_amt, nbt_net_amt, nbt_error_msg);

   --Check for errors in the called package.
   if nbt_error_msg is not null then
      user_error_message('E', nbt_error_msg);
      return;   -- Stops the procedure here
   end if;
```

```
htp.htmlOpen;
-- This is where we would display all the information we calculated
-- back to the browser. This would simply use htp.prints,
-- tableOpen,…

htp.htmlClose;

--Commit transaction
commit;

exception
  when others then
    rollback;
    log_error (nbt_code_section,
               sqlerrm,
               'Runtime error doing payroll calculation for emp #'||
               in_emp);
end accept_emp_info;
```

Technically, this code works, but it's seriously flawed because it relies on programming logic to maintain the error condition identified in the stored program unit. A preferred approach is to use the error propagation mechanism at the foundation of PL/SQL—the exception. Rewriting the preceding code using *raise_application_error* provides a mechanism for returning custom error messages to the user's browser. This removes the dependency on logic to maintain the error condition identified in the stored program unit. The following example illustrates the *web_payroll_calc* routine with exception logic instead of simply setting an error message.

```
create or replace procedure web_payroll_calc(in_emp     in number,
                                out_gross  out number,
                                out_ded    out number,
                                out_net    out number,
                                out_error  out varchar2) is
  no_timesheet        exception;
  nbt_timesheet_found boolean        := false;
  nbt_code_section    varchar2(4000);

  cursor timesheet_cur (in_id in number) is
    select *
      from  web_timesheet
      where emp_id        = in_id
      and   processed_flag = 'N';
begin
  --Access all outstanding timesheet entries for the employee
  --and process.
```

```
  nbt_code_section := 'Before timesheet_rec loop';
  for timesheet_rec in timesheet_cur(in_emp) loop
    nbt_code_section := 'In timesheet_rec loop';
    nbt_timesheet_found := true;
    --Call incremental payroll logic here...

  end loop;
  nbt_code_section := 'After timesheet_rec loop';

  --Prevent check creation if no timesheet records were found.
  if not nbt_timesheet_found then
    raise no_timesheet;
  end if;
exception
  when no_timesheet then
    raise_application_error(-20000, 'Check not created - no timesheet
                                    records found.');

  when others then
    rollback;
    log_error (nbt_code_section,
               sqlerrm,
               'Runtime error doing payroll calculation for emp #'||to_char(in_emp));
end web_payroll_calc;
```

Notice the effect on the *accept_emp_info* routine—no longer does an obligation exist to check the error text to verify if it's NULL (or empty) and user-defined exceptions are implemented to process accordingly:

```
create or replace procedure accept_emp_info
(in_emp number) is
-- User-defined exception to prevent exception raised in
-- stored program units (by raise_application_error) from being
-- handled by others clause.
pu_failure      exception;
pragma          exception_init(pu_failure, -20000);
nbt_gross_amt   number(10,2);
nbt_ded_amt     number(10,2);
nbt_net_amt     number(10,2);
nbt_error_msg   varchar2(4000);
nbt_code_section varchar2(4000);
begin

  -- Perform payroll calculations and populate the payroll tables.
  -- The gross, deduction, and net check amounts will be returned.
  -- Use these to complete the payroll check record and display
  --  to the browser
  web_payroll_calc(in_emp, nbt_gross_amt, nbt_ded_amt, nbt_net_amt, nbt_error_msg);
```

```
-- This is where we would display all the information we calculated
-- back to the browser. This would simply use htp.prints, tableOpen
htp.htmlOpen;

htp.htmlClose;

--Commit transaction
commit;

exception
  when PU_FAILURE then
    user_error_message('E', sqlerrm);
  when others then
    rollback;
    log_error (nbt_code_section,
               sqlerrm,
               'Runtime error doing payroll
                calculation for emp #'||to_char(in_emp));
end accept_emp_info;
```

Preparing for Production Problems by Designing Enhanced Debugging/ Tracing Logic into Application

Debugging is often thought of as a task that occurs only during an application's development phase. Code in the development phase is littered with *htp.comment, dbms_output, text_io,* and *file_io* commands for the sole purpose of tracing bugs and logic errors. Removing these debugging statements from the production code seems unfortunate because they'll likely be needed if the subject code begins to encounter run-time problems, such as abnormal terminations, excessive execution times, or undesired output.

Logically removing the debugging statements—through comments—from the code is a good compromise, but this technique requires the code to be edited (to restore the statements) before debugging can begin.

An ideal solution would be to design debugging statements into the application and enable them dynamically with a Debug Control option. If the setting for the debug control variable (or column data) is stored within a table as data, the application can be placed in to a debugging/tracing mode without touching a single line of code. The other option is to set the variable in the package body's init procedure.

TIP
Package body units can be recompiled without invalidating the procedures dependent on the package. When a package specification is recompiled, every program unit referencing this package becomes invalid. If you use this procedure throughout your application, a blunder like that (recompiling the package specification when it's unnecessary) could invalidate your entire application! Oracle attempts to revalidate (recompile) an invalid procedure (or function) on the next execution. For deeply nested procedures, the first Web user to access a page must wait several extra seconds for all invalid stored modules to be recompiled.

The immediate advantages to an application that supports dynamic debugging/ tracing are as follows:

■ The application can be debugged/traced while executing without interfering with the actual execution. Thus, debugging can be performed in the environment where the problem is occurring. This can help those "it worked on the development server" types of problems and the intermittent types of problems only the user community seems to generate.

■ The application can be debugged without spending time and money hacking the code to insert debugging statements. This eliminates that feel of "it seems like we were here before (during development) and now we're expecting someone to pay us to duplicate earlier work."

■ If the debugging log includes time information (identical to the *web_debug* procedure, illustrated in the following example), the log can be used to trace slow-running routines. The right combination of debugging statements can help identify the exact statement affecting performance.

■ If you want to extend the debug mode power further, set *debug_mode* to be a number, rather than a Boolean variable. This enables you to turn on different levels of debug messaging.

■ The log can be written to a file or table. The following script directs logging information to a table:

```
create or replace package web_debug is
   debug_mode boolean;
```

```
  start_time integer;
  procedure init;
  procedure write_log(in_location varchar2,
                      in_debug_text in varchar2);
  procedure really_write_log(in_location varchar2,
                             in_debug_text in varchar2);
end web_debug;
/

create or replace package body web_debug is
  procedure init is
    -- We could store the debug value in a table, but for this
    -- example, to shorten the code, we're just going to
    -- hardcode this. It's important to put this in the package
    -- body so that the value can be changed, the package body
    -- recompiled without invalidating all referencing
    -- procedures.
  begin
    web_debug.debug_mode := true;
    if web_debug.start_time is NULL then
       web_debug.start_time := dbms_utility.get_time;
    end if;
  end init;

  procedure write_log
    (in_location varchar2,
     in_debug_text in varchar2) is
  begin
    -- Only write the log, if we are in debug mode
    web_debug.init;
    if web_debug.debug_mode then
       really_write_log(in_location, in_debug_text);
    end if;
  end write_log;

  procedure really_write_log
    (in_location varchar2,
     in_debug_text in varchar2) is
  nbt_log_time        date           := sysdate;
  nbt_start_time      integer        := dbms_utility.get_time;
  nbt_program_unit    varchar2(4000);
  nbt_unit_type       varchar2(4000);
  nbt_unit_owner      varchar2(4000);
  nbt_unit_line       number;
  nbt_browser         varchar2(4000) :=
                      owa_util.get_cgi_env('HTTP_USER_AGENT');
  nbt_server_software varchar2(4000) :=
                      owa_util.get_cgi_env('SERVER_SOFTWARE');
```

```
   nbt_server_name      varchar2(4000) :=
                        owa_util.get_cgi_env('SERVER_NAME');
   nbt_server_port      varchar2(4000) :=
                        owa_util.get_cgi_env('REMOTE_HOST');
   nbt_remote_host      varchar2(4000) :=
                        owa_util.get_cgi_env('REMOTE_ADDR');
   nbt_remote_addr      varchar2(4000) :=
                        owa_util.get_cgi_env('SERVER_PORT');
   nbt_script_name      varchar2(4000) :=
                        owa_util.get_cgi_env('SCRIPT_NAME');
   nbt_path             varchar2(4000) :=
                        owa_util.get_owa_service_path;
begin
   owa_util.who_called_me(nbt_unit_owner, nbt_program_unit,
                      nbt_unit_line, nbt_unit_type);

   -- Insert the date and time of the log entry, the time the
   -- grand (the one called from the user's browser) procedure
   -- started (in 100ths of a second), the time this call was
   -- made (in 100ths of a second) and the debug text.
   insert into debug_log
     (log_time, grand_start_time, debug_start_time,
      debug_text, program_unit_name, unit_type, unit_owner,
      execution_location, browser, server_software,
      server_name, server_port, remote_host, remote_addr,
      path, script_name, log_user)
   values
     (nbt_log_time, web_debug.start_time, nbt_start_time,
      in_debug_text, nbt_program_unit, nbt_unit_type,
      nbt_unit_owner, in_location, nbt_browser,
      nbt_server_software, nbt_server_name, nbt_server_port,
      nbt_remote_host, nbt_remote_addr, nbt_path,
      nbt_script_name, user);
exception
   when others then
     raise_application_error(-20000,
           'Error in write_log procedure');
   end really_write_log;
end web_debug;
```

This package assists you in debugging your code at any time. You can log as
much or as little debugging information as you deem necessary. In the preceding
example, we captured a significant amount of information. An important piece of
information captured is the time the Web procedure started and the time each
debug statement was captured. By subtracting these two numbers, you can track
execution speed down to the hundredth of a second. The following procedure is
an example of a procedure using the preceding *web_debug* package.

TIP
Use dbms_utility.get_time to retrieve time down
to the hundredth of a second.

```
create or replace procedure web_submit
    (in_emp_no     integer,
     in_name       varchar2,
     in_address    varchar2,
     in_address_2  varchar2,
     … ) is
    insert_counter integer;
    update_counter integer;
    nbt_code_section varchar2(4000);
begin
    nbt_code_section := 'Procedure web_submit starting';
    web_debug.write_log(nbt_code_section, 'Incoming Args - Emp No: '||
                        in_emp_no||…);

    nbt_code_section := 'Validation';
    web_debug.write_log(nbt_code_section,'Starting');
    web_validate(in_emp_no, …);

    --Begin calculation routines.
    nbt_code_section := 'Calculation';
    web_debug.write_log(nbt_code_section,'Starting');
    web_calc(in_emp_no, …);

    --Create transaction records.
    nbt_code_section := 'Transaction Creation';
    web_debug.write_log(nbt_code_section,'Starting');

    insert into order_header...
    web_debug.write_log(nbt_code_section,'Order Header: '||
        sql%rowcount||' records inserted.');

    insert into order_detail...
    web_debug.write_log(nbt_code_section,'Order Detail: '||
        sql%rowcount||' records inserted.');

    update inventory...
    web_debug.write_log(nbt_code_section,' Inventory: '||
        sql%rowcount||' records inserted.');

    nbt_code_section := 'Procedure web_submit ending normally';
    web_debug.write_log(nbt_code_section,NULL);
exception
    when others then
```

```
    rollback;
    log_error (nbt_code_section,
               sqlerrm,
               'Processing emp #'||to_char(in_emp_no));
end web_submit;
```

Presenting All Validation Errors Simultaneously Using an Error Array

Most Web applications rely on server-side code to validate user input to some extent. While performing as much validation as possible within the Web page (with JavaScript) is customary, certain types of validations, such as checking stock quantities, can only be performed on the server. When performing these server-side validations, a couple of key advantages are apparent when performing a complete validation and returning a complete list of problems to the user.

Most users seem to prefer an all-inclusive list of errors prior to attempting another submit. An application that forces the user to fix one validation error only to warn of another can quickly affect the user's patience. Add a slow Internet connection to this type of validation logic and the user can quickly become frustrated.

You can reduce network communication by providing an exhaustive list of errors to the user. The user can work from the error list to correct all identified errors prior to performing subsequent commits. If the user has properly corrected all error conditions, the next submission will most likely succeed. Compare this to a piecemeal validation routine that requires repeated submits for the user to be warned of all data validation errors. If validation can be performed on the client, it should be. Client-side validation is usually accomplished with JavaScript. For more information about using JavaScript for your client-side validation, refer to Chapter 7.

Our all-inclusive validation can be implemented using a simple PL/SQL table (similar to an array in most languages) serving as an error stack, which the validation routines can push messages into. The algorithm is as follows:

- The server-side submission procedure receives a submission from the Web application

- It calls validation/processing routines

- These routines push messages into the array as problems are encountered

- On completion of the validation/processing routines, the array is checked for contents (using the count property)

  - If the error array is empty, no errors were encountered and the transaction can be finalized

■ If the array contains any data, the transaction may need to be rolled back and the array contents sent back to the user as a Web page

The following sample code demonstrates the technique. The following *web_validation* package contains the validation routines. Notice the *io_error_array* is declared at the package level, and is passed in and out of each of the other procedures, all of which build on the error messages.

```
create or replace package web_validation is
    type error_type is table of varchar2(4000) index by binary_integer;
    io_error_array web_validation.error_type;
    procedure check_customer (
                in_cust        in      number,
                in_total       in      number,
                io_error_array in out web_validation.error_type);
    procedure check_stock (
                in_item        in owa_util.ident_arr,
                in_qty_wanted  in owa_util.ident_arr,
                io_error_array in out web_validation.error_type);
end web_validation;
/

create or replace package body web_validation is
    -- This procedure validates the customer account.
    procedure check_customer (
      in_cust        in      number,
      in_total       in      number,
      io_error_array in out web_validation.error_type) is
      nbt_cust_found boolean := false;
      cursor cust_cur(in_id in number) is
        select credit_amt
        from   web_cust
        where  cust_id = in_id;
    begin
      for cust_rec in cust_cur (in_cust) loop
        nbt_cust_found := true;
        if cust_rec.credit_amt < in_total then
          io_error_array(io_error_array.count + 1) :=
              'Your credit limit ('||cust_rec.credit_amt||
              ') is insufficient to complete order - '||
              'please reduce items and/or quantities.';
        end if;
      end loop;
      if not nbt_cust_found then
        io_error_array(io_error_array.count + 1) :=
              'Incorrect account number - please re-enter.';
      end if;
    exception
```

```
      when others then
         io_error_array(io_error_array.count + 1) :=
           'Unable to access your account. Please call customer service.';
   end check_customer;

   --This procedure verifies that the item is still available.
   procedure check_stock (
      in_item        in owa_util.ident_arr,
      in_qty_wanted  in owa_util.ident_arr,
      io_error_array in out web_validation.error_type) is
      nbt_item_found boolean;
      cursor stock_cur(in_id in number) is
         select on_hand
         from   web_stock
         where  item_id = in_id;
   begin
     for nbt_item_no in 1 .. in_item.count loop
        nbt_item_found := false;
        for stock_rec in stock_cur (in_item(nbt_item_no)) loop
          nbt_item_found := true;
          if stock_rec.on_hand < in_qty_wanted(nbt_item_no) then
            io_error_array(io_error_array.count + 1) :=
                 'Only '||stock_rec.on_hand||' units of item '||
                 in_item(nbt_item_no)||
                 'are available - please re-enter quantity.';
          end if;
        end loop;
        if not nbt_item_found then
          io_error_array(io_error_array.count + 1) :=
               'Incorrect item number - please re-enter.';
        end if;
     end loop;
   exception
     when others then
        io_error_array(io_error_array.count + 1) :=
          'Unable to verify inventory. Please call customer service.';
   end check_stock;
end web_validation;
```

This package performs the data validation. The following code is an example of a procedure called from the user's browser, calling each of the validation routines to build the error array:

```
create or replace procedure web_process_order
    (in_cust  number,
     in_total number,
     in_item  owa_util.ident_arr,
     in_qty   owa_util.ident_arr) is
```

```
  done              exception;
  io_error_array    web_validation.error_type;
  nbt_code_section varchar2(4000);
begin
  --Validate the customer.
  nbt_code_section := 'Validate customer';
  web_validation.check_customer(in_cust, in_total, io_error_array);

  --Validate the selected items.
  nbt_code_section := 'Checking Stock';
  web_validation.check_stock(in_item, in_qty, io_error_array);

  --If any of the validation procedures encountered errors then
  --put all error messages in a Web page and send back to the user.
  --Otherwise, process the order.
  if io_error_array.count > 0 then
    for loopctr in 1 .. io_error_array.count loop
      user_error_message('E', io_error_array(loopctr));
    end loop;
    raise done;
  end if;

  --Code to actually process order should be placed here.
  --The same error array should be used to record processing errors
  --and present them to the user.

exception
  when done then
    null;
  when others then
    rollback;
    log_error (nbt_code_section,
               sqlerrm,
               'Runtime error processing order for cust #' ||
                to_char(in_cust));
end web_process_order;
```

Confirming Proper Code Installation Using Version Reporting Packages

Determining whether the changes made to a package's source code were ever compiled into the database might become difficult. In addition, stored program units undergo minor formatting changes as source code is moved into the database, thus making it impossible to check the compiled code by extracting it and comparing it to the source script. The simple solution is to add a versioning variable to the package body and updating it to the current date whenever the source code is changed. This versioning can provide the first line of offense to tackle a production problem by verifying the compiled versions of program units are the correct versions.

```
create or replace package body my_package is
    -- Always maintain version when making coding changes
    -- This variable should be clearly visible near the top of the package
    -- as a reminder to developers to keep it updated.
    pg_version_c constant varchar2(30) := '19991230.1';
end my_package;
```

A decimal addition to the timestamp value enables tracing of multiple changes within the same day. The variable should be highlighted with a comment and kept near the top of the package body or the developers might forget to update it. A simple query against the *user_source* table yields the version of a package compiled into the database. The SELECT statement appears identical to the following snippet of code:

```
select  text
from    user_source
where   name = 'MY_PACKAGE'
and     type = 'PACKAGE BODY'
and     upper(text) like '%PG_VERSION_C%CONSTANT%';
```

The results of the preceding query are neither user-friendly nor terribly effective:

```
    pg_version_c constant varchar2(30) := '19991230.1';
```

TIP
Never recompile the package specification unless you're making a change to the definition of the program units (procedures or functions) therein.

Taking this tip and our versioning approach one step further, a simple *what_version* function can be added to the package to set and return the contents of the version variable:

```
create or replace package my_package is
   function what_version return varchar2;
   pragma restrict_references (what_version, WNDS);
end my_package;

create or replace package body my_package is
   pg_version_c constant varchar2(30) := '19991230.1';
   function what_version return varchar2 is
   begin
```

```
      return pg_version_c;
    end what_version;
end my_package;
```

The packages can be probed individually to return the version string or a simple PL/SQL block, such as the following *check_versions* procedure, can be used to probe all packages at once. The *user_objects* table contains two important columns, *created* and *last_ddl_time*. The *last_ddl_time* column identifies the date and time the program unit was last recompiled. In the following procedure, the *last_ddl_time* column is converted to the character format of yyyymmdd (same format as our version number) and compared with our version variable to provide the developer with further information:

```
create or replace procedure check_versions
    (in_program_unit      varchar2 default '%') is
    nbt_dml_statement    varchar2(4000);
    nbt_package_version  varchar2(4000);
    nbt_record_count     integer;
    nbt_version_cursor   integer;
    cursor source_cur is
      select distinct name
      from   user_source
      where  type    = 'PACKAGE'
      and    name like in_program_unit;

cursor object_cur (in_object varchar2) is
      select to_char(last_ddl_time, 'YYYYMMDD') last_ddl_time
      from   user_objects
      where  object_name = in_object
      and    object_type = 'PACKAGE BODY';
begin
  htp.htmlOpen;
  htp.headOpen;
  htp.title('View Program Unit Versions');
  htp.headClose;
  htp.bodyOpen;
  htp.tableOpen('BORDER=1');
  htp.tableRowOpen;
  htp.tableHeader('Program Unit');
  htp.tableHeader('Version');
  htp.tableHeader('Last DDL Date');
  htp.tableHeader('Notes');
  htp.tableRowClose;
  for source_rec in source_cur loop
    nbt_version_cursor := dbms_sql.open_cursor;
    nbt_dml_statement := 'select '||source_rec.name||
                          '.what_version from dual';
    begin
```

```
      dbms_sql.parse(nbt_version_cursor, nbt_dml_statement,
                dbms_sql.native);
      dbms_sql.define_column(nbt_version_cursor, 1,
                nbt_package_version, 100);
      nbt_record_count := dbms_sql.execute(nbt_version_cursor);
      if dbms_sql.fetch_rows(nbt_version_cursor) > 0 then
          dbms_sql.column_value(nbt_version_cursor, 1,
                nbt_package_version);
      else
        nbt_package_version := 'Version Reporting Failed';
      end if;
    exception
      when others then
        nbt_package_version := 'Version Reporting Not Supported';
    end;
    htp.tableRowOpen;
    htp.tableData(lower(source_rec.name));
    htp.tableData(nbt_package_version);
    for object_rec in object_cur (source_rec.name) loop
      htp.tableData(object_rec.last_ddl_time);
      if substr(nbt_package_version,1,8) !=
              object_rec.last_ddl_time then
        htp.tableData('*** Versions do not match ***');
      else
          htp.tableData;
      end if;
    end loop;
    htp.tableRowClose;
    dbms_sql.close_cursor(nbt_version_cursor);
  end loop;
  htp.tableClose;
  htp.bodyClose;
  htp.htmlClose;
end check_versions;
```

Marking Your Trail
with Application Tracing

Application Tracing is functionality for developers, DBAs, and support staff to
determine rapidly what users and automated agents/daemons are doing at a given
point in time. Through application tracing, answering rudimentary questions that
cannot be answered easily otherwise becomes possible, such as

■   How many users are currently running the User Maintenance Form?

■ How many records has the Payroll Calculation procedure processed so far?

■ One of Brad's procedures is stuck in an infinite loop again! How can we determine which database session to kill without a DBA to figure this out for us?

In addition, application tracing provides for advanced performance tuning and resource use analysis via the Oracle Trace and SQL Trace utilities.

Application tracing should be enabled for all applications via the *dbms_application_info* package. This package provides the capability to update the *Module, Action,* and *Client_Info* columns of the *v$session* table; as the following example shows:

```
select userenv ('sessionid') from dual;
USERENV ('SESSIONID')
-------------------
              62743
select module, action, client_info from v$session where audsid = 62743;
MODULE              ACTION              CLIENT_INFO
------------------- ------------------- -------------------------
SQL*Plus
exec dbms_application_info.set_module('package1', 'procedure1');
select module, action, client_info from v$session where audsid = 62743;
MODULE              ACTION              CLIENT_INFO
------------------- ------------------- -------------------------
package1            procedure1
exec dbms_application_info.set_action('procedure2');
select module, action, client_info from v$session where audsid = 62743;
MODULE              ACTION              CLIENT_INFO
------------------- ------------------- -------------------------
package1            procedure2
exec dbms_application_info.set_client_info('Web Session=123456');
select module, action, client_info from v$session where audsid = 62743;
MODULE              ACTION              CLIENT_INFO
------------------- ------------------- -------------------------
package1            procedure2          Web Session=123456
exec dbms_application_info.set_client_info('Records Processed=945');
select module, action, client_info from v$session where audsid = 62743;
MODULE              ACTION              CLIENT_INFO
------------------- ------------------- -------------------------
package1            procedure2          Records Processed=945
select module, action, client_info
from v$session
where module = 'tsc_spu_pkg';
MODULE              ACTION            CLIENT_INFO
------------------- ----------------- --------------------------------
tsc_spu_pkg         messaging_daemon  Name="0009DE0A0001" Checkpoint="4"
```

The following guidelines should be used to determine which column (*Module, Action,* or *Client_Info*) to set and when:

- The *Module* column always carries the name of the currently active exposed module. *Exposed modules* are those high-level application modules with which the user community interacts directly. In a Forms application, the exposed modules are Forms. In a dynamically generated Web application, the exposed modules are Packages.

- The *Action* column always carries the name of the currently active program unit in package.program format. The package.program format is needed, as the currently executing program unit might not exist within the exposed module identified by the *Module* column. This is true in the case of supporting program units, such as data lookup routines or modularized data processing routines. Because supporting program units aren't considered exposed modules, the package in which they exist would never be placed into the *Module* column solely because of the execution of said program unit.

- When application authentication is being used, the *Client_Info* column must always contain some type of reference (*User Key, Web Session Key,* and so forth) to the user connected to the database.

- When database authentication is being used, the *Client_Info* column shouldn't contain a reference to the current user. Doing so would be redundant because the *Username* column provides this information.

- Processes that run continuously (such as agents and daemons) must update the *Client_Info* column on a regular basis as a sign they're functioning properly. The update frequency should never be more than 15 minutes. Because these types of process are always run using database authentication, the *Client_Info* column needn't identify the executing user.

- Long running processes (such as Payroll Jobs, Import Routines, and Data Scrubbers) must update the *Client_Info* column on a regular basis as a sign they're functioning properly. When possible, the number of records processed must also be included. The update frequency should never be more than five minutes. If the process isn't being run using database authentication, the *Client_Info* column must also include the user reference as previously defined.

Applications served completely out of the database must constantly maintain the tracing columns as previously detailed.

Agents and daemons that run server side must constantly maintain the tracing columns as previously detailed.

Client applications (Forms, Reports, and so forth) need only maintain the tracing columns for primary objects (a Form, a Report, and so forth). Client-side code executing within these primary modules won't attempt to maintain the tracing columns because this would generate excessive network traffic. Server-side code being executed from client applications should maintain the tracing columns, however.

Keep Production Code Wrapped

The wrapping of PL/SQL program units has long been used as a means of protecting intellectual property. With the introduction of in-place editors (such as PL/SQL Developer, TOAD, and SQL*Navigator), however, the PL/SQL Wrapper can be used as a safeguard to prevent in-place editing of code. Once a program unit is wrapped, it can no longer be edited by any code editor. This forces the development community into the source code control system for all code maintenance.

Summary

In this chapter, you learned about numerous debugging tips for your Web applications. Topics included general debugging techniques, determining table/row locks, debugging tools, debugging without interfering with a users' view, how to look up general Oracle errors, reviewing the log files, and heavier topics. The deeply technical topics included the following:

- Using proper error-handling techniques to decrease bug recovery time
- Sending error messages to a user interface using raise_application_error
- Preparing for production problems by designing enhanced debugging/ tracing logic into an application
- Presenting all validation errors simultaneously using an error array
- Confirming proper code compilation using a version reporting package
- Securing production code with the PL/SQL wrapper

CHAPTER
23

Logging and Site Analysis

hen it comes to developing Web sites, understanding your customers is important. Who are your customers? What are their personalities? What's the best way to communicate with them? How can you tell them more about your company? How can you offer them more services?

Who your customers are can typically be answered by demographics-type questions, such as gender, race, age, education, home value, family size, income level, and so forth. *Pyschographics* measure your customers self-concept, attitude, interests, opinions, beliefs, preferences, and personality traits. *Communigraphics* information, such as understanding your customers' communication skills, cooperation, and participation, is another component that must be understood. These traits (demographics, pyschographics, and communigraphics) are strategic components you need to build in to your application.

The final component to understanding your customers could be called *clickographics,* which is their attention span, focus, appetite, impulsiveness, judgment, and analytical skills. Web logs can help you understand this customer component.

Understanding all these components results in predictive marketing. You'll know which customers you should cross-sell (such as selling you another product along with the product you wanted to purchase—a case with your new camera) versus up-sell (for example, you asked about our low end camera, but we're going to show you the one you asked for, plus one just a little better—because you always have to have the best of the best). Your sales group will no longer use assumptive marketing techniques. It's a one-on-one sales method for every unique customer. When you're successful at understanding your customers and how they find you, you'll see more page hits, increased editorial exposure, increased feedback, shortened sales cycle, increased sales, and decreased lead costs.

All Web servers generate log files recording requests made to the Web server and *i*AS is no exception. *i*AS performs several types of logging, each of which is discussed in this chapter.

Measuring the success of your Web site can be attributed primarily to the visitors it receives and *i*AS server use logs are the main focus of this chapter. Adequate analysis of the value and impact of your site requires monitoring and accumulating user activity. Most HTTP listeners, including the *i*AS HTTP Listener, provide activity logs to support your analysis requirements. The HTTP Listener accepts HTTP requests, forwards them to the *i*AS modules for dynamic content generation, or simply retrieves static content from an operating system file. *i*AS processes the dynamic requests in a third-party module (aka mod) and generates a result to be redirected back to the client. With most Web server installations, the capability exists to write log information about requests to standard text files. Interpreting the data within the accumulated log files to represent your Web server's activity involves creating programs (perhaps in Java, Perl, or C). Or, you could purchase a program specifically designed to do this. I highly recommend the latter. Why reinvent the wheel when low-cost (and even no-cost shareware) solutions are available? The information in the log files is parsed and subjected to programmatic analysis. The data is presented in a specific text or graphic report format. Typically, this analysis process is completed as a batch operation with little capability of ad hoc query operations on the data. A good tool also enables you to query the data.

So, what is all this hype over log files? The log files contain information providing factual answers to business questions, such as

- Who is hitting my Web site?

- Which pages are requested the most?

- What are the top paths through the site?

- Which files are downloaded the most?

- What is the activity of my site by day?

- What is the activity level by day of the week/hour?

- What is my best advertising source?

- What type of browser is being used?

Beyond marketing, advertising, and sales information, log information can be used to tune the server properly, identify a timeframe when your site can afford to be down, forecast the adding of new machines, and, perhaps, justify expanding Web-based services. Some of the newer analysis reports a promise to analyze how users are actually using your site. For example, are users stuck in Web page jail (an infinite loop on the site) or are they *pogo-sticking* (going up and down the site's structure) to find information?

This chapter will discuss the following topics:

- Getting a basic understanding of *i*AS use logging

- Resetting or rolling the log files

- Retrieving further information on log file formats

- Looking for Web Site Management tools

- Reviewing WebTrends SM solution

Getting a Basic Understanding of *i*AS Use Logging

Every time a user hits *i*AS (with a browser via the HTTP protocol), by default *i*AS places a record in your access log. Beyond the current date and time, the record stores information about the URLs requested and provides you with some basic information about the browser, such as the hostname, IP address, and so forth. By counting records, you can quickly assess how many hits your Web site received. Considerably more information is readily available that you can gather on each request. For example, if you want to know which browser is most commonly used to access your site or what languages your readers speak, you can log this information.

*i*AS uses the TransferLog Directive to create a single log file that stores the details of every request. As noted, *i*AS's logging capabilities are far more advanced than this. *i*AS can write the log file in any format. *i*AS can also write multiple log files, each with a different format, and can send log messages to an external process via a pipe.

The standard format for *i*AS log files looks like this:

```
192.168.0.2 - - [04/Mar/2001:00:39:01 -0700]
                "GET / HTTP/1.1" 200 2123
192.168.0.2 - - [04/Mar/2001:00:39:02 -0700]
                "GET /logo.gif HTTP/1.1" 200 1725
```

This standard format is called the common log format. You can customize the format of the log file that *i*AS writes as you see fit. People often customize the format to place a better delimiter (other than a space) between the fields. More often, the logs are customized to log additional information, such as the browser type, referring page (the page that linked the user to the current page), and so on. This additional information is usually placed at the end of each line, so standard log analysis programs can still analyze the file.

Special character sequences are used to represent specific information components to include in the *i*AS logs. For example, the character sequence %h is replaced with the name of the remote host. Table 23-1 shows a complete explanation of the escape sequences and the order of the fields to be placed into the Common Log Format (CLF). As you can see, many additional information components can be included.

Value	Description	Order in CLF
%a	Remote IP-address.	
%A	Local IP-address.	
%B	Bytes sent, excluding HTTP headers.	
%b	Bytes sent, excluding HTTP headers. In CLF format (i.e., a '-' rather than a 0 when no bytes are sent).	7
%c	Connection status when response is completed. 'X' = connection aborted before the response completed. '+' = connection may be kept alive after the response is sent. '-' = connection will be closed after the response is sent.	
%{ANYENV}e	The contents of the environment variable ANYENV.	
%f	Filename.	
%h	The fully-qualified domain name of the client, or its IP number if the name is not available.	1
%H	The request protocol.	
%{Header}i	The contents of any Header: header line(s) in the request sent to the server.	
%{user-agent}i	The type of browser that the user made the request using.	
%{referer}i	The URL of the page the user was on that contained the link to this URL—the referring page.	
%{accept-language}i	Client language preference.	
%l	Remote username—if IdentityCheck is enabled and the client machine runs identd, then this is the identity information reported by the client.	2

TABLE 23-1. *Log File Format Reference*

Value	Description	Order in CLF
%m	The request method.	
%{Note}n	The contents of note "Note" from another module.	
%{Header}o	The contents of Header: header line(s) in the reply.	
%p	The canonical Port of the server serving the request.	
%P	The process ID of the child that serviced the request.	
%q	The query string (prepended with a ? if a query string exists, otherwise an empty string).	
%r	The request line from the client, enclosed in double quotes (").	5
%s	The three digit status code returned to the client. For requests that got internally redirected, this is the status of the *original* request --- %>s for the last.	6 (%>s)
%t	Date and time of the request, in common log format time format, which is in the following format [day/month/ year:hour:minute:second zone] which can be broken down as follows: day = 2*digit month = 3*letter year = 4*digit hour = 2*digit minute = 2*digit second = 2*digit zone = (`+' | `-') 4*digit	4
%{format}t	The time, in the form given by format, which should be in strftime(3) format (potentially localized).	

TABLE 23-1. *Log File Format Reference* (continued)

Value	Description	Order in CLF
%T	The time taken to serve the request, in seconds.	
%u	Remote user (from auth; may be bogus if return status (%s) is 401)—if the request was for a password protected document, then this is the userid used in the request.	3
%U	The URL path requested.	
%v	The canonical ServerName of the server serving the request.	
%V	The server name according to the UseCanonicalName setting.	

TABLE 23-1. *Log File Format Reference* (continued)

iAS performs several types of logging. There are several logging directives, each of which is defined in the following in greater detail, including

- ■ LogFormat Directive
- ■ CustomLog Directive—Access Logs
- ■ ErrorLog Directive—Error Logs
- ■ TransferLog Directive—Similar to CustomLog
- ■ Unique Directives—Third-Party Modules
- ■ CookieLog Directive—Cookie Logs

The iAS logging module provides a centralized location for collecting and examining alert, warning, and error messages from all components of iAS applications.

LogFormat Directive

The *LogFormat Directive* specifies the format of the access log files. The default delimiter is a space. The delimiter you use in your LogFormat Directive is the delimiter to be used to write the log file.

The LogFormat Directive can either specify the default log file format (the log files specified after the LogFormat Directive) or provide an alias (that is, a nickname) for the defined log file format. As you can see by the syntax, the nickname is optional. The syntax for the LogFormat Directive is

```
LogFormat format|nickname [nickname]
```

The default LogFormat (if one isn't specified for a CustomLog or ErrorLog Directive) is

```
LogFormat "%h %l %u %t \"%r\" %>s %b"
```

The following LogFormat command defines a log format using the @ sign as the delimiter and includes the browser and referring page in the format specification. This example directive uses a nickname for the format myFormat. Note, when the definition includes a nickname, the format specified doesn't become the default format, it only defines a format alias or nickname.

```
LogFormat "%h@%l@%u@%t@\"%r\"@%>s@%b@{user-agent}i@{referer}i" myFormat
```

Reference the myFormat LogFormat in a CustomLog Directive using this command:

```
CustomLog logs/myLog.log myFormat
```

iAS creates the following aliases (combined, common, referrer, and agent) by default:

```
LogFormat "%h %l %u %t \"%r\" %>s %b \
          "%{Referer}i\" \"%{User-Agent}i\"" combined
LogFormat "%h %l %u %t \"%r\" %>s %b" common
LogFormat "%{Referer}i -> %U" referer
LogFormat "%{User-agent}i" agent
```

CustomLog Directive—Access Logs

The iAS access log (CustomLog Directive) collects data specific to who is hitting the server and how the Web site is being used. Every time an HTTP request is made, information is collected about the connection. For all Web servers generating log files that record requests made to the Web server, the HTTP server log files contain the time of the request, the source IP address of the request, the URL requested, the response code, and the size of the response block.

Web servers typically perform logging of an HTTP request in either the Common Log File format or the Extended Log File (XLF) format. XLF is a superset of CLF because XLF includes logging of HTTP request and response headers. The CLF log file format was developed by the National Center for Supercomputing Applications (NCSA) and has become the standard logging format for most Web servers. The XLF format isn't yet a recognized standard. If you purchase a Site Management (SM) tool and plan to process XLF logs, be sure the tool you're planning to purchase supports XLF logs. *iAS* provides you with the option to write the logs in either XLF (your own custom format) or CLF (a common format).

The access log is specified using the CustomLog Directive. The syntax for this directive is

```
CustomLog filename|pipe format|nickname [env=[!]environment-variable]
```

The CustomLog Directive can be used at the server or virtual host configuration level. Conditional logging (using the environment attribute is available in Apache 1.3.5 or later (*iAS* 1.0.2.1 is based on Apache 1.3.12 and 1.0.2.2 is based on 1.3.19, so both versions support this feature). The module that performs the logging is mod_log_config.

The first argument (filename|pipe), specifies the location to which the logs will be written. This argument can take on two different forms:

■ **file**   A filename, relative to the ServerRoot directory

■ **pipe**   The pipe character |, followed by the path to a program to receive the log information on its standard input

The second argument specifies the format of the data to be written to the log file. This can specify either a nickname defined by a previous LogFormat Directive (discussed in the following) or it can be an explicit format string as described in the log formats section.

The third argument is optional. This argument determines whether a particular request is logged, based on the presence or absence of a particular server environmental variable. If the specified environment variable is set for the request (or isn't set, in the case of a 'env=!name' clause), the request is logged. Environment variables can be set on a per-request basis using the mod_setenvif and/or mod_rewrite modules. For example, if you want to record requests for all GIF images on your server in a separate logfile, but not in your primary logfile, you could use the following directives. The SetEnvIf Directive checks the Request_URI environmental variable (which contains the URL the user or browser called on the Web server) to see if it ends with .gif. If it does, it sets the gif-image environmental variable to true. The first CustomLog Directive checks to see if the gif-image environmental variable is set to true. If it is "true", it writes the log record to the gif-request.log file. The final CustomLog Directive checks to make sure the gif-image environmental variable isn't true. If it is "not true," it writes the log record to the nongif-requests.log file.

```
SetEnvIf Request_URI \.gif$ gif-image
CustomLog gif-requests.log common env=gif-image
CustomLog nongif-requests.log common env=!gif-image
```

*i*AS contains a number of commented-out CustomLog Directives, so you can easily capture additional log information with predefined LogFormat nicknames. After installing *i*AS, the following directive is uncommented:

```
CustomLogs logs\access_log common
```

Because it is uncommented, the default log file contains CLF data. The configuration file also contains commented-out lines for separate agent and referer logfiles. If you want to create these separate files, you can uncomment the following directives:

```
CustomLog logs\referer_log referer
CustomLog logs\agent_log agent
```

As noted in the configuration file, if you prefer to maintain a single log file with access, agent, and referer information, uncomment the following line:

```
CustomLog logs\access_log combined
```

TIP
You can create as many log files as you want by simply including additional CustomLog Directives. Remember, though, writing data out to an operating system file affects performance, so each additional log file decreases the performance of iAS.

As discussed in Chapter 3, directives are context-sensitive. So, for each virtual host, you can define an error and access log file similar to the following example:

```
<VirtualHost 192.143.2.45>
      ServerAdmin webmaster@rentcondo.com
      DocumentRoot /www/docs/rentcondo
      ServerName www.rentcondo.com
      ErrorLog logs/rentcondo_error.log
      CustomLog logs/rentcondo_access.log combined
</VirtualHost>
```

If a CustomLog or ErrorLog Directive isn't inside the Virtual Host Directive, log requests for the Virtual Host are placed in to the logs defined in the main server.

TIP
You can choose to log particular fields when the response status is (or isn't) a particular value. For example, to log the browser for 200 or 304 statuses only, the following syntax would be used for this attribute:

```
%200,304{User-agent}i
```

TIP
You can put an exclamation point (!) immediately after the percent sign (%) to mean "not" (that is, only log if the status isn't 200 or 304):

```
%!200,304{User-agent}i
```

TIP
The strings in the directives can contain literal characters. For example, the character sequence \n and \t represent new line and new tab. Literal quotes and backslashes should be escaped with backslashes, as previously shown in the CLF format.

ErrorLog Directive—Error Logs

Another type of logging is error logging. The *error log* contains information logged by the HTTP server and by specific modules. The messages in the error log enable you to trace or debug a specific component that's providing information for your analysis.

The syntax of the ErrorLog Directive is

```
ErrorLog filename
```

The default ErrorLog Directive on installation of *iAS* is

```
ErrorLog logs/error_log
```

The LogLevel Directive is a supplemental directive for the ErrorLog and is used to control the number of messages logged to the error_log file. Possible values include debug, info, notice, warn, error, crit, alert, and emerg.

TIP
The default LogLevel is set to warn. To save processing time, the recommendation is that you change to a LogLevel of error, which can improve performance as much as 150 percent on some servers.

TransferLog Directive—Similar to CustomLog

The *TransferLog Directive* is a directive that was used prior to nicknames in the LogFormat syntax. While this is still supported, it's recommended you use the CustomLog Directive. The TransferLog Directive has exactly the same arguments and effect as the CustomLog Directive. It doesn't, however, enable you to specify the log format explicitly and you can't use it for conditional logging of requests. With the TransferLog Directive, the log format is determined by the most recently specified LogFormat Directive (that doesn't define a nickname). The CLF is used if no other format was specified.

The syntax of the TransferLog Directive is

```
TransferLog file|pipe
```

The following is an example LogFormat and TransferLog Directive:

```
LogFormat "%h %l %u %t \"%r\" %>s %b \"%{Referer}i\" \"%{User-agent}i\""
TransferLog logs/access_log
```

Unique Directives—Third-Party Modules

*i*AS supports logging for third-party modules, such as Oracle's Java Servlet engine (mod_ose). The third-party module logs can provide you with information specific to the module.

The modules (mods) may have their own log directives, which can be found in the module configuration file (for example, the jserv.conf file), along with documentation in the comments of the configuration file. For example, the jserv.conf documents that "Log file for this module operation relative to Apache root directory. Set the name of the trace/log file. To avoid possible confusion about the location of this file, an absolute pathname is recommended. This log file is different than the log file that is in the jserv.properties file; it is the log file for the C portion of Apache JServ." The syntax and defaults are also documented in these files. Important to note is that when these logs are set to DISABLED, the log is redirected to the Apache error log.

The warning found in the jserv.properties file is worth noting. "WARNING: logging is a very expensive operation in terms of performance. You should reduce the generated log to a minimum or even disable it if fast execution is an issue. Note that if all log channels (see below) are enabled, the log may become really big since each servlet request may generate many Kb of log. Some log channels are mainly for debugging purposes and should be disabled in a production environment." This is absolutely true. The default is that logging is on.

TIP
In a production environment, turn logging off by setting the parameter "log=false."

Another warning found in the jserv.properties file is this: "WARNING: Default values are lousy, you probably want to tweak them and report the results back to the development team." That sums it all up, doesn't it? Take the time to go through the configuration files of any and all third-party modules your application is using and tune them. Many of the parameters in these modules are discussed in great detail in Chapter 3.

CookieLog Directive—Cookie Logs

The *CookieLog Directive* sets the filename for the logging of cookies. Cookies are passed as header information, so you can log cookies using the %{Cookie}i character sequence. The filename is relative to the ServerRoot. This directive is included for compatibility with *mod_cookies* only and is deprecated. If you're migrating from OAS to *i*AS, it's unlikely you'll need this directive.

The module also implements the CookieLog Directive, used to log user-tracking information created by mod_usertrack.

The syntax for the CookieLog Directive is

```
CookieLog filename
```

Resetting or Rolling the Log Files

OAS provides you with automatic log-rolling capabilities, but *i*AS doesn't. The access log file grows typically at a rate of 1MB or more for each 10,000 requests (based on the CLF). Moving or deleting the log file on a regular basis is necessary. If you're only going to delete the log files, then you might consider not even writing them. Most people like to have at least a minimal log (the last few hours), however, to monitor for attacks or other special situations.

To handle this, you need to set up a scheduled job (cron on Unix) that will run at a regular interval. You can also write a script that monitors the size of the file. *i*AS continues writing to the old log file even if you move the file. Therefore, the server must be restarted after the log file is moved or deleted, so it will open a new log.

The following is a sample cron script—you could take this a step further and increment the filename with numbers, dates, or some other value to make the filenames unique:

```
mv access_log archive/access_log.old
apachectl graceful
```

Or, log files can be rotated automatically by writing them through a pipe to a program designed for that purpose. The *rotatelogs* utility, for example, provides this functionality. You can find the complete documentation on rotatelogs in the Unix manuals. This file exists in the src/support/ directory. The rotatelogs utility can be used like this:

```
CustomLog "|/src/support/rotatelogs
           /$ORACLE_HOME/Apache/logs/access_log 86400"
```

The previous syntax enables daily rotation of the log files. The logs are rotated every 86,400 seconds (24 hours in a day, 60 seconds in a minute, 60 minutes in an hour).

A more sophisticated log file rotation is available under the name "cronolog" from Andrew Ford's site at **http://www.ford-mason.co.uk/resources/cronolog/**. Andrew's cronolog can automatically create logfile subdirectories based on time and date, and can have a constant symbolic link point to the rotating logfiles. The sample using cronolog is

```
CustomLog "|/src/support/cronolog
           --symlink=/$ORACLE_HOME/Apache/logs/access_log
           /$ORACLE_HOME/Apache/logs/%Y/%m/access_log" combined
```

Retrieving Further Information on Log File Formats

For technical information on log file formats, consult the World Wide Web Consortium (W3C) Web site at **http://www.w3.org**. The working draft for the Extended Log File format can be found at the following URL: **http://www.w3.org/pub/WWW/TR/WD-logfile.html**. The **http://www.apache.org** site also contains information about log files.

Looking for Web Site Management Tools

Site Management (SM) tools are used to gather and report statistical data regarding activity on your Web server. The tools use swift analysis of the raw data from the *iAS* logs. In today's competitive marketplace, any information that can be learned about a customer visiting your Web site can be of great worth. Essentially, the SM user can learn what people are looking for on a Web site, how the contents of a Web site are being accessed, who the most common visitors are, and which links are repeatedly accessed. Armed with this information, you can organize a Web site more efficiently.

In today's highly competitive electronic commerce and dot-com information technology market, any information collected about your public audience can serve invaluably for strategizing a solid marketing campaign. Because advertising is a large portion of the budget of most Internet-based businesses, the analysis of this information can be exceptionally valuable.

SM tools have even found their place within our criminal justice system. Investigators revealed that Web management tools help them to identify perpetrators of electronic viruses quickly (for example, the Melissa virus in 1999). The power driving these tools comes from their capability to crunch data stored within the Web server's log files. Furthermore, these tools generate sophisticated graphical reports with an array of choices for customizing output. Features common to the leading SM tools include multilanguage reporting, scheduled reporting, and several reporting platform options: Excel, Word, HTML, text file format, and e-mail.

Too many SM vendors exist to list within this chapter. When shopping for a SM tool, narrow the selection by comparing the business needs (for example, volume of log files, frequency of reporting, and OS platform) to the core features offered by the tools. Particular mention is given later in this chapter to Oracle's SM tool of choice, WebTrends Log Analyzer. If you want to find a list of available SM tools through a search engine, search for Site Management. SM vendors are extending the product scope to merge technology with consumer demand. These tools have become strong and dependable for advanced reporting on the activity of your Web server. WebTrends is only one example of a SM product with feature offerings that continue to grow. As discussed in Chapter 16, Portal provides a simplified, but built-in SM tool.

Reviewing WebTrends SM Solution

Once you determine you want to create reports based on the data coming from your Web server's log files, you can create a profile in WebTrends, and then away you go. The product is truly that simple! A WebTrends profile points to where your log files are stored. WebTrends supports analysis of access, referrer, and agent log files. You can also specify how you want these log files analyzed and whether you want any filters applied to the data. The profile settings are reflected in the generated output in the form of a Web log analysis report.

WebTrends provides a number of key features and products to help you analyze your Web logs. These tools and features are listed in Table 23-2. The log analysis of WebTrends provides roughly 100 reports for your review. WebTrends produces a number of valuable reports, including the following:

- **General statistics reports** Introduction, general statistics, server statistics

- **Resources accessed** Most requested pages, most requested content groups, least requested pages, entry pages, exit pages, single access pages, most accessed directories, paths through site, most downloaded file, most uploaded file, submitted forms, and dynamic page parameters

- **Dynamic page details** Downloaded file types

- **Advertising** Top advertising, advertising views, and clicks

- **Visitors and demographics** Visits per user, new versus returning users, authenticated users, users most active, countries, North American states and provinces, most active cities, most active organizations, and organization breakdown

- **Activity statistics** Summary of activity for report, period summary of activity by time, increment activity level by day of week, activity level by hour, and bandwidth

- **Technical statistics** Web server/technical information, server cluster load-balance (server cluster add-on), forms submitted by users, browser/client errors, page not found (404) errors, and server errors

- **Referrers and keywords** Referring sites, referring URLs, search engines, search phrases, search phrases by engine, search keywords, search keywords by engine, search keywords, and phrases by engine

- **Browsers and platforms** All browsers, Netscape browsers by version, Microsoft browsers by version, visiting spiders, most-used platforms, and operating systems

Do you want to reinvent all these reports? Table 23-2 contains a list of features that SM vendors, such as WebTrends, provide.

Component Name	Component Description
Web Server Traffic Analysis	Provide detailed Web site analysis and traffic reporting to others in your organization
Streaming Media Server Analysis	Understand the details of streaming media usage on your site, including the most popular clips, stops, starts, replays, and so forth
Proxy Server Analysis	Track the usage trends of your intranet and better understand your users' productivity
Link Analysis and Quality Control	Improve the quality, performance, and integrity of your Web site
Site Manager	Gain a visual understanding of your Web site's structure and layout
Monitoring, Alerting, and Recovery	Keep your Web site up and running at all times
ClusterTrends Server Cluster Add-On (Optional)	Accurately analyze Web site traffic and technical performance across clusters of local or geographically dispersed servers
DBTrends technology	Correlate information from existing ODBC databases with results from WebTrends data analysis
FastTrends ODBC technology	Export results from WebTrends FastTrends database to high-end Oracle, Microsoft SQL, Sybase, Informix, and other ODBC-compliant databases for further data analysis

TABLE 23-2. *WebTrends Components*

As previously mentioned, WebTrends communicates an overall focus on delivering finite statistics and advanced reporting on every component of your Web server. On the other hand, iLux, another SM vendor, has placed great emphasis on how its total product can help you to strategize a marketing campaign better.

WebTrends Log Analysis

With a brief overview of how WebTrends acts as a reporting mechanism for your Web logs, let's analyze *i*AS log extracts from actual access, referrer, and agent file reports. Web servers typically generate an access log automatically. The Web server records information, such as the user and the URL requested.

Access Log: Activity Level by Hour of the Day

The *Activity Level by Hour of the Day* report shows the most and the least active hours of the day for the report period. The report also includes a table that breaks down activity to show the average for each individual hour of the day. If several days exist within the report period, the value presented is the sum of all hits during that period of time for all days. This information determines whether the Web site is being hit 24 hours a day and if a pattern of downtime exists (for backups and so forth). It also provides you with insight into how "globally" your site is accessed. If peak hours tend to be obvious and quite close to your business hours, then your site probably isn't "global."

Access Log: Most Active Organizations

The *Most Active Organizations* report identifies the companies or organizations that access your Web site most often. Without this report, we'd never have known Oracle was the number one company hitting our Web site. This report can also help you judge what you want to include on the next revision of your Web site. Based on the domain, you can direct people to a specific portion of your site. For example, a major hardware vendor once directed every request coming from its competitors' domain to its job listings.

Access Log: Most Downloaded Files

The *Most Downloaded Files* report identifies the most popular file downloads from your Web site. If an error occurred during the transfer, that transfer isn't counted. TUSC has hundreds of documents available for download on our site. Understanding which papers and presentations people are downloading is helpful, so we can plan future presentations on the key topics of interest to people. Our mission is to make a difference. This report helps us measure exactly how effective we are in making a difference for people and their companies.

Access Log: Bandwidth

The *Bandwidth* report helps you understand the bandwidth requirements of your site by indicating the volume of activity as kilobytes transferred. This is useful information for judging your telecommunications requirements if you host your site internally. The Bandwidth report is also useful for determining your ISP bandwidth requirements.

Referrer Log Analysis

Referrer is defined as the URL of an HTML page from which a visitor clicks to access your site. A *referrer log file* is generated by the Web server. The data contained within this log file is used to identify who is accessing your Web site. What sites are people coming from to access your site (referring URLs)? What are they searching for? What search engines are they using to hit your site?

Referrer Log: Top Referring Sites

The *Top Referring Sites* report identifies the domain names or numeric IP addresses with links to your site. This information is only displayed if your server is logging this information. The data is useful for determining how effectively your advertising dollars are spent and whom you should thank for providing a link to your site.

Referrer Log: Top Search Engines By Keyword

How about finding out what search engines are returning your Web site as the result of a keyword search? This information provides you with valuable information for your metatags and keywords when submitting to the search engines.

Agent Log Analysis

The Web server can generate an *Agent Log* that maintains information on the operating system and browser used by visitors to your Web site. The following subsections are a few reporting samples from this particular log file.

Agent Log: Most Used Browsers

The *Most Used Browsers* report identifies the most popular WWW browsers used by visitors to your site. This information is only displayed if your server is logging the browser/platform information. With this knowledge, you can take measures to ensure your Web site is compliant with these browsers. WebTrends breaks down each of the browser versions visitors use to access your site.

Agent Log: Most Used Platforms

The *Most Used Platforms* report identifies the operating systems most used by the visitors to your Web site. This information is useful for determining compliance with these platforms.

Link Analysis

WebTrends can crawl through your site and offer suggestions for repairing and optimizing your site. As you add more links, the task of testing your site may become time-consuming. A Web site analysis tool can save you time by automating the task.

Within your link analysis profile, you indicate the location of the Web site you want to analyze to WebTrends and how you want the site checked. WebTrends locates the starting URL and walks through the site, checking all internal and external links according to your profile settings.

The following subsections are sample extracts from a WebTrends Link Analysis report. Information from these reports proves helpful in debugging and improving your site.

Link Analysis: Broken Pages

The Link Analysis: Broken Pages report provides information similar to the following: "2 pages (.01%) contain broken links. Refer to the Broken Pages section for further details."

Link Analysis: Suggestions for Improvements

The *Link Analysis: Suggestions for Improvements* report provides you with a number of suggestions on how to improve your Web site. For example, "Of the 90 pages on this site, 5 could be improved by adding titles, ALT attributes, or height and width attributes to images. ALT attributes give a description of the image for visitors who view the page in text mode (this description is also displayed while the page loads, and before the image appears). Height and width attributes enable browsers to load images faster."

TIP
Always use height/width attributes for images embedded within HTML tables. A browser won't display an HTML table until it knows how to size its borders. Without the height/width tag attributes, the browser waits until all images are completely downloaded before displaying the table.

Link Analysis: Site Statistics by Link Types

The *Link Analysis: Site Statistics by Link Types* report provides you with an analysis of your link types. For example, "Of the 5,268 total links on this site, 95 percent are HTTP, 0 percent are FTP, and the remaining are of e-mail, news, gopher, or other types."

Link Analysis: Oldest and Newest Pages

The *Link Analysis: Oldest and Newest Pages* report provides information about the oldest and newest pages on your Web site. For example, "The oldest HTML page was last modified on Wed Nov 30 19:02:52 1999. The most recent change was made on Tue Nov 24 17:54:15 2000 at page: **http://www.tusc.com/consulting/emrgtech.html**."

Link Analysis: Biggest (Slowest) Pages

The *Link Analysis: Biggest (Slowest) Pages* report provides statistics about the slowest pages throughout your site. For example, "This site contains 90 HTML pages, with a combined total size of 5,021 kilobytes (including all graphics and other linked files). The bigger the pages, the slower they load, which may be a problem if the majority of your visitors use dial-up connections. Refer to the Biggest Pages section for further details."

Summary

*i*AS provides a comprehensive output enabling you to fully monitoring activity on your Web server. Whether it's logging information about the visitors to your Web site(s), specific requests, or individual *i*AS component logging, the capability to capture this information is integrated into *i*AS, so take full advantage of the information you need.

CHAPTER
24

Search Engine
Ranking Secrets

et's face it. This whole Web site marketing thing is only a game—a war game with players that number at about 100 million publicly available Web pages! To narrow the playing field, you must understand how search engines work, how to select and use keywords, and how to use your best offense—metatags and titles. This chapter discusses how powerful metatags can make your site a winner in the search-engine game. Because this is a game where you want to be caught, a number of metatag strategies are covered in detail, along with nine other strategies for winning not only the game, but also the championships. Think of metatags as the secret ringer, but you should know *much* more.

Certainly, no lack of information exists on the subject of search-engine ranking or getting your site submitted to the search engines. In other words, the problem isn't finding information on these subjects. The real problem is boiling all this information down to the top items you need to do to promote your site. After considerable research, I limited all the material down to the following list:

- Keyword Writing and Placement

- Talking to the Robots

- Achieving Link Popularity

- Gaining Click Popularity

- Don't Spam Anyone or Anything

- Building Trojan "Doorway" Pages

- Reviewing Manual Submission

- Paying for Rank

- Buying Submission Software and Services

- Avoiding Lawsuits

- Don't Forget about Offline Promotion

- Beware of Other Pitfalls

As you might have noticed from the previous list, life exists beyond keywords. In fact, keywords are important, but they aren't the be-all, end-all answers to your woes. As in any industry where everybody thinks they're smarter than everyone else (sometimes called the NIH factor or Not Invented Here), the search engine companies are no exception. In fact, more than 2000 search engines exist today and each search engine uses its own set of rules for ranking sites. Most sites do place high value on the metatags (primarily via Inktomi's database, which is used by most of the major search engines, such as Yahoo!, Hotbot, AOL Search, and GoTo). But others rank sites based on click popularity (DirectHit), link popularity (Excite, Go, Google), directory listed priority (Go), fee-based (GoTo), and human-compiled methods (LookSmart, which is used by

MSN, Excite, and Open Directory). Open Directory's data is used by a number of search engines, including AOL, Lycos, Netscape, Hotbot, and AltaVista. Several search engines use other search engines as their driving force based on the search type, but almost every company also uses some proprietary component to their site's *spider,* an automated program that searches the Internet for new Web documents, or collection facility.

Note, although these are all commonly referred to as "search engines," three different kinds of search sites exist: search engines, search directories, and metasearchers.

Search engines are typically automated. They include sites like AltaVista, Hotbot, and Lycos. Search engines are composed of a large database that's queried by users through a Web page. You can add your site to the database by filling in a form or two, which instructs their spider to visit the submitted URL. This spider then scans the document(s) for relevant information, such as keywords, metatags, and so forth and passes the appropriate information back to the search engine database for the listing. When someone uses the engine to search for information, the database is then queried using various criteria to determine what listings are returned and in what order.

Search directories work a lot like search engines, but rather than a spider or robot adding your URL to a database, a *person* does it. In other words, the information is compiled by a human. Search directories include the always popular Yahoo! Like search engines, you submit your URL to search directories to be added to a directory. Because people review Web sites, these indices typically take much longer than their spidered counterparts to get submissions listed. Directories usually only index one (your main) page, as opposed to all the various pages throughout your site. And, because someone actually *looks* at your site, many directories take this opportunity to filter out sites they don't feel offer the type of content they'd like to provide to users. In other words, submitting a link to Yahoo! doesn't necessarily mean the link will get listed on Yahoo!

Metasearchers don't actually have their own database. Instead, they use a program to query numerous databases (from other search engines and directories) to provide users with URLs that match their search. Metasearchers include Ask Jeeves and Dogpile. Because metasearches only query *other* databases, you cannot add your URL to their engine. If your URL is listed in the databases it checks, however, your site comes up in relevant searches.

Keyword Writing

Keywords are critically important to your search-engine ranking success, so it's important to understand exactly what a keyword is. A great place to start is with your favorite search engine. Perform a search using a keyword you feel should lead you to the site or page(s) you want to index. Find a competitor who is at or near the top of the search result, and then go to your competitor's site. View the source for the page to see what your competitor is doing with their metatags and keywords that got the page at the top of the list. Use this information as a valuable learning exercise only, but do *not* copy from your competitor.

You can look in many places to find out what people are typically searching for, but the most common general searches may not apply to your business. In fact, picking more unique words for your search keywords is often best. If you're curious, however, here are some sites that show you the commonly typed keyword searches:

- Ask Jeeves Peek Through The Keyhole (**http://www.askjeeves.com/docs/peek/**) shows top searches at this popular question-answering search engine.

- MetaCrawler MetaSpy (**http://www.metaspy.com/**) enables you to see either a filtered or nonfiltered sample of top, real-time search terms from this popular metasearch service.

- Search.com Snoop (**http://savvy.search.com/snoop**) shows recent searches on this popular metasearch service.

- Kanoodle Search Spy (**http://www.kanoodle.com/spy/**) displays live searches on this pay-for-placement search engine.

- Fireball LiveSuche (**http://www.fireball.de/voyeur-fireball.fcg**) lets you see— in German—what people are searching for. Hier können Sie live sehen, was gerade in Fireball gesucht wird. Fireball is one of Germany's major search services.

- Mopilot LiveSearch (**http://mopilot.com/index.htm?go=live.php3**) shows you what queries those with WAP or wireless browsers at this WAP search engine are making.

Keyword Placement

I can assure you that keywords in specific metatags (that is TITLE, KEYWORDS, and DESCRIPTION) are big keys to your success with the search engines. The top places to put your keywords in your HTML are:

- Document title
- Description metatag
- Keyword metatag
- Headlines
- Links
- Body copy
- Alternate image tags
- Comments

- Hidden fields

- URL or site address

TITLE Tag

One of the most common oversights people make when creating a Web site is they don't think too much about the title of their page(s). Titles are important because when people bookmark your site, the default bookmark is the page title. More important, however, is that search engines look at this information as well. Not all search engines use your title as criteria in determining your relevancy for any given search, but most do! The TITLE of your home page is extremely important. The *TITLE tag* displays the header that is displayed in your browser.

At *TUSC*, an Oracle consulting, product, and software firm, we sell posters and books from our Web site. For this example, let's say this is all we want to achieve with our site. Based on this brief description, what would the best title be for our home page?

- <TITLE>TUSC—Home</TITLE>

- <TITLE>TUSC—Oracle Posters, Oracle Books, and more</TITLE>

- <TITLE>Oracle, Consulting, Posters, Books, Performance Tuning, PL/SQL, Web Development, OAS, The Ultimate Software Consultants, DBA, Remote DBA,…</TITLE>

- <TITLE>Sex, Pictures, Naked, XXX…</TITLE>

- <TITLE>TUSC—Oracle Posters, Oracle Books, Performance Tuning, PL/SQL, Web Development and more.</TITLE>

- <TITLE>TUSC—Better than Company X at Posters and Books</TITLE>

Starting with the first title (<TITLE>TUSC—Home</TITLE>)—this is probably one of the most common ways people title their pages. Although this is a functional title because it tells users where they are on your site, what happens when a search engine is indexing your site through keywords found in your title? Nothing. What words are a user likely to type in when searching for posters or books that would lead them to the TUSC site? TUSC? Home? Probably not. So, while benefits do exist for visitors in using this kind of title, it's a definite search engine no-no, unless someone is looking specifically for your name (and it's a unique word), the first title isn't going to help anyone find your site.

The second title (<TITLE>TUSC—Oracle Posters, Oracle Books, and more</TITLE>) is a little better. In addition to providing the company name for our site, the title references the kinds of posters and books available, specifically Oracle. If a user were to search for either specific (Oracle Posters or Oracle Books), a page with that title would likely receive a better listing.

The third title (<TITLE>Oracle, Consulting, Posters, Books, Performance Tuning, PL/SQL, Web Development, OAS, The Ultimate Software Consultants, DBA, Remote DBA,...</TITLE>) makes use of an extensive list of keywords. While using keywords is a good idea in titles, you should limit yourself to a few important ones rather than typing in every word that has anything to do with your site. Be concise! A long title is a bad thing.

The fourth title (<TITLE>Sex, Pictures, Naked, XXX...</TITLE>) makes use of all too commonly used keywords in searches. These keywords have nothing to do with either posters or books, however. Therefore, not only is this a deceptive title, it's unlikely to produce positive results. If users notice the misleading keywords, they can even have you removed from search engines and directories! Using misleading keywords is a bad idea.

The fifth title (<TITLE>TUSC—Oracle Posters, Oracle Books, Performance Tuning, PL/SQL, Web Development and more.</TITLE>) is the best. This title uses a number of relevant keywords users are likely to use in searches, it makes sense when read, and it's short and to the point. So, the bottom line is this: keep your title short and accurate. Think long and hard about your keywords, and don't forget to check good listings on other people's sites to see what they did with their titles.

Title six (<TITLE>TUSC—Better than Company X at Posters and Books</TITLE>) can create a legal issue for you.

TIP

Few search engines alphabetize their listings, but several do pay attention to alphabetical and symbol characters. All other page indicators being equal, a TITLE and a metadescription tag beginning with the letter A will come before others. Symbol and number characters are ranked before A and can be used to push your site a few places higher in the search engines. Similarly, the inclusion of an extra space in front of the letter A may push a site up one position. If your TITLE starts with the letter O, substitute the 0 (zero) character to see your site displayed above all the sites beginning with A.

The search engines revisit Web sites on a regular basis to update their database. If you have pages that are getting lots of hits, leave the TITLE tag alone. If not, fine-tune the TITLE tag and the search engine robots will see it as a new page. Combined with your fine-tuning of keywords in the TITLE, the net effect can push your page higher in the search engines' listings. If you do change the TITLE tag, check to make sure the rest of the page supports and amplifies the new TITLE.

Stacking the TITLE tag involves repeating the TITLE tag five to seven times. This can give your site a small advantage over others, all else being equal, though you run the risk of having the TITLE tag ignored by some search engines (considered spam by some). Use this strategy only if you have similar pages listed that don't use stacked TITLE tags. For example:

```
<HTML>
<HEAD>
<TITLE>TUSC - PL/SQL Poster</TITLE>
<TITLE>TUSC - PL/SQL Poster</TITLE>
<TITLE>TUSC - PL/SQL Poster</TITLE>
<TITLE>TUSC - PL/SQL Poster</TITLE>
<TITLE>TUSC - PL/SQL Poster</TITLE>
</HEAD>
```

DESCRIPTION Tag

The *DESCRIPTION tag* is used by search engines to describe your document and should contain a short, plain language description of the document or page. This is particularly important if your document has little text, is a frameset, or has extensive scripts at the top. Enter a brief description of this page because search engines vary on the maximum number of characters allowed in a description. The range of characters indexed is from 150 characters to 395 characters. For example:

```
<META NAME="description" CONTENT="Free Oracle Posters from TUSC">
```

KEYWORDS Tag

The *KEYWORDS metatag* should contain keywords used by search engines to index your document, in addition to words from the title and document body. Keywords are typically used for synonyms and alternates of title words. Enter the strategic keywords and phrases that people would most likely enter in a search engine query when searching for information about the topic on the page. For example, if your site sells office supplies, your keywords might be "office supplies," "paper," "pencil," "pen," or "stapler" to name a few. The following is an example:

```
<META NAME="keywords" CONTENT="office supplies, paper, pencil, pen, stapler">
```

When developing your home page, try to place a variation of your keywords throughout the page. You should place the keywords as many times as you can, but do it throughout the entire Web page and make sure it sounds professional. Keywords determine how your site will rank. Be cautious about choosing a single keyword that 100,000 other sites are using. Otherwise, you'll get lost in the lists. Instead, narrow your choice of a keyword into something less general and more targeted or unique. Did you know you could get the search engines to help you choose a targeted keyword? For example, the following sites can help you generate the keywords for a page:

- **http://goto.com/linead/getlisted.cgi**

- **http://www.excite.com/** (search for keywords)
- **http://www.keywordcount.com/**
- **http://www.webtrends.net/**

Submission of keywords is only possible for 10 percent of the search engines. Top search engine positioning depends a lot on having the correct mix of keywords. In other words, the number of times your keyword or key phrase appears versus the total number of words on your Web page is extremely important—commonly called *keyword density*. If your keyword density is too high, however, your page is penalized in the scoring (considered spam, as defined in the following). On the other hand, if the score is too low, your page can be lost in obscurity. Depending on the size of the page, a good range is 2 to 25 percent of the page. Keyword relevance may change with search engine changes. Total keyword relevance guarantees a high position in search engines' listings.

TIP
A keyword's relevance that's too high may spam some search engines, returning a lower position in their listings.

Pages with keywords appearing in the title are assumed to be more relevant than others. Search engines also check to see if the keywords appear near the top of a Web page, such as in the headline or in the first few paragraphs of text. They assume any page relevant to the topic will mention those words right from the beginning.

Keyword frequency is another major factor in how search engines determine relevancy. A search engine analyzes how often keywords appear in relation to other words in a Web page. Those with a higher frequency are often deemed more relevant than other Web pages.

Some search engines index more Web pages than others, while some search engines also index Web pages more often than others. In other words, no two search engines have exactly the same collection of Web pages to search through. Search engines may also give Web pages a "boost" for certain reasons. For example, Excite uses link popularity as part of its ranking method. It can tell which of the pages in its index have many links pointing at them. These pages are given a slight boost during ranking because a page with many links to it is probably well regarded on the Internet. Be sure to link all your affiliates together—again and again.

Headers

Headers were originally intended to emphasize certain words on a page, allowing a quick way to bold and enlarge text without having to change font tags. While they're less common these days, search engines will sometimes use the text found within these tags to determine the page's relevancy for a search. In other words, these tags are seen as superkeywords. Make your headings count. Be sure to place your keywords in them!

Links

Another excellent place to put keywords is within your anchor links. For example:

```
<A HREF="http://yourcompany.com/oracle poster.htm">Oracle PL/SQL
Posters</A>
```

Keywords Throughout the Page

In addition to keywords found in metatags and titles, search engines often look through your page for keywords relevant to the search. This is sometimes referred to as *full-page indexing.* This logic prevents people from using irrelevant keywords throughout the hidden elements of their page to receive better listings because the body of their document will lack the false keywords. If you want to enhance your search engine listings, definitely consider using relevant keywords throughout your document, but don't simply throw them throughout your page for the sake of having extra keywords. Do keep keywords in mind when writing your text. Use keywords when appropriate and when they flow with the body of your document.

People often ask, "How many times should keywords appear in your document to help enhance your listings?" The answer is "Quite a few!" Because it's logical for a page about computers to use the word "computers" on any given page quite a few times, search engines aren't likely to consider a word repeated throughout your document as spam unless you really overdo it. Putting relevant keywords in the first paragraph of your document is also important. Some search engines may give the first paragraph priority over the rest of the document. Remember, your "home" or gateway page is probably the most important page of all for your keywords.

Alternate Image Tags

Using image tags gives you the option of providing users with images turned off with alternate text. Newer browsers typically show this text as *hint text,* a tip or hint that pops up when the mouse pointer is held over an image. Because search engines cannot look at pictures, the alternate text for images is one of the ways they can identify a page's content. Most people don't bother typing in the alternative text when inserting pictures into a document, but if you want to better index them as keywords, you should. For example:

```
<img src=http://images.mysite.com/rdba.gif alt="Remote Oracle Database
Administration">
```

In the Comments

Another great place to put keywords is within the HTML comments. Including keywords in this context is easy. For example:

```
<-- Oracle Posters and Oracle Books can be found here -->
```

Using Hidden Fields in Forms

Using keywords in the FORM tag's hidden fields offers yet another place to include keywords. For example:

```
<FORM METHOD="POST" ACTION="doesnotmatter">
<input type="hidden" name="movemeup" VALUE="TUSC,Oracle,Consulting,PL/
SQL Poster,....">
</FORM>
```

URL or Site Address

Another fine place to put your keywords is within the URL. For some search engines, putting your keywords in the URL can provide the highest impact of any part of your page. Keywords can include:

- The host name (for example, posters.oracle.tusc.com)

- The virtual path (for example, /oracle/posters/)

- The filename (for example, oracle posters.htm)

Talking to the Robots

You can control the Web robots (or search engine spiders) on a per-page basis or at the directory level.

Robots Metatag

To control the robots on a per-page basis, use the *Robots metatag*. The following example contains the tags necessary to instruct robots (spiders and search engines) to traverse beyond the current page, but not to index the current page:

```
<META NAME="ROBOTS" CONTENT="NOINDEX,FOLLOW">
```

Other possible Robots content values for the Robots metatag include the following:

- **NOINDEX**   Prevents anything on the page from being indexed

- **NOFOLLOW**   Prevents the crawler from following the links on the page and indexing the linked pages

- **NOIMAGEINDEX**   Prevents the images on the page from being indexed, but the text on the page can still be indexed

- **NOIMAGECLICK**   Prevents the use of links directly to the images; instead, there will only be a link to the page

Robots.txt File

The robots.txt file is used to prevent search engine spiders from indexing your entire Web site, or specific pages and/or directories, usually in one quick grouping. The following robots.txt file would prevent your entire Web site from being indexed:

```
User-agent: *
Disallow: /
```

This tag is perfect for sites under construction. If you want to disallow a specific search engine from indexing your site, you can prevent specific spiders from indexing your site, as in the following example, which simply uses the spider's name:

```
User-agent: spider-name
     Disallow: /
```

Remember, not *all* search engines heed the robots.txt file. Some may just ignore your guidance, in which case you need to restrict access from that IP address or domain.

Achieving Link Popularity

Many search engines rank the more popular Web sites higher. If you wrote a search engine, wouldn't you want to rank the popular ones higher? Popularity is determined by how many sites are linked to your site. You can get other sites to link to your site in a few ways. For example, you can trade links with other Web sites. You can also submit your Web site to the pages people call Free For All links (FFA). Two good resources you can use to get your site listed on hundreds or even thousands of pages are:

- http://www.linkomatic.com

- http://www.linksrx.com

The more pages linked to your Web site, the better off you are! You can check your link popularity (and other great information about your site) at the following Web site:

- http://www.Websitegarage.com

The concept of link popularity is similar to Metcalfe's theory about the power of the Internet, which is equal to the number of endpoints times the number of endpoints.

The more people who link to your site, the more popular you become—this is like the viral effect that Napster has (or maybe once) enjoyed! The only problem with Napster's primary "business" concept is it isn't legal.

The concept of exchanging reciprocal links is a simple one: you give someone a link from your page in exchange for a link from his or her page. Exchanging links with the right kind of page can bring in just as much traffic as good listings on search engines, if not more. Generally speaking, you want to find sites with some kind of relationship to what you have to offer, but don't offer exactly the same thing. For example, because TUSC is offering Oracle consulting services, another commercial site offering Oracle consulting isn't likely to link to our site because that might result in a loss of sales for them. Likewise, offering a link to them on your site would be like sending customers somewhere else to shop. Other sites, however, might not be in direct competition with you, but offer something that could be of interest to your visitors and vice versa. In TUSC's case, companies like Compaq, Veritas, and RevealNet are perfect companies for us to have such a relationship with. Let's say you have a site for your go-cart company. Why not trade links with a racetrack site? Trying to sell used cars? Swap with an insurance company. These are the best kinds of links for commercial sites and they can significantly increase your traffic if done properly.

Initiating a link swap is fairly simple. Find the appropriate contact at the site you want to trade links with and tell them why you feel an exchange would be mutually beneficial. Don't just say, "You wanna trade links?" and expect people to jump at the opportunity. Nobody wants to get involved in a one-sided trade, so make a compelling case for what you can do for their company and why you want a link from their site. A little flattery never hurt either.

Be careful! Try to avoid getting involved in one-sided trades. Ask how much traffic the site is receiving before agreeing to anything and monitor traffic received from the link if possible. Check occasionally to ensure the link is available on the site because some people remove links after the exchange has been agreed on, thinking you won't notice.

TIP

The Google search engine enables you to quickly check all sites that link to your site, so you might consider using its tool for this search. This tool is also useful to see who's referencing your site that you aren't aware of. By checking each of those sites, you can quickly confirm that everyone's links to you are appropriate. Additionally, I encourage you to use the search engines to find other information about your company—things people are saying about your company—good and bad.

Links can be in any form—banner ads, buttons, text links, and so forth. A properly used text link can be just as effective as a banner ad, if not more. In fact, studies have discovered that most people ignore banner ads. In one study, the OK button was a *huge* banner on the page. When asked for comments about the application, the users said their primary complaint was that no "OK" button was there. Discuss the available options and, remember, some links work better than others, depending on the forum.

If you want to swap links with a site receiving much more traffic than you do, you might want to try offsetting the difference by offering a more prominent link, that is, a banner ad for a text link.

Gaining Click Popularity

Some sites rank sites based on click popularity. In other words, based on how many people select your site after searching. Click popularity isn't something you can have much effect on unless you direct everyone to the search engine instead of your site. In theory, you might be able to fool these search engines by using an automated program—for example, Perl (LWP) or UTL_HTTP—to call the search engine link over and over, but you might have to spoof the IP address or find other ways to gain link popularity. Otherwise, this is a difficult one to manipulate. Click popularity might not be in your control, but you can always experiment.

Don't Spam Anyone or Anything

If you're unclear about the definition of *spamming* the search engines, this is the alteration or creation of a document with intent to deceive an electronic catalog or filing system. In other words, attempting to fool the search engine to better your ranking odds (as the previous click popularity tip suggests). Any technique that increases the potential position of a site at the expense of the quality of the search engine's database can also be regarded as *spamdexing*—also known as *spamming* or *spoofing*. Most every search engine will demote your site ranking if they suspect your site of spamming them. Some sites will remove your site entirely!

You should be aware of what constitutes spamming to avoid trouble with the search engines. If you have a page with a white background, for example, and you have a table that has a blue background and white text in it, you are actually spamming the engine without even knowing it! Infoseek (now **go.com**) will see white text and a white page background, concluding your background color and your page color are the same, so you're spamming! It won't be able to tell the white text is actually within a blue table and is perfectly legible. This is silly, but it will cause that page to be dropped off the index. You can get this page back on by changing the text color in the table to say, yellow, and resubmitting the page to Infoseek. See what a difference a small change can make? Yet, you probably had no idea your page was considered spam! Generally, it's easy to know what to avoid to keep from being labeled a spammer and having your pages or your site penalized. By following a few simple rules, you can safely improve your search engine rankings without unknowingly spamming the engines and getting penalized for it. Some techniques are clearly considered as an attempt to spam the engines. Where possible, you should avoid the following:

- Keyword stuffing. This is the repeated use of a word to increase its frequency on a page. Search engines now have the capability to analyze a page and determine whether the frequency is above a "normal" level in proportion to the rest of the words in the document.

- Invisible text. Some Webmasters stuff keywords at the bottom of a page and make their text color the same as the page background. This is also detectable by the engines.

- Tiny text. Same as invisible text but with tiny, illegible text.

- Page redirects. Some engines, especially GoTo, don't like pages that take the user to another page without his or her intervention, for example, using metarefresh tags, cgi scripts, Java, JavaScript, or server-side techniques. Use a refresh with a one-second timer on the page, but include a link for good measure.

- Metatag stuffing. Don't repeat your keywords in the metatags more than once and don't use keywords that are unrelated to your site's content.

- Don't create too many doorways with similar keywords.

- Don't submit the same page more than once on the same day to the same search engine.

- Don't submit virtually identical pages, that is, don't simply duplicate a Web page, give the copies different filenames, and submit them all. This will be interpreted as an attempt to flood the engine.

- Avoid code swapping. In other words, don't optimize a page for top ranking, and then swap another page in its place once a top ranking is achieved.

- Don't submit doorways (discussed in the following) to submission directories like Yahoo!

- Don't submit more than the allowed number of pages per engine per day or week. Each engine has a limit on how many pages you can manually submit to it using its online forms. Currently, these are the limits: AltaVista, 1-10 pages per day; Hotbot, 50 pages per day; Excite, 25 pages per week; GoTo, 50 pages per day, but unlimited when using e-mail submissions. Please note, this isn't the total number of pages that can be indexed, it's just the total number that can be submitted. If you can only submit 25 pages to Excite, for example, and you have a 1,000-page site, that's no problem. The search engine will come crawling to your site and index all pages, including those you didn't submit.

Certain practices can be considered spam by the search engine when they're simply part of honest Web site design. For example, Infoseek doesn't index any page with a fast page refresh. Yet, refresh tags are commonly used by Web site designers to produce visual effects or to take people to a new location of a page that has been moved. Also, some engines look at the text color and background color and, if they match, that page is considered spam. But you could have a page with a white background and a black table somewhere with white text in it. Although perfectly legible and legitimate, that page will be ignored by some engines. Another example is GoTo advises against (but doesn't seem to drop from the index) having many pages with links to one page. Even though this is meant to discourage spammers, it also places many legitimate Webmasters in the spam region (almost anyone with a large Web site or a Web site with an online forum always has their pages linking back to the home page).

These are only a few examples of gray areas in the search engine ranking games. Fortunately, because the search engine people know people are trying to fool them and that honest mistakes occur as well, they won't penalize your entire site just because you included things they consider gray areas.

Building Trojan "Doorway" Pages

How do you position your Web site at the top of search engine results? Use Trojan or doorway pages. *Doorway pages,* also known as *entry* or *bridge pages,* are Web pages designed specifically to rank highly on the unique ranking algorithms of each search engine. The two best things about using doorway pages is they cost far less than other promotional tools, such as banner ads, and they work better when properly designed.

To put this simply, a doorway page is created using the kind of text statistics and factors that make a page rank highly on a particular engine for a particular keyword or phrase. As you can imagine, determining, and then creating, hundreds or even only one doorway page that's "attractive" to a search engine is a mind-intensive and time-consuming matter. Companies do offer services to help you create these pages.

A doorway is designed for the search engines, to make the search engines happy. The doorway page links to your main site and takes your visitors there. A Web site is designed for people, to make people happy, to fill a need, make money, or whatever your goals may be. What's good for people, however, isn't always good for the search engine. If, for example, you have a Web site that

- has a lot of graphics and hardly any text

- runs on a database and creates dynamically generated pages

- is in a highly competitive area

- deals with a wide variety of general topics

chances are your pages will rank poorly on search engine rankings.

This creates a serious dilemma: how to make Web pages that are pleasing, useful and logical to humans and, at the same time, super-friendly to search engines.

Doorway pages help you solve these troubling dilemmas. You want to keep your current Web site as is and create dozens of doorway pages, each optimized to rank well for a different keyword in a different engine. Typically, when targeting ten keywords across five search engines, you end up with 50 pages pointing to your home page or other sections on your site. This isn't unusual and search engines won't penalize you as long as your doorway pages are professional and honest, and so is your submission. You want your Web site to be found under several keywords your prospects are likely to search by.

For this reason, create separate pages that emphasize each of those keywords/ phrases that rank well for each search engine. On average, to cover all possibilities, you need to make doorways for about 50 keywords or phrases related to your product or service for each of the top search engines. Although this can be time-consuming, it's an extremely powerful online marketing tool.

Assuming you want to make sure you're ranked highly on the five top engines (AltaVista, Hotbot, Lycos, GoTo, and Excite—Yahoo! doesn't accept doorway pages), you have to make five versions of each doorway page, each optimized for a particular engine.

What goes into making a doorway page? First, you need to know that ranking criteria varies from search engine to search engine. Most evaluate the placement of keywords or keyword phrases on various parts of your pages based simultaneously on all these criteria:

- **Prominence of the keyword searched** How early in a page a keyword appears.

- **Frequency of the keyword searched** Number of times the keyword appears. Be careful about this. Simply repeating the keyword won't work because grammatical structure and keyword weight also play a role.

- **"Weight" of the Keywords** This is the ratio of keywords to all other words. Each search engine has a threshold. If your page crosses that threshold, the engine labels it as spam and ignores it.

- **Site Popularity** A few search engines consider how popular your site is when ranking.

- **Proximity of Keywords** How close together the keywords are to each other, especially when the item searched for is a phrase.

- **Keyword Placement** The locations where an engine looks for the keyword, for example, in the body, title, metatags, and so forth.

- **Grammatical Structure** Some engines consider grammar in their calculations. They do this to make it harder for spammers to do their thing.

- **Synonyms** Some engines look for words similar in meaning to the keyword.

As you can see, the ranking criteria are highly dynamic, using a complex algorithm that integrates all the previous factors in various proportions and with various maximum and minimum values. An important criterion to look deeper into is the keyword placement criteria.

Reviewing Manual Submission

To get listed in each of the search engines and ranked highly, make sure you manually submit with the following major search engines. A good idea is to submit your Web site once every few weeks to keep your listing fresh. As mentioned, for the best results, I recommend doing this manually, so you know your site was submitted properly and accepted. If you don't have the time (or staff) to accomplish this, however, the following tools are also effective.

Things *not* to do to get listed:

- Tell their staff to "Hurry up already!"

- Submit your URL repeatedly. Because a listing can take up to two months before it goes in, wait at least six weeks before requesting a listing a second time.

- Submit your URL to regional indexes and categories that have nothing to do with your site.

- Spam keywords in your titles and description when submitting.

Things you should do:

- Wait until your site is done before submitting.

- Read submission rules at least twice.

- Find the appropriate category for your site (or categories, you can have two listings).

- Review your submission carefully before sending it off.

A good idea is to double-check your site to make sure everything is up-to-snuff before submitting your URL to any search engines, directories, awards sites, and so forth. Remember, getting things right the first time is much easier than having to go back and correct your mistakes, so take the time before you submit. What do you check for before you submit? Here are some suggestions:

- Research keyword combinations of sites with good listings on various search engines.

- Use meta keyword tags on *each* page within the site, using different combinations to get better listings for various searches.

- Use metadescription tags on each page.

- Use Robot metatags to protect any pages you don't want indexed from being spidered and to ensure others are listed.

- Use keywords in the page content to ensure better listings in various search engines that spider content.

- Make sure the site is finished (or nearly finished) before submitting it.

- Test the compatibility of the site on various platforms with various browsers.

- Validate the code to make sure no errors exist.

Paying for Rank

Search engines generally are in the business of making money, so with many search engines, money talks. In other words, you can pay for your ranking on search engines to generate your traffic. If you don't want to fight the search engine war or if you have some spare money, you might want to check this out. The leading pay-ranking search engine on the market today is **GoTo.com**, which was the first company to start this type of service. Another one following in its footsteps is **http://www.findwhat.com**. This type of search engine can be an effective way to market your Web site because you can get targeted visitors as cheaply as one cent per click! The top positions are ranked accordingly to who wants to pay more.

Buying Submission Software and Services

Should you submit your site manually, pay someone to do it, or buy a tool? Manual submission can often be the most effective method but, as suggested, you might not have the time or staff to accomplish this. You may want to consider software or services. Many of the services are as effective as manual submissions. The least costly method is via an automated search engine submission software product.

Automated Submission Software

You can purchase software to help you keep up your rankings with the major search engines. A highly rated program that can help you succeed with the search engine war is TopDogg. More information on this software is available at **http://www.topdogg .com/cgi-bin/click?id=4**.

Search engines are the key to Web site traffic, but manually submitting your site to every one is a headache. Intelliquis is hoping to cure what ails you with its Web site, *Traffic Builder*. According to *PC Week,* though, Traffic Builder is fraught with enough problems to send you out for aspirin. With the tool, just enter your site's URL and other pertinent data into Traffic Builder's forms, select the engines you want to hit, and you're off. According to *PC Week,* while Traffic Builder features an astonishing 900+ engines (a list you can easily update), 100+ of tested submissions were rejected (because of time-outs or out-of-date forms) during a multihour run. Traffic Builder also froze in midsession more than once, forcing annoying reboots. The flood of confirmations and upsells *PC Week* got back from many of the search engines left them wishing for something more intelligent.

AddWeb Pro is an impressively enhanced Web site-submission application that can increase your Web site traffic and improve your search-engine ranking. This Pro version features support for up to 100 simultaneous submissions, the capability to import Web profiles, and the AddWeb Engine Builder, an application for maintaining a customized database that includes automatic gathering of form fields, category translation, and testing. With nine step-by-step tutorials covering Page Building, Profile Setup, Submission, Ranking, Searching, Reporting, and Auto-Reporting, even the fledgling Webmaster can take advantage of the many excellent tools available in the package. Just fill in a simple form and the program uses your Internet connection to batch-process submissions to an impressive number of sites, displaying progress in real time. When the submission process is complete, you can check your ranking with a built-in utility. This program performs quickly and efficiently, and even includes a tool for keyword searches. The trial version disables some features, limits submissions to the top ten search engines, and lets you create only one profile. Don't require high-volume submissions? Try *AddWeb Standard,* also available in their library.

JOC Web Promote is a simple Web site promotion program that announces your Web pages to search engines and link indexes. The search engine database includes more than 700 engines in this version. The straightforward interface consists of three panes. In the first pane, you enter site information, such as metadescription and keywords. In the second, you choose which engines to submit to. And, in the third pane (new to this version), you can generate an entrance page to your site. Until you register, you can submit only to AltaVista, AOL Netfind, Excite, Hotbot, GoTo, Lycos, Magellan, Webcrawler and Yahoo!. When we ran it, the program took only about 20 seconds to submit a test homepage successfully to the "big eight" search engines. JOC Web Promote automatically prints a text report of each submission session and it can also save your submission sessions in its proprietary .jwp format. We did run into some typographical errors in the interface. Note, because search engines can take as long as a month to index a new site, the outcome of our test submissions isn't known yet. Help is included with the software.

The Web site Promoter Engine (WSPE) can help you post your site to the dozens of Web search engines in operation, including Yahoo!, InfoSeek, AltaVista, and Lycos. You fill out an onscreen form of descriptive information about your site and WSPE becomes a spider, automatically submitting the information in the proper format for each search engine. WSPE creates a run-time log of its success (or failure), so you know what engines have accepted your information. You can create files of site information to handle multiple sites. The evaluation version is limited to submission to only ten sites. Registration enables you to download a larger site list.

Increase the visibility of your Web site with *Accutagger,* an easy-to-use application that provides a complete solution for adding and managing Web page metatags. Its attractive, tabbed interface enables you to step comfortably through the process. Add a title, description, keywords, author, copyright, e-mail, language, and more. Classification, distribution, links, rating, PICS rating, revisit, and refresh are also among the available tags. Keyword and Description Managers are available for you to manage information easily in these key fields. You can retrieve keywords from an existing HTML document and rearrange keyword order. Once you're satisfied with your efforts, you can have Accutagger write the metatag results to one or more local Web pages. You can also use it to analyze your use of metatags (local or remote) and recommend adjustments to your strategy. Other features include comprehensive report generation, automatic backups of modified Web pages, a built-in spelling checker, and more. A fine tutorial and excellent online help are available.

Submission Services

Many companies offer services to submit your site to the search engines. *@Submit!* (**http://www.usWeb sites.com/submit/**) is a free service provided by United States Web sites to help give you a quick start with promoting your Web site. Their free service is used thousands of times every month. Many Webmasters and site owners have reported excellent results after using this service. They provide you with a quick and easy way to submit your URL to the most important directories and search engines. Scroll down the page and start promoting now!

Ei Web Promotion's (**http://www.ei-Web.com/**) search engine positioning and search engine submission services are designed to help Webmasters promote their sites to the major search engines, and to take advantage of the Internet's primary advertising vehicle. Their search engine experts pride themselves on their ability to gain top search engine rankings successfully, without using deceptive or unethical methods of promotion. Ei's search engine positioning service is guaranteed. Fees are based entirely on results and, if their promotion team fails to obtain top rankings for your site, you pay nothing. Because many search engines and directories reject submissions from automated processes or software, all search engines submissions are performed manually by a search engine promotion specialist.

Avoiding Lawsuits

Is it illegal to use trademarked terms in your metatags? Not necessarily. Can you get sued? Yes, and people have. Trouble can come your way, depending on why and how you're using the tags. Those who used the tags in what was deemed a deceptive manner have lost in court. However, legal action was halted (so far) against one defendant who proved to a judge that she had a legitimate reason to use the terms.

Key cases about this issue are summarized here, but you can get considerably more information about these cases on the searchenginewatch site (**http://www .searchenginewatch.com**):

The Cases So Far

Filed/Settled (mm/dd/yy)	Case	What's Important	Result
07/23/97 02/06/98	Oppedahl & Larson v. Advanced Concepts	First case dealing with the issue of misleading metatags. Terms appeared only in the tags and spamming was involved.	Permanent Injunction
07/01/97 08/27/97	Insituform Technologies v. National Envirotech	First legal ruling in a case involving metatags.	Settlement and Permanent Injunction
09/08/97	Playboy v. Calvin Designer Label	First legal ruling that didn't also involve a settlement.	Preliminary Injunction (issued on filing)
04/22/98	Playboy v. AsiaFocus and Internet Promotions	First legal ruling resulting in a cash award.	$3 million award
04/23/98	Playboy v. Terri Welles	First legal ruling supporting the use of trademark terms in metatags.	Denied Preliminary Injunction; Appeal rejected

Don't Forget Offline Promotion

Don't forget about promoting your site offline. The majority of people promoting their online presence don't have the financial resources to promote their Web site offline. For those who do, a number of ways exist that commercial sites are able to bring attention to their Internet venture outside the World Wide Web. Have you ever seen a television commercial for a radio station? How about an advertisement in the newspaper for a television show? Promoting your Internet venture through alternative mediums can often be a wise alternative to advertising exclusively via the Web. The number of ways through which this "offline" promotion can be accomplished is endless. Rather than attempting to list all the available methods here, let's go over some of the more common and effective advertising alternatives available. Remember, most offline promotion requires some kind of advertising budget.

Business Cards

Businesses often neglect to advertise their online presence on business cards, which is surprising considering what an effective method this can be for attracting visitors to a company's Web site.

People are often less hesitant to look up information on a company's products and/or services through the Internet than they would be if forced to call or meet with a business representative.

Company Literature

Business cards are a great place to start, but don't stop there if your organization distributes any additional literature to potential or existing customers. Don't forget about

- Brochures/Pamphlets
- Videos
- Invoices/Estimates
- Address Labels
- Calendars/Mugs/Other promotional items
- Letterhead

Listing your URL anywhere you would place your organization's address or telephone number is advantageous. Including your URL in your printed advertising is a cost-effective, common sense way to advertise.

Direct Reference

Don't be reluctant to mention your organization's Web site when speaking with clientele. Your Web site provides 24-hour instant access to a wealth of information that customers should be able to access. Unless you tell them where to find it, they won't know where to go for more information during "off" hours.

Targeted Advertising

If you conduct business directly through your Web site or if you feel your organization's online presence is a good way to promote your business, why not refer good prospects to your Web site via mail, telephone, or fax? Obviously, contacting everyone with an Internet connection isn't feasible, but many people are often less reluctant to look into your offerings if they can do so in the privacy of their own office or home. What you can do offline to promote your online venture depends on the size of your organization, what you offer, your budget, and a number of other factors. Ease into it at first. Compare the costs of the promotion with the benefits received and stick with what works for you.

Other Pitfalls

You also need to know things that can get you into trouble. The following sections cover a few things *not* to do.

Beware of Banner Ads

Be careful about putting a banner ad at the top of your page. By doing this, you take the chance of having the search engine read the banner ad code before it reads your content. You don't want your Web page indexed by the search engines based on the banner ad's code, so put the banner ad at the bottom of your page.

Avoid Search Engine Stumbling Blocks

Some search engines view Web pages the way someone using an extremely old browser might see it. They might not read image maps or JavaScript links or frames. You need to anticipate these problems or a search engine might not index any or all of your Web pages.

Image Maps Might Not Be Followed—Provide HTML Links

Often, designers create only image map links from the home page to inside pages. A search engine that cannot follow these links cannot get "inside" the site. Unfortunately, the most descriptive, relevant pages are more often the inside pages than the home page.

Solve this problem by adding some HTML hyperlinks to the home page that lead to major inside pages or sections of your Web site. This is also something to help some of your human visitors. You can put these links at the bottom of the page. The search engine can find them and follow them.

Also consider making a site map page with text links to everything in your Web site. You can submit this page to the search engines, which helps the engines locate important pages within your Web site.

Finally, be sure to do a good job of linking between your pages internally. If you point to different pages from within your site, you increase the odds that search engines will follow links, and then find and index more of your Web site.

Beware of Frames—They Can Kill

Some of the major search engines cannot follow links in frames. Make sure an alternative method exists for the engines to enter and index your site, either through metatags or smart design.

Dynamic Doorblocks

Are you generating dynamic pages via CGI or database delivery? If you are, expect that some of the search engines won't be able to index them. Consider creating static pages whenever possible, perhaps by using the database to update the pages, not to generate them on-the-fly. If the pages are generated by the PL/SQL module, you can spool the HTML to a file using UTL_HTTP or from SQL*Plus using the owa_util.showpage procedure. Search engines tend to choke on question marks, so avoid using symbols, especially the question mark (?) in your URLs.

Summary

Make sure those looking for your site find it as uncomplicated as possible. Now that you're armed with metatag ringers and the top strategies you need to promote your site, you should be well on your way to a victory in the Web ranking games.

References

I researched a lot of information on the Web to write this chapter. The sites I visited, where possible, are listed in the following. The articles listed were also found on the Internet. I'd like to give a special thanks to Danny Sullivan, editor of **SearchEngineWatch.com**, for providing me with an in-depth article on metatags.

Web Sites

- **http://vancouver-webpages.com/META/**
- **http://www.searchenginewatch.com**
- **http://www.usWeb sites.com/submit/**
- **http://www.ei-web.com/**—Ei Web Promotion
- **http://Zdnetcomputershopper.com**
- **http://www.upenn.edu/computing/web/webdev/meta/metarobot.html**
- **http://whatis.techtarget.com/**
- **http://www.quinion.com/words/turnsofphrase/tp-spa1.htm**
- **http://www.usc.edu/isd/publications/networker/98-99/v9n1-Sept_Oct_98/sidebar-spamdexing.html**
- **http://jbmarketingtips.com/**

Articles

- "Avoid Spamming the Search Engines," by David Gikandi.
- "The War on Spamdexing," by Christopher Stamper, special to **abcnews.com**.
- "Back to Basics: Meta Tags," by Scott Clark.
- "The New Meta Tags Are Coming—Or Are They?" *The Search Engine Report,* Dec. 4, 1997.
- "PC Computing Traffic Builder Or Traffic Jam?" by Christopher Null, *Smart Business,* October 26, 1999.

CHAPTER
25

Oracle Text and
Ultra Search

hen it comes to building Web applications, the job isn't done until you add search capabilities. Oracle has some amazing tools to accomplish this on your own, specifically, Oracle Ultra Search. Many tools also exist within the marketplace, but Oracle's tool comes with Oracle9i, so how can you pass it up? Oracle Text (formerly Oracle interMedia) is at the foundation of Oracle Ultra Search. Other free tools are out there, including Master.com, which I also discuss in this chapter.

In this chapter, you learn about the following topics:

- Oracle Text
- Oracle Ultra Search
- Master.com

Oracle Text

When I first asked Omar Alonso, the Oracle Product Manager for Oracle Text, about the product, he described it this way: "It's part of enterprise and standard editions of 9i. Just create a table with some data, create a text index, and try some text queries." So I did exactly that. It truly is that simple!

The Web page for Oracle Text can be found at **http://technet.oracle.com/ products/text/content.html**. The pages at this location provide you with all kinds of information about Oracle Text. Oracle Text uses standard SQL to index, search, and analyze text and documents stored in the Oracle database, as well as files and data on the Web. Oracle Text can

- analyze document themes and gists
- search text using a variety of strategies, including:
  - full-text (Boolean, exact phrase, proximity, section searching, misspellings, stemming, wildcard, thesaurus, word equivalence, and scoring)
  - mixed (text index plus relational attributes)
  - thematic (search HTML and XML sections and tag values; render search results in various formats including unformatted text, HTML with automatic keyword highlighting)
- analyze the original document format
- analyze and index most document formats with over 150 document filters

Oracle Text supports 39 languages and performs bulk loading of documents in Oracle9*i* with SQL*Loader.

To demonstrate how Oracle Text works, suppose we have a table of financial market articles we've built using utl_http to extract these stories from a financial Web site. The table contains news stories about specific companies we're tracking. The table is named "story," the long column that contains the actual story (or article) is named "story_text." To create a text index on our long field, we need to use the following syntax:

```
create index storyidx on story(story_text)
indextype is ctxsys.context;
```

Wow, that was easy! Now we need to execute the following query, which retrieves a specific story:

```
select story_text
from    story
where   contains (story_text,
                  '(global or (revenue and president)) and Hewlett') > 0
```

You can see our query uses Boolean logic to find specific queries meeting these criteria. The following output shows the results of the query:

Hewlett-Packard Warns Tech Slowdown Global By Peter Henderson PALO ALTO, Calif.

Printer and computer maker Hewlett-Packard Co. (NYSE:HWP - news) said on Wednesday that May sales were weaker-than-expected as the economic slowdown encircled the globe, casting doubt on hopes for recovery in the technology sector.

We are now more cautious about our revenue guidance, Chairman, President, and Chief Executive Carly Fiorina told analysts. No. 3 personal computer maker Hewlett-Packard had previously forecast that revenue would be flat to down 5 percent for the fiscal third quarter, which ends on July 31.

It doesn't get any easier, now does it? Oracle Text offers a vast array of features and services. In fact, an entire book could be written about Oracle Text. The important thing to know for this chapter is that Oracle Text is the basic foundation for the Ultra Search features for *i*AS.

Oracle Ultra Search

You can find a lot of information about Oracle Ultra Search (formerly *i*Search) on Oracle's site (**http://technet.oracle.com/products/ultrasearch/content.html**).

At first I found the tool to be in its early stages but, then again, maybe that was only my learning curve. Once I finally figured out how to get the data into Ultra Search, I couldn't actually perform a search; however, I did get the search functionality to work and I documented how I accomplished this in this chapter.

Oracle also provides an API to extract the data and a number of resources to get you going with Ultra Search. The interface is a bit difficult to figure out at first and it has some limitations, as you see in the following.

Ultra Search is available only with version 9*i* of the database. It doesn't come with 9*i*AS. To get to administration functionality of Ultra Search, I went to the following page on my 9*i*AS server (with 9*i* running as my database):

```
http://tuscil-sun6.tuscil.com:7777/ultrasearch/admin/control/login.jsp
```

You might have noticed that I hadn't yet moved my primary port to port 80. This became a problem later, as you'll see. The previous URL displays the page shown in Figure 25-1.

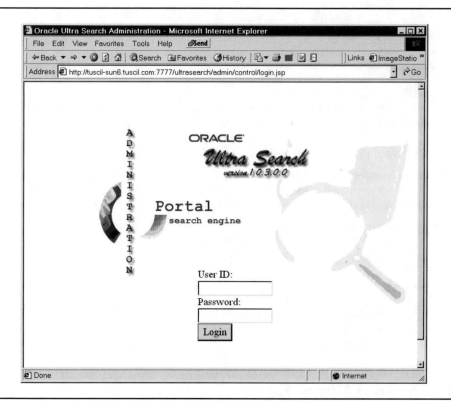

FIGURE 25-1. *Login for Administration*

NOTE
To use the administration tool, your browser must be Netscape version 4.0 or Microsoft Internet Explorer version 4.0 or higher.

You're required to provide a user name and a password to administer Ultra Search. Ultra Search uses database authentication, but the user must be granted the WKADMIN role to administer Ultra Search. To login as the administrator, I created an account—named EXAMPLES—and then granted the WKUSER and WKADMIN roles to EXAMPLES. WKUSER is the role needed by the JSP query, as you see in the following.

Before you can login to Ultra Search, you must perform a few more setup steps. First, you must edit the database.properties file (which can be found in the $ORACLE_HOME/ultrasearch/jsp/admin/config/ directory). You must specify the host name, port, and SID of the Oracle instance and listener. Ultra Search uses JDBC to connect to your Oracle database. In the database.properties file, edit the line that begins with "connection.url" as follows:

```
"connection.url=jdbc:oracle:thin:@<hostname>:<port>:<SID>"
```

My host is named tuscil-sun6, SQL*Net runs on port 1521, and the SID for this machine is dev2. I changed the connection.url string as follows:

```
connection.url=jdbc:oracle:thin:@tuscil-sun6:1521:dev2
```

Once I made these changes (and saved the file), I stopped 9*i*AS, and then restarted it. I could then log in to the Ultra Search administration tool. To stop and start 9*i*AS on UNIX, invoke the Apachectl program as follows:

```
$WEB_ORACLE_HOME/Apache/Apache/bin/apachectl stop
$WEB_ORACLE_HOME/Apache/Apache/bin/apachectl start
```

After logging in to Ultra Search, the initial page is displayed, as shown in Figure 25-2. I first needed to define an instance to allow Ultra Search to work with. I clicked the Instance tab, and then I clicked Create. As you can see in Figure 25-3, I specified the name of my instance (this is an arbitrary name you select), and the schema (and password) to place the Ultra Search data into. This is the same schema I defined

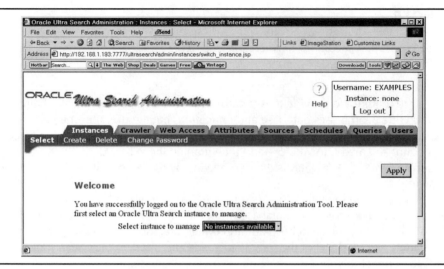

FIGURE 25-2. *Logged in to Ultra Search*

FIGURE 25-3. *Creating an Ultra Search Instance*

previously. This step takes some time to process because it creates all the underlying or supporting tables and indexes needed for Ultra Search to perform its duties.

As you can see in Figure 25-4, I was successful in creating this instance. Next, you need to click Select and choose this instance to work with. Optionally, you could create additional instances but, typically, one is enough.

Next, I need to tell Ultra Search where to pull its content. I add my site's URL (**www.tusc.com**) to the seed list under the Web Access tab, as shown in Figure 25-5. This information feeds the scheduler that will crawl through the sites.

Now I was ready for Ultra Search to build its repository of searchable data. I clicked the Schedules tab and tried to execute the Primary Schedule. The default schedule implicitly crawls the Default Web Source (under Web Access). User-defined schedules are for user-defined Web sources. The scheduler couldn't run the job, however, because my job_process_queue (init.ora parameter) was set to 0. You'll want to change this in your init.ora but, until you can get it changed there, you can issue the following command from a DBA account (this is a 9*i* database feature):

```
alter system set job_queue_processes = 10
```

After executing this statement, I could Execute Immediately the Primary Schedule that indexes all Web sources. Important to note is failure to run the primary schedule first renders the synchronization of other Web sources

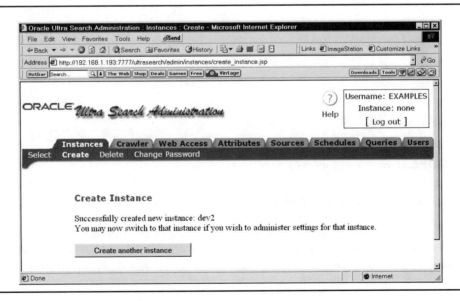

FIGURE 25-4. *Successful Instance creation*

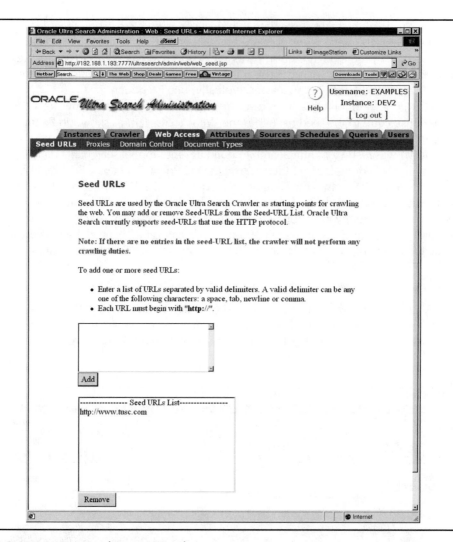

FIGURE 25-5. *Web Access Seeds*

ineffective—in other words, they won't work. Figure 25-6 shows the execution of the schedule at its completion. It sure was fast! In less than six minutes, it found more than 24,000 documents. I had restricted the index to consume 5MB of disk space, so it only fetched 551 documents. You can also see the number of documents it was planning to fetch, the average document size, the speed of retrieving the documents, failures, rejections, and so on.

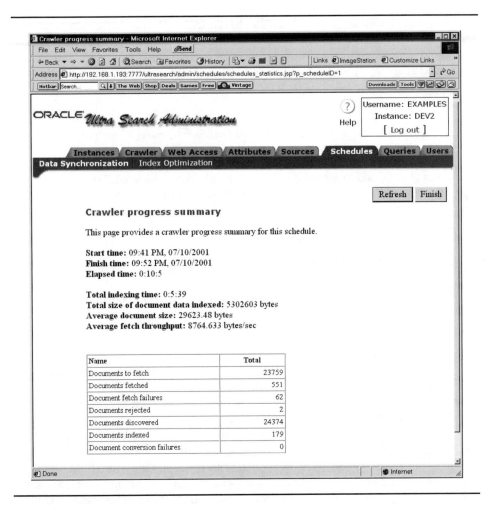

FIGURE 25-6.   *Primary Schedule in progress*

Ultra Search uses a Crawler to index the documents. Documents stay in their original repositories and the *crawled* information is used to build an index that stays within your firewall in a designated Oracle9*i* database. The high-performance, scalable crawler searches Web pages, databases (Oracle and non-Oracle), IMAP mail servers, and HTML documents. The goal is to provide the best relevance ranking and globalization support in the industry—all in a flexible, easy-to-integrate query framework.

To use the query feature of Ultra Search, it appeared I must be logged in to the tool first, but this didn't seem right. Why would a user need to log in to do a search? I continued to play with gsearch.jsp, but I couldn't get it working. I typically received an error saying I was using incompatible versions of PL/SQL and Java. I couldn't figure out how I could be doing that. Then I executed the following URL for the gsearchf.jsp:

```
http://tuscil-sun6.tuscil.com:7777/ultrasearch/query/jsp/gsearchf.jsp
```

The *f* stands for the "Frames-based" version of Ultra Search. This seemed to work, but I continued to get exceptions when I executed a search. So, I dug into the gsearch.jsp and I noticed it was setting a username and password—wk_test. I had placed my instance in to the examples schema, not wk_test, so I modified the following lines:

```
qt.setUser("wk_test");
qt.setPassword("wk_test");
```

to the following text, where "examples" is my username with the same password:

```
qt.setUser("examples");
qt.setPassword("examples");
```

Wow! After about six days of fighting with Ultra Search, it was, in fact, more than "Ultra Store". Once I realized the problem, I modified exactly the same lines in gsearchf.jsp. In fact, I also needed to modify mail.jsp, display.jsp, and gutil.jsp. The results of my search are shown in Figure 25-7.

You can see the results include the title of the HTML page, the URL, a description of the page's contents, the size of the page, and a rating. The rating indicates how accurate this page is likely to be in serving your request. One more field I like is the Last Modified Date. This field indicates how current the content is on the page. Ultra Search also uses this date when it updates your Ultra Search database. Ultra Search queries the HTTP headers for this information. If the page isn't new, it won't refresh the content. In fact, Ultra Search doesn't even retrieve the content of the page (only the header), saving considerable network traffic. This feature is like a fast refresh of a materialized view.

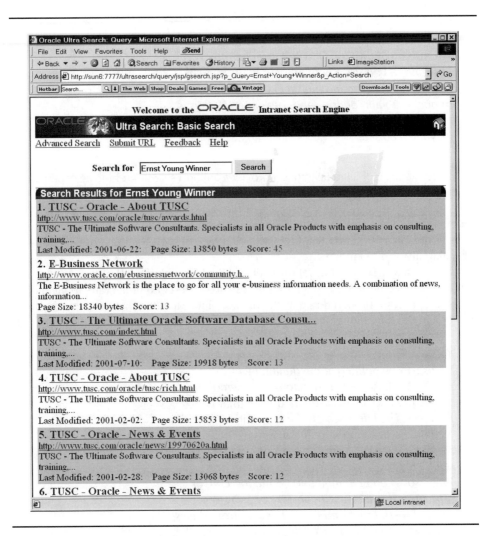

FIGURE 25-7. *Ultra Search Java Server Page demonstration*

TIP

All the search capabilities provided with Oracle Text are available for Oracle Ultra Search. Therefore, I can use Boolean logic in my search. For example, (ioug and niemiec) or (brown and rmoug) is a valid query—and, better yet, it returns valid results. This makes for a powerful search engine for your Web site!

The advantage of Ultra Search is it provides uniform search-and-locate capabilities over multiple repositories: multiple Oracle databases, IMAP mail servers, HTML documents served up by a Web server, or files on disk. Ultra Search is geared to be an out-of-the-box application that enables a Portal search across the content assets of your organization. Ultra Search takes advantage of the Oracle9i core capabilities of scalability and reliability.

The Ultra Search Administration Tool and the Ultra Search JSP Query Application are Java Server Page Web applications. These are three-tier architecture applications. The three tiers are broken down as the browser interface (the first tier), the Web server and the JSP engine (the middle tier), and the Oracle9i database (the third tier).

TIP

Seeds can be defined at the default level (that is, Web Access) as previously shown or they can be defined at a user-defined level (that is, Sources). The Ultra Search documentation provides a complete description of the difference between these, but I couldn't specify a port for a user-defined seed. I left my Web server on the default port of 7777, so when I attempted to define the URL of **http://tuscil-sun6 .tuscil.com:7777/** *as a user-defined seed, I received the following error. This is one reason that I concluded this product is still in the early adopter stage:*

```
Oracle Ultra Search Error
Invalid URL: http://tuscil-sun6.tuscil.com:7777/
```

Master.com

If you don't want to use Ultra Search, I have an easy, no-cost solution for you. A while ago, I evaluated a number of search engines available on the market today. You can buy a search engine from Yahoo!, Excite, Goto, or pretty much anybody. They range in price from $1,000 to hundreds of thousands of dollars. Some provide only custom consulting solutions, and so forth, but Master.com is different. *Master.com* sells its search engine, but it also provides a hosted version of its search engine, which is *very* easy to use and quite powerful. In fact, we use this search engine on the TUSC site. If you go to our site and type in your search criteria, you might not even be able to tell we're using Master.com's search engine, unless you look closely. In Figure 25-8, you can see the search block on our page.

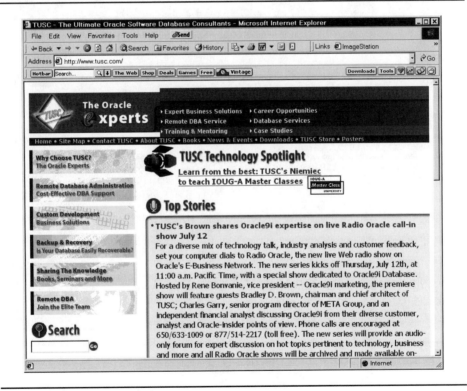

FIGURE 25-8. *TUSC Web site—notice the search block*

When I search from the site, it actually searches a subdomain on Master.com, which is **tusc.master.com**. Figure 25-9 shows the results produced from the Master.com site.

A configuration page is within the site that enables me to add new subdomains and search criteria. It also lets me see exactly what people are searching for.

The site provides you with a number of configuration pages and reports to see who is hitting your search page and what they're searching for. Master.com scans our site weekly for new changes. Figure 25-10 shows a report displaying search hits per day, services requested, the IP addresses that hit the search site, top client queries, and query words. You can also view historical data.

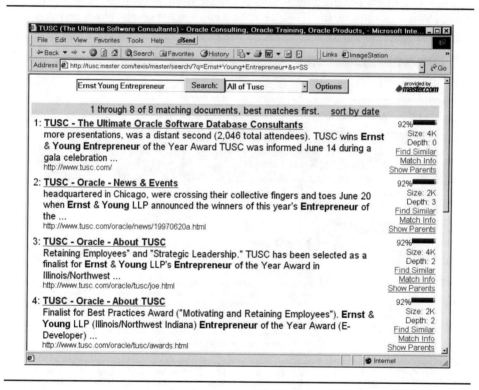

FIGURE 25-9. *Master.com search results*

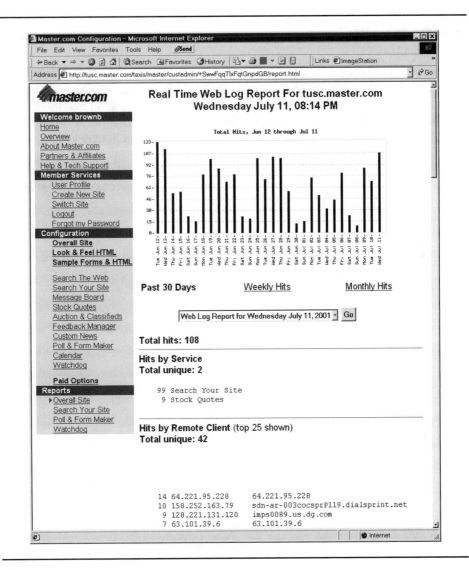

FIGURE 25-10.   *Master.com entire site report*

Summary

Oracle Text is the basis for a number of Oracle components today. It is a powerful tool for searching your Oracle database. Oracle Ultra Search is a new product that has provided added value for Oracle Text. I look forward to continued enhancements to Ultra Search and the administrative portions of the product, and I'm confident we'll see this product evolve as an important part of every *iAS* application. In fact, by the time you check out the TUSC Web site's search engine, it may just be changed to Ultra Search. Master.com provides a simple, free solution for your search needs. All these tools can enhance your Web site by providing powerful search engines. Now go enable your site visitors to search, search, search the Web!

CHAPTER
26

Load and
Application Testing

very application requires thorough testing. Both the application functionality and performance are keys to the success of any application. I once asked a CEO for his top two priorities for the application we were building. He rated speed number one and accuracy of the information number two. When I heard this, I had to stop and think. Then, I asked another question for clarity: "So, you would rather the information show quickly than be correct?" Again, to my surprise, he said, "yes!" Personally, I disagree. I believe the application should be fast, but the information must also be accurate. Load testing can tell you how fast your application is and how it will perform under stress. The same software often tests your application's functionality, confirming the desired data results, and performs load testing.

In this chapter, you learn about the following topics:

- Load and Application Testing Software

- Writing Your Own Load Tester

- Load-testing Services

Load and Application Testing Software

When you search for software to meet your needs, like anything that demonstrates a demand, you can find an overabundance of supply. Mercury and Rational are the two leading companies in this space—and their price tags reflect this. Depending on your needs, you can find a number of possible solutions.

Mercury's Topaz (formerly LoadRunner)

To measure the end-user experience of your Web applications accurately, you must be able to record and measure complete business processes, not only single URLs. Complete business processes span multiple pages. To monitor your entire business process accurately, you must be able to emulate and verify each step, as well as the dynamic content for each page. Mercury's Topaz enables you to do just that.

The complexity of Web applications provides an additional monitoring challenge. These applications are built with sophisticated Web technologies that process information on the browser, server, or both. In fact, a typical Web application includes JavaScript, Active Server pages, pop-up windows, cookies, and frames. Topaz supports the following technologies:

- JavaScript

- Active Server Pages

- Java applets

- Cookies

- Standard logins

- Plug-ins

- Pop-up windows

TUSC has been involved with clients using Mercury WinRunner and LoadRunner. We had excellent success with both of these products. Mercury recently purchased FreshWater Software to further enhance their Web site monitoring capabilities.

Rational's (formerly SQA) Robot

TUSC also had excellent success using Rational Robot. A great (and short) article titled "SQA Robot—A Summary and Evaluation" can be found at **http://www.wisc.edu/testsoft/t11r.html**. The first paragraph sums up the product well: "SQA Robot is a tool developed by Rational Software Corporation for automating the testing of Microsoft Windows client/server applications. It runs under Windows 3.1*x*, 95, and NT. With SQA Robot, you can record keystrokes and mouse movements while running applications and later play them back." Remembering that a browser runs on a client, Web applications can also be tested using Rational Robot.

As Rational put it, the concept behind this product is to reduce testing time and effort. Your e-commerce and e-business applications need thorough functional testing, but testing time is almost nonexistent. Rational Robot can cut the amount of time, money, and manpower your company expends performing functional tests on your Web applications.

Rational Robot is an object-oriented tool that enables you to create, modify, and run automated functional, regression, and smoke tests for e-applications built using a wide variety of independent development environments. Rational TestManager and Rational SiteCheck are included with Rational Robot, giving you, respectively, the capability to manage all test assets and have them available to all team members, as well as a robust tool for Web site link management, site monitoring, and more.

With Rational Robot, you can test beyond an application's GUI to the hundreds of properties of an application's component objects with just the click of a mouse. You can record and replay test scripts that recognize the objects in your various applications. You can also track, report, and chart all the information about your quality assurance testing process. And, you can detect and repair problems associated with the various elements of your Web site.

Rational Robot can be purchased as a single product or as a component of Rational Suite TestStudio.

Web Performance Trainer

Another piece of software we've used is Web Performance Trainer (**http://webperformanceinc.com/**). We used *Web Performance Trainer* and found it was effective because it allowed the use of business cases and profiles. We could set up a business case for a customer service user, another for a sales rep user, and yet another for a customer—all performing actions the particular user would normally perform. Then, we could put these business cases all into a Profile. One great thing is that among the "run" options is the option to tell the software to start with any number of users and gradually add however many users you want after a specific time period. The demo limits you to a total of 25 users hitting the server at once, however. We eventually had two profiles (one for the development server and another for the production server). We could use the cases in the profiles to run tests over a specific amount of time and with a specific amount of users.

As Web Performance tells you, when developing distributed applications on Internet time, load testing and performance tuning can often be left until the last minute or even put off until it becomes a problem. When you're in the last stages of creating a distributed application or working hard to add features to an existing site, you don't have time to delay your deadline a week to configure and learn how to use a testing tool.

If Web sites contained only static HTML, performance wouldn't be so much of an issue. Server performance for static content is largely limited by bandwidth, and the technology to scale by adding more Web servers is well known. The picture changes greatly, however, with the addition of scripts and a database on the back end. Writing or buying a back-end script that's either too slow or doesn't scale is quite easy, in which case adding more servers simply masks the underlying bottleneck.

The good news is this: with Web Performance Trainer, you can find performance bottlenecks early during the development or configuration process so they can be fixed before your users complain. Within minutes, you'll be simulating hundreds of users a second, hitting your Web server at connection speeds from 14.4 Kbps to 100 Mbps. But easy to use doesn't mean unsophisticated—WP Trainer uses the same multithreading technology found in $100,000 load-testing tools, while giving you control to monitor and edit the data stream.

Web Performance's research shows the currently available performance-testing tools are so cumbersome to install and use, they're rarely used after the initial purchase. To be effective, performance tools should be used during the development process and anytime a change is made to the back-end software. Web Performance Trainer is so convenient, you'll find yourself going back to it again and again to see if you can tweak that extra little bit of performance from your code.

The software for Web Performance Trainer includes the following features:

- Supports all browsers
- Supports all Web servers
- Simulates up to 400 users/playback machine
- Runs on Windows NT, Linux, Solaris, and most UNIX variants
- Simulates users at variable connection speeds
- Reports statistics at the transaction, Web page, and hit level
- Requires no scripting—simply click your browser

LoadTesting.com's Portent Supreme

With hundreds of load-testing software packages available, *Portent* provides another solution. For more information, see **http://www.loadtesting.com**. As Portent asks on its site: "Why is load testing important?" Portent promises that with its tool, you can increase uptime and availability of mission-critical Internet systems. Load testing increases your uptime of your mission-critical systems by helping you spot bottlenecks in your system under large-user stress scenarios before they happen in a production environment. Watch your system handle (or not) the load of thousands of concurrent users hitting your site before you deploy and launch it for all the world to visit. When so much effort is put into building a Web project, it's a shame to realize the site won't scale after it's been deployed. Avoid project failures because of not testing high-load scenarios. IT projects are expensive. The hardware, the staffing, the consultants, the bandwidth, and more add up quickly. Avoid wasting money on expensive IT resources and ensure it will all scale with load testing.

Writing Your Own Load Tester

Reinventing the wheel isn't usually a good idea, but if you have simple needs for load (and application) testing, you can write your own custom piece of software to do this. Most any language could be used to develop a load tester. The following subsections show a few examples. You can use these programs to test the performance of your own site, to compare your performance to your competitors, or for fun (slowing down your competitors—just kidding, of course).

PL/SQL Using UTL_HTTP

The following PL/SQL procedure executes a series of URLs. In this example, the URLs are hard coded into the program (in a PL/SQL table—that is, array), but they could be placed into a database table. This program does nothing with the HTML it retrieves. You can enhance this program to compare the results to HTML stored in another table (that is, the desired_results table). You can also enhance the procedure to check other database tables to make sure the desired database modifications are made. To test the load effectively, you need to execute this procedure from multiple stations or sessions. Running this procedure as it stands (in single stream) analyzes the performance per execution. This specific procedure was used to test the same code (select * from scott.emp) written in four different languages (PL/SQL, Perl, PHP, and Java). The test_all procedure generates an HTML table as its output, all nicely formatted.

```
PROCEDURE test_all
(in_loops number default 1)
AS
    end_time     owa_util.num_arr;
    end_time2    owa_util.num_arr;
    min_time     number := 99999999;
    max_time     number := 0;
    lang         owa_text.vc_arr;
    all_lang     varchar2(1000);
    url          owa_text.vc_arr;
    html         utl_http.html_pieces;
BEGIN

-- Define Languages and URLs to execute for language
lang(1) := 'Start';
lang(2) := 'PL/SQL';
url(2)  := 'http://tuscbdb/pls/examples/get_emp';
lang(3) := 'Perl';
url(3)  := 'http://tuscbdb/perl/get_emp.pl';
lang(4) := 'PHP';
url(4)  := 'http://tuscbdb/php/get_emp.php3';
lang(5) := 'Java';
url(5)  := 'http://tuscbdb/jsps/getemp.jsp';

    -- Build a string containing the languages (for printing)
    for i in 2 .. lang.count loop
        all_lang := all_lang || ', ' || lang(i);
    end loop;

  -- Start by printing the header information
    htp.htmlOpen;
    htp.headOpen;
    htp.title( 'Testing'||all_lang);
    htp.headClose;
    htp.bodyOpen( cattributes => ' BGCOLOR=#FFFFFF' );
    htp.header( 3, 'Testing'||all_lang);
    htp.hr;
    htp.tableOpen( cattributes => ' border=1' );
```

```
htp.tableRowOpen;
htp.tableData;
for i in 2 .. lang.count loop
    htp.tableHeader(lang(i));
end loop;
htp.tableRowClose;

-- Set the starting time
end_time(1) := dbms_utility.get_time;

-- Now execute the URLs for each language (100 times or however many
-- were passed in), calculating the min and max as you go.
for i in 2 .. lang.count loop
    for j in 1 .. in_loops loop
        html := utl_http.request_pieces(url(i));
        if j = 1 then
            end_time2(i-1) := dbms_utility.get_time;
        end if;
        null;
    end loop;
    end_time(i) := dbms_utility.get_time;
    if end_time(i) - end_time(i-1) < min_time then
        min_time := end_time(i) - end_time(i-1);
    end if;
    if end_time(i) - end_time(i-1) > max_time then
        max_time := end_time(i) - end_time(i-1);
    end if;
    end_time(i) := dbms_utility.get_time;
end loop;
htp.tableRowClose;

-- Now print the times for total executions
htp.tableRowOpen;
htp.tableHeader('Total Time (w/ first execution)');
for i in 2 .. lang.count loop
    htp.tableData((end_time(i) - end_time(i-1))/100);
end loop;
htp.tableRowClose;
-- Now print the times for total executions (less 1st execution)
htp.tableRowOpen;
htp.tableHeader('Total Time (excluding first execution)');
for i in 2 .. lang.count loop
    htp.tableData((end_time(i) - end_time2(i-1))/100);
end loop;
htp.tableRowClose;
-- Now print the times per execution
htp.tableRowOpen;
htp.tableHeader('Avg Time per Execution');
for i in 2 .. lang.count loop
```

```
        htp.tableData((end_time(i) - end_time(i-1))/100/in_loops);
    end loop;
    htp.tableRowClose;

    -- Now show the best and worst time
      htp.tableRowOpen;
    htp.tableData;
    for i in 2 .. lang.count loop
        htp.print('<TD>');
        if end_time(i) - end_time(i-1) = max_time then
            htp.print('Worst Time');
        end if;
        if end_time(i) - end_time(i-1) = min_time then
            htp.print('Best Time');
        end if;
        htp.print('</TD>');
  end loop;
      htp.tableRowClose;

    -- Close up the HTML
    htp.tableClose;
    htp.header(3,'Executed '||to_char(in_loops)||' times each.');
    htp.bodyClose;
    htp.htmlClose;
END;
```

Figure 26-1 demonstrates the previous test_all procedure when used to test PL/SQL, Thin JDBC, and Thick JDBC's performance.

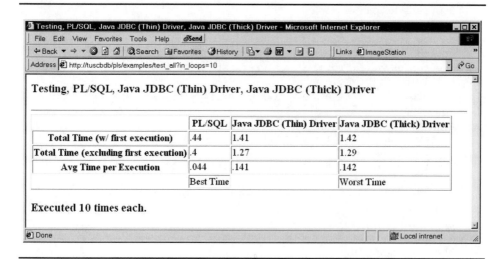

FIGURE 26-1.   *Test_All procedure in action*

Perl Using LWP

The following Perl program uses *LWP* (an open-source Perl program that reads Web pages, just like utl_http). LWP can be enhanced just like the previous procedure can be enhanced. This Perl program can be executed from the command prompt (using Perl). Again, to simulate multiple users, you need to start background processes to emulate the number of users you want to simulate. The following example also tests the same programs as the previous *test_all* procedure. This program doesn't report the output formatted in HTML; instead, it simply displays the output to standard output.

```perl
#!/usr/bin/perl
use LWP::Simple;
use Text::Wrap;
@url=("http://tuscbdb/pls/examples/get_emp",
      "http://tuscbdb/perl/get_emp.pl",
      "http://tuscbdb/php/get_emp.php3",
      "http://tuscbdb/jsps/getemp.jsp");
foreach $url (@url) {
  print $url;
  $_ = get($url); #First time don't count in time
  print "*";
  $currtime = time();
  for ($i=1; $i<=100; $i++) {
    $_ = get($url);
    print ".";
  }
  $nowtime = time();
  print $nowtime-$currtime;
  print "\n";
}
```

JavaScript Load Tester

This *JavaScript* executes a number of URLs simultaneously. It doesn't compute load times, but you can do that with your stopwatch or from your application if you want this information. What it does do for you, however, is execute a set of URLs a set number of times, simultaneously. In other words, it generates a concurrent load on a number of URLs, all from one browser! The output is broken into multiple frames, so you can watch the pages display as they're retrieved from the URLs requested. Again, modify this JavaScript as you want.

```html
<HTML>
<HEAD>
<TITLE>Build a load tester script</TITLE>
<SCRIPT Language=JavaScript>
<!--
```

```
urls = window.prompt('How many URLs would you like to hit?','1');
url = new Array(100);
for (i=1; i<=urls; i++) { url[i] =
  window.prompt('Enter URL '+i,'http://'); };
times = window.prompt('How many times would
  you like to hit each URL?','1');
totalTimes = urls * times;
// Number of columns is the square root rounded up
cols = Math.round(Math.sqrt(totalTimes));
// Number of rows is the number of columns divided by columns
rows = Math.round(totalTimes / cols);
document.write("<HTML>");
document.write("<HEAD><TITLE>Load Test</TITLE></HEAD>");
rowText = "";
for (r=1; r<=rows; r++) {
  rowText = rowText + "1";
  if (r<rows) rowText = rowText + ", ";
};
colText = "";
document.write('<FRAMESET ROWS="'+rowText+
  '" border=1 frameborder=0 sizable=0>');
for (c=1; c<=cols; c++) {
  colText = colText + "1";
  if (c<cols) colText = colText + ", ";
};
rc = 0;  // Record count for looping through URLs
trc = 0;  // Keep track of total URLs and
          // times hit, may end up with blank cells
for (r=1; r<=rows; r++) {
  document.write('<FRAMESET COLS="'+colText+'" border=1 frameborder=0 sizable=0>');
  for (c=1; c<=cols; c++) {
  rc++;
  if (rc>urls) {rc=1};
  trc++;
  if (trc <= totalTimes) { document.write('<FRAME SRC="'+url[rc]+'">');};
  };
  document.write('</FRAMESET>');
  };
  document.write('</FRAMESET>');
  document.write('</HTML>');
//-->
</SCRIPT>
</HEAD><BODY>Please answer these questions for load testing...
</BODY></HTML>
```

Figure 26-2 demonstrates the loadtest JavaScript program as it's executing two different URLs while breaking the page into a series of frames.

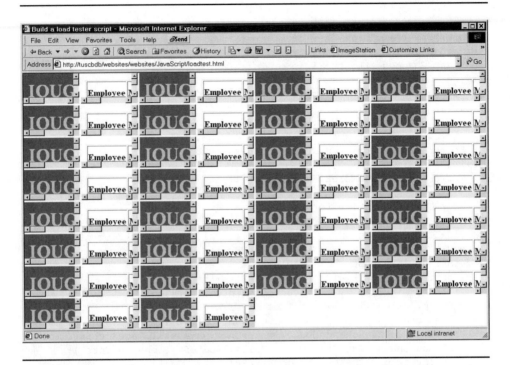

FIGURE 26-2. *JavaScript loadtest concurrently executing 60 requests*

Java Using Acme's Spider

Acme Software (**http://www.acme.com/java/software/Acme.Spider.html**) provides a class for Java that enables you to traverse the Web starting at a given URL. It fetches HTML files and parses them for new URLs to look at. This class can also be used to report timings, just like the previous programs. The example provided here simply reads through a Web site displaying the title of each page it encounters. You can modify this program as you choose. My Java program also uses the ConnectionBean Java bean, which is discussed in Chapter 13.

```
<! PageReader.jsp >
<%@ page import="java.sql.*, Acme.Spider, java.net.*, java.io.*"%>
<jsp:useBean id="connection" class="ConnectionBean" scope="session"/>
<html>
<title>Read a series of Web Pages</title>
```

```
<body bgcolor="#0000FF" text="#FFFFFF"
  link="#FFFF00" vlink="#FFFF99" alink="#CCFF66">
<table border=1>
<tr><th>URL</th><th>Content Type</th>
<th>Last Changed</th><th>Title or Full Page</th></tr>
<%
    String inURL = request.getParameter("inURL");
    if (inURL == null)
       {inURL = "http://www.tusc.com/";}
    String inHTML = request.getParameter("inHTML");
    Enumeration spider = new Acme.Spider(inURL);
    int i = 0;
    while (spider.hasMoreElements() && i<100)
     {
      // Limiting to 100 for testing
      i++;
      URLConnection conn     = (URLConnection) spider.nextElement();
      URL thisURL            = conn.getURL();
      String thisURLStr      = thisURL.toExternalForm();
      out.println("<TR><TD>" + thisURLStr + "</TD>");
      String mimeType        = conn.getContentType();
      out.println("<TD>" + mimeType + "</TD>");
      long changed           = conn.getLastModified();
      java.util.Date changedDate      = new java.util.Date( changed );
      String changedDateStr = Acme.Utils.lsDateStr( changedDate );
      out.println("<TD>" + changedDateStr + "</TD>");
      // If changed = 0, then this is a CGI or a directory, not a file
      try {
        InputStream s        = conn.getInputStream();
           if (mimeType.startsWith("text/html") && changed != 0) {
           BufferedReader fromServer =
             new BufferedReader(new InputStreamReader(s));
           out.println("<TD><base href=\"" + thisURLStr + "\">");
           for (String l = null; (l = fromServer.readLine()) != null; ) {
        if (inHTML != null) {
        out.println(l);
        }
        int titlePos = l.indexOf("<TITLE>");
        if (titlePos > -1) {
           int titleEnd = l.indexOf("</TITLE>");
            out.println(l.substring(titlePos + 7,titleEnd));
        }
           }
           out.println("</TD>");
           }
      s.close();    //Make sure it really exists by opening and closing
     }
      catch ( IOException e ) {}
  }
```

```
%>
</table>
<%= i %>
</body>
</html>
```

Figure 26-3 demonstrates the output of PageReader.jsp.

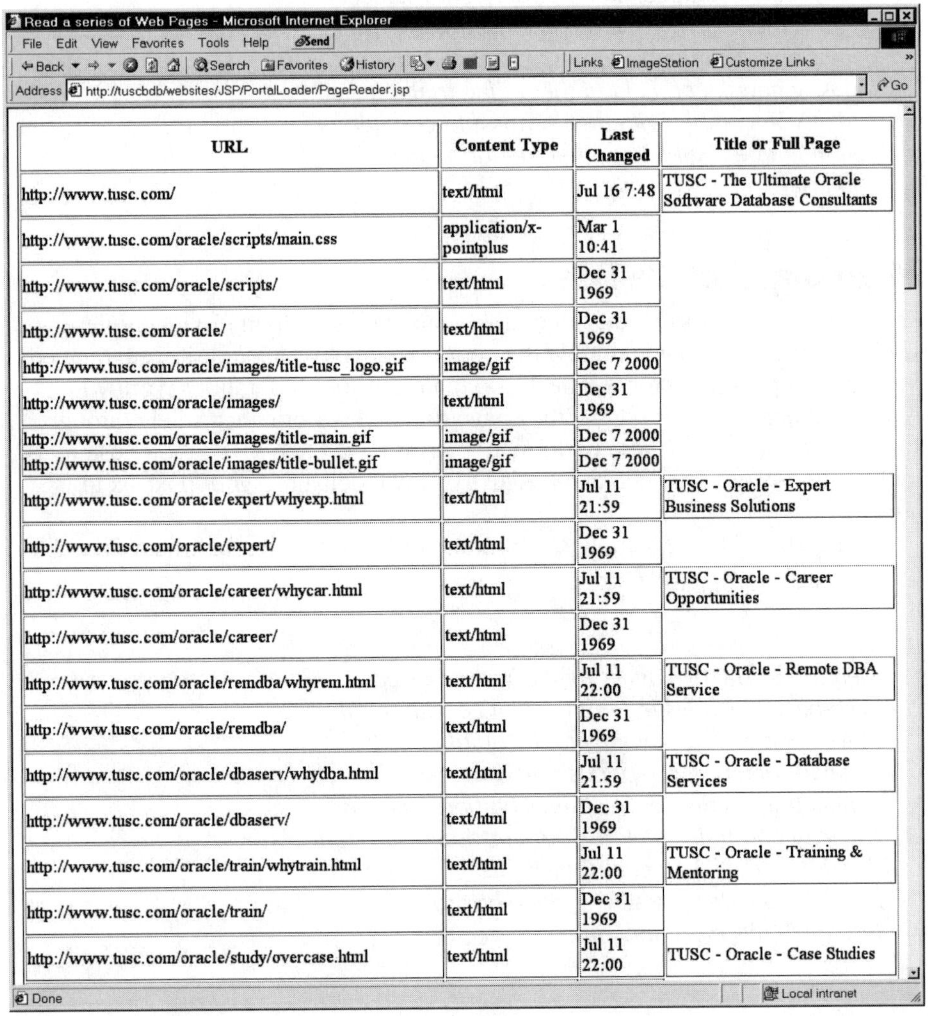

URL	Content Type	Last Changed	Title or Full Page
http://www.tusc.com/	text/html	Jul 16 7:48	TUSC - The Ultimate Oracle Software Database Consultants
http://www.tusc.com/oracle/scripts/main.css	application/x-pointplus	Mar 1 10:41	
http://www.tusc.com/oracle/scripts/	text/html	Dec 31 1969	
http://www.tusc.com/oracle/	text/html	Dec 31 1969	
http://www.tusc.com/oracle/images/title-tusc_logo.gif	image/gif	Dec 7 2000	
http://www.tusc.com/oracle/images/	text/html	Dec 31 1969	
http://www.tusc.com/oracle/images/title-main.gif	image/gif	Dec 7 2000	
http://www.tusc.com/oracle/images/title-bullet.gif	image/gif	Dec 7 2000	
http://www.tusc.com/oracle/expert/whyexp.html	text/html	Jul 11 21:59	TUSC - Oracle - Expert Business Solutions
http://www.tusc.com/oracle/expert/	text/html	Dec 31 1969	
http://www.tusc.com/oracle/career/whycar.html	text/html	Jul 11 21:59	TUSC - Oracle - Career Opportunities
http://www.tusc.com/oracle/career/	text/html	Dec 31 1969	
http://www.tusc.com/oracle/remdba/whyrem.html	text/html	Jul 11 22:00	TUSC - Oracle - Remote DBA Service
http://www.tusc.com/oracle/remdba/	text/html	Dec 31 1969	
http://www.tusc.com/oracle/dbaserv/whydba.html	text/html	Jul 11 21:59	TUSC - Oracle - Database Services
http://www.tusc.com/oracle/dbaserv/	text/html	Dec 31 1969	
http://www.tusc.com/oracle/train/whytrain.html	text/html	Jul 11 22:00	TUSC - Oracle - Training & Mentoring
http://www.tusc.com/oracle/train/	text/html	Dec 31 1969	
http://www.tusc.com/oracle/study/overcase.html	text/html	Jul 11 22:00	TUSC - Oracle - Case Studies

FIGURE 26-3.   *PageReader JSP after reading through the TUSC site*

Load-Testing Services

If you don't have the resources or you don't want to buy a tool to perform your load testing, you can outsource this task. Again, the demand for this service is high, so a number of providers exist for these services.

TIP

*Keynote (**http://www.keynote.com**) offers load testing, site assurance, and Internet performance measurements. Their site offers everything from demos and downloads, to white papers, to a free industry newsletter. Fill out the online trial request and, if you comply with their terms and conditions, you might be eligible for a free performance appraisal.*

Mercury ActiveTest

The folks at Mercury say they can double your Web site's performance today. Their experts can help you double the performance of your Web site, guaranteed! Mercury has performed more than 1,000 load tests for corporations worldwide. And, in 98 percent of their tests, they have doubled performance solely through software optimization. These performance gains have often saved their customers millions of dollars. They guarantee ActiveTest will deliver or your next six tests are FREE.

Figure 26-4 shows a sample report of the findings and saving from Mercury to one of their clients.

TIP

*Mercury Interactive offers ActiveTest, a hosted, Web-based load-testing service that conducts full-scale stress testing of your site. By emulating the behavior of thousands of customers using your Web application, ActiveTest identifies bottlenecks and capacity constraints before your customers do. Your first test is free if you comply with its terms, which are listed on Mercury's Web site—**http:// testyourlimits.merc-int.com**.*

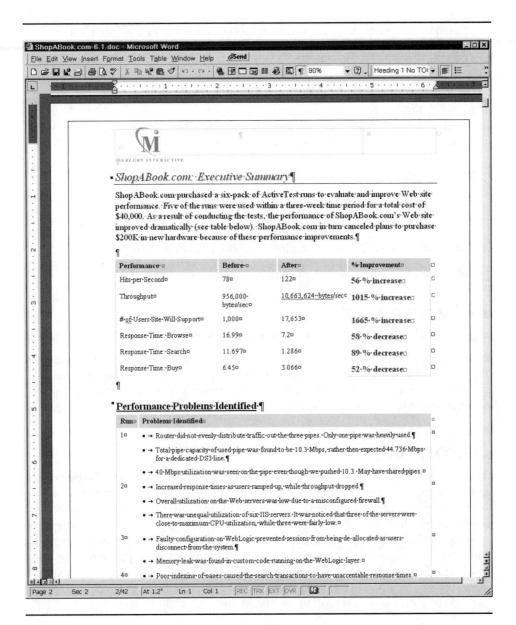

FIGURE 26-4. *Sample report of findings from Mercury*

Go to the Mercury Web site, create an account (ID and password), fill in a bunch of demographic information, accept the terms, and you're off to load testing six times, IF Mercury cannot double your performance. Not only does Mercury do a load check, it also does a security check. Their consultants must generate a load-test script, so it takes a few days before you can do the tests. This isn't 100 percent automated, but it works.

Figure 26-5 shows another look at the level of detail provided by Mercury—from the architecture to detailed statistics—it's all in their report.

How does this work? Within six tests, the ActiveTest team can help you improve your site's performance by

- Doubling the maximum number of concurrent users that can access the site; or

- Cutting the average transaction response time in half; or

- Doubling your system's maximum throughput (Kbps).

IT Service Firms (Consultants, ASPs, and so forth)

Numerous consulting firms and ASPs have purchased testing software. Many of these firms offer testing services to companies like yours. Select a consulting firm you trust to get the job done. Verify the firm's references and review their prior successes in this specific area before signing a contract.

Summary

Your application must serve your customers with accurate information; otherwise, good information can result in garbage out. Application testing is of the utmost importance for every application. Take the time and effort to do this for your applications. These software packages enable you to perform regression testing quickly to make sure ongoing application maintenance won't affect prior program functionality. If your application provides the exact results desired, it must also be able to perform under stress or load. Does your application scale linearly? Does performance die when you hit a certain threshold (that is, once you reach the 598th user, does performance drop off to nil)? Load and application testing are a must!

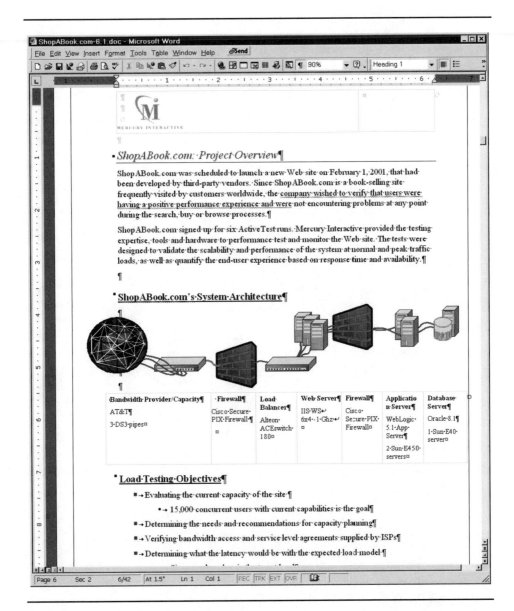

FIGURE 26-5.   *Architecture analysis by Mercury*

Index

Symbols and Numbers

Index

A

F

K

V

X

INTERNATIONAL CONTACT INFORMATION

AUSTRALIA
McGraw-Hill Book Company Australia Pty. Ltd.
TEL +61-2-9417-9899
FAX +61-2-9417-5687
http://www.mcgraw-hill.com.au
books-it_sydney@mcgraw-hill.com

CANADA
McGraw-Hill Ryerson Ltd.
TEL +905-430-5000
FAX +905-430-5020
http://www.mcgrawhill.ca

GREECE, MIDDLE EAST, NORTHERN AFRICA
McGraw-Hill Hellas
TEL +30-1-656-0990-3-4
FAX +30-1-654-5525

MEXICO (Also serving Latin America)
McGraw-Hill Interamericana Editores S.A. de C.V.
TEL +525-117-1583
FAX +525-117-1589
http://www.mcgraw-hill.com.mx
fernando_castellanos@mcgraw-hill.com

SINGAPORE (Serving Asia)
McGraw-Hill Book Company
TEL +65-863-1580
FAX +65-862-3354
http://www.mcgraw-hill.com.sg
mghasia@mcgraw-hill.com

SOUTH AFRICA
McGraw-Hill South Africa
TEL +27-11-622-7512
FAX +27-11-622-9045
robyn_swanepoel@mcgraw-hill.com

UNITED KINGDOM & EUROPE (Excluding Southern Europe)
McGraw-Hill Education Europe
TEL +44-1-628-502500
FAX +44-1-628-770224
http://www.mcgraw-hill.co.uk
computing_neurope@mcgraw-hill.com

ALL OTHER INQUIRIES Contact:
Osborne/McGraw-Hill
TEL +1-510-549-6600
FAX +1-510-883-7600
http://www.osborne.com
omg_international@mcgraw-hill.com

☑ YES! Please send me a FREE subscription to *Oracle Magazine*. ☐ NO

To receive a free bimonthly subscription to *Oracle Magazine*, you must fill out the entire card, sign it, and date it (incomplete cards cannot be processed or acknowledged). You can also fax your application to **+1.847.647.9735**. Or subscribe at our Web site at www.oracle.com/oramag/

SIGNATURE (REQUIRED) X _____   DATE _____

NAME _____   TITLE _____

COMPANY _____   TELEPHONE _____

ADDRESS _____   FAX NUMBER _____

CITY _____   STATE _____

COUNTRY _____   POSTAL CODE/ZIP CODE _____

E-MAIL ADDRESS _____

☐ From time to time, Oracle Publishing allows our partners exclusive access to our e-mail addresses for special promotions and announcements. To be included in this program, please check this box.

You must answer all eight questions below.

1 What is the primary business activity of your firm at this location? *(check only one)*
- ☐ 03 Communications
- ☐ 04 Consulting, Training
- ☐ 06 Data Processing
- ☐ 07 Education
- ☐ 08 Engineering
- ☐ 09 Financial Services
- ☐ 10 Government—Federal, Local, State, Other
- ☐ 11 Government—Military
- ☐ 12 Health Care
- ☐ 13 Manufacturing—Aerospace, Defense
- ☐ 14 Manufacturing—Computer Hardware
- ☐ 15 Manufacturing—Noncomputer Products
- ☐ 17 Research & Development
- ☐ 19 Retailing, Wholesaling, Distribution
- ☐ 20 Software Development
- ☐ 21 Systems Integration, VAR, VAD, OEM
- ☐ 22 Transportation
- ☐ 23 Utilities (Electric, Gas, Sanitation)
- ☐ 98 Other Business and Services

2 Which of the following best describes your job function? *(check only one)*
CORPORATE MANAGEMENT/STAFF
- ☐ 01 Executive Management (President, Chair, CEO, CFO, Owner, Partner, Principal)
- ☐ 02 Finance/Administrative Management (VP/Director/ Manager/Controller, Purchasing, Administration)
- ☐ 03 Sales/Marketing Management (VP/Director/Manager)
- ☐ 04 Computer Systems/Operations Management (CIO/VP/Director/ Manager MIS, Operations)

IS/IT STAFF
- ☐ 07 Systems Development/ Programming Management
- ☐ 08 Systems Development/ Programming Staff
- ☐ 09 Consulting
- ☐ 10 DBA/Systems Administrator
- ☐ 11 Education/Training
- ☐ 14 Technical Support Director/ Manager
- ☐ 16 Other Technical Management/Staff
- ☐ 98 Other _____

Form 5

3 What is your current primary operating platform? *(check all that apply)*
- ☐ 01 DEC UNIX
- ☐ 02 DEC VAX VMS
- ☐ 03 Java
- ☐ 04 HP UNIX
- ☐ 05 IBM AIX
- ☐ 06 IBM UNIX
- ☐ 07 Macintosh
- ☐ 09 MS-DOS
- ☐ 10 MVS
- ☐ 11 NetWare
- ☐ 12 Network Computing
- ☐ 13 OpenVMS
- ☐ 14 SCO UNIX
- ☐ 24 Sequent DYNIX/ptx
- ☐ 15 Sun Solaris/SunOS
- ☐ 16 SVR4
- ☐ 18 UnixWare
- ☐ 20 Windows
- ☐ 21 Windows NT
- ☐ 23 Other UNIX _____
- ☐ 98 Other _____
- 99 ☐ **None of the above**

4 Do you evaluate, specify, recommend, or authorize the purchase of any of the following? *(check all that apply)*
- ☐ 01 Hardware
- ☐ 02 Software
- ☐ 03 Application Development Tools
- ☐ 04 Database Products
- ☐ 05 Internet or Intranet Products
- 99 ☐ **None of the above**

5 In your job, do you use or plan to purchase any of the following products or services? *(check all that apply)*
SOFTWARE
- ☐ 01 Business Graphics
- ☐ 02 CAD/CAE/CAM
- ☐ 03 CASE
- ☐ 05 Communications
- ☐ 06 Database Management
- ☐ 07 File Management
- ☐ 08 Finance
- ☐ 09 Java
- ☐ 10 Materials Resource Planning
- ☐ 11 Multimedia Authoring
- ☐ 12 Networking
- ☐ 13 Office Automation
- ☐ 14 Order Entry/Inventory Control
- ☐ 15 Programming
- ☐ 16 Project Management

- ☐ 17 Scientific and Engineering
- ☐ 18 Spreadsheets
- ☐ 19 Systems Management
- ☐ 20 Workflow
HARDWARE
- ☐ 21 Macintosh
- ☐ 22 Mainframe
- ☐ 23 Massively Parallel Processing
- ☐ 24 Minicomputer
- ☐ 25 PC
- ☐ 26 Network Computer
- ☐ 28 Symmetric Multiprocessing
- ☐ 29 Workstation
PERIPHERALS
- ☐ 30 Bridges/Routers/Hubs/Gateways
- ☐ 31 CD-ROM Drives
- ☐ 32 Disk Drives/Subsystems
- ☐ 33 Modems
- ☐ 34 Tape Drives/Subsystems
- ☐ 35 Video Boards/Multimedia
SERVICES
- ☐ 37 Consulting
- ☐ 38 Education/Training
- ☐ 39 Maintenance
- ☐ 40 Online Database Services
- ☐ 41 Support
- ☐ 36 Technology-Based Training
- ☐ 98 Other _____
- 99 ☐ **None of the above**

6 What Oracle products are in use at your site? *(check all that apply)*
SERVER/SOFTWARE
- ☐ 01 Oracle8
- ☐ 30 Oracle8*i*
- ☐ 31 Oracle8*i* Lite
- ☐ 02 Oracle7
- ☐ 03 Oracle Application Server
- ☐ 04 Oracle Data Mart Suites
- ☐ 05 Oracle Internet Commerce Server
- ☐ 32 Oracle *inter*Media
- ☐ 33 Oracle JServer
- ☐ 07 Oracle Lite
- ☐ 08 Oracle Payment Server
- ☐ 11 Oracle Video Server
TOOLS
- ☐ 13 Oracle Designer
- ☐ 14 Oracle Developer
- ☐ 54 Oracle Discoverer
- ☐ 53 Oracle Express
- ☐ 51 Oracle JDeveloper
- ☐ 52 Oracle Reports
- ☐ 50 Oracle WebDB
- ☐ 55 Oracle Workflow
ORACLE APPLICATIONS
- ☐ 17 Oracle Automotive

- ☐ 35 Oracle Business Intelligence System
- ☐ 19 Oracle Consumer Packaged Goods
- ☐ 39 Oracle E-Commerce
- ☐ 18 Oracle Energy
- ☐ 20 Oracle Financials
- ☐ 28 Oracle Front Office
- ☐ 21 Oracle Human Resources
- ☐ 37 Oracle Internet Procurement
- ☐ 22 Oracle Manufacturing
- ☐ 40 Oracle Process Manufacturing
- ☐ 23 Oracle Projects
- ☐ 34 Oracle Retail
- ☐ 29 Oracle Self-Service Web Applications
- ☐ 38 Oracle Strategic Enterprise Management
- ☐ 25 Oracle Supply Chain Management
- ☐ 36 Oracle Tutor
- ☐ 41 Oracle Travel Management
ORACLE SERVICES
- ☐ 61 Oracle Consulting
- ☐ 62 Oracle Education
- ☐ 60 Oracle Support
- ☐ 98 Other _____
- 99 ☐ **None of the above**

7 What other database products are in use at your site? *(check all that apply)*
- ☐ 01 Access
- ☐ 02 Baan
- ☐ 03 dbase
- ☐ 04 Gupta
- ☐ 05 IBM DB2
- ☐ 06 Informix
- ☐ 07 Ingres
- ☐ 08 Microsoft Access
- ☐ 09 Microsoft SQL Server
- ☐ 98 Other _____
- ☐ 10 PeopleSoft
- ☐ 11 Progress
- ☐ 12 SAP
- ☐ 13 Sybase
- ☐ 14 VSAM
- 99 ☐ **None of the above**

8 During the next 12 months, how much do you anticipate your organization will spend on computer hardware, software, peripherals, and services for your location? *(check only one)*
- ☐ 01 Less than $10,000
- ☐ 02 $10,000 to $49,999
- ☐ 03 $50,000 to $99,999
- ☐ 04 $100,000 to $499,999
- ☐ 05 $500,000 to $999,999
- ☐ 06 $1,000,000 and over

If there are other Oracle users at your location who would like to receive a free subscription to *Oracle Magazine*, please photocopy this form and pass it along, or contact Customer Service at **+1.847.647.9630**

OPRESS

Get Your FREE Subscription to *Oracle Magazine*

Oracle Magazine is essential gear for today's information technology professionals. Stay informed and increase your productivity with every issue of *Oracle Magazine*. Inside each **FREE,** bimonthly issue you'll get:

- Up-to-date information on Oracle Database Server, Oracle Applications, Internet Computing, and tools
- Third-party news and announcements
- Technical articles on Oracle products and operating environments
- Development and administration tips
- Real-world customer stories

Three easy ways to subscribe:

1. Web Visit our Web site at **www.oracle.com/oramag/.** You'll find a subscription form there, plus much more!

2. Fax Complete the questionnaire on the back of this card and fax the questionnaire side only to **+1.847.647.9735.**

3. Mail Complete the questionnaire on the back of this card and mail it to P.O. Box 1263, Skokie, IL 60076-8263.

If there are other Oracle users at your location who would like to receive their own subscription to *Oracle Magazine*, please photocopy this form and pass it along.

Knowledge is power. To which we say,

crank up the power.

Are you ready for a power surge?

Accelerate your career—become an **Oracle Certified Professional (OCP)**. With Oracle's cutting-edge *Instructor-Led Training*, *Technology-Based Training*, and this *guide*, you can prepare for certification faster than ever. Set your own trajectory by logging your personal training plan with us. Go to **http://education.oracle.com/tpb**, where we'll help you pick a training path, select your courses, and track your progress. We'll even send you an email when your courses are offered in your area. If you don't have access to the Web, call us at 1-800-441-3541 (Outside the U.S. call +1-310-335-2403). **Power learning has never been easier.**

ORACLE
University